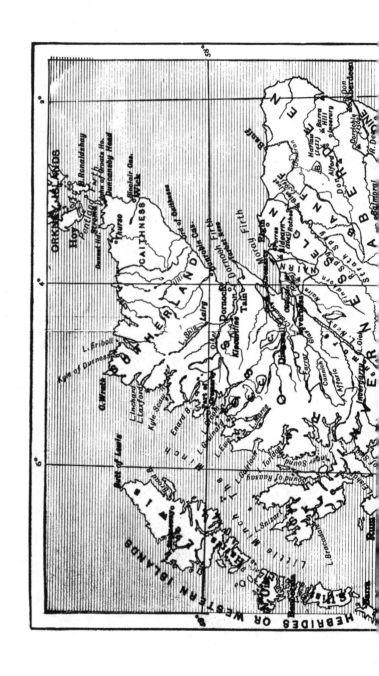

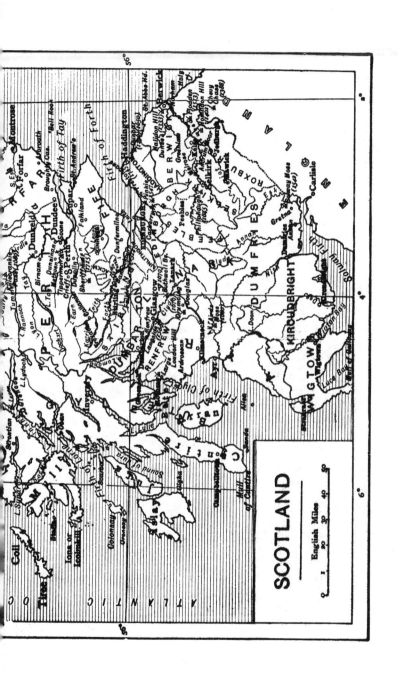

SCOTLAND

English Miles

THE SCOTCH-IRISH

OR

THE SCOT IN NORTH BRITAIN, NORTH IRELAND, AND NORTH AMERICA

BY

CHARLES A. HANNA

VOLUME I

Originally published: New York, 1902.
Reprinted by Genealogical Publishing Co., Inc.
1001 N. Calvert St., Baltimore, MD 21202
1968, 1985, 1995
First paperback reprint, 2005
Library of Congress Catalogue Card Number 68-18634
International Standard Book Number, Volume I: 0-8063-1133-9
Set Number: 0-8063-0168-6
Made in the United States of America

PREFACE

THESE volumes are designed to serve as an introduction to a series of Historical Collections which the writer expects hereafter to publish, relating to the early Scotch-Irish settlements in America. They are not intended as a history of the Scotch-Irish people, for such a work would require more time and labor than have been expended upon the present undertaking.

The subject is one, like that of the history of America itself, which must wait for some future gifted historian; but unlike the subject of American history in general, it is also one concerning which no comprehensive treatment has ever been attempted. Such being the case, in order to enable the reader to understand the relation of the Scotch-Irish to American history, it has seemed necessary to make a brief general survey of the origin and old-world history of the race to which the Scotch-Irish belong.

In doing this, it has not been his purpose to attempt even an outline sketch of the history of Scotland, but merely to condense and connect the record of its most important events, and indicate some of the principal writers upon different aspects of its history.

The fact is, that the lack of acquaintance of many native-born Americans with the details of Scottish history is such that they require an elementary grounding even in the annals of its most noteworthy events. Such a primer the writer has undertaken to prepare. In doing so, he has found it advisable to compile, epitomize, and consolidate a number of the most compact of the sketches of Scottish history which have appeared in Great Britain, using for this purpose the writings of William F. Skene and of E. William Robertson, the *Annals* of Lord Hailes, the brief history of Mackintosh and, for the topographical and ethnographical description of Scotland of the present day, the works of the French geographer and traveller, J. J. E. Reclus, of which an edition in English has been published by Messrs. D. Appleton & Company.

The written history of the Scots in Ireland is in very much the same condition as their history in America. Few attempts have been made to record it; and for this reason, very little of their history can be presented. What is given has been condensed chiefly from Harrison's monograph on *The Scot in Ulster;* from Latimer's and Reid's histories of the Irish Presbyterians; and from Hill's *Plantation of Ulster.* The most valuable features of the present volumes in this connection will be found to be the contemporary documents and reports relating to the inception and progress of the colonization of Northern Ireland by the Scots.

Scottish history, as has been intimated, is as a sealed book to the great majority of American readers. In the United States, outside of the public

libraries in perhaps two or three of the larger cities, it is difficult to find
reprints of any of the original sources of information on the history of Scotland, or indeed any commentaries on the subject, except occasional copies
of the histories of Dr. William Robertson and Mr. John Hill Burton, neither
of which is adapted to present requirements. For this reason, it has been
deemed essential by the writer, in giving his references, to print the citations
in full; as it seems probable that that is the only means of making them
available to the greater part of his readers.

NEW YORK, Dec. 1, 1901.

CONTENTS

Contents

ACKNOWLEDGMENTS

ACKNOWLEDGMENTS are due to the publishers hereinafter named for their courtesy in permitting the use. in text and notes, of extracts from their publications, as follows :

To Messrs. D. Appleton & Co., publishers of Reclus's *The World and Its Inhabitants*, Bancroft's *History of the United States*, and Lecky's *England in the XVIIIth Century*.

To Messrs. William Blackwood & Sons, publishers of Burton's *History of Scotland*, Harrison's *Scot in Ulster*, MacKerlie's *Galloway : Ancient and Modern*, and Maxwell's *History of Dumfries and Galloway*.

To James Cleland, publisher, and W. T. Latimer, author, of Latimer's *History of the Irish Presbyterians*.

To David Douglas, publisher of Robertson's *Scotland under Her Early Kings*, and Skene's *Celtic Scotland*.

To Joseph Foster, editor of *Members of the Scottish Parliament*.

To Samuel Swett Green, author and publisher of *The Scotch-Irish in America*.

To Messrs. Macmillan & Co., Limited, London, publishers of Green's *Short History of England*, *Making of England*, *Conquest of England*, and *General History of England*.

To Messrs. Harper & Brothers, publishers of Campbell's *The Puritan in Holland, England, and America*, Freeman's *Origin of the English Nation*, and Green's *Short History of England*, *Conquest of England*, and *Making of England*.

To Messrs. Houghton, Mifflin & Co., publishers of Adams's *Massachusetts : Its Historians and Its History*, Fiske's *Critical Period of American History*, and Winsor's *Narrative and Critical History of America*.

To Messrs. J. B. Lippincott & Co., publishers of Fisher's *Evolution of the Constitution of the United States*.

To Messrs. Longmans & Co. and Messrs. Charles Scribner's Sons, publishers of Froude's *English in Ireland*.

To Messrs. Longmans & Co., publishers of Lecky's *England in the XVIIIth Century*.

To the Presbyterian Board of Publication, publishers of Breed's *Presbyterians and the Revolution*, Craighead's *Scotch and Irish Seeds in American Soil*, and Moffat's *The Church in Scotland*.

To Oliver P. Temple, author of *The Covenanter, Cavalier, and Puritan*.

To James Thin, publisher of Cunningham's *Church History of Scotland*.

To T. Fisher Unwin, publisher of Rhys's *The Welsh People*.

AMERICA'S DEBT TO SCOTLAND

CHAPTER I

THE SCOTCH-IRISH AND THE REVOLUTION

THE term "Scotch-Irish" is peculiarly American, and in tracing its origin we have, epitomized, the history of the people to whom it is now applied. The word seems to have come into general use since the Revolution, having been first taken as a race-name by many individuals of a very large class of people in the United States, descendants of emigrants of Scottish blood from the North of Ireland. The name was not used by the first of these emigrants, neither was it generally applied to them by the people whom they met here.[1] They usually called themselves "Scotch," just as the descendants of their former neighbors in Northern Ireland do to-day; and as do some of their own descendants in this country, who seemingly are averse to acknowledging any connection with Ireland.[2] The Quakers and the Puritans generally spoke of them as "the Irish,"[3] and, during the Revolutionary period, we find a large and influential body of these people joined together at Philadelphia, in the formation of a patriotic association to which they gave the distinctively Irish title, "The Society of the Friendly Sons of St. Patrick."[4]

The appellation "Scotch-Irish" is not, as many people suppose, an indication of a mixed Hiberno-Scottish descent; although it could be properly so used in many cases. It was first appropriated as a distinctive race-name by, and is now generally applied to, the descendants in America of the early Scotch Presbyterian emigrants from Ireland. These Scotch people, for a hundred years or more after 1600, settled with their wives and families in Ulster, in the North of Ireland, whence their descendants, for a hundred years after 1700,—having long suffered under the burdens of civil and religious oppression imposed by commercial greed and despotic ecclesiasticism, — sought a more promising home in America.

It has been remarked by some recent observers in this country that while American history has been chiefly written in New England, that section has not been the chief actor in its events.

No doubt the second part of this proposition would be disputed by a large number of American people as not substantiated, who would perhaps claim that their position was supported by the testimony of a majority of the writers on the subject. With the latter claim it is not my purpose to take issue. Yet the first part of the proposition is more lacking in substantiation than the second. For, while it is apparent that the natural spirit of self-assertion, so early manifested by the descendants of the English Puritans, has found expression in a lengthy series of recitals of the doings and virtues of New England men, it is no less evident that these portrayals are largely of restricted application, and, for the most part, can only be considered as contributions to that portion of American history which is called local.

That these writings have ever been taken as national history arises perhaps from a conjunction of two causes, or conditions. The first of these, and one that naturally would have been ineffective without the other, is the marked tendency on the part of many New England writers to ignore or belittle the presence of any element not within the range of their own immediate horizon. In this they are peculiarly English, and exhibit that trait which has become so characteristic of the native English as to take its name from their geographical situation, namely,—insularity. The second cause, which will be more fully adverted to hereafter, arises from the comparative dearth of historical writings originating outside of the Puritan colonies.

The New England fathers came to a strange coast and found stretching back from the shore a forbidding wilderness, to them of such unknown depth that it was not until after a slow and gradual pushing forward of the frontier line for a period extending over a century and a half that their children found this wilderness was unsubdued only as far west as the Hudson River ; and fully another century elapsed before many of them were willing to acknowledge this to be the case. To the fathers, accordingly, New England meant America, and to some of the sons who stayed at home it is not unnatural that the western boundary line of America should seem to be fixed at the point where the early Dutch settlements began.

In the examination of the contributions of the New England writers to the " history of America," therefore, it is only necessary to bear in mind the restricted sense in which so many of them use this term, and to observe their superficial treatment of men and affairs not within their own provincial boundaries, to enable us to accept these contributions at their true value. Hence we can take pride with the New Englanders in the noble deeds which they narrate of their fathers and of the good these fathers wrought for their own communities, and can thus understand the nature and extent of New England's contribution to the good of our country as a whole.

It is, however, this inevitable disposition on the part of New England writers in their treatment of American history to magnify local at the expense of national affairs, to which may be attributed so much of the present adverse criticism of their authority. If it be said that this tendency is only a natural manifestation of the dominating Anglo-Saxon spirit, which brooks no rivalry and sees no good in anything foreign to itself, it may properly be answered that the page of impartial history is no place for such display.⁶ The share of New England in making American history is great ; but it is perhaps not so great as its chroniclers would have us believe. Neither can it be said by any fair-minded student that the events which took place on the soil of New England are of chief interest or importance in connection with the progress and success of the American War of Independence, and the foundation of our present system of government subsequent thereto, even though the record of those events forms the substance of a majority of the books which have been called American history.

A notable instance of this one-sided treatment of our country's history, if not of its actual perversion, on the part of all but the most recent writers, treating the subject from a New England standpoint, is that furnished by certain tables purporting to give the numbers of troops supplied by the different colonies in the Revolutionary War. These tables have appeared in whole or in part a great many times during the past sixty years, and until recently have been quite generally cited to show the superior patriotism of New Hampshire, Massachusetts, Rhode Island, and Connecticut over that of the other colonies, and to sustain the claim, repeatedly made, that New England furnished more than half the soldiers in that struggle. The tables first appeared in the *Collections of the New Hampshire Historical Society for 1824*, vol. i., p. 236 ; then in the *American Almanac for 1830*, p. 187, and *for 1831*, p. 112; in *Niles's Register* for July 31, 1830 ; in Sabine's *Loyalists of the Revolution*, in 1847, p. 31 ; in Lossing's *Field Book of the Revolution*, vol. ii., p. 837 ; in Hildreth's *History of the United States*, vol. iii., p. 441 ; in Barry's *Massachusetts*, vol. ii., p. 304 ; in Greene's *Historical View of the American Revolution*, p. 455 ; etc.⁷

They are supposed to be founded on a report made to Congress, May 11, 1790, by Henry Knox, then Secretary of War ; but they contain only a portion of the figures given in that report, and utterly ignore and omit the part relating to the enlistment and service of certain southern troops composing, perhaps, one fourth of the entire army. The compilers of the tables also attempt to summarize the portion given, by adding up the aggregates of the various enlistment rolls for the whole Revolutionary period (many of which in the early part of the war were duplicated more than four times in a single year, the same names appearing at every ninety-days' re-enlistment), and then claiming that the results reached give the total number of Regulars furnished by the different colonies in the struggle. This erroneous summary appears as follows :

```
New Hampshire......................12,496
Massachusetts........................67,807
Rhode Island ........................ 5,908
Connecticut..........................31,939
New York ...........................17,781
New Jersey..........................10,726
      Carried forward.................146,657
```

```
Brought forward................146,657
Pennsylvania........................25,678
Delaware........................... 2,386
Maryland............................13,912
Virginia.............................26,678
North Carolina...................... 7,263
South Carolina...................... 6,417
Georgia............................. 2,679
```
                                    —————
                                    231,670

The report on which these tables are said to be founded is published in the *American State Papers*, vol. i., pp. 14–19, of the series relating to Military Affairs ; and in order to show the falsity of the statements based upon the garbled and incomplete extract made from it in the aforesaid tables, the report is here given in full and the figures accompanying the same appear in tabulated form on the opposite page. This tabulation, it may be remarked, shows the form in which the incomplete statement appears, as well as the full report,— the figures here printed in heavy-faced type being omitted from all of the former tables since the first report of Knox.

TROOPS, INCLUDING MILITIA, FURNISHED BY THE SEVERAL STATES
DURING THE WAR OF THE REVOLUTION.

Communicated to the House of Representatives, May 11, 1790.

WAR OFFICE OF THE UNITED STATES, May 10, 1790.

In obedience to the order of the House of Representatives, the Secretary of War submits the statement hereunto annexed of the troops and militia furnished from time to time by the several States, towards the support of the late war.

The numbers of the regular troops having been stated from the official returns deposited in the War Office, may be depended upon ; and in all cases where the numbers of militia are stated from the returns, the same confidence may be observed.

But *in some years of the greatest exertions of the Southern States there are no returns whatever of the militia employed.* In this case recourse has been had to letters of the commanding officer, and to well informed individuals, in order to form a proper estimate of the numbers of the militia in service ; and although the accuracy of the estimate cannot be relied on, yet it is the best information which the Secretary of War can at present obtain. When the accounts of the militia service of the several States shall be adjusted it is probable that the numbers will be better ascertained.

There are not any documents in the War Office from which accurate returns could be made of the ordnance stores furnished by the several States during the late war. The charges made by the several States against the United States, which have been presented by the commissioners of accounts, are, probably, the only evidence which can be obtained on the subject.

All of which is humbly submitted to the House of Representatives.

H. KNOX, Secretary of War.

A STATEMENT OF THE TROOPS, CONTINENTAL AND MILITIA, FURNISHED BY THE RESPECTIVE STATES DURING THE REVOLUTIONARY WAR, FROM 1775 TO 1783 INCLUSIVE.

(From *American State Papers*, vol. i., Military Affairs, pp. 14-19.)

STATES	1775 Militia	1776 Continental	1776 Militia	1777 Continental	1777 Militia	1778 Continental	1778 Militia	1779 Continental	1779 Militia	1780 Continental	1780 Militia	1781 Continental	1781 Militia	1782 Continental	1783 Continental	Incorrect "Aggregate of Regulars Furnished"
New Hampshire	2824	3019	**1000**	1172	1111 / **2200**	1283	**500**	1004	222	1017	760	700		744	733	12,496 / **3,700**
Massachusetts	16444	13372	4000 / **3000**	7816	2775 / **2000**	7010	1927 / **4500**	6287	1451	4453	3436	3732	1566	4423	4370	67,807 / **9,500**
Rhode Island	1193	798	1102	548	**1500**	630	2426	507	756	915	554	464	1501	481	372	5,908 / **1,500**
Connecticut	4507	6390	5737 / **1000**	4563	**2000**	4010		3544		3133	668	2420		1732	1740	31,939 / **3,000**
New York	2075	3629	1715 / **2750**	1903	929 / **2500**	2194		2256	**1500**	2179	**2000**	1778		1198	1169	17,781 / **8,750**
New Jersey		3193	5893	1408	**1500**	1586	**1000**	1276		1105	162	823		660	675	10,726 / **2,500**
Pennsylvania	400	5519	4876	4983	2481 / **2000**	3684		3476		3337		1346		1265	1598	25,678 / **2,000**
Delaware		609	145	299	**1000**	349		317		325	231	89		164	235	2,386 / **1,000**
Maryland		637	2592	2030	1535 / **4000**	3307		2849		2065		770	1337	1280	974	13,912 / **4,000**
Virginia	**3180**	6181		5744	1269 / **4000**	5230	**2600**	3973	**4600**	2486	**4500**	1225	2894 / **2000**	1204 / **1000**	629	26,678 / **21,880**
North Carolina	2000	1134	**3000**	1281		1287		1214	2706 / **1000**		**3000**	545	3000	1105	697	7,263 / **12,000**
South Carolina	4000	2069	**4000**	1650	**350**	1650	**2000**	909	**4500**		**6000**		3000	2000	139	6,417 / **25,850**
Georgia	1000	351	**1950**	1423	**750**	673	**3200**	87	**750**		750		750	750	145	2,679 / **9,900**
Total	37623	46901	42760	34820	33900	32893	18153	27699	17485	21015	22061	13892	16048	18006	13476	337,250

It should be observed that the column of aggregate footings which appears at the right side of the table is not to be found in the original report of General Knox. This column gives the erroneous summary of the successive enlistment rolls, already referred to; but these rolls cannot be added together for the purpose of showing the number of troops furnished with any more propriety than we can add the population of Massachusetts in 1776 to that of the same State in 1777, 1778, 1779, 1780, and 1781 for the purpose of finding out the number of people who lived there during the Revolution. We might attempt to make an approximation of the average number of troops from each State by dividing the aggregates of the complete returns by the total number of years, but this would only afford a conjectural average upon which no reliance could be placed ; for besides the fact that Knox's militia returns are mainly estimated, many of the early Continental enlistments, as has been already stated, were made for only three months at a time, and either renewed at the expiration of the term by re-enlistment, or the ranks filled by fresh levies ; or, as was more generally the case during 1775 and 1776, the Continental ranks were so frequently depleted by desertions that to ascribe an average service of one month to each man enlisted therein during the first eighteen months of the war would perhaps be nearer a true statement of the fact than to set the service of each individual at from three to twelve months. The militia estimates, however, as General Knox states, approximate the numbers actually serving, and are not, as in the case of the Continentals, merely records of enlistments. It will also be noticed that these militia reports do not refer to the minutemen or militiamen who did not serve, but the estimates are of those who were actually called out and saw service in the field. In the South this service was perhaps harder and more fatal— and relatively much more effective—than that of the Continental line in the North, for the reason that the patriots of the South had to contend not only with the invading armies from abroad, but also with the armed forces of their Tory neighbors at home, whose numbers often exceeded their own, and the cruelty and brutality of whose attacks were surpassed only by the savage atrocities of another of Great Britain's hired auxiliaries—the native Indians.[8]

The fact is that these tables of Knox, as they now exist, are of little or no value whatever in giving a correct idea of the proportionate number of troops furnished by the different colonies. We know that Pennsylvania, for instance, had more than twenty thousand men in the Flying Camp, who saw service about New York, in 1776 ; yet Knox's tables show from Pennsylvania but little more than half that number, including both Continentals and militia. And that almost as many as twenty-five thousand were under arms in that State the year before is apparent from the testimony of Richard Penn given before Parliament in 1775.[9]

The following letter, received by the writer from the War Department at Washington in response to an inquiry for some explanation of Knox's figures, will serve to show how little reliance can be placed upon them :

September 2, 1897.

SIR:

Referring to your letter of the 26th ultimo, and its two enclosures, relative to the number of men in service during the War of the Revolution, I have the honor to advise you as follows:

Various tables and statements have been made up from the report of the Secretary of War of May 10, 1790, referred to in your letter, but I do not know of any one of them that is of any value or is entitled to any weight whatever. There is nothing on file in this Department which suggests any interpretation of the figures given in that report, and it is impossible to ascertain whether those figures represent the number of new enlistments during each year, or whether they include men who were in service at some time during the year but who enlisted in a prior year. In other words, it cannot be positively determined whether the figures merely represent *additions* to the force during each year, or whether they represent these additions together with the force *remaining in service from a prior year*. It is certain that, in either case, they do not represent the total number of individuals added to the force in any year, or the total number of individuals in service in any year, because there must have been many duplications caused by counting the same man over again for each successive enlistment. As pointed out in the letter addressed to you by this office on the 9th ultimo, it is well known that a very large proportion of the men who served during the Revolution rendered two, three, or more terms, or "tours," of service. This was notably the case in militia organizations, in which men frequently served tours of a few days each at comparatively short intervals. . . .

It will never be possible to determine with any approximation to accuracy the number of individuals who actually rendered military service during the Revolution. The records that have survived destruction and have been handed down to us are meagre in the extreme, but I do not believe that if every military record that was made during the Revolution had been preserved so as to be available for reference at the present time, it would be possible to make even a reasonably accurate estimate of the number of men in service from any State or from all the States together. The records of that time were comparatively few, were imperfectly kept, and contained but little of the statistical information which is to be found in the records of later wars. But even in the case of the War of the Rebellion of 1861 to 1865 it has been found impossible to determine accurately from all of the voluminous records that were kept the number of individuals who were in service from any State or from all the States. . . .

No returns or other documents have been found in this Department from which the missing information, indicated on the list of organizations which accompanied your letter, can be supplied.

The term "on command," as given on the published returns of the Revolutionary Army, is understood to be equivalent to the term "on detached service," as used at the present day, and the number of men so reported should be included with the number of "present and fit for duty" to determine the effective force of the Army. . . .

Regretting my inability to be of more material service to you in connection with the subject of your inquiry, I am

Very respectfully,

F. C. AINSWORTH,
Colonel, U. S. Army,
Chief, Record and Pension Office.

Concerning the matter of desertions, the correspondence of Washington, in the latter part of 1776, contains numerous complaints of this evil, and in some of his letters of that period to Governor Trumbull he specifies the districts whose troops were most faulty in this respect. In the same connection, the following excerpt from an incomplete memorial prepared by General Steuben on the subject, and printed in Kapp's *Life of Steuben* (pp. 704, 705), is of great importance as presenting an official statement of the composition of the army from the Inspector-General himself. This memorial also shows that Steuben accounted for the frequent re-enlistments by suggesting the frequency of desertions :

The respectable citizens who entered the lists with so much ardor, quitted their cabins with more regret to answer to the second call. Those who were in more easy circumstances emptied their purses to induce those who were poorer to take their places. The rotation of service soon became a speculation, and before the end of the second campaign there were very few rich enough to pay a substitute to serve in their stead. Associations were formed, and, by the force of money, children, invalids, and vagrants were engaged to complete the number of the contingents. These men were engaged for such short terms that one recruit soon took the place of another, and the country became quickly destitute of money. They then began to pay in produce. Negroes, cattle, produce, even lands, were given to recruits who were utterly useless to the army.

Congress and the commander-in-chief remonstrated. The evil had become incurable. The soldiers whose term had expired could not be kept on at any price ; several withdrew in the middle, others at the end of the campaign. The enemy was always in full force, while the American Army was almost insufficient to furnish the guards for our advanced posts. The new recruit generally arrived when the operations of the war were far advanced. He arrived in a wretched condition, destitute of every article of clothing, and utterly ignorant of a soldier's duty. Often a third of these new levies was totally unfit for service ; another third soon went into hospital ; and the remaining third was slightly trained during the time that the enemy employed in making his dispositions.

In the third campaign the government was compelled to reduce to a considerable extent the number of regiments, from inability to recruit them. If the fate of America could have been decided in one day by a general engagement, it is possible that the enthusiasm of our valorous citizens might have achieved a victory over an army as brave as it was well disciplined. But a war is seldom finished by one or two battles. It is necessary to keep the field, and the hope of regaining advantages on another occasion tends to prolong the operations of the war.

The citizen who had braved death at Bunker Hill could not resist the desire to see his family and take charge of his household. The hero in the battle of to-day became a deserter to-morrow, perfectly confident that he was not guilty of any impropriety. " I have had my turn," he used to say ; " I have fought bravely, let my neighbor do likewise. If five hundred thousand of my fellow citizens fire as many shots at the enemy as I have fired in the last battle, the enemy would be soon annihilated, and my country would be free." The neighbor, animated by the same sentiments, puts on his arms, joins the army, fills the vacancy, and asks nothing better than to fight and distinguish himself. But a battle is not fought every day. He waits a week, two, three, perhaps a month. He begins to long to see his family, his cabin, his land, which requires his presence to sow the crop or make his harvest. He fears to lose the produce of an entire year. His anxiety affects his health. There is nothing left for him but to go into hospital or go home. He returns to require some other neighbor to take his turn, and so on indefinitely. This rotation soon exhausts the village, but the war is not ended, and the enemy is getting ready for another campaign.

The military establishment in 1775 consisted of three battalions of infantry from New Hampshire, as follows : those of Colonels Enoch Poor, James Reed, and John Stark ; twenty-seven from Massachusetts, as follows : Colonels Daniel Brewer, Jonathan Brewer, Theophilus Colton, Timothy Danielson, Ephraim Doolittle, John Fellows, James Frye, Thomas Gardner, Samuel Gerrish, John Glover, William Heath, Ebenezer Learned, Moses Little, John Mansfield, John Nixon, John Paterson, Edmund Phinney, William Prescott, Joseph Reed, Paul D. Sargent, James Scammon, John Thomas, Timothy Walker, Artemas Ward, Asa Whitcomb, Benjamin Woodbridge ; three from Rhode Island, as follows : Colonels Thomas Church, Daniel Hitchcock, James Varnum ; eight from Connecticut, as follows : Colonels Benjamin Hinman, Jedediah Huntington, Samuel H. Parsons, Israel Putnam, Joseph Spencer, David Waterbury, David Wooster, Charles Webb ; four from New York, as follows : Colonels James Clinton, James Holmes, Alexander McDougall, Gosen Van Schaick ; two from New Jersey, as follows: Colonels William Alexander and William Maxwell; two from Pennsylvania, as follows: Colonels John Bull and William Thompson; two from North Carolina, as follows : Colonels Robert Howe and James Moore ; and two from South Carolina, as follows : Colonels Christopher Gadsden and William Moultrie. There was also, besides these fifty-four battalions of infantry, one artillery regiment from Massachusetts under command of Colonels Joseph Gridley and Henry Knox.

The infantry establishment of 1776 consisted of twenty-seven regiments of " Continentals " so-called, composed of one regiment from Pennsylvania : the 1st, under Colonel William Thompson ; three from New Hampshire : the 2d, Colonel James Reed ; 5th, Colonel John Stark ; 8th, Colonel Enoch Poor ; sixteen from Massachusetts : the 3d, Colonel Ebenezer Learned ; 4th, Colonels John Nixon and Thomas Nixon ; 6th, Colonel Asa Whitcomb ; 7th, Colonel William Prescott ; 12th, Colonel Moses Little ; 13th, Colonel Joseph Reed ; 14th, Colonel John Glover ; 15th, Colonel John Paterson ; 16th, Colonel Paul D. Sargent ; 18th, Colonel Edmund Phinney ; 21st, Colonel Jonathan Ward ; 23d, Colonel John Bailey ; 24th, Colonel John Greaton ; 25th, Colonel William Bond ; 26th, Colonel Loammi Baldwin ; 27th, Colonel Israel Hutchinson ; two from Rhode Island : 9th, Colonel James Varnum ; 11th, Colonel Daniel Hitchcock ; and five from Connecticut : 10th, Colonels Samuel H. Parsons and John Tyler ; 17th, Colonel Jedediah Huntington ; 19th, Colonel Charles Webb ; 20th, Colonels Benedict

Arnold and John Durkee ; 22d, Colonel Samuel Wyllys. There were also an additional regiment from New Hampshire, Colonel Seth Warner's, and one from Pennsylvania and Maryland, Colonel Nicholas Hausegger's, both afterwards included in the sixteen additional regiments raised under resolve of Congress of 27th December, 1776. Besides the Continental Line of 1776, the following States also furnished Continental troops in that year : New York Line, five regiments : 1st, Colonels Rudolphus Ritzema and Gosen Van Schaick ; 2d, Colonels G. Van Schaick and James Clinton ; 3d, Colonels James Clinton, Rudolphus Ritzema, and Peter Gansevoort ; 4th, Colonels Cornelius Wynkoop and Henry Livingston ; 5th, Colonel Lewis Dubois ; New Jersey Line, four regiments : 1st, Colonels William Alexander, William Winds, and Silas Newcomb ; 2d, Colonels William Maxwell and Israel Shreve ; 3d, Colonel Elias Dayton ; 4th, Colonels Ephraim Martin and David Brearley (Lieutenant-Colonel); Pennsylvania Line, seven battalions: 1st, Colonel John P. De Haas; 2d, Colonels Arthur St. Clair and Joseph Wood; 3d, Colonels John Shee and Lambert Cadwallader ; 4th, Colonel Anthony Wayne ; 5th, Colonel Robert Magaw ; 6th, Colonel William Irvine ; 7th, Colonel Samuel Miles, Rifle Battalion; and five additional regiments : 8th, Colonel Æneas Mackay ; 9th, Colonel James Irvine ; 10th, Colonel Joseph Penrose ; 11th, Colonel Richard Humpton ; 12th, Colonel William Cook ; Delaware Line, one regiment: Colonel John Haslet; Maryland Line, seven regiments : 1st, Colonels William Smallwood and Francis Ware ; 2d, Colonel Thomas Price ; 3d, Colonel Mordecai Gist ; 4th, Colonel Josiah C. Hall ; 5th, Colonel William Richardson ; 6th, Colonel Otho H. Williams ; 7th, Colonel John Gunby ; Virginia Line, fifteen regiments : 1st, Colonel James Reed : 2d, Colonel William Woodford ; 3d, Colonels Hugh Mercer and George Weedon ; 4th, Colonels Adam Stephen and Thomas Elliott ; 5th, Colonels William Peachy and Charles Scott ; 6th, Colonel Mordecai Buckner ; 7th, Colonel William Dangerfield and William Crawford ; 8th, Colonel Peter Muhlenberg ; 9th, Colonels Charles Fleming and Isaac Reed ; 10th, Colonel Edward Stevens ; 11th, Colonel Daniel Morgan ; 12th, Colonel James Wood ; 13th, Colonel William Russell ; 14th, Colonel Charles Lewis ; 15th, Colonel David Mason ; North Carolina Line, nine regiments : 1st, Colonels James Moore and Francis Nash ; 2d, Colonels Robert Howe and Alexander Martin ; 3d, Colonel Jethro Sumner ; 4th, Colonel Thomas Polk ; 5th, Colonel John A. Lillington ; 6th, Colonel Edward Buncombe ; 7th, Colonel James Hogan ; 8th, Colonel James Armstrong ; 9th, Colonel Abraham Shephard ; South Carolina Line, five regiments : 1st, Colonels Christopher Gadsden and Charles C. Pinckney ; 2d, Colonels William Moultrie and Isaac Motte ; 3d, Colonel William Thompson ; 4th, ——————————— ; 5th, Colonel Isaac Huger ; Georgia Line, two regiments : 1st, Colonel Lachlan McIntosh ; 2d, Colonel Joseph Habersham. Besides these eighty-nine regiments of infantry there were two artillery regiments : Colonels Richard Gridley and Henry Knox's Massachusetts Artillery and Colonel Charles Harrison's Virginia

Artillery. There was also a regiment of light horse organized in Connecticut by Colonel Elisha Sheldon.

In 1777 the New Hampshire Line contained three regiments under Colonels John Stark and Joseph Cilley, Enoch Poor, and Alexander Scammell ; the Massachusetts Line, sixteen, under Colonels Joseph Vose, John Bailey, John Greaton, William Shepard, Rufus Putnam, Thomas Nixon, Ichabod Allen, Michael Jackson, James Wesson, Thomas Marshall, Ebenezer Francis and Samuel Carlton (Lieutenant-Colonel), Edward Wigglesworth, Gamaliel Bradford, and Timothy Bigelow ; the Rhode Island Line, two, under Colonels Christopher Greene and Israel Angell ; the Connecticut Line, eight, under Colonels Jedediah Huntington and Josiah Starr, Charles Webb, Samuel Wyllys, John Durkee, Philip B. Bradley, William Douglas and Return J. Meigs, Heman Swift, John Chandler ; the New York Line, five, under Colonels Gosen Van Schaick, Peter Van Cortland, Peter Gansevoort, Henry B. Livingston, and Lewis Dubois ; the New Jersey Line, four, under Colonels Mathias Ogden, Israel Shreve, Elias Dayton, and David Rhea (Lieutenant-Colonel) ; the Pennsylvania Line, thirteen, under Colonels Edward Hand and James Chambers, John P. De Haas, James Irvine and Henry Bicker, Joseph Wood and Thomas Craig, Lambert Cadwallader, Francis Johnston, Robert Magaw, William Irvine, Æneas Mackay and Daniel Brodhead, James Irvine and Anthony J. Morris and Richard Butler, Joseph Penrose and James Chambers and Adam Hubley (Lieutenant-Colonel), Richard Humpton, William Cook and John Bull ; the Delaware Line, one, under Colonel David Hall ; the Maryland Line, seven, under Colonels John H. Stone, Thomas Price, Mordecai Gist, Josias Hall, William Richardson, Otho H. Williams, and John Gunby; the Virginia Line, fifteen, under Colonels James Reed and James Hendricks, William Woodford and Alexander Spotswood, George Weedon and Thomas Marshall, Thomas Elliott and Robert Lawson and Isaac Reed, Charles Scott and Josiah Parker, Mordecai Buckner and John Gibson, William Crawford and Alexander McClanachan, Peter Muhlenberg and Abraham Bowman and John Neville, Isaac Reed and George Matthews, Edward Stevens, Daniel Morgan, James Wood, William Russell, Charles Lewis, and David Mason ; the North Carolina Line, ten, under Colonels Francis Nash and Thomas Clarke, Alexander Martin and John Patton, Jethro Sumner, Thomas Polk, Edward Buncombe, Gideon Lamb, James Hogan, James Armstrong, John Williams, and Abraham Shephard ; the South Carolina Line, five, under Colonels Charles C. Pinckney, Isaac Motte, William Thompson, ———— (4th), and Isaac Huger (5th) ; and the Georgia Line, four, under Colonels ———— (1st), Samuel Elbert (2d), ———— (3d), and John White (4th). Lieutenant-Colonel John McIntosh commanded one of the Georgia regiments.

In 1778 there were three infantry regiments from New Hampshire under Colonels Joseph Cilley, ·Nathan Hale, and Alexander Scammell ; fifteen from Massachusetts, all but the 11th under the same colonels as in 1777 ;

two from Rhode Island, under Greene and Angell ; eight from Connecticut, with the same colonels as in 1777, with the exception of the 2d, in which Zebulon Butler succeeded Charles Webb, and the 8th, in which Giles Russell succeeded John Chandler ; five from New York, under the colonels of 1777 ; four from New Jersey, under the colonels of 1777 ; thirteen from Pennsylvania, under the colonels of 1777, with the exception of the 2d, in which Walter Stewart succeeded Henry Bicker, the 10th, in which George Nagel first, and afterwards Richard Humpton, succeeded to the command, and the 11th, which was disbanded and its place taken by Colonel Thomas Hartley's 4th Additional Continental Regiment ; one from Delaware, under Lieutenant-Colonel Joseph Vaughan ; seven from Maryland ; fifteen from Virginia, under Richard Parker (1st), Christopher Febiger (2d), William Heath (3d), Isaac Reed and John Neville (4th), Josiah Parker and Richard Russell (5th), John Gibson and John Greene (6th), Alexander McClanachan and Daniel Morgan (7th), John Neville and James Wood (8th), George Matthews and John Gibson (9th), John Green and William Davies (10th), Daniel Morgan and Abraham Buford (11th), James Wood (12th), William Russell (13th), Charles Lewis and William Davies (14th), and David Mason and Abraham Buford (15th) ; North Carolina, eight ; South Carolina, five ; Georgia, four, Lieutenant-Colonel John McIntosh succeeding to command of the 3d, where he remained until the close of the war.

In 1779, and thereafter, of the sixteen additional regiments raised under resolution of Congress of 27th December, 1776, the 2d and 3d (Virginia) were united under Nathaniel Gist ; the 4th (Pennsylvania) was designated as the 11th Pennsylvania ; the 5th, 6th, and 7th (Massachusetts) were united under Henry Jackson, and became the 16th Massachusetts in 1780 ; the 8th and 12th (New Jersey) were united under Oliver Spencer, and the remainder seem mostly to have been continued by their respective States as additional regiments until 1781. The Massachusetts Line (fifteen regiments) remained substantially intact until 1781 ; as did those of New Hampshire (three regiments), Rhode Island (two regiments), and Connecticut (eight regiments), until the end of 1780. Lieutenant-Colonel Isaac Sherman succeeded Giles Russell in command of the 8th Connecticut in October, 1779 ; and the names of John Bailey (in 1780), Ichabod Allen (in 1778), Samuel Carlton (in 1778), and Edward Wigglesworth (in 1779) disappear as commanders of regiments from Massachusetts. There was no change in the number or commanders of the five regiments of New York from 1778 to 1781, excepting in the case of the 5th, where Marinus Willet succeeded Lewis Dubois in December, 1779. In New Jersey, the 4th was probably incorporated with one of the additional regiments after 1778. In Pennsylvania, Morgan Connor succeeded William Irvine as commander of the 7th in May, 1779, and he was succeeded in January, 1780, by Josiah Harmar ; the 12th and 13th were disbanded before the close of 1778. In Delaware, Joseph Vaughan continued in command of the one regiment from that State to the close of the war. In

Maryland, Otho H. Williams was transferred to the command of the 1st and John Gunby to that of the 2d, in January, 1781 ; Lieutenant-Colonels John E. Howard and Thomas Woolford serving successively in the 5th up to October, 1779, under Colonel William Richardson ; and Lieutenant-Colonel N. Ramsay succeeding Mordecai Gist as commander of the 3d at the beginning of 1779. In Virginia, the 12th, 13th, 14th, and 15th regiments were disbanded towards the close of 1778 ; William Davies became colonel of the 1st, Abraham Buford of the 2d, and John Gibson of the 7th, in February, 1781 ; the 9th, 10th, and 11th having also been disbanded. In North Carolina there are no returns from the 5th, 6th, 7th, 8th, after 1778. In South Carolina, the 2d regiment seems to have been under command of Major Isaac Harleston after December, 1778, the 1st and 3d remaining unchanged to 1781 ; there are no returns, lists, or rolls of the 4th to be found, but Isaac Huger continued as colonel of the 5th to June, 1779, and the regiment remained in service until 1781. The names of Colonels Francis Marion and David Hopkins also appear in orders. In Georgia, the 1st, 2d, and 3d regiments remained in service to the close of the war ; the 4th probably not later than 1779.

RETURNS OF THE CONTINENTAL LINE REGIMENTS IN 1776, OFFICERS AND RANK AND FILE PRESENT AND FIT FOR DUTY, OR ON COMMAND.

The following returns are from the volumes of the Fifth Series of *American Archives :*

July, 1776. Monthly return of forces in South Carolina, vol. i., p. 632.

September 27th. Return of Colonel William Smallwood's Maryland Regiment, vol. ii., p. 567.

October 5th. Return of forces under Washington at Harlem Heights, vol. ii., p. 907.

November 9th. Return of the forces in Northern Department under Gates, vol. iii., pp. 701, 702.

December 1st. Return of forces under Washington at Trenton, vol. iii., p. 1035.

December 22d. Return of the forces under Washington on the banks of the Delaware, vol. iii., pp. 1401, 1402.

CONTINENTALS :		TOTAL.
1. Edward Hand, Pa.......Oct.	5,	367
2. James Reed, N. H.......Nov.	9,	221
3. Ebenezer Learned, Mass.Oct.	5,	474
4. Thomas Nixon, Mass....Oct.	5,	386
5. John Stark, N. H........Nov.	9,	258
6. Asa Whitcomb, Mass.....Nov.	9,	308
7. William Prescott, Mass...Oct.	5,	318
8. Enoch Poor, N. H......Nov.	9,	274
9. James Varnum, R. I.....Oct.	5,	330
10. Sam'l H. Parsons, Ct....Oct.	5,	448
11. Daniel Hitchcock, R. I.. Oct.	5,	312
12. Moses Little, Mass.......Oct.	5,	347
13. Joseph Read, Mass......Oct.	5,	424
14. John Glover, Mass.......Oct.	5,	384
15. John Paterson, Mass.....Nov.	9,	249
16. Paul D. Sargent, Mass...Oct.	5,	398

TOTAL.

17. Jedediah Huntington, Ct.Oct. 5, 230
18. Edmund Phinney, Mass..Nov. 9, 301
19. Charles Webb, Conn.....Oct. 5, 428
20. John Durkee, Conn......Dec. 22, 371
21. Jonathan Ward, Mass....Oct. 5, 435
22. Samuel Wyllys, Conn.....Oct. 5, 391
23. John Bailey, Mass.......Oct. 5, 394
24. John Greaton, Mass......Nov. 9, 476
25. William Bond, Mass.....Nov. 9, 164
26. Loammi Baldwin, Mass...Oct. 5, 378
27. Israel Hutchinson, Mass..Oct. 5, 489
     Knox's Artillery.........Oct. 5, 341
                                    ─────
                                    9,896

NEW YORK LINE :

1. Gosen Van Schaick......Nov. 9, 231
2. James Clinton...........Oct. 5, 253
3. Rudolphus Ritzema......Oct. 5, 338
4. Cornelius Wynkoop......Nov. 9, 114
5. Lewis Dubois...........

NEW JERSEY LINE :

1. Silas Newcomb..........Nov. 9, 165
2. Israel Shreve..........Nov. 9, 225
3. Elias Dayton...........Nov. 9, 540
4. Ephraim Martin........Oct. 5, 277

PENNSYLVANIA LINE :

1. John P. De Haas........Nov. 9, 393
2. Joseph Wood...........Nov. 9, 262
3. Lambert Cadwallader....Oct. 5, 336
4. Anthony Wayne.........Nov. 9, 394
5. Robert Magaw..........Oct. 5, 343
6. William Irvine.........Nov. 9, 277
   Miles's Rifle Regiment...Oct. 5, 105
   Pennsylvania and Maryland
     German Regiment, Hau-
     segger's (one half)......Dec.22, 197

DELAWARE LINE :

1. John Haslet...........Oct. 5, 479

MARYLAND LINE :

1. William Smallwood......Sept. 27, 592
2. Maryland and Pennsylvania
     German Regiment, Hau-
     segger's (one half).....Dec. 22, 197

VIRGINIA LINE :

1. James Read............Oct. 5, 379
2. William Woodford.......
3. George Weedon.........Oct. 5, 510
4. Thomas Elliott..........Dec. 1, 263
5. Charles Scott...........Dec. 1, 184
6. Mordecai Buckner.......Dec. 1, 313
7. William Crawford.......
8. Peter Muhlenberg.......July   381
9. Isaac Reed.............July 12, 120
10. Edward Stevens.........
11. Daniel Morgan..........
12. James Wood.. ....
    Harrison's Artillery......

NORTH CAROLINA LINE :

1. Francis Nash...........July   357
2. Alexander Martin.......July   306
3. Jethro Sumner.........July   342
4. Thomas Polk...........
5. Edward Buncombe.......
6. John A. Lillington.......
7. James Hogan...........
8. James Armstrong........
9. John Williams..........
   3d Company Horse......July   36

SOUTH CAROLINA LINE :

1. Christopher Gadsden.....July   326
2. William Moultrie........July   392
3. William Thompson.......July   414
4. Artillery................
5. Isaac Huger............July   297
6. ....July   299

GEORGIA LINE :

1. Lachlan McIntosh.......
2. Samuel Elbert..........

CANADIAN REGIMENTS :

1. James Livingston........
2. Moses Hazen...........

These returns, complete for all the New England regiments, show a total number in the Continental Line from that section in the fall of 1776 of about 9500 men, or an average of 353 men to each of the twenty-seven New England regiments. The incomplete returns from the fifty-two regiments outside of New England show a total of 11,004 men in thirty-four regiments, an average of 323 men in each. There are no returns in the archives of the War Department from the remaining eighteen regiments, but estimating that they contained an average of 300 men each, or 5400 in all, it would give a total effective force of " Regulars " in the American Army, before the loss of Fort Washington, of about 26,000 men, of whom thirty-seven per cent. were from New England.

In the collections of the Historical Society of Pennsylvania is a folio manuscript volume, *Abstracts of Muster-Rolls*, prepared by direction of Deputy Muster-Master-General William Bradford, Jr., which contains the names of the field officers and officers commanding companies, with the strength of each company and regiment. This invaluable book, the cover of which is largely composed of muster-rolls dated at Valley Forge, gives the musters for the months of June, July, August, September, and October of 1778, and January of 1779. The following is the muster for July of 1778, as it is in a more perfect condition than any of the others.

PARTIAL ROSTER OF OFFICERS UNDER WASHINGTON, JULY, 1778.

NORTH CAROLINA.

First Regiment. — Colonel, Thomas Clark ; Lieutenant-Colonel, Mabane ; Major, Ashe ; Captains, Tatum, Dixon, Bowman, Read, McRees, Moore ; commissioned officers, 26 ; staff, 4 ; non-commissioned and privates, 658.

Second Regiment.—Colonel, John Patten ; Lieutenant-Colonel, Harney ; Major, Murpee ; Captains, Englis, Tenner, Coleman, Hall, Armstrong, Williams ; commissioned officers, 27 ; staff, 5 ; non-commissioned and privates, 647.

DELAWARE.

Delaware Battalion. — Colonel, David Hall ; Captains, Patten, Anderson, Leavmonth, Kirkwood, Jaquett ; Lieutenants, Wilson, Powell, Rhodes ; commissioned officers, 29 ; staff, 5 ; non-commissioned and privates, 351.

AT LARGE.

Lieutenant-Colonel, Aaron Burr ; Captains, Tom, Sandford, Hallet ; Lieutenants, Dove, Neely ; commissioned officers, 11 ; staff, 5 ; non-commissioned and privates, 88.

Major, William Harrison ; Captains, Wikoff, Burrows, Forman, Combs ; commissioned officers, 6 ; staff, 2 ; non-commissioned and privates, 73.

Colonel, Oliver Spencer ; Captains, Broderick, Weatherby, Striker, Edsell, Pierson, Bommel ; Lieutenants, Meiker, Ogden ; commissioned officers, 14 ; staff, 4 ; non-commissioned and privates, 157.

First Regiment. —Colonel, Joseph Cilley ; Captains, Taswell, Scott, Fry, Hutcheson, Wail, House, Emmerson, Morrell ; commissioned officers, 26 ; staff, 4 ; non-commissioned and privates, 476.

Second Regiment. — Major, Benjamin Titcomb ; Captains, Drew, Carr, Norris, Rowell, Clay, Blodgett, Robinson ; Lieutenant, Hardy ; commissioned officers, 27 ; staff, 3 ; non-commissioned and privates, 368.

Third Regiment. — Colonel, Alexander Scammell ; Captains, Livermore, Gray, Weiser, Fry, Stone, McClary, Bealls, Ellis ; commissioned officers, 26 ; staff, 3 ; non-commissioned and privates, 333.

Independent Corps. —Captain, Selir ; commissioned officers, 5 ; non-commissioned and privates, 44.

CONNECTICUT.

First Regiment. — Colonel, Heman Swift ; Captains, Woodbridge, Watson, Hill, Converse, Beardsley, Chapman, Hale, Steven ; commissioned officers, 25 ; staff, 4 ; non-commissioned and privates, 398.

Second Regiment. — Lieutenant-Colonel, Isaac Sherman ; Captains, Parsons, Beebe, Manning, Hinkly, Betts, Walbridge, Mills, Parker ; commissioned officers, 16 ; staff, 5 ; non-commissioned and privates, 289.

Third Regiment. — Major, David Sill ; Captains, Haney, Troop, Shumway, Ely, Perkins, Richards, Darrow, Home ; commissioned officers, 23 ; staff, 5 ; non-commissioned and privates, 434.

Fourth Regiment. — Colonel, Philip Bradley ; Captains, Strong, Lacey, Wright, Sandford, Prior, Catlin, Childs, Harts ; commissioned officers, 23 ; staff, 4 ; non-commissioned and privates, 386.

Fifth Regiment. — Major, Joseph Hait ; Captains, Monson, Brown, Rice, Brigham, Sandford, Smith, Comstock, Mattocks ; commissioned officers, 21 ; staff, 4 ; non-commissioned and privates, 336.

Sixth Regiment. — Colonel, John Durkee (two companies detached) ; Captains, Bacon, Fitch, McGuire, Lee, Webb, Bile, Hallam, Harmar ; commissioned officers, 26 ; staff, 5 ; non-commissioned and privates, 348.

NEW YORK.

First Regiment. — Colonel, Gosen Van Schaick ; Captains, Finch, Hicks, Sherwood, Hogkish, Copp, McCracky, Graham, Wendall ; commissioned officers, 28 ; staff, 5 ; non-commissioned and privates, 454.

Second Regiment. — Colonel, Philip Cortland ; Captains, Wright, Ten Eyk, (late) Graham, Riker, (late) Hallet, Pell, Lounsbery ; Lieutenant, French ; commissioned officers, 23 ; staff, 4 ; non-commissioned and privates, 413.

Fourth Regiment. — Colonel, Henry Livingston ; Captains, Titus, Sackett, Gray, Strong, Smith, Walker, Davis ; Lieutenant, Elsworth ; commissioned officers, 20 ; staff, 4 ; non-commissioned and privates, 383.

RHODE ISLAND.

Second Regiment.—Colonel, Israel Angell; Captains, C. Olney, S. Olney, Dexter, Potter, Humphreys, Tew, Hughes, Allen (detachment of Colonel Green); commissioned officers, 27; staff, 4; non-commissioned and privates, 469.

PENNSYLVANIA.

First Regiment.—Colonel, James Chambers; Captains, Grier, Buchanan, Wilson, Hamilton, Simpson, Doyle, Craig, Wilson, Parr; Lieutenant, Hughes; commissioned officers, 25; staff, 2; non-commissioned and privates, 331.

Second Regiment.—Colonel, Walter Stewart; Lieutenant-Colonel, Henry Miller; Major, Murray; Captains, Marshall, Ashmead, Howell, Bankson, Tolbert, Patterson; commissioned officers, 24; staff, 3; non-commissioned and privates, 437.

Third Regiment.—Colonel, Thomas Craig; Captains, Craig, Moore, S. Moore, Butler, Rees, Christie, Holling, Epple; commissioned officers, 12; staff, 4; non-commissioned and privates, 204.

Fourth Regiment.—Lieutenant-Colonel, William Butler; Captains, Connelly, Means, Burd, Williams, McGowan, Fishburn, Scull, Gray; commissioned officers, 19; staff, 3; non-commissioned and privates, 217.

Fifth Regiment.—Colonel, Francis Johnston; Captains, Oldham, Christy, Smith, McHenry, Gregg, Seely, Potts, Bond, Bartholomew; commissioned officers, 24; staff, 2; non-commissioned and privates, 300.

Sixth Regiment.—Colonel, Josiah Harmar; Captains, Mouser, Cruise, McCowan, Waugh, Humph, Bower, ———; commissioned officers, 15; staff, 5; non-commissioned and privates, 194.

Seventh Regiment.—Colonel, William Irvine; Captains, Bratton, Wilson, Alexander, J. Alexander, Parker, Montgomery, Irwin, Miller; commissioned officers, 26; staff, 1; non-commissioned and privates, 201.

Ninth Regiment.—Colonel, Richard Butler; Captains, Bowen, Irwin, Davis, Henderson, Grant, McClelland; Lieutenant, Bickham; commissioned officers, 21; staff, 5; non-commissioned and privates, 210.

Tenth Regiment.—Colonel, Richard Humpton; Lieutenant-Colonel, Hubley; Major, Grier; Captains, Stake, Lang, Sample, Weaver, Stout, Colhoon; commissioned officers, 22; staff, 3; non-commissioned and privates, 342.

Twelfth Regiment.—(Late William Cook); Captains, McElhatton, Lincoln, Patterson, Bohn, Miller, Ruby; commissioned officers, 9; staff, 4; non-commissioned and privates, 146.

NEW JERSEY.

First Regiment.—Colonel, Mathias Ogden; Captains, Mead, Piatt, Polhemus, Longstreet, Morrison, Baldwin, Angell; Lieutenant, D. Hart; commissioned officers, 22; staff, 5; non-commissioned and privates, 532.

Second Regiment.—Colonel, Israel Shreve; Captains, Redding, Hollingshead, Sparks, Holmes, Cummings, Lucy, one company wanting; commissioned officers, 20; staff, 5; non-commissioned and privates, 365.

Third Regiment.—Colonel, Elias Dayton; Captains, Ballard, Ross, Anderson, Patterson, Grifford (vacant), Cox, Mott; commissioned officers, 23; staff, 4; non-commissioned and privates, 473.

Fourth Regiment.—Colonel, Ephraim Martin; Captains, Anderson, Mitchell, Lyon, Forman; Lieutenants, Johnston, Lloyd, Barton; commissioned officers, 19; staff, 5; non-commissioned and privates, 321.

MARYLAND.

First Regiment.—Colonel, John H. Stone; Captains, Gaither, Roxborough, Ewing, Winder; Lieutenants, Smith, Bruce, Farnadis, Peal; commissioned officers, 19; staff, 5; non-commissioned and privates, 374.

Second Regiment.—Colonel, Thomas Price; Captains, Anderson, Long, Davidson, Eccleston, Williams, Dent, Dorsey; Lieutenant, Hardman; commissioned officers, 16; staff, 4; non-commissioned and privates, 526.

Third Regiment.—Colonel, Mordecai Gist; Captains, Smith, Gist, Brice, Griffiths, Marbury, Brooks; Lieutenants, Armstrong, Deaver, Clagett, Smith; commissioned officers, 31; staff, 6; non-commissioned and privates, 461.

Fourth Regiment.—Colonel, Josiah C. Hall; Captains, Oldham, Selman, Lansdale, Goodman, Burgess, Smith, Norwood; Lieutenants, Reilly, Smith; commissioned officers, 23; staff, 5; non-commissioned and privates, 517.

Fifth Regiment.—Colonel, William Richardson; Captains, Hawkins, Hardey, Lynch, Johnston; Lieutenants, Hamilton, Emory, Hand; Ensign, Jones; commissioned officers, 19; staff, 5; non-commissioned and privates, 457.

Sixth Regiment.—Colonel, Otho Williams; Captains, Harris, Hyres, Dobson, D. Beal, Lawrence, Freeman, Myle, Ghislin; commissioned officers, 20; staff, 5; non-commissioned and privates, 391.

Seventh Regiment.— Colonel, John Gunby; Captains, Jones, Stull, Spyker, Grost, Morris, Bayley, Anderson; Lieutenant, Beatty; commissioned officers, 23; staff, 4; non-commissioned and privates, 369.

German Battalion.—Lieutenant-Colonel, Ludwig Weltner; Captains, Hubley, Bunner, Boyer, Baltzell; Lieutenants, Cramer, Rice, Shugart, Boyer, Meyer; commissioned officers, 20; staff, 4; non-commissioned and privates, 385.

VIRGINIA.

First Regiment.—Colonel, Richard Parker; Captains, Minnes, Conyngham, Lawson, Lewis; commissioned officers, 22; staff, 5; non-commissioned and privates, 243.

Second Regiment.—Colonel, Christian Febiger; Captains, Harrison, Mc-

Calmis, Taylor, W. Taylor, Willis, Upshaw, Holmes, Parker ; commissioned officers, 23 ; staff, 5 ; non-commissioned and privates, 253.

Third and Seventh Regiments.—Lieutenant-Colonel, William Heath ; Captains, Young, Hill, Blackwell, Peyton, Lipscomb, Powell, Briscoe ; Captain-Lieutenant, Baylor ; Lieutenant, Sayres ; commissioned officers, 27 ; staff, 9 ; non-commissioned and privates, 556.

Fourth and Twelfth Regiments.—Colonel, James Wood ; Lieutenant-Colonel, Nevil ; Major, Clark ; Captains, Lapsley, Still, Wall, Kirkpatrick, Waggoner, Croghan, Bowyer ; commissioned officers, 30 ; staff, 13 ; non-commissioned and privates, 752.

Fifth Regiment.—Colonel, Joseph Parks ; Captains, Fowler, Anderson, Colston, Fauntleroy ; commissioned officers, 23 ; staff, 4 ; non-commissioned and privates, 182.

Sixth Regiment.—Colonel, John Gibson ; commissioned officers, 17 ; staff, 5 ; non-commissioned and privates, 85.

Ninth Regiment.—Lieutenant-Colonel, Burgess Ball ; commissioned officers, 10 ; staff, 1 ; non-commissioned and privates, 53.

Tenth Regiment.—Colonel, John Greene ; Captains, Shelton, West, Stephens, Mountjoy, Spotswood, Blackwell, Gillison ; Lieutenant, Lamne ; commissioned officers, 23 ; staff, 4 ; non-commissioned and privates, 380.

Eleventh and Fifteenth Regiments.—Colonel, David Meson ; Captains, Porterfield, Gregory, Ree, Gray ; Colonel, Cropper ; Major, Wallace ; Captains, Will, Johnston ; commissioned officers, 26 ; staff, 10 ; non-commissioned and privates, 584.

Fourteenth Regiment.—Colonel, William Davis ; Captains, Conway, Reid, Robert, Winston, Overton, Marks, Jones, Thweat ; commissioned officers, 26 ; staff, 4 ; non-commissioned and privates, 390.

First State Regiment.—Colonel, George Gibson ; Captains, Brown, Hamilton, Ewell, T. Ewell, Shields, Valentine, Armistead, Crump, Hoffler, Nicholas; commissioned officers, 29 ; staff, 4 ; non-commissioned and privates, 329.

Second State Regiment.—Colonel, Gregory Smith ; Captains, Spiller, Dudley, Talifero, Quarles, Busse, Garnet, Barnard, Lewis ; commissioned officers, 26 ; staff, 4 ; non-commissioned and privates, 418.

At Large.—Colonel, John Parke ; Captains, Bicker, Prowel, Keen, Dennis, Grubb, Redman ; commissioned officers, 16 ; staff, 2 ; non-commissioned and privates, 89. (Captain McLean's company not mustered.)

At Large.—Colonel, William Grayson ; Captains, Mitchell, Smith, Triplett, Jones, Moore, McGuire, Smallwood, Willis, (late) Grant ; commissioned officers, 17 ; staff, 3 ; non-commissioned and privates, 189.

MASSACHUSETTS.

First Regiment.—Colonel, Thomas Marshall ; Captains, Wolcut, Soper, Warner, Marshall, Smith, Thomas, King, Wales ; commissioned officers, 25 ; staff, 5 ; non-commissioned and privates, 277.

Second Regiment.—Colonel, G. Bradford ; Captains, Wadsworth, Cooper, Warner, Marshall, Smith, Thomas, King, Wales ; commissioned officers, 22 ; staff, 5 ; non-commissioned and privates, 311.

Third Regiment.—Colonel, Benjamin Tupper ; Captains, Thorne, May- bury, Farnum, White, Wheelwright, Page, Porter, Greenleaf ; commissioned officers, 30 ; staff, 5 ; non-commissioned and privates, 342.

Fourth Regiment.—Colonel, Samuel Brewer ; Captains, Watkins, Bur- bank, Jenkins, Merrel, Stones, Chadwick, Donnel, Brewer ; commissioned officers, 29 ; staff, 5 ; non-commissioned and privates, 313.

Fifth Regiment.—Colonel, James Wesson ; Captains, Pettengill, Child, Bartlet, Blanchard, Cogswell, Ward, Dix ; commissioned officers, 22 ; staff, 5 ; non-commissioned and privates, 336.

Sixth Regiment.—Colonel, John Bailey ; Captains, Darby, Maxwell, Drew, Alden, Dunham, Burr, Allen, Warren ; commissioned officers, 24 ; staff, 5 ; non-commissioned and privates, 384.

Seventh Regiment.—Colonel, Michael Jackson ; Captains, Keith, Burnam, Brown, Varnum, Wiley, Cleveland, Eb. Cleveland, Bancroft ; commissioned officers, 25 ; staff, 4 ; non-commissioned and privates, 315.

His Excellency's Body-Guard.—Captain, Gibbs ; commissioned officers, 4 ; staff, 1 ; non-commissioned and privates, 148.

LIGHT DRAGOONS.

Colonel, Stephen Moylan ; Captains, Moore, Plunket, Hopkins, Heard, Pike, Gray ; commissioned officers, 15 ; staff, 5 ; non-commissioned and privates, 187.

Colonel, Theo. Bland ; Captains, Jones, Belfield, Call, Harrison, Dan- dridge ; commissioned officers, 15 ; staff, 5 ; non-commissioned and privates, 165.

Colonel, George Blaylor ; Captains, Lewis, Jones, Smith, Cad. Jones ; commissioned officers, 15 ; staff, 6 ; non-commissioned and privates, 129.

ARTILLERY.

Colonel, Ch. Harrison ; Captains, Brown, ———, ———, Dandridge, Singleton, Carter, Pendleton, Henry, Baylop, Eddens ; commissioned officers, 42 ; staff, 5 ; non-commissioned and privates, 432.

Colonel, John Crane ; Captains, Burbeck, Eustice, Wills, Trothengha, Sergeant, Treadwell, Seward ; commissioned officers, 36 ; staff, 2 ; non- commissioned and privates, 295.

Colonel, John Lamb ; Captains, Lee, Jnoa. Gibb, Clark, Randall, Porter, Doughty, Bauman, Mansfield ; commissioned officers, 34 ; staff, — ; non-commissioned and privates, 203.

SUMMARY.

New Hampshire, total	officers	and	men,	1,315
Massachusetts	"	"	"	2,642
Rhode Island	"	"	"	500
Connecticut	"	"	"	2,352

Total in New England regiments,	6,809

New York, total	officers	and	men,	1,334
New Jersey	"	"	"	1,794
Pennsylvania	"	"	"	2,811
Delaware	"	"	"	385
Maryland	"	"	"	3,689
Virginia	"	"	"	4,891
North Carolina	"	"	"	1,367

Total in all State regiments,	23,080

Artillery,	1,049
Light Dragoons,	542
At Large,	358

Grand total	25,029

We can gain considerable knowledge of the American Army in 1778 and 1779 from the reports of Baron Steuben, its Inspector-General, some of which, printed in Kapp's *Life of Steuben*, can be profitably repeated at this time :

The effective strength of the army was divided into divisions, commanded by major-generals ; into brigades, commanded by brigadier-generals ; and into regiments, commanded by colonels. The number of men in a regiment was fixed by Congress, as well as in a company — so many infantry, cavalry, and artillery. But the eternal ebb and flow of men engaged for three, six, and nine months, who went and came every day, rendered it impossible to have either a regiment or a company complete ; and the words company, regiment, brigade, and division were so vague that they did not convey any idea upon which to form a calculation, either of a particular corps or of the army in general. They were so unequal in their number, that it would have been impossible to execute any manœuvers. Sometimes a regiment was stronger than a brigade. I have seen a regiment consisting of *thirty men*, and a company of one *corporal!* Nothing was so difficult, and often so impossible, as to get a correct list of the State or a return of any company, regiment, or corps. . . . General Knox assured me that, previous to the establishment of my department, there never was a campaign in which the military magazines did not furnish from five thousand to eight thousand muskets to replace those which were lost in the way I have described above. The loss of bayonets was still greater. The American soldier, never having used this arm, had no faith in it, and never used it but to roast his beefsteak, and indeed, often left it at home. This is not astonishing when it is considered that a majority of the States engaged their soldiers for from six to nine months. Each man who went away took his musket with him, and his successor received another from the public store. No captain kept a book. Accounts were never furnished nor required. As our army is, thank God, little subject to desertion, I venture to say that during an entire campaign there have not been twenty muskets lost since my system came into force. It was the same with the pouches and other accoutrements, and I do not believe that I exaggerate when I state that my arrangements have saved the United States at least eight hundred thousand French livres a year.

The arms at Valley Forge were in a horrible condition, covered with rust, half of them without bayonets, many from which a single shot could not be fired. The pouches were quite as bad as the arms. A great many of the men had tin boxes instead of pouches, others had cow-horns ; and muskets, carbines, fowling-pieces, and rifles were to be seen in the same company.

The description of the dress is most easily given. The men were literally naked, some of them in the fullest extent of the word. The officers who had coats, had them of every color and make. I saw officers, at a grand parade at Valley Forge, mounting guard in a sort of dressing gown, made of an old blanket or woollen bed-cover. With regard to their military discipline, I may safely say no such thing existed. In the first place there was no regular formation. A so-called regiment was formed of three platoons, another of five, eight, nine, and the Canadian regiment of twenty-one. The formation of the regiments was as varied as their mode of drill, which only consisted of the manual exercise. Each colonel had a system of his own, the one according to the English, the other according to the Prussian or French style. There was only one thing in which they were uniform, and that was the way of marching in the manœuvers and on the line of march. They all adopted the mode of marching in files used by the Indians.

I have not been able to find any correct statement of the strength of the southern army [10] ; but without doing injustice to the South, we may reasonably suppose that matters stood much worse there than in the North, because the South was more divided in itself, and less enthusiastic for the cause of Independence. On the other hand, we find, in the Steuben Papers, the strength of the principal army exactly stated.

General Washington's army, at the beginning of the campaign of 1779, consisted of six divisions, of two brigades each, numbering in all 11,067 men — forty-six regiments. These regiments had from one hundred and fifty (Seventh Virginia) to four hundred and thirty (Sixth Connecticut) rank and file. Steuben selected from each regiment, in proportion to its strength, a number of picked men, to form eight light-infantry companies, and then, where they were too weak, united the regiments into one battalion. Thus, the whole army consisted of thirty-five battalions (9,755 men), making two hundred and seventy-eight the average strength of each battalion, and the eight companies of light infantry before mentioned in addition. Each of the latter had one field officer, four captains, eight subalterns, twelve sergeants, and 164 rank and file. The divisions were severally known as the Virginia, Maryland, Pennsylvania, Connecticut, Massachusetts, and North Carolina.

FORMATION OF THE ARMY COMMANDED BY HIS EXCELLENCY GENERAL
WASHINGTON, FOR THE BEGINNING OF THE PRESENT
CAMPAIGN [1779].

VIRGINIA.

First Brigade, Woolford [Woodford?] — 2d Regiment, 175 ; 5th and
11th, 223 ; 8th, 182 ; 7th, 150 ; 3d and 4th, 245. Total, 975.
Second Brigade, Muhlenberg.—6th, 168 ; 2d State, 230 ; Gist's, 153 ;
1st State, 209 ; 1st and 10th, 270. Total, 1030.

MARYLAND AND DELAWARE.

First Brigade, Smallwood.— 1st, 260 ; 5th, 220 ; 7th, 230 ; 3d, 270.
Total, 980.
Second Brigade, Guest [M. Gist].— 2d, 280 ; 6th, 230 ; 4th, 320 ;
Delaware, 220. Total, 1050.

PENNSYLVANIA.

First Brigade, Irvine.— 1st, 210 ; 7th, 170 ; 10th, 240 ; 2d, 340. Total,
960.
Second Brigade, Johnson.— 3d, 260 ; 6th, 180 ; 9th, 180 ; 5th, 240.
Total, 860.

CONNECTICUT.

First Brigade, Huntington.— 4th, 184 ; 8th, 232 ; 6th, 430 ; 3d, 367.
Total, 1213.
Second Brigade, Parsons.—1st, 289 ; 5th, 220 ; 2d, 206 ; 7th, 295. Total,
1010.

MASSACHUSETTS.

First Brigade, Nixon.— 2d, 224 ; 5th, 263 ; 4th, 313. Total, 800.
Second Brigade, Learned.— 1st, 277 ; 7th, 212 ; 8th, 248. Total, 737.
Pettason's [Paterson's] Brigade.—9th, 192 ; 12th, 184 ; 10th, 179 ; 15th,
260. Total, 815.

NORTH CAROLINA.

1st, 328 ; 2d, 298. Total, 626.

Return of the number of men enlisted during the war, and for shorter
periods in the army under the immediate command of His Excellency
General Washington, December, 1779 :

1st Maryland Brigade	1416
2d " "	1497
1st Pennsylvania "	1253
2d " "	1050
New Jersey "	1297
New York "	1267
1st Connecticut "	1680
2d " "	1367
Hand's "	1033
Stark's "	1210
Total,	13,070

It would appear from the figures given in the preceding pages that the New England element in the American Army, subsequent to the withdrawal of the British from New England territory, was under forty per cent. of the whole native force, or but little more than proportionate to its relative population. In like manner, it appears that the leaders of the army were no less representative of its true constitution than the rank and file. Of Washington's twelve generals at the beginning of the war, Nathanael Greene, William Heath, Seth Pomeroy, Israel Putnam, Joseph Spencer, John Sullivan, John Thomas, Artemas Ward, and David Wooster were New England men—Charles Lee of Virginia, and Richard Montgomery and Philip Schuyler of New York completing the staff. But the majority of the New Englanders dropped out of sight before the conflict was fairly begun ; and besides Greene, the only general officers from that section who achieved renown during the progress of the war were the Scotch-Irishmen, Henry Knox and John Stark, and the Irishman, John Sullivan. The New England general in command of the forces on Long Island seems to have been relegated mainly to garrison duty after the retreat from that place, and Benjamin Lincoln's campaign in the South resulted most disastrously. When the army was discharged in 1783, we find that among the fifteen major-generals, New England was represented by five — Greene, Heath, Putnam, Lincoln, and Knox. Of the remainder, there were, of Scottish descent, besides Knox :   William Alexander (N. J.), Alexander McDougall (N. Y.), Arthur St. Clair (Pa.) ; of English descent, in addition to the four first named : Horatio Gates (Va.), Robert Howe (N. C.), William Smallwood (Md.), and William Moultrie (?) (S. C.); of French birth: Lafayette and Du Portail ; and of German: Steuben. Of the twenty-two brigadiers at that time—six from New England—there were of Scottish blood : William Irvine (Pa.), Lachlan McIntosh (Ga.), John Paterson (Mass.), Charles Scott (Va.), John Stark (N. H.); of Anglo-Scottish : George Clinton (N. Y.), James Clinton (N. Y.), Edward Hand (Pa.), Anthony Wayne (Pa.); of French : Isaac Huger (S. C.); of German : Johann De Kalb (France), Peter Muhlenberg (Va.); of Welsh : Daniel Morgan (Va.), O. H. Williams (Md.); and of English : Elias Dayton (N. J.), Mordecai Gist (Md.), John Greaton (Mass.), Moses Hazen (Mass.), Jedediah Huntington (Conn.), Rufus Putnam (Mass.), Jethro Sumner (?) (S. C.), George Weedon (Va.). Out of the thirty-seven names on these two lists of 1783, eleven were from New England ; and of the total list about one half were of English descent, while two fifths were to a large degree Celtic in their descent.

Proceeding to analyze the list of the other generals created during the Revolutionary period, we further find as of probable Scottish blood : John Armstrong (Pa.), Francis Barber (N. J.), William Campbell (Va.), George Rogers Clark [11] (Va.), William Davidson (N. C.), John Douglas (Conn.), James Ewing (Pa.), Robert Lawson (Va.), Andrew Lewis (Va.), William Maxwell (N. J.), Hugh Mercer (Va.), James Moore (N. C.), John Nixon

(Pa.), Andrew Pickens (S. C.), James Potter (Pa.), Joseph Reed (Pa.), Griffith Rutherford (N. C.), John Morin Scott (N. Y.), Adam Stephen (Va.), Thomas Sumter (?) (Va.), William Thompson (Pa)., a total of twenty-one ; of Welsh blood : John Cadwallader (Pa.), William Davies (Va.), James Varnum (Mass.); of French : P. H. De Barre (France), Philip De Coudray (France), A. R. De Fermoy (France), John P. De Haas (Pa., Holland-French), Francis Marion (S. C.); of Dutch: Nicholas Herkimer (N. Y.), Abraham Ten Broeck (N. Y.), Philip Van Cortlandt (N. Y.), Gosen Van Schaick (N. Y.); of German : Frederic W. de Woedtke ; of Irish : Thomas Conway (Ireland), James Hogan (N. C.), Stephen Moylan (Pa.); of Polish : Casimir Pulaski (Poland); and of probable English descent : Benedict Arnold (Conn.), William Blount (N. C.), Philemon Dickinson (N. J.), Samuel Elbert (Ga.), John Fellows (Mass.), Joseph Frye (Mass.), John Frost (Maine), Christopher Gadsden (S. C.), John Glover (Mass.), John Lacey (Pa.), Ebenezer Learned (Mass.), Thomas Mifflin (Pa.), Francis Nash (?) (Va.), William North (Maine), Samuel Parsons (Conn.), Enoch Poor (N. H.), James Reed (N. H.), Gold S. Silliman (Conn.), Edward Stevens (Va.), James Wadsworth (Conn.), Joseph Warren (Mass.), John Whitcomb (Mass.), James Wilkinson (Md.), William Woodford (Va.), Nathaniel Woodhull (N. Y.), a total of twenty-five ; making with the other names mentioned in this paragraph a list of sixty-three names in all, less than half of which are English, and about one fourth from New England.

Taking all the lists together, we have an aggregate of one hundred and nine names, which include practically all of Washington's generals ; and it appears that but thirty-one of them came from the New England States, and that less than half were of English descent—about sixty being non-English.

An examination of the lists of colonels, captains, lieutenants, and minor commissioned officers will show a like distribution. The names of 2310 of those who were in the Continental service are printed in the *American State Papers*, vol. iii., Military Affairs, pp. 529 to 559, under the heading, " Schedule of the names and rank of most of the officers of the War of Independence, chiefly returned as belonging to the lines or corps of the thirteen original United States soon after said army was disbanded in 1783, arranged alphabetically and numbered distinctly according to the States."

This schedule is prefaced by the following communication to Congress from the Secretary of War :

NINETEENTH CONGRESS : SECOND SESSION : 342. STATEMENT OF THE NAMES AND RANK OF THE OFFICERS OF THE REVOLUTIONARY WAR, &C.

Communicated to the House of Representatives, January 10, 1827.

DEPARTMENT OF WAR, January 10, 1827.

SIR :
    In compliance with the resolution of the House of Representatives of the 8th instant, directing the Secretary of War " to report to their House

the name and rank of each officer of the Continental army who served to the end of the Revolutionary War, and who were by the resolution of Congress entitled to half-pay during life ; and also, as nearly as practicable, the names of the remaining officers and their places of residence," I transmit herewith a list of the names and rank of the officers of the Revolutionary War, as complete as the records of the Department will furnish, with the exception of foreign officers. There is no evidence in the Department to show which of them " were by the resolution of Congress entitled to half-pay during life," nor is it known which of them are still living, with their places of residence, except those who are on the pension list.

Very respectfully, etc.,

JAMES BARBOUR, Secretary of War.

To the Speaker of the House of Representatives.

The list of names sent with this report shows the State to which each officer is credited, and the regiment to which he belonged. In the final years of the war, with very few exceptions, the officers commanded troops raised by their own States. Of these 2310 officers, 79 were from New Hampshire, 445 from Massachusetts, 44 from Rhode Island, 254 from Connecticut, 200 from New York, 92 from New Jersey, 421 from Pennsylvania, 32 from Delaware, 166 from Maryland, 337 from Virginia, 99 from North Carolina, 93 from South Carolina, and 48 from Georgia. Less than forty per cent. of these were from New England.

It will be seen from the heading of the list that these officers principally belonged to the Continental Army. Militia officers are not, as a rule, mentioned, unless they also served in the Continental or State lines. As the most of the troops of the Southern States did not belong to the Continental establishment, but were simply State militiamen, their officers would have no place in this list.

NOTES TO CHAPTER I.

[1] As early as 1763–64 we find them mentioned by the name " Scotch-Irish " in the Legislature of the Province of Pennsylvania, when one Nathaniel Grubb, a member of the Assembly from Chester County so denominated the Paxtang settlers. These people had petitioned the Quaker government in vain for protection from the murderous attacks of the savages ; and finally, despairing of help from that source, some of them took the law into their own hands and made an indiscriminate slaughter of such Indians as they could find in their neighborhood. In denouncing this action to his fellow Quakers, Grubb referred to these settlers as "a pack of insignificant Scotch-Irish, who, if they were all killed, could well enough be spared." (See, William H. Egle, *History of Dauphin County, Penna.*,p. 60.)

Rev. John Elder, also, in a letter written from Paxtang, under date of February 7, 1764, to Col. Edward Shippen, of Lancaster, relative to the killing of the Conestoga Indians in December, 1763, says : " The Presbyterians, who are the most numerous I imagine of any Denomination in the Province, are enraged at their being charged in bulk with these facts, under the name of Scotch-Irish, and other ill-natured titles, and that the killing of the Conestogoe Indians is compared to the Irish massacres and reckoned the most barbarous of either, so that things are grown to that pitch now that the country seems determined that no Indian Treaties shall be held, or savages maintained at the expense of the Province, unless his Majestie's pleasure on these heads is well known ; for I understand,.

to my great Satisfaction that amidst our great confusions there are none even of the most warm and furious tempers, but what are firmly attached to his Majesty, and would cheerfully risk their lives to promote his service."

Edmund Burke, writing in 1757, says: "The number of white people in Virginia is between sixty and seventy thousand; and they are growing every day more numerous, by the migration of the Irish, who, not succeeding so well in Pennsylvania as the more frugal and industrious Germans, sell their lands in that province to the latter, and take up new ground in the remote countries in Virginia, Maryland, and North Carolina. These are chiefly Presbyterians from the Northern part of Ireland, who in America are generally called Scotch-Irish."—*European Settlements in America*, vol. ii., p. 216.

[2] Although they came to this land from Ireland, where their ancestors had a century before planted themselves, yet they retained unmixed the national Scotch character. Nothing sooner offended them than to be called Irish. Their antipathy to this appellation had its origin in the hostility existing in Ireland between the Celtic race, the native Irish, and the English and Scotch colonists. Mr. Belknap quotes from a letter of Rev. James MacGregor to Governor Shute, in which he says: "We are surprised to hear ourselves termed Irish people, when we so frequently ventured our all for the British crown and liberties against the Irish Papists and gave all tests of our loyalty which the government of Ireland required, and are always ready to do the same when required."—Parker's *History of Londonderry, New Hampshire*, p. 68.

[3] As against the more or less willing adoption of the name "Scotch-Irish" in the middle of the last century we may contrast the following citations, gathered by Mr. Thomas Hamilton Murray, a more recent emigrant from Ireland, who argues that a man born in a stable must be a horse. Mr. Murray says:

"The colonial records repeatedly mention the 'Irish,' not the Scotch-Irish. Cotton Mather, in a sermon in 1700, says: 'At length it was proposed that a colony of Irish might be sent over to check the growth of this country.' . . . The party of immigrants remaining at Falmouth, Me., over winter, and which later settled in Londonderry, N. H., were alluded to in the records of the general court as 'poor Irish.'

"On St. Patrick's day, the Irish of Portsmouth, N. H., instituted St. Patrick's Lodge of Masons. Later we find Stark's Rangers at Fort Edward requesting an extra supply of grog so as to properly observe the anniversary of St. Patrick.

"Marmion's *Maritime Ports of Ireland* states that 'Irish families' settled Londonderry, N. H. Spencer declares that 'the manufacture of linen was considerably increased by the coming of Irish immigrants.' In 1723, says Condon. 'a colony of Irish settled in Maine.' Moore, in his sketch of Concord, N. H., pays tribute to the 'Irish settlers' in that section of New England. McGee speaks of 'the Irish settlement of Belfast,' Me. The same author likewise declares that 'Irish families also settled at Palmer and Worcester, Mass.' Cullen describes the arrival at Boston in 1717 of Capt. Robert Temple, 'with a number of Irish Protestants.' Capt. Temple was, in 1740, elected to the Charitable Irish Society. In another place Cullen alludes to 'the Irish spinners and weavers, who landed in Boston in the earlier part of the 18th century.' . . .

"Among those who have been wrongly claimed [as Scotch-Irish] are Carroll, Sullivan, . . . Moylan, Wayne, Barry, . . and . . . of a later period, . . . Meade and Sheridan. . . .

"Of the Revolutionary heroes mentioned above, Charles Carroll was of old Irish stock. His cousin, John Carroll, was a Roman Catholic clergyman, a Jesuit, a patriot, a bishop, and archbishop. Daniel Carroll was another sterling patriot.

"The Sullivans, James and John, were also of ancient Irish stock, the name having been O'Sullivan even in their father's time.

"Gen. Knox and his father were both members of the Charitable Irish Society, of Boston. The General also belonged to the Friendly Sons of St. Patrick, Philadelphia.

"Moylan was a brother of the Roman Catholic bishop of Cork.   . . .
"Wayne was of Irish [English] descent and proud of his Irish lineage.   He was an active member of the Friendly Sons of St. Patrick.
"Barry was an Irish Roman Catholic."
(T. H. Murray, in Appendix to Samuel Swett Green's monograph on *The Scotch-Irish in America*, read before the American Antiquarian Society in Boston, April 24, 1895.)

⁴ The members of this organization were as follows : Isaac All, John Barclay, Thomas Barclay, William Barclay, Commodore John Barry, Thomas Batt, Colonel Ephraim Blaine, John Bleakly, William Bourke, Dr. Robert Boyd, Hugh Boyle, John Boyle, John Brown, William Brown, General Richard Butler, Andrew Caldwell, David Caldwell, James Caldwell, John Caldwell, Samuel Caldwell, William Caldwell, George Campbell, James Campbell, Samuel Carson, Daniel Clark, Dr. John Cochran, James Collins, John Connor, William Constable, D. H. Conyngham, James Crawford, George Davis, Sharp Delany, John Donnaldson, John Dunlap, William Erskine, Thomas Fitzsimmons, Tench Francis, Turbutt Francis, Benjamin Fuller, George Fullerton, Archibald Gamble, Robert Glen, Robert Gray, John Greene, General Edward Hand, William Hamilton, James Hawthorn, Charles Heatly, George Henry, Alexander Holmes, Hugh Holmes, George Hughes, Genl. William Irvine, Francis Johnston, Genl. Henry Knox, George Latimer, Thomas Lea, John Leamy, James Logan, Ulysses Lynch, Blair M'Clenachan, George Meade, James Mease, John Mease, Matthew Mease, John Mitchell, John Mitchell, Jr., Randle Mitchell, William Mitchell, Hugh Moore, Major James Moore, Patrick Moore, Col. Thomas Moore, James Moylan, Jasper Moylan, John Moylan, Genl. Stephen Moylan, John Murray, John M. Nesbitt, Alexander Nesbitt, Francis Nichols, John Nixon, Michael Morgan O'Brien, John Patton, Capt. John Patterson, Oliver Pollock, Robert Rainy, Thomas Read, Genl. Thomas Robinson, John Shee, Hugh Shiell, Charles Stewart, Walter Stewart, William Thompson, George Washington (an adopted member), Genl. Anthony Wayne, Francis West, Jr., John West, William West, William West, Jr., John White, Joseph Wilson. The Moylans, Barry, Fitzsimmons, Leamy, and Meade, all brave and active patriots, are said to have been Catholic Irish, and probably also were Bourke, Connor, Lynch, O'Brien, and Shee. The others, with very few exceptions, were Scotch-Irish. When Robert Morris organized the Bank of Pennsylvania in 1780 for the purpose of furnishing funds to keep the army in food, more than one third of its £300,000 capital was subscribed for and paid in by twenty-seven members of this Society.   The society is still in existence.

⁵ Two notable exceptions were those of the settlement of Luzerne County (Wyoming), Penna., by 117 colonists from Connecticut in 1762–63 and by 196 in 1769 ; and the settlement at Marietta, Ohio, of the Massachusetts colonists in 1788. Small colonies were also planted in Maryland, South Carolina, and Georgia by settlers from New England.

⁶ More than sixty years ago Dr. Charles Hodge found occasion to rebuke an indiscreet exhibition of this same spirit in connection with the early church history of the country. His remarks, at that time so pertinent to the point in question, have ever since been so generally applicable to the majority of New England attempts at American history that they cannot be said to have lost any of their force since 1839.   He says (*Constitutional History of the Presbyterian Church*, vol. i., pp. 60, 61) :

"Nothing but a sectional vanity little less than insane, could lead to the assertion that Congregationalism was the basis of Presbyterianism in this country, and that the Presbyterian Church never would have had an existence, except in name, had not the Congregationalists come among us from New England.   The number of Puritans who settled in New England was about twenty-one thousand.   If it be admitted that three-fourths of these were Congregationalists, (which is a large admission,) it gives between fifteen and sixteen thousand. The Presbyterian emigrants who came to this country by the middle of the last century, were between one and two hundred thousand.   Those from Ireland alone, imperfect as are the records of emigration, could not have been less than fifty thousand, and probably were far more numerous. . . .

" It is to be remembered that the emigration of New England men westward did not take place, to any great extent, until after the Revolutionary War ; that is, until nearly three-fourths of a century after the Presbyterian Church was founded and widely extended. At that time western New York, Ohio, and the still more remote west was a wilderness. Leaving that region out of view, what would be even now the influence of New England men in the Presbyterian Church ? Yet it is very common to hear those who formed a mere handful of the original materials of the Church, speaking of all others as foreigners and intruders. Such representations would be offensive from their injustice, were it not for their absurdity. Suppose the few (and they were comparatively very few) Congregationalists of East Jersey had refused to associate with their Dutch and Scotch Presbyterian neighbours, what great difference would it have made ? Must the thousands of Presbyterians already in the country, and the still more numerous thousands annually arriving, have ceased to exist ? Are those few Congregationalists the fathers of us all ? The truth is, it was not until a much later period that the great influx of Congregationalists into our Church took place, though they are now disposed to regard the descendants of its founders as holding their places in the Church of their fathers only by sufferance."

[7] The falsity of these tables was first clearly pointed out by Mr. Justin Winsor, in an address delivered before the Historical Society of Massachusetts, in January, 1886. See *Proceedings* of that Society, Second Series, vol. ii., pp. 204-207.

[8] The backwoodsmen were engaged in a threefold contest. In the first place, they were occasionally, but not often, opposed to the hired British and German soldiers of a foreign king. Next, they were engaged in a fierce civil war with the Tories of their own number. Finally, they were pitted against the Indians, in the ceaseless border struggle of a rude, vigorous civilization to overcome an inevitably hostile savagery. The regular British armies, marching to and fro in the course of their long campaigns on the seaboard, rarely went far enough back to threaten the frontiersmen ; the latter had to do chiefly with Tories led by British chiefs, and with Indians instigated by British agents.—Roosevelt, *Winning of the West*, vol. i., p. 276.

Dr. Thomas Smythe gives a careful statement of the activity of Presbyterian elders in the War of Independence in the province of South Carolina : " The battles of the ' Cowpens,' of ' King's Mountain,' and also the severe skirmish known as ' Huck's Defeat,' are among the most celebrated in this State as giving a turning-point to the contests of the Revolution. General Morgan, who commanded at the Cowpens, was a Presbyterian elder. . . . General Pickens . . . was also a Presbyterian elder, and nearly all under their command were Presbyterians. In the battle of King's Mountain, Colonel Campbell, Colonel James Williams (who fell in action), Colonel Cleaveland, Colonel Shelby, and Colonel Sevier were all Presbyterian elders ; and the body of their troops were collected from Presbyterian settlements. At Huck's Defeat, in York, Colonel Bratton and Major Dickson were both elders in the Presbyterian Church. Major Samuel Morrow, who was with Colonel Sumter in four engagements, and at King's Mountain, Blackstock, and other battles, and whose home was in the army till the termination of hostilities, was for about fifty years a ruling elder in the Presbyterian Church. It may also be mentioned in this connection that Marion, Huger, and other distinguished men of Revolutionary memory were of Huguenot . . . descent."—Thomas Smythe, *Presbyterianism, the Revolution, the Declaration, and the Constitution*, pp. 32 *seq.*

[9] Examination of Richard Penn before Parliament, November 1, 1775 :

" Q. What force has the Province of Pennsylvania received ? A. When I left Pennsylvania they had 20,000 men in arms, imbodied but not in pay ; and 4500 men since raised. Q. What were these 20,000 ; militia, or what ? A. They were volunteers throughout the Province. Q. What were the 4500 ? A. They were Minute-men, when upon service in pay."

[10] Greene's army at the battle of Guilford Court-House (N. C.), March 15, 1781, consisted of 4243 foot and 201 cavalry. It was composed of Huger's brigade of Virginia Continentals, 778 ; Williams's Maryland brigade and a company from Delaware, 630 ; infantry of Lee's partisan legion, 82 ; total of Continentals, 1490. There were also 1060 North Carolina militia, under Brigadier-Generals Butler and Eaton ; 1693 militia from Augusta and Rockbridge counties, Virginia, under Generals Stevens and Lawson ; in all, 2753. Washington's light dragoons, 86 ; Lee's dragoons, 75 ; Marquis de Bretagne's horse, 40 ; total, 201.

[11] Mr. Reuben G. Thwaites, of the State Historical Society of Wisconsin, writes to the author of this paper as follows : " According to all family traditions, John Clark, great-grandfather of George Rogers Clark, came to Virginia, in 1630, from the southwest part of Scotland. According to one tradition, a few years later, he visited friends in Maryland, and married there ' a red-haired Scotch woman.' George Rogers Clark himself had ' sandy ' hair ; another tradition has it that the woman was a Dane. Their one son, William-John, died early, leaving two sons, John (2) and Jonathan. Jonathan was a bachelor, and left his estate to his brother's son, John (3). One of William-John's daughters married a Scotch settler, McCloud, and their daughter married John Rogers, the father of the Ann Rogers who married John Clark (4), her cousin, and thus she became the mother of George Rogers Clark. So George Rogers Clark had Scotch ancestry on both sides of the house."—Samuel Swett Green, *The Scotch-Irish in America.*

CHAPTER II

THE SCOTCH-IRISH AND THE CONSTITUTION

L ET us now examine the composition of the Continental Congress of
1776, the fifty-six members of which were the signers of the Declaration. So far as can at this time be ascertained, that body consisted of
thirty-four of English descent, as follows: John Adams (Mass.), Samuel
Adams (Mass.), Josiah Bartlett (N. H.), Carter Braxton (Va.), Samuel
Chase (Md.), George Clymer (Pa.), William Ellery (R. I.), Benjamin
Franklin (Pa.), Elbridge Gerry (Mass.), Lyman Hall (Ga.), John Hancock
(Mass.), Benjamin Harrison (Va.), Thomas Heyward, Jr. (S. C.), Joseph
Hewes (N. C.), Stephen Hopkins (R. I.), Francis Hopkinson (N. J.),
Samuel Huntington (Conn.), F. L. Lee (Va.), R. H. Lee (Va.), Arthur
Middleton (S. C.), Robert Morris (Pa.), Lewis Morris (N. Y.), William
Paca (Md.), Robert Treat Paine (Mass.), John Penn (N. C.), Cæsar Rodney (Del.), Benjamin Rush (Pa.), Roger Sherman (Conn.), Richard Stockton (?) (N. J.), Thomas Stone (Md.), George Walton (Ga.), William Whipple
(N. H.), Oliver Wolcott (Conn.), George Wythe (Va.) ; eleven of Scottish:
William Hooper (N. C.), Philip Livingston (N. Y.), Thomas McKean (Pa.),
Thomas Nelson, Jr. (Va.), George Ross (Del.), Edward Rutledge (S. C.),
James Smith (Pa.), George Taylor (Pa.), Matthew Thornton (N. H.), James
Wilson (Pa.), John Witherspoon (N. J.) ; five of Welsh : William Floyd
(N. Y.), Button Gwinnett (?) (Ga.), Thomas Jefferson (Va.), Francis Lewis
(N. Y.), William Williams (Conn.) ; one of Swedish : John Morton (Pa.);
two of Irish: Charles Carroll (Md.), Thomas Lynch, Jr. (S. C.). The father
of George Read (Del.) was born in Ireland and his mother in Wales ;
Abraham Clark, of Elizabethtown, and John Hart, of Hunterdon County,
both from strong Scottish settlements in New Jersey, are difficult to place.

On the whole, the Continental Congress of 1776 was a fairly representative body, being two thirds English and one third non-English ; although it
may be observed that the Dutch of New York, the Germans of Pennsylvania, and the Huguenots of the South are not represented by members of
their own races. The first two classes, however, were generally, and to a considerable degree erroneously, regarded as unfavorable to the American cause.

A similar examination of the membership of the Constitutional convention, which completed its labors at Philadelphia, September 17, 1787, shows
a like mixed composition to that of the Continental Congress.

Of the fifty-four members representing the colonies in that body, we
find that, besides Washington, probably twenty-nine of them were English,
as follows : Abraham Baldwin (Ga.), Richard Bassett (Del.), Gunning
Bedford, Jr. (Del.), William Blount (N. C.), David Brearly (N. J.), George

Clymer (Pa.), William R. Davie (N. C.), Jonathan Dayton (N. J.), John Dickinson (Del.), Oliver Ellsworth (Conn.), William Few (Ga.), Benjamin Franklin (Pa.), Elbridge Gerry (Mass.), Nicholas Gilman (N. H.), Nathaniel Gorham (Mass.), Jared Ingersoll (Pa.), William Johnson (Conn.), Rufus King (Mass.), John Langdon (N. H.), George Mason (Va.), Thomas Mifflin (Pa.), Gouverneur Morris (Pa.), Robert Morris (Pa.), William Pierce (Ga.), Charles Pinckney (S. C.), Charles C. Pinckney (S. C.), Roger Sherman (Conn.), Caleb Strong (Mass.), George Wythe (Va.) ; twelve were Scottish : John Blair (Va.), Alexander Hamilton (N. Y.), W. Churchill Houston (N. J.), William Livingston (N. J.), James McClurg (Va.), James McHenry (Md.), John Mercer (Md.), William Paterson (N. J.), John Rutledge (S. C.), Richard Dobbs Spaight (?)(N. C.), James Wilson (Pa.), Hugh Williamson (N. C.) ; three were Irish : Pierce Butler (S. C.), Daniel Carroll (Md.), Thomas Fitzsimmons (Pa.) ; two French : Daniel Jenifer (?) (Md.), Henry Laurens (S. C.) ; one German : Jacob Broom (?) (Del.) ; George Read (Del.) was Welsh-English ; James Madison's ancestry was mixed — English, Welsh, and Scottish, and that of Edmund Randolph (Va.) English and Scottish ; John Lansing (N. Y.) and Robert Yates (N. Y.) were Dutch, and the descent of Luther Martin (Md.) is uncertain.

When the independent State governments were formed after the adoption of the Declaration of Independence, and their governors chosen, then, in the words of the ablest and most recent historian of the Puritans,[1] "the Scotch-Irish gave to New York her first governor, George Clinton. . . . To Delaware they gave her first governor, John MacKinley. To Pennsylvania they gave her war governor, Thomas McKean, one of the signers of the Declaration of Independence. To New Jersey Scotland gave her war governor, William Livingston, and to Virginia, Patrick Henry, not only her great war governor but the civil leader who, supported by his Scotch-Irish brethren from the western counties, first carried and then held Virginia for the cause of Independence. To North Carolina the Scotch-Irish gave her first governor, Richard Caswell, and to South Carolina they gave another signer of the Declaration, Edward Rutledge, and another great war governor in the person of John Rutledge. . . . What those men did for the cause of American Independence is known to every student, but their un-English origin is not so generally recognized. In the colonial wars their section furnished most of the soldiers of Virginia.

"It is a noteworthy fact in American history, that of the four members of Washington's Cabinet, Knox, of Massachusetts, the only New Englander was a Scotch-Irishman ; Alexander Hamilton, of New York, was a Scotch-Frenchman ; Thomas Jefferson was of Welsh descent, and the fourth, Edmund Randolph, claimed among his ancestors the Scotch Earls of Murray. New York also furnished the first chief justice of the United States, John Jay, who was a descendant of French Huguenots ; while the second chief justice, John Rutledge,[2] was Scotch-Irish, as were also Wilson and Iredell, two of the four original associate justices ; a third, Blair, being of Scotch origin. John Marshall,' the great chief justice, was, like Jefferson, of Scotch and Welsh descent."

Jonathan Trumbull, Connecticut's war governor (the original " Brother Jonathan"), was descended from a member of the ancient Scottish border clan of Turnbull.' Archibald Bulloch, the Scottish ancestor of Theodore Roosevelt, was likewise the Revolutionary Governor of Georgia in 1776–77.

To pursue the subject further, it appears that of the twenty-five Presidents of the United States down to the present time, less than half the number were of purely English extraction. Of predominating English blood may be counted Washington, the two Adamses, Madison, William Henry Harrison, Tyler, Pierce, Fillmore, Lincoln, and, perhaps, Taylor. Cleveland's father was of English descent, but the name of his mother's father (Abner Neal), who was born in Ireland, indicates a Celtic origin, possibly Scottish. Benjamin Harrison and Theodore Roosevelt both had Scotch-Irish mothers. Of the remaining twelve Presidents, Monroe, Hayes, Jackson, Polk, Buchanan, Johnson, Grant, Arthur, and McKinley (nine) have been of Scottish descent — the last seven largely Ulster Scotch. Jefferson was of Welsh ancestry ; Van Buren, Dutch ; and Garfield a mixture of Welsh and Huguenot French. This list is instructive, in showing that one-half our Presidents have been to a large extent of Celtic extraction. (For notes on the Genealogies of the Presidents, see Appendix N.)

Of the great statesmen connected with the period immediately following the Revolution, perhaps the four most eminent names are those of Thomas Jefferson, James Madison,' John Adams, and Alexander Hamilton : the first of Welsh origin, the second and third English, and the fourth Scotch. Next to these four may be mentioned the names of James Wilson, the Scotsman, whom Bancroft pronounces to have been the most learned civilian of the Constitutional Convention, than whom none were more influential, sagacious, or far-seeing ; John Jay, the French Huguenot ; John Dickinson, the English Quaker ; Roger Sherman, the English Connecticut compromiser ; and John Rutledge, the Ulster Scot. Of the members of the Convention of 1787, nine were graduates of Princeton, some of them pupils of the venerable Witherspoon, four were from Yale (including Livingston), three from Harvard, two from Columbia (including Hamilton), two from Glasgow, one from Oxford, one from Pennsylvania (Williamson), and five, six, or seven from William and Mary (including Blair and Jefferson — the latter of whom had there as his chief instructor Dr. William Small, the Scottish teacher from whom he imbibed so many of his own liberal views).' Of the college-bred men in the convention, therefore, it would seem that more than half were either of Scottish descent or educational training ; and this fact could not have been without some influence in the result of its deliberations.'

3

So far as their theories of government went, it would appear that the members of the convention were influenced more by the French writers than by the English exemplars. Montesquieu was the oracle of Washington ; and Madison and Jefferson freely acknowledged their debt to Scottish and Continental influences. Hamilton's allusion to the English system as a model, and his first plan of an elective monarchy, were both alike repugnant to the views of his colleagues. In the words of Yates, "he was praised by everybody, but supported by none."

The most judicial mind in the Constitutional Convention was undoubtedly that of the Scottish James Wilson, from Pennsylvania, the leader in the debates. Madison has been called the Father of the Constitution ; Wilson breathed into it the breath of life. "Of the fifty-five delegates," says McMaster, "Wilson was undoubtedly the best prepared, by deep and systematic study of the history and science of government, for the work that lay before him." His learning Wilson had in times past turned to excellent use, and in the Convention he became one of the most active members. None, with the exception of Gouverneur Morris, was so often on his feet during the debates, and none spoke more to the purpose. He supported direct popular suffrage and a single executive. He probably exercised more influence than any other single member in determining the character of the Constitution, and to him is due the honor of securing later the ratification of that instrument by the State of Pennsylvania. He clearly foresaw and warned his colleagues against the evils which would and did result from the pernicious New England principle of State sovereignty—a principle that, notwithstanding his earnest protests, was given undue acknowledgment and strength by the Connecticut compromise. This measure decided the question of representation in and election to the Senate.

Representing the most democratic State in the confederation, Wilson, more than any other one man in that assemblage, strove for the adoption of a purely democratic form of government, one that would be entirely of the people, wholly for the people, and truly by the people. Opposed to him at times were Roger Sherman, the New England leader, John Dickinson, the Pennsylvania Quaker who spoke for Delaware, Luther Martin, the leader of the Maryland delegation, Alexander Hamilton, the sole acting member from New York, John Rutledge, the foremost citizen of South Carolina, William Paterson, who voiced the sentiments of New Jersey, and even Edmund Randolph, the eloquent advocate of the Virginia Plan.

Wilson successfully refuted the arguments of his adversaries, and had his judgment been followed in every question as it was in most of them, the least satisfactory features of our Constitution would have been kept out, and the Republic might have been spared the loss of countless lives and treasure. From first to last, he was the chief opposer of the plan of equal representation of the States in the Senate, and did everything in his power to procure the election of senators by a direct vote of the people.[1]

From time to time claims have been made by overzealous members of the Presbyterian Church that the Federal Constitution was modelled upon their form of Church government — a system which requires each congregation to be represented in the general assemblies of that Church by delegates chosen by its own congregational members.[9] Evidently these claims are as far out of the way in one direction as are in another the similar claims to the effect that our Constitution was copied from that of England.[10] The Presbyterian Church was probably no more a factor in forming the constitutional government of the United States than was the church of the Congregationalist, the Lutheran, the Baptist, or the Quaker. The most that can be said to this end is that many men who had been brought up under Scottish ideals of freedom and duty took a prominent part in the Convention of 1787, and that the result of their deliberations bears a resemblance to the system of government laid down by the canons of the Scottish Church. This resemblance may result from the fact that the Presbyterian form of church government is a mean between the Congregational, or Puritan, plan—which involves the entire independence and sovereignty of each community,[11] and the Episcopalian, or Cavalier, plan—which would aim at the centralization of power in the hands of one man.

In Pennsylvania, the opposition to the adoption of the Constitution came chiefly from some of the Presbyterians ; and in Virginia, also, a large number of them stood behind Patrick Henry in his opposition to that instrument. At the same time, it is probable that if a vote could have been taken in the Presbyterian Church it would have shown many more of its adherents favorable to the Constitution than opposed to it. In the Pennsylvania convention held for its ratification, an examination of the list of delegates shows that considerably more than one half the number present and voting were of Presbyterian proclivities ; yet when the final vote for the adoption of the Constitution was taken, but twenty-three votes were cast against it, and forty-six in its favor. The Anti-Federalists in the Pennsylvania convention had for their leaders in the debate the three Scotch Presbyterians, Whitehill, Findley, and Smilie, who came from the counties of Cumberland, Westmoreland, and Fayette ; while the Federalists also looked for leadership to the two Scotch Presbyterians, Wilson and McKean. The final vote was as follows :

Yeas. — George Latimer, Benjamin Rush, Hilary Baker, James Wilson, Thomas McKean, William MacPherson, John Hunn, George Gray, Samuel Ashmead, Enoch Edwards, Henry Wynkoop, John Barclay, Thomas Yardley, Abraham Stout, Thomas Bull, Anthony Wayne, William Gibbons, Richard Downing, Thomas Cheyney, John Hannum, Stephen Chambers, Robert Coleman, Sebastian Graff, John Hubley, Jasper Yeates, Henry Slagle, Thomas Campbell, Thomas Hartley, David Grier, John Black, Benjamin Pedan, John Arndt, Stephen Balliet, Joseph Horsfield, David Deshler, William Wilson, John Boyd, Thomas Scott, John Neville, John Allison, Jonathan

Roberts, John Richards, F. A. Muhlenberg, James Morris, Timothy Picker-
ing, Benjamin Elliott.—Total, 46.

Nays. — John Whitehill, John Harris, John Reynolds, Robert Whitehill,
Jonathan Hoge, Nicholas Lutz, John Ludwig, Abraham Lincoln, John
Bishop, Joseph Hiester, James Martain, Joseph Powell, William Findley,
John Bard, William Todd, James Marshall, James Edgar, Nathaniel Bread-
ing, John Smilie, Richard Baird, William Brown, Adam Orth, John Andre
Hanna. — Total, 23.

A very full account of the proceedings of the Pennsylvania convention
was printed in 1888 by the Historical Society of Pennsylvania, under the
title, *Pennsylvania and the Federal Constitution*, edited by John Bach McMaster and Frederick D. Stone. The following statement from that work (pp.
21, 22) may enable us to comprehend some of the motives which influenced
the twenty-three members who comprised the opposition :

An examination of this list reveals the fact that the little band of malcontents was made up of all the delegates from the counties of Cumberland, Berks, Westmoreland, Bedford, Dauphin, Fayette, half of those from
Washington, half from Franklin, and John Whitehill, of Lancaster. The
reason is plain. The constitution proposed for the United States was in
many ways the direct opposite of the constitution of Pennsylvania. The
legislature of Pennsylvania consisted of a single house. The legislature
of the United States was to consist of two houses. The President of Pennsylvania was chosen by the Assembly. The President of the United States
was chosen by special electors. The constitution of Pennsylvania had a
bill of rights, provided for a body of censors to meet once each seven years
to approve or disapprove the acts of the legislature ; for a council to advise
the President ; for annual elections ; for rotation in office, all of which were
quite unknown to the proposed constitution for the United States. But the
Pennsylvania constitution of 1776 was the work of the Patriot party ; of this
party a very considerable number were Presbyterians ; and the great Presbyterian counties were Cumberland, Westmoreland, Bedford, Dauphin, and
Fayette. In opposing the new plan these men simply opposed a system of
government which, if adopted, would force them to undo a piece of work
done with great labor, and beheld with great pride and satisfaction. Every
man, therefore, who gave his vote for the ratification of the national constitution, pronounced his State constitution to be bad in form, and this its
supporters were not prepared to do. By these men, the refusal of the con·
vention to accept the amendments they offered was not regarded as ending
the matter. They went back to the counties that sent them more determined
than ever, but failed to gain to their side the great body of Presbyterians.

A perusal of the journal of the Federal Convention and of the various private accounts of the debates [12] will sufficiently indicate how far New England in 1787 was behind the middle colonies and Virginia in its conception
of what constitutes a democracy.

John Adams contended that the English Constitution was the "most
stupendous fabric of human invention" (*Works*, vol. iv., p. 358), a declaration which seems to have been the source of amusement to many of his

contemporaries.[13] Thomas Jefferson explained Mr. Adams's attitude on the subject in this way :

Adams had originally been a republican. The glamour of royalty and nobility during his mission to England had made him believe their fascination a necessary ingredient in government. . . . His book on the American Constitution having made known his political bias, he was taken up by the monarchical Federalists in his absence, and on his return to the United States he was made by them to believe that the general disposition of our citizens was favorable to monarchy.[14]

Even so usually careful a reader as John Fiske fails to recognize fully the various influences which were at work in the framing of the Constitution. In seeking to present what may appear to some to be rather too flattering a portrayal of the attitude and share of the New England delegates in the deliberations of the convention, he follows John Adams in ascribing everything to the supposed influence of the British Constitution. Fiske says :

The most curious and instructive point concerning the peculiar executive devised for the United States by the Federal Convention is the fact that the delegates proceeded upon a thoroughly false theory of what they were doing. . . . They were trying to copy the British Constitution, modifying it to suit their republican ideas ; but curiously enough, what they copied in creating the office of President was not the real English executive or prime minister, but the fictitious English executive, the sovereign. And this was associated in their minds with another profound misconception, which influenced all this part of their work. They thought that to keep the legislative and executive offices distinct and separate was the very palladium of liberty ; and they all took it for granted, without a moment's question, that the British Constitution did this thing. England, they thought, is governed by a King, Lords, and Commons, and the supreme power is nicely divided between the three, so that neither one can get the whole of it, and that is the safeguard of English liberty. So they arranged President, Senate, and Representatives to correspond, and sedulously sought to divide supreme power between the three, so that they might operate as checks upon each other. If either one should ever succeed in acquiring the whole sovereignty, then they thought there would be an end of American liberty.
. . . But in all this careful separation of the executive power from the legislative they went wide of the mark, because they were following a theory which did not truly describe things as they really existed. And that was because the English Constitution was, and still is, covered up with a thick husk of legal fictions which long ago ceased to have any vitality. . . .
In our time it has come to be perfectly obvious that so far from the English Constitution separating the executive power from the legislative, this is precisely what it does not do. In Great Britain the supreme power is all lodged in a single body : the House of Commons.[16]

Let us examine these statements in the light of Madison's and Hamilton's elucidation of the same subject and see if those two delegates—themselves originally strong admirers of the English Constitution—were really so entirely ignorant of its distinctions. On this subject Madison says :

One of the principal objections inculcated by the more respectable adversaries of the Constitution, is its supposed violation of the political maxim that the legislative, executive, and judiciary departments ought to be separate and distinct. In the structure of the Federal Government, no regard, it is said, seems to have been paid to this essential precaution in favor of liberty. The several departments of power are distributed and blended in such a manner as at once to destroy all symmetry and beauty of form ; and to expose some of the essential parts of the edifice to the danger of being crushed by the disproportionate weight of other parts. . . .

The oracle who is always consulted and cited on this subject is the celebrated Montesquieu. . . . Let us endeavor in the first place to ascertain his meaning on this point.

The British Constitution was to Montesquieu what Homer has been to the didactic writers on epic poetry. . . .

On the slightest view of the British Constitution, we must perceive that the legislative, executive, and judiciary departments are by no means totally separate and distinct from each other. . . .

From these facts, by which Montesquieu was guided, it may clearly be inferred that, in saying " there can be no liberty where the legislative and executive powers are united in the same person, or body of magistrates," or " if the power of judging be not separated from the legislative and executive powers," he did not mean that these departments ought to have no partial agency in, or no control over, the acts of each other. . . .

If we look into the constitutions of the several States, we shall find, notwithstanding the emphatical, and, in some instances, the unqualified terms in which this axiom has been laid down, that there is not a single instance in which the several departments of power have been kept absolutely separate and distinct. (James Madison, *Federalist*, No. xlvii.)

It was shown in the last paper, that the political apothegm there examined does not require that the legislative, executive, and judiciary departments should be wholly unconnected with each other. I shall undertake in the next place to show that, unless these departments be so far connected and blended as to give to each a constitutional control over the others, the degree of separation which the maxim requires, as essential to a free government, can never in practice be duly maintained. (*Ibid.*, No. xlviii).

Hamilton's comparison of the executives under the two constitutions is as follows :

I proceed now to trace the real characters of the proposed executive, as they are marked out in the plan of the Convention. This will serve to place in a strong light the unfairness of the representations which have been made in regard to it.

The first thing which strikes our attention is, that the executive authority, with few exceptions, is to be vested in a single magistrate. This will scarcely, however, be considered as a point upon which any comparison can be grounded ; for if, in this particular, there be a resemblance to the king of Great Britain, there is not less a resemblance to the Grand Signior, to the Khan of Tartary, to the Man of the Seven Mountains, or to the governor of New York. . . .

The President is to be the " commander-in-chief of the army and navy of the United States, and of the militia of the several States, when called into the actual service of the United States. He is to have power to grant reprieves and pardons for offences against the United States, except in cases of impeachment ; to recommend to the consideration of Congress such measures as he shall judge necessary and expedient ; to convene, on extraordinary occasions, both houses of the legislature, or either of them, and in case of disagreement between them with respect to the time of adjournment, to adjourn them to such time as he shall think proper ; to take care that the laws be faithfully executed ; and to commission all officers of the United States." In most of these particulars, the power of the President will resemble equally that of the king of Great Britain and of the governor of New York. The most material points of difference are these : — First: — The President will have only the occasional command of such part of the militia of the nation as by legislative provision may be called into the actual service of the Union. The king of Great Britain and the governor of New York have at all times the entire command of all the militia within their several jurisdictions. . . . Second : — The President is to be commander-in-chief of the army and navy of the United States. In this respect his authority would be nominally the same with that of the king of Great Britain, but in substance much inferior to it. It would amount to nothing more than the supreme command and direction of the military and naval forces, as first general and admiral of the confederacy ; while that of the British king extends to the declaring of war, and to the raising and regulating of fleets and armies ; all which by the Constitution under consideration would appertain to the legislature. . . . Third : — The power of the President in respect to pardons would extend to all cases except those of impeachment. The governor of New York may pardon in all cases, even in those of impeachment, except for treason and murder. . . . Fourth : — The President can only adjourn the national legislature in the single case of disagreement about the time of adjournment. The British monarch may prorogue or even dissolve the Parliament. . . .

Hence it appears, that, except as to the concurrent authority of the President in the article of treaties, it would be difficult to determine whether that magistrate would in the aggregate possess more or less power than the governor of New York. And it appears yet more unequivocally, that there is no pretence for the parallel which has been attempted between him and the king of Great Britain. But to render the contrast in this respect still more striking, it may be of use to throw the principal circumstances of dissimilitude into a closer group.

The President of the United States would be an officer elected by the people for four years : The king of Great Britain is a perpetual and hereditary prince.

The one would be amenable to personal punishment and disgrace : The person of the other is sacred and inviolable.

The one would have a qualified negative upon the acts of the legislative body : The other has an absolute negative.

The one would have a right to command the military and naval forces of the nation : The other, in addition to this right, possesses that of declaring war, and of raising and regulating fleets and armies by his own authority.

The one would have a concurrent power with a branch of the legislature in the formation of treaties : The other is the sole possessor of the power of making treaties.

The one would have a like concurrent authority in appointing to offices : The other is the sole author of all appointments.

The one can confer no privileges whatever : The other can make denizens of aliens, noblemen of commoners ; can erect corporations, with all the rights incident to corporate bodies.

The one can prescribe no rules concerning the commerce or currency of the nation : The other is in several respects the arbiter of commerce, and in this capacity can establish markets and fairs ; can regulate weights and measures ; can lay embargoes for a limited time ; can coin money ; can authorize or prohibit the circulation of foreign coin.

The one has no particle of spiritual jurisdiction : The other is the supreme head and governor of the national church.

What answer shall we give to those who would persuade us that things so unlike resemble each other ? The same that ought to be given to those who tell us that a government, the whole power of which would be in the hands of the elective and periodical servants of the people, is an aristocracy, a monarchy, and a despotism. (Alexander Hamilton, *Federalist*, No. lxix.)

It is only necessary to compare these statements with those of Mr. Fiske to see that some of our modern commentators on the Constitution have discovered a great many more things in that instrument than its authors were aware they had put there when drafting it.

Just what were the contributions of England to the American Constitution, is somewhat difficult to determine. There was certainly no manner of resemblance in form between the unwritten Constitution of Great Britain and the voluminous written instrument subscribed at Philadelphia by the delegates from the American colonies in September, 1787. It is true, the first ten amendments, proposed by Congress in 1789, may be said to constitute a Bill of Rights, having been adopted with that end in view. In form they do bear an outward resemblance to those limitations upon kings which, until recently, were regarded in England as the foundation and chief bulwark of liberty. But the vital substance of the ten amendments to our Constitution finds few counterparts in similar enunciations of the British legislature. In this day some of the minor provisions of these amendments, which no doubt seemed vital to our fathers, appear to us to be chiefly valuable as reminders of the excesses of tyranny from which they had escaped, and of the kind of constitutional government under which those excesses had been committed. As a matter of fact, the adoption of the first ten amendments to the American Constitution by Congress was due chiefly to popular clamor, and not from conviction on the part of the legislators that they were necessary in order to complete the Constitution. The framers of the original document almost without exception deemed most of the provisions of these amendments superfluous.

The declarations of the Bill of Rights passed by the English Parliament in 1689 were as follows :

1.   That the pretended power of suspending of laws, or the execution of laws by regal authority without consent of Parliament, is illegal.

2.   That the pretended power of dispensing with laws, or the execution of laws by regal authority, as it hath been assumed and exercised of late, is illegal.

3. That the commission for erecting the late court of commissioners for ecclesiastical causes, and all other commissions and courts of like nature, are illegal and pernicious.

4. That levying money for or to the use of the Crown, by pretence of prerogative, without grant of Parliament, for longer time or in other manner than the same is or shall be granted, is illegal.

5. That it is the right of subjects to petition the king, and all commitments and prosecutions for such petitioning are illegal.

6. That the raising or keeping a standing army within the kingdom in time of peace, unless it be with consent of Parliament, is against law.

7. That the subjects which are Protestants may have arms for their defence suitable to their conditions, and as allowed by law.

8. That elections of members of Parliament ought to be free.

9. That the freedom of speech, and debates or proceedings in Parliament, ought not to be impeached or questioned in any court or place out of Parliament.

10. That excessive bail ought not to be required, nor excessive fines imposed, nor cruel and unusual punishments inflicted.

11. That jurors ought to be duly impanelled and returned, and jurors which pass upon men in trials for high treason ought to be freeholders.

12. That all grants and promises of fines and forfeitures of particular persons before conviction are illegal and void.

13. And that for redress of all grievances, and for the amending, strengthening, and preserving of the laws, Parliament ought to be held frequently.

We have but to read over the amendments to the American Constitution and compare them with the foregoing English Bill of Rights to perceive how much they are opposed, both in letter and spirit, to the whole theory and practice of the science of government as applied by England during the whole of the eighteenth and the greater part of the nineteenth century. In doing this we realize that the amendments are not so much limitations restricting the operation of government under the American Constitution as they are eternal protests against a recurrence of the evils which had been suffered under the Constitution of Britain.

The first amendment provides that—

Congress shall make no law respecting an establishment of religion.

Or abridging the freedom of speech, or of the press.

The absence of the first of these provisions from the constitution of England, even to this day, is what, perhaps, more than any one thing else, led to the early and rapid British settlement of America, and drove to its shores such a large proportion of the bravest and noblest of the English and Scottish people. The necessity for the second provision was probably first impressed upon the minds of Americans by the prosecution, on information, of the printer, John Peter Zenger, for libelling the English governor of New York in 1735.

The second amendment announces that " A well-regulated militia being necessary to the security of a free state, the right of the people to keep and bear arms shall not be infringed." The English Bill of Rights permits only those who are Protestants to "have arms for their defence."

The third amendment provides that no soldier in time of peace shall be quartered in any house without the consent of the owner. This corresponds with a provision in the English Petition of Rights passed by Parliament and approved by Charles I. in 1628. The only provision in the English Bill of Rights bearing on this subject is, that a standing army shall not be kept within the kingdom without consent of Parliament.

The fourth amendment relates to the right of search or seizure, and requires all warrants for arrest or search to be specific, and supported by oath. There is no corresponding clause in the English Bill of Rights.

The fifth amendment requires all criminal indictments to be made by a grand jury ; and provides that no person shall for the same offence twice be put in jeopardy of life or limb ; nor be deprived of life, liberty, or property without due process of law. The nearest corresponding provision in the Bill of Rights is that contained in the eleventh clause, suggesting "That jurors ought to be duly impanelled and returned," instead of being creatures of the judge or prosecutor.

The sixth amendment gives the accused the right of a speedy trial before witnesses in criminal cases.

The seventh amendment assures the right of trial by jury. It appears from Olaus Wormius that this system was first introduced into Denmark by Regnerus, surnamed Lodborg, who began to reign in the year 820, from whom Ethelred of England is said to have borrowed it. It was Henry II. who brought into general use in England the trial by jury, afterwards incorporated in Magna Charta and confirmed by King John.

The eighth amendment is a counterpart of the tenth provision of the English Bill of Rights, prohibiting excessive bail or fines, or cruel and unusual methods of punishment.

The ninth amendment states that the enumeration in the Constitution of certain rights shall not be construed as a denial or disparagement of others "retained by the people." This, of course, would be an anomaly in the constitution of a monarchical government, where all rights possessed by the people have first to be granted by the supreme power, the Crown.

The tenth amendment reserves to the States and to the people all powers not delegated to the general government.

A comparison of all these amendments with the English Bill of Rights, therefore, shows that one only out of the ten is copied from the charter of British constitutional privileges. Nearly all the amendments show in themselves that they were devised and worded to meet conditions which were either pertinent or peculiar to American life and experience. To a large extent they form an embodiment of certain features of the common law as it had been applied in America to American conditions for more than a hundred years before 1787. The provisions for free speech, a free press, freedom of religion, freedom to bear arms, freedom from unwarranted search or seizure, freedom from indictment on secret information, and freedom from the usurpation of the people's natural rights, were all of American origin. They were attached to the Constitution because Americans had learned by bitter experience, in the century between the enactment of the English Bill of Rights and the adoption of the American Constitution, that their absence from the British charter led to numerous abuses and perversions of justice on the part of imported judges and governors.

In short, the difference between the British and the American Constitutions is a fundamental one. The former is a concession of privileges to the people by the rulers : the latter, a grant of authority by the people to the rulers.

But before leaving our original Scotch commentator, let us see just what his views were on the question of the kinship between the British and American Constitutions. Some expression of these views is to be found in No. lxxxiv. of the *Federalist :*

The several bills of rights, in Great Britain, form its constitution. . . .
It has been several times truly remarked, that bills of rights are, in their origin, stipulations between kings and their subjects, abridgments of prerogative in favor of privilege, reservations of rights not surrendered to the prince. Such was Magna Charta, obtained by the barons, sword in hand, from King John. Such were the subsequent confirmations of that charter by succeeding princes. Such was the Petition of Right assented to by Charles the First, in the beginning of his reign. Such also was the declaration of rights presented by the Lords and Commons to the Prince of Orange in 1688, and afterwards thrown into the form of an act of Parliament, called the Bill of Rights. It is evident, therefore, that according to their primitive signification, they have no application to constitutions professedly founded upon the power of the people, and executed by their immediate representatives and servants. Here, in strictness, the people surrender nothing ; and as they retain everything, they have no need of particular reservations. "We, the People of the United States, to secure the blessings of liberty to ourselves and our posterity, do ordain and establish this constitution for the United States of America." This is a better recognition of popular rights than volumes of those aphorisms which make the principal figure in several of our State bills of rights, and which would sound much better in a treatise of ethics than in a constitution of government.

While it may be a fact that the New England members, and especially the Massachusetts members of the convention, were imbued with the truly English idea of uniting the executive and legislative branches by making the executive head merely the creature of the legislature,[16] yet that this plan was not adopted is perhaps due to the efforts of those members whose birth or training had not been such as to bring them into accordance with English traditions. The idea of a representative form of government was novel to the men from New England, and contrary to their accustomed methods ; so that from the date of the first gathering it took several days' time to win them over to it. James Wilson, the Pennsylvania Scotsman, led in the opposition to the English and New England plan of vesting the executive power mainly in the legislature ; and to say, as Mr. Fiske does, that Wilson did not know at what he was aiming is to belittle the intelligence of the convention's clearest mind. The chief contribution of New England was the essentially English suggestion of compromise. The conditions under which one of these compromises was made were so unwise, though so characteristic of the typical English commercial spirit actuating its promoters, as to make it a matter of doubt whether on the whole the evil consequences arising from the compromises were not greater than the benefits which they secured. These conditions involved the demand for special privileges by the shipping interest of New England, and the prohibition of a tax on exports, coupled with the recognition of the right of the southern states to continue for twenty years the importation of negroes, and to maintain indefinitely the institution of slavery. A bargain was made between the two sections, and all three propositions were carried by the united votes of New England and all the southern states save Virginia.

Certainly, the one republican institution which forms the chief glory and boast of New England, that of local self-government, cannot be clearly traced back to England. Where it did originate is a disputed question. Mr. Douglas Campbell, in his inquiry into the origin of certain American institutions, has traced the beginnings of many of them to Holland. While there is some doubt as to the sufficiency of his proof in the case of township organization,[17] he has at least made it apparent that at the time the Pilgrims left Holland that country and its institutions were infinitely more analogous to the government established at Plymouth than to any like institutions in England.[18] In concluding his review of some of the Dutch contributions to America, Mr. Campbell sums them up as follows[19] :

Such are the leading institutions, political and legal, for which the American Republic is indebted, directly or indirectly, to the Netherland Republic, itself the heir of all the ages. Some of them, especially our written constitutions, have been greatly improved upon ; but at the time of their introduction into America few, if any, of them could be found in any country of Europe except the Netherlands. Having completed our sketch of their history, let us now bring them together, in order that we may appreciate their combined importance.

First comes the Federal Constitution, a written instrument as opposed to the unwritten English Constitution. Next are the provisions of this instrument placing checks on the power of the President in declaring war and peace, and in the appointment of judges and all important executive officers. Then comes the whole organization of the Senate — a mutable and yet a permanent body, representing independent bodies politic, and not caste in State and Church. After these features of the national system, but not less important, follow our State constitutions, our freedom of religion, our free press, our wide suffrage, and our written ballot. With these come the free schools, for boys and girls alike, the township system (with its sequence of local self-government in county and State), the independence of the judiciary, the absence of primogeniture, the subjection of land to execution for debt, and the system of recording deeds and mortgages. Added to these are our public prosecutors of crime in every county, the constitutional guarantee that every accused person shall have subpœnas for his witnesses and counsel for his defence, the reforms in our penal and prison system, the emancipation of married women, and the whole organization of our public charitable and reformatory work.

Taking these institutions all together, is there any cause for wonder that they excite astonishment among modern English scholars and statesmen who, looking beneath the mere surface resemblances of language and domestic habits, seek an explanation of the manifest difference between the people of England and a people in the United States assumed by them to be of the same blood? These observers, unlike some of our American writers, see plainly enough that our institutions are not inherited from England, however much we may have of English characteristics.

The simple fact is, that the whole theory of society and government in the two countries has always been radically different. Under such conditions, it was but natural that our forefathers should turn for their precedents, not to a monarchy or an aristocracy, but to a republic — a republic which was the beacon-light of the English Commonwealth, and whose people were our warmest unselfish sympathizers throughout the Revolution, as they also proved themselves to the Union cause during our late struggle for a national existence.

The latest writer on the subject, Mr. Sydney George Fisher, in his book on *The Evolution of the Constitution of the United States*, takes issue with Mr. Campbell and with all other writers who attribute the origin of American institutions for the most part to European influences. In an exhaustive examination of early trading and colonial charters and laws, he presents a great many facts tending to prove that the American system of government is not copied from others at all, but is the result of a slow and gradual period of evolution and growth which took place on this continent for two hundred years after 1584. This is both a philosophical and a satisfactory explanation of the origin of our institutions, and Mr. Fisher's book goes far toward making the reader believe that it is also the true one. In referring to English sources of the Constitution, this writer says [20]:

After reading the assertions of learned writers that our Constitution was modelled on the British government as it existed in 1787, I have sometimes turned to the words of the Constitution to see the resemblance, and have never been able to find it. As one reads along, sentence after sentence, everything seems so un-English and so original and so peculiar to our own locality that the mind is forced to the conclusion that it either grew up as a natural product of the soil or was invented offhand — struck off at a given time, as Mr. Gladstone says. I recommend to those who believe in the British model theory to adopt this simple plan : Read our Constitution, sentence by sentence, from beginning to end, and see how many sentences they can trace to an origin in the British government.

I do not deny that in a certain sense it is all English. . . . I would be the last person in the world to dispute the Anglo-Saxon influence in our civilization. But all this is very different from the dogma some wish to establish, that our Constitution was taken or copied from or suggested by the forms of the British government as it existed in 1787. . . .

In the first eleven amendments to the Constitution, a number of the provisions about trial by jury and freedom of speech were doubtless evolved from the experience of the race in England. But even these, as already shown, were worked out slowly and re-evolved on American soil. In the body of the Constitution itself — the political framework proper — there is little or nothing that can be traced to the forms of the British government as it existed in 1787 or at any other time for hundreds of years previous.

I do not deny that the framers of our Constitution considered and discusssed the forms of the British Constitution. But they considered them principally, as the minutes of their debates will show, for the purpose, or at any rate with the result, of avoiding them. They were intelligent men,—a large number of them were college-bred, — and they discussed the forms of government of all countries. They were not unmindful of the example of Holland, the democracies of Greece, the Roman republic and empire, and the free republics of the Middle Ages. They took what light they could from them all ; and I think as good an argument could be framed to show that they were guided by what they knew of classic antiquity as could be brought forward to prove that they were guided by the British Constitution.

But the foundation for all their final decisions, the basis which the forms of government in Europe merely illustrated or made more certain, was their own experience of nearly two hundred years with the colonial charters and constitutions and the constitutions of 1776. What they took from England went back through that two hundred years, and then not to the British government, but to the forms of the old trading charters. What had been envolved from the trading charters had been so long with us that it was completely Americanized, and it was valued by the framers of the Constitution for that reason, and because it had been tested by two hundred years of American life.

They did not commit the absurdity of skipping those two hundred years of their history, or of crossing an ocean and entering other countries to copy constitutions. . . . They. took their own experience as it was up to that date in the place and community for which they were making a frame of government. They made no skips or jumps, but went backward in the past directly from themselves and in their own line, taking for their guide that which was nearest to them and latest developed, provided it had ,been tested in that line of their own past.[1]

NOTES TO CHAPTER II.

[1] Douglas Campbell, *The Puritan in Holland, England, and America*, vol. ii., pp. 481, 487, 488.

[2] Bancroft speaks of him as the ablest man south of the Potomac.

[3] Marshall's mother was of the Scotch family of Keith.

[4] See *Autobiography of John Trumbull*, p. 12. New York, 1841.

[5] On the twenty-seventh of May [1776], Cary from the committee presented to the [Virginia] convention the declaration of rights which Mason had drafted. For the next fortnight the great truths which it proclaimed, and which were to form the groundwork of American institutions, employed the thoughts of the convention. One clause only received a material amendment. Mason had written that all should enjoy the fullest toleration in

the exercise of religion. . . . A young man, then unknown to fame, . . . proposed an amendment. He was James Madison, the son of an Orange County planter, bred in the school of Presbyterian dissenters under Witherspoon at Princeton, trained by his own studies, by meditative rural life in the Old Dominion, by an ingenuous indignation at the persecution of the Baptists, and by the innate principles of right, to uphold the sanctity of religious freedom. He objected to the word "toleration," because it implied an established religion, which endured dissent only as a condescension ; and as the earnestness of his convictions overcame his modesty, he proceeded to demonstrate that "all men are equally entitled to the free exercise of religion, according to the dictates of conscience." . . . This was the first achievement of the wisest civilian of Virginia.—Bancroft, vol. iv., p. 417.

[6] In the spring of 1760 I went to William and Mary College where I continued two years. It was my great good fortune, and what probably fixed the destinies of my life, that Dr. William Small of Scotland was then professor of Mathematics, a man profound in most of the useful branches of science, with a happy talent of communication, correct and gentlemanly manners, and an enlarged and liberal mind. He most happily for me became soon attached to me and made me his daily companion when not engaged in the school ; and from his conversation I got my first views of the expansion of science, and of the system of things in which we are placed.—Jefferson's *Autobiography*, p. 2.

[7] Bancroft, vol. vi., p. 211.

[8] See Appendix A (James Wilson and the Convention of 1787).

[9] Grouping together, then, these facts among others—the fact that Presbyterianism is in its own nature a system of pure representative republican government, and as such in striking harmony, both in form and spirit, with that of the State and nation ; that it has always been peculiarly odious to tyrants ; the numerous patriotic deliverances of the Synod of New York and Philadelphia and of some of the Presbyteries of our Church ; the fact that "the first voice publicly raised in America to dissolve all connection with Great Britain," was that of the Presbyterians, the Westmoreland County resolutions and the Mecklenburg Declaration ; the fact that Witherspoon, a Presbyterian of the most authentic type, represented in the Continental Congress the compact Presbyterianism of the land, and that (besides his other numerous and exceedingly important services) he threw the whole weight of his own personal influence and that of those he represented, first in favor of the Declaration of Independence and then in favor of the organization of the States into a confederate union—and we have some of the grounds upon which to base an estimate of the share which Presbyterians had in building and launching that national vessel that now rides so proudly upon the billows with forty millions of voyagers on board.—W. P. Breed, *Presbyterians and the Revolution*, pp. 177-179.

[10] See *Letters and Other Writings of James Madison*, vol. ii., p. 144; vol. iv., pp. 469–475, 480, 482 ; *Works of John Adams*, vol. iv., p. 358 ; *Works of Thomas Jefferson*, vol. ix., p. 97.

[11] The choice between a confederacy and a republic was very much the same as a choice between Congregationalism and Presbyterianism ; for Congregationalism is a confederacy of independent churches, but Presbyterianism is an organized representative and constitutional government. The Presbyterian form of government was familiar to the great mass of the inhabitants in the middle and southern colonies ; it was the form of government which Puritan Episcopacy has ever preferred. The Congregationalism of Connecticut and of other parts of New England tended in the same direction. There is no reason to doubt that Presbyterianism influenced the framers of the Constitution in their efforts to erect a national organism,—a constitutional republic. But Congregationalism also had its influence in defining the limitations of the supremacy of the general government and in the reservation of the sovereignty of the States in all those affairs which were not assigned to the general government. It is true, Presbyterianism was prepared for such limitations by the Scotch Barrier Act of 1697, which prevented hasty legislation by an appeal to all the Presbyteries

of the Church ; and still more by the persistent resistance of American Presbyterianism to any legislative power in the Synod, without the consent of the Presbyteries.   But the limitations of the general government in the American Constitution were beyond anything known to Presbyterianism before, and the reserved rights of the States were vastly in excess of any rights ever claimed or exercised by Presbyteries.   The American form of civil government was a happy combination of some of the best features presented in Presbyterianism and in Congregationalism.—Briggs, *American Presbyterianism*, pp. 356, 357.

[12] See Bancroft, vol. vi., book iii.

[13] See Madison's *Works*, vol. ii., p. 144 ; vol. iv.,   pp. 469–475, 480–482.

[14] *Writings of Thomas Jefferson*, vol. ix., p. 97.

[15] *Critical Period of American History*, p. 289.

[16] See extracts from debates in the Constitutional Convention, and particularly the words of Sherman and Gerry (Appendix A).

[17] Campbell, *The Puritan in Holland, England, and America*. vol. ii., pp. 426–430.

[18] *Ibid.*, vol. ii., chap. xxii.

[19] *Ibid.*, vol. ii., pp. 465–467 (by permission of Messrs. Harper & Brothers).

[20] *The Evolution of the Constitution of the United States*, pp. 90–93.

[21] See Appendix B (Pennsylvania's Formative Influence).

CHAPTER III

THE SCOTCH-IRISH IN AMERICAN POLITICS

IN more recent years Scotland's contribution to the United States has been no less remarkable in the number and high standing of the Scottish names which appear on America's Roll of Honor than it was in the early days of the Republic.

Starting with the governors of the States and Territories, a brief examination of the civil lists published in Lanman's *Biographical Annals of the Civil Government*, a semi-official work, shows that up to the year in which that book was printed (1886) there have been about half a dozen more than one thousand State or Territorial governors in office since 1789. Of these, judging from the names alone, more than two hundred are of evident Scottish descent, and it is altogether probable that if a closer inspection were to be made a great many more would be found of that race, although bearing names alike common to Scotland and England. In connection with the same subject it may be remarked that, of the colonial governors sent from England to the American colonies before 1776, and of the provincial governors from that time to 1789, upwards of forty were of Scottish blood, among them being Robert Hunter (1710), William Burnett (1720), John Montgomerie (1728), John Hamilton (1736), Cadwallader Colden (1760), John, Earl of Dunmore (1770), James Robertson (1780), all of New York ; Robert Barclay (1682), John Skene (1686), Lord Neil Campbell (1687), Andrew Hamilton, John Hamilton (1736), William Livingston (1776), all of New Jersey ; Andrew Hamilton (1701), Sir William Keith (1717), Patrick Gordon (1726), James Logan (1736), James Hamilton (1748), Joseph Reed (1778), all of Pennsylvania ; and all, except the one last named, governors of Delaware also ; John McKinley (1777), of Delaware ; Alexander Spotswood (1710), William Gooch (?) (1727), Robert Dinwiddie (1752), John Campbell (1756), John Blair (1767), William Nelson (1770), Lord Dunmore (1772), Patrick Henry (1776), Thomas Nelson (1781), all of Virginia ; William Drummond (1663), Gabriel Johnston (1734), Matthew Rowan (1753), Alexander Martin (1782), Samuel Johnston (1788), all of North Carolina ; Joseph Morton (?) (1682), Richard Kirk (1684), James Moore (1719), William Campbell (1775), John Rutledge (1779), all of South Carolina ; William Erwin (1775), Archibald Bulloch (1776), John Houston (1778), Edward Telfair (1786), all of Georgia ; and George Johnstone (1763), of Florida.

Of the State governors from 1789 to 1885, the Scotch furnished to Pennsylvania nearly one-half her chief executives ; to Virginia, nearly one-third ; to North Carolina, more than one-fourth ; to South Carolina, nearly

4

one-third ; to Georgia, more than one-half ; to Alabama, more than one-fifth ; to Mississippi, about one-fifth ; to Louisiana, more than one-fifth ; to Texas, about one-third ; to Tennessee, nearly one-half ; to Kentucky, about one-third ; to Ohio, one-half ; to Indiana, more than one-third ; to Illinois, nearly one-third ; to Missouri, nearly one-half.

Among other celebrated Scottish characters of colonial times may be mentioned Captain William Kidd, the notorious pirate, Major Richard Stobo, and possibly Sir William Johnson, Great Britain's celebrated Indian agent in the Mohawk valley.

Of Scotch descent, also, on both sides of his house, was General George Rogers Clark, the record of whose daring and successful campaigns north of the Ohio River in 1778, is not surpassed in American history. To this man alone the United States owes that part of its territory lying between the Ohio and Mississippi rivers ; and had it not been for the conquest of this empire from the British by Clark and his Scotch-Irish soldiers, the States of Ohio, Indiana, Michigan, Illinois, Iowa, Wisconsin, and Minnesota might have been to-day a portion of the Dominion of Canada.[1]

In the naval wars of 1776 and later, we find among the most celebrated commanders the following of Scottish birth or descent :   John Paul Jones, Samuel Nicholson, Richard Dale, Alexander Murray, Charles Stewart, James Barron, John Rodgers, Sr., John Rodgers, Jr., Thomas McDonough, Matthew Galbraith Perry, Oliver Hazard Perry,[2] Franklin Buchanan.

Some well-known border heroes of Scottish descent, besides George Rogers Clark, were Adam and Andrew Poe, Samuel Brady, Captain Jack, Simon Kenton, Kit Carson, David Crockett, and Samuel Houston.

Among the American generals and warriors since the Revolution none rank higher than Andrew Jackson, Winfield Scott, Hugh Brady, Zachary Taylor, U. S. Grant, James B. McPherson, George B. McClellan, J. E. Johnston, Stonewall Jackson, J. E. B. Stuart, James Longstreet, John A. Rawlins, Robert H. Milroy, Lew Wallace, Irvin McDowell, Q. A. Gilmore, Hugh Kilpatrick, Francis P. Blair, John F. Reynolds, Fitz-John Porter, David Hunter, William H. Jackson, Alexander W. Campbell, David Bell, William Birney, Horace Porter, John A. McNulta, Alexander Hays, Lafayette McLaws, D. M. Gregg, Schuyler Hamilton, John J. Abercrombie, William H. Lytle, John B. S. Todd, Winfield S. Hancock, Clement A. Finley, Isaac Ridgeway Trimble, James Ronald Chalmers, George A. McCall, John A. McClernand, Nathan B. Forrest, Benjamin McCulloch, John B. Magruder, John B. Gordon, John A. Logan, Theodore Roosevelt,[3] Henry W. Lawton, Frederick Funston, and Daniel, George W., Robert L., Alexander McD., Daniel, Jr., Edwin S., Edward M., and Anson G. McCook, all of Scottish blood.

In American politics this race has been represented by such individuals as Thomas H. Benton, John C. Calhoun,[4] Jefferson Davis, James G. Blaine, Thomas A. Hendricks, Joseph E. McDonald, John Bell, Alexander H.

Stephens, Samuel Randall, J. C. Breckenridge, John G. Carlisle, Simon Cameron, the Livingstons of New York, William B. Allison, John B. Gibson, Matthew S. Quay, Calvin S. Brice, Marcus A. Hanna, Whitelaw Reid, J. Sterling Morton, Wayne McVeagh, Chauncey Mitchell Depew, Robert Todd Lincoln, Stephen A. Douglas, Adlai E. Stevenson, Stephen B. Elkins, Daniel S. Lamont, Arthur P. Gorman, William McKinley.[5]

In the Presidents' Cabinets, the Scotch have been represented as Secretaries of State by Edward Livingston, Louis McLane, John Forsyth, John C. Calhoun, James Buchanan, Jeremiah S. Black, James G. Blaine, John Hay ; Secretaries of the Treasury, Alexander Hamilton, George W. Campbell, Alexander J. Dallas, William H. Crawford, Louis McLane, Thomas Ewing, Thomas Corwin, James Guthrie, Howell Cobb, Salmon P. Chase, Hugh McCulloch ; Secretaries of War, Henry Knox, James McHenry, John Armstrong, James Monroe, William H. Crawford, George Graham, John C. Calhoun, James Barbour, Peter B. Porter, John Bell, James M. Porter, George W. Crawford, Jefferson Davis, Simon Cameron, U. S. Grant, James D. Cameron, George W. McCrary, Alexander Ramsey, Robert Todd Lincoln, Daniel S. Lamont ; Secretaries of the Navy, Paul Hamilton, Thomas W. Gilmer, William A. Graham, John P. Kennedy, James C. Dobbin, George M. Robeson, Nathan W. Goff ; Secretaries of the Interior, Thomas Ewing, Alexander H. H. Stuart, Robert McClelland, James Harlan, Henry M. Teller ; Postmasters-General, John McLean, James Campbell, Montgomery Blair, Frank Hatton ; Attorneys-General, John Breckenridge, Felix Grundy, Jeremiah S. Black, James Speed, John W. Griggs ; United States Senators, (since 1860), Blair (2), Cameron (2), Cockrell, Gibson, Logan, McMillan, McPherson, Mitchell (2), Stewart, Teller, McEnery, Caffery, Butler, McLaurin, Cannon, Vance, Johnston, Houston, Bailey, Blaine, Burnside, Gordon, Sharon, Armstrong, Beck, Wallace, Thurman, Patterson (2), Oglesby, McDonald (2), McCreery, Brownlow, Caldwell, Kelly, Ramsey, Robertson, Scott (2), Tipton, Corbett, Harlan, Hill, Pomeroy, Wilson, Ross, Dixon, Davis (2), Guthrie, Grimes, Welch, Cowan, McDougall, Henderson, Hendricks, Nesmith, Carlisle, Breckenridge, Kennedy, Johnson, Hunter, Hemphill, Douglas, Morton, McComas, Ross, Clark, Foster, McCumber, Hanna, Culberson, Hamilton (2), Mills, Kyle, McBride, Brice, Lindsay, Blackburn, Palmer, Cullom, Call, Kenney, Beveridge, and others ; Speakers of the House, John Bell, James K. Polk, Robert M. T. Hunter, Howell Cobb, James L. Orr, James G. Blaine, Michael C. Kerr, Samuel J. Randall, John G. Carlisle, David B. Henderson.

In literature may be named Washington Irving, Edgar Allan Poe, Herman Melville, Joel Chandler Harris, Lew Wallace, Marion Crawford,Thomas Nelson Page, Maurice Thompson ; in art, Gilbert Stuart, J. McNeil Whistler, Walter MacEwen, George Inness, J. Q. A. Ward, James Wilson McDonald, James D. Smillie, Alexander Doyle, E. F. Andrews, Thomas Crawford, Frederick MacMonnies, John W. Alexander ; in music, Edward MacDowell.

In practical science, whether the credit for the invention of the telegraph be given to Charles Morrison, to Joseph Henry, or to Samuel Finley Morse, each of whom contributed towards it, the honor still belongs to the Scotch. Edison's mother was Mary Elliott, of Scottish blood ; and John Ericsson had in his veins a strain of the same virile current. Likewise, William Henry, James Rumsey, and Robert Fulton, who each had a share in the invention of the steamboat, were all three Scotch ; as well as Alexander Graham Bell and Elisha Gray, the inventors of the telephone, and the McCormicks, who did so much for the improvement of harvesting machinery. Drs. D. Hayes Agnew and Frank Hamilton the eminent surgeons, Alexander Wilson the ornithologist, and Asa Gray the botanist, all of Scottish descent, are also ranked among the greatest in their respective professions.

In no departments of American civil life, however, is the Scottish influence more marked and dominating than in those of the judiciary and the press. The interpretation of law in America has been chiefly the work of non-English judges ; and perhaps it is not too much to say that the distinctive character of American jurisprudence is due to the preponderating influence of men of Celtic blood at the bench and bar.

Of the fifty judges of the United States Supreme Court from 1789 to 1882, we find not more than twenty-two of probable English blood ; Jay and Duval, of French ; Marshall, of Welsh and Scotch ; Rutledge, Wilson, Blair, two Johnsons, Paterson, Moore, Livingston, Todd, Thompson, Trimble, McLean, Barbour, McKinley, Daniel, Nelson, Grier, Campbell, Miller, Davis, Harlan, of Scottish ; and Wayne, Catron, and Chase of mixed descent.

The first newspaper printed in America—the *Boston News-Letter*—was the enterprise of a Scotchman bearing the characteristic name of John Campbell.   In recent times, among editors of the first rank, we find as representatives of the Scottish race : James Gordon Bennett, Horace Greeley, Henry W. Grady, Murat Halstead, Samuel Medary, Joseph Medill, James W. Scott, Alexander K. McClure, John A. Cockerill, Whitelaw Reid, Washington and John R. McLean, Joseph B. McCullagh, Richard Smith, John Russell Young, Henry Watterson, "Richelieu" Robinson, Beriah Wilkins, Robert W. Patterson.

Among America's prominent business men of Scottish descent may be named A. T. Stewart, Robert Stuart, Peter Cooper, John I. Blair, John Crerar, James Lenox, Andrew Carnegie, John Davison Rockefeller.

Daniel Webster, the most brilliant statesman New England has given to the country, was likewise not of English origin in the paternal line, but came from the New Hampshire Scotch.[6]

In view of these facts can it not with propriety be contended that the Scottish race, in proportion to its relative strength in the New World, has contributed to America a vastly greater number of her leaders in thought and action than has any other ?

NOTES TO CHAPTER III.

[1] A list of the officers of the Illinois Regiment and of the Crockett Regiment :
Brig.-General — George Rogers Clark. Lieut.-Col. — John Montgomery. Majors
— Thomas Quirk, George Slaughter. Captains — John Bailey, Richard Brashear, Abraham
Chaplin, Benjamin Fields, Robert George, John Gerault, Richard Harrison, Abraham Kellar,
Richard McCarty, John Rogers, Benjamin Roberts, Mark Thomas, Isaac Taylor, Robert
Todd, John Williams. Lieutenants — Richard Clark, William Clark, James Merriweather,
James Montgomery, James Robertson, William Roberts, Joseph Saunders, Jarret Williams.
Ensigns — William Asher, Laurence Slaughter. Cornet — John Thurston.
Crockett's Regiment : Lieut.-Col. — Joseph Crockett. Major — George Walls. Surgeon — Charles Greer. Captains — John Chapman (killed), William Cherry, John Kerney, Benjamin Kinley (died), Peter Moore, Abraham Lipton, Thomas Young. Ensigns —
Henry Daring, Samuel Ball Greene, Hugh McGavock.
For George Rogers Clark's descent, see p. 30, note 11.
The names of the following Scotch-Irishmen and others are taken from a list of the
" Noncommissioned Officers and Soldiers of the Illinois Regiment and the Western Army
under the Command of General George Rogers Clark." The full list appears in the *Virginia Historical Magazine*, vol. i., pp. 131–141 :
John Allen, Sr., John Allen, Jr., John Anderson, Samuel Allen (Sergeant), David Allen,
Isaac Allen, Francis Adams, Wm. Bell, John Blair, David Bailey, Richard Breeden, James
Brown (S.), Wm. Berry, James Bentley, John Bentley, Lon Brown, James Baxter (Corporal),
J. B. Biron (S.), Colin Brown, Wm. Barry, Thos. Benton or Bernton, John Breeden (S.),
Samuel Bird, Wm. Bowen (C.), John Barber, Robert Burnett (died), James Bryant, George
Burk, John Burris, John Boyles, Ebenezer Bowing, Asher Brown, Adam Bingoman, Samuel
Blackford, Simon Burney, Lewis Brown, Collin Brown, Daniel Bolton, John Clark, Andrew
Clark, Richard Chapman, Edward Chapman, Wm. Chapman, Patrick Cornelia, Wm.
Crassley, John Cowan, Andrew Cannon, James Curry, Patrick Conroy, Joseph Cooper,
Ramsey Cooper, Thomas Connolly, John Conn, George Campbell (S.), John Campbell, John
Cowdry, Andrew Cowan, Daniel Calvin, James Corder, Rice Curtis, Ellick Chamber,
Edward Cockran, George Cockran, Dennis Coheron, James Cameron (C.), Daniel Cowgill,
James Cox, Andrew Cocles, James Dawson, James Dawson, John Doyle, Benj. Duncan,
Archibald Duncan, Charles Duncan, David Duncan, Nimrod Duncan, Joseph Duncan,
Samuel Duncan, John Duff, Joseph Donon, Abraham Frazier (S.), Henry Foster, John
Grimes, John Gordon, John George, John Garret, Samuel Gibbons, David Glenn, James
Graham, Samuel Humphries, Thomas Hays, Barney Higgons, Miles Hart, James Hays,
Wm. Hall, Wm. Huin, Andrew Hendrix, John Johnston, Edward Johnston, Samuel
Johnston, Thos. Jamison (S.), David Kennedy, James Kincaid, James Kirkley, Thomas
Kirk, Wm. Kerr, Robert Kidd, George Key, Thomas Key, John Lasley, Peter Laughlin,
John Levinston, Richard Lovell, Benjamin Lewis, Jacob Lyon, John Lyons, Wm. Long,
Pleasant Lockhert, Archibald Lockhart, Hugh Logan, James Lewis, Edward Murray, John
Montgomery, Francis McDermot, John Moore (S.), John McMickle, Abraham Miller (C.),
John Montgomery, Wm. Montgomery, Chas. McLockland, Edward Matthews (S.), John
McGuire, James McIntosh, Patrick Marr (C. and S.), John McMichaels, James McMullen,
Patrick McClure, Wm. Merriweather, John Miller, Charles Martin, David McDonald, John
Murphy, Thomas Murray, Thomas McClain, Wm. Munrony (S.), Sylvestor Munrony,
Thomas McQuiddy, Thomas McDaniel, James McDonald, Elijah Martin, James McKin,
Solomon Martin, John McKinney, John Moore, Thomas Moore, Thomas McDonald, Wm.
Marshall, John McGann, Enock Nelson, Moses Nelson, John Nelson, John Neal, Ebenezer
Ozburn, John Patterson, James Potter, Edward Parker, Wm. Patterson, David Pagan,
Ebenezer Potter, Samuel Pickens, John Ross, Andrew Ryan, Lazarus Ryan, James Ramsay,
John Robertson (S.), James Ross (S.), John Rice (S.), David Rogers (S.), Joseph Rogers,

Larkin Rutherford, Richard Robinson, Joseph Ross (C.), Benjamin Russell, Robert Randal, Patrick Riley, David Smith, Randal Smith, Joseph Smith, John Spencer, Wm. Shannon, John Stephenson (S.), Samuel Stephenson, James Thompson, James Taylor, Edward Taylor, Wm. Thompson, Daniel Tygard, Thomas Taylor, Robert Whitehead, Wm. Whitehead, Randal White, Robert White, David Wallace, Wm. Wilkerson, John Wilson, Thomas Wray.

[2] " Going out from Put-in-Bay the tenth of September, 1813, with his whole squadron, Perry met the British fleet in a memorable naval contest.   Himself a young man of twenty-eight years of age, he was opposed to one of Nelson's veterans.   Himself a Scotch-Irishman, his opponent, Captain Robert H. Barclay, was a Scotchman.   The engagement was hot, but at three o'clock in the afternoon the gallant Perry saw the British flag hauled down.   For the first time since she had created a navy, Great Britain lost an entire squadron.   "We have met the enemy and they are ours," is the familiar line in which Perry announced his victory, in a despatch to General William Henry Harrison.   Commodore Perry's mother was Sarah Wallace Alexander, a Scotch woman from the north of Ireland. She became the mother of five sons, all of whom were officers in the United States Navy. Two daughters married Captain George W. Rogers and Dr. William Butler of the United States Navy.   Dr. Butler was the father of Senator Matthew Galbraith Butler, of South Carolina.   After the victory at Lake Erie, some farmers in Rhode Island declared, such was the estimation in which they held this woman, that it was 'Mrs. Perry's victory.' "—S. S. Green, *The Scotch-Irish in America.*

[3] Theodore Roosevelt's father, bearing the same name, was of Dutch descent ; his mother, a native of Georgia, of Scottish.   Theodore Roosevelt, Sr., married Martha Bulloch on December 22, 1853.   Martha Bulloch's parents were Major James Stephens Bulloch and Martha Stewart, the latter a daughter of Daniel Stewart (an officer of the Revolution) and Susan Oswald.   James Stephens Bulloch was a son of James and Ann Irvine Bulloch, the latter a daughter of Dr. John and Ann Elizabeth Baillie Irvine.   James Bulloch (b. 1765 ; d. Feb. 9, 1806) was a son of Archibald and Mary De Veaux Bulloch, the latter a daughter of James De Veaux, of French Huguenot descent, and senior judge of the King's Court in the province of Georgia.   Archibald Bulloch was president and commander-in-chief of the colony of Georgia, 1776–1777 ; delegate to the Continental Congress of 1775, and elected to the one of 1776 ; signed the first constitution of the State of Georgia as president ; and died in 1777.   He was a son of James and Jean Stobo Bulloch, the latter a daughter of Rev. Archibald Stobo, who sailed from Scotland with the Darien colonists in 1698, and subsequently (in 1700) settled at Charleston, S. C.   James Bulloch, Sr., b. about 1701, in Scotland, came from Glasgow to Charleston about 1728, where, in 1729, he married Jean Stobo. The Bullochs appear to belong to Baldernock, in Stirlingshire, where the name appears on the records for some four hundred years back.   See *A History and Genealogy of the Families of Bellinger and De Veaux*, etc., by Joseph Gaston Bulloch, Savannah, 1895.

[4] John C. Calhoun was the grandson of James Calhoun, who is said to have emigrated from Donegal, Ireland, in 1733 (*John C. Calhoun*, by Dr. H. von Holst, p. 8).   John C. Calhoun was the son of Patrick Calhoun, whom James Parton, in his *Famous Americans of Recent Times*, speaks of (pp. 117, 118) as a Scotch-Irishman, who, with Andrew Jackson and Andrew Johnson, other Scotch-Irishmen, illustrates well the " North of Ireland " character. Patrick Calhoun was a Presbyterian like his father (J. Randolph Tucker, in article " John Caldwell Calhoun," in Appleton's *Cyclopædia of American Biography*).   In 1770, Patrick Calhoun married (von Holst. p. 8) Martha Caldwell, who, says John S. Jenkins in his *Life of John Caldwell Calhoun* (p. 21), was a daughter of a Scotch-Irish Presbyterian, who, according to Tucker, was an emigrant from Ireland.

[5] Henry Clay has been classed with the Scotch-Irish by Mr. Elbert Hubbard.

[6] Lodge, *Daniel Webster*, p. 5 ; Curtis, *Life of Daniel Webster*, vol. i., p. 2.

CHAPTER IV

NEW ENGLAND NOT THE BIRTHPLACE OF AMERICAN LIBERTY

ANOTHER instance of the effect of continuous advertising by New England's historians of the superlative and exclusive patriotism of her sons may be noted in the claims so frequently made, that the American people were first prepared for the idea of resistance to the arbitrary measures of Great Britain, and for independence, by a few of the citizens of Massachusetts. These claims seem first to have been given prominence by the discussion that arose among some of the surviving leaders of the Revolutionary period, in 1817 and 1818, upon the appearance of William Wirt's *Life of Patrick Henry.* On page 41 of that book,[1] the biographer cites Thomas Jefferson as saying that " Mr. Henry certainly gave the first impulse to the ball of the Revolution."[2]

This statement by Mr. Wirt led to several appeals being made to Mr. Jefferson by correspondents from New England for its verification ; and in answering such communications, its distinguished author uniformly disclaimed any thought of the general application of his remark to the country at large, and very properly limited its range to the development of the Revolutionary movement within his own State.

The spirit of sectional pride had been aroused, however, and an extensive epistolary discussion followed, in which some of the foremost citizens of the Republic took part. New England's chief advocate was John Adams, doubtless the original " Honest John " of American politics. With his natural garrulousness, he had written at great length the history of the origin of independence in Massachusetts, going into minute detail to show how it all developed from the Boston speech made by James Otis in 1761. While Mr. Adams's report of and commentary upon this famous argument, written so many years after it occurred, reminds the reader somewhat of the eloquent and lengthy speeches which the Roman and mediæval historians put into the mouths of warrior heroes about to engage in some great battle, there can be no doubt as to the general correctness of his statements regarding the effect of Otis's words in crystallizing public sentiment in Massachusetts and turning it definitely against the encroaching tendencies of Great Britain's commercial policy. It goes without saying, that the beginning of resistance on the part of John Adams dates from that time. His description of the incident, given in a letter to William Tudor, written March 29, 1817, begins as follows[3] :

The scene is the Council Chamber in the old Town House in Boston. The date is in the month of February, 1761. . . .

In this chamber, round a grate fire, were seated five Judges with Lieu-tenant-Governor Hutchinson at their head as Chief Justice, all arrayed in their new fresh, rich robes of scarlet English broadcloth ; in their large cambric bands, and immense judicial wigs. In this chamber were seated at a long table all the barristers-at-law of Boston, and of the neighboring county of Middlesex, in gowns, bands, and tie wigs. . . . In this chamber you have now the stage and the scenery ; next follows a narrative of the subject. . . .

When the British ministry received from General Amherst his despatches announcing the conquest of Montreal, and the consequent annihilation of the French government in America, in 1759, they immediately conceived the design and took the resolution of conquering the English colonies, and sub-jecting them to the unlimited authority of Parliament. With this view and intention they sent orders and instructions to the collector of customs in Boston, Mr. Charles Paxton, to apply to the civil authority for writs of assist-ance, to enable the custom-house officers, tide-waiters, land-waiters, and all, to command all sheriffs and constables to attend and aid them in breaking open houses, stores, shops, cellars, ships, bales, trunks, chests, casks, pack-ages of all sorts, to search for goods, wares, and merchandises, which had been imported against the prohibition or without paying taxes imposed by certain acts of Parliament, called the acts of trade. . . .

Now for the actors and performers. Mr. Gridley argued with his charac-teristic learning, ingenuity, and dignity. . . . Mr. Thacher followed him on the other side, and argued with the softness of manners, the ingenuity and cool reasoning, which were remarkable in his amiable character.

But Otis was a flame of fire !—with a promptitude of classical allusions, a depth of research, a rapid summary of historical dates and events, a pro-fusion of legal authorities, a prophetic glance of his eye into futurity, and a torrent of impetuous eloquence, he hurried away everything before him. American Independence was then and there born ; the seeds of patriots and heroes were then and there sown, to defend the vigorous youth, the *non sine Diis animosus infans*. Every man of a crowded audience appeared to me to go away, as I did, ready to take arms against Writs of Assistance. Then and there was the first scene of opposition to the arbitrary claims of Great Britain. Then and there the child Independence was born. In fifteen years, namely, in 1776, he grew up to manhood, and declared himself free.[4]

After reading Mr. Wirt's *Life of Patrick Henry*, and comparing the date of his famous speech before the Virginia Assembly with that of James Otis's argument against the Writs of Assistance, Mr. Adams valiantly took up his pen in defence of the honor of his native State, and at once indited a notice of infringement to the panegyrist of the Virginia orator in this fashion[5] :

I envy none of the well-merited glories of Virginia, or any of her sages or heroes. But, Sir, I am jealous, very jealous, of the honor of Massachu-setts.

The resistance to the British system for subjugating the colonies began in 1760, and in the month of February, 1761, James Otis electrified the town of Boston, the province of Massachusetts Bay, and the whole continent more than Patrick Henry ever did in the whole course of his life. If we must have panegyric and hyperbole, I must say that if Mr. Henry was Demos-thenes and Mr. Richard Henry Lee, Cicero, James Otis was Isaiah and Eze-kiel united.[6]

Basing chiefly on this, and on other hasty and ill-considered statements of a like tenor, made at about the same time, New England's historians, as a rule, have since accepted as final and authoritative this claim of her foremost Revolutionary statesman as to the beginnings in America of resistance to the repressive measures of Great Britain ; and with one voice they ascribe to Massachusetts, and to Massachusetts alone, the inauguration of the movement which led to final independence.

That the deliberate judgment of Adams did not confirm the drawing of such a broad conclusion from the statement first put forth by himself under the impulse of feelings aroused by wounded State pride, may be reasonably demonstrated by an examination of some of his later writings.

As tending to show this more impartial attitude on the part of the amiable and impulsive Adams, his correspondence with Madison in the same year may be cited, in which some observations of the latter afford a convincing proof, as well of Adams's ultimately just conception as of the insufficiency of any view of the matter in which the range is limited to individuals. Madison's letter to Adams of August 7, 1818, is in part as follows [7] :

> Your remark is very just on the subject of Independence. It was not the offspring of a particular man or a particular moment. . . . Our forefathers brought with them the germ of Independence in the principle of self-taxation. Circumstances unfolded and perfected it.
> The first occasion which aroused this principle was, if I can trust my recollection, the projected union at Albany in 1754, when the proposal of the British Government to reimburse its advances for the colonies by a parliamentary tax on them was met by the letter from Dr. Franklin to Governor Shirley, pointing out the unconstitutionality, the injustice, and the impolicy of such a tax.
> The opposition and discussions produced by the Stamp and subsequent Acts of Parliament, made another stage in the growth of Independence. . . .

Franklin's letters to Governor Shirley written in December, 1754, to which reference is made by Madison, contain such expressions as these [8] :

> I apprehend that excluding the people of the colonies from all share in the choice of the grand council will give extreme dissatisfaction, as well as the taxing them by act of Parliament, where they have no representation. . . .
> That it is supposed an undoubted right of Englishmen not to be taxed but by their own consent, given through their representatives.
> That the colonies have no representatives in Parliament.
> That to propose taxing them by Parliament, and refuse them the liberty of choosing a representative council to meet in the colonies and consider and judge of the necessity of any general tax and the quantum, shows a suspicion of their loyalty to the Crown, or of their regard for their country, or of their common sense and understanding which they have not deserved.

In Pennsylvania, the matter of taxation had been a constant source of dispute between the Assembly and the Proprietary government for many years prior to 1760. In that State, more than ten years before the battle of

Lexington, an armed uprising took place on the part of the Scotch-Irish against the principle of taxation without representation or protection.

The inciting causes of this hostile demonstration against the provincial government of Pennsylvania grew out of the continued and studied neglect, by the Quaker oligarchy then controlling the Pennsylvania Assembly, of that primary essential of all organized governments, namely, the ability and disposition to defend its citizens against the murderous invasions of an armed foe. The Quaker government not only failed to furnish protection to its citizens, but made a virtue of its own shortcomings in that respect.

Along the thinly settled borders, in 1762–63, two thousand persons had been killed or carried off, and nearly an equal number of families driven from their homes. "The frontier people of Pennsylvania," says Parkman, "goaded to desperation by long-continued suffering, were divided between rage against the Indians, and resentment against the Quakers, who had yielded them cold sympathy and inefficient aid. The horror and fear, grief and fury, with which these men looked upon the mangled remains of friends and relatives, set language at defiance." On one occasion, the frontiersmen sent to Philadelphia a wagon laden with the mangled corpses of their friends and relatives, who had fallen by Indian butchery. These were carried along the streets, with many people following, cursing the Indians, and also the Quakers because they would not join in war for the destruction of the savages. But the hideous spectacle failed of the intended effect, and the Assembly still turned a deaf ear to all entreaties for more effective aid. The Scotch-Irish of the frontier were the chief sufferers from the depredations of the Indians. They were of a rude and hardy stamp,—hunters, scouts, rangers, Indian traders, and backwoods farmers,—who had grown up with arms in their hands, and been trained under all the influences of the warlike frontier. They fiercely complained that they were interposed as a barrier between the rest of the province and a ferocious enemy, and that they were sacrificed to the safety of men who looked with indifference on their miseries, and lost no opportunity to extenuate and smooth away the cruelties of their destroyers.

Along the western frontiers of Pennsylvania, Maryland, and Virginia, in the summer of 1763, terror reigned supreme. Indian scalping parties were ranging everywhere, laying waste the settlements, destroying the harvests, and butchering men, women, and children, with ruthless fury. Many hundreds of wretched fugitives flocked for refuge to Carlisle and the other towns of the border, bringing tales of inconceivable horror. Strong parties of armed men, who went out to reconnoitre the country, found every habitation reduced to cinders, and the half-burned bodies of the inmates lying among the smouldering ruins ; while here and there was seen some miserable wretch, scalped and tomahawked, but still alive and conscious. As the summer passed, the frontiers of Cumberland County were completely abandoned by the Scotch-Irish settlers, many of whom, not content with seeking refuge at Carlisle, continued their flight to the eastward, and pushed on to Lancaster and Philadelphia. Carlisle presented a most deplorable spectacle. A multitude of the refugees, unable to find shelter in the town, had encamped in the woods, or on the adjacent fields, erecting huts of branches and bark, and living on such charity as the slender means of the townspeople could supply. The following is an extract from a letter dated at Carlisle, July 5, 1763 (Hazard's *Pennsylvania Register*, iv., 390) :

Nothing could exceed the terror which prevailed from house to house, from town to town. The road was near covered with women and children flying to Lancaster and Philadelphia. The pastor of the Episcopal Church went at the head of his congregation, to protect and encourage them on the way. A few retired to the breastworks for safety. The alarm once given could not be appeased.

The letter from which the following extract is taken appears in the *Pennsylvania Gazette*, No. 1804, the letter being dated at Carlisle, July 12, 1763 :

I embrace this first leisure since yesterday morning to transmit you a brief account of our present state of affairs here, which indeed is very distressing ; every day, almost, affording some fresh object to awaken the compassion, alarm the fears, or kindle into resentment and vengeance every sensible breast, while flying families, obliged to abandon house and possessions, to save their lives by an hasty escape ; mourning widows, bewailing their husbands surprised and massacred by savage rage ; tender parents, lamenting the fruits of their own bodies, cropt in the very bloom of youth by a barbarous hand ; with relations and acquaintances pouring out sorrow for murdered neighbors and friends, present a varied scene of mingled distress.

To-day a British vengeance begins to arise in the breasts of our men. One of them that fell from among the twelve, as he was just expiring, said to one of his fellows, "Here, take my gun, and kill the first Indian you see, and all shall be well."

In October, 1763, several companies of Rangers were formed by the Scotch-Irish in Lancaster and Cumberland counties, for the purpose of patrolling the borders and giving such protection as they were able to the scattered inhabitants. One of these companies, starting from Paxtang in Lancaster County, marched to the relief of the Connecticut settlers at Wyoming, but arrived two days after that settlement had been burned, and its inhabitants killed, imprisoned, or driven off by the Indians. They buried the dead bodies of those who had fallen in the massacre, and returned to the southern settlements. The Quakers, who seemed resolved that they would neither defend the people of the frontier nor allow them to defend themselves, vehemently inveighed against the several expeditions up the Susquehanna, and denounced them as seditious and murderous. "Urged by their blind prejudice in favor of the Indians," says Parkman, "they insisted that the bands of the Upper Susquehanna were friendly to the English ; whereas, with the single exception of a few Moravian converts near Wyoming, who had not been molested by the whites, there could be no rational doubt that these savages nourished a rancorous and malignant hatred against the province. But the Quakers, removed by their situation from all fear of the tomahawk, securely vented their spite against the borderers, and doggedly closed their ears to the truth." Meanwhile, the people of the frontier besieged the Assembly with petitions for relief ; but little heed was given to their complaints.

At this time, the provincial government had the custody of some twenty Iroquois Indians, who were seated on Conestoga Manor, in Lancaster County, not far from the Susquehanna. The men spent part of their time in hunting, and lounged away the rest of it in idleness and dissipation. They lived by beggary, and the sale of brooms, baskets, and wooden ladles, made by the women. In the immediate vicinity they were commonly regarded as vagabonds, but in the neighboring settlements they were looked upon as secretly abetting the enemy, acting as spies, giving shelter to scalping parties, and aiding them in their depredations. Their chief had repeatedly threatened to kill various white men and women of the neighborhood.

About the middle of December, word was brought to the settlers living at Paxtang (now Harrisburg), that an Indian, known to have committed depredations in the vicinity, had been traced to Conestoga. Matthew Smith, a man of influence and popularity among his associates, called together a number of the Paxtang Rangers, and led them to the Conestoga settlement. One of the men saw an Indian issuing from a house, and thought that he recognized him as the savage who had killed his own mother. Firing his rifle, he brought the Indian down. Then, with a loud shout, the furious mob rushed into the cabins, and killed all the Indians whom they found there, some six in number. Fourteen of the Conestogas managed to escape, and, fleeing to Lancaster, were given a place of refuge in the county jail. While there, word was again carried to the Paxtang men that an Indian, known to have murdered the relatives of one of their number, was among those who had received the protection of the Lancaster magistrates. This again aroused a feeling of rage and resentment amongst the Rangers. On December 27th some fifty of them, under the leadership of Lazarus Stewart, marched to Lancaster, broke open the jail, and with the fury of a mob massacred every Indian contained therein, man, woman, and child.

This is said by some to have been the first instance of the operation of lynch law in America ; and many blame the Scotch-Irish for its introduction. Doubtless the odium is merited ; as a similar incident occurred nearly twenty years later, when some of the Scotch-Irish of Washington County, Pennsylvania, under far less extenuating circumstances, murdered in cold blood upwards of ninety men, women, and children of the community of Moravian Indians at Gnadenhutten, west of the Ohio. This atavistic tendency is further illustrated in our own day by the lynching of negroes in the South, the frequency of which is probably due to the fact that the southern white population is chiefly of Scotch-Irish descent ; these examples of perverted administration of justice finding many parallels in the annals of mediæval Scotland. The family feuds of Kentucky, which for the most part seem peculiar to families bearing Scottish names, may also be cited as examples and counterparts in America of the clan and family feuds formerly so common in Scotland. The case of the Regulators of North Carolina is another well-known instance in American history of the Scotch-Irish backwoodsmen taking the administration of justice into their own hands, when their rulers had failed to provide for them a safe government.

But the uprising of the "Paxtang Boys" was more than that of a mere lynching mob, bent on the immediate extermination of all redskins who came within its reach. It was a protest, bloody and atrocious, it is true, made by the harassed frontiersmen against the cowardly policy of the Quaker government. The Scotch-Irish had suffered grievously from the Indian outrages, caused in a great measure by the neglect of that government to provide adequately for the defence of the province. They had repeatedly appealed to the Assembly, and their petitions for help had been rejected with contempt. They were unable to bring about a change for the better, as all the political power was in the hands of a small number of people. They determined finally to appeal to force, and, in doing so, thought in their first blind rage that they might strike a blow at the Quakers, and at the same time rid themselves of probable enemies, by killing the Quakers' wards. The Assembly, they argued, had shown infinitely more consideration for the feelings of the Indians than it had for the wounds of the Scotch-Irish. It had voted the savages large sums of money as presents, and indirectly enabled them to carry on an exterminating warfare against the whites ; while at the same time it refused to make any proper defence of the province against the marauders. If the Quakers were unmoved by the killing of hundreds of their Scotch-Irish fellow citizens, whom they hated, perhaps they could be made to realize the condition of the frontiers by the killing of their own Indian wards, whom they loved and cherished.

The Paxtang Rangers, in their bitter resentment against the government, lost sight of the fact that it is better for twenty guilty men to escape than for one innocent man to suffer. Their own miseries made them believe in all sincerity that the only good Indian is a dead one ; and that they themselves were the agents appointed of Providence to make all Indians good.

The Reverend John Elder was captain of the Paxtang Rangers, and minister of Paxtang and Derry congregations, from which the Rangers were enlisted. He tried in vain to dissuade his men from going to Conestoga on their bloody errand, and desisted only after they had broken away from him in anger. On the 27th December, 1763, the reverend captain wrote to Governor Penn as follows :

The storm which had been so long gathering, has at length exploded. Had Government removed the Indians from Conestoga, as was frequently urged without success, this painful catastrophe might have been avoided.

What could I do with men heated to madness? All that I could do was done. I expostulated, but life and reason were set at defiance, and yet the men, in private life, were virtuous and respectable — not cruel, but mild and merciful. . . . The time will arrive when each palliating circumstance will be calmly weighed. This deed, magnified into the blackest of crimes, shall be considered one of those youthful ebullitions of wrath caused by momentary excitement, to which human infirmity is subjected.

The different proclamations of Governor Penn, and the action of the Assembly relative to this transaction, created intense excitement on the frontiers of Lancaster, Berks, and Northampton counties, and meetings were held at which the provincial authorities were severely condemned. Representatives were appointed to proceed to Philadelphia and demand redress and protection. Accompanying them were large delegations from the "back inhabitants."

The approach of the frontiersmen caused great uneasiness in Philadelphia. Their force was magnified by rumor to many thousands. Six companies of foot, one of artillery, and two troops of horse were formed to oppose them : and some thousands of the inhabitants, including many Quakers, were prepared to render assistance, in case an attempt should be made upon the town. The barracks, which were under the protection of the regular troops, were fortified, several works being thrown up about them, and eight pieces of cannon mounted.

On arriving at Germantown, the Paxtang men were met by commissioners to whom they made known their grievances. Colonel Matthew Smith and James Gibson then accompanied the commissioners to Philadelphia, where they met the Governor and the Assembly, and presented their demands. In the meantime, with few exceptions, the frontiersmen who accompanied them returned home.

The memorial of Gibson and Smith was sustained by a "Declaration" bearing fifteen hundred signatures.

In a letter written at this time, Governor Penn says : "We expect a thousand of back inhabitants in town, *to insist upon the Assembly granting their request with regard to the increase of representatives, to put them upon an equality with the rest of the counties.* They have from time to time presented several petitions for the purpose, which have been always disregarded by the House ; for which purpose they intend to come in person. I am of opinion they [the Assembly] will never come into [agreement], as it will be the means of lessening the power of the governing few in this Province."

The petition presented by these Scotch-Irish citizens, in enumerating their grievances, mentions as the chief one the fact that they were not permitted a proportionate share in the government of the province. This petition is printed in full in the *Colonial Records of Pennsylvania*, vol. ix., pp. 138–145, and its principal contents are as follows :

We, Matthew Smith and James Gibson, in behalf of ourselves and his

Majesty's faithful and loyal subjects, the inhabitants of the frontier counties of Lancaster, York, Cumberland, Berks, and Northampton, humbly beg leave to remonstrate and lay before you the following grievances, which we submit to your wisdom for redress.

First, We apprehend that, as freemen and English subjects, we have an indisputable title to the same privileges and immunities with his Majesty's other subjects who reside in the interior counties of Philadelphia, Chester, and Bucks, and therefore ought not to be excluded from an equal share with them in the very important privilege of legislation : nevertheless, contrary to the Proprietor's charter, and the acknowledged principles of common justice and equity, our five counties are restrained from electing more than ten representatives, viz., four for Lancaster, two for York, two for Cumberland, one for Berks, and one for Northampton, while the three counties and city of Philadelphia, Chester, and Bucks elect twenty-six. This we humbly conceive is oppressive, unequal, and unjust, the cause of many of our grievances, and an infringement of our natural privileges of freedom and equality ; wherefore, we humbly pray that we may no longer be deprived of an equal number with the three aforesaid counties, to represent us in Assembly.[9]

Secondly, We understand that a bill is now before the House of Assembly, wherein it is provided that such persons as shall be charged with killing any Indians in Lancaster county, shall not be tried in the county where the fact was committed, but in the counties of Philadelphia, Chester, or Bucks. This is manifestly to deprive British subjects of their known privileges, to cast an eternal reproach upon whole counties, as if they were unfit to serve their country in the quality of jurymen, and to contradict the well-known laws of the British nation in a point whereon life, liberty, and security essentially depend, namely, that of being tried by their equals, in the neighborhood where their own, their accusers, and the witnesses' character and credit, with the circumstances of the fact are best known, and instead thereof putting their lives in the hands of strangers, who may as justly be suspected of partiality to as the frontier counties can be of prejudices against Indians. . . .

Thirdly, During the late and present Indian War, the frontiers of this Province have been repeatedly attacked and ravaged by skulking parties of the Indians, who have with the most savage cruelty murdered men, women, and children, without distinction, and have reduced near a thousand families to the most extreme distress. It grieves us to the very heart to see such of our frontier inhabitants as have escaped savage fury with the loss of their parents, their children, their wives, or relatives, left destitute by the public, and exposed to the most cruel poverty and wretchedness, while upwards of an hundred and twenty of these savages, who are with great reason suspected of being guilty of these horrid barbarities, under the mask of friendship, have procured themselves to be taken under the protection of the Government with a view to elude the fury of the brave relatives of the murdered, and are now maintained at the public expense. Some of these Indians, now in the Barracks at Philadelphia, are confessedly a part of the Wyalusing Indians, which tribe is now at war with us, and the others are the Moravian Indians, who, living with us under the cloak of friendship, carried on a correspondence with our known enemies on the Great Island. We cannot but observe, with sorrow and indignation, that some persons in this Province are at pains to extenuate the barbarous cruelties practised by these savages on our murdered brethren and relatives, which are shocking to

human nature, and must pierce every heart but that of the hardened perpe-
trators or their abettors; nor is it less distressing to hear others pleading
that although the Wyalusing tribe is at war with us, yet that part of it which
is under the protection of the Government, may be friendly to the English,
and innocent. In what nation under the sun was it ever the custom that
when a neighboring nation took up arms, not an individual should be
touched but only the persons that offered hostilities? Who ever proclaimed
war with a part of a nation, and not with the whole? Had these Indians
disapproved of the perfidy of their tribe, and been willing to cultivate and
preserve friendship with us, why did they not give notice of the war before
it happened, as it is known to be the result of long deliberations, and a pre-
concerted combination among them? Why did they not leave their tribe
immediately, and come among us before there was ground to suspect them,
or war was actually waged with their tribe? No, they stayed amongst
them, were privy to their murders and ravages, until we had destroyed
their provisions, and when they could no longer subsist at home, they come,
not as deserters but as friends, to be maintained through the winter, that
they may be able to scalp and butcher us in the spring.

And as to the Moravian Indians, there are strong grounds at least to
suspect their friendship, as it is known that they carried on a correspondence with our enemies on the Great Island. We killed three Indians going
from Bethlehem to the Great Island with blankets, ammunition, and provisions, which is an undeniable proof that the Moravian Indians were in
confederacy with our open enemies; and we cannot but be filled with
indignation to hear this action of ours painted in the most odious and
detestable colors, as if we had inhumanly murdered our guides, who preserved us from perishing in the woods, when we only killed three of our
known enemies, who attempted to shoot us when we surprised them. And,
besides all this, we understand that one of these very Indians is proved, by
the oath of Stinson's widow, to be the very person that murdered her husband. How, then, comes it to pass, that he alone, of all the Moravian
Indians, should join the enemy to murder that family? Or can it be supposed that any enemy Indians, contrary to their known custom of making
war, should penetrate into the heart of a settled country to burn, plunder,
and murder the inhabitants, and not molest any houses in their return, or
ever be seen or heard of? Or how can we account for it, that no ravages
have been committed in Northampton county since the removal of the
Moravian Indians, when the Great Cove has been struck since? These
things put it beyond doubt with us that the Indians now at Philadelphia are
his Majesty's perfidious enemies, and, therefore, to protect and maintain
them at the public expense, while our suffering brethren on the frontiers
are almost destitute of the necessaries of life, and are neglected by the public, is sufficient to make us mad with rage, and tempt us to do what nothing
but the most violent necessity can vindicate. We humbly and earnestly
pray, therefore, that those enemies of his Majesty may be removed as soon
as possible out of the Province.

Fourthly, We humbly conceive that it is contrary to the maxims of good
policy, and extremely dangerous to our frontiers, to suffer any Indians, of
what tribe soever, to live within the inhabited parts of this Province while
we are engaged in an Indian war, as experience has taught us that they are
all perfidious, and their claim to freedom and independency puts it in their
power to act as spies, to entertain and give intelligence to our enemies, and
to furnish them with provisions and warlike stores. To this fatal intercourse

between our pretended friends and open enemies, we must ascribe the greatest part of the ravages and murders that have been committed in the course of this and the last Indian war. We therefore pray that this grievance be taken under consideration and remedied.

Fifthly, We cannot help lamenting that no provision has been hitherto made, that such of our frontier inhabitants as have been wounded in defence of the Province, their lives and liberties, may be taken care of, and cured of their wounds at the public expense. We therefore pray that this grievance may be redressed.

Sixthly, In the late Indian war, this Province, with others of his Majesty's colonies, gave rewards for Indian scalps, to encourage the seeking them in their own country, as the most likely means of destroying or reducing them to reason, but no such encouragement has been given in this war, which has damped the spirits of many brave men, who are willing to venture their lives in parties against the enemy. We therefore pray that public rewards may be proposed for Indian scalps, which may be adequate to the dangers attending enterprises of this nature.

Seventhly, We daily lament that numbers of our nearest and dearest relatives are still in captivity among the savage heathen, to be trained up in all their ignorance and barbarity, or to be tortured to death with all the contrivances of Indian cruelty, for attempting to make their escape from bondage ; we see they pay no regard to the many solemn promises they have made to restore our friends who are in bondage amongst them. We therefore earnestly pray that no trade may hereafter be permitted to be carried on with them until our brethren and relatives are brought home to us.

Eighthly, We complain that a certain society of people in this Province [meaning the Quakers] in the late Indian war, and at several treaties held by the King's representatives, openly loaded the Indians with presents, and that I[srael] P[emberton], a leader of the said society, in defiance of all government, not only abetted our Indian enemies, but kept up a private intelligence with them, and publicly received from them a belt of wampum, as if he had been our Governor, or authorized by the King to treat with his enemies. By this means, the Indians have been taught to despise us as a weak and disunited people, and from this fatal source have arose many of our calamities under which we groan. We humbly pray, therefore, that this grievance may be redressed, and that no private subject be hereafter permitted to treat with, or carry on a correspondence with, our enemies.

Ninthly, we cannot but observe with sorrow, that Fort Augusta, which has been very expensive to this Province, has afforded us but little assistance during this or the last war. The men that were stationed at that place neither helped our distressed inhabitants to save their crops, nor did they attack our enemies in their towns, or patrol on our frontiers. We humbly request that proper measures may be taken to make that garrison more serviceable to us in our distress, if it can be done.

N. B. We are far from intending any reflection against the commanding officer stationed at Augusta, as we presume his conduct was always directed by those from whom he received his orders.

Signed on behalf of ourselves, and by appointment of a great number of the frontier inhabitants.

February 13th, 1764.

MATTHEW SMITH,
JAMES GIBSON. [10]

No action on the two memorials was taken by the Assembly, but a bill was passed granting supplies for the ensuing campaign ; and the consequent military preparations, together with a threatened renewal of the war on the part of the Indians, engrossed the minds of the frontier people, and caused the excitements of the winter to be forgotten.

The nature of some earlier conflicts between the Assembly and the State Government of Pennsylvania is thus alluded to by Franklin in chapter nine of his *Autobiography* :

These public quarrels were all at bottom owing to the Proprietaries, our hereditary governors ; who, when any expense was to be incurred for the defence of their province, with incredible meanness instructed their deputies to pass no act for levying the necessary taxes, unless their vast estates were in the same act expressly exonerated ; and they had even taken the bonds of these deputies to observe such instructions. . . . The Assemblies for three years held out against this injustice, though constrained to bend at last.

The significance of the contest between the Assembly and the Proprietary may be inferred from a perusal of the message sent to the Assembly by Governor Morris, May 16, 1755, which charges some of its members, among other things, with a *desire for independence*.[11] This portion of the message may well be reproduced in connection with the present consideration of its subject. It is to be found in volume vi. of the *Colonial Records of Pennsylvania*, at pp. 386, 387 :

GENTLEMEN :

When I summoned You together on the Seventeenth of March last I was in Hopes You would bring with you Inclinations to promote the Publick Service by Granting the Supplies expected by the Crown and by putting this Province into a Posture of Defence ; but I am sorry to find that neither the Danger to which this Country stands exposed, nor his Majesty's repeated and affectionate calls, have had any Weight with You.

The Bill you sent me for striking Twenty-Five Thousand Pounds was of a more extraordinary Nature than that I refused my Assent to in the Winter Sessions, as it gave General Braddock a Power over no more than Five Thousand Pounds, and subjected the remaining Twenty Thousand and all the Surplus of the Excise for Eleven Years to come to the Disposition of some of the Members of your House, and to the Assembly for the Time being.

The offering Money in a Way and upon Terms that You very well knew I could not consistent with my Duty to the Crown consent to, is in my Opinion trifling with the King's Commands, and amounts to a Refusal to give at all, and I am satisfied will be seen in this Light by my Superiors, who by your Bill above mentioned, which I shall lay before them, and by the whole of your Conduct since You have been made acquainted with the designs of the French, will be convinced that your Resolutions are and have been to take Advantage of your Country's Danger, to aggrandize and render permanent your own Power and Authority, and to destroy that of the Crown. That it is for this Purpose and *to promote your Scheme of future Independency* You are grasping at the Disposition of all Publick Money and at the Power of filling all the offices of Government especially those of the Revenue, and when his Majesty and the Nation are at the Expense of sending Troops for the Protection of these Colonies, You refuse to furnish them with Provisions and necessary Carriages tho' your country is full of both, unless You can at the same Time encroach upon the Rights of the Crown and increase your own Power, already too great for a Branch of a Subordinate dependant Government so remote from the principal Seat of Power.

In an address delivered before the Historical Society of Pennsylvania, in 1882, upon "Pennsylvania's Formative Influence upon Federal Institutions," Mr. William A. Wallace presented some facts which may well be given a place in connection with the subject of taxation without representation :

The earliest instance that I can find in which the issue of no taxation without representation was sharply defined in America was that of 1740, between the city of Philadelphia and the Provincial Assembly. The city corporation, consisting of the mayor and common council, possessed extensive powers of taxation, and it was proposed to take them away and vest them in commissioners and assessors, to be elected by the people. A bill for that purpose was passed by the Assembly, but the Governor refused to sign it. The quarrel was really between the proprietary party and the people. The city corporation was a close body, originally composed of persons nominated by William Penn, and keeping up succession by the election of councilmen and aldermen by those already in office, so that the policy of the corporation guarded from the interference of persons whose views might have differed from the councilmen. In the controversy the Assembly struck the key-note which sounded thirty-six years afterward in the Declaration of Independence. The ground was taken that as the inhabitants of the city had no right to choose members of the city corporation, the latter should not have the power of taxing the people without their own consent ; that the King claimed no power of levying taxes without the consent of Parliament, and that there should be no taxation without representation.[12]

This action was twenty-five years before the resolutions of the House of Burgesses of Virginia, introduced by Patrick Henry, were passed, and, whilst it may be true, as Mr. Jefferson states, that Mr. Henry certainly gave the "first impulse to the ball of the Revolution" by these resolutions, yet the people of the colonies were familiar with the controversies in Pennsylvania, and these and the teachings of Franklin prepared the public mind for its final attitude of resistance to the death. Mr. Graham, in his history of the colonies, says that when in the beginning of 1764, Lord Granville informed the colonies of his purpose to procure an Act of Parliament, imposing a stamp duty on the colonies, which ultimately was carried into execution, and aroused the patriotic fervor and indignation of all of the people, the Pennsylvania Assembly "was distinguished above all others by the temperate, firm, dignified, and consistent strain of its debates and proceedings." It was declared there that this proposition was a deviation from national usage, unconstitutional, unjust, and unnecessary, and that Parliament had no right to tax the colonies at all. They recognized the right of the Crown to ask for supplies, and expressed their willingness to grant them, but utterly denied the power and authority of the ministers and Parliament to tax them. Virginia and New York also gave positive contradiction to this claim of right to tax the colonies, and affirmed its unconstitutionality. Differing from Pennsylvania in her dignified silence, they sent petitions to both King and Parliament, but that of Virginia weakened its force by distinguishing between the power and the right to tax, for, while denying the right, the exertion of the supposed power was deprecated in a manner which indicated that no opposition beyond remonstrance was intended. They denied the right, recognized the power, and breathed not a syllable that implied either the power or the will to resist the infliction. The petition of New York was not presented. No member of Parliament was found willing to present it, and it reached England after the Stamp Act was in progress.

Massachusetts, on the contrary, amid her divided councils, not only did not boldly stand against the right to tax, but addressed the House of Commons by a petition imploring for favor. The practical effect was to sanction the pretensions of Parliament to enforce its right to enact and execute the Stamp Act, and to place the hope of the colonies upon the lenity and indulgence of the British Government. The bold and unhesitating declaration announced in our Assembly under the lead of Dickinson and Franklin against the right, and the denial of the power by its record, was followed by no other of the colonies, but Franklin in advocating the doctrine thus laid down, in his controversy with British authority, as our representative, quoted Philip De Comines and the famous declaration : " There is neither King nor sovereign lord on earth, who has beyond his own domain power to lay the imposition of one farthing on his subjects, without the consent of those who pay it, unless he does it by tyranny and violence." Here, as in other things, we find Pennsylvania and her sons in the advance, and this, too, in face of the fact that the charter to Penn at least impliedly recognized the right of Parliament to tax. When this first step in the oppressive statutes of the mother country, which ultimately brought armed resistance and independence, was taken, and the Stamp Act was a fixed fact, Virginia, under the fiery lead of Henry, declared through a small majority of its House of Burgesses that " the most substantial and distinguished part of their political birthright was the privilege of being taxed exclusively by themselves, or their representatives," and thus primarily voiced the universal thought. Massachusetts, following Otis, Adams, and Hancock, at the same hour initiated her call for a convention of the colonies for unity and resistance. Our Assembly with unanimous voice placed upon record their protest, that " the only legal representatives of the people were the persons elected to serve as members of the Assembly, and that the taxation of the Province by any other persons whatsoever was unconstitutional, unjust, subversive of liberty, and destructive of happiness."

The firm and decided attitude of the colonies, and the representations and genius of Franklin, then the agent of Pennsylvania at London, so prevailed upon Pitt and those in power, that the Stamp Act was repealed within two years from its enactment, and the opening of the bloody drama of the Revolution was postponed for further contests between prerogative and arbitrary power on the one hand, and patriotic independence and personal right on the other. They soon came, and in them we trace the spirit of feudal control combating the rights of the individual, which, since the foundation of the colony, had been struggling for the mastery.

NOTES TO CHAPTER IV.

[1] P. 59, 25th edition.

[2] In his conversation with Webster in 1824, Jefferson pronounced a further eulogy on the character of Patrick Henry in these words : " It is not now easy to say what we should have done without Patrick Henry. He was far before all in maintaining the spirit of the Revolution. His influence was most extensive with the members from the upper counties ; and his boldness and their votes overawed and controlled the more timid and aristocratic gentlemen of the lower part of the State. . . . After all, it must be allowed that he was our leader in the measures of the Revolution in Virginia, and in that respect more is due to him than to any other person. If we had not had him we should have got on pretty well as you did by a number of men of nearly equal talents but he left all of us far behind."—Curtis, *Life of Daniel Webster*, vol. i., p. 585.

[3] *Works*, vol. x., pp. 244, 245, 247.

[4] See, also, *Works of John Adams*, vol. x., pp. 274, 277, 279, 280, 282, 289, 292, 298, 314, 317, 320.

[5] *Works*, vol. x., p. 272.

[6] The influence of this controversy [over the Writs of Assistance in 1761] in producing the Revolution, is not wholly due to the fiery eloquence of Otis, whose words, said John Adams, " breathed into the nation the breath of life," nor to the range of his argument . . . but to their effect upon the commercial interest — then the leading one — of New England ; for if the latent powers of these writs were set free and used by the revenue officers, the commerce of Boston, Salem, and Newport would have been effectually crippled.— *Narrative and Critical History of America*, vol. vi., pp. 11, 12. Mellen Chamberlain, *The Revolution Impending*.

In the debate in the Commons on the Boston Port Bill and the infraction of the charter of Massachusetts, Sir Richard Sutton said that " even in the most quiet times the disposition to oppose the laws of this country was strongly ingrafted in the Americans, and all their actions conveyed a spirit and wish for independence. If you ask an American who is his master, he will tell you he has none, nor any governor but Jesus Christ." (*Adolphus*, ii., 108)—*N. and C. Hist.*, vi., p. 232, note.

[7] *Life and Writings of James Madison*, vol. iii., p. 105.

[8] See Franklin's *Works*, vol. ii., pp. 376, 377 ; and for the whole history of his plan of union and its attendant circumstances, *ibid.*, pp. 343 to 387, and his *Autobiography*, ch. ix.

[9] The number of taxables in Lancaster, Cumberland, York, Northampton, and Berks counties in 1760 was 15,437, and in Bucks, Chester, and Philadelphia, 16,230.

[10] See Parkman, *Conspiracy of Pontiac*, ch. xxv., and his Appendix E.

[11] On this subject see also Appendix E (Examination of Joseph Galloway).

[12] See *Colonial Records of Pennsylvania*, vol. iv., pp. 375-420. The principle is laid down in a message from the Assembly to the Governor in May, 1740, as follows (p. 408) : " Nor would any part of the bill, if passed into a law, debar them from levying money on the inhabitants to these purposes, if they were authorized by their charter so to do, altho' in our opinion, it ought not nor cannot give any such power, for the following reasons : 1. The members of the corporation were originally named by the Proprietor, and have since chosen their successors ; and as the inhabitants of the city have not any right to chuse them, it is not reasonable they should have the power of levying money on the inhabitants without their consent. 2. The King himself claims no power of laying and levying taxes on his subjects but by common consent in Parliament ; and as all the powers of government in this province are derived under him, they cannot be greater in this respect than those from which they are derived," etc.

CHAPTER V

LIBERTY OF SPEECH AND CONSCIENCE DEFINITELY ESTAB-
LISHED IN AMERICA BY MEN OF SCOTTISH BLOOD

WE have now cited some authentic instances of vigorous and prolonged resistance to the monarchical principle of taxing the many for the benefit of the few, as well as the promulgation of the doctrine of no taxation without representation, all of which occurred many years before the passage of the Stamp Act. We have also had the example of an armed demonstration on the part of the Scotch-Irish of Pennsylvania in opposition to the first-named principle, at a time when the Massachusetts Independence "infant" was yet in its swaddling clothes.

Nor are these all. The early pages of American colonial history contain numerous like instances of resistance to arbitrary power ever since the time of the first great outbreak of the American spirit in opposition to old-world traditions and oppressions which took place in 1676 in the revolt of the English Nathaniel Bacon and the Scottish William Drummond and their followers against the royal government as then administered by Governor Berkeley in Virginia.

Let us now consider another of these vital principles of human liberty, one in the development of which Americans boast themselves as being foremost among the nations of the world, — that is, liberty of speech and the freedom of the press.

This principle was, perhaps, first effectively contended for and successfully established in the hearts of the American public twenty-six years before James Otis's speech at Boston, in the trial of John Peter Zenger, a printer of New York, and it was then done chiefly by the eloquence and persistence of the Scottish Attorney-General of Pennsylvania, a man named Andrew Hamilton, who was aided by two Presbyterian lawyers of New York, James Alexander and William Smith. Hamilton was the chief actor in this affair, which has been cited by Gouverneur Morris as the beginning of American liberty, and no early moulder of public opinion on the questions involved in that struggle deserves a higher place in the affections of the American people than this Scotch attorney, the first "Philadelphia lawyer" to give that appellation international renown.[1]

The occasion of his appearance was a memorable one, and the incident is not unlike that narrated by John Adams in telling of the argument over the Writs of Assistance in Massachusetts; the scene in this case being the highest court of the neighboring colony of New York, and the leading actors the chief justice and attorney-general of that province with the aged and fearless lawyer from the Quaker colony. Its action took place on August 4, 1735, and the incident is narrated at length in a pamphlet issued soon afterwards by two of the defendant's attorneys. Zenger's defence was undertaken by the Presbyterian Junta, which later became so famous in the Revolutionary history of New York.[2]

Zenger was the publisher of the *New York Journal*, and had printed in its columns some strictures on William Cosby, the royal governor of the province. These criticisms were for the most part true, and for that reason very unpalatable to their subject. As a warning to others, as much as for his own offences, Zenger was arrested. It was proposed to deal summarily with the prisoner, but public interest was aroused in his casè, and it was seen that if he was convicted all hope of free speech would for the time be gone. As the public became interested, the authorities became determined and harsh. In pursuance of his rights, Zenger's counsel made an objection to the judges who were to try the case, and they were promptly disbarred, while a lawyer was assigned by the Court to carry on the defence. When Zenger was finally called on to face a jury, the authorities were confident of making short work of his case, and of establishing a precedent which would crush out in the future what they termed "sedition." Through the instrumentality of James Alexander and William Smith, who were the chief spirits in a society known as the "Sons of Liberty," Andrew Hamilton was induced to appear as counsel for the prisoner. The fame of this venerable attorney, his standing at the bar, the prominent offices he had held, and his position as a member of the Pennsylvania Assembly, forbade his being treated in the summary fashion of Zenger's earlier counsel, so the representatives of the prosecution could do nothing but submit. They had hopes from the jury, and knew that the judges were with them.

The prosecution claimed that all the jury had to determine was, whether the publication which was scheduled as libellous had appeared, and that they had nothing to do with the truth or falsity of the libel. Hamilton demurred from this, saying he was prepared to admit the publication of the strictures, and to prove their truth, leaving the issue to the jury to be whether truth was a libel or not. He was overruled by the Court on the inferred ground that anything reflecting on the King was a libel. Hamilton then denied that the King's representative had the same prerogatives as the sovereign himself, and claimed the right of proving the truth of every statement that had been made in Zenger's paper. This the Court again overruled, and Hamilton then confined his attention to the jury, and made a glowing speech on behalf of personal liberty and the right of free criticism, which still ranks as one of the masterpieces of American eloquence. "His speech," says Dr. Peter Ross, whose account has been chiefly followed,[3] "was productive of effect far beyond the limits of the court-room in which it was delivered, or the case in which it was used. It started a train of thought which fired men's minds, and did more than anything else to give expression to the popular desire for freedom." Hamilton admitted again the publication of the words deemed libellous, and urged the jury, even though the Court might decide otherwise, to consider the words for themselves, and put their own construction upon them. In closing, he said : " You see I labor under the weight of many years, and am borne down by many infirmities of body ; yet old and weak as I am, I should think it my duty, if required, to go to the uttermost part of the land where my service could be of any use in assisting to quench the flame of prosecutions upon informations set on foot by the Government to deprive a people of the right of remonstrating, and complaining, too, against the arbitrary attempts of men in power. Men who oppress and injure the people under their administration provoke them to cry out and complain, and then make that very complaint the foundation for new oppressions and persecutions. . . . The question before the Court is not of small or private concern. It is not the cause of a poor printer, nor of New York alone, which you are now trying. No ! It may in its consequences affect every freeman that lives under the British Government upon the main of America. It is the best cause. It is the cause of liberty. And I make no doubt but your upright conduct this day will not only entitle you to the love and esteem of your fellow-citizens, but every man who prefers freedom to a life of slavery will bless and honor you, as men who have baffled the attempts of tyranny, and by an impartial and incorrupt verdict have made a noble foundation for securing to ourselves and our posterity and our neighbors that to which nature and the laws of our country have given us a right — the liberty of both exposing and opposing arbitrary power, in these parts of the world, at least, by speaking and writing truth."

The prosecution replied, and the Court gave his charge against the prisoner ; but Hamilton's eloquence proved irresistible, and the jury, after a few minutes' deliberation, brought in a verdict of " Not Guilty."

How this verdict was received by the citizens of New York who were present at Zenger's trial is related by an early historian of that State [1]:

Shouts shook the hall. The judges threatened the leader of the tumult with imprisonment, when a son of Admiral Norris declared himself the leader and invited a repetition of the huzzas. The judges had no time for a reply, for the shouts were instantly repeated, and Mr. Hamilton was conducted from the hall by the crowd to a splendid entertainment. The whole city renewed the compliment at his departure the next day. He entered the barge under a salute of cannon, and the corporation presented him with the freedom of the city in a gold box, on which its arms were engraved, encircled with the words, "Demersæ Leges, Timefacta Libertas, Hæc Tandem Emergunt."

Dr. John W. Francis states in his description of the city of New York (printed in the American edition of *Brewster's Encyclopedia*, and on page 400 of Hinton's *History of the United States*), that Gouverneur Morris told him that " the trial of Zenger in 1735 was the germ of American freedom — the morning star of that liberty which subsequently revolutionized America."

The origin of the so-called Presbyterian, or liberal, party in New York, which first committed and then held that colony to the American cause during the Revolution, dates from the time of this trial ; and its importance in forming and influencing public sentiment in the middle colonies is well indicated by the view of the trial generally taken by writers on the opposite side since that time.

In the memoir of Chief Justice James De Lancey, prepared by Edward F. De Lancey, and published in the *Documentary History of New York*, vol. iv., pp. 1037–1059, the Zenger case is referred to as follows :

About two years afterwards came on before the Supreme Court the famous trial of John Peter Zenger for a series of libels on the governor and chief officers of the colony. He was a printer by trade, in arrears to a small amount as collector of taxes in the city, and the Assembly had refused to allow him to discharge the small debt by doing public printing enough to cover it.

He subsequently published a small paper entitled the *New York Weekly Journal*, at the instance of the opposition, in which the libels complained of were published. His counsel were James Alexander and William Smith, the elder, the supposed authors of the libels, two gentlemen of ability and intellect, both politically opposed to Chief Justice De Lancey.

Aware that the law would certainly convict their client, they attempted to destroy the court by excepting to the commissions of the judges as invalid and illegal ; though they knew them to be in the usual form, and such as their predecessors had always held, and under which they had acted for a number of years. Their objections, if valid, would have destroyed the court as well as the commissions, for it existed, not by force of any statute, as they contended, but by virtue of an ordinance of the governor and council, dated May 15, 1699. A formal denial of its existence deliberately made was therefore a gross contempt of court, and the Chief Justice from the bench warned the counsel of the consequences. But they persisted in tendering the exceptions, upon which the court made an order, striking their names from its rolls and excluding them from further practice. Zenger, being unable to procure other counsel, the court assigned him Mr. Joseph Murray, with whom the silenced lawyers associated Mr. Hamilton, of Philadelphia, who made so artful an address to the jury at the trial a few days afterwards that, in the words of one of their own [Tory] friends (Smith, *History of New York*, ii., 22), "when he left his client in those hands, such was the fraudful dexterity of the orator, and the severity of his invectives upon the governor and his adherents, that the jury, missing the true issue before them, they, as if triers of their rulers, rather than of Zenger, pronounced the criminal innocent because they believed them to be guilty."

Chief Justice De Lancey's course on this occasion has been much misunderstood, owing to the fact that the only report of the trial was that published by Zenger himself, written by the silenced lawyers, and printed, not in New York, but in Boston, in 1738, three years after the trial, which of course represents him in the worst possible light. Taking the facts of the case, however, as given even there, it would be difficult to point out any other course which the court could have taken consistently with its own dignity and self-respect.

At this period, and from these controversies and others allied to them, arose the two great parties which ever afterwards divided the people of the province : the one maintaining principles moderate and conservative ; the other, those of a more radical tendency.

Both professed the strongest attachment and loyalty to the British constitution, and vied with each other in claiming and upholding all the rights of Englishmen.

In New York, as in some of the other colonies, the religious element entered largely into politics. In point of wealth and influence the Episcopalians were the leading denomination, the Dutch Reformed Church came next, and the Presbyterians last ; while in point of numbers their positions were exactly reversed, the Presbyterians outnumbering the Dutch, and the Dutch the Episcopalians. The last, with most of the Dutch, chiefly belonged to the conservative party ; while the remainder of the Dutch and the Presbyterians almost to a man were found in the ranks of the opposition.

Another and very striking peculiarity in the composition of the colonial parties was the remarkable preponderance of the wealth and social position of the province on the side of the conservatives [the Loyalist party of 1776]. In their ranks were found the Philipses, Van Cortlandts, De Lanceys, Bayards, Crugers, Wattses, Waltons, Van Rensselaers, Beekmans, Bleeckers, Barclays, Joneses of Long Island, Jays, Verplancks, Harrisons, and other substantial families ; while in those of the opposition the Livingstons, Morrises, Alexanders, and perhaps the Smiths and one or two more were probably all that belonged to the same class.

Here, then, we find the contest for freedom of public utterance and the liberty of the press waged and won in America at least forty years before Lexington, and at a time when James Otis and Samuel Adams themselves were not long out of their swaddling clothes. Yet, concerning these things, the pages of so-called American histories, of the New England school, in nine cases out of ten are silent.

Finally, let us revert to a much earlier period and consider for a moment the founding in America of what, with civil liberty, is the twin support of the structure of all just and lasting governments, namely, the principle of religious freedom.[b]

In Penn's colony liberty of worship was permitted from the beginning of his government. In Maryland and in one or two others of the southern colonies, for a short time at the beginning there was the same beneficent provision made by their laws or charters, but statutory enactment soon destroyed it. Outside of Pennsylvania and Rhode Island, at the beginning of the eighteenth century, the English Church had been established by law in most of the middle and southern governments, and the Congregational Church in those of New England. The Revolution of 1689 had brought to Britain, among other blessings, that of the Toleration Act, but its provisions had not yet been fully or definitely extended to the American colonies. Rev. Francis Makemie, the Scotch-Irish founder of American Presbyterianism, had come from County Donegal, Ireland, to the island of Barbadoes about 1683, and thence proceeded to the eastern shore of Maryland. There and along the Elizabeth River in Virginia he began to labor in establishing missionary stations among the Scotch and Scotch-Irish families who had settled in those parts. In the course of twenty years he had helped to build up two or three church organizations in that territory, and in 1706 their ministers united with those of other churches of Maryland, Delaware, and Pennsylvania in forming the Presbytery of Philadelphia. After this organization had been made, Makemie undertook a journey to Boston. While on the way he stopped and preached in New York, and there the opportunity came to him for making that first fight against the encroachments of the English Church establishment in America, which resulted in restricting and minimizing its power forever afterwards.

After the adjournment of the Presbytery of Philadelphia, October 27, 1706, Francis Makemie took with him John Hampton and set out on his journey, probably to consult with the Boston ministers. They stopped at New York on their way. They were invited by the Puritans of the city to preach for them. The Consistory of the Dutch Church, in accordance with their generous custom, offered their church edifice for the purpose. But their kindness was frustrated by the refusal of Governor Cornbury to permit it. Makemie, therefore, preached, January 20, 1706–7, in the private house of William Jackson, in Pearl Street.* The same day, John Hampton preached at Newtown, Long Island. On the following Tuesday, Makemie and Hampton went to Newtown intending to preach the next day, according to appointment; but they were there arrested on a warrant from Governor Cornbury, on the ground that they had preached without his permission. They were detained until March 1st, when they were brought before the Supreme Court on a writ of habeas corpus.

The charge against Hampton was not pressed, but Makemie was released on bail to appear for trial June 3d. He immediately returned to Philadelphia with Hampton for the meeting of the Presbytery of Philadelphia, March 22, 1707. From thence he writes to Benjamin Colman, of Boston :

Since our imprisonment we have commenced a correspondence with our rev. breth. of the ministry at Boston, which we hope according to our intention has been communicated to you all, whose sympathizing concurrence I cannot doubt of, in an expensive struggle, for asserting our liberty against the powerful invasion of Lord Cornbury, which is not yet over. I need not tell you of a picked jury, and the penal laws, are invading our American sanctuary without the least regard to the toleration, which should justly alarm us all.

The New England ministers immediately wrote to Sir Henry Ashurst, Sir Edmund Harrison, and other London agents, April 1, 1707 :

Except speedy relief be obtained, the issue will be, not only a vast oppression on a very worthy servant of God, but also a confusion upon the whole body of Dissenters in these colonies, where they are languishing under my Lord Cornbury's arbitrary and unaccountable government. We do therefore earnestly solicit you, that you would humbly petition the Queen's Majesty on this occasion, and represent the sufferings of the Dissenters in those parts of America which are carried on in so direct violation of her

Majesty's commands, of the laws of the nation, and the common rights of Englishmen. (Hutchinson, *History of the Province of Massachusetts Bay,* 2d edition, London, 1768, ii., p. 125.)

Makemie returned to New York and sustained his trial. He was defended by three of the ablest lawyers in the province—James Reigniere, David Jameson, and William Nicholl, made an elaborate and convincing argument in defence of his own religious rights, and was acquitted on the ground that he had complied with the Toleration Act and had acted within his rights as a Presbyterian minister. He produced his license to preach under the Toleration Act in Barbadoes, and this was recognized as valid throughout the Queen's dominions. The claim of Cornbury, that it was necessary that he should have a special license from the governor of New York, was simply ridiculous. But, notwithstanding his acquittal, Makemie was obliged to pay the costs of the prosecution as well as the defence, amounting to the large sum of £83 7s. 6d. "This trial," says Professor Briggs, "followed by the bitter pursuit of the acquitted man on the part of the wrathful governor, was the culmination of a series of tyrannical acts which aroused the entire Puritan body of the colonies and of Great Britain to action. The arbitrary acts of Governor Cornbury were indefensible. He had exceeded his prerogative, transgressed the provisions of the Toleration Act, and violated the liberties of the Dissenters, and indeed twisted and perverted the royal instructions to himself. He even intermeddled with the missionaries of the Society for the Propagation of the Gospel in Foreign Parts, and gained the hostility of all the better elements in the Church of England." The New York Assembly, in April, 1707, remonstrated against Cornbury's actions, charged him with bribery, with encroachment on the liberties of the people, and finally expressed their determination to redress the miseries of their country. He was recalled, and in 1709 Lord Lovelace took his place.[1]

An account of Makemie's trial was first printed in 1707, and a second publication was made in 1755. The former account was reprinted in Force's *Tracts* in 1846 (vol. iv.), and the latter in Hill's *American Presbyterianism* (1839). For Makemie's argument, see Appendix D.

NOTES TO CHAPTER V.

[1] Of this event, Gouverneur Morris said : " Instead of dating American liberty from the Stamp Act, I trace it to the persecution of Peter Zenger, because that event revealed the philosophy of freedom both of thought and speech as an inborn human right, so nobly set forth in Milton's *Treatise on Unlicensed Printing.*"—Lossing, *The Empire State,* Hartford, 1888, p. 147. For Hamilton's argument, see Appendix C.

[2] The account of Zenger's trial was first printed in Boston in 1738, and passed through several editions, two of which appeared in London in 1738, and another in Lancaster, Pa., in 1756. See *Documentary History of New York,* vol. iv., p. 104.

[3] *The Scot in America,* pp. 302–307.

[4] William Dunlap, *History of New Netherlands, Province of New York, and State of New York*, vol. i., pp. 298–310.

[5] " Where is the man to be found at this day . . . who will believe that the apprehension of Episcopacy contributed fifty years ago, as much as any other cause, to arouse the attention not only of the inquiring mind, but of the common people, and urge them to close thinking on the constitutional authority of Parliament over the colonies ? This, nevertheless, was a fact certain as any in the history of North America. . . .

" The opinion, the principles, the spirit, the temper, the views, designs, intrigues, and arbitrary exertions of power displayed by the Church of England at that time towards the Dissenters, as they were contemptuously called, though in reality the churchmen were the real dissenters, ought to be stated at full length. . . .

" In Virginia, the Church of England was established by law in exclusion and without toleration."—John Adams, *Works*, vol. x., pp. 185, 186.

At the commencement of the Revolution, public feeling in the eastern colonies was excited by the fears of the spiritual jurisdiction of the British ecclesiastics. Elbridge Gerry and Samuel Adams, for political effect, led off with predictions as groundless as they were vain. Plain facts demonstrated that, notwithstanding these misrepresentations, Episcopalians were the leading architects of the great work of American Independence. Franklin, Laurens, the Pinckneys, Wythe, Marshall, Pendleton, the Randolphs, Hamilton, Washington, Jefferson, Patrick Henry, Monroe, Rutledge, the Lees, Jay, Williams, Gen. Wayne, Robt. R. Livingston, Gouverneur, Lewis, and Robert Morris, Duer, Duane, Lord Stirling, William Samuel Johnson, Chase, Madison, and a host of others, distinguished patriots of the Revolution, were of the Episcopal Church. — Opdike, *History of the Episcopal Church in Providence, R. I.*, pp. 241, 242.

[6] This sermon was printed at Boston in 1707. A reprint of the Boston edition may be found in the *Collections of the New York Historical Society for the Year 1870*, pp. 409-453.

[7] *American Presbyterianism*, pp. 152-155.

CHAPTER VI

THE AMERICAN PEOPLE NOT RACIALLY IDENTICAL WITH THOSE OF NEW ENGLAND

THE second reason for the undue prominence of New England in the popular conception of American history, to which reference was made in the introductory chapter, is found in the absence, for a long time, of any systematic or comprehensive treatment by the writers of the middle and southern colonies of the history of their own districts.[1] A start was made in this direction, it is true, by Dr. David Ramsay in his *History of South Carolina* (1789), followed, with less degrees of excellence, by Hugh Williamson's *History of North Carolina*, Gordon's Histories of *Pennsylvania* and *New Jersey*, and Day's, Howe's, and Barber's *Historical Collections of Pennsylvania, Virginia*, and *New Jersey ;* but these books were all written at a date when there was little material collected or available, and before the inception of modern methods of historic inquiry and analysis ; and they are only good examples of what can be done by conscientious workmen without proper tools, or suitable material at hand on which to work. Bancroft was the first American historian to do even partial justice to the subject from a national standpoint. Foote's *Sketches of Virginia* and of *North Carolina* are among the most valuable contributions to the early history of these States that we have, but these works were written nearly fifty years ago. Bishop Meade's *Churches and Families of Virginia* also contains a vast amount of local and family history in connection with that of the Episcopal churches.

In New England, from the time of its first settlement, more or less ample and detailed records of the political and social history of nearly every community, however small, have been preserved in written form, as well as much of personal history. The publication of these records, which has been carried on for many years by public and private agencies, and their use as the bases for many of our popular histories, has served to disseminate a vastly greater amount of information about the people and events with which these records are concerned than those of any other part of America.

Literary genius, likewise, has aided materially in forming our popular ideals of characters and events in connection with certain phases of American history, particularly with those of New England. Indeed, certain literary productions may have been the sole sources of information regarding occurrences which are now reputed historic. This has been true in all ages. *The Arabian Nights*, in the incidental evidence which it affords, as well as by reason of its own intrinsic merit, must always be our chief authority for the high degree of civilization attained by the early Mohammedans ; just as the military prowess of ancient Greece has from time immemorial been best appreciated through the glowing imageries of the minstrel poet, and the glory of English history been best expressed in the imaginary conceptions of an obscure playwright. Shakspeare has given us an idea of the character of Richard III. and his predecessors and followers, as well as of that of Macbeth, which a more thorough investigation — while showing it to be in a large measure false — can never completely correct. In like manner, Walter Scott has typified in the personality of the first Richard all the romantic tendencies of the age of the Crusaders, with the result that his highly idealized portrait will ever be preferred to the less flattering though more honest delineation of history. So it is that the best-known pictures of early American life and character presented in our romantic literature, being taken for the most part through New England lenses, can be considered, from an historical standpoint, only with due allowance for that fact. Hawthorne has immortalized the Puritan, just as Cooper has created the American Indian of the popular mind ; yet, however true the former's characterization of the early New Englander may be, it has but little more value, as a type of the true American eponym, than that of the latter.

These various aids and influences, either of a literary or historic nature, have not until quite recently been available for the study of American history in its broader sense ; and we are only just beginning to get the benefit of their assistance in the examination of other than the New England portion of it. But this examination can never be carried on with entire satisfaction, until the complete publication of the early records of the general government. An attempt was made to this end some fifty or sixty years ago, which began quite favorably, and resulted in the publication of Force's series of *Archives* pertaining to affairs at the beginning of the Revolutionary struggle, and the projection of other series. But that work was dropped long before completion, and beyond nine volumes of *Archives* of the years 1775 and 1776, and the several volumes of *State Papers* of later date, very little other data has been printed. There is a vast amount of material relating to the colonial period and to the progress of the war and the subsequent formation of our system of government which still remains to be published.

It is, however, to the recent enlightened policy of many of the State governments of the original colonies that we are indebted for the inauguration of a movement looking to the conservation of the materials for their early history in a form that makes them at once both accessible and capable of preservation. This consists in the publication of various volumes of State archives, Revolutionary rosters, and documentary and other records, of which many series have already been issued by the States of New York, New Jersey, Pennsylvania, Maryland, Virginia, and North Carolina, and others are in course of preparation. Of these, by far the most useful and comprehensive in their preparation are the fifty volumes of *Archives* brought out by the State of Pennsylvania under the capable editorship of Dr. William H. Egle, for many years the State librarian.

In New York, up to 1887, there had been published a *Documentary History* (4 vols., 1850) and seventeen volumes (1856–1887) of documents relating to the colonial history, including a roster of Revolutionary soldiers. New Jersey published twenty volumes of *Archives* between 1872 and 1893, and also a Revolutionary roster.

Besides these State publications, the various State historical societies of the older colonies have also awakened in late years to the fact that, in order to justify their right to existence, it will be necessary for them to do something of a less trivial nature than merely to publish reports of their business meetings and lengthy obituaries of their deceased members. In consequence we are beginning to benefit by their labors. The New York society gives the best promise of future accomplishments, if the industry of its members is at all equal to the opportunities afforded in the wealth of documentary material now undergoing classification by the State officials.

The Historical Society of the State of Pennsylvania is unfortunate in being located away from the seat of the State government. Its headquarters are in Philadelphia, where live most of its members, and consequently its work is directed more along the line of local investigation than concerned with the history of the State at large. It might more appropriately be called the Historical Society of Philadelphia. In that field its labors are invaluable. Its chief publication is the *Pennsylvania Magazine*, a large quarterly, established in 1877, and a model periodical of the class. In the Society's early days a number of volumes relating to the history of the State were also issued, but few in recent years. The inattention on the part of this Society to that portion of the State outside of Philadelphia, however, is more than made up by the private enterprise of Dr. Egle, already mentioned in connection with the publication of the State *Archives*. During the past twenty years this gentleman, in addition to his work on the State *Archives*, published on his own behalf more than a dozen volumes of historical collections relating to interior Pennsylvania. The debt owed to him by all students of that part of early American history is one that will steadily increase with the passing years. The chief work of the Maryland society up to this date has been the preparation of sixteen volumes of *Maryland Archives* (1883–1897), which were printed by the State, and nine or ten volumes of *Collections*. The Historical Society of Richmond has also contributed nearly a dozen volumes (1882–1891) of *Collections* relating to Virginia. There is a rich field in that State for the future historian of America, but up to the present time a comparative dearth of published material. Some early history of North Carolina, including a roster of Revolutionary soldiers, has been given in the *Colonial Records* of that State (18 vols., 1886–1900) ; but South Carolina has produced only a few small volumes of *Collections*, issued by its Historical Society some forty years ago (1857–59) ; and Georgia still less.

In addition to the various general historical societies in these States, there are also many other organizations devoted to the collection of historical matter relating to special classes of the population. Of these may be mentioned the Holland Society of New York, the Huguenot Society, and the Scotch-Irish Society of America. The one last named held an annual congress each year from 1889 to 1897, and published nine volumes of its *Collections*. Their contents are chiefly made up from the addresses delivered at the annual meetings; hence there is considerable difference in their degrees of merit.

None of these works compare in thoroughness or scope with the publications of the New England State governments and of their various historical and antiquarian societies. There is nothing in the Middle States equal to the *Plymouth* or *Suffolk Records* of Massachusetts, for instance ; or the *Provincial, State*, or *Town Papers* of New Hampshire ; or the *New England Historical and Genealogical Register*.

As another result of the fecundity and one-sidedness of the New England writers before 1870, it has been long customary to ascribe to the English element in the American population the credit not only for all the early achievements of the nation in war and peace,[2] but also for having furnished practically all the colonists who settled in the country before the Revolution.[3] As a matter of fact, nothing could be more erroneous. The population of the New England States at the date of the first general census (1790) was 1,009,408, and the total white population of the country, 3,172,006. Bancroft estimated the white population of the colonies in 1775 to have been about 2,100,000; and as it is probable that the New England population did not increase so rapidly between 1775 and 1790 as that of the other States, we may safely estimate it at one-third of the total population in 1775.

Of the total white population at the outbreak of the Revolution there is abundant evidence to show that at least one-third was not of English descent or sympathies at all, but consisted of a variety of nationalities, including the Germans, French, Hollanders, Swedes, and others. The Germans and Swiss comprised nearly a third of the population of Pennsylvania in 1776,[4] and they likewise had formed many communities in western Maryland and northern Virginia, as well as in the lower country of South Carolina. The Swedes made the first settlements in Pennsylvania and Delaware; but these were afterwards overrun by the Dutch, who acquired most of the territory along the Delaware River, as well as that of the Hudson and Mohawk valleys in New York, and a considerable portion of New Jersey. The Welsh had large grants of land and numerous settlements in Delaware and southeastern Pennsylvania. The French, usually Huguenot refugees from the German Palatine, or from Holland or Ireland, were likewise among the early colonizers of Pennsylvania, and the same people formed a large part of the first European population of the Carolinas. But the settlements of all these different nationalities taken together did not begin to equal in number or importance those of another class of people with which we now have to deal — a class that was as distinctly non-English as many of those just named ;

6

and one that had infinitely greater reason than any of the others for resenting the course of injustice and oppression so long pursued in the administration of the British Government.[5]

These were the Scots of North Britain and North Ireland, a composite race, even at that time having in the organic make-up of each individual a combination of the several racial elements which were almost identical with those now forming the present collective population of America, and from which the American of the future is gradually being evolved. Theirs was the one representative and typical race in America with which all others are coming more and more to conform. That is to say, these Attacot-Goidelic-Cymro-Anglo-Norse-Danish Scots of colonial times, these Celto-Teutonic emigrants to America of the eighteenth century, combined in their individual bodies the physical attributes of the Angle, the Gael, the Norse, and the Brython. In their veins was already blended the blood of the various peoples which in the past hundred years have been pouring millions of individuals into the race alembic called America ; and to a far greater extent than any of their neighbors were these Scottish emigrants of the eighteenth century the true prototypes of the typical American of the twentieth.[6]

Their settlements in America began in the seventeenth century but were made chiefly in the eighteenth. At the time of the Revolution these people comprised fully forty per cent. of the patriotic population of the country south of New England.

The Continental Congress of 1776 made an estimate of the population of the thirteen original colonies as a basis from which to apportion the expense of the war.[7] The figures of this conjectural census of Congress are as follows :

New Hampshire	102,000
Massachusetts (including Maine)	352,000
Rhode Island	58,000
Connecticut	202,000
New York (including Vermont)	238,000
New Jersey	138,000
Pennsylvania	341,000
Delaware	37,000
Maryland	174,000
Virginia (including Kentucky)	300,000
North Carolina (including Tennessee)	181,000
South Carolina	93,000
Georgia	27,000
Total white population	2,243,000
Slave population	500,000
	2,743,000[8]

This estimate is now generally conceded to have been too large, since the census of 1790 showed a total white population of only 3,172,006 ; and as the average normal rate of increase of population in America ever since we have had any data to enable us to strike an average has been about three per cent. a year, the population doubling about every twenty-three years, it would appear that the actual population of the colonies in 1776 was about ten per cent. less than the congressional estimate. For the purpose of lessening its proportion of the general tax, New Hampshire caused a State census to be taken in 1782, and as a result of that census reported its population at 82,000, but this figure was in all probability as far below the true number as that of the congressional estimate was above it. Pennsylvania had not quite 40,000 taxables in 1770. Counting six persons to one taxpayer, the population then would have been about 240,000, and, with an annual increase of three per cent., about 280,000 in 1776. There was, however, a very large immigration of Ulster Scots into this province in 1773 and it is probable the report made by Governor Penn to Lord Dartmouth, January 30, 1775,[9] fixing the white population at 300,000, was not far from the truth. Bancroft, as stated before, estimated the total white population of the colonies in 1775 to have been 2,100,000.[10] It would seem that we can safely follow this estimate, and assign 700,000, or one-third, to the territory east of the Hudson.[11] Of the 1,400,000 west of the Hudson and south of the St. Lawrence, the following is probably as close and accurate an estimate as can be made from the data now available, the estimated 1,400,000 of inhabitants being apportioned among the nine States in accordance with their relative populations in 1790 :

New York (excluding Vermont)	202,000
New Jersey	109,000
Pennsylvania	273,000
Delaware	30,000
Maryland	134,000
Virginia (including Kentucky)	325,000
North Carolina (including Tennessee)	206,000
South Carolina	90,000
Georgia	34,000
Total	1,403,000

Now, we may safely estimate the proportion of inhabitants of Scottish blood or descent to have been one-eighth of the whole white population in New York ; one-fifth to one-fourth in the States of New Jersey, Maryland, and Virginia ; more than one-third in Pennsylvania, Delaware, North Carolina, and Georgia ; and one-half in South Carolina.[12]

Using the census of 1790 as a basis on which to apportion the population in 1775, we find from the foregoing estimates that the number of inhabitants of Scottish ancestry at that time in the nine colonies south of New England (there were probably 25,000 in New England) was close to 385,000, as follows:

New York	25,000
New Jersey	25,000
Pennsylvania	100,000

Delaware...	10,000
Maryland..	30,000
Virginia...	75,000
North Carolina..................................	65,000
South Carolina..................................	45,000
Georgia...	10,000
Total.............................	385,000

Of the 1,400,000 total white population of these States it is probable that nearly one-third were in open or secret sympathy with the Crown during the Revolution, and did not voluntarily contribute either men or means to the American cause. Many of these were engaged in active hostilities against the patriotic party, particularly in New York and North and South Carolina, in the latter of which States at times more than half the population is said to have been on the English side. John Adams estimated that about one-third of the Americans were Loyalists in the first years of the struggle, though he sometimes reduced this figure considerably.[13] It would perhaps be not an exaggeration to say that in Maryland and Virginia in 1776 one-sixth of the white population was opposed to the war and to independence, and was to a greater or less extent Loyalist; in New Jersey, Pennsylvania, and Delaware, one-third; and in New York, Georgia, and the Carolinas, two-fifths.[14] If these figures may be taken as fairly accurate in the aggregate, they would reduce the patriotic population to somewhat below a million, outside of New England; and of that number it is altogether likely that less than half were of English extraction.

Concerning the patriotism of the Scotch-Irish, the general testimony of contemporary and later writers is to the effect that there were no Tories among them, and that they were found uniformly arrayed against the British; but it is probable this statement can be taken as applicable only in a general way and one to which many individual exceptions may be noted. One of these exceptions was that of the notorious renegade, Simon Girty and his brothers, who were probably Scotch-Irish on their mother's side. The Scotch (Jacobite) Highlanders of North Carolina principally settled along the Cape Fear River, were nearly all active Tory partisans,[15] as were also the Scotch Catholics of New York. Many Scottish names appear in Sabine's list of Loyalists, principally from these two States; and some also from Pennsylvania, among which may be mentioned that of Galloway.[16]

Among the British and Tory leaders in the South during the Revolutionary War may be mentioned Colonel Patrick Ferguson, Major James Dunlap, Captains Patrick and John Moore, Captain Peter Campbell, Captain Cunningham, Major Fraser, Lieutenant John McGinnis, Captain Walter Gilkey, Captain Grimes, Captain Wilson, Lieutenant Lafferty, Captain Alexander Cameron, Captain James Kerr, Lieutenant-Colonel Alexander Innes, all apparently of Scotch or Scotch-Irish origin, and many of them born in America. In the West were Governor Hamilton, Dr. John Connolly, the

Girty brothers, McKee, Elliott, and others ; while with Howe's northern army undoubtedly the greatest soldier was General James Grant.

NOTES TO CHAPTER VI.

[1] " A good deal of surprise was expressed at the Congress [of the Scotch-Irish Society of America, held in 1889] that a history of the Scotch-Irish had never been attempted ; but we do not have to seek far for the reason. There is ample material from which to speak in a general way of their origin and of their existence in Ireland, but when we come to their emigration to America, excepting the causes which led to it, it is meagre in the extreme. Coming from one part of Great Britain to another, no record has been preserved of their arrivals as would have been the case had they been of alien origin ; and all we know is that while a large majority came to Pennsylvania, others settled in Virginia and the Carolinas. The country along the Atlantic coast was then comparatively thickly settled, and the Scotch-Irish took up their abodes on the outskirts of civilization. This was not because the Quakers sent them there, as has been asserted, to protect their own settlements from the Indians, or because the Scotch-Irish did not wish to live near the Quakers, who were continually finding fault with them, but *for* the same reason that now takes the emigrants to the West,—*i. e.*, because there good land is cheap, and large families can be supported at a small expense. They took with them their religion and their schools, and those in Pennsylvania extended their settlements across the mountains and down the valley into Maryland and Virginia. There they met with their brethren from Virginia and Carolina, and penetrated into the country now included in the States of Kentucky and Tennessee. Excepting in a general way the records of this emigration are difficult to trace, and are only found by examining old deeds, wills, and family tradition.

" It must also be remembered that in no way, in the same sense of the word, did the Scotch-Irish Presbyterians *settle* a colony as the Puritans *settled* Massachusetts, the Quakers Pennsylvania, the Catholics Maryland, or the Episcopalians Virginia. They belonged to a later wave of emigration than any of the above, and when they arrived on this side of the Atlantic, governments were firmly established. The consequence is that there are no early governmental records that can be quoted as giving expression to their views. Besides this, the worldly condition of many of the emigrants was not such as would permit them to take an active part in political affairs, as the elective franchise was then limited by a property qualification, and some of those who might have claimed the right to vote were too deeply engaged in providing for their families to take an active part in politics. It was not, therefore, until they gained a foothold, and by their thrift, energy, and enterprise made their settlements important, that they exercised any influence in colonial affairs. When this point was gained they brought into public life an element directly antagonistic to the established order of things, and no one can deny that they were instrumental in bringing about the War for Independence, which they loyally supported. What the result of their influence would have been in Kentucky and Tennessee, where they were pioneer settlers, had it not been for the Revolution, we can only surmise. After that, civil and religious liberty were such cardinal principles of government, that it is not safe to attribute them to any one class. The material for the history of the Scotch-Irish in this country we fear has been largely destroyed. Some portion of it may yet exist in private letters, in church records, and in the diaries that some of their ministers wrote while travelling from one settlement to another. Much can also be accomplished by preparing memoirs, as full of original material as possible, of early settlers in various parts of the country."—Frederick D. Stone, in *The Pennsylvania Magazine*, January, 1890.

[2] The trouble with the historical writers who have taken upon themselves the defence of the founders of Massachusetts is that they have tried to sophisticate away the facts. In so

doing they have of necessity had recourse to lines of argument which they would not for an instant accept in defence or extenuation of those who in the Old World pursued the policy with which they find themselves confronted in the early record of the New. But there that record is : and it will not out. Roger Williams, John Wheelwright, and Anne Hutchinson come back from their banishment, and stand there as witnesses ; the Quakers and Baptists, with eyes that forever glare, swing from the gallows or turn about at the cart's tail. In Spain it was the dungeon, the rack, and the fagot ; in Massachusetts it was banishment, the whip, and the gibbet. In neither case can the records be obliterated. Between them it is only a question of degree,—one may in color be a dark drab, while the other is unmistakably a jetty black. The difficulty is with those who, while expatiating with great force of language on the sooty aspect of the one, turn and twist the other in the light, and then solemnly asseverate its resemblance to driven snow. Unfortunately for those who advocate this view of the respective Old and New World records, the facts do not justify it. On the contrary, while the course in the matter of persecution pursued by those in authority in the Old World was logical and does admit of defence, the course pursued by the founders of Massachusetts was illogical, and does not admit of more than partial extenuation. — Charles Francis Adams, *Massachusetts : Its Historians and Its History*, p. 34.

³ See *New Englander Magazine*, vol. x., pp. 393-414, for an elaborate example of this false enumeration.

⁴ Proud, *History of Pennsylvania*, vol. ii., p. 273.

⁵ Driven from their adopted home in the north of Ireland by English persecution, there was burned into their very souls the bitter recollection of English ingratitude and English broken faith. They were un-English in their origin, and they came to America — which they have always looked upon as their only country — hating England, her Church, and her form of government with the intensest hatred. They contributed as little which was original to American institutions as did the Puritans of New England ; but they were also as willing to accept new ideas from other quarters, and they contributed elements to American thought and life without which the United States of to-day would be impossible. By them American independence was first openly advocated, and but for their efforts, seconding those of the New England Puritans, that independence would not have been secured.— Campbell, *The Puritan in Holland, England, and America*, vol. ii., p. 471.

⁶ " The backwoods mountaineers . . . were all cast in the same mould, and resembled each other much more than any of them did their immediate neighbors of the plains. The backwoodsmen of Pennsylvania had little in common with the peaceful population of Quakers and Germans who lived between the Delaware and the Susquehanna ; and their near kinsmen of the Blue Ridge and the Great Smoky Mountains were separated by an equally wide gulf from the aristocratic planter communities that flourished in the tide-water regions of Virginia and the Carolinas. . . .

" The backwoodsmen were Americans by birth and parentage, and of mixed race ; but the dominant strain in their blood was that of the Presbyterian Irish — the Scotch-Irish as they were often called. . . . Mingled with the descendants of many other races, they nevertheless formed the kernel of the distinctively and intensely American stock who were the pioneers of our people in their march westward, the vanguard of the army of fighting settlers, who with axe and rifle won their way from the Alleghanies to the Rio Grande and the Pacific. . . . The Presbyterian Irish stock furnished Andrew Jackson, Samuel Houston, David Crockett, James Robertson, Lewis, the leader of the backwoods hosts in their first great victory over the northwestern Indians, and Campbell, their commander in their first great victory over the British. . . .

" That these Irish Presbyterians were a bold and hardy race is proved by their at once pushing past the settled regions, and plunging into the wilderness as the leaders of the white advance. They were the first and last set of immigrants to do this ; all others have merely followed in the wake of their predecessors. But indeed, they were fitted to be Americans from the very start; they were kinsfolk of the Covenanters; they deemed it a religious duty to interpret their own Bible, and held for a divine right the election of their own clergy. For generations their whole ecclesiastic and scholastic systems had been fundamentally democratic. . . ."—Roosevelt, *Winning of the West*, vol. i., pp. 102–106.

[7] Pitkin's *Statistics*, p. 583; *Harper's Magazine*, vol. li., p. 399.

[8] John Adams gives the following estimate as one made by Congress in 1774: "In the year 1774 there was much private conversation among the members of Congress concerning the number of souls in each colony. The delegates of each were consulted, and the estimates made by them were taken down as follows: New Hampshire, 150,000; Massachusetts, 400,000; Rhode Island, 59,678; Connecticut, 192,000; New York, 250,000; New Jersey, 130,000; Pennsylvania and Delaware, 350,000; Maryland, 320,000; Virginia, 640,000; North Carolina, 300,000; South Carolina, 225,000; total, 3,016,678."—*Works*, vol. vii., p. 302. "Governor Pownall thinks that 2,142,037 would come nearest to the real amount [of whites] in 1774."—*Ibid.*, vol. vii., p. 304. See, also, Holmes's *Annals*, vol. ii., p. 533, etc. "An estimate of the white population of the States made in 1783 for purposes of assessment gives the number as 2,389,300 (*American Remembrancer*, 1783, part ii., p. 64)."—McMaster, *History of the United States*, vol. i., p. 9.

[9] *Pennsylvania Archives*, First Series, vol. iv., p. 597.

[10] *History of the United States* (1888), vol. iv., p. 62.

[11] The population of the New England States in 1790 was 1,009,408, or a little less than one-third of the total white population of 3,172,006. It is reasonable to assume that the population of the newer middle colonies increased more by immigration between 1776 and 1790 than that of New England, and we know that many New England people moved into the western colonies, particularly to New York and Ohio. It is therefore probable that an estimate of New England's population in 1776 fixing it at one-third of the whole cannot be far out of the way.

[12] The following estimate of the white population in 1775, which does not vary much from that given in the table quoted, is found in Seaman's *Essays on the Progress of Nations*, New York, 1852, pp. 579–583: "Maine, 45,000; New Hampshire, 90,000; Vermont, 40,000; Massachusetts, 280,000; Rhode Island, 50,000; Connecticut, 195,000 [total for New England, 700,000]; New York, 175,000; New Jersey, 120,000; Pennsylvania, 275,000; Delaware, 35,000; Maryland, 160,000; Virginia, 360,000; North Carolina, 200,000; South Carolina, 90,000; Georgia, 25,000 [total, outside of New England, 1,440,000]; total for the thirteen colonies, 2,140,000." Mr. Seaman's estimate of the population of Maryland is perhaps based on a census taken in 1755, giving it 107,208 white inhabitants; but as there were but 208,649 whites in 1790, the population could not have increased as rapidly during the interim as in the other States, where it usually doubled in from twenty to twenty-five years. Hence, it is probable that 160,000 is too large an estimate for the population of Maryland in 1775, and, on the other hand, 134,000 (about 64 per cent. of the population in 1790) may be somewhat below the true figures. In New Jersey in 1830, out of a total white population of 299,667, there were about 44,000 communicants in the various churches, representing with their families perhaps 200,000 persons. Of these, 13,517 were Presbyterians; 15,567, Methodists; 6,000, Quakers; 4,173, Dutch Reformed; 3,981, Baptists; and 900, Episcopalians. It is safe to say the Presbyterians were chiefly Scottish; and likewise a considerable proportion of the Methodists and Baptists, because in the South, for instance, there are more persons of that blood in those two churches than in the whole membership of the Presbyterian Church. Smith, in his *History of the Province of New Jersey*, published in 1765, gives information respecting the number of the various congregations in the province, from which the following table is compiled: Episcopalians, 21; Presbyterians, 65; Quakers, 39; Baptists, 20; Seventh-Day Baptists, 2; Low Dutch Calvinists, or Reformed, 21; Dutch Lutherans, 4; Swedish Lutherans, 4; Moravians, 1; German Lutherans, 2; Separatists, 1; Rogerians, 1; Lutherans, 1; total, 179. In Pennsylvania in 1760 there were 31,667 taxables

(*Colonial Records*, vol. xiv., p. 336).   At that time a large part of the frontier inhabitants were not entered on the tax-lists (see Proud's *History of Pennsylvania*, vol. ii., p. 275, note).   Delaware formed part of Pennsylvania prior to 1776, and was largely overrun by the Scotch-Irish before they reached the Susquehanna valley.   A considerable part of western Maryland was settled by Scottish emigrants, as well as Cecil and Somerset counties on the Eastern Shore, and many districts around Baltimore.   Jefferson states in his *Autobiography* (p. 31), that in 1776 a majority of the inhabitants of Virginia were Dissenters (at that time chiefly Presbyterians and Baptists), and as one-fourth of the total white population was in the upper country and west of the mountains (see Virginia Militia returns in 1782, annexed to chapter ix., Jefferson's *Notes* on Virginia), and that fourth almost to a man of Scottish ancestry, we may safely conclude that of the whole white population those people comprised nearly one-fourth.   Williamson (*History of North Carolina*, vol. ii., p. 68) says that the Scottish race was the most numerous in the northwestern part of Carolina; and we know that they comprised nearly the whole of the population of Tennessee (then part of North Carolina).   Ramsay says they were more numerous than any other race in South Carolina (*History of South Carolina*, vol. i., p. 20); and they likewise formed, if not a majority, at least a controlling element in the population of Georgia.   To-day their descendants in the Carolinas, Georgia, Tennessee, Kentucky, and West Virginia form the most influential and presumably the most numerous element in the white population of those States; and in all probability the same thing is true of the native-born population of Ohio, Indiana, and Illinois.

" When the first Continental Congress began its sittings, the only frontiersmen west of the mountains, and beyond the limits of continuous settlement within the old thirteen colonies, were the two or three hundred citizens of the little Watauga commonwealth.   This qualification is put in because there were already a few families on the Monongahela [this is incorrect, because there were 7500 to 10,000 settlers in Westmoreland County, Pa., before 1776], the head of the Kanawha, and the Upper Holston ; but they were in close touch with the people behind them.   When peace was declared with Great Britain, the backwoodsmen had spread westward in groups, almost to the Mississippi, and they had increased in number to some twenty-five thousand souls, of whom a few hundred dwelt in the bend of the Cumberland, while the rest were about equally divided between Kentucky and Holston.   These figures are simply estimates ; but they are based on careful study and comparison, and, though they must be some hundreds, and maybe some thousands, out of the way, are quite near enough for practical purposes."—Roosevelt, *Winning of the West*, vol. ii., p. 370.

[13] " New York and Pennsylvania were so nearly divided — if their propensity was not against us — that if New England on one side and Virginia on the other had not kept them in awe, they would have joined the British."—*Works of John Adams*, vol. x., p. 63.   This opinion of John Adams, which he affirmed more than once in the latter part of his life, was on one occasion mentioned by him in a letter to his old compatriot, Thomas McKean, Chief Justice of Pennsylvania, a signer of the Declaration of Independence, and a member of every American Congress from that of 1765 to the close of the Revolution.   " You say," wrote McKean in reply, " that . . . about a third of the people of the colonies were against the Revolution.   It required much reflection before I could fix my opinion on this subject ; but on mature deliberation I conclude you are right, and that more than a third of influential characters were against it " (Adams's *Works*, vol. x., pp. 63, 110).—Sparks, *Washington*, vol. ii., p. 496.

John Adams was of the opinion that only about a third of the people were averse to the Revolution, but in 1780 in his letters to Calkoen, written to secure Dutch sympathy, he flatly affirms that the Tories constituted not a twentieth of the population, which may mean that he thought the French alliance and the progress of the war had diminished at that time the body of its opponents.—Winsor, *Narrative and Critical History of America*, vol. vii., p. 187.

It is probably below the truth to say that a full half of the more honorable and respected

Americans was either openly or secretly hostile to the Revolution.—Lecky, *England in the Eighteenth Century*, vol. iv., p. 153.

[14] " Of the New England colonies Connecticut had the greatest number of Tories, and next in proportion to population was the district which was afterwards known as the State of Vermont.

". . . In Virginia, especially after hostilities began, the Tories were decidedly less in number than the Whigs. In North Carolina, the two parties were about evenly divided. In South Carolina, the Tories were the numerous party; while in Georgia their majority was so great that, in 1781, they were preparing to detach that colony from the general movement of the rebellion, and probably would have done so, had it not been for the embarrassing accident which happened to Cornwallis at Yorktown in the latter part of that year."—Moses Coit Tyler, in *American Historical Review*, vol. i., p. 28 (October, 1895).

Considerable information in regard to the Loyalists may be found in Winsor's *Narrative and Critical History of America*, vol. vii., pp. 185–214, and in Sabine's *Loyalists of the Revolution*.

[15] A strong contrast to the political apathy of these worthy men [the Germans of South Carolina] was to be found in the rugged population of the upland counties. Here, the small farmers of Scotch-Irish descent were, every man of them, Whigs, burning with a patriotic ardor that partook of the nature of religious fanaticism; while on the other hand the [Highland] Scotsmen who had come over since Culloden were mostly Tories, and had by no means as yet cast off that half-savage type of Highland character which we find so vividly portrayed in the Waverley novels.—Fiske, *American Revolution*, vol. ii., p. 165.

The single exception was that of some of the Highlanders in North Carolina at the beginning of the Revolution. Banished from Scotland for taking up arms for the Pretender, their pardon was conditioned on a solemn oath of allegiance to their sovereign. Such obligations they regarded with peculiar sacredness, and they had required the king to swear to the Solemn League and Covenant. Not feeling to any great degree the evils complained of by the other colonists, they were slow to engage in the contest. Some of them at first sympathized with and aided the royalists ; but when the monarchical government came to an end, they became the fast friends and supporters of republican institutions. We may respect their moral principles, while we deplore their error of judgment, that led them at first to battle with freemen who were only demanding their rights.—Craighead, *Scotch and Irish Seeds in American Soil*, p. 315. See also *Colonial Records of North Carolina*, vol. v., pp. 1194–98.

[16] See Appendix E (Parliamentary Examination of Joseph Galloway, March, 1779).

CHAPTER VII

AMERICAN IDEALS MORE SCOTTISH THAN ENGLISH

IT is difficult to understand the grounds for claiming that the credit for the conception or development of the principle of man's equality belongs to the English. So far as history and the observation of life reveal, that principle is not established in England to-day, nor even recognized by any more than a small part of its population. Still less was it the case more than a hundred years ago, either in England or in English colonies. The distinctions of caste remained longer as bitter realities in Massachusetts than they did in Virginia ; and so far from either of those States being the first to introduce the principles of democracy, it does not seem to be overstating it to say that Quaker Pennsylvania, with two-thirds of its population non-English, had more real freedom and political equality twenty years before 1787, than Massachusetts or Virginia had twenty years after that date. Neither can it be considered an exaggeration to say that those embryonic principles of civil liberty which first were brought to New England by the Pilgrims from Holland, then for one hundred and thirty years buried and forgotten in the sterile soil of later New England Puritanism, and which finally seemed to germinate spontaneously and produce such abundant fruit during the Revolutionary period, did not come chiefly from England, but came rather from the influence of the French writers, and from Switzerland and the Dutch Republic.

Prior to 1850 Massachusetts remained essentially English, and would be so to-day were it not for the large influx of foreign population during the past fifty years. If there is any one characteristic that distinguishes the Englishman more than another, it is his persistent assertion — and, where he is able, the maintenance — of his own rights. This is doubtless a consequence of his Teutonic nature. It comes from the realization of his own intrinsic excellence, and from that spirit which prompts him to go out and subdue the earth. Unless constantly held in check, however, it is very easy for him to overstep the line between his own rights and the rights of others ; and so far as he is free to act upon his own racial instincts, he does overstep this line. This is strictly in accordance with the theory of evolution. If the Englishman did not do so unto others it might be so done unto him. We see manifestations of this encroaching spirit, in all aspects of English life or history, from the time of Hengist and Horsa down to the time of Jameson's Raid, and from the days of John Smith and John Winthrop down to the days of the year 1901. It is this aggressive spirit which proudly points the way to the universal dominion of the so-called Anglo-Saxon race ; and it is the one attribute without which the Anglo-Saxon's further racial progress, according to his own view, would be impossible. Hence, to repeat, the Englishman has a greater regard for his own rights than for those of others. So truly is this the case, that the rights of his weaker neighbor are invariably sacrificed, whenever the two clash together. As a result, there can be no real equality among the English. There is not such a thing in England to-day, nor indeed any pretence of it. Socially, the distinctions of caste and rank are perhaps not so strongly marked there between the various classes as were those between master and slave in early America, but the distance between the high and the low is almost as great,— and the abject wretchedness of the poorest class in England is far more noticeable. The opportunities of the individual are likewise restricted wholly to those of his particular class, and it is only by a miracle that he can ever hope to break through into a higher and better association.

Down to a few years before the Revolutionary War, the Englishman of New England did not differ greatly from his kinsmen at home. He had the same aggressive and independent nature, the same reverence for ecclesiastical and political power, the same suspicion, jealousy, and hatred of things not English, and the same bitter intolerance and persecuting spirit for all opinions not identical with his own. The Puritans who came to Massachusetts before 1640 soon forgot the lessons of forbearance and justice they had learned at home when persecuted for conscience' sake. They and their children retained the pride of caste, the arrogance, the narrow-mindedness, and the bigotry of the ruling class at home. They made laws prohibiting people of the poorer classes from wearing as good clothing as their superiors in wealth and position. They established a State church, and enforced conformity to its worship and universal contributions to its support, by means of the whipping-post, the jails, and the gibbet.[1] They limited suffrage to the members of the Established Church ; and during most of the time they required qualifications for church-membership which were wholly secular and which had no connection whatever with religion.[2]

In all respects, their government prior to 1760 partook only of the nature of an ecclesiastical and aristocratic oligarchy, and it was more than sixty years after that time before the principle of equal rights became fully established in Massachusetts.[3]

In America, as in every other country, the first to appreciate the necessity for man's equality before the law were those who had suffered most from the perversions of justice. These were the early Pilgrims, the Quakers, the Catholics, the Baptists, and the Scotch-Irish Presbyterians. As a rule, the oppressed can better be relied upon to distinguish between right and wrong than the oppressors. They have a keener moral sense, and their more active exercise of nature's first instinct teaches them the necessity of giving due deference to the rights of their fellow men.

As we know, laws are but limitations upon arbitrary power ; and the battle for man's industrial, political, and religious freedom has ever been a contest between vested interests and highly privileged power on the one side, and unaided, suffering, and burden-bearing humanity on the other. Injustice must be long endured and its oppressions made intolerable before the weaker masses who suffer from its burdens can acquire enough intelligent strength to resist, and to bring about reforms. Reforms rarely originate with the power-holding classes ; but are granted by them as concessions — indeed, usually wrung from them by repeated and urgent protests, prayers, and, at certain long intervals, by the sword of the revolutionist.

The oppressed and persecuted, therefore, are those to whom mankind owes its greatest social blessings. They ever stand as living witnesses against injustice and tyranny. They are the first to demand reforms. In the days of Rome, they raised the standard of the Cross, around which in due time the men of all nations gathered. Under this standard was erected later the most effective system ever devised by the genius of man for curbing the despots of paganism—a system so well organized, indeed, that when the evils which it was created to destroy had been wellnigh stamped out it gave those evils a new lease on life by introducing their spirit into its own religious polity, resulting in the massacres of the Reformation period.

So, in the days of John Knox, the blood of the early Scottish martyrs was the seed not only of the British Protestant Church, but of the greater tree of human liberty, which grew up and flourished under his fostering care; yielding its fruits in abundant measure when the time came for Scotland to take the lead against tyranny and to preserve for herself, for England, and for all mankind the threatened heritage of granted liberties.[4]

To a vastly greater extent does America owe her love of liberty to those who had suffered from persecution. At an early day becoming the harbor and home of the oppressed of all nations, its shores ever received the exiles, the refugees, and the proscribed of the monarchies of Europe. Here came the Pilgrim, the Puritan, the Baptist, the Quaker, the Mennonite, the Moravian, the Catholic, the Huguenot, and the Presbyterian. Here these people felled the forests, subdued the wilderness, planted the soil, established towns, raised schoolhouses, built churches, and in every way prepared themselves to guard the precious treasure of civil and religious liberty which they had crossed unknown seas to obtain. However, with the lapse of years and the coming of children and grandchildren, some of them grew to forget the lessons of liberty which they had learned in the old world, and remembered only the deeper-grounded hereditary admonitions of their earlier persecuting forefathers. These colonists reverted to the same life of injustice and oppression which their cousins still lived at home.

This, as has been already intimated, and as we shall more fully perceive in the pages following, was particularly the case in New England and Virginia. In the former colony, the retrogression was rapid and marked. To use the expression of its most candid native expositor, the period between 1637 and 1760 was the "glacial" age of Massachusetts.[5] In early Virginia there never was much of Freedom's light let in. Its early settlers were English Royalists, so-called Cavaliers, who were Episcopalian conformists, and dissent of any kind was prohibited by the severest penalties. The institution of slavery was established there before the expulsion of the Stuarts from England, and the slave trade was encouraged and maintained by British adventurers and Yankee skippers,' notwithstanding the protest of many of Virginia's most eminent men.'

In New England, until the Scotch came, the sole guardians of liberty were the Separatists, the Quakers, and the Baptists. The first, because of their liberal views, were forced to remove from Massachusetts to Connecticut and Maryland, and the others were driven into Rhode Island and New Jersey. In the central colonies, those who kept alive the sacred flame were found at first in Maryland, but later chiefly in Pennsylvania and New Jersey, where the Quakers had early settled and where afterwards came the Moravians, the Lutherans, the Huguenots, the Catholics, and the Covenanters. These two colonies became the only secure retreats for all the persecuted of Europe, of Britain, of New England, and of the Episcopalian colonies of the South.' Here was the landing-place of more than three-fourths of the Protestant emigrants from Ireland, and here they lived, increased, spread out over the south and west, and carried into Maryland, Virginia, and the Carolinas their democratic principles of human equality, of the responsibility of the governor to the governed, and of the supremacy of conscience over all established forms of thought, government, or worship.

It was not until a long time after the beginning of the present century that freedom of worship prevailed in Massachusetts. Up to the middle of the preceding one, it was not safe for a visiting Presbyterian minister to preach in that colony or in Connecticut. In 1740, a few Scotch-Irish families lived in Worcester. After infinite labor and pains, and with considerable sacrifice on their part, they began the erection of a small meeting-house within the confines of that village. The framework of the building had been reared, and the structure was being pushed to completion, when, one dark night, a body of citizens, representing the majesty of the State and the Puritan Church, secretly assembled before the partially erected building. Having made all preparations, they began to demolish the structure, and before morning had razed it to the ground. The offensive Presbyterians were not permitted to rebuild, but were obliged to remove to the frontiers. These Scots, and their fellow-colonists in Londonderry, New Hampshire, gave to America Matthew Thornton, Hugh McCulloch, Salmon P. Chase, Charles Foster, George B. McClellan, Asa Gray, Horace Greeley, General John Stark, and perhaps, also, Henry Knox, the Boston bookseller, whom Washington so highly honored. Reverend Samuel Finley, a Scotch-Irish Presbyterian, afterwards president of Princeton College, was arrested and imprisoned in Connecticut in 1742–43, because he ventured to preach in that colony without an invitation from a minister of one of the established churches. Francis Makemie, the father of American Presbyterianism, was likewise arrested and imprisoned in New York, in 1707, because he held services in the city of that name as a Presbyterian minister. New Jersey, Rhode Island, Pennsylvania, and Maryland were the only colonies in which there was any approach to freedom of worship during the first half of the eighteenth century. Down to the beginning of the Revolutionary period, Virginia was, if anything, more intolerant than Massachusetts. Dissenting ministers were imprisoned there after the year 1760, according to Patrick Henry's reading of their bill of indictment, for "preaching the gospel of Jesus Christ." That State was the first, however, to adopt a constitution declaring for a total separation of Church and State ; and it was owing to the earnest fight against the intolerable inflictions of the old laws, a fight made chiefly by the Scotch-Irish composing the Presbytery of Hanover,[9] that, beginning in 1776, these laws were finally swept from the statute-books. In contrasting the New England and the Southern colonies, Mr. Douglas Campbell points out the racial differences in their respective populations, and thus reveals the true reason for the differences in their treatment of the matter of religious liberty. He says [10] :

The New England Colonies were republics, but not democracies. Most of them had state churches ; their suffrage, though broad, was restricted, and among their people social distinctions were very marked. When these colonies became States they clung, with true English tenacity, to their old traditions, and looked with horror upon the levelling democratic theories advanced in other quarters. In the South, on the other hand, with its large and influential Scotch-Irish population, the natural tendency was to get as far as possible from the past. These men hated England as the New Englanders never did, and they also hated all her institutions. Their religion had taught them the absolute equality of man, and on this point they were in full accord with men like Jefferson, who had learned the same principle from the philosophers of France. Here, then, in this difference of race we may perhaps find an explanation of the fact that Virginia, formerly the most aristocratic, became the most democratic in theory of all the States ; while Massachusetts, standing on old conservative ways, became the chief exponent of the opposing theories. One thing is very clear — from no English element of the population, except the Separatists, would have come the ideas of human equality, freedom of religion, separation of Church and State, and universal suffrage.

Peculiarly appropriate to the consideration of these questions are the lectures delivered by Charles Francis Adams, at Cambridge, in 1893, which have since been published in an enlarged form, under the title of *Massachusetts : Its Historians and Its History*. Some of Mr. Adams's observations may be cited here :

So far as the principles of civil liberty and human right are concerned, Massachusetts has always been at the front. . . . The backbone of the movement which preceded the French Revolution, she inspired the agitation which ended in the fall of African slavery.

Such has been the Massachusetts record as respects equality before the law ; as respects religious toleration, it has been of a character wholly different. Upon that issue, indeed, not only has Massachusetts failed to make herself felt, but her record as a whole, and until a comparatively recent period, has been scarcely even creditable. This, too, was the case from the beginning.

The story opens with the contested charter election of 1637, as a result of which Governor John Winthrop replaced Governor Sir Harry Vane as chief executive of the colony. This election took place . . . on the 27th day of May. Four months later it was followed by the gathering of the first Synod of Massachusetts churches. . . . The Synod sat through twenty-four days, during which it busied itself unearthing heterodox opinions and making the situation uncomfortable for those suspected of heresy. . . . Finally . . . took place the trial of the arch-heretic, Mistress Anne Hutchinson ; and on the 18th of November, 1637, she was condemned to banishment.

As the twig is bent, the tree inclines. The Massachusetts twig was here and then bent ; and, as it was bent, it during hard upon two centuries inclined. The question of Religious Toleration was, so far as Massachusetts could decide it, decided in 1637 in the negative. On that issue Massachusetts then definitely and finally renounced all claim or desire to head the advancing column, or even to be near the head of the column ; it did not go to the rear, but it went well towards it, and there it remained until the issue was decided. But it is curious to note from that day to this how the exponents of Massachusetts polity and thought, whether religious or historical, have, so to speak, wriggled and squirmed in the presence of the record. . . . They did so in 1637, when they were making the record up ; they have done so ever since. There was almost no form of sophistry to which the founders of Massachusetts did not have recourse then,—for they sinned against light, though they deceived themselves while sinning ; and there is almost no form of sophistry to which the historians of Massachusetts have not had recourse since,—really deceiving themselves in their attempt to deceive others. . . .

The first decision, and the policy subsequently pursued in accordance with it, were distinct, authoritative, and final,—against religious toleration. . . . The offence, as well as the policy to be pursued by the government, was explicitly and unmistakably set forth by the chief executive and the presiding official at the trial of Mrs. Hutchinson, when Governor Winthrop said to her,—" Your course is not to be suffered ; . . . we see not that any should have authority to set up any other exercises besides what authority hath already set up." . . .

I have cited Urian Oakes, President of Harvard College from 1675 to 1681. He was succeeded by Increase Mather, who was President from 1685 to 1701 ; and in 1685 Increase Mather thus delivered himself on the subject of religious liberty :

" Moreover, sinful Toleration is an evil of exceeding dangerous consequence : Men of Corrupt minds though they may plead for Toleration, and Cry up Liberty of Conscience, etc., yet if once they should become numerous and get power into their hands, none would persecute more than they. . . . And indeed the Toleration of all Religions and Perswasions, is the way to have no true Religion at all left. . . . I do believe that Antichrist hath not at this day a more probable way to advance his Kingdom of Darkness, than by a Toleration of all Religions and Perswasions." (*A Call to the Rising Generation*, 1685, pp. 107, 108.) . . .

So far as America is concerned, it is greatly to be feared that we in the matter of historical work are yet in the filio-pietistic and patriotic stage of development. "Ancestor worship" is the rule, and an excellent illustration of the results to which that worship leads those given to it is afforded in the treatment which has been accorded to that portion of the Massachusetts record which relates to religious toleration. It is not too much to say that the resources of sophistry and special pleading have been exhausted in the attempt to extenuate or explain it away. On its face it presents difficulties of an obvious nature : wholesale proscription ; frequent banishment under penalty of death in case of return ; the infliction of punishments both cruel and degrading, amounting to torture, and that regardless of the sex of those punished ; the systematic enforcement of rigid conformity through long periods of time ;—all these things are part of the record :—and in these bad respects it is not at once apparent how the Massachussets record differs from those of Spain or France or England. But the Massachusetts school of historians, undismayed by the difficulties which confronted it, has addressed itself to the task in such a blind sense of filial devotion that the self-deception of many, and not the least eminent of those composing the school, has been complete. It is not pleasant to have such remarks made, but there is a certain justice in Sir Henry Maine's reference, to " the nauseous grandiloquence of the American panegyrical historian " (*Popular Government*, p. 222) ; and J. A. Doyle might have extended his criticism of the early New England chroniclers,— that in reading their writings " we are reading not a history but a hagiology,"— so as to include not a few later investigators. . . .

Again, approaching a yet larger question,— the question of Toleration. Confronted with the record on that matter, the Massachusetts historian, so free and frank in his denunciation of English and Italian and Spanish ecclesiastical bigotry and intolerance, proceeds to argue that, after all, " religious intolerance, like every other public restraint, is criminal wherever it is not needful for the public safety : it is simply self-defence whenever toleration would be public ruin." (Palfrey, *History of New England*, 1864, i., 300.) These words from the latest and most elaborate history of New England sound like an echo,— loud, reverberating, close at hand,— of the utterance of two centuries before. Thus Increase Mather, later president of Harvard College, expressed himself in 1681 : " The place may sometimes make a great alteration, as to indulgence to be expected. It is evident, that that Toleration is in one place not only lawful, but a necessary duty, which in another place would be destructive, and the expectation of it irrational." . . .

The stronger and more stimulating the food, the sooner any undue quantity of it is felt ; until, in the case of wine, while a carefully measured use may stimulate the healthy and nourish the sick, excess brings on fever and delirium. Rhode Island went through this experience in its early days. It was, so to speak, the dumping-ground for the surplus intellectual activity of New England. . . . Thus what was a good and most necessary element in the economy of nature and the process of human development was an excess in Rhode Island ; and the natural result followed,— a disordered community. . . . But it by no means followed that what disordered infant Rhode Island would have proved more than a healthy stimulant for larger and more matured Massachusetts. In its spirit of rigid conformity, Massachusetts rejected and expelled whatever did not immediately assimilate ; and so did Spain. Indeed, Spain regarded Holland much as Massachusetts regarded Rhode Island . . . the only trouble was that while Massachusetts did not have enough of the stimulant, Rhode Island had too much. . . .

But, as I have observed, this fact the inhabitants of Massachusetts could not see then, and the Massachusetts school of historians has refused to see it since. Those composing that school have systematically narrowed their vision ; and denouncing the rulers of Spain and France and England for bigotry, intolerance, and cruelty,—shutting their eyes to Holland . . . they have pointed to Rhode Island as an example of what must inevitably have ensued had the rulers of Massachusetts in its formative period not pursued that policy of which Philip II. was the great and only wholly successful expositor. In other words, they insist that in the seventeenth century toleration meant chaos,—" had our early ancestors . . . placed their government on the basis of liberty for all sorts of consciences, it would have been in that age a certain introduction of anarchy " (Ellis, *Memorial History of Boston,* i., 127) ; and in proof of this they point to Rhode Island. . . .

It was not until after the adoption of the Federal Constitution in 1787 that the political agitation which for Massachusetts began in 1760 can be said to have practically subsided. . . . During that period, nearly the lifetime of a generation, the glacial mass of superstition and terrorism had been gradually but imperceptibly receding and disappearing. It was still potent, but in an inert sort of way. . . . When the constitution of 1780 was framed, it yielded a grudging and reluctant consent to limited concessions of nonconformity ; but it was then so potent and so rife that the framer of the instrument abandoned in despair the attempt to put his idea of religious freedom in any form of words likely to prove acceptable to those who were to pass upon his work (*Works of John Adams,* iv., p. 222, n.). . . .

The phase of political activity has already been alluded to. In that field Massachusetts was always at home — it enjoyed an easy American supremacy which even its ice age did not wholly arrest. And now, when the struggle against superstition had drawn to a close, that against caste came again to the front, with Massachusetts still in the van. Indeed, on this issue, in 1837 as in 1635, the proper and natural place for the Puritan commonwealth was in the van. It stood there ; indeed it was the van.

The record, opened at Plymouth in December, 1620, closed as a distinct and independent record in April, 1865. That long struggle for the recognition of the equality of man before the law, of which Massachusetts was the peculiar and acknowledged champion, came to its close at Appomattox.

Frank and novel, indeed, are these confessions of Puritan shortcoming from a scion of one of New England's most noted families. While one cannot but feel that Mr. Adams has rendered an inestimable service to the cause of truth, it is yet to be questioned whether in his concluding sentences he does not himself fall under the filio-pietistic influence when speaking of the Massachusetts monopoly of the principles of civil liberty. Claiming descent from John Cotton, as Mr. Adams does, it is not strange that the inquiry arises whether the fact of that descent, and the desire to condone the bigotry of that ancestor, may not have led him to take a broader and more philosophical survey of the subject of religious liberty in New England than has been taken by any of his predecessors. It may also be questioned whether his estimate as to the perniciousness of the early Puritan ecclesiastical system may not have been reached through a realization of the inadequacy of any other conclusion to rightly explain the Jesuitical polity developed and practised by that Puritan ancestor. John Cotton was a man who argued that, "to excommunicate an Heretick, is not to persecute ; that is, it is not to punish an innocent, but a culpable and damnable person, and that not for conscience, but for persisting in error against light of conscience, whereof it hath been convinced." [11]

Would that some equally worthy descendant of John Winthrop or Edmund Andros might give us a like demagnetized and impartial account of the history of civil liberty in Massachusetts.

Lacking this, we have, however, from an outside source, a very clear and forceful criticism of those portions of Mr. Adams's addresses which partake of tendencies the opposite of the liberal ones just indicated. This criticism is to be found in Oliver Perry Temple's little volume on *The Covenanter, Cavalier, and Puritan*, [12] and is as follows :

The truth is, from the beginning "caste" was in higher favor and more regarded in this [Massachusetts] than in any of the Colonies, except possibly in Virginia. The distinction between the "better class"—those "above the ordinary degree"—and those of "mean condition," was expressly pointed out and declared by the General Court in 1651. Under the law enacted by it, regulating the kind of dress to be worn, and other things, magistrates, civil and military officers, persons of education and employment "above the ordinary degree," those who were worth two hundred pounds, and those whose estates had been considerable, but had decayed,—all those in a word called the better class, were exempt from the operation of these sumptuary laws. But the court declared most earnestly, almost pathetically, its "utter detestation and dislike that men or women of mean condition, educations, and callings, should take upon them the garbe of gentlemen, by the wearing of gold or silver lace, or buttons or poynts at their knees, to walke in great bootes ; or women of the same ranke to weare silk or tiffany hoodes or scarfes, which, though allowable to persons of greater estates, or more liberal education, yet we cannot but judge it intolerable in persons of such like condition." (Bryant's *History of the United States*, vol. ii., 63.)

Most reluctantly do I attempt to take from "Puritan Massachusetts" any of the honors she so gracefully and complacently wears, won in the long contest over the abolition of slavery, but the truth of history compels my doing so. That State was not "in the van" ; much less "was she the van" on that question until after 1836. The leading men of Virginia condemned the institution of slavery both before and immediately after the Revolution. In 1804 a number of Baptist ministers in Kentucky started a crusade against the institution, which resulted in a hot contest in the denomination, and the organization of the "Baptist Licking Locust Association Friends of Humanity." In 1806 Charles Osborne began to preach "immediate emancipation" in Tennessee. Ten years later he started a paper in Ohio, called the *Philanthropist*, devoted to the general cause of humanity. In 1822 a paper was started at Shelbyville (no State mentioned, probably Kentucky), called the *Abolition Intelligencer*.

Osborne probably went from Jefferson County, eastern Tennessee, the same county from which John Rankin,* the noted abolitionist, went, since his was the first name on the roll of the " Lost Creek Manumission Society" of that county in 1815.

Twenty years before Massachusetts took her stand at all on this subject, there were eighteen manumission, or emancipation, societies in eastern Tennessee, organized by the Covenanters, the Methodists, and the Quakers of that region, which held regular meetings for a number of years in the interest of emancipation or abolitionism. In 1822 there were five or six abolition societies in Kentucky. In 1819 the first distinctively emancipation paper in the United States was published in Jonesborough, eastern Tennessee, by Elihu Embree, a Quaker, called the *Manumission Intelligencer*. In 1821 Benjamin Lundy purchased this paper, and published it for two years in Greenville, East Tennessee, under the title of the *Genius of Universal Emancipation*. Lundy was merely the successor of Embree. At and previous to this time, the Methodist Church in Tennessee, at its conferences, was making it hot for its members who held or who bought or sold slaves, by silencing or expelling them.

On the other hand, as late as 1835, William Lloyd Garrison was mobbed in the streets of Boston, because he was an abolitionist. About 1827, Benjamin Lundy could not find an abolitionist in that city. In 1826, of the one hundred and forty-three emancipation societies in the United States, one hundred and three were in the South, and not one, so far as I know, in Massachusetts. John Rankin, the noted abolitionist of Ohio, who went from East Tennessee in 1815 or 1816,—a Covenanter and from a Covenanter neighborhood,—declared in the latter part of his life that it was safer in 1816 to 1820 to make abolition speeches in Tennessee or Kentucky than it was in the North.

In 1833, the poet Whittier and George Thompson, the celebrated English abolitionist, were mobbed and narrowly escaped with their lives, in attempting to make abolition speeches in one of the towns of Massachusetts.†

In 1833, Governor Everett, of Massachusetts, suggested the expediency of prosecuting abolitionists. Mr. Garrison said, in the first number of the *Liberator*, that he found in the North "contempt more bitter, prejudice more stubborn, and apathy more frozen than among slave-owners themselves." It was estimated, in 1828, that in Tennessee three-fifths of the people were favorably disposed toward the principle of emancipation.

In the Constitutional convention of Tennessee, in 1834, a proposition was made to emancipate the slaves of the State, and it received over one-third of the votes of the members, and the favorable indorsement of all, those opposing it approving the principle, but insisting that the time for that step had not yet arrived.

It is well known that Henry Clay commenced his political career in Kentucky by an effort to secure the emancipation of the slaves of that State. The fact is, the emancipation movement seems to have gotten its first start and strength in Virginia, Tennessee, and Kentucky, though the Quakers of Pennsylvania made feeble efforts in that direction before the Revolution.[13]

It thus appears that Massachusetts was a long way behind even some of

---

* John Rankin's father was a Pennsylvanian and was in the Revolutionary War. John was the founder of the Free Presbyterian Church and organized the first " underground railway " in Ohio.

† This is likewise true of Benjamin Lundy, who first interested Garrison in abolition.

the slave States in the struggle for "man's equality before the law." It was not until 1836 that she led in the abolition movement.

From the very beginning, as we have seen, there has always been a tendency toward caste in Massachusetts. Her people were Englishmen. They had English ideas. Ideas of caste were a part of their heritage. I have already quoted one of their early statutes showing that a clear distinction was drawn between the "better class," those "above the ordinary degree," and those of "mean condition." Those of the latter class were not to wear the same clothing that the former did.   . . .

I refer to one more fact on this subject. In the discussion over the formation of the Federal Constitution, and during the twelve years following its adoption, the Federal and the Anti-Federal parties were formed and came into being ; the one, thoroughly democratic, was led by Mr. Jefferson ; the other, led by Mr. Hamilton and John Adams, leaned toward a strong central government. Massachusetts and New England, following the lead of Mr. Adams, ranged themselves on the Federal side, while the Southern States followed the leadership of Mr. Jefferson. Massachusetts became a Federal State, while Virginia became thoroughly Democratic.

As the logical conclusion of the discussions in the last four chapters, and the underlying thought running through them all, it is affirmed as almost an undeniable proposition that the advanced theories and the liberal ideas, in reference to both political and religious liberty, which, like threads of gold, were woven into the institutions of the country and the life of the people, and which gave them their chief glory, were of Covenanter, and not of Puritan or Cavalier, origin. This is so manifestly true as to religious liberty that the reader has only to recall the facts already given in order to command his ready assent to the truth of the proposition. For it will be remembered that until after the coming of the Covenanters there was not one gleam of light in all the dreary regions dominated by the Puritans and the Cavaliers. The despotism and the gloom of intolerance reigned supreme. A narrow bigotry and superstition cast their blighting shadows over the minds of men. Notwithstanding the bold and never-ceasing teachings of the Covenanters, from the day of their arrival in the country until they had aroused the storm of the Revolution, so difficult was it to induce the Puritans and the Cavaliers to relax their deadly grasp on the consciences of men that eleven years passed away after the inauguration of hostilities in the colonies before universal religious liberty prevailed in the Cavalier State, and nearly sixty years before complete religious emancipation was accomplished in Massachusetts.

The struggles for political and personal liberty are always easily remembered. The glare and the thunders of war are never forgotten. But the quiet, the persistent, and the courageous warfare waged by the Covenanters, everywhere and at all times, for the right of conscience, while it was effecting a revolution as important for the happiness of mankind as the great one settled by arms, did not appeal to the senses and the imagination of men, and hence it has been but little noted by speakers or by historians.

To prove the correctness of the other branch of my summary, or proposition, in reference to political freedom, it is only necessary to refer to the facts already given, to show the deeply rooted ideas of caste and social distinction existing in the minds of the ruling classes, and in the society of Virginia and Massachusetts, previous to and at the date of the Revolution. These caste ideas and social distinctions did not prevent those favorable to

Independence from doing their duty in the great contest of arms, but they did have a most important influence in shaping the institutions of the country, and in giving tone and coloring to its thought afterward.   And in this second stage of the Revolution, these Covenanters, dwelling in large numbers in all the States south of New England, with their liberal and advanced ideas, learned in their bitter experience of nearly two centuries, and with their creed of republicanism, were ready to infuse their spirit and inject their ideas of equality into the constitutions, the institutions, and into the life of that vast region.   Under this influence even aristocratic Cavalier Virginia became, as we have seen, the most democratic of all the States. Under this influence, also, the constitution of Tennessee was framed, which was pronounced by Mr. Jefferson the most republican in its spirit of all the American constitutions.   And this same spirit pervaded the institutions of all the Southern States, excepting South Carolina.   I do not withhold from Mr. Jefferson the high meed of praise he so richly merits for his magnificent work in behalf of liberal ideas and republican institutions in Virginia.   But Mr. Jefferson was always a Covenanter in his opinions as to political and religious liberty.   Besides this, we have seen that he would have failed in his great reforms, except for the powerful aid he received from the Covenanters.

Nor do I ignore the teachings of Roger Williams, nor the liberal ideas of the Dutch of New York, nor the conservative opinions of the Quakers, nor the tolerant spirit of the Catholics of Maryland, in accomplishing these great results, but these were insignificant in their influence in comparison with the widely extended power of the great Covenanter race.

NOTES TO CHAPTER VII.

[1] See Alexander Johnston's " History of Parties," in *Nar. and Crit. History of America*, vol. vii., and Bryant's *History of the United States*. " Ministers of the Gospel would have a poor time of it if they must rely on a free contribution of the people for their maintenance. . . . The laws of the province [Massachusetts] having had the royal approbation to ratify them, they are the king's laws. By these laws it is enacted that there shall be public worship of God in every plantation ; that the person elected by the majority of inhabitants to be so, shall be looked upon as the minister of the place ; and that the salary for him, which they shall agree upon, shall be levied by a rate upon all the inhabitants. In consequence of this, the minister thus chosen by the people is (not only Christ's, but also) in reality the king's minister, and the salary raised for him is raised in the king's name, and is the king's allowance unto him."— Cotton Mather, *Ratio Disciplinæ ; or, Faithful Account of the Discipline Professed and Practised in the Churches of New England*, p. 20.

[2] " The constancy of the Quakers under their sufferings begot a pity and esteem for their persons, and an approbation of their doctrines ; their proselytes increased ; the Quakers returned as fast as they were banished ; and the fury of the ruling party was raised to such a height that they proceeded to the most sanguinary extremities. Upon the law they had made, they seized at different times upon five of those who had returned from banishment, condemned, and hanged them. It is unknown how far their madness had extended, if an order from the King and Council in England about the year 1661 had not interposed to restrain them.

" It is a task not very agreeable to insist upon such matters ; but, in reality, things of this nature form the greatest part of the history of New England, for a long time. They persecuted the Anabaptists, who were no inconsiderable body amongst them, with almost an equal severity. In short, this people, who in England could not bear being chastised with rods, had no sooner got free from their fetters than they scourged their fellow refugees with scorpions ; though the absurdity, as well as the injustice of such a proceeding in them, might stare them in the face."—Burke, *European Settlements in America*, vol. ii., p. 151.

³ Most of the States [at the time of Jefferson's inauguration] had had property qualifications as limitations either on the right of suffrage or on the composition of the legislature. The Republican policy had been to remove such limitations in the States which they controlled, and to diminish the time of residence required for naturalization. The bulk of the new voters, therefore, went to them, and they were continually making their hold stronger on the States which had come under their control. New England and Delaware remained Federalist, and Maryland was doubtful ; the other States could be counted on almost certainly as Republican. Under the New England system, governmental powers were practically divided among a multitude of little town republics ; and restriction on the right of suffrage, intrenched in these towns, had to be conquered in a thousand successive strongholds. The towns, too, sufficient to themselves, cared little for the exclusion from national life involved in their system ; and for nearly twenty years New England was excommunicated from national politics. It was not until the rise of manufactures and of dissenting sects had reinforced continuous agitation that the Republican revolution penetrated New England and overcame the tenacious resistance of her people.— Alexander Johnston, "History of Parties," in *Narrative and Critical History of America*, vol. vii., p. 272.

⁴ " Knox, under God, made the Scotch and the Scotch-Irish. . . .

"Observe well, the influence of this prophetic patriot was felt most at St. Andrews, through the long Strathclyde, in the districts of Ayr, Dumfries, and Galloway, the Lothians and Renfrew. There exactly clustered the homes which thrilled to the herald voice of Patrick Hamilton ; there were the homes which drank in the strong wine of Knox ; there were the homes of tenacious memories and earnest fireside talk ; there were the homes which sent forth once and again the calm, shrewd, iron-nerved patriots who spurned as devil's lie the doctrine of ' passive resistance ' ; and there — mark it well —were the homes that sent their best and bravest to fill and change Ulster ; thence came in turn the Scotch-Irish of the *Eaglewing ;* thence came the settlers of Pennsylvania, Virginia, the Carolinas, Tennessee, and Kentucky ; and the sons of these men blush not as they stand beside the children of the *Mayflower* or the children of the Bartholomew martyrs. I know whereof I affirm. My peculiar education and somewhat singular work planted me, American-born, in the very heart of these old ancestral scenes ; and from parishioners who held with deathless grip the very words of Peden, Welsh, and Cameron, from hoary-headed witnesses in the Route of Antrim and on the hills of Down, have I often heard of the lads who went out to bleed at Valley Forge,— to die as victors on King's Mountain,—and stand in the silent triumph of Yorktown. We have more to thank Knox for than is commonly told to-day.

" Here we reach our Welshes and Witherspoons, our Tennents and Taylors, our Calhouns and Clarks, our Cunninghams and Caldwells, our Pollocks, Polks, and Pattersons, our Scotts and Grays and Kennedys, our Reynoldses and Robinsons, our McCooks, McHenrys, McPhersons, and McDowells.

" But the man behind is Knox. Would you see his monument? Look around. Yes : To this, our own land, more than any other, I am convinced must we look for the fullest outcome and the yet all unspent force of this more than royal leader, this masterful and moulding soul. . . . Carlyle has said : ' Scotch literature and thought, Scotch industry ; James Watt, David Hume, Walter Scott, Robert Burns. I find Knox and the Reformation at the heart's core of every one of those persons and phenomena ; I find that without Knox and the Reformation, they would not have been. Or what of Scotland ?' Yea, verily ; no Knox, no Watt, no Burns, no Scotland, as we know and love and thank God for : And must we not say no men of the Covenant ; no men of Antrim and Down, of Derry and Enniskillen ; no men of the Cumberland valleys ; no men of the Virginian hills ; no men of the Ohio stretch, of the Georgian glades and the Tennessee Ridge ; no rally at Scone ; no thunders in St. Giles ; no testimony from Philadelphian Synod ; no Mecklenburg declaration ; no memorial from Hanover Presbytery ; no Tennent stirring the Carolinas ; no Craighead sowing the seeds of the coming revolution ; no Witherspoon pleading for the signing of our great charter ; and no such declaration and no such constitution as are ours, — the great Tilghman himself being witness in these clear words, never by us to be let die : ' The framers of the Constitution of the United States were greatly indebted to the standards of the Presbyterian Church of Scotland in modelling that admirable document.'— Rev. John S. McIntosh, *Proceedings Scotch-Irish Society of America*, vol. i., pp. 199–201.

"In the history of Scotland, too, I can find properly but one epoch : we may say, it contains nothing of world-wide interest at all but this Reformation by Knox. A poor, barren country, full of continual broils, dissensions, massacrings ; a people in the last state of rudeness and destitution, little better perhaps than Ireland at this day. Hungry, fierce barons, not so much as able to form any arrangement with each other *how to divide* what they fleeced from these poor drudges ; but obliged, as the Columbian Republics are at this day, to make of every alteration a revolution ; no way of changing a ministry but by hanging the old ministers on gibbets : this is a historical spectacle of no very singular significance : ' Bravery ' enough, I doubt not ; fierce fighting in abundance : but not braver or fiercer than that of their old Scandinavian Sea-king ancestors ; *whose* exploits we have not found worth dwelling on ! It is a country as yet without a soul : nothing developed in it but what is rude, external, semi-animal. And now at the Reformation, the internal life is kindled, as it were, under the ribs of this outward material death. A cause, the noblest of causes, kindles itself, like a beacon set on high ; high as Heaven, yet attainable from Earth ;—whereby the meanest man becomes not a Citizen only, but a Member of Christ's visible Church ; a veritable Hero, if he prove a true man !

"This that Knox did for his nation, I say, we may really call a resurrection as from death. It was not a smooth business ; but it was welcome, surely, and cheap at that price, had it been far rougher. On the whole, cheap at any price ;—as life is. The people began to *live:* they needed first of all to do that, at what cost and costs soever. Scotch Literature and Thought, Scotch Industry ; James Watt, David Hume, Walter Scott, Robert Burns : I find Knox and the Reformation acting in the heart's core of every one of these persons and phenomena ; I find that without the Reformation they would not have been."—Thomas Carlyle, *On Heroes and Hero Worship*, iv.

[5] So much for the early clergy. As to the magistrates, in the mouths of James I. and Charles I., of Philip II. of Spain, or Louis XIV. of France, the words : "We see not that any should have authority to set up any other exercises besides what authority had already set up,"— these words in those mouths would have had a familiar as well as an ominous sound. To certain of those who listened to them, they must have had a sound no less ominous when uttered by Governor John Winthrop in the Cambridge meeting-house on the 17th of November, 1637. In them was definitely formulated and clearly announced the policy thereafter to be pursued in Massachusetts. It was thereafter pursued in Massachusetts. John Winthrop, John Endicott, and Thomas Dudley were all English Puritans. As such they had sought refuge from authority in Massachusetts. On what ground can the impartial historian withhold from them the judgment he visits on James and Philip and Charles and Louis ? The fact would seem to be that the position of the latter was logical though cruel ; while the position of the former was cruel and illogical.— C. F. Adams, *Massachusetts : Its Historians and Its History*, p. 38.

[6] See letter of Col. William Byrd, written from Virginia to Lord Egmont, July 12, 1730, printed in *American Historical Review* for October, 1895, vol. i., p. 88 ; also, W. E. B. DuBois, *The Suppression of the African Slave-Trade to the United States of America, 1638–1870*, chapter iv. (*Harvard Historical Studies*, vol. i.).

[7] Bancroft, vol. ii., pp. 276–279, 549, 550 ; vol. iii., pp. 410–413 ; vol. iv., p. 34 ; vol. v., p. 329.

"I have found no mention of negroes in the colony until about 1650. The first brought here as slaves were in a Dutch ship ; after which the English commenced the trade, and continued it until the Revolutionary War. That suspended, *ipso facto*, their further importation for the present, and the business of the war pressing constantly on the Legislature, this subject was not acted on finally until the year '78, when I brought in a bill to prevent their further importation. This passed without opposition, and stopped the increase of the evil by importation, leaving to future efforts its final eradication. In 1769 I became a member of the Legislature by the choice of the county in which I lived, and so continued until it was closed by the Revolution. I made one effort in that body for the permission of the emancipation of slaves, which was rejected; and indeed, during the regal government nothing liberal could expect success."—Jefferson's *Autobiography*, pp. 3, 38.

[8] "In 1681, William Penn received from Charles II. a grant of the Province of Pennsylvania, including what is now the State of Delaware. Penn's mother was a Dutch woman from Rotterdam, and one very prominent in her generation. His peculiar religious ideas, as we have already seen, were derived from his mother's country. He travelled extensively in Holland, and spoke the language so well that he preached to the Dutch Quakers in their native tongue. Finally, before coming to America, he took up his residence for some time at Emden, in democratic East Friesland. Under all these influences, he sat down in 1682, and prepared a "Frame of Government" for his dominion, and a "Code of Laws," which was afterwards adopted by the General Assembly. In their preparation he was assisted by Algernon Sidney, who had lived many years upon the Continent, who was perfectly familiar with the institutions of the Netherland Republic and on most intimate terms with its leading statesmen. How much they borrowed from Holland we shall see hereafter. [The registration of land titles; that all prisons should be workhouses for felons, vagrants, etc., and should be free to others as to fees, board, and lodgings; that landed estate should be liable for a descendant's debt (one-third in cases where issue was left); that one-third the estate of a murderer passed to the next of kin of his victim ; that all children in the province over the age of twelve were to be taught a trade ; religious toleration.]

"With Pennsylvania, we reach the most southern point to which a Dutch influence upon the early settlers of America can be traced, as we also reach the limit of the colonies whose institutions, except that of slavery, have affected the American Commonwealth. Virginia alone contributed an idea, that of the natural equality of man ; but this was borrowed by her statesmen from the Roman law.

"One fact in connection with the Southern colonies, which in early days were almost wholly under an English influence, is very significant. In 1669, John Locke, with the aid of the Earl of Shaftesbury, prepared a frame of government for Carolina. None of the provisions of this constitution, except that for recording deeds and mortgages, were borrowed from Holland, and not one of them, with this exception, has found a permanent place among American Institutions. *The Puritans in Holland, England, and America*, vol. ii., pp. 418–420 (by permission of Messrs. Harper & Brothers).

[9] This Presbytery furnished 10,000 names to a petition, which was the force back of Jefferson's bill for religious freedom (1785), an enactment of which he was so proud that he had a statement of the fact that he was its author engraved upon his tombstone. The petition is printed herein as Appendix F.

[10] *The Puritan in Holland, England, and America*, vol. ii., p. 502.

[11] Cotton's "Answer to Williams," *Narragansett Club Publications*, vol. iii., pp. 48–49 ; also vol. ii., p. 27.

[12] See Appendix L (Tithes in Ulster).

[13] The first printed protest in America against slavery, issued by Rev. George Keith, a Scotch Quaker, October 13, 1693, and published at New York by William Bradford, is reproduced in the *Pennsylvania Magazine*, vol. xiii., pp. 265–270.

CHAPTER VIII

THE SCOTTISH KIRK AND HUMAN LIBERTY

IT may seem a reiteration of the words of Mr. Henry Thomas Buckle to say that the history of Scotland during the century and a half from 1550 to 1700 is almost completely merged in the history of the Scottish Church.[1] He who would form a just conception of the forces in operation in that country, during the period when the Middle Ages passed away and the modern era began, must study them chiefly in connection with their bearing on religion. But it will not suffice in such an investigation to assume that ecclesiasticism means religion. In his elaborate and, in some respects, highly philosophical analysis of civilization in Scotland,[2] it seems to the writer that Mr. Buckle has failed to reach a wholly true and satisfactory estimate of Scottish character, and that in just so far as he has neglected to discriminate in this regard. It is true he approaches the subject from the logical English point of view. Looking upon the institution of the Church with strictly utilitarian eyes, he fails to perceive the spiritual life of its people, of which the Church in Scotland may in all seriousness be considered merely the medium of expression. Long accustomed by heredity, training, and experience to the ecclesiastical system at home, which, even down to his own time, was wont to administer to its adherents only such theological pabulum as would nourish doctrines according with the views and vices of its reigning head, it is at least not surprising that the great mind which produced the Introduction to the *History of Civilization in England* should fail to strike the keynote of that part of its theme which relates to North Britain. Nor can it be greatly wondered at, in view of the history of the English Church establishment, that one of its native observers should formulate a judgment against the religious system of the neighboring country, finding evidences in it of the same spirit which dominated the Church at home, and denouncing it as the chief hindrance to its country's progress ; even though in so doing his gravest charge against the Scottish Church is, that its votaries have too much superstitious reverence for God and the Bible.

It will ever be a matter of regret that Mr. Buckle passed away just as he had fairly entered upon the prosecution of his great work. Still more is it to be regretted that he died before the full promulgation of our modern theories of science and philosophy. Had he lived to-day it is not unlikely that his name would have been linked with that of Herbert Spencer, and his methods in historical analysis become analogous in nature and merit to those of that master-thinker in matters of speculative philosophy. He might, in some respects, have excelled that philosopher had he enjoyed the fuller knowledge of the present day instead of beginning to unfold and develop his theories of the philosophy of history by the light of the first fitful and half-clouded rays of forty years ago. In that event, being a student of history, it is possible Buckle might have taken a different view of the part religion has played in the progress of the world from that expressed in his work. He might, also, afterwards have based his theory as to Scottish progress or retro-gression upon a different premise from the one which he has used. Whether he would have done so or not, however, it is reasonably certain that, if living to-day, he would have seen a gradual change of public opinion between the years 1861 and 1900 as to the correctness of his original hypothesis. Nor could he have failed to perceive a slowly growing conviction on the part of fair-minded thinkers — a conviction that, after all, some of the chief ele-ments of human progress are bound up with the phenomena of religion; that human nature does not reach its highest development under a strictly intel-lectual standard of morality ; that human reason is not yet sufficiently acute to classify, much less to harmonize, the incongruities of daily life and expe-rience ; in short, that the permanency of nations and the endurance of the race itself depends not so much upon intellectual development as upon the cultivation, to a greater or less extent, of those restraining influences of religion which the able author of the *History of Civilization in England* has denominated a "mixture of wonder and fear." [3]

Mr. Buckle has failed to grasp the one salient point necessary for a right understanding of the history of religion and its effects in Scotland. Or, noting the results of a certain moving cause, he has so clouded and distorted the evidences of its presence that we can only reach a true apprehension of the cause by reasoning backward from his luminous and eulogistic summary of its effect.

This cause or principle of action in the Scottish people, the workings of which have been so beneficial to the growth of human liberty and to man's progress, this divine afflatus which Mr. Buckle seeks to stigmatize by the use of that much-abused term "superstition," and to classify as an emanation from the caverns of darkness and ignorance, is the principle of conscience. It is this which is the guiding light of the Scottish soul and intellect. With-out the full and just recognition of its pervading influence among that people, it were vain for us to attempt to read aright the lessons of Scottish history ; and idle to seek for explanation of the reasons for Scottish pre-eminence, of which we see so many proofs in the mental and material subjugation of the earth.

Probably the most noticeable instance of the blindness of the author of the *History of Civilization in England* is afforded in the conclusion reached by him in the following passage [4] :

By this union of ignorance with danger, the clergy had, in the fifteenth century, obtained more influence in Scotland than in any other Euro-pean country, Spain alone excepted. And as the power of the nobles had increased quite as rapidly, it was natural that the Crown, completely over-shadowed by the great barons, should turn for aid to the Church. During the fifteenth century and part of the sixteenth, this alliance was strictly preserved, and the political history of Scotland is the history of a struggle by the kings and clergy against the enormous authority of the nobles. The contest, after lasting about one hundred and sixty years, was brought to a close in 1560, by the triumph of the aristocracy and the overthrow of the Church. With such force, however, had the circumstance just narrated engrained superstition into the Scotch character, that the spiritual classes quickly rallied, and, under their new name of Protestants they became as formidable as under their old name of Catholics. . . . The great Protestant movement which, in other countries, was democratic, was, in Scotland, aristocratic. We shall also see, that, *in Scotland, the Reformation, not being the work of the people, has never produced the effects which might have been expected from it, and which it did produce in England.* It is, indeed, but too evident that, while in England Protestantism has diminished superstition, has weakened the clergy, has increased toleration, and, in a word, has secured the triumph of secular interests over ecclesiastical ones, its result in Scotland has been entirely different; and that in that country the Church, changing its form without altering its spirit, not only cherished its ancient pretensions but unhappily retained its ancient power; and that, although that power is now dwindling away, the Scotch preachers still exhibit, whenever they dare, an insolent and domineering spirit, which shows how much real weakness there yet lurks in the nation, where such extravagant claims are not immediately silenced by the voice of loud and general ridicule.

The inadequacy and perniciousness of Mr. Buckle's conception of the real bearing of religion upon the national life and character of the Scottish people cannot perhaps be better shown than by such a disingenuous statement as this. In it he deliberately ignored the facts, and falsified and reversed the verdict of modern history. Messrs. Freeman and Gardiner, in their sketch of English history contained in a recent edition of the standard reference manual of Great Britain,[5] only voice the opinion of all honest students when they say:

The English Reformation then, including in that name the merely ecclesiastical changes of Henry as well as the more strictly religious changes of the next reign, was not in its beginning either a popular or a theological movement. In this it differs from the Reformation in many continental countries, and especially from the Reformation in the northern part of Britain. The Scottish Reformation began much later; but, when it began, its course was far swifter and fiercer. That is to say, it was essentially popular and essentially theological. The result was, that, of all the nations which threw off the dominion of the Roman See, England, on the whole, made the least change, while Scotland undoubtedly made the most. (On the whole, because, in some points of sacramental doctrine and ritual, the Lutheran churches, especially in Sweden, have made less change than the Church of England has. But nowhere did the general ecclesiastical system go on with so little change as it did in England.) In England change began from above. . . . The small party of theological reform undoubtedly welcomed the changes of Henry, as being likely in the end to advance their own cause; but the mass of the nation was undoubtedly favorable to Henry's system of Popery without the Pope.

On the same subject, Green says [6] :

Knox had been one of the followers of Wishart ; he had acted as pastor to the Protestants who after Beaton's murder held the Castle of St. Andrews, and had been captured with them by a French force in the summer of 1547. The Frenchmen sent the heretics to the galleys ; and it was as a galley slave in one of their vessels that Knox next saw his native shores. . . . Released at the opening of 1549, Knox found shelter in England, where he became one of the most stirring among the preachers of the day, and was offered a bishopric by Northumberland. Mary's accession drove him again to France. But the new policy of the Regent now opened Scotland to the English refugees, and it was as one of these that Knox returned in 1555 to his own country. Although he soon withdrew to take charge of the English congregations at Frankfort and Geneva, his energy had already given a decisive impulse to the new movement. In a gathering at the house of Lord Erskine he persuaded the assembly to " refuse all society with idolatry, and bind themselves to the uttermost of their power to maintain the true preaching of the Evangile, as God should offer to their preachers an opportunity." The confederacy woke anew the jealousy of the government, and persecution revived. But some of the greatest nobles now joined the reforming cause. The Earl of Morton, the head of the house of Douglas, the Earl of Argyle, the greatest chieftain of the west, and above all a bastard son of the late King, Lord James Stuart, who bore as yet the title of Prior of St. Andrews, but who was to be better known afterwards as the Earl of Murray, placed themselves at the head of the movement. The remonstrances of Knox from his exile at Geneva stirred them to interfere in behalf of the persecuted Protestants ; and at the close of 1557 these nobles united with the rest of the Protestant leaders in an engagement which became memorable as the first among those Covenants which were to give shape and color to Scotch religion.

" We," ran this solemn bond, " perceiving how Satan in his members, the Antichrists of our time, cruelly doth rage, seeking to overthrow and to destroy the Evangel of Christ, and His Congregation, ought according to our bounden duty to strive in our Master's cause even unto the death, being certain of our victory in Him. The which our duty being well considered, we do promise before the Majesty of God and his Congregation that we, by His grace, shall with all diligence continually apply our whole power, substance, and our very lives to maintain, set forward, and establish the most blessed Word of God and His Congregation, and shall labor at our possibility to have faithful ministers, purely and truly to minister Christ's Evangel and Sacraments to his people. We shall maintain them, nourish them, and defend them, the whole Congregation of Christ and every member thereof, at our whole power and wearing of our lives, against Satan and all wicked power that does intend tyranny or trouble against the foresaid Congregation. Unto the which Holy Word and Congregation we do join us, and also do forsake and renounce the congregation of Satan with all the superstitious abomination and idolatry thereof : and moreover shall declare ourselves manifestly enemies thereto by this our faithful promise before God, testified to His Congregation by our subscription at these presents."

The Covenant of the Scotch nobles marked a new epoch in the strife of religions. Till now the reformers had opposed the doctrine of nationality to the doctrine of Catholicism. In the teeth of the pretensions which the Church advanced to a uniformity of religion in every land, whatever might be its differences of race or government, the first Protestants had advanced the principle that each prince or people had alone the right to determine its form of faith and worship. " Cujus regio " ran the famous phrase which embodied their theory, " ejus religio." It was the acknowledgment of this principle that the Lutheran princes obtained at the Diet of Spires ; it was on this principle that Henry based his Act of Supremacy. Its strength lay in the correspondence of such a doctrine with the political circumstances of the time. It was the growing feeling of nationality which combined with the growing development of monarchical power to establish the theory that the political and religious life of each nation should be one, and that the religion of the people should follow the faith of the prince. Had Protestantism, as seemed at one time possible, secured the adhesion of all the European princes, such a theory might well have led everywhere as it led in England to the establishment of the worst of tyrannies, a tyranny that claims to lord alike over both body and soul. The world was saved from this danger by the tenacity with which the old religion still held its power. In half the countries of Europe the disciples of the new opinions had soon to choose between submission to their conscience and submission to their prince ; and a movement which began in contending for the religious supremacy of kings ended in those wars of religion which arrayed nation after nation against their sovereigns. In this religious revolution Scotland led the way. Her Protestantism was the first to draw the sword against earthly rulers. The solemn " Covenant " which bound together her " Congregation " in the face of the regency, which pledged its members to withdraw from all sub-mission to the religion of the State and to maintain in the face of the State their liberty of conscience, opened that vast series of struggles which ended in Germany with the Peace of Westphalia and in England with the Toleration Act of William the Third.

The " Covenant " of the lords sounded a bold defiance to the Catholic reaction across the border. While Mary replaced the Prayer-book by the Mass, the Scotch lords resolved that wherever their power extended the Common Prayer should be read in all churches. While hundreds were going to the stake in England, the Scotch nobles boldly met the burning of their preachers by a threat of war. " They trouble our preachers," ran their bold remonstrance against the bishops in the Queen-mother's presence ; " they would murder them and us ! shall we suffer this any longer ? No, madam, it shall not be ! " and therewith every man put on his steel bonnet.

The testimony of Froude is likewise equally direct and positive [1] :

But in England the Reformation was more than half political. The hatred of priests and popes was more a predominant principle than specialty of doctrine. . . . What kings and Parliament had done in England, in Scot-land had to be done by the people, and was accompanied therefore with the passionate features of revolt against authority. . . . John Knox became thus the representative of all that was best in Scotland. He was no narrow fanatic, who, in a world in which God's grace was equally visible in a thousand creeds, could see truth and goodness nowhere but in his own for-mula. He was a large, noble, generous man, with a shrewd perception of actual fact, who found himself face to face with a system of hideous iniquity.

Here, then, we have the direct refutation of Buckle's statements as to the origin of the Scottish Reformation, by four leading authorities on British history, and their opinions are merely confirmatory of the judgment of all observing and unprejudiced men.

Much in the same line with Mr. Buckle's theory of the origin and accomplishment of the Reformation in Scotland is the oft-repeated assertion that the Scottish Church was as relentless and unceasing a persecutor of dissenters as were those of the Papacy or Episcopacy.[8] This assertion, likewise, is not sustained by the facts. Bigoted and intolerant as the Scottish Church became after it was made a part of the machinery of State, its methods were mild and innocuous compared with those of its rivals.[9] The one solitary case where death was inflicted by the authorities for heresy, at the instigation or with the approval of the Kirk, was that of Thomas Aikenhead, who was hanged in 1697 on the charge of atheism and blasphemy against God. While this was a wholly unjustifiable and villainous act of cruelty, it can hardly be classed with those persecutions from which the Presbyterians had suffered. It would seem to belong rather to that class of religious perversities of which the most familiar example was the burning of witches. In this latter diabolism Scotland engaged with perhaps greater zest than either England or Massachusetts. The distinction between the crime of the hanging of Thomas Aikenhead and that of the burning of George Wishart, by the Catholics, or the drowning of Margaret Wilson, by the Episcopalians, therefore, is probably to be found by a contrast of motive rather than of degree ; at most it is the difference between fanaticism and tyranny. In the latter cases, the sufferers had denied the authority of the bishops. These prelates aimed at preferment by mixing politics with religion, and could not be wholly sincere or disinterested. George Wishart and Margaret Wilson were slain by them because the bishops could brook no limitations upon their own power. In the case of Thomas Aikenhead, the authority of God had been questioned, and the fanatical zealotry of the ministers permitted the application of John Cotton's law, without the apparent intervention of any personal motives.[10] If such a distinction should at first appear too finely drawn, an examination of the workings of the two principles thus suggested will show that their results are, as a rule, widely different. Indeed, in some aspects, their dissimilarity is almost of equal extent and correspondence with that existing between the two churches of North and South Britain; and the divergence of their ends but little short of that which marks the two opposite principles of democracy and despotism. In New England, where the Calvinistic theory of the supremacy of God and the Bible over man's conscience was at first as fully carried out as in Scotland, a system of democracy was inaugurated which, until its progress became retarded by the union of Church and State, reached a higher degree of perfection than had been the case in any other English community. This system, but for the entrance and long-continued presence of the fatally defective policy of ecclesiastical usurpation in secular affairs, might have developed into an ideal form of government. In Old England, on the contrary, where the authority of the bishops over man's conscience was ever maintained and the theory fully developed by Laud and Sharp and the Stuarts, a highly despotic form of government resulted, from which mankind had occasionally to find relief by "blood-letting," as in the revolutions of 1638 and 1688. The only similarity apparent in the ultimate workings of these two principles, therefore, would seem to be that identical results have sometimes been reached by the action of one and reaction from the other.

No theological system has yet been devised that is able to sustain this dual relation—secular and spiritual—without deteriorating ; and the history of the Presbyterian Church in Scotland after 1690, when it became the established Church of the State, marks a rapid change in spirit and a steady decadence in spiritual power and influence, only paralleled, perhaps, by that of the kindred Church of New England after 1640.

Charles II., at the time of his father's death, was a friendless fugitive. The Scotch offered to receive him as their king, on condition that he should pledge himself by oath to regard and preserve their Presbyterian form of Church government. To this he assented. When he arrived in the kingdom he subscribed the covenant ; and again at his coronation, under circumstances of much more than usual solemnity, he swore to preserve it inviolate. The Scotch accordingly, armed in his defence ; but, divided among themselves, and led by a general very unfit to cope with Cromwell, they were soon defeated, and Charles was again driven to the Continent. When he returned in 1660, he voluntarily renewed his promise to the Scotch, by whom his restoration had been greatly promoted, not to interfere with the liberty of their Church. No sooner, however, was he firmly seated on his throne than all these oaths and promises were forgotten. Presbyterianism was at once abolished, and Episcopacy established ; not such as it was under James I. when bishops were little more than standing moderators of the Presbyteries, but invested, by the arbitrary mandate of the King, with the fulness of prelatical power. An act was passed making it penal even to speak publicly or privately against the King's supremacy, or the government of the Church by archbishops and bishops. A court of high commission, of which all the prelates were members, was erected and armed with inquisitorial powers. Multitudes of learned and pious ministers were ejected from their parishes, and ignorant and ungodly men, for the most part, introduced in their stead. Yet the people were forced, under severe penalties, to attend the ministrations of these unworthy men. All ejected ministers were prohibited preaching or praying except in their own families ; and preaching or praying in the fields was made punishable with death. Any one, though the nearest relative, who should shelter, aid, or in any way minister to the wants of those denounced, was held liable to the same penalty as the person assisted. All landholders were required to give bond that their families and dependants should abstain from attending any conventicle. To enforce these wicked laws torture was freely used to extort evidence or confession ; families were reduced to ruin by exorbitant fines ; the prisons were filled with victims of oppression ; multitudes were banished and sold as slaves ; women and even children were tortured or murdered for refusing to take an oath they could not under-stand ; soldiers were quartered upon the defenceless inhabitants and allowed free license ; men were hunted like wild beasts, and shot or gibbeted along the highways.   Modern history hardly affords a parallel to the cruelty and oppression under which Scotland groaned for nearly thirty years.   And what was the object of all this wickedness ?   It was to support Episcopacy. It was done for the bishops, and, in a great measure, by them.   They were the instigators and supporters of these cruel laws, and of the still more cruel execution of them.   Is it any wonder, then, that the Scotch abhorred Episco-pacy ?   It was in their experience identified with despotism, superstition, and irreligion.   Their love of Presbyterianism was one with their love of liberty and religion.   As the Parliament of Scotland was never a fair representation of the people, the General Assembly of their Church became their great organ for resisting oppression and withstanding the encroachments of their sovereigns.   The conflict, therefore, which in England was so long kept up between the Crown and the House of Commons, was in Scotland sustained between the Crown and the Church.   This was one reason why the Scotch became so attached to Presbyterianism ; this, too, was the reason why the Stuarts hated it, and determined at all hazards to introduce prelacy as an ally to despotism.[11]

The chief period of the so-called Presbyterian persecution in Scotland was that immediately succeeding the Revolution of 1688, when we do find a wholesale expulsion of the Episcopal clergy, and, so far as it could be done without the use of measures involving the loss of life and limb, an earnest attempt to suppress Episcopacy in Scotland.   This, it should be remem-bered, was immediately at the close of a reign of terror which had existed in that country for twenty-five or thirty years, and was but the fuller carry-ing out for Scotland of the work of the Revolution.   As the calling of the Prince of Orange and the expulsion of James II. was first made possible through the fear of Papacy on the part of the English, so the progress and success of the Revolution was finally assured only by the fixed determination of the Scots to rid themselves of Episcopacy, and to re-establish the popular religion which had been overthrown by Charles.   They had infinitely greater cause to fear the bishops of the Anglican Church than their southern neigh-bors had to fear those of St. Peter's.   They had suffered tenfold more from the oppressions of the British pope and his bishops than had the English from those of the pontiff of Rome.   In the annals of religious persecution in the British Islands, the crimes of the Roman Catholic Church were but venial compared with the enormities perpetrated through the ambition and malignancy of the prelates and heads of the Established Church of England, by which the Scots were the chief sufferers.[12]

So far as Scotland was concerned, therefore, the benefits of the Revolu-tion, the success of which that country had rendered possible, would have been wholly lost to it, had the chief provoking cause been left unmolested.

and entrenched in a position for working further harm to the cause of human liberty. All the legitimate arguments which may be made to justify the overthrow of papal authority in England, apply with thrice-augmented force to sustain the action of the Scottish people in breaking the wings of those ecclesiastical vampires who had been draining the life-blood of Scotland. Nay, the whole force of the argument in favor of the Protestant Reformation of Christendom must be broken before it can successfully be maintained that the action of the Scottish people in uprooting the Episcopal system was inconsistent with their professed devotion to the cause of religious liberty."[13]

The extent to which the cause of the Covenanters was bound up with that of human liberty and opposed to the united despotism of king and prelate may be shown by the reproduction of the celebrated Queensferry Paper, for their approval of the revolutionary sentiments of which so many of the Scottish martyrs suffered death. The substance of the contents of this document, and the accompanying account of its origin, are copied from the appendix to the *Cloud of Witnesses* (15th edition, pp. 343–348), as follows :

A brief relation of the persecutions and death of that worthy gentleman, Henry Hall of Haughhead, who suffered martyrdom at Queensferry, June 3, 1680.[14]

Henry Hall of Haughhead, having had religious education, began early to mind a life of holiness ; and was of a pious conversation from his youth ; he was a zealous opposer of the public resolutions, insomuch that when the minister of the parish where he lived complied with that course, he refused to hear him, and went to Ancrum, to hear Mr. John Livingston. Being oppressed with the malicious persecutions of the curates and other malignants for his nonconformity with the profane courses of abomination, that commenced at the unhappy restoration of that most wicked tyrant Charles II. he was obliged to depart his native country, and go over the border into England in the year 1665, where he was so much renowned for his singular zeal in propagating the gospel among the people, who before his coming among them were very rude and barbarous ; but many of them became famous for piety after. In the year 1666, he was taken in his way to Pentland, coming to the assistance of his convenanted brethren, and was imprisoned with some others in Sessford castle, but by the divine goodness he soon escaped thence through the favour of the Earl of Roxburgh, to whom the castle pertained, the said earl being his friend and relation ; from which time, till about the year 1679, he lived peaceably in England, much beloved of all that knew him, for his concern in propagating the knowledge of Christ in that country ; insomuch that his blameless and shining christian conversation, drew reverence and esteem from his very enemies. But about the year 1678, the heat of the persecution in Scotland obliging many to wander up and down through Northumberland and other places ; one colonel Struthers intended to seize any Scotsman he could find in those parts ; and meeting with Thomas Ker of Hayhope, one of Henry Hall's nearest intimates, he was engaged in that encounter upon the account of the said Thomas Ker, who was killed there : upon which account, he was forced to return to Scotland, and wandered up and down during the hottest time of the persecution, mostly with Mr. Richard Cameron and Mr. Donald Cargil, during which time, besides his many other christian virtues, he signalized himself for a real zeal in defence of the persecuted gospel preached in the fields, and gave several proofs of his valour and courage, particularly at Rutherglen, Drumclog, Glasgow, and Bothwell-bridge ; whereupon being forefaulted and violently pursued, to eschew the violent hands of his indefatigable persecutors, he was forced to go over to Holland ; where he had not stayed long, when his zeal for the persecuted interest of Christ, and his tender sympathy with the afflicted remnant of his covenanted brethren in Scotland, then wandering through the desolate caverns and dens of the earth, drew him home, choosing rather to undergo the utmost efforts of persecuting fury, than to live at ease when Joseph was in affliction, making Moses' generous choice, rather to suffer affliction with the people of God, that he might be a partaker of the fellowship of Christ's sufferings, than to enjoy that momentary pleasure the ease of the world could afford ; nor was he much concerned with the riches of the world, for he stood not to give his ground to hold the prohibited field-preachings upon, when none else would do it ; he was a lover and follower of the faithfully preached gospel, and was always against the indulgence ; he was with Mr. Richard Cameron at those meetings where he was censured.

About a quarter of a year after his return from Holland, being in company with the Rev. Mr. Donald Cargil, they were taken notice of by two blood-hounds the curates of Borrowstounness and Carridden, who went to Middleton, governor of Blackness-castle, and informed him of them ; who having consulted with these blood-thirsty ruffians, ordered his soldiers to follow him at a distance by two or three together, with convenient intervals for avoiding suspicion ; and he (the said Middleton) and his man riding up, observed where they alighted and stabled their horses ; and coming to them, pretended a great deal of kindness and civilities to Mr. Donald Cargil and him, desiring that they might have a glass of wine together. When they were set, and had taken each a glass, Middleton laid hands on them, and told them they were his prisoners, commanding in the king's name all the people of the house to assist, which they all refused, save a certain waiter, through whose means the governor got the gates shut till the soldiers came up ; and when the women of the town, rising to the rescue of the prisoners, had broke up the outer gate, Henry Hall, after some scuffle with the governor in the house, making his escape by the gate, received his mortal blow upon his head, with a carbine by Thomas George, waiter, and being conveyed out of the town by the assistance of the women, walked some pretty space of way upon his feet, but unable to speak much, save only that he made some short reflection upon a woman that interposed between him and the governor, hindered him to kill the governor, and so to make his escape timeously. So soon as he fainted, the women carried him to a house in the country, and notwithstanding the care of surgeons, he never recovered the power of speaking more. General Dalziel being advertised, came with a party of the guards, and carried him to Edinburgh ; he died by the way : his corpse they carried to the Cannongate tolbooth, and kept him there three days without burial, though a number of friends convened for that effect, and thereafter they caused bury him clandestinely in the night. Such was the fury of these limbs of antichrist, that having killed the witnesses, they would not suffer their dead bodies to be decently put in graves.

There was found upon him the rude draught of a paper containing a mutual engagement to stand to the necessary duty of the day against its stated enemies ; which was called by the persecutors, Mr. Cargil's convenant, and frequently in the foregoing testimonies, the Queensferry paper, because

there it was seized by the enemies. This paper Divine Providence seems to
have made as it were the dying words and testimony of that worthy gentleman ; and the enemies made it one of the captious and ensnaring questions
they constantly put to the sufferers, and therefore it will not be impertinent
here to insert the heads of it, as they are compendized by the learned author
of *The Hind Let Loose*, page 133. For it was still owned by Mr. Donald
Cargil, that the draught was not digested and polished, as it was intended,
and therefore it will be so far from being a wrong to recite the heads of it
only, that it is really a piece of justice done him, who never intended it
should see the world as it was when the enemies found it. I shall not pretend
to justify every expression in it, but rather submit it entirely to better judgments ; nor did the sufferers for most part adhere to it, without the limitation
(so far as it was agreeable to the Word of God, and our national covenants)
and in so far as it seems to import a purpose of assuming to themselves a
magistratical authority, their practice declares all along, that they did not
undertand it in that sense :

The tenor of it was an engagement,

1st, To avouch the only true and living God to be their God, and to close
with his way of redemption by his son Jesus Christ, whose righteousness is
only to be relied upon for justification ; and to take the Scriptures of the
Old and New Testament to be the only object of faith, and rule of conversation in all things. 2d, To establish in the land righteousness and religion,
in the truth of its doctrine, purity and power of its worship, discipline and
government, and to free the church of God of the corruption of Prelacy, on
the one hand, and the thraldom of Erastianism on the other. 3d, To persevere
in the doctrine of the reformed churches, especially that of Scotland, and in
the worship prescribed in the Scriptures, without the inventions, adornings,
and corruptions of men ; and in the Presbyterian government, exercised in
sessions, presbyteries, synods and general assemblies, as a distinct government from the civil, and distinctly to be exercised, not after a carnal manner,
by plurality of votes, or authority of a single person, but according to the
Word of God, making and carrying the sentence. 4th, To endeavour the
overthrow of the kingdom of darkness, and whatsoever is contrary to
the kingdom of Christ, especially idolatry and popery in all its articles, and
the overthrow of that power that hath established and upheld it—And to
execute righteousness and judgment impartially, according to the Word of
God, and degree of offences, upon the committers of these things especially,
to-wit, blasphemy, idolatry, atheism, buggery, sorcery, perjury, uncleanness,
profanation of the Lord's day, oppression and malignancy. 5th, Seriously
considering,—there is no more speedy way of relaxation from the wrath of
God, than hath ever lien upon the land since it engaged with these rulers,
but of rejecting them, who hath so manifestly rejected God,—disclaiming his
covenant—governing contrary to all right laws, divine and human—and contrary to all the ends of government, by enacting and commanding impieties,
injuries and robberies, to the denying of God his due, and the subjects theirs ;
so that instead of government, godliness, and peace, there is nothing but
rapine, tumult, and blood, which cannot be called a government, but a lust-
ful rage—and they cannot be called governors, but public grassators and
land judgments, which all ought to set themselves against, as they would do
against pestilence, sword, and famine, raging amongst them—Seeing they
have stopped the course of the law and justice against blasphemers, idolaters, atheists, buggerers, murderers, incestuous and adulterous persons
— and have made butcheries on the Lord's people, sold them as slaves,

imprisoned, forfeited, &c. and that upon no other account, but their maintaining Christ's right of ruling over their consciences, against the usurpations of men. Therefore, easily solving the objections : First, Of our ancestors obliging the nation to this race and line ; that they did not buy their liberty with our thraldom, nor could they bind their children to anything so much to their prejudice, and against natural liberty, (being a benefit next to life, if not in some regard above it) which is not an engagement to moral things : they could only bind to that government, which they esteemed the best for common good ; which reason ceasing, we are free to choose another, if we find it more conducible for that end. Second, Of the covenant binding to defend the king ; that that obligation is only in his maintenance of the true covenanted reformation,—which homage they cannot now require upon the account of the covenant which they have renounced and disclaimed ; and upon no other ground we are bound to them—the crown not being an inheritance, that passeth from father to son, without the consent of tenants. Third, Of the hope of their returning from these courses, whereof there is none, seeing they have so often declared their purposes of persevering in them. And suppose they should dissemble a repentance,—supposing also they might be pardoned for that which is done — from whose guiltiness the land cannot be cleansed, but by executing God's righteous judgments upon them, —yet they cannot now be believed after they have violated all that human wisdom could devise to bind them.

Upon these accounts they reject that king, and those associate with him in the government,—and declare them henceforth no lawful rulers, as they had declared them to be no lawful subjects,—they having destroyed the established religion, overturned the fundamental laws of the kingdom, taken away Christ's church-government, and changed the civil into tyranny, where none are associate in partaking of the government, but only those who will be found by justice guilty as criminals.—And declare they shall, God giving them power, set up government and governors according to the Word of God, and the qualifications required, Exodus xviii. 20—And shall not commit the government to any single person or lineal succession, being not tyed as the Jews were to one single family,—and that kind being liable to most inconveniences, and aptest to degenerate tyranny.—And moreover, that these men set over them, shall be engaged to govern, principally by that civil and judicial law, (not that which is any way typical) given by God to his people Israel—as the best, so far as it goes, being given by God—especially in matters of life and death, and other things so far as they reach, and are consistent with christian liberty—exempting divorces and polygamy, &c.

6th, Seeing the greatest part of ministers not only were defective in preaching against the rulers for overthrowing religion—but hindered others also who were willing, and censured some that did it—and have voted for acceptation of that liberty, founded upon, and given by virtue of that blasphemously arrogate and usurped power—and appeared before their courts to accept of it, and to be enacted and authorized their ministers—whereby they have become ministers of men, and bound to be answerable to them as they will.—And have preached for the lawfulness of paying that tribute, declared to be imposed for the bearing down of the true worship of God.— And advised poor prisoners to subscribe that bond,—which if it were universally subscribed,—they should close that door, which the Lord hath made use of in all the churches of Europe, for casting off the yoke of the whore, —and stop all regress of men, when once brought under tyranny, to recover their liberty again.—They declare they neither can nor will hear them &c.,

nor any who encouraged and strengthened their hands, and pleaded for them, and trafficked for union with them. 7th, That they are for a standing gospel ministry, rightly chosen, and rightly ordained,—and that none shall take upon them the preaching of the word, &c., unless called and ordained thereunto.

And whereas separation might be imputed to them, they repel both the malice, and the ignorance of that calumny.—For if there be a separation, it must be where the change is ; and that was not to be found in them, who were not separating from the communion of the true church ; nor setting up a new ministry, but cleaving to the same ministers and ordinances that formerly they followed, when others have fled to new ways, and a new authority, which is like the old piece in the new garment. 8th, That they shall defend themselves in their civil, natural and divine rights and liberties. —And if any assault them, they shall look on it as a declaring a war, and take all advantages that one enemy does of another—But trouble and injure none, but those that injure them.

NOTES TO CHAPTER VIII.

[1] During the first fifty years of this time, the Scottish Kirk was practically supreme. What it then did to "retard human progress," as Mr. Buckle would say, is best summed up in the words of its enemy, King James VI., spoken when he first went down into England, and presided at the Hampton Court Conference, held in January, 1604. See pp. 434–36.

[2] *History of Civilization in England*, vol. ii., ch. ii.–v.

[3] What may be termed, in its broadest sense, the utilitarian tendency of modern religious thought, may be noted in some of the popular writings of Alfred Russell Wallace, S. Laing, A. J. Balfour, Benjamin Kidd, Matthew Arnold, John Fiske, etc.

[4] Vol. ii., ch. ii. (vol. ii., pp. 152, 153, American edition).

[5] See also Gardiner's *History of England*, 1603–1642, vol. i., pp. 22–26 ; vol. viii., pp. 373–375.

[6] *History of England*, book vi., ch. ii.

[7] *History of England*, vol. vi., ch. xxxvii., pp. 220, 221.

[8] The Scotch have been greatly, and, to a certain extent, justly blamed, because, instead of being satisfied with securing the liberty of their own church, they insisted on the overthrow of that of England. It should be remembered, however, that intolerance was the epidemic of the age. The Episcopalians enforced the prayer-book, the Presbyterians the covenant, the Independents the engagement. The last being more of a political character than either of the others, was, so far, the least objectionable. It was, however, both in design and in fact, what Neal calls it, "a severe test for the Presbyterians." Besides, the rigid doctrine of the exclusive divine right of Presbyterianism, and an intolerant opposition to Prelacy, did not prevail among the Scotch until they were driven, by persecution, into extreme opinions. When they found Episcopacy, in their own bitter experience, associated with despotism and superstition, and, in their firm belief, with irreligion and Popery, it is not wonderful that they regarded it as a bitter root which could bear nothing good. Their best apology is that which they themselves urged at the time. They considered it essential to the liberty of their church and country that the power of the bishops should be destroyed in England. The persecutions which they had already endured, and their just apprehensions of still greater evils, sprang from the principles and conduct of the English prelates. How well founded this opinion was, the atrocities consequent on the restoration of Charles II. and the re-establishment of Episcopacy, abundantly proved.—Hodge, *History of the Presbyterian Church*, vol. i., pp. 46, 47.

[9] See Lecky, *England in the Eighteenth Century*, vol. ii., ch. v.

[10] The Assembly which met in the beginning of 1696 passed an act against the atheistical opinions of the Deists, which received a melancholy comment in an occurrence which took place during the same year. A student of eighteen, named Thomas Aikenhead, had unfortunately imbibed sceptical opinions, and had been imprudent enough to spout them to some of his companions. Trinity in unity, he said, was a contradiction. Moses had learned magic in Egypt, and this was the secret of his miracles. Ezra was the author of the Pentateuch ; Theanthropas was as great an absurdity as Hirco-Cervus. These sceptical commonplaces reached the ears of the authorities, and the youth was indicted under an old statute which made it a capital crime to curse the Supreme Being. He was convicted and sentenced to be hanged. It was in vain that the poor lad with death before his eyes, recanted his errors and begged for his life. Even a reprieve for a few days was denied him, and the clergy of the city . . . gave their voice for his death. He died with a Bible in his hand in token of his change of mind.—Cunningham, *Church History of Scotland*, vol. ii., pp. 197, 198.

[11] Hodge, *History of the Presbyterian Church in America*, pp. 47–50.

[12] The enormities of this detestable government are far too numerous, even in species, to be enumerated in this slight sketch ; and of course, most instances of cruelty have not been recorded. The privy council was accustomed to extort confessions by torture—that grim divan of bishops, lawyers, and peers, sucking the groans of each undaunted enthusiast, in hopes that some imperfect avowal might lead to the sacrifice of other victims, or at least warrant the execution of the present. . . . It was very possible that Episcopacy might be of apostolical institution ; but for this institution houses had been burned and fields laid waste, and the gospel been preached in the wilderness, and its ministers had been shot in their prayers, and husbands had been murdered before their wives, and virgins had been defiled, and many had died by the executioner, and by massacre, and imprisonment, and in exile and slavery, and women had been tied to stakes on the sea-shore till the tide rose to overflow them, and some had been tortured and mutilated ; it was a religion of the boots and the thumbscrew, which a good man must be very cool-blooded indeed if he did not hate and reject from the hands which offered it. For, after all, it is much more certain that the Supreme Being abhors cruelty and persecution, than that he has set up bishops to have a superiority over Presbyters.—Hallam, *Constitutional History*, vol. iii., pp. 435, 442. The wonderful subserviency and degradation of the Scottish parliament during this period must strike all readers with astonishment. This fact is partially explained, and the disgrace in some measure palliated by the peculiarity of its constitution. The controlling power was virtually in the hands of the bishops, who were the creatures, and of course, the servants of the crown. The lords of the articles were originally a committee chosen by the parliament for the preparation of business. But Charles I, without any authority from parliament, had the matter so arranged, that "the bishops chose eight peers, the peers eight bishops ; and these appointed sixteen commissioners of shires and boroughs. Thus the whole power was devolved upon the bishops, the slaves and sycophants of the crown. The parliament itself met only on two days, the first and last of their pretended session, the one time to choose the lords of the articles, the other to ratify what they proposed."—Hallam, vol. iii., p. 428. This arrangement was renewed after the restoration of Charles II.

[13] "So soon as it was known in Scotland that William of Orange had landed at Torbay ; that he was slowly advancing toward London ; that the English nobility were flocking to him ; that the royal army was deserting to him, that the bewildered James had attempted to flee the country, the people began to show how ready they were to concur with the prince in shaking off the burdens under which they had groaned.

"Meanwhile there were wild rumors afloat of an army of Irish Papists that had landed, or was about to land, on the coast of Galloway. Some said it was already at Kirkcudbright and had burned it. . . . In such times rumors are rife. People began to dread a massacre. The Council had dissolved. The military had been marched into England.

There was a dissolution of all authority. The peasantry of the western counties began to collect in large crowds, armed with such weapons as they could procure, and to take the law into their own hands. Their wrath vented itself on the unhappy curates. They resolved to purge the temple of them without waiting for the decision of the legislature. They began their work upon Christmas, which seems to have been thought an appropriate day. In some cases the curates saved themselves from insult by timely flight. In other cases they were laid hold of by the rabble, carried about in mock procession, had their gowns torn over their heads, their Prayer-Books burned before their eyes, and then were told to be off, and never to show themselves in the parish again. When done with the minister, the mob frequently entered the manse, tumbled the furniture out at the windows, marched the inmates to the door, took possession of the keys ; and on next Sunday a preacher who had till lately been skulking among the hills, was found in the pulpit thundering against persecuting prelatists. These rabblings went on for two or three months ; every now and then an instance was occurring till almost every parish in the south and west was cleaned of its Episcopal incumbent. Upwards of two hundred clergymen were thus rabbled out of their manses, their parishes, and their livings (Somers's *Tracts*, coll. iii., vol. iv., p. 133. " Case of the Episcopal Clergy in Scotland Truly Represented." " Case of the Afflicted Clergy," etc., Burnet's *History*, vol. ii., p. 444).

" The wives and families of these men shared in their misfortunes. Many must have been rendered homeless ; some reduced to absolute beggary. . . . Still no life was lost. The only martyrdom these men underwent was a little rough usage from an ignorant rabble, and the loss of their livings. And it must be remembered that in the districts of the country where these things happened the curates occupied their pulpits in opposition to the will of the people, and enjoyed stipends of which others had been tyrannically deprived. They had no root in the soil ; they were aliens in their own parishes. What is more, they were suspected of having abetted the persecution of those who preferred their old Presbyterian ministers to them. They had their roll of absentees from church to hand to the military officers commanding in the district. . . .

" For twenty-five long years, the Presbyterians had been cruelly oppressed ; and yet when times of revolution came, they did not rise and murder their oppressors. Even the rabblings were conducted chiefly by the Cameronians and the lowest of the people, and many of the Presbyterians strongly condemned them."—Cunningham, *Church History of Scotland*, vol. ii., pp. 151–153.

[14] See Appendix R (The Scottish Martyrs.)

CHAPTER IX

RELIGION IN EARLY SCOTLAND AND EARLY ENGLAND

THE real differences between the religious life of Scotland and that of England are not wholly those of creed and polity, brought about by the Reformation of the sixteenth century. They would seem to go back much farther than that period, and to have given evidence of existence more than nine hundred years before. They may have originated from the radical differences between the ancient pagan mythology of the Druids and that of the Teutons. The religious genius of early Scotland was, of course, largely Celtic, and there is no reason for believing that the more or less complete but very gradual amalgamation of the early race with that of the Norse and the Angle has essentially altered the inherent racial tendency toward emotional fervor and intensity. Going from a warmer climate into the comparatively bleak and northern country of Caledonia, the early Celt doubtless became more "hard-headed," and lost much of that exuberance of emotion which to-day is so characteristic of his cousins in France and Ireland, and, perhaps, also in Wales. His peculiar traits were modified later by the commingling of his blood with that of the Northmen. But his early racial point of view was far distant from that of the pagans who brought the worship of Woden into Britain, and the assimilating influences of climate and intermarriage, even to this day, have not sufficed to break down the barrier between the two cults. Christianity was probably planted in Great Britain long before the Romans left. The first native account we have of its early history there is that of Bede, in his allusions to the conversion (176–190) of Lucius, King of the Britons, and to the establishment by Ninian of the Church of Candida Casa at Whithorn, in Galloway. This foundation is supposed to have been made about the year 397, and Ninian (who died about 432) was therefore the precursor and contemporary of St. Patrick (396–469 ?). More than a hundred and sixty years later, Columba, the Scot, came from the island of Iona to North Britain, and converted the Picts, as Bede tells us in the following passage (*Eccl. Hist.*, bk. iii., ch. iv.) :

In the year of our Lord 565, when Justin, the younger, the successor of Justinian, had the government of the Roman Empire, there came into Britain a famous priest and abbat, a monk by habit and life, whose name was Columba, to preach the word of God to the provinces of the northern Picts, who are separated from the southern parts by steep and rugged mountains ; for the southern Picts, who dwell on this side of those mountains, had long before, as is reported, forsaken the errors of idolatry, and embraced the truth, by the preaching of Ninias, a most reverend bishop and holy man of the British nation, who had been regularly instructed at Rome, in the faith and mysteries of the truth ; whose episcopal see, named after St. Martin the bishop, and famous for a stately church, (wherein he and many other saints rest in the body,) is still in existence among the English nation. The place belongs to the province of the Bernicians, and is generally called the White House, because he there built a church of stone, which was not usual among the Britons.

Columba came into Britain in the ninth year of the reign of Bridius, who was the son of Meilochon, and the powerful king of the Pictish nation, and he converted that nation to the faith of Christ, by his preaching and example, whereupon he also received of them the aforesaid island for a monastery, for it is not very large, but contains about five families, according to the English computation. His successors hold the island to this day ; he was also buried therein, having died at the age of seventy-seven, about thirty-two years after he came into Britain to preach. Before he passed over into Britain, he had built a noble monastery in Ireland, which, from the great number of oaks, is in the Scottish tongue called Dearm-ach — The Field of Oaks [now Derry]. From both which monasteries, many others had their beginning through his disciples, both in Britain and Ireland ; but the monastery in the island where his body lies, is the principal of them all.

Columba's religion was the same as that of St. Patrick. It had been brought from the East at a time when the early Church retained its primitive simplicity, and before it had become corrupted through the acquisition of that temporal power which came to it upon the dissolution of the Roman Empire.[1]

The English were converted by St. Augustine, who came from Rome to Britain in 597.[2] He was followed in 625 by Paulinus. The success of their missions is related by Bede in his *Ecclesiastical History*, bk. i., ch. xxv., and bk. ii., ch. ix.

The first conflict between the primitive Christianity of the Celts and the more secularized ecclesiasticism of Rome occurred in England about the year 604, and in all its aspects is typical of the struggle which took place in North Britain between the latter-day representatives of the two systems in the time of the Stuarts. Bede's narrative,[3] therefore, needs no commentary :

In the meantime, Augustine, with the assistance of King Ethelbert, drew together to a conference the bishops, or doctors, of the next province of the Britons, at a place which is to this day called Augustine's Ac, that is, Augustine's Oak, on the borders of the Wiccii and West Saxons ; and began by brotherly admonitions to persuade them, that preserving Catholic unity with him, they should undertake the common labour of preaching the Gospel to the Gentiles. For they did not keep Easter Sunday at the proper time, but from the fourteenth to the twentieth moon ; which computation is contained in a revolution of eighty-four years. Besides, they did several other things which were against the unity of the church.[4] When, after a long disputation, they did not comply with the entreaties, exhortations, or rebukes of Augustine and his companions, but preferred their own traditions before all the churches in the world, which in Christ agree among themselves, the holy father, Augustine, put an end to this troublesome and tedious contention, saying, "Let us beg of God, who causes those who are of one mind to live in his Father's house, that he will vouchsafe, by his heavenly tokens, to declare to us, which tradition is to be followed ; and by what means we are to find our way to his heavenly kingdom. Let some infirm person be brought, and let the faith and practice of those, by whose prayers he shall be healed, be looked upon as acceptable to God, and be adopted by all." The adverse party unwillingly consenting, a blind man of the English race was brought, who having been presented to the priests of the Britons, found no benefit or cure from their ministry ; at length, Augustine, compelled by real necessity, bowed his knees to the Father of our Lord Jesus Christ, praying that the lost sight might be restored to the blind man, and by the corporeal enlightening of one man, the light of spiritual grace might be kindled in the hearts of many of the faithful.   Immediately the blind man received sight, and Augustine was by all declared the preacher of the Divine truth. The Britons then confessed, that it was the true way of righteousness which Augustine taught ; but that they could not depart from their ancient customs without the consent and leave of their people.   They therefore desired that a second synod might be appointed, at which more of their number would be present.

This being decreed, there came (as is asserted) seven bishops of Britons, and many most learned men, particularly from their most noble monastery, which, in the English tongue, is called Bancornburg [Bangor], over which the Abbat Dunooth is said to have presided at that time.   They that were to go to the aforesaid council, repaired first to a certain holy and discreet man, who was wont to lead an eremitical life among them, advising with him, whether they ought, at the preaching of Augustine, to forsake their traditions.   He answered, " If he is a man of God, follow him."—" How shall we know that ? " said they.   He replied, " Our Lord saith, ' Take my yoke upon you, and learn of me, for I am meek and lowly in heart ' ; if therefore, Augustine is meek and lowly of heart, it is to be believed that he has taken upon him the yoke of Christ, and offers the same to you to take upon you.   But, if he is stern and haughty, it appears that he is not of God, nor are we to regard his words."   They insisted again, " And how shall we discern even this ? "—" Do you contrive," said the anchorite, " that he may first arrive with his company at the place where the synod is to be held ; and if at your approach he shall rise up to you, hear him submissively, being assured that he is the servant of Christ ; but if he shall despise you, and not rise up to you, whereas you are more in number, let him also be despised by you."

They did as he directed ; and it happened, that when they came, Augustine was sitting on a chair, which they observing, were in a passion, and charging him with pride, endeavoured to contradict all he said.   He said to them, " You act in many particulars contrary to our custom, or rather the custom of the universal church, and yet, if you will comply with me in these three points, viz., to keep Easter at the due time ; to administer baptism, by which we are again born to God, according to the custom of the holy Roman Apostolic Church ; and jointly with us to preach the word of God to the English nation, we will readily *tolerate* all the other things you do, though contrary to our customs."   They answered they would do none of those things, *nor receive him as their archbishop;* for they alleged among themselves, that " if he would not now rise up to us, how much more will he contemn us, as of no worth, *if we shall begin to be under his subjection ?*"   To whom the man of God, Augustine, is said, in a threatening manner, to have foretold, that in case they would not join in unity with their brethren, they should be warred upon by their enemies ; and, if they would not preach the way of life to the English nation, they should at their hands undergo the vengeance of death. All which, through the dispensation of the Divine judgment, fell out exactly as he had predicted.

For afterwards the warlike king of the English, Ethelfrid, of whom we have already spoken, having raised a mighty army, made a very great slaughter of that perfidious nation, at the City of Legions, which by the English is called Legacestir, but by the Britons more rightly Carlegion [Chester]. Being about to give battle, he observed their priests, who were come together to offer up their prayers to God for the soldiers, standing apart in a place of more safety ; he inquired who they were ? or what they came together to do in that place ? Most of them were of the monastery of Bangor in which, it is reported, there was so great a number of monks, that the monastery being divided into seven parts, with a ruler over each, none of those parts contained less than three hundred men, who all lived by the labour of their hands. Many of these, having observed a fast of three days, resorted among others to pray at the aforesaid battle, having one Brocmail appointed for their protector, to defend them whilst they were intent upon their prayers, against the swords of the barbarians. King Ethelfrid being informed of the occasion of their coming, said, " If then they cry to their God against us, in truth, though they do not bear arms, yet they fight against us, because they oppose us by their prayers." He, therefore, commanded them to be attacked first, and then destroyed the rest of the impious army, not without considerable loss of his own forces. About twelve hundred of those that came to pray are said to have been killed, and only fifty to have escaped by flight. Brocmail turning his back with his men, at the first approach of the enemy, left those whom he ought to have defended, unarmed and exposed to the swords of the enemies. Thus was fulfilled the prediction of the holy Bishop Augustine, though he himself had been long before taken up into the heavenly kingdom ; that those perfidious men should feel the vengeance of temporal death also, because they had despised the offer of eternal salvation.

In Northumbria, also, some of the Scottish missionaries, later, had labored and made converts. When King Oswy was asked to join the communion of Rome, the Scots sought to have him continue in their own as being that of the more ancient British Church. He accordingly appointed a synod to be held at Whitby in the year 664, and there, like James I. at the Hampton Court Conference 940 years later, the king was won over by the " superior arguments " of the bishops and decided to accept their innovations, and to give up the less formal and more primitive church system of the Scots. For the account of this conference let us again have recourse to Bede [b]:

In the meantime, Bishop Aidan being dead, Finan, who was ordained and sent by the Scots, succeeded him in the bishopric, and built a church in the Isle of Lindisfarne, the episcopal see; nevertheless, after the manner of the Scots, he made it, not of stone, but of hewn oak, and covered it with reeds; and the same was afterwards dedicated in honour of St. Peter the Apostle, by the reverend Archbishop Theodore. Eadbert, also bishop of that place, took off the thatch, and covered it, both roof and walls, with plates of lead.

At this time, a great and frequent controversy happened about the observance of Easter, those that came from Kent or France affirming, that the

Scots kept Easter Sunday contrary to the custom of the universal church. Among them was a most zealous defender of the true Easter, whose name was Ronan, a Scot by nation, but instructed in ecclesiastical truth, either in France or Italy, who, disputing with Finan, convinced many, or at least induced them to make a more strict inquiry after the truth; yet he could not prevail upon Finan, but, on the contrary, made him the more inveterate by reproof, and a professed opposer of the truth, being of a hot and violent temper. James, formerly the deacon of the venerable Archbishop Paulinus, as has been said above, kept the true and Catholic Easter, with all those that he could persuade to adopt the right way. Queen Eanfleda and her followers also observed the same as she had seen practised in Kent, having with her a Kentish priest that followed the Catholic mode, whose name was Romanus. Thus it is said to have happened in those times that Easter was twice kept in one year; and that when the king having ended the time of fasting, kept his Easter, the queen and her followers were still fasting and celebrating Palm Sunday. This difference about the observance of Easter, whilst Aidan lived, was patiently tolerated by all men, as being sensible, that though he could not keep Easter contrary to the custom of those who had sent him, yet he industriously laboured to practise all works of faith, piety, and love, according to the custom of all holy men; for which reason he was deservedly beloved by all, even by those who differed in opinion concerning Easter, and was held in veneration, not only by indifferent persons, but even by the bishops, Honorius of Canterbury, and Felix of the East Angles.

But after the death of Finan, who succeeded him, when Colman, who was also sent out of Scotland, came to be bishop, a greater controversy arose about the observance of Easter, and the rules of ecclesiastical life. Whereupon this dispute began naturally to influence the thoughts and hearts of many, who feared, lest having received the name of Christians, they might happen to run, or to have run, in vain. This reached the ears of King Oswy and his son Alfrid; for Oswy, having been instructed and baptized by the Scots, and being very perfectly skilled in their language, thought nothing better than what they taught. But Alfrid, having been instructed in Christianity by Wilfrid, a most learned man, who had first gone to Rome to learn the ecclesiastical doctrine, and spent much time at Lyons with Dalfin, archbishop of France, from whom also he had received the ecclesiastical tonsure, rightly thought this man's doctrine ought to be preferred before all the traditions of the Scots. For this reason he had also given him a monastery of forty families, at a place called Rhypum; which place, not long before, he had given to those that followed the system of the Scots for a monastery; but forasmuch as they afterwards, being left to their choice, *prepared to quit the place rather than alter their opinion,* he gave the place to him, whose life and doctrine were worthy of it.

Agilbert, bishop of the West Saxons, above-mentioned, a friend to King Alfrid and to Abbat Wilfrid, had at that time come into the province of the Northumbrians, and was making some stay among them; at the request of Alfrid, made Wilfrid a priest in his monastery. He had in his company a priest, whose name was Agatho. The controversy being there started, concerning Easter, or the tonsure, or other ecclesiastical affairs, it was agreed, that a synod should be held in the monastery of Streanehalch, which signifies the Bay of the Lighthouse, where the Abbess Hilda, a woman devoted to God, then presided; and that there this controversy should be decided. The kings, both father and son, came thither, Bishop Colman with his

Scottish clerks, and Agilbert with the priests Agatho and Wilfrid ; James
and Romanus were on their side; but the Abbess Hilda and her followers
were for the Scots, as was also the venerable Bishop Cedd, long before
ordained by the Scots, as has been said above, and he was in that council a
most careful interpreter for both parties.

King Oswy first observed, that it behoved those who served one God
to observe the same rule of life; and as they all expected the same kingdom
in heaven, so they ought not to differ in the celebration of the Divine mysteries; but rather to inquire which was the truest tradition, that the same
might be followed by all; he then commanded his bishop, Colman, first to
declare what the custom was which he observed, and whence it derived its
origin.   Then Colman said: " The Easter which I keep, I received from
my elders, who sent me bishop hither; all our forefathers, men beloved of
God, are known to have kept it after the same manner; and that the same
may not seem to any contemptible or worthy to be rejected, it is the same
which St. John the Evangelist, the disciple beloved of our Lord, with all
the churches over which he presided, is recorded to have observed."   Having said thus much, and more to the like effect, the king commanded Agilbert to show whence his custom of keeping Easter was derived, or on what
authority it was grounded.   Agilbert answered : " I desire that my disciple,
the priest Wilfrid, may speak in my stead; because we both concur with
the other followers of the ecclesiastical tradition that are here present, and
he can better explain our opinion in the English language, than I can by an
interpreter."

Then Wilfrid, being ordered by the king to speak, delivered himself
thus:—" The Easter which we observe, we saw celebrated by all at Rome,
where the blessed apostles, Peter and Paul, lived, taught, suffered, and
were buried; we saw the same done in Italy and in France, when we travelled through those countries for pilgrimage and prayer.   We found the
same practised in Africa, Asia, Egypt, Greece, and all the world, wherever
the church of Christ is spread abroad through several nations and tongues,
at one and the same time; except only these and their accomplices in obsti-
nacy, I mean the Picts and the Britons, who foolishly, in these two remote
islands of the world, and only in part even of them, oppose all the rest of
the universe.   . . .

" But as for you, Colman, and your companions, you certainly sin, if, having heard the decrees of the Apostolic See, and of the universal church, and
that the same is confirmed by holy writ, you refuse to follow them; for, though
your fathers were holy, do you think that their small number, in a corner of
the remotest island, is to be preferred before the universal church of Christ
throughout the world? And if that Columba of yours, (and, I may say, ours
also, if he was Christ's servant,) was a holy man and powerful in miracles,
yet could he be preferred before the most blessed prince of the apostles, to
whom our Lord said, ' Thou art Peter, and upon this rock I will build my
church, and the gates of hell shall not prevail against it, and to thee I will
give the keys of the kingdom of heaven ' ? "

When Wilfrid had spoken thus, the king said, " Is it true, Colman, that
these words were spoken to Peter by our Lord ? " He answered, " It is true,
O king! " Then says he, " Can you show any such power given to your
Columba ? " Colman answered, " None." Then added the king, " Do
you both agree that these words were principally directed to Peter, and that
the keys of heaven were given to him by our Lord ? " They both answered,
" We do." Then the king concluded, " And I also say unto you, that he

is the door-keeper, whom I will not contradict, but will, as far as I know and am able, in all things obey his decrees, lest, when I come to the gates of the kingdom of heaven, there should be none to open them, he being my adversary who is proved to have the keys." The king having said this, all present, both great and small, gave their assent, and renouncing the more imperfect institution, resolved to conform to that which they found to be better.

The disputation being ended, and the company broken up, Agilbert returned home. Colman, perceiving that his doctrine was rejected, and his sect despised, took with him such as would not comply with the Catholic Easter and the tonsure, (for there was much controversy about that also,) and went back into Scotland, to consult with his people what was to be done in this case. Cedd, forsaking the practices of the Scots, returned to his bishopric, having submitted to the Catholic observance of Easter. This disputation happened in the year of our Lord's incarnation 664, which was the twenty-second year of the reign of King Oswy, and the thirtieth of the episcopacy of the Scots among the English; for Aidan was bishop seventeen years, Finan ten, and Colman three.

The matter of religion came up again in North Britain in 717, when Nechtan, King of the Picts, yielding to the southern influence then becoming powerful at his court, accepted the tonsure, and replaced the Scottish clergy with that of Rome (Bede, bk. v., ch. xxi.):

At that time, [716] Naitan, king of the Picts, inhabiting the northern parts of Britain, taught by frequent meditation on the ecclesiastical writings, renounced the error which he and his nation had till then been under, in relation to the observance of Easter, and submitted, together with his people, to celebrate the Catholic time of our Lord's resurrection. For performing this with the more ease and greater authority, he sought assistance from the English, whom he knew to have long since formed their religion after the example of the holy Roman Apostolic Church. Accordingly he sent messengers to the venerable Ceolfrid, abbat of the monastery of the blessed apostles, Peter and Paul, which stands at the mouth of the river Wear, and near the river Tyne, at the place called Jarrow, which he gloriously governed after Benedict, of whom we have before spoken; desiring that he would write him a letter containing arguments, by the help of which he might the better confute those that presumed to keep Easter out of the due time; as also concerning the form and manner of tonsure for distinguishing the clergy; not to mention that he himself possessed much information in these particulars. He also prayed to have architects sent him to build a church in his nation after the Roman manner, promising to dedicate the same in honour of St. Peter, the prince of the apostles, and that he and all his people would always follow the custom of the holy Roman Apostolic Church, as far as their remoteness from the Roman language and nation would allow. The reverend Abbat Ceolfrid, complying with his desires and request, sent the architects he desired.

This action of Nechtan, as we shall see in a later chapter, had a great deal to do in bringing about the ultimate overthrow of the Pictish dynasty by Kenneth McAlpine, and the re-installation of the Scottish forms of worship.[6] The Roman Church was set up in Scotland again after 1068, through the influence of Queen Margaret[7] and during the feudal period of Britain it remained in the ascendancy, although for some time before its final overthrow the clergy seem to have lost their influence with the masses.[8]

Surely it is more reasonable to account for the greater influence of the early Scottish clergy over the people by ascribing it to their less autocratic manners and simpler lives, rather than to "Scottish superstition."

In examining into the differences between the Scottish and English views of things religious, we shall find also that they have ever been influenced and controlled by the diverse forces originating from differences of race, climate, and physical environment. Stated broadly, the two contrary social systems in which they are embodied may be said to symbolize the operation of two important but opposing influences of nature, both constantly working for the development and betterment of the race of man. These influences may be denominated, for lack of better terms, knowledge and environment; the first, perhaps, closely related to or even generated by the second, yet, nevertheless, ceaselessly exercising itself against it, and seeking to secure its subordination and control. The second, as constantly pursuing its blind course, and except in so far as it is guided and restrained by the first, wholly impassive as to whether its casualties elevate or ruin. One comprehends all the outward material forces of nature; the other, the inherent consciousness of organic existence. One wields the fate-hammer of life, under whose blows individual character is either shaped into a noble and beautiful form, or beaten into a base and ignoble counterfeit. The other serves both as a die and a buffer, by which the crushing power of the hammer is at the same time moderated and rightly directed. These two influences constitute the mainsprings of action in mankind, and working together they have raised man so far above the level of the first created being as to lead us to infer that their ultimate accomplishment may some day realize all the latent aspirations of the human soul. The social organism of England, with reference to the individual, is not unlike the phenomena of natural environment with relation to its effects on organic life. The operation of the forces of both proceeds with little regard to the value of the unit. Neither takes account of the individual as such, but only through his relation to the whole, and then under certain fixed and immutable laws governing his status with respect to his surroundings, any infraction of which involves immediate punishment. In both cases the controlling force is from without. In Scotland, on the other hand, the individual is everything. The unit instinctively seeks to stand alone, and to stand up as a unit wherever it may be placed. Verily, each man is a law unto himself; although, in most cases, he exercises sufficient self-control to make him mindful of the rights of his neighbor. In that way, the Scot practically rises above the restrictions of set forms of law, or stipulated rules of conduct. In his case there is little necessity for these restrictions. In express terms, he governs himself and is no longer the slave to his political or social environment, but independent of it, if not its master.   Conscience has become the touchstone to character, and the controlling force is from within.

In a broader sense, these distinctions apply to the whole scheme of man's development.   In the evolution of human society the joint work of this inward and outward force may well be traced in the phenomena of war and labor.

War is the natural environment of society, ever threatening its destruction : industrial activity, or labor, is the inherent safeguard of society, and its heritage from the slave.   The transition of the European proletariat from a state of savagery to one of civilized industry began with the subjection of conquered peoples by Grecian and Roman warriors ; and had it not been for the universal spread of slavery which took place under the Roman Empire, the civilization of the Caucasian to-day might differ but little from that of his darker-skinned brothers the world over.   It was through slavery that natural man, constrained, first learned to toil, and so began to work out the salvation of his race.   The twin supporting pillars of ancient society were predatory warfare and the enslavement, or robbery, of labor.   On these the fabric of Roman power and civilization mainly rested.   Taken together, they likewise formed the chief corner-stone of the institution of feudalism.   Naturally, therefore, they became, in part, the inheritance of Rome's chief legatee and feudalism's great ally, master, and successor — the Church of the Middle Ages.[9]   In the childhood of the world, man's instinct, begotten of experience, became sufficiently developed to enable him to guard against the ordinary destructive forces of nature.   But instinct alone was powerless to save his race from the terrible agency invoked when some, desiring to reap where they had not sown, made war on their fellow-men.   It then became necessary for men to battle, and the victory always went to the stronger.   The killing of the vanquished, which in the early days of the race would appear to have been common both in plundering and in bullying warfare, would largely tend to prevent population from increasing beyond a point where the natural products of the earth and the prey of the hunter were sufficient to sustain it.   In the occasional sparing of female lives and the carrying off and subsequent debasement of an enemy's women-folk doubtless is to be found the origin of human slavery.   After that, men's lives came at times to be spared, and domestic slavery was instituted.[10]   From this it was but a few steps to industrial slavery, and then began the operation of those influences which have since produced our modern civilization.   As men were conquered and enslaved the necessity for war grew less imperative; and as men began to labor and to reap, the value of a man's life became greater and life's problems took on a new meaning.   Hundreds of years after the building of the pyramids man was still learning the lesson of patience and endurance, of labor and of hope, of right and of wrong, under the lash of the taskmaster, at the oar of the galley, or in the ranks of his lord's army.   In time, warriors came to see the superior advantages of peace, and indiscriminate warfare ceased. Conscience was born and free labor inaugurated. As the moral sense developed, the lot of the slave became less hard. Laws were made to mitigate the suffering of the oppressed. Gradually the form of slavery was modified, and ultimately it was changed to serfdom, vassalage, and tenantry. Finally its most objectionable features were done away with, and to-day they practically cease to exist.

But the force of despotic authority which established slavery as an institution still remains, and its burdens have not yet been completely removed from the shoulders of mankind. In feudal Europe the fitting complement, guide, and accessory to this force was the power of the mediæval Church, serving as a check, it is true, upon certain excesses of tyranny, yet without which it would have been impossible for absolutism to have restrained so long the rising power of conscience. In England—is it unfair to say it ?—the Church Establishment during the past three hundred and sixty years has stood in a like relation to kingly authority, and is to-day the emblem and memorial of a once all-powerful but now impotent and fast-disappearing institution of monarchy, just as the Roman Church system is a surviving relic of the drawn sword and the mailed hand of the age of iron. Both alike belong to despotism, feudalism, and those other early stages of development which European civilization has passed through and left behind.

On the other hand, can it be truthfully denied that the theological system which, in matters religious, takes as its chief tenet the theory of the supremacy of the individual conscience over the voice of earthly authority—that makes man's accountability to a God a more imperative obligation than his accountability to a prince, and controverts the divine right of kings — can it be denied that this system on which the polity of England has ever sought to cast odium by the use in pulpit and statute of such invidious terms as " dissent," " nonconformity," " toleration," " heresy, " merely embodies the accumulated protest of man's conscience against the oppressions of tyranny; and that it constituted the first and only effective barrier that has ever been erected to save the race from the encroachments of that force most antagonistic to human welfare — man's unrestricted exercise of arbitrary power ?

Verily, the chief distinction between the Scottish and English character *is* that arising from the two different conceptions of religion. The Scotch make of religion their main guiding standard of life and rule of conduct. Its requirements are supreme over those of any temporal or political consideration. Its functions and obligations are superior to those of any secular authority, often, indeed, more sacredly regarded than the bond which holds together the social fabric. Among the English, on the contrary, religion has ever been of secondary importance, and subordinate to the secular State, and to the needs and requirements of the existing organization of society, whatever it might for the time be — allodial, feudal, monarchical, or constitutional. The promptings, hopes, aspirations, and advancements of the

9

individual English conscience, therefore, are entirely limited by considerations for the rights of existing society as a whole, however irrationally constituted. The good of the individual is set aside for the good of the state. Existing institutions, vested rights, and unequal concentrations of power, rank, or privilege, are to be sustained, and their claims demand and receive at least equal consideration with the highest claims of humanity. Hence arises the necessity for compromise; concessions have to be made on both sides. The strong must yield a little of his substance to the weak. His vested rights must suffer that their opportunities may be enlarged. But the weak can never expect full justice from the strong. They must always act on the rule that half a loaf is better than no bread. Hence, the history of civilization and human progress in England, from the time when the land was seized by the strong hand of the Norman, has been merely a story of continually growing demands on the part of the increasing masses; continual repulse and rejection on the part of the power-holding classes; and final concessions and mutual compromise on the part of both. The body of English laws, in consequence, is chiefly the record of half-acquired demands on the part of the people and half-granted concessions on the part of their lords. By far the greater portion of the power still remains in the hands of the representatives of those who first seized it, and the part received by the people is but a fraction of what would result from a justly proportioned division.

We find, therefore, that the word " compromise " is written, cross-written, and under-written on almost every page of the record of English history, English legislation, and English statesmanship. The English statute-book is one long, unvarying repetition of the story of evils partially cured, of wrongs half-righted, and of the attempts of the framers of laws to please all parties concerned. The British Constitution is proverbially a patchwork composition, in which every man can claim that his rights are given recognition, and no two men can tell alike just what those rights are.

The germination and growth of English liberty may be likened to that of a hardy oak, planted within the walls of a strong tower. In the course of time it grew and filled the whole of the tower, although ever circumscribed and prevented from reaching its full stature and extent by the impassable walls of stone. A day may come when it will force the foundations from the ground, and reach the freedom of the open air by breaking asunder the confining walls of its prison. Or, possibly, since the ecclesiastical mortar has lost its bond, the walls may fall of their own weight; for, indeed, to-day, monarchy in England stands much like other of the crumbling and ivy-covered ruins of feudal power and grandeur—slowly but surely disintegrating and passing away.

In America, of course, the conditions were vastly different. Here was a primeval state of nature. Here began the childhood of a new world. Here, at the first, were none of man's injustices to man; no castles; no oppressions of tyranny; no burdens of bishops. Naturally, the plant of liberty thrived and flourished from the start; and the enemies it has had since have been those of parasitical growth, such as become threatening only when suffered for too long a time to remain undisturbed.

In Scotland, also, the liberty tree had a more favorable soil and less burdensome bonds than in England, and it was watered and nourished by the blood of many martyrs. The power of the nobles was more frequently opposed to that of the king, and as a result there was often a division and sometimes a disregard of authority. Under these conditions, the rights of the people were more fully regarded. Then, when John Knox stirred the soil and fertilized the roots with his Calvinistic doctrines of equality and liberty, the result was a rapid growth and a complete bursting of restricting bonds.

Thus we may conclude that the difference between Scottish and English character, in its ultimate analysis, is this: the former has been developed chiefly by the exercise of self-control, guided by the individual conscience; the latter, by the discipline of authority, imposed by feudal and monarchical power. While it is sometimes contended that monarchy is more favorable to the exceptional few, and offers better promise to ambitious men, it is generally admitted that democracy affords more opportunity for progress to the average man, and is therefore better in its results for the masses. However, the history of America shows that more of her *leaders* have come from the democratic Scotch, in proportion to their number, than from the king-loving English. Hence, it is to be inferred that that system of government is better both for leaders and followers which gives the greatest possible amount of individual liberty, not inconsistent with the rights of others. This insures perfect equality of rank and opportunity, without offering undue incentive to the ambition of its leading citizens. Consequently, such a system is not only the most desirable for the common people, but, by elevating the average standard of humanity, serves also to offer broader and higher aims for the worthy efforts of the ambitious.

NOTES TO CHAPTER IX.

[1] See Appendix G (Christianity in Early Britain).

[2] It is usual for native writers on English Church history, who seek to minimize the influence of Rome on their religion, to ascribe the conversion of the Angles and Saxons almost wholly to the labors of the Scottish missionaries and the Christianized Britons who remained alive after the Anglian conquest. On the other hand, in recent years, Freeman and other native writers on English secular history attempt to show that practically none of the eastern Britons survived the exterminating wars of the English invaders. While these two theories are wholly inconsistent with one another, the evidence shows the former to be no less erroneous than the latter.

[3] Book ii., ch. ii.

[4] Although Bede and other writers make most mention of the disputes and controversies respecting the celebration of Easter, and the peculiar form of clerical tonsure, and such like

fooleries, from which some have hastily concluded that there was, after all, nothing but the most trifling and unessential distinctions between the Culdees [Columbans] and their Anglo-Roman opponents; yet a closer examination may enable us to discover . . . that they differed in some points of vital importance. . . . From incidental notices . . . it may be gathered that the Culdees were opposed to the Church of Rome in such essential doctrines as the following: They rejected . . . auricular confession, penance . . . authoritative absolution . . . transubstantiation . . . the worship of angels, saints, and relics, . . . praying to saints for their intercession, prayers for the dead, . . . works of supererogation, . . . confirmation.—Hetherington, *History of the Church of Scotland*, pp. 15, 16. The vital point of their difference, as stated by their representatives at the Whitby conference, in 664, will be found in the next succeeding extract from Bede. It was that they would not accept Augustine as their superior.

[5] Bk. iii., ch. xxv.

[6] See p. 218, Note 43.

[7] See p. 305.

England's influence and example were the direct causes of the subservience of Scotland's more ancient and purer faith. This might be rendered evident did our limits permit us to trace minutely the successive events which led to this disastrous result; such as the residence for a time in England of some of our most powerful kings, especially Malcolm Canmore and David I., who, returning to Scotland with their minds filled with prejudices in behalf of the pomp and splendor of the English Prelacy, made it their utmost endeavor to erect buildings and organize and endow a hierarchy which might vie in dignity and grandeur with those of their more wealthy neighbors. The ruinous effects were soon apparent. In vain did the best of the Scottish clergy oppose these innovations; their more ambitious brethren were but too ready to grasp at the proffered wealth and honor; and at length, to save themselves from the usurpations of the Archbishop of Canterbury, who strove to assert supremacy over the Scottish church, they yielded up their spiritual liberty to the Roman pontiff in the year 1176.—Hetherington, *History of the Church of Scotland*, p. 14.

[8] See Knox's *History of the Reformation*, bk. i.

[9] Slavery under the Roman empire was carried on to an excess never known elsewhere, before or since. Christianity found it permeating and corrupting every domain of human life, and in six centuries of conflict succeeded in reducing it to nothing. . . . Christianity in the early ages never denounced slavery as a crime, never encouraged or permitted the slaves to rise against their masters and throw off the yoke; yet she permeated the minds of both masters and slaves with ideas utterly inconsistent with the spirit of slavery. Within the Church, master and slave stood on an absolute equality.—W. R. Brownlow, *Lectures on Slavery and Serfdom in Europe*, lecture 1, 2.

[10] It has been often shown . . . that slavery was introduced through motives of mercy, to prevent conquerors from killing their prisoners. Hence the Justinian code and also St. Augustine (*De Civ. Dei.*, xix., 15) derived *servus* from *servare*, to preserve, because the victor preserved his prisoners alive.—Lecky, *History of European Morals*, vol. i., pp. 101, 102.

CHAPTER X

SCOTTISH ACHIEVEMENT

WITH the Scotch, the expression of the spiritual has ever been through religion. In art and literature they have produced less relatively than the English — in the North of Ireland, almost nothing. Yet it is far from the truth to say that Celtic genius has not found expression in literature or art. More than once it has been pointed out that Shakespeare himself was born near the forest of Arden, close to the border-line between England and Wales. The people of the West of England to-day are probably as much Celtic as Teutonic, and it would seem that there are at least no better grounds for claiming their greatest genius as a Saxon than for assuming that he may have been a Briton. He is as likely to have been the one as the other; though if the truth could be known, it would probably be found that he had received an infusion of the blood and the spirit of both.[1]

Of the second greatest poet of Britain, it may be said there is vastly more reason for believing him to have been of purely Celtic extraction than there is for asserting Shakespeare's genius to have been wholly Teutonic. It is possible, however, that Burns, also, was of mixed descent. Rare Ben Jonson, likewise, although himself born in England, was the grandson of an Annandale Scotchman.

Walter Scott, James Boswell, Lord Byron, Robert L. Stevenson, Edgar Allan Poe, James M. Barrie, Thomas Carlyle, Washington Irving, Hall Caine, Robert Barr, John M. Watson, S. R. Crockett, David Christie Murray, and William Black are writers of Scottish blood who have been given a high place in English literature, and some of them classed as English. In their days, Buchanan, Robertson, Hume, and Macaulay were perhaps the greatest historians Britain had produced. Those Scots have since been eclipsed by other writers of a more English origin; but the latter, in turn, have been outdone by a Celt — one whose work, so far as it has gone, shows the most philosophical, judicious, and enlightened treatment of the subject of English history that it has yet received. This historian is Mr. W. E. H. Lecky.

Other Scottish writers who have helped to make the fame of " English " literature world-wide are Tobias Smollett, William E. Aytoun, Joanna Baillie, M. O. W. Oliphant, Alexander Barclay, John Stuart Blackie, James Beattie, Robert Buchanan, John Hill Burton, Thomas Campbell, Jane Porter, Andrew Lang, Archibald Forbes, Benjamin Kidd, George Farquhar (of Londonderry), John Galt, George MacDonald, John Barbour, James Hogg (the *Ettrick Shepherd*), John Wilson (*Christopher North*), Allan Ramsay, William Drummond, James Pollok, William Dunbar, James Thomson (who wrote *Rule, Britannia*), James Macpherson, Charles Mackay, F. W. Robertson.

Among the great thinkers in the fields of political and practical science Scotland has given to the world James Watt (the inventor of the steam-engine), Adam Smith, Hugh Miller, William Thomson (Lord Kelvin), Joseph Black, Robert Simson, John Robinson, Sir James Mackintosh, Sir Alexander Mackenzie, Morell Mackenzie, William Murdoch (the inventor of illuminating-gas), John Napier (the inventor of logarithms), James Bruce, the two Rosses, Mungo Park, James Grant, Dugald Stewart, and David Livingstone, besides a legion of American scientists of the first rank. William Ewart Gladstone was of purely Scottish parentage. His father, born in Leith, was descended from a Lanarkshire farmer, and his mother, Ann Robertson, belonged to the Ross-shire Robertsons.[2] James Bryce likewise is of Scottish descent.[3] In America, during the past ten years, these two men were the best known and most popular Britons of the decade, and Gladstone's death was mourned as generally on this side of the Atlantic as in Great Britain. Lord Rosebery, the present leader of the Liberal party in Great Britain, is also a Scotchman.

Ulster can boast of the names of some of the best of the captains who served under Wellington; and she gave to India two men who helped materially to save that empire for England during the great mutiny—Henry and John Lawrence. Of the blood of the Ulster settlers sprang Lord Castlereagh, George Canning, Sir Henry Pottinger, and Lord Cairns; and also one of the most brilliant and successful of modern administrators, Lord Dufferin, the inheritor of the title of one of the first of the Scottish settlers, James Hamilton, Lord Clannaboye, and the possessor of part of the old Scottish settlement on the south shore of Belfast Lough.[4]

In art, Scotland has produced little that is worthy; but the same remark applies with equal force to England. British art, as a rule, is built on foundations of conventionality rather than inspiration. Here, as in some certain other attributes of a refined civilization, the best examples are produced by Celtic France. Nevertheless, critics to-day are coming to class the Scottish artist, Henry Raeburn, with the world's greatest portrait painters. George Cruikshank, also, was the son of a father born north of the Tweed. To America, France, more than England, represents all that is most excellent in modern art. As a consequence, American artists of Scottish and English ancestry are producing more excellent work than their British cousins of native stock.[5]

In connection with the subject of Scottish achievement, it will be appropriate to give in condensed form the results of an investigation made by Mr. William H. Hunter, a diligent and painstaking student, who presented the following facts in an address delivered before the West Florida Pioneer Scotch Society on January 25, 1895:

It has been said that opportunity is the father of greatness; but the opportunity for inventing the steam-engine obtained before the boy Watt

played with the vapor from his mother's kettle.   A Scotchman saw the opportunity and grasped it, and revolutionized the forces in the hands of man.
    When we study race-building, we can understand why a Scotchman
(Cyrus McCormick) invented the mowing-machine.   John Sinclair, a Scotchman of wonderful perception, organized the British Board of Agriculture.
John Caird's writings added not a little to the advancement of agriculture.
Henry Burden invented the cultivator, and Thomas Jefferson gave us the
modern plough.   I am also told that Longstreet, who improved the cotton-
gin, and made possible its operation by means of steam power, was of Scottish blood.   I take it that there are men here to-day who remember the
revolution made in American farming by the introduction of the double
Scotch harrow.
    When Michael Menzies and Andrew Meikle invented the threshing-ma-
chine in 1788, they made it so nearly perfect in all its workings that little
room for improvement was left for latter-day genius.   The improved roads
in most general use are made after the systems introduced by the eminent
Scotch engineers, MacAdam and Telford.
    Watt made the first electrical apparatus, and would have continued ex-
periments along this line, but dropped electricity to give his whole time to
perfecting the steam-engine. . . .   The honor for harnessing lightning
to serve man as a swift messenger belongs to one through whose veins
coursed Scotch blood — Samuel Finley Breese Morse. . . .   The old-
time telegraphers, James D. Reid, Andrew Carnegie, Robert Pitcairn, Kenneth McKenzie, and David McCargo, the men who aided Morse, and made
his system successful, are of Scotch blood.   The Wizard of Menlo Park is of
the same blood [Edison's mother was Mary Elliott].   Sir William Thomson,
a native of Scotch-Ireland, made possible the successful operation of the
ocean electric cables by invention of the mirror-galvanometer, which reflects
the words noted by the electric sparks as they flash under the sea.   The
telephone was invented by Alexander Graham Bell, a Scotchman, while
Elisha Gray, of the same blood, is at work perfecting a telotograph. . . .
John Ericsson was born a Swede, but his biographer says of him that he
got his genius from his mother, who was of Scottish descent. . . .   In
speaking of the steamship, how many Scotch names come to mind!   Newcomen, Watt, Patrick Miller, Symington, Henry Burden, Bell, Roach, the
American shipbuilder, and Fulton, distinguished as the first person to successfully propel a boat by steam.   The first steam vessel to cross the Atlantic
from America was built by a Scotchman.   The *Great Western*, constructed
by Henry Burden, was the first steamship to cross the ocean from Europe to
America.   The modern mariner's compass was invented by Sir William
Thomson.
    The possibility of a railway was first suggested by Watt.   Henry Burden
first made the peculiar spike, used to this day to fasten the rail to the cross-
tie.   Peter Cooper built the first locomotive in America.   The Pennsylvania
Railroad Company, the greatest and most powerful railroad corporation in
the world, was brought to its present stage by the skilled efforts of such
Scotchmen as Thomas A. Scott, William Thaw, J. N. McCullough, James
McCrea, and Robert Pitcairn [to these names should now be added those of
Frank Thomson and A. J. Cassatt]; while General Campbell, the manager
of the Baltimore & Ohio system, is also a Scotchman [later John K. Cowen,
also of Scottish blood].   During the late war between the States, the Federal
railroad military service was under the generalship of D. C. McCullum.
The Canadian Pacific Railroad was built by a Scotchman.

It is a fact that Puritan ladies were taught to spin, on Boston Common, by Scottish immigrants from Northern Ireland; and the great textile industry was given impetus by the invention of carding and spinning machines by Alexander and Robert Barr, which machines were introduced by a Mr. Orr, also a New England Scotchman.   And the inventor of the mule spinning machine was a Scot.   Gordon McKay invented the sole-stitching that revolutionized shoemaking in New England.

The first iron-furnace west of the Alleghany Mountains was erected by a Scotchman named Grant, in 1794.   At this mill, the cannon-balls used by Perry in the battle of Lake Erie were made.   John Campbell, a stalwart Ohio Scot, first employed the hot-blast in making pig-iron.

The Scotch author is eminent in every line of literary production.   We could rest our honors with Hume, Carlyle, Scott, and Burns, and hold a high place in the world of letters.   Adam Smith was the first person to write of political economy as a science, which theme has been also treated by Samuel Baily, J. R. McCullough, Chalmers, and Alison.   Scotland gave the literary world Barbour, Blind Harry, Gavin Douglas, Wyntoun, Dunbar, McKenzie, Wilson, Grant, Barrie, George MacDonald, and John Stuart Blackie.   .   .   . Scotland gave to America Washington Irving.   .   .   .   Mrs. Margaret Wilson Oliphant is of our blood, and also Robert Louis Stevenson.   What author of fiction has received fuller attention than John Maclaren Watson ?

The Scot has been a voluminous writer of theology from the days of John Knox, the real hero of the Reformation.   You all know that, of the six ablest British sermonizers — Alison, Irving, Chalmers, Robertson, Robert Hall, and Spurgeon — the first four mentioned were Scotch.

Hugh Miller told us the story of the rocks.   To Scotland we are indebted for William McLuce, the father of American geology, undertaking, as he did, as a private enterprise, the geological survey of the United States, visiting each State and Territory, and publishing his maps six years prior to publication of the Smith geological map of England.   The Owens — David, Richard, and Robert Dale—were men of the highest attainments in the field of American geology, the latter, at his death, having the finest museum and laboratory on the Western Continent.   Andrew Ramsey, who was the director-general of the Geological Survey of Great Britain, was a Scot.

Nicholl, Keill, and Ferguson, the noted astronomers, were Scotchmen. The most learned of American astronomers was General Armsby McKnight Mitchell.   .   .   .   Maria Mitchell, another Scotch-American astronomer, had the distinction of receiving a medal from the King of Denmark.

No other race has produced a greater mathematician than John Napier, the most distinguished of the British writers on the science of numbers. Has Germany produced men of larger grasp of thought along this line than James Beattie or Andrew Baxter, than Sir William Hamilton or Doctor Abercrombie ?   Neil Arnott was the first person to illustrate scientific principles in the language of common life, his work being so popular that it ran through five editions in six years.   Robert and James Holdams, the philosophers, Spencer Fullerton Baird, the most noted American naturalist, Alexander Wilson, the ornithologist, Samuel Mitchell, who published the first scientific periodical in the United States, Lindley Murray, the philologist — all were Scots, and all authorities in their respective fields of research.   Dr. Clay McCauley, the noted Scotch Unitarian of Boston, is at the head of the Senshin Sacknin, or school of advanced learning belonging to this church in Japan.   Who has written on the science of botany with greater clearness than John H. Balfour ?   Was there ever a scholar of wider distinction for comprehensive treatment of botany than Asa Gray, the descendant of a New England Scotch family ? W. R. Smith, a Scotchman, has been for years superintendent of the Government Botanical Gardens.

That distinguished Scotch anatomist, John Abernethy, the father of modern surgery, revolutionized this science. Dr. J. Y. Simpson was the first person to use chloroform as an anæsthetic in the practice of surgery. Ephraim McDowell's skill found new fields in operative surgery, and he became noted in Europe as well as in America. No race has given to medicine the superiors of William and John Hunter, of Matthew Bailie, or John Barclay. If one were to ask who have been the four most noted surgeons and medical doctors in America, the answer would be: Hamilton, Hammond, Hays Agnew, and Weir Mitchell, all of Scotch blood.

As early as 1795, Dr. Thornton called attention to the possibility of teaching the deaf and dumb to talk, and Alexander Bell introduced the system for instructing the deaf and dumb, invented by his Scotch father. John Alston was the inventor of the blind alphabet, and John Gall printed in English the first book for the blind.

Gedd, the inventor of stereotyping, was a Scotchman. The Scot also gave us the lightning presses. Scott, Gordon, and Campbell are of our blood. David Bruce, the pioneer type-maker, the inventor of the type-casting machine, introduced the Gedd process in America. Archibald Binney and James Ronaldson established the first type foundry in Philadelphia. To Bruce and the McKellars we are greatly indebted for the advanced position our country holds to-day in this great industry. The first American newspaper, the *News-Letter*, was published in Boston by John Campbell. William Maxwell, a Scotchman, published at Cincinnati the first newspaper in the Northwest Territory; and the first religious paper in the United States was published at Chillicothe, Ohio, by a Scotchman.

In sculpture, Scotland has given to England and America their finest artists. William Calder Marshall, and not an Englishman, won the prize offered by the British government for a design for the Wellington monument. Sir John Steele executed the colossal statue of Burns that adorns New York's beautiful park. John C. King, the New England sculptor, whose busts of Adams and Emerson are masterpieces of plastic art, and whose cameos of Webster and Lincoln are magnificent gems, was a Scot; as was Joel Hart, whose statues of Clay at Richmond and New Orleans are extensively admired. Crawford and Ward are of our blood; and where is there a Scot whose heart does not beat with pride in the knowledge that Scotch blood courses in the veins of Frederick Macmonnies ? There is no end to Scotch painters. Sir David Wilkie was perhaps the most noted of British artists. Then there were Francis Brant and William Hart. Some of the works of Alexander Johnston are among the world's masterpieces. David Allan's pen drew the familiar illustrations to Burns's lyrics. There was an academy of art in Glasgow before there was one in London. Guthrie, Mac-Gregor, Walton, Lavery, Patterson, Roche, and Stevenson all have been eminent painters. Gilbert Stuart, who left us portraits of prominent actors in early American history, was a Scot, as was E. F. Andrews, who has given America its best portraits of Jefferson, Martha Washington, and Dolly Madison, those which hang in the White House. Alexander Anderson was the first American wood-engraver, inventing, as he did, the tools used by those pursuing this art.

No other race has produced explorers of greater achievement than Mackenzie, Richardson, Ross, Collison, McClintock [Melville, Greely], or Hays.

John and Clark Ross made the only valuable discoveries ever made in the Antarctic region; while David Livingstone, Mungo Park, Doctor Johnson [James Grant], and Doctor Donaldson penetrated Darkest Africa. Thomas Hutchins, the first geographer of the United States, was Scotch. So were James Geddes and Samuel Forrer, the pioneer engineers of the Northwest Territory. Commodore Matthew Galbraith Perry, one of the famous family of sailors, broke down the walls of Japan, and let in the light of Western civilization. The Perrys got their great force of character from their mother, who was Scotch. For thirty years Sir Robert Hart was at the head of the Chinese financial system, and opened to commerce many Chinese ports, while Samuel M. Bryan was for a dozen years the Postmaster-General of Japan, and introduced into that empire the Western postal system.

Do we speak of war, a thousand Scotch names rise above all the heroes: Wallace at Stirling; Bruce at Bannockburn; Wolfe's Scottish soldiers at the Heights of Abraham; Forbes at Fort Duquesne; Stark at Bennington; Campbell at King's Mountain; Scott at Lundy's Lane; Perry on Lake Erie; Grant at Appomattox. Were not Wellington and Napier Scotch? The latter was.

Paul Jones was only one of the naval heroes of our blood. Oliver Hazard Perry captured a whole British fleet in the battle of Lake Erie, building his own ships on the bank of the lake. Perry's mother was an Alexander; and it is a fact not mentioned in histories published in New England, that for years after, the victory on Lake Erie was called Mrs. Perry's victory, by neighbors of the family in Rhode Island. Thomas McDonough, of Lake Champlain, Stewart, and Bailey were Scots. Isaac Newton, who had charge of the turret and engine of the *Monitor*, in its clash with the *Merrimac*, was of the same blood. Alexander Murray commanded the *Constitution ;* and William Kidd, the daring pirate, was also a Scotchman.

In the American Civil War the Scotch-American generals of the Federal Army from Ohio alone made our race conspicuous in skill at arms. Grant was a Scotchman. His [father's] people came direct to America, and first settled in Connecticut [his mother's people were of Pennsylvania Scotch-Irish stock]. New England gave the country not only Stark and Knox, but Grant and McClellan, as well as Salmon P. Chase and Hugh McCulloch. But I was speaking of Ohio. The McDowells, the Mitchells, the McPhersons, the Fighting McCooks (two families having nine general officers in the field), the Gibsons, the Hayeses, the Gilmores, all were Ohio Scots. General Gilmore, you will remember, revolutionized naval gunnery in his cannonade and capture of Fort Pulaski, which extended his fame throughout Europe. Gilmore, the " Swamp Angel," as he was called, was an Ohio Scotchman. A majority of the Indian fighters in the Northwest during the Revolutionary period were Scotchmen and Scotch-Irishmen, whose achievements are history. The McCullochs, the Lewises, the McKees, the Crawfords, the Pattersons, the Johnstons, and their fellow Scots won the West. George Rogers Clark made complete conquest of the Northwest, giving to free government five great States that otherwise would have been under the British flag. The truth about Ohio is, it has been Scotch from its first governor, Arthur St. Clair, down to the present [1895] chief executive, William McKinley. In the list of governors, we find Duncan McArthur, Jeremiah Morrow (or Murray), the father of the national road and of Ohio's internal improvements, Allen Trimble, who introduced the public-school system into Ohio, Rutherford B. Hayes, who became President of the United States, James E. Campbell, and William McKinley, who is likely to be a candidate of one of the political parties for the office of President [of the six Presidents born in, or who were elected to office from, Ohio — Harrison, Grant, Hayes, Garfield, Harrison, and McKinley — four were of Scottish descent].

Professor Hinsdale, an Ohio historian of Puritan extraction, wrote this bit of truth: " The triumph of James Wolfe and his Highlanders on the Heights of Abraham, and not the embattled farmers of Lexington, won the first victory of the American Revolution." And did it come by mere chance that another Scotchman, in the person of General John Forbes, at about the same time, led the English forces that reduced Fort Duquesne at the confluence of the three rivers, and opened the gateway to the boundless west for the forward march of Anglo-Saxon civilization ? Did it come by chance that James Grant was the commander in the relief of Lucknow; that the unmatched Havelock led Scottish soldiers in his Asiatic campaigns which brought such lustre to British arms ? We have a right to manifest pride in the fact that of the four field commanders-in-chief in the Civil War, three were Scotch — Scott, McClellan, and Grant. Chinese Gordon was a Scot. Through the veins of Robert E. Lee flowed the blood of Robert Bruce. Ulysses S. Grant and Jefferson Davis were descendants of the same Scotch family of Simpson.

Statesmen ? If Scotland had given to civil government only the name of Gladstone, she might ever glow with a mother's pride. Erskine, too, was a Scotchman, and considered by many writers the ablest and most eloquent of the long line of British jurists whose influence was most potent in giving England freer government, and withal the most vigorous defender of constitutional liberty born on British soil. Jefferson, the author of the Declaration of Independence, and of the law providing for religious tolerance; Madison, the father of the Constitution, Monroe, [Jackson], Polk, [Taylor], Buchanan, Johnson, Grant, Hayes, [Arthur, Harrison, McKinley], are Presidents our race has given to the United States. Daniel Webster was of Scottish blood; so were the intellectual giants, Benjamin Wade and Joshua Giddings. Wade's Puritan father was so poor in purse that the son was educated at the knee of his Scotch Presbyterian mother. McLean and Burnet, two of the ablest lawyers and statesmen of the West, were Scots. With one exception, all the members of Washington's Cabinet were of the same virile blood; as were likewise three out of four of the first justices of the United States Supreme Court.

In finance, the Scotch are no less distinguished than in other lines of endeavor. William Paterson was the founder of the Bank of England, and Alexander Hamilton established the American system of finance. Both were Scots.

The accepted notion that all the Scotch get their theology from Calvin is incorrect. Charles Pettit McIlvaine, perhaps the ablest bishop of the Protestant Episcopal Church in America, and certainly one of the most profound educators on this continent, was a Scotchman by descent. Bishop Matthew Simpson was without question the ablest prelate of the Methodist Episcopal Church in America. James Dempster, whom John Wesley sent to America as a missionary, was a Scotchman, and his son, John Dempster, was the founder of the school of theology of the Boston University. " Father McCormick," as he was called, organized the first Methodist Episcopal church in the Northwest Territory. John Rankin was the founder of the Free Presbyterian, and Alexander Campbell of the Christian Disciples' Church. Robert Turnbull was the most scholarly divine of the New England Baptist Church. Edward Robinson, of the Puritan Church, was recognized as the ablest American biblical scholar. While referring to scholars,

I must not neglect to mention the fact that James Blair founded William and Mary College in Virginia; that Princeton is a Scotch institution; that Doctor Alexander founded Augusta Academy, now the great Washington and Lee University; that Jefferson gave the South the University of Virginia; that Doctor John McMillan and the Finleys established more than a dozen colleges in the West and South; that Doctor Charles C. Beatty established the first woman's college west of the Alleghany Mountains; and that Joseph Ray, William H. McGuffey, and Lindley Murray were three of America's most prominent educators.

NOTES TO CHAPTER X.

[1] It seems certain that William Shakespeare was at least in part of Celtic descent. He was a grandson of Richard Shakespeare, Bailiff of Wroxhall, by Alys, daughter of Edward Griffin of Berswell. Edward Griffin was of the Griffin or Griffith family of Baybrook in Northamptonshire, who claimed descent from Griffith, son of Rhysap Tudor, King of South Wales. See *The Gentle Shakespeare: A Vindication*, by John Pym Yeatman, of Lincoln's Inn, London, 1896. See also p. 314, Note 13.

[2] John Gladstanes, of Toftcombes, near Biggar, in the upper ward of Lanarkshire, was a small farmer, who married Janet Aitken; their son, Thomas, who died in 1809, settled in Leith, where he was a prosperous merchant, and where he married Helen Neilson, of Springfield; their son John, born in 1764, married, 1800, Ann Robertson, daughter of Andrew, a native of Dingwall, in Ross-shire; John and his wife settled in Liverpool, where, in 1809, their son, William Ewart Gladstone, was born.

[3] Rev. James Bryce (1767–1857) went from Scotland, where he was born, to Ireland, and settled in 1805, as minister of the anti-burgher church in Killaig, County Londonderry. His son, James Bryce (1806–1877) was born in Killaig (near Coleraine). In 1846, appointed to the High School, Glasgow. (See *Dictionary of National Biography*, to which the information contained in the article on the Bryces was furnished by the family.) James Bryce, the writer of *The American Commonwealth*, the son and grandson of the persons just mentioned, was born in Belfast, Ireland, May 10, 1838. His mother was Margaret, eldest daughter of James Young, Esquire, of Abbeyville, County Antrim. (See *Men and Women of the Time*, thirteenth edition, 1891.)—Samuel Swett Green, *The Scotch-Irish in America*, p. 34.

[4] "T—— C——," a writer in *Fraser's Magazine* for August, 1876, makes the following observations on the character and achievements of the Scotch in Ulster:

"Ulstermen have been described as a mongrel community. This is true in a sense. They are neither Scotch, English, nor Irish, but a mixture of all three; and they are an ingredient in the Irish population distinguished by habits of thought, character, and utterance entirely unlike the people who fill the rest of the island. It is easy to see, however, at a single glance that the foundation of Ulster society is Scotch. This is the solid granite on which it rests. There are districts of country—especially along the eastern coast, running sixty or seventy miles, from the Ards of Down to the mouth of the Foyle—in which the granite crops out on the surface, as we readily observe by the Scottish dialect of the peasantry. Only twenty miles of sea separate Ulster from Scotland at one point; and just as the Grampians cross the channel to rise again in the mountains of Donegal, there seems to be no break in the continuity of race between the two peoples that inhabit the two opposite coasts. Thus it comes to pass that much of the history of Ulster is a portion of Scottish history inserted into that of Ireland; a stone in the Irish mosaic of an entirely different color and quality from the pieces that surround it. James I., colonized Ulster in the seventeenth century, not with the Gaelic Scots, who might have coalesced with their kindred Celts in Ireland, but with that Lowland rural population who from the very first fixed the moral and religious tone of the entire province. Ireland was then called ' the back door of Great Britain '; and

James I. was anxious to place a garrison there that would be able not only to shut the door, but to keep it shut, in the face of his French or Spanish enemies ; and, accordingly, when an attempt was made at the Revolution to force the door, the garrison was there—the advanced outpost of English power—to shut it in the face of the planter's grandson, and so to save the liberties of England at the most critical moment in its history. One may see (as Hugh Miller did) in the indomitable firmness of the besieged at Derry the spirit of their ancestors under Wallace and Bruce, and recognize in the gallant exploits of the Enniskillen men under Gustavus Hamilton, routing two of the forces despatched to attack them, and compelling a third to retire, a repetition of the thrice-fought and thrice-won battle of Roslin. . . .

"It is now time to notice the character and ways of the Ulsterman, not the Celt of Ulster, who gives nothing distinctive to its society,—for he is there what he is in Munster or Connaught, only with a less degree of vivacity and wit,—but the Scotch-Irishman, inheriting from Scotland that Norse nature often crossed no doubt with Celtic blood, the one giving him his persistency, the other a touch of impulsiveness to which Ulster owes so much of its progress and prosperity. He represents the race which has been described as ' the vertebral column of Ulster, giving it at once its strength and uprightness'—a race masculine alike in its virtues and faults—solid, sedate, and plodding—and distinguished both at home and abroad by shrewdness of head, thoroughgoing ways, and moral tenacity. The Ulsterman is, above all things, able to stand alone, and to stand firmly on his own feet. He is called 'the sturdy Northern,' from his firmness and independence and his adherence to truth and pro-bity. He is thoroughly practical. He studies uses, respects common things, and cultivates the prose of human life. The English despise the Irish as aimless, but not the man of Ulster, who has a supreme eye to facts, and is ' locked and bolted to results.' There is a business-like tone in his method of speaking. He never wastes a word, yet on occasion he can speak with volubility. He is as dour and dogged on occasion as a Scotchman, with, how-ever, generally less of that infusion of sternness—so peculiarly Scotch—which is really the result of a strong habitual relation between thought and action. English tourists notice the stiff and determined manner of the Ulsterman in his unwillingness to give way to you at fair or market, on the ground that one man is as good as another. The Ulsterman, no matter what his politics, is democratic in spirit ; and his loyalty is not personal, like that of the Celt, but rather a respect for institutions. He has something, too, of the Scotch pugnacity of mind, and always seems, in conversation, as if he were afraid of making too large admissions. Mr. Matthew Arnold speaks of ' sweet reasonableness' as one of the noblest elements of cul-ture and national life. The Ulsterman has the reasonableness, but he is not sweet. A southern Irishman says of him : ' The Northerns, like their own hills, are rough but health-some, and, though often plain-spoken even to bluntness, there is no kinder-hearted peasantry in the world.' But he is certainly far inferior to the Celtic Irishman in good manners and in the art of pleasing. Though not so reserved or grave as the Scotchman, and with rather more social talent, he is inferior to the Southern in pliancy, suppleness, and bonhomie. He hates ceremony and is wanting in politeness. He is rough and ready, and speaks his mind without reserve. He has not the silky flattery and courteous tact of the Southern. A Killarney beg-garman will utter more civil things in half an hour to a stranger than an Ulsterman in all his life ; but the Ulsterman will retort that the Southern is ' too sweet to be wholesome.' Cer-tainly, if an Ulsterman does not care about you, he will neither say nor look as if he did. You know where to find him ; he is no hypocrite. The Celt, with his fervent and fascinating manner, far surpasses him in making friends whom he will not always keep ; while the Ulster-man, not so attractive a mortal at the outset, improves upon acquaintance, and is considera-bly more stanch in his friendships. Strangers say the mixture of Protestant fierte with good-nature and good-humor gives to the Ulsterman a tone rather piquant than unpleasing. Like some cross-grained woods, he admits of high polish, and when chastened by culture and religion, he turns out a very high style of man. He differs from the Celt, again, in the way he takes his pleasures ; for he follows work with such self-concentration that he never thinks of looking about him, like the Celt, for objects to amuse or excite. He has few holidays (unlike the Celt, whose holidays take all the temper out of labor), and he hardly knows how to employ them except in party processions.

"The Ulsterman is not imaginative or traditional, chiefly, because his affections strike no deep root into Irish history. The Celt is more steeped in poetry and romance ; the Ulsterman knows almost nothing of fairy mythology, or of the love of semi-historic legend which fires the imagination of the Celt. The ghost is almost the exclusive property of the ancient race. The Ulsterman has certainly lost his share, or at least his interest, in such things, although he is surrounded, like the Celt, by all the old monuments of pagan times, each with a memory and a tale as gray as the stone itself. It is probably because he is so imaginative that the Celt has not such a real possession of the present as the Ulsterman ; for those who think too much of a splendid past, whether it be real or imaginary, are usually apt to think too little of the present, and the remark has been made that the poetry of the Celt is that of a race that has seen better days, for there is an almost total want of the fine old Norse spirit of self-reliance, and of making the best possible use of the present. In one of his fits of despondency, Goethe envied America its freedom from ruined castles, useless remembrances, and vain disputes, which entangle old nations and trouble their hearts while they ought to be strong for present action. Certainly the Ulsterman has not allowed himself to be encumbered in any such way.

"People have said of Ulstermen, as they have said of the Scotchmen, that they are destitute of wit and humor ; but they certainly have wut, if they have not wit, and as practised in the northeastern part of the province, it corresponds very nearly with what is properly humor. It has not the spontaneity, the freshness, the oddity, the extravagance of Celtic humor, which upsets our gravity on the instant ; it has not the power of ' pitching it strong' or ' drawing the long-bow' like the humor of America ; nor has it the sparkling and volatile characteristics of French wit. It is dry, caustic, and suggestive, on the whole rather reticent of words, and, in fact, very Scotch in character ; and the fun is contained rather in the whole series of conceptions called up by a set of anecdotes and stories than by any smart quip or flash at the close. Often the humor, as in Scotland, lies not in what is said but in what is suggested, the speaker all the while apparently unconscious of saying anything to excite amusement or laughter. Many of the illustrations are, like those of Dean Ramsay, of an ecclesiastical character ; for the Ulsterman, like the Scotchman, makes religion a condition of social existence, and demands with an unsparing rigor, on the part of all his neighbors, a certain participation in the ordinances of religion. . . .

"We need hardly say that Presbyterianism runs strong in the native current of Ulster blood. It has a good deal of the douce Davie Dean type, and is resolutely opposed to all religious innovations. It was Dean Swift who said, when he saw the stone-cutters effacing the cherub faces from the old stonework of an Episcopal church which was to do duty as a Presbyterian edifice, ' Look at these rascally Presbyterians, chiselling the very Popery out of the stones !' Mr. Froude says it was the one mistake of Swift's life, that he misunderstood the Presbyterians. It is not generally known that there was a Janet Geddes in Ulster. At the Restoration, the celebrated Jeremy Taylor appointed an Episcopal successor at Comber, County Down, to replace an excellent Presbyterian worthy, who refused conformity. The women of the parish collected, pulled the new clergyman out of the pulpit, and tore his white surplice to ribbons. They were brought to trial at Downpatrick, and one of the female witnesses made the following declaration : ' And maun a' tell the truth, the haile truth, and naethin but the truth ?' ' You must,' was the answer. ' Weel, then,' was her fearless avowal, ' these are the hands that poo'd the white sark ower his heed.' It is Presbyterianism that has fixed the religious tone of the whole province, though the Episcopalians possess, likewise, much of the religious vehemence of their neighbors, and have earned among English High Churchmen the character of being Puritan in their spirit and theology.

"Arthur Helps, in one of his pleasant essays, says that the first rule for success in life is to get yourself born, if you can, north of the Tweed ; and we should say it would not be a bad sort of advice to an Irishman to get himself born, if possible, north of the Boyne. . . . He might have to part with something of his quickness of perception, his susceptibility to external influence, and his finer imagination ; but he would gain in working-power, and especially in the one great quality indispensable to success—self-containedness, steadiness, impassibility to outward excitements or distracting pleasures. It is this good quality, together with his adaptability, that accounts for the success of the Ulsterman in foreign countries. He may be hard in demeanor, pragmatical in mind, literal and narrow, almost without a spark of imagination ; but he is the most adaptable of men, and accepts people he does not like in his grave, stiff way, reconciling himself to the facts or the facts to himself. He pushes along quietly to his proper place, not using his elbows too much, and is not hampered by traditions like the Celt. He succeeds particularly well in America and in India, not because Ulstermen help one another and get on like a corporation ; for he is not clannish like the Scottish Highlanders or the Irish Celts, the last of whom unfortunately stick together like bees, and drag one another down instead of up. No foreign people succeed in America unless they mix with the native population. It is out of Ulster that her hardy sons have made the most of their talents. It was an Ulsterman of Donegal, Francis Makemie, who founded American Presbyterianism in the early part of the last century, just as it was an Ulsterman of the same district, St. Columbkille, who converted the Picts of Scotland in the sixth century. Four of the Presidents of the United States and one Vice-president have been of Ulster extraction : James Monroe [?], James Knox Polk, John C. Calhoun, and James Buchanan. General Andrew Jackson was the son of a poor Ulster emigrant who settled in North Carolina towards the close of the last century. ' I was born somewhere,' he said, ' between Carrickfergus and the United States.' Bancroft and other historians recognize the value of the Scotch-Irish element in forming the society of the Middle and Southern States. It has been the boast of Ulstermen that the first general who fell in the American war of the Revolution was an Ulsterman—Richard Montgomery, who fought at the siege of Quebec ; that Samuel Finley, president of Princeton College, and Francis Allison, pronounced by Stiles, the president of Yale, to be the greatest classical scholar in the United States, had a conspicuous place in educating the American mind to independence ; that the first publisher of a daily paper in America was a Tyrone man named Dunlap ; that the marble palace of New York, where the greatest business in the world is done by a single firm, was the property of the late Alexander T. Stewart, a native of Lisburn, County Down ; that the foremost merchants, such as the Browns and Stewarts, are Ulstermen ; and that the inventors of steam-navigation, telegraphy, and the reaping machine — Fulton, Morse, and McCormick — are either Ulstermen or the sons of Ulstermen.

"Ulster can also point with pride to the distinguished career of her sons in India. The Lawrences, Henry and John,— the two men by whom, regarding merely the human instruments employed, India has been preserved, rescued from anarchy, and restored to a position of a peaceful and progressive dependency,— were natives of County Derry. Sir Robert Montgomery was born in the city of Derry ; Sir James Emerson Tennant was a native of Belfast ; Sir Francis Hincks is a member of an Ulster family remarkable for great variety of talent. While Ulster has given one viceroy to India, it has given two to Canada in the persons of Lord Lisgar and Lord Dufferin. Sir Henry Pottinger, who attained celebrity as a diplomatist, and was afterward appointed governor-general of Hong Kong, was a native of Belfast. Besides the gallant General Nicholson, Ulster has given a whole gazetteful of heroes to India. It has always taken a distinguished place in the annals of war. An Ulsterman was with Nelson at Trafalgar, another with Wellington at Waterloo. General Rollo Gillespie, Sir Robert Kane, Lord Moira, and the Chesneys were all from County Down. Ulstermen have left their mark on the world's geography as explorers, for they furnished Sir John Franklin with the brave Crozier, from Banbridge, his second in command, and then sent an Ulsterman, McClintock, to find his bones, and another Ulsterman, McClure, to discover the passage Franklin had sought in vain. . . .

"We have already spoken of the statesmanlike ability of Ulstermen abroad. Mention may now be made of at least one statesman at home — Lord Castlereagh — who was a native of County Down, and the son of the first Marquis of Londonderry, who was a Presbyterian elder till the day of his death. The name of Castlereagh may not be popular in any part of Ireland on account of the bloody recollections of the rebellion of 1798 ; but his reputation as a statesman has undoubtedly risen of late years, for it is now known that he was not such an absolutist or ultraist as has been generally imagined. He possessed in perfection the art of managing men, and excelled as a diplomatist, while he had an enormous capacity for work as an administrator. For most of his career he had a very remarkable man for his private secretary, Alexander Knox, a native of Derry, whose literary remains have been edited by Bishop Jebb, and whose conversational powers are said to have recalled those of Dr. Johnson himself. Lord Macaulay calls him ' an altogether remarkable man.' George Canning, the statesman who detached England from the influences of Continental despotism and restored her to her proper place in Europe, who was the first minister to perceive the genius and abilities of Wellington, and who opened that ' Spanish ulcer ' which Napoleon at St. Helena declared to be the main cause of his ruin, was the son of a Derry gentleman of ancient and respectable family. Lord Plunket, who was equally celebrated in politics, law, and oratory, was a native of Enniskillen, where his father, the Rev. Thomas Plunket, was a minister of the Presbyterian Church. To come down nearer to our own times, three men who have made their mark on the national politics of Ireland — John Mitchell, Charles Gavan Duffy, and Isaac Butt — belong to Ulster. The first was the son of a Unitarian minister, and was born in County Derry ; the second is the son of a County Monaghan farmer ; the third, the son of the late rector of Stranorlar parish in County Donegal. An Ulsterman — Lord Cairns — now [1876] presides over the deliberations of the House of Lords.

"But we must speak of the more purely intellectual work of Ulstermen, in the walks of literature, science, and philosophy. It has been remarked that, though their predominant qualities are Scotch, they have not inherited the love of abstract speculation. Yet they have produced at least one distinguished philosopher in the person of Sir Francis Hutchison, professor of moral philosophy in the University of Glasgow in the last century, and, if we may follow the opinion of Dr. McCosh, the true founder of the Scottish school of philosophy. He was born at Saintfield, County Down, where his father was a Presbyterian minister. In natural science, Ulster can boast of Sir Hans Sloane, a native of Killyleagh, County Down ; of Dr. Black, the famous chemist, a native of Belfast ; of Dr. James Thompson and his son, Sir William Thompson, both natives of County Down ; and of William Thomson and Robert Patterson, both of Belfast. In theology and pulpit oratory, Ulstermen have always taken a distinguished place. If Donegal produced a deistical writer so renowned as John Toland, Fermanagh reared the theologian who was to combat the whole school of Deism in the person of the Rev. Charles Leslie, the author of *A Short and Easy Method with the Deists*. The masterly treatise of Dr. William Magee, Archbishop of Dublin, on the doctrine of the atonement still holds its place in theological literature. He was an Enniskillener, like Plunket, and his grandson, the present bishop of Peterborough, is one of the most eloquent divines on the English bench. There is no religious body, indeed, in Ulster, that cannot point to at least one eminent theologian with a fame far extending beyond the province. The Presbyterians are proud of the reputation of the Rev. Henry Cooke, of Belfast ; the Unitarians, of the Rev. Henry Montgomery, of Dunmurry, near Belfast ; the Baptists of the Rev. Alexander Carson, of Tubbermore, County Derry, the author of the ablest treatise ever written on behalf of Baptist principles ; the Methodists, of Dr. Adam Clarke, the learned commentator on the Scriptures, who was born at Maghera, in the same county ; and the Covenanters, of the Rev. John Paul, who had all the logical acuteness of a schoolman. In oratory, Ulstermen are proud of the great abilities of Plunket, Cooke, Montgomery, Isaac Butt, and Lord Cairns. In pure scholarship they name Dr. Archibald Maclaine, chaplain at The Hague, and translator of Mosheim's *History* ; Dr. Edward Hincks, of Killyleagh, County Down, the decipherer of the Nineveh tablets ; and Dr. Samuel Davidson, the eminent biblical scholar and critic. . . .

" Ulster claims the sculptor, Patrick McDowell ; and Crawford, whose works adorn the Capitol at Washington, was born, we believe, at sea, his parents being emigrants from the neighborhood of Ballyshannon, County Donegal. But we cannot remember a single painter, or musical composer, or singer, who belongs to Ulster. In the art of novel-writing there is William Carleton, already referred to, the most realistic sketcher of Irish character who has ever lived, and who far excels Lever, and Lover, and Edgeworth in the faithfulness of his pictures, though he fails in the broader representations of Hibernian humor. No one has so well sounded the depths of the Irish heart, or so skilfully portrayed its kinder and nobler feelings. Ulster was never remarkable for pathos. Carleton is an exception ; but he belonged to the ancient race, and first saw the light in the home of a poor peasant in Clogher, County Tyrone. The only other novel-writers that Ulster can boast of — none of them at all equal in national flavor to Carleton — are Elizabeth Hamilton, the author of *The Cottagers of Glenburnie*, who lived at the beginning of this century ; William H. Maxwell, the author of *Stories of Waterloo ;* Captain Mayne Reid, the writer of sensational tales about Western America ; Francis Browne ; and Mrs. Riddle, the author of *George Geith*. In dramatic literature, Ulster can boast of George Farquhar, the author of *The Beaux' Stratagem*, who was the son of a Derry clergyman, and of Macklin, the actor as well as the author, known to us by his play *The Man of the World*. The only names it can boast of in poetry are Samuel Ferguson, the author of *The Forging of the Anchor ;* William Allingham, the author of *Laurence Bloomfield*, with two or three of lesser note."

[5] The affinity between France and America is not limited to the latter's appreciation and imitation in matters of art alone. At an early day in the history of this country, that affinity extended far beyond the bounds of æsthetical amenities. It included the fields of politics, of science, and of warfare. The reason for this is not far to seek. There are many people in America who never will, nor do they care to, understand aright the history of the building of the American nation ; and to these people the idea of such a thing as a close bond of union and sympathy with France, which for so long a time obviously existed in America, is one of the things which they cannot explain, and for which they can only account by classing it as an anomaly. To honest students of their country's history, however, and to all who can see beyond their own immediate community or horizon, it is evident that there was no anomaly in a Franco-American alliance ; and that to a very large proportion of the American people whose forefathers were here in pre-Revolutionary days, such a union was quite as much to be expected as, at other times, would be an alliance with England. The Ancient League between Scotland and France, which existed from before the time of Bruce until the days of Knox, was an alliance for defence and offence against the common enemy of both ; and that League was the veritable prototype of the later alliance between America and France against the same enemy.

10

CHAPTER XI

THE TUDOR-STUART CHURCH RESPONSIBLE FOR EARLY AMERICAN ANIMOSITY TO ENGLAND

THE English Church Establishment owed its origin primarily to the vices of Henry VIII.,[1] a prince whose abnormal appetite for new wives led him into excesses too great even for the absolution of the Roman pontiff ; though it is altogether likely that Henry's divorce of Catherine of Aragon was refused by the Pope more because it menaced the papal ascendancy than because it troubled the papal conscience. Organized under such circumstances, Henry's " Church " naturally obeyed in all things the will of its creator; and, as the conditions required, it was afterwards the pander, flatterer, or main coadjutor of his various successors; so that, down to the beginning of the present century the religion of the loyal Englishman, as compared with that of others, had in it more that was of a secular nature, and in all things subordinate to the State. The English Episcopalian has until recently been taught that the king is the supreme head of the " Church," and his universal worship of the royal fetich is, perhaps, nothing more than a manifestation of the same emotions which in other religious establishments differently constituted find expression in the worship of departed ancestors, of the saints, of the Virgin Mary, or of the Deity. As a result of this teaching, the Englishman's veneration for British royalty became almost as strong as that with which other men regard things holy, and was certainly more far-reaching in its effects. The compact between the Church Establishment and royalty was in the nature of a close partnership, with the terms and conditions clearly laid down and accepted on both sides. The kings have ever since relied chiefly upon their bishops to maintain the loyalty of the common people to the crown, and to that end the bishops have heretofore effectively used that most powerful agency, religion.

At the same time, the Church soon secured from the king a division of the power thus obtained and a goodly share of the material acquisitions resulting from its exercise. It has been necessary for both parties to the compact, as a matter of self-preservation, to prevent the intrusion of new elements into the field, and so long as it could possibly be done they were kept out. Early manifestations of spiritual religion, accordingly, were viewed with alarm and abhorrence by bishop and king alike, stigmatized as dissension by the one and sedition by the other, and repressed as treason by both. It is only during the present century, with the spread of knowledge among the masses, that the great body of the English people has learned that there is not necessarily any more than a nominal kinship between the terms " bishop " and " religion "; and that the consequent decadence of the Anglican Church has resulted. The crimes of the founder of that Church, connived at and participated in by Cranmer, Archbishop of Canterbury,² have scarcely a parallel in any history but that of the Turk; and to call Henry a reformer of religion is analogous to saying that the fear of the devil is the beginning of godliness. The vain Elizabeth, likewise, committed so many heinous offences in the name of religion, that their aggregate evil would far outweigh the good of her reputed contribution to its reformation.³ Therefore, when the Scottish nation of God-worshippers became associated with the English nation of king-worshippers, under James Stuart's rule, it is not surprising that the English " spiritual lords " should find nothing but error and treason in the teachings of the Scottish system of religion, a system which did not recognize the king as the supreme head and fountain of the Church.

Under such an institution, then, as Henry founded,—not truly a spiritual church, but an offshoot of despotism,—the persecutions of the Presbyterians in Scotland followed the succession of James Stuart to the throne of Elizabeth as a matter of course. Hence, it was to be expected that in Scotland should be fought and won the first battles that established the principle for which the Scottish martyrs died—that in matters of conscience the king was not supreme,⁴ and that the State and Church were distinct and separate institutions, and not to be joined together as one.⁵

In England and in English history it is customary to speak of Henry VIII.'s Roman Catholic daughter as " Bloody Mary " because she burned some scores of Protestants and one or two Episcopalian bishops.⁶ Compared with many of the successors of those bishops, however, and with some of her own successors, Queen Mary was as red to black. Where she killed scores, they destroyed thousands; while she was a wronged, superstitious, sickly, and unbalanced woman,— a daughter of Spain and of Henry Tudor,— brooding over and avenging the barbarities inflicted upon herself, her mother, and her mother's Church,— they were set up as teachers, exemplars, and rivals of Christ and the prophets.⁷ Her crimes were those of retaliation, ignorance, and superstition; theirs were deep-planned, self-seeking, and malicious. The English Church Establishment, for its years, has fully as much to answer for that is evil as any like organization by which the name of religion has ever been disgraced. It is not surprising, therefore, that in all the history of the inception and progress of those movements which have given to England her boasted boon of British liberty and to the world at large the beneficent results arising from the victories of the British conscience, we find their first chief opposer and vilifier in the Established Church.⁸

However, the murdering missionaries of this Establishment, turned loose in Scotland by the Stuarts in the seventeenth century, did not all pursue their bloody work of destruction unmolested. One of the chief agents of the persecution, Archbishop Sharp, met his death at the point of the sword, and died even as Cardinal Beaton had died in Scotland more than a century before, with no time for repentance, and no chance for an earthly benediction.   Neither can their course be regarded as productive of results ultimately disastrous to the cause of humanity, however great the sufferings of their immediate victims; but rather, on the contrary, it proved to be the means of hastening the coming of some of mankind's greatest blessings.   It was the inciting cause of the great revolution that began in Scotland in 1638, spread over England a few years later, and reached its culmination when the head of the Anglican Church's earthly god was cut off.   Afterwards, it drove thousands of the Scottish Presbyterians into Ireland.   Without the presence of these refugees in Ulster in 1689 the complete success of the revolution of that period would have been impossible.

Yet, notwithstanding the fact that the Scots saved Ireland to William, and made it possible for him to succeed to the English crown, the measure of their cup of persecution was not yet filled; and for more than half a century afterwards the British Government, chiefly through the Episcopal Establishment, continued to run up a debt of hatred with these Scottish emigrants — a debt that accumulated rapidly during the first years of the eighteenth century, and the evidences of which were handed down from father to son and added to in each succeeding generation.   After 1689, it received its first fresh increments in Ireland by the passage of certain Parliamentary acts, tending to the restriction and resulting in the destruction of the woollen industry; they being the final ones in a series of discriminating enactments which began at the Restoration in favor of the English manufacturers as against those of Ireland.[9]

This was followed in 1704 by the passage of the bill containing the English Test Act.   This act practically made outlaws of the Presbyterians in Ireland, and was one of the chief inciting causes of the emigration to America which increased with such rapidity during the first twenty years after its enactment.[10]

The next infliction to which the Ulster Scots were subjected was that of rack-renting landlordism, by which thousands of families were driven out of the country after 1718.   Rents were increased to two or three times their former amounts; and in addition to this extortion the Dissenters were still obliged to pay the blood-money exacted by the Established Church in the form of tithes.[11]

These galling and unjust discriminations continued with more or less modified severity during the whole period between the passage of the Test Act and the time of the final throwing off of the British yoke by those whom its operation had driven to America.

It is said by most American historians that the War of Independence was not a suddenly conceived movement; that it resulted from repeated acts of injustice on the part of Great Britain toward the American colonies subsequent to and resulting from the French and Indian wars of 1755 and 1763; that the arbitrary action of the king's representatives in America began to be resented by some of the citizens fifteen years before the battle of Lexington;

that in Massachusetts the necessity for some measure of relief from ecclesiastical and governmental tyranny became apparent as early as 1761; and that the political agitation of the next decade and a half was what stirred the people up to a sufficiently adequate realization of the meaning of the oppressive measures inflicted upon New England by Great Britain, and made them ready to accept the issue when it was finally drawn, and to abide by its consequences when they became apparent.   All this is very true, so far as it goes.   It is also true that the concentration of the disciplinary measures upon the devoted patriots of Boston, and their being the first to suffer from those measures and the results following upon their attempted enforcement, may to a great extent account for the eagerness and intensity with which those people precipitated and entered upon the conflict.   But these are only portions of the truth, and he who would read American history aright must first take into account the aggregate value of the contributions to America in men and measures of the Holland and Palatinate Dutch, the Huguenot French, and the Lowland and Ulster Scotch, decide just how much greater, if any, is America's eighteenth-century debt to England and the English than her obligation to non-English men and ideas of other countries, and learn the whole truth — that to no one man or set of men, and to no one exclusive creed, community, race, nationality, or sectional division, is due the credit for those institutions and that liberty which came to be called American after the events of 1776.

He is, indeed, a superficial student of American history and of human nature, who can see the workings of no other influences at that time than those which immediately led up to the conflict at Lexington.[12]

In New England, to be sure, there was no long-seated bitterness against the British Government.   England was truly the mother country of that province.   Their grievances were recent; their wounds fresh.   Great Britain in its restrictive measures against Boston Port touched their pockets as well as their persons, and like true Englishmen they were bound to fight against any encroachments upon their guaranteed rights of person or property.

But in a great body of the people outside of New England the causes were deeper and of more ancient origin.   Their enmity to England and the English government dated far back from the beginning of history.   It was not unlike the feeling of the Roman Catholic Irish in America toward England at the present day.   The Scots were the hereditary foes of the English kings. Their battles with the English had made of the Scottish Lowlands one vast armed camp and battle-field during the larger part of a period of five centuries after the year 1000.[13]   Their forbears were "Scots who had wi' Wallace bled." They were children of the men who had fought the English at Stirling Bridge, at Bannockburn, and "on Flodden's dark field."   Their fathers also had perished in countless numbers before the malignant fury of the Anglican Establishment.   For worshipping God as their consciences dictated they had been hunted like wild beasts by the merciless dragoons of the bishops;

pursued from moor to glen by armed bands of the king's soldiers, their children shot down like dogs by the ferocious ruffians employed by the English Church, or doomed to a fate worse than death by savage Highlanders, sure of a promised immunity, whom that Church had turned loose upon their defenceless homes.

The Scotch were not of a cowardly race, nor were they weak and spiritless louts, subject to their masters for life or death, like dumb, driven cattle. They cannot be judged by modern standards, but must be compared with people of other races who were their contemporaries.   It is true they endured unjust persecutions and grievous oppressions for long periods without open complaint or effective resistance.   But they rebelled against their tyrants and oppressors earlier, and more often, and more efficaciously than did the people of any other nation.   They anticipated the English by a full century in their revolutions, and their claim for the rights of the individual. They were more than two centuries ahead of the French in fighting and dying for the principles of the French Revolution.   They were farther advanced three centuries ago than the Germans are to-day in their conceptions and ideals of individual liberty.   Buckle well says, in speaking of his own English race, " If we compare our history with that of our northern neighbors, we must pronounce ourselves a meek and submissive people."   There have been more rebellions in Scotland than in any other country, excepting some of the Central and South American republics.   And the rebellions have been very sanguinary, as well as very numerous.   The Scotch have made war upon most of their kings, and put to death many.   To mention their treatment of a single dynasty, they murdered James I. and James III. They rebelled against James II. and James VII.   They laid hold of James V. and placed him in confinement.   Mary they immured in a castle, and afterwards deposed.   Her successor, James VI., they imprisoned; they led him captive about the country, and on one occasion attempted his life. Towards Charles I. they showed the greatest animosity, and they were the first to restrain his mad career.   Three years before the English ventured to rise against that despotic prince, the Scotch boldly took up arms and made war on him.   The service which they then rendered to the cause of liberty it would be hard to overrate.   They often lacked patriotic leaders at home, and their progress was long retarded by internecine and clan strife.   They were hard-headed, fighting ploughmen.   Though with a deep religious character, and conscientiousness to an extreme that often has seemed ridiculous to outsiders, their material accomplishments as adventurers, pioneers, and traders, in statesmanship, in science, in metaphysics, in literature, in commerce, in finance, in invention, and in war, show them to be the peers of the people of any other race the world has ever known.

Hence, they entered upon the American Revolutionary contest with a deep-seated hatred of England inherited from the past, with a passionate desire for vengeance, and with that never-ceasing persistence which is their chief characteristic as a race [14]; and in tracing their history down to this point it would seem as if we could see the working of some inscrutable principle of Divine compensation; for without the later presence in America of these descendants of the martyred Scottish Covenanters — doubly embittered by the remembrance of the outrageous wrongs done their fathers and the experience of similar wrongs inflicted upon themselves and their families—the Revolution of 1776 would not have been undertaken, and could not have been accomplished. [1b]

NOTES TO CHAPTER XI.

[1] See Appendix H (Henry VIII.'s Reformation and Church).

[2] Cranmer first suggested to Henry a means by which he might free himself from Catherine without waiting for a papal divorce ; namely, that if he could obtain opinions from the learned of the universities of Europe to the effect that his marriage was illegal because of Catherine's having been his deceased brother's wife, then no divorce would be necessary. Just how these opinions were obtained is told in letters of Richard Croke and others in Nos. xcix., cxxvi., cxxviii., cxlvi., clvii., and cciii., of Pocock's *Records of the Reformation ;* and also by a contemporary of Cranmer (Cavendish, *Life of Wolsey*, Singer's edition, p. 206) in these words : " There was inestimable sums of money given to the famous clerks to choke them, and in especial to those who had a governance and custody of their universities' seals." Later, Cranmer pronounced the divorce between Catherine and Henry, when it became apparent that the Pope would not consent to it ; and he likewise arbitrarily divorced Anne and Henry, and declared the children of both consorts of that king to be bastards. When finally brought to punishment by Mary for the many injuries done to her mother, herself, and her church, and for his share in the execution of the Catholics, he basely recanted his Protestantism in the vain hope of saving his life.

"The courage that Cranmer had shown since the accession of Mary gave way the moment his final doom was announced. The moral cowardice with the lust and despotism of Henry displayed itself again in six successive recantations by which he hoped to purchase pardon."—Green, *History of the English People*, book vi., ch. ii.

[3] " Upon the approach of the Armada many of the Catholics had been placed in prison as a precautionary measure. Even this hardship did not turn them against the government. Those confined in Ely for their religion signed a declaration of their " readiness to fight till death, in the cause of the queen, against all her enemies, were they kings, or priests, or popes, or any other potentate whatsoever." Before 1581, three Catholics had been executed for their religion, and after the landing of Campian and Parsons, a few Jesuits were added to the number. Now, directly after the destruction of the Armada, which proved how little danger there was from Rome, a selection of victims was made from the Catholics in prison, as if to do honor to the victory.

" Six priests were taken, whose only alleged crime was the exercise of their priestly office ; four laymen who had been reconciled to Mother Church, and four others who had aided or harbored priests. They were all tried, convicted, and sentenced to immediate execution. Within three months, fifteen more of their companions were dealt with in the same manner, six new gallows being erected for their execution. It was not so much as whispered that they had been guilty of any act of disloyalty. Upon their trials nothing was charged against them except the practice of their religion. This was called treason, and they met the barbarous death of traitors, being cut down from the gallows while alive, and disembowelled when in the full possession of their senses. But this was only the beginning of the bloody work. In the fourteen years which elapsed between the attempted invasion by Spain and the death of Elizabeth, sixty-one Catholic clergymen (few of whom were Jesuits), forty-seven laymen, and two gentlewomen suffered capital punishment for some one or other of the spiritual felonies and treasons which had been lately created, most of the victims being drawn and quartered.

"Many writers, when alluding to this butchery, make the statement that it was not a religious persecution ; that these victims were punished for treason and not for their religion. But when a statute, in defiance of all principles of law, makes the mere practice of a religious rite punishable as an act of treason, it is the paltriest verbal quibble to say that it is not a religious persecution. Under such a definition, all of Alva's atrocities in the Netherlands could be justified, and the Inquisition would take the modest place of a legitimate engine of the State."—Douglas Campbell, *The Puritan in Holland, England, and America*, vol. ii., pp. 110–112 (by permission of Messrs. Harper & Brothers).

In the elections for the New Parliament [1661] the zeal for church and king swept all hope of moderation and compromise before it. . . . The new members were yet better Churchmen than loyalists. . . . At the opening of their session they ordered every member to receive the communion, and the League and Covenant to be solemnly burned by the common hangman in Westminster Hall. The bishops were restored to their seats in the House of Lords. The conference at the Savoy between the Episcopalians and Presbyterians broke up in anger. . . . . The strongholds of this party were the corporations of the boroughs ; and an attempt was made to drive them from these by the Test and Corporation Act, which required a reception of the communion according to the rites of the Anglican Church, a renunciation of the League and Covenant, and a declaration that it was unlawful on any grounds to take up arms against the King, before admission to municipal offices. A more deadly blow was dealt at the Puritans in the renewal of the Uniformity Act. Not only was the use of the Prayer-book and the Prayer-book only, enforced in all public worship, but an unfeigned consent and assent was demanded from every minister of the Church to all which was contained in it ; while for the first time since the Reformation, all orders save those conferred by the hands of bishops were legally dissolved. . . . It was the close of an effort which had been going on ever since Elizabeth's accession to bring the English communion into closer relations with the reformed communions of the Continent, and into greater harmony with the religious instincts of the nation at large. The Church of England stood from that moment isolated and alone among all the churches of the Christian world. The Reformation had separated it irretrievably from those which still clung to obedience of the Papacy. By its rejection of all but Episcopal orders, the Act of Uniformity severed it as irretrievably from the general body of Protestant churches, whether Lutheran or Reformed. And while thus cut off from all healthy religious communication with the world without, it sank into immorality within. With the expulsion of the Puritan clergy, all change, all efforts after reform, all national development, suddenly stopped. From that time to this, the Episcopal Church has been unable to meet the varying spiritual needs of its adherents by any modification of its government or its worship. It stands alone among all the religious bodies of Western Christendom in its failure through two hundred years to devise a single new service of prayer or of praise.—Green's *Short History*, pp. 606, 607.

[4] See Appendix I (Scotland *vs*. The Divine Right of Kings).

[5] This is said to be the one original principle contributed by America to the science of government, but whether that be true or not, it came wholly and solely from that part of the American people whose forefathers had died for it in Scotland. The doctrine of the responsibility of kings to their subjects, as widely disseminated through America by Thomas Paine in his *Common Sense* in 1774, and by Jefferson afterwards made a chief corner-stone of the Declaration, is likewise of Scottish rather than English origin. See Appendix F. (Separation of Church and State.)

[6] The executions of Protestants which took place in "Bloody Mary's" reign were, in 1555, seventy-five ; in 1556, eighty-three ; in 1557, seventy-seven ; in 1558, fifty-one ; a total of 286.

[7] The religious changes had thrown an almost sacred character over the " majesty " of the King. Henry was the Head of the Church. From the primate to the meanest deacon every minister of it derived from him his sole right to exercise spiritual powers. The voice of its preachers was the echo of his will. He alone could define orthodoxy or declare heresy. The forms of its worship and beliefs were changed and rechanged at the royal caprice. Half of its wealth went to swell the royal treasury, and the other half lay at the King's mercy. It was this unprecedented concentration of all power in the hands of a single man that over-awed the imagination of Henry's subjects. He was regarded as something high above the laws which govern common men. The voices of statesmen and priests extolled his wisdom and authority as more than human. The Parliament itself rose and bowed to the vacant throne when his name was mentioned. An absolute devotion to his person replaced the old loyalty to the law. When the Primate of the English Church described the chief merit of Cromwell, it was by asserting that he loved the King " no less than he loved God."—John Richard Green, *History of the English People*, book vi., ch. i.

[8] This was particularly true at the time of the Revolutions of 1638, 1688, and 1775.

[9] See Appendix J (Repression of Trade in Ireland).

[10] No Presbyterian could henceforth hold any office in the army or navy, in the customs, excise, or post office, nor in any of the courts of law, in Dublin or the provinces. They were forbidden to be married by their own ministers ; they were prosecuted in the ecclesiastical courts for immorality because they had so married. The bishops introduced clauses into their leases forbidding the erection of meeting-houses on any part of their estates and induced many landlords to follow their example. To crown all, the Schism Act was passed in 1714, which would have swept the Presbyterian Church out of existence, but Queen Anne died be-fore it came into operation, but not before the furious zeal of Swift had nailed up the doors and windows of the Presbyterian meeting-house at Summer Hill, in the neighborhood of Laracor. Similar scenes occurred at three other places. The immediate effect of these proceedings was to estrange the Presbyterian people ; and, soon after, when they saw that all careers were closed against them, wearied out with long exactions, they began to leave the country by thousands. The destruction of the woollen trade sent 20,000 of them away. The rapacity and greed of landlords, and especially the Marquis of Donegal, the grandson of Sir Arthur Chichester, the founder of the Ulster plantation, caused the stream of emigration to America to flow on for nearly forty years without intermission.—Thomas Croskery, *Irish Presbyterianism*, Dublin, 1884, pp. 13, 14.

See Appendix K (The Test Act).

[11] " It would be difficult indeed to conceive a national condition less favourable than that of Ireland [in 1717] to a man of energy and ambition. . . . If he were a Presbyterian he was subject to the disabilities of the Test Act. . . . The result was that a steady tide of emi-gration set in, carrying away all those classes who were most essential to the development of the nation. The manufacturers and the large class of energetic labourers who lived upon manufacturing industry were scattered far and wide. Some of them passed to England and Scotland. Great numbers found a home in Virginia and Pennsylvania, and they were the founders of the linen manufacture in New England (*Burke's Settlements in America*, ii., 174, 175, 216).

" The Protestant emigration which began with the destruction of the woollen manufacture, continued during many years with unabated and even accelerating rapidity. At the time of the Revolution, when great portions of the country lay waste, and when the whole framework of society was shattered, much Irish land had been let on lease at very low rents to Eng-lish, and especially to Scotch, Protestants. About 1717 and 1718 these leases began to fall in. Rents were usually doubled, and often trebled. The smaller farms were generally put up to competition, and the Catholics, who were accustomed to live in the most squalid misery, and to forego all the comforts of life, very naturally outbid the Protestants. This fact, added to the total destruction of the main industries on which the Protestant population subsisted, to the disabilities to which the Protestant nonconformists were subject on account of their religion, and to the growing tendency to throw land into pasture, produced a great social revolution, the effects of which have never been repaired."—Lecky, *Ireland in the Eighteenth Century*, vol. i., pp. 245, 246.

Mr. Robert Slade, Secretary to the Irish Society of London in 1802, who had been sent to Londonderry to inspect the property of that Society, in the report of his journey writes as follows : " The road from Down Hill to Coleraine goes through the best part of the Cloth-workers' proportion, and was held by the Right Hon. Richard Jackson [he was nominated for Parliament by the town of Coleraine in 1712], who was the Society's general agent. It is commonly reported in the country, that, having been obliged to raise the rents of his tenants very considerably, in consequence of the large fine he paid, it produced an almost total emigration of them to America, and that they formed a principal part of that undisciplined body which brought about the surrender of the British army at Saratoga." This undoubtedly refers to the emigration of those colonists who, in 1718–19, founded the town of Londonderry, New Hampshire, from which place were recruited Stark's Rangers, who fought the battle of Bennington, and also many of those who took part in the battles which led to Burgoyne's surrender. Five ship-loads, comprising about one hundred and twenty families, sailed from Ulster in the summer of 1718, reaching Boston on August 4th. Here they were not long permitted to remain by the Puritan Government, owing to the fact that they had come from Ireland, but were granted a portion of the township in which they afterwards built the town of Londonderry, the site then being far out on the frontier. These emigrants were accompanied by four ministers, among whom was the Reverend James Macgregor. He had been ordained at Aghadoey in 1701, and served as their first minister in America. Their motives in emigrating may be gathered from a manuscript sermon of Mr. Macgregor's, addressed to them on the eve of their embarkation. · These reasons he states as follows : " 1. To avoid oppression and cruel bondage. 2. To shun persecution and designed ruin. 3. To withdraw from the communion of idolators. 4. To have an opportunity of worshipping God according to the dictates of conscience and the rules of His inspired Word."

See also Appendix L (Tithes in Ulster).

[12] Mr. Adolphus, in his book on the Reign of George III., uses the following language : " The first effort toward a union of interest was made by the Presbyterians, who were eager in carrying into execution their favorite project of forming a synod. Their churches had hitherto remained unconnected with each other, and their union in synod had been considered so dangerous to the community that in 1725 it was prevented by the express interference of the lords-justices. Availing themselves, with great address, of the rising discontents, the convention of ministers and elders at Philadelphia enclosed in a circular-letter to all the Presbyterian congregations in Pennsylvania the proposed articles of union. . . . In consequence of this letter, a union of all the congregations took place in Pennsylvania and the Lower Counties. A similar confederacy was established in all the Southern provinces, in pursuance of similar letters written by their respective conventions. These measures ended in the establishment of an annual synod at Philadelphia, where all general affairs, political as well as religious, were debated and decided. From this synod orders and decrees were issued throughout America, and to them a ready and implicit obedience was paid.

" The discontented in New England recommended a union of the Congregational and Presbyterian interests throughout the colonies. A negotiation took place, which ended in the appointment of a permanent committee of correspondence, and powers to communicate and consult on all occasions with a similar committee established by the Congregational churches in New England. . . .

" By this union a party was prepared to display their power by resistance, and the Stamp law presented itself as a favorable object of hostility."

Equally explicit testimony is borne in a published address of Mr. William B. Reed of Philadelphia, himself an Episcopalian : " The part taken by the Presbyterians in the contest with the mother-country was indeed, at the time, often made a ground of reproach, and the connection between their efforts for the security of their religious liberty and opposition to the oppressive measures of Parliament, was then distinctly seen." Mr. Galloway, a prominent advocate of the government, in 1774, ascribed the revolt and revolution mainly to the action of the Presbyterian clergy and laity as early as 1764. Another writer of the same period says : " You will have discovered that I am no friend to the Presbyterians, and that I fix all the blame of these extraordinary proceedings upon them."—J. G. Craighead, *Scotch and Irish Seeds in American Soil*, pp. 322–324.

[13] The two nations in the long course of their history had met each other in three hundred and fourteen pitched battles, and had sacrificed more than a million of men as brave as ever wielded claymore, sword, or battle-axe.—Halsey, *Scotland's Influence on Civilization*, p. 14.

[14] " Call this war, my dearest friend, by whatsoever name you may, only call it not an American Rebellion, it is nothing more nor less than an Irish-Scotch Presbyterian Rebellion." —Extract from a letter of Captain Johann Heinrichs of the Hessian Jager Corps, written from Philadelphia, January 18, 1778 ; see *Pennsylvania Magazine of History and Biography*, vol. xxii., p. 137.

General Wayne had a constitutional attachment to the decision of the sword, and this cast of character had acquired strength from indulgence, as well as from the native temper of the troops he commanded. They were known by the designation of the Line of Pennsylvania ; whereas they might have been with more propriety called the *Line of Ireland*. Bold and daring, they were impatient and refractory ; and would always prefer an appeal to the bayonet to a toilsome march. Restless under the want of food and whiskey, adverse to absence from their baggage, and attached to the pleasures of the table, Wayne and his brigade were more encumbered with wagons than any equal portion of the army. The General and his soldiers were singularly fitted for close and stubborn action, hand to hand, in the centre of the army ; but very little adapted to the prompt and toilsome service to which Lafayette was and must be exposed, so long as the British general continued to press him. Cornwallis therefore did not miscalculate when he presumed that the junction of Wayne would increase rather than diminish his chance of bringing his antagonist [Lafayette] to action.—Gen. Henry Lee, *Memoirs of the War in the Southern Department*, ch. xxxi., p. 203, vol. ii., first edition ; p. 292, second edition.

Dr. Charles Janeway Stille, in his work on *Major-General Anthony Wayne and the Pennsylvania Line in the Continental Army*, in commenting on this passage speaks as follows : " A curious error has been fallen into by many historians, including Mr. Bancroft, in speaking of the Pennsylvania Line, that ' it was composed in a large degree of new-comers from Ireland.' . . . These writers are evidently thinking of the characteristic qualities of the Celtic Irishman in war ; but there were not, it is said on good authority [*i. e.*, Dr. William H. Egle and John Blair Linn, editors of the Pennsylvania *Archives*], more than three hundred persons of Irish birth (Roman Catholic and Celtic) in the Pennsylvania Line. Two-thirds of the force were Scotch-Irish, a race with whose fighting qualities we are all familiar, but which are quite opposite to those which characterize the true Irish Celt. Most of them were descendants of the Scotch-Irish emigrants of 1717–1730, and very few of them were ' new-comers.'" In making the statement last quoted, Dr. Stille evidently overlooked the large emigration of Scotch-Irish from Belfast to Pennsylvania which took place in 1772–73. These emigrants left Ulster with a bitter animosity to England, brought on in a large measure by the same causes which afterwards led to the Protestant Irish Rebellion of 1798.

[15] See Appendix M (The Scotch-Irish and the Revolution).

THE SCOT IN NORTH BRITAIN

CHAPTER XII

WHO ARE THE SCOTCH-IRISH?

THE North of Ireland is divided into the counties of Antrim, Down, Armagh, Londonderry (formerly Coleraine), Tyrone, Monaghan, Donegal, Fermanagh, and Cavan. These nine counties comprise the ancient province of Ulster, which includes a fourth part of the island, and contains 8567 square miles of territory, an area equal to nearly one-fifth that of Pennsylvania, or of about the same extent as the portion of that State lying south and east of the Blue Ridge Mountains.

At the present time, one-third of the land in Ulster is under cultivation ; somewhat more than a third is in pasturage ; and a little less than one-fourth is classed as waste land—mountains and bogs : in all 5,321,580 acres. Such of this land as was not laid off into towns and roads was held, in 1881, by 22,000 owners—3,766,816 acres, or 72 per cent., belonging to 477 individuals, of whom 95 owned 2,088,170 acres, or 40 per cent. of the whole.

In 1891, the population of the province was 1,619,814, of whom 45.98 per cent. are classified in the Census Report of Great Britain as Roman Catholics ; 22.39 per cent. as Episcopalians ; and 26.32 per cent. as Presbyterians. These proportions bear a close affinity to those of the various racial elements of which the population is composed. In this respect, the Roman Catholic Church represents approximately the ancient Irish element; the Episcopalian Church, the English or Anglo-Irish ; and the Presbyterian, the Scotch or Scotch-Irish. In those districts where one element predominates over another, we find a majority of the people identified, to a greater or less extent, with the corresponding religious sect. This has been the case for nearly three hundred years, or ever since the foreign elements were first introduced, and is so generally recognized that it is perhaps not too much to say that in no other mixed population in the world has church affiliation been so characteristic of race and nationality as in the North of Ireland since the beginning of the seventeenth century.[1] This circumstance being kept in mind, does much to simplify the work of tracing the various elements of the population to their original sources.

The Presbyterian Church of Ireland now numbers over 550 congregations, and there are, besides, several United Presbyterian and Reformed Presbyterian congregations. The Presbyterians number nearly half a million—about one-tenth of the population of the country. The Episcopalian Church claims over 600,000 adherents. The Presbyterian Church doubtless includes more than four-fifths of the Scots of Ulster. The manner in which the membership of that church is distributed affords ample proof of this. Ulster claims fifteen-sixteenths of them, and they are found in those identical

localities where we know that the Scots settled.   In Antrim they constitute
38 per cent. of a total population of 428,000 ; in Down, 38 per cent. of a
total population of 267,000 ; while in Londonderry they form 30 per cent.,
in Tyrone, 19, and in Armagh 15 per cent. of the population.   But it is when
we come to examine the details of the census of 1881 that the clearest traces
of the Scottish emigration are to be found.   Down has only 38 per cent. of
Presbyterians, but that is because the south of the county was never colonized, and is still Roman Catholic.   The old Scottish colony in Upper Clannaboye and the Great Ards is still nearly as Presbyterian as in 1630.   James
Hamilton, immediately after settling there in 1606, raised churches and
placed "learned and pious ministers from Scotland" in the six parishes of
his, estate — Bangor, Killinchy, Holywood, Ballyhalbert, Dundonald, and
Killyleagh.   These parishes have gone on flourishing, so that when the census
collector did his rounds through Hamilton's old estate in 1881, he found
that it contained 29,678 inhabitants ; and that although it was situated in
what has been called the most Catholic country in Europe, only 3444 Roman
Catholics were there to be found, as against 17,205 Presbyterians.   For
nearly three centuries these "Westlan' Whigs" have stood true to their Scottish Church.   The record of Hugh Montgomery's settlement is quite as
curious.   His old headquarters, Newtown-Ards, has grown into a flourishing little manufacturing town ; and Donaghadee is a big village well known
as a ferry-port for Scotland.   Still they remain "true blue" Presbyterian.
Montgomery's estate is pretty well covered by the four parishes of Newtown-
Ards, Grey Abbey, Comber, and Donaghadee.   These have a united population
of 26,559 ; the Presbyterians number 16,714, and the Roman Catholics only
1370 — the balance being mainly Episcopalians and Methodists.   In Armagh
and in Fermanagh, on the other hand, the Episcopalians are more numerous
than the Presbyterians.   In the former there are 32 per cent. belonging to
the Church of Ireland, and only 15 to the Presbyterian Church ; while in
the latter there are only 2 per cent. of Presbyterians, as against 36 of Episcopalians.   The balance of nationalities and of religions remains to all
appearance what the colonization of the seventeenth century made it, and
that notwithstanding the great emigration from Ulster during the eighteenth
century.   The only strange change is, that Belfast, which was at its foundation an English town, should so soon have become in the main Scottish, and
should remain such unto this day.

There is another point that may be mentioned in this connection — one,
indeed, on which the foregoing conditions may be said quite largely to
depend.   That is, the fact that intermarriages between the natives and the
Scotch settlers of the seventeenth century, and their descendants in Ulster,
have been so rare and uncommon as to be practically anomalous, and in
consequence can hardly be said to enter into the general question of race
origin ; or at most, only in an incidental way.[2]

It is true, this cannot be said of the English colonists of Elizabeth's time, nor of Cromwell's soldiers, who settled in the southern provinces of Ireland after 1650. Concerning these two latter classes of settlers, as the most recent authoritative writer[3] on Ireland has said : " No feature of Irish history is more conspicuous than the rapidity with which intermarriages had altered the character of successive generations of English colonists. . . . The conquest of Ireland by the Puritan soldiers of Cromwell was hardly more signal than the conquest of these soldiers by the invincible Catholicism of the Irish women." But in the case of the Scotch colonists planted by James in Ulster, and of those who followed them, we find none of the results attributed by Lecky to the intermarriages of the English soldiers with the Irish. And while it is true that the influence of religion in keeping up the lines of race distinction has been at times overestimated, yet in the case of the Ulster Scots, it cannot be maintained that propinquity and the associations of daily life made it " absolutely certain that attachments would be formed, that connections would spring up, that passion, caprice, and daily association would . . . prove too strong for religious or social repugnance " to an extent sufficient to change or perceptibly influence the character of their descendants. These Scottish people in Ireland to-day exhibit all the distinctive racial characteristics of their Scottish forefathers ; and have none of the peculiar qualities attributed by the two leading writers on the subject to the offspring of mixed marriages between Irish Protestants and Roman Catholics. Thus we are led to conclude that inasmuch as the Ulster Scots have not been overcome by the invincible Roman Catholicism of the Irish women, and since they remain Presbyterians, as their early Scotch ancestors were before them, they are likewise of unmixed Scottish blood.

Concerning the correctness of this conclusion, we have the recent testimony of two distinguished Americans, one of them a native and the other for many years a resident of Ulster. And, considering the well-known prominence of these two gentlemen as clergymen, it cannot be supposed that their denominational proclivities would lead them to give any other than an accurate statement of facts so readily capable of verification. One of these witnesses, the late Dr. John Hall of New York, said : " I have sometimes noticed a little confusion of mind in relation to the phrase, ' Scotch-Irish,' as if it meant that Scotch people had come over and intermarried with the native Irish, and that thus a combination of two races, two places, two nationalities had taken place. That is by no means the state of the case. On the contrary, with kindly good feeling in various directions, the Scotch people kept to the Scotch people, and they are called Scotch-Irish from purely local, geographical reasons, and not from any union of the kind that I have alluded to. I have n't the least doubt that their being in Ireland and in close contact with the native people of that land, and their circumstances there, had some influence in the developing of the character, in the broadening of the sympathies, in the extending of the range of thought and action of the Scotch-Irish people ; but they are Scotch through and through, they are Scottish out and out, and they are Irish because, in the providence of God, they were sent for some generations to the land that I am permitted to speak of as the land of my birth."

The second authority is the Rev. John S. MacIntosh of Philadelphia, who, by reason of his many years of close observation spent amongst the people of Ulster, and his extended research into their earlier history, is perhaps better qualified to speak conclusively on the subject than any other living person. His testimony is that : " Our American term — the Scotch-Irish — is not known even in Ulster, save among the very few who have learned the ways of our common speech. The term known in Britain is the Ulsterman ; and in Ireland, it is the 'sturdy Northern,' or at times the 'black Northern.' What changed the Lowlander, and what gave us the Ulsterman ? In this study I have drawn very largely upon the labors of two friends of former years — Dr. William D. Killen of the Assembly's College, one of the most learned and accurate of historians, and the Rev. George Hill, once Librarian of Queen's College, Belfast, Ireland, than whom never was there more ardent student of old annals and reliable of antiquarians. But more largely still have I drawn on my own personal watch and study of this Ulster folk in their homes, their markets, and their churches. From Derry to Down I have lived with them. Every town, village, and hamlet from the Causeway to Carlingford is familiar to me. Knowing the Lowlander and the Scotch-Irish of this land, I have studied the Ulsterman and his story of rights and wrongs, and that eagerly, for years. I speak that which I have seen, and testify what I have heard from their lips, read from old family books, church records, and many a tombstone in kirk-yards. . . .

" This fact, that the Ulster colonist was a stranger, and the favorite, for the time, of England and her government, wrought in a twofold way ; in the Ulsterman and against him. . . .

" Again, the fact that he was the royal colonist wrought in him the pride, the contempt, the hauteur and swaggering daring of a victorious race planted among despised savages. What at a later day was seen here may be seen down all the stretch of Ulster history. I have myself seen it, and heard time and again he would 'lord it ower the mere Eerish.' And the rulers of that hour both cultivated that feeling and enforced it. The Celt of that day had nothing to make him winsome or worthy of imitation. Romance and sentiment may as well be dropped. We have the hard facts about the clansmen of the O'Neill. The glory and the honor were with England. The times were big with the fresh British life. The men and women of that age and the age just closed are mighty by their witching force of greatness in good and evil. It is the era of Britain's bursting life and greatening soul. Song and statesmanship, the chiefs of the drama, and the captains of daring are telling mightily on our forefathers in England and in Ulster. The new 'Plantation' itself is full of enchantment when contrasted with the old state of internecine war. . . . But those proud and haughty strangers, with high heads and their new ways, were hated as aliens and harried from the beginning by 'the wild Irish.'

"The scorn of the Scot was met by the curse of the Celt. The native chiefs and their clansmen did not distinguish between the government and the colonists ; nor had they the right ; nor did the colonists give them any cause. The hate and the harrying of the Irish were returned, and with compound interest, by the proud Ulsterman. I neither approve nor apologize : I simply state what I find. To him the 'redshanks' of the 'wild Earl' of Tyrone were exactly as the redskins of our forests to the men of New England and the Susquehanna and the Ohio. The natives were always 'thae Eerish !' and the scorn is as sharp to-day on the tongue of a Belfast Orangeman as two centuries ago. It has been said that the Ulster settlers mingled and married with the Irish Celt. The Ulsterman did not mingle with the Celt. I speak, remember, chiefly of the period running from 1605 to 1741. There had been in Ireland before the 'Plantation' some wild Islanders from the west of Scotland, whose descendants I have found in the Antrim 'Glynnes' ; they did marry and intermarry with the natives ; but King James expressly forbade any more of these island-men being taken to Ulster ; and he and his government took measures that the later settlers of the 'Plantation' should be taken 'from the inward parts of Scotland,' and that they should be so settled that they 'may not mix nor intermarry' with 'the mere Irish.' The Ulster settlers mingled freely with the English Puritans and with the refugee Huguenots ; but so far as my search of state papers, old manuscripts, examination of old parish registers, and years of personal talk with and study of Ulster folk disclose—the Scots did not mingle to any appreciable extent with the natives. I have talked with three very old friends, an educated lady, a shrewd farmer's wife, and a distinguished physician ; they could each clearly recall their great-grandfathers ; these great-grandparents told them their fathers' tales ; and I have kept them carefully as valuable personal memoirs. These stories agree exactly with all we can get in documents. With all its dark sides, as well as all light sides, the fact remains that Ulsterman and Celt were aliens and foes.

"Hence came constant and bitter strife. . . . In both Lowlander and Ulsterman is the same strong racial pride, the same hauteur and self-assertion, the same self-reliance, the same close mouth, and the same firm will—'the stiff heart for the steek brae.' They are both of the very Scotch, Scotch. To this very hour, in the remoter and more unchanged parts of Antrim and Down, the country-folks will tell you : 'We're no Eerish bot Scoatch.' All their folk-lore, all their tales, their traditions, their songs, their poetry, their heroes and heroines, and their home-speech, is of the oldest Lowland types and times."

Again, we have some supplementary evidence to the same effect from a recent Scottish author, John Harrison, who, in his account of the native

Irish-Scots, gives a brief and characteristic description of an Ulster grave-yard. This author says :

Two miles south from Donaghadee, on the shore road into the Upper Ards, that narrow peninsula between Strangford Lough and the Irish Sea, there lies a little enclosure which must arrest the stranger's attention. It is a graveyard, and is called Temple-patrick. It is surrounded by low stone walls ; no church or temple is now within its confines ; no trees or flowers give grateful shade, or lend colour and tender interest ; it is thickly covered with green mounds, and with monumental slabs of gray slaty stone,—the graves are packed close together. Read the simple "headstones," and you discover no trace of sentiment ; few fond and loving words ; no request for the prayers of the passer-by for the souls of those who sleep below ; nothing more akin to sentiment than "Sacred to the memory of." Above, great masses of gray clouds, as they go scudding past, throw down on the traveller, as he rests and thinks, big drops of rain ; and before him is spread out, north, south, and east, the sullen sea, whose moan fills all his sense of hearing. It is not the spot which a man would love to picture to himself as his last resting-place. Read the names on the stones, and you discover why here in Ireland there is to be found nothing of tender grace to mark the higher side, nothing of tinsel to show the lower, of Irish character. The names are very Scottish—such as Andrew Byers, John Shaw, Thomas MacMillan, Robert Angus ; it is a burying-place of the simple peasants of County Down, who are still, in the end of the nineteenth century, as Scottish as they were when they landed here nearly three centuries ago.   .   .   .

It is difficult to bring home to men who do not know Ireland and its history, the fact that there is a deep, strongly marked difference between the Ulstermen and the Irish, and that that difference is not accidental, not the divergence arising out of different surroundings, not even that springing from antagonistic religious training, but is the deeper, stronger-marked cleavage of differing race. It is as distinct as that between any two varieties of any other animal—say between mastiff and stag-hound. Of course, intermarriage gradually shades off the difference of type ; but take the Scots of the Ards of Down, who have probably scarcely intermarried with the Irish during the three hundred years they have been in the island, and contrast them with the inhabitants of West Donegal, who have probably scarcely mixed their blood with the English, and you see the race difference. It is strange for any man who is accustomed to walk through the southern districts of Scotland, and to meet the country people going about their daily work in their everyday clothes and everyday manner, to cross into Ireland and wander through the country roads of Down or Antrim. He is in a country which is supposed to be passionately anxious to set up a separate nationality, and yet he cannot feel as if he were away from his own kith and kin. The men who are driving the carts are like the men at home ; the women at the cottage doors are in build and carriage like the mothers of the southern Highlands ; the signs of the little shops in the village bear well-known names—Paterson, perhaps, or Johnstone, or Sloan ; the boy sitting on the "dyke" with nothing to do is whistling "A man 's a man for a' that." He goes into a village inn, and is served by a six-foot, loosely-hung Scottish Borderer, worthy to have served "drams" to "the Shepherd and Christopher North" ; and when he leaves the little inn he sees by the sign that his host bears the name of "James Hay," and his wonder ceases.

The want of strangeness in the men and women is what strikes him as so strange. Then he crosses the Bann, and gets into a different region. He leaves behind him the pleasant green hills which shut in Belfast Lough, the great sweep of rich plain which Lough Neagh may well ask to show cause why it should not be annexed to its inland sea ; he gets within sight of the South Derry hills, and the actors in the scene partly change. Some are very familiar ; the smart maid at his inn is very like the housemaid at home, and the principal grocer of the little village is the "very image" of the elder who taught him at the Sunday School ; but he meets a donkey-cart, and neither the donkey nor its driver seem somehow or other to be kin to him ; and the "Father" passes him, and looks at him as at a stranger who is visiting his town,—then the Scotsman knows that he is out of Scotland and into Ireland. It is not in Belfast that he feels the likeness to home so much, for everybody is walking fast just as they are in Glasgow, so he cannot notice them particularly, and, of course, the "loafers" at the public-house doors, who are certainly not moving smartly, do not count for anything in either town ; but it is in the country districts—at Newtown Ards, or Antrim, where life is leisurely, that he recognizes that he is among his own people ; while it is in a town which is in the border-land between Scottish and Irish, say at Coleraine, on a Saturday market-day, that he has the difference of the two types in face and figure brought strongly before him. Some seem foreign to him, others remind him of his "ain countrie," and make him feel that the district he is in, is in reality the land of the Scot.

A contributor to the *Edinburgh Review* for April, 1869, in writing on this subject, says :

Another effect of the Plantation [of Ulster] was that it effectually separated the two races, and kept them apart. It planted a new race in the country, which never coalesced with the native population. There they have been in continual contact for more than two centuries ; and they are still as distinct as though an ocean rolled between them. We have seen that all former schemes of plantation failed, because the new settlers became rapidly assimilated to the character, manners, and faith of the native inhab- itants ; even the descendants of Oliver's Puritan troopers being as effectually absorbed in the space of forty years as to be undistinguishable from the Celtic mass. The Ulster settlement put an end to the amalgamation of races ; difference of creed, difference of habits, difference of tradition, the sundering effects of the penal laws, kept them apart. The Presbyterian settlers preserved their religious distinctness by coming in families, and the intense hatred of Popery that has always marked the Scottish mind was an effective hindrance to intermarriage. It is a curious fact, that the tra- ditions of the Ulster Presbyterians still look back to Scotland as their home, and disclaim all alliance with the Celtic part of Ireland. Indeed, the past history of Ulster is but a portion of Scottish history inserted into that of Ireland ; a stone in the Irish mosaic of an entirely different quality and color from the pieces that surround it.

Hence it is that in Ulster of the present day there is little difficulty in distinguishing the citizen of Scottish blood from the Episcopalian of English and the Roman Catholic of Irish descent. In the towns and districts where the Presbyterians are most numerous we find that, so far as names, language, habits of thought and action, and the testimony of recorded history can be taken, the population bears the most characteristic marks of a Scottish origin.[4] In the country districts, the peasant still retains the Scotch "bur" in his speech [5]; devoutly believes in the doctrines of John Calvin and John Knox ; is firmly committed against everything allied with Popery or Prelacy ; and usually emphatic in his claims to a Scottish and his disavowal of an Irish descent.[6]

Not that all the Irish Scots are Presbyterians, however, nor all the Presbyterians Scotch. From the days of Echlin and Leslie down, some of the most bitter opponents and persecutors of Ulster Presbyterianism and its adherents have been Scotchmen ; while some of its most useful and influential supporters have come from the ranks of the English Puritans and the French Huguenots.[7] Nevertheless, the great bulk of the Presbyterian settlers in Ulster were from Scotland, and of this class was composed nearly the whole emigration from that country. In inquiring into the origin of these people, therefore, we must seek for it on the other side of the Irish Channel.

NOTES TO CHAPTER XII.

[1] The rector of the parish of Dungiven, in county Derry, writing in 1814, says : "The inhabitants of the parish are divided into two races of men, as totally distinct as if they belonged to different countries and regions. These, in order that we may avoid the invidious names of Protestant and Roman Catholic, which indeed have little to say in the matter, may be distinguished by the usual names of Scotch and Irish, the former including the descendants of all the Scotch and English colonists who have emigrated hither since the time of James I., and the latter comprehending the native and original inhabitants of the country. Than these, no two classes of men can be more distinct : the Scotch are remarkable for their comfortable houses and appearance, regular conduct, and perseverance in business, and their being almost entirely manufacturers ; the Irish, on the other hand, are more negligent in their habitations, less regular and guarded in their conduct, and have a total indisposition to manufacture. Both are industrious, but the industry of the Scotch is steady and patient, and directed with foresight, while that of the Irish is rash, adventurous, and variable."—*Statistical Account of Ireland*, Dublin, 1814, vol. ii., p. 307.

[2] The numerous Protestant Kellys, Sullivans, Murphys, McMahons, and others show that there are exceptions to this general proposition.

[3] W. E. H. Lecky, *England in the Eighteenth Century*, vol. ii., p. 404.

[4] The two counties which have been most thoroughly transformed by this emigration are the two which are nearest Scotland, and were the first opened up for emigrants. These two have been completely altered in nationality and religion. They have become British, and in the main, certainly Scottish. Perhaps no better proof can be given than the family names of the inhabitants. Some years ago, a patient local antiquary took the voters' list of county Down "of those rated above £12 for poor-rates," and analyzed it carefully. There were 10,028 names on the list, and these fairly represented the whole proper names of the county. He found that the following names occurred oftenest, and arranged them in order of their frequency : Smith, Martin, M'Kie, Moore, Brown, Thompson, Patterson, Johnson, Stewart, Wilson, Graham, Campbell, Robinson, Bell, Hamilton, Morrow, Gibson, Boyd, Wallace, and Magee. He dissected as carefully the voters' list for county Antrim, in which there were 9538 names, and found that the following were at the top : Thompson, Wilson, Stewart,

Smith, Moore, Boyd, Johnson, M'Millan, Brown, Bell, Campbell, M'Neill, Crawford, M'Alister, Hunter, Macaulay, Robinson, Wallace, Millar, Kennedy, and Hill. The list has a very Scottish flavor altogether, although it may be noted that the names that are highest on the list are those which are common to both England and Scotland : for it may be taken for granted that the English " Thompson " has swallowed up the Scottish " Thomson," that " Moore " includes the Ayrshire " Muir," and that the Annandale " Johnstones " have been merged by the writer in the English " Johnsons." One other point is very striking — that the great Ulster name of O'Neill is wanting, and also the Antrim " Macdonnel." . . . Another strong proof of the Scottish blood of the Ulstermen may be found by taking the annual reports presented to the General Assembly of the Presbyterian Church of Ireland, held in June, 1887. Here are the names of the men, lay and clerical, who sign these reports, the names being taken as they occur : J. W. Whigham, Jackson Smith, Hamilton Magee, Thomas Armstrong, William Park, J. M. Rodgers, David Wilson, George Macfarland, Thomas Lyle, W. Rogers, J. B. Wylie, W. Young, E. F. Simpson, Alexander Turnbull, John Malcolm, John H. Orr. Probably the reports of our three Scottish churches taken together could not produce so large an average of Scottish surnames.—*The Scot in Ulster*, Edinburgh, 1888, pp. 103-105.

[5] Many of the settlers were English, but the larger and more influential element came from the Calvinists of Scotland. . . . To-day the speech of Ulster is Scotch rather than English, showing which nationality has predominated.—Douglas Campbell, *The Puritan in Holland, England, and America*, vol. ii., p. 474.

[6] Towards the end of the last century " in all social and political matters the native Catholics, in other words the immense majority of the people of Ireland, were simply hewers of wood and drawers of water for Protestant masters, for masters who still looked on themselves as mere settlers, who boasted of their Scotch or English extraction, and who regarded the name of ' Irishman ' as an insult." — J. R. Green, *History of the English People*, book ix., ch. ii.

Most of the great evils of Irish politics during the last two centuries have arisen from the fact that its different classes and creeds have never been really blended into one nation, that the repulsion of race or of religion has been stronger than the attraction of a common nationality, and that the full energies and intellect of the country have in consequence seldom or never been enlisted in a common cause.—Lecky, *England in the Eighteenth Century*, vol. ii., p. 505. Am. ed., pp. 440 and 441. Travellers tell us that to-day in sections of Ulster the population is Scotch and not Irish.

[7] A considerable portion of the English colonists, especially those who came to the London settlement in Londonderry county, were Puritans, and joined with the Scots in church affairs. A strong Calvinistic element was also afterwards infused into the district by the French Huguenots, who settled in different parts of Ireland after the Revocation of the Edict of Nantes.—Harrison, *The Scot in Ulster*, p. 21.

" While along the shores of Down and Antrim, and by the banks of the Six-Mile Water and the Main, the colonists are almost wholly from the Lowlands of Scotland ; upon the shores of Derry and Donegal, and by the banks of the Foyle and the Bann, were planted by the action of the same far-seeing James Stuart, bands of English colonists. Large grants of land in the escheated counties of Ulster were bestowed upon the great London companies, and on their vast estates by the Foyle and the Bann were settled considerable numbers of fine old English families. The Englishmen may be easily traced to this very day in Derry, and Coleraine, and Armagh, and Enniskillen. Groups of these Puritans dotted the whole expanse of Ulster, and in a later hour, when the magnificent Cromwell took hold of Ireland, these English colonists were reinforced by not a few of the very bravest and strongest of the Ironsides. To this very hour I know where to lay my hands on the direct lineal descendants of some of Cromwell's most trusted officers, who brought to Ireland blood that flowed in the purest English veins. The defiant city of Derry was the fruit of the English settlement, the royal borough of Coleraine, the cathedral city of Armagh, the battle-swept Enniskillen, and several towns and hamlets along the winding Bann.   Among these English settlers were not a few who were ardent followers of George Fox, that man who in many respects was Cromwell's equal, and in some his master ; these Friends came with a man of great force of character, Thomas Edmundson, who bore arms for the Parliament, and has left behind him a singularly interesting diary.   The Friends came to Antrim in 1652, and settled in Antrim and Down ; hence come the Pims, the Barclays, the Grubbs, and Richardsons, with many another goodly name of Ulster.

" The name of this Irish province was spreading over Europe by the second decade of the seventeenth century as the ' shelter of the hunted ' ; and soon the Puritan and the Quaker are joined in Ulster by another nobleman of God's making — the Huguenot from France. Headed by Louis Crommellin they came a little later and settled in and around Lisburn, founding many of the finest industries of Ulster, and giving mighty impulse to those already started.   And still later, following the ' immortal William ' came some brave burghers from Holland and the Netherlands.   Thus Ulster became a gathering ground for the very finest, most formative, impulsive, and aggressive of the free, enlightened, God-fearing peoples of Europe."—J. S. MacIntosh, " The Making of the Ulsterman," *Scotch-Irish Society of America Proceedings*, vol. ii., pp. 98, 99.

CHAPTER XIII

SCOTLAND OF TO-DAY

IT has been said of the modern Scottish race by some of its enthusiastic sons that, in proportion to its numbers, that race has produced more men who have taken a prominent part in the affairs of the English speaking world than has any other. Whether this be true or not, there are two facts bearing upon that phase of Scottish race-history to which attention may propèrly be called. The first and most important fact is, that nearly all the men of Scottish birth or descent who are renowned in history trace their family origin back to the western Lowlands of Scotland. That is to say, the district comprising the counties of Lanark, Renfrew, Ayr, Dumfries, Wigtown, Kirkcudbright, and Dumbarton—in area about the same as Connecticut, and the most of which was formerly included in the Celto-British kingdom of Strathclyde,—has produced a very large proportion of the men and families who have made the name of Scotland famous in the world's history.[1]

In this district are to be found the chief evidences in Scotland of the birth or residence of King Arthur and his Knights of the Round Table. Dumbartonshire is the reputed birthplace of St. Patrick, Ireland's teacher and patron saint. Elderslie, in Renfrewshire, is said to have been the birthplace of Scotland's national hero, William Wallace. Robert Bruce also, son of Marjorie, Countess of Carrick and daughter of Nigel or Niall (who was himself the Celtic Earl of Carrick and grandson of Gilbert, son of Fergus, Lord of Galloway), was, according to popular belief, born at his mother's castle of Turnberry, in Ayrshire. The seat of the High Stewards of Scotland, ancestors of the royal family of the Stuarts, was in Renfrewshire. The paternal grandfather of William Ewart Gladstone was born in Lanarkshire. John Knox's father is said to have belonged to the Knox family of Renfrewshire. Robert Burns was born in Ayrshire. The sect called the "Lollards," who were the earliest Protestant reformers in Scotland, appear first in Scottish history as coming from Kyle in Ayrshire, the same district which afterwards furnished a large part of the leaders and armies of the Reformation. The Covenanters and their armies of the seventeenth century were mainly from the same part of the kingdom. Glasgow, the greatest manufacturing city of Europe, is situated in the heart of this district. These same seven counties also furnished by far the greater part of the Scottish colonists of Ulster, in Ireland, from whom are descended a large proportion of the Scotch-Irish who have become famous in American history.[2]

The second fact about the race-history of Scotland and one that in a measure accounts for the first, is, that the population of the western Lowlands during the past six hundred years has consisted of a mixed or composite race, made up of a number of different and originally very dissimilar racial elements. The basis of the race was the Romanized Briton who lived " between the walls," built by the Romans across the island of Great Britain in the time of the Emperor Hadrian.* Chiefly from these early Britons— or *Welsh* (*i. e.*, " aliens "), as they were called by the Anglic invaders,— the Ulster Scot gets his Celtic blood, and not from the Gaels of modern Ireland. The Britons were in part Brythonic or Cymric Celts, identical with some of the tribesmen of Gaul who are described by Cæsar ; in part Gaelic Celts, who had preceded the Cymri some centuries in their migration to the islands ; in part non-Celtic and non-Aryan Aborigines, whom the Gaels found there ; and in part a blended race, comprising all these basic elements, with an additional Roman element furnished from the Roman legions (provincial and imperial), which for four centuries traversed, harried, and dominated the island of Great Britain. As time passed, there came marked departures from the original type, occasioned by intermarriages, first with the Picts and Scots, then with the Angles and Danes who occupied and largely peopled the eastern coast of Scotland, and with the Norsemen, who settled in the southwest.² From the last-named stock comes most of the Teutonic blood of the Ulster Scots, or Scotch-Irish. After the eleventh century, the Normans came from England into Scotland in large numbers, and occupied much of the land, their leaders frequently intermarrying with the daughters of native Celtic chieftains. Long before the seventeenth century, in the early years of which the Scottish emigration to Ireland began, the various race-groups of the western Lowlands of Scotland had become fused into one composite whole, having the attributes of the Celt, the Norse, the Angle, and the Norman ; thus typifying many centuries ago the identical race which the world to-day is beginning to recognize as the American—an amalgamation of the Teutonic and the Celtic, having the staying qualities of the one, with the grace, adaptability, and mental brilliancy of the other.

" The Scottish Lowlanders are a very mixed race," says Reclus, the French traveller and geographer, " and even their name is a singular proof of it. Scotland was originally known as Hibernia, or Igbernia,⁴ whilst the name of Scotia, from the end of the sixth to the beginning of the eleventh century, was exclusively applied to modern Ireland. The two countries have consequently exchanged names."

John of Fordun, the first of the early historians of Scotland whose writings can even in part be relied upon, has given us the following description of Scotland as it existed in his day (he died shortly after 1384) :

Scotia is so named after the Scottish tribes by which it is inhabited. At first, it began from the Scottish firth on the south, and, later on, from the

* One wall ran east from the Clyde and the other from the Solway.

river Humber, where Albania also began. Afterwards, however, it commenced at the wall Thirlwal, which Severus had built to the river Tyne.
But now it begins at the river Tweed, the northern boundary of England,
and, stretching rather less than four hundred miles in length, in a north-
westerly direction, is bounded by the Pentland Firth, where a fearfully
dangerous whirlpool sucks in and belches back the waters every hour. It is
a country strong by nature, and difficult and toilsome of access. In some
parts, it towers into mountains ; in others, it sinks down into plains. For
lofty mountains stretch through the midst of it, from end to end, as do the
tall Alps through Europe ; and these mountains formerly separated the Scots
from the Picts, and their kingdoms from each other. Impassable as they are
on horseback, save in very few places, they can hardly be crossed even on
foot, both on account of the snow always lying on them, except in summer-
time only ; and by reason of the boulders torn off the beetling crags, and the
deep hollows in their midst. Along the foot of these mountains are vast
woods full of stags, roe-deer, and other wild animals and beasts of various
kinds ; and these forests oftentimes afford a strong and safe protection to the
cattle of the inhabitants against the depredations of their enemies ; for the
herds in those parts, they say, are accustomed, from use, whenever they hear
the shouts of men and women, and if suddenly attacked by dogs, to flock
hastily into the woods. Numberless springs also well up, and burst forth
from the hills and the sloping ridges of the mountains, and, trickling down
with sweetest sound, in crystal rivulets between flowery banks, flow together
through the level vales, and give birth to many streams ; and these again to
large rivers, in which Scotia marvellously abounds, beyond any other country;
and at their mouths, where they rejoin the sea, she has noble and secure
harbors.

Scotia, also, has tracts of land bordering on the sea, pretty, level, and rich,
with green meadows, and fertile and productive fields of corn and barley, and
well adapted for growing beans, peas, and all other produce ; destitute, however, of wine and oil, though by no means so of honey and wax. But in the
upland districts, and along the highlands, the fields are less productive, except
only in oats and barley. The country is, there, very hideous, interspersed
with moors and marshy fields, muddy and dirty ; it is, however, full of pasturage grass for cattle, and comely with verdure in the glens, along the water-
courses. This region abounds in wool-bearing sheep, and in horses ; and its
soil is grassy, feeds cattle and wild beasts, is rich in milk and wool, and manifold in its wealth of fish, in sea, river, and lake. It is also noted for birds of
many sorts. There noble falcons, of soaring flight and boundless courage,
are to be found, and hawks of matchless daring. Marble of two or three
colors, that is, black, variegated, and white, as well as alabaster, is also
found there. It also produces a good deal of iron and lead, and nearly all
metals.

The manners and customs of the Scots vary with the diversity of their
speech. For two languages are spoken amongst them, the Scottish and the
Teutonic ; the latter of which is the language of those who occupy the seaboard and plains, while the race of Scottish speech inhabit the highlands and
outlying islands.[b] The people of the coast are of domestic and civilized
habits, trusty, patient, and urbane, decent in their attire, affable, and peaceful, devout in Divine worship, yet always prone to resist a wrong at the hand
of their enemies. The highlanders and people of the islands, on the other
hand, are a savage and untamed nation, rude and independent, given to
rapine, ease-loving, of a docile and warm disposition, comely in person, but

unsightly in dress, hostile to the English people and language, and, owing to diversity of speech, even to their own nation, and exceedingly cruel. They are, however, faithful and obedient to their king and country, and easily made to submit to law if properly governed.

The Picts or Caledonians, who lived in the country at the time of its conquest by the Romans, do not appear to have formed a strong element of the actual population of the Scottish Lowlands.[6]   The inhabitants of that part of the country seem for the most part to be of British and Anglo-Celtic race.   The line which separated the Britons from the Picts runs, approximately, across the isthmus of the Clyde and Forth ; the ancient wall of Antoninus thus marking an ethnological frontier no less than a political one.   But Angles and Britons were compelled to share their territory with emigrants of various races, including the Scots of Ireland, Frisians, Northmen, and Danes.   " At some places," says Reclus, "and more especially along the coast, people of different origin live in close contact with each other, and yet remain separate.   Their blood has not mingled ; habits, customs, and modes of thought and action have remained distinct.   Along the whole of the coast, on that of the German Ocean, no less than on that of the Irish Sea, we meet with colonies of fishermen, some of whom claim descent from the Northmen, whilst others look upon the Danes as their ancestors. There are even colonies which tradition derives from Flanders.   Several of the maritime villages consist of two portions like the towns on the coasts of Catalonia, Liguria, and Sicily, the upper part being inhabited by Saxon artisans and agriculturists, while the lower part forms the ' Marina ' of Scandinavian fishermen.   These various elements of the population have, however, become fused in the greater part of the country.   Physically the Scotchman resembles the Norwegian, and this is not solely due to a similarity of climate, but also to the numerous unions between Scandinavian invaders and the daughters of the country.   The languages of the two countries also possess more features in common than was formerly believed.   The Scotch speak English with a peculiar accent which at once betrays their origin.   Their intonation differs from that of the English, and they suppress certain consonants in the middle and at the end of words.   They still employ certain old English terms, no longer made use of to the south of the Tweed, and, on the strength of this, patriotic Scotchmen claim to speak English with greater purity than their southern neighbors.   Amongst the many words of foreign derivation in common use, there are several French ones, not only such as were introduced by the Normans, but also others belonging to the time when the two peoples were faithful allies, and supplied each other with soldiers.

" The Scotch Lowlander is, as a rule, of fair height, long-legged, strongly built, and without any tendency to the obesity so common amongst his kinsmen of England.   His eye is ordinarily brighter than that of the Englishman, and his features more regular ; but his cheeks are more prominent, and the leanness of the face helps much to accentuate these features. In these respects he bears a striking resemblance to his American cousins. Comparative inquiries instituted by Forbes prove that physical development is somewhat slower amongst Scotchmen than amongst Englishmen ; the former comes up to the latter in height and strength only at the age of nineteen, but in his ripe age he surpasses him to the extent of about five per cent. in muscular strength.[7] Of all the men of Great Britain, those of southwestern Scotland are distinguished for their tall stature. The men of Galloway average 5 feet 7 inches in height, which is superior to the stature attained in any other district of the British Islands. The Lowlander is intelligent, of remarkable sagacity in business, and persevering when once he has determined upon accomplishing a task ; but his prudence degenerates into distrust, his thrift into avarice. As in America, there is not a village without one or more banks. When abroad he seeks out his fellow-countrymen, derives a pleasure in being useful to them, and helps their success in life to the best of his ability.

" The achievements of Scotch agriculturists, who are so little favored by climate, must appear marvellous to the peasants of Italy and of many parts of France. Under the fifty-sixth degree of latitude they secure crops far more abundant than those obtained from the fertile lands on the Mediterranean, which are nine hundred miles nearer to the equator. Human labor and ingenuity have succeeded in acclimatizing plants which hardly appear to be suited to the soil and climate of Scotland. About the middle of the eighteenth century a patch of wheat was pointed out near Edinburgh as a curiosity, whilst now that cereal grows in abundance as far north as the Moray Firth. And yet it appears as if the climate had become colder, for it is no longer possible to cultivate the poppy or tobacco, as was done in the beginning of the century. Several varieties of apples, pears, and prunes, formerly in high repute, no longer arrive at maturity, and the horticultural societies have ceased offering prizes for these productions, because it is no longer possible to grow them in the open air. The manufacturing triumphs of Scotland have been quite equal to those achieved in agriculture, and it is on Scottish soil that Glasgow, the foremost manufacturing town of the United Kingdom, has arisen, with a population greater than that of either Manchester, Leeds, or Birmingham. Scotland, through her numerous emigrants who live in London and the other great towns, has also largely contributed towards the prosperity of England. The hawkers in the English manufacturing districts are usually known as 'Scotchmen.' The Scotch colonists in New Zealand and Canada are amongst the most active and industrious, and the young Lowlanders who go out to India as government officials are far more numerous in proportion than those from England.

" The love of education for its own sake, and not merely as a means to an end, is far more widely spread in Scotland than in England. The lectures at the universities are attended with a zeal which the students of Oxford or Cambridge seldom exhibit.   It is by no means rare to meet pupils in elementary schools who are passionately fond of study, and the humble homes of artisans and laborers frequently contain a select library which would do credit to a wealthy English tradesman.   At the same time there are not wanting young men who accelerate their studies in order that they may secure the certificates which form their passport to lucrative employment. They work hard, no doubt, but they strive not after knowledge, but for material gain.   The students of Edinburgh have little time to devote to those exercises of strength and skill which are so highly cultivated at Oxford and Cambridge.[8]   By a curious contrast, these Scotchmen, so practical and full of common sense, have an extraordinary love for the supernatural.   They delight in stories of terror and of ghosts.   Though clever architects of their own fortunes, they are yet fatalists, and the religious sects of which most of them are members defend with singular fervor the doctrine of predestination.   Thousands amongst the peasants, dressed in clerical black, are veritable theologians; and know how to discuss the articles of their faith with a great luxury of Scripture texts.   As Emerson says, they allow their dialectics to carry them to the extremes of insanity.   In no other country of the world is the Sabbath observed with such rigor as in Scotland.   On that day many of the trains and steamers cease running, and silence reigns throughout the land.   There are even landed proprietors who taboo their hills on that day, and if a tourist is found wandering amongst them he is treated as a reckless violator of the proprieties."

Who were the earliest inhabitants of the Scottish Highlands?   Of what race were the Picts, who formerly inhabited the country, and over whom even the Romans could not triumph?   Were they pure Celts, or had their blood already mingled with that of Scandinavia?   It is usually believed that the Picts had preceded the other Britons in their migration to the island, coming at a very early age, and that their idioms differed much more from the dialect spoken in Gaul than did Cymric.   They originally inhabited, perhaps, the whole of Great Britain, and were pushed to the northward by the Britons, who in turn were displaced by Romans and Angles.[9]

Numerous stone monuments, known as Picts' " houses," or weems, and invariably consisting of a chamber or centre passage surrounded by smaller apartments, are attributed to these aborigines.   The mainland, and to a great extent the islands, abound in *broughs*, or *borgs*—that is, towers of defence, resembling, at least externally, the nuraghe of Sardinia.   On the Shetland Islands there are seventy-five of these towers, and in the Orkneys seventy.   Petrie, who has examined forty of them, looked upon them as fortified dwelling-houses.   Their circular walls are twelve feet and more in thickness ; their original height is not known, for every one of them has reached us in a partial state of demolition.   Pestles for crushing corn, stone lamps, and vessels made of the bone of whales testify to the rudimentary state of civilization which the inhabitants had attained.   The Brough of

Mousa, to the south of Lerwick, bulges out near its base, probably to prevent the use of scaling ladders, and recesses occur at regular intervals on the inside of the wall.   Cromlechs, cairns, standing stones, symbolical sculptures, circles of stones, pile dwellings, and vitrified forts are found in several localities both on the mainland and the islands.   Primitive monuments of this kind form one of the most salient landscape features in the Orkneys.   On Pomona there is a district of several square miles in area which still abounds in prehistoric monuments of every description, although many stones have been carried away by the neighboring farmers.   In the tumulus of Meashow, opened in 1861, were discovered over nine hundred Runic inscriptions, and the carved images of fanciful animals.   On the same island are the standing stones of Stennis ; and on Lewis, twelve miles to the west of Stornoway, the " gray stones of Callernish."   These latter, forty-eight in number, are also known as Tuirsachan, or " Field of Mourning," and they still form a perfect circle, partly buried in peat, which has grown to a height of from six to twelve feet around them.[10]   We know that these constructions belong to different ages, and that now and then the stones raised by the earliest builders were added to by their successors.   Christian inscriptions in *oghams* and *runes*, in characters not older, according to Munch, than the beginning of the twelfth century, have been discovered on these monuments.   At Newton, in Aberdeenshire, there is a stone inscribed in curiously shaped letters, not yet deciphered.

Notwithstanding a change of religion, these sacred places of the ancient inhabitants still attract pilgrims.   On South Uist the people until recently walked in procession around a huge pile of rocks, turning thrice in following the apparent path of the sun.   The small island of Iona at the western extremity of Mull is one of those places which have been held sacred for generations.   Various stone monuments prove that this spot was held in veneration at the dawn of history, and this probably induced the Irish apostle, St. Columba, to found here a monastery—the " light of the western world "—which soon became the most famous in Great Britain.   Hence went forth those ascetic Culdees whom the jealousy of the clergy caused to disappear in the course of the thirteenth century.[11]   In the ruined ecclesiastical buildings of this islet are buried more than sixty kings of Scotland, Ireland, and the Hebrides, the last interred here having been Macbeth.   A prophecy says that one day the whole earth will be swallowed up by a deluge, with the exception of Iona.   There was a time when this venerated island was interdicted to women, as Mount Athos is at the present day.   Not far from the church lay the " black stones," thus called on account of the malediction attaching to him who foreswore himself by their side.   It was here that the " Lords of the Isles," kneeling on the ground with their hands raised to heaven, were bound to swear to maintain intact the rights of their vassals.[12]   Among the heaps of rocks piled up on the beach, it is said by monks in expiation of their trespasses, are found fine fragments of granite, porphyry, and serpentine, which the inhabitants employ Scotch workmen to cut and polish, in order that they may sell them as amulets to their visitors. Formerly these stones were looked upon throughout the Hebrides as the most efficacious medicine against sorcery ; and when about to be married a bridegroom, to insure happiness, placed a stone of Iona upon his bare left foot.[13]

The Scotch Highlanders are more or less mixed with Scandinavians, for the Northmen, who for centuries held possession of the Orkneys, gained a footing also upon the mainland, where they founded numerous colonies. Scandinavian family names are frequent in the Orkneys, but the type of the inhabitants is nevertheless Scotch.[14] The geographical nomenclature of the Shetland Isles is wholly Norwegian. The names of farms terminate in *seter* or *ster*, and those of hills in *hoy* or *hole*. In 1820 the sword dance of the ancient Norwegians might still be witnessed on one of the islands, and, according to Gifford,[15] Norse was spoken in a few families as recently as 1786. Sutherland clearly formed part of the old domain of the Northmen. That county lies at the northern extremity of Scotland ; but to the inhabitant of the Orkneys it was a Southern Land, and the name which they gave to it has survived to our own time.

A few Scandinavian colonies on the mainland have retained their distinct character. As an instance may be mentioned the village of Ness on Lewis, the inhabitants of which are distinguished for their enterprise, presenting a singular contrast to the sluggishness of their Gaelic neighbors. The descendants of these hostile races have, like oil and water, long refused to mingle. It would nevertheless be next to impossible to define the boundaries between the various races throughout the country. Language certainly would prove no safe guide, for many of the Gaels have given up their language and speak English. Out of 5,000,000 Scotchmen, only 350,000 are able to express themselves in Gaelic, and of these only 70,000 are ignorant of English.[16] As to the Scandinavians, not one amongst their descendants now speaks Old Norse. The greater number of them speak English, but many, too, have adopted Gaelic. In most of the islands the names of places are Danish, although Gaelic has for centuries been the spoken language. Even in St. Kilda, remote as is its situation, an intermingling of Gaels and Northmen has been recognized.

The use of Gaelic was discontinued at the court of Scotland about the middle of the eleventh century, and it is doomed to disappear. Far poorer in its literature and less cultivated than Welsh, its domain diminishes with every decade, for English is now almost universally spoken in the towns, and the Highland valleys are becoming depopulated, or invaded by Saxon sportsmen and graziers. If Caledonia really stands for Gael-Dun, or " Mountain of the Gael," then its limits are becoming narrower every time the meshes of the network of railroads are drawn tighter. But though Celtic may disappear as a spoken language, the geographical nomenclature of Scotland will for all time bear witness to its ancient domination.   Those acquainted with Gaelic may obtain a tolerably correct notion of the relief of the ground by merely studying the names upon a map.   Names like *ben, carn, carr, carragh, cnoc, creag, cruach, dun, mam, meal, monadh, sguir, sith, sithean, sliabh, stob, stuc, tolm, torr,* and *tullich,* will suggest to their minds variously shaped mountains ; *eye, i,* and *innis* denote islands ; *linne* and *loch* represent lakes or gulfs ; *abh, abhuinn, uisge, esk,* and *buinne,* stand for rivers or torrents.   *Inver* in the west, and *Aber* in the east, indicate the mouths of rivers.   The names *Albainn, Albëinn,* or *Albion,* by which the Gaels were formerly designated, are now applied to all Britain.   The Gaelic bards speak of their fellow-countrymen by preference as *Albannaich,* or " Mountaineers." [17] The Albannaich of the Grampians and the Albanians of the Pindus are thus known by a similar name, having possibly the same meaning.

The translation of one of John Knox's religious works was the first book printed in Gaelic, and thus, as in Wales, the Reformation conferred upon the language of the people an importance which it had not possessed before. But whilst in Wales religious zeal, through its manifestation in the pulpit and the press, has contributed in a large measure to keep alive the native idiom, the division of the Highlanders into Roman Catholics and Protestants has resulted in a diminution of the collective patriotism of the people, as it reveals itself in language.   Roman Catholics are numerous in the county of Inverness, and it merely depended upon the chief of a clan whether his followers remained true to the old faith or embraced the new.   Canna and Eigg are the only Hebrides the inhabitants of which remained Roman Catholics.   Those of the larger island of Rum, it is said, hesitated what to do, when the chief of the MacLeods, armed with a yellow cudgel, threw himself in the way of a procession marching in the direction of the Romish church, and drove the faithful to the temple which he patronized. Hence Protestantism on that island is known to the present day as the " Religion of the Yellow Cudgel." [18]   But notwithstanding these changes of religion many superstitions survive amongst the people.   In Lewis, " stone " and " church " are synonymous terms, as they were in the time when all religious ceremonies were performed around sacred megaliths. [19]

The fame of the Highlanders had been sung by poets and novelists, until they came to be looked upon as typical for bravery, loyalty, and all manly virtues.   The soldiers in their strange and showy garb have so frequently won distinction upon the field of battle that all their panegyrists said about their native virtues was implicitly believed ; and on the faith of poets we admired their pipers, the successors of the ancient bards, who accompanied their melancholy chants on the harp.   In reality, however, the Highlanders, until recently, were warlike herdsmen, as the Montenegrins, Mirdits, and Albanians are even now, always at enmity with their neighbors. It was only after forts had been built at the mouths of the valleys, and military roads constructed through their territories, that they were reduced to submission.   The members of each family were closely united, and, like American Indians, they had their war cries, badges, and distinctly patterned tartans.   The people were thus split up into about forty clans, or, including the Lowland families, into about one hundred, and several of these clans consisted of more than 10,000 individuals.   The principal Highland clans in 1863 were: MacGregors, 36,000 ;   MacKenzies, 21,000 ;   MacLeans, 16,000 ;   MacLeods, 14,000 ;   MacIntoshes, 11,000 ;   MacDonalds, 10,000. The members of each clan, though sometimes only cousins a hundred times removed, all bore the same name, and they fought and worked together. The land was originally held in union, being periodically divided amongst the clan.   The honor of the tribe was dear to every one of its individual members, and an injury done to one amongst them was avenged by the entire community.   When the kings of Scotland had to complain of a Highland chief, they attacked his clan, for they well knew that every member of it would embrace the cause of the chief.   There existed no courts of justice in the Highlands, but blood was spilt for blood.   Various monuments recall such acts of savage vengeance, and as recently as 1812 a Highland family set up seven grinning heads as a trophy to commemorate a sevenfold murder committed by its ancestors.   A cavern on Eigg Island is strewn with human bones, the relics of the ancient inhabitants of the island, two hundred in number, who are said to have been suffocated within the cavern by a neighboring chief, MacLeod, in retaliation for some private injury.[20]

As long as every member of the community possessed a share in the land, Scotland was spared the struggle between rich and poor.   But by the close of the eighteenth century, the poorer members of the clan, though still claiming cousinship with their chief, had lost all proprietary rights in the land, and the lairds, when remonstrated with by the clan, responded in the words of the device adopted by the earls of Orkney, " Sic fuit, est, et erit! "   They were even then able to drive away the ancient inhabitants from the plots of land they occupied, in order that they might transform them into pasturing or shooting grounds.   Several landlords even burned down the cabins of their poor " cousins," thus compelling them to leave the country.   Between 1811 and 1820, 15,000 tenants were thus evicted from the estates of the Duchess of Stafford.

Entire villages were given up to the flames, and on a single night three hundred houses might have been seen afire.   Nearly the whole population of four parishes was in this way driven from its homes. Since the middle of the century about one million acres in the Highlands have been cleared of human beings and sheep, to be converted into shooting grounds.[21]   Thus, contrary to what may be usually witnessed in civilized countries, the Highland valleys are returning to a state of nature, and wild beasts taking the place of domesticated animals.   The country formerly almost bare of trees has been largely planted, and from Black Mount in Argyleshire to Marr Forest in Aberdeen there now extends an almost unbroken belt of verdure.   Already the shooting grounds cover over two million acres, and they are continually extending. Scotland has emphatically become a sporting country, and many a large estate is managed as a shooting ground, that proving more profitable to its proprietor than would its cultivation. There are not wanting sportsmen willing to pay £400 for a salmon stream, £1000 for the right of shooting over a moor, or £4000 for a deer park. With these rents a salmon may cost £8 and a stag £40. In 1877, 2060 shooting grounds in Scotland were let for £600,000.[22] Scotland, even more than England, is a land of wide demesnes, and twenty-one individuals share between them the third of the kingdom, seventy the half, and one thousand and seven hundred nine-tenths of it. The Duke of Sutherland alone owns about the fifteenth part of Scotland, including nearly the whole county from which he derives his title. Domains of such vast extent cannot be properly cultivated, and heaths and swamps which would repay the labor bestowed upon them by peasant proprietors are allowed by their wealthy owners to remain in a state of nature.

In the Orkneys, a portion of the land is still owned by *odallers*, or peasant proprietors ; but the Shetland Islands and several of the Hebrides, including Lewis, the largest amongst them, belong to a single proprietor, who thus disposes indirectly of the lives of the inhabitants, whom he can compel to abandon their homes whenever it suits his interests. Several islands, such as Barra and Rum, which formerly supported a considerable population, have in this way become almost deserts ; and amongst the inhabitants left behind there are even now many who live in a state of extreme poverty, who look upon *carrageen*, or Iceland moss, as a luxury, and who are dependent upon seaweeds and fish for their daily sustenance. Owing to the inferiority of the food, dyspepsia is a common complaint, and certain physicians declare that the gift of " second sight," which plays so prominent a part in the history of the Highlanders, is traceable to a disorder of the organs of digestion. The villages of Lewis are perhaps unique of their kind in Europe. The inhabitants gather the stones embedded in the peaty soil to construct rough concentric walls, filling the space between them with earth and gravel. A scaffolding made of old oars and boughs supports a roof covered with earth and peat, leaving a wide ledge on the top of the circular wall, upon which vegetation soon springs up, and which becomes the favorite promenade and playground of children, dogs, and sheep. A single door gives access to this unshapely abode, within which a peat fire is kept burning throughout the year, in order that the damp which perpetually penetrates through the wall and roof may evaporate. Horses, cows, and sheep, all of diminutive stature, owing to the want of nourishment, occupy one extremity of this den, while the fowls roost by the side of the human inhabitants, or perch near the hole left for the escape of the smoke. To strangers the heat and smoke of these dwellings are intolerable, but the former is said to favor the laying of eggs.[23] Such are the abodes of most of the inhabitants of Lewis. Yet the claims to comfort have increased since the commencement of the nineteenth century, and a porringer is no longer looked upon as a veritable curiosity.

NOTES TO CHAPTER XIII

[1] It may be not without interest to note here the names of the twenty-nine American Immortals, for whom memorial tablets have been placed in the Hall of Fame, erected during the year 1900 on University Heights in the city of New York. The names were selected by a jury of ninety-seven members, composed of twenty-five college presidents, twenty-six professors of science and history, twenty-three publicists, editors, and authors, and twenty-three justices of state and national supreme courts. The result of this selection was as follows, the number of votes cast for each candidate being appended :

George Washington (97), Abraham Lincoln (96), Daniel Webster (96), Benjamin Franklin (94), Ulysses S. Grant (92), John Marshall (91), Thomas Jefferson (90), Ralph Waldo Emerson (87), Henry W. Longfellow (85), Robert Fulton (85), Washington Irving (83), Jonathan Edwards (81), Samuel Finley Breese Morse (80), David G. Farragut (79), Henry Clay (74), Nathaniel Hawthorne (73), George Peabody (72), Robert E. Lee (69), Peter Cooper (69), Horace Mann (67), Eli Whitney (67), John James Audubon (67), Henry Ward Beecher (66), James Kent (65), Joseph Story (64), John Adams (61), William Ellery Channing (58), Gilbert Stuart (52), Asa Gray (51),

Of the twenty-nine names given above, the bearers of seven were of Scottish descent in the male line—Webster, Grant, Fulton, Irving, Cooper, Stuart, and Gray ; Marshall was Welsh and Scotch ; Morse, English and Scotch ; Jefferson, Welsh, English, and Scotch ; Farragut, Spanish ; Audubon, French and Spanish : Clay, uncertain ; Edwards, Welsh ; Adams, English and Welsh ; and the remaining fourteen English. Of the other names voted on by the jury, the fifteen receiving the most votes under the number necessary to elect (fifty-one) were as follows, the names of those of Scottish descent (six out of fifteen) being printed in italics : *John C. Calhoun* (49), *Andrew Jackson* (49), John Quincy Adams (48), William Cullen Bryant (48), James Madison (48), Rufus Choate (47), Mark Hopkins (47), Elias Howe (47), *Horace Greeley* (45), *Joseph Henry* (44), James B. Eads (42), Benjamin Rush (42), John Lothrop Motley (41), *Patrick Henry* (39), *Edgar Allan Poe* (37).

Thus of the forty-four Americans receiving the highest number of votes, sixteen were of Scottish origin in whole or part, thirteen being of Scottish descent in the male line.

[2] The ancient Celto-Scottish kingdom of Strathclyde, which, as late as the eleventh century, extended from the Clyde to the river Ribble, in Lancashire, England, and formed part of the domain of Malcolm Canmore, King of the Scots in the time of William the Conqueror, was the ancestral home, not only of the Scotch-Irish and many of the heroes of Scotland, but also of the families of Washington, Jackson, and Taylor, which have furnished three presidents to the United States.

[3] The reader will of course remark that of the four kingdoms—Dalriadic Irish, Pictish, British of Strathclyde, and English of Bernica—the two latter realms extended far south beyond the line of modern Scotland. This fact had remarkable consequences in Scottish history. Otherwise the existence of these four kingdoms mainly interests us as showing the nature of the races—Pictish, British, Irish, and English—who were, then, the inhabitants of various parts of Scotland, leaving, doubtless, their strain of blood in the population. A Dumfries, Ayr, Renfrew, Lanark, or Peebles man, as a dweller in Strathclyde, has some chance of remote British (Brython) ancestors in his pedigree ; a Selkirk, Roxburgh, Berwickshire, or Lothian man is probably for the most part of English blood ; an Argyleshire man is or may be descended from an Irish Scot or Dalriad ; the northern shires are partly Pictish, as also is Galloway, always allowing for the perpetual mixture of races in really historical and in prehistoric times.—Andrew Lang, *History of Scotland*, vol. i., p. 31.

[4] See Strabo, book i., ch. iv.; book ii., ch. i., v.; book iv., ch. v.

[5] If a line is drawn from a point on the eastern bank of Loch Lomond, somewhat south of Ben Lomond, following in the main the line of the Grampians, and crossing the Forth at Aberfoil, the Teith at Callander, the Almond at Crieff, the Tay at Dunkeld, the Ericht at Blairgowrie, and proceeding through the hills of Brae Angus till it reaches the great range of the Mounth, then crossing the Dee at Ballater, the Spey at Lower Craigellachie, till it reaches the Moray Firth at Nairn—this forms what was called the Highland Line and separated the Celtic from the Teutonic-speaking people. Within this line, with the exception of the county of Caithness, which belongs to the Teutonic division, the Gaelic language forms the vernacular of the inhabitants.—*Celtic Scotland*, ii., 453.

The Scottish Highlands are sometimes spoken of so as to convey the impression that there is a clearly defined mountain district, contrasted with "the Lowlands," as though the latter were a vast plain. There could hardly be a greater mistake. From Kirkcudbright to Caithness, there is hardly a county without its hill ranges ; and without leaving the Southern district, the lover of mountain beauty will find noble heights and solitary glens, with many a rippling burn from tarns among the hills.—Samuel G. Green, *Scottish Pictures*, p. 117.

[6] This description of the present inhabitants of the Lowlands and Highlands of Scotland is chiefly taken from Elisée Reclus's *La Terre*, Appleton's American edition, 1883. Reclus bases on Kemble, *Saxons in England*; Latham, *Ethnology of the British Isles ;* Murray, in *Philological Society's Transactions*, 1873; etc.

[7] Forbes ; Hugh Miller, *First Impressions of England and the English*.

[8] Demogeot and Montucci, *De l' enseignement superieur en Angleterre et en Ecosse*.

[9] Just as Highland scenery has come to be reckoned peculiarly Scottish scenery, not only by Englishmen and foreigners, but even by the inhabitants of the Lowlands themselves, to whom its lakes and glens, its stony precipices and wind-swept isles are as familiar and dear as they were once dreaded and disliked ; so in some important aspects, of which war is perhaps the chief, the Highlander has become the typical Scot, and the Lowlander, who mainly shaped the fortunes of the nation and gave it its place in history, has acquiesced in the representation and is proud of the disguise. No harm can follow from this if we only keep steadily in view the true ethnological condition of Scotland, and realize the fact that while in Southern Britain the Saxons and Angles almost wholly superseded the original Cymric population, there is no evidence that a similar act ever took place in North Britain ; there is no record of a Teutonic settlement except in the southeast, and there is no probability that the Picts between Drumalban and the eastern sea, or even the Cymry of Strathclyde, though they lost their language and their independence, were ever expelled from their original seats, or transformed in character by any extraordinary infusion of a Teutonic element.—J. M. Ross, *Scottish History and Literature*, p. 15.

[10] Wilson's *Prehistoric Annals of Scotland*.

[11] Jameson's *History of the Culdees*.

[12] Forbes Leslie, *Early Races of Scotland*.

[13] Mercey, *Revue des Deux Mondes*, Sept., 1838.

[14] Hugh Miller, *Footprints of the Creator*.

[15] *Historical Description of Zetland*.

[16] E. G. Ravenstein, *On the Celtic Languages in the British Isles*.

[17] Forbes Leslie, *Early Races of Scotland*.

[18] Dr. Johnson, *Tour in the Western Hebrides*.

[19] Anderson Smith, *Lewisiana*.

[20] Hugh Miller, *Cruise of the "Betsey."*

[21] Hugh Miller, *Sutherland as it Was and Is*.

[22] *Official Journal*, Nov. 16, 1877.

[23] Anderson Smith, *Lewisiana*.

CHAPTER XIV

THE CALEDONIANS, OR PICTS

OF the inhabitants of Britain in prehistoric times we can learn but little, and that only in the most general way. While the literature on the subject is quite extensive, and, so far as it records the results of archæological investigation, not without considerable value, yet the data thus far made available are so fragmentary as to form a basis for hardly anything more than a probable supposition as to who they were and whence they came.[1] The following summary by one of the recent English authorities[2] gives us a hint of the progress thus far made in this line of inquiry :

From the bones which have been taken from the tombs, and from the ancient flint-mines uncovered in Sussex and Norfolk, the anatomists have concluded that the Neolithic Britons were not unlike the modern Eskimo. They were short and slight, with muscles too much developed for their slender and ill-nurtured bones ; and there is that marked disproportion between the size of the men and women, which indicates a hard and miserable life, where the weakest are overworked and constantly stinted of their food. The face must have been of an oval shape, with mild and regular features : the skulls, though bulky in some instances, were generally of a long and narrow shape, depressed sometimes at the crown and marked with a prominent ridge, "like the keel of a boat reversed."[3] . . .
The oldest races were in a pre-metallic stage, when bronze was introduced by a new nation, sometimes identified with the oldest Celts, but now more generally attributed to the Finnish or Ugrian stock. When the Celts arrived in their turn, they may have brought in the knowledge of iron and silver ; the Continental Celts are known to have used iron broad-swords at the battle of the Anio in the fourth century before Christ, and iron was certainly worked in Sussex by the Britons of Julius Cæsar's time ; but as no objects of iron have been recovered from our Celtic tumuli, except in some instances of a doubtful date, it will be safer to assume that the British Celts belonged to the later Bronze Age as well as to the Age of Iron.[4]

With reference to the earliest population of Scotland, the following hypothesis given by Samuel Laing in his work on *Prehistoric Remains of Caithness* may be taken as a fairly comprehensive statement :

Our population contains three distinct ethnological elements : I. Xanthochroi brachycephali (the fair, broad-headed type) ; II. Xanthochroi dolichocephali (the fair, long-headed type); III. Melanchroi (the dark type). In Cæsar's time, and for an indefinitely long period, Gaul contained the first and third of these elements, and the shores of the Baltic presented the second. In other words, the ethnological elements of the Hiberno-British islands are identical with those of the nearest adjacent parts of the continent of Europe, at the earliest period when a good observer noted the characters of their population.

Dr. Thurnam has adduced many good reasons for believing that the "Belgic" element intruded upon a pre-existing dolichocephalic "Iberian" population; but I think it probable that this element hardly reached Ireland at all, and extended but little into Scotland. However, if this were the case, and no other elements entered into the population, the tall, fair, red-haired and blue-eyed dolichocephalia, who are, and appear always to have been, so numerous among the Irish and Scotch, could not be accounted for.

But their existence becomes intelligible at once, if we suppose that long before the well-known Norse and Danish invasions a stream of Scandinavians had set into Scotland and Ireland, and formed a large part of our primitive population. And there can be no difficulty in admitting this hypothesis when we recollect that the Orkneys and the Hebrides have been, in comparatively late historical times, Norwegian possessions. . . . In another fashion, the fair and broad-headed "Belgæ" intruded into the British area; but meeting with a large dolichocephalic population, which at subsequent times was vastly reinforced by Anglo-Saxon, Norse, and Danish invasions, this type has been almost wiped out of the British population, which is, in the main, composed of fair dolichocephalia and dark dolichocephalia. . . . But language has in no respect followed these physical changes. The fair dolichocephali and fair brachycephali of Germany, Scandinavia, and England speak Teutonic dialects; while those of France have a substantially Latin speech; and the majority of those of Scotland, and, within historic times, all those of Ireland, spoke Celtic tongues. As to the Melanchroi, some speak Celtic, some Latin, some Teutonic dialects; while others, like the Basques (so far as they come under this category) have a language of their own.

So far as any definite conclusions can be deduced from the work of the ethnologists and archæologists, it appears that the first Celtic invaders to enter Scotland (whether at a period simultaneous with or prior or subsequent to the advent of the Stone-Age Britons in that part of the island cannot perhaps be definitely told) were the Gaels, or Goidels, who had crossed over into Britain from Gaul, first settling on those portions of the coast most easy of access from the points of embarkation, thence pushing into the interior, and gradually spreading to the west and north. In their progress they must have encountered and, to a greater or less extent, superseded the aborigines — the Britons of the Stone Age. This may have been done by exterminating them, by driving them off towards the west, or by assimilating them with themselves. Probably all of these methods of race extinction were brought into operation. In such a primitive age, these tribes, native and foreign, cannot be conceived to have been other than loosely organized hordes of wandering savages, preying upon one another, without fixed habitations, and to whom all weaker strangers were foredoomed enemies. The Celts, bringing with them from the Continent the knowledge of bronze and iron, would have considerable advantage in battle over the aborigines, who had no more effective weapons than sharpened stones. In those days, also, it is reasonable to suppose that the country was so sparsely populated that for centuries after the first coming of the Gaels, there would be room enough on the island for both races ; and many bodies of the aborigines no doubt remained unmolested long after the extinction of their race had been in part accomplished.[5] As fresh waves of invasion swept over the eastern shores, the Celts first coming would be apt to be driven farther and farther inland from the coast, and would in turn displace the natives — who, to escape death or slavery, would be obliged to push farther westward and northward. Some of these (supposed) aborigines, however, seem to have made a successful stand against the encroachments of the newcomers, and among them we find two tribes who were identified with portions of Scotland down to a date long after the beginning of the historic era. These were the Novantæ and Selgovæ mentioned by Ptolemy, whose territory in his time (the early part of the second century) embraced the country west of the river Nith and south of the Ayr — Kirkcudbrightshire and Galloway — and possibly, also, the peninsula of Kintyre, in Argyle. Toward the end of the Roman occupation they seem to have coalesced, and became known as the Attecotti, a "fierce and warlike tribe," who gave the Romans a great deal of trouble. They afterwards appear in history as the Galloway Picts, and seem to have remained a distinct people under that name down to a comparatively recent date.[6]

The Gaelic Celts of the first migrations were in time followed by other bodies of their own tribesmen, and later by large incursions of invaders of a kindred race—the Cymric Celts.[7] The first comers, accordingly, seem to have been pushed on to the west and north, overrunning the west of England and Wales, entering Scotland, and some of them, more venturesome than others, crossing over into Northern Ireland, and making that country their own.[8] In the course of time, various tribes of the Cymric Celts acquired the most of Southern Britain and not a small portion of Scotland, spreading over the island in considerable numbers, and leaving few parts unoccupied save the hills and highlands of Scotland, which became the final retreat and stronghold of their Gaelic cousins.[9]

Cæsar was the first observer who has left any record of these early Cymro-Celtic Britons. Of their origin and manner of living he speaks as follows (*De Bello Gallico*, book v., ch. xii., xiv.) :

The interior portion of Britain is inhabited by those of whom they say that it is handed down by tradition that they were born in the island itself ; the maritime portion by those who had passed over from the country of the Belgæ for the purpose of plunder and making war ; almost all of whom are called by the names of those states from which being sprung they went thither, and having waged war, continued there and began to cultivate the lands. The number of the people is countless, and their buildings exceedingly numerous, for the most part very like those of the Gauls ; the number of cattle is great. They use either brass or iron rings, determined at a certain weight, as their money. Tin is produced in the midland regions ; in the maritime, iron ; but the quantity of it is small ; they employ brass, which is imported. There, as in Gaul, is timber of every description except beech and fir. They do not regard it lawful to eat the hare, and the cock, and the goose; they, however, breed them for amusement and pleasure. The climate is more temperate than in Gaul, the colds being less severe.

The most civilized of all these nations are they who inhabit Kent, which is entirely a maritime district, nor do they differ much from the Gallic customs. Most of the island inhabitants do not sow corn, but live on milk and flesh, and are clad with skins. All the Britons, indeed, dye themselves with woad, which occasions a bluish color, and thereby have a more terrible appearance in fight. They wear their hair long, and have every part of their body shaved except their head and upper lip. Ten and even twelve have wives common to them, and particularly brothers among brothers, and parents among their children; but if there be any issue by their wives, they are reputed to be the children of those by whom respectively each was first espoused when a virgin.

A description of the several peoples inhabiting Britain at this time, or shortly after, is found in Ptolemy's *Geography*, written about A.D. 121. According to Professor Rhys's interpretation of Ptolemy, most of the country between the Humber and Mersey and the Caledonian Forest belonged to a tribe or confederation known as the Brigantes. The Novantæ and Selgovæ, occupying the district on the Solway west of the Nith, appear, however, to have been independent of them; as were also the Parisi, between the Humber and the Tees. The Otadini (occupying a portion of Lothian and the coast down to the southern Wall) and the northern Damnonii (inhabiting the district north of the Novantæ, the Selgovæ, and the Otadini, and to a considerable distance beyond the Forth and Clyde—the present counties of Ayr, Renfrew, Lanark, Dumbarton, Stirling, and the western half of Fife) were either distinct peoples subject to the Brigantes, or included in the tribes that went under that name.[10]

Aside from the Novantæ and Selgovæ, these various tribes are now generally supposed to have belonged to the Cymric Celts, being part of the same people who, since the time of Julius Cæsar, have been popularly known as "Britons," at the present day sometimes called "Brythons," to distinguish them from the "Goidels," or Gaelic Celts of Britain. Freeman includes with the Brythons nearly all the tribes of North Britain, a classification which seems entirely too comprehensive; he says of the latter:

On the whole, it is most likely that they belonged to the same branch of the Celtic race as the southern Britons, and that they differed from them chiefly as the unsubdued part of any race differs from the part which is brought into subjection. In the later days of the Roman power in Britain, these northern tribes, under the name of Picts, appear as dangerous invaders of the Roman province, invaders whose inroads were sometimes pushed even into its southern regions.[11]

The connection of these different divisions of the early races with our subject is quite important, for, as we shall see later on, that portion of Britain inhabited for so long a time by the Novantæ, the Selgovæ, the Otadini, the Damnonii, the Brigantes, and the Galloway Picts of later writers is the part from which Ireland received the largest proportion of her Scottish immigrants.[12]

Up to the close of the tenth century, the name "Scotland" was applied solely to the Hibernian island. The present Scotland was then known as Caledonia, or by its ancient Gaelic name of Alban, or Albania. Before that period, and, indeed, for some time afterwards, its boundaries did not extend south of the Forth and Clyde. That part of the country south of these estuaries was included in the Roman province, and its inhabitants for the most part were Romanized Britons. During their wars with the Brigantes in the first century, the Romans learned of a people to the north of that nation, whom they termed Caledonian Britons. Lucan first mentions them A.D. 65 : "Unda Caledonios fallit turbata Britannos." They are alluded to by Tacitus some fifteen years later (*Life of Agricola*, c. xi.), who says :

Who were the first inhabitants of Britain, whether indigenous or immigrants, is a question involved in the obscurity usual among barbarians. Their temperament of body is various, whence deductions are formed of their different origin. Thus, the ruddy hair and large limbs of the Caledonians point out a German derivation.[13] The swarthy complexion and curled hair of the Silures, together with their situation opposite to Spain, render it probable that a colony of the ancient Iberi possessed themselves of that territory. They who are nearest Gaul resemble the inhabitants of that country; whether from the duration of hereditary influence, or whether it be that when lands jut forward in opposite directions, climate gives the same condition of body to the inhabitants of both. On a general survey, however, it appears probable that the Gauls originally took possession on the neighboring coast. The sacred rites and superstitions of these people are discernible among the Britons. The languages of the two nations do not greatly differ. The same audacity in provoking danger, and irresolution in facing it when present, is observable in both. The Britons, however, display more ferocity, not being yet softened by a long peace ; for it appears from history that the Gauls were once renowned in war, till, losing their valor with their liberty, languor and indolence entered among them. The same change has also taken place among those of the Britons who have been long subdued ; but the rest continue such as the Gauls formerly were.

Tacitus's account of the campaigns carried on against the Caledonians by Agricola sufficiently illustrates the spirit and valor of these early Scotchmen. Though often defeated in battle, they were never subdued ; and when unable to withstand the charges of the Roman legions in the open, they fell back to their retreats in forest and mountains, where they were able to hold the Romans at bay.

Dion Cassius, the historian (about A.D. 155–230), brings them to our attention again, when in the year 201 we find the Caledonians joined with the Mæatæ in preparation for an attack on the Roman province. This was postponed, however, by the action of the Roman Governor, Virius Lupus, who purchased peace at a great price from the Mæatæ. Dion, writing before the year 230, gives the following description of these Mæatæ, which, while in some respects evidently founded upon fable, yet as a whole corresponds with like accounts which have come down to us of the neighboring tribes (l. lxxvi., ch. xii.) :

Of the Britons, the. two most ample nations are the Caledonians and the Mæatæ ; for the names of the rest refer for the most part to these. The Mæatæ inhabit near the very wall which divides the island in two parts ; the Caledonians are after those. Each of them inhabits mountains, very rugged, and wanting water, also desert fields full of marshes ; they have neither castles nor cities, nor dwell in any ; they live on milk, and by hunting, and maintain themselves by the fruits of trees : for fishes, of which there is a very great and numberless quantity, they never taste ; they dwell naked in tents, and without shoes ; they use wives in common, and whatever is born to them they bring up.[14] In the popular state they are governed as for the most part ; they rob on the highway most willingly ; they war in chariots ; horses they have, small and fleet ; their infantry, also, are as well most swift at running as most brave in pitched battle. Their arms are a shield and a short spear, in the upper part whereof is an apple of brass, that while it is shaken it may terrify the enemies with sound ; they have likewise daggers ; they are able to bear hunger, cold, and all afflictions ; for they merge themselves in marshes, and there remain many days having only their heads out of water ; and in woods are nourished by the barks and roots of trees. But a certain kind of food they prepare for all occasions, of which if they take as much as the size of a single bean, they are in nowise ever wont to hunger or thirst.

The nation of the Mæatæ (*i.e.*, " Men of the Midlands ") embraced those tribes immediately north of the Roman wall between the Forth and the Clyde, while the Caledonians were to the north and east. This division of the people into two nations or septs seems to have continued for some centuries. In 380, they were known as the Dicalidones and the Vecturiones. By Bede they appear to have been distinguished as the Northern Picts and the Southern Picts.[15]

In the year 208, Severus penetrated into their country as far as the river Tay. By great exertions in clearing the country of forests and undergrowth, and the construction of roads and bridges, he acquired a limited district beyond that Wall of Antoninus which he had reconstructed between the Clyde and the Forth. This territory the Romans afterwards garrisoned, and retained for a few years. Severus is said to have fought no battles, on this march, but his loss in men was very great, owing to the destructive guerilla warfare carried on by the natives during the progress of the work of clearing. In 211, the Mæatæ and Caledonians prepared again for an attack on the Romans. The death of Severus in that year preventing his conduct of the operations against them, his son and successor was forced to make peace with these tribes on terms which it would seem eventually involved the withdrawal of the Roman garrisons to the south of the Wall.

After this we learn nothing more of the Caledonians from the Roman writers until near the beginning of the following century, when they are brought to our attention again under a new name, and one by which the early inhabitants of Scotland have become best known in history. Eumenius, the panegyrist, in his oration to Constantius Chlorus delivered at Autun, in

Gaul, A.D. 296, on the occasion of the victory of the latter over Allectus, compares the victor with the former leaders who had fought against the Britons, and adds : " The nation Cæsar attacked was then rude, and the Britons, used only to the Picts and Hibernians,—enemies then half naked,— easily yielded to the Roman arms and ensigns." At the same place some years later (309-10) Eumenius pronounced a second panegyric on Constantius Chlorus, before Constantine, the son of Constantius, in which he said : "The day would fail sooner than my oration were I to run over all the actions of thy father, even with this brevity. His last expedition did not seek for British trophies (as is vulgarly believed), but, the gods now calling him, he came to the secret bounds of the earth. For neither did he by so many and such actions, I do not say the woods and marshes of the Caledonians and other Picts, but not Hibernia [Scotland ?], near at hand, nor farthest Thule," etc.

These, and similar brief allusions on the part of later writers, are all that we get from the pages of early history concerning a subject which, towards the close of the last century, gave rise to the famous Pictish Controversy, a dispute that was carried on in Scotland for many years, and with extreme bitterness on both sides, but which did not result in adding much information to that imparted by Eumenius in the passage quoted above : namely, that the Caledonians were Picts.[16] For a full consideration of these discussions, the reader is referred to the works of Pinkerton, Ritson, Chalmers, Prichard, Grant, Betham, and others. While we cannot but agree with Mr. Hill Burton in concluding that the labor of those writers has been without avail, and are entirely willing to "content ourselves with the old and rather obvious notion that by *Picti* the Romans merely meant painted people,'' without any consideration about their race, language, or other ethnical specialties," yet the efforts of our modern workers in the same field have been more fruitful of results, so far as the ethnology of these painted people is concerned. It is now generally believed that they were primarily descended from the aborigines of Britain, who were non-Celtic and non-Aryan. Later, in accordance with the usually adopted view as to the priority of the Gaelic emigration to Britain, its subsequent movement northward, and the facility with which the Picts afterwards coalesced with the Scots, they must also have become to a large extent Gaelic. Yet, the presence of known Cymric peoples in the Pictish territories in Roman times,—one instance being that of the northern Damnonii, who were cut off from their own nation by the building of the first Wall,—together with the many proofs of Brythonic occupation shown in the topographical nomenclature of the northern Lowlands, lead us to the conclusion that, so far as the Southern Picts were concerned, their peculiar characteristics had to a considerable extent been modified by the infusion of Cymric elements. In other words, the Northern Picts seem to have been largely of the aboriginal type, more or less modified by fusion with the Gaelic, while those of the south were a mixed Gaelic, Cymric, and aboriginal people. This view harmonizes with the distinction nearly always made by the early historians in their references to the inhabitants of Caledonia—as instanced by the Mæatæ and Caledonians of Dion Cassius, the Caledonians and " other Picts " of Eumenius, the Dicalidones and Vecturiones of Ammianus, and, somewhat later, the Northern and Southern Picts of Bede.[18]

The Picts were converted to Christianity by the preaching of St. Columba in the latter half of the sixth century (after A.D. 565) ; and they were ruled over by a line of Pictish kings down to the year 842, when Kenneth MacAlpin, king of the Dalriada Scots, brought them under subjection, and united the two kingdoms under one crown.

The chief original sources of information about the Pictish kingdom and its rulers are the *Ulster Annals*, the *Annals of Tighernac*, and the *Pictish Chronicle*, of which the best editions are those contained in Mr. William F. Skene's *Chronicles of the Picts and Scots*. English translations of portions of the first two of these have been printed in the *Collectanea de Rebus Albanicis* of the Iona Club (see Appendix O).

The names of the Pictish kings from the beginning of the fifth century, with the dates of the commencement of their reigns, duration of same, and dates of death, are as follows :

About A.D. 406, Drust (or Drest) I., son of Irb (or Erp, or Wirp).

451, Talore I., son of Aniel, reigned four years.

455–57, Nechtan I., surnamed Morbet, son of Irb (or Erp); reigned twenty-four years.

480, Drest (or Drust) II., surnamed Gurthinmoch ; reigned thirty years.

510, Galanau ; reigned twelve years.

522, Dadrest ; reigned one year.

523, Drest (or Drust) III., son of Gyrom ; reigned eleven years.

524, the same, with Drust IV., son of Udrust (or Wdrost).[19]

529, Drust III. (alone).

534, Gartnaoch I., son of Gyrom ; reigned seven years.

541, Giltram (or Cailtram), son of Gyrom ; reigned one year.

542, Talorg II., son of Muircholaich ; reigned eleven years.

553, Drest V., son of Munait ; reigned one year.

554, Galam,[20] son of Cendaeladh ; reigned two years ; died (probably) 580.

555, the same, with Bridei.

556, Bridei (or Bruidi, or Brudei, or Brude) I., son of Mailcon (Bruidi mac Mailochon) ; reigned thirty years ; died 583.

586, Gartnard (or Gartnaidh) II., son of Domelch (or Domlech or Donald) (Gartnay mac Donald) ; reigned eleven years ; died 599.

597, Nechtan II., grandson (or nephew) of Uerd (Nechtan Hy Firb) ; reigned twenty years.

612 (or 617), Cinioch (or Cinaeth, or Kenneth, or Cinadon), son of Luchtren (or Lachtren) ; reigned fourteen to nineteen years ; died 631.

631, Gartnard (or Gartnaidh) III., son of Wid (or Foith) (Gartnay macFoith) ; reigned four years ; died 635.

635, Breidei (or Bruidi) II., son of Wid (or Foith) (Bruidi mac Foith) ; reigned five years ; died 641.

641, Talorc (or Talore, or Talorcan) III., son of Wid (or Foith) (Talorcan mac Foith) ; reigned twelve years ; died 653.

653, Talorcan, son of Ainfrait (or Anfrith,[21] or Eanfred) ; reigned four years ; died 657.

657–63, Gartnait (or Gartnaidh) IV., son of Donnell (or Domhnaill) (Gartnay mac Donald) ; reigned six and a half years ; died 663.

665, Drest (or Drust, or Drost) VI., son of Donnell and brother of Gartnach (Drust mac Donald) ; reigned seven years ; expelled 672.

672, Bredei (or Bruidi, or Bruidhe,[22] or Bredei) III., son of Bili (or Bile or Beli) (Bruidi mac Bili) ; reigned twenty-one years ; died 693.

693, Taran (or Gharan), son of Entefedich (or Enfisedech) (Gharan mac Enfisedech) ; reigned four years ; expelled 697.

695–7, Brudei (or Bredei, or Bruidi, or Brude) IV., son of Derili (or Derelei) (Brudei mac Derili) ; reigned eleven years ; died 706.

709, Nechtan III., son of Derili ; reigned fifteen years ; resigned 724 ; returned 728 ; died 729.

724, Drest (or Druxst or Drost) VII.; expelled 726 ; died, 729.

726, Alpin, son of Eachaidh ; expelled 728 ; died 741.

729–31, Angus (or Hungus) I., son of Fergus (or Wirgust) ; reigned thirty years ; died 761.

761, Brudei (or Bruidi) V., son of Fergus ; reigned two years ; died 763.

763, Kenneth (or Cinaedh, or Ciniod), son of Feredach (or Wirdech, or Wredech) ; reigned twelve years ; died 775.

775, Alpin, son of Wroid ; reigned three years ; died 780.

777–8, Drust (or Drost), son of Talorgen (or Talorcan) ; reigned four to five years ; and Talorgan (or Talorcan), son of Angus ; reigned two and a half years ; died about 782.

784, Conall, son of Taidg (or Canaul, son of Tarl'a) ; reigned five years ; expelled 789–90.

790, Constantine, son of Fergus (or Wirgust) ; reigned thirty years ; died 820.

820, Angus (brother of Constantine), son of Fergus ; reigned twelve years ; died 834.

834, Drust (or Drost), son of Constantine, and Talorcan (or Talorgan), son of Uitholl (or Wthoil) ; reigned about three years.

836, Eoganan, son of Angus ; reigned three years ; died 839.

839, Wrad (or Fered), son of Bargoit ; reigned about three years.

842, Bred (or Bruidi), son of Ferat ; reigned one year.

842–4, Kenneth II., surnamed mac Alpin, King of Albany.

NOTES TO CHAPTER XIV.

[1] One of the most useful books on this subject is Dr. Daniel Wilson's *Prehistoric Annals of Scotland.*

[2] Charles I. Elton, *Origins of English History*, London, 1890.

[3] Dr. Thurnam was the first to recognise that the long skulls, out of the long barrows of Britain and Ireland, were of the Basque or Iberian type, and Professor Huxley holds that the river-bed skulls belong to the same race. We have therefore proofs that an Iberian or Basque population spread over the whole of Britain and Ireland in the neolithic age, inhabiting caves, and burying their dead in caves and chambered tombs, just as in the Iberian peninsula also, in the neolithic age.—*Cave Hunting*, p. 214, by W. Boyd Dawkins, M.A., 1874.

[4] " The site of the prehistoric Celtic village near Glastonbury has been further excavated since July last under the superintendence of the discoverer, Arthur Bullied. The sites of the dwellings are marked by mounds. One of these contained the greatest depth of clay yet found, no less than nine feet, the accumulation of successive hearths, which were found necessary as the weight of the clay gradually compressed the peat beneath. This mound contained three hundred tons of clay, all of which must have been brought in their boats by the inhabitants from the neighboring hills. Under the mound was found the framework of a loom with brushwood and wattlework to form the foundation. That the inhabitants were much engaged in spinning is clear from the fact that in addition to other things connected with the craft no fewer than forty horn and bone carding combs have been unearthed· Strangely enough, no two of these are exactly of the same pattern. As in previous seasons, a large number of bone articles has been discovered. The number of broken bone needles and splinters of bone found in one mound seems to indicate that it was utilized as a needle factory.

" Another mound was very rich in fragments of pottery and other evidences of the manufacture of hardware. No fewer than ten bronze fibulæ were found, these being fashioned almost exactly like the modern safety-pin. Two bronze studs, probably a part of harness or for fastening clothing, were also found, together with other small bronze articles. A neatly cut iron file about eight inches long was found. As usual, very few human remains were discovered, part of the skeleton of a very young child being all that was brought to light this summer. With the exception of the cracked skulls of a few unfortunate warriors, the remains of very young children have chiefly been found in past years, Mr. Bullied being of the opinion that these primitive people conveyed their dead to the neighboring hills for interment.

" Parts of three broken millstones were unearthed and in one mound a clay oven, measuring two feet by nine inches. One glass article only was brought to light this year, a blue glass bead with a wavy line of dark blue running around it."—*London Times*, *circa* January, 1898.

[5] As for Britain, one of the most thoroughly non-Celtic portions of it south of the Clyde was probably that of the Selgovæ or hunters, in Roman times, and later the more limited Pictish district beyond the Nith.—J. Rhys, *Celtic Britain*, p. 270.

[6] The name of the Nith in Ptolemy's time was Novios, and it is from it that this people got the name of Novantæ, given them probably by Brythons. . . . To the east and northeast of the Novantæ dwelt the Selgovæ, protected by thick forests and a difficult country. They have left their name in the modern form of Solway to the moss and to the firth called after them. The word probably meant hunters, and the people to whom it applied may be supposed, not only to have been no Brythons, but to have been to no very great extent Celtic at all, except perhaps as to their language, which they may have adopted at an early date from the Goidelic invaders ; in a great measure they were most likely a remnant of the aboriginal inhabitants, and the same remark may be supposed to be equally applicable to the Novantæ. . . . They lived between the Walls, and appeared in history

as Genunians, we think, and Attecotti. . . . The struggle in which they took part against the Romans ended in their ultimately retaining only the country behind the Nith, where the name of the Novantæ becomes in Bede's mouth, that of the Niduarian Picts, known as the Picts of Galloway for centuries afterwards.—*Celtic Britain*, pp. 220–221.

The name "Picti" was likewise applied to the inhabitants of Galloway, comprising the modern counties of Kirkcudbright and Wigton, till a still later period, and survived the entire disappearance of the name as applied to any other portion of the inhabitants of Scotland, even as late as the twelfth century.   This district was occupied in the second century by the tribe termed by Ptolemy the "Novantæ," with their towns of Rerigonium and Lucopibia, and there is nothing to show that the same people did not occupy it throughout, and become known as the Picts of Galloway, of which "Candida Casa," or Withern, was the chief seat, and occupied the site of the older Lucopibia.—*Celtic Scotland*, vol. i., p. 131.

The Picts of Galloway are occasionally confounded with or included amongst the Southern Picts, though when Bede describes the latter people as dwellers beyond the Forth, at the foot of the lofty range of mountains separating them from the northern division of their race, he places them in a very different part of the country from Galloway.   Ritson maintains that Galloway was a province of the Southern Picts, laying it down, in his dogmatic manner, "as an incontrovertible fact, for which we have the express authority of Bede."   In support of this assertion he quotes Bede, *Hist. Eccl.*, l. iv., ch. xxvi., which, unfortunately for his argument, proves exactly the contrary, as the seat of Trumwine's bishopric is there said to have been placed at Abercorn on the Forth, which divides the territories of the Picts and the Angles—a very long way from Galloway.   Bede was very well acquainted with this latter district under the name of the diocese of Candida Casa, as it belonged, when he wrote, to the kingdom of Northumbria ; and in his last chapter he commemorates the establishment of an Anglian bishop within its boundaries.   As he distinctly says that the Picts, after their victory at Nectan's Mere, recovered from the Angles all that they had previously lost, it is plain that the diocese of Candida Casa, which remained in possession of the Northumbrians, could not have belonged to the Picts, but must have been conquered from another race, the Britons.   The authority of Bede is quite sufficient to refute the account of Jocelin, a monk who in the twelfth century ascribed the conversion of the Picts of Galloway to a certain shadowy St. Kentigern in the seventh ; this very district having been, upwards of two centuries before, the seat of a Christian bishop, the British Ninian.   A still more apocryphal story occurs in the *Acta Sanctorum* (11th March), that St. Constantine of Cornwall (the contemporary of Gildas) was martyred in Kintyre about the year 570, when preaching to the heathen Galwegians and pagan Scots ; or exactly at the same time when Columba was converting the Northern Picts from his asylum of Iona, which he received from the Christian King of the Dalriads.   Another argument has been brought forward to place the Picts in Galloway in the days of Bede, because the venerable historian has said that St. Cuthbert, on an excursion from Melrose, was driven by stress of weather to the territory of the Picts called Niduari— "ad terram Pictorum qui Niduari vocantur."   "The Picts inhabiting the banks of the Nith in Dumfriesshire," say Smith and Pinkerton, "whither the holy man could not have gone in a boat," retorts Ritson—with much truth—suggesting in his turn Long Niddry in Linlithgowshire, to reach which place, however, the holy man's boat must have been driven by stress of weather across a considerable tract of dry land.   The explanation of the difficulty seems to be that Cuthbert, sailing from some point on the eastern coast, was driven northwards by contrary winds into the Firth of Tay, landing near Abernethy on the coast of Fife, the inhabitants of the banks of the Nethy probably being the "Picti qui Niduari vocantur".— *Scotland under her Early Kings*, vol. ii., p. 382.   See Note 12, p. 214.

[7] As early as the middle of the fourth century the British provinces were already persistently attacked by sea and land.   The Picts and Scots, and the warlike nation of the "Attecotti," from whom the Empire was accustomed to recruit its choicest soldiers, the fleets of Irish pirates in the north, the Franks and Saxons on the southern shores, combined to-

gether, whenever a chance presented itself, to burn and devastate the country, to cut off an outlying garrison, to carry off women and children like cattle captured in a foray, and to offer the bodies of Roman citizens as sacrifices. . . . The "Notitia Dignitatum" [compiled about A.D. 400] mentions several regiments of Attecotti serving for the most part in Gaul and Spain. Two of their regiments were enrolled among the "Honorians," the most distinguished troops in the Imperial armies. Though their country is not certainly known, it seems probable that they inhabited the wilder parts of Galloway.—Elton, *Origins of English History*, p. 338. After the building of the Roman wall by which those south of it were severed from their kinsmen north of it the former probably soon lost their national characteristics and became Brythonicized, while the Selgovæ remained to form, with the Novantæ, the formidable people of the Attecotti, who afterwards gave Roman Britain so much to do, until their power was broken by Theodosius, who enrolled their able-bodied men in the Roman army, and sent them away to the continent, where no less than four distinct bodies of them served at the time when the Table of Dignities was drawn up. They were a fierce and warlike people, but by the end of the Roman occupation they seem to have been subdued or driven beyond the Nith: . . . here the language of the inhabitants down to the sixteenth century was Goidelic.—*Celtic Britain*, pp. 233–234.

Upon the whole it seems highly probable—and these Gaulish inscriptions add to the weight of probability—that the Galli of Cæsar were in the same line of Celtic descent with the Irish, and that the name is preserved to this day in Gadhel and Gael, and commemorated also in the triad Galedin, Celyddon, and Gwyddyl, as well as in Caledonia, Galatas, Keltai, and Celtæ. It is also nearly certain that these Galli or Gaels were the first to colonize Britain, and probably that they were the first to colonize Gaul, and that in both cases they were closely followed by a people of the same original stock and using a similar language, called Cymry, Cimri, and in earlier times Kimmerioi, Cimmerii.—Thomas Nicholas, *Pedigree of the English People*, p. 43.

There also cannot be a doubt that the statement which eminent writers have handed down is virtually correct, that the Goidels or Gaels were the first Celtic inhabitants, who absorbed the aborigines as the situations or circumstances demanded, and who in turn were next dislodged by the Cymri, and other Celtic fresh hordes who flocked into Britain, driving the said Goidels northwards, and across to Ireland. If other proof were wanting, we have it in the surnames, and the names of places, many of which are common to both Galloway and Ireland, being found on both sides of the Channel. It is also not to be forgotten that, as Roger de Hovedon relates, the Galwegians, at the battle of the Standard in A.D. 1138, used the war-cry "Albanach! Albanach!" thus identifying themselves as Irish-Scots; for to the present time the Irish call the people of Scotland Albanach and Albanaigh. It also extends further, for as Irish-Scots its use implied that they considered they had returned to the land of their fathers, and were entitled to be Scotsmen, which is the Gaelic meaning of the word. Hovedon, having lived at the time, is thus contemporary evidence and it is related that he was sent on a mission to Scotland.—MacKerlie, *Galloway, Ancient and Modern*, p. 62.

[8] "That this is so may be inferred with a reasonable degree of certainty from the inauguration and progress of the English conquest of a later age, which, beginning at nearly the same point on the eastern coast that Cæsar had found most convenient to reach from Gaul, gradually extended westward and northward, driving the Celts before until they reached the western shore.

"The early separation of these pioneers of the Gaelic race through their crossing into Ireland, whether from Scotland or Wales, is quite sufficient to account for the marked difference now existing between the Gaelic, or Irish, language and the Welsh."—Nicholas, *Pedigree of the English People*, London, 1873, p. 46.

Diodorus Siculus, a contemporary of Cæsar, states that Ireland was inhabited by "Britains." Camden thinks they first emigrated from Galloway. Spain was at least five hundred miles distant ; and the nearest promontory of Gaul lay about three hundred miles from the shores of Ireland.

[9] Professor Rhys, in his latest work (*The Welsh People*, New York and London, 1900, written in collaboration with Dr. David Brynmor-Jones), has applied the name "Goidelo-Celtic," or "Celtican," to the language of the Gaelic Celts, and "Galato-Celtic," or "Galatic," to that of the Brythonic Celts. On this subject, he says :

"The ancient distinction of speech between the Celts implies a corresponding difference of race and institutions, a difference existing indeed long before Celts of any description came to these islands. . . .   The two peoples are found to have differed largely in their manner of disposing of their dead, and each had weapons characteristic of its own civilization. The interments with the most important remains of the older stock are found mostly in the neighborhood of the Alps, including the upper portions of the basin of the Danube and the plains of North Italy (see Bertrad and Reinach's volume on *Les Celtes dans les Vallées du Po et du Danube*, Paris, 1894). This older Celtic world began, about the sixth century B.C., to be invaded by the Galatic Celts, whose home may be inferred to have consisted of Central and Northern Germany and of Belgium ; and the remains of these Galatic Celts are to be studied in the great burial places between the Seine, the Marne, and the Rhine—in the country, in short, from which they invaded Britain. It has been surmised that this movement was begun by the Brythons between the time of Pytheas, in the fourth century B.C., and the visits of Julius Cæsar. The latter mentions, (ii., 4.) a certain Diviciacos, king of the Suessiones, a Belgic people which has left its name to Soissons, as the most powerful prince in Gaul, and as ruling also over Britain. This was, moreover, late enough to be within the memory of men living in Cæsar's time. . . .

"When, it may be asked, did the other Celts, the Goidels, whom the Brythons found here, arrive in this country ? It is impossible to give any precise answer to such a question, but it may be supposed that the Goidels came over not later than the great movements which took place in the Celtic world of the Continent in the fifth and sixth centuries before our era (see the *Premiers Habitants de l'Europe*, vol. i., p. 262, and Zimmer's *Mutterrecht der Pikten* in the *Zeitschrift für Rechtsgeschichte*, vol. xv., pp. 233, 234). We mean the movements which resulted in the Celts reaching the Mediterranean and penetrating into Spain, while others of the same family began to press towards the east of Europe, whence some of them eventually crossed to Asia Minor and made themselves a home in the country called after them Galatia. On the whole, we dare not suppose the Goidels to have come to Britain much later than the sixth century B.C. ; . . .   rather should we say that they probably began to arrive in this country earlier. Before the Brythons came the Goidels had presumably occupied most of the island south of the firths of the Clyde and Forth. So when the Brythons arrived and began to press the Goidels in the west, some of the latter may have crossed to Ireland ; possibly they had begun still earlier to settle there. The portion of Ireland which they first occupied was probably the tract known as the kingdom of Meath, approximately represented now by the diocese of that name ; but settlements may have also been made by them at other points on the coast.

"We have next to consider the question whether the first Celtic comers, the Goidels, were also the first inhabitants of this country. This may be briefly answered to the effect that there seems to be no reason to think so, or even to suppose that it may not have been uninterruptedly inhabited for a time before it ceased to form a continuous portion of the continent of Europe. . . .   It is but natural to suppose that the Goidels, when they arrived, subjugated the natives, and made slaves of them and drudges. From the first the fusion of the two races may have begun to take place. . . .   The process of fusion must have been quickened by the advent of a third and hostile element, the Brythonic . . .   and under the pressure exerted by the Brythons the fusion of the two other nations may have been so complete as to produce a new people of mixed Goidelic and native origin. . . .   Accordingly, supposing the Aborigines not to have been Aryans, one might expect the language of the resultant

Goidelic people to show more non-Aryan traits than the language of the Brythons ; as a matter of fact, this proves to be the case."

[10] The southern Damnonii, inhabiting as they did what was later the nucleus of the kingdom of the Cumbrians, must undoubtedly be regarded as their ancestors and as Brythons. So were the Otadini Brythons . . . they disappeared early, their country having been seized in part by the Picts from the other side of the Forth, and in part by Germanic invaders from beyond the sea.—*Celtic Britain*, p. 271.

Over the ethnography of Selgovæ and Novantæ much controversy has taken place. It is probable that on the shores of Solway, as in the rest of the British Isles, there was at one time an aboriginal race, small and dark-haired, which early Greek writers describe as being replaced by the large-limbed, fairer-skinned Celts. The early Irish historical legends contain numerous allusions to this people, generally known as Firbolg. But as it cannot be affirmed that any trace of these has been identified, either in the traditions or sepulchral remains of this particular district, further speculation about them is for the present futile. The fairest inference from the majority of place-names in Novantia — now Galloway — as well as from the oldest recorded personal names, is that it was long inhabited by people of the Goidelic or Gaelic branch of Celts, speaking the same language, no doubt with some dialectic variation, as the natives of Ireland and the rest of what is now Scotland. The Cymric or Welsh speech, which was afterwards diffused among the Britons of Dumfriesshire and Strathclyde, did not prevail to dislodge innumerable place-names in the Goidelic language which still remain within the territory of the Strathclyde Britons. That the people who dwelt longest in Galloway spoke neither the Welsh form of Celtic nor the Pictish dialect of Gaelic, may be inferred from the absence of any certain traces of either of these languages among their names of places. Yet, as will be shown hereafter, they bore the name of Picts long after it had fallen into disuse in other parts of Scotland. They were Picts, yet not the same as Northern Picts dwelling beyond the Mounth, nor as the Southern Picts, dwelling between the Mounth and the Forth ; Gaels, yet not of one brotherhood with other Gaels — a distinction emphasized by the name given to them of *Gallgaidhel* or stranger Gaels. This term became in the Welsh speech *Gallwyddel* (*dd* sounds like *th* in "this"), whence the name Galloway, which still denotes the Stewartry of Kirkcudbright and the shire or county of Wigtown. Reginald of Durham, writing in the twelfth century, has preserved one word of Galloway Pictish. He says that certain clerics of Kirkcudbright were called *scollofthes* in the language of the Picts. This is a rendering of the Latin *scolasticus*, differing not greatly from the Erse and Gaelic *scolog*, more widely from the Welsh *yscolheic*.—Maxwell, *History of Dumfries and Galloway*, pp. 4, 5.

[11] "One may say that the Welsh people of the present day is made up of three elements : the Aboriginal, the Goidelic, and the Brythonic. And it would be unsafe to assume that the later elements predominate ; for the Celtic invaders, both Goidels and Brythons, may have come in comparatively small numbers, not to mention the fact that the aboriginal race, having been here possibly thousands of years before the first Aryan arrived, may have had such an advantage in the matter of acclimatization, that it alone survives in force. This is now supposed to be the case with France, whose people, taken in the bulk, are neither Frankish nor Celtic so much as the representatives of the non-Aryan populations which the first Aryans found there. It thus becomes a matter of interest for us to know all we can about the earliest inhabitants of this country. Now, the question of the origin of that race is, according to one view taken of it, inseparably connected with the Pictish question ; and the most tenable hypothesis may be said to be, that the Picts were non-Aryans, whom the first Celtic migrations found already settled here. The Picts appear to have retained their language and institutions latest on the east coast of Scotland in portions of the region between Clackmannan and Banff. But Irish literature alludes to Picts here and there in Ireland, and that in such a way as to favor the belief that they were survivals of a race holding possession at one time of the whole country. If the Picts were not Aryans, we could hardly suppose them to have been able to acquire possession of extensive tracts of these islands after

the arrival of such a powerful and warlike race as the early Aryans.   The natural conclusion is, that the Picts were here before the Aryans came, that they were, in fact, the aborigines.

" Now, something is known of the manners and customs of the ancient Picts ; for one of them at least was so remarkable as to attract the attention of the ancient authors who mention the peoples of this country.   It was the absence among them of the institution of marriage as known to men of the Aryan race.   This is illustrated by the history of the Picts in later times, especially in the case of their kings, for it is well known that a Pictish king could not be succeeded by a son of his own, but usually by a sister's son.   The succession was through the mother, and it points back to a state of society which, previous to the conversion of the Picts to Christianity, was probably based on matriarchy as distinguished from marriage and marital authority. . . .

" The same conclusion as to the probable non-Aryan origin of the Picts is warranted by facts of another order, namely, those of speech ; but the Pictish question is rendered philologically difficult by the scantiness of the remains of the Pictish language. . . . Failing to recognize the borrowing of Goidelic and Brythonic words by the Picts, some have been led to regard Pictish as a kind of Gaelic, and some as a dialect akin to Welsh.   The point to have been decided, however, was not whether Gaelic or Welsh explains certain words said to have been in use among the Picts, but whether there does not remain a residue to which neither Gaelic nor Welsh, nor, indeed, any Aryan tongue whatsoever, can supply any sort of key.   This is beginning of late to be perceived. . . .   It is not too much to say that the theory of the non-Aryan origin of the Pictish language holds the field at present."—Rhys, *The Welsh People*, pp. 13-16.

[12] Some information in regard to the early inhabitants of the district west of the Nith may be found in the works of Mr. P. H. MacKerlie, chief of which is *Lands and their Owners in Galloway*.   In speaking of the language, he says : " It is also found that the Lowland Scottish was not derived from the Saxon, from which it differs in many respects, but appears to have had its origin from the language of the Northern Picts and Norwegian settlers.   It is true that there are no means of distinctly tracing this ; but the belief of some writers that the Picts were originally Britons, and became mixed with Norse blood, is more than probable. The Pictish language, so far known as Celtic, is considered as having been nearer to the dialects of the Britons than to those of the Gael, which coincides with the above account of their origin — hence the characteristics of both, blended with the Goidel or Gaelic, to be found in the Scots.   There can be little doubt that the Scottish language had its foundation principally from these sources.   Chalmers gives many Scottish words as decidedly British or Cymric. In addition there are many Goidelic or Gaelic words, as can be traced by any one possessed of Gaelic and Scottish dictionaries.   It is historical that in the eleventh century Gaelic was in use at the Court of Malcolm Canmore, and also in the Church at that period.   This continued until Edgar succeeded as king in 1098, when Norman French (not Saxon) displaced the Gaelic at Court."—*Galloway, Ancient and Modern*, p. 79.

Mr. MacKerlie's work is chiefly valuable for its local features, and he cannot be too closely followed in his general conclusions.   His statement as to the origin of the Scottish language must be taken with considerable allowance.   Mr. Hill Burton, however, takes an equally extreme position on the other side of the question.   In speaking of the Lowlanders, he says : " How far Celtic blood may have mingled with their race we cannot tell, but it was the nature of their language obstinately to resist all admixture with the Gaelic.   The broadest and purest Lowland Scotch is spoken on the edge of the Highland line.   It ought, one would think, to be a curious and instructive topic for philology to deal with, that while the established language of our country — of England and Scotland — borrows at all hands — from Greek, from Latin, from French, — it takes nothing whatever, either in its structure or vocabulary, from the Celtic race, who have lived for centuries in the same island with the Saxon-speaking races, English and Scots."—*History of Scotland*, vol. i., p. 200.

[13] In elucidation of this passage no less reputable an authority than Thomas H. Huxley

is named by Mr. Skene as sponsor for his proposition that "the people termed Gauls and those called Germans by the Romans did not differ in any important physical character." This, indeed, coincides with the usual description given by the Romans.

[14] This subject has been discussed in connection with the succession of the Pictish kings. The names of the reigning kings are in the main confined to four or five names, as Brude, Drust, Talorgan, Nechtan, Gartnaidh, and these never appear among the names of the fathers of kings, nor does the name of a father occur twice in the list. Further, in two cases we know that while the kings who reigned were termed respectively Brude and Talorcan, the father of the one was a Briton, and of the other an Angle. The conclusion which Mr. McLennan in his very original work on primitive marriage draws from this is, that it raises a strong presumption that all the fathers were men of other tribes. At any rate, there remains the fact, after every deduction has been made, that the fathers and mothers were in no case of the same family name ; and he quotes this as a reason for believing that exogamy prevailed among the Picts. But this explanation, though it goes some way, will not fully interpret the anomalies in the list of Pictish kings. The only hypothesis that seems to afford a full explanation is one that would suppose that the kings among the Picts were elected from one family, clan, or tribe, or possibly from one in each of the two divisions of the Northern and Southern Picts ; that there lingered among the Picts the old custom among the Celts, who, to use the language of Mr. McLennan, "were anciently lax in their morals, and recognized relationship through mothers only ; that intermarriage was not permitted in this royal family tribe, and the women had to obtain their husbands from the men of other tribes, not excluding those of a different race ; that the children were adopted into the tribe of the mother, and certain names were exclusively bestowed on such children."—*Celtic Scotland*, vol. i., pp. 233–234 ; John F. McLennan, *Origin of the Form of Capture in Marriage Ceremonies.*

[15] These Britons, known by the name of Mæatæ, included under them several lesser people, such as the Otadini, Selgovæ, Novantes, Damnii, etc.—T. Innes, *Critical Essay on the Ancient Inhabitants of the Northern Parts of Britain or Scotland*, book i., ch. ii., art. i.

[16] Herodian (lib. iii.), in his account of Severus's expedition, written about 240, calls the same inhabitants of Caledonia simply Britons, but he describes them as Picts, or painted, in these words : "They mark their bodies with various pictures of all manner of animals, and therefore they clothe not themselves lest they hide the painted outside of their bodies."—Innes, book i., ch. iii., art. i.

[17] "The Scots, in their own tongue, have their name for the painted body [Cruithnigh], for that they are marked by sharp-pointed instruments of iron, with black pigments, with the figures of various animals. . . .

"Some nations, not only in their vestments, but also in their bodies, have certain things peculiar to themselves . . . nor is there wanting to the nation of the Picts the name of the body, but the efficient needle, with minute punctures, rubs in the expressed juices of a native herb, that it may bring these scars to its own fashion : an infamous nobility with painted limbs."—Isadore of Seville, *Origines*, l. ix., ch. ii.; and l. xix., ch. xxiii.

[18] The Picts and Scots have usually been associated with Caledonia. These names are recent in origin, being used only by later Roman writers. Bede (sixth cent.) calls Caledonia "Provincia Pictorum"; and it would seem that in his time the name Picts, or Pehts, had nearly superseded the older term Caledonii—derived from the Cymric Celydon, and this related to the generic Galatæ, Celtæ, Galli.—Nicholas, *Pedigree of the English People*, p. 49.

The proper Scots, as no one denies, were a Gaelic colony from Ireland. The only question is as to the Picts or Caledonians. Were they another Gaelic tribe, the vestige of a Gaelic occupation of the island earlier than the British occupation, or were they simply Britons who had never been brought under the Roman dominion ? The geographical aspect of the case favors the former belief, but the weight of the philological evidence seems to be on the side of the latter.—Freeman, *Norman Conquest*, ch. ii., sec. 1.

The Picts were simply Britons who had been sheltered from Roman conquest by the fastnesses of the Highlands, and who were at last roused in their turn to attack by the weakness of the province and the hope of plunder.   Their invasions penetrated to the heart of the island.   Raids so extensive could hardly have been effected without help from within, and the dim history of the time allows us to see not merely an increase of disunion between the Romanized and un-Romanized population of Britain, but even an alliance between the last and their free kinsfolk, the Picts.—J. R. Green, *Short History of the English People*, ch. i., sec. I.

The Southern Picts are said by Bede to have had seats within these mountains. . . . These districts consist of the Perthshire and Forfarshire Highlands, the former of which is known by the name of Atholl.   The western boundary of the territory of the Southern Picts was Drumalban, which separated them from the Scots of Dalriada, and their southern boundary the Forth.   The main body of the Southern Picts also belonged no doubt to the Gaelic race, though they may have possessed some differences in the idiom of their language ; but the original population of the country, extending from the Forth to the Tay, consisted of part of the tribe of Damnonii, who belonged to the Cornish variety of the British race, and they appear to have been incorporated with the Southern Picts, and to have introduced a British element into their language.   The Frisian settlements, too, on the shores of the Firth of Forth may also have left their stamp on this part of the nation.—*Celtic Scotland*, vol. i., p. 231.

[19] This Drust is clearly connected with Galloway ; and we thus learn that when two kings appear in the *Pictish Chronicle* as reigning together, one of them is probably king of the Picts of Galloway.

"Near to the parish church of Anwoth, in Galloway, is a low undulating range of hills, called the Boreland hills.   One of these goes by the name of Trusty's Hill, and round its top may be traced the remains of a vitrified wall."—Stuart's *Sculptured Stones*, vol. i., p. 31.

[20] He, too, was probably a king of the Picts of Galloway, and traces of his name also can be found in the topography of that district.   The old name of the parish of New Abbey, in Kirkcudbright, was Loch Kendeloch.

[21] Skene says that Talorcan was obviously the son of that Ainfrait, the son of Aedilfrid, an elder brother of Osuald, who on his father's death had taken refuge with the Picts, and his son Talorcan must have succeeded to the throne through a Pictish mother.   At the time, then, when King Oswiu extended his sway over the Britons and Scots, there was a king of the Anglic race by paternal descent actually reigning over the Picts.   Tighernac records his death in 657, and Bede tells us that within three years after he had slain King Penda, Oswiu subjected the greater part of the Picts to the dominion of the Angles.   It is probable, therefore, that he claimed their submission to himself as the cousin and heir on the paternal side of their king, Talorcan, and enforced his claim by force of arms.

[22] Brudei (Bredei, or Brude) was paternally a scion of the royal house of Alclyde, his father, Bili, appearing in the Welsh genealogies annexed to Nennius as the son of Neithon and father of that Eugein who slew Domnall Brec in 642.   His mother was the daughter of Talorcan mac Ainfrait, the last independent king of the Picts before they were subjected by Oswiu.

CHAPTER XV

THE SCOTS AND PICTS

THE Scots of Dalriada acquired possession of the peninsula of **Kintyre** and adjacent territory in Argyle at the beginning of the sixth century. About 503 Loarn More, son of Erc, settled there with his brothers, Angus and Fergus, and some of their followers. They came from Irish Dalriada— a district in Ireland approximately corresponding to or included in the northern portion of the present county of Antrim.

Of the Scots of Ireland we have frequent mention by the Roman historians. As we have seen, their island was for some centuries known by the name of Scotia,[1] and after the Scots had settled in Albania, it continued to be called Scotia Major in distinction from Scotia Minor, which was the first form of the present name, "Scotland," as applied to North Britain.

The following references to the Scots are found in the *History* of Ammianus Marcellinus (written between 380 and 390), and they are the first accounts that we have of these people under that name, although they may have been of the same race with the " Hibernians " mentioned by Eumenius in 296, who, with the Picts, were said by him to have been the hereditary enemies of the Britons in Cæsar's time. It seems more probable, however, that the term " Hibernians " was first applied by the Romans to the inhabitants of Western Scotland.

These were the events which took place in Illyricum and in the East. But the next year, that of Constantius's tenth and Julian's third consulship [A.D. 360], the affairs of Britain became troubled in consequence of the incursions of the savage nations of Picts and Scots, who, breaking the peace to which they had agreed, were plundering the districts on their borders, and keeping in constant alarm the provinces exhausted by former disasters.— (Book xx., ch. i.)

At this time [A.D. 364], the trumpet, as it were, gave signal for war throughout the whole Roman world ; and the barbarian tribes on our frontier were moved to make incursions on those territories which lay nearest to them. The Allemanni laid waste Gaul and Rhætia at the same time. The Sarmatians and Quadi ravaged Pannonia. The Picts, Scots, Saxons, and Attecotti harassed the Britons with incessant invasions.[2]

It will be sufficient here to mention that at that time [A.D. 368] the Picts, who were divided into two nations, the Dicalidones and the Vecturiones, and likewise the Attecotti, a very warlike people, and the Scots were all roving over different parts of the country, and committing great ravages.— (Book xxvi., ch. iv.)

Theodosius, father of the emperor of that name, finally succeeded in driving the invaders north of Severus's wall, and the country between that and the Wall of Hadrian was added to the Roman Empire about 368 as the fifth province in Britain, and called Valentia, after the reigning emperor. The legions becoming reduced by the revolt of Maximus about 390, however, further incursions of the Picts and Scots took place ; and though fresh troops were sent against them and the territory again recovered, the final withdrawal of the garrisons during the next twenty years left the province wellnigh defenceless and exposed to the raids of the savages, who from that time on broke through the walls with impunity and overran and destroyed the Roman settlements at will (Ammianus, book xxvii., ch. viii.).

The early attacks on Britain by the Scots seem to have been made directly from Ireland, and were more in the nature of predatory forays than permanent territorial conquests.   They first appear to have come through Wales.'

The *History* of Nennius, so-called ' (a mixture of fables and half-truths), tells us :

§ 11.   Æneas reigned over the Latins three years ; Ascanius, thirty-three years ; after whom Silvius reigned twelve years, and Posthumus thirty-nine years : the former, from whom the kings of Alba are called Silvan, was brother to Brutus, who governed Britain at the time Eli, the high-priest, judged Israel, and when the ark of the covenant was taken by a foreign people.   But Posthumus, his brother, reigned among the Latins. [Fabulous.]

§ 12.   After an interval of not less than eight hundred years, came the Picts, and occupied the Orkney Islands [?] : whence they laid waste many regions, and seized those on the left-hand side of Britain, where they still remain, keeping possession of a third part of Britain to this day.

§ 13.   Long after this, the Scots arrived in Ireland from Spain. [?]   . . .

§ 14.   . . .   The sons of Liethali obtained the country of the Dimetæ where is a city called Menavia [St. David's] and the province Guiher and Cetguela [Caer Kidwelly, in Carmarthenshire], which they held till they were expelled from every part of Britain, by Cunedda and his sons.

§ 15. . . .   The Britons came to Britain in the third age of the world ; and in the fourth, the Scots took possession of Ireland.   The Britons who, suspecting no hostilities, were unprovided with the means of defence, were unanimously and incessantly attacked, both by the Scots from the west and by the Picts from the north.   A long interval after this, the Romans obtained the empire of the world.

§ 62. . . .   The great king, Mailcun, reigned among the Britons, *i. e.*, in the district of Guenedota, because his great-great-grandfather Cunedda, with his twelve sons, had come before from the left-hand part, *i. e.*, from the country which is called Manau Gustodia, one hundred and forty-six years before Mailcun reigned, and expelled the Scots with much slaughter from those countries, and they never returned again to inhabit them.

The invasions of the Scots and Picts after the departure of the Romans from Britain (418–426) are thus described by Gildas, who wrote in the middle of the sixth century :

§ 13.   At length also, new races of tyrants sprang up, in terrific numbers, and the island, still bearing its Roman name, but casting off her institutes and laws, sent forth among the Gauls that bitter scion of her own planting, Maximus, with a great number of followers, and the ensigns of royalty, which he bore without decency and without lawful right, but in a tyrannical manner, and amid the disturbances of the seditious soldiery. . . .

§ 14.   After this, Britain is left deprived of all her soldiery and armed bands, of her cruel governors, and of the flower of her youth, who went with Maximus, but never again returned ; and utterly ignorant as she was of the art of war, groaned in amazement for many years under the cruelty of two foreign nations—the Scots from the northwest, and the Picts from the north.

§ 15.   The Britons, impatient at the assaults of the Scots and Picts, their hostilities and dreaded oppressions, send ambassadors to Rome with letters, entreating in piteous terms the assistance of an armed band to protect them, and offering loyal and ready submission to the authority of Rome, if they only would expel their invading foes.   A legion is immediately sent, forgetting their past rebellion, and provided sufficiently with arms.   When they had crossed over the sea and landed, they came at once to close conflict with their cruel enemies, and slew great numbers of them.   All of them were driven beyond the borders, and the humiliated natives rescued from the bloody slavery which awaited them.   . . .

§ 16.   The Roman legion had no sooner returned home in joy and triumph, than their former foes, like hungry and ravening wolves, rushing with greedy jaws upon the fold which is left without a shepherd, and wafted both by the strength of oarsmen and the blowing wind, break through the boundaries, and spread slaughter on every side, and like mowers cutting down the ripe corn, they cut up, tread under foot, and overrun the whole country.

§ 17.   And now again they send suppliant ambassadors, with their garments rent and their heads covered with ashes, imploring assistance from the Romans, and like timorous chickens, crowding under the protecting wings of their parents, that their wretched country might not altogether be destroyed, and that the Roman name which now was but an empty sound to fill the ear, might not become a reproach even to distant nations.   Upon this, the Romans, moved with compassion, as far as human nature can be, at the relations of such horrors, send forward, like eagles in their flight, their unexpected bands of cavalry by land and mariners by sea, and planting their terrible swords upon the shoulders of their enemies, they mow them down like leaves which fall at the destined period ; and as a mountain-torrent swelled with numerous streams, and bursting its banks with roaring noise, with foaming crest and yeasty wave rising to the stars, by whose eddying currents our eyes are as it were dazzled, does with one of its billows overwhelm every obstacle in its way, so did our illustrious defenders vigorously drive our enemies' band beyond the sea, if any could so escape them ; for it was beyond those same seas that they transported, year after year, the plunder which they had gained, no one daring to resist them.

§ 18.   The Romans, therefore, left the country, giving notice that they could no longer be harassed by such laborious expeditions, nor suffer the Roman standards, with so large and brave an army, to be worn out by sea and land by fighting against these unwarlike, plundering vagabonds ; but that the islanders, inuring themselves to warlike weapons, and bravely fighting, should valiantly protect their country, their property, wives, and children, and, what is dearer than these, their liberty and lives.   . . .

§ 19.   No sooner were they gone, than the Picts and Scots, like worms which in the heat of mid-day come forth from their holes, hastily land again from their canoes, in which they had been carried beyond the Cichican valley, differing one from another in manners, but inspired with the same avidity for blood, and all more eager to shroud their villainous faces in bushy hair than to cover with decent clothing those parts of their body which required it.   Moreover, having heard of the departure of our friends, and their resolution never to return, they seized with greater boldness than before on all the country towards the extreme north as far as the wall. To oppose them there was placed on the heights a garrison equally slow to fight and ill adapted to run away, a useless and panic-struck company, who slumbered away days and nights on their unprofitable watch. Meanwhile the hooked weapons of their enemies were not idle, and our wretched countrymen were dragged from the wall and dashed against the ground. Such premature death, however, painful as it was, saved them from seeing the miserable sufferings of their brothers and children. But why should I say more? They left their cities, abandoned the protection of the wall, and dispersed themselves in flight more desperately than before. The enemy, on the other hand, pursued them with more unrelenting cruelty than before, and butchered our countrymen like sheep, so that their habitations were like those of savage beasts; for they turned their arms upon each other, and for the sake of a little sustenance, imbrued their hands in the blood of their fellow countrymen. Thus foreign calamities were augmented by domestic feuds; so that the whole country was entirely destitute of provisions, save such as could be procured in the chase.

§ 20. Again, therefore, the wretched remnant, sending to Ætius, a powerful Roman citizen, address him as follows: "To Ætius, now consul for the third time: the groans of the Britons." And again, a little further, thus: "The barbarians drive us to the sea; the sea throws us back on the barbarians: thus two modes of death await us, we are either slain or drowned." The Romans, however, could not assist them, and in the meantime the discomfited people, wandering in the woods, began to feel the effects of a severe famine, which compelled many of them without delay to yield themselves up to their cruel persecutors, to obtain subsistence; others of them, however, lying hid in mountains, caves, and woods, continually sallied out from thence to renew the war. And then it was, for the first time, that they overthrew their enemies, who had for so many years been living in their country; for their trust was not in man, but in God; according to the maxim of Philo, "We must have divine assistance, when that of man fails." The boldness of the enemy was for a while checked, but not the wickedness of our countrymen; the enemy left our people, but the people did not leave their sins.

§ 21. For it has always been a custom with our nation, as it is at present, to be impotent in repelling foes, but bold and invincible in raising civil war, and bearing the burdens of their offences. They are impotent, I say, in following the standard of peace and truth, but bold in wickedness and falsehood. The audacious invaders therefore return to their winter quarters, determined before long again to return and plunder. And then, too, the Picts for the first time seated themselves at the extremity of the island, where they afterwards continued, occasionally plundering and wasting the country.

As already stated, about the year 503 the sons of Erc, a descendant of Cairbre Riadhi (founder of the kingdom of Dalriada in the northern part of the present county Antrim), passed from Ireland to Scotland with a body of their followers, and established a government over some of their countrymen who had previously settled in the southwest of Argyle. One of these sons, Fergus More, succeeded his brother Loarn in the chiefship, and is generally esteemed the founder of the dynasty.[5]

Fergus was followed by his son, Domangart (died 505), by the latter's sons, Comgall (died 538) and Gabhran (died 560), and by Comgall's son, Conal (died 574). Ædan, son of Gabhran, seized the succession after the death of his cousin, Conal, and during his long reign did much to increase the power and influence of the colony and to create a respect for the Scots' arms, by making war against the Picts, the Britons of Strathclyde, and the Saxons.⁶ He lived to see his dominion independent of the Irish Dalriada, to which it had before been tributary, and is usually esteemed the founder of the kingdom of the Scots, having been the first to form the families and tribesmen of his race into a compact and united people.

St. Columba settled in Iona about 565, and the colony of Dalriada in the time of Ædan was, in consequence, the centre and chief source of the Christian faith and propaganda in Britain. From thence missionaries travelled to many parts of the island and to the Continent ; and the conversion of the Gaelic Picts of the north by the preaching and ministrations of Columba no doubt prepared the way for the union of the Scots and Picts, which, more than two centuries later, followed the conquering career of the most renowned of Ædan's successors.

Ædan ascended the throne of Dalriada in 574 ; or perhaps it would be more correct to say that he became chief of the Dalriad tribe. In 603 he led a numerous force — recruited largely from the Britons of Strathclyde — against Æthelfrid, the Anglian king of Bernicia.⁷ Meeting him in Liddesdale, near the frontier line of the kingdoms of Bernicia and Strathclyde (in the present Roxburghshire), a decisive battle was fought at Degsastan, which resulted in the utter defeat and rout of Ædan's army, and the extension of the western boundary of the Anglian kingdom to the river Esk.⁸ The annalist, Tighernac, records Ædan's death in 606, at the age of seventy-four.

He was succeeded by his son, Eocha Buidhe, who resigned the throne to his son, Conadh Cerr. In the year 629, the latter was slain in the battle of Fedhaeoin, fought in Ireland between the Irish Dalriads and the Irish Picts, or Cruithne. Both parties to this contest received auxiliaries from Scotland ; Eocha Buidhe appears also in this battle, on the side of the Picts, and opposed to his son, Conadh, the leader of the Dalriad Scots.⁹ Mr. Skene infers from this, and from other confirmatory circumstances, that Eocha, at this time having withdrawn from Dalriada, must have been ruler of the Galloway Picts.¹⁰ He died later in the same year.

Domnall Brecc, or Breac, brother to Conadh Cerr, succeeded to the throne of Dalriada on the death of the latter. In 634, he fought the Northumbrians at Calathros (now Callender, in Stirlingshire), and was defeated.¹¹ Three years later he was again defeated with great loss in the battle of Mag Rath, in Ireland, whither he had gone as an ally of the Cruithne, or Irish Picts, in their contest with Domnall mac Aed, king of the Irish Dalriads. In 638, Tighernac records another battle and defeat, being that of Glinnemairison, or Glenmureson, which name has been identified with that of the present Mureston Water, south of the river Almond, in the parishes of Mid and West Calder (Edinburghshire).   As the siege of Etin (Edinburgh) is mentioned in the same reference, and as this was the second defeat which the Dalriad king had suffered at the hands of the Angles within the space of four years in contiguous territory, it is to be supposed that these battles may have resulted from the efforts of Domnall Brecc to dispossess the Angles of that portion of their dominions in or near which the battles were fought.   The battle of Degsastan, near the Esk, in 603, and these fights on both sides of the Avon in 634 and 638, would seem to fix these streams as at that time marking the extremities of the frontier line between Northumbria and Strathclyde.[12]

While the Britons were naturally allied with the Scots in these wars against the common enemy of both, it appears that the circumstances of their union were not otherwise sufficiently favorable to insure more than the temporary ascendancy of the Dalriad chief as their leader at this time.   It is possible he may have taken the opportunity of his leadership as an occasion for seeking permanent rule ; but if this were so, he could not have met with much encouragement from the Britons ; for in the year 642, Tighernac tells us, he was slain at Strathcawin (or Strath Carron), by Oan, king of the Britons.[13]

In 654, Penda, king of the Angles of Mercia, with his British or North Welsh allies, was defeated by Oswiu, King of Northumbria, in a battle fought near the Firth of Forth.[14]   Penda and nearly all of his leaders were slain. This victory not only established Oswiu firmly upon the Northumbrian throne, but also enabled him to bring under his rule the dominions of the Strathclyde Britons and of the Scots and Southern Picts.[15]   In 672, after Ecgfrid had succeeded Oswiu on the Northumbrian throne, the Picts attempted to regain their independence, but without success.[16]

After the death of Domnall Brecc in 642, and the successes of Oswiu, which must indirectly at least have influenced Dalriada, that kingdom seems to have remained for a long time broken up into rival clans, the Cinel Loarn, or Race of Loarn, and the Cinel Gabhran being the two most important.[17]   It was not until 678 that these clans again appear united in offensive warfare.   In that year they fought against the Britons, but were defeated.[18] Afterwards, in union with the Picts, they seem to have made attempts at recovering their independence, and so far succeeded that Ecgfrid, then king of the Northumbrians, felt obliged to enter Pictland with an invading army to reduce them.   This was in 685.   On June 20th of that year a great battle was fought at Duin Nechtan, or Nechtansmere (Dunnichen, in Forfarshire ?), in which the English king and his entire force perished.[19]

"From that time," in the words of Bede, "the hopes and strength of the English kingdom began to waver and retrograde ; for the Picts recovered their own lands, which had been held by the English and the Scots that were in battle, and some of the Britons their liberty, which they have now enjoyed for about forty-six years. Among the many English who then either fell by the sword, or were made slaves, or escaped by flight out of the country of the Picts, the most reverend man of God, Trumwine, who had been made bishop over them, withdrew with his people that were in the monastery of Abercurnig."

The king of the Picts at this time was an Anglo-Briton, Brudei, son of Bili, King of Strathclyde,[20] and grandson through his mother of that Pictish king, Talorcan, who was called the son of Ainfrait (Eanfrid), the Angle. Ainfrait was the brother of King Oswiu, and uncle to King Ecgfrid. On the death of Æthelfrid, father to Ainfrait and Oswiu, in 617, his throne had been seized by Ædwine. Bede tells us[21] that during all the time King Ædwine reigned in Northumbria, Ainfrait, with his brothers and many of the nobility, lived in banishment among the Scots, or Picts.

During the forty-six years between the defeat of the Angles at Nechtansmere and the period at which Bede's history is brought to a close, two conflicts took place between the Dalriads and the Strathclyde Britons, in both of which the latter were defeated.[22] These occurred in the neighboring territories of the Picts, during the reign of Nechtan, son of Derili, who ruled from before 710 to 724. It was this Nechtan who, as Bede states,[23] was persuaded to forsake the teachings and customs of the Scottish Church, which had been established in Pictland by St. Columba, and to conform to those of Rome. In 717 he expelled the Columban priests from his kingdom and gave their possessions and places to such of the clergy as had conformed to Rome.

Shortly after this date, Selbhac, son of Farchar Fata, and leader of the Dalriad tribe known as Cinel Loarn, seems to have obtained the ascendancy over the rival tribe of Gabhran, and succeeded in uniting the Dalriad Scots again into one great clan, of which he became the head. Selbhac is the first chief after the death of Domnall Brecc in 642 to acquire the title of King of Dalriada. In 723 he resigned the throne to his son, Dungal, and became a cleric.

In 724, Nechtan, king of the Picts, also having become a cleric, was succeeded by Druxst (or Drust). The latter was expelled from Pictland in 726 by Alpin, son of Eachaidh (or Eachach) by a Pictish princess.[24] At the same time, Dungal, the Cinel Loarn chieftain, who occupied the throne of Dalriada, was expelled from that dominion and succeeded by Eochaidh (or Eochach), the head of the rival Scottish clan Gabhran. Eochaidh was a brother or half-brother to Alpin, then king of the Picts, both being sons of Eachaidh, Domnall Brecc's grandson.[25]

Dungal's father, Selbhac, in 727, made an unsuccessful attempt to restore his son to the Scottish throne, but Eochaidh seems to have continued in power until 733, in which year Tighernac records his death.

In Pictavia also, at this time, the right to the throne was disputed by several powerful rivals. Nechtan, who had resigned his rule to Druxst in order that he himself might experiment with monastic life, now returned to contest the claims of Alpin, the Dalriadic aspirant who had driven out Nechtan's legatee. Angus of Fortrenn, son of Fergus, also appeared as a claimant. Alpin was defeated by Angus in a battle fought in 728 at Monaigh Craebi (Moncrieff), and the territory west of the river Tay was lost to him in consequence. Not long afterwards, Nechtan also met Alpin in battle at Scone, completely overthrew his forces and partially recovered the Pictish kingdom and title for himself.[26]

In 729 Angus and Nechtan met and contested for the supreme leadership. A battle was fought at Loch Inch, near the river Spey, which resulted in the defeat and rout of Nechtan's forces and the assumption of kingly authority and title by Angus. Soon after this battle, Angus encountered and slew Druxst; and in 732, the last of his rivals was removed by the death of Nechtan. Angus ruled Pictland for thirty years.

In 733, Eochaidh, King of Dalriada, having died, Selbhac's son, Dungal, regained the throne of that kingdom. During the next year, Dungal having aroused the anger of Angus by an attack upon the latter's son, Brude, the Pictish king invaded Dalriada, and put its ruler to flight. Two years later (in 736), Angus destroyed the Scots' city of Creic, and taking possession of Donad, the capital, he laid waste all Dalriada, put in chains the two sons of Selbhac,[27] and appears to have driven out the fighting men of the two leading clans. One of these, the Cinel Loarn, was then under the chiefship of Muredach, and the other, the Cinel Gabhran, was ruled by that Alpin mac Eachaidh who had been driven from the Pictish throne by Nechtan in 728. Both of these chieftains attempted to free their country from the grasp of the invader by carrying the war into Pictland. Muredach fought the Picts on the banks of the Avon (at Carriber), where he was opposed by Talorgan, brother to Angus, and was completely defeated and routed by that lieutenant.[28] Alpin himself, about 1740, likewise invaded Ayrshire, the country of the Galloway Picts, and though he succeeded in "laying waste the lands of the Galwegians," he met his death the following year while in their territories.[29] In the same year in which Alpin was killed (741), Angus is said to have completed the conquest of Dalriada. Its subjection to the Picts must have continued at least during the period of his life.

The existing authentic records for the century following the death of Alpin in 741 give but little information as to Dalriada, beyond the names of some of its clan chieftains. It may reasonably be supposed to have remained during that time a subject state of the then powerful Pictish kingdom.

Simeon of Durham tells us that a battle was fought in 744 between the Picts and the Britons,[30] and in 750, the Picts, under the leadership of Talorgan, the brother of Angus, met the Britons in a great battle at Magedauc (in Dumbartonshire), in which Talorgan was slain.[31] Eadberht, Anglic king of Northumbria, in 750, added to his Galloway possessions the plain of Kyle (in Ayrshire) and "adjacent regions." He formed an alliance with Angus a few years later against the Britons of Strathclyde, and in 756 received the submission of that kingdom.[32]

Five years later (761) Angus mac Fergus died, and his brother, Brude, came to the Pictish throne. He died in 763, and was succeeded by Ciniod (Kenneth), son of Wirdech, who reigned twelve years.[33] Alpin, son of Wroid, followed Kenneth, and his death is recorded in 780 as king of the Saxons,[34] which would seem to point to his acquisition of more or less of the Northumbrian territory south of the Forth.

Drust, son of Talorgan, succeeded Alpin, and reigned for five years, his succession being disputed by Talorgan, son of Angus, who also reigned in part of the Pictish kingdom for two years and a half. Conal, son of Tarla, then held the throne for about five years, when he was overthrown and succeeded by Constantine, son of Fergus.[35]

Conal fled to Dalriada, then under the government of Constantine, son of Domnall, whom he seems later to have succeeded, for in 807 Conal's assassination is reported as that of one of the rulers of Dalriada. After that date the name of Constantine, son of Fergus, appears as King of Dalriada for the nine years following, so that during that period this kingdom was doubtless united with Pictland under the one ruler. The two Constantines may have been identical.

For some years after 816 Constantine's brother, Angus mac Fergus (2d), governed Dalriada, and on the death of the former in 820, Angus succeeded him as ruler over both kingdoms. After 825 Dalriada was governed by Aed, son of Boanta ; and then for a term by Angus's own son, Eoganan.

In 834 Angus died, when Drust, son of Constantine, and Talorgan, son of Wthoil, are said to have reigned jointly for the space of two or three years, the former probably ruling the Southern Picts, and the latter those of the North. It is likely that this joint reign arose from a disputed succession, for about the same time another aspirant to the throne appeared in the person of Alpin, who was called king of the Scots, and apparently must have claimed title to the Pictish throne through maternal descent. He fought the Picts near Dundee in 834, and was successful in his first battle ; but later in the same year was defeated and slain.[36]

In 836 Eoganan, son of Angus, is recorded in the *Pictish Chronicle* as the successor to Drust and Talorgan. He reigned for three years, and in 839 was slain by the Danes, who had invaded the kingdom. On his death, Kenneth (son of Alpin, king of the Scots), who had been chief of the Dalriad clans since the death of his father in 834, made war against the Picts. Taking advantage of the presence of the Danish pirates, and perhaps possessing some inherited title to the Pictish throne, he succeeded in establishing himself first as the supreme ruler of Dalriada (839) and then, four or five years later, became also the king of the Picts.[37] Between the death of Eoganan and the accession of Kenneth mac Alpin, there were two intermediate kings of Pictland. These were Wrad, son of Bargoit, who reigned three years, and Bred, son of Ferat, who reigned one year.

When Kenneth mac Alpin became king of the Picts in 844, his territories embraced that part of Scotland now included in the counties of Perth, Fife, Stirling, Dumbarton, and Argyle.[38]   North and west of this district the country continued in a state of practical independence for a long time afterward, being in part occupied by the Northern Picts, and in part by the Norsemen.   South of Kenneth's territories the Northumbrian Angles occupied the province of Bernicia, which included most of the present counties of Scotland south of the Forth and east of the Avon and Esk.   They also maintained lordship over part of the district now known as Galloway and Ayr.   The Cymric Britons of Strathclyde lived and ruled where are now the counties of Renfrew, Lanark, Dumfries, Peebles (Clydesdale, Nithsdale, and Annandale) ; the adjacent portions of Ayr and Galloway and also for a considerable distance to the south of Solway Firth.

The reasons for the success of Kenneth in establishing himself and the small and numerically insignificant [39] colony of Dalriad Scots who inhabited the southwestern portion of Argyle as the ruling element in the land of the Picts have never been very clearly understood.   Superior prowess,[40] maternal ancestry,[41] favorable matrimonial alliances,[42] the labors of missionaries,[43] the wars of the Picts with other intruders,[44] the higher culture of the Scots,[45] and various other causes have been surmised and assigned in explanation. Our present knowledge of the period will not justify more than a tentative acceptance of these several theories as a whole, with the allowance that each one probably accounts in part, or, might account in part, for the result.

Kenneth died in 858, and his brother Donald succeeded him, who reigned four years.   On Donald's death, Constantine, the son of Kenneth, came to the throne.   After a reign of some fifteen years, he was killed in battle with the Norsemen, who fought the Scots [46] at Inverdufatha (Inverdovet) near the Firth of Forth, in 876-7.   Constantine was succeeded by his brother, Aedh, or Hugh, who reigned as king of the Picts for one year, when he was killed by his own people.

While, under the law of Tanistry, which governed the descent of the crown among the Scots, Donald, son of Constantine, was entitled to rule, yet by the Pictish law, Eocha (son of Constantine's sister and of Run, king of the Britons of Strathclyde) was the next heir ; and as the Pictish party at this time seems to have been in the ascendancy, Eocha was made king. Being too young to reign, however, another king was associated with him as governor.[47]   This governor, or regent, was Grig, or Ciric, son of Dungaile. While the earlier *Pictish Chronicle* gives no account of this reign beyond the statement that after a period of eleven years Eocha and Grig were both expelled from the kingdom, the later writers have made a popular hero of Grig ; and his virtues and achievements are magnified to most gigantic proportions.[48]   Grig, having been forced to abdicate, was succeeded in 889 by Donald, son of Constantine, who reigned for eleven years.   Donald was also chosen as King of Strathclyde, which henceforth continued to receive its princes from the reigning Scottish family until it was finally merged into the Scottish kingdom. During Donald's reign his kingdom ceased to be called Pictland or Pictavia and became known as the kingdom of Alban or Albania, and its rulers were no longer called kings of the Picts, but kings of Alban.[49] Donald was slain in battle with the Danes, probably at Dunotter in Kincardineshire.[50]

From 900 to 942 the throne was held by Constantine, son of Aedh, and cousin to Donald. During his reign, Æthelstan, King of Mercia, became ruler of Wessex (in 925), and at once set about to extend his power northward from the Humber. He first arranged for a marriage between his sister and Sihtric, the Danish ruler of Deira, the southern province of Northumbria. On Sihtric's death (926), Æthelstan immediately seized his kingdom and annexed it to his own, driving out Guthferth, the son of Sihtric, who had succeeded his father, and forming an alliance for peace with Ealdred, ruler of Bernicia, the northern province of Northumbria, and with Constantine, King of Alban.[51] A little later, however, Aulaf, or Olaf, the eldest son of Sihtric, having in the meantime married King Constantine's daughter, and thereby secured the co-operation of the Scottish ruler, succeeded also in enlisting in his behalf Olaf of Dublin, a leader of the Danes, or Ostmen, of Ireland, and Owin, king of the Cumbrians.[52] Together these allies prepared for an attempt to recover Olaf's heritage. But Æthelstan, anticipating them, invaded Alban by sea and land and ravaged a great part of that kingdom.[53]

Three years afterwards the confederated forces again assembled and made a descent upon Deira. At first they were successful in their attacks, but finally encountered Æthelstan with all his army on the field of Brunanburgh, and there fought the great battle which takes its name from that place. Æthelstan was victorious and drove the allied forces of the Scots and Danes from the field with great losses, among the slain being the son of the Alban king, with many of his bravest leaders.[54]

In 942 Constantine, having retired to a monastery, was succeeded by Malcolm, son of Donald, who also acquired sovereignty over Cumbria,[55] and reigned until 954, when he was killed in a battle with the Norsemen near Fodresach, now Fetteresso, in Kincardineshire. The next king, Indulf, was also killed by the Norsemen in 962, at Cullen, in Banffshire.[56] During his reign the kingdom seems first to have been extended south of the Forth, Edinburgh for a time being added to its territory. Duff, or Dubh, son of Malcolm, next occupied the throne, but he was expelled about 967 by Cuilean, or Colin, son of Indulf, who succeeded him as king, and was slain himself four years later (971) in a quarrel with the Strathclydensians.

Kenneth II., brother of Duff, and son of the first Malcolm, then gained the crown. He is said to have greatly ravaged the territory of the Strathclyde Welsh; and then, in order to protect himself against their counterattacks, to have fortified the fords of the river Forth, which separated the two kingdoms.[57] Immediately after his attack on Strathclyde, he also invaded Saxonia, as the northern part of Northumbria was then called. The following year, Kenneth MacMalcolm made a second attempt against the same district. At that time, Domnall, or Dunwallaun, son of Eoain, was king of the Strathclyde Britons.[58] Edinburgh is supposed to have been permanently ceded to the Scots during the reign of Kenneth MacMalcolm, as a result of his continued operations against the territory south of the Forth.[59] Kenneth was slain by some of his subjects at Fettercairn in Kincardineshire, 995.[60]

He was succeeded by Constantine, son of Colin MacIndulf, who, after a reign of two years, was killed by Kenneth MacMalcolm (2d) and succeeded by Kenneth MacDuff (Kenneth III.), surnamed Grim, who retained the throne for some eight or nine years.

In 997, the death of Malcolm MacDonald, king of the northern Britons, is recorded.[61]

Kenneth MacDuff was defeated in battle and slain at Strathern in 1005, by his cousin, Malcolm, son of King Kenneth MacMalcolm. He was known as Malcolm II., or Malcolm MacKenneth, and reigned from 1005 until 1034, when he is said to have been assassinated at Glamis, in Angus. He is accused of having procured, about 1033, the death of a son of Boete MacKenneth, and grandson of Kenneth II. (or of Kenneth III.)[62] The claim of Kenneth MacDuff's grandson to the crown, under the Pictish law of succession,* was superior to that of King Malcolm's own grandson, Duncan. In 1006, shortly after the commencement of his reign, King Malcolm II. invaded Northumbria, but was defeated and driven out with the loss of many of his best warriors.[63] Twelve years later (1018), in conjunction with Owen the Bald, king of the Strathclyde Britons, Malcolm made a second attempt against Northumbria, which proved more successful. In a battle fought at Carham, on the Tweed, he defeated the Northumbrians and Danes with great loss.[64] In consequence, they were obliged to cede to the victor all of Northumbria lying north of the Tweed, which territory from that time became a part of Scotland.[65]

The kingdom of Strathclyde, or Cumbria, also, was now completely absorbed into Scotland. Its ruler, Owen, having been slain in the year of the battle of Carham, the union with Scotland took place through the succession of Duncan, grandson of Malcolm, to the lordship of Strathclyde. For that portion of his domain which extended south from the Solway Firth, to the river Ribble, in Lancashire, Duncan continued to do homage to the King of England, as his predecessors before him had done, since the time (945) when the English king, Eadmund, had given it "all up to Malcolm, king of the Scots, on condition that he should be his fellow-worker as well by sea as by land."[66] This Prince Duncan was the son of Bethoc, or Beatrice, Malcolm's daughter, who had married Crinan of the House of Athol, lay Abbot of Dunkeld, said by Fordun to have been also the Steward of the Isles. On

---

* The early Picts had no institution of marriage, succession passing through the maternal line alone. See note 11, p. 196.

the death of Malcolm, his grandfather, in 1034, Duncan, King of Strathclyde, ascended the Scottish throne, thus completely uniting the subkingdom of Strathclyde with Scotia.

Another daughter of Malcolm had been given in marriage to Sigurd, the Norse jarl, ruler of the Orkney Islands. By her Sigurd had a son, Thorfinn, cousin to Duncan, born about 1009, who, on the death of his father, some five years later, succeeded to the lordship of Caithness, Sutherland, and other districts, including Galloway.[67]   In this capacity, he was also over-lord of the tributary provinces of Moray and Ross, which at the time of Earl Sigurd's death were ruled over by the Mormaor Finleikr, or Finley (father of Macbeth).[68]

Duncan, king of the Scots, married the sister[69] of Siward, the Danish Earl of Northumbria; and reigned for about five years. He became involved in a war with his cousin, Thorfinn, over the sovereignty of the northern districts of Scotland, and was slain at Bothgowan in 1039–40 by Macbeth, who had by that time succeeded to the mormaorship of Ross and Moray.[70] Upon the supposed circumstances of Duncan's tragic death, as depicted by Boece and copied by Holinshed, Shakspeare constructed his play of *Macbeth*.

Before going into the details of that tragedy, it will be well to pause and take a glance at the surroundings and condition of the Scottish kingdom at the beginning of Duncan's brief reign.   There are three things connected with the preceding reign of his grandfather, Malcolm II., which mark it as a distinctive and important epoch in Scottish history. The first and most notable of these was the cession to Malcolm by its Danish ruler of that portion of the Anglo-Danish kingdom of Northumbria known as Lothian — being all that part of eastern Scotland lying north of the Tweed and south of the Forth.   This cession resulted from the victory of the Scots at Carham in 1018, to which allusion has already been made.[71] The next important event was the marriage of Malcolm's daughter with Sigurd, the Norse over-lord of the northern regions of Scotland, and the establishment of their son, Thorfinn, as ruler of that domain on the death of his father.   This marriage eventually proved to be an effective step toward bringing the whole country north of "Scot's Water,"[72] under the rule of one king.   The third event was the accession of Duncan to the kingship or lordship of Strathclyde after the death of Owen the Bald, in 1018, and the subsequent peaceful union of that kingdom with Scotland on the ascension of Duncan to the Scottish throne.   It is proper, therefore, to give a brief summary of the circumstances leading up to this conjunction of conditions which ultimately resulted in the amalgamation of the various racial elements of Scotland into one people. The Cumbrian and Norse districts will first be taken up, as being more intimately associated with the history of Malcolm's nearest male heirs ; and the Anglo-Danish province will afterwards be considered in connection with the reign of Duncan's son, Malcolm Canmore — in whom its possession may be said first to have been definitely confirmed.[73]

NOTES TO CHAPTER XV.

[1] Ireland is first mentioned as being also called Scotia by Isadore of Seville, 580–600.

[2] The first recorded appearance of the Saxons off the coast of Gaul is in A.D. 287. Eutropius, ix., 21. (*Monum. Hist. Brit.*, p. lxxii.)

The boats of Irish pirates—or, as they were then called, Scots—ravaged its western shores, while a yet more formidable race of freebooters pillaged from Portsmouth to the Wash. In their homeland between the Elbe and the Ems, as well as in a wide tract across the Ems to the Rhine, a number of German tribes had drawn together into the people of the Saxons, and it was to this people that the pirates of the Channel belonged.—J. R. Green, *Making of England*, p. 15.

[3] " We learn from the account given by the historian of their eventual recovery, that the districts ravaged by the Picts were those extending from the territories of the independent tribes to the Wall of Hadrian between the Tyne and the Solway, and that the districts occupied by the Scots were in a different direction. They lay on the western frontier, and consisted of part of the mountain region of Wales on the coast opposite to Ierne, or the island of Ireland, from whence they came.

" Unaided as she was left, Britain held bravely out as soon as her first panic was over ; and for some thirty years after the withdrawal of the legions the free province maintained an equal struggle against her foes. Of these she probably counted the Saxons as still the least formidable. The freebooters from Ireland were not only scourging her western coast, but planting colonies at points along its line. To the north of the Firth of Clyde these " Scots" settled about this time in the peninsula of Argyle. To the south of it they may have been the Gaels, who mastered and gave their name to Galloway ; and there are some indications that a larger though a less permanent settlement was being made in the present North Wales." —Green, *Making of England*, p. 23.

[4] Written not long before the ninth century, and, so far as its record of earlier events goes, chiefly useful in giving us the form in which they were current in the time of the author.

[5] Though, as we have seen, his eldest brother Loarn ruled before him, yet Fergus holds a more conspicuous position as the father of the dynasty, since it was his descendants, and not those of Loarn, who afterwards ruled in Dalriada. It is in him, too, that the scanty broken traces of genuine history join the full current of the old fabulous conventional history of Scotland. Thus Fergus may be identified with Fergus II.—the fortieth king of Scotland, according to Buchanan and the older historians. This identity has served to show with singular clearness the simple manner in which the earlier fabulous race of Scots kings was invented. A Fergus was still the father of the monarchy, but to carry back the line to a respectable antiquity, a preceding Fergus was invented, who reigned more than 300 years before Christ — much about the time when Babylon was taken by Alexander, as Buchanan notices. To fill up the intervening space between the imaginary and the actual Fergus, thirty-eight other monarchs were devised, whose portraits may now be seen in the picture-gallery of Holyrood.—Burton, *History of Scotland*, vol. i., p. 287.

[6] Wales, or the country of the Cymri, at this time extended from the Severn to the Clyde, and comprised all modern Wales, Cheshire, Lancashire, part of Westmoreland, Cumberland, Dumfriesshire, Ayrshire, Lanarkshire, and Renfrewshire. Novantia, however, remained Pictish—*i. e.*, Goidelic—in speech and race. Thus, whatever had been the affinity in earlier centuries between the Selgovæ of Dumfriesshire and the Novantæ, or Attecotts, of Galloway, it had been replaced in the sixth century by hereditary racial enmity. Galloway was peopled by Attecott Picts ; Annandale, Nithsdale, and Strathclyde by Britons, Cymri, or Welshmen. . . . In the sixth century, then, there were four races contending for what was formerly the Roman province of Valencia—(1) the Britons, Cymri, or Welsh, ancient subjects of Rome, who may be regarded as the legitimate inhabitants ; (2) the Northern and

Southern Picts, representing the older or Goidelic strain of Celts, with an admixture, perhaps, of aboriginal Ivernians, with whom may be associated the Attecott Picts west of the
Nith ; (3) the Scots from Erin, also Goidelic, but distinct from the Picts, not yet firmly settled in Lorn and Argyle under Ædan, the [great-] grandson of Fergus Mor Mac Eirc, but
making descents wherever they could find a footing, and destined to give their name to Alban
in later centuries as "Scotland" ; and (4) the Teutonic colonists.—Herbert Maxwell, *History
of Dumfries and Galloway*, pp. 32, 33.

  [7] *Celtic Scotland*, vol. i., p. 163.

  [8] " Alban, or, as we now call it, Scotland, had by this time resolved itself into four dominions, each under its separate line of kings. The Picts held the country north of the Forth,
their chief town being near the mouth of the Ness ; Argyle and Lorn formed the kingdom of
Dalriada, populated by the Scottish (that is, Irish) descendants of the colony of Fergus Mor.
The British kingdom of Alclut or Strathclyde was the northern portion of the Cymric territory, or old Wales, once extending from Cornwall to Dunbarton, but permanently severed
first by the Saxon king, Ceawlin, who in 577 took possession of the country round Bath and
Gloucester ; and second by Edwin, King of Bernicia, at the great battle of Chester, in 613.
Strathclyde, then, comprised a tract extending from the Derwent in Cumberland to Loch
Lomond, the capital being called in Welsh Alclut, or the cliff on the Clyde, but known to
the Dalriadic and Pictish Gaels as dun Bretann, the fort of the Welshmen.

  " On the east the Saxon realm of Bernicia stretched from the Humber to the Forth under
King Edwin, who has left his name in Edinburgh, the Saxon title of the town which the
Gaels called Dunedin, but whose seat of rule was Bamborough. Just as the territory of the
Attecott Picts was separated from Strathclyde by the rampart now known as the De'il's Dyke,
so Bernicia was separated from Strathclyde by the Catrail, an earthwork crossing the upper
part of Liddesdale. Besides these four realms there was a debatable strip of country between
the Lennox Hills and the Grampians, including the carse of Stirling and part of Linlithgowshire, chiefly inhabited by the Southern Picts or Picts of Manau ; and lastly, the old territory
of the Niduarian or Attecott Picts, who had managed to retain autonomy under native princes,
and a degree of independence, by means of powerful alliances.

  " At the beginning of the seventh century, then, Dumfriesshire was under the rule of the
Welsh kings of Strathclyde, while Wigtonshire and Kirkcudbright, soon to acquire the name
of Galloway, were under their native Pictish princes."—Maxwell, *History of Dumfries and
Galloway*, pp. 35, 36.

  [9] A. D. 629, Cath Fedhaeoin in quo Maelcaith mac Scandail Rex Cruithnin victor erat.
Concad Cer Rex Dalriada cecidit et Dicuill mac Eachach Rex Ceneoil Cruithne cecedit et
nepotes Aidan, id est, Regullan mac Conaing et Failbe mac Eachach (et Osseric mac Albruit
cum strage maxima suorum). Eochadh Buidhi mac Aidan victor erat.—Tighernac.

  [10] *Celtic Scotland*, vol. i., p. 242.

  [11] In the same year in which the battle was fought which placed Osuald on the throne of
Bernicia, Domnall Brecc, king of the Scots of Dalriada, appears to have made an attempt to
wrest the district between the Avon and the Pentland Hills from the Angles, whether as
having some claim to it through his grandfather, Aidan, or what is more probable, as a leader
of the Britons, is uncertain.—*Celtic Scotland*, vol. i., p. 247.

  [12] " In the centre of Scotland, where it is intersected by the two arms of the sea, the
Forth and the Clyde, and where the boundaries of these four kingdoms approach one another,
is a territory extending from the Esk to the Tay, which possessed a very mixed population,
and was the scene of most of the conflicts between these four states. Originally occupied by
the tribe of the Damnonii, the northern boundary of the Roman province intersected it for
two centuries and a half, including part of this tribe and the province, and merging the rest
among the barbarians. On the fall of the Roman power in Britain, it was overrun by the
Picts, and one of the earliest settlements of the Saxons, which probably was composed of
Frisians, took place in the districts about the Roman wall. It was here that, during the

sixth century, the main struggle took place. It falls naturally into three divisions. The first extends from the Esk and the Pentland Hills to the Roman wall and the river Carron. This district we find mainly peopled by Picts, the remains probably of those who once occupied the eastern districts to the southern wall, and preserved a kind of independence, while the rest were subjected by the Angles.

"From the Picts the Angles give the hills which formed its southern boundary the name of the Pehtland, now Pentland Hills. Near its southeastern boundary was the strong natural position called by the Britons Mynyd Agned and also Dineiddyn, and by the Gaels Dunedin. Nine miles farther west, the Firth of Forth is narrowed till the coast approaches to within two miles of that of Fife, and affords a ready means of access ; and on the south shore of the upper basin of the Forth, and near the termination of the Roman wall, was the ancient British town of Caeredin, while in the Forth itself opposite this district was the insular town of Guidi. The western part of this territory was known to the Welsh by the name of Manau Guotodin, and to the Gael as the plain or district of Manann, a name still preserved in Sliabhmanann, now Slamanan, and this seems to have been the headquarters of these Picts.

"Between them and the kingdom of the Picts proper lay a central district, extending from the wall to the river Forth, and on the bank of the latter was the strong position afterwards occupied by Stirling Castle ; and while the Angles of Bernicia exercised an influence and a kind of authority over the first district, this central part seems to have been more closely connected with the British kingdom of Alclyde. The northern part, extending from the Forth to the Tay, belonged to the Pictish kingdom, with whom its population, originally British, appears to have been incorporated, and was the district afterwards known as Fortrein and Magh Fortren.

"Finally, on the north shore of the Solway Firth, and separated from the Britons by the lower part of the river Nith, and by the mountain range which separates the counties of Kirkcudbright and Wigton from those of Dumfries and Ayr, were a body of Picts, termed by Bede Niduari ; and this district, consisting of the two former counties, was known to the Welsh as Galwydel, and to the Irish as Gallgaidel, from which was formed the name Gallweithia, now Galloway."—*Celtic Scotland*, vol. i., pp. 237–239. See Note 6, p. 192.

[13] During these wars there appears to have been hitherto a combination of the Britons of Alclyde and the Scots of Dalriada against the Angles and the Pictish population subject to them. It was, in fact, a conflict of the western tribes against the eastern, and of the Christian party against the pagan and semi-pagan, their common Christianity forming a strong bond of union between the two former nations, and after the death of Rhydderch Hael in 603 the Dalriadic kings seem to have taken the lead in the command of the combined forces.—*Celtic Scotland*, vol. i., p. 249.

[14] Oswy . . . held the same dominions for some time, and for the most part subdued and made tributary the nations of the Picts and Scots, which possess the northern parts of Britain : but of these hereafter.—Bede, book ii., ch. v.

[15] The same King Oswy governed the Mercians, as also the people of the other southern provinces, three years after he had slain King Penda ; and he likewise subdued the greater part of the Picts to the dominion of the English.—Bede, book iii., ch. xxiv.

The Scots of Dalriada naturally fell under his [Oswiu's] dominion along with the Britons, and we have the testimony of Adamnan that they were trodden down by strangers during the same period. But while these nations became tributary to the Angles during this period of thirty years, the mode in which the kings of Northumbria dealt with the Picts shows that their dominion over them was of a different kind, and that they viewed that part of the nation which was subject to them as now forming part of the Northumbrian kingdom. The way for this was prepared by the accession of Talorcan, son of Ainfrait, to the throne of the Picts on the death of Talore, son of Wid, or Ectolairg mac Foith, as Tighernac calls him, in 653. Talorcan was obviously the son of that Ainfrait, the son of Ædilfrid, and elder brother of Osuald, who on his father's death had taken refuge with the Picts, and his son

Talorcan must have succeeded to the throne through a Pictish mother. At the time, then, when Oswiu thus extended his sway over the Britons and Scots there was a king of the Anglic race by paternal descent actually reigning over the Picts. Tighernac records his death in 657, and Bede tells us that within three years after he had slain King Penda, Oswiu subjected the greater part of the Picts to the dominion of the Angles. It is probable, therefore, that he claimed their submission to himself as the cousin and heir on the paternal side of their king Talorcan, and enforced his claim by force of arms. How far his dominion extended it is difficult to say, but it certainly embraced, as we shall see, what Bede calls the province of the Picts on the north side of the Firth of Forth, and, nominally at least, may have included the whole territory of the Southern Picts ; while Gartnaid, the son of Donnell, or Domhnaill, who appears in the *Pictish Chronicle* as his successor, and who from the form of his father's name must have been of pure Gaelic race, ruled over those who remained independent.—*Celtic Scotland*, vol. i., pp. 257-258.

[16] In the first years of his [Ecgfrid's] reign the bestial people of the Picts, despising their subjection to the Saxons, and threatening to throw off the yoke of servitude, collected together innumerable tribes from the north, on hearing which Ecgfrid assembled an army, and at the head of a smaller body of troops advanced against this great and not easily discovered enemy, who were assembled under a formidable ruler called Bernaeth, and attacking them made so great a slaughter that two rivers were almost filled with their bodies. Those who fled were pursued and cut to pieces, and the people were again reduced to servitude, and remained under subjection during the rest of Ecgfrid's reign.—Eddi, *Life of St. Wilfrid*, ch. xix. (written before 731).

[17] In the meantime the little kingdom of Dalriada was in a state of complete disorganization. We find no record of any real king over the whole nation of the Scots, but each separate tribe seems to have remained isolated from the rest under its own chief, while the Britons exercised a kind of sway over them, and, along with the Britons, they were under subjection to the Angles.— *Celtic Scotland*, vol. i., p. 263.

[18] A. D. 678, Interfectio generis Loairn itirinn, id est, Feachair fotai et Britones qui victores erant.—Tighernac.

Bellum Duinlocho et bellum Liaccmaelain et Doirad Eilinn—*Annals of Ulster*.

[19] Bede, book iv., ch. xxvi.

[20] Brudei was paternally a scion of the royal House of Alclyde, his father Bili appearing in the Welsh genealogies annexed to Nennius as the son of Neithon and father of that Eugein who slew Domnall Brecc in 642.

[21] Book iii., ch. i.

[22] 711, Congressio Brittonum et Dalriadha for Loirgeclat ibu Britones devicti. 717, Congressio Dalriada et Brittonum in lapide qui vocatur Minvircc et Britones devicti sunt.—Tighernac.

[23] Book v., ch. xxi. See p. 126.

[24] 726, Nechtain mac Derili constringitur apud Druist regem. Dungal de regno ejectus est et Druist de regno Pictorum ejectus et Elphin pro eo regnat. Eochach mac Eachach regnare incipit.—Tighernac.

[25] 697, Euchu nepos Domhnall jugulatus est.—*Annals of Ulster*.

[26] 728, Cath Monaigh Craebi itir Piccardachaib fein (*i. e.*, between the Picts themselves), Aengus et Alpine issiat tuc in cath (fought that battle), et ro mebaigh ria (the victory was with) n Aengus et ro marbhadh mac Alpin andsin (and the son of Alpin was slain there) et ro gab Aengus nert (and Angus took his person). Cath truadh itir (an unfortunate battle between the) Piccardachaebh ac Caislen Credhi et ro mebaigh ar in (and the victory was against the same), Alpin et ro bearadh a cricha et a daine de uile (and his territories and all his men were taken), et ro gab Nechtan mac Derili Righi na Picardach (lost the kingdom of the Picts).—Tighernac. The *Ulster Annals* add : '' ubi Alpinus effugit.''

[27] 736, Aengus mac Fergusa rex Pictorum vastavit regiones Dailriata et obtinuit Dunad

et compulsit Creich et duos filios Selbaiche catenis alligavit, id est, Dongal et Feradach, et Paulo post Brudeus mac Aengusa mic Fergusa obiit.—Tighernac.

[28] 736, Bellum Cnuicc Coirpri i Calathros uc etar Linndu inter Dalriatai et Fortrenn et Talorgan mac Ferguso filium Ainbhceallach fugientum cum exercitu persequitur in qua congressione multi nobiles ceciderunt.—*Annals of Ulster.*

[29] One of the chronicles appears to have preserved the traditionary account of his death when it tells us that he was slain in Galloway, after he had destroyed it, by a single person who lay in wait for him in a thick wood overhanging the entrance of the ford of a river as he rode among his people. (Cesty fust tue en Goloway, com il le avoit destruyt, de un soul hom qi ly gayta en un espesse hoys en pendaunt al entree dun ge de un ryvere, com chevaucheoit entre ses gentz.—*Scala Chron.*) The scene of his death must have been on the east side of Loch Ryan, where a stream falls into the loch, on the north side of which is the farm of Laight, and on this farm is a large upright pillar stone, to which the name of Laight Alpin, or the Grave of Alpin, is given.

[30] By the Picts, Simeon usually understands the Picts of Galloway, and this battle seems to have followed the attack upon them by Alpin and his Scots.

[31] 750, Cath etir Pictones et Britones, id est a Talorgan mac Fergusa et a brathair et ar Piccardach imaille friss (and his brother and a slaughter of Picts with him).—Tighernac.

750, Bellum inter Pictos et Brittonis, id est, Gueith Mocetauc et rex eorum Talorgan a Brittonibus occiditur.—*An. Cam.*

[32] 756, Eadberht rex, xviii. anno regni sui et Unust rex Pictorum duxerunt exercitum ad urbem Alcluth. Ibique Brittones in deditionem receperunt prima die mensis Augusti. Decima autem die ejusdem mensis interiit exercitus pene omnis quem duxit. (Eadberhtus) de Ouania ad Niwanbirig, id est, ad novam civitatem.—Simeon of Durham.

[33] 775, Rex Pictorum Cynoth ex voragine hujus cœnulentis vitæ eripitur.—Simeon of Durham.

" After the death of Angus MacFergus, king of the Picts, who is stigmatized by a Saxon writer as ' a bloody tyrant,' the history of the succeeding period again becomes obscure. Bruidi, his brother, followed him on the throne, which, after the death of Bruidi, and an interval of fifteen years, during which it was again occupied in succession by two brothers, reverted once more to the family of Angus in the persons of his son and grandson—Constantine MacFergus, also probably a member of the same race, acquiring the supreme power towards the close of the century by driving out Conal MacTeige, who lost his life a few years later in Kintyre. The names of three kings of Dalriada attest the existence of the little kingdom, without throwing any further light upon its history, though from the character of a subsequent reference to Aodh, ' the Fair,' it may be conjectured that he was in some sense the restorer of the line of Kintyre. After the death of Doncorcin, the last of these three princes, which happened shortly after the accession of Constantine, no further mention of the province will be found in any of the Irish annals which have hitherto been published.

" For thirty years and upwards, the supremacy of Constantine was undisputed, and he was succeeded upon his death by his brother Angus, his son Drost, and his nephew Eoganan in the same regular order which is subsequently observable amongst the early kings of Scotland. His reign was unquestionably an era of considerable importance, tradition connecting it with the termination of the Pictish monarchy, and representing Constantine as the last of the Pictish kings — a tradition which must have owed its origin to a vague recollection of some momentous change about this period. He and his brother Angus are numbered most suspiciously amongst the immediate predecessors of Kenneth MacAlpin in the ' Duan of Alban,' the oldest known genealogy of the early kings of Scotland ; whilst the name of Constantine, unknown amongst the paternal ancestry of Kenneth, was borne by his son and many of his race, who would thus appear to have looked for their title to the throne quite as much to their maternal as to their paternal line of ancestry — for the mother of Alpin, Kenneth's father, was traditionally a daughter of the House of Fergus. (Innes, book i., art. viii. *Cale-*

donia, book ii., ch. vi., p. 302, note A, with other authorities cited by both.) The marriage of Kenneth's grandfather with a sister of Constantine and Angus rests solely on tradition, but it appears the most probable solution of his peaceful accession to the throne. The examples of Talorcan, son of Eanfred, perhaps also of his cousin Bruidi, son of Bili, which is a British name, shows that the alien extraction of the father was no bar to the succession of the son. Such a succession would be exactly in accordance with the old custom mentioned by Bede, that 'in cases of difficulty' the female line was preferred to the male, *i. e.*, a near connection in the female line to a distant male heir. From not attending to the expression 'in cases of difficulty,' the sense of Bede's words has been often misinterpreted."—*Scotland under her Early Kings*, vol. i., pp. 18, 19.

[34] 780, Elpin rex Saxonum moritur.—*Annals of Ulster*.

[35] 789, Bellum inter Pictos ubi Conall mac Taidg victus est et evasit et Constantin victor fuit.

790, Vel hic bellum Conall et Constantin secundum alios libros.—*Annals of Ulster*.

[36] Anno ab incarnatione Domini octingentesimo tricesimo quarto congressi sunt Scotti cum Pictis in sollempnitate Paschali. Et plures de nobilioribus Pictorum ceciderunt. Sicque Alpinus Rex Scottorum victor extitit, unde in superbiam elatus ab eis, altero concerto bello, tercio decimo kal. Augusti ejusdem anni a Pictis vincitur atque truncatur.—*Chronicles of the Picts and Scots*, p. 209.

[37] The *Chronicle of Huntingdon* tells us that Kynadius succeeded his father Alpin in his kingdom, and that in the seventh year of his reign, which corresponds with the year 839, while the Danish pirates, having occupied the Pictish shores, had crushed the Picts who were defending themselves, with a great slaughter, Kynadius, passing into their remaining territories, turned his arms against them, and having slain many, compelled them to take flight, and was the first king of the Scots who acquired the monarchy of the whole of Alban, and ruled in it over the Scots.

Cujus filius Kynadius successit in regno patris qui vii° regni sui anno, cum piratæ Danorum, occupatis littoribus, Pictos sua defendentes, straga maxima pertrivissent, in reliquos Pictorum terminos transiens, arma vertit et multis occisis fugere compulit, sicque monarchiam totius Albaniæ, quæ nunc Scotia dicitur, primus Scottorum rex conquisivit et in ea primo super Scottos regnavit.—*Chronicles of the Picts and Scots*, p. 209.

[38] *Chronicles of the Picts and Scots*, edited by Wm. F. Skene, pp. 9, 21, 65, 84, 102, 135, 154, 184, 361, 362 : E. W. Robertson, *Scotland under her Early Kings*, vol. i., pp. 23-39.

[39] In the *Tract of the Men of Alban* we are told that "the armed muster of the Cineal Loarn was seven hundred men ; but it is of the Airgialla that the seventh hundred is."—*Chron. Picts and Scots*, p. 313. This name (Airgialla) was therefore likewise applied to two districts whose people were subject to the Cineal Loarn, and contributed one hundred men to their armed muster, and were probably the "Comites" who fought along with Selbhac in 719.

[40] It is utterly impossible that the Picts could have been exterminated and their language eradicated by the broken remnants of the insignificant tribe of Kintyre, and it is equally improbable that such a conquest, if it ever took place, should have escaped the notice of every contemporary writer. The Pictish name disappeared, but the Pictish people and their language remained as little influenced by the accession of Kenneth MacAlpin, apparently in right of his maternal ancestry, as they were at a later period by the failure of the male line of the same family in the person of Malcolm the Second, and by the similar accession, in right of his maternal ancestors, of a prince of the Pictish House of Athol.—*Scotland under her Early Kings*, vol. ii., p. 373.

At this time the Picts were the chief power in Scotland ; but, like the Scots of Argyle, they were divided among themselves. . . . The Picts were rather living in a rude confederacy than under a fixed monarchy ; and, besides the domestic feuds and broils incident to tribunal communities, the Britons, Picts, Saxons, Scots, and finally the Danes, carried on an intermissive warfare with one another, often showing little result. Throughout the seventh and eighth centuries, the first four tribes frequently met in deadly conflict on a sort of debatable land, extending from the river Forth to the river Almond, in the counties of Stirling and Linlithgow. This region seems to have been occupied by a mixed population of Picts, Angles, and Britons ; and here the chief tribes encountered each other, and fought most of their battles.—John Mackintosh, *History of Civilization in Scotland*, vol. i., p. 111.

[41] See Note 33, p. 217.

[42] War was declared against the Picts ; and he [Kenneth] gathered his forces together, and made his way into the country. So furiously, then, did he rage not only against the men, but even the women and little ones, that he spared neither sex nor holy orders, but destroyed, with fire and sword, every living thing which he did not carry off with him. Afterwards, in the sixth year of his reign, when the Danish pirates had occupied the coast, and, while plundering the seaboard, had, with no small slaughter, crushed the Picts who were defending their lands Kenneth, likewise, himself also turned his arms against the remaining frontiers of the Picts, and, crossing the mountain range on their borders, to wit, the backbone of Albania, which is called Drumalban in Scottish, he slew many of the Picts, and put the rest to flight ; thus acquiring the sole sovereignty over both countries. But the Picts, being somewhat reinforced by the help of the Angles, kept harassing Kenneth for four years. Weakening them subsequently, however, by unforeseen inroads and various massacres, at length, in the twelfth year of his reign, he engaged them seven times in one day, and swept down countless multitudes of the Pictish people. So he established and strengthened his authority thenceforth over the whole country from the river Tyne, beside Northumbria, to the Orkney Isles — as formerly St. Adamnan, the Abbot of Hy (Iona), had announced in his prophecy. Thus, not only were the kings and leaders of that nation destroyed, but we read that their stock and race, also, along with their language or dialect, were lost ; so that whatever of these is found in the writings of the ancients is believed by most to be fictitious or apocryphal.—John of Fordun's *Chronicle*, book iv., ch. iv.

[43] During the entire period of a century and a half which had now elapsed since the Northern Picts were converted to Christianity by the preaching of St. Columba (565), there is hardly to be found the record of a single battle between them and the Scots of Dalriada. Had they viewed each other as hostile races, it is difficult to account for the more powerful nation of the Picts permitting a small colony like the Scots of Dalriada to remain in undisturbed possession of the western district where they had settled ; and prior to the mission of St. Columba we find the king of the Northern Picts endeavoring to expel them ; but after that date there existed a powerful element of peace and bond of union in the Columban Church.—*Celtic Scotland*, vol. i., p. 276.

The Scottish clergy, no doubt, never lost the hope of regaining their position as the Church of Pictavia, and of recovering their possessions there. The occurrence of a Scottish prince having a claim to the Pictish crown by the Pictish law of succession, accompanied by the invasion of the Danes, and the crushing defeat sustained by the Pictish army which opposed them, probably afforded a favorable opportunity.—Skene, Introduction to John of Fordun's *Chronicle*, p. xlix.

[44] The causes of this revolution are obscure ; but the defeat of the Picts by the Danes (in 839) must have facilitated the accession of a king of Scottish descent ; and the natural outcome of the long struggle among the various tribes, which we dimly discern through the mist, had a tendency towards a greater concentration of power somewhere—one or other of the chief tribes would gradually obtain an ascendancy. It is to these circumstances we should look for an explanation of the foundation of the monarchy. Other explanations have been offered, such as royal marriages, the efforts of the Scots clergy, and so on, but none of them are satisfactory. It is safer, and probably nearer the truth, to rely on the accumulating force of the surrounding circumstances.—Mackintosh, *History of Civilization in Scotland*, vol. i., p. 112.

[45] " We cannot thoroughly understand the significance of the ascendancy so acquired by the kings of the Dalriadic race, without realizing to ourselves, what is not to be done at once, the high standard of civilization which separated the Scots of Ireland and Dalriada from the other nations inhabiting the British Isles. . . . We have no conspicuous memorials of such a social condition, such as the great buildings left by the Romans and the Normans. Celtic civilization took another and subtler, perhaps a feebler shape. It came out emphatically in dress and decoration. Among Irish relics there are many golden ornaments of exquisitely beautiful and symmetrical pattern. Of the trinkets too, made of jet, glass, ornamental stone, and enamel, the remnants found in later times belong in so preponderating a proportion to Ireland, as to point to the centre of fashion whence they radiated being there. There seems to have been a good deal of what may be called elegant luxury : the great folks, for instance, lay or ecclesiastic, had their carriages and their yachts. Especially the shrines, the ecclesiastical vestments, and all the decorations devoted to religion were rich and beautiful. They had manuscripts beautifully written and adorned, which were encased in costly and finely worked bindings. It is to this honor done to sacred books, of which the finest specimens belong to Ireland, that we may attribute the medieval passion for rich bindings.

" The high civilization of the Celtic Scots, indeed, was received with a becoming deference all around. . . . Among the nations around, whether of Teutonic or Celtic origin, the civilization of the Scots, then a rising and strengthening civilization, raised them high in rank, and gives us reason to believe that the Picts, instead of mourning the loss of independence, felt their position raised by counting the Dalriadic sovereign as their own too."—Burton, *History of Scotland*, vol. i., pp. 294, 295, 297.

[46] Paulo post ab eo bello in xiiij ejus facto in Dolair inter Danarios et Scottos. Occisi sunt Scotti co Ach Cochlam.—*Pictish Chronicle*. This is the first appearance in the *Pictish Chronicle* of the term " Scotti " or Scots being applied to any portion of the inhabitants of Pictavia, and it seems to have been used with reference to those of the province of Fife in particular, but the *Ulster Annals* record the death of Constantine as king of the Picts.

[47] Eochodius autem filius Run regis Britannorum nepos Cinadei ex filia regnavit annis xi. Licet Ciricium filium alii dicunt hic regnasse ; eo quod alumpnus ordinatorque Eochodio fiebat.—*Pictish Chronicle*.

[48] In their hands he becomes Gregorius Magnus, or Gregory the Great, and in his person restores the true line of Scots royalty, which had been perverted to serve the claims of powerful collaterals. He is the great hero-king of his age. He drives out the Danes, he humbles England, he conquers Ireland ; but his magnanimity will permit him to take no more advantage of his success than to see that these two kingdoms are rightly governed, that they are rid of the northern invaders, and that their sceptres are respectively wielded by the legitimate heir. All this is just about as true as the story of the king of Scotland with five royal companions rowing the barge of King Edgar in the Dee. When the two countries afterwards had their bitter quarrel, such inventions were the way in which the quarrel was fought in the cloister.—Burton, *History of Scotland*, vol. i., p. 331.

[49] See *Chronicles of the Picts and Scots*, pp. 9, 209 ; Robertson's *Scotland under her Early Kings*, vol. i., pp. 54, 55; *Celtic Scotland*, vol. i., p. 335.

" Though we know less of his diplomacy in the states to the northward of the Danelaw, we can see that Ælfred was busy both with Bernicia and the kingdom of the Scots. The establishment of the Danelaw in Mid-Britain, the presence of the pirates in Caithness and the Hebrides, made these states his natural allies ; for, pressed as they were by the vikings alike from the north and from the south, their only hope of independent existence lay in the help of Wessex. Of the first state we know little. The wreck of Northumbria had given freedom to the Britons of Strathclyde, to whom the name of Cumbrians is from this time transferred. The same wreck restored to its old isolation the kingdom of Bernicia. Deira formed part of the Danelaw, but the settlement of the Danes did not reach beyond the Tyne, for Bernicia, ravaged and plundered as it had been, still remained English, and governed, as it would seem, by the stock of its earlier kings. The weakness of this state drew it to Ælfred's side ; and we know that the Bernician ruler, Eadwulf of Bamborough, was Ælfred's friend.

" The same dread of the Danes drew to him the kingdom of the Scots. The Scot kingdom, which at its outset lurked almost unseen among the lakes of Argyle, now embraced the whole of North Britain, from Caithness to the firths, for the very name of the Picts had disappeared at a moment when the power of the Picts seemed to have reached its height. The Pictish kingdom had risen fast to greatness after the victory of Nechtansmere in 685. In the century which followed Ecgfrith's defeat, its kings reduced the Scots of Dalriada from nominal dependence to actual subjection ; the annexation of Angus and Fife carried their eastern border to the sea, while to the south their alliance with the Northumbrians in the warfare which both waged on the Welsh extended their bounds on the side of Cumbria or Strathclyde. But the hour of Pictish greatness was marked by the extinction of the Pictish name. In the midst of the ninth century the direct line of their royal house came to an end, and the under-king of the Scots of Dalriada, Kenneth MacAlpin, ascended the Pictish throne in right of his maternal descent. For fifty years more Kenneth and his successors remained kings of the Picts. At the moment we have reached, however, the title passed suddenly away, the tribe which had given its chief to the throne gave its name to the realm, and ' Pict-land' disappeared from history to make room first for Alban or Albania, and then for ' the land of the Scots.' "—Green, *Conquest of England*, ch. iv., secs. 39, 40.

[50] A.D. 900, Domhnall mac Constantin Ri Alban moritur.—*Annals of Ulster*.

[51] *English Chronicle*, Anno 926. See p.

[52] The men of the northern Danelaw found themselves backed not only by their brethren from Ireland, but by the mass of states around them — by the English of Bernicia, by the Scots under Constantine, by the Welshmen of Cumbria or Strathclyde. It is the steady recurrence of these confederacies which makes the struggle so significant. The old distinctions and antipathies of race must have already, in great part, passed away before peoples so diverse could have been gathered into one host by a common dread of subjection, and the motley character of the army pointed forward to that fusion of both Norman and Briton in the general body of the English race, which was to be the work of the coming years.—Green, *Conquest of England*, ch. v., sec. 42.

[53] Deinde hostes subegit, Scotiam usque Dunfœder et Wertermorum terrestri exercitu vastavit, navali vero usque Cateness depopulatus est.—Simeon of Durham, di Gestis Reg. Fugato deinde Owino rege Cumbrorum et Constantino rege Scotorum, terrestri et navali exercitu Scotiam sibi subjugando perdomuit.—Simeon of Durham, *Ecclesiastical History of Durham*. See also *English Chronicle*, Anno 933.

[54] Florence of Worcester, Anno 937 ; the Egill's Saga ; *Anglo-Saxon Chronicle*, Anno 937 ; Simeon of Durham says, in his *History of the Kings*, that " Æthelstan fought at Wendune, and put King Oulaf with six hundred and fifteen ships, Constantin, king of the Scots, and the king of the Cumbrians with all their forces, to flight." And in his *History of the Church of Durham* he says : " Æthelstan fought at Weondune, which is also called Aetbrunnanmere or Brunnanbyrig, against Oulaf, the son of Guthred, the late king, who had arrived with a fleet of six hundred and fifteen ships, supported by the auxiliaries of the kings recently spoken of, that is to say, of the Scots and Cumbrians."

[55] In 945 Eadmund conquered Cumberland. It might not be easy to say exactly what territory is meant by that name ; but it was clearly the whole or a part of the ancient Strathclyde. This territory Eadmund bestowed on Malcolm, king of Scots, distinctly as a territorial fief. . . . The northern kingdom of the Britons now became the ordinary appanage of the heirs of the Scottish crown . . . and soon after the Scottish kings themselves made their way south of the Forth. In the reign of Eadred, Edinburgh, the border fortress of Northumberland to the north, became a Scottish possession . . . it was the beginning of the process which brought the lands between Forth and Tweed into the possessions of the Scottish kings, and which thereby turned them into English kings of a Northern England,

which was for a while more English than the southern England itself.—Freeman's *Sketch of English History*.

⁵⁶ *Chronicles of the Picts and Scots*, pp. 10, 151, 174, 302.

⁵⁷ *Chronicles of the Picts and Scots*, p. 10.

⁵⁸ He is the same Domnaldus who was king of the Cumbrians when Eadmund ravaged the country in 945, and was the son of that Eugenius, king of the Cumbrians, who fought in the battle of Brunanburgh.

975, Domnall mac Eoain Ri Bretain in ailitri.—Tighernac.

974, Dunwallawn, King of Strathclyde, went on a pilgrimage to Rome (*Brut y Tywysogion*).— *Chronicles of the Picts and Scots*, pp. 77, 124.

⁵⁹ In the north the settlement effected by Eadmund still held good, in spite of a raid into which the Scots seem to have been tempted by a last rising of the Danelaw. The bribe of the Cumbrian realm sufficed to secure the Scot king as a fellow-worker with Eadgar, as effectively as it had secured him as a fellow-worker with Eadmund, while a fresh bond was added by the cession during this reign of the fortress of Edinburgh with the district around it, along with the southern shore of the Forth, to the Scottish king.—Green, *Conquest of England*, ch. vii., sec. 12.

⁶⁰ Interfectus est a suis hominibus in Fotherkern per perfidiam Finvelæ filiæ Cunchar comitis de Engus, cujus Finvelæ unicum filium predictus Knyeth interfecit apud Dunsinoen. —*Chronicles of the Picts and Scots*, pp. 175, 289.

⁶¹ A.D. 997, Maelcolaim mac Domnall Ri Breatan Tuaiscert moritur.—Tighernac.

⁶² See note 1, Chapter XX.

⁶³ Fordun, book iv., ch. xli. Malcolm appears to have died in 1029 and to have then been succeeded by another Malcolm—so at least the Danish authorities tell us ; but the Scots' chronicles give the whole of the period of the united reigns to one Malcolm ; and in using any lights they give us, it is necessary to speak of them as one, since there are no means of separating their two reputations. It was the younger Malcolm, however, according to the same authorities, who was the son of Kenneth,— the other, who had the longer reign, being called " Mac Malbrigid Mac Ruaidhri."— Burton, *History of Scotland*, vol. i., p. 341. This theory was first suggested by Skene in his *Highlanders of Scotland*, published in 1837, but was afterwards considered by him to be untenable (*Celtic Scotland*, vol. i., p. 400). See p. 238.

⁶⁴ *Chronicles of the Picts and Scots*, p. 366.

⁶⁵ A comet appeared for thirty nights to the people of Northumbria, a terrible presage of the calamity by which that province was about to be desolated. For, shortly afterwards (that is, after thirty days), nearly the whole population, from the river Tees to the Tweed and their borders, were cut off in a conflict in which they were engaged with a countless multitude of Scots at Carrun.—Simeon of Durham, *Ecclesiastical History of Durham*, ch. v.

1018, a great battle was fought at Carham between the Scots and the English, between the son of Waltheof, earl of the Northumbrians, and Malcolm, the son of Kenneth, king of the Scots ; with whom in battle was Owen the Bald, king of the Clutinians.— Simeon of Durham, *Hist. Reg.*

Which [Uchtred] being slain [by King Cnut] his brother Eadulf, surnamed Cudel, very slothful and timid, succeeded him in *comitatum*. But fearing lest the Scots should revenge upon him the death of those whom his brother, as is above said, had slain, gave all Lothian for satisfaction and firm concord. In this manner was Lothian added to the kingdom of the Scots.—Simeon *De Obsess. Dun.*

We have the authority of the *Saxon Chronicle* for the fact that Uchtred was slain two years before and that Cnut had made Eric, a Dane, his successor, while Simeon makes his brother, Eadulf Cudel, succeed him.—*Celtic Scotland*, vol. i., p. 393.

⁶⁶ *English Chronicle*, Anno 945. See p. 300.

⁶⁷ *Orkneyinga* Saga, *Collectanea de Rebus Albanicis*, pp. 340, 346. See Appendix P.

[68] The same Finleikr who appears in Tighernac as Findlaec mac Ruaidhri, Mormaer Moreb, and in the *Ulster Annals* as " Ri Alban," indicating that he claimed a position of independence both from the earls of Orkney and the kings of the Scots. — *Celtic Scotland*, p. 389.

[69] Fordun says, " cousin."

[70] He was, however, murdered through the wickedness of a family, the murderers of both his grandfather and great-grandfather, the head of which was Machabeus, son of Finele, by whom he was privily wounded unto death at Bothgofnane ; and, being carried to Elgin, he died there, and was buried, a few days after, in the island of Iona. — Fordun, book iv., ch. xliv.

[71] Innes, Ap. 4. Sim., *Hist. Dun.*, i., 3, c. 5, 6 ; *Ibid.*, *De Obs. Dun.*, p. 81 ; *De Gestis*, 1018. On comparing the passages of Simeon it is impossible to doubt that the cession of Lothian by Eadulf Cudel was the result of the battle of Carham, though there is an evident reluctance in the English chronicler to allude to the defeat and its consequences. The men of the Lothians, according to Wallingford, retained their laws and customs unaltered, and though the authority is questionable, the fact is probably true, for Lothian law became eventually the basis of Scottish law. Conquest indeed in these times did not alter the laws and customs of the conquered,unless where they come into contact and into opposition with those of the conquerors, and the men of the Lothians remained under the Scottish kings in much the same position as the men of Kent under the kings of Mercia and Wessex, probably exchanging the condition of a harassed for that of a favored frontier province. — *Scotland under her Early Kings*, vol. i., p. 96.

[72] The Firth of Forth.

[73] Scotland had now reached her permanent and lasting frontier towards the south, the dependent principality of Strathclyde, having, apparently, during the course of this reign, been finally incorporated with the greater kingdom. When Donald, son of the Eogan who shared in the bloody fight of Brunanburgh, died on a pilgrimage in 975, he seems to have been succeeded by his son Malcolm, whose death is noticed by the Irish Tighernac under the date of 997. The last king of Strathclyde, who has found a place in history, is Eogan " the Bald," who fought by the side of the Scottish king at Carham, probably a son of the British Malcolm whose family name he bears ; and in the person of this Eogan the line of Aodh's son, Donald, appears to have become extinct. The earliest authorities of the twelfth century give the title of " king of the Cumbrians," meaning undoubtedly the northern Cumbria or Strathclyde, to Malcolm's grandson, Duncan, and it is probable that upon the failure of the line of Scoto-British princes, the King of Scotland placed his grandson over the province, which from that time, losing the last semblance of independence, ceased to be ruled by a separate line of princes. — Robertson, *Scotland under her Early Kings*, vol. i., p. 98.

" We have already seen how the political relations of the Scots with their southern neighbors had been affected by the action of the Danes. Pressed between the Norse jarls settled in Caithness and the Danelaw of Central England, the Scot kings were glad to welcome the friendship of Wessex ; but with the conquest by the house of Ælfred of the Danelaw, and the extension of the new English realm to their own southern border, their dread of English ambition became in its turn greater than their dread of the Dane. In the battle of Brunanburgh the Scot king, Constantine, fought side by side with the Northmen against Æthelstan. Eadmund's gift of southern Cumbria showed the price which the English kings set upon Scottish friendship. The district was thenceforth held by the heir of the Scottish crown, and for a time at least the policy of conciliation seems to have been successful, for the Scots proved Eadred's allies in his wars with Northumbria. But even as allies they were still pressing southward on the English realm. Across the Forth lay the English Lowlands, that northern Bernicia which had escaped the Danish settlement that changed the neighboring Deira into a part of the Danelaw. It emerged from the Danish storm as English as before, with a line of native ealdormen who seem to have inherited the blood of its older kings. Harassed as the land had been, and changed as it was from the Northumbria of Baeda or Cuthbert, Bernicia was still a tempting bait to the clansmen of the Scottish realm.

"One important post was already established on Northumbrian soil. Whether by peaceful cession on Eadred's part or no, the border fortress of Edinburgh passed during his reign into Scottish hands. It is uncertain if the grant of Lothian by Eadgar followed the acquisition of Edinburgh; but at the close of his reign the southward pressure of the Scots was strongly felt. 'Raids upon Saxony' are marked by the *Pictish Cronicle* among the deeds of King Kenneth; and amidst the troubles of Æthelred's reign a Scottish host swept the country to the very gates of Durham. But Durham was rescued by the sword of Uhtred, and the heads of the slain marauders were hung by their long, twisted hair round its walls. The raid and the fight were memorable as the opening of a series of descents which were from this time to form much of the history of the north. Cnut was hardly seated on the throne when in 1018 the Scot king, Malcolm, made a fresh inroad on Northumbria, and the flower of its nobles fell fighting round Earl Eadwulf in a battle at Carham, on the Tweed. . . .

"Few gains have told more powerfully on the political character of a kingdom than this. King of western Dalriada, king of the Picts, lord of Cumbria, the Scot king had till now been ruler only of Gaelic and Cymric peoples. 'Saxony,' the land of the English across the Forth, had been simply a hostile frontier — the land of an alien race — whose rule had been felt in the assertion of Northumbrian supremacy and West-Saxon over-lordship. Now for the first time Malcolm saw Englishmen among his subjects. Lothian, with its Northumbrian farmers and seamen, became a part of his dominion. And from the first moment of its submission it was a most important part. The wealth, the civilization, the settled institutions, the order of the English territory won by the Scottish king, placed it at the head of the Scottish realm. The clans of Kintyre or of the Highlands, the Cymry of Strathclyde, fell into the background before the stout farmers of northern Northumbria. The spell drew the Scot king, in course of time, from the very land of the Gael. Edinburgh, an English town in the English territory, became ultimately his accustomed seat. In the midst of an English district the Scot kings gradually ceased to be the Gaelic chieftains of a Gaelic people. The process at once began which was to make them Saxons, Englishmen in tongue, in feeling, in tendency, in all but blood. Nor was this all. The gain of Lothian brought them into closer political relations with the English crown. The loose connection which the king of Scots and Picts had acknowledged in owning Eadward the Elder as father and lord, had no doubt been drawn tighter by the fealty now owed for the fief of Cumbria. But Lothian was English ground, and the grant of Lothian made the Scot king 'man' of the English king for that territory, as Earl Eadwulf was Cnut's 'man' for the land to the south of it. Social influences, political relations, were henceforth to draw the two realms together; but it is in the cession of Lothian that the process really began." — Green, *Conquest of England*, ch. ix., secs. 38–40.

It should be borne in mind that Mr. Green writes from the customary English point of view in stating that the conquest of Lothian by Malcolm made the Scottish kings the liege men of the rulers of England. Scottish historians contend that the record of their king having acknowledged Eadward the Elder as "father and lord" is a fabricated one; and the evidence seems to be with them. See p. 359.

CHAPTER XVI

THE BRITONS

OF the Romanized Britons after the departure of the imperial legions in the early part of the fifth century, we have no definite record until the time of Gildas,[1] who wrote about 556. His description of the conquest of the island by the Saxons is more particularly confined to the events which took place in Kent. However, he gives a brief account of the inhabitants "between the Walls," and of their weak and inadequate defence against the Picts and Scots.[2] The legendary accounts of the battles of King Arthur with the Saxons, as given in the compilation of Nennius, while no doubt to a certain degree mythical, at least show us that the portion of Britain with which Arthur's name and achievements were earliest connected was not within the bounds of the present Wales; but in the vicinity of Carlisle, and to a great extent north of Solway Firth. These accounts of Nennius are as follows:

§ 38. Hengist, after this, said to Vortigern, "I will be to you both a father and an adviser; despise not my counsels, and you shall have no reason to fear being conquered by any man or any nation whatever; for the people of my country are strong, warlike, and robust: if you approve, I will send for my son and his brother, both valiant men, who at my invitation will fight against the Scots, and you can give them the countries in the north, near the wall called Gual [Antoninus's wall]." The incautious sovereign having assented to this, Octa and Ebusa arrived with forty ships. In these they sailed round the country of the Picts, laid waste the Orkneys, and took possession of many regions, even to the Pictish confines. . . .

§ 50. St. Germanus, after Vortigern's death, returned into his own country. At that time the Saxons greatly increased in Britain, both in strength and numbers. And Octa, after the death of his father Hengist, came from the sinistral part of the island to the kingdom of Kent, and from him have proceeded all the kings of that province, to the present period.

Then it was that the magnanimous Arthur, with all the kings and military force of Britain, fought against the Saxons. And though there were many more noble than himself, yet he was twelve times chosen their commander, and was as often conqueror. The first battle in which he was engaged was at the mouth of the river Gleni. The second, third, fourth and fifth, were on another river, by the Britons called Dubglas, in the region Linnius. The sixth on the river Bassas. The seventh in the wood Celidon, which the Britons call Cat Coit Celidon. The eighth was near Guinnion Castle, where Arthur bore the image of the Holy Virgin, mother of God, upon his shoulders, and through the power of our Lord Jesus Christ, and the holy Mary, put the Saxons to flight, and pursued them the whole day with great slaughter. The ninth was at the city of Legion, which is called Cair Lion. The tenth was on the banks of the river Tribruit. The eleventh was on the mountain Breguoin, which we call Agned. The twelfth was a most severe contest, when Arthur penetrated to the hill of Badon. In this engagement, nine hundred and forty fell by his hand alone, no one but the Lord

affording him assistance. In all these engagements the Britons were successful. For no strength can avail against the will of the Almighty.

The more the Saxons were vanquished, the more they sought for new
supplies of Saxons from Germany ; so that kings, commanders, and military
bands were invited over from almost every province. And this practice they
continued till the reign of Ida, who was the son of Eoppa ; he, of the Saxon
race, was the first king of Bernicia, and in Cair Ebrauc [York].

The "river Gleni " has been usually identified with the Glen, a river in
the northern part of Northumberland ; the " Dubglas, in the region of
Linnius," with the two streams called Douglas, or Dubhglass, in Lennox,
which fall into Loch Lomond, and also with the Dunglas, which formed
the southern boundary of Lothian ; the Bassas, with an isolated rock in the
Firth of Forth, near the town of North Berwick, called " The Bass " ; the
" wood Celidon," with the Caledonian forest ; the fastness of " Guinnion,"
with the church of Wedale, in the vale of the Gala Water ; the mount
called " Agned " with Edinburgh. In the chronicle attached to Nennius,
Arthur is said to have been slain at the battle of Camlan in 537, in which he
fought Medraud. This Medraud was the son of Lleu of Lothian. It is true,
Mr. Guest has located the sites of many of these battles in the south ; but
the preponderance of evidence favors the northern localities as given above.[3]

The Arthurian romances, which appeared at a later date than the Nennius fragments, also pertain largely to Arthur's adventures in the north, and
this to a far greater extent than is generally realized, even by those who are
familiar with that romantic literature.[4]

The district in Scotland occupied by the Britons at this time comprised
all that part of the country between the Clyde and the Solway lying west of
the Esk,[5] excepting that southern portion west of the Nith, occupied in
Ptolemy's time by the Novantæ, the supposed progenitors of the Niduarian
or Galloway Picts. Later, the British territory was reduced through the
partial subjugation of Galloway by the Northumbrians, mention of which
is made as early as 750.[6] During the next hundred years, probably about
the time of Kenneth MacAlpin's accession to the Pictish throne, 843-44, there
seem also to have been settlements made by the Irish or Dalriada Scots or
Picts along the western and southern coasts of Galloway.[7]

Ida, the Angle, who built the strong citadel of Bamborough, on the
northeast coast of England in 547, reigned over Bernicia for twelve years.[8]
His successors are described by Nennius as follows :

§ 63. Adda, son of Ida, reigned eight years ; Ethelric, son of Adda,
reigned four years. Theodoric, son of Ida, reigned seven years. Freothwulf
reigned six years ; in whose time the kingdom of Kent, by the mission of
Gregory, received baptism. Hussa reigned seven years. Against him
fought four kings, Urien, and Ryderchen, and Guallauc, and Morcant.
Theodoric fought bravely, together with his sons, against that Urien. But
at that time sometimes the enemy and sometimes our countrymen were defeated, and he shut them up three days and three nights in the island of

Metcaut ; and whilst he was on an expedition he was murdered, at the instance of Morcant, out of envy, because he possessed so much superiority over all the kings in military science.   Eadfered Flesaurs reigned twelve years in Bernicia, and twelve others in Deira, and gave to his wife, Bebba, the town of Dynguoaroy, which from her is called Bebbanburg[9] [Bamborough].

The British king, Ryderchen (or Rhydderch) mentioned in this passage, fought a great battle against some of the other Welsh[10] chiefs in 573, at Arddyred (now Arthuret) on the river Esk, about eight miles north of Carlisle.[11]   Rhydderch was victorious, and became sovereign ruler of all the northern Britons, with his capital established at Alclyde.[12]   Adamnan, who was born in 624, mentions him in his *Life of Columba*,[13] as Rodericus, son of Tothail, who reigned at the rock of Cluaithe (Petra-Cloithe, Alclyde, or Dumbarton.)[14]   Adamnan states also that Rhydderch was a friend and correspondent of St. Columba.   His death is said to have occurred in 603.[15]

In 642, the *Annals* of Tighernac record the killing of Domnall Brecc, king of the Dalriad Scots, at Strathcawin, by Oan (Owen, or Eugein), king of the Britons.[16]

In 654, Oswiu, King of Bernicia, defeated the Britons and Mercians, under the command of Penda the Mercian king, in a battle fought in Lothian, and thus obtained supremacy over the Strathclyde people.   Their subjection to the Angles continued for about thirty years, until the disastrous defeat and death of Ecgfrid at Nechtansmere (Dunnichen) in 685.[17]   In the year 658, the *Ulster Annals* record the death of Guiret, King of Alclyde.   There is then an interval of thirty-six years before another death record appears.   In 694, Tighernac mentions the death of Domnall mac Avin, King of Alclyde, whom Mr. Skene supposes to have been the son of that Owen who is said to have slain Domnall Brecc in 642.   Domnall mac Avin was succeeded by Beli or Bili, son of Alpin, and grandson of the same Owen.   In 752, Tighernac refers to the death of "Tuadar mac Bili Ri Alochlandaih" (Tuadubr, son of Bili, King of Alclyde).[18]   Four years later, Eadberht, King of Northumbria, and Angus, King of the Picts, led an army to Alclyde, and there compelled the submission of the British.[19]

It is probable that Strathclyde remained under the rule of Northumbria for some time after this conquest.   The *Annals of Ulster* record the burning of Alclyde in the calends of January, 780 ; and in 828, King Ecgbryht is said to have overrun and subdued the North Welsh.[20]   From that time there is but little record of the kingdom until nearly half a century later, when it again appears as the British kingdom of Strathclyde.   In the year 872, the *Ulster Annals* inform us that Artgha, king of the Britons of Strathclyde, was put to death, at the instigation of Constantine (son of Kenneth mac Alpin), then king of the Picts.   The descent of this Artgha from Dunnagual, whose death is recorded in 760, is given in the Welsh genealogies attached to Nennius.

Simeon of Durham records the invasion of the Strathclyde district by the

Danes in 875, under the leadership of Halfdan, who brought the whole of Northumbria under subjection, and destroyed great numbers of the Picts (of Galloway) and people of Strathclyde.[21] Artgha left a son, Run, who succeeded to the government, and married a daughter of Kenneth MacAlpin. On the death of Kenneth's son, Aedh, king of the Picts, in 878, Eocha, the son of Run, came to the throne of Alban, which he held for eleven years, having associated with him another Briton, Ciric, or Grig, the Gregory the Great of some of the later Scottish historians. During this reign a large party of the Britons are said to have left Strathclyde for the south and to have finally settled in Wales.[22] Eocha and Grig seem to have ruled jointly for a time over Strathclyde and Pictland, until they were both expelled in 889.[23] They were succeeded by Donald in the sovereignty of Strathclyde. The latter died in 908.[24] He is said by Skene to have been the last of the family claiming Roman descent which had hitherto given its kings to Alclyde. Donald was succeeded by another Donald — a brother of Constantine II., King of Alban, and son to that Aedh mac Kenneth whose sister had married Run, the former King of Strathclyde.

The next ruler of whom we have a record was Owen, or Eugenius, who is mentioned by Simeon of Durham, in connection with Constantine, King of Alban, as having been defeated by the Saxon Æthelstan in 934.[25] He was the son of the same Donald who became king in 908. Owen's son, Donald, succeeded him, and was king in 945, when the kingdom was invaded and conquered by Eadmund, the Northumbrian ruler, who gave it up to Malcolm, king of the Scots.[26] Donald, however, continued as the nominal ruler. He apparently recovered his independence after Malcolm's death, and reigned for upwards of thirty years. The *Pictish Chronicle* states that in 971, Cuilean, King of Alban, and his brother, Eochodius, or Eocha, were slain by the Britons, who were under the leadership of Ardach. Kenneth, Cuilean's successor, attempted to avenge the latter's death by laying waste the British territories ; but succeeded in doing this only after considerable loss to himself,[27] and in the following year was obliged to fortify the fords of the river Forth in order to protect himself from the counter-attacks of the Britons.

Tighernac records a pilgrimage made by Domnall, son of Eoain, king of the Britons, in 975, and the same event is mentioned in the British chronicle the *Brut y Tywysogion*, which calls him Dunwallaun, King of Strathclyde, and states that he went on a pilgrimage to Rome. Tighernac's record is followed by another in 997, mentioning the death in that year of Malcolm, son of Donald, and king of the northern Britons.[28] Malcolm seems to have been succeeded by his brother, as the next reference to the Strathclyde kings mentions Owen (or Eugenius), surnamed The Bald, son of Domnall, as ruler in 1018, in which year he fought with Malcolm, King of Alban, at the battle of Carham, against their common enemy, the Northumbrian Danes. On Owen's death in the same year,[29] he was succeeded by Duncan, the grandson of the Scottish Malcolm. This Duncan on ascending the throne of Scotland in 1034 permanently united the kingdoms under a single ruler, and merged the two into one.

NOTES TO CHAPTER XVI.

[1] The genuineness of Gildas, which has been doubted, may now be looked on as established (see Stubbs and Haddan, *Councils of Britain*, i., 44). Skene (*Celtic Scotland*, i., 116, note) gives a critical account of the various biographies of Gildas. He seems to have been born in 516, probably in the North-Welsh valley of the Clwyd; to have left Britain for Armorica when thirty years old, or in 546 : to have written his *History* there about 556 or 560; to have crossed to Ireland between 566 and 569; and to have died there in 570. For the nature and date of the compilation which bears the name of Nennius, see Guest, *Early English Settlements*, p. 36, and Stevenson's introduction to his edition of him. In its earliest form, it is probably of the seventh century. Little, however, is to be gleaned from the confused rhetoric of Gildas; and it is only here and there that we can use the earlier facts which seem to be embedded among the later legends of Nennius.—J. R. Green, *The Making of England*, p. 23.

St. Gildas, the author of a querulous treatise, *De excidio Britanniæ*, is said, in his *Life*, by an anonymous monk of Ruys, in Brittany, about 1040, to have been born at Alcluyd, or, as he calls it, in the most fertile region of Arecluta (A.D. 520); his father, according to his other biographer, Caradoc of Llancarvan, a writer of the following century, called Nau, (or Kau,) and being the King of Scotland, the most noble of the northern kings; meaning, it is presumed, that he was a king or prince of Strathclyde. The monk of Ruys, however, only calls the father " nobilissimus et catholicus vir," though he says that " Cuillus " (Hueil, Caradoc) " post mortem patris, ei in regno successit."—Ritson, *Annals of Strathclyde*, p. 142.

[2] See p. 201, sec. 19.

On their departure from Britain in 407 the Roman Government probably calculated on re-establishing their authority at no distant day, and left certain officials of native birth to administer the government, which for a time they had been forced to relinquish. For some time previous to this Britain had been divided into five provinces, of which Valentia, the northernmost, so named by Theodosius in honour of the Emperor Valentinian, was left under the rule of Cunedda or Kenneth, the son of Edarn or Aeternus. Tradition says that his mother was a daughter of Coel Hen, British King of Strathclyde, whose name is preserved in that of the district of Kyle in Ayrshire, and in our nursery rhyme of " Old King Cole." (Coel Hen signifies Old Cole.) Cunedda's official title as ruler of Valentia was Dux Britanniarum, or Duke of the Britons. He left eight sons, some of whom became, like their father, very powerful and distinguished. From one of these, Meireon, the county of Merioneth is named; from another, Keredig, the county of Cardigan.—Maxwell, *History of Dumfries and Galloway*, pp. 31, 32.

The five Romanized tribes of North Britain continued to occupy their respective districts, and were known in history as the Cumbrians, or Walenses. They remained divided, as formerly, in clanships, each independent of the other, and an almost constant civil war was the consequence. They were exposed to repeated inroads from the Scots and Picts; and to the invasion of a still more dangerous enemy—the Saxons—who, in the fifth century, extended their conquests along the east coast of North Britain, from the Tweed to the Forth; the defeated Otadini and Gadeni falling back among their countrymen, the Damnonii, and other tribes who occupied the Lothians. Seeing the peril by which they were surrounded—the Picts and Scots on the north, and the Saxons on the south—the inhabitants of Ayrshire, Renfrewshire, Lanarkshire, Dumfriesshire, Liddesdale, Teviotdale, Galloway, and the greater part of Dumbartonshire and Stirlingshire, formed themselves into a distinct kingdom called Alcluyd. The metropolis of the kingdom—Alcluyd—was, no doubt, situated on the banks of the Clyde, but the precise locality is not now known. Dumbarton rock was the main place of strength, and the seat of the *reguli*. The history of the Alcluyd kingdom presents a series of wars domestic and foreign, throughout the greater portion of its existence—sometimes with the Picts, sometimes with the Scots, oftener with the Saxons, and not less frequently one clan against another. Though repeatedly defeated and overrun, they continued to defend themselves with great spirit ; and more than once their restless enemies felt the weight of their sword.—Paterson, *History of the County of Ayr*, vol. i., p. 13.

[3] Mr. Nash, in his introduction to *Merlin, or the Early History of King Arthur*, makes a statement which appears to me to be well founded : " Certain it is," he says, " that there are two Celtic—we may perhaps say two Cymric—localities, in which the legends of Arthur and Merlin have been deeply implanted, and to this day remain living traditions cherished by the peasantry of these two countries, and that neither of them is Wales or Britain west of the Severn. It is in Brittany and in the old Cumbrian kingdom south of the Firth of Forth that the legends of Arthur and Merlin have taken root and flourished." To Cumbria, however, may be added Cornwall, where the Arthurian romance places the scene of many of its adventures ; and it is rather remarkable that we should find in the second century a tribe termed Damnonii possessing Cornwall and a tribe of the same name occupying the ground which forms the scene of his exploits in the north.—Skene, *Celtic Scotland*, vol. i., pp. 154-55.

[4] " If any reality could be extracted from them, Scotland would have full share in it, since much of the narrative comes northward of the present border. Berwick was the Joyeuse garde of Sir Lancelot, and Aneurin describes a bloody battle round Edinburgh Castle. Local tradition and the names of places have given what support such agencies can to the Scottish claims on the Arthurian history. So the curious Roman edifice on the bank of the Carron was called Arthur's Oon or Oven ; and we have Arthur's Seat, Ben Arthur, Arthurlee, and the like. The illustrious ' Round Table ' itself is at Stirling Castle. The sculptured stones in the churchyard of Meigle have come down as a monument to the memory and crimes of his faithless wife. A few miles westward, on Barry Hill, a spur of the Grampians, the remnants of a hill-fort have an interest to the peasant as the prison of her captivity. In the pretty pastoral village of Stowe there was a ' Girth ' or sanctuary for criminals, attributed to the influence of an image of the Virgin brought by King Arthur from Jerusalem, and there enshrined. . . .

" The parish of Meigle, in Forfarshire, is the spot most richly endowed with these monuments ; and Boece tells us that they commemorate Arthur's false queen, here known by the name of Guanora, who fell a captive to the Picts in their contest with the Britons."—Burton, *History of Scotland*, vol. i., pp. 143, 177.

See *Arthurian Localities, their Historical Origin, Chief Country, and Fingalian Relations*, by John Stuart Glennie, M.A., 1869.

[5] Cornwall was subsequently occupied by the [Saxon] strangers, and the place of the Britons to the south of present Scotland became limited to what was afterwards known as the principality of Wales. The narrow part of North England, Lancashire and Yorkshire, being occupied by the Saxons there was thus a gap between the Southern Britons and those of Scotland. These latter became a little independent state, known as Strathclyde, endowed with a sort of capital and national fortress at Dumbarton. This country is now known as the shires of Ayr, Renfrew, Lanark, Stirling, and Dumbarton. It had its own small portion in the events of the time through which it existed in independence, and became at last, as we shall see, absorbed in the aggregation that made the kingdom of Scotland. Such was one of the early elements of this aggregation.—Burton, *History of Scotland*, vol. i., p. 82.

[6] The same natural boundary which separated the eastern from the western tribes afterwards divided the kingdom of the Strathclyde Britons from that of the Angles ; at a subsequent period, the province of Galweia from that of Lodoneia in their most extended sense ; and now separates the counties of Lanark, Ayr, and Dumfries from the Lothians and the

Merse. Galloway in its limited sense was not more clearly separated by this mountain barrier on the north from Strathclyde than were the Pictish races from the British race by the same chain, and the earlier tribes of the Selgovæ and Novantæ from the Damnonii.

[7] See pp. 242–43.

[8] See pp. 269–70.

[9] Ida, the son of Eoppa, possessed countries on the left-hand side of Britain, *i. e.*, of the Humbrian sea, and reigned twelve years, and united Dynguayth Guarth-Berneich [Deira and Bernicia].—*Nennius*, § 61.

[10] The name Welsh, or *Wealas*, meaning "strangers," or "foreigners," was applied by the English to all the Celtic inhabitants of Britain.

[11] See *Proceedings Scottish Antiquarian Society*, vol. vi., p. 91.

[12] "We arrive at something like historic certainty of events in the southwest. The Angles were pagans. The Picts of Novantia had generally relapsed from Christianity into their original cult, of which the traditions had been kept alive by the native bards, and a large part of the Welsh population, in the valleys of Annan, Nith, and Clyde, had followed them. The Welsh leader was Gwendolew, who claimed descent from Coel Hen—Old King Cole. But there was still a Roman party among these northern Britons, led by Rydderch Hael—that is, Roderick the Liberal—who adhered to Christianity.

"The great issue between the pagans and Christians was fought out on the borders of Dumfriesshire in 575, at a place called Ardderyd, now Arthuret, on the Scottish bank of the Esk. Gwendolew's camp was about four miles north of this, and gave the name still borne by a stream called Carwhinelow—that is, caer Gwendolew, Gwendolew's camp. (The parish of Carruthers in Dumfriesshire probably takes its name from caer Rydderch, Roderich's camp.) The Christian champion Rydderch was completely victorious, and became ruler of the Strathclyde Britons, under the title of King of Alclut."—Maxwell, *History of Dumfries and Galloway*, p. 34.

[13] Reeves's edition, 1874, pp. 15, 136, 224.

[14] It is called likewise, by Adamnan, Petra-Cloithe, and by other ancient writers, Arecluta, Alcwith, Aldclyhit, and Alcluth ; all implying a rock, or elevation, upon the Clyde, now Dumbarton, a corruption of Dunbritton. The foundation of the monarchy cannot be ascertained. If, however, we may credit the *Life of St. Ninian* [written in the twelfth century], it existed so early as the fourth.; whence it can be traced, with sufficient certainty, down to nearly the close, at least, of the tenth.—Ritson, *Annals of the Caledonians, Picts, etc.*, vol. ii., p. 132.

[15] The population of this kingdom seems to have belonged to the two varieties of the British race—the southern half, including Dumfriesshire, being Cymric or Welsh, and the northern half having been occupied by the Damnonii, who belonged to the Cornish variety. The capital of the kingdom was the strongly fortified position on the rock on the right bank of the Clyde, termed by the Britons Alcluith, and by the Gadhelic people Dunbreatan, or the fort of the Britons, now Dumbarton ; but the ancient town called Caer Luel or Carlisle in the southern part must always have been an important position. The kingdom of the Britons had at this time no territorial designation, but its monarchs were termed kings of Alcluith, and belonged to that party among the Britons who bore the peculiar name of Romans, and claimed descent from the ancient Roman rulers in Britain. The law of succession seems to have been one of purely male descent.—*Celtic Scotland*, vol. i., p. 236.

[16] 642, Domnall-brecc in cath Strathacauin in fine anni in Decembre interfectus est xv regni sui ab Ohan rege Britonum.—Tighernac.

[17] Bede, book iv., ch. xxvi. See p. 204.

[18] 722, Beli filius Elfin moritur.—*An. Cam.* Bili mac Elphine rex Alochluaithe moritur. —Tighernac.

The author of *Galloway, Ancient and Modern*, in his reading of the early annalists has fallen into the rather careless error of confusing the fathers of the Strathclyde kings with the kings themselves. For instance, at page 91, he says: "The next king of Strathcluyd was Owen, who was ruling in 694 when his son Daniel (Domnall) died. He was succeeded by Elphin (Alpin), who appears as king in 772 when his son Bili died." The record of Tighernac for 694 is as follows: "Domnall mac Avin [Owen] rex Alochluaithne moritur," and for 722 (not 772) the same record reads, "Bili mac Elphin rex Alochluaithe moritur."

[19] 756, Eadberht, rex, xviii. anno regni sui et Unust rex Pictorum duxerunt exercitum ad urbem Alcluth. Ibique Brittones in deditionem receperunt prima die mensis Augusti.— Simeon of Durham.

The successes of Eadbert reduced the fortunes of the Britons in this quarter to the lowest ebb. Kyle was rendered tributary to Northumbria, which already included Cunningham; and shortly after the middle of the century, Alclyde or Dumbarton, the strongest bulwark of the Northern Britons, surrendered to the united forces of the Northumbrians and the Picts. The capture of Alclyde must have thrown the whole of the ancient British territories in the Lennox, which were subsequently included in the diocese of Glasgow, into the power of Angus, together with a great portion of the "debateable land" between the Forth and Clyde, similarly included in the "Cumbrian" diocese; and the little principality of Strathclyde was now completely hemmed in and surrounded by hostile territories, though the gradual decline of the Northumbrian power towards the close of the eighth century enabled the petty state to struggle on for another hundred years in a precarious species of nominal independence.— Robertson, *Scotland under her Early Kings*, vol. i., p. 18.

[20] *English Chronicle*, An. 828. See p. 298.

[21] See also the *English Chronicle*, Anno 875, p. 298, where in describing the same event, the people of Strathclyde are called the Strathclyde Welsh. The name *Straecled Wealas* is rendered by Æthelwerd into the Latin *Cumbri*, which Mr. Skene notes as the first appearance of the term *Cumbri*, or *Cumbrians*, as applied to the people of Strathclyde.

"Much confusion has arisen from the ambiguous use of the appellations of Cumbria and Cumberland. The former name was undoubtedly applied at one time to a wide extent of country stretching at least from Dumbartonshire to North Wales, from which district it was early separated when the greater part of modern Lancashire was added to the Northumbrian dominions. A little later the grants of Ecgfrith to St. Cuthbert must have severed the modern counties of Cumberland and Westmoreland from the northern Cumbria or Strathclyde, which was still further curtailed by the settlements of the Angles in the diocese of Candida Casa, a district of which the greater part, if not the whole, had by this time probably fallen into the hands of the ancestors of the Picts of Galloway.

"Southern Cumbria or Cumberland does not appear to have been included amongst the conquered districts recovered by the Britons after the defeat and death of Ecgfrid at the battle of Nechtan's Mere. When Eardulf the bishop carried off the relics of St. Cuthbert and St. Oswald from the profane violence of a pagan as fierce as Penda, the most trusted companion of his hurried flight was Edred, the Saxon Abbot of Carlisle; and there is little reason to doubt that at this time the descendants of the men who won the land in the days of Ecgfrid still peopled the broad acres granted to the monastery of St. Cuthbert. Forty years later it is told how Edred, the son of Rixinc, the foremost chieftain amongst the nobility of Deira, rode 'westward over the hills,' and slew the Lord Eardulf, a prince of the Bernician race of Ida, carried off his wife 'in spite of the Frith and the people's wishes,' and held forcible possession of territories reaching from Chester le Street to the Derwent, till he lost both lands and life in the battle of Corbridge Moor. All these names are genuine Saxon, and though the original British population may still have lingered amidst the lakes and mountains of their picturesque region, it may be safely doubted whether they paid either tribute or submission to the Scoto-British prince who yet retained some vestiges of authority over the fertile valley of the Clyde; and whilst Scottish Cumbria, or Strathclyde, continued under the rule of a branch of the MacAlpin family from the opening of the tenth century till the reign of Malcolm the Second, English Cumbria, or Cumberland, when it was not under the authority of the Northumbrian earls, in whose province it was included, may be said to have remained in a state of anarchy till the conquest."—*Scotland under her Early Kings*, vol. i., p. 70.

" The last retreat of the Romanized Britons was called originally Strathclyde, but in later times more frequently Cumbria. . . .

" In the scanty notices of the chroniclers the district is generally called a kingdom, but this may have been more from the habit of using that term towards the neighboring nations, than because there was any fixed form of monarchical government in Strathclyde."—Burton, *History of Scotland*, vol. i., pp. 182, 278, 279.

²² Again, in 875, the same restless enemy, sallying forth from Northumberland, laid waste Galloway, and a great part of Strathcluyd. Thus harassed by the insatiable Northmen, many of the inhabitants of Alcluyd resolved upon emigrating to Wales. Under Constantin, their chief, they accordingly took their departure ; but were encountered by the Saxons at Lochmaben, where Constantin was slain. They, however, repulsed their assailants, and forced their way to Wales, where Anarawa, the king, being at the time hard pressed by the Saxons, assigned them a district which they were to acquire and maintain by the sword. In the fulfilment of this condition, they aided the Welsh in the battle of Cymrid, where the Saxons were defeated and driven from the district. The descendants of these Strathcluyd Britons are said to be distinguished from the other inhabitants of Wales at the present day. The Strathcluyd kingdom was, of course, greatly weakened by the departure of so many of the best warriors ; and it continued to be oppressed both by the Scots and Anglo-Saxon princes. The judicious selection of a branch of the Scottish line as their sovereign had the effect of securing peace between the two nations for some time. Hostilities, however, at length broke out with great fury, in consequence of Culen — who ascended the Scottish throne in 965 — having dishonored his own relative, a granddaughter of the late King of Strathcluyd. Incensed at the insult, the inhabitants flew to arms, under King Ardach, and marching into Lothian, there encountered the Scots. The battle was a fierce one, and victory declared for the Alcluydensians. Both Culen and his brother Eocha were slain. This occurred in 971. The Scottish throne was ascended by Kenneth III. [II.] ; and the war between the Scots and Cumbrians continuing, the latter, under Dunwallin—the successor of Ardach—were at length overpowered on the bloody field of Vacornar ; where, the *Welsh Chronicle* states, the victors lost many a warrior. Dunwallin retired to Rome in 975. The Strathcluyd kingdom, now fairly broken up, was annexed to the Scottish crown, and the inhabitants became mixed with the Scots and Picts. This was a successful era for the Scots. Though the country had been overrun by Æthelstan, the Saxons gained no permanent advantage. On the contrary, Eadmund, in 945, ceded Cumberland, in England, to Malcolm I., on condition of unity and aid. Lothian, which had previously been held by England, was also delivered up to Malcolm III., in 1018, after the battle of Carham with Uchtred of Northumberland.—Paterson, *History of the County of Ayr*, p. 15.

" An occasional brief entry in the early chronicles reveals the anxiety of the rulers of the Picts and Scots to avail themselves of the gradual decline of the Northumbrian power for the purpose of extending their own influence over the neighboring province of Strathclyde. Some such motives may have instigated Kenneth to seek for his daughter the alliance of a British prince ; and a few years later, the death of Artgha, King of Strathclyde, which is attributed by the Irish annalists to the intrigues of Constantine the First, may have been connected with the same policy of aggrandizement, and have furthered the claims of Eocha, the son of Constantine's sister. The advancement of Eocha to the Scottish throne was shortly followed by important consequences to his native province, and after the flight and death of the Welsh prince Rydderch ap Mervyn had deprived the northern Britons of one of their firmest supporters, a considerable body of the men of Strathclyde, relinquishing the ancient country of their forefathers, set out, under a leader of the name Constantine, to seek another home amongst a kindred people in the south. Constantine fell at Lochmaben in attempting to force a passage through Galloway ; but his followers, undismayed at their loss, persevered in their enterprise, arriving in time to assist the Northern Welsh at the great battle of the Con-way, where they won the lands, as the reward of their valor, which are supposed to be occupied by their descendants at the present day. (*An. Ult.*, 876, 877 ; *An. Camb.* and *Brut y Tywys.* 880 ; *Caledonia*, vol. i., book iii., ch. v., p. 355.)

"Chalmers gives the name of Constantine to their first leader, whilst, according to Caradoc, Hobart was their chief when they reached Wales. To some old tradition of this migration, and to the encroachments of the Galwegians, the *Inquisitio Davidis* probably alludes : 'Diverse seditiones circumquaque insurgentes non solum ecclesiam et ejus possessiones destruxerunt verum etiam totam regionem vastantes ejus habitatores exilio tradiderunt.' (*Reg. Glasg*) In fact it would appear as if a Scottish party had dated its rise from the days of Kenneth MacAlpin, and secured a triumph by the expulsion of its antagonists, on the accession of Eocha to the Scottish throne, and by the election of Donald in the reign of the second Constantine.

"With the retreating emigrants, the last semblance of independence departed from the Britons of the north ; and upon the death of their king Donald, who was probably a descendant of Kenneth's daughter, Constantine the Second experienced little difficulty in procuring the election of his own brother Donald to fill the vacant throne. Henceforth a branch of the MacAlpin family supplied a race of princes to Strathclyde ; and although for another hundred years the Britons of that district remained in a state of nominal independence, they ceased to exist as a separate people, appearing, on a few subsequent occasions, merely as auxiliaries in the armies of the Scottish kings."—*Scotland under her Early Kings*, vol. i., p. 54.

The Angles only retained their power over the Picts of Galloway and the Cumbrians south of the Solway, together with the city of Carlisle, which Ecgfrith, shortly before his death, had given to St. Cuthbert, with some of the land around it. The Cumbrians north of the Solway became independent, and had kings of their own again, of whom one is recorded as dying in 649, and another in 722. But the Picts of Galloway continuing under the yoke of the Northumbrians, the king of the latter managed in 750 to annex to Galloway the district adjoining it on the north and west, which was then a part of the land of the Cumbrians, though it may have long before belonged to the Picts. In the same year, a war took place between the former and the Picts of Lothian, who suffered a defeat and lost their leader, Talorgan, brother to the King of Alban, in a battle at a place called Mocetauc in the *Welsh Chronicle*, and supposed to be in the parish of Strathblane in the county of Stirling ; but in 756 we read of the Picts and the Northumbrians joining, and pressing the Cumbrians sorely. Afterwards little is known of them (except that Alclyde was more than once destroyed by the Norsemen) until we come down to the end of the ninth century, when we meet with a Welsh tradition that the Cumbrians who refused to submit to the English were received by the King of Gwynedd into the part of North Wales lying between the Dee and the Clwyd, from which they are made to have driven out some English settlers who had established themselves there. How much truth there may be in this story is not evident, but it is open to the suspicion of being based to some extent on the false etymology which identifies the name of the Clwyd with that of the Clyde. It is needless to say that the latter, being Clota in Roman times, and Clut in old Welsh, could only yield Clud in later Welsh. Harassed and weakened on all sides, the Cumbrians ceased to have kings of their own race in the early part of the tenth century, when a Scottish line of princes established itself at Alclyde ; and in 946 the kingdom was conquered by the English king Eadmund, who bestowed the whole of it from the neighborhood of the Derwent to the Clyde [?] on the Scottish king Maelcoluim or Malcolm, on condition that he should assist him by land and sea, the help anticipated being intended against the Danes. . . . William the Red made the southern part of Cumbria, including the city of Carlisle, an earldom for one of his barons ; and thus it came to pass that the name of Cumberland has ever since had its home on the English side of the border, while the northern portion, of which the basin of the Clyde formed such an important part, is spoken of in the *Saxon Chronicle* as that of the Strathclyde Welshmen.   It may here be added that this last was still more closely joined to the Scottish crown when David became king in 1124; but its people, who formed a distinct battalion of Cumbrians and Teviotdale men in the Scotch army at the battle of the Standard in 1130, preserved their Cymric characteristics long afterwards.   How late the Welsh language lingered between the Mersey and the Clyde we have, however, no means of discovering, but, to judge from a passage in the *Welsh Triads*, it may be surmised to have been spoken as late as the fourteenth century in the district of Carnoban (see Gee's *Myvyrian Archæology*, p. 401, triad 7), wherever between Leeds and Dumbarton that may turn out to have been.—Rhys, *Celtic Britain*, pp. 146–148.

[23] On the west were the districts occupied by the Britons of Strathclyde.   In the previous century and a half these had been narrowed to the vale of the Clyde, with Alclyde or Dumbarton as its stronghold, and the rest of the British districts had, along with Galloway, been under the dominion of the Angles of Northumbria; but their rule had been relaxed during the period of disorganization into which the Northumbrian kingdom had fallen, and had by degrees become little more than nominal, when the invasion of Bernicia by the Briton Giric, who for a time occupied the Pictish throne, led to the severance of these districts from Northumbria, and the whole of the British territory from the Clyde to the river Derwent in Cumberland became once more united under the rule of an independent king of the Britons. —*Celtic Scotland*, p. 346.

[24] Et in suo octavo anno cecidit excelsissimus rex Hibernensium et archiepiscopus apud Laignechos id est Cormac mac Cuilennan.   Et mortui sunt in tempore hujus Donevaldus rex Britannorum et Duvenaldus filius Ede rex eligitur.—*Chronicles of the Picts and Scots*, p. 9.

[25] Fugato deinde Owino rege Cumbrorum et Constantino rege Scotorum, terrestri et navali exercitu Scotiam sibi subjugando perdomuit.—Simeon of Durham, *Hist. de Dun. Ec.*

[26] *English Chronicle*, Anno 945.

944, Strathclyde was ravaged by Saxons.—*Brut y Tywysogion.*

946, Stratclut vastata est a Saxonibus.—*An. Camb.*

The life of St. Cadrœ gives us almost a contemporary notice of the Cumbrian kingdom. St. Cadrœ was a native of Alban, and flourished in the reign of Constantin who fought at Brunanburgh, and leaves him to go on a foreign mission.   He comes to the " terra Cumbrorum," and Dovenaldus, the king who ruled over this people, receives him gladly and conducts him " usque Loidam civitatem quæ est confinium Normannorum atque Cumbrorum." —*Chronicles of the Picts and Scots*, p. 116.

[27] Statim predavit Britanniam ex parte Pedestres Cinadi occisi sunt maxima cede in Moin na Cornar.—*Pictish Chronicle.*

[28] He was, no doubt, the son of that Donald who was king of the Cumbrians when his kingdom was overrun by King Eadmund and bestowed upon Malcolm, King of Alban, and this shows that though the sovereignty was now vested in the Scottish kings, the line of provincial kings still remained in possession of their territory.—*Celtic Scotland*, vol. i., p. 382.

[29] With him ended the kingdom of Strathclyde.   Galloway as a portion of it then fell into the full possession of the Norsemen.—Mac Kerlie, *Galloway, Ancient and Modern*, p. 92.

CHAPTER XVII

THE NORSE AND GALLOWAY

THE Norwegian and Danish invasions of Britain began in 793. In that year the Northmen made an attack upon the island of Lindisfarne, which lies a little south of Tweedmouth. Their raid is thus described by Simeon of Durham :

In the same year [793] of a truth, the pagans from the northern region came with a naval armament to Britain like stinging hornets, and overran the country in all directions like fierce wolves, plundering, tearing, and killing not only sheep and oxen, but priests and levites, and choirs of monks and nuns. They came, as we before said, to the church of Lindisfarne, and laid all waste with dreadful havoc, trod with unhallowed feet the holy places, dug up the altars, and carried off all the treasures of the holy church. Some of the brethren they killed, some they carried off in chains, many they cast out naked and loaded with insults, some they drowned in the sea.

The following year a party of Norsemen plundered the monastery at the mouth of the Wear, where their chief was killed, and their fleet afterwards wrecked by a storm. In the same year one of their fleets laid waste the Western Isles and sacked the church of Iona. Four years later they again visited the Western Isles. In 802 they burned the Iona church ; and in 806 killed the inhabitants of that island, numbering sixty-eight persons. These pirates were distinguished by the Irish as belonging to two races, the Finngaill—white, or fair-haired strangers (Norse),—and the Dubhgaill,—black, or dark-haired strangers (Danes).

While it has been generally customary to speak of them as Northmen, yet so far as Scotland was concerned they approached it from the east — and in the case of the Danes from the southeast — the distance between Norway and Scotland being but about two hundred miles. First sailing to the Orkneys these invaders proceeded down along the west coast into the Irish Sea, and made their landings in Ireland, Cumberland, or Galloway [1] as the hope of plunder might lead them. The Irish gave to the Danes the name of Ostmen, or Men of the East, which properly described them ; but that point of the compass from which they approached Normandy and the southern coast of England is the one that furnished them with the name by which they are best known.

The following account of the operations of the Norse in Northern, Western, and Southwestern Scotland is based chiefly on the *Orkneyinga* and other Norse sagas, and on the *Annals* of Tighernac and of Ulster (see Appendixes O and P).

In 825, Blathmhaic, son of Flann, was killed by the Norse in Iona. In

839, the Danes came to Dublin with sixty-five ships. After plundering Leinster, they entered Scotland through Dalriada, and, in a battle with the Picts and Scots, killed their ruler, Eoganan, son of Angus. This helped to open the way for the accession of Kenneth MacAlpin to the Pictish throne.[2]

During Kenneth's reign his country was often harassed by these troublesome visitors. Later they seem to have made permanent settlements in some parts of the island, particularly in the north and in Galloway.[3] In the latter district they intermarried with and made allies of the natives, who in time became known along the western coast of Scotland and in Ireland as the "Gallgaidhel", or "stranger (*i. e.*, renegade) Gaels."

The fragments of *Irish Annals* published by the Irish Archæological Society state that in 852 a battle was given by Aedh, King of Ailech, to the fleet of the Gallgaidhel, who were said to be Scots and foster-children of the Northmen, and who themselves were formerly called Northmen. They were defeated and slain by Aedh, many heads being carried off as trophies by himself and Niall. The Irish justified their action on this occasion by saying that "these men were wont to act like Lochlans" (Northmen). Again it is stated of them in 858 that the Gallgaidhel were "a people who had renounced their baptism, and were usually called Northmen, for they had the customs of the Northmen, and had been fostered by them, and though the original Northmen were bad to the churches, these were by far worse in whatever part of Erin they used to be." In 866 a large fleet of Danish pirates, under command of Halfdan and his two brothers, arrived off the coast of England. After spending the winter in East Anglia, they invaded Northumbria, took the city of York, killed the two rival claimants to the Northumbrian throne, and made Ecgberht king. He ruled for six years, and was succeeded by Ricsig.

In the same year in which occurred Halfdan's invasion of Northumbria, Olaf the White, the Norwegian king of Dublin, who had married a daughter of Kenneth MacAlpin and may have had designs upon the latter's throne, invaded Pictavia with the "Galls" of Erin and Alban, laid waste all the country, and occupied it from the kalends of January to the feast of St. Patrick (March 17th). On returning to Ireland, he took with him both booty and hostages.[4] From the same source we learn that in the year 870 Alclyde was invested by the Northmen under Olaf and Imhair, and destroyed after a four months' siege ; much booty and a great host of prisoners being taken. Olaf and Imhair seem also to have attacked both the Picts of Galloway and the Angles of Bernicia, for they are said to have returned to Dublin with two hundred ships and great booty of men, Angles, Britons, and Picts, as captives.[5] In 875 a Danish army under command of Halfdan again ravaged Northumbria, Galloway, and Strathclyde,[6] and made great slaughter of the Picts. In the same year, Thorstein the Red (son of Olaf the White by Audur, daughter of the Norseman, Kettil Flatnose), who had succeeded to his father's rule, attacked the northern provinces of Scotland and added Caithness, Sutherland, Ross, and Moray to his dominion. He was slain soon after by the Albanians. In the year 877 the Danes and Norwegians of Ireland contested for the mastery. The Finngaill being successful, the Danes were driven out of Ireland and entered Scotland. Here they attacked the Scots in Fifeshire and slew a great multitude of them, together with Constantine, their king. Between 885 and 890 the Norwegians colonized the Orkney Islands, and Harold Harfagr, King of Norway, having taken possession, gave them to Rognwald, Earl of Maeri. He relinquished to his brother, Sigurd, on whom the King bestowed the title of jarl. Sigurd soon after invaded Scotland and reconquered Caithness, Sutherland, Ross, and Moray. He was killed in an encounter with Maelbrigda, a Scottish jarl. His son, Guthorn, succeeded to his estates, but died within a year. Earl Rognwald then sent his own sons, Hallad and Einar, to rule the Orkneys, the latter of whom retained the government until his death in 936.

About 900 a Danish army, having invaded and plundered Ireland, came into Scotland and overran the southern districts, fighting several battles with the Scots, in one of which King Donald was slain. At this time the Norse influence was very strong in Caithness and Sutherland, those provinces being ruled from the Orkneys. The Norse also established themselves in the Western Isles and in Man, and soon came to exert almost as great an influence there as in Galloway. In 912 Rognwald, with a powerful band of Danish pirates, invaded Scotland and ravaged Dunblane. He returned again in 918, having visited and plundered in Ireland in the meantime. The Scots' king, Constantine, having united his forces with those of Ealdred, ruler of Bernicia, met the Danes in battle, and succeeded in routing them. Notwithstanding this, they soon afterwards secured possession of Bernicia, where Rognwald established himself as king.' In 937 the Scots, having united with the Danes of Northumbria and those of Dublin in making war against Æthelstan, shared in the disastrous defeat inflicted by that king upon his enemies at the battle of Brunanburgh. Soon after this event, Eric of the Bloody Axe, son of Harold Harfagr, King of Norway, came to the coasts of England on a plundering expedition. Having been offered a settlement in Northumberland by King Æthelstan, he seated himself there with his followers. After his death, his sons removed to the Orkneys, and in the reign of the Scottish king Indulf (954–962), they are said to have been the leaders of a Norwegian fleet which made a descent upon Buchan.

Upon the death of Einar, Earl of the Orkneys, in 936, he was succeeded by his son Thorfinn, called the "Skull-cleaver," who married Grelauga, daughter of Dungadr, or Duncan, the Jarl of Caithness, and thus confirmed the possession of that province to his descendants. His eldest son, Havard, having succeeded to the rule, was slain by his own wife; and Liotr, the second son, assumed the title and domain. Another brother, Skuli, disputed the succession. Having secured the support of the Scottish king, he gave battle to Liotr and was slain. Liotr fought a second battle with the Scots, and killed Earl Maelbrigdi, their leader ; but received a wound himself from which he afterwards died. Hlodver, the surviving son of Thorfinn Einarson, then became Earl of Orkney. Upon his death, which occurred about the year 980, Sigurd, his son, became ruler. Soon after, Finley (or Finleikre or Finlaec—son of Ruaidhri and brother to Maelbrigdi) who was the Scottish Mormaor (Earl) of Moray, made war against Sigurd, but was defeated by him in battle. The latter, in consequence, gained possession of Moray, Ross, Sutherland, and "Dali," all of which provinces he ruled over in 989. However, Finley mac Ruaidhri eventually recovered Moray at a later date, and continued as lord of that distiict until 1020, when he was slain by the sons of his brother, Maelbrigdi.

These sons of Maelbrigdi appear to have been Malcolm, who died in 1029, and Gilcomgain, who was killed in 1032. The latter had married Gruoch, daughter of Boete (son of King Kenneth MacMalcolm), or according to some authorities, a granddaughter of Boete other than Gruoch. After the death of Gilcomgain, his widow married Macbeth (son of Finley), who doubtless had a hand in the killing of her first husband, in retaliation for the killing of Finley by Gilcomgain and his brother. Malcolm mac Maelbrigdi (so-called by Tighernac), who died in 1029, is spoken of by the annalist as " *ri* (or king) of Scotland." Undoubtedly at that time the mormaors of Moray were the virtual rulers of the greater part of Scotland lying north of the Grampians. Under the Pictish system of descent, the rights of a deceased king's brother were superior to those of the king's son ; and as that system prevailed in the Highlands long after the tenth century, Finley would be the natural successor to the mormaorship on the death of his brother Maelbrigdi. This succession, however, as indicated above, was disputed by the sons of Maelbrigdi, and they succeeded in settling the title for the time being by killing their uncle. After their own deaths, Macbeth was the next in succession, notwithstanding Gilcomgain had left an infant son (Lulach).

A few years after the beginning of the eleventh century (about 1008), the *Orkneyinga Saga* tells us, Sigurd, Earl of Orkney, married the daughter of Melkolf (Malcolm) " King of the Scots," and by her had a son, Thorfinn. When the latter was five years old, " the King of Scots gave to Thorfinn, his relation, Katanes [Caithness] and Sutherland, and an earl's title along with it, and gave him men to rule the domain along with him." [8] While this King Malcolm, has been identified with Malcolm MacKenneth (grandfather of Duncan), King of Southern Scotland, by Messrs. Skene and Robertson and by all later writers founding on them, there is no certainty that they were the same. In some points the probabilities favor the view taken originally by Mr. Skene in his *Highlanders*, that the Norse sagas, in their first mention of King Malcolm, really referred to Malcolm mac Maelbrigdi, Mormaor of

Moray, the " ri " who died in 1029, and who was the ruler of the Scotland best known to Earls Sigurd and Thorfinn. (See " The Norse Sagas," Appendix P.)

Five years after Thorfinn's birth (in 1014), in the final struggle which took place between the Irish and the Danes, Earl Sigurd went to Dublin as an ally of the latter, and there met his death at the battle of Clontarf. Before embarking for Ireland, Sigurd had sent his young son Thorfinn to the child's grandfather, Malcolm, King of Scotland. Upon the death of the father, Malcolm bestowed Caithness and Sutherland upon Thorfinn, with the title of earl, and gave him men to enable him to establish his authority. Sigurd had three sons by a former wife—Sumarlidi, Brusi, and Einar — among whom the Orkneys were divided. They all died prior to 1029, however; and before King Malcolm's death in 1034, Thorfinn, their half-brother, had succeeded to the earldom of Orkney. On Duncan's accession to the Scottish throne, after the death of Malcolm, that king assumed full authority over Caithness, and bestowed it upon his nephew, Moddan, with the title of earl. Duncan's cousin, Thorfinn, naturally looked upon this as an abrogation of his own rights, and the two became enemies. When Moddan came north with his men from Sutherland to take possession of the earldom, he was met by a superior force under Thorfinn and compelled to retire. Duncan at once organized a considerable army, and having sent Moddan to the north overland, sailed from Berwick to Caithness with a fleet of eleven vessels. Thorfinn met the fleet in the Pentland Firth, and though having with him only five warships, defeated Duncan, and obliged the latter to retire to the Moray Firth, where he landed, and started for the south to get together a new army. Earl Moddan, who in the meantime had entered Caithness, was followed by Thorfinn's lieutenant, and surprised and slain at Thurso. Duncan collected as large an army as possible, and having entered Moray again, met Thorfinn in battle at Torfness, or Broghead, where, the second time, he was completely defeated and his forces routed. Earl Thorfinn then overran and subdued the country as far south as Fife.[9] Soon after, Duncan was slain by Macbeth, the Mormaor of Moray, whose father, Finley, had regained the mormaorship after the death of Earl Sigurd. Macbeth at the time may have been operating as an ally of Thorfinn[10]; or, according to some accounts, endeavoring to make good his own wife's claim to the Scottish throne—a claim which seems to have been at least of equal merit with that of Duncan himself.

After Duncan's death, Macbeth succeeded to his crown ; yet the power of Earl Thorfinn at this time was nearly as great as his own. Thorfinn possessed the nine earldoms of Sutherland, Ross, Moray, " Dali," Buchan, Mar, Mearns, Angus, and Galloway[11] ; and without his assistance the Mormaor of Moray could hardly have succeeded in establishing himself upon the Scottish throne.[12] It is probable, therefore, that Macbeth's reign marked the highest point ever reached by Norse influence in Scotland.[13] As that influence has a considerable interest in connection with the genesis and development of the people of Galloway, and one that has not until recently been clearly recognized, it may at this period properly be considered.

The part of Scotland now known by the name of Galloway embraces the counties of Kirkcudbright and Wigton, which lie west of the lower Nith valley, and south of the range of high hills or mountains that form the southern boundary of Ayr and Dumfries. In earlier times, after its separation from Strathclyde, Galloway probably included Annandale (in Dumfries), the two southern districts of Ayr (Kyle and Carrick), and perhaps also a great part of the northern district of Ayr (Cuninghame) in addition.[14] It thus embraced within its bounds nearly the whole of the southern and western coast of Scotland from the mouth of the Nith to the Clyde.

St. Columba preached to the Northern Picts as early as 565 ; but long before that St. Ninian had converted the Galloway Picts,[15] and built the mission station or monastery of Candida Casa, or White House, at Whithorn on the southeastern coast of Wigtonshire.

Ninian is said to have been born on the shore of Solway Firth,[16] to have been the son of a king, or nobleman, and to have studied at Rome, where he was consecrated as Bishop by Pope Siricius. He started in 395 on a mission to convert the Attecotts.[17]

Now, he chose his seat in a place which is now called Withern [Whithorn] ; which place, situate upon the shore of the ocean, while the sea stretches far from the east, west, and south, is inclosed by the sea itself ; from the north part a way is opened for those only who are willing to enter. There, then, by the command of the man of God, the masons, whom he had brought with him, erect a church ; before which they say there was none in Britain built of stone.[18]

This stone church presented such a contrast to the customary oaken structures of the surrounding country that it soon became known far and wide as the White House. Ninian is said to have died and been buried here about 432.[19]

In Bede's time, Whithorn had been erected into an Episcopal See under the fostering care of the Northumbrian kings. The Lord of Northumbria likewise maintained dominion over more or less of the territory and people of Galloway.[20] Such districts as did not acknowledge his sovereignty remained either under their own independent chiefs or were included in the kingdom of Strathclyde, which, after the victory of the Picts at Nechtansmere in 685, had been freed from the Northumbrian yoke.

In 740, Alpin (son of Eachaidh by a Pictish mother), who had been successively king of the Northern Picts (726) and king of the Scots (729) and who later was driven out of those kingdoms by Angus, entered Galloway (Ayrshire) with an army and laid its territory waste. In 741 he was defeated by Innrechtach near the Dee,[21] and obliged to retreat to Loch Ryan, where he was assassinated.[22]

In 750 Eadberht, King of Northumbria, added the plain of Kyle and other regions to his Galloway domain.²³ These "other regions" are generally supposed to have been portions of the adjacent districts of Cuninghame and Carrick in Ayrshire.²⁴ They were retained as dependencies until the close of the same century, when by reason of civil feuds at home, and the increasing invasions of the Norsemen from without, the Angles were compelled to withdraw from Galloway and their suzerainty was given up.²⁵

It has usually been assumed by modern historians, founding on George Chalmers, that there were repeated invasions of Galloway from Ireland during the seventh and eighth centuries, and that this district was then, like Argyle in the sixth, largely colonized by emigrants from Ulster. This assumption has been in a great measure refuted by Mr. Skene,²⁶ and as the question is one of considerable interest at this point, it will not be amiss to give his argument some consideration. It is as follows :

Chalmers, in his *Caledonia* (i., p. 358), states dogmatically that Galloway was colonized in the eighth century by Cruithne [Picts] from Ireland, and that they were followed by fresh " swarms from the Irish hive during the ninth and tenth centuries," and this statement has been accepted and repeated by all subsequent writers as if there were no doubt about it. There is not a vestige of authority for it. Galloway belonged during these centuries to the Northumbrian kingdom, and was a part of Bernicia. Bede, in narrating the foundation of Candida Casa by St. Ninian (Book iii., ch. iv.), says, " qui locus ad provinciam Berniciorum pertinens " ; and there is abundant evidence that Galloway was under the rule of the Northumbrian kings after his time. It is antecedently quite improbable that it could have been colonized from Ireland during this time without a hint of such an event being recorded either in the Irish or English annals.

The only authorities referred to by Chalmers consist of an entire misapplication of two passages from the *Ulster Annals*. He says : " In 682 A.D., Cathasao, the son of Maoledun, the Mormaor of the Ulster Cruithne, sailed with his followers from Ireland, and landing on the Firth of Clyde, among the Britons, he was encountered and slain by them near Mauchlin, in Ayr, at a place to which the Irish gave the name of Rathmore, or great fort. In this stronghold Cathasao and his Cruithne had probably attacked the Britons, who certainly repulsed them with decisive success."—*Ulster An.,* sub. an. 682. " In 702 the Ulster Cruithne made another attempt to obtain settlement among the Britons on the Firth of Clyde, but they were again repulsed in the battle of Culin."—*Ib.,* sub. an. 702. The original texts of these passages is as follows : " 682. Beltum Rathamoire Maigiline contra Britones ubi ceciderunt Catusach mac Maelduin Ri Cruithne et Ultan filius Dicolla. 702. Bellum Campi Cuilinn in Airdo nepotum Necdaig inter Ultu et Britones ubi filius Radgaind cecidit. Ecclesiarum Dei Ulait victores erant." Now, both of these battles were fought in Ulster. Rathmore, or great fort of Maigiline, which Chalmers supposed to be Mauchlin, in Ayr, was the chief seat of the Cruithne in Dalaraidhe, or Dalaradia, and is now called Moylinny. See Reeves's *Antiquities of Down and Connor,* p 70. Airdo nepotum Necdaig, or Arduibh Eachach, was the Barony of Iveagh, also in Dalaradia, in Ulster (*Ib.,* p. 348) ; and these events were attacks by the Britons upon the Cruithnigh of Ulster, where the battles were fought, and not attacks by the latter upon the British inhabitants of Ayrshire

Now, while it must be admitted that the case against the relevancy of Mr. Chalmers's citations and his theory of an eighth century settlement of the Irish in Galloway is a very clear one, the fact remains that for several hundred years past, and certainly as far back as the time of Kenneth MacAlpin (840), there have been apparent in the people themselves direct indications of large Gaelic infusions into the Galloway population, whether their origin be Ireland or the north of Scotland. The most noticeable of these evidences are to be found in the language and in the names of the people. Up to and beyond the twelfth century the Picts of Galloway spoke the Gaelic tongue. At the battle of the Standard in 1138 the war-cry of the Galwegians, who were in the van of the Scottish army, was "Albanaich! Albanaich!" the Gaelic name for Scotland ; and the English on the other side are said to have answered back in derision, "Yry! Yry!" (Irish! Irish!) To this day, "Eerish" is a term of contempt in Galloway.[27]

Mr. Skene, while fully acknowledging the presence of a considerable Gaelic element in the Galloway population, and while eyer alive to the important bearing which language sustains to racial questions, handles it in this case more with reference to its efficacy as a refutation of the claim for a Cymro-Celtic origin of the Galloway Picts.[28] But in doing so he incidentally presents some testimony which, if it proves no one thing in particular, at least shows what was the vulgar opinion of the origin of the Galwegians, about the time of John Knox. This testimony is as follows :

If any part of the Pictish people might be expected to retain their peculiar language and characteristics, it would be the Picts of Galloway ; and if that language had been a Cymric dialect, it must have merged in the speech of the British population around them. In one of the legends which seems peculiarly connected with them, Gaedel Ficht or the Gaelic Pict appears as the "eponymus" of the race ; and Buchanan tells us that in his day, that is, in the reign of Queen Mary, "a great part of this country still uses its ancient language." What that language was we learn from a contemporary of Buchanan, William Dunbar, the poet, who, in the "Flyting" between him and Kennedy, taunted his rival with his extraction from the natives of Galloway and Carrick, and styles him "Ersch Katheraine," "Ersch brybour baird," and his poetry as "sic eloquence as they in Erschert use." This word "Ersch" was the term applied at the time to Scotch Gaelic, as when Sir David Lyndesay says —

> Had Sanct Gerome bene borne intil Arygle,
> Into Irische toung his bukis had done compyle.

And Kennedy retorts upon Dunbar—

> Thow luvis nane Erische, enf I understand,
>   But it sowld be all trew Scottismenn is leid ;
> It was the gud langage of this land.

Mr. Mac Kerlie, in Paterson's *History of the County of Ayr* (pp. 14, 16), explains the reasons for the similarity between the Gaelic tongue of Galloway and that of Ulster, in this wise :

In 740, however, the Alcluydensians of Kyle were invaded by Alpin, king of the Scots, who landed at Ayr with a large body of followers. He is said to have wasted the country between the Ayr and the Doon as far inland as the vicinity of Dalmellington, about sixteen miles from the sea. There he was met by an armed force under the chiefs of the district, and a battle having ensued, Alpin was slain, and his army totally routed. The spot where the king was buried is called at this day Laicht-Alpin, or the Grave of Alpin. Chalmers observes that this fact is important, as showing that the Gaelic language was then the prevailing tongue in Ayrshire. No doubt it is : but it is one of the strongest arguments that could be urged against his theory that the Gaelic was superinduced upon the British, which he holds was the language of the Caledonian Picts, as well as the Romanised tribes. If the Damnonii of Ayrshire spoke Gaelic in 836, they must have done so long before ; because at that period, as we have seen, the Scots of Argyle had made no settlement in Ayrshire.

But the fact that there is a considerable difference between the Gaelic of the Galloway Cruithne and the Gaelic of the Scots — that the former bears a much closer affinity to the Irish as it now exists — is strong evidence that the Scottish Gaelic was not a direct importation from Ireland, and that the Dalriads of Argyle were not purely Irish. Though originally from North Britain, the Cruithne had been long resident in Ireland, and did not settle in Galloway till about four centuries later than the return of Fergus to Argyleshire ; consequently the greater similarity in language and customs can easily be accounted for.[29]

The evidences of a considerable Gaelic admixture in the blood of the early southwestern Scotchmen are also shown in their place-names and surnames. This is particularly the case in Ayrshire, which was the native county of the first emigrants to Antrim and Down in the seventeenth century. To again quote the author of the *History of the County of Ayr* (vol. i., pp. 9, 16, 17) :

In so far as Ayrshire is concerned, there can be no doubt that the early inhabitants were purely Celtic ; whether called Britons, Belgæ, Scots, Picts, or Cruithne, they must all have been of Gallic extraction. This is apparent in the topography of the country, the hill-forts, stone-monuments, and Druidical and other remains which have everywhere been found. Even yet, notwithstanding the frequent accessions, in later times, of Saxons, Normans, and Flemings, the bulk of the population retains much of its original features. This appears in the prevailing patronymics, many of which preserve their Celtic prefixes, such as M'Culloch, M'Creath, M'Crindle, M'Adam, M'Phadric, or M'Phedries ; or have dropped them like the Alexanders, Andrewses, Kennedies, and Bones, within these few centuries. Campbell is a numerous surname. The Celtic lineaments are perhaps not so strong in Cuninghame, at least in the middle portion of it, as in the other districts ; but this is easily accounted for by the early settlements of the De Morville, and other great families from England, in the richest parts of it. In Pont's maps, drawn up at the commencement of the seventeenth century, the Celtic names are more numerous both in Kyle and Cuninghame than in the maps of the present day. The Gaelic language is said [by Buchanan] to have been spoken in some quarters of Ayrshire so late as the sixteenth century. . . .

The main topographical argument of Chalmers in favor of the Scoto-Irish theory, is the circumstance of *Inver*, in two instances, having been substituted for *Aber*. Now, as formerly shown, there are only two solitary instances of *Inver* in the whole topography of Ireland, and not one throughout the range of Galloway. The word, therefore, seems to have been peculiar to the Scottish Gael. In Kyle, on the contrary, we have several samples of it in old charters. Ayr itself is called *Inver-ar* in some instances, while we have *Inverpolcurtecan* and *Inverdon*. Another distinction between the Gaelic, Welsh, and Irish, worthy of being taken notice of, is the patronymic mark. In the Scots it is *Mac ;* in Welsh, *Ap ;* and in Irish, *O'*. Now, if the Scots had been thoroughly Irish in their descent, as Chalmers affirms they were in their manners, laws, and customs, it is difficult to understand why they should have differed so widely upon so common a point ; and it is equally strange that, in the oldest charters, where the Walenses, the remains of the Alcluyd Britons, are distinctly mentioned, there should not occur a single Welsh patronymic mark, if the language of the North Britons and the Welsh were so congenerous as he supposed. If we take, according to Chalmers, the British words in the topography of Scotland as a proof that the inhabitants spoke Welsh, the same rule would apply equally to Ireland, where the same British words are prevalent.

The lists of the Scottish and Pictish kings are adduced by Chalmers as another proof of the British speech of the Picts, the names of the latter having no meaning unless in the British. Now this is not the case. Most of the Pictish names are just as capable of being explained by a Gaelic dictionary as those of the Scots. The difference lies chiefly in the spelling, a circumstance which is not to be wondered at.

The Gaelic was not a written language. The earliest verses known are the *Duan*, a sort of genealogy of the Scottish kings, composed in the eleventh century, during the reign of Malcolm Canmore. The Irish *Annals of Ulster* and Tighernach were not written before the thirteenth [?] century, so that any writings at all extant — even where Gaelic names of places occur in the earliest charters — all make a nearer approach to the language as it is now spoken and understood than the Welsh authorities, to whose records of facts we are chiefly indebted for any knowledge which has been preserved of the Picts or Alcluydensians, and who wrote at a much earlier period. The annals of the latter came to us through an ancient Cambro-British medium, those of the Scots through a recently written, and no doubt much changed branch of a kindred tongue.

Another argument against the Irish extraction of the Scots may be drawn from the statement of Chalmers, that the Scoto-Irish brought the custom of war-cries with them. Now, in the first place, we know that war-cries were not peculiarly Irish ; and, in the second, that the Scots did not use the affix *abo*, to their cries, such as Butler-*abo*, or Crom-*abo*, which was general over Ireland. Their national war-cry was simply *Albanich* from Albyn, the ancient name of North Britain. Thus we see there was nothing Irish even in the style of their war-cry, while the cry itself shows that they were of Albyn, not of Ireland. Even the Cruithne, or " the wild Scots of Galloway," as they were termed in the twelfth century, used the same war-cry. At the battle of the Standard, in 1136, they led the van,[30] and rushing on to battle, the cry was " Albanich ! Albanich ! Albanich ! " Thanks to Hoveden, who has recorded the circumstance, we have here strong presumptive proof that both the Dalriads of Argyle and the Cruithne of Galloway were originally from Albyn, and had preserved the same national war-cry throughout their long pilgrimage in the North of Ireland. As the term Albyn only applied in ancient times to the Pictish country north of the Forth, the cry would not have been locally appropriate in Galloway; hence it was not likely to have been adopted after their arrival. The war-cry in ancient, like armorial bearings in more modern times, may be regarded as strong evidence of descent.

Taking all things into consideration, it is difficult to avoid the conclusion that there was, in reality, very little difference originally between the language of the Scots, Picts, and Alcluydensians. If there had been as great a distinction between the Gaelic and the Pictish language as the apocryphal specimen left by Merlin, a poet of the sixth century, would lead us to suppose, there would have been little use in appointing Gaelic clergymen over a Pictish people. That what is now the Lowland dialect had its rise during the Scottish period there can be little doubt. The annexation of Lothian, occupied for centuries chiefly by the Angles, brought them into closer contact with the inhabitants of the adjacent districts; while a body of Saxons actually effected a settlement in Kyle and Cuninghame. Though these, it may be inferred, did not long retain possession, owing to the decline of the Northumbrian power, still the probability is that a portion both of their lineage and language remained. The many Saxons brought into Scotland by Malcolm Canmore — though numbers of them were expelled by the Scots after his death — must have tended greatly to disseminate a language already constituting the vernacular tongue of the east coast from the Forth to the Tweed.

The Lowland dialect, originating in a combination of the oldest and purest Teutonic with the native Gaelic or British, owes to this union much of that peculiar softness, copiousness, and graphic power for which it is distinguished. One-third of the language, upon careful examination, will be found to be Celtic. It has also a considerable admixture of French, the acquisition of which can easily be accounted for by the number of Norman settlers who came amongst us, and the subsequent intercourse which took place between France and Scotland. In the next, or Anglo-Saxon period of our history, the growth of the Scottish dialect can be still more distinctly traced.

In reference to the laws during the era of which we are now writing, Chalmers shows that they were Celtic, and very different from the Saxon; but that they were peculiarly Scoto-Irish, as in accordance with his system, he affirms, is by no means so clear. It is not at all proved that the laws of the Scots were different from those of the Picts, or Lowland Britons. The predominance of the Scots brings them down more nearly to written evidence; and therefore we have a better knowledge of the customs which prevailed under their rule. On the contrary, we are almost in total ignorance of the laws by which the Picts or Alcluydensians were governed.

The law of tanistry — by which the succession of the crown was regulated — existed apparently amongst the Picts as well as the Scots. Bede casually informs us that it was a rule with the Picts, when the succession came to be disputed, that the preference should be given to the nearest claimant by the female side. It was this law which placed Kenneth on the throne, in opposition to the other competitor, Bred.

That the customs of the Scots and Picts were the same is apparent from an ordinance of Edward I., issued with a view to the settlement of Scotland, in which he says, " the custom of the Scots and Picts shall for the future be prohibited, and be no longer practised." *Customs*, not *custom*, would have been the phrase if there had been different customs prevailing among the Scots and Britons.   During the Scottish period the country had been ecclesiastically divided into parishes, but the introduction of sheriffdoms and justiciaries belongs to a later age.

Mr. MacKerlie refers to the same conditions in the district of modern Galloway (*Galloway, Ancient and Modern*, pp. 62–63) :

> The distance between the county Down and Galloway is twenty-two miles, and thus only eight miles farther off than Antrim from Kintyre, and both to be seen from Ireland.   The emigration to Galloway must have been gradual, and spread over centuries, until the Ulster settlers were so numerous as to become the dominant people.   It is to be remembered that the Strathclyde kingdom came into existence about A.D. 547–8, which fully accounts for the absence of information in regard to the erroneous supposition that Galloway was an independent district, with rulers of its own.   This continued until A.D. 1018, when Strathclyde as a kingdom came to an end ; but the Norsemen then got full possession of and sway over Galloway, which continued for about two centuries, until the kings of Scotland were fully established, and ruled over the whole kingdom, as since known.
>
> The popular idea that Galloway was all along a kingdom in itself is purely ideal, and without the slightest basis for it.   We wish to direct attention to the close communication which evidently existed between Galloway and Ireland from the earliest times.   It is easily understood from being such close neighbours.   There also cannot be a doubt that the statement which eminent writers have handed down is virtually correct, that the Goidels or Gaels were the first Celtic inhabitants, who absorbed the aborigines as the situations or circumstances demanded, and who in turn were next dislodged by the Cymri, and other Celtic fresh hordes who flocked into Britain, driving the said Goidels northwards, and across to Ireland.   If other proof were wanting, we have it in the surnames, and in the names of places, many of which are common to both Galloway and Ireland, being found on both sides of the Channel.

There was a more or less considerable Teutonic element introduced into the population of Galloway at an early date not only by the Angles who occupied it in Bede's time, but to a far greater extent by the Norse sea-kings and their followers, who settled there in large numbers during the latter part of the tenth and first half of the eleventh centuries.   This conquest of Galloway and northern Scotland has been briefly sketched in the preceding pages.   Let us now consider the results of that conquest.   This subject has been treated at some length by the author last quoted, who says :

> The idea has also largely prevailed that Galloway was for long under Saxon rule, with no other basis, so far as we can trace, than that in A.D. 723 commenced a succession of bishops connected with the Anglo-Saxon Church. This, however, was of short duration, as the last bishop was elected in 790. He was still there in 803, but the line ended with him.[91]   This ecclesiastical establishment, which did not exist for a century, was distinct from district rule.   The power of the Church of Iona extended to Northumberland, until the Anglo-Saxons conformed to Rome in 664.   This latter was the church

thrust on the Galwegians, and failed at that period. Afterwards, when King David I., with his Anglo-Normans, etc., succeeded in establishing the Anglo-Church of Rome in Scotland without an archbishop, the Pope directed that the Primate of York should consecrate, and this was continued until an archbishop was established at St. Andrews in A.D. 1472. During that period, however, Scotland as a country was not subject to England, and so it was with Galloway, an ecclesiastical union only existing with Northumberland.

That Galloway was overrun and devastated on different occasions is to be believed, but permanent settlement does not appear. The confusion, however, about the district was kept up; and under date 875 we are told that the Britons of Strathclyde and the Picts of Galloway were ravaged by the Danes of Northumberland.[32] This is correct in one sense, as the Irish-Scots in Galloway, through Bede, had their name stamped in history as Picts; but we have mentioned in its proper place how it arose. The statement under date 875 conveys that Galloway and Strathclyde were not united, which is erroneous.

Mackenzie, in his *History of Galloway*, while joining in the usual opinion (taken from uninvestigated writings), yet admits that few traces are left in support of Anglo-Saxon occupation, and at Whithorn specially, the place where such should be found. In the absence of facts, he therefore had recourse to making out something from the names of places, in which he was singularly unfortunate. His examples were *Boreland, Engleston*, and *Carleton*, as now spelled. The first he describes as the habitations of the slaves who were employed by the Anglo-Saxons to till the ground, termed boors, and hence Boreland. The next, Engleston, or Ingleston, is described as applied to farms which had been occupied by the Angles. The last is Carleton, which lands he states were so called from the ceorles, or middle-class Saxons, who were the owners.

We thus have Galloway and Ayrshire transformed into an Anglo-Saxon province, as having been fully in their possession. The meanings given of all three are entirely erroneous. Boreland, as Bordland, is to be found as "lands kept by owners in Saxon times for the supply of their own board or table, but it referred specially to the Norsemen, from the Orkneys to Galloway, as lands exempt from *skatt*, the land-tax, for the upholding of Government. Ingleston has been corrupted by some writers to Englishtoun, the abode of the English, whereas it is also from the Norse and refers to land of a certain character or quality. Under our reference to the Norse occupation of Galloway, we will enter into more particulars in regard to the names Boreland and Engleston. Lastly, Carleton, being from ceorles, is very farfetched. If it had been from a Saxon source as indicated, the class from whom it is said to have been derived must have been very few (three or four) in number. . . . Other lands in Wigtonshire, and Borgue parish, Kirkcudbrightshire, got the same designation from descendants who removed there.

In fact, all the erroneous exaggerations in regard to the Anglo-Saxon occupation of Galloway have arisen from the Norse rule being overlooked. The supposition has been that the latter only held the coast, whereas their rule of the district was thorough.[33]

The earliest record of the appearance of the Norsemen in British waters is to be found in the Anglo-Saxon *Chronicles*. They are stated to have come from Haeretha-land, now Hordaland, on the west coast of Norway. The Irish *Annals* and Welsh *Chronicles* give the date of their first appearance on

the Irish coast as A.D. 795, but it is clear enough that they were known centuries previously. . . . About 872, King Harold, aided by Earl Rognwald, subdued the Hebrides, inclusive of the Isle of Man. Thorstein the
Red, son of Olaf the White, King of Dublin, and Earl Sigurd, subdued
Caithness and Sutherland, as far as Ekkielsbakkie, and afterwards Ross and
Moray, with more than half of Scotland, over which Thorstein ruled, as
recorded in the *Landnama-bok*.

About 963, Sigurd, son of Earl Hlodver, and his wife Audna (the daughter of the Irish king Kiarval), became ruler over Ross and Moray, Sutherland and the Dales (of Caithness), which seems also to have included old
Strathnavar. Sigurd married, secondly, the daughter of Malcolm (Malbrigid),
called King of Scotland. He was slain at Clontarf near Dublin, in 1014.
By his first marriage he left issue, Sumarlidi, Brusi, and Einar, who divided
the Orkneys between them. By his second marriage he had issue, Thorfinn,
on whom King Malcolm bestowed the earldom of Caithness.

To quote from the introduction, *Njal Saga*, by Dasent [*Saga of Burnt
Njal*, George Webbe Dasent, 1861], " Ireland knew them [the Vikings]
Bretland or Wales knew them, England knew them too well, and a great part
of Scotland they had made their own. To this day the name of almost every
island on the west coast of Scotland is either pure Norse, or Norse distorted,
so as to make it possible for Celtic lips to utter it. The groups of Orkney
and Shetland are notoriously Norse ; but Lewis and the Uists, and Skye
and Mull are no less Norse, and not only the names of the islands themselves, but those of reefs and rocks, and lakes, and headlands, bear witness
to the same relation, and show that, while the original inhabitants were not
expelled, but held in bondage as thralls, the Norsemen must have dwelt and
dwelt thickly too, as conquerors and lords."

The foregoing extract gives a description which investigation corroborates. The blank in the history of Galloway after the termination of the
Strathcluyd kingdom is now fully met. The only difficulty is to determine
at what date Galloway became separated from Strathcluyd. Earl (Jarl)
Malcolm, who lived near Whithorn in 1014, is the first Norseman specially
named. His place of residence is believed to have been Cruggleton Castle,
of historic renown in after-times. Eogan the Bald, who fought at Carham,
and died in 1018, was the last King of Strathcluyd. We have thus only a
difference of four years, and certain it is that Earl Malcolm was in Galloway,
and evidently located there as one in possession. In the *Burnt Njal* we find
the following : " They (Norsemen) then sailed north to Berwick (the Solway), and laid up their ship, and fared up into Whithorn in Scotland, and
were with Earl Malcolm that year." . . .

Another point certain from close investigation is, that Jarl (Earl) Thorfinn (son of Sigurd II.) ruled over Galloway in 1034, the time mentioned,
and continued to do so until his death in 1064 or 1066 [1057]. In 1034
he was twenty-seven years of age. In Scottish history we learn nothing of
him, although in possession of a large part of Scotland. During his lifetime
he ruled Galloway from Solway to Carrick. The *Flateyjarbok* contains the
Orkneyinga Saga complete in successive portions : and in Munch's *Historie
et Chronicon Manniæ*, Earl Thorfinn is distinctly mentioned.

It is also related that the Earl Gille had married a sister of Sigurd II.,
and acted as his lieutenant in the Sudreys. He is said to have resided at
Koln, either the island of Coll or Colonsay ; and when Sigurd fell at Clontarf in 1014, he took Thorfinn, the youngest son, under his protection, while
the elder brothers went to the Orkneys, and divided the northern dominions

amongst them. The two elder brothers died early in life, and Brusi accepted a pension for his claim ; therefore, when Thorfinn grew up he found himself possessed of nine earldoms in Scotland, to which he added all Galloway. Munch thinks they were Caithness, Sutherland, Ross, Moray, Buchan, Athol, Lorn, Argyle, and Galloway. To quote from Munch : "The *Orkneyinga Saga* says so expressly."

Outliving his elder brothers, he (Thorfinn) became the Lord of Orkney and Shetland ; Caithness was given to him by his maternal grandfather, and after the death of Malcolm . . . he . . . conquered Sutherland and Ross, and made himself lord of Galloway, in the widest sense of this denomination — viz., from Solway to Carrick — where he resided for long periods, and whence he made successful inroads, sometimes on Cumberland, sometimes upon Ireland. He possessed, besides the Sudreys and part of Ireland, not less than nine earldoms in Scotland, etc. As Munch further states, all the Hebrides and a large kingdom of Ireland were also his. The Skeld Arnor, who personally visited him, and made a poem in his honour, testifies in it that his kingdom extended from Thurso rocks to Dublin. He also mentions that Thorfinn obtained possession of eleven earldoms in Scotland, all the Sudreyar (Hebrides), and a large territory in Ireland. He further states that Thorfinn sent men into England to foray, and then, having collected a force from the places named, he sailed from England, where he had two pitched battles : as Arnor gives it — "South of Man did these things happen."

This is contemporary evidence. In 1035, when Rognwald arrived from Norway, Thorfinn was much occupied in Scotland, and they made an alliance by which Rognwald was to have his part of Orkney free of contest, under condition of assisting Thorfinn with all the forces he could command. This alliance lasted ten years, and during that time Thorfinn made many incursions into England and Ireland. He generally resided in the south during the summer months, and in Caithness, or rather the Orkney and Shetland Isles, during the winter. They quarrelled, however, and Rognwald was slain in 1045. Thorfinn died about 1064 [?],[34] says Munch, or sixty years after King Malcolm . . . so far as the exact dates can be ascertained. . . .

In regard to Thorfinn, it is stated that he "resided long at Caithness in a place called Gaddgedlar, where England and Scotland meet." Munch correctly insists that Gaddgedlar meant Galloway,[35] which at the period extended to Annan on one side and Carrick on the other, in its widest sense — or, in other words, the south-western part of Scotland, from Annandale on the Solway to Carrick opposite Kintyre — and therefore, in the true sense of the word, the boundary towards England. Munch was too careful a writer to confuse such a subject, and gave as his opinion that the sentence was incomplete, having been incorrectly copied from the original MS. This belief has been proved to be correct, as we will hereafter show. . . .

We have had much assistance from other eminent Norse scholars, but that Gaddgedlar meant Galloway has been confirmed beyond dispute by the late G. Vigfusson, who communicated to us privately the missing passage before his *Collection of Sagas* was in the press. He found it in a Danish translation, made in A.D. 1615, and preserved in Stockholm, from an ancient Icelandic vellum, which is no longer in existence. The existing printed text of the *Orkneyinga Saga* was founded on the *Flateyensis* only. The passage in its purity is, "Sat Þorfinner jarl longum a Katanesi en Rognvaldr i Eyjum. Þat var a einu sumri at Þorfinnr jarl herjadi um Sudreyjar ok

vestan um Skotland. Hann la par sem Gaddgedlar heita, par maetist Skotland ok England. Hann hafdi giork fra ser lid sudr a England at Strand-
hoggi." The rough translation is : " Earl Thorfinn dwelt for the most part
in Caithness, but Rognwald in the Isles. One summer Earl Thorfinn made
war in the Hebrides and the west of Scotland. He lay at the place called
Gaddgedlar, where Scotland and England meet. He had sent some from
himself men to England for a strand-head (coast foray)." We will give Mr.
Vigfusson's notes, which he sent to us in regard to the foregoing : (1) " ' En
Rognwaldr. Hann la,' is taken from the translation — the careless copyist of
the *Flateyensis* having here omitted and transposed a whole important passage. The suggestion of the late Norse historian, P. A. Munch, is thus
conclusively proved to be true, both as to the identification of Gaddgedlar-
Galloway (the translator spells it Gaardgellar), as also the unsound state of
the text. Munch surmised that after ' Katanesi' something, the copula
' ok ' or the like, had been dropped out. It now is found that a whole sentence has been omitted or transposed. (2) We have followed the translator,
where the text runs thus : ' Gaardgellar der modis Engeland oc, Scotland
da haff de han Sendt nogen af sin Krigs folck hen paa Engeland, etc.' The
Flateyensis is here all confusion. As we have shown, Thorfinn ruled over a
large part of Scotland and a part of Ireland. He also carried his sway to
portions of England, and at one time was chief of the Thingmen. He went
to Rome, supposed about A.D. 1050, saw the Pope, and obtained absolution
for all his sins. His position is thus shown to have been not only that of a
warrior, but also of a conqueror."

That Galloway was under his sway is clear. This opinion is fully entertained among the learned in Copenhagen ; and as mentioned to us, arising
from our investigations, great interest has been evinced in the universities
there in regard to Galloway, considering it at one time to have belonged to
the sea-kings. It thus appears to us as very strange how the occupation of
the districts, in the full sense, by the Norsemen has escaped the notice of
those who have entered on Galloway history.

The desire to make the Fergus line of lords of Galloway the ancient
inheritors has blinded research. If the character of the people had only
been considered, such an omission would not have occurred ; for we think
no one will be bold enough to dispute the fact that the fortresses on the
coast were built by the Norsemen. Having incurred such labor, is it to be
supposed for one moment that they were erected as coast ornaments, or that
the fierce natives of Galloway would have permitted such erections if they
had not been subdued ? All the Danish records tell us of a conquered
people. The fortresses never could have been built under other circumstances. . . .

There can, we think, be no question that the principal fortresses in
Galloway were erected in the time of Jarls, or Earls, Malcolm and Thorfinn,
long before the appearance of King Magnus, styled in the annals, *Chronicum Scotorum*, as King of Lachlann. His descent was in 1093. He
returned to Norway in 1099. In 1102 he came back, and was killed in
Connaught, Ireland, in 1103. He was buried in St. Patrick's Church, Down.
He only reigned over the Western Isles for six years, when he was succeeded
by Olave, who was a pacific prince, and his confederacy with Ireland and
Scotland so close, that no one presumed to disturb the peace of these isles
while he lived. He married Affrica, daughter of Fergus, Lord of Galloway.
The *Inquisitio Davidis*, a nearly contemporary document, particularly notices
the influx of a Gentile, *alias* heathen, population, and this could only be the

Norsemen, as both Irish, Scots, and Saxons (so-called) were Christians, in theory at least, for two or three centuries before that time. . . .

The Northern sagas, 870–75, show that the mass of the population then in Galloway was of the Cymric race, sometimes called Brythons ; but the Irish-Scots or Gaels, from the counties Antrim and Down, the particulars in regard to whom we have already given, must also have been numerous, for in 876 the Cymri were under their rule, and those who would not submit to the yoke retreated to Wales to rejoin their countrymen in that quarter. . . . The Norsemen have left various marks of their occupation of Galloway in the names of places and also in surnames.

Under the alleged Saxon occupation, which is erroneous, we have referred to Boreland, Ingleston, and Carleton, at pp. 87, 88. The first two are from the Norse, and the last from an Irish personal name. The Lothians were for a time in the possession of the Anglo-Saxons (so-called), and yet, after careful investigation, the first is not to be found there, and the second, only once, in West Lothian. We find a Boreland in Peeblesshire, a property so called in Cumnock parish, and Boarland in Dunlop parish, Ayrshire. There are also lands so called in Dumfriesshire, near the mouth of the Nith, which Timothy Pont gives in his survey as North, Mid, and South Bordland. The Borelands in Galloway are so numerous that we must deal with them as one, for there are fourteen farms with the name in the Stewartry, and three in Wigtonshire.

In Brewer's *Dictionary of Phrase and Fable*, Bordlands is interpreted to mean "lands kept by lords in Saxon times for the supply of their own board or table." This approaches the true meaning, and is all that can be found until we come to the Norse, when it is cleared up. We find in the Orkneys, where the Norsemen's headquarters were, that part of the ancient estate of the jarls (earls) of Orkney and Shetland consisted of the "bord-lands," which were the quarters of the jarls when occasionally travelling through the islands, and therefore exempt from *skatt*, the tax upon all land occupied by the Udellers or Odellers, for the expense of government. This *skatt*, or *scat*, was an ancient land-tax payable to the Crown of Norway. *Skatt* in Norse is to make tributary, and *skatt*-land is tributary land. The Udellers held land by uninterrupted succession without any original charter, and without subjection to feudal service, or the acknowledgment of any superior. The exemption of the "bordlands" from *skatt* or land-tax is shown in some old rentals of Orkney. In a rental dated 30th April, 1503, there is the following entry : "Memorandum, That all the Isle of Hoy is of the ald Erldome and Bordland, quhilk payit nevir scat." There are several similar entries relating to other Bordlands in the same rental. In a later rental, bearing date 1595, there are several farms entered—viz., "Hanga-back, na scat, quia Borland," etc. Numerous other entries of the same description are given. . . . That the Borelands in Galloway have a similar derivation as those in the Orkneys cannot be doubted. The old spelling in Galloway is "Bordland," as the old deeds will show. The same refers to the lands already mentioned at the mouth of the Nith, Dumfries-shire side. Bordland, in fact, appears to be the proper spelling throughout Scotland. . . .

The other special name is Engleston or Ingleston, which we mentioned at p. 87. In regard to it there are at least two opinions, one being that it is derived from "English," and another from the Scottish "ingle," a chimney, or rather fireplace. There are several farms bearing the name in Galloway, and one so called in West Lothian. In a charter granted by King David II., lands so called have it spelled Inglynstoun, and in another charter by Robert II., it is Inglystoun (Robertson's *Index of Charters*). Pont, in his map drafted between 1608–20, spells it " Englishtoun," which cannot be accepted, for it is obviously incorrect. The surname of Inglis found in Scotland is the root of this error, as the assumption has been that it is a corruption of " English " ; but opposed to this idea is the fact that although several individuals named Inglis are to be found in the possession of lands at an early period, not one of them is styled of Ingliston or Inglystoun. The Inglises of Manner seem to have been the chief family, and they held the lands of Branksome or Branksholm, afterwards possessed by the Scotts (Buccleuch). The Ingliston in West Lothian probably got the name from Inglis of Cramond, the first of which family was a merchant in Edinburgh about 1560, the Reformation time. It has also been overlooked that " English " is a distinct English surname borne by families in England, and any affinity with it and Inglis has no other basis than some similarity in sound. We still adhere to the same opinion as given by us in *Lands and their Owners in Galloway*, that the farms in Galloway called Engleston or Ingleston have nothing to do with the surname Inglis, or as Englishtoun ; but were given from the nature or character of the land, and are from the Norse *engi* for meadow-land, or a meadow, which is also found in Anglo-Saxon as *ing* or *inge*, a pasture, a meadow. . . .

Worsaae mentions that the names of places ending in " by " are to be found only in the districts selected by the Norsemen for conquest or colonization—as Lockerby, in Dumfriesshire, Appleby and Sorby (a parish, and some farms corrupted to " bie "), in Wigtonshire, etc. Sorby is also to be found in North Yorkshire and Cumberland, where settlements existed. Camden mentions a peninsula called " Flegg," in Norfolk, where the Danes had settled, and that in a little compass of ground there were thirteen villages ending in " by," a Danish word signifying a village or dwelling-place ; and hence the *bi-lagines* of the Danish writers, and the "by-laws" in England, come to signify such laws as are peculiar to each town or village. It is also sometimes in the form of *bui*, a dweller, an inhabitant, whereas *baer* or *byr* or *bae* means a village, etc. Pollbae, in Wigtonshire, should in correct form be Pollrbae, the marshy or boggy farm. We entered on this subject in our historical sketch to vol. ii. of *Lands and their Owners in Galloway*. It is of importance, as it goes to prove with other evidence what we have held to all along, that instead of a mere coast occupation, as generally believed, Galloway was in the full possession of the Norsemen. We were therefore glad to find in Professor MacKinnon's article, No. VI., on " The Norse Elements," published in the *Scotsman*, December 2, 1887, the following from his pen : " *Beer, byr,* ' a village,' becomes *by*, and marks the Danish settlement in England—Whitby, Derby, Selby, Appleby ; and in the Isle of Man, Dalby, Salby, Jurby. This form is not common in the Isles. There is Europie, ' beach village,' in Lewis, hence the ' Europa Point ' of the maps. There is Soroby in Tyree, and Soroba near Obam. Shiaba (Schabby in old records), on the south of Mull, contains the root. So do Nereby and Connisby (*konung*, a ' king's village ') in Islay, Canisby in Caithness, and Smerby in Kintyre." . . .

To continue the general subject the word *flow*, well known in Galloway as donating marshy moorland, is from the Norse *floi*, for a marshy moor.

The names of places beginning or ending with *garth* or *guard* show where the Scandinavians were settled in *gaarde* or farms, which belonged to the

Danish chiefs, or Udellers (*holdus* from old Norsk *holldr*). Worsaae mentions that these seem to have been the property of the peasants, on condition of their paying certain rents to their feudal lords, and binding themselves to contribute to the defence of the country. In Galloway we have Garthland and Cogarth as examples. Worsaae does not seem to have visited the district, but to have been in Dumfriesshire, as he refers to Tundergarth, Applegarth, and Huntgarth.

The Holms he also notices, which are to be found in Galloway and other parts of Scotland, also in England where the Norsemen had settlements. The name is from the Norse *holmr*, meaning an island in a loch or river, or a plain at the side of a river. In Orkney there are the parish and Sound so-called, also four islands. In Shetland there are three small islands, and at Skye there is one, etc.

Among many other Norse names in Galloway, there is Tung or Tongue. Worsaae calls the " Kyles of Tongue," in Sutherlandshire, pure Norwegian.

Fleet, the name of a river in Anwoth parish, is from the Norse *fljot*, pronounced in Anglo-Saxon *fleot*. In the parish at Stoneykirk are the farms and bay of Float, locally stated to have been so called from the wreck of one of the ships of the Spanish Armada ; and to make it complete, the headland close to, corrupted from the Gaelic word *monadh*, the hill-head, to " Moneyhead," from money supposed to have been lost from the wreck. Such derivations are erroneous. The name Float is from the Norse *flott*, which means a plain ; and the access from the bay, with the character of the farms so called, together with the history of the lands adjoining, fully bear out the Norse meaning. One of the Orkney Isles is called Flotta. It was the residence of the historiographer appointed by the Crown of Norway to gather information ; his work was therefore called *Codex Flotticenses*.

The Norse word Borg, given to a parish, is now spelled Borgue ; and Gata corrupted to Galtway.

In the bay of Luce, or rather in the offing, are the " Scar Rocks," and without reference to them, Worsaae mentions *sker* or *skjaer* as the Norse for isolated rocks in the sea, which those we refer to truly are. Begbie (Bagbie) and Killiness are also Norse.

The Norse names in Galloway are far from being exhausted, as will be found by reference to the parishes and lands given in *Lands and their Owners in Galloway*.

Worsaae refers to Tinwald in Dumfriesshire as undoubtedly identical with Thingvall or Tingvold, the appropriate Scandinavian or Norse term for places where the Thing was held. Elsewhere he states that they settled their disputes and arranged their public affairs at the Things. In connection with this he mentions Dingwall in Cromarty, Tingwall in the Shetland Isles, and Tynewald or Tingwall in the Isle of Man.

We will only add here one other word, and a well-known one over Scotland—viz., kirk, which is from *kirke*, the Danish for church. In the old Norse it is *kirkja*. In the same language there is *kirke-gaard* or *garth* and *kirkju-gardr*, a kirk or churchyard. In the German it is *kirche*, and in Anglo-Saxon, *church*.

Worsaae correctly mentions that old Irish authors called the inhabitants of Denmark *Dublochlannoch*—dark Lochlans—the word *Lochlan* with them being the usual appellation for Scandinavia. It is also given as *Lochlin* and *Lochlann*. In the Gaelic it is somewhat similar, as in that language *Dubh-Lochlinneach* means a Dane, and *Fionn-Lochlinneach*, a Norwegian. The latter are also found called *Finngheinte* in Gaelic. Worsaae repeats that the best and oldest Irish chronicles distinguish between the light-haired *Finn-Lochlannoch* or *Fionn-Lochlannaigh*, the Norwegians, and the dark-haired *Dubh-Lochlannoch* or *Dubh-Lochlannaigh*, the Danes ; or, what is the same, between *Dubhgall, Dubh-Ghoill*, and *Finngall, Fionn-Ghoill*.³⁶

NOTES TO CHAPTER XVII.

¹ During the latter years of Kenneth's reign, a people appear in close association with the Norwegian pirates, and joining in their plundering expeditions, who are termed Gall-gaidhel. This name is formed by the combination of the two words " Gall," a stranger, a foreigner, and " Gaidhel," the national name of the Gaelic race. It was certainly first applied to the people of Galloway, and the proper name of this province, Galweitha, is formed from Galwyddel, the Welsh equivalent of Gallgaidhel. It seems to have been applied to them as a Gaelic race under the rule of Galle or foreigners : Galloway being for centuries a province of the Anglic kingdom of Northumbria, and the term " Gall " having been applied to the Saxons before it was almost exclusively appropriated to the Norwegian and Danish pirates. Towards the end of the eighth century the power of the Angles in Galloway seems to have become weakened, and the native races began to assert their independent action. —*Celtic Scotland*, vol. i., p. 311.

² See p. 208.

³ " Deira was the district thus portioned out amongst the Northmen who peopled the ancient kingdom of Northumbria, whilst Bernicia and the territory of St. Cuthbert, between Tees and Tyne, seem to have been still occupied by a Saxon proprietary, to a certain extent in a dependent condition, as exemplified in the *Wergilds* of the *Northern Leod*, in which the *Holdr* is reckoned at twice the value of the *Thegn*. A sure and certain test of a colonization of this description is afforded by the topography of the districts thus allotted, the *Caster* and the *By* invariably marking the presence of the Northmen, not only as a dominant, but as an actual occupying class ; and as only four *Bys* are to be found to the northward of the Tees, whilst the *chester* is traceable from Tees to Tweed, and in a few instances even beyond that river, it may be safely assumed that though the territory of St. Cuthbert was divided by Reginald Hy Ivar between his followers Skuli and Olaf, the Tees was the northern boundary of the actual settlement, and that Deira alone was ' roped out ' amongst the Danes.

" The *Caster* and the *By* in Cumberland and Westmoreland tell at the present day of a considerable colonization amidst the bleak moorlands of the west, unconnected apparently with the Danes of the Yorkshire Trythings. . . . whilst beyond the Solway not a few *Bys* between the Annan and the Esk mark the encroachments of the Northmen in the eastern division of modern Dumfriesshire, a few settlers penetrating into Galloway. Cannoby, Dunnaby, Wyseby, Perceby, Middleby, Lockerby, and Sibalby occur in Dumfriesshire, and Sorby and Appleby in Wigtonshire."—*Scotland under her Early Kings*, vol. ii., pp. 432, 437.

⁴ *Annals of Ulster.*

⁵ 871, Amlaiph et Imhar do thuidhecht a frithisi du Athacliath a Albain dibhcedaib long (came again to Athacliath from Alban with 200 ships), et praeda maxima hominum Anglorum et Britonum et Pictorum deducta est secum ad Hiberniam in captivitate.—*Annals of Ulster.*

⁶ Predictus exercitus [Danorum] se in duas partes divisit, una pars cum Haldene ad regionen Nordanhymbrorum secessit et eam vastavit et hyemavit juxta flumen quod dicitur Tine et totam gentem suo dominetui subdidit et Pictos atque Strathduccenses depopulati sunt.—Sim. Dun. 875, Congressio Pictorum for Dubgallu et strages magna Pictorum facta est.—*An. Ult.*

⁷ *English Chronicle*, Anno 924. See p. 298.

[8] *Orkneyinga Saga, Coll. de Rebus Albanicis.* See Appendix P.

[9] " So it was that Scotland received a population of immigrants from Norway along the seaboard from Caithness to Fife. In Lothian and Northumberland they met and mingled with the people of a kindred race who had crossed from Jutland, Zealand, and Friesland to the coast of England. It is from the change that domesticated each successive horde of new-comers, that we lose all historical hold upon their coming as a separate fact, and have so much difficulty in identifying the leaders who brought them over. We cannot say where it was that the first man of Teutonic northern race set foot in Scotland, and whether he found the land empty or inhabited by Celts. But we know pretty well that from the fourth century to the tenth this race spread over the land that is now Lowland Scotland, and that if they found Celts there, these were pressed westwards to join the community of their fellow-Celts that had crossed over from Ireland.

" Of the stormy history of which such scattered fragments only can be recovered, the general influence on the future of Scotland may be thus abbreviated : As far as the Firth of Forth stretched Northumbria, where the Norse element predominated. It gradually combined with kindred elements on the side of England, while northward of the firth there was a combination with fresh invaders from Scandinavia, and a general pressure on any remains of Celtic inhabitancy, if there were such remains, along the north-eastern districts — a pressure driving them westward into the mountain district peopled by their Irish kindred. Orkney became a province of Norway, with a tendency to stretch the power of that state over the adjoining mainland. The Hebrides and other islands along the west coast, so far as they held out any inducement for permanent settlement to the Scandinavian colonists, had a seat of government in the Isle of Man."—Burton, *History of Scotland*, vol. i., pp. 317, 330.

[10] " Such is the account given us by the saga of this war. Marianus supplements it by telling us that in the year 1040, Donnchad, King of Scotia, was slain in autumn, on the 14th of August, by his general, Macbethad, son of Finnlaech, who succeeded him in the kingdom. Macbeth was at this time the Ri or Mormaor of the district of Myrhaevi or Moray, which finally became the seat of war, and when Duncan sent far and wide to the chieftains for aid, he probably came to his assistance with the men of Moray, and filled the place which Moddan had formerly occupied as commander of his army ; but the tie which united the mormaors of Moray with the kings of the Scots was still a very slender one. They had as often been subject to the Norwegian earls as they had been to the Scottish kings ; and when Duncan sustained this crushing defeat, and he saw that Thorfinn would now be able to maintain possession of his hereditary territories, the interests of the Mormaor of Moray seem to have prevailed over those of the commander of the king's army, and he was guilty of the treacherous act of slaying the unfortunate Duncan, and attaching his fortunes to those of Thorfinn.

" The authorities for the history of Macbeth knew nothing of Earl Thorfinn and his conquests. On the other hand, the sagas equally ignore Macbeth and his doings, and had to disguise the fact that Thorfinn was attacking his own cousin, and one who had derived his right to the kingdom from the same source from which Thorfinn had acquired his to the earldom of Caithness, by concealing his identity under the contemptuous name of Karl or Kali Hundason, while some of the chronicles have transferred to Macbeth what was true of Thorfinn, that he was also a grandson of King Malcolm, and a *Welsh Chronicle* denominates him King of Orkney. The truth seems to be that the conquest of the provinces south of Moray, which took place after this battle, was the joint work of Thorfinn and Macbeth, and that they divided the kingdom of the slain Duncan between them ; Thorfinn receiving the districts which had formerly been under his father, with the addition of those on the east coast extending as far as Fife or the Firth of Tay. According to the *Orkneyinga Saga*, he possessed ' nine earldoms in Scotland, the whole of the Sudreys, and a large riki in Ireland,' and this is confirmed by the *St. Olaf's Saga*, which tells us that ' he had the greatest riki of any earl of Orkney ; he possessed Shetland and the Orkneys, the Sudreys, and likewise a great riki in Scotland and Ireland.' Macbeth obtained those in which Duncan's strength mainly lay —

the district south and west of the Tay, with the central district in which Scone, the capital, is situated. Cumbria and Lothian probably remained faithful to the children of Duncan."— *Celtic Scotland*, vol. i., pp. 403–405.

To the existence of a Norwegian kingdom at this period lasting for thirty years, during which Macbeth ruled as a tributary of Thorfinn, I must equally demur. The chronicles of England, Scotland, and Ireland are silent upon this subject, whilst the sagas only say that Thorfinn plundered the country as far as Fife and returned to Caithness, where he dwelt " amongst the Gaddgedlar," every year fitting out a fleet for a course of piracy — the normal summer occupation of an Orkney jarl in that age. They make no allusion to his placing officers over the conquered districts, according to the invariable custom of the time ; and in describing his proceedings after his victory, their expressions are no stronger than upon the occasion of his marauding incursion upon England, with his nephew Rognwald, in the days of Hardacanute, when after a great victory the jarls are said to have ranged over all England in arms, slaying and burning in every quarter. The conqueror of Scotland, the main support of Macbeth, would have scarcely been obliged to yield a share in the Orkneys to his nephew Rognwald, backed by a force of *three ships ;* nor does Thorfinn seem to have been of a character to allow his dependent to assume the title of *king*, whilst he was contented with that of *jarl*. A king ruling under a jarl would have been a novelty in history. The support given to Macbeth by the Norwegians, and the presence of a Saxon army at Lumphanan, are equally dubious ; for the *Normans* mentioned in connection with Siward's expedition four years before, were Osbern Pentecost, Hugh, and others, who had sought refuge at the Court of Macbeth about two years before the appearance of the Anglo-Danish Earl. (Flor. Wig., 1054).—*Scotland under her Early Kings*, vol. ii., p. 478, 479.

[11] *Celtic Scotland*, vol. i., pp. 411–413. Professor Munch, in his *Histori et Chronicon Manniæ*, names these districts as Caithness, Sutherland, Ross, Moray, Buchan, Athol, Lorn, Argyle, and Galloway.

[12] It is hardly possible that the tangled tale of Macbeth's murder of Duncan and his usurpation of the throne of Scotia will ever be clearly unravelled, but this much seems tolerably certain, that Macbeth ruled in concert with the powerful Norse Earl Thorfinn, who succeeded Earl Melkoff or Malcolm at Whithorn, and, according to the *Chronicum Regum Manniæ*, " lived long at Gaddgeddli [Galloway], the place where England and Scotland meet." — Maxwell, *History of Dumfries and Galloway*, p. 43.

[13] We know, historically, that in the west, group after group of Norse invaders were absorbed into the Irish-speaking population. Although the Norsemen were conquerors of the Highland region, and gave it monarchs and lords, the more civilized language absorbed the ruder though fundamentally stronger, and all spoke the Irish tongue together. Thus, in language, the Teutonic became supreme in the eastern Lowlands, the Celtic among the western mountains. From a general view of the whole question, an impression — but nothing stronger than an impression — is conveyed, that the proportion of the Teutonic race that came into the use of the Gaelic is larger than the proportion of the Celtic race that came into the use of the Teutonic or Saxon. Perhaps students of physical ethnology may thus account for the contrasts of appearance in the Highlands ; in one district the people being large-limbed and fair, with hair inclined to red ; in others, small, lithe, and dusky, with black hair. — Burton, *History of Scotland*, vol. i., p. 207.

It is remarked by Worsaae [Jeus Jacob Asmussen Worsaae, *Account of the Danes and Northmen in England, Scotland, and Ireland*, 1851], that the language of the Lowlands of Scotland is so much like that of Scandinavia that seamen wrecked on the coasts of Jutland and Norway [are reputed to] have been able to converse without difficulty in their mother tongue with the people there [?]. Also, that the popular language of the Lowlands contains a still greater number of Scandinavian words and phrases than even the dialect of the North of England. He states, in addition, that the near relationship of the North Englishmen with the Danes and other Scandinavians is reflected both in popular songs and in the folk-lore, and is even more so in the Scottish Lowlands, whither great immigrations of Northmen took place. Modern Scandinavian has changed considerably ; but in the Icelandic, which is pure, its affinity with the ancient Scottish is great. The Lord's Prayer in the two languages, as given by Pinkerton, will show this. The orthography and pronunciation constitute the principal difference. It is obvious that the assimilation of Icelandic into Scottish was attended with no difficulty. It was considered by some writers — and truly so, we think, from the character and customs of the people, — that the Scandinavian poetry gave to the Scottish some of its wildness, added greatly to by the Celtic element. It is stated that the Scandinavian and the Scottish music scales are very similar. Worsaae mentions, as we have already stated, that it was a special trait of the Scandinavians that they very quickly accommodated themselves to the manners and customs of the countries where they settled. They even sometimes quite forgot their mother tongue, without, however, losing their original and characteristic national stamp. The well-known " raven," called the Danebrog of heathenism, which was borne for centuries, and viewed with superstitious awe in the British Isles as well as elsewhere, was not put aside for long after they became Christianized. According to Worsaae, it was borne until about A.D. 1100 ; but a Galloway legend brings it to a date some years later. — *Galloway, Ancient and Modern*, p. 112.

[14] Ayrshire is divided by the rivers Doon and Irvine into three districts — Carrick, Kyle, and Cunninghame. At what period these three were erected into a sheriffdom is not precisely known. Wyntoun, the venerable and generally accurate chronicler of Scotland, speaking of the wars of Alpin with the Picts, says :

> " He wan of were all Galluway ;
> Thare wes he slayne, and dede away."

As the death of Alpin occurred in 741, near Dalmellington, on the north banks of the Doon, it may be inferred that Ayrshire was then an integral part of Galloway. Yet, though this was the case, it is well known that there were no sheriffs under the purely Celtic rule of the country, which prevailed until the eleventh century ; and from charters of David I. it is evident that in his reign, if not previously, the boundaries of Galloway had been greatly limited. — Paterson, *History of the County of Ayr*, p. 1.

" Galloway anciently comprehended not only the country now known by that name, and the Stewartry of Kirkcudbright, but also the greatest part, if not the whole, of Ayrshire. It had its own princes and its own laws. It acknowledged, however, a feudatory dependence on Scotland. This dependence served only to supply the sovereign with rude undisciplined soldiers, who added rather to the terror than to the strength of his armies.

" Even at so late a period as the reign of Robert Bruce, the castle of Irvine was accounted to be in Galloway. There is reason to suppose that a people of Saxon origin encroached by degrees on the ancient Galloway. The names of places in Cuningham are generally Saxon. The name of the country itself is Saxon. In Kyle there is some mixture of Saxon. All the names in Carrick are purely Gaelic." — Lord Hailes, *Annals of Scotland*, vol. i., p. 118.

[15] We cannot, certainly, infer, from this *Life* [of Ninian] that there were any Picts in Galloway, at this period. Ninian, as will be elsewhere seen, goes from Whithorn into the country of the Southern Picts to convert that idolatrous people. . . . " There is extant," says Usher, " among our Irish, a *Life* of the same Ninian, in which he . . . is reported to have had, also, a brother, St. Plebeia by name, as we read in his *Life* by John of Tinmouth." — Ritson, *Annals of the Caledonians, Picts, etc.*, vol. ii., pp. 140, 141.

[16] In that region it is supposed in the western part of the island of Britain where the ocean stretching as an arm, and making, as it were, on either side two angles, divideth at this day [1150] the realms of the Scots and Angles, which, till these last times belonging to the Angles, is proved not only by historical record, but by actual memory of individuals to have had a king of its own.—Ailred, *Vita Niniani*, ch. i.

[17] Ailred, *Life of Ninian*, ch. iv.

[18] It is perhaps to Whithorn, therefore, alone among the towns of Scotland, that honour is due for having maintained the worship of the Almighty uninterrupted for fifteen hundred years.—Maxwell, *History of Dumfries and Galloway*, p. 3.

Whit-herne (Saxon) implies the white-house ; the signification, likewise, of *Louko-pibia* and *Candida-casa*. This famous mansion was situate upon the continental peninsula of Galloway, now Wigtonshire, where, or near which, Fergus, Lord of Galloway, between seven and eight centuries afterward, founded a priory of the same name ; and not (as has been asserted) upon the little island at the point of it. "Candida casa vocatur locus in extremis Angliæ juxta Scotiam finibus, ubi beatus Ninia requiescit, natione Britto, qui primus ibidem Christi prædicationem evangelizavit. Sanctum hunc Ninian præclarum virtutibus experta est antiquitas. Scribit, Alcuinus, in epistola ad fratres ejusdem loci dicens : Deprecor vestræ pietatis unanimitatem ut nostri nominis habeatis memoriam in ecclesia sanctissimi patris vestri Niniæ episcopi, qui multis claruit virtutibus, sicut mihi nuper delatum est per carmina matricæ artis, quæ nobis per fideles nostros discipulos Eboracensis ecclesiæ scholastica directa sunt, in quibus et facientis cognovi eruditionem, et facientis miracula sanctitatem." (William of Malmesbury, *De Ges. Pon.*, book iii.)—Ritson, *Annals of Galloway.*

[19] Maxwell, *History of Dumfries and Galloway*, p. 29.

[20] Bede, book v., ch. xxiii.

But the Attecott Picts did undergo about this time a very important change in their foreign relations. The successors of Edwin, King of Bernicia, became, as the price of their alliance, *ard-righ* or over-lords of Galloway, and under them the native chiefs ruled the people.—Maxwell, *History of Dumfries and Galloway*, p. 36.

That part of Galloway which lay along the sea-coast, or at the greatest distance from the seat of government, was now overrun by the Northumbrian Saxons who made settlements in it. The farms which are still styled Inglestons are thought to have derived their name from the Angles who then possessed them, and motes seem generally to have been in their vicinity. Those slaves whom they employed in tilling the ground were termed boors, and the places which they inhabited or occupied are still named Boorlands. The lands called "Carletons" also obtained their name from the ceorles, or middle class of society among the Saxons ; the thanes being the highest and the slaves the lowest.—Mackenzie, *History of Galloway*, vol. i., p. 130. These derivations are discussed by Mr. MacKerlie, who ascribes them to the Norse and Gaelic settlers, rather than to the Angles. See p. 247.

[21] 741, battle of Drum Cathmail between the Cruithnigh and the Dalriads against Innrechtach.—*Annals of Ulster.*

[22] While riding through a ford in Glenapp he was killed by a man hidden in a wood, and his burial-place is marked to this day by a large stone called *Laicht Alpin*, Alpin's Grave, which gives the name to the farm of Laicht on which it stands.—Maxwell, *History of Dumfries and Galloway*, p. 37.

He crossed from Kintyre to Ayr, and then moved southwards. A great deal of misconception has accompanied his movements. Wyntoun has been implicitly believed, who wrote his *Chronicle* about 700 years after the event, and has not been considered altogether trustworthy in regard to other matters. And he has rendered it—

> " He wan of werre all Galloway,
> There wes he slayne, and dede away."

The story of the devastation of the district rests on these lines. There is no doubt that he never overran Wigtonshire, nor was even in it. He was only on the borders of present Galloway, and there was slain, not in battle, as is generally supposed, but by an assassin who lay in wait for him at the place, near Loch Ryan, where the small burn separates Ayrshire from Wigtonshire. An upright pillar stone marks the spot, and was called Laicht Alpin, which in the Scoto-Irish means the *stone* or *grave of Alpin.*—*Galloway, Ancient and Modern*, p. 65.

[23] Bede, continuation of *Chronicle*, Anno 750.

Kyle, according to Buchanan, was so designated from Coilus, King of the Britons, who was slain and interred in the district.   The learned historian informs us that a civil war having ensued between the Britons who occupied the south and west of Scotland, and the Scots and the Picts, who were settled in the north and north-west, the opposing armies met near the banks of the Doon ; and that, by a stratagem, Coilus, who had dispatched a portion of his forces northward, was encompassed between the Scots and Picts, and completely routed.   He was pursued, overtaken, and slain in a field or moor, in the parish of Tarbolton, which still retains the name of Coilsfield, or Coilus's field.   Modern inquirers have regarded this as one of the fables of our early history.   Tradition corroborates the fact of some such battle having been fought.—Paterson, *History of the County of Ayr*, vol. i., p. 2.

[24] Eadberct's forces arrived in time to reinforce Innrechtach in pursuing Alpin's defeated army.   The result was that all Carrick and Kyle were added to the Northumbrian realm.   This was the high-tide mark of Saxon dominion in the north.   Its chronicles during the latter half of the eighth century show that the domestic difficulties of the Northumbrian over-lords of Galloway had become so pressing as to divert them from all thought of further conquest. —Maxwell, *History of Dumfries*, p. 38.

These nations had now resumed their normal relation to each other — east against west — the Picts and Angles again in alliance, and opposed to them the Britons and the Scots. Simeon of Durham tells us that in 744 a battle was fought between the Picts and the Britons, but by the Picts, Simeon usually understands the Picts of Galloway, and this battle seems to have followed the attack upon them by Alpin and his Scots.   It was followed by a combined attack upon the Britons of Alclyde by Eadberct of Northumbria, and Angus, king of the Picts.   The chronicle annexed to Bede tells us that in 750 Eadberct added the plain of Cyil with other regions to his kingdom.   This is evidently Kyle in Ayrshire, and the other regions were probably Carrick and Cuninghame, so that the king of Northumbria added to his possessions of Galloway on the north side of the Solway the whole of Ayrshire.—*Celtic Scotland*, vol. i., pp. 294–5.

Connected with the three divisions of Ayrshire there is the old rhyme of

> " Kyle for a man,
>   Carrick for a coo,
> Cuninghame for butter and cheese,
>   And Galloway for woo."

These, and similar popular and traditionary lines, are worthy of preservation ; as they constitute, as it were, popular landmarks in statistics, which supply a ready test to the changes that come over a district.   Some contend for a different reading, making

> " Carrick for a man,
>   Kyle for a cow,"

but the first would seem to be the proper one.   It is the one most general, and as old as the days of Bellenden.—Paterson, *History of the County of Ayr*, vol. i., p. 4.

[25] Gradually the Viking pirates crept round the Caledonian shores ; their black *kyuls* found as good shelter in the lochs of the west as in the fiords of Norway and the Baltic, whence they had sailed.   Iona fared no better than Lindisfarne, and now it seemed as if the pagan torch must fire the sacred shrine of St. Ninian at Whithorn.   But to the warlike prowess of their Attecott ancestors these Picts of Galloway seem to have added the talent of far-seeing diplomacy, by means of which the Norsemen, instead of desolating their land like the rest with fire and sword, were induced to fraternise with them and make common cause. What were the terms paid by Christians for their alliance with pagans can never now be revealed.   It is plain from the place-names of Norse origin scattered through the Stewartry and the shire, among those in Gaelic and Saxon speech, that there was a permanent Scandinavian settlement there, but we are left to imagine whether the relations between the two

races were those of over-lords and tributary, or whether they merely became fellow-pirates. At all events the connection cost the Galloway men the respect of other Celtic communities. The Irish chronicler, MacFirbis, declares that they renounced their baptism and had the customs of the Norsemen, and it is in the ninth century that they first appear mentioned as *Gallgaidhel*, or foreign Gaels, taking with the Vikings part in plundering and devastation. So it came to pass that their monastery of Candida Casa was spared.—Maxwell, *History of Dumfries and Galloway*, pp. 38, 39.

"What most hindered the complete reduction of the Danelaw was the hostility to the English rule of the states north of it, the hostility of Bernicia, of Strathclyde, and, above all, of the Scots. The confederacy against Æthelstan had been brought together by the intrigues of the Scot king, Constantine ; and though Constantine, in despair at his defeat, left the throne for a monastery, the policy of his son Malcolm was much the same as his father's. Eadmund was no sooner master of the Danelaw than he dealt with this difficulty in the north. The English blood of the Bernicians was probably drawing them at last to the English monarch, for after Brunanburh we hear nothing of their hostility. But Cumbria was far more important than Bernicia, for it was through Cumbrian territory that the Ostmen [of Ireland] could strike most easily across Britain into the Danelaw. . . .

"Under Eadberht the Northumbrian supremacy had reached as far as the district of Kyle in Ayrshire ; and the capture of Alclwyd by his allies, the Picts, in 756, seemed to leave the rest of Strathclyde at his mercy. But from that moment the tide had turned ; a great defeat shattered Eadberht's hopes ; and in the anarchy which followed his reign district after district must have been torn from the weakened grasp of Northumbria, till the cessation of the line of her bishops at Whithern (Badulf, the last bishop of Whithern of the Anglo-Saxon succession whose name is preserved, was consecrated in 791. Sim. Durh. *ad. ann.*) tells that her frontier had been pushed back almost to Carlisle. But even after the land that remained to her had been in English possession for nearly a century and a half it was still no English land. Its great land-owners were of English blood, and as the Church of Lindisfarne was richly endowed here, its priesthood was probably English too. But the conquered Cumbrians had been left by Ecgfrith on the soil, and in its local names we find few traces of any migration over moors from the east. . . .

"Along the Irish Channel the boats of the Norwegian pirates were as thick as those of the Danish corsairs on the eastern coast ; and the Isle of Man, which they conquered and half colonized, served as a starting-point from which the marauders made their way to the opposite shores. Their settlements reached as far northward as Dumfriesshire, and southward, perhaps, to the little group of northern villages which we find in the Cheshire peninsula of the Wirral. But it is the lake district and in the north of our Lancashire that they lie thickest. . . . While this outlier of northern life was being planted about the lakes, the Britons of Strathclyde were busy pushing their conquests to the south ; in Eadmund's day, indeed, we find their border carried as far as the Derwent ; but whether from the large space of Cumbrian ground they had won, or no, the name of Strathclyde from this time disappears, and is replaced by the name of Cumbria. Whether as Strathclyde or Cumbria, its rulers had been among the opponents of the West-Saxon advance ; they were among the confederates against Eadward as they were among the confederates against Æthelstan ; and it was no doubt in return for a like junction in the hostilities against himself that Eadmund, in 945, 'harried all Cumberland.' But he turned his new conquest adroitly to account by using it to bind to himself the most dangerous among his foes ; for he granted the greater part of it to the Scottish king, on the terms that Malcolm should be 'his fellow-worker by sea and land.' In the erection of this northern dependency we see the same forces acting, though on a more distant field, which had already begun the disintegration of the English realm in the formation of the great earldormanries of the eastern coast. Its immediate results, however, were advantageous enough. Scot and Welshman, whose league had till now formed the chief force of opposition to English supremacy in the north, were set at variance ; the road of the Ostman was closed, while the fidelity of the Scot king seemed to be secure by the impossibility of holding Cumbria against revolt without the support of his ' fellow-worker' in the south."—Green, *Conquest of England*, ch. vi., secs. 14–17.

[26] *Celtic Scotland*, vol. i., p. 132.

[27] Sir Herbert Maxwell, *History of Dumfries and Galloway*, p. 51.

In this battle, says Lambarde, " After that the bishop of Durham had exhorted the soldiers to fighte, the Scottes cryed out ' Albany ! Albany !' after their own manner, as thoughe al had bene theires. But the Englishe souldyours sent amongst them suche hayle of schott that after a whyle they turned their backes, and, in fine, theare was slayne of theim to the number of 11,000, and they weare, for their brag of Albany, mocked with ' Yry, Yry, Standard !' a terme of great reproach at that time, as Matthew Paris witnesseth " ; in whose work, however, no such thing is to be found.—Ritson, *Annals of Galloway*, p. 264.

[28] The enmity between the Strathclyde Britons and Ulstermen would tend to make the Galloway Picts throw in their lot with their congeners of Ulster, and no doubt intercourse between them was frequent and generally amicable, leading to intermarriage and relationship of blood. But there is not the least ground for believing that Galloway was overrun at this time in a hostile sense by the people from the opposite Irish coast.—Maxwell, *History of Dumfries and Galloway*, p. 36.

" The portion of the Pictish people which longest retained the name were the Picts of Galloway. Completely surrounded by the Britons of Strathclyde, and isolated from the rest of the Pictish nation, protected by a mountain barrier on the north, and the sea on the west and south, and remaining for centuries under the nominal dominion of the Angles of Northumbria, they maintained an isolated and semi-independent position in a corner of the island, and appear as a distinct people under the name of Picts as late as the twelfth century, when they formed one division of the Scottish army at the battle of the Standard. . . .

" We find, therefore, that in this remote district, in which the Picts remained under their distinctive names as a separate people as late as the twelfth century, a language considered the ancient language of Galloway was still spoken as late as the sixteenth century, and that language was Gaelic."—*Celtic Scotland*, vol. i., pp. 202–204.

[29] It will thus be seen that to those in North Antrim, the Mull of Kintyre, only fourteen miles distant, being in sight, and with countrymen already settled in Argyleshire, easy means offered for leaving Hibernia ; and, as recorded, a colony passed over in A.D. 498, under the leadership of Fergus Mor Mac Earca. . . . There is not such special mention to be found of the southern movement, but there cannot be a doubt that in the same way the Irish Scoti in Down, etc.—southern Dalriada—being opposite to Galloway, only twenty-two miles distant, and always more or less to be seen, except in thick weather, it offered an inducement for them to pass over there, and more particularly as communication seems to have existed previously with Galloway, which there is reason to believe was constant. That such an exodus took place is supported by the people found in Galloway after the Roman period. As we have already mentioned, Chalmers, in his *Caledonia*, gives the period of the settlement in the ninth and tenth centuries. We consider that it must have begun about the same time as the emigration to Argyleshire, while it was of a more gradual character, extending over several centuries, and not an immediate rush, which will account for not a vestige of authority as argued by Dr. Skene. It is, however, mentioned in the *Pictish Chronicle* that the settlement was made about A.D. 850 by stratagem, when they slew the chief inhabitants, which latter statement is likely enough ; but this conveys that they had been in Galloway for some time, and had become numerous, thus supporting what we have mentioned, that the colonization had been gradual.—*Galloway, Ancient and Modern*, pp. 52, 53.

[30] " Alpin, king of the Scots of Dalriada (not to be confused with him who perished in Glenapp in 741), had been expelled from his kingdom by the Northern Picts. His son Kenneth (in Gaelic, *Cinaedh*), afterwards renowned as Kenneth MacAlpin, had taken refuge in Galloway. By the help of his relatives there, and the co-operation of the Norsemen, he

was able to regain his kingdom of Dalriada and afterwards defeat the Northern Picts in the epoch-making battle of Fortrenn. . . .

"It has been plausibly suggested that the right which for many centuries afterwards was undoubtedly claimed by and conceded to the men of Galloway to march in the van of Scottish armies, was conferred on them by Kenneth MacAlpin in recognition of their services at this momentous time. The new king certainly gave proof of the value set upon these services by giving his daughter in marriage to a Galloway chief called Olaf the White.

"In the same year, 844, in which Kenneth was crowned King of Alban, the Gallgaidhel, or Picts of Galloway, assisted Olaf to seize the throne of Dublin.

"On the death of Kenneth MacAlpin in 860, Olaf made a determined attempt on the crown of Alban. Inheritance among the Picts was invariably through the female line. Olaf's wife, being daughter to Kenneth, gave him a better claim under Pictish law than Kenneth's son Constantin. In company with Imhair, Olaf captured Dumbarton in 872, and held a great part of Alban, retreating with much booty and many captives to Galloway, whence the whole party sailed in two hundred ships to Dublin."—Maxwell, *History of Dumfries and Galloway*, pp. 40, 41.

[31] The name of Heathored occurs as the last amongst the bishops of Whithern in Flor. Wig. App., and his predecessor, Badwulf, is alluded to by Sim. Dun. under 796. The topography of Galloway and the language once spoken by the Galwegians (who acknowledged a Kenkinny — Cen-Cinnidh — not a Pen-cenedl) distinguish them from the British race of Strathclyde—the Walenses of the early charters as opposed to the Galwalenses. Beda, however, knew of no Picts in the diocese of Candida Casa (*v.* Appendix K), and consequently they must have arrived at some later period, though it would be difficult to point with certainty to their original home. Some authorities bring them from Dalriada, making them Cruithne or Irish Picts; and the dedication of numerous churches in Galloway to saints popular in the northeast of Uladh seems to favor their conjecture. The name of Galloway is probably traceable to its occupation by Gall, in this case Anglian strangers.—Robertson, *Scotland under her Early Kings*, vol. i., p. 21.

[32] A mighty devastation of Strathclyde and Galloway is recorded in 875 by Simeon of Durham, and this is corroborated in the *Annals of Ulster*, where reference is made to a bloody defeat of the Picts by the Dubhgall or Danes.

[33] "The next important personage to appear in Galloway history is Ronald the Dane, titular King of Northumbria, styled also Duke of the Galwegians, in right of the ancient superiority of the Saxon kings over the Picts. With Olaf of the Brogues (Anlaf Cuaran), grandson of Olaf the White, as his lieutenant, he drove the Saxons before him as far south as Tamworth. This was in 937, but in 944 the tide of victory rolled north again. King Eadmund drove Ronald out of Northumbria to take refuge in Galloway. Of this province he and his sons continued rulers till the close of the tenth century. But these were Dubhgalls or Danes, and they now fell to war with the Fingalls or Norse, who possessed themselves of the province. Galloway, on account of its central position between Ireland, Cumbria, and Strathclyde, and still more because of its numerous shallow bays and sandy inlets, so convenient for Viking galleys, was then in higher esteem than it has ever been since among maritime powers.

"Sigurd the Stout, Earl of Orkney, grandson of Thorfinn the Skull-cleaver, was Lord of Galloway in 1008. His resident lieutenant was a native prince, Malcolm, whose name appears in the sagas as Earl Melkoff."—*History of Dumfries and Galloway*, p. 42.

[34] "In 1057 Malcolm Canmore—son of the murdered Duncan,—attacked the usurper Macbeth, defeated and slew him and became King Malcolm III., of Scotia. The great Earl Thorfinn having died in the same year, Malcolm most prudently married his widow Ingibiorg, of the Pictish race, thereby bringing under his rule the Norse districts of Scotland, including Galloway. Consolidation was now the order of the day. The Norse influence, undermined by the effects of the battle of Clontarf, was steadily on the wane. The island

of Britain, soaked as it was with centuries of bloodshed, was resolving itself into the two main dominions of England and Scotland — a process which the Church, relieved from oppression by the pagan Norsemen, lent her influence to accelerate. The native rulers of Galloway showed some hesitation as to the realm into which they would seek admission. Tradition and custom tempted them to union with their old over-lords the Saxon earls of Northumbria ; but the Saxon power was waning, as the Roman and the Norse had waned before. Geography as well as linguistic and racial affinity turned the scale, and the Galwegians became lieges of the Scottish king.

"In this manner closed the dominion of the Norsemen over Galloway, and such parts along the Solway shore of Dumfriesshire as they had been able to hold by force. Their strength ever lay in their ships, but of their handiwork some traces probably remain in a peculiar kind of cliff tower, which may be seen at various parts of the coast, such as Castle Feather and Cardhidoun near the Isle of Whithorn, and Port Castle on the shore of Glasserton parish."—Maxwell, pp. 43, 44.

[35] "Gallwallia or Galwedia is termed in the *Irish Annals* Gallgaedhel, a name also applied to the people of the Isles. The name of Galwedia in its more extended sense consisted of the districts extending from Solway to the Clyde ; but in its limited sense, in which it is used here, it is co-extensive with the modern counties of Wigton and Kirkcudbright. In the Norse sagas it is termed Gaddgeddli.

"Both districts of Ergadia and Gallwallia appear to have been to a great extent occupied by the Norwegians down to the period when these 'reguli' first appear. At the battle of Cluantarf in 1014, there is mention of the Galls or foreigners of Man, Sky, Lewis, Cantire, and Airergaidhel (*Wars of Gaedel with the Galls*, p. 153). Thorfinn, the Earl of Orkney, when he conquered the nine 'rikis' in Scotland in 1034, included in his possessions Dali or Ergadia, and Gaddgedli or Galloway, and in the same year the *Irish Annals* record the death of 'Suibhne mac Cinaeda ri Gallgaidel.' Though Thorfinn's kingdom in Scotland terminated in 1604, when it is said that 'many rikis which he had subjected fell off, and their inhabitants sought the protection of those native chiefs who were territorially born to rule over them' (*Coll. de Reb. Alb.*, p. 346), the Norwegians appear to have retained a hold of Ergadia and Galwedia for nearly a century after, as we find in the *Irish Annals* mention made in 1154 of the fleets of Gallgaedel, Arann, Cintyre, Mann, and the Centair Alban, or seaboard of Alban, under the command of Macscelling, a Norwegian (*Annals of the Four Masters*, 1154). Mac Vurich likewise states that before Somerled's time, 'all the islands from Mannan (Man) to Arca (Orkneys), and all the bordering country from Dun Breatan (Dumbarton) to Cata (Caithness) in the north, were in the possession of the Lochlannach (Norwegians), and such as remained of the Gaedel of those lands protected themselves in the woods or mountains'; and in narrating the exploits of Somerled, he says 'he did not cease till he had cleared the western side of Alban from the Lochlannach.'

"It seems probable, therefore, that the natives of Ergadia and Gallwallia had risen under Somerled and Fergus, and had finally expelled the Norwegians from their coasts, and that owing to the long possession of the country by the Norwegians, all trace of their parentage had disappeared from the annals of the country, and they were viewed as the founders of a new race of native lords.

"The two districts appear, however, closely connected with each other in the various attempts made by the Gaedheal against the ruling authority in Scotland."—Skene, *Fordun*, vol. ii., p. 431.

[36] Much less equivocal are the remains of Scandinavian occupation preserved in the place-names of the south-west. Many hills still bear the title "fell"—the Norse *fjall*— often pleonastically prefixed to the Gaelic *barr*, as in Fell o' Barhullion, in Glasserton parish, or disguised as a mere suffix, as in Criffel. The well-known test-syllable *by*, a village, farm, or dwelling, so characteristic of Danish rather than of Norse occupation, takes the place in southern districts which *bolstadr* holds in northern. Lockerby, the dwelling of Locard or

Lockhart, Canonbie, and Middlebie in Dumfriesshire—Busby, Sorby, and Corsbie in Wigtonshire—are instances in point. *Vik*, a creek or small bay, gives the name to Southwick parish and Senwick (*sand vik*, sandy bay); and *n'es*, a cape, appears in Sinniness (*sunnr n'es*, south point) and Borness (*borh n'es*, burgh or fort point); but Auchness is in another language, being the Gaelic *each inis*, horse-pasture. Pastoral occupation is implied in Fairgirth (*faer gardr*, sheep-fold); but Cogarth, the cow-pen, is more probably Saxon than Scandinavian, for though in modern Danish "cow" is *ko*, in old Norse it was *kyr*. Tinwald, like Dingwall in the north, is *þinga vollr*, the assembly-field, and Mouswald, *mosi vollr*, the moss-field.—Maxwell, *Dumfries and Galloway*, pp. 44, 45.

CHAPTER XVIII

THE ANGLES

RETURNING again to the subject of Macbeth's so-called usurpation, it may be stated that, in addition to the causes already suggested as leading to his revolt, we find another reason given by some of the early chroniclers in apparent justification of his conduct in slaying Duncan and possessing himself of that ruler's kingdom. This explanation is, that Macbeth's wife, Gruoch, was the daughter of that Boete (or Boedhe) MacKenneth whose son was slain by King Malcolm MacKenneth about 1033, in order to prepare the way for the peaceable ascension to the throne of his own daughter's son, Duncan.[1]

The title of Boete's heirs to the crown, according to the customary order of descent at that time, was superior to that of Malcolm's heirs. Therefore, it has been contended that, as Malcolm had wrongfully removed Boete's son by killing him, and thus made the way clear for the succession of his own grandson, it was not unnatural that the claims of the latter should be contested by the other heirs of Boete and their representatives.[2] Besides the son whom Malcolm killed, Boete had left also a daughter, Gruoch, who married into the family of the Mormaors of Moray, carrying her claims with her. Her husband, Gilcomgain mac Maelbrigdi mac Ruaidhri, was slain in a family quarrel, but left a son by Gruoch, named Lulach, an infant, who thus represented the line of King Kenneth MacDuff. Gruoch next married Macbeth mac Finley mac Ruaidhri, (second cousin to Gilcomgain) who had succeeded to the mormaorship of Moray. By the hitherto prevalent Pictish system of alternation, Lulach was the rightful king; and as guardian and representative of his stepson, Macbeth stood for the child's claims on the Scottish crown, as against Duncan, son of Malcolm's daughter, Bethoc, by Crinan.[3]

Macbeth reigned for about seventeen years, and the contemporary records of the period all seem to indicate that his rule was one of considerable benefit to the kingdom.[4] In 1045 an attempt was made by Crinan, the father of Duncan, to dethrone Macbeth; but it proved abortive, resulting in the death of Crinan [5] and, in consequence, the more secure possession of the crown by Macbeth. In 1050 the latter made a pilgrimage to Rome.[6]

In 1054, Siward, the Danish earl of Northumbria, a close connection of the family of Duncan,[7] led an army into Scotland against Macbeth, in the interests of Duncan's son, Malcolm, and perhaps at the instance of Edward, King of England.[8] Although not then successful in recovering the central kingdom, Siward succeeded in confirming Malcolm as ruler of all that portion of Scotland south of the Clyde and Forth.[9] Siward died in 1055, however, and Malcolm was not able to push his cause further until 1057. In that year he formed an alliance with Tostig, who was the son of Earl Godwin and successor to Siward as ruler of Northumberland.   Then taking advantage of the death of Thorfinn, Macbeth's most powerful coadjutor, the allies again entered the domain of the latter and on the 15th of August, 1057, Malcolm killed Macbeth in battle at Lumphanan.[10]

Malcolm then ascended the throne.   Having married Ingiborg, widow of Thorfinn, he seems soon afterwards to have united the different states of the north into the single kingdom of Scotia.   Within a few years he became so powerful as to attempt the invasion of England.[11]   In 1068-9, Ingiborg apparently having died in the meantime, he married Margaret,[12] sister of Edgar Ætheling, the Saxon heir to the English crown, who with his family and followers, had been driven out of England after the coming of the Normans in 1066, and had taken refuge in Scotland.

This King Malcolm is known in history as Malcolm Canmore, so named from the size of his head, the Celtic words " cean mohr " meaning " head big."   The possession of the Anglian province of Northumbria known as Lothian, which had been ceded to his great-grandfather, Malcolm mac Kenneth, after the battle of Carham in 1018, in Malcolm Canmore, became definitely confirmed to the crown of Scotland.[13]   This union resulted in bringing under one government the Teutonic races of the eastern, northern, and western coasts, and the Celtic Gaels and Cymri of Galloway, Strathclyde, and Scotia proper.   Malcolm's marriages, first with Ingiborg the Norse jarl's widow, and secondly, with Margaret, daughter of the Saxon royal family, may be taken as presaging the union of races that was to follow in Scotland.[14]   As the most substantial and enduring attributes of Scottish civilization owe their origin to this amalgamation, and are in a great measure due to the infusion of Teutonic blood into the veins of the Celt, we cannot do better in this connection than to consider at length the nature and extent of the English elements entering into the composition of the feudal Scotchman.

Having already sketched the rise and progress of the Norwegian power in the north and west, one considerable source of the Teutonic stream, it now remains only to inquire into the history of Northumbria, the northern province of which in Malcolm's time became firmly united with Scotland, forming the modern counties of Haddington, Roxburgh, Linlithgow, Edinburgh, Berwick, etc.   It has been deemed proper to give this history in the form of extracts from the early annals relating to Britain and Northumbria, so far as these are preserved in the history of Gildas, the works of Bede, and in the *English Chronicle*, these three being our chief authorities for early English history.   Inasmuch as the record of the English conquest of North Britain does not begin until the year 547, the history of the preceding century—aside from the brief descriptions of Nennius already given, and similar references to be found in the Welsh Book of the Princes (*Brut y Tywysogion*), and the *Annales Cambriæ* — can only be inferred from such records as remain of the earlier English conquest of the southern portions of the island.

The history of Gildas was written about 556–560 ; that of Bede about 731 ; and the English or Anglo-Saxon Chronicle is the work of various hands between Bede's time and the middle of the twelfth century, the earliest copies extant bearing evidences of a date some years prior to 900.

GILDAS — HISTORY OF BRITAIN *

§ 23. Then all the councillors, together with that proud tyrant Gurth-rigern [Vortigern], the British king, were so blinded, that, as a protection to their country, they sealed its doom by inviting in among them (like wolves into the sheep-fold) the fierce and impious Saxons, a race hateful both to God and men, to repel the invasions of the northern nations. Nothing was ever so pernicious to our country, nothing was ever so unlucky. What palpable darkness must have enveloped their minds — darkness desperate and cruel ! Those very people whom, when absent, they dreaded more than death itself, were invited to reside, as one may say, under the selfsame roof. Foolish are the princes, as it is said, of Thafneos, giving counsel to unwise Pharaoh. A multitude of whelps came forth from the lair of this barbaric lioness, in three *cyuls*, as they call them, that is, in three ships of war, with their sails wafted by the wind and with omens and prophecies favorable, for it was foretold by a certain soothsayer among them, that they should occupy the country to which they were sailing three hundred years, and half of that time, a hundred and fifty years, should plunder and despoil the same. They first landed on the eastern side of the island, by the invitation of the unlucky king, and there fixed their sharp talons, apparently to fight in favor of the island, but, alas ! more truly against it. Their mother-land, finding her first brood thus successful, sends forth a larger company of her wolfish offspring, which, sailing over, join themselves to their bastard-born comrades. From that time the germ of iniquity and the root of contention planted their poison amongst us, as we deserved, and shot forth into leaves and branches. The barbarians being thus introduced as soldiers into the island, to encounter, as they falsely said, any dangers in defence of their hospitable entertainers, obtain an allowance of provisions, which, for some time being plentifully bestowed, stopped their doggish mouths. Yet they complain that their monthly supplies are not furnished in sufficient abundance, and they indus-triously aggravate each occasion of quarrel, saying that unless more liberality is shown them, they will break the treaty and plunder the whole island. In a short time, they follow up their threats with deeds.

§ 24. For the fire of vengeance, justly kindled by former crimes, spread from sea to sea, fed by the hands of our foes in the east, and did not cease, until, destroying the neighboring towns and lands, it reached the other side of the island, and dipped its red and savage tongue in the western ocean. In these assaults, therefore, not unlike that of the Assyrian upon Judea, was fulfilled in our case what the prophet describes in words of lamentation : " They have burned with fire the sanctuary ; they have polluted on earth the tabernacle of thy name." And again, " O God, the Gentiles have come into thine inheritance ; Thy holy temple have they defiled," etc. So that all the columns were levelled with the ground by the frequent strokes of the

* See also pp. 200–202.

battering-ram, all the husbandmen routed, together with their bishops, priests, and people, whilst the sword gleamed, and the frames crackled around them on every side. Lamentable to behold, in the midst of the streets lay the tops of lofty towers, tumbled to the ground, stones of high walls, holy altars, fragments of human bodies, covered with livid clots of coagulated blood, looking as if they had been squeezed together in a press ; and with no chance of being buried, save in the ruins of the houses, or in the ravening bellies of wild beasts and birds ; with reverence be it spoken for their blessed souls, if, indeed, there were many found who were carried, at that time, into the high heaven by the holy angels. So entirely had the vintage, once so fine, degenerated and become bitter, that, in the words of the prophet, there was hardly a grape or ear of corn to be seen where the husbandman had turned his back.

§ 25. Some, therefore, of the miserable remnant, being taken in the mountains, were murdered in great numbers ; others, constrained by famine, came and yielded themselves to be slaves for ever to their foes, running the risk of being instantly slain, which truly was the greatest favor that could be offered them : some others passed beyond the seas with loud lamentations instead of the voice of exhortation. "Thou hast given us as sheep to be slaughtered, and among the Gentiles hast thou dispersed us." Others, committing the safeguard of their lives, which were in continual jeopardy, to the mountains, precipices, thickly wooded forests, and to the rocks of the seas (albeit with trembling hearts), remained still in their country.[15] But in the meanwhile, an opportunity happening, when these most cruel robbers were returned home, the poor remnants of our nation (to whom flocked from divers places round about our miserable countrymen as fast as bees to their hives, for fear of an ensuing storm), being strengthened by God, calling upon him with all their hearts, as the poet says, "With their unnumbered vows they burden heaven," that they might not be brought to utter destruction, took arms under the conduct of Ambrosius Aurelianus, a modest man, who of all the Roman nation was then alone in the confusion of this troubled period by chance left alive. His parents, who for their merit were adorned with the purple, had been slain in these same broils, and now his progeny in these our days, although shamefully degenerated from the worthiness of their ancestors, provoke to battle their cruel conquerors, and by the goodness of our Lord obtain the victory.

§ 26. After this, sometimes our countrymen, sometimes the enemy, won the field, to the end that our Lord might in this land try after his accustomed manner these his Israelites, whether they loved him or not, until the year of the siege of Bath-hill, when took place also the last almost, though not the least slaughter of our cruel foes, which was (as I am sure) forty-four years and one month after the landing of the Saxons, and also the time of my own nativity. And yet neither to this day are the cities of our country inhabited as before, but being forsaken and overthrown, still lie desolate ; our foreign wars having ceased, but our civil troubles still remaining. For as well the remembrance of such a terrible desolation of the island, as also of the unexpected recovery of the same, remained in the minds of those who were eye-witnesses of the wonderful events of both, and in regard thereof, kings, public magistrates, and private persons, with priests and clergymen, did all and every one of them live orderly according to their several vocations. But when these had departed out of this world, and a new race succeeded, who were ignorant of this troublesome time, and had only experience of the present prosperity, all the laws of truth and justice were so shaken and subverted that not so much as a vestige or remembrance of these virtues remained among the above-named orders of men, except among a very few who, compared with the great multitude which were daily rushing headlong down to hell, are accounted so small a number, that our reverend mother the church, scarcely beholds them, her only true children, reposing in her bosom.

NENNIUS — GENEALOGIES OF THE KINGS, ETC.

§ 57. (Bernicia)—Woden begat Beldeg, who begat Beornec, who begat Gethbrond, who begat Aluson, who begat Ingwi, who begat Edibrith, who begat Esa, who begat Eoppa, who begat Ida. But Ida had twelve sons, Adda, Belric, Theodric, Ethelric, Theodhere, Osmer, and one queen, Bearnoch, Ealric. Ethelric begat Ethelfrid : the same is Aedlfred Flesaur. For he also had seven sons, Eanfrid, Oswald, Oswin, Oswy, Oswudu, Oslac, Offa. Oswy begat Alfrid, Elfwin, and Ecgfrid. Ecgfrid is he who made war against his cousin Brudei, king of the Picts, and he fell therein with all the strength of his army, and the Picts with their king gained the victory ; and the Saxons never again reduced the Picts so as to exact tribute from them. Since the time of this war it is called Gueithlin Garan.

But Oswy had two wives, Riemmelth, the daughter of Royth, son of Rum ; and Eanfled, the daughter of Edwin, son of Alla.

§ 58. (Kent)—Hengist begat Octa, who begat Ossa, who begat Eormenric, who begat Ethelbert, who begat Eadbald, who begat Ercombert, who begat Egbert.

§ 59. (East Anglia)—Woden begat Casser, who begat Titinon, who begat Trigil, who begat Rodmunt, who begat Rippa, who begat Guillem Guercha, [Uffa, or Wuffa] who was the first king of the East Angles. Guercha begat Uffa, who begat Tytillus, who begat Eni, who begat Edric, who begat Aldwulf, who begat Elric.

§ 60. (Mercia)—Woden begat Guedolgeat, who begat Gueagon, who begat Guithleg, who begat Guerdmund, who begat Ossa, who begat Ongen, who begat Eamer, who begat Pubba. This Pubba had twelve sons, of whom two are better known to me than the others, that is Penda and Eawa. Eadlit is the son of Pantha, Penda, son of Pubba, Ealbald, son of Alguing, son of Eawa, son of Penda, son of Pubba. Egfert son of Offa, son of Thingferth, son of Enwulf, son of Ossulf, son of Eawa, son of Pubba.

§ 61. (Deira)—Woden begat Beldeg, Brond begat Siggar, who begat Sibald, who begat Zegulf, who begat Soemil, who first separated Deur from Berneich [Deira from Bernicia]. Soemil begat Sguerthing, who begat Giulglis, who begat Ulfrea, who begat Iffi, who begat Ulli, Edwin, Osfrid, and Eanfrid. There were two sons of Edwin, who fell with him in battle at Meicen, and the kingdom was never renewed in his family, because not one of his race escaped from that war ; but all were slain with him by the army of Catguollaunus, king of the Guenedota [Cadwalla, king of the western Britons], Oswy begat Ecgfrid, the same is Ailguin, who begat Oslach, who begat Alhun, who begat Adlsing who begat Echun, who begat Oslaph. Ida begat Eadric, who begat Ecgulf, who begat Leodwald, who begat Eata, the same is Glinmaur, who begat Eadbert and Egbert, who was the first bishop of their nation.

Ida, the son of Eoppa, possessed countries on the left-hand side of Britain, *i. e.*, of the Humbrian sea, and reigned twelve years, and united Dynguayth Guarth-Berneich [Deira and Bernicia].

§ 62. Then Dutigirn at that time fought bravely against the nation of the Angles. At that time Talhaiarn Cataguen was famed for poetry, and Neirin, and Taliesin, and Bluchbard, and Cian, who is called Guenith Guaut, were all famous at the same time in British poetry.

The great king, Mailcun, reigned among the Britons, *i. e.*, in the district of Guenedota, because his great-great-grandfather, Cunedda, with his twelve sons, had come before from the left-hand part, *i. e.*, from the country which is called Manau Gustodin, one hundred and forty-six years before Mailcun reigned, and expelled the Scots with much slaughter from those countries, and they never returned again to inhabit them.

§ 63. Adda, son of Ida, reigned eight years ; Ethelric, son of Adda, reigned four years. Theodoric, son of Ida, reigned seven years. Freothwulf reigned six years. In whose time the kingdom of Kent, by the mission of Gregory, received baptism. Hussa reigned seven years. Against him fought four kings, Urien, and Ryderthen, and Guallauc, and Morcant. Theodoric fought bravely, together with his sons, against that Urien. But at that time sometimes the enemy and sometimes our countrymen were defeated, and he shut them up three days and three nights in the island of Metcaut ; and whilst he was on an expedition he was murdered, at the instance of Morcant, out of envy, because he possessed so much superiority over all the kings in military science. Eadfered Flesaurs reigned twelve years in Bernicia, and twelve others in Deira, and gave to his wife, Bebba, the town of Dynguoaroy, which from her is called Bebbanburg [Bamborough].

Edwin, son of Alla, reigned seventeen years, seized on Elmete, and expelled Cerdic, its king. Eanfled, his daughter, received baptism, on the twelfth day after Pentecost, with all her followers, both men and women. The following Easter Edwin himself received baptism, and twelve thousand of his subjects with him. If any one wishes to know who baptized them, it was Rum Map Urbgen [Rhun, son of Urien] : he was engaged forty days in baptizing all classes of the Saxons, and by his preaching many believed on Christ.

§ 64. Oswald, son of Ethelfrid, reigned nine years ; the same is Oswald Llauiguin ; he slew Catgublaun [Cadwalla], king of Guenedot, in the battle of Catscaul, with much loss to his own army. Oswy, son of Ethelfrid, reigned twenty-eight years and six months. During his reign there was a dreadful mortality among his subjects, when Catgualart [Cadwallader] was king among the Britons, succeeding his father, and he himself died amongst the rest. He slew Penda in the field of Gai, and now took place the slaughter of Gai Campi, and the kings of the Britons, who went out with Penda on the expedition as far as the city of Judeu, were slain.

§ 65. Then Oswy restored all the wealth, which was with him in the city, to Penda ; who distributed it among the kings of the Britons, that is, Atbert Judeu. But Catgabail alone, king of Guenedot, rising up in the night, escaped, together with his army, wherefore he was called Catgabail Catguommed. Ecgfrid, son of Oswy, reigned nine years. In his time the holy bishop Cuthbert died in the island of Medcaut. It was he who made war against the Picts, and was by them slain.

Penda, son of Pybba, reigned ten years ; he first separated the kingdom of Mercia from that, of the Northmen, and slew by treachery Anna, king of the East Anglians, and St. Oswald, king of the Northmen. He fought the battle of Cocboy, in which fell Eawa, son of Pybba, his brother, king of the Mercians, and Oswald, king of the Northmen, and he gained the victory by diabolical agency. He was not baptized, and never believed in God.

§ 66. From the beginning of the world to Constantius and Rufus, are found to be five thousand, six hundred and fifty-eight years.

Also from the two consuls, Rufus and Rubelius, to the consul Stilicho, are three hundred and seventy-three years.

Also from Stilicho to Valentinian, son of Placida, and the reign of Vortigern, are twenty-eight years.

And from the reign of Vortigern to the quarrel between Guitolinus and Ambrosius, are twelve years, which is Guoloppum, that is Catgwaloph. Vortigern reigned in Britain when Theodosius and Valentinian were consuls, and in the fourth year of his reign the Saxons came to Britain, in the consulship of Felix and Taurus, in the four hundredth year from the incarnation of our Lord Jesus Christ.

From the year in which the Saxons came into Britain, and were received by Vortigern, to the time of Decius and Valerian, are sixty-nine years.

THE VENERABLE BEDE'S ECCLESIASTICAL HISTORY

Bede, or Beda, surnamed, on account of his learning and piety, " Venerable," was born about the year 673, probably in what is now the parish of Monkton, near Wearmouth, in Durham. He was educated in the monastery of St. Peter at Wearmouth, and after his twentieth year removed to the neighboring monastery of St. Paul at Jarrow, where he died about 735. His most valuable work is the *Historia Ecclesiastica Gentis Anglorum*, an ecclesiastical history of England in five books, to which we are indebted for almost all our information on the early history of England before the year 731. Bede gained the materials for this work partly from Roman writers, but chiefly from native chronicles and biographies, records, and public documents, and oral and written communications from his contemporaries. King Ælfred translated it into Anglo-Saxon.

Bede's chief sources for the description of Britain are Pliny, Solinus, Orosius, and Gildas; St. Basil is also cited; and the traditions which were current in Bede's own day are occasionally introduced. The history of the Romans in Britain is founded chiefly upon Orosius, Eutropius, and Gildas, corrected in some places by the author, apparently from tradition or local information. Documents pre-existing in an historical form are occasionally quoted, among those of which use has been made being the *Life of Gregory the Great*, written by Paulus Diaconus; the *Miracles of Ethelberga, Abbess of Barking ;* the *Life of Sebbi,* king of the East Saxons ; the *Legend of Fursey ;* the *Legend of Cuthbert of Lindisfarne ;* and the *Treatise* of Arculf *De Locis Sanctis.*

The author seems to have been at work on his History down to the time of his death. The following extracts are made from Giles's translation :

BOOK I., CHAPTER I.—This island at present, following the number of the books in which the Divine law was written, contains five nations, the English, Britons, Scots, Picts, and Latins, each in its own peculiar dialect cultivating the sublime study of Divine truth. The Latin tongue is, by the study of the Scriptures, become common to all the rest. At first this island had no other inhabitants but the Britons, from whom it derived its name, and who, coming over into Britain, as is reported, from Armorica, possessed themselves of the southern parts thereof. When they, beginning at the south, had made themselves masters of the greatest part of the island, it happened, that the nation of the Picts, from Scythia, as is reported, putting to sea, in a few long ships, were driven by the winds beyond the shores of Britain, and arrived on the northern coasts of Ireland, where, finding the nation of the Scots, they begged to be allowed to settle among them, but could not succeed in obtaining their request. Ireland is the greatest island next to Britain, and lies to the west of it ; but as it is shorter than Britain to the north, so, on the other hand, it runs out far beyond it to the south, opposite to the northern parts of Spain, though a spacious sea lies between them. The Picts, as has been said, arriving in this island by sea, desired to have a place granted them in which they might settle. The Scots answered that the island could not contain them both ; but "We can give you good advice," said they, "what to do ; we know there is another island, not far from ours, to the eastward, which we often see at a distance, when the days are clear. If you will go thither, you will obtain settlements ; or, if they should oppose you, you shall have our assistance." The Picts, accordingly, sailing over into Britain, began to inhabit the northern parts thereof, for the Britons were possessed of the southern. Now the Picts had no wives, and asked them of the Scots ; who would not consent to grant them upon any other terms, than that when any difficulty should arise, they should choose a king from the female royal race rather than from the male : which custom, as is well known, has been observed among the Picts to this day. In process of time, Britain, besides the Britons and Picts, received a third nation, the Scots, who, migrating from Ireland under their leader, Reuda, either by fair means, or by force of arms, secured to themselves those settlements among the Picts which they still possess. From the name of their commander, they are to this day called Dalreudins ; for, in their language, Dal signifies a part. Ireland, in breadth, and for wholesomeness and serenity of climate, far surpasses Britain. . . . It is properly the country of the Scots, who migrating from thence, as has been said, added a third nation in Britain to the Britons and the Picts. There is a very large gulf of the sea which formerly divided the nation of the Picts from the Britons ; which gulf [the Firth of Clyde] runs from the west very far into the land, where, to this day, stands the strong city of the Britons, called Alcluith. The Scots arriving on the north side of this bay, settled themselves there.

CHAPTER XI.—In the year 407, Honorius, the younger son of Theodosius, and the forty-fourth from Augustus, being emperor, two years before the invasion of Rome by Alaric, king of the Goths, when the nations of the Alani, Suevi, Vandals, and many others with them, having defeated the Franks and passed the Rhine, ravaged all Gaul, Gratianus Municeps was set up as tyrant and killed. In his place, Constantine, one of the meanest soldiers, only for his name's sake, and without any worth to recommend him, was chosen emperor. As soon as he had taken upon him the command, he passed over into France, where being often imposed upon by the barbarians with faithless treaties, he caused much injury to the Commonwealth. Whereupon Count Constantius, by the command of Honorius, marching into Gaul with an army, besieged him in the city of Arles, and put him to death. His son Constans, whom of a monk he had created Cæsar, was also put to death by his own Count Gerontius, at Vienne.

Rome was taken by the Goths, in the year from its foundation, 1164.

Then the Romans ceased to rule in Britain, almost 470 years after Caius Julius Cæsar entered the island. They resided within the rampart, which, as we have mentioned, Severus made across the island, on the south side of it, as the cities, temples, bridges, and paved roads there made, testify to this day ; but they had a right of dominion over the farther parts of Britain, as also over the islands that are beyond Britain.

CHAPTER XII.—From that time, the south part of Britain, destitute of armed soldiers, of martial stores, and of all its active youth, which had been led away by the rashness of the tyrants, never to return, was wholly exposed to rapine, as being totally ignorant of the use of weapons. Whereupon they suffered many years under two very savage foreign nations, the Scots from the west, and the Picts from the north. We call these foreign nations, not on account of their being seated out of Britain, but because they were re- mote from that part of it which was possessed by the Britons ; two inlets of the sea lying between them, one of which runs in far and broad into the land of Britain, from the Eastern Ocean, and the other from the Western, though they do not reach so as to touch one another. The eastern has in the midst of it the city Giudi. The western has on it, that is, on the right hand thereof, the city Alcluith, which in their language signifies the Rock Cluith [Clyde], for it is close by the river of that name.

On account of the irruption of these nations, the Britons sent messengers to Rome with letters in mournful manner, praying for succours, and promis- ing perpetual subjection, provided that the impending enemy should be driven away. An armed legion was immediately sent them, which, arriving in the island, and engaging the enemy, slew a great multitude of them, drove the rest out of the territories of their allies, and having delivered them from their cruel oppressors, advised them to build a wall between the two seas across the island, that it might secure them, and keep off the enemy ; and thus they returned home with great triumph. The islanders raising the wall, as they had been directed, not of stone, as having no artist capable of such a work, but of sods, made it of no use. However, they drew it for many miles between the two bays or inlets of the seas, which we have spoken of ; to the end that where the defence of the water was wanting, they might use the rampart to defend their borders from the irruptions of the enemies. Of which work there erected, that is, of a rampart of extra- ordinary breadth and height, there are evident remains to be seen at this day. It begins at about two miles' distance from the monastery of Aber- curnig, on the west, at a place called in the Pictish language, Peanfahel, but in the English tongue, Penneltun, and running to the westward, ends near the city Alcluith.

But the former enemies, when they perceived that the Roman soldiers were gone, immediately coming by sea, broke into the borders, trampled and overran all places, and like men mowing ripe corn, bore down all before them. Hereupon messengers are again sent to Rome, imploring aid, lest their wretched country should be utterly extirpated, and the name of a Roman province, so long renowned among them, overthrown by the cruelties of barbarous foreigners, might become utterly contemptible. A legion is accordingly sent again, and, arriving unexpectedly in autumn, made great slaughter of the enemy, obliging all those that could escape, to flee beyond the sea ; whereas before, they were wont yearly to carry off their booty without any opposition. Then the Romans declared to the Britons, that they could not for the future undertake such troublesome ex- peditions for their sake, advising them rather to handle their weapons, like men, and undertake themselves the charge of engaging their enemies, who would not prove too powerful for them, unless they were deterred by cowardice ; and, thinking that it might be some help to the allies, whom they were forced to abandon, they built a strong stone wall from sea to sea, in a straight line between the towns that had been there built for fear of the enemy, and not far from the trench of Severus. This famous wall, which is still to be seen, was built at the public and private expense, the Britons also lending their assistance. It is eight feet in breadth, and twelve in height, in a straight line from east to west, as is still visible to beholders. This being finished, they gave that dispirited people good advice, with patterns to furnish them with arms. Besides, they built towers on the sea-coast to the southward, at proper distances, where their ships were, because there also the irruptions of the barbarians were apprehended, and so took leave of their friends, never to return again.

After their departure, the Scots and the Picts, understanding that they had declared they would come no more, speedily returned, and growing more confident than they had been before, occupied all the northern and farthest part of the island, as far as the wall. Hereupon a timorous guard was placed upon the wall, where they pined away day and night in the utmost fear. On the other side, the enemy attacked them with hooked weapons, by which the cowardly defendants were dragged from the wall, and dashed against the ground. At last, the Britons, forsaking their cities and wall, took to flight and were dispersed. The enemy pursued, and the slaughter was greater than on any former occasion ; for the wretched natives were torn in pieces by their enemies, as lambs are torn by wild beasts. Thus, being expelled their dwellings and possessions, they saved themselves from starvation by robbing and plundering one another, adding to the calamities occasioned by foreigners, by their own domestic broils, till the whole country was left destitute of food, except such as could be procured in the chase.

CHAPTER XIII.—In the year of our Lord 423, Theodosius, the younger, next to Honorius, being the forty-fifth from Augustus, governed the Roman empire twenty-six years. In the eighth year of his reign, Palladius was sent by Celestinus, the Roman pontiff, to the Scots that believed in Christ, to be their first bishop. In the twenty-third year of his reign, Ætius, a renowned person, being also a patrician, discharged his third consulship with Symmachus for his colleague. To him the wretched remains of the Britons sent a letter, which began thus :—" To Ætius, thrice Consul, the groans of the Britons." And in the sequel of the letter they thus expressed their calamities :—" The barbarians drive us to the sea ; the sea drives us back to the barbarians : between them we are exposed to two sorts of death ; we are either slain or drowned." Yet neither could all this procure any assistance from him, as he was then engaged in most dangerous wars with Bledla and Attila, kings of the Huns. And, though the year before this, Bledla had been murdered by the treachery of his brother Attila, yet Attila himself remained so intolerable an enemy to the Republic, that he ravaged almost all Europe, invading and destroying cities and castles. At the same time there was a famine at Constantinople, and shortly after, a plague followed, and a great part of the walls of that city, with fifty-seven towers, fell to the ground. Many cities also went to ruin, and the famine and pestilential state of the air destroyed thousands of men and cattle.

CHAPTER XIV.—In the meantime, the aforesaid famine distressing the Britons more and more, and leaving to posterity lasting memorials of its mischievous effects, obliged many of them to submit themselves to the depredators ; though others still held out, confiding in the Divine assistance, when none was to be had from men. These continually made excursions from the mountains, caves, and woods, and, at length, began to inflict severe losses on their enemies, who had been for so many years plundering the country. The Irish robbers thereupon returned home, in order to come again soon after. The Picts, both then and afterwards, remained quiet in the farthest part of the island, save that sometimes they would do some mischief, and carry off booty from the Britons.

When, however, the ravages of the enemy at length ceased, the island began to abound with such plenty of grain as had never been known in any age before ; with plenty, luxury increased, and this was immediately attended with all sorts of crimes ; in particular, cruelty, hatred of truth, and love of falsehood ; insomuch, that if any one among them happened to be milder than the rest, and inclined to truth, all the rest abhorred and persecuted him, as if he had been the enemy of his country. Nor were the laity only guilty of these things, but even our Lord's own flock, and his pastors also, addicting themselves to drunkenness, animosity, litigiousness, contention, envy, and other such like crimes, and casting off the light yoke of Christ. In the meantime, on a sudden, a severe plague fell upon that corrupt generation, which soon destroyed such numbers of them, that the living were scarcely sufficient to bury the dead : yet, those that survived, could not be withdrawn from the spiritual death, which their sins had incurred, either by the death of their friends, or the fear of their own. Whereupon, not long after, a more severe vengeance, for their horrid wickedness, fell upon the sinful nation. They consulted what was to be done, and where they should seek assistance to prevent or repel the cruel and frequent incursions of the northern nations ; and they all agreed with their king Vortigern to call over to their aid, from the parts beyond the sea, the Saxon nation ; which, as the event still more evidently showed, appears to have been done by the appointment of our Lord himself, that evil might fall upon them for their wicked deeds.

CHAPTER XV.—In the year of our Lord 449, Martian being made emperor with Valentinian, and the forty-sixth from Augustus, ruled the empire seven years. Then the nation of the Angles, or Saxons, being invited by the aforesaid king, arrived in Britain with three long ships, and had a place assigned them to reside in by the same king, in the eastern part of the island, that they might thus appear to be fighting for their country, whilst their real intentions were to enslave it. Accordingly they engaged with the enemy, who were come from the north to give battle, and obtained the victory ; which, being known at home in their own country, as also the fertility of the country, and the cowardice of the Britons, a more considerable fleet was quickly sent over, bringing a still greater number of men, which, being added to the former, made up an invincible army. The new comers received of the Britons a place to inhabit, upon condition that they should wage war against their enemies for the peace and security of the country, whilst the Britons agreed to furnish them with pay. Those who came over were of the three most powerful nations of Germany—Saxons, Angles, and Jutes. From the Jutes are descended the people of Kent, and of the Isle of Wight, and those also in the province of the West-Saxons who are to this day called Jutes, seated opposite to the Isle of Wight. From the Saxons, that is, the country which is now called Old Saxony, came the East-Saxons, the South-Saxons, and the West-Saxons. From the Angles, that is, the country which is called Anglia, and which is said, from that time, to remain desert to this day, between the provinces of the Jutes and the Saxons, are descended the East-Angles, the Midland-Angles, Mercians, all the race of the Northumbrians, that is, of those nations that dwell on the north side of the river Humber, and the other nations of the English. The two first commanders are said to have been Hengist and Horsa. Of whom Horsa, being afterwards slain in battle by the Britons, was buried in the eastern part of Kent, where a monument, bearing his name, is still in existence. They were the sons of Victgilsus, whose father was Vecta, son of Woden; from whose stock the royal race of many provinces deduce their original. In a short time, swarms of the aforesaid nations came over into the island, and they began to increase so much, that they became terrible to the natives themselves who had invited them. Then, having on a sudden entered into league with the Picts, whom they had by this time repelled by the force of their arms, they began to turn their weapons against their confederates. At first, they obliged them to furnish a greater quantity of provisions; and, seeking an occasion to quarrel, protested that, unless more plentiful supplies were brought them, they would break the confederacy, and ravage all the island; nor were they backward in putting their threats into execution. In short, the fire kindled by the hands of these pagans, proved God's just revenge for the crimes of the people; not unlike that which, being once lighted by the Chaldeans, consumed the walls and city of Jerusalem. For the barbarous conquerors acting here in the same manner, or rather the just Judge ordaining that they should so act, they plundered all the neighboring cities and country, spread the conflagration from the eastern to the western sea, without any opposition, and covered almost every part of the devoted island. Public as well as private structures were overturned; the priests were everywhere slain before the altars; the prelates and the people, without any respect of persons, were destroyed with fire and sword; nor was there any to bury those who had been thus cruelly slaughtered. Some of the miserable remainder, being taken in the mountains, were butchered in heaps. Others, spent with hunger, came forth and submitted themselves to the enemy for food, being destined to undergo perpetual servitude, if they were not killed even upon the spot. Some, with sorrowful hearts, fled beyond the seas. Others, continuing in their own country, led a miserable life among the woods, rocks, and mountains, with scarcely enough food to support life, and expecting every moment to be their last."[15]

CHAPTER XVI.—When the victorious army, having destroyed and dispersed the natives, had returned home to their own settlements, the Britons began by degrees to take heart, and gather strength, sallying out of the lurking places where they had concealed themselves, and unanimously imploring the Divine assistance, that they might not utterly be destroyed. They had at that time for their leader, Ambrosius Aurelius, a modest man, who alone, by chance, of the Roman nation had survived the storm, in which his parents, who were of the royal race, had perished. Under him the Britons revived, and offering battle to the victors, by the help of God, came off victorious. From that day, sometimes the natives, and sometimes their enemies, prevailed, till the year of the siege of Baddesdown-hill, when they made no small slaughter of those invaders, about forty-four years after their arrival in England. But of this hereafter. . . .

CHAPTER XXIII.—In the year of our Lord 582, Maurice, the fifty-fourth from Augustus, ascended the throne, and reigned twenty-one years. In the tenth year of his reign, Gregory, a man renowned for learning and behavior, was promoted to the apostolical see of Rome, and presided over it thirteen years, six months and ten days. He, being moved by Divine inspiration, in the fourteenth year of the same emperor, and about the one hundred and fiftieth after the coming of the English into Britain, sent the servant of God, Augustine, and with him several other monks, who feared the Lord, to preach the word of God to the English nation. They having, in obedience to the pope's commands, undertaken that work, were, on their journey, seized with a sudden fear, and began to think of returning home, rather than proceed to a barbarous, fierce, and unbelieving nation, to whose very language they were strangers ; and this they unanimously agreed was the safest course. In short, they sent back Augustine, who had been appointed to be consecrated bishop in case they were received by the English, that he might, by humble entreaty, obtain of the holy Gregory, that they should not be compelled to undertake so dangerous, toilsome, and uncertain a journey. The pope, in reply, sent them a hortatory epistle, persuading them to proceed in the work of the Divine word, and rely on the assistance of the Almighty. . . .

CHAPTER XXV.—Augustine, thus strengthened by the confirmation of the blessed Father Gregory, returned to the work of the word of God, with the servants of Christ, and arrived in Britain. The powerful Ethelbert was at that time king of Kent ; he had extended his dominions as far as the great river Humber, by which the Southern Saxons are divided from the Northern. On the east of Kent is the large Isle of Thanet containing according to the English way of reckoning, 600 families, divided from the other land by the river Wantsum, which is about three furlongs over, and fordable only in two places, for both ends of it run into the sea. In this island landed the servant of our Lord, Augustine, and his companions, being, as is reported, nearly forty men. They had, by order of the blessed Pope Gregory, taken interpreters of the nation of the Franks, and sending to Ethelbert, signified that they were come from Rome, and brought a joyful message, which most undoubtedly assured to all that took advantage of it everlasting joys in heaven, and a kingdom that would never end, with the living and true God. The king having heard this, ordered them to stay in that island where they had landed, and that they should be furnished with all necessaries, till he should consider what to do with them. For he had before heard of the Christian religion, having a Christian wife of the royal family of the Franks, called Bertha ; whom he had received from her parents, upon condition that she should be permitted to practise her religion with the Bishop Luidhard, who was sent with her to preserve her faith. Some days after, the king came into the island, and sitting in the open air, ordered Augustine and his companions to be brought into his presence. For he had taken precaution that they should not come to him in any house, lest, according to an ancient superstition, if they practised any magical arts, they might impose upon him, and so get the better of him. But they came furnished with Divine, not with magic virtue, bearing a silver cross for their banner, and the image of our Lord and Saviour painted on a board ; and singing the litany, they offered up their prayers to the Lord for the eternal salvation both of themselves and of those to whom they were come. When he had sat down, pursuant to the king's commands, and preached to him and his attendants there present, the word of life, the king answered thus :—"Your words and promises are very fair, but as they are new to us, and of uncertain import, I cannot approve of them so far as to forsake that which I have so long followed with the whole English nation. But because you are come from far into my kingdom, and, as I conceive, are desirous to impart to us those things which you believe to be true, and most beneficial, we will not molest you, but give you favorable entertainment, and take care to supply you with your necessary sustenance ; nor do we forbid you to preach and gain as many as you can to your religion." Accordingly he permitted them to reside in the city of Canterbury, which was the metropolis of all his dominions, and, pursuant to his promise, besides allowing them sustenance, did not refuse them liberty to preach. . . .

CHAPTER XXVI.—As soon as they entered the dwelling-place assigned them, they began to imitate the course of life practised in the primitive church ; applying themselves to frequent prayer, watching and fasting ; preaching the word of life to as many as they could ; despising all worldly things, as not belonging to them ; receiving only their necessary food from those they taught ; living themselves in all respects conformably to what they prescribed to others, and being always disposed to suffer any adversity, and even to die for that truth which they preached. In short, several believed and were baptized, admiring the simplicity of their innocent life, and the sweetness of their heavenly doctrine. There was on the east side of the city, a church dedicated to the honor of St. Martin, built whilst the Romans were still in the island, wherein the queen, who, as has been said before, was a Christian, used to pray. In this they first began to meet, to sing, to pray, to say mass, to preach, and to baptize, till the king, being converted to the faith, allowed them to preach openly, and build or repair churches in all places.

When he, among the rest, induced by the unspotted life of these holy men, and their delightful promises, which, by many miracles, they proved to be most certain, believed and was baptized, greater numbers began daily to flock together to hear the word, and, forsaking their heathen rites, to associate themselves, by believing, to the unity of the church of Christ. Their conversion the king so far encouraged, as that he compelled none to embrace Christianity, but only showed more affection to the believers, as to his fellow citizens in the heavenly kingdom. For he had learned from his instructors and leaders to salvation, that the service of Christ ought to be voluntary, not by compulsion. Nor was it long before he gave his teachers a settled residence in his metropolis of Canterbury, with such possessions of different kinds as were necessary for their subsistence.[16] . . .

CHAPTER XXXIV.—At this time [603], Ethelfrid, a most worthy king, and ambitious of glory, governed the kingdom of the Northumbrians, and ravaged the Britons more than all the great men of the English, insomuch that he might be compared to Saul, once king of the Israelites, excepting only this, that he was ignorant of the true religion. For he conquered more territories from the Britons, either making them tributary, or driving the inhabitants clean out, and planting English in their places, than any other king or tribune.[17] To him might justly be applied the saying of the patriarch blessing his son in the person of Saul, "Benjamin shall ravin as a wolf ; in the morning he shall devour the prey, and at night he shall divide the spoil." Hereupon, Ædan, king of the Scots that inhabit Britain, being concerned at his success, came against him with an immense and mighty army, but was beaten by an inferior force, and put to flight ; for almost all his army was slain at a famous place, called Degsastan, that is, Degsastone. In which battle also Theodbald, brother of Ethelfrid, was killed, with almost all the forces he commanded. This war Ethelfrid put an end to in the year 603 after the incarnation of our Lord, the eleventh of his own reign, which lasted twenty-four years, and the first year of the reign of Phocas, who then governed the Roman empire. From that time, no king of the Scots durst come into Britain to make war on the English to this day.[18]

In the province of the Northumbrians, where King Ceolwulf reigns, four bishops now preside ; Wilfrid in the church of York, Ethelwald in that of Lindisfarne, Acca in that of Hagulstad, Pechthelm in that which is called the White House, which, from the increased number of believers, has lately become an episcopal see, and has him for its first prelate. The Picts also at this time are at peace with the English nation, and rejoice in being united in peace and truth with the whole Catholic Church. The Scots that inhabit Britain, satisfied with their own territories, meditate no hostilities against the nation of the English. The Britons, though they, for the most part, through innate hatred, are adverse to the English nation, and wrongfully, and from wicked custom, oppose the appointed Easter of the whole Catholic Church ; yet, from both the Divine and human power withstanding them, can in no way prevail as they desire ; for though in part they are their own masters, yet elsewhere they are also brought under subjection to the English. Such being the peaceable and calm disposition of the times, many of the Northumbrians, as well of the nobility as private persons, laying aside their weapons, rather incline to dedicate both themselves and their children to the tonsure and monastic vows, than to study martial discipline. What will be the end hereof, the next age will show. This is for the present the state of all Britain ; in the year since the coming of the English into Britain about 285, but in the 731st year of the incarnation of our Lord, in whose reign may the earth ever rejoice ; may Britain exult in the profession of his faith ; and may many islands be glad, and sing praises in honor of his holiness !

BOOK V., CHAPTER XXIV.—I have thought fit briefly to sum up those things which have been related more at large, according to the distinction of times, for the better preserving them in memory.

In the sixtieth year before the incarnation of our Lord, Caius Julius Cæsar, first of the Romans, invaded Britain, and was victorious, yet could not gain the kingdom.

In the year from the incarnation of our Lord, 46, Claudius, second of the Romans, invading Britain, had a great part of the island surrendered to him, and added the Orkney Islands to the Roman empire.

In the year from the incarnation of our Lord, 167, Eleutherius, being made bishop at Rome, governed the Church most gloriously fifteen years. Lucius, king of Britain, writing to him, requested to be made a Christian, and succeeded in obtaining his request.

In the year from the incarnation of our Lord 189, Severus, being made emperor, reigned seventeen years ; he enclosed Britain with a trench from sea to sea.

In the year 381, Maximus, being made emperor in Britain, sailed over into Gaul, and slew Gratian.

In the year 409, Rome was crushed by the Goths, from which time Roman emperors began to reign in Britain.

In the year 430, Palladius was sent to be the first bishop of the Scots that believed in Christ, by Pope Celestine.

In the year 449, Martian being made emperor with Valentinian, reigned seven years ; in whose time the English, being called by the Britons, came into Britain.

In the year 538, there happened an eclipse of the sun, on the 16th of February, from the first to the third hour.

In the year 540, an eclipse of the sun happened on the 20th of June and the stars appeared during almost half an hour after the third hour of the day.

In the year 547, Ida began to reign ; from him the royal family of the Northumbrians derives its original ; he reigned twelve years.

In the year 565, the priest, Columba, came out of Scotland, into Britain, to instruct the Picts, and he built a monastery in the isle of Hii.

In the year 596, Pope Gregory sent Augustine with monks into Britain, to preach the word of God to the English nation.

In the year 597, the aforesaid teachers arrived in Britain ; being about the 150th year from the coming of the English into Britain.

In the year 601, Pope Gregory sent the pall into Britain, to Augustine, who was already made bishop ; he sent also several ministers of the word, among whom was Paulinus.

In the year 603, a battle was fought at Degsastane.

In the year 604, the East Saxons received the faith of Christ, under King Sabert, and Bishop Mellitus.

In the year 605, Gregory died.

In the year 616, Ethelbert, king of Kent, died.

In the year 625, the venerable Paulinus was, by Archbishop Justus, ordained bishop of the Northumbrians.

In the year 626, Eanfleda, daughter to King Edwin, was baptized with twelve others, on Whit-Saturday.

In the year 627, King Edwin was baptized, with his nation, at Easter.

In the year 633, King Edwin being killed, Paulinus returned to Kent.

In the year 640, Eadbald, king of Kent, died.

In the year 642, King Oswald was slain.

In the year 644, Paulinus, first bishop of York, but now of the city of Rochester, departed to our Lord.

In the year 651, King Oswin was killed, and Bishop Aidan died.

In the year 653, the Midland Angles, under their prince, Penda, received the mysteries of the faith.

In the year 655, Penda was slain, and the Mercians became Christians.

In the year 664, there happened an eclipse of the sun ; Earconbert, king of Kent, died ; and Colman returned to the Scots ; a pestilence arose ; Ceadda and Wilfrid were ordained bishops of the Northumbrians.

In the year 668, Theodore was ordained bishop.

In the year 670, Oswy, king of the Northumbrians, died.

In the year 673, Egbert, king of Kent, died, and a synod was held at Hertford, in the presence of King Egfrid, Archbishop Theodore presiding : the synod did much good, and its decrees are contained in ten chapters.

In the year 675, Wulfhere, king of the Mercians, dying, when he had reigned seventeen years, left the crown to his brother Ethelred.

In the year 676, Ethelred ravaged Kent.

In the year 678, a comet appeared ; Bishop Wilfrid was driven from his see by King Egfrid ; and Bosa, Eata, and Eadhed were consecrated bishops in his stead.

In the year 679, Elfwine was killed.

In the year 680, a synod was held in the field called Hethfeld, concerning the Christian faith, Archbishop Theodore presiding ; John, the Roman abbot, was also present. The same year also the Abbess Hilda died at Streaneshalch.

In the year 685, Egfrid, king of the Northumbrians, was slain.

The same year, Lothere, king of Kent, died.

In the year 688, Cædwalla, king of the West Saxons, went to Rome from Britain.

In the year 690, Archbishop Theodore died.

In the year 697, Queen Ostritha was murdered by her own people, that is, the nobility of the Mercians.

In the year 698, Berthred, the royal commander of the Northumbrians, was slain by the Picts.

In the year 704, Ethelred became a monk, after he had reigned thirty years over the nation of the Mercians, and gave up the kingdom to Ceolred.

In the year 705, Alfrid, king of the Northumbrians, died.[19]

In the year 709, Ceolred, king of the Mercians, having reigned six years, went to Rome.

In the year 711, Earl Bertfrid fought with the Picts.

In the year 716, Osred, king of the Northumbrians, was killed ; and Ceolred, king of the Mercians, died ; and Egbert, the man of God, brought the monks of Hii to observe the Catholic Easter and ecclesiastical tonsure.

In the year 725, Withred, king of Kent, died.

In the year 729, comets appeared ; the holy Egbert departed ; and Osric died.

In the year 731, Archbishop Bertwald died.

The same year Tatwine was consecrated ninth archbishop of Canterbury, in the fifteenth year of Ethelbald, king of Kent.

(What follows appears to be by another hand. Bede died in the year 735.)

In the year from the incarnation of our Lord 732, Egbert was made bishop of York, in the room of Wilfrid ; Cunebert, bishop of Lindisfarians, died.

A.D. 733, there happened an eclipse of the sun, on the 18th day before the kalends of September, about the third hour of the day ; so that almost all the orb of the sun seemed to be covered with a black and horrid shield.

In the year from the incarnation of our Lord 733, Archbishop Tatwine having received the pall by apostolical authority, ordained Alwich and Sigfrid bishops.

A.D. 734, the moon, on the 2d before the kalends of February, about the time of cock-crowing, was, for about a whole hour, covered with a bloody red, after which a blackness followed, and she regained her light.

In the year from the incarnation of our Lord 734, Bishop Tatwine died.

In the year from the incarnation of our Lord 735, Nothelm was ordained archbishop ; and Bishop Egbert, having received the pall from the apostolic see, was the first confirmed archbishop after Paulinus, and ordained Frithbert and Frithwald bishops ; and the priest Bede died.

A.D. 737, too much drought rendered the land unfruitful, and Ceolwulf, voluntarily receiving the tonsure, left the kingdom to Eadbert.

A.D. 739, Ethelard, king of the West Saxons, died, as did Archbishop Nothelm.

A.D. 740, Cuthbert was consecrated in Nothelm's stead. Ethelbald, king of the Mercians, through impious fraud, wasted part of the Northumbrians, their king Eadbert, with his army, being employed against the Picts. Bishop Ethelwald died also, and Conwulf was consecrated in his stead. Amwin and Eadbert were slain.

A.D. 741, first a great drought happened in the country. Charles, king of the Franks, died ; and his sons, Caroloman and Pepin, reigned in his stead.

A.D. 745, Bishop Wilfrid and Ingwald, bishop of London, departed to our Lord.

A.D. 747, the man of God, Herefrid, died.

A.D. 750, Cuthred, king of the West Saxons, rose up against King Ethelbald and Angus ; Theneorus and Eanred died ; Eadbert added the plain of Kyle and other places to his dominions.[20]

A.D. 756, in the fifth year of King Eadbert, on the ides of January, there happened an eclipse of the sun ; afterwards, the same year and month, on the 9th before the kalends of February the moon suffered an eclipse, being most horridly black.

A.D. 756, Boniface, called also Winfrid, bishop of the Franks, received the crown of martyrdom, with fifty-three others ; and Redger was consecrated archbishop in his stead, by Pope Stephen.

A.D. 757, Ethelbald, king of the Mercians, was miserably murdered, in the night, by his own tutors ; Beonred began his reign ; Cynewulf, king of the West Saxons, died ; and the same year, Offa, having vanquished Beonred, in a bloody manner, sought to gain the kingdom of the Mercians.

A.D. 758, Eadbert, king of the Northumbrians, receiving St. Peter's tonsure, for the love of God and to gain the heavenly country by violence, left the kingdom to his son Oswulph.

A.D. 759, Oswulph was wickedly murdered by his own servants ; and Ethelwald, being chosen the same year by his people, entered upon the kingdom ; in whose second year there happened a great tribulation of mortality, and continued almost two years, several grievous distempers raging, but more especially the dysentery.

A.D. 761, Angus, king of the Picts, died ; who, from the beginning to the end of his reign, continued a bloody tyrannical butcher : Oswin was also slain.

A.D. 765, King Alcred was advanced to the throne.

NOTES TO CHAPTER XVIII.

[1] The *Ulster Annals* have in 1033 " Mac meic Boete meic Cinaedha do marbhadh la (slain by) Maelcolaim meic Cinaedha." It has usually been assumed that this Boete was the son of Kenneth, son of Dubh, the predecessor of Maelcolm mac Kenneth, and thus represented a rival branch of the house ; but the dates will not admit of this, and his father Kenneth must be placed a generation farther back. He may either have been the same Kenneth who was father of Malcolm, thus making Boete his brother, or the Kenneth, son of Malcolm who slew Constantin, son of Cuilein, in 997, and who is supposed by Fordun to be his illegitimate brother. Fordun tells us that " the old custom of the succession of kings lasted without a break until the time of Malcolm, son of Kenneth, when, for fear of the dismemberment of the kingdom, which might perhaps result therefrom, that king by a general ordinance decreed as a law forever that henceforth each king after his death should be succeeded in the government of the kingdom by whoever was at the time being the next descendant — that is, a son or a daughter, a nephew or a niece, the nearest then living. Failing in these, however, the next heir begotten of the royal or collateral stock should possess the right of inheritance."—(Fordun, *Chron.*, Ed. 1872, b. iv., c. i.) Whether Malcolm actually issued a formal decree to this effect rests on the authority of Fordun alone, which can hardly be accepted for the events of this early period. Malcolm seems to have taken the readier mode of removing from life any competitor who should claim as a male descendant.—*Celtic Scotland*, p. 399.

[2] At his death, in 1033, there was no powerful adult collateral to seize on the succession. He is said to have provided for this by putting to death the grandson of Kenneth IV. [III.]

The charge stands on very faint evidence; and were it not that it adds an item to the long catalogue of royal crimes, the tenuity of the evidence might be regretted, since such a death would help to clear up the tragic mysteries of the next reign.—Burton, *History of Scotland*, vol. i., p. 343.

³ It appears from the chartulary of St. Andrews that Gruoch, *filia Bodhe*, was the wife of Macbeth, son of Finnloech, and reigned along with him, while Lulach, his successor, is termed in one of the Latin lists *nepos filii Boede.*—*Chronicles of the Picts and Scots*, p. 147.

The foundation for Shakespeare's tragedy is the account given by Hector Boece, which was copied into *Holinshed's Chronicle* and thence came to the hands of the poet. Boece's story is as follows:

"Nocht lang eftir, hapnit ane uncouth and wonderful thing, be quhilk followit sone, ane gret alteration in the realme. Be aventure, Makbeth an Banquho wer passand to Fores, quhair King Duncane hapnit to be for the time, and met be the gait thre wemen, clothit in elrage and uncouth weid. Thay wer jugit, be the pepill, to be weird sisteris. The first of thaim said to Makbeth, 'Hale, Thane of Glammis!' the second said, 'Hale, Thane of Cawder!' and the third said, 'Hale, King of Scotland!' Then said Banquho, 'Quhat wemen be ye, sa unmerciful to me, and sa favorabil to my companyeon? For ye gaif to him nocht onlie landis and gret rentis, bot gret lordschippis and kingdomes; and gevis me nocht.' To this, answerit the first of thir weird sisteris, 'We schaw more felicite appering to the than to him; for thoucht he happin to be ane king, his empire sall end unhappelie, and nane of his blude sall eftir him succeid; be contrar, thow sall nevir be king, bot of the sal cum mony kingis, quhilkis, with lang progressioun, sall rejose the croun of Scotland.' Als sone as thir wourdis wer said, thay suddanlie evanist out of sicht. This prophecy and divinatioun wes haldin mony dayis in derision to Banquho and Makbeth. For sum time Banquho wald call Makbeth, King of Scottis, for derision; and he on the samin maner, wald call Banquho, the fader of mony kingis. Yit, becaus al thingis succedit as thir wemen devinit, the pepill traistit and jugit thame to be weird sisteris. Not lang after it hapnit that the Thane of Cawder was disherist and forfaltit of his landis, for certane crimes of lese majeste; and his landis wer gevin be King Duncane to Makbeth. It hapnit in the nixt nicht, that Banquho and Makbeth wer sportand togiddir at thair supper. Than said Banquho, 'Thow hes gottin all that the first two weird sisteris hecht. Restis nocht bot the croun, quhilk wes hecht be the third sister.' Makbeth, revolving all thingis as thay wer said be thir weird sisteris, began to covat the cround; and yit he concludit to abide quhil he saw the time ganand thairto, fermelie believing that the third weird suld cum, as the first two did afore.

"In the mene time, King Duncane maid his son Malcolme prince of Cumbir, to signify that he suld regne eftir him. Quhilk wes gret displeseir to Makbeth; for it maid plane derogatioun to the third weird, promittit afore to him be thir weird sisteris. Nochteles, he thocht, gif Duncane wer slane, he had maist richt to the croun, becaus he wes nerest of blude theirto, be tennour of the auld lawis maid eftir the deith of King Fergus, 'Quhen young children wer unabil to govern the croun, the nerrest of thair blude sall regne.' Als, the respons of thir weird sisteris put him in belief, that the third weird suld cum as weill as the first two. Attour, his wife, impacient of lang tary, as all wemen ar, specially quhare thay ar desirus of ony purpos, gaif him gret artation to persew the third weird, that scho micht be ane quene; called him, oft timis, febil cowart, and nocht desiris of honouris; sen he durst not assailye the thing with manheid and curage, quhilk is offerit to him be benivolence of fortoun; howbeit sindry otheris hes assailyeit sic thingis afore, with maist terribil jeopardyis, quhen thay had not sic sickernes to succeid in the end of thair laubouris as he had.

"Makbeth, be persuasion of his wife, gaderit his freindis to ane counsall at Innernes, quhare King Duncane happinit to be for the time. And becaus he fand sufficient oportunite, be support of Banquho and otheris his freindis, he slew King Duncane, the VII. yeir of his regne. His body was buryit in Elgin, and efter tane up and brocht to Colmekill, quhare it remains yit, amang the sepulturis of uthir kingis; fra our redemption MXLVI.

yeris."—Bellenden's *Croniklis of Scotland*, book xii., chap. iii., Edinburgh, 1822, translated from Boece's *History and Croniklis of Scotland*.

⁴ " Machbet filius Finlach contulit per suffragiis orationum et Gruoch filia Bodhe rex et regina Scotorum, Kyrkness Deo omnipotenti et Kaledeis, prefatæ insulæ Lochlevine cum suis finibus et terminis.

" Cum omni libertate collata fuit villa de Kyrkenes Deo omnipotenti et Kaledeis, alique omni munere et onere et exaccione regis et filii regis, vice comitis et alicujus et sine refectione pontis et sine exercitu et venatione, sed pietatis intuitu et orationum suffragiis fuit Deo omni potenti collata.   Cum summa veneratione et devotione Makbeth rex contulit Deo et Sancto Servano de Lochlevyn et heremitis ibidem Deo servientibus Bolgyne filii Torfyny cum omni libertate et sine onere exercitus regis et filii ejus, vel vicecomitis, et sine exactione alicujus, sed caritatis intuitu et orationum suffragiis."—*Chr. of St. Andrews*, p. 114, 12.

⁵ A. D. 1045 Cath etir Albancho araenrian cur marbadh andsin Crinan Ab. Duincalland ocus sochaighe maille fris. i. nae xx laech.—*Annals of Tighernac.*

⁶ Probably to obtain absolution for the murder of Duncan, as Marianus tells us that in the year 1050 the king of Scotia, Macbethad, freely distributed silver to the poor at Rome. According to the *Orkneyinga Saga* (Mr. Anderson's edition, p. 43), Thorfinn, earl of Orkney, went to Rome in the same year, " and saw the Pope, from whom he obtained absolution for all his sins."

There is a singular passage concerning Macbeth in *Florence of Worcester*, p. 626 " Anno 1050, Rex, Scotorum Macbethad " Romæ argentum spargendo distribuit." Fordun simply adds " Pauperibus " ; L. v., c. 9, because that word follows in the text, Ps. 112. From the words of Fordun, Goodall draws this notable inference. " Machebeda Roman profectus " ; Index ad Fordun. Thus from Fordun, and his publisher, we learn, " that Macbeth went to Rome, and there distributed ' alms to the poor ' " ; whereas the original insinuated " that ' Macbeth bribed the court of Rome.' "—Hailes, *Annals of Scotland*, vol. i., p. 4.

⁷ Siward was doubly connected with the house of Crinan, the abbot of Dunkeld, for his wife's aunt, Aldgitha, half-sister of Earl Ealdred, was married to Maldred, son of Crinan, and King Duncan himself married either the sister or the cousin of Earl Siward, by whom he had a son, Malcolm.—*Celtic Scotland*, vol. i., p. 408.

⁸ In 1054 Siward, the valiant duke of the Northumbrians, by the command of King Edward, with both an army of horse, and a powerful fleet, went into Scotland and fought a battle with Macbeth, king of Scots, and many thousand of the Scots and all the Normans, of whom we have above made mention, being killed, put him to flight, and constituted King Malcolm, son of the king of the Cumbrians, as the king had commanded. In that battle, however, his son and many of the English and Danes fell.—*Florence of Worcester.*

Under the year 1054 the chronicle contains two separate accounts of the expedition of Earl Siward, in which he defeated Macbeth and returned with enormous booty. Such were the only results, according to the contemporary chronicler, of an expedition which appears to have been directed against Macbeth on account of the protection he had afforded to the Norman favorites of the Confessor. Tighernac, the contemporary Irish annalist, alludes to this defeat of Macbeth under the same year ; and four years later, in 1058, he notices an abortive attempt of the Norwegians, which is also entered in the *Saxon Chronicle* under the same date, placing the defeat and death of Macbeth, which raised Malcolm Ceanmore to the throne, in the same year. In later chroniclers the events of both these years have been purposely confounded, and Siward has been, for obvious reasons, represented as defeating and killing Macbeth, and restoring Malcolm to his father's throne at the command of the English king — all which, as he died in 1055, he must have risen from his grave (like Reginald Hy Ivar) to effect. That the defeat of Macbeth in 1054 contributed eventually to the success of Malcolm in 1058 is highly probable ; but the misrepresentations of the Anglo-Norman writers cannot stand for a moment against the account of the contemporary and more impartial authorities.—E. William Robertson, *Scotland under her Early Kings*, vol. ii., p. 400.

A new cause for action had now made itself felt. The flight of a body of Normans to the Scottish court on Godwine's return from exile forced on the struggle. The power of Macbeth had been doubled by his close alliance with the Orkney jarls, and his reception of the Normans threatened danger to the English realm. It was " by the king's order " that Siward marched over the border to fight Macbeth. The danger was soon dispelled. In 1054 a Northumbrian fleet appeared off the Scottish coast, and a Northumbrian army met Macbeth and his Orkney allies in a desperate battle. The English victory was complete ; the Normans were cut to pieces, and Macbeth fled to his Norse allies, to perish after four years of unceasing struggle with Duncan's son, Malcolm, whom Siward placed on the Scottish throne.—Green, *Conquest of England*, ch., xi., § 8.

[9] The *Saxon Chronicle* makes no mention of Malcolm in connection with this expedition ; but Florence of Worcester adds to an account, apparently taken from the *Saxon Chronicle*, that it was made *jussu regis*, that the forces on the one side were " Scoti et Normanni," on the other " Angli et Dani," and that Siward " Malcolmum regis Cumbrorum filium ut rex jusserat regem constituit." Macbeth, however, appears in the *Irish Annals* as Ri Alban till 1057, and Marianus states distinctly that he reigned till that year, which is conclusive as to Malcolm not having been made king of Scotland in 1054. It is remarkable, however, that in this passage he is not called " filius regis Scottorum " but " filius regis Cumbrorum ; " and Simeon seems not to have recognized Duncan as king of the Scots, for he makes Macbeth the immediate successor of Malcolm, son of Kenneth, " Anno mxxxiiij Malcolm rex Scottorum obiit cui Macbethad successit." The solution seems to be that he was established in 1054 as king of Cumbria, and at this time Lothian seems to have been included in the territories under the rule of the rex Cumbrorum.—*Celtic Scotland*, p. 410.

[10] Marianus has in 1057 " Macfinlaeg occiditur in Augusto ; " and again, " Inde Macfinlaeg regnavit annis 17 ad eandem missam Sanctæ Mariæ " (15th August). Tighernac under 1057, " Macbethadh mic Findlaich Airdri (sovereign of) Alban domarbad do (slain by) Mælcolaim mic Dondcadha, to which the *Ulster Annals* add " i cath " (in battle).—*Chron. Picts and Scots*, pp. 65, 78, 369.

" Mony Jnglishmen in lyke maner of hich kin and blude followeat him [Malcolm Canmore] into Scotland, quhome the king of his liberalitie promouet til Dignities, because stoutlie thay had stande with him in his defence against his ennimies of quhilkes war Calder, Lockhart, Gordoun, Setoun, Lauder, Wawn, Meldroun, Schaw, Lermont, Libertoun, Straquhin, Rotray, Dundas, Cockburne, Myrtom, Jnglis, Leslye, Cargill, Cuilra, Mar, Meinzies, Abbercrummie, the chiefest : of thir mony nobile houses have tane the beginning. The name lykewyse mony have receivet frome their fortitude and mony fra the land quhair thay duell.

" The same tyme was Waltir Fleanthie, his sone decoret with the honor of chiefe Merchal, because in Galloway and in the hilandes he dantounet had the rebellis ; of quhome cam the familie of the Stuartis."—John Lesley, (1571) *Historie of Scotland*, vol., i. b. vi. Lesley's account of the English origin of so many Scottish families is not based on any information or record more authentic than that of Boece.

[11] " Simeon of Durham too tells us that in the year 1061 ' Aldred, archbishop of York, went to Rome with Earl Tostig and received the pall from Pope Nicholas. Meanwhile Malcolm, king of Scots, furiously ravaged the earldom of his sworn brother Earl Tostig, and violated the peace of St. Cuthbert in the island of Lindisfarne.'

" From this date may be traced the beginning of the long warfare which for so many centuries desolated the borderland of England and Scotland. Malcolm, claiming in the name of Edgar the right of rule over all Cumbria and part of Northumbria, overran all that country, which brought him into contact with William Rufus. This led to the invasion of Scotland by William, and ended in Malcolm doing homage to the English king for the territories of Lothian and Cumbria."—Maxwell, *Dumfries and Galloway*, p. 45.

[12] See *English Chron.*, Anno 1067.

The connection of Malcolm with this family by marriage with his sister was a very important one for him, and he now combined in his own person advantages which gave him a claim to the obedience of each of the different races now united under his rule.   In the male line he represented the powerful lay abbots of Dunkeld, and inherited their influence over the ecclesiastical foundations dependent upon that monastery.   In the female, he possessed the more important representation of the Scottish royal house who had ruled for a century and a half over the kingdom of Scotland.   His father Duncan had been recognized for twenty years by the Welsh population of Cumbria and Strathclyde as their king, and by his mother he was connected with the Danes of Northumbria and their powerful Earl Siward.   His marriage with Ingibiorg gave him a claim to the good will at least of the Norwegians, and the Anglic population of Lothian and Northumbria would look upon his marriage with the daughter of the Ætheling as giving him an additional right to their steadfast support.   The northern province of Moray alone, whose hereditary rulers were of the same family as Macbeth, would probably render but an unwilling submission to his authority, and his rule over them would be but little more than nominal.—*Celtic Scotland*, vol. i., p. 415.

" Quhen Wilyeam of Normandie knew this, [the marriage of Margaret to Malcolm] he commandet to pass out of Jngland all Edgar his freindes and of his kin ; of quhome sprang up Lindsay, Vaus, Ramsay, Loual, Toures, Prestoun, Sandelandis, Bissatt, Foulis, Wardlaw, Maxwell, and mony vthiris of grett nobilitie, that tyme cam first in Scotland. . . .   With Agatha [mother of Edgar and Margaret], lykewyse cam out of Wngre [Hungary] mony, as Crychtoun, Fodringhame, Giffert, Manlis, Borthik, and vthiris ; amang quhon war Bartholomew Leslie. . . .   About this tyme lykwyse cam out of France ane innumerable multitude of Nobles of quhome we have Freser, Sanschir, Montgomerie, Campbell, Brise,Betoun, Tailyefer, Bothwell, and vthiris diueris."—*Historie of Scotland*, by John Lesley, vol. i., b. vi. This account is probably without much foundation in fact. See p. 330, note 3.

[13] See *English Chronicle*, Anno 1072.

[14] The form in which the influence of the Conquest was first felt in Scotland, was by a steady migration of the Saxon people northward.   They found in Scotland people of their own race, and made a marked addition to the predominance of the Saxon or Teutonic element. About the year 1068 there came among these emigrants a group whose flight from England, and reception in the court of Malcolm, make a turning-point in history.   Edgar, the Ætheling, the heir of the Saxon line of kings, came over, bringing with him his mother and two sisters, and such a body of retainers as an exiled court might command.   One of the sisters, Margaret, was afterwards married to Malcolm ; and thus it behoved the king of Scotland, whether from chivalrous sympathy or from self-interest, to be the champion of the Saxon claims, and the Conqueror's enemy.—Burton, *History of Scotland*, vol. i., p. 373.

[15] The caves of the Yorkshire moorlands preserve traces of the miserable fugitives who fled to them for shelter.   Such a cave opens on the side of a lonely ravine, known now as the King's Scaur, high up in the moors beside Settle.   In primeval ages it had been the haunt of hyenas, who dragged thither the mammoths, the reindeer, the bisons, and the bears that prowled in the neighboring glens.   At a later time it became a home of savages, whose stone adzes and flint knives and bone harpoons are still embedded in its floor.   But these, too, vanished in their turn, and this haunt of primitive man lay lonely and undisturbed till the sword of the English invaders drove the Roman provincials for shelter to the moors.   The hurry of their flight may be gathered from the relics their cave-life has left behind it.   There was clearly little time to do more than to drive off the cattle, the swine, the goats, whose bones lie scattered round the hearth fire at the mouth of the cave, where they served the wretched fugitives for food.   The women must have buckled hastily their brooches of bronze or particolored enamel, the peculiar workmanship of Celtic Britain, and snatched up a few household implements as they hurried away.   The men, no doubt, girded on as hastily the swords whose dainty sword-hilts of ivory and bronze still remain to tell the tale of their doom, and, hiding

in their breast what money the house contained, from coins of Trajan to the wretched "minims" that told of the Empire's decay, mounted their horses to protect their flight. At nightfall all were crouching beneath the dripping roof of the cave, or round the fire that was blazing at its mouth, and a long suffering began in which the fugitives lost year by year the memory of the civilization from which they came. A few charred bones show how hunger drove them to slay their horses for food; reddened pebbles mark the hour when the new vessels they wrought were too weak to stand the fire, and their meal was cooked by dropping heated stones into the pot. A time seems to have come when their very spindles were exhausted, and the women who wove in that dark retreat made spindle whorls as they could from the bones that lay about them.—Green, *Making of England*, p. 64.

[16] " In other matters the conversion left our Teutonic institutions to themselves to abide or to change according to influences on which the change of religion had no direct bearing. . . .

" War did not cease, whether wars with the Britons or wars among the rival English kingdoms. But here came in the most direct effect of the conversion on the general history of the island. The wars of the converted Teuton ceased to be wars of extermination : therefore, in those parts of Britain which the English won after their conversion, a real British element was assimilated into the English mass."—Freeman, *English People in Its Three Homes*, p. 145.

[17] " He wasted the race of the Britons more than any chieftain of the English had done," says Bæda, " for none drove out or subdued so many of the natives, or won so much of their land for English settlement, or made so many tributary to Englishmen." The policy of accepting the submission and tribute of the Welsh, but of leaving them on the conquered soil, became indeed, from this moment, the invariable policy of the invaders ; and as the invasion pushed farther and farther to the west, an ever-growing proportion of the Britons remained mingled with the conquerors.—Green, *Making of England*, p. 192.

[18] Of Ædilfrid, who at this time ruled over Bernicia, and soon after extended his sway over Deira also, it is told us by Bede that he " conquered more territories from the Britons, either making them tributary, or expelling the inhabitants and planting Angles in their places, than any other king " ; and to his reign we attribute the greatest extension of the Anglic power over the Britons. He appears to have added to his kingdom the districts on the west between the Derwent and the Mersey, thus extending Deira from sea to sea, and placing the Northumbrian kingdom between the Britons of the north and those of Wales. The river Tees appears to have separated Deira from Bernicia, and the Angles of Bernicia, with whom we have more immediately to do, were now in firm possession of the districts extending along the east coast as far as the Firth of Forth, originally occupied by the British tribe of the Ottadeni and afterwards by the Picts, and including the counties of Berwick and Roxburgh and that of East Lothian or Haddington, the rivers Esk and Gala forming their western boundary. The capital of Deira was York, and that of Bernicia the strongly-fortified position on the coast nearly opposite the Farne Islands, crowning a basaltic rock rising 150 feet above the sea, and accessible only on the southeast, which was called by the Britons, Dinguayridi, by the Gael, Dunguaire, and by the Angles Bebbanburch after Bebba the wife of Ædilfrid, now Bamborough. About half way along the coast, between Bamborough and Berwick-on-Tweed, lay parallel to the shore, the long flat island called by the Britons, Ynys Medcaud, and by the Angles, Lindisfarne.—*Celtic Scotland*, vol. i., p. 236.

[19] Aldferth, king of Northumbria, died in 705, and was succeeded by his son, Osred, a boy eight years old ; and in the following year Tighernac records the death of Brude, son of Dereli, who was succeeded by his brother Nectan, son of Dereli, according to the Pictish law of succession. Five years after his accession, the Picts of the plain of Manann, probably encouraged by the success of the neighboring kingdom of the Picts in maintaining their independence against the Angles, rose against their Saxon rulers. They were opposed by Berctfrid, the prefect or Alderman of the Northumbrians, whose king was still in only his fourteenth year. The Picts, however, were defeated with great slaughter, and their youthful

leader Finguine, son of Deleroith, slain. The *English Chronicle* tells us that this battle was fought between Haefe and Caere, by which the rivers Avon and Carron are probably meant, the plain of Manann being situated between these two rivers. These Picts appear to have been so effectually crushed that they did not renew the attempt, and we do not learn of any further collision between the Picts and the Angles during this period.

The Scots of Dalriada and a part of the British nation, we are told, recovered their freedom, the Angles still maintaining the rule over the rest of the Britons. The portion of their kingdom which became independent consisted of those districts extending from the Firth of Clyde to the Solway, embracing the counties of Dumbarton, Renfrew, Lanark, Ayr, and Dumfries—with the stronghold of Alclyde for its capital ; but the Angles still retained possession of the district of Galloway with its Pictish population, and Whithorn as their principal seat, as well as that part of the territory of the Britons which lay between the Solway Firth, and the river Derwent, having as its principal seat the town of Carlisle, which Ecgfrid had, in the same year in which he assailed the Picts, given to Saint Cuthbert, who had been made bishop of Lindisfarne in the previous year, that is in 684.

[20] In the same year the Picts of the plain of Manann and the Britons encountered each other at Mocetac or Magdedauc, now Mugdoc in Dumbartonshire, where a great battle was fought between them, in which Talorgan, the brother of Angus, who had been made king of the outlying Picts, was slain by the Britons. Two years after Tuadubr, the son of Bili, king of Alclyde, died, and a battle was fought between the Picts themselves at a place called by Tighernac " Sreith," in the land of Circin, that is in the Strath in the Mearns, in which Bruidhi, the son of Maelchu, fell. As his name is the same as the Brude, son of Mailcu, who was king of the northern Picts in the sixth century, this was probably an attack upon Angus's kingdom by the northern Picts.

Eadberht, king of Northumbria, and Angus, king of the Picts, now united for the purpose of subjecting the Britons of Alclyde entirely to their power, and in 756 they led an army to Alclyde, and there received the submission of the Britons on the first day of August in that year. Ten days afterwards, however, Simeon of Durham, records that almost the whole army perished as Eadberht was leading it from Ovania, probable Avondale or Strathaven in the vale of the Clyde, through the hill country to Niwanbyrig or Newburgh. The Britons of Alclyde thus passed a second time under subjection to the Angles, which continued some time, as in 760 the death of Dunnagual, the son of Tuadubr is recorded, but he is not termed king of Alclyde.

CHAPTER XIX

SCOTTISH HISTORY IN THE ENGLISH OR ANGLO-SAXON CHRONICLE

THE work which passes under the name of the *English Chronicle* is a continued narrative written at different times, and in the Anglo-Saxon language, of the most important events of English history from the earliest period to the year 1154. It is evident, both from the antiquity of the manuscripts of the *Chronicle* now extant, as well as from certain allusions and forms of speech which occur in it, that the latter part, at least, was written by a person contemporary with the events which he relates. In all probability the earlier part of the chronicle is also of a contemporary character, and therefore ascends to a very early period of English history, even to the time of the Heptarchy itself. This opinion rests upon the fact that, while the dialect of the latter portion of the chronicle approaches very nearly to our modern English, the early part of it bears the impress of times much more rude and ancient, and the language in which it is written is unintelligible to the modern reader who has not made the Anglo-Saxon tongue an object of study.

The best edition of the work is that of Benjamin Thorpe, published by the British Government in the *Rolls Series*, 1861.

There are now but six ancient copies of the *English Chronicle* known to be in existence, which may be described as follows :

A. The first copy of this chronicle is generally known by the name of the Benet or Plegmund Manuscript, so called because it is preserved in Benet (now Corpus Christi) College, Cambridge, and because Plegmund, Archbishop of Canterbury, in the reign of King Ælfred, is thought to have had some hand in compiling the first part of it.

" From internal evidence of an indirect nature," says Dr. Ingram, " there is great reason to presume that Archbishop Plegmund transcribed or superintended this very copy of the *Saxon Annals* to the year 891, the year in which he came to the See. Wanley observes it is written in one and the same hand to this year, and in hands equally ancient to the year 924, after which it is continued in different hands to the end.

" At the end of the year 890 is added, in a neat but imitative hand, the following interpolation, which is betrayed by the faintness of the ink, as well as by the Norman cast of the dialect and orthography :

" ' Her wæs Plegemund gecoron of gode and of eallen his halechen.'

" There are many other interpolations in this MS.; a particular account of which, however curious, would necessarily become tedious."

Prefixed to this manuscript is a genealogy of the West Saxon kings from the landing of Cerdic and his son Cynric to the accession of Ælfred.

B. The second copy of the *English Chronicle* is in the British Museum. (MS. Cotton, *Tiberius* A. vi.) It is " written in the same hand with much neatness and accuracy, from the beginning to the end," and " is of very high authority and antiquity. It was probably written about 977, where it terminates. The hand-writing resembles that ascribed to St. Dunstan. It narrowly escaped destruction in the fire at Westminster, previous to its removal to its present place of custody, being one of Sir R. Cotton's MSS., formerly belonging to the monastery of St. Augustine's, Canterbury."

C. A third manuscript is also in the British Museum. (Cotton, *Tiberius* B. i.)

" This manuscript contains many important additions to the former chronicles, some of which are confirmed by Cotton, *Tiberius* B. iv.; but many are not to be found in any other manuscript, particularly those in the latter part of it. These are now incorporated with the old materials. Wanley considers the hand-writing to be the same to the end of the year 1048. The orthography, however, varies about the year 890 (889 of the printed chronicle). There is a break between the years 925 and 934, when a slight notice is introduced of the expedition of Æthelstan into Scotland. The manuscript terminates imperfectly in 1066, after describing most minutely the battle of Stanford-bridge ; the few lines which appear in the last page being supplied by a much later hand."

D. A fourth copy of the *English Chronicle* also is found in the British Museum. (Cotton, *Tiberius* B. iv.)

" This manuscript is written in a plain and beautiful hand, with few abbreviations, and apparently copied in the early part, with the exception of the introductory description of Britain, from a very ancient manuscript. The defective parts, from A.D. 261 to 693, were long since supplied from four excellent manuscripts by Josselyn ; who also collated it throughout with the same ; inserting from them, both in the text and in the margin, such passages as came within his notice ; which are so numerous, that very few seem to have eluded his vigilant search. A smaller but elegant hand commences fol. 68, A.D. 1016 ; and it is continued to the end, A.D. 1079, in a similar hand, though by different writers. Wanley notices a difference in the year 1052."

E. The fifth manuscript is in the Bodleian Library at Oxford. (*Laud* E, 80.)

" It is a fair copy of older chronicles, with a few inaccuracies, omissions, and interpolations, to the year 1122 ; therefore no part of it was written before that period. The next ten years rather exhibit different ink than a different writer. From 1132 to the end, A.D. 1154, the language and orthography became gradually more Normanized, particularly in the reign of King Stephen ; the account of which was not written till the close of it.

The dates not being regularly affixed to the last ten years, Wanley has inadvertently described this manuscript as ending A.D. 1143; whereas it is continued eleven years afterwards."

F. The sixth and last copy is in the British Museum. (Cotton, *Domitian* A. viii.)

This is a singularly curious manuscript, attributed generally to a monk of Christ Church, Canterbury, on account of the monastic interpolations. It is often quoted and commended by H. Wharton, in his *Anglia Sacra*, because it contains much ecclesiastical and local information. It is considered, however, of the least authority among the Cotton manuscripts, because the writer has taken greater liberties in abridging former chronicles, and inserting translations of Latin documents in his own Normanized dialect. Towards the end the writer intended to say something about Prince Eadward, the father of Edgar and Margaret; but it is nearly obliterated and the manuscript soon after concludes, A.D. 1056. It is remarkable for being written both in Latin and Saxon; but for what purpose it is now needless to conjecture. It is said to have been given to Sir Robert Cotton by Camden.

G. Besides these six, no other ancient copy is known to exist; but there is a single leaf of an ancient copy in the British Museum. (Cotton, *Tiberius* A. iii.) There are also three modern transcripts, two of which are in the Bodleian Library (Junian MSS. and *Laud* G. 36) and one in the Dublin Library. (E 5, 15.) The Bodleian transcripts are taken from two of the Cotton manuscripts, and therefore are of little critical value; but the Dublin transcript appears to be taken from an original, now lost (Cott., *Otho* B. xi.), and therefore it possesses an independent authority.

At the end of the Dublin transcript is this note, in the hand-writing of Archbishop Usher: "These Annales are extant in Sr R. Cotton's Librarye at the ende of Bede's Historye in the Saxon Tongue." This accords with the description of the manuscript in Wanley's *Catalogue*, p. 219; to which the reader is referred for more minute particulars. As this manuscript was therefore in existence so late as 1705, when Wanley published his *Catalogue*, there can be little doubt that it perished in the lamentable fire of 1731, which either destroyed or damaged so many of the Cotton manuscripts while deposited in a house in Little Dean's Yard, Westminster.

This transcript is become more valuable from the loss of the original. It appears from the dates by William Lambard himself, at the beginning and the end, that it was begun by him in 1563, and finished in 1564, when he was about the age of twenty-five.

Of these six, or if we include the Dublin Manuscript, seven copies of the *English Chronicle*, no two of them agree in the date at which they terminate. Thus:

B comes down no later than A.D. 977.

G ends at A.D. 1001.

F ends imperfectly at 1056.

C ends at 1066.

A ends at 1070.

D ends abruptly at 1079.

E ends imperfectly at 1154.

The following extracts from the *English Chronicle*, relating to Scottish history, are made from Giles's edition of that work, corrected by comparison with Thorpe's edition :

EXTRACTS FROM THE ENGLISH, OR ANGLO-SAXON CHRONICLE.

A. 449. This year Martian and Valentinian succeeded to the empire, and reigned seven winters. And in their days Hengest and Horsa, invited by Wyrtgeorn [Vortigern], king of the Britons, sought Britain on the shore which is named Ypwines fleot ; first in support of the Britons, but afterwards they fought against them. King Wyrtgeorn gave them land in the southeast of this country, on condition that they should fight against the Picts. Then they fought against the Picts, and had the victory wheresoever they came. They then sent to the Angles ; desired a larger force to be sent, and caused them to be told the worthlessness of the Britons, and the excellencies of the land. Then they soon sent thither a larger force in aid of the others. At that time there came men from the three tribes in Germany ; from the Old Saxons, from the Angles, from the Jutes. From the Jutes came the Kentishmen and the Wightwarians, that is, the tribe which now dwells in Wight, and that race among the West Saxons which is still called the race of Jutes. From the Old Saxons came the men of Essex and Sussex and Wessex. From Anglia, which has ever since remained waste betwixt the Jutes and Saxons, came the men of East Anglia, Middle Anglia, Mercia, and all Northumbria. Their leaders were two brothers, Hengest and Horsa : they were the sons of Wihtgils ; Wihtgils son of Witta, Witta of Wecta, Wecta of Woden : from this Woden sprang all our royal families, and those of the Southumbrians also.

A. 455. This year Hengest and Horsa fought against king Vortigern at the place which is called Ægels-threp [Aylesford], and his brother Horsa was there slain, and after that Hengest obtained the kingdom, and Æsc his son.

A. 457. This year Hengest and Æsc his son fought against the Britons at the place which is called Crecganford [Crayford], and there slew four thousand men ; and the Britons then forsook Kent, and in great terror fled to London.[1]

A. 465. This year Hengest and Æsc fought against the Welsh [*i. e.*, "the enemy," or British] near Wippedes fleot [Ebbsfleet ?], and there slew twelve Welsh aldormen, and one of their thanes was slain there, whose name was Wipped.

A. 473. This year Hengest and Æsc fought against the Welsh, and took countless booty ; and the Welsh fled from the Angles as fire.

A. 477. This year Ælle came to Britain, and his three sons, Cymen, and Wlencing, and Cissa, with three ships, at a place which is named Cymenes-ora, and there slew many Welsh, and drove some in flight into the wood which is named Andredes-lea.

A. 488. This year Æsc succeeded to the kingdom, and for twenty-four years was king of the Kentish people.

A. 491. This year Ælle and Cissa besieged Andredes-ceaster, and slew all that dwelt therein, not even one Briton was there left.[2]

A. 495. This year came two aldormen to Britain, Cerdic and Cynric his son, with five ships, at the place which is called Cerdices ora, and on the same day they fought against the Welsh.

A. 508. This year Cerdic and Cynric slew a British king, whose name was Natan-leod, and five thousand men with him. After that the land was named Natan-lea, as far as Cerdicesford.

A. 514. This year came the West Saxons to Britain with three ships at the place which is called Cerdices ora, and Stuf and Wihtgar fought against the Britons and put them to flight.

A. 547. This year Ida began to reign, from whom arose the royal race of the Northumbrians; and reigned twelve years, and he built Bebbanburh, which was at first enclosed by a hedge, and afterwards by a wall.[3] Ida was the son of Eoppa, Eoppa of Esa, Esa of Ingwi, Ingwi of Angewit, Angewit of Aloc, Aloc of Benoc, Benoc of Brand, Brand of Baeldeg, Baeldeg of Woden, Woden of Freothelof, Freothelof of Freothewulf, Freothewulf of Finn, Finn of Godulf, Godulf of Geat.

A. 560. This year Ceawlin succeeded to the kingdom of the West Saxons, and Ælle assumed the kingdom of the Northumbrians, Ida being dead; each of them reigned thirty winters. Ælle was the son of Yffe, Yffe of Uxfrea, Uxfrea of Wilgils, Wilgils of Westerfalcna, Westerfalcna of Saefugl, Saefugl of Saebald, Saebald of Sigegeat, Sigegeat of Swebdaeg, Swebdaeg of Sigegar, Sigegar of Waegdaeg, Waegdaeg of Woden, Woden of Freothewulf.

A. 565. This year Æthelberht succeeded to the kingdom of the Kentish people, and held it fifty-three winters. In his days the holy Pope Gregory sent us baptism, that was in the two and thirtieth year of his reign: and Columba, a mass-priest, came to the Picts, and converted them to the faith of Christ: they are dwellers by the northern mountains. And their king gave him the island which is named Ii [Iona]: where there are five hides of land, from what men say. There Columba built a monastery, and he was abbot there thirty-two winters, and there he died when he was seventy-two winters. His inheritors yet have the place. The South Picts had been baptized long before: to them bishop Nina, who had been taught at Rome, preached baptism, whose church and his monastery is at Whiterne, hallowed in the name of St. Martin: there he rests, with many holy men. Now in Ii there must ever be an abbot, not a bishop; and to him must all the Scot bishops be subjects, because Columba was an abbot, not a bishop.

A. 588. This year king Ælle died, and Æthelric reigned after him for five years.

A. 593. This year Ceawlin, and Cwichelm, and Cryda perished; and Æthelfrith succeeded to the kingdom of the Northumbrians; he was the son of Æthelric, Æthelric of Ida.

A. 597. This year Ceolwulf began to reign over the West Saxons; and he constantly fought and strove against either the Angle race, or against the Welsh, or against the Picts, or against the Scots. He was the son of Cutha, Cutha of Cynric, Cynric of Cerdic, Cerdic of Elesa, Elesa of Esla, Esla of Giwis, Giwis of Wig, Wig of Freawine, Freawine of Freothogar, Freothogar of Brand, Brand of Baeldaeg, Baeldaeg of Woden. This year Augustine and his companions came to the land of the Angles.

A. 603. This year Ægthan, king of the Scots, fought against the Dalreods and against Æthelfrith, king of the Northumbrians, at Dægsanstan, and almost all his army was slain.   There was slain Theodbald, Æthelfrith's brother, with all his host.   Since then no king of Scots has dared to lead an army into this nation.   Hering, the son of Hussa, led the army hither.

A. 606.   .   .   .   In this year Æthelfrith led his army to Chester, and there slew numberless Welsh : and so was fulfilled the prophecy of Augustine, which he uttered, " If the Welsh refuse peace with us, they shall perish at the hands of the Saxons."   There also were slain two hundred priests, who came that they might pray for the army of the Welsh : their chief was named Scromail [Brocmail], who escaped thence with some fifty.'

A. 607.   This year Ceolwulf fought with the South Saxons.

A. 617.   This year Æthelfrith, king of the Northumbrians, was slain by Raedwald king of the East Angles, and Ædwine the son of Aelle succeeded to the kingdom, and ravaged all Britain, save the Kentish people only.'   And drove out the æthelings, sons of Æthelfrith ; that was, first Eanfrith and Oswald, then Oswiu, Oslac, Oswudu, Oslaf, and Offa.

A. 627.   This year, at Easter, Paulinus baptized Ædwine king of the Northumbrians, with his people : and earlier in the same year, at Pentecost, he had baptized Eanflaed, daughter of the same king.

A. 633.   This year king Ædwine was slain by Cadwalla and Penda at Heathfield [Hatfield Chase ?] on the second of the Ides of October, and he reigned seventeen years ; and his son Osfrith was also slain with him.   And then afterwards Cadwalla and Penda went and laid waste all the land of the Northumbrians.   When Paulinus saw that, then took he Æthelburh, Ædwine's widow, and withdrew in a ship to Kent.   And Eadbald and Honorius received him very honorably, and gave him a bishop's see at Rochester ; and he there continued to his end.

A. 634.   .   .   .   This year Osric, whom Paulinus had previously baptized, succeeded to the kingdom of Deira ; he was the son of Ælfric, Ædwine's paternal uncle.   And to Bernicia succeeded Eanfrith the son of Æthelfrith.   And this year also bishop Birinus first preached baptism to the West Saxons under king Cynegils.   Birinus went thither by command of Honorius the Pope, and he there was bishop until his life's end.   And this year also Oswald succeeded to the kingdom of the Northumbrians, and he reigned nine winters ; the ninth being reckoned to him on account of the heathenship which they had practised, who ruled them for one year between him and Ædwine.

A. 642.   This year Oswald, king of the Northumbrians, was slain by Penda the Southumbrian at Maserfield on the day of the Nones of August, and his corpse was buried at Bardney, whose holiness and his miracles were afterwards variously made known throughout this island, and his hands are at Bamborough, uncorrupted.   And the same year that Oswald was slain, Oswiu his brother succeeded to the kingdom of the Northumbrians, and he reigned thirty years less two.'

A. 670.   This year Oswiu king of the Northumbrians died, on the 15th of the Kalends of March, and Ecgferth his son reigned after him ; and Hlothhere, the nephew of bishop Æthelbyrht, succeeded to the bishopric over the West Saxons, and held it seven years, and Bishop Theodore consecrated him.   And Oswiu was the son of Æthelfrith, Æthelfrith of Æthelric, Æthelric of Ida, Ida of Eoppa.

A. 684.   In this year Ecgferth sent an army against the Scots, and Berht his aldorman with it and miserably they afflicted and burned God's churches.

A. 685.   .   .   .   This year Ceadwalla began to strive for the kingdom.

Ceadwalla was the son of Coenbryht, Coenbryht of Cadda, Cadda of Cutha, Cutha of Ceawlin, Ceawlin of Cynric, Cynric of Cerdic. And Mul was the brother of Ceadwalla, and he was afterwards burned in Kent. And the same year, on the 13th of the Kalends of June, king Ecgferth was slain, near the North sea, and a great army with him. He had been king fifteen winters, and Aldferth his brother succeeded to the kingdom after him. Ecgferth was the son of Oswiu, Oswiu of Æthelfrith, Æthelfrith of Æthelric, Æthelric of Ida, Ida of Eoppa.

A. 688. This year Ine succeeded to the kingdom of the West Saxons, and held it thirty-seven winters; and he built the monastery at Glaston-bury; and afterwards withdrew to Rome, and there dwelt until his dying days: and the same year Ceadwalla went to Rome, and received baptism from the Pope, and the Pope named him Peter; and after seven nights he died. Now Ine was the son of Cenred, Cenred of Ceolwald, Ceolwald was Cynegils' brother, and they were sons of Cuthwine the son of Ceawlin, Ceawlin of Cynric, Cynric of Cerdic.[7]

A. 705. This year Aldferth, king of the Northumbrians, died on the nineteenth of the Kalends of January at Driffield; and bishop Saxwulf. Then Osred his son succeeded to the kingdom.

A. 716. This year Osred king of the Northumbrians was slain on the southern border; he had the kingdom seven [?] winters after Aldferth; then Cenred succeeded to the kingdom, and held it two years, then Osric, and held it eleven years; and the same year Ceolred king of the Mercians died, and his body lies at Lichfield, and Æthelred's, the son of Penda, at Bardney. Then Æthelbald succeeded to the kingdom of the Mercians, and held it forty-one winters. Æthelbald was the son of Alweo, Alweo of Eawa, Eawa of Pybba, whose kin is before written. And the pious man Ecgberht turned the monks in the island of Iona to right, so that they observed Easter rightly, and the ecclesiastical tonsure.

A. 731. This year Osric, king of the Northumbrians, was slain, and Ceolwulf succeeded to the kingdom and held it eight years, and Ceolwulf was the son of Cutha, Cutha of Cuthwine, Cuthwine of Leodwald, Leodwald of Ecgwald, Ecgwald of Aldhelm, Aldhelm of Ocga, Ocga of Ida, Ida of Eoppa. And archbishop Beorhtwald died on the Ides of January; he was bishop thirty-seven years six months and fourteen days. And the same year Tatwine was consecrated archbishop; he had before been a priest at Breo-dun in Mercia. Daniel bishop of Winchester, and Ingwald bishop of London, and Aldwine bishop of Lichfield, and Aldwulf bishop of Rochester consecrated him on the tenth of June; he had the archbishopric three years.

A. 737. This year bishop Forthere and queen Frejthogitha went to Rome. And king Ceolwulf received St. Peter's tonsure, and gave his kingdom to Eadberht, his paternal uncle's son; he reigned twenty-one winters; and bishop Æthelwold and Acca died, and Cynewulf was consecrated bishop. And the same year king Æthelbald ravaged the land of the Northumbrians.

A. 738. This year Eadberht the son of Eata, Eata being the son of Leodwald, succeeded to the kingdom of the Northumbrians, and held it twenty-one winters. His brother was archbishop Ecgberht the son of Eata; and they both rest in one porch at York.[8]

A. 755. This year Cynewulf, and the West Saxon witan deprived his kinsman Sigebryht of his kingdom, for his unrighteous deeds, except Hampshire, and that he held until he slew the aldorman who had longest remained with him. And then Cynewulf drove him into Andred, and he there abode until a swine-herd stabbed him at Pryfetes flod, and he avenged the aldorman Cumbra.

And Cynewulf fought often in great battles against the Brito-Welsh; and after he had held the kingdom about one and thirty years, he would drive out an ætheling, who was named Cyncheard; and Cyncheard was Sigebryht's brother. And he then learned that the king with a small company was on a visit to a woman at Merantun [Merton]; and he there beset him and surrounded the bower, before the men discovered him who were with the king. And when the king perceived that, he went to the door, and then gallantly defended himself, until he looked on the ætheling, and then rushed out on him and sorely wounded him; and they were all fighting against the king until they had slain him. . . .

A. 757. This year Eadberht king of the Northumbrians assumed the tonsure, and his son Oswulf succeeded to the kingdom, and reigned one year; and he was slain by his household on the eighth of the Kal. of August.⁹

A. 759. This year Bregowin was ordained archbishop at St. Michael's-tide, and held the see four years. And Moll Æthelwald succeeded to the kingdom of the Northumbrians, and reigned six winters, and then left it.

A. 761. This year was the great winter; and Moll king of the Northumbrians slew Oswine at Ædwin's Cliff on the eighth of the Ides of August.¹⁰

A. 765. This year Alchred succeeded to the kingdom of Northumbria, and reigned nine winters.

A. 774. This year at Eastertide, the Northumbrians drove their king Alchred from York, and took Æthelred, the son of Moll, for their lord, who reigned four winters.¹¹

A. 778. This year Æthalbald and Heardberht slew three high-reeves; Ealdulf, the son of Bosa, at Kings-cliff, and Cynewulf and Ecga at Helathyrn, on the eleventh of the Kalends of April: and then Alfwold succeeded to the kingdom and drove Æthelred from the land; and he reigned ten winters.

A. 787. This year king Beorhtric took Eadburh, king Offa's daughter, to wife; and in his days first came three ships of Northmen, from Hæretha-land [in Norway]. And then the reve rode thereto, and would drive them to the king's vill, for he knew not what they were: and they there slew him. Those were the first ships of Danishmen that sought the land of the English race.¹²

A. 789. This year Alfwold, king of the Northumbrians, was slain by Sicga on the 8th of the Kalends of October; and a heavenly light was frequently seen there where he was slain; and he was buried at Hexham within the church; and Osred, the son of Alcred succeeded to the kingdom after him; he was his nephew. And a great synod was assembled at Aclea.

A. 790. This year archbishop Ianbryht died, and the same year abbot Æthelheard was chosen archbishop. And Osred, king of the Northumbrians, was betrayed, and driven from the kingdom; and Æthelred, the son of Æthelwald afterwards succeeded to the kingdom.

A. 791. This year Baldwulf was hallowed bishop of Whiterne, on the 16th of the Kalends of August, by archbishop Eanbald and by bishop Æthelberht.

A. 792. This year Offa, king of the Mercians, commanded the head of king Æthelbryht to be struck off. And Osred, who had been king of the Northumbrians, having come home from exile, was seized and slain on the 18th of the Kalends of October; and his body rests at Tynemouth. And king Æthelred took a new wife, who was called Ælfled, on the 3rd of the Kalends of October.

A. 793. This year dire forewarnings came over the land of the North-umbrians, and miserably terrified the people; these were excessive whirl-winds, and lightnings; and fiery dragons were seen flying in the air. A great famine soon followed these tokens; and a little after that, in the same year, on the 6th of the Ides of January, the havoc of heathen men miser-ably destroyed God's church at Lindisfarne through rapine and slaughter. And Sicga died on the 8th of the Kalends of March.

A. 794. This year Pope Adrian and king Offa died, and Æthelred, king of the Northumbrians, was slain by his own people on the 13th of the Kalends of May; and bishop Ceolwulf and bishop Eadbald departed from the land. And Ecgferth succeeded to the kingdom of the Mercians, and died the same year. . . . And the heathens ravaged among the Northum-brians, and plundered Ecgferth's monastery at Donemuth [Wearmouth]; and there one of their leaders was slain, and also some of their ships were wrecked by a tempest; and many of them were there drowned, and some came to shore alive, and they were forthwith slain at the river's mouth.

A. 795. This year the moon was eclipsed between cock-crowing and dawn, on the 5th of the Kalends of April; and Eardwulf succeeded to the kingdom of the Northumbrians on the 2d of the Ides of May; and he was afterwards consecrated king, and raised to his throne on the 8th of the Kalends of June, at York, by archbishop Eanbald, and bishop Æthel-berht, and bishops Higbald and Badwulf.

A. 798. This year there was a great fight at Whalley in the land of the Northumbrians, during Lent, on the 4th of the Nones of April, and there Alric, the son of Heardberht, was slain, and many others with him.

A. 806. This year the moon was eclipsed on the Kalends of September; and Eardwulf king of the Northumbrians was driven from his kingdom; and Eanberht, bishop of Hexham, died.

A. 823. This year there was a fight of the Welsh and the men of Devon at Gafulford: and the same year Ecgbryht king of the West Saxons and Beornwulf king of the Mercians fought at Ellendun, and Ecgbryht gained the victory, and a great slaughter was there made. He then sent from the army his son Æthelwulf, and Ealhstan his bishop, and Wulfheard his aldor-man to Kent with a large force and they drove Baldred the king north over the Thames. And the men of Kent, and the men of Surrey, and the South Saxons, and the East Saxons, turned to him; because they had formerly been unjustly forced from his kinsmen. And the same year the king of the East Angles and the nation sought Ecgbryht for peace and as protection from dread of the Mercians; and the same year the East Angles slew Beornwulf king of the Mercians.

A. 825. This year Ludecan king of the Mercians was slain, and his five aldormen with him; and Wiglaf succeeded to the kingdom.

A. 827. This year the moon was eclipsed on the massnight of midwinter. And the same year king Ecgbryht subdued the kingdom of the Mercians, and all that was south of the Humber; and he was the eighth king who was *Brytenwalda*. Ælle king of the South Saxons was the first who had thus much sway; the second was Ceawlin king of the West Saxons; the third was Æthelbryht king of the Kentishmen; the fourth was Redwald king of the East Angles; the fifth was Ædwine king of the Northumbrians; the sixth was Oswald who reigned after him; the seventh was Oswiu, Oswald's brother; the eighth was Ecgbryht king of the West Saxons. And Ecgbryht led an army to Dore against the Northumbrians, and they there offered him obe-dience and concord, and thereupon they separated."

A. 828.   This year Wiglaf again obtained the kingdom of the Mercians, and bishop Æthelwald died ; and the same year king Ecgbryht led an army against the North Welsh, and he reduced them to humble obedience.

A. 833.   This year king Ecgbryht fought against the crews of thirty-five ships at Carrum, and there was great slaughter made, and the Danishmen held possession of the battle-place.   And Hereferth and Wigthun, two bishops, died ; and Dudda and Osmod, two aldormen, died.

A. 866.   This year Ætheldred, Æthelbryht's brother, succeeded to the kingdom of the West Saxons : and the same year a great heathen army came to the land of the Angle race, and took up their winter quarters among the East Angles, and were there horsed ;   and the East-Angles made peace with them.

A. 870.   This year the army rode over Mercia into East Anglia, and took up their winter quarters at Thetford : and the same winter king Ædmund fought against them, and the Danes gained the victory, and slew the king, and subdued all that land, and destroyed all the monasteries which they came to.

A. 873.   This year the army went into Northumbria, and took up winter quarters at Torksey in Lindsey : and then the Mercians made peace with the army.

A. 875.   This year the army went from Repton ; and Halfdan went with some of the army into Northumbria, and took up winter quarters by the river Tyne.   And the army subdued the land, and often harried on the Picts, and the Strathclyde Welsh.   And the three kings, Guthorm, and Oskytel, and Amund, went with a large army from Repton to Cambridge, and sat down there one year.   And that summer king Ælfred went out to sea with a fleet, and fought against the crews of seven ships, and one of them he took, and put the rest to flight.

A. 924.   In this year, before midsummer, king Eadweard went with his forces to Nottingham, and commanded the burgh to be built on the south side of the river, over against the other, and the bridge over the Trent, between the two burghs : and then he went thence into Peakland, to Bakewell, and commanded a burgh to be built nigh thereunto, and manned.   And then chose him for father and for lord, the king of the Scots and the whole nation of the Scots, and Ragnold and the sons of Eadulf and all those who dwell in Northumbria, as well English as Danish, and Northmen and others, and also the king of the Strathclyde Welsh, and all the Strathclyde Welsh.[14]

A. 925.   This year king Eadweard died, and Æthelstan his son succeeded to the kingdom.   And St. Dunstan was born and Wulfhelm succeeded to the archbishopric of Canterbury.   This year king Æthelstan and Sihtric, king of the Northumbrians, came together at Tamworth, on the 3d of the Kalends of February ; and Æthelstan gave him his sister.

A. 926.   This year fiery lights appeared in the north part of the heavens. And Sihtric died, and King Æthelstan assumed the kingdom of the Northumbrians.   And he subjugated all the kings who were in this island ; first, Howel, king of the West Welsh ; and Constantine, king of the Scots ; and Owen Gwent; and Ealdred, son of Ealdulf, of Bamborough ; and they confirmed the peace by pledge, and by oaths, at the place which is called Eamot, on the 4th of the Ides of July ; and they renounced all idolatry, and after that departed in peace.

A. 933.   This year . . . king Æthelstan went into Scotland, as well with a land army as with a fleet, and ravaged a great part of it.

A. 937.   This year king Æthelstan and Eadmund his brother led a force to Brunanburh, and there fought against Olaf ; and, Christ helping, had the victory : and they there slew five kings and seven jarls.

 Here Æthelstan, king, of earls the lord, of warriors the ring giver, and his brother eke, Eadmund Ætheling, life-long glory

in battle won
with edges of swords
at Brunanburh
The board-walls they clove,
they hewed the war-linden,
 with hammas' leavings,
offspring of Eadweard,
such was their noble nature
from their ancestors,
that they in battle oft
'gainst every foe
the land defended,
hoards and homes.
The foe they crushed,
the Scottish people
and the shipmen
fated fell.
The field streamed
with warriors' blood,
since the sun up
at morning-tide,
mighty planet,
glided o'er grounds,
God's candle bright,
the eternal Lord's,
till the noble creature
sank to its setting.
There lay many a warrior
by javelins strewed,
northern man
over shield shot ;
so the Scots eke,
weary, war-sad.
West Saxons onwards
throughout the day,
in bands,
pursued the footsteps
of the loathed nations.
They hewed the fugitives
behind, amain,
with falchions mill-sharp.
Mercians refused not
the hard hand-play
to any heroes
who with Olaf,
over the ocean,
in the ship's bosom,
this land sought
fated to the fight.

Five lay
on the battle-stead,
youthful kings,
by swords in slumber laid :
so seven eke
of Olaf's jarls ;
of the army countless,
shipmen and Scots.
There was made flee
the Northmen's prince,
by need constrained,
to the ship's prow
with a little band.
The bark drove afloat :
the king departed
on the fallow flood,
his life preserved.
So there eke the aged
came by flight
to his country north,
Constantine,
hoary warrior.
He had no cause to exult
in the falchions' intercourse.
Here was his kindred band
of friends o'erthrown
on the folk-stead,
in battle slain ;
and his son he left
on the slaughter-place,
mangled with wounds,
young in the warfare.
He had no cause to boast,
hero grizzly-haired,
of the bill-clashing,
the old deceiver ;
nor Olaf the more,
with the remnant of their armies ;
they had no cause to laugh
that they in war's works
the better men were
in the battle-stead,
at the rush of banners,
meeting of javelins,
tryst of men,
the clash of weapons ;
that they on the slaughter-field
with Eadweard's
offspring played.

The North men departed
in their nailed barks ;
bloody relic of darts,
on roaring ocean
o'er the deep water
Dublin to seek,
again Ireland,
shamed in mind.
  So too the brothers,
both together,
king and ætheling,
their country sought,
West Saxons' land,
in the war exulting.
They left behind them,
the carcasses to share,
with pallid coat
and the swarty raven
with horned neb,
and him of goodly coat,
the eagle white tailed,
the carrion to devour,
greedy war-hawk,
and the grey beast,
wolf of the wood.
Carnage greater has not been
in this island
ever yet
of people slain,
before this,
by edges of swords,
as books us say,
old chroniclers,
since from the east hither,
Angles and Saxons
came to land,
o'er the broad seas
Britain sought,
proud war-smiths,
the Welsh o'ercame,
men for glory eager
the country obtained.

A. 940. This year King Æthelstan died at Gloucester on the 6th of the Kal. of November, forty-one years save one night after King Ælfred died. And Eadmund the ætheling, his brother, succeeded to the kingdom, and he was then eighteen winters old. And King Æthelstan reigned fourteen years and ten weeks.

A. 944. This year King Eadmund subdued all Northumberland under his power, and expelled two kings, Olaf, son of Sihtric, and Rainald, son of Guthferth.

A. 945. This year King Eadmund harried over all Cumberland, and gave it all up to Malcolm king of the Scots, on the condition, that he should be his co-operator, both on sea and on land.¹⁶

A. 946. This year King Eadmund died on St. Augustine's mass-day. It was widely known how he his days ended : that Liofa stabbed him at Puckle-church. Æthelflaed at Domerham, Ælfgar's daughter, the aldorman, was then his queen : and he had the kingdom six years and a half. And then after him his brother Eadred the ætheling succeeded to the kingdom, and reduced all Northumberland under his power : and the Scots gave him oaths, that they would all that he would.¹⁶

A. 947. This year King Eadred came to Taddenes Scylf, and there Wulfstan the archbishop and all the Northumbrian witan swore fealty to the king : and within a little while they belied it all, both pledges and also oaths.

A. 948. This year king Eadred harried over all Northumberland, because they had taken Eric to be their king : and then, in that harrying, was the famous monastery burned at Ripon that St. Wilfrid built. And as the king went homewards, the army within York overtook him (the rear of the king's forces was at Chesterford) and there they made great slaughter. Then was the king so wroth that he would have marched his forces in again and wholly destroyed the land. When the Northumbrian witan understood that, then forsook they Eric, and made compensation for the deed to king Eadred.

A. 949. This year Olaf Cwiran came to Northumberland.

A. 952. In this year king Eadred commanded archbishop Wulfstan to be brought into the fastness at Jedburgh, because he had been oft accused to the king : and in this year also the king commanded great slaughter to be made in the town of Thetford, in revenge for the abbat Eadelm, whom they had before slain. This year the Northumbrians expelled king Olaf, and received Eric, Harold's son.

A. 954. This year the Northumbrians expelled Eric, and Eadred assumed the kingdom of the Northumbrians. . . .

A. 972. This year Eadgar the ætheling was hallowed king, on Pentecost's mass-day, on the 5th of the Ides of May, the thirteenth year since he had obtained the kingdom, at the Hot-baths ; and he was then one less than thirty years of age. And soon after that, the king led all his ship-forces to Chester ; and there came to meet him six kings, and they all swore fealty to him, that they would be his fellow-workers by sea and by land.

A. 975. The 8th of the Ides of July. Here Eadgar died, ruler of Angles, West Saxons' joy, and Mercians' protector, . . . and this year Eadward, his son, succeeded to the kingdom.

A. 978. . . . In this year was King Eadward martyred ; and Æthelred the ætheling, his brother, succeeded to the kingdom, and he was in the same year consecrated king.

A. 993. In this year came Olaf with ninety-three ships to Staines, and ravaged there about, and then went thence to Sandwich, and so thence to Ipswich, and that all over-ran ; and so to Maldon. And there Brithnoth the alderman came against them with his forces, and fought against them : and they there slew the alderman, and had possession of the place of carnage. And after that peace was made with them ; and him [Olaf] the king afterwards received at the bishop's hands, through the instruction of Sigeric bishop of the Kentishmen, and Ælfheah [II.] of Winchester.

A. 994. In this year came Olaf and Svein to London, on the nativity of St. Mary, with ninety-four ships ; and they then continued fighting stoutly against the town, and would also have set fire to it. But there they sustained more harm and evil than they ever supposed that any townsmen would be able to do unto them.

A. 1014. In this year king Svein ended his days, at Candlemas, on the third of the Nones of February. And that same year Ælfuig was consecrated bishop of London, at York, on St. Juliana's mass-day. And all the fleet then chose Cnut for king. Then counselled all the witan who were in England, clergy and laity, that they should send after king Æthelred ; and they declared that no lord was dearer to them than their natural lord, if he would rule them more justly than he had before done. Then sent the king his son Eadward hither with his messengers, and bade them to greet all his people ; and said that he would be to them a loving lord, and amend all those things which they all abhorred, and all of those things should be forgiven which had been done or said to him, on condition that they all, with one consent, would be obedient to him, without deceit. And they then established full friendship, by word and by pledge, on each side, and declared every Danish king an outlaw from England for ever. Then, during Lent, king Æthelred came home to his own people ; and he was gladly received by them all. Then, after Svein was dead, Cnut sat with his army at Gainsborough until Easter ; and it was agreed between him and the people of Lindsey that they should find him horses, and that afterwards they should all go out together, and plunder. Then came king Æthelred thither, to Lindsey, with his full force, before they were ready : and then they plundered, and burned, and slew all the people whom they could reach. And Cnut went away with his fleet, and thus the poor people were deceived through him, and then he went southward until he came to Sandwich ; and there he caused the hostages to be put on shore who had been delivered to his father, and cut off their hands, and ears, and noses. And besides all these evils, the king ordered the army which lay at Greenwich to be paid twenty-one thousand pounds.

A. 1017. In this year king Cnut obtained the whole realm of the English race, and divided it into four parts : Wessex to himself, and East Anglia to Thorkell, and Mercia to Eadric, and Northumbria to Eric.'' And in this year was Eadric the aldorman slain in London, very justly, and Northman, son of Leofwine the aldorman, and Æthelweard, son of Æthelmaer, the great, and Brihtric, son of Ælfeah, in Devonshire. And king Cnut banished Eadwig the ætheling, and afterwards commanded him to be slain, and Æadwig king of the churls. And then, before the Kalends of August, the king commanded the relict of king Æthelred, Richard's daughter, to be fetched for his wife ; that was Ælfgyfu in English, Ymma in French.

A. 1031. This year Cnut went to Rome. And as soon as he came home then went he into Scotland and the king of the Scots, Malcolm, submitted to him, and became his man, but that he held only a little while ; and two other kings, Maelbaethe and Iehmarc. And Robert, count of Normandy, went to Jerusalem, and there died ; and William, who was afterwards king of England, succeeded to Normandy, although he was a child.

A. 1036. This year died king Cnut at Shaftesbury, and he is buried in Winchester in the old monastery: and he was king over all England very nigh twenty years. And soon after his decease there was a meeting of all the witan at Oxford ; and Leofric the earl, and almost all the thanes north of the Thames, and the " lithsmen " at London, chose Harold for chief of all England, him and his brother Harthacnut who was in Denmark. And Godwine the earl and all the chief men of Wessex withstood it as long as they could ; but they were unable to effect any thing in opposition to it. And then it was resolved that Ælfgyfu, Harthacnut's mother, should dwell at Winchester with the king her son's, " huscarls " [the Danish body-guard] and hold all Wessex in his power ; and Godwine the earl was their man. Some men said of Harold that he was son of king Cnut and of Ælfgyfu daughter of Ælfhelm the aldorman, but it seemed quite incredible to many men ; and he was nevertheless full king over all England.

A. 1037. This year was Harold chosen king over all, and Harthacnut forsaken, because he stayed too long in Denmark ; and then they drove out his mother Ælfgyfu, the queen, without any kind of mercy, against the stormy winter : and she came then to Bruges beyond the sea ; and Balwine the count there well received her, and there kept her the while she had need. And before, in this year, died Æfic the noble dean at Evesham.

A. 1039. This year king Harold died at Oxford, on the 16th of the Kalends of April, and he was buried at Westminster. And he ruled England four years and sixteen weeks ; and in his days to sixteen ships eight marks were paid for each rower, in like manner as had been before done in the days of king Cnut. And in this same year came king Harthacnut to Sandwich, seven nights before midsummer. And he was immediately received as well by Angles as by Danes.

A. 1040. This year died king Harold. Then sent they after Harthacnut to Bruges ; thinking that they did well. And he then came hither with sixty ships before midsummer, and then imposed a very heavy tribute so that it could hardly be levied; that was eight marks for each rower, and all were then averse to him who before had desired him; and moreover he did nothing kindly during his whole reign. He caused the dead Harold to be taken up, and had him cast into a fen. This year archbishop Eadsige went to Rome. This year was the tribute paid; that was twenty-one thousand and ninety-nine pounds. And after that they paid to thirty-two ships, eleven thousand and forty-eight pounds. And, in this same year, came Eadward, son of king Æthelred, hither to land, from Normandy; he was brother of king Harthacnut: they were both sons of Ælfgyfu, who was daughter of count Richard.

A. 1042. This year died king Harthacnut as he stood at his drink, and he suddenly fell to the earth with a terrible convulsion.

A. 1043. This year was Eadward consecrated king at Winchester on the first day of Easter. And this year, fourteen nights before St. Andrew's mass, the king was advised to ride from Gloucester, and Leofric the earl, and Godwine the earl, and Sigwarth [Siward] the earl, with their followers, to Winchester, unawares upon the lady [Emma]; and they bereaved her of all the treasures which she possessed, they were not to be told, because before that she had been very hard with the king her son; inasmuch as she had done less for him than he would, before he was king, and also since: and they suffered her after that to remain therein.

This year king Eadward took the daughter [Edgitha] of Godwine the earl for his wife.

A. 1051. . . . And in this same year were banished Godwine, the earl, and all his sons from England; and he and his wife, and his three sons, Sweyen, and Tostig, and Gyrth went to Bruges: and Harold and Leofwine went to Ireland, and there dwelt during the winter.

A. 1052. This year came Harold, the earl, from Ireland, with his ships to the mouth of the Severn, nigh the boundaries of Somerset and Devonshire, and there greatly ravaged; and the people of the land drew together against him, as well from Somerset as from Devonshire; and he put them to flight, and there slew more than thirty good thanes, besides other people: and soon after that he went about Penwithsteort. And then king Eadward caused forty smacks to be fitted out. They lay at Sandwich many weeks; they were to lie in wait for Godwine, the earl, who had been at Bruges during the winter; and, notwithstanding, he came hither to land first, so that they knew it not. And during the time that he was here in the land, he enticed to him all the men of Kent, and all the boatmen from Hastings and everywhere there by the sea-coast, and all the East end, and Sussex, and Surrey, and much else in addition thereto. Then all declared that they with him would die and live. . . . And Godwine landed, and Harold his son, and from their fleet as many as to them seemed fitting. Then there was a general council: and they gave his earldom clean to Godwine, as full and as free as he before possessed it, and to his sons also all that they before possessed, and to his wife and his daughter as full and as free as they before possessed it.

A. 1053. In this year was the king at Winchester at Easter, and Godwine, the earl, with him, and Harold, the earl, his son, and Tostig. Then, on the second day of Easter, sat he with the king at the feast; then suddenly sank he down by the footstool, deprived of speech, and of all his power, and he was then carried into the king's chamber, and they thought it would pass over: but it did not so: but he continued on, thus speechless and powerless, until the Thursday, and then resigned his life: and he lies there within the old monastery. And his son Harold succeeded to his earldom, and resigned that which he before held ; and Ælfgar succeeded thereto.

A. 1054. This year went Siward the earl [of Northumbria] with a great army into Scotland, and made much slaughter of the Scots and put them to flight ; and the king escaped. Moreover, many fell on his side, as well Danishmen as English, and also his own son.

A. 1065. And king Eadward came to Westminster at midwinter, and there caused to be consecrated the monastery which himself had built to the glory of God and of St. Peter, and of all God's saints ; and the church hallowing was on Childermass-day. And he died on Twelfth-day eve, and him they buried on Twelfth-day eve, in the same minster, as it hereafter sayeth. . . . And this year also was Harold consecrated king.

A. 1066. In this year king Harold came from York to Westminster at Easter which was after the midwinter in which the king died, and Easter was then on the day the 16th of the Kalends of May. . . . And soon after came in Tostig the earl from beyond sea into the Isle of Wight, with so great a fleet as he might procure ; and there they yielded him as well money as food. And king Harold, his brother, gathered so great a ship-force, and also a land-force, as no king here in the land had before done ; because it was made known to him that William the Bastard would come hither and win this land ; all as it afterward happened. And the while, came Tostig the earl into Humber with sixty ships ; and Eadwine the earl came with a land-force and drove him out. And the boatmen forsook him ; and he went to Scotland with twelve smacks. And there met him Harald king of Norway with three hundred ships ; and Tostig submitted to him and became his man. And they then went both into Humber, until they came to York ; and there fought against them Eadwine the earl, and Morkere the earl, his brother: but the Normen had the victory. Then was it made known to Harold king of Angles that this had thus happened : and this battle was on the vigil of St. Matthew. Then came Harold our king unawares on the Northmen, and met with them beyond York, at Stanford-bridge, with a great army of English people ; and there during the day was a very severe fight on both sides. There was slain Harald Harfagri ["the Fairhaired"], and Tostig the earl ; and the Northmen who were there remaining were put to flight ; and the English from behind hotly smote them, until they came, some, to their ships, some were drowned, and also burned ; and thus in divers ways they perished, so that there were few left : and the English had possession of the place of carnage. The king then gave his protection to Olaf, son of the king of the Norwegians, and to their bishop, and to the earl of Orkney, and to all those who were left in the ships : and they then went up to our king and swore oaths that they ever would observe peace and friendship towards this land ; and the king let them go home with twenty-four ships. These two great battles were fought within five days. Then came William count of Normandy into Pevensey, on the eve of St. Michael's mass : and soon after they were on their way, they constructed a castle at Hasting's-port. This was then made known to king Harold, and he then gathered a great force, and came to meet him at the hoar apple-tree ; and William came against him unawares, before his people were set in order. But the king nevertheless strenuously fought against him with those men who would follow him ; and there was great slaughter made on either hand. There was slain king Harold, and Leofwine the earl, his brother, and Gyrth the earl, his brother, and many good men ; and all the Frenchmen had possession of the place of carnage, all as God granted them for the people's sins. Archbishop Ealdred and the townsmen of London would then have child Eadgar for king, all as was his true natural right : and Eadwine and Morkere vowed to him that they would fight together with him. But in that degree that it ought ever to have been forwarder, so was it from day to day later and worse ; so that at the end all passed away. This fight was done on the day of Calixtus the Pope. And William the count went afterwards again to Hastings, and there awaited to see whether the people would submit to him. But when he understood that they would not come to him, he went upwards with all his army which was left to him, and that which afterwards had come from over the sea to him ; and he harried all that part which he over-ran, until he came to Berkhampstead. And there came to meet him archbishop Ealdred, and child Eadgar, and Eadwine the earl, and Morkere the earl, and all the chief men of London ; and then submitted, for need, when the most harm had been done : and it was very unwise that they had not done so before ; since God would not better it, for our sins : and they delivered hostages, and swore oaths to him ; and he vowed to them that he would be a kind lord to them : and nevertheless during this, they harried all that they over-ran. Then, on mid-winter's day, archbishop Aldred consecrated him king at Westminster ; and he gave him a pledge upon Christ's book, and also swore, before he would set the crown upon his head, that he would govern this nation as well as any king before him had at the best done, if they would be faithful to him. Nevertheless, he laid a tribute on the people, very heavy ; and then went, during Lent, over sea to Normandy, and took with him archbishop Stigand, and Aegelnoth, abbot of Glastonbury, and child Eadgar, and Eadwine the earl, and Morkere the earl, and Waltheof the earl, and many other good men from England. And bishop Odo and William the earl remained here behind, and they built castles wide throughout the nation, and poor people distressed ; and ever after it greatly grew in evil. May the end be good when God will.

A. 1067. This year the king came back to England on St. Nicholas's mass-day, and on that day Christ's Church, Canterbury, was consumed by fire. Bishop Wulfwig also died, and lies buried at his see of Dorchester. Child Eadric and the Britons were hostile this year, and fought with the men of the castle at Hereford, to whom they did much harm. The king this year imposed a heavy tax on the unfortunate people ; but, notwithstanding, he let his men plunder all the country which they passed through : after which he marched to Devonshire and besieged Exeter eighteen days. Many of his army were slain there : but he had promised them well and performed ill : the citizens surrendered the city, because the thanes had betrayed them. This summer the child Eadgar, with his mother Agatha, his sisters Margaret and Christina, Maerleswegen and several good men, went to Scotland under the protection of king Malcolm, who received them all.[16] Then it was that king Malcolm desired to have Margaret to wife : but the child Eadgar and all his men refused for a long time ; and she herself also was unwilling, saying that she would have neither him nor any other person, if God would allow her to serve him with her carnal heart, in strict continence, during this short life. But the king urged her brother until he said yes ; and indeed he did not dare to refuse, for they were now in Malcolm's power. So that the marriage was now fulfilled, as God had foreordained, and it could not be otherwise, as he says in the Gospel, that not a sparrow falls to the ground, without his foreshowing. The prescient Creator knew long before what he would do with her, namely that she should increase the Glory of God in this land, lead the king out of the wrong into the right path, bring him and his people to a better way, and suppress all the bad customs which the nation formerly followed. These things she afterwards accomplished. The king therefore married her, though against her will, and was pleased with her manners, and thanked God who had given him such a wife. And being a prudent man he turned himself to God and forsook all impurity of conduct, as St. Paul, the apostle of the Gentiles, says : " *Salvabitur vir,*" *&c.* which means in our language " Full oft the unbelieving husband is sanctified and healed through the believing wife, and so belike the wife through the believing husband." The queen above-named afterwards did many things in this land to promote the glory of God, and conducted herself well in her noble rank, as always was her custom. She was sprung from a noble line of ancestors, and her father was Eadward Ætheling, son of king Eadmund. This Eadmund was the son of Æthelred, who was the son of Eadgar, the son of Eadred ; and so on in that royal kin. Her maternal kin traces up to the emperor Henry, who reigned at Rome.

This year Harold's mother, Githa, and the wives of many good men with her, went to the Flatholm, and there abode some time ; and afterwards went from thence over the sea to St. Omer's.

This Easter the king came to Winchester ; and Easter was then on the tenth day of the Kalends of April. Soon after this the lady Matilda came to this country, and archbishop Ealdred consecrated her queen at Westminster on Whitsunday. It was then told the king, that the people of the North had gathered together and would oppose him there. Upon this he went to Nottingham, and built a castle there, and then advanced to York, where he built two castles : he then did the same at Lincoln, and everywhere in those parts. Then earl Gospatric and all the best men went into Scotland. During these things one of Harold's sons came with a fleet from Ireland unexpectedly into the mouth of the river Avon, and soon harried all that neighborhood. They went to Bristol, and would have stormed the town, but the inhabitants opposed them bravely. Seeing they could get nothing from the town, they went to their ships with the booty they had got by plundering, and went to Somersetshire, where they went up the country. Eadnoth, the constable fought with them, but he was slain there, and many good men on both sides ; and those who were left departed thence.

A. 1068. This year king William gave the earldom of Northumberland to earl Robert, but the men of that country surrounded him in the burgh at Durham and slew him and 900 others with him. And then Eadgar ætheling marched with all the Northumbrians to York, and the townsmen treated with him ; on which king William came from the south with all his army, and sacked the town, and slew many hundred persons. He also profaned St. Peter's monastery, and all other places, and the ætheling went back to Scotland.

After this came Harold's sons from Ireland, about midsummer, with sixty-four ships and entered the mouth of the Taw, where they incautiously landed. Earl Brian came upon them unawares with a large army, and slew all their bravest men : the others escaped to their ships, and Harold's sons went back again to Ireland.

A. 1069. This year died Ealdred archbishop of York, and he lies buried in his episcopal see. He died on the festival of Prothus and Hyacinthus, having held the see with much honor ten years, all but fifteen weeks.

Soon after this, three of the sons of king Svein came from Denmark with 240 ships, together with jarl Asbiorn and jarl Thorkell, into the Humber ; where they were met by child Eadgar and earl Waltheof, and Maerleswegen, and earl Gospatric with the men of Northumberland and all the landsmen, riding and marching joyfully with an immense army ; and so they went to York, demolished the castle, and gained there large treasures. They also slew many hundred Frenchmen, and carried off many prisoners to their ships ; but, before the shipmen came thither, the Frenchmen had burned the city, and plundered and burnt St. Peter's monastery. When the king heard of this, he went northward with all the troops he could collect, and laid waste all the shire ; whilst the fleet lay all the winter in the Humber, where the king could not get at them. The king was at York on midwinter's day, remaining on land all the winter, and at Easter he came to Winchester.

A. 1072. This year king William led an army and fleet against Scotland, and he stationed the ships along the coast and led his land force in at the ford ; but he found nothing to reward his pains. And king Malcolm came and made peace with king William, and delivered hostages, and was his man. And king William returned home with his forces.

A. 1075. This year king William went over sea to Normandy ; and child Eadgar came into Scotland from Flanders on St. Grimbald's mass-day. King Malcolm and Margaret his sister received him there with much pomp. Also Philip, king of France, sent him a letter inviting him to come, and offering to give him the castle of Montreuil, as a place to annoy his enemies from. After this, king Malcolm and his sister Margaret gave great presents and much treasure to him and his men, skins adorned with purple, marten-skin, weasel-skin and ermine-skin-pelisses, mantles, gold and silver vessels, and escorted them out of their dominions with much ceremony. But evil befell them at sea ; for they had hardly left the shore, when such rough weather came on, and the sea and wind drove them with such force upon the land, that their ships went to pieces and they saved their lives with much difficulty. They lost nearly all their riches and some of their men were taken by the French : but the boldest of them escaped back to Scotland, some on foot and some mounted on wretched horses. King Malcolm advised Eadgar to send to king William beyond the sea, and pray his peace. Eadgar did so, and the king acceded to his request and sent to fetch him. Again, king Malcolm and his sister made them handsome presents, and escorted them with honor out of their dominions. The shire-reeve of York met him at Durham, and went all the way with him, ordering him to be provided with food and fodder at all the castles which they came to, until they reached the king beyond the sea. There king William received him with much pomp, and he remained at the court, enjoying such privileges as the king granted him.

A. 1079. This year, between the two festivals of St. Mary, Malcolm, king of Scotland, invaded England with a large army, and harried Northumberland as far as the Tyne ; and he slew many hundred men, and carried home much money and treasure and many prisoners.

A. 1091. This year king William [Rufus] held his court at Westminster at Christmas, and the following Candlemas he departed from England to Normandy, bent on his brother's ruin ; but whilst he was in the country peace was made between them. . . . During this peace Eadgar ætheling was dispossessed of those lands which the count had granted him, and he departed and went from Normandy into Scotland, to the king his brother-in-law, and his sister. Whilst king William was out of England, Malcolm king of Scotland invaded this country, and harried great part of it, till the good men to whom the keeping of the land was entrusted, sent their troops against him and drove him back. When king William heard this in Normandy he hastened to return, and he came to England and his brother, count Robert, with him. And they called out a fleet and army, but almost all the ships were lost, a few days before Michaelmas ere they reached Scotland. And the king and his brother proceeded with the army : and when king Malcolm heard that they sought to attack him, he marched with his array out of Scotland into Leeds in England, and remained there. And when king William approached, count Robert and Eadgar ætheling mediated a peace between the kings, on condition that king Malcolm should repair to our king, and become his man, and in all the like subjection as to his father before him ; and this he confirmed by oath. And king William promised him all the lands and possessions that he held under his father. By this peace Eadgar ætheling was reconciled to the king. And the kings separated in great friendship, but this lasted during a short time only. Earl Robert abode here with the king till Christmas drew near, and in this time he found little good faith as to the fulfilment of the treaty, and two days before the feast he took ship from the Isle of Wight and sailed to Normandy, and Eadgar ætheling with him.

A. 1092. This year king William went northward to Carlisle with a large army, and he repaired the city, and built the castle. And he drove out Dolphin, who had before governed that land ; and having placed a garrison in the castle, he returned into the south, and sent a great number of country folk thither, with their wives and cattle, that they might settle there and cultivate the land.

A. 1093. This year, in Lent, king William was very sick at Gloucester, insomuch that he was universally reported to be dead : and he made many good promises in his illness. . . . After this the king of Scotland sent desiring that the stipulated conditions might be performed ; and king William summoned him to Gloucester, and sent hostages to him in Scotland, and afterwards Eadgar ætheling and others met him, and brought him with much honor to the court. But when he came there, he could neither obtain a conference with our king nor the performance of the conditions formerly promised him, and therefore they departed in great enmity : and king Malcolm returned home to Scotland, and as soon as he came thither, he assembled his troops and invaded England, harrying the country with more fury than behooved him : and Robert, earl of Northumberland, with his men, lay in wait for him, and slew him unawares.[19] He was killed by Morel of Bamborough, the earl's steward, and king Malcolm's gossip ; his son Edward, who, had he lived, would have been king after his father, was killed with him. When the good queen Margaret heard that her most beloved lord, and her son, were thus cut off, she was grieved in spirit unto death, and she went with her priest into the church, and having gone through all befitting rites, she prayed of God that she might give up her spirit. And then the Scots chose Donald, the brother of Malcolm, for their king, and drove out all the English who had been with king Malcolm. When Duncan, the son of king Malcolm, heard all this, for he was in king William's court, and had remained here from the time that his father gave him as an hostage to our king's father, he came to the king, and did such fealty as the king required ; and thus, with his consent, he departed for Scotland, with the aid that he could muster, both English and French, and he deprived his kinsman Donald of the throne, and was received as king. But then some of the Scotch again gathered themselves together, and slew nearly all his men, and he himself escaped with few others. They were afterwards reconciled on this condition, that Duncan should never more bring English or Frenchmen into that country.

NOTES TO CHAPTER XIX

[1] There is no need to believe that the clearing of the land meant so impossible a thing as the general slaughter of the men who held it. Slaughter there was, no doubt, on the battle-field or in towns like Anderida, whose resistance woke wrath in their besiegers. But for the most part the Britons were not slaughtered; they were defeated and drew back. — Green, *History of the English People*, vol. i., ch. ii.

[2] At the fate of the greater portion of the Britons of the Roman provinces we can only guess. . . . The Saxons, we know, had multitudes of slaves, and as they would follow the ordinary old rules of conquest, we may suppose that their earliest stock of this commodity was acquired in the conquests by which they gained their lands. In this shape and in others a great proportion of the British people seem to have become absorbed into the Saxon. — Burton, *History of Scotland*, vol. i., p. 182.

I have no doubt that the warfare waged by our forefathers, as long as they clave to their heathen worship, was strictly a war of extermination, so far as there can be such a thing as a war of extermination at all. I do not mean that every Briton was actually swept from the face of the earth by the English of those times, as the English of our times have swept away the natives of Tasmania. There is, however, one difference between the two cases. The Britons, aliens in blood, language, and religion, were at least men of our own color. The two races, therefore, could mingle, and they could mingle without leaving any sensible trace of the mixture. And to some extent, no doubt, they did mingle. The pedigree of no nation is absolutely pure. The women, it is obvious, would often be spared, and Celtic mothers might hand on some drops of Celtic blood to English sons. So, too, some of the conquered would doubtless be allowed to live as slaves of their conquerors. This sort of thing happens in every conquest; it must have happened when the Welsh settled in Britain, just as much as when the English did. I believe that, speaking in the rough way which is the only way in which we can speak of such matters, the Welsh vanished from the land and the English took their places. — Freeman, *Origin of the English Nation*, pp. 113–115.

[3] Here, however, they seem, by the middle of the sixth century, to have made themselves masters of the ground. Along Lothian or the coast between Lammermoor and the Forth, they had pushed to the little stream of the Esk, where their way was barred by the rock-fortress of Myned Agned, the site of the later Edinburgh: while south of the Lammermoor they had advanced along the loops of the Tweed as far as the vale of the Gala Water, and up the dales and streamlets which lie to the south and to the north of it, till their advance was thrown back from the wilder hill country on the west. Here the border line of the Cattrail, as it strikes through Ettrick Forest, marks the border of Welsh and Engle. A barrier as difficult curved round to the south in the line of the Cheviots; but between the extremity of this range and the sea a thin strip of coast offered an open pathway into the country beyond the Tweed; and Ida — "the Flamebearer," as the Britons called him — a chieftain of the invaders, whom they raised in 547 to be their king, seized in this quarter a rock beside the shore, and established a base for further conquest in the fortress of Bamborough. — Green, *Making of England*, p. 69.

After the departure of the Romans, the first germs of events that can be called national history appear in the sixth century. The partition of the country, such as we have seen it, had not greatly varied. On the east side, the Saxon invaders pressed hard on the Britons between the walls; and when the terrible Ida at that time built himself a fortress at Bam-burgh, within twenty miles of the Tweed, he seems to have ruled the country northwards to the Tay. The Britons continued to maintain an independent territory in the west, from the Solway to the Clyde; and northward the country was divided between the Picts on the east and north, and the Irish Scots on the west. — Burton, *History of Scotland*, vol. i., p. 278.

[4] I do not think that we shall find that in any of the Mercian lands east of the Severn the Briton has left more traces behind him than he has in Kent or Norfolk. When we cross the

Severn the case is different. We then get into the real Welsh march. One of the greatest English conquests of the eighth century was that which changed the Welsh town of Pen-y-wern into the English Shrewsbury. Hereford was long an English outpost against the Welsh, and indeed in parts of Herefordshire the names of places are Welsh, and it is not so very long since the Welsh language died out there. The Severn, I think, must be taken as the extent of complete English conquest, of utter annihilation of older inhabitants and older systems, in that part of Britain. . . . There is a certain Celtic element in Devonshire, though it is much less strong than in Cornwall, and there is a certain Celtic element in Somersetshire, though it is much less strong than in Devonshire. Any one who knows the country, any one who, even at a distance, looks carefully at the map, will be able to make out a sprinkling of Celtic names and other Celtic indications, beginning at the Axe, and getting thicker and thicker till we cross the Tamar into the strictly Celtic land of Cornwall. In these districts there can be no doubt that, just as in Cornwall, the population is very largely of Celtic descent, and has been simply assimilated to the English. . . . With the introduction of Christianity our forefathers ceased to be mere destroyers ; they were satisfied with being conquerors. Instead of dealing with the vanquished as with wild beasts, they were now content to receive them, not indeed as their political equals, but still as fellow-Christians and fellow-subjects. — Freeman, *Origin of the English Nation*, pp. 151–154.

[5] In these earlier conquests of the Bernicians, as Ida's folk were called, the settlement was as complete as in the rest of Britain. Their homes, indeed, must have been scantily sprinkled over the wild and half-reclaimed country ; but, scant as they were, these " hams " and " tons " told as plainly as in other districts the tale of English colonization. Dodings and Livings left their names to hamlets like Doddington and Livingston : along the wild coast Tynings and Coldings made their fisher-villages at Tyningham and Coldingham ; while Elphinston and Edmonston preserve the memory of English Elphins and Edmonds who raised their homesteads along the Teviot and the Tweed. Nowhere, indeed, has the English tongue been preserved in greater purity than in the district which now calls itself Southern Scotland. But the years that had been spent in winning this little tract show that the Bernician force was but a small one ; and the continued slowness of their southward advance from Bamborough proves that even after the union under Ida their strength was but little increased. — Green, *Making of England*, p. 70.

[6] Bede ranks Osuiu as the seventh king of the nations of the Angles who possessed imperial power, and sums up the result of his reign by saying that " he held nearly the same dominions for some time as his predecessors, and subdued and made tributary the greater part of the nations of the Picts and Scots which possess the northern parts of Britain." He thus not only freed his own kingdom from the incursions of the Mercians, and found himself at last in the full and quiet possession of it, but he materially added to his dominions. In the south he obtained possession of Mercia for three years, and in the north extended his sway not only over the Britons but over the Picts and Scots ; and thus commenced the dominion of the Angles over the Britons of Alclyde, the Scots of Dalriada, and the southern Picts, which was destined to last for thirty years. By the fall of Penda and the defeat and slaughter of his British allies, the Britons of Alclyde naturally fell under his sway. Tighernac records the death of no king of Alclyde during this period till the year 694, and the *Ulster Annals*, after recording in 658 the death of Gureit or Gwriad, king of Alclyde, have also a blank during the same time. — *Celtic Scotland*, vol. i., p. 256.

[7] " The fact which I am supposed to admit grudgingly is in truth one of the greatest importance for a right knowledge of the progress of the English Conquest and of its results. The laws of Ine, King of the West Saxons, dating from the eighth century, set before us a state of things in the West Saxon kingdom which has nothing like it either in our earlier or our later records. It is very likely that, if we had any laws of Offa, King of the Mercians, later in the same century, they would set before us nearly the same state of things ; but unluckily we have not got any such laws to make us quite sure. That state of things is one

in which Briton and Englishman appear as living side by side in the land, subjects of the same king, protected by the same law, but still marked off in everything, the one as the conquering, the other as the conquered race.

" Now, in the laws of Ine, the blood and the oath of a Briton of a certain rank is systematically rated at a lower price than the blood and the oath of an Englishman of the same rank. And there are provisions in the same code which show us Britons, not as slaves, not as strangers, as men fully under the living protection of the law, but still as forming a class distinct from Englishmen and inferior to Englishmen. Now what does all this prove ? We must remember that there is nothing like this legislation of Ine's either in the earlier or in the later laws, neither in the older laws of Kent nor in the later laws of Wessex. The picture of a land inhabited by two nations still keeping perfectly distinct belongs only to the legislation of Wessex at one particular time, the time which followed the first conquests made by the West Saxons in their new character of Christians. The lawgivers of Kent had no Britons to legislate about ; in Kent, a land conquered in the days of heathendom, the British inhabitants had been rooted out. The later lawgivers of Wessex might have to legislate about British enemies or British captives ; they had not to legislate about a settled British population in their own kingdom. It is plain that conversion to Christianity, though it did not stop warfare, made warfare less frightful. The Christian conqueror did not seek the extermination of his conquered enemies ; he was satisfied with their political subjection. In the lands conquered after the conversion the Briton lived on much as the Roman lived on in Gaul. We see him there in the time of Ine, free, protected by the law, but marked as the inferior of his conqueror. When Ælfred gave laws to Wessex, things had changed ; the conquerors had assimilated the conquered ; the British inhabitants of Wessex had passed into Englishmen.

" It is plain, then, that, in the shires of Somerset and Devon, the lands for which this legislation of Ine must have been mainly meant, a considerable part of the people must be English by adoption only. Cornwall, I need hardly say, was a strictly British land, with a British nomenclature, and a British speech which lingered on into the last century. These lands were long known as the Wealh-cyn, the land of the Welsh or British people. There is then an undoubted British fusion in the English people, an infusion dating from the seventh century. The fact is undoubted ; it is open to any one to make what inferences he chooses from it. Only let him stop and think whether the lands from Elbe to Niemen have not poured a greater foreign infusion into the blood of Germany than the lands from Axe to Tamar have poured into the blood of England. My inferences are these : The presence of legislation about Britons in the laws of Ine, compared with its absence in the earlier laws, points to the difference between heathen conquest, which involved the extermination of the conquered, and Christian conquest, which did not. And it thereby teaches us how thoroughly the extermination was in the days of heathendom. On the other hand, the fact that the conquered were thoroughly assimilated by the conquerors between the beginning of the eighth century and the end of the ninth shows that the speech and the civilization of Rome had utterly passed away from Western Britain in the seventh century." — Freeman, *English People in its Three Homes*, pp. 147–149.

[8] At this time the Northumbrians were at enmity with the Picts. Ceolwulf, the king of Northumbria, had followed the fashion of the time and become a monk in Lindisfarne in the year 737. He was succeeded by his cousin Eadberht, the son of his father's brother ; and we are told, in the short chronicle annexed to Bede, that in 740 Ædilbald, king of Mercia, unfairly laid waste part of Northumbria, its king, Eadberht, being occupied with his army against the Picts. It is probable that Angus had excited the hostility of the king of Northumbria by stirring up the Picts of Lothian and Galloway to revolt, and that Eadberht may have encouraged if not invited the Scots of Dalriada to occupy their country. Alpin is said by all authorities to have reigned four years after Dungal, which brings us to the year 740, when he invaded Galloway with the part of the Dalriadic nation which followed him, and was slain there, after having laid waste and almost destroyed the country of the Picts. The *Ulster*

Annals thus record it in 741 : " Battle of Drum Cathmail between the Cruithnigh and the Dalriads against Innrechtach." The locality of this battle appears to have been in Galloway, not far from Kirkcudbright, and Innrechtach was probably the leader of the Galloway Picts. One of the chronicles appears to have preserved the traditionary account of his death when it tells us that Alpin was slain in Galloway, after he had destroyed it, by a single person who lay in wait for him in a thick wood overhanging the entrance of the ford of a river as he rode among his people. The scene of his death must have been on the east side of Loch Ryan, where a stream falls into the loch, on the north side of which is the farm of Laight, and on this farm is a large upright pillar stone, to which the name of Laight Alpin, or the grave of Alpin, is given. In the same year we have the short but significant record of the crushing of the Dalriads by Angus, son of Fergus.—*Celtic Scotland*, vol. i., pp. 291–292.

⁹ Edbert, king, in the eighteenth year of his reign, and Unust, king of the Picts, led an army to the city of Alcluyd, and there the Britons thereof received [*i. e.*, surrendered upon] conditions, the first day of August.—*Annals of Ulster*.

During the reign of Eadberht in the middle of the eighth century, the kingdom of Northumbria had apparently attained to a position of as great power as that to which it had been raised in the previous century by Ecgfrid. The two provinces of Deira and Bernicia were united under his rule ; the territories of the Britons south of the Solway Firth and the province of Galloway on the north were parts of his kingdom ; he had himself added to it Kyle and the adjacent districts, and in conjunction with Angus, the equally powerful king of the Picts, had enforced the submission of the Britons of Alclyde when, after a reign of twenty-one years, he, in the year 758, abdicated his throne in favor of his son Oswulf, and took the tonsure. His son was in the following year treacherously slain by his own people, and with him ended the direct descendants of Ida. The kingdom seems then to have fallen into a state of disorganization, and has thus been well described : " One earldorman after another seized on the government, and held it till his expelled predecessors returned with a superior force, or popular favor or successful treason had raised up a new competitor." And thus it continued till the end of the century, when the arrival of the Northmen added an additional element of confusion. In 867 the monarchy completely broke down. In the previous year a large fleet of Danish pirates, under the command of Halfdan, Inguar, and Hubba, the sons of Ragnar Lodbrog, had arrived on the coast of England, and had wintered in East Anglia, and this year they invaded Northumbria, and took possession of the city of York. The Northumbrians had just expelled their king Osbryht, and placed Alla on the throne, but the former was now recalled, and the two kings, uniting their forces, attempted to wrest the city of York from the Danes, and were both slain. The Danes then took possession of the whole of Northumbria as far as the river Tyne, and placed Ecgbert as king over the Northumbrians north of the Tyne. After a reign of six years Ecgbert died, and was succeeded by Ricsig. It was in his time that, in 875, Halfdan, with his Danes, again entered Northumbria, and brought the whole country under his dominion. In the following year Ricsig died, and Halfdan is said by Simeon of Durham to have placed a second Ecgbert over the Northumbrians beyond the Tyne. He is said to have reigned only two years. But notwithstanding, in 883, or seven years after, when Halfdan dies, we are told by Simeon that by the advice of the abbot Eadred, Guthred, son of Hardicnut, was made king, and reigned at York ; but Ecgbert ruled over the Northumbrians. There is no mention of this second Ecgbert either in his *History of Durham* or of the Archbishops of York, and he appears with his inconsistent dates to be a mere reproduction of the Ecgbert who was placed over the Northumbrians north of the Tyne in 867, introduced to fill up a period when the historian did not know or did not care to tell who really ruled over Bernicia at that time. This is, however, the period of Girig's reign, and he may, like his predecessor Kenneth, have overrun Lothian and obtained possession of Bamborough, the chief seat of the Bernician kings, which lies at no great distance from the south bank of the Tweed ; and Simeon himself indicates this when he tells us in his *History of the Church of Durham* that during the reign of Guthred "the nation of the Scots had collected a numerous army and, among other deeds of cruelty, had invaded and plundered the monastery of Lindisfarne." His object, too, may have been to free the Britons, his own countrymen, from the Anglic yoke, and certainly, if he conquered Bernicia, and perhaps that part of Anglia which consisted of the British possessions extending from the Solway to the Derwent, their reunion with the kingdom of the Strathclyde Britons, as well as the freedom of Galloway from Anglic supremacy, would be the natural result.—*Celtic Scotland*, vol. i., pp. 331–333.

[10] Eadberht, the king of Northumbria, abdicated his throne in 758, and was succeeded by his son Osulf, who had reigned only one year when he was slain, and by his own people ; and in 759, Æthelwald, called Moll, became king ; and in the third year, Simeon tells us, a battle was fought between him and Oswine, one of his generals, at Eldun near Melrose, in which Oswine was slain, which shows that Æthelwald's kingdom still extended at least as far as East Lothian. The place meant is the Eildon Hill near Melrose. The *English Chronicle* calls the place Ædwine's Cliffe.

[11] Simeon of Durham tells us that in 774 King Alchred, by the design and consent of all his connections, being deprived of the society of the royal family and princes, changed the dignity of empire for exile. He went with a few of the companions of his flight first to the city of Bamborough, and afterwards to the king of the Picts, Cynoht by name ; and Æthelred, the son of his predecessor, occupied the throne of Northumbria for six years.

[12] "Presently, in the ninth and tenth centuries, the English who had thus invaded the land of the Britons were themselves invaded in the land which they had made their own. In a considerable part of England the conquerors themselves became the conquered. A new nomenclature was brought in ; through a large part of several English shires the names which the English had given to the spots which they wrested from the Briton gave way to new names which marked the coming of another race of conquerors. Wherever names end in *by*, we see the signs of this new revolution, the signs of the coming of a new element in the land, and an element which indeed supplied a wide field for adoption, but which hardly stood in need of assimilation. As the English came on the Britons, so the Danes came on the English ; they occupied a considerable part of England ; in the end they placed a Danish king on the throne of what by that time had become the united English kingdom. Such an event as this is a mighty one, filling no small space in a narrative history of the English people. . . .

"But, in such a sketch as I am now setting before you, the great tale of the Danish invasions goes for but little. Misleading as such a view would be in an ordinary history, I might for my present purpose almost venture to speak of the Danish conquest as the last wave of the English conquest, as the coming of a detachment who came so late that they could settle only at the expense of their comrades who had settled already. For the Danes were a kindred folk to the English, hardly differing more from some of the tribes which had taken a part in the English conquest than those tribes differed from one another. The coming of the Dane hardly amounted to more than the addition of a fourth Teutonic element to the Angles, Saxons, and Jutes who had come already."— Freeman, *The English People in its Three Homes*, p. 150.

[13] "In Ecgberht's day Britain had come to consist of three long belts of country, two of which stretched side by side from the utmost north to the utmost south, and the population of each of which was absolutely diverse. Between the eastern coast and a line which we may draw along the Selkirk and Yorkshire moorlands to the Cotswolds and Selwood, lay a people of wholly English blood. Westward again of the Tamar, of the western hills of Herefordshire, and of Offa's Dyke, lay a people whose blood was wholly Celtic. Between them, from the Lune to the coast of Dorset and Devon, ran the lands of the Wealh-cyn — of folks, that is, in whose veins British and English blood were already blending together and presaging in their mingling a wider blending of these elements in the nation as a whole.

"The winning of Western Britain opened, in fact, a way to that addition of outer elements to the pure English stock which has gone on from that day to this without a break. Celt and Gael, Welshman and Irishman, Frisian and Flamand, French Huguenot and German Palatine, have come successively in, with a hundred smaller streams of foreign blood. . . . So far as blood goes, few nations are of an origin more mixed than the present English nation; for there is no living Englishman who can say with certainty that the blood of any of the races we have named does not mingle in his veins. As regards the political or social structure of the people, indeed, this intermingling of blood has had little or no result. They remain purely English and Teutonic.

"The firm English groundwork which had been laid by the character of the early conquest has never been disturbed. Gathered gradually in, tribe by tribe, fugitive by fugitive, these outer elements were quietly absorbed into a people whose social and political form was already fixed. But though it would be hard to distinguish the changes wrought by the mixture of race from the changes wrought by the lapse of time and the different circumstances which surround each generation, there can be no doubt that it has brought with it moral results in modifying the character of the nation. It is not without significance that the highest type of the race, the one Englishman who has combined in their largest measure the mobility and fancy of the Celt with the depth and energy of the Teutonic temper, was born on the old Welsh and English borderland, in the forest of Arden."—Green, *Conquest of England*, ch. i., §§ 2, 3.

[14] The king of Scots with his whole nation, and Reginald, the king of the Danes, with the English and Danes inhabiting Northumberland, the king also of the Strathclyde Britons with his people, chose the elder king for their father and lord, and contracted with him a firm league.—*Florence of Worcester*. (Anno 921). See p. 359.

[15] It has usually been assumed that this refers to the district in England afterwards called Cumberland alone, but the people termed by the same chronicle the Strathclyde Welsh had now come to be known under the Latin appellation of *Cumbri*, and their territory as the land of the Cumbrians, of which "Cumbraland" is simply the Saxon equivalent. Their king at this time was Donald, the son of that Eugenius or Owin, who was at the battle of Brunanburh. He is called king of the Northern Britons, and his kingdom extended from the Derwent in Cumberland to the Clyde. Accordingly we find in the British annals that at this time Strathclyde was ravaged by the Saxons. There can be little question that the tenure by which the Cumbrian kingdom was held by Malcolm, was one of fealty towards the king of England, and this seems to be the first occasion on which this relation was established with any reality between them, so far, at least, as this grant is concerned.—*Celtic Scotland*, vol. i., p. 362.

Cumbria, or Cambria, was the name given to the northern territory retained by the Romanized Britons—a territory described as a continuation northward of their Welsh territory. Gradually, however, the name of Strathclyde was given to that portion reaching from the Solway northwards—in fact, the portion within modern Scotland. The word Cumbria continued to be frequently used as equivalent to Strathclyde, but about the period of the gift, it had come to apply to the English portion only of the old British territory—a portion in which Saxons and Norsemen had successively planted themselves. If what King Edmond handed over to the King of Scots was Strathclyde, he professed to give a territory that was not his own, but was, indeed, naturally lapsing into the other dominions of the King of Scots. Whatever meaning, then, we are to give to the passage in the chronicle, must connect it with the country now known as Cumberland and Westmoreland. Of these territories it can only be said, that at this period, and for long afterwards, they formed the theatre of miscellaneous confused conflicts, in which the Saxons, the Scots, and the Norsemen, in their turn, partake. Over and over again we hear that the district is swept by the Saxon kings' armies, but it did not become a part of England until after the Norman Conquest. Meanwhile, to the King of Scots it was not so much an object of acquisition as the more accessible territory of Northumberland.—Burton, *History of Scotland*, vol. i., p. 337.

[16] It has yet to be recorded, nine years later, in 946, that Æthelstane's successor reduced all Northumberland under his power; and the Scots gave him oath that they would all that he would. It happens, however, that the year before this we have an entry which the tenor of those we have been dealing with renders still more inexplicable than they are themselves : "Anno 945.—In this year King Eadmond harried over all Cumberland, and gave it all up to Malcolm, King of the Scots, on the condition that he should be his co-operator both on sea and on land." Three years before this, Constantine had retired from his throne, and became abbot of the Culdees at St. Andrews—an office, as we shall see, not unworthy of a tired king. It was to his successor, Malcolm, that this strange gift was made.—*Burton*, vol. i., p. 336.

[17] Worsaæ states that the Northmen, by the Danish conquests, became the progenitors of as much as half of the present population of England. The Saxon race in the north has been greatly exaggerated. They were principally located in the south of England, and, in proof of this, the dialects in the north and south were always different. The first has much of the Scandinavian, while the latter is considered to have more of the Belgian or Low Dutch. There are in England specimens of written Saxon as early as the seventh century. From ritual books it is seen that Saxon of about A.D. 890 and Dano-Saxon of about 930 differ to a considerable extent.—*Galloway, Ancient and Modern*, p. 78.

[18] " Edmond Ironside left two infant sons, Edwin and Edward. By order of Canute, they were conveyed out of England in 1017 (*Chron. Sax.*). At length they found an asylum in Hungary. Edwin died there. Edward was recalled by Edward the Confessor in 1057. He only lived to see the land of his nativity, from which he had been exiled during forty years (*Ibid.*, p. 169). The Children of Edward were Edgar Ætheling, Margaret, and Christian.

" There is a confusion, hardly to be unravelled, as to the time and manner of Edgar's retreat into Scotland, and his sister's marriage. In *Chron. Sax.* (pp. 173, 174) it is said that Edgar went into Scotland in 1067, with Maerleswegen, and the other malcontents. S. Dunelm places this event in 1068 (p. 197). According to *Chr. Melrose.* (p. 158), the nuptials of Margaret were solemnized in 1067 ; but, according to the same history (p. 160), in 1070. Fordun, l. v., c. 16, relates from Turgot, that Edgar, with his mother and sisters, had embarked, in order to return to the place of his nativity, but that he was driven to Scotland by a tempest. With him Aldred concurs (*De Genealogia Regum Anglorum*, p. 367). Fordun adds, that the place where the ship anchored was called Sinus S. Margaretæ (now St. Margaret's Hope) ; and (c. 17), that the nuptials were solemnized at Dunfermline. Hovedon (p. 226) relates the same story of the tempest ; but places it in 1067. He adds, that, at that time, the marriage of Margaret and the King of Scots was agreed on, ' hac quoque occasione actum est, ut Margareta Regi Malcolmo nupta traderetur.' "—*Hailes, Annals of Scotland*, vol. i., p. 7.

[19] On his death he left the kingdom in possession for the first time of the same southern frontier which it ever after retained. It was now separated from the kingdom of England by the Solway Firth, the range of the Cheviot Hills and the River Tweed. From the Solway to the Clyde extended that portion of Cumbria which still belonged to the Scottish king ; from the Tweed to the Forth, the district of Lothian. From the Forth to the Spey was Alban or Albania, now called Scotia. Beyond it, on the north, the province of Moravia ; on the west, Airergaidhel or Argathelia ; while beyond these were, on the north, Caithness and the Orkney Isles forming the Norwegian earldom of Orkney ; and, on the west, the Sudreys or Western Islands still occupied by the Norwegians, though since the death of Thorfinn belonging nominally to Scotland.—*Celtic Scotland*, vol. i., p. 432.

CHAPTER XX

FROM MALCOLM CANMORE TO KING DAVID

W E now have our annals brought down to a period where the written history of Scotland may be said to begin. From this time on, we have accessible what are practically contemporary records of the events occurring in and after the reign of Malcolm Canmore. There is no early connected account of Scottish history before his time that can be taken as authentic. Such records of events as are preserved are to be found only in the brief and ofttimes contradictory notices of the Irish, Welsh, and English annalists. There have already been given such references as are contained in the English chronicles, and the substance of the contents of the others. It only remains to add a short account of the Irish and Welsh chronicles in order that we may know what are the foundations for that portion of Scottish history now passed in outline, and which at this late day can only be tentatively constructed from their meagre and fragmentary details.

The oldest of these records is the *Pictish Chronicle*, compiled in the reign of Kenneth Mac Malcolm (971–995), the contents of which consist mainly of a list of the Pictish kings, with the dates of commencement of their respective reigns. The latter portion of this list has already been given.[1] One edition of the same exists in Latin, which is said to have been translated from a Gaelic original ; and a version may also be found in the Irish *Nennius*.

In the reign of Kenneth's son, Malcolm (1004–1034), between the years 1014 and 1023, appeared the *Synchronisms* of Flann Mainistrech, or Flann, the Ferleighin of the monastery called Mainister Boice, which contains a list of the kings of Ireland synchronized with contemporary rulers of other countries, including many who ruled in Scotland ; the chronicle being brought down to the early part of the eleventh century. Flann died in 1056.

The third chronicle is that of Marianus Scotus, who was born in 1028, and died in 1082–83. This covers a period extending from the creation of the world to the year 1082.

Another list of the early rulers of Scotland is given in the Irish version of the British, or Welsh, chronicle which goes by the name of *Nennius*. This book was translated from the Latin into Irish by Gillacaemhan, who died in 1072, and considerable additions were made to it by him from Irish and Pictish sources.

Gillacaemhan is also reputed to have been the author of a brief historical poem known as the *Albanic Duan*, which probably appeared between the time of Malcolm Canmore's accession to the throne (1057) and the death of its author (1072).

The last of these early Gaelic chronicles is that of Tighernac of Cloinmacnois, who died in 1088. His work is known as the *Annals of Tighernac*, and it probably contains a greater number of references to Scottish affairs than any of the others that have been named. (See Appendix O.)

Besides these may be mentioned the *Annales Cambriæ* and the *Brut y Tywysogion*, being the two Cymric chronicles next in date and importance to those of Gildas and Nennius. They give much incidental information of the British kingdom of Strathclyde after the time of Bede. The first extends from 447 to 1288, and the second from 681 to 1282. There are also the *Annals of Innisfallen* and the *Annals of Ulster*, both extremely valuable for the light they throw upon the early history of Scotland. Of secondary importance to the foregoing is the *Leabhar Gabhala*, or *Book of Conquests*, by Michael O'Clery, founded upon a more ancient book of invasions, of which a fragment is contained in the *Leabhar na Huidhri* and the *Book of Leinster*, and complete editions in the *Books* of *Ballimote* and *Leacan*.

Concerning the *Annals of the Four Masters* (written 1632–1636), a work often quoted as the basis of ancient Irish history, every indication connected with its appearance points to its having an origin similar to that of the artificially constructed Scottish histories of Hector Boece, John Major, and George Buchanan, namely, the lively imagination and clever pen of the authors. The earlier part of the *Annals of the Four Masters* comprises a narrative of the fabulous history of Ireland in the form of a chronicle, and, like the similar works of Giraldus de Barri Cambrensis and Geoffrey of Monmouth, is interesting from a literary standpoint only. The latter parts are said in the preface to be taken from other and more ancient documents. The authority for each event not being stated, however, and the lack of substantiation for a great part of the records given, throws the whole work open to suspicion ; and it has practically no value as history.

"We have no extant Scotch writing so early as the reign of Malcolm Canmore, who died in the year 1093," says Cosmo Innes, in his essay on *Scotland in the Middle Ages*. "That the art of writing was known and practised among us to a small extent before, we cannot doubt ; but it was probably used only for books connected with the Church, its forms and service. At least there is no evidence of the existence, so early as that reign, of any charter, record, or chronicle. The oldest Scotch writing extant is a charter by King Duncan (not 'the gracious Duncan,' murdered by Macbeth, but his grandson, who reigned in 1095), granted to the monks of St. Cuthbert of Durham. It is kept in the treasury of Durham, and is in perfect preservation. The rude pinning of a seal to it has raised some suspicion with regard to its genuineness ; but I think without foundation. The appending of the seal is apparently a modern and clumsy attempt to add a sort of authentication, which the charter did not want. It is executed in the Anglo-Saxon manner, by the granter and the several witnesses affixing their crosses, and in most Anglo-Saxon charters seals were not used. We have several charters still preserved of Edgar, the brother and successor of Duncan, who reigned till 1106, and who used a seal after the Norman fashion, on which he takes the barbaric style of *Basileus*. From his time, that is, from the beginning of the twelfth century, we have charters of all the Scotch kings, in an unbroken series, as well as of numerous subjects, and derive from them more information for public and domestic history, than is at all generally known.

"There is still preserved a poor fragment of a Scotch chronicle, which appears to have been written about the year 1165. It is a single leaf, now inserted in the MS. of the *Chronicle of Melrose*, in the Cottonian library. The rest of that venerable chronicle, written in the thirteenth century, in the Abbey of Melrose, is the most ancient Scotch writing of the nature of continuous history that is now extant. A few other fragments of chronicles of that century perhaps, but being for the most part bare lists of the Scotch and Pictish kings, are now deposited in the royal library at Paris. When used by Camden and other historians, they were in the library of Cecil, Lord Burleigh.

"Of the collections of the laws of Scotland, the oldest is one which has been lately restored to this country, from the public library at Berne. It is a fine and careful MS., written about 1270 ; and, what adds greatly to its interest, containing an English law treatise and English styles, as well as some of the most ancient laws of Scotland, particularly David I.'s venerable code of Burgh laws ; and last of all, the ancient laws of the Marches, concerted by a grand assize of the borderers of the two kingdoms in 1249. This singular mixture of the laws of two countries (which might have served as materials for the mysterious fabrication of a so-called Scotch code) excites our curiosity as to the owner of the book ; but the only clue we find to guide us is a memorandum scribbled on the last leaf, of an account of sheep taken from John, the shepherd of Malkariston, on Sunday next before the feast of St. Andrew, in the year 1306, when the flock is counted in ewes, dynmouts, and hogs. Next in interest to the Berne MS. is a book of Scotch laws, chiefly Burghal, which was picked up in a book-stall in Ayr in 1824, and its previous history cannot be traced. It is a fine MS., of the age of Robert I., or at least of the early half of the fourteenth century. After that period there is no want of MS. collections of our laws, but all of the character of private and unauthentic compilations.

"State papers, properly so-called, few, but of great importance, begin in the reign of Alexander III., or the latter half of the thirteenth century, and there are still preserved imperfect records of parliamentary proceedings, from the age of Robert Bruce downwards.

"These are all the materials of the civil history of Scotland which we still possess, previous to the work of John Barbour, of which I shall have occasion to speak hereafter. Soon after his time, Andrew Wyntoun, prior of Loch Leven, wrote his rhyming chronicle, and John Fordun laid the foundation of Scotch history in his *Scoti-Chronicon.* These two writers were engaged upon their works at the same time, about the latter years of the fourteenth century ; but neither seems to have been aware of the other's undertaking.

"There was only one province of the Scotch king's dominions that we find asserting peculiar customary laws. We know little of the early history of the district now called Galloway. It had scarcely come under the confirmed dominion of the kings of Scotland in the reign of Malcolm Canmore. We have seen the rude insubordination of its people, under his son David at the Battle of the Standard. The native lords were still too powerful for the distant authority of the sovereign. William the Lion had a code of laws for its government (*assisa Mea de Galweia*), and judges for administering them. They met at several places, and we have still records of a few of their decisions, some of which are remarkable. Among other places, the judges of Galloway are found at Lanark prescribing rules to the Mairs of the province regarding the mode of collecting the king's *Kane.*

"For long after that time, Galloway continued to be governed according to its own peculiar laws. In the reign of Robert Bruce, its people had not yet acquired, nor perhaps desired, the right of trial by jury, but practised the mode of purgation and acquittance according to their ancient laws — those very laws of the Brets and Scots which Edward in vain endeavored to abolish. As late as 1385, Archibald Douglas, lord of Galloway, while undertaking in Parliament to further the execution of justice within his territory, protested for the liberty of the law of Galloway in all points."

From the various accounts of the early peoples of Scotland given in the foregoing pages, and which are to some extent based on these Celtic records, we may conclude that in the time of Malcolm Canmore there were five or more distinct races inhabiting his domain.

Of these, no doubt the most numerous were the Gaels and aborigines of Scotia proper, known in ancient times as Caledonians and Picts. They occupied in Malcolm's time the most of eastern Scotland north of the Firth of Forth. Along the entire eastern coast and in the northern provinces of Caithness, Sutherland, and Ross, they were more or less mingled and mixed with the Norse. They probably did not become a lettered race until some centuries after the advent of St. Columba. Therefore we have no early native accounts of their history; or, indeed, any written records of any kind in their primitive language. But because there are no written remains of the Pictish language as such (beyond the list of their kings and one or two words preserved in the writings of outsiders), it does not necessarily follow that that language and the people who spoke it have been obliterated, even though such an idea was once generally accepted.

Next to the Picts was the kindred race of Gaelic Scots of the western Highlands, descendants of the Dalriad emigrants from Ireland, who had a written Gaelic language. These Scots had perhaps become so largely interfused with the aboriginal Gaelic Picts as not only to bestow upon them their own distinctive name, but also to so modify, establish, and conform with their own the unwritten Pictish language, as to save the latter from being obliterated by that of the more civilized and lettered Cymric people to the south of the Clyde.

The part of Scotland lying between the Clyde and Forth, and west of the Avon and the Esk, was occupied chiefly by the Cymric or Brythonic Celts of Strathclyde, being the remnant outside of Wales of those Britons whose ancestors in the fourth century had been, at least in name, citizens of the Roman empire.

Adjoining the Cymric Celts on the west and south were the Attecott Picts of Galloway (probably the descendants of the Stone-Age, non-Celtic aborigines), together with the Gaelic inhabitants of the districts of Cunningham and Kyle, then also in Galloway, but now in Ayrshire. Both of these races were more or less mixed with the Norse ; and the Norse likewise occupied the greater part of Caithness and Sutherland, with portions of the western coast, Ross, and Moray. They also doubtless formed a considerable part of the population all along the eastern shore as far south as the Forth— and in the southern districts they may have been largely mixed with the Anglic population from Bernicia.[2]

East of the Britons were the Angles of Bernicia, who occupied all the country between the Tweed and the Forth. Their numbers were twice largely augmented, first by the immigration of the disaffected English who followed Edgar Ætheling from England on the advent of the Normans,[3] and later by the large number of captives who were taken into Scotland by Malcolm Canmore after his numerous invasions of Northumberland.

Malcolm first invaded England in 1061. In that year he entered and wasted the dominion of his friend and ally, Earl Tostig, brother of King Harold, during the earl's absence on a pilgrimage to Rome. This invasion was due to some differences between the two, but does not appear to have been followed by a counter-attack on the part of the Danes. A more extensive foray was made in 1070. At that time Malcolm ravaged all northern England, taking an army through Cumberland into Teesdale, and penetrating to the vicinity of Durham, where he laid waste all the country, and for a while carried on a savage war of extermination. But later, changing his policy, he directed that all the young people of both sexes be driven as captives into Scotland. "So great was the number of these captives that for many years they were to be found in every Scottish village, nay, even in every Scottish hovel," are the words in which our chronicler describes this invaluable accession to the population of Malcolm's kingdom.[4] This attack was followed by reprisals on the part of William the Conqueror, who entered Northumberland with an army, laid waste all the country between the Humber and the Tees, and obliged such of the inhabitants as were not destroyed by the sword or famine to seek refuge in Scotland.

In 1072, William the Conqueror led an army into Scotland, but his expedition appears to have been fruitless, although the *English Chronicle* tells us that he afterwards met King Malcolm and made an agreement with him, by the terms of which Malcolm became William's liege for at least such of his possessions as lay within the English kingdom. Malcolm at the same time may have become confirmed in his sovereignty over that portion of Northumberland north of the Tweed, which has ever since remained an integral part of Scotland.

The Scottish king invaded England again in 1079 and wasted the country as far as the river Tyne. The following year William sent an army against the Scots under the leadership of his son Robert, who, after meeting with some reverses, was fain to content himself with the erection of a fortress near the Tyne, which was called New Castle. William died in 1087, and four years later the king of the Scots again invaded England, taking his army some distance south of New Castle. In the same year (1091) William Rufus, son and successor of the Conqueror, prepared to invade Scotland with a large fleet and army. His ships were destroyed by a storm before they reached Scotland, but the army proceeded by land, and on nearing the borders of the two kingdoms, was confronted at " Lothene in England " [5] by Malcolm, in command of a large force. Here, through the efforts of Edgar Ætheling and Earl Robert, brother of William Rufus, a treaty of peace was concluded between the two monarchs and the armies were both withdrawn from the border.

However, the conditions of this peace not being carried out by William Rufus to the entire satisfaction of Malcolm, an interview for a further consideration of the matter was arranged between the two kings, which took place at Gloucester in August, 1093. At this meeting William desired Malcolm to do homage to him as liegeman for the territories which the latter held in England. Malcolm declined to perform homage in the interior of England, such a course being derogatory to his dignity as an independent sovereign ; but offered to do so on the frontiers, and in presence of the chief men of both kingdoms. This proposition not being satisfactory to William, the interview was accordingly terminated, with bitter feeling on both sides. Malcolm, on returning home, immediately assembled an army and again invaded Northumberland with his wonted ferocity. On this occasion, while besieging the castle of Alnwick in that country, he was slain by Robert de Moubray. His second son, Edward, perished with him. Malcolm's surviving children by his second wife were Ethelred, Edmund, Edgar, Alexander, David, Matildis, or Maud, who afterwards became the wife of Henry I. of England, and Mary, who married Eustace, Count of Boulogne.

Donald Bane, the brother of Malcolm, who for many years had made his home in the Hebrides, seized the occasion of that king's death to invade Scotland with a numerous following collected from the Western Isles. None of Malcolm's children being of mature years he usurped the throne, but was driven out the next year by Duncan, the eldest son of Malcolm by his first wife, Ingiborg, the widow of Thorfinn. Duncan had been left in England as a hostage by his father. With the help of William Rufus he raised an army, largely composed of English and Norman adventurers, and soon expelled the usurper. Duncan then ascended the throne and reigned for one year, when he was assassinated by a partisan of Donald Bane, and the latter regained the crown.[6] In 1097, Edgar Ætheling, with the assistance of William Rufus, raised a second English army, marched into Scotland, and again dethroned Donald, placing Edgar, another son of Malcolm, in his stead.

In 1100, William Rufus having been slain, the English crown passed to his brother, Henry, who in the same year, as already stated, married Matildis, sister to King Edgar of Scotland. Two years later, Mary, another sister, was married to Eustace, Count of Boulogne.

Edgar died in 1106, and was succeeded as king by his brother, Alexander I., their younger brother, David, at the same time being given possession of that part of the kingdom called Cumberland.[7] Alexander married Sibilla, a natural daughter of Henry I., and his reign was a peaceful one, terminating at his death without issue in 1124.

The crown then passed by inheritance to David, the youngest son of Malcolm Canmore. He had spent the early years of his life at the court of the English king, and in England married Matilda, daughter of Waltheof (son of Siward), Earl of Northumberland and of Huntingdon. David afterwards succeeded to the earldom of Huntingdon.

The early years of his reign were marked with few events of importance until 1130, when a formidable revolt arose in Moray. It was speedily crushed, and Angus, Earl of that province, was slain.[8]

In 1135, Henry I. died, and his nephew, Stephen, seized the throne in usurpation of the rights of Matilda, Henry's daughter.[9] Matilda's uncle, King David, accordingly marched into England with an army, and occupied the northern portions of that country, nominally in the interest of Matilda.[10] Stephen took the field against him with a superior force, but before coming to blows a peace was made, and David's possessions in England were confirmed to his son Henry, the latter undertaking to do homage to King Stephen for them.

The next year, Stephen being absent in Normandy, David again prepared to invade Northumberland, claiming the lordship of that district in the name of his son, Prince Henry, by right of his descent from Waltheof, the deceased Earl of Northumberland, father of David's wife. However, he was prevailed upon to grant a truce until Stephen should return out of Normandy. The latter, on reaching England, rejected David's claim, and in 1137 the king of the Scots invaded Northumberland with a large army, one division being under command of his nephew, William, son of Duncan, and the other commanded by the king in person and his son. They assaulted the Castle of Wark but were unable to carry it. The army was then turned loose on the defenceless people of the country, who were massacred with merciless barbarity.[11]

In 1138, Stephen approached Scotland with an army, and forced David to retire to the north of the Tweed, where he encamped near Roxburgh. The English king, after wasting the Scottish borders, withdrew his forces without coming into conflict with David's army. Shortly after, Stephen being called to the south of England to repress a rebellion there, David took advantage of his absence to invade Northumberland again, this time with an army of 26,000 men. Here, after repeating the excesses of the former campaign and wasting the country for a period of several weeks, the army finally marched into Yorkshire, where it was opposed only by a small body of English cavalry, headed by several of the Norman barons of the north.

On the 22d of August, 1138, the armies met near North Allerton, and the celebrated Battle of the Standard was fought, which resulted in the defeat of the Scottish army. [12] David retired to Carlisle with his depleted forces; but shortly afterwards led them to the siege of Wark Castle, and succeeded in reducing that stronghold by famine.

There are two or more lengthy contemporary accounts of this invasion. That of Richard of Hexham has been selected as giving the most detailed description of the progress of David's motley and unmanageable force in its devastating march through the English territories. A better-written but perhaps somewhat less accurate account is that of Ailred of Rivaulx. The following is Hexham's :

1138. William, the son of Duncan, nephew of David king of Scotland, with part of the army of the same David, assailed, with nocturnal treachery, the castle which is called Carrum, in the land of the king of England, and, destroying the country all around, began to attack it by storm. Afterward, the king himself, with Henry his son, and a greater army, coming thither, and trying the endeavours of all their force, attempted to carry the town by engines which throw stones and other machines, and, by various attacks, and thereafter besieged it three weeks. But he profited nothing, nay rather, God assisting, each of his attempts was turned against himself. Now the king, perceiving his labour there to be fruitless, and a grievous loss to him and his from day to day to grow, inflamed with indignation and anger ; at length, leaving the town, hastened, with all his multitude, to destroy Northumberland. Therefore that detestable army, more atrocious than every kind of pagans, carrying reverence neither to god nor to men, having plundered the whole province, everywhere killed persons of each sex, of every age and condition, destroyed, pillaged, burned towns, churches, houses. For men sick in bed, and women pregnant, and in the act of delivery, and infants in cradles, and other innocents, between the breasts and in the bosoms of their mothers, with the mothers themselves, and decrepit old men, and worn out old women, and all other feeble persons from whatever cause where they were found, they killed with the point of the sword, or thrust through with their lances : And by how much the more miserable kind of death they could destroy them, by so much the more they rejoiced. . . . Now this abominable army was composed of Normans, Germans, English, of Northumbrians and Cumbrians, from Teviotdale and

Lothian, of Picts, who are vulgarly called Galwegians, and Scots ; nor was there any who knew their number.

Therefore, running up and down through the province, and sparing no one, they wasted almost all Northumberland, as far as the river Tyne, with sword and fire. Now, in this madness of stormy time, that noble monastery of Hexham, although being placed in the middle concourse, and as it were in the way of that abominable army, and of the above mentioned evils, it was straightened by them on every side, yet, god assisting, it offered to its own people and all flying to it, a most firm peace, and remained to all those a most safe asylum against all hostile attacks. Nevertheless, at first the Picts making an irruption, with very great violence, to the river Tyne flowing hard by the same town, had proposed to destroy the same like other places. But by and by before they could pass the aforesaid river, two of their number were killed by the country people : which the rest perceiving, they departed back terrified. Moreover two of the same nation of Picts came to a certain oratory of St. Michael situate on the same north part of the river Tyne, which belonged to the aforesaid church of Hexham. Breaking therefore the door thereof, what they there found they took away with them. But the vengeance of God was not wanting. For presently, being delivered to the devil, they are deprived of sense, and as madness agitated them, running up and down in the sight of all through the woods and country by night and day, one of them at first bruising his mouth with stones, afterward his thighs being cut off by some one, the other drowning himself in the Tyne, each damned by either death miserably perished. In the meantime, about the purification of St. Mary, Stephen king of England, with a very great army of horse and foot, came : which when the king of Scotland knew, leaving Northumberland, he hastened with his own army to his own land. . . . But the paschal solemnity being accomplished, presently in the next week on Saturday, the often mentioned king of Scotland with his abominable army returned again into Northumberland, and, afterward, destroyed the greatest part of the land of St. Cuthbert in the eastern part between Durham and the sea, with no less fury and cruelty than is above said. But the holy Cuthbert, at length, had compassion on his people. For, while his soldiers did these things, the king, with his knights, remained not far distant from Durham : where, a serious sedition having arisen, on account of a certain woman, the Picts threatened to destroy the king with his attendants : with which fear while he was greatly troubled, behold by a false rumour it is published that a great army is approaching from South England. Therefore, leaving his victuals, which were then ready, no one pursuing, he fled with all his people to his own country, and turned aside to the town of Norham, and laying siege thereto, tried, by various means and machines, to conquer and take it : And while he there stayed in the siege, he sent William MacDuncan his nephew, with the Picts, and part of his army, on an expedition into Yorkshire : whither arriving, and by reason of the sins of the people, obtaining a victory, the possessions of a certain noble monastery, which is situated in Furness, and the province which is called Craven, for a great part, they with sword and fire destroyed. Therefore, sparing no rank, no age, no sex, no condition, children and relations in sight of their parents, and lords in the sights of their servants, and vice versa, and husbands before the eyes of their wives, by how much the more miserable they were able, they at first slew, then, alas ! noble matrons alone and chaste virgins mixed with other women and at the same time with the plunder they carried off. Naked also and in troops, tied and coupled together with ropes and thongs, and pricking them with their lances and darts, they drove them before them.   Afterward, these being divided with the booty, some of them moved by compassion delivered certain of them free to the church of St. Mary of Carlisle.   But the Picts and many others led those which came to them along with them to their own country.   Finally those bestial men, esteeming adultery, and incest, and all other crimes, for nothing, after, in the manner of brute animals, they were weary of abusing those most wretched creatures, either made them hand-maids for themselves, or sold them to other barbarians for cows.   Now king David, having committed the siege of Carrum to two of his thanes, that is, barons, with their followers, with the greatest part of his army marched to the town which is called Bamburgh ; And, entering into the land of St. Cuthbert, waited for that part of his army which had not yet come to him : And presently, at his proclamation, the Picts and Cumbrians, and the men of Carlisle, of the circumjacent region came together to him. Therefore his whole army being assembled, because it appeared to him ex-ceedingly great, and unconquerable, for, in truth, it was considerable, hav-ing more than 26,000 men, he rejoiced with exceeding great joy.   Now, these things being done before the octave of the nativity of St. Mary, the king, with his army, passing by Durham to the Tees, caused the cornfields to be destroyed, the towns and churches, which on another occasion he left untouched, after his manner, to be broken, plundered, and burned.   Pass-ing also over the Tees, he began to do the same thing.   But divine piety, affected by the tears of numberless widows, orphans, and wretched persons, did not suffer him longer to exercise such impiety.   For, whilst he was pre-paring himself and his followers to this sort of wickedness, all his prepara-tion, and what he proposed to do, and whither to go, both by proclaiming fame, and by certain messengers running between, was not concealed from the men of Yorkshire.   Therefore the barons of that province assembled at York, and diligently considered amongst themselves what council they ought to take in this crisis.   .   .   .   But they went to the town which is called Thirsk.   While, therefore, they waited for the approach of the Scots, behold they learn that the king, with his army, has already passed the river Tees, and is now, in his manner, destroying their province.   Therefore with the utmost haste, they go to meet them : and passing through the town called North-Allerton, they came early in the morning to a field which was distant therefrom two miles.   Presently some of them erected in the midst of a certain machine which they had brought thither the mast of a ship, which they called Standard.   Afterward they had scarcely instructed them-selves in warlike arms, when behold the king of Scotland, with his whole army well prepared and most ready to fight, is announced to be near.   There-fore the greatest part of the horsemen, leaving their horses, became footmen. In like manner, on the part of the adversaries, the king himself and all his people, became footmen.   In the front of the battle were the Picts, in the midst the king with his knights and English, the rest of the barbarians, dispersed round about on every side, roared like beasts.

The king, in the meantime, the earls and best men of his realm being assembled together, began to treat with them concerning the order of the battle, and it pleased a great many, that, as many as had come up, the armed men, knights, and bowmen, should precede the whole army, inasmuch as armed men would attack armed men, knights encounter with knights, and arrows with arrows.   The Galwegians resisted, saying, that it was their right to construct the first battalion, and give the first assault unto the enemy, to animate by their bravery the rest of the army.   Others said, it would be dangerous, if, in the first attack, the unarmed should meet with the armed, forasmuch, as, if the first battalion, not sustaining the shock of war, should fall into flight, even the hearts of the brave would be easily dissolved.   The Galwegians, nevertheless, insisted, requiring their right to be granted to them :   " For why," they said, " O King, dost thou fear, and art too much frightened, at those iron coats which thou perceivest at a distance?   To us, certainly, are iron sides, a breast of brass, a mind void of fear, whose feet have neither felt flight, nor, ever, their backs a wound.   How far did these mail-coats profit the French at Clithero?   Whether did not these unarmed, as they call them, compel them to cast off their hauberks, and neglect their helmets, and abandon their shields?   Let your wisdom, therefore, O King, see how little confidence there is in these things, which, in need, are more for burthen than for comfort.   We at Clithero carried off the victory from these mail-coats, and we shall prostrate them to-day with our lances, using the valour of the mind for a shield."   These things being said, when the king seemed to acquiesce in the counsels of the knights, Malisse, earl of Strathern, very much enraged, said, " Why is it, O King, that thou rather committest thyself to the will of the Normans, when none of them with his arms is about to surpass me unarmed to-day in battle?"   These words Allan de Percy, bastard son of the great Allan, a most brave knight and very much approved in military affairs, hardly bearing, says, turning to the earl, " A grand word hast thou spoken, and which, to-day, for thy life, thou wilt not be able to perform."   Then the king, appeasing both, lest a tumult should, suddenly, be born of this altercation, yielded to the will of the Galwegians.

Therefore, in the octave of the assumption of saint Mary, on the eleventh of the calends of September, on Monday, between the first hour and the third the conflict of this battle was begun and ended.   For, immediately, on the first encounter, numberless Picts being slain, the rest, their arms being thrown away, took to flight.   The field is filled with carcasses, a great many are taken, the king, and all the others, turn their backs :   Finally of such an army, all being either killed or taken, or scattered like sheep without a shepherd.   For the English, and Scots, and Picts, and the other barbarians, wherever they accidentally found themselves, whosoever prevailed, either killed or wounded, or, at least, plundered each other, and so, by the just judgment of God, were equally oppressed by their own people as by strangers.   (Ricard. prior Hagiustal. co. 315, &c.)

Finally, in 1139, a treaty of peace was concluded between Stephen and David, by the terms of which Stephen yielded to David's son, Henry, his birthright, the earldom of Northumberland.

In 1142, Harold, brother of the King of Man, raised a fleet and made a descent upon Galloway ; but the inhabitants of that province, long accustomed to war, were successful in repelling the invaders, and put them to flight.[13]

The remainder of David's reign was passed in comparative peace, which was interrupted only by the occasional invasions of an impostor called Malcolm Mac Heth.   He was a pretended son of the Earl of Moray, but in reality an English monk, whose name seems to have been Wimund.   Having married the daughter of Somerled, Thane of Argyle, he organized a party in

Man and made repeated descents upon the Scottish coasts, slaying the inhabitants and plundering the country. David sent forces after him at different times, but they were unable to effect his capture, and when the King's soldiers left one district to pursue him in another, the adventurer returned and renewed his attacks. He was finally granted certain territories by the Scottish king as the price of peace ; but afterwards he was blinded and imprisoned.

A considerable influx of Normans took place during the time of David, numbers of them following him out of England when he succeeded to the throne, and many more entering Scotland afterwards at the invitation of this hospitable monarch.[14] Their settlement in the West is thus outlined by the author of the *History of the County of Ayr* (pp. 18, 19) although it is likely that more than half of those whose names are mentioned were of native Celtic families :

When David I., who married an English countess who had numerous vassals, ascended the throne in 1124, he is said to have been followed at successive periods, by no fewer than a thousand Anglo-Normans. During the reign of this monarch, Hugh de Morville, amongst others, came to Scotland, and, besides being appointed High Constable, was endowed with vast grants of land. He possessed the greater part of Cuninghame, and, under his auspices, a number of families, who afterwards rose to high feudal distinction, were settled in that district. The Loudoun family, who assumed the name of the lands as their patronymic, were Anglo-Normans. So were the progenitors of the Cuninghames. The Rosses were also vassals of Hugh de Morville. Godfrey de Ros acquired the lands of Stewarton from Richard de Morville. Stephen, the son of Richard, obtained lands in Cuninghame, which he called Stephen's-tun (Stephenston of the present day). The Lockharts of Lanarkshire and Ayrshire are of Anglo-Norman descent. Simond, the son of Malcolm, who settled in Lanarkshire, held lands under the Stewart family in Kyle, which he called Syming-tun, now Symington. The Colvilles, who possessed Ochiltree for some time, were from England. The Montgomeries of Eaglesham, and subsequently of Eglintoun, were Norman, and vassals of Walter the High Steward, who obtained the greater part of Renfrewshire. A brother of Walter is conjectured, upon good grounds, to have been the ancestor of the Boyds. The Stewarts were themselves Anglo-Normans, as were also the Bruces of Annandale and Carrick. The Wallaces of Kyle are supposed to have been of Norman descent [very improbable], from one Eimerus Galleius, whose name appears as a witness to the charter of the Abbey of Kelso, founded by David I. That the progenitors of the Hero of Scotland came from England is further held to be countenanced by the fact that there existed in London, in the thirteenth century, certain persons of the name of *Waleis ;* but none of our historians or genealogists have been able to trace the slightest family connection between them ; neither is it known at what period, if Norman or English, they settled in Scotland. The first of the name on record is Richard Walense, who witnesses a charter to the monks of Paisley, by Walter the High Steward, before the year 1174. The name came to be afterwards softened to *Waleys* or Wallace. In the absence of direct proof to the contrary, it is not unreasonable to conjecture that the Wallaces were native Scots. Some consider them to have been Welsh, apparently without reference to the fact that the Alcluydensians are often confounded in history by the terms British and Welsh. Long after the

Alcluyd kingdom had been destroyed, the inhabitants — the descendants of the Damnii — were known by the appellation of *Walenses*. It is therefore probable that the ancestors of Wallace adopted the patronymic of *Walense*, in the same way that *Inglis* is known to have been assumed from English, or *Fleming* from the Flemings. This is strongly countenanced by the fact that the name of the family was originally Walens. The coincidence is at all events curious, and not without interest. The property of Richard Walens may have been called Richard*tun*, in accordance with the prevailing Saxon custom of the time — not because he was himself of English extraction. The Flemings, who were all foreigners, came to be so numerous in Scotland that they were privileged to be governed by their own laws. The list of lowland clans, amounting in all to thirty-nine, if it is authentic, which is very doubtful, as given in the recently published MS. of Bishop Leslie, who wrote during the reign of Queen Mary, shows that the greater number were of Saxon or Norman extraction. The following is the list: Armstrong, Barclay, Brodie, Bruce, Colquhoun, Comyn, Cuninghame, Cranstoun, Crawford, Douglas, Drummond, Dunbar, Dundas, Erskine, Forbes, Gordon, Graham, Hamilton, Hay, Home, Johnstone, Kerr, Lauder, Leslie, Lindsay, Maxwell, Montgomerie, Murray, Ogilvie, Oliphant, Ramsay, Rose, Ruthven, Scott, Seton, Sinclair, Urquhart, Wallace, Wemyss.

There were also the Boyles, Blairs, Dunlops, Fullartons, Hunters, Fairlies, Linns, Eglintouns, Fergushills, Muirs, Monfoids, Auchinlecks, etc., who rose out of Ayrshire; and the Stewarts, Sempills, Caldwells, Ralstouns, Walkinshaws, Brisbanes, Dennistouns, Porterfields, Lyles, Houstouns, Cathcarts, Pollocks, Whytefuirds, Knoxes, Cochranes, etc., out of Renfrewshire — all of whom were of considerable status.

There was one Alan le Fenwick, connected, no doubt, with the parish in this county of that name, who swore fealty to Edward I. It is rather surprising that neither the Kennedies, a very extensive and old Celtic clan in Carrick, nor the Boyds, are mentioned amongst the foregoing. Whether *Vestiarium Scoticum* be a forgery or not, the families enumerated are well known to have flourished in the Lowlands; and, indeed, most of them are in existence at this moment. It is obvious, therefore, that the Celtic population, at least the chiefs, had been superseded to a great extent. In Ayrshire, as already stated, the mass of the inhabitants, were purely Celtic; but, as in other districts, the bulk of the property passed into the hands of Norman and Saxon emigrants, with whose followers the towns and villages were crowded. This infusion of foreign blood was not effected without some difficulty. The Celtic population were greatly opposed to the new system, and they broke out into frequent insurrections. When William was made prisoner at Alnwick in 1174, a general rising took place against the strangers, who were compelled to take shelter in the king's castles. During the reigns of Edgar, Alexander I., David I., and Malcolm IV., various disturbances occurred in consequence of the prejudices entertained by the old against the new race. The repeated irruptions of the Galwegians, whose territory included not only Carrick but Kyle and Cuninghame, at the commencement of the reign of David I., must of course have involved what now constitutes Ayrshire in the struggle. On the captivity of William, Galloway rose in revolt, slew the English and Normans, expelled the king's officers, and destroyed his castles.

In 1149, Henry of Anjou, son of Matilda of England, attempted to overthrow King Stephen, and to that end enlisted the aid of his mother's uncle, the

Scottish king.   Having entered into correspondence with the Earl of Chester, David and Henry together marched to Lancaster, but not being seconded by their English ally, they were obliged to retreat without having accomplished anything.

David's son, Henry, died in 1152, and his death was followed a year later by that of David himself, which occurred May 24, 1153, at Carlisle, a town then within his dominions.[15]

Malcolm IV., son of Prince Henry, succeeded to his grandfather's throne, being at that time twelve years of age.   His reign was inaugurated by an insurrection which was organized by Somerled, the father-in-law of Malcolm Mac Heth, who invaded Scotland with the sons of that Malcolm, and committed many depredations.   One of these sons, Donald, was captured at Whithorn in Galloway, in 1156, and imprisoned with his father in Roxburgh castle.   In 1157 King Malcolm surrendered to Henry II., then king of England, all Crown possessions in the northern counties of that country, including the earldoms of Northumberland, Cumberland, and Huntingdon, and received in return Henry's acknowledgment of his own title to Huntingdon, which presumably belonged by inheritance to Malcolm's youngest brother, David.

Malcolm's brother, William, held the earldom of Northumberland at this time, and his loss of that province naturally imbued him with a feeling of resentment against the English.   Two years later Malcolm visited France, and there fought under the English Henry's banners.   His nobles, however, jealous of the growing influence of the English king over their young sovereign, sent a deputation to urge his return, and the king accordingly hastened home.[16]

In 1160 an insurrection took place in Galloway.   It was not until after three successive invasions of that district that the rebellion was finally crushed.   Thereupon Fergus, Lord of Galloway, having given his son, Uchtred, to Malcolm as a hostage, himself retired to an abbey, and the kingdom was again at peace.[17]

In 1162, Malcolm expelled many of the rebellious inhabitants of Moray, and planted new colonists in their place.   Chief among these newcomers seem to have been the Flemings or natives of Flanders (Belgium), whose name is preserved to this day in that of many worthy families of Scottish descent.[18]   Two years later, Somerled, Thane of Argyle, again invaded Scotland, landing at Renfrew, where he was opposed by the inhabitants, and himself and his son, Gillacolane, were slain.

NOTES TO CHAPTER XX

[1] See pp. 189–90.

[2] Overlying the little that we absolutely know of the people called Picti there is a great fact that at a very early period — whenever, indeed, the inhabitants of Scotland come forward in European history — the territory of old assigned to the Picts was occupied by a people

thoroughly Gothic or Teutonic, whether they were the descendants of the large-limbed and red-haired Caledonians of Tacitus, or subsequently found their way into the country.   To the southward of the Forth, we know pretty well that they were the Saxons of Deira and Bernicia, superseding the Romanised Britons ; but all along northwards the Lowlands were covered with people of the same origin.   Those who see their descendants at the present day acknowledge the Teutonic type to be purer in them than in the people of England.—Burton, *History of Scotland*, vol. i., p. 200.

[3] The overthrow of the Saxon dynasty in England by the Normans, the consequent exile of many of the Saxon families of distinction, who took refuge in Scotland, and Malcolm's marriage with Margaret, all tended to create a partiality for the habits of the South. . . . The Saxon language, which, as we have seen, was previously spoken in the east of Scotland, and partially in the south, was first introduced at the court, in compliment to the queen, in the region of Malcolm Canmore.   Under Edgar, the Saxon mania made still greater strides. Large bodies of emigrants were settled throughout the kingdom, both north and south of the Forth.—Paterson, *History of the County of Ayr*, vol. i., p. 18.

Boece (l. xii., fol. 258, a.) says, that the partisans of Edgar Ætheling were outlawed by William the Conqueror, sought a retreat in Scotland, and all received grants of lands from Malcolm.   Of them Boece mentions the following families : Lindsay, Vaux, Ramsay, Lovel, Tours, Preston, Sandilands, Bisset, Soulis, Wardlaw, and Maxwell.   But I consider this list as drawn up from the imagination of Boece, without any regard to historical truth.   Some of the names in it are Norman, others local.   Boece also gives a list of families who came from Hungary with Queen Margaret, and settled in Scotland : As Crichton, Fotheringham, Giffard, Maul, Borthwick ; how Crichton, Fotheringham, and Borthwick, should happen to be Hungarian names, I know not.   Giffard was a Norman, and came over with the Conqueror ; (Du Chesne, p. 1126.)   Everyone knows that the family of Maul was greatly distinguished in France before the conquest.—Hailes, *Annals of Scotland*, vol. i., p. 39.

[4] " Amid these depredations inflicted by the Scots, Earl Cospatric, who, as already mentioned, had purchased the earldom of Northumbria of King William for a sum of money, having obtained the aid of some active allies, ravaged Cumberland with dreadful havoc ; and then, having laid waste the country with fire and sword, returned with a large quantity of spoil, and shut himself and his followers within the strong fortifications of Bebbanburgh ; whence frequently sallying forth, he greatly weakened the enemy's strength.   At this period Cumberland was subject to King Malcolm ; not by rightful possession, but in consequence of having been subjugated by force.

" Malcolm, on hearing what Cospatric had done (while he was still looking at the church of Saint Peter burning amid the flames kindled by his own men), could hardly contain himself for anger, and commanded his men no longer to spare any individual of the English nation, but either to strike them to the earth and slay them, or making them prisoners, carry them off, doomed to the yoke of perpetual slavery.   The troops having received this sanction, it was dreadful even to witness the cruelties they were guilty of towards the English.   Some aged men and women were decapitated with the sword ; others, like swine intended for food, were pierced through and through with lances ; infants were torn from the breasts of their mothers, thrown aloft into the air, and on falling, received upon the points of lances, sharp weapons being thickly planted in the ground.

" The Scots, more savage than wild beasts, took delight in these cruelties, as though a spectacle of games ; and thus did the age of innocence, destined to attain heaven, breathe its last, suspended between heaven and earth.   But the young men and young women, and whoever besides seemed adapted for toil and labor, were driven away in fetters in front of the enemy, to endure a perpetual exile in captivity as servants and handmaids.   Some of these, while running before those who drove them on, became fatigued to a degree beyond what their strength could endure, and, as they sank to the ground on the spot, the same was the place of their fall and of their death.   While beholding these scenes, Malcolm was moved to compassion by no tears, no groans of the wretched creatures; but, on the contrary, gave orders that they should be perseveringly driven onward in their course.

"In consequence of this, Scotland became filled with men-servants and maid-servants of English parentage; so much so, that even at the present day not only not even the smallest village, but not even the humblest house is to be found without them."—Simeon of Durham.

Besides the Saxons, many of the Norman nobility, who were dissatisfied with the rule of the Conqueror, retired to Scotland, where they were encouraged by every mark of distinction which could be heaped upon them. It seemed to be the policy of the Scottish kings to encourage the settlement of foreigners, with a view to consolidate the authority of the crown, and enable them to overcome the dangerous power of the native clans whose genius and habits were by no means favourable to concentrated government or the cultivation of commerce. —Paterson, *History of the County of Ayr*, vol. i., p. 18.

[5] He for mid his fyrde ut of Scotlande into Lothene on England, and thaerabad (*Sax. Chr.* p. 197). The words of S. Dunelm, (p. 216,) are, "Cui rex Malcholmus cum exercitu in provincia Loidis occurrit." The question is, what we are to understand by "Lothene on England," and "provincia Loidis." Some writers think that Lothene on England means what is now called Lothian in Scotland; others, that provincia Loidis means the territory of Leeds in Yorkshire; and that Lothene on England must be understood of the same place. I am not satisfied with either hypothesis. 1. There is no reason to believe, that the *Chr. Sax.* by Lothene on England, meant what is now called Lothian; the word Lothene occurs but twice in *Chr. Sax.* at this place, and at p. 229, where "se Bishop of Lothene J." is mentioned. J. Bishop of Lothene could not mean J. Bishop of Lothian, as has been elsewhere shewn, (*Remarks on the History of Scotland*, p. 81); and if Lothene put simply does not mean Lothian in Scotland, it would be strange if Lothene in England did. There is the highest probability that *Chr. Sax.* understood the passage into Scotland to be at Solway, or at the Tweed. This is inconsistent with the idea of Lothian being in England, or of its being distinguished from Scotland as a kingdom, in the days of Malcolm III. But, 2. There is no reason to believe, that by provincia Loidis, S. Dunelm meant the territory of Leeds in Yorkshire. It will be remarked, that Malcolm invaded England in May, 1091, that he retreated from Chester le Street, and that the meeting between Malcolm and William Rufus must have been as late as October, 1091; for it happened after the destruction of William's fleet by a tempest in the end of September: If then Loidis provincia means Leeds, it follows, that Malcolm must have invaded England a second time, in autumn, 1091, and must have penetrated farther south than he did in his expedition in May, 1091. Now, this is inconsistent with the general report of historians, who agree that Malcolm invaded England five times; 1, in 1061; 2, in 1070; 3, in 1079; 4, in May, 1091; 5, in autumn, 1093. Had he invaded England in autumn, 1091, and proceeded into Yorkshire the number of his invasions would have been six, not five. I have sometimes thought that there is an error either in the MSS., or printed copies of the *Saxon Chronicle*, and that the word should be Lothere, not Lothene: the difference between the Anglo-Saxon n and r is very minute, and might be easily mistaken; the r is formed by drawing the first stroke of the n a little below the line. If this conjecture could be admitted the place where the two kings met may have been Lothere, now Lowther, in the north parts of Westmoreland, near the borders of that district of Cumberland which Malcolm possessed, and in the neighbourhood of Penrith, the place concerning which, as I imagine, the controversy then was.—Hailes, *Annals of Scotland*, vol. i., pp. 24, 25.

[6] A.D. 1094. . . . This year also the Scots conspired against their king Duncan, and slew him, and they afterwards took his uncle Dufenal a second time for their king; through whose instructions and instigation Duncan had been betrayed to his death.—*English Chronicle*.

[7] "Six years after he obtained these lands, he founded, in the year 1113, a monastery of Benedictine monks of Tyron, at Selkirk, on the banks of the Ettrick, and his foundation-charter will still further indicate the extent of his possessions as earl. In this charter he calls himself Earl David, son of Malcolm, king of Scots, and addressed it to all his adherents,

Normans, Angles, and Scots, and gives the monks the lands of Selkirk and other lands in Teviotdale, a ploughgate in Berwick, and a croft in the burgh of Roxburgh, the tenth of his 'can' or dues from Galweia or Galloway, and in addition some lands in his English lordship of Northampton ; and he shows his independent position by adding that this grant was made while Henry was reigning in England and Alexander in Scotia, or Scotland proper. Not long after he refounded the bishopric of Glasgow, to which he appointed John as first bishop, who had been his tutor.   The instrument which records the restoration of the diocese, and an investigation ordered by Earl David into the possessions of the see, is still preserved, and may probably be dated some time between the years 1116 and 1120.   In this document it was stated that ' in the time of Henry, king of England, while Alexander, king of Scots, was reigning in Scotia, God had sent them David, brother-german of the king of Scotia, to be their prince and leader ;' and, ' David, prince of the Cumbrian region, causes inquisition to be made into the possessions of the church of Glasgow in all the provinces of Cumbria which were under his dominion and power, for he did not rule over the whole of the Cumbrian region.'   The kingdom of Cumbria originally extended from the Firth of Clyde to the river Derwent, including what was afterwards the dioceses of Glasgow, Galloway, and Carlisle. That portion, however, which extended from the Solway Firth to the river Derwent, and afterwards formed the diocese of Carlisle was wrested from the Scots by William Rufus in 1092, and was bestowed by Henry the First upon the Ranulf de Meschines.   David's possessions in Cumbria consisted, therefore, of the counties of Lanark, Ayr, Renfrew, Dumfries, and Peebles, and the inquisition contains lands in these counties.   He was, as we have seen, overlord of Galloway, and his rule extended also over Lothian and Teviotdale, in the counties of Berwick, Roxburgh, and Selkirk ; for, in a charter by Earl David to the monks of Durham of the lands of Swinton in Berwickshire, he addresses it to Biship John of Glasgow, to Gospatric, Colban and Robert his brothers, and to his thanes and drengs of Lothian and Teviotdale ; and, in another, Thor of Ednam in Berwickshire calls him his overlord, or the superior of his lands.

   " From these deeds we not only learn the extent of David's possessions, but we also see that he had attached to himself not only his Anglic vassals but a large following of Norman barons.   Of the witnesses to the inquisition there are, besides his countess Matilda, his nephew William, son of his brother Duncan, eight of Anglic race and fourteen who are Normans.   In his foundation charter of Selkirk, besides Bishop John of Glasgow, his countess Matilda, his son Henry, his nephew William, and three chaplains, there are eleven Norman witnesses, nine Anglic, and a solitary Gillemichel to represent the Celtic race.   The native Cumbrians nowhere appear as witnessing his grants, and it seems plain enough that he had largely introduced the Norman element into his territories, and ruled over them as a feudal superior basing his power and influence upon his Norman and Anglic vassals, of whom the former were now the most prominent both in the weight and number."—*Celtic Scotland*, vol. i., pp. 455-457.

   [8] An. 1130 . . .   This year was Angus slain by the Scottish army, and a great number of persons with him.   There was God's right wrought upon him, for that he was all forsworn.—*English Chronicle*.

   Malcolm, a bastard son of Alexander, attempted to deprive his uncle of the crown, and involved him in two rather severe contests ; but David, who was his superior in talent as well as in wealth and power, defeated him and his party.   In the year of our Lord 1130, while King David was ably applying himself to a cause in King Henry's court, and carefully examining a charge of treason which, they say, Geoffrey de Clinton had been guilty of, Angus, earl of Moray, with Malcolm and five thousand men, entered Scotia [or Scotland proper] with the intention of reducing the whole kingdom to subjection.   Upon this Edward, who was a cousin of King David and commander of his army, assembled troops and suddenly threw himself in the enemy's way.   A battle was at length fought, in which Earl Angus was slain and his troops defeated, taken prisoners, or put to flight.   Vigorously pursuing the fugitives with his soldiers elated with victory, and entering Morafia, or Moray, now deprived of its lord and protector, he obtained, by God's help, possession of the whole of that large territory. Thus David's dominions were augmented, and his power was greater than that of any of his predecessors.—*Ordericus Vitalis*, b. viii., c. xxii.

1130. Battle between the men of Alban and the men of Moray, in which fell four thousand of the men of Moray, with their king, Oengus, son of the daughter of Lulag, a thousand also of the men of Alban in heat of battle.—*Annals of Ulster*.

[9] "An. 1135. This year, at Lammas, king Henry went over sea: and on the second day, as he lay asleep in the ship, the day was darkened universally, and the sun became as if it were a moon three nights old with the stars shining round it at mid-day. Men greatly marvelled, and great fear fell on them, and they said that some great event should follow thereafter—and so it was, for the same year the king died in Normandy, on the day after the feast of St. Andrew. Soon did this land fall into trouble, for every man greatly began to rob his neighbour as he might. Then king Henry's sons and his friends took his body, and brought it to England, and buried it at Reading. He was a good man, and great was the awe of him ; no man durst ill treat another in his time ; he made peace for men and deer. Whoso bare his burden of gold and silver, no man durst say to him aught but good. In the meantime his nephew Stephen de Blois had arrived in England, and he came to London, and the inhabitants received him, and sent for the archbishop, William Corboil, who consecrated him king on midwinter-day. In this king's time was all discord, and evil-doing, and robbery ; for the powerful men who had kept aloof, soon rose up against him ; the first was Baldwin de Redvers, and he held Exeter against the king, and Stephen besieged him, and afterwards Baldwin made terms with him. Then the others took their castles, and held them against the king, and David, king of Scotland, betook him to Wessington [Derbyshire], but nowithstanding his array, messengers passed between them, they came together, and made an agreement, though it availed little.

"An. 1137. This year king Stephen went over sea to Normandy, and he was received there because it was expected that he would be altogether like his uncle, and because he had gotten possession of his treasure, but this he distributed and scattered foolishly. King Henry had gathered together much gold and silver, yet did he no good for his soul's sake with the same. When king Stephen came to England, he held an assembly at Oxford ; and there he seized Roger bishop of Salisbury, and Alexander bishop of Lincoln, and Roger the chancellor his nephew, and he kept them all in prison till they gave up their castles. When the traitors perceived that he was a mild man, and a soft, and a good, and that he did not enforce justice, they did all wonder. They had done homage to him, and sworn oaths, but they no faith kept ; all became forsworn, and broke their allegiance, for every rich man built his castles, and defended them against him, and they filled the land full of castles. They greatly oppressed the wretched people by making them work at these castles, and when the castles were finished they filled them with devils and evil men.

"Then they took those whom they suspected to have any goods, by night and by day, seizing both men and women, and they put them in prison for their gold and silver, and tortured them with pains unspeakable, for never were any martyrs tormented as these were. They hung some up by their feet, and smoked them with foul smoke ; some by their thumbs, or by the head, and they hung burning things on their feet. They put a knotted string about their heads, and twisted it till it went into the brain. They put them into dungeons wherein were adders and snakes and toads, and thus wore them out. Some they put into a crucet-house, that is, into a chest that was short and narrow, and not deep, and they put sharp stones in it, and crushed the man therein so that they broke all his limbs. There were hateful and grim things called Sachenteges in many of the castles, and which two or three men had enough to do to carry. The Sachentege was made thus : it was fastened to a beam, having a sharp iron to go around a man's throat and neck, so that he might noways sit, nor lie, nor sleep, but that he must bear all the iron. Many thousands they exhausted with hunger. I cannot and I may not tell of all the wounds and all the tortures that they inflicted upon the wretched of this land ; and this state of things lasted the nineteen years that Stephen was king, and ever grew worse and worse.   They were continually levying an exaction from the towns, which they called *Tenserie*, and when the miserable inhabitants had no more to give, then plundered they, and burnt all the towns, so that well mightest thou walk a whole day's journey nor ever shouldst thou find a man seated in a town, or its lands tilled.

"Then was corn dear, and flesh, and cheese, and butter, for there was none in the land —wretched men starved with hunger—some lived on alms who had been erewhile rich ; some fled the country—never was there more misery, and never acted heathens worse than these. At length they spared neither church nor churchyard, but they took all that was valuable therein, and then burned the church and all together.   Neither did they spare the lands of bishops, nor of abbots, nor of priests ; but they robbed the monks and the clergy, and every man plundered his neighbour as much as he could.   If two or three men came riding to a town, all the township fled before them, and thought that they were robbers.   The bishops, and clergy were ever cursing them, but this to them was nothing, for they were all accursed, and forsworn, and reprobate.   The earth bare no corn, you might as well have tilled the sea, for the land was all ruined by such deeds, and it was said openly that Christ and his saints slept.   These things, and more than we can say, did we suffer during nineteen years because of our sins."—*English Chronicle.*

[10] " At length he received letters from King Henry's daughter, complaining that she had been excluded from her father's will, robbed of the crown which had been secured to her and her husband by solemn oaths ; that the laws were set aside, and justice trodden under foot ; and the sworn fealty of the English barons was broken and disregarded.   She therefore earnestly and sorrowfully implored him, as her kinsman, to succor her in her need ; as her liege vassal, to aid her in her distress.   The king was deeply grieved ; and inflamed with zeal for a just cause, the ties of blood and regard for his oath induced him to foment insurrections in England, that by so doing, by God's help, Stephen might be compelled to resign the crown, which it appeared to him had been unjustly acquired, to the rightful owner.   The King of Scots entertained at his court the English exiles who continually urged him to these measures. Among these were Robert de Baddington's son, and his collateral kinsmen, who have been mentioned before as having, on their banishment, taken refuge in Scotland, with the hope of re-establishing themselves in their own country.   There were also Eustace Fitz-John, an intimate friend of King Henry, with some others, who, in the desire of advancing themselves, or of defending what appeared to them the right cause, sought every opportunity of promoting a rupture.   King David, therefore, for that was his name, published an edict throughout Scotland, calling his people to arms, and, changing his line of conduct, let loose without mercy a most fierce and destructive storm on the English people.

" Scotland, called also Albany, is a country overspread by extensive moors, but containing flourishing woods, and pastures, which feed large herds of cows and oxen.   It has safe harbours, and is surrounded by fertile islands.   The natives are savage, and their habits uncleanly ; but they are neither stunted by extremity of cold, nor debilitated by severe want. Swift of foot and lightly armed, they make bold and active soldiers.   Among themselves, they are so fearless as to think nothing of death ; among strangers, their cruelty is brutal, and they sell their lives dearly.   A confused multitude of this people being assembled from the Lowlands of Scotland, they were formed into an irregular army, and marched for England.   Crossing the borders they entered the province of Northumbria, which is very extensive, and abounds with all necessary supplies, and there they pitched their camp.   Being now mustered in regular companies [incursions were made] over the face of the country, which extended round in great fertility."—*Chronicle of the Acts of King Stephen.*

[11] An. 1138.   This year David, King of Scotland, entered this land with an immense army resolving to conquer it, and William Earl of Albemarle, to whose charge the king had committed York, and other trusty men, came against him with a few troops, and fought with him,

and they put the king to flight at the Standard, and slew a great part of his followers.—*English Chronicle.*

"At length that hostility to the aggressive Normans, which had spread so far and sunk so deep, took practical shape in the memorable invasion which was stopped by the battle of the Standard in 1138. This affair thoroughly alarmed the Norman party throughout all England. It was not the usual plundering raid or foray, but an invasion in which, as the *Saxon Chronicle* says, the King of Scots 'thought he would win this land.' We are fortunate in having the story of this invasion told to us by one who was present and able to describe what he saw—Ailred, abbot of Rievaulx, in Yorkshire. He was a wonderful Latinist for his age, and a devotee of study and the pen, insomuch that he refused a bishopric which his eminence as a scholar and author had brought in his way, preferring to follow his favourite pursuits in the retirement of his abbey. What we see is, a country with many wealthy ecclesiastical establishments and powerful baronies, into which there drifts a huge countless host of men—a few disciplined soldiers among them, but the great body a wild diversified horde, such as we may suppose to have been commanded by Attila or Genseric. There are among them not only the Scots and the wild Picts of Galloway, but it is said men from that distant Orkney over which the King of Scots had no control. All this motley host assembled round him, although his position as a belligerent was, that he was fighting for the province of Northumberland, of which his son was heir by inheritance. As he marches on in the midst of them, he is rather borne along by the current, than the commander of an army. If fear and hatred of the Norman aggressors was the leading idea that united elements so discordant, there is little doubt that a zest for plunder had the more powerful influence in keeping the host together.

"When Stephen came he broke into the Scots' border while David's army continued pillaging in England. But Stephen had troubles in the South to which he had to turn quickly, leaving the country to defend itself as the great host advanced southward in the direction of York. . . . The Norman barons gathered into a group, among whom we find William of Albemarle, Walter of Ghent, with De Moubrays, De Percys, De Coucys, Nevilles, and Ferrers. Two Norman knights, with names afterwards familiar in history, were selected to reason with King David, because they held lands of him as well as of the English king. They were Robert de Bruce and Bernard de Baliol, both men whose descendants became well known in Scotland. Their mission was ineffective, and they returned to their comrades, withdrawing allegiance from King David, and leaving their Scots estates to be forfeited, if need be."—Burton, *History of Scotland*, vol. i., pp. 435-437.

[19] From the harangue which Ailred supposes Walter L'Espec, the English general, to have pronounced before the battle of the Standard, we learn that the Scottish infantry were altogether without armour, that they used spears of an enormous length, and that their swords were ill tempered and brittle; that their only implement of defence was a target of leather, and that in their camp there were jesters or buffoons, and dancers, both male and female.—Hailes, *Annals of Scotland*, vol. i., p. 325.

"Fordun notices very shortly the battle of the Standard at Allerton or Northallerton, in which David I. was defeated in 1138, but Ailred's fuller account of it gives a curious picture of the various populations which made up the kingdom of Scotland, and still remained distinct. The army was arranged in the following bodies:

Prima acies—
  1. Galwenses.
Altera acies. Filius regis et milites sagittarii cum eo—
  2. Cumbrenses.
  3. Tevidalenses.
Tertius cuneus—
  4. Laodonenses.
  5. Insulani.
  6. Lavernani.

Rex in sua acie retinuit—

7. Scotti.
8. Muravenses.
9. De militibus Anglis et Francis ad sui corporis custodiam.

" The Galwenses were the Picts of Galloway ; the Cumbrenses, the Welsh population of Strathclyde ; the Tevidalenses, the people of Teviotdale ; the Laodonenses, the Anglic population of Lothian ; the Insulani, the Gael of the Isles ; the Lavernani were probably the people of the Lennox. This word is a corruption of Levenach, or, according to Gaelic orthography, Leamhainach, and the Leamhnaigh, or men of the Lennox, often appear in the Irish records as acting separately ; thus, in the ' Wars of the Gaedhil with the Gaill,' we have a statement that the Gael, in 1005, levied tribute from the Saxons and Britons [Strathclyde], and Leamhnaigh, and Alban, and Airergaedhil [Argyle] (p. 137). The Leamhnaigh also took part in the battle of Cluantarff. The Scotti were the inhabitants of Alban or Scotia in its confined sense, viz., the districts extending from the Forth to the river Spey on the north and Drumalban on the west ; the Muravenses, the people of Moray, beyond the Spey ; the Milites Franci were the Norman soldiers."—Skene, *Notes and Illustrations to Fordun*, vol. ii., p. 425.

[13] 1142. The three sons of Harold, the brother of Olave, a fleet being assembled, passed over to Galloway, willing to subdue it. The Galwegians, however, forming a circle, and a great effort being made, encountered with them. They, immediately, turning their backs, fled with great confusion to Man, and all the Galwegians, who inhabited therein, some of them they slew, others they banished.—*Chron. Reg. Man.*

[14] First of all, who and what were the Normans ? May I answer in an epigrammatic saying of my own, which is already in print, but which I am vain enough to think will bear saying twice ? The Norman, then, was a Dane who had stayed a little time in Gaul to put on a slight French varnish, and who came into England to be washed clean again. The Dane who came straight from Denmark had put on no such varnish, and needed no such cleaning. The Danes who had wrested the coast of the French duchy from its own dukes and kings, who had shut up those dukes and kings in an inland city, but who in so doing had taken to the tongue and the manners of the land in which they had settled—those, in short, who had changed from Northmen into Normans,—still remained kinsmen, though they may have forgotten the kindred ; but they had put on the garb of strangers, and in that garb they came among us. Our work was to strip them of that foreign garb, to bring to light the true brotherhood that lurked beneath, to bring back the Saxon of Bayeux and the Dane of Coutances to his natural place alongside of the Saxon of Winchester and the Dane of York, to teach even the more deeply Romanized Norman of Rouen to come back once more to the Teutonic hearth which he had forsaken.—Freeman, *The English People in Its Three Homes*, p. 154.

[15] David is often represented, in modern times, as the exterminator of his fellow-countrymen, granting their lands to foreigners, and driving out the native Scottish race, or enslaving them beneath the yoke of alien masters — a course that could have hardly earned the character ascribed to him by his friend and biographer Ailred, " he was beloved by his own people, the Scots, and feared by the men of Galloway." It would be nearer the truth, perhaps, to describe him as the great confirmer of proprietary right throughout the settled portion of his kingdom.—*Scotland under Her Early Kings*, vol. i., p. 288.

[16] At length the Scottish lords, seeing their king's too great intimacy and friendship with Henry, King of England, were sore troubled, and all Scotland with them. . . . So they sent an embassy after him. . . . Thereupon, he returned from the army at Toulouse, and came to Scotland, on account of divers pressing matters ; and by his authority as king, he bade the prelates and nobles meet together at his borough of Perth. Meanwhile the chief men of the country were roused. Six earls—Ferchard, Earl of Stratherne, to wit, and five other earls—being stirred up against the king, not to compass any selfish end, or through treason, but rather to guard the common weal, sought to take him, and laid siege to the keep

of that town. God so ordering it, however, their undertaking was brought to naught for the nonce; and after not many days had rolled by, he was, by the advice of the clergy, brought back to a good understanding with his nobles.—Fordun, *Annals*, iii.

[17] " King Malcolm the Fourth, three times, with a great army, marched into Galloway, and, at length, subjugated it to himself."

" Fergus, prince of Galloway, took the canonical habit in the church of the Holy-rood of Edinburgh ; and gave to them the town which is called Dunroden."—Roger de Hoveden.

This Fergus was the husband of Elizabeth, a natural daughter of Henry I.

[18] " One great cause of the wealth and prosperity of Scotland during these early times was the settlement of multitudes of Flemish merchants in the country, who brought with them the knowledge of trade and manufactures and the habits of application and industry which have so long characterized this people. In 1155 Henry II. banished all foreigners from his dominion, and the Flemings, of whom there were then great numbers in England, eagerly flocked into the neighboring country, which offered them a near and safe asylum.

" We can trace the settlement of these industrious citizens, during the twelfth and thirteenth centuries, in almost every part of Scotland, in Berwick, in St. Andrews, Perth, Dumbarton, Ayr, Peebles, Lanark, Edinburgh, and in the districts of Renfrewshire, Clydesdale, and Annandale, in Fife, in Angus, in Aberdeenshire, and as far north as Inverness and Urquhart."—Tytler, *History of Scotland*, vol. ii., chap. iii., § 4.

CHAPTER XXI

WILLIAM THE LION

MALCOLM died December 28, 1164, and was succeeded by his brother William, known in history as William the Lion. Almost immediately after his coronation, William made a demand on King Henry for the restitution of Northumberland, which had been so indiscreetly surrendered to the English by the youthful Malcolm a few years before. William, like his predecessor, fought under the banners of Henry in his wars with France; perhaps with the hope of recovering his inheritance there by acts of feudal vassalage, as well as to perform the service due from him for Huntingdon.

His humility not availing, however, he entered into negotiations with France in 1168, with the object of forming an alliance against the English. This was the first step taken by the Scottish kings towards the formation of the famous Ancient League between Scotland and France which continued down to the time of Mary Stuart. Soon afterwards William bestowed Huntingdon upon his brother David, and in 1173 joined with King Henry's son (Henry III.) in that prince's rebellion against his father, having been promised the earldom of Northumberland for his assistance. William laid siege to Wark and Carlisle, but could not force those garrisons to capitulate. Meanwhile his army, which contained a large body of the savage Galwegians, ravaged Northumberland with excessive cruelty, spreading terror among the inhabitants and slaughtering without mercy old men, women, and children.

The following year William, while still in Northumberland, was one day riding with a small party of mounted attendants in a field near Alnwick Castle, when he came up with a body of horsemen whom at first he mistook for Scots; but who proved to be a company of Yorkshire barons. They had ridden to the North, intending to render such assistance as they could in opposing the Scots, and now bore down upon the Scottish knights, making some of them prisoners. Among these captives they were astonished to find King William himself.[1] They immediately carried him off to the South and delivered him to the English king.

Henry was fully aware of the value of such a capture, and had had sufficient provocation to lead him to make the most of it. Accordingly he had the Scots' king conveyed to the strong castle of Falaise in Normandy, where he would be unable to communicate with his subjects in Scotland. Henry then proposed, as the condition for William's release, that he himself be given sovereignty over all Scotland; and that William should become Henry's vassal for that country, as he was already for his English earldoms. Although this involved an entire surrender of independence on the part of Scotland, the King of the Scots was fain to accept the terms proposed; and a treaty to that effect was accordingly executed between the two, which was afterwards ratified by an assemblage of the Scottish nobles and clergy. William, after formally doing homage to Henry, delivered to him his brother David and twenty-one of his nobles as hostages, together with the keeping of the castles of Roxburgh, Jedburgh, Berwick, Edinburgh, and Stirling.

Immediately after the king's capture the Galwegians, on returning home, had risen in revolt and undertaken to kill or drive out all the Norman barons and other foreigners who had been settled in their country.

These foreigners during the reigns of the two preceding monarchs had come into Scotland in great numbers, many young men of the noble Norman families of the South having accompanied David north of Tweed on his return home from England to assume the crown. Others resorted to the courts of David and Malcolm at the invitation of those kings ; who appear to have bestowed upon them vast grants of lands and many titular honors.[2]

The revolting Galwegians were under the command of the two sons of Fergus, Uchtred and Gilbert, who besought Henry to receive their homage and become Lord Superior of their country. In the same year, a quarrel having arisen between these two brothers as to the division of their inheritance, Gilbert, through the instrumentality of his son, Malcolm, made a prisoner of Uchtred, and put him to a cruel death, first causing his tongue to be cut off, and his eyes to be torn out. He then sought to make himself master of Uchtred's portion but was resisted by the latter's son, Roland. Gilbert then asked the protection of Henry, and again offered him his submission, but the English king refused to accept it.[3] On William's return from Falaise in 1175, he led an army into Galloway to punish Gilbert, but the latter made the King pecuniary satisfaction. The following year, having accompanied William to York, Gilbert was received into Henry's favor and did homage to that ruler.[4]

In 1179, William, with his brother David, marched a large army into Ross-shire, to suppress a revolt that had arisen there. The leader of the insurgents was called MacWilliam or Donald Bane, and claimed to be the grandson of Duncan, Malcolm Canmore's oldest son. The King was unable to bring the rebels to bay, so, after fortifying two castles, he returned to the South. Some seven years later MacWilliam was surprised and slain by King William's army in Moray.

In 1184, Gilbert, lord of Galloway, invaded Scotland, committing many depredations. His death took place in the following year ; and on that occasion Roland, son of the murdered Uchtred, rose against Gilbert's adherents. Having slain their commander, Gilpatrick, he possessed himself of all Galloway. His action was favored by William, but opposed by their Lord Superior, King Henry. The latter, in 1186, brought an army to Carlisle, and prepared to invade Galloway for the purpose of punishing the vassal who had dared to possess himself of another's territory without first obtaining permission from and making terms with his feudal superior.

Roland fortified all the passes into Galloway, and prepared himself for a desperate resistance; but before extremities were reached, the differences were adjusted by agreement, and the armies withdrawn. Roland was permitted to retain what had formerly belonged to his father, Uchtred, and Duncan, Gilbert's son, was confirmed in the possession of Carrick, which was then a district of Galloway.[5]

Henry, King of England, died in 1189. In the same year, his son and successor, Richard I., needing money to help him fit out a contemplated expedition to the Holy Land, arranged with William to restore the independence of Scotland for a consideration of 10,000 merks. Accordingly, this sum was paid by the Scottish people for their freedom.

In 1196 William De Moreville, constable of Scotland, having died, Roland, lord of Galloway, who had married De Moreville's sister, succeeded him. The same year a revolt occurred in Caithness, some of the Norse inhabitants having arisen under the lead of Harald, Earl of Orkney and Caithness. William suppressed the rebellion by marching an army into that district; but the attempt was repeated the following year, when the rebels appeared in arms under the command of Torfin, son of Harald. William again marched to the North, and having seized Harald held him until his son Torfin surrendered himself as a hostage. The same year (1197) William built the castle of Ayr, as a menace to the turbulent Galwegians.

In 1209, Alan, son of Roland of Galloway,[6] married Margaret, the daughter of William's brother David, Earl of Huntingdon.

In 1211, Guthred, a member of the family of MacWilliam, invaded Ross-shire from Ireland. After wasting it for a time he was finally captured and executed.

During the reign of William and of his two immediate predecessors, as has been already stated, a new element was introduced into the population of the country by reason of the large emigration of Norman noblemen, who were invited into Scotland by those kings, established at their courts, and given liberal grants of territory and titles.[7]

There has been considerable controversy over the question of the settlement of the Anglo-Normans in Scotland, some writers going so far as to claim that in a large measure they displaced the original inhabitants of the Lowlands. Others contend that their immigration was numerically so insignificant that it had practically no part in the composition of the Scottish nation. Or, granting that numbers of them came into Scotland in the beginning, the frequent revolts on the part of the natives against the rule of the foreigners, and the consequent expulsion of many of them, are instanced as grounds for the belief that the Normans did not become incorporated into the population.

By far the best statement of the case that has come under the observation of the writer is that contained in Mr. E. William Robertson's essay on the subject of Displacement, published in the appendix to his *Scotland under Her Early Kings.* As his treatment of the case is so admirable and his conclusions so reasonable and just, their claims to our consideration are of primary importance. Mr. Robertson writes as follows :

Different opinions are current in different ages, and there was a time when it would have been considered a heresy to trace a great Scottish name to any but a strictly Scottish source, the Norman *Flahald* being accordingly renamed *Fleance,* and assigned as an heir to Banquo, figuring as Thane of Lochaber. Since that time the tide has flowed in the opposite direction, and it has been argued as if every Scottish name of note were to be traced to a foreign settler ; whilst it appears to have been the singular destiny of that part of Scotland answering to ancient *Scotia,* that the real ancestry of the bulk of its population should be invariably ignored. Here were the *Gwyddel Ffichti,* pre-eminently the Gaelic *Picts,* and the leading division of the Pictish people, whose descendants, devoting their ancestry to extermination, resolutely declared themselves Gaelic *Scots.* Time passed away, and after the Lowland Scottish dialect penetrated over all this portion of northern Scotland, its inhabitants, forgetting the language of their forefathers, called all who spoke it *Erse* or Irish ; the mountaineers were looked upon as an Irish race, and at length the very citadel and stronghold of Alban's Gaelic kings was supposed to have been peopled by a race akin to the population of the Lothians—though totally unknown to Beda. Keating's convenient theory of a pestilence that swept away every plebeian of *Milesian* origin, thus leaving Ireland to the nobility alone, will now probably only provoke a smile ; they were an inconvenient race for genealogists, these plebeians, and were thus summarily dealt with. But the theory is scarcely less extravagant which supposes ancient *Scotia* to have been filled with a population unknown to history—for when did they arrive ? Untraceable in topography—for where are their vestiges ? and who, if they ever really existed in this quarter, must have exhibited the unwonted spectacle of a dominant people, strong enough to hold their ground throughout the leading provinces of the kingdom, yet submitting to the rule of a king and a nobility sprung from the very race which they are supposed to have driven from the soil ? Where was the strength of the ancient Gaelic kingdom of Scotland if it were not in this very quarter ?

Extermination seldom, if ever, follows upon a conquest. Roving and savage tribes, deprived of their hunting grounds by the encroachments of far more highly civilized races, may gradually disappear, dying out like the aborigines upon the continent of America : but when a settled population is conquered, the proprietary either emigrate, disappear, or sink into a subordinate situation, whilst the bulk of the people remain under the invaders in a position comparatively slightly altered. It is only, however, after a conquest of a certain character that any change of this description occurs at all ; for where a settled proprietary is not thus displaced, it may become absorbed amongst another race, and all difference of origin be thus forgotten ; but it will certainly not die out and perish of itself, nor will Scotland afford any instance to the contrary. No conquest of any description, that could account for a wide displacement of the native population in favor of foreign settlers is traceable at any period of authentic history when such a settlement is supposed to have taken place. The northern wars of Malcolm Canmore represent a struggle between *Scotia* and her southern dependencies against *Moravia* — between the population of the South and East against the people of the North and West : but of the foreign bands, who are sometimes supposed

to have secured the victory for Malcolm, where is there a trace in history?
Where are the lands with which they are rewarded, and by what tenure did
they hold them? Moray, the great hereditary province of the rival family,
was not forfeited before the reign of David; and it was scarcely out of the
property of his own adherents that Malcolm distributed his rewards. Mar,
Buchan, Angus, Strathern, and Menteith, with the great lay Abbacy of
Brechin, are found long after this period in the hands of native magnates;
whilst Athol and Fife were conferred, not upon the supporters of a policy
hostile to the native race, but upon branches of the reigning family, or upon
a family devoted to its support. Malcolm may have availed himself of
foreign assistance, and there was undoubtedly an immigration in his days
into his kingdom; but to judge from the example of Cospatric, the majority
of his new subjects were planted upon the southern frontiers, amidst a
population of kindred origin and customs, where the same hostility to the
Norman rule which prompted their emigration, would secure their fidelity
as watchful guardians of the English marches. Twice subsequently were
"foreigners" expelled,— from northern Scotland, probably; not a numerous population, who would unquestionably have defended their rights,—and a
sanguinary struggle would have arisen from such a measure,—but the Court
and personal friends of Margaret, and the immediate followers of Duncan
II. — just as "the Normans" were driven, some thirty years before, from
the kingdom of the Confessor. Edgar was reinstated by his kinsman the
Ætheling, but it will scarcely be asserted that the army provided by Rufus
was settled permanently upon the soil of Scotland; and nothing more is
known of his uneventful career. Alexander resented a conspiracy against
his own person by a *Northern* war; the Spey, the frontier river between
Scotia and *Moravia*, was again the scene of the contest, and the king drove
his enemies "over the Stockford into *Ross*." There is an indistinct vision
of the forfeiture of one great magnate on this occasion, Malpeder MacLoen,
styled "Mormaor of the Merns," and henceforth there is not a trace of
treasonable disaffection or forfeiture on a great scale throughout the whole
extent of *Scotia*. The Earl of Strathern, indeed, participated in the mysterious conspiracy of Perth, but he was not forfeited, as the *Moravian* Earl
of Ross appears to have been — probably because his share in the attempt
may have been limited to changing the counsellors of the sovereign — and
Galloway was the seat of the war which followed upon the defeat of the
attempt.

No better test can be applied in a question of this description than
the composition of the *juries* which pronounced "the verdict of the neighborhood," and were always made up of the *probi homines*, the gentry and proprietary of the district. The earl's son, the thane's son, the abbot and his
son, the judge or his brother, and other similar notabilities of native origin
appear in Angus, and generally along the eastern coast and in *Scotia ;* whilst
in Renfrew, when Patrick de Blantyre was served heir to his ancestral
barony, the jury to a man were of Gaelic origin, and must have been "his
peers," barons, or freeholders by charter. Renfrew had been given as a
barony to the Steward, but the *probi homines* seem to have been little affected
by the grant. The instances thus quoted are all taken from the age succeeding the reigns of David and William, affording ample testimony that the
native proprietary in the settled districts of Scotland had been little interfered with by the measures of those sovereigns. The case was different in
eastern Ross and Moray, where the disaffected had been rooted out, their
lands forfeited, and settlers planted widely in their place. Here the juries

were of a mixed character, Norman and other names mingling with, and generally, indeed, predominating amongst, those that testify to a native extraction. But the confiscations in *Moravia* were local and partial, and can scarcely be supposed to have affected the loyal proprietary upon the eastern coast, and in other parts of *Scotia*. The destructive northern wars of the Conqueror have stamped their results in letters of blood upon the Yorkshire survey in Domesday, but what effect did they produce upon the allodial Gavellers of Kent, or even upon the neighboring Ridings of Lincolnshire?

It was the charter and feudal tenure which gradually converted the native proprietary of *Scotia* into "lairds of that ilk," henceforth undistinguishable amongst the general feudal baronage. At the battle of the Standard, Earl Malise of Strathern was the champion of the anti-feudal combatants. Forty years later his grandson, Gilbert, was as thoroughly a feudal baron as the latest Norman settler, granting charters sealed with the device of a mounted knight in armor, and with a novelty yet more unusual, a shield emblazoned with arms. It is scarcely possible to doubt that a similar change was in progress in many other parts of the kingdom besides Strathern. Not only in Scotland, but throughout Europe the shifting patronymic marks the prevalence of the early benefice, when all who claimed a provision in right of their birth and descent were known by the name of their immediate ancestors, the *vier anen* giving the title to the birthright which was subsequently founded on the charter. It was not until the benefice became the feud, after the temporary and renewable provision became the inalienable and hereditary property, that it conferred a more or less permanent name upon its owner, all early surnames being invariably "of that ilk" — the proprietor being named from his property. At the opening of the twelfth century, or at any rate at the close of the eleventh, the territorial surname was unknown throughout Scotland from the Pentland Firth to the Tweed ; and the same might also be said of England. Very few names, indeed, of this description were brought into England by the followers of the Conqueror,—none certainly existed before their arrival,—and wherever a Norman name is found that does not occur in Domesday, it may be safely assumed that, however old its standing, it represents a later emigrant from the Continental duchy rather than one of the combatants at Hastings. The descendants of the latter generally adopted the names of those properties in England which they had won with the sword. Many a Norman name penetrated into Scotland, the majority territorial, whether derived from English or Norman fiefs, which would seem to place their arrival in the reigns of David and William. Others again settled in Scotland before they had acquired a name of this description, the race of *Flahald* assuming a name from their hereditary office of steward — for the son of Walter Fitz Alan was known as Alan Fitz Walter — whilst the appellation of *Masculus, la Mâle,* attached to a family of great importance in early times, seems to have been perpetuated with the old broad pronunciation under the form of *Maule.* The race often gave the name ; *Fleming* and *Inglis* would have appeared in the charters as *Flandrensis* and *Anglicus ;* the first ancestor of the great border clan of *Scot* must have stood out amongst the Saxons of the Lothians as *Scotus,* the Gael ; whilst the name of *Walensis,* or *le Waleys,* given to the progenitors of Wallace, marks the forefathers of the great Scottish champion to have been Cumbro-Britons of Strathclyde. From the frequent occurrence of an addition, such as Flandrensis, to the name of the first recipient of a charter, it may be assumed, that in its absence, and where no district

territorial surname is attached, the recipient was usually of native extraction, especially if in a well-affected district — the first holder by charter,
but not necessarily the first of the race in Scotland.

It is sometimes, indeed, rather hastily assumed that every territorial
surname denotes the presence of a foreign settler, when in reality it is only
the mark of tenure by charter.   There can, of course, be no doubt about
names brought from another land, whilst in the case of many a surname
derived from places in Scotland, it would be not a little difficult to pronounce
with any certainty an absolute opinion.   There are sufficient instances, however, to show the rashness of any sweeping conclusion such as that to which
allusion has been made.   The family of *de Strathbogie* sprung from a son of
the Earl of Fife ; that of *de Ogilvie* from a junior branch of the earls of
Angus, whose representative at present in the male line is the Earl of Airlie.
Roland de Carrick received a grant of the Seneschalship and Kenkynol of
that district from Earl Nigel when the earldom passed with his daughter to
another race, and the name of *de Carrick* appears amongst the settlers
planted in Moray.   Roland was scarcely of foreign origin, but rather a near
relative of the Earl, and probably the heir male of the family.   The *de
Abernethies* and the earlier *de Brechins* were lay Abbots of their respective
districts.   Were Abbacies conferred in this manner upon the Norman followers of David and William ?   Names like *de Ergaedia, de Insulis, de Atholia,
de Galloway*, speak for themselves.   In many others, again, there is a strong
presumption of native origin, as, for instance, in *de Scone*, a name often
occurring in the earlier charters.   Malothen appears in the reign of Alexander I. as the first known *Vice-Comes* of Scone, and the family of *de Scone*
were probably descendants of the hereditary Sheriff.   The first known
ancestor of the Durwards was Malcolm de Lundin, whose son Thomas, the
first Durward, confirmed the grant of his mother and grandfather—the
father's name is not mentioned—to the Culdees of Moneymusk.   The name
of Malcolm, and the connection with the Culdees, point apparently to a
native origin ; whilst the office of Durward, which raised the family to
distinction, was acquired, probably, by the union of Malcolm with Thomas's
mother.*

There are many other territorial surnames which there seem the strongest
reasons for assigning to native Scots.   *Dufyth* de Conan, for instance,
Duncan de Fernival, *Macbeth* de Dych, *Angus* de Auchenross, amongst the
probi homines already quoted ; *Macbeth* de Libberton, *Gilbert* de Cles,
Gilbert de Smitheston, *Constantine* de Lochore, all of which I have taken
at random from a page in the Dunfermlyn Registry.   The bulk of the *Mesne*-
tenants were probably the original proprietary, whether to the north or south
of the Forth ; whilst great Norman barons, personal friends of David and
his successors, received large grants, and were placed upon a footing with
the earls as *majores barones*.

It will scarcely be disputed that in later times the Scottish *laird* was
often better known by the name of his property than by his own surname,
and nowhere was this custom more prevalent than in the Highlands
after the earlier patronymic had been superseded.   Centuries before the
patronymic had thus disappeared from *Moravia* it had been displaced
throughout the feudalized portion of ancient *Scotia;* but as the change
occurred before the rise of surnames, the fief supplied the family name, and
after the lapse of a few generations all recollection of kindred origin was
obliterated, or survived only in vague local tradition.   *Stewart* of Appin and

*Reg. Prior. St. And., p. 369.

Stewart of Garth must once have had a common ancestor, but had they received their fiefs before the establishment of surnames, who would have known, after the lapse of a few generations, that the *de Garth* of Perthshire was akin to *de Appin* of Argyle? Three great families in succession held the lordship of Lorne, and all Argyleshire is still full of MacDougals, Stewarts, and Campbells, offshoots of the families in question. The same may be said of Athol, in which the Robertsons, the Stewarts, and the Murrays, names long prevalent in the district, represent the families which once held the earldom, one of them still holding the dukedom. Many a Sutherland has branched off similarly in the North, and the western coasts are peopled with the descendants of different Lords of the Isles. The greater the name in Scotland the more numerous it is, and more widely spread, and it can be hardly doubted that a similar process must at one time have been going on all over feudalized *Scotia*, before the establishment of separate surnames; for it would be strange indeed if no offshoots branched off from families which sometimes held their earldoms for centuries. A faint clue exists in Fife through the old privileges of the "clan MacDuff," which were certainly claimed by the families of *de Spens* and *de Arbuthnot*, whilst the Seneschalship was held by *de Blair* and *de Balfour*. The latter office seems to have been invariably conferred upon a near kinsman, though in either case it may, of course, have been acquired by marriage. Little more can be said on the subject, but had the surname existed in Scotland distinct and separate from the territorial appellation two or three centuries before it actually arose, many of the old Fifeshire families would, I should imagine, have had little difficulty in tracing their descent from the Premier Earls of Scotland.

The whole policy of David and his successors appears to have been founded on a principle diametrically opposed to this "theory of displacement." It was his object to introduce but not to enforce feudal tenure; to tolerate rather than perpetuate Scottish service. He never made his Norman nobles earls, but barons, "with the rights and custom of an earl;" and there must surely have been a reason for adopting such a course—for giving "brevet rank," if I may so express myself, to his foreign nobles, instead of making them earls at once. This reason will probably be found in the characteristics of the different tenures. When Alexander II. levied fines for non-attendance in the host, those fines were only exacted from tenants by Scottish service, earls, Thanes, and Ogtierns, for the baron is not alluded to. The earl was answerable to the king alone; the Thane to the king or earl; the Ogtiern to the Thane or *Miles*. Hence it may be gathered that the introduction of the feudal tenure of knight-service would at that time have reduced the Thanes to the footing of Ogtierns. An alien earl, holding by feudal tenure, would have had to conquer his earldom from the proprietary.

No such result followed from the earlier tenure of the earl, count, or mormaor, who was simply a royal deputy interposed between the proprietary and the sovereign, and not interfering in any way with existing tenures. He was necessarily, however, a man of influence enough to enable him to carry out effectually the authority thus delegated to him; and such influence could only have been acquired in one of two ways. A newly created earl must either have been a member of some native race to which the native proprietary were accustomed, or willing, to look for their *Cen-cinnœth* — he must have been in some way united to them by the tie of blood: or, if an alien, he must have been supported by an alien force—a *feudal* force, after the reign of David—and the result would have been a rising amongst the proprietary. Such was probably the true reason why Bruce, Fitz-Alan, De Moreville, and other great Norman nobles never appear as earls, but only with "the rights and custom of an earl." Holding by Scottish service they would have been powerless without a kindred "following": whilst a feudal tenure would have interfered with the proprietary rights of the very class which formed the military strength of the earldom. History clearly shows that, as the power of the sovereign extended over the west, it was his policy, not to eradicate the old ruling families, but to retain them in their native provinces, rendering them more or less responsible for all that portion of their respective districts which was not placed under the immediate authority of the royal sheriffs or baillies. In Galloway, Argyle, and Ross, the old races were thus confirmed in authority, and the result was comparative peace. In Moray the old race was proscribed; feudal tenure was purposely introduced, wherever it was possible; and the result was *rebellion for a century*. Elsewhere a similar policy would have unquestionably produced corresponding results. Confiscation would have been followed by rebellion, and the policy which spared the native races in the once disaffected districts of Galloway, Argyle, and Ross would have scarcely risked such an alternative amongst the loyal proprietary of *Scotia*. Intermarriage gradually familiarized the Scots with the feudal barons holding earldoms, and knights holding thanedoms; but I think it very doubtful if either earldom or thanedom were originally conferred upon baron or knight; or if any earldom was held by feudal tenure until Bruce gave Moray to Randolf, to be held by *both* knight service and Scottish service.

The theory of displacement, however, is not confined to Scotland beyond the Forth, and it is equally assumed that the Lothians were thoroughly resettled and colonized by a tide of immigrants from beyond the southern frontier. Orm, Leving, Doding, Edulf, Edmund, and Elfin — though the latter name, like that of Dunwallon "the faithful thegn," who figures in so many of the Kentish charters, has rather a British sound—are all brought from the south to fix their abode at, and stamp their names upon, Ormiston, Levingston, Duddingston, Edilston, Edmonston, and Elphinston. Thor, the ancestor of the Ruthvens, Warnebald of the Cunninghams, Maccus or Magnus of the Maxwells, are equally traced to a foreign stock. But where, may it be asked, were the descendants of the men who had held the land as their own from the days when Edwin built his *Burh* upon the Forth, full five hundred years before? The topography, charters, etc., according to Mr. Innes, "leave no doubt that a Teutonic dialect was the universal spoken language of Lothian, Merse, and Teviotdale, from the time of David I." I should be inclined to extend this remark considerably farther back—at least five centuries, probably six. When Abercorn, Cunningham, and the diocese of Whithern were in the possession of the Angles at the time of Beda, and when they added Kyle to their dominions soon after his death, their language must have been spoken over a far wider extent of country. The diocese of Whithern fell into other hands at the opening of the ninth century; Strath Clyde was gradually absorbed amongst the dominions of the Scottish kings; and the Anglian population either receded or remained in a subordinate position attached to the soil. Nothing of this sort, however, happened in the eastern districts of southern Scotland, and I should imagine that the dialect of the Bernician Angles, which subsequently became the basis of Lowland Scotch, continued to be spoken uninterruptedly in this quarter from the close of the sixth, or the opening of the seventh century. The charters show that, in this quarter, the agricultural population attached to the soil bore Teutonic names ; whilst toward the west and beyond the Forth they were generally Celtic. This is always a sign of lengthened occupation. Beyond the river the Highlands form a convenient receptacle into which all the dispossessed proprietary of native Gaelic origin are supposed to have been "pushed" — such is the word sometimes used. It is not specified, however, where the native proprietary of Teutonic origin were "pushed" out of the Lothians, perhaps because it might be inconvenient to find a place for them. When David laid down the enactment that if a man were *disseized*, or dispossessed of his property, he was no longer to challenge the aggressor, but to appeal to the verdict of the neighborhood, it may be gathered that there were rights of property before his reign ; and that the loss of such rights in individual cases was resented by an appeal to the sword. Yet are we called upon to believe that, whilst such was the legal custom in individual cases, a general measure of *disseisin* was gradually carried out amongst a population never backward, but rather overready, in making such an appeal, and over the whole face of Scotia and the Lothians —over the whole of the well-affected portion of the kingdom ! a measure so vast that not a name of any note has come down to the present day that can be traced to the old Bernician Angles, whilst the shattered remnants of the Gaelic proprietary sheltered themselves amidst the Highlands and in Galloway ! The whole theory is mythical. Such a measure would have raised all Scotia to the Forth, all Lothian to the Tweed, in one general blaze of insurrection. The earls were never "pushed out," and if the remaining proprietary were dispossessed, where would have been the use of legislating for thanes and ogtierns in the reign of Alexander II.? What fees could the Earls of Fife have shared with the king, if there had been no proprietary in the earldom holding by the ancient tenure ? If they had not been dispossessed in the thirteenth century, when did the displacement begin ? The demesne lands of the crown were wide enough to admit of many an acre being granted away without dispossessing a single well-affected subject either in *Scotia* or the Lothians. Wide baronies were made over to the great Norman feudatories, in which, as in Renfrew, the *probi homines* remained undisturbed ; and the true result of the measures of David and his successors was to feudalize the settled portion of the kingdom, not to convert it into a desert by the extermination or displacement of the original proprietary.

NOTES TO CHAPTER XXI

[1] "1174. Immediately after the close of Easter, the King of Scotland marched his army into Northumberland, and there, by his Scots and Galwegians, acted execrably. For they divided pregnant women, and threw the extracted fœtuses upon the points of their lances. They slew boys, young and old, and infants of each sex, from the greatest to the least, without any ransom or mercy. They also mangled the priests and clerks, in the very churches, upon the altars. Whatever things, therefore, the Scots and Galwegians reached, all were full of horror and cruelty. In the meantime the king of Scotland with his army besieged Carlisle. . . . And thence departing, besieged the castle of Prudehou, of Ordenel de Dunfranville ; but was not able to take it : For the army of Yorkshire made ready to come upon him. Now the leaders of this army were Robert de Stuteville, and William his son, and William de Vesci, and Randal de Glanvilla, and Randal de Thilli ; and Bernard de Balliol, and Odenel de Dunfranville. When this was announced to the king of Scotland, he left the castle, which he had besieged, and flying thence came to Alnwick, and besieged it, and sent thence the Earl Duncan, and the Earl of Angus, and Richard de Morville, with

almost all his army through the circumjacent provinces to waste them ; and the king of Scotland remained there with his private attendants.   The Earl Duncan straightway divided his army again into three parts: One he retained with him, and the remaining two he sent to burn the circumjacent towns, and to kill the men from the greatest to the least, and to bring off booty.   And he with the part of the army which he had chosen for himself, entered the town of Warkworth, and burned it, and killed therein all whom he found, men and women, great and small: and made his guards break open the church of St. Leonard, which was there, and kill therein, and in the house of the clerk of that town, more than 100 men, besides women and children, alas for pity ! . . .   But almighty God on the same day avenged the injury and violence offered to the church of his martyr ; for the aforesaid leaders of the army of Yorkshire, when they had heard that the king of Scotland had retired from Prudehou, and besieged Alnwick, and so had sent his army from him, followed him with haste ; and unawares found him before Alnwick playing with his soldiers, as if secure and fearing nothing.   For he himself, when he had seen them coming from afar, thought them to be the Earl Duncan and those who were with him.   But when they had approached him, they rushed upon him, and straightway took him ; and his soldiers, leaving him, fled."—*Gesta Henrici Secundi.*

2 " The history of the contests in the outlying districts has shown the difficulties which the authority of the King of Scots had in extending to certain territories in the north and the west, which, in the end, came under his rule, We have seen how the term Scots was first applicable only to natives of Ireland ; how it crossed the Channel, and included the descendants of those Irish who had settled in Argyle ; and how, at last, the monarch ruling from the Tweed and the Solway northward was named the ' King of the Scots.' Still that was a colloquial expression, such as we use when we designate the United Kingdom of Great Britain and Ireland by the word Britain, or England.   The King of the Scots, when he issued his charters as a notification to all classes among whom he held rule, called them Francs and Angles, Scots and Galwegians. The Francs were the Norman settlers, and had become so numerous as to be a great element in the population. The Angles were the refugee families who had fled from Norman tyranny in England, and perhaps the whole population of the Lothians was so called.   The term Scotia or Scotland at this time (1150) meant the country north of the Forth.   This river, with its Firth, was called ' the Scots Water,' and Lothian and Galloway were as yet countries only united with Scotland under the same crown.   Thus, among the earliest of the public laws—those attributed to William the Lion—there is a regulation by which an inhabitant of Scotland, making a seizure or distraint beyond—that is, south of—the Forth, must bring it under the notice of the sheriff of Stirling—spoken of sometimes as a town on the border of Scotland—and convey it to Haddington, where it may be redeemed."—Burton, *History of Scotland*, vol. ii., p. 50.

" The house of Bruce was a fine type of those Norman races in whose hands were the destinies of so many European communities. Why they should have been so loved and courted, is one of the mysteries in the histories of social influences. What they were at the Court of Edward the Confessor, they became in the courts of the Scots kings from David downwards.

" Sir Thomas Gray, in his Chronicle written early in the fourteenth century, tells how William the Lion brought with him, when returning to Scotland from his captivity, younger sons of the families to whom he was indebted for courtesies, and how he endowed them with lands. We cannot take the passage as precise statistics. We may get more from it by counting it as the shape into which the chronicler put the traditions of the migration of the great Norman houses to Scotland.   In this view the list of names is instructive : ' Il enprist od ly en Escoce plusours dez fitzpusnes dez seygnours Dengleterre qi ly estoient beinuoillauntz, et lour dona lez terres des autres qy ly estoient rebelis. Si estoint dez Baillolfs, de Bruys, de Soulis, et de Moubray, et les Saynclers ; lez Hayes, les Giffardis, les Ramesays, et Laundels : les Biseys, les Berkleys, les Walenges, lez Boysis, lez Mountgom-

eris, lez Vaus, lez Colevyles, lez Frysers, lez Grames, lez Gourlays, et plusours autres?"—
Burton, *History of Scotland*, vol. ii., p. 14.

The same passage is noted by Lord Hailes : " There is a passage in *Scalæ Chronica*, preserved by Leland (*Collectanea*, t. i., p. 533), which deserves to be remembered, though its truth may be questioned. ' The nobilles of Scotland cam no nearer than Pembles (r. Peebles) yn Scotland to mete with theyr King. Wherefore he toke with hym many of the younger sunnes of the nobyl men of England that bare hym good wylle, and gave them landes in Scotland of them that were rebelles to hym. These were the names of the gentilmen that he toke with hym : Bailliol, Breuse, Soully, Moubray, Sainctclere, Hay, Giffard, Ramesey, Laundel, Bysey, Berkley, Walenge, Boys, Montgomery, Vaulx, Coleville, Fresir, Grame, Gurlay, and dyverse other."—*Annals of Scotland*, vol. i., p. 131.

[3] " There were in this army two brothers, Gilbert, that is, and Uchtred, lords of the province of Galloway, with a numerous body of their proper nation. These were the sons of Fergus, formerly prince of the same province, and had succeeded to their father, yielding to the fates, the king of Scotland, who is the chief lord of that land, dividing between them the inheritance. But Gilbert, the elder by birth, being displeased that he was defrauded of the entirety of his paternal right, had always hated his brother in his heart, while, however, the fear of the king restrained the violence of his conceived fury.

" Uchtred, the son of Fergus, and Gilbert, his brother, when they heard that their lord the king of Scotland was taken [at Alnwick], straightway returned, with their Galwegians, into their country, and forthwith expelled from Galloway all the bailiffs and wardens which the king of Scotland had put over them, and killed all the English and French whom they were able to apprehend ; and took and destroyed all the fortresses and castles which the King of Scotland erected in their land, and killed all those whom they had taken within them.

" Uchtred and Gilbert, the sons of Fergus, contending that each of them should be lord and have dominion over the Galweigans, had great hatred between themselves ; so that each of them lay in wait to kill the other : And in process of time, Gilbert, the son of Fergus, assembled his men, and went to council with them, that Uchtred his brother should be taken and killed ; and at the time fixed they came together, that they might take and kill him : and Malcolm, the son of Gilbert, the son of Fergus, came and besieged the island, in which Uchtred the brother of his father, and the cousin of Henry King of England the son of Maud the Empress, dwelled, and took him, and sending his executioners, commanded that they should pluck out his eyes, and cut off his testicles and his tongue ; and it was so done : and leaving him half alive, departed : and he, a little after, ended his life. While these things were done, the lord the king sent into England one of his chaplains, named Roger de Hoveden, to Robert de Vaux, that they two should agree with Uchtred and Gilbert, and entice them into his service. When they had come about the feast of St. Clement to a conference between them and Gilbert the son of Fergus, the same Gilbert and the other Galwegians offered them, for the use of the king, 2000 marks of silver, and 500 hogs, rent by the year, upon this condition, that the king should receive them in his hand, and take them from the servitude of the king of Scotland. But the aforesaid messengers of the king of England would not make this end with the Galwegians, until they had spoken with the king : and when it was shown to the king, how Uchtred, the son of Fergus, his cousin, was killed, he would not make any peace with those Galwegians."—*Gesta Henrici Secundi*.

[4] " 1175. The lord the King [Henry II.] gave and granted to the king of Scotland license to march an army into Galloway, to subdue Gilbert, son of Fergus, for this reason, that he revolted from his fealty and maliciously killed his brother Uchtred.

" The King [Henry] about the feast of St. Dennis came as far as Feckham : and there came to him William king of Scotland ; and brought with him Gilbert the son of Fergus, who had killed his brother Uchtred. And this Gilbert, having made peace with the lord the king concerning the death of his brother, who was the king's cousin, became his man and swore fealty to him against all men ; and for having his good will, gave him a thousand marks of silver (and Duncan his son as a hostage for keeping the peace); And so, his peace being made, he came home, and commanded that all foreigners, who held any tenement in Galloway by the king of Scotland should be banished : and he who would not submit to this proclamation, should suffer capital punishment."—*Gesta Henrici Secundi.*

ˢ "1185. On the day of the circumcision, died Gilbert, the son of Fergus, prince of the Galwegians, enemy of the king of Scotland, his lord ; whose son and heir, Duncan, the lord the king of England held in the custody of Hugh de Morwic, upon the engagements contracted between them, for keeping the peace." . . .

" Roland, the son of Uchtred, the son of Fergus, immediately after the death of Gilbert, his father's brother, having collected to his assistance a copious multitude of horse and foot, invaded the land of the aforesaid Gilbert ; and killing all that willed to resist him, subjugated that whole land to himself ; he likewise killed all the more powerful and rich inhabitants of all Galloway ; and occupied their lands ; and made therein a great many castles and fortresses, in order to strengthen his government."—*Ibid.*

Roland had a battle against Gillecolm, in which the brother of Roland fell, and Gillecolm perished.—Chronicle of Melrose.

" 1186. William, king of Scotland, and David, his brother, at the command of the King [Henry] came to his court, bringing with them Josceline, bishop of Glasgow, and Arnold, abbot of Melros, and earls and barons from the kingdom of Scotland ; whom the lord the king honourably received : and after a few days, having taken from the above said earls and barons of Scotland security for keeping faith to him, and taken hostages from them, he sent them into their own country, and commanded them, that they should subdue Roland the son of Uchtred ; unless he would come to his court, and stand to right upon this, that against the prohibition of himself and his judges he had entered the land of Gilbert the son of Fergus, and other barons of Galloway, with a hostile hand, and had occupied or obtained it subject to himself. When the aforesaid Roland had heard these things, collecting a large multitude of horsemen and footmen, he rendered unpassable, as much as he could, the entrances of Galloway, and the ways thereof, cut and half-cut trees being placed across the ways. Without delay, Henry king of England assembled a great army from all the provinces of England ; and coming as far as Carlisle, sent thence William king of Scotland and David, his brother, that they might bring Roland to him. But when he would not come, he sent again for him the same messengers, and with them Hugh bishop of Durham, and Randal de Glanville the justiciary : who, giving hostages to the aforesaid Roland, and making him security for safe conduct in going and returning, brought him to the king unto Carlisle : which Roland made peace with the lord the king, in this manner, to-wit, That the land which was of Uchtred the son of Fergus his father, should remain to him in quiet, as he had the same on the day in which he was alive and dead. And concerning the land, which was of Gilbert the son of Fergus his uncle ; which Duncan the son of the aforesaid Gilbert claimed against him, he should stand to right in the court of the lord the king of England at his summons. And for keeping these conditions Roland swore, and gave his three sons hostages. He also swore fealty to the king of England and his heirs, by the command of the king of Scotland, against all men. William, king of Scotland, and David, his brother, and all the earls and barons of Scotland likewise swore, that if Roland should go back from the aforesaid convention and from the king of England, they themselves with the king of England would faithfully hold to confound the same Roland, until he should thereof satisfy the lord the king of England. Josceline, also, bishop of Glasgow, promised on the word of truth before all and on the relicks of the saints, that unless Roland kept the aforesaid convention unshaken, he himself against him and his land would publish the sentence of excommunication."—*Gesta Henrici Secundi.*

" In the moneth of August, at Cairluel, Rouland Talvaten, lord of Galway, did homage and fealtie to king Henry, withe al that held of hym."—Leland's *Collectanea,* ii., 5.

[6] " 1200. In the month of December, Roland, prince of Galloway, died in England at Northampton, the 14th of the kalends of January, on Tuesday, and was there buried at the abbey of St. Andrew.

" In the same year Duncan, son of Gilbert, son of Fergus, ravished Aveline, daughter of Alan, son of Walter, lord of Renfrew, before William king of Scotland returned out of England : Whence the same king, greatly enraged, took from Alan the son of Walter 24 pledges for keeping the peace to him and his land, and doing right upon that calumny."—Roger de Hoveden.

[7] " The extent to which the feudal and Norman element had already been introduced into the south of Scotland, while under the rule of earls, by David, will be apparent when we examine the relation between the Norman barons who witness his charters and the land under his sway. The most prominent of those who witness the foundation charter of Selkirk are four Norman barons, who possessed extensive lordships in the north of England. The first was Hugo de Moreville, and we find him in possession of extensive lands in Lauderdale, Lothian, and Cuningham in Ayrshire. The second was Paganus de Braosa. The third Robertus de Brus, who acquired the extensive district of Annandale in Dumfriesshire ; and the fourth Robertus de Umfraville, received grants of Kinnaird and Dunipace in Stirlingshire. Of the other Norman Knights who witness this charter, and also the inquisition, Gavinus Ridel, Berengarius Engaine, Robertus Corbet, and Alanus de Perci possess manors in Teviotdale. Walterus de Lindesaya has extensive possessions in Upper Clydesdale, Mid and East Lothian and in the latter districts Robertus de Burneville is also settled. In Scotland proper the character in which David ruled will be best seen by contrasting his charters with those of his predecessors. Eadgar, who possessed the whole kingdom north of the Tweed and the Solway, addresses his charters to all his faithful men in his kingdom, Scots and Angles. Alexander, who possessed the kingdom north of the Firths of Forth and Clyde alone, to the bishops and earls, and all his faithful men of the kingdom of Scotia. A charter granted by David, in the third year of his accession to the throne, to the monks of Durham, of lands in Lothian, is addressed to all dwelling throughout his kingdom in Scotland and Lothian, Scots and Angles ; but when we enter Scotland proper, and compare his foundation charter of Dunfermline with that of Scone by his predecessor Alexander I., there is a marked contrast between them. Alexander grants his charter to Scone, with the formal assent and concurrence of the seven earls of Scotland ; and it is confirmed by the two bishops of the only dioceses which then existed in Scotland proper, with exception of St. Andrews, which was vacant, and the witnesses are the few Saxons who formed his personal attendants, Edward the constable, Alfric the pincerna, and others. King David's charter to Dunfermline, a foundation also within Scotland proper, is granted ' by his royal authority and power, with the assent of his son Henry, and with the formal confirmation of his queen Matilda, and the bishops, earls, and barons of his kingdom, the clergy and people acquiescing.' Here we see the feudal baronage of the kingdom occupying the place of the old constitutional body of the seven earls, while the latter appear only as individually witnessing the charter. David's subsequent charters to Dunfermline show this still more clearly, for they are addressed to the ' bishops, abbots, earls, sheriffs, barons, governors, and officers, and all the good men of the whole land, Norman, English, and Scotch ' ; in short, the feudal community or ' communitas regni,' consisting of those holding lands of the crown, while the old traditional earls of the Celtic kingdom appear among the witnessess only."— *Celtic Scotland*, vol. i., 458–459.

CHAPTER XXII

THE SECOND AND THIRD ALEXANDERS TO JOHN BALIOL

WILLIAM the Lion died in 1214, and was succeeded by his son, Alexander II. As was not unusual in those times, the beginning of his reign was marked by conflicts with England, and efforts at revolt in various parts of his own kingdom. In 1215, Donald MacWilliam, with some Irish allies, invaded Moray, but was driven out. The following year, Alexander sided with the English barons against King John in the hope of recovering his family's title to Northumberland. The English king, by way of reprisal, wasted Yorkshire and Northumberland, stormed and burned Berwick, and, entering Scotland, burned the priory of Coldingham, and the towns of Dunbar and Haddington.

Alexander retaliated by laying waste the western borders with fire and sword. He burned the monastery of Holmcultram in Cumberland, took possession of Carlisle, and assaulted Bernard Castle. King John's death occurring shortly afterwards, the war was soon brought to a close ; and Carlisle was surrendered back to the English.

In 1219, David, Earl of Huntingdon, died, leaving a son John, (who afterwards became the Earl of Chester), and three daughters : Margaret, married to Alan of Galloway ; Isabella, married to Robert Bruce ; and Ada, married to Henry de Hastings. The union of Isabella with Robert Bruce, gave the family of the latter its title to the crown. In 1221, King Alexander married Princess Joan of England, sister of Henry III. The following year, an insurrection having occurred in Argyle, many of the native leaders were forced to leave that district, and their estates were distributed among the king's followers. In 1228, Gillescop rose in insurrection and ravaged portions of Moray and Inverness. He was slain in 1229. Shortly before that time the Isle of Man had become subject to Alan, Lord of Galloway.[1]

In 1233, John de Baliol, Lord of Bernard Castle, married Dervergoyll, daughter of Alan, Lord of Galloway, and of Margaret, cousin to King Alexander. Through this union arose the claim of the Baliols to the Scottish throne. The same year Alan of Galloway died, leaving three heiresses : Helen, wife of Roger de Quincy, Earl of Winchester ; Dervergoyll, wife of John Baliol ; and Christian, wife of William des Forts, son of the Earl of Albemarle. The Galwegians, unwilling to have their country parcelled out to the various Anglo-Norman barons who had married the heiresses, now besought the king to attach that district to the possessions of the Scottish Crown. Failing in this, they next requested that Thomas, the bastard son of Alan, who had married the daughter of the king of Man, be appointed as his father's successor. This also having been refused, the Galwegians broke out into rebellion and under the lead of the bastard Thomas and a Gaelic chief named Gilrodh, wasted Scotland with savage ferocity. Alexander brought an army against them and put them to flight ; but was afterwards prevailed upon to pardon the insurgents.[2]

Historians all concur in ascribing to the reign of this king a period of unexampled growth and prosperity for the material interests of the country, and even down to the seventeenth century Alexander II's reign was spoken of as the Golden Age of Scotland.[3]

In 1237, a treaty was made between Henry and Alexander by the terms of which the latter released his hereditary claim to the counties of Northumberland, Cumberland, and Westmoreland, and the English king settled on him lands in Northumberland and Cumberland of an annual value of two hundred pounds. Two years later, Alexander's wife having died, he married Mary, daughter of Ingelram de Couci. In 1241 a son was born to them, who was also named Alexander.

The next year was distinguished in Scotland by the revival of a feud that had some time previously existed between the houses of Bisset and Murray. Henry Murray, Earl of Athole, was murdered at Haddington. Suspicion having fallen on Walter Bisset, he was forced to flee the kingdom and his estates were confiscated. Making his way to the English court he sought retaliation ; and, by representing that Alexander was harboring Henry's enemies, so far succeeded in poisoning the mind of the latter against the Scottish king as to induce him to organize an expedition for the purpose of invading Scotland. To that end an army was accordingly assembled at Newcastle ; and Alexander is said by Matthew of Paris to have gathered together a force of nearly 100,000 men to oppose them ; although this is evidently an exaggeration.

No doubt the formidable array of Scottish warriors made it an easy matter for Henry's nobles, nearly all of whom were friendly to Alexander, to dissuade their king from pushing hostilities farther. Through the mediation of the English barons a peace was arranged at Newcastle, and the proposed invasion abandoned.

In 1249, while on an expedition to compel the submission of Angus, Lord of Argyle, who at that time was a liege of the king of Norway, Alexander died. He was succeeded by his eight-year-old son, who was crowned as Alexander III. In 1251, when the king was but ten years old, his marriage with Margaret, daughter of Henry III., took place at York. At this time Alexander did homage to Henry for his possessions in England ; and the English ruler thereupon took occasion to demand homage also for the kingdom of Scotland. To this request the young Alexander, prepared by his counsellors for such an emergency, replied that he had been invited to York to marry the Princess of England, and not to treat on affairs of state ; and that he could not take such a step as that now proposed by Henry

23

without the advice and counsel of his people. Accordingly, for the time being, the matter of homage for Scotland was dropped.

During Alexander III.'s minority the kingdom was governed by successive cliques of his nobles. According to Fordun, there were as many kings as counsellors, and the nation was universally oppressed. In the beginning of the reign, the Comyns were the most powerful family in Scotland. Two barons of their party, Robert de Ros and John de Baliol were regents, and there were more than thirty knights of the name of Comyn in the kingdom.

In 1255, the leaders of the opposition party, among whom were Patrick, Earl of March, Malise, Earl of Strathern, Nigel, Earl of Carrick, Robert de Brus, Alexander the Steward, and Alan Durward, having surprised Edinburgh Castle and seized the persons of the king and queen, constituted themselves wardens of the royal couple and regents of the kingdom. In this they had the active coöperation of Henry III. of England, who with an army marched toward the Scottish borders. An interview between the two kings was held at Roxburgh in September, 1255, when it was arranged that the following persons should act as regents of the kingdom during the Scottish king's minority: Richard Inverkeithen, Bishop of Dunkeld ; Peter de Ramsay, Bishop of Aberdeen ; Malcolm, Earl of Fife ; Patrick, Earl of Dunbar or March ; Malise, Earl of Strathern ; Nigel, Earl of Carrick ; Alexander the Steward of Scotland ; Robert de Brus ; Alan Durward ; Walter de Moray ; David de Lindesay ; William de Brechin ; Robert de Meyners ; Gilbert de Hay ; and Hugh Gifford.

At the same time Gamelin, Chancellor of Scotland and Bishop-elect of St. Andrews, William de Bondington, Bishop of Glasgow, Clement, Bishop of Dunblane, William Comyn, Earl of Mentieth, Alexander Comyn, Earl of Buchan, William de Mar, Earl of Mar, John de Baliol, Robert de Ros, John Comyn, William Wisheart, Archdeacon of St. Andrews, and others were removed from the king's council and deprived of their civil offices. Bishop Gamelin offered opposition to the proceedings of the new regents, and later was made the object of their attacks. He journeyed to Rome, in 1256, enlisted the Pope on the side of his party, and the following year had sentence of excommunication pronounced against his enemies. William Comyn, Earl of Mentieth, took this opportunity to organize a party of his friends, seized the king at Kinross, in his name deposed the recently appointed regents, and prepared to meet their forces on the field of battle.

Before coming to blows, a compromise was effected by which a new regency was established and both parties were given representation in its composition. It consisted of Mary, the Queen-dowager ; John de Brienne, her second husband ; Gamelin, Bishop of St. Andrews ; William, or Walter Comyn, Earl of Mentieth ; Alexander Comyn, Earl of Buchan ; William, Earl of Mar ; Alexander the Steward of Scotland ; Robert de Meyners ; Gilbert de Hay; and Alan Durward. As constituted, each party had nominally four representatives, and the Queen-dowager and her husband increased the number to ten. As these latter two were already firm partisans of the Comyn interest, it really left the control of the kingdom in the hands of that faction.

In 1260, the king and queen of the Scots visited London, and during the queen's stay there an heiress was born to them. This daughter was named Margaret. She was afterwards (in 1281) married to Eric, ruler of Norway.

In 1263, the Norwegian king, Haco, built and manned a large fleet at Bergen. Sailing westward to the Orkneys, he levied additional forces there and from his vassals in the Western Isles. Thence sailing south along the western coast of Scotland he entered the Firth of Clyde, and approached the coast of Ayrshire, having with him about 160 vessels. The Norwegians prepared to disembark at Largs in Cuningham, with the intention of invading Scotland. Here, a tempest having arisen and raged for some days, many of the ships were disabled or lost, and the army became disheartened; so that when they were attacked by the Scots of the surrounding country, their resistance was not sufficient to withstand the first onset. They were scattered and fled; such as could make good their retreat returned with Haco to the Orkneys, where that defeated and disappointed sea-king immediately afterwards sickened and died.

The defeat of Haco was followed, in 1264, by the subjection of Man and the Western Isles to Alexander. Two years later, in consideration of the payment of four thousand merks, Magnus, King of Norway, ceded to Scotland all his rights to these western possessions, only reserving to himself the Shetlands and the Orkneys.

Henry III., King of England, died in 1272, and was afterwards succeeded by his son Edward I. (that is, first of the Norman Edwards). About this time (1274) was born in Annandale a son and heir to Robert Brus II. The latter had married Martha, Countess of Carrick, a daughter of Adam, Earl of Carrick. The father was a son of that older Robert Brus who had married Isabella, daughter of David, Earl of Huntingdon, and niece to William the Lion.

The circumstances of the union of Robert Brus II. with Martha, Countess of Carrick, as given by Fordun, were as follows:

In the year 1271, Louis, King of France, after he had won from the discomfited Saracens a certain very large island named Barbary, met his doom; as did his first-born son Louis, and much people of the Christians with them — among others, David, Earl of Athol, and Adam, Earl of Carrick, and a great many other Scottish and English nobles. Now Adam, Earl of Carrick, left an only daughter, named Martha, as his heiress; and she succeeded him in his domain and earldom. After she had, therefore, become mistress of her father's domain, as she was, one day, going out hunting at random, with her esquires and handmaidens, she met a gallant knight riding across the same country — a most seemly youth, named Robert of Bruce, son of Robert, surnamed the Bruce, the noble lord of Annandale in Scotland, and of Cleveland in England. When greetings and kisses had been given on each side, as is the wont of courtiers, she besought him to stay and hunt, and walk about ; and seeing that he was rather unwilling to do so, she by force, so to speak, with her own hand, made him pull up, and brought the knight, although very loath, to her castle of Turnberry with her.   After dallying there, with his followers, for the space of fifteen days or more, he clandestinely took the countess to wife ; while the friends and well-wishers of both knew nothing about it, nor had the king's consent been got at all in the matter.   Therefore the common belief of the whole country was that she had seized — by force, as it were — this youth for her husband.   But when this came to King Alexander's ears, he took the castle of Turnberry, and made all her other lands and possessions be acknowledged as in his hands, because she had wedded with Robert of Bruce without having consulted his royal majesty.   By means of the prayers of friends, however, and by a certain sum of money agreed upon, this Robert gained the king's goodwill, and the whole domain.   Of Martha, by God's providence, he begat a son, who was to be the savior, champion, and king of the bruised Scottish people, as the course of the history will show forth ; and his father's name, Robert, was given him.

> In twelve seven four since Christ our manhood wore,
> And at the feast when Benedict deceased,
> That noble knight, King Robert, saw the light,
> Called from the womb by Heaven's almighty doom.

In 1278, Alexander appeared in the English Parliament and in general terms swore fealty to Edward I.   The English king accepted Alexander's fealty, " saving the claim of homage for the kingdom of Scotland whenever he or his heirs should think proper to make it."

In 1283, Alexander's son, Prince Alexander (born 1263), died without issue ; and his daughter, Margaret, Queen of Norway, also died the following year (January 28th), leaving an only daughter, Margaret, who has become known in Scottish history as the Maid of Norway.   On this child the right to the throne was settled by Alexander and his Parliament shortly after the death of her mother.   Margaret of Norway became queen by succession in 1286, when Alexander met his death by being thrown from his horse.

The infant queen being still in Norway, in her father's care, a regency was established, consisting of six lords : William Fraser, Bishop of St. Andrews ; Duncan, Earl of Fife ; Alexander, Earl of Buchan ; Robert Wisheart, Bishop of Glasgow ; John Comyn, Lord of Badenoch ; and James, the Steward of Scotland.   This regency continued for two years ; when, upon the murder of the Earl of Fife by Sir Patrick Abernethy and Sir Walter Percy, succeeded by the death of Buchan, a quarrel arose amongst the remaining regents, and their number was reduced to three by the separation of James the Steward.

In 1289, Eric, King of Norway, sent an embassy to Edward I. of England to secure his assistance in harmonizing the dissensions existing in his daughter's kingdom.   Edward, having first procured a dispensation from Pope Nicholas for the marriage of his eldest son to Scotland's queen, undertook to assume also a fatherly interest in the affairs of Margaret's kingdom.

To this end he called a convention composed of three representatives from each of the three kingdoms of Norway, England, and Scotland, which met at Salisbury in the latter part of the year 1289 to arrange for the conveyance of the infant queen to her dominions. At another convention held at Brigham in July of the following year, a treaty was concluded between the English and Scottish representatives, confirming the proposed marriage of Margaret to Edward's son, Edward II.

In the month of September the young queen sailed from Norway, but having sickened on the passage the ship landed at Orkney, where the queen died.

This death, terminating the direct line of Alexander III., left the succession open to numerous collateral claimants, chief of whom were John de Baliol, claiming by right of his descent from Margaret, the oldest daughter of David, Earl of Huntingdon, through her daughter, Dervergoyll (Baliol's mother); and Robert Brus (II.), son of David's second daughter, Isabella. Bruce's claim was based upon the fact of his being the nearest male descendant of David, as opposed to that of Baliol, who was one generation farther removed from David, although himself the descendant of David's eldest daughter. Besides these two there were eight other competitors for the crown, their titles all being more remote than those of Baliol and Bruce.

Edward, the English king, thereupon assumed to be arbiter between the claimants. Having ordered his northern barons with all their forces to assemble at Norham on the first of June, he invited the Scottish nobles and clergy to meet him there about a month before that time. This preliminary meeting was accordingly held at Norham, May 10, 1291, and there Edward for the first time announced his own pretensions to the title of Lord Paramount of Scotland, and laid claim to the power which such a title implied.

The Scots desired a delay to consider whether or not they should accept Edward as their monarch. After three weeks had elapsed the second meeting was held, this time on the north bank of the Tweed, at which were present seven of the claimants to the throne: Robert Bruce; Florence, Count of Holland; John de Hastings, Lord of Abergavenny; Patrick de Dunbar, Earl of March; William de Ross; Robert de Pinkeny; and Nicholas de Soulis.

These persons, being first questioned as to whether they acknowledged the competency of Edward, as Lord Paramount of Scotland, to pass upon the question of succession, severally gave their assent. Another competitor, William de Vesci, present by an attorney, likewise acquiesced, and the next day John Baliol appeared and made a similar answer. Eric of Norway was the tenth claimant.

Following this, Edward suggested the formation of a commission to consider the various claims presented. This commission was to consist of 104 members, forty of whom were to be named by Bruce and his party, forty by Baliol and his party, and twenty-four by the king of England. Upon their appointment the cause was submitted, and about a year later their findings were made known to the Lord Paramount.

In the meantime a general homage to the king of England was required on the part of the Scottish nobles, and during the summer of 1291 many of the barons, the clergy, and the burgesses swore fealty to Edward I.

Toward the end of the year 1292, the finding of the commissioners on the vital point in question between Bruce and Baliol was announced. It was to the effect that, "by the laws and usages of both kingdoms, in every heritable succession, the more remote in one degree lineally descended from the eldest sister, was preferable to the nearer in degree issuing from the second sister."

As Baliol was the grandson of the eldest sister, and Bruce the son of the second sister of the daughters of Earl David, this answer was favorable to the former, and in November, 1292, Edward rendered judgment accordingly. John Baliol was therefore crowned at Scone on the 30th day of the same month, becoming king of Scotland by grace of his Lord Paramount, Edward I.; and doing homage to that ruler for his kingdom before the end of the year.

Concerning the justice of Edward's claim to the supremacy of Scotland, innumerable pages have been written on the one side or the other. The case naturally furnished grounds for fierce and unceasing disputation between the historians of both countries for many centuries after. In that age, the right of possession was largely determined by the power of the possessor. The fact that Edward was wise enough to grasp the opportunity for asserting his intangible claim to superiority at the particular time when every one of the competitors for the throne was willing to sacrifice his nation's integrity for personal advantage must ever be considered the strongest proof of his title as Lord Paramount. Had his successors been equally fortunate in retaining for England what had been won by the masterful policy of this greatest of the Edwards, it is doubtful if the justice of his course would in later ages have been seriously questioned.

However, the international code of his age admitted not only the right of him to seize who had the power, but also involved the necessity for him to hold that could. After events proved the inadequacy of Edward's main title to superiority. Hence the pursuit of the English claims was transferred from the field to the study, and their consideration there has ever since been fruitful of many ingenious arguments.

The most instructive of these arguments, for the light it throws upon the conditions surrounding the presentation of the original English claim to the sovereignty of Scotland, is that of Mr. Edward A. Freeman, contained in the first volume of his *History of the Norman Conquest*. While the main point at issue cannot be said to be satisfactorily established by Mr. Freeman's argument, yet the value of his attempt as a contribution to that part of Scottish history with which we are here immediately concerned is very great.

Inasmuch as the gist of Mr. Freeman's contention as to the ancient vassalage of Scotia proper rests upon the supposed submission of Constantine II. to Edward the Elder in the year 924, considerable importance attaches to the record of that event. Indeed, it has been the cause of continual controversy between the writers on the opposite sides of the question from the time when King Edward first made his claim of superiority in 1290 down to the present day. The passage in the *English Chronicle* on which this claim of submission is based reads as follows: " 924. . . . He [Eadweard] went thence into Peakland, to Bakewell, and commanded a *Burh* to be built nigh thereunto and manned. And then chose him to father and lord the king of Scots, and the whole nation of the Scots, and Ragnold, and Eadulf's son, and all those who dwell in Northumbria, as well English as Danes, and Northmen, and others ; and also the king of the Strathclyde Welsh, and all the Strathclyde Welsh." This passage has been thoroughly demolished by Mr. E. William Robertson, who best presents the Scottish side of the case in his essay on *The English Claims*. While it may never be possible to get an unprejudiced conclusion as to the merits of the case from an English or Scottish source, we submit that Mr. Robertson's argument has so far destroyed the credibility of the passage in the *English Chronicle*, on which that of Mr. Freeman mainly rests, as to render it inadmissible as trustworthy evidence. In consequence, Mr. Freeman's arguments, being based upon what are, to say the least, doubtful and uncertain premises, cannot be given that consideration to which their comprehensive statement of tenth-century conditions in the North, and the eminence of the author, would otherwise entitle them.

Mr. Robertson's particular criticism of the passage in question is as follows :

How far does this passage agree with the true history of the period as far as that can be ascertained ? Alfred's rule never extended over the Danes. When Guthrum and his *Here* " gave hostages, and swore with many oaths that they would leave his *kingdom*," the agreement was fulfilled by their departure from Chippenham, in *Wessex*, to Cirencester in *Mercia*—across the Thames,—and though Alfred's kingdom was subsequently enlarged, at his death he only ruled over all "Angel-cyn, except that part under the Danes." The earlier years of Edward were passed in frequent struggles against the same people, nor was it until within a few years of his death that the Danes of Mercia and East Anglia " sought him as lord "—the Southumbrian Danes, in other words, for all the early authorities agree that Æthelstan was the first king who united Angles, Danes, and Britons under one sceptre. "In uno solidantur Britannidis arva," wrote Æthelwald, profoundly ignorant of the passage which now appears in the Saxon Chronicle attributing this union to Edward ; an ignorance in which the author of the old poem to which Malmesbury alludes also shared, when he described the Northumbrian Sitric as one " qui antecessorum regum potentiam rugatis naribus derisissit." The

contempt of the Northumbrian Danes for the authority of Æthelstan's ancestors is scarcely consistent with their voluntary submission to his father in
the preceding year.   The ignorance of the earlier authorities about this
passage is justified by the authentic charters of the reign of Æthelstan, in
which the names of the Danish Eorls occur for the first time amongst the attest-
ing witnesses.   It was not till after Sitric's death in 927 that the submission
of the *Northumbrian* Danes to an Anglo-Saxon king was first brought about,
Æthelstan possessing himself of the kingdom of his sister's husband, and
defeating all the attempts of Godfrey, the survivor of Ivar's grandsons, to
establish himself in the territories of his brothers.

But not only is the passage inconsistent with the history of the period as
it appears to have been known to the earlier authorities of the tenth century ;
it contains internal evidence of its untruth.   That such acts of submisssion
were made upon a frontier is a fact notorious from all the tenor of contemporary history ; and when Edward received the submission of the Southumbrian Danes, the *Eorls*, the *Holds*, and the *Here* tendered their allegiance
each in their respective neighborhood, a course rendered still more imperative from their tendering it in a body, according to the older form of
Leudisamium.   Every Danish freeman swore *personally* to be true to his
Anglo-Saxon " *Hlaford* and *Mundbora*," and the oath was of course taken at
some neighboring place at which every freeholder could attend.   The
words which Simeon and Florence place in the mouth of Malcolm Ceanmore show that, in the opinion of that age, no Scotttish king had ever met
an Anglo-Saxon sovereign except upon their mutual frontiers, and all authentic history proves such meetings to have invariably been the result of a
march to the north.   But Bakewell in the Peak is hardly upon the Scottish,
nor even upon the Northumbrian frontiers, and the construction of a *Burh*
in the north of Derbyshire would have scarcely brought the Danes to terms ;
much less would it have gathered the whole free population of Scotland,
Northumbria, and Strath-Clyde around their respective leaders, to take the
oaths of fealty at such a distance from their homes, and to place themselves
within the *socn* of the English king !

Nor is this all.   Three years before his supposed appearance at Bakewell,
Reginald Hy Ivar was in his grave.   The Irish Annals, at this period most
accurate and trustworthy authorities in all connected with the Hy Ivar
family, place his death in 921 (An. Ult. 920).[4]   Undoubtedly the English
chronology of this era is hopelessly confused, and Florence places these
events under that year ; but if his date is preferred, the last three and most
important years of Edward's reign are left a blank, and the authority of the
best and oldest MSS. of the *Chronicle* must be impugned.   I cannot think
that this is necessary.   Edward built a *Burh* at Bakewell in the last year of
his reign, and the chronicler faithfully recorded it as his latest act ; but of
the vast assemblage of all Scotland, Northumbria, and Strath-Clyde, which
gathered around that place to tender allegiance to Edward as their overlord,
both king and chronicler were equally ignorant.

The claims grounded in the feudal era on the *chronicled* dependance of the Scots upon the Anglo-Saxon monarchy before the Conquest, may
be said to rest either upon passages interpolated in a true text ; actual forgeries and fabrications ; or else upon amplifications and exaggerations of the
truth.   An instance of the first class is afforded in Simeon of Durham, according to whose authority in Twysden, under the date 1059, " Kinsi, Archbishop of York, Aylwin, Bishop of Durham, and Tosti, Earl of Yorkshire,
conducted King Malcolm to King Edward."   This passage is correctly de-

scribed in *Mon. Hist. Brit.*, p. 609, as entered *on the margin of the MS.*, and as Roger Hoveden, who, at the opening of the thirteenth century, copied the whole of Simeon's chronicle word for word into his own, has omitted all notice of it, the entry—of which the object is unmistakable—must have been added to the original MS. at a very late date, and, once incorporated with the body of the work, has been falsely stamped with the almost contemporary authority of Simeon.

The reign of Edgar, as depicted in the Anglo-Norman chronicles, is fertile in examples of the second description. After the coronation of that king at Bath, he is said by three MSS. of the *Saxon Chronicle* to have sailed to Chester, where he was met by *six* kings, who all pledged themselves to be his "efen-wyrhtan," or allies by sea and by land. Æthelward, in the chronicle which he compiled for the use of his cousin, the Emperor Otho's daughter, though he alludes to Edgar's coronation in 973, takes no notice of the meeting at Chester; but in the twelfth century, and in the pages of Florence of Worcester, the coronation, which alone appears to have stimulated the poetic energy of the Anglo-Saxon bards, is completely eclipsed in importance by the subsequent progress on the Dee. Eight kings now meet the English monarch, rowing him submissively to the monastery of St. John, and upon his return to his palace, Edgar turns to his nobles with the remark that none of his successors ought to vaunt himself king of the Angles until he had enjoyed a similar triumph. It is easier to understand the process by which the *six* kings grew into *eight*, with Kenneth of Scotland in the van, than to account for the silence of the contemporary Æthelward, and of every Saxon chronicler before the Conquest, about a triumph to which Edgar himself is supposed to have attached so much importance.

In his anxiety to render his narrative as circumstantial as possible, the original framer of the story has committed the error of *naming* the eight kings—Kenneth, King of Scotland; Malcolm, King of the Cumbrians; Maccus, King of the Isles; and Duffnal, Siferth, Howel, Jacob, and Jukill—thus laying himself open to be convicted of inaccuracy. There could have been no "king of the Cumbrians" at this time, for the grant of *Cumbra-land*, made to Malcolm the First in 945, and for which he renewed his oaths upon the accession of Edred, ceased upon the death of the Scottish king, and the feudal subinfeudation of that province as a fief held by the Scottish Tanist is totally contrary to the real history of the period. Donald, son of the Eogan who appears to have fallen at Brunanburgh, was king of Strath-Clyde during the whole of Edgar's reign, dying in the same year as the English king, whilst on a pilgrimage to Rome; and if the "rex Cumbrorum" means "king of Strath-Clyde," no *Malcolm* could have appeared at Chester in that capacity. Malcolm, King of the Cumbrians, is indubitably a *myth*. Of the other five kings, Siferth, Howel, and Jacob are unquestionably meant for Jevaf ap Idwal, his son Howel, and his brother Iago, princes of North Wales; and Jukill, or Juthael, may be intended for another of the same race, Idwal ap Idwal. Five years before the meeting at Chester, Jevaf was imprisoned, blinded, and hanged by his brother Iago, and could scarcely have been in a condition to "grace the triumph on the Dee." The name of Duffnal was utterly unknown amongst the contemporary princes of the Welsh, and is only applicable to the king of Strath-Clyde, adding another element to the confusion. This is scarcely the handiwork of a contemporary chronicler.

The five princes of the Welsh, however, had not yet played their part, for subsequently to the earliest edition of the progress on the Dee it became the object of the king of England to assert the dependence of the lords of Galloway upon his crown, and accordingly it will scarcely excite surprise to find that province enumerated amongst the " kingdoms " which Roger of Wendover was the first to attach to their names. His selection, however, was most unfortunate, for to Duffnal he has given South Wales, the undoubted appanage of Owen, or his son Einion, of the family of Howel Dha, whilst for Galloway he has chosen Iago, as unquestionably a prince of North Wales. With his donation of Westmoreland to Jukill I need hardly interfere.

Two charters are connected with the supposed occurrences of this period, both of which have been condemned as spurious by Mr. Kemble. The first was evidently intended to pass for a donation made at Edgar's coronation, for it is witnessed by the eight kings " at Bath in the Feast of Pentecost," but dated unluckily in 966, five years before Kenneth could sign himself " Rex Scotorum," or Edgar was crowned at " the city of sick men ! " The second is framed far more skilfully, but bears evident marks of the Norman era of its composition and some circumstances connected with it are especially worthy of notice. Malmesbury, in his *Antiquities of Glastonbury*, mentions certain privileges and grants made to the monastery by Edgar, and the text goes on thus: " Hoc donum, ne instabile vel inglorium sit, lituo eburneo, quem linibus auri prætexebat, super altare dato confirmavit. *Dedit etiam aliud privelegium in hæc verba*—[here follows the charter in question, concluding] *Acta est hæc privelegii pagina et confirmata apud Londonium . . . anno 971 indictione 14*. . . . Ad supplementum vero securitatis ne tanta liberalitas nutaret, Johanne . . . Papa persuaso, donum suum Apostolico suffulsit edicto, cujus hæc est series. Noverit cunctorum, etc. . . . Actum tempore Egelwardi, ejusdem monasterii Abbatis, hoc Apostolicum decretum anno 965." In other words, a charter dated in 971 and attested amongst other witnesses by Abbot Sigegar, was confirmed by the Pope in 965, in the time of Sigegar's predecessor, Abbot Aylward! The interpolation is unmistakable ; but by omitting the words in italics, the sense is restored as Malmesbury wrote it, Edgar's original gift, attested by placing the ivory horn on the altar, having been confirmed by the Pope in 965. The same interpolation is traceable in nearly every MS. of the *Gesta Regum*, in which this identical charter reappears, to be invariably confirmed by the Pope five years before it was granted by the king. It would be unjust to attribute this questionable transaction to Malmesbury. In his *Gesta Regum* he writes thus : " Arturis sepulchrum nusquam visitur unde antiquitas næniarum adhuc eum venturum fabulatur " ; and again, in a passage copied from his *Antiquities of Glastonbury*, " Illud quod pene clam omnibus est, libenter prædicarem, si veritatem exculpere possem, quid illæ pyramides sibi velint quæ . . . cimeterium monachorum prætexant" ; yet in the same *Antiquities* some one has not hesitated to interpolate the following : " Prætermitto de Arturo, inclyto rege Brittonum, in cimeterio monachorum inter duas Pyramides cum sua conjuge tumulato ! " The body of Arthur was discovered, according to Wendover, in 1191, and the hand of Malmesbury had long been mouldering in the grave when this passage, and the charter, of which he was equally ignorant, were inserted in his works by some unscrupulous fabricator.

Another fabrication which has been inserted amongst the events of this reign is the cession of Lothian to Kenneth of Scotland, to be held of the English crown as a hereditary feudal fief. This first appears in the pages generally attributed to John of Wallingford, who filled the office of abbot of St. Albans—the same monastery in whose chronicles " the five kings " first appear with kingdoms—from 1195 to 1214 ; though they would appear rather to have been the work of another John of Wallingford who died in 1258. According to this authority, on the death of Osulf, unwilling that any part of Northumbria should pass hereditarily, Edgar created an earldom for Oslac, extending from Humber to Tees, and erected the sea-coast of *Deira*, reaching from Tees to *Mireforth*,—meaning probably the Firth of Forth,—into another earldom for Eadulf Ewelchild, which must have interfered considerably with the grant to Oslac.   Lothian, always open to the incursions of the Picts and Scots, was little cared for by the English kings, and Kenneth, hearing of the liberality of Edgar, and hoping to profit by it, was conducted to the English court by the two earls and Elfsi, Bishop of Durham—a proceeding not a little suggestive of the marginal addition to Simeon of Durham, to which allusion has been already made.   Arrived there, Kenneth suggests to Edgar that this neglected Lothian had always belonged of hereditary right to the kings of Scotland, a claim which Edgar refers to his council, who assent to it, with the reservation that it was always held by homage, assigning as a reason that it was a worthless province, and difficult of access to defend.   Kenneth accordingly consents to hold Lothian as a fief "sub nomine homagii . . . sicque determinata vetus querela de Louthian, et adhuc nova sæpe intentatur."

It is scarcely necessary to remark, about a tale so redolent of the age in which it was first put forth, that it will not be found in a single authority of an earlier date than the thirteenth century.   Every chronicler before that epoch, Norman as well as Saxon, was ignorant of " the old quarrel about Lothian," yet it is strange that Æthelward, at least, should not have celebrated its cession during his kinsman's reign in some of those unpolished periods that excited the contemptuous pity of the fastidious Malmesbury. Simeon, the best authority for Northumbrian history, writing a hundred years and upwards before Wallingford, tells how Lothian was ceded to the Scots through the pusillanimity of Eadulf Cudel in the days of Canute, ignorant alike of the previous cession to Kenneth and of the existence of " the old quarrel" in the time of Edgar.   Yet Simeon's earls—Osulf, Oslac, Waltheof, Uchtred—are historical characters, whose names appear in authentic charters ; " Oslac Eorl with the *Here* dwelling in the Eorldordom " is mentioned in the laws of Edgar, but the name of his companion in the pages of Wallingford, Eadulf Ewelchild, is never found except in two spurious charters—once in the appropriate company of another *myth*, Malcolm Dux,—and, in fact, is nothing else than a blundering attempt at adapting the real ceder of Lothian, *Child Eadulf Cudel*, to the time of Edgar as *Eadulf* Ewelchild.   Wendover has improved upon the account attributed to his abbot, mentioning the conditions on which Lothian was to be held :   Kenneth and his successors were to attend the court of the English kings on every solemn festival when the latter " wore the crown," and *mansiones* were assigned for the support of the Scottish train on these continual progresses, which remained in the possession of the Scottish kings until the reign of Henry the Second.   The addition of Wendover, with the *mansiones* held to the days of the second Henry, was purposely framed to correspond with the supposed cession of Lothian, which the same chronicler has added to the fiefs surrendered by Malcolm IV. to the English king in 1157; a cession which has not only been overlooked by every contemporary authority, but was also totally ignored by the English kings themselves, who showed an unaccountable negligence in exercising the right, which they would unquestionably have acquired by such an act, of summoning the baronage of the Lothians to perform the military service due to their English overlord.

NOTES TO CHAPTER XXII

[1] "1224. Reginald [King of the Isles], taking with him Alan, lord of Galloway, with the Manks, proceeded to the insular parts ; that the part of the land which he had given to Olave his brother he might take from him and subjugate it to his own dominion.   But forasmuch as the Manks did not choose to fight against Olave or the islanders, because they loved them, Reginald and Alan, doing no good, returned home.   After a short time, Reginald, under pretence of going to the court of the lord the king of England, received from the people of Man one hundred marks, and proceeded to the court of Alan lord of Galloway. At the same time he gave his daughter in marriage to the son of Alan ; which the Manks hearing were very angry, and sending for Olave constituted him their king.

"1228.   Olave, with all the great men of Man, and the braver part of the people sailed to the Isles.   Shortly after, Alan, lord of Galloway, and Thomas, earl of Athol, and Reginald the king, came to Man with a great army, wasted all the southern part of Man, and plundered churches, and killed as many men as they could take ; and the southern part of Man was reduced almost into a desert :   And after this Alan returned with his army into his own land, and left his bailiffs in Man, who should render him the tribute of the country."— *Chron. Regum Manniæ.*

[2] The Norman barons divided the territory between them ; "but," we are told in the *Chronicle of Melrose*, "the inhabitants of that land preferring one master rather than several went to our lord the king with the request that he himself would accept the lordship of that inheritance, but the king was too just to do this.   Thereupon the Galwegians were angry beyond measure, and prepared for war.   Moreover, they devastated with fire and sword some of the royal lands contiguous to themselves," and the king resolved to make a final effort to reduce it entirely to obedience.

"In the following year our lord the king," says the chronicler, "mustered an army, and entered Galloway.   Having reached a spot convenient for the purpose, he determined there to pitch his tents, for the day was now drawing toward evening.   The Galwegians, however, who had all day been hiding among the mountains, knew the place better, and, trusting to their local acquaintance with its difficulties, offered the king battle.   In truth, the place was filled with bogs, which were covered over with grass and flowers, amongst which the larger portion of the royal army had involved itself.   At the beginning of the battle the earl of Ross, called Makintagart, came up and attacked the enemies in the rear, and as soon as they perceived this they took to flight, and retreated into the woods and mountains, but they were followed up by the earl and several others, who put many of them to the sword, and harassed them as long as daylight lasted.   On the next day the king, acting upon his accustomed humanity, extended his peace to as many as came to him, and so the surviving Galwegians, with ropes around their necks, accepted his offer."

[3] The time of peace with England, of plenty in the land, of foreign trade flourishing, of internal peace, of law and justice, was the period of a full century following the treaty between William the Lion and Richard Cœur-de-Lion, comprehending the reign of William and the long reigns of the second and third Alexanders.—Cosmo Innes, *Scotland in the Middle Ages*, p. 296.

In a material point of view, it may safely be affirmed that Scotland at the death of King Alexander III. was more civilized and more prosperous than at any period of her existence, down to the time when she ceased to be a separate kingdom in 1707.—Innes, *Sketches of Early Scottish History and Social Progress*, p. 157.

"Castles, which had begun to be erected in the reign of Malcolm Canmore, were rapidly multiplied by those Norman barons and their followers who, as we have already seen, obtained large grants of land from the Scottish monarchs.   Various strongholds along the sea-coasts, supposed to have been built by the Vikings, as well as cells or religious houses, are known to have previously existed.   But it was chiefly under the protection of the baronial towers that hamlets and towns sprung up ; and in less than two centuries a vast change was produced. Ayrshire, notwithstanding the attachment of the inhabitants to their Celtic habits, seems to have made considerable progress in the new order of things, though most of the towns and principal villages are of Celtic origin : for example, Ayr, Irvine, Kilmarnock, Kilmaurs, Mauchline, Ochiltree, Auchinleck, Cumnock, Ballantrae, Girvan, Maybole, &c., no doubt took their rise prior to the Saxon era of our history. Those of more recent times are easily known by the Teutonic affix *tun* or *ton*. They are ten in number : Coylton, Dalmellington, Galston, Monkton, Richarton, Stevenston, Stewarton, Straiton, Symington, and Tarbolton ; and even these are not all wholly Saxon. . . .

" Though it is thus apparent that the majority of the towns and villages of the county took their rise in Celtic times, and while the Gaelic continued to be the prevailing language, there can be little doubt that the introduction of foreigners, especially the mercantile Flemings, whom the mistaken policy of the English monarchs drove from the south, tended greatly to promote that mercantile prosperity for which the country was distinguished in the reign of Alexander. In ship-building, in fishing, in agriculture, and commerce, Scotland was considerably in advance of England in the twelfth century. The Saxons, Flemings, and other foreigners, are known to have been settled chiefly in the towns ; yet, in Aryshire at least, they seem to have constituted but a small body in comparison with the other inhabitants. The names, so far as they have been preserved in the municipal records of Ayr, for instance, show that Celtic patronymics were by far the most numerous."—Paterson, *History of the County of Ayr*, pp., 22, 23.

[4] Mr. Robertson was not the first to see the fatal objection to the statement in the *Saxon Chronicle* that Regnwald, king of Northumbria, took Eadward for his father and lord in 924, while he died in 921. Florence of Worcester saw it before him, and places the event under the year 921. The most recent discussion of the question of the English Supremacy is that by Mr. Charles Truman Wyckoff, entitled, *Feudal Relations between the Kings of England and Scotland.* Chicago University Press, 1897.

CHAPTER XXIII

WALLACE AND BRUCE

IN accordance with Edward's order, the accession of Baliol to the crown of Scotland was followed by a transfer of the right of final appeal from the Scottish to the English king in all causes brought in the courts of Scotland. The first important case to come up after this arrangement had been made was one relating to the lands of Duncan MacDuff, then a minor, whose guardian had been dispossessed by Baliol, and imprisoned. The guardian appealed to the Lord Paramount, and the Scottish king was summoned to appear before Edward and answer his complaint. This Baliol failed to do, and a second summons was sent. Baliol appeared. When questioned in regard to MacDuff's cause, he replied that he was king of Scotland, and could not answer without the advice of his people. When reminded that he was Edward's liegeman and angrily questioned by his master, Baliol persisted in his refusal to answer without the advice of his counsellors. The English Parliament then adjudged him guilty of contempt; and, as a penalty, ordered that the three principal castles of Scotland be surrendered to King Edward. The latter, however, wishing to avert an open conflict at that time, stayed the whole of the proceedings until the following year. When the English Parliament met again in May, 1294, Baliol appeared, and apparently made his peace. A war with France having broken out in the meantime, Baliol likewise agreed to yield up the entire revenues of his English possessions for three years to assist in fighting the French.

Edward ordered an embargo to be laid on all vessels trading at Scottish ports; but this was evaded by the Scots, and that nation made a secret treaty of alliance with Philip, King of France. In the latter part of the next year (1295) Baliol, moreover, engaged with King Philip to assist him with his whole power in case Edward invaded France; while the French king agreed, on his part, to render like succor to Baliol if the English should enter Scotland.

March 26, 1296, the king of the Scots having assembled a large force, and relying too strongly upon the fair promises of his new ally, began open hostilities against the English by an invasion of Cumberland. He assaulted Carlisle, but was obliged to retreat without effecting its reduction. About ten days later his army entered Northumberland, whence, after burning some ecclesiastical posts and making an unsuccessful attempt against the castle of Harbottle, it retired empty-handed. Edward, in the meantime, led a strong sea and land force against Berwick. After capturing that town and butchering the garrison and inhabitants,[1] he forced the capitulation of the castle. Baliol at this time formally renounced his allegiance to Edward.

The latter soon afterwards sent a strong body of troops under Earl War-ren to invest Dunbar Castle ; and the Scottish army, marching to its relief, encountered the English before that stronghold. Warren's forces repulsed and defeated the Scots with great slaughter. King Edward and the remainder of his army coming up the next day, the garrison of the castle surrendered. Roxburgh Castle was soon afterwards yielded up to the English by James, the Steward of Scotland. The castles of Edinburgh and Stirling were like-wise surrendered with little resistance. These operations placed Edward in control of the kingdom ; and before the middle of the following July (1296) Baliol surrendered, acknowledged himself a rebel, went through a humiliat-ing public penance, and resigned the government of Scotland entirely to Edward.

The English king now proceeded through Scotland as far north as Moray Firth, and all classes of the inhabitants came forward at his stopping-places and swore fealty to their new master. The detailed record of this and the previous submissions has been preserved to us in the so-called " Ragman Roll," which contains numerous and lengthy lists of the names of those who thus subjected themselves to King Edward during the time of his sovereignty over Scotland.[2]

Edward appointed John de Warren, Earl of Surrey, as governor of Scotland and returned into England.

Not long afterwards, the peace of the newly established English depend-ency was disturbed by rumors of disorders in the west. It was said that one William Wallace, a native of the ancient kingdom of Strathclyde,[3] had there slain the sheriff of Lanark, a high officer of the English crown. Having committed some offence for which he became an object of suspicion to the English authorities, according to the legendary accounts, the sheriff of Lanark attacked his place of abode and killed his wife or mistress. Wallace is said to have retaliated by killing the sheriff, and thus to have become an outlaw. Associating with himself some friends of kindred spirit, he soon gave the English authorities more abundant cause for believing him to be a man of desperate character. Having received numerous accessions to his little band of warriors, and aided by the presence and support of a brave knight named Sir William Douglas, Wallace, in May, 1297, planned to capture the English High Justiciary, who was then holding his court at Scone (Perth). That official saved himself from being taken by a hurried departure from the country. Thereupon, a season of war and anarchy ensued in western Scotland. Armed bands ravaged the country, killing and driving out the English officials ; and, where there was show of success, storming and destroying their abodes. The insurrection seems to have arisen mainly in the western Lowlands, in that district comprising Galloway and Strath-clyde, which had ever been the most turbulent and troublesome part of the kingdom south of the Highlands. Toward Galloway the most of the rebel-lious bands accordingly made their way. Many of the Scottish barons also joined the standard of revolt, among them being Robert Wisheart, Bishop of Glasgow ; Alexander de Lindesay, the Steward of Scotland and his brother, Sir Richard Lundin, and Robert de Brus (Bruce). The patriots soon had a considerable army gathered, which was posted in the vicinity of Irvine in Ayrshire. Here, Henry de Percy, having marched to the scene of the uprising with a considerable force, found them.

By reason of the jealousies entertained by many of the Scottish nobles against one another, it was impossible for them to offer effective resistance to the experienced and disciplined soldiers of England. Eventually all but one of the barons withdrew from the Scottish army with their followers and again submitted to Edward.[4] That monarch pardoned them, and also released such of the nobles as he had imprisoned during the former year.

In William Wallace, however, his countrymen found the incarnation of all those noble and heroic traits apotheosized in the reputed character of the mythical Tell. Scorning submission to the English, resolutely determined to free his country from Edward's grasp, and perhaps lacking only the opportunity to mete out fitting punishment to those barons who had deserted their nation's cause,[5] Wallace did not for a moment relax his efforts to make the revolution general, nor cease in his hostile operations against the invaders. Notwithstanding the defection of the barons, his army continued daily to increase in strength and numbers. He laid siege to the castle of Dundee. While there, he received intelligence of the English army's movement toward Stirling. Hastening with all his forces to the passage of the Forth, he there posted his troops on the north bank of the river and prepared to intercept the progress of the enemy. On September 12, 1297, the English approached, fifty thousand strong,[6] and attempted to cross over on the long, narrow bridge which at that place spanned the channel. They were led by Hugh de Cressingham, King Edward's Treasurer for Scotland. A considerable body, consisting of about half the English force, soon passed the bridge, and then made ready to form on the other side. Wallace, awaiting this opportunity, instantly pounced down upon them with the Scots, cut off their communication with the other side, and at once charged on the divided body with all his forces. Taking them at such a disadvantage, his onslaught was irresistible and proved sufficient to carry the day. Cressingham was slain ; his troops were mown down like blades of grass ; and such as escaped death by the sword were pushed into the river and drowned. A panic seized the remainder of the English soldiers on the south bank of the river. They burned the bridge, abandoned their baggage, fled in terror to Berwick, hastened on into England, and Scotland was once more free.

This brilliant success was immediately followed by the surrender of Dundee Castle and the evacuation of Berwick ; and then Wallace led his victorious army into England and wasted all the country as far south as Newcastle. Soon returning, he organized a regency, proclaimed himself governor of Scotland in the name of King John de Baliol (then a prisoner in England), and assumed and administered the government.

During the progress of these operations Edward had been absent in Flanders. Upon his return in the early part of the year 1298, having first vainly summoned the Scottish barons to meet him in a Parliament at York, he assembled an army and marched toward the Border.[7] At this time, as we have seen, Wallace had the active support of but a few of the Scottish noblemen, the great majority being deterred from taking up arms through fear of Edward or by reason of their jealousy of Wallace. Among his followers, however, were John Comyn of Badenoch, Sir John Stewart of Bonkill, brother to the Steward, Sir John Graham of Abercorn, Macduff, the granduncle of the Earl of Fife, and young Robert Bruce, Earl of Carrick. The leader last named guarded the castle of Ayr.

Edward first sent a fleet around through the Firth of Forth under the command of the Earl of Pembroke. A landing was made in Fife, where Wallace attacked and defeated the force in the battle of Black Ironside Forest, June 12, 1298.[8]

Edward, meanwhile having occupied Berwick, advanced to the vicinity of Edinburgh, the Scots retiring before him and wasting the country as they proceeded, in order that it might afford no subsistence to their enemy. Having despatched a fleet with provisions, to pass around the north of Scotland and down to the mouth of the Clyde, Edward made ready to march into the West. The fleet being delayed, however, he did not deem it safe to proceed ; and, his supplies running low, he was forced to order a retreat to the eastern border. The Scots prepared to take advantage of the condition in which the English army was now placed, and advanced in considerable force to the vicinity of Falkirk. Edward, changing his plans, immediately marched against them. The armies met at Falkirk, July 22, 1298. Wallace's army was composed mainly of spearmen and bowmen, who were sustained by a body of but a thousand horsemen. The English relied chiefly upon their cavalry. At the first encounter the Scottish cavalry, many times outnumbered by that of the English, became panic-stricken and fled. Then the Scotch archers were soon decimated by the incessant discharge of stones and arrows on the part of the English infantry ; and the spearmen, having no support from cavalry or archers, had their front broken by the fierce and repeated onslaughts of Edward's horse. In the end a complete defeat and rout ensued, the Scottish loss being exceedingly great.[9]

Edward now marched into the West, stopping first to repair Stirling Castle which had been burned by the Scots, and then proceeding into Annandale. At his approach, it is said, Bruce burned the castle of Ayr and retired.[10] Edward thereupon seized Bruce's castle of Lochmaben in Dumfries, wherein were confined the hostages given in 1297 as pledges for the loyalty of Galloway.[11]

Crossing the Solway, the English king and his army now passed out of

24

Scotland. He returned again, however, by the Western Marches in 1300, and completely subdued Dumfriesshire and Galloway.

After the disastrous defeat at Falkirk, Wallace resigned his office as governor of Scotland, and in the summer of 1299, William Lamberton, Bishop of St. Andrews, Robert Bruce, Earl of Carrick, and John Comyn of Badenoch, the younger, were chosen guardians of the kingdom in his place. Soon afterwards they besieged and took Stirling Castle. From this time on the name of Wallace as a national leader disappears from the records of the councils and conflicts of Scotland.

After Edward had again conquered the greater part of the kingdom, he assembled a Parliament at St. Andrews which pronounced sentence of outlawry against Scotland's hero, and a price was set upon his head. Wallace was afterwards betrayed to the English, in 1303, by a false friend, Sir John, son of Walter Stewart, Earl of Mentieth. Having been arraigned at Westminster as a traitor to Edward and a destroyer of the lives and property of many of the English king's subjects, he was sentenced to death, August 23, 1305, and immediately executed under circumstances of the most barbaric and revolting cruelty.

He was first hung up, but cut down alive; and then disembowelled and the contents of his abdomen burned before his face. The executioner then beheaded him and his body was quartered. One arm was sent to Newcastle and there fixed above the bridge; another was sent to Berwick; the right leg was exposed at Perth, and the left at Aberdeen. His head Edward caused to be set on a pole and raised above London Bridge.

Shocking as the recital of these atrocities may be, they had altogether a contrary effect from the one intended by their perpetrator. Instead of striking terror to the hearts of Scotland's friends, they excited only feelings of profound pity for the martyred patriot, and engendered a deep-seated resentment against their cruel and merciless perpetrator.

Wallace's torture added one more item, and that a very heavy one, to the list of Scottish grievances against the English. No doubt it had a full and lasting effect in arousing the national spirit for that supreme contest with the invaders which almost immediately followed. Thus even by his death Wallace served the cause of his country in a degree by no means the least.

We now approach the most interesting period of Scotland's early history. It is one in which for the first time become apparent the evidences of the gradual amalgamation of the many dissimilar racial elements composing its population into one compact and united whole. The Scottish people as known in modern times may be said to date their national existence from their War of Independence. For two hundred years before the year 1314, Scotland was composed of a series of petty subkingdoms under the rule of powerful barons, who had practically sovereign authority over their respective territories. It is true they all owned allegiance to the reigning king; but unless that overlord was himself a most capable and resourceful leader his government was little more than a nominal one. The nobles were bound to furnish the king with an agreed number of soldiers in case of war, but their own jurisdiction over the rights and liberties of their vassals and followers was well-nigh supreme. Indeed, this authority continued, though in a more restricted degree, for nearly two centuries after the War of Independence ; and it was not until the time of the later Stuarts that the power of the nobles was appreciably lessened. The career of Wallace, however, and the success of his volunteer armies is the first recorded instance we have of any great national assertion on the part of the people themselves, aside from the personal wars of their hereditary masters.[12]

The period of Wallace and Bruce also marks the close in Scotland of the Feudal Era, which had been inaugurated by David and his successors somewhat more than a century before. The plan of campaigning necessarily carried on by the Scots in their contests with the vastly superior forces of Edward's armored knights was probably the inception in Great Britain of our modern system of warfare, wherein more attention is paid to ensuring the intelligence and efficiency of the individual soldier in the ranks, together with his proper arming, than to the construction of massive fortifications or the glorification of knightly valor.

To this end, Bruce set a notable example by appearing at the battle of Bannockburn practically without armor, and inaugurating that contest by crushing, with a single blow of his axe, the heavily armored English knight who rode out from the ranks to oppose him. And on the death of King Robert, after Scotland had finally established her independence, he is said to have left a memorable legacy to his fellow-countrymen ; one which has never been made use of by them but with advantage. This was in the shape of a code of rules or instructions for the defence of their mountainous kingdom from the invasions of the English ; and it has come down to us in the following modified form, styled "Good King Robert's Testament" :

> On fut suld all Scottis weire
> Be hyll and mosse thaimself to weire,
> Let wod for wallis be bow and speire
> That innymeis do thaim na dreire ;
> In strait placis gar keip all stoire,
> And byrn the planen land thaim befoire ;
> Thanen sall they pass away in haist
> Quhen that they find naithing bot waist,
> With wyllis and waikenen of the nicht
> And mekill noyes maid on hycht,
> Thanen sall they turnen with great affrai,
> As they were chasit with swerd away,
> This is the counsall and intent
> Of gud King Robert's testament.

From this stage of our narrative we may begin to make use of the contemporary chronicles of native origin ; inasmuch as Scotland's earliest historians belong to the fourteenth century.   As the period now under consideration is one of extreme interest, it merits a more detailed examination than can be given in a sketch like the present.   The latest and best account of Bruce and of the Scottish War of Independence is that of Herbert Maxwell (New York and London, 1897).   For our purpose, however, we may view Bruce's career and the events succeeding from the standpoint of Fordun's *Annals*.   Before doing this it may be well to examine briefly the sources from which his history is drawn, and also to glance at some of the authorities for the preceding and subsequent periods.

The materials for Scottish history of the middle ages are to be found mainly in the writings of the early chroniclers, Scottish and English, in the registers and chartularies of the ancient ecclesiastical establishments, many of which have been published by the Bannatyne, Hunterian, and Maitland Book Clubs of Scotland, in the manuscript records and charter chests of private families, and in the published records of the British Government.

The chief Scottish chronicles of the reign of Malcolm Canmore and the next four hundred years succeeding, are as follows :

1. The *Chronicle of Melrose*.   This begins at the year 735, and down to the end of the twelfth century is based on the chronicles of the northern writers who succeeded Bede—closely following that of Simeon of Durham, until the year 1121.   It is continued as an original narrative to 1270, when the manuscript breaks off.   Its value as an original record is very great, and it forms the basis of Fordun's history for that period.   The text of the manuscript was printed by the Bannatyne Club in 1835.

2. The *Chronicon Sanctæ Crucis*, or *Holyrood Chronicle* (Edinburgh), extends from 1124 to 1165, and is a contemporary account of the reigns of David and Malcolm IV.   This manuscript has also been printed by the Bannatyne Club (1828).

3. The *Chronicon de Lanercost*, one of the most interesting of the northern chronicles, was probably written by a Minorite friar of the convent at Carlisle.   It covers the period from 1201 to 1346, being a contemporary account of events during the time of Wallace and Bruce, and is considered one of the most valuable records of border history (Bannatyne Club, 1839).

4. The *Scalacronica* of Sir Thomas Gray of Heton.   This is a chronicle of England and Scotland from 1066 to 1362.   The author's father was an esquire under the Sheriff of Lanark at the time of his encounter with William Wallace; and the son has preserved an account of that affair.   The book is especially useful for the period of the Scottish wars with England.   The writer died about 1369.   Probably the best edition is that printed by the Maitland Club in 1836.

5. John of Fordun's *Chronicle of the Scottish Nation*.   This was written in the latter part of the fourteenth century, being brought down in an unfinished state to the year 1385, when its completion was prevented by the death of the author.   The earlier part of the work, being founded to a great

extent on the fictitious chronicles that were written during the twelfth and thirteenth centuries for the main purpose of establishing the remote antiquity of the royal line of Scotland,[13] is largely artificial and not to be depended upon. The authenticated portions of Fordun's history comprise the most of Books IV. and V., and nearly the whole of the *Annals* of Mr. Skene's edition. These are based largely upon the Melrose Chronicle, referred to above.

6. The *Scoti Chronicon* of Walter Bower, or Walter Bowmaker, appeared in 1441, and comprises Fordun's *Chronicle* down to the year 1153, with a continuation by Bower to 1436. It is more especially useful as a contemporary account of the events occurring in the author's lifetime (1385–1449).

7. The *Original Chronicle of Scotland*, by Andrew of Wyntoun. This begins at the Creation and comes down to the year 1408. Its author, born about the middle of the fourteenth century, was elected prior of the monastery of St. Serf's Inch in Loch Leven about 1395, where he continued for nearly twenty years, and afterwards became canon of St. Andrews. The *Chronicle* was completed between the years 1420 and 1424. It is written in verse, and for that reason is not so valuable as it would have been in another form. Still, this writer is more often quoted than any other Scottish historian of the period. Like Bower, he gives a contemporary account of events in the latter half of the fourteenth and beginning of the fifteenth century.

8. The *Book of the Brus*, by John Barbour. The author was born about 1316, and died March 13, 1395, some twenty years after the completion of his book. This work also is in metrical form, but, notwithstanding, it is a most useful contribution to historical literature, and a chief source for the details of the Scottish War of Independence, and of the life of Scotland's greatest warrior and king. It is the great national epic of the country, and occupies a similar place in the literature of Scotland to the *Odyssey* in that of Greece; although perhaps never so popular with the people as the legendary narrative of the achievements of Wallace, which appeared about a century later. Barbour's very full and spirited description of the battle of Bannockburn, by which independence was won, is followed closely by later historians in giving the details of that event.[14] The *Acts and Deeds of Wallace* was the production of a writer who goes by the name of Henry the Minstrel, or Blind Harry. His work consists of a rhyming and fabulous account of the achievements of Scotland's national hero. The full name of the author is unknown. He is supposed to have been a wandering minstrel who, about 1460, set down in writing a connected series of the rhyming doggerel verses which he had been accustomed to sing from house to house. Being written about a century and a half after Wallace's death, the work no doubt embodied all the accumulated traditions and embellishments of the period in which it appeared.[15]

9. The *Auchinleck Chronicle*. This embraces the reign of James II. (1437–1460), and is about the only contemporary record we have of the events of that period. It was preceded by the interesting contemporary

account of the murder of the first James a reprint of which appears in the Appendix to Pinkerton's *History of Scotland.*

NOTES TO CHAPTER XXIII

[1] In this carnage 4000 men perished, according to Langtoft, although his translator says 40,000; 7500 perished, according to Fordun, l. xi., c. 20. Upwards of 8000, according to Hemingford, t. i., p. 91. Matthew Westm., p. 427, says 60,000; but this may have been an error of the transcriber for 6000.

[2] See Appendix Q (The Ragman Roll).

[3] Of Wallace of Elderslie, near Paisley, in Renfrewshire. Such is the opinion generally received. His *Achievements*, written by Blind Harry, has been long a popular book in Scotland. It would be lost labour to search for the age, name, and condition of an author who either knew not history, or who meant to falsify it. (See M'Kenzie, *Lives of Scots Writers,* vol. i., p. 422.) A few examples may serve to prove the spirit of this romancer. He always speaks of Aymer de Valloins, Earl of Pembroke, as a false Scottish knight. He mentions Sir Richard Lundin as one of Wallace's coadjutors at the battle of Stirling, whereas he was of the opposite party, and indeed was, to all appearance, the only man of true judgment in the whole English army. B. vi., c. 4, he says that one Sir Hugh, sister's son of Edward I., went, in the disguise of a herald, to Wallace's camp, was detected, and instantly beheaded; that Wallace surprised Edward's army at Biggar, and with his own hand slew the Earl of Kent; that many thousands of the English fell in the engagement, particularly the second son of the King of England, his brother Sir Hugh, and his two nephews.—Hailes, *Annals of Scotland*, vol. i., p. 269.

[4] Their names were John Comyn, Earl of Buchan, Constable of Scotland; Alexander Comyn of Buchan; Alexander and Robert, the brothers of John Comyn of Badenoch; John Comyn the younger of Badenoch (he became bound to give his son as an hostage); John Comyn of Kilbride; John, Earl of Athole; John de Mentieth, brother of the Earl of Mentieth; Richard Siward, late governor of Dunbar; David de Brechin; William Biset, son and heir of the deceased Robert Biset; Richard Lovel, son and heir of the deceased Hugh Lovel; Godefroy and William de Ros; David the son, and David the brother, of Patrick Graham; John de Glenurhard; Hugh de Airth; John and Randulph de Grant; Laurence de Angus; Alexander Corbet; Brice Tailor; Alan de Lasceles; Herbert de Morhan; Alexander M'Glay (filius Glay); William Mareschal; and John de Drummond.

[5] Those who submitted at Irvine were Robert Bruce, The Steward and his brother, Alexander de Lindesay, Sir Richard de Lundin, and Sir William Douglas. Robert Wisheart, Bishop of Glasgow, negotiated the treaty. Wallace ascribed the conduct of Wisheart to traitorous pusillanimity. In the first heat of resentment, he flew to the Bishop's house, pillaged its effects, and led his family captive.

[6] Quoniam, ut dicebant quidam, qui in eodem conflictu fuerant, si a summo mane usque ad horam undecimam, absque ulla interruptione vel impedimento, transissent, adhuc extrema pars exercitus in parte magna remansisset; nec fuit aptior locus in regno Scotiæ ad concludendum Anglicos in manus Scotorum, et multos in manus paucorum.—W. Hemingburgh (t. i., p. 128). The same writer says that the English army consisted of 1000 horsemen and 50,000 foot (*ibid.*, p. 127).

[7] W. Hemingford says that this army excelled in cavalry. There were 3000 horsemen armed at all points, and upwards of 4000 horsemen in armor, but whose horses were not armed: "Tria millia electorum in equis armatis, præter equitantes armatos in equis non armatis, qui numerabantur plusquam quattuor millia electa." The king desired no infantry except volunteers: their number amounted to 80,000 (t. i., p. 159).

[8] This is related on the credit of the Scottish historians. The English mention it not.

The story, however, is not inconsistent with probability. I cannot say so much for the famous story of the barns of Ayr. It is asserted that Wallace, accompanied by Sir John Graham, Sir John Mentieth, and Alexander Scrymgeour, Constable of Dundee, went into the west of Scotland to chastise the men of Galloway, who had espoused the party of the Comyns and the English ; that, on the 28th August, 1298, they set fire to some granaries in the neighbourhood of Ayr, and burnt the English cantoned in them (A. Blair, p. 5 ; J. Major, fol. 70). This relation is liable to much suspicion. 1. Sir John Graham could have no share in the enterprise, for he was killed at Falkirk 22d July, 1298. 2. Comyn the younger, of Badenoch, was the only man of the name of Comyn who had any interest in Galloway, and he was at that time of Wallace's party. 3. It is not probable that Wallace would have undertaken such an enterprise immediately after the discomfiture at Falkirk. I believe that this story took its rise from the pillaging of the English quarters about the time of the treaty of Irvine in 1297, which, as being an incident of little consequence, I omitted in the course of this history. (See W. Hemingford, t. i., p. 123.)—Hailes, *Annals of Scotland*, vol. i., p. 280.

[9] Walsingham (p. 42) computes the number slain at 60,000 ; W. Hemingford (t. i., p. 165), at 50,000 ; M. Westm. (p. 431), at 40,000 ; Trivet (p. 313), at 20,000 ; Buchanan (l. viii., p. 139), at 10,000.

" It would be tedious and unprofitable to recite all that has been said on this subject by our own writers from Fordun to Abercrombie : How Wallace, Stewart, and Comyn quarreled on the punctilio of leading the van of an army which stood on the defensive ; how Stewart compared Wallace to " an owl with borrowed feathers " ; how the Scottish commanders, busied in this frivolous altercation, had no leisure to form their army : how Comyn traitorously withdrew 10,000 men ; how Wallace, from resentment, followed his example ; how, by such disastrous incidents, the Scottish army was enfeebled, and Stewart and his party abandoned to destruction. Our histories abound in trash of this kind : there is scarcely one of our writers who has not produced an invective against Comyn, or an apology for Wallace, or a lamentation over the deserted Stewart. What dissensions may have prevailed among the Scottish commanders, it is impossible to know. It appears not to me that their dissensions had any influence on their conduct in the day of battle. The truth seems to be this : The English cavalry greatly exceeded the Scottish in numbers, were infinitely better equipped, and more adroit : the Scottish cavalry were intimidated, and fled. Had they remained on the field, they might have preserved their honour ; but they never could have turned the chance of that day. It was natural, however, for such of the infantry as survived the engagement, to impute their disaster to the defection of the cavalry. National pride would ascribe their flight to treachery rather than to pusillanimity. It is not improbable that Comyn commanded the cavalry ; hence a report may have been spread that Comyn betrayed his country ; this report has been embellished by each successive relator. When men are seized with a panic, their commander must from necessity, or will from prudence, accompany them in their flight. Earl Warrenne fled with his army, from Stirling to Berwick ; yet Edward I. did not punish him as a traitor or a coward.

" The tale of Comyn's treachery, and Wallace's ill-timed resentment, may have gained credit, because it is a pretty tale, and not improbable in itself. But it amazes me that the story of the congress of Bruce and Wallace, after the battle of Falkirk, should have gained credit. I lay aside the full evidence which we now possess, ' that Bruce was not, at that time, of the English party, nor present at the battle.' For it must be admitted that our historians knew nothing of those circumstances which demonstrate the impossibility of the congress. But the wonder is, that men of sound judgment should not have seen the absurdity of a long conversation between the commander of a flying army and one of the leaders of a victorious army. When Fordun told the story, he placed ' a narrow but inaccessible glen ' between the speakers. Later historians have substituted the river Garron in the place of the inaccessible glen, and they make Bruce and Wallace talk across the river like two young declaimers from the pulpits in a school of rhetoric."—Hailes, *Annals of Scotland*, vol. i., pp. 286-288.

[10] For some time after that the Earl of Carrick acted a very dubious part. Hemingburgh says that " when he heard of the king's coming [westward, after Falkirk], he fled from his face and burnt the castle of Ayr which he held." But the testimony of both English and Scottish chroniclers is of little value, for it was the object of both, with different motives, to make it appear that Bruce attached himself early to the national cause. There is extant a letter written by Bruce from Turnberry Castle on July 3d, apparently in this year, to Sir John de Langton, Chancellor of England, begging a renewal of the protection to three knights who were with him on the king's service in Galloway. Again, in another document, undated, but apparently written in the late autumn of 1298, Bruce is commanded by King Edward to bring 1000 picked men of Galloway and Carrick to join an expedition about to be made into Scotland. However, as there is some doubt about the date of these papers, Bruce's attitude during 1298 must be held to be uncertain. It is to be noted, however, that when Edward, on returning to England after his victory at Falkirk, made grants of land in Scotland to his followers, Annandale and Carrick, held by the elder and younger Bruce, were not among the lands so disposed of. Nevertheless, the Bruces do not seem to have been in possession of Annandale at this time, for in 1299 Sir Alan FitzWarin defended Lochmaben Castle against the Earl of Carrick from 1st to 25th August. This was the immediate outcome of a notable arrangement come to during that summer, whereby the Earl of Carrick (whom, to avoid confusion, I may hereafter designate by his modern title of Bruce), William de Lamberton, Bishop of St. Andrews, and John Comyn of Badenoch (the " Red Comyn ") constituted themselves guardians of Scotland in the name of King John (de Balliol). Bruce, as the principal guardian, was to have custody of the castles, but he appears to have been still wavering, for we hear nothing definite of his movements till after the year 1300, when Edward led the flower of his chivalry to the invasion of Dumfries and Galloway.—Maxwell, *Dumfries and Galloway*, pp. 77-78.

[11] There were eleven hostages originally, but their ill treatment and sufferings were such that before September 8, 1300, all but one had perished. Their names were : Lachlan Maclachlan ; Donald, son of Thomas Acarson ; Martin, son of Yvo of Slotham ; John MacWilliam, " Brownbeard " ; Gilpatrick Macbreck, son of MacRory ; Niven MacThomas, son of MacRory ; Andrew MacEwen MacGill Rory ; Mathew Macmorris MacSalvi ; Yvo filius Schephert de Killo Osbern (Closeburn); John, son of Duncan Makhou ; and (the sole survivor) Robert MacMaster.

[12] " It cannot be denied that this political and ecclesiastical feeling of nationality was mainly a defensive foreign policy on the part of Scotland. She knew perfectly well that her people were not as homogeneous in their origin as those of England ; that while they might fight under one banner, and call themselves Scots, for the honour and independence of the kingdom, they were internally separated by the most startling differences and discords. In great international conflicts, like Bannockburn or Flodden, the Scottish Celt and the Scottish Teuton might combine to resist or assail a formidable opponent ; but within the realm of Scotland itself the antagonism of race and the difference in their modes of life engendered the fiercest animosities, and made peace and security impossible along the line of the Grampians. The way in which the " Highland Host " went to work among the Covenanters of the western shires is a conspicuous instance of the utter absence of any feeling of kinship or inward national sympathy between the savage marauders of the northern glens and the industrious farmers and traders of the southern plains.

" Not till well on in the eighteenth century — till Jacobitism was no longer a source of alarm to the mass of the people, and only a poetic grief to its adherents — did the sense of distinction of race become dim, and Scotchmen generally begin to imagine that even the uncouth native of a remote Hebridean isle, to whom English was an unknown tongue, was somehow more akin to the weaver of Glasgow or the farmer of the Merse, than was the miner of Durham or the cattle-feeder of Northumberland."—J. M. Ross, *Scottish History and Literature*, p. 12.

[13] It is thus only the early part of Fordun's work which is tainted with this artificially constructed history. With the reign of Kenneth mac Alpin the historical period of Scottish history, in the true sense of the term, may be said to commence, and he had little motive to pervert the history of his successors, while that part of his history which is based upon the work he originally compiled, extending from the accession of Malcolm Canmore to the year 1363 when he put it together, and contained in his fifth book, and in the annals which follow, is one of great value and authority, and must form the basis of any continuous narrative of the history of that period.—Skene, *Introduction to Fordun*, vol. ii., p. lxxviii.

[14] The Brus is a poem, but not a fiction. We conceive that the author has worked up into epic shape and form the proud traditions of an emancipated people, the numberless stories of suffering and success that were then floating about in hall and hut, in monastery and burg. Sometimes he had even conversed with hoary veterans who had survived the agony of the strife.—J. M. Ross, *Scottish History and Literature*, p. 55.

[15] It is difficult from our point of view to approach Blind Harry's poem seriously ; but it would certainly be a mistake to consider it a mere fabricated romance of a peasant minstrel. It is much more than that. It is the garner into which has been gathered all that harvest of popular legend about Wallace which had been ripening for nearly two centuries. We do not suppose that the author was at all scrupulous in his treatment of traditions, or that he shrank from contributing his quota to the general sum of patriotic fiction. Everywhere in the work there is evidence of more than poetical license ; but we are convinced that in the main it recites and re-echoes the "gests" that had enraptured and amazed successive generations of his countrymen. This, we have seen, was the opinion of the learned and critical Major, in whose boyhood Blind Harry wrote ; but no criticism can possibly determine to what extent its "gests" are genuine deeds, or where its history ends and mythology begins. Its outrageous perversions of public and ascertained facts throw a cloud of suspicion over every incident and circumstance in the poem, even when they are of such a nature as not to forbid belief.—J. M. Ross, *Scottish History and Literature*, p. 76.

CHAPTER XXIV

JOHN OF FORDUN'S ANNALS OF WALLACE AND BRUCE

XCVIII

RISE AND FIRST START OF WILLIAM WALLACE

THE same year [1296] William Wallace lifted up his head from his den—as it were—and slew the English sheriff of Lanark, a doughty and powerful man, in the town of Lanark. From that time, therefore, there flocked to him all who were in bitterness of spirit, and weighed down beneath the burden of bondage under the unbearable domination of English despotism; and he became their leader. He was wondrously brave and bold, of goodly mien, and boundless liberality; and, though, among the earls and lords of the kingdom, he was looked upon as low born, yet his fathers rejoiced in the honour of knighthood. His elder brother, also was girded with the knightly belt, and inherited a landed estate which was large enough for his station, and which he bequeathed, as a holding, to his descendants. So Wallace overthrew the English on all sides; and gaining strength daily, he, in a short time, by force, and by dint of his prowess, brought all the magnates of Scotland under his sway, whether they would or not. Such of the magnates, moreover, as did not thankfully obey his commands, he took and browbeat, and handed over to custody, until they should utterly submit to his good pleasure. And when all had thus been subdued, he manfully betook himself to the storming of the castles and fortified towns in which the English ruled; for he aimed at quickly and thoroughly freeing his country and overthrowing the enemy.

XCIX

BATTLE OF STIRLING BRIDGE

In the year 1297 the fame of William Wallace was spread all abroad, and, at length, reached the ears of the king of England; for the loss brought upon his people was crying out. As the king, however, was intent upon many troublesome matters elsewhere, he sent his treasurer, named Hugh of Cressingham, with a large force to repress this William's boldness, and to bring the kingdom of Scotland under his sway. When, therefore, he heard of this man's arrival, the aforesaid William, then busy besieging the English who were in Dundee Castle, straightway intrusted the care and charge of the siege of the castle to the burgesses of that town on pain of loss of life and limb, and with his army marched on, with all haste, towards Strivelyn [Stirling] to meet this Hugh. A battle was then fought, on the 11th of September near Strivelyn, at the bridge over the Forth. Hugh of Cressingham was killed, and all his army put to flight; some of them were slain with the sword, others taken, others drowned in the waters. But, through God, they were all overcome; and the aforesaid William gained a happy victory, with no little praise. Of the nobles, on his side, the noble Andrew of Moray alone, the father of Andrew, fell wounded.

C

WILLIAM WALLACE WINTERS IN ENGLAND

The same year, William Wallace, with his army, wintered in England, from Hallowmas to Christmas; and after having burnt up the whole land of Allerdale, and carried off some plunder, he and his men went back safe and sound. The same year, moreover, on the 20th of August, all the English—regular and beneficed clergy, as well as laymen—were, by this same William, again cast out from the kingdom of Scotland. And the same year, William of Lamberton was chosen bishop of Saint Andrews.

CI

BATTLE OF FALKIRK

In the year 1298, the aforesaid king of England, taking it ill that he and his should be put to so much loss and driven to such straits by William Wallace, gathered together a large army, and, having with him, in his company, some of the nobles of Scotland to help him, invaded Scotland. He was met by the aforesaid William, with the rest of the magnates of that kingdom; and a desperate battle was fought near Falkirk, on the 22nd of July. William was put to flight, not without serious loss both to the lords and to the common people of the Scottish nation. For, on account of the ill-will, begotten of the spring of envy, which the Comyns had conceived towards the said William, they, with their accomplices, forsook the field, and escaped unhurt. On learning their spiteful deed, the aforesaid William, wishing to save himself and his, hastened to flee by another road. But alas! through the pride and burning envy of both, the noble Estates [communitas] of Scotland lay wretchedly overthrown throughout hill and dale, mountain and plain. Among these, of the nobles, John Stewart, with his Brendans; Macduff, of Fife; and the inhabitants thereof, were utterly cut off. But it is commonly said that Robert of Bruce,—who was afterwards king of Scotland, but then fought on the side of the king of England—was the means of bringing about this victory. For, while the Scots stood invincible in their ranks, and could not be broken by either force or stratagem, this Robert of Bruce went with one line, under Anthony of Bek, by a long road round a hill, and attacked the Scots in the rear; and thus these, who had stood invincible and impenetrable in front, were craftily overcome in the rear. And it is remarkable that we seldom, if ever, read of the Scots being overcome by the English, unless through the envy of lords, or the treachery and deceit of the natives, taking them over to the other side.

CII

WILLIAM WALLACE RESIGNS THE OFFICE OF GUARDIAN

But after the aforesaid victory, which was vouchsafed to the enemy through the treachery of Scots, the aforesaid William Wallace, perceiving, by these and other strong proofs, the glaring wickedness of the Comyns and their abettors, chose rather to serve with the crowd, than to be set over them, to their ruin, and the grievous wasting of the people. So, not long after the battle of Falkirk, at the water of Forth, he, of his own accord, resigned the office and charge which he held, of guardian.

CIII

JOHN COMYN BECOMES GUARDIAN OF SCOTLAND

The same year, John Comyn, the son, became guardian of Scotland; and remained in that office until the time when he submitted to the king of England — to-wit., the next year after the struggle at Roslyn. But, within that same time, John of Soulis was associated with him, by John of Balliol, who had then been set free from prison, and was dwelling on his lands of Balliol. Soulis did not long keep his charge and governance; but as he was simple-minded, and not firm enough, bearing many a rebuff, he was looked down upon; so he left Scotland, and withdrew to France, where he died.

CIV

TRUCE GRANTED AT THE INSTANCE OF THE KING OF FRANCE TO THE ESTATES OF THE KINGDOM OF SCOTLAND

In the year 1300, Philip, king of France, sent a cleric, named Pierre de Muncy, and one knight, Jean de Barres, to Edward, king of England, to obtain a truce between Edward himself and the Estates of Scotland. At his instance, the king of England granted a truce to the kingdom of Scotland, from Hallowmas, in the above mentioned year, to the next following Whitsunday. And it was at the instance of the king of France, not as in any way the ally of the kingdom of Scotland, but as his cousin and particular friend, and the friendly peacemaker between the two sides, that he granted this truce. This, moreover, he forced the aforesaid ambassadors to own before he granted the truce.

CV

JOHN OF SOULIS

The same year, John of Soulis, the guardian of Scotland, without mentioning the other guardian, with the advice of the prelates, earls, barons, and other nobles of the Estates of the kingdom of Lothian, despatched the Lord William, Archdeacon of Lothian, Master Baldred Bisset, and William of Eglisham, as commissioners and special envoys to Boniface VIII., then sovereign Pontiff, to break and lay bare unto him the sundry and manifold hardships brought upon the kingdom of Scotland by the enmity of the said king of England; and to get meet relief against his harassing outrages—as is more fully contained in the commission of those ambassadors, a copy whereof, together with that Baldred's pleading against the king of England, and many letters bearing on that lawsuit, is in a pamphlet written by Alan of Montrose.

CVI

THE KING OF ENGLAND SUMMONED TO THE COURT OF ROME

Now the king of England, having been summoned by the Pope, in the year 1301, sent two proofs patent to that same sovereign Pontiff, in order to give him a clear insight into the right which he averred was vested in him, from days of old, to the throne of Scotland. But Baldred, in a lucid discourse, shortly answered all his arguments, plainly showing, by strong proofs and very clear evidence, that they were utterly devoid of truth—as may be seen in his pleading. The same year, a castle, viz., the Pel de Lithcu [Peel of Linlithgow], was built by the king of England.

CVII

CONFLICT OF ROSLYN

On the 27th of July, 1302, took place the great and famous engagement between the Scots and English, at Roslyn, where the English were defeated, though with great difficulty. From the beginning of the first war which ever broke out between the Scots and English, it is said, there never was so desperate a struggle, or one in which the stoutness of knightly prowess shone forth so brightly. The commander and leader in this struggle was John Comyn, the son. Now this was how this struggle came about, and the manner thereof. After the battle fought at Falkirk, the king of England came not in person, for the nonce, this side of the water of Forth; but sent a good large force, which plundered the whole land of Fife, with all the lands lying near the town of Perth, after having killed a great many of the dwellers in those lands. On the return of this force, with countless spoils, that king hied him home again with his host. Now this was brought about, doubtless, by God's agency: for had he made a lengthened stay then, or after the battle of Dunbar and the seizure of King John, he would either have subjugated the whole land of Scotland, and the dwellers therein, to his sway, or made it a waste with naught but floods and stones. But the goodness of God, Who alone tends and heals after wounds, so governed the actions and time of that king, that, being stirred up to battle, and engrossed with sundry wars, he could not put off all other matters, and give himself up to subduing this kingdom. So that king of England went back with his men, having first appointed the officers of the sheriffdoms, and the wardens of the castles, in the districts beyond the water of Forth, which were then fully and wholly subject unto his sway—with the exception of a few outlaws (or, indeed, robbers) of Scottish birth, who were lurking in the woods, and could not, because of their misdeeds, submit to the laws. But John Comyn, then guardian of Scotland, and Simon Fraser, with their followers, day and night did their best to harass and annoy, by their great prowess, the aforesaid king's officers and bailiffs; and from the time of that king's departure, four years and more, the English and the Anglicized Scots were harried by them, in manifold ways, by mutual slaughter and carnage, according to the issue of various wars.

CVIII

When the aforesaid king had got news of this, he sent off a certain nobleman, Ralph Confrere, his treasurer [Ralph de Manton, the Cofferer], a man stout in battle, and of tried judgment and wisdom, with a certain body of chosen knights, thoroughly well armed, to seek out, in every hole and corner, those who troubled and disturbed the king's peace, and not to forbear punishing them with the penalty of death. So they entered Scotland, and went about ranging through the land, until they, at Roslyn, pitched their tents, split up into three lines apart, for want of free camping room. But the aforesaid John Comyn and Simon, with their abettors, hearing of their arrival, and wishing to steal a march rather than have one stolen upon them, came briskly through from Biggar to Roslyn, in one night, with some chosen men, who chose rather death before unworthy subjection to the English nation; and, all of a sudden, they fearlessly fell upon the enemy. But having been, a little before, roused by the sentries, all those of the first line seized their weapons, and manfully withstood the attacking foe. At length, however, the former were overcome. Some were taken, and some slain, while some, again, fled to the other line. But, while the Scots were sharing the booty, another line straightway appeared, in battle-array; so the Scots, on seeing it, slaughtered their prisoners, and armed their own vassals with the spoils of the slain; then, putting away their jaded horses, and taking stronger ones, they fearlessly hastened to the fray. When this second line had been, at length, overcome, though with difficulty, and the Scots thought they had ended their task, there appeared a third, mightier than the former, and more choice in their harness. The Scots were thunderstruck at the sight of them; and being both fagged out in manifold ways,—by the fatigues of travelling, watching, and want of food — and also sore distressed by the endless toil of fighting, began to be weary, and to quail in spirit, beyond belief. But, when the people were thus thrown into bewilderment, the aforesaid John and Simon, with hearts undismayed, took up, with their weapons, the office of preachers; and, comforting them with their words, cheering them with their promises, and, moreover, reminding them of the nobleness of freedom, and the baseness of thraldom, and of the unwearied toil which their ancestors had willingly undertaken for the deliverance of their country, they, with healthful warnings, heartened them to the fray. So, being greatly emboldened by these and such-like words, the Scots laid aside all cowardice, and got back their strength. Then they slaughtered their prisoners, with whose horses and arms they were again — as it were — renewed; and, putting their trust in God, they and their armed vassals marched forward most bravely and dashingly to battle. The shock was so mighty and fierce, that many were run through, and bereft of life; and some of either host, after awful spear-thrusts, savage flail-strokes, and hard cudgelling, withdrew from the ranks, by hundreds, forties, and twenties, to the hills, time after time, fagged out and dazed by the day's fighting. There they would throw back their helmets, and let the winds blow upon them; and after having been thus cooled by the breeze, they would put away their wounded horses, and, mounting other fresh ones, would thus be made stronger against the onslaughts of the foe. So, after this manifold ordeal and awful struggle, the Scots, who, if one looked at the opposite side, were very few in number—as it were a handful of corn or flour compared with the multitude of the sea-sand—by the power, not of man, but of God, subdued their foes, and gained a happy and gladsome victory.

CIX

THE KING OF ENGLAND SCOURS THE PLAINS AND HILLS AND BRINGS THE KINGDOM OF SCOTLAND UNDER PEACEFUL SUBJECTION TO HIMSELF

In revenge for the foregoing outrages, the king of England, with a very large force, both by sea and by land, entered Scotland, in the year 1303, with the deliberate design of once for all fully bringing it and the dwellers therein, under his yoke; or, of sweeping out the inhabitants altogether, and reducing the land itself to an utter and irreclaimable wilderness. Having, therefore, scoured the hills and plains, both on this side of the hills and beyond them, he, in person, reached Lochindorb; and, after making some stay there, he received the submission of the northern districts, and appointed officers of his in all the castles and fortified towns surrendered to him. Returning thence leisurely, he received the submission of all the communities, as well as fortresses and castles they passed through, with none to withstand or attack him; and, after much winding about through the land, he got to Dunfermline, where he lingered a long time, wintering there until Candlemas.[1] The same year, his son and heir, Edward of Carnarvon, Prince of Wales, made a long stay in the town of Perth. Food was in such plenty there, for the whole of the aforesaid time, that a laggen, Scottish measure, of good wine sold for fourpence.

CX

THE ESTATES OF SCOTLAND MAKE THEIR SUBMISSION TO THE KING OF ENGLAND

The same year, after the whole Estates of Scotland had made their submission to the king of England, John Comyn, then guardian, and all the magnates but William Wallace, little by little, one after another, made their submission unto him; and all their castles and towns — except Strivelyn [Stirling] Castle, and the warden thereof — were surrendered unto him. That year, the king kept Lent at Saint Andrews, where he called together all the great men of the kingdom, and held his parliament; and he made such decrees as he would, according to the state of the country—which, as he thought, had been gotten and won for him and his successors forever—as well as about the dwellers therein.

CXI

STIRLING CASTLE BESIEGED BY THE KING OF ENGLAND

Just after Easter, in the year 1304, that same king besieged Strivelyn [Stirling] Castle for three months without a break. For this siege, he commanded all the lead of the refectory of Saint Andrews to be pulled down, and had it taken away for the use of his engines. At last, the aforesaid castle was surrendered and delivered unto him on certain conditions, drawn up in writing, and sealed with his seal. But when he had got the castle, the king belied his troth, and broke through the conditions : for William Oliphant, the warden thereof, he threw bound into prison in London, and kept him a long time in thrall. The same year, when both great and small in the kingdom of Scotland (except William Wallace alone) had made their submission unto him; when the surrendered castles and fortified towns which had formerly been broken down and knocked to pieces, had been all rebuilt, and he had appointed wardens of his own therein; and after all and sundry of Scottish birth had tendered him homage, the king, with the Prince of Wales, and his whole army, returned to England. He left, however, the chief warden as his lieutenant, to amend and control the lawlessness of all the rest, both Scots and English. He did not show his face in Scotland after this.

CXII

RISE OF ROBERT OF BRUCE, KING OF SCOTLAND

After the withdrawal of the king of England, the English nation lorded it in all parts of the kingdom of Scotland, ruthlessly harrying the Scots in sundry and manifold ways, by insults, stripes, and slaughter, under the awful yoke of slavery. But God, in His mercy, as is the wont of His fatherly goodness, had compassion on the woes, the ceaseless crying and sorrow, of the Scots; so He raised up a savior and champion unto them—one of their own fellows, to-wit., named Robert of Bruce. This man, seeing them stretched in the slough of woe, and reft of all hope of salvation and help, was inwardly touched with sorrow of heart; and, putting forth his hand unto force, underwent the countless and unbearable toils of the heat of day, of cold and hunger, by land and sea, gladly welcoming weariness, fasting, dangers, and the snares not only of foes, but also of false friends, for the sake of freeing his brethren.[2]

CXIII

LEAGUE OF KING ROBERT WITH JOHN COMYN

So, in order that he might actually give effect to what he had gladly set his heart upon, for the good of the commonwealth, he humbly approached a certain noble, named John Comyn (who was then the most powerful man in the country), and faithfully laid before him the unworthy thraldom of the country, the cruel and endless tormenting of the people, and his own kind-hearted plan for giving them relief. Though, by right, and according to the laws and customs of the country, the honour of the kingly office and the succession to the governance of the kingdom were known to belong to him before any one else, yet, setting the public advantage before his own, Robert, in all purity and sincerity of purpose, gave John the choice of one of two courses: either that the latter should reign, and wholly take unto himself the kingdom, with its pertinents and royal honours, forever, granting to the former all his own lands and possessions; or that all Robert's lands and possessions should come into the possession of John and his forever, while the kingdom and the kingly honour were left to Robert. Thus, by their mutual advice as well as help, was to be brought to maturity the deliverance of the Scottish nation from the house of bondage and unworthy thraldom; and an indissoluble treaty of friendship and peace was to last between them. John was perfectly satisfied with the latter of the aforesaid courses; and thereupon a covenant was made between them, and guaranteed by means of sworn pledges, and by their indentures with their seals attached thereto. But John broke his word; and, heedless of the sacredness of his oath, kept accusing Robert before the king of England, through his ambassadors and private letters, and wickedly revealing that Robert's secrets. Although, however, Robert was more than once sounded thereupon by the aforesaid king, who even showed him the letters of his adversary who accused him, yet, inspired by God, he always returned an answer such that he over and over again softened the king's rage by his pleasant sayings and skilful words. The king, however, both because he was himself very wily and shrewd, and knew full well how to feign a sham friendship, and also because Robert was the true heir of the kingdom of Scotland, looked upon the latter with mistrust,—the more so because of John's accusations. So, because of his aforesaid grounds for mistrust, Edward bade Robert stay always at court; and he delayed putting him to death — or, at least in prison — only until he could get the rest of this Robert's brothers together, and punish them and him at once, in one day, with sentence of death.

CXIV

KING ROBERT ACCUSED BEFORE THE KING OF ENGLAND BY JOHN COMYN

As the said John's accusations were repeated, at length, one night, while the wine glittered in the bowl, and that king was hastening to sit down with his secretaries, he talked over Robert's death in earnest,—and shortly determined that he would deprive him of life on the morrow. But when the Earl of Gloucester, who was Robert's true and tried friend in his utmost need, heard of this, he hastily, that same night, sent the aforesaid Robert, by his keeper of the wardrobe, twelve pence and a pair of spurs. So the keeper of the wardrobe, who guessed his lord's wishes, presented these things to Robert, from his lord, and added these words: " My lord sends these to you, in return for what he, on his side, got from you yesterday." Robert understood, from the tokens offered him, that he was threatened by the danger of death; so he discreetly gave the pence to the keeper of the wardrobe, and forthwith sent him back to the Earl with greeting in answer, and with thanks. Then, when twilight came on, that night, after having ostentatiously ordered his servants to meet him at Carlisle, with his trappings, on the evening of the following day, he straightway hastened towards Scotland, without delay, and never stopped travelling, day or night, until he was safe from the aforesaid king's spite. For he was under the guidance of One of whom it is written:—" There is no wisdom, no foresight, no understanding against the Lord, Who knoweth how to snatch the good from trial, and mercifully to deliver from danger those that trust in Him."

CXV

DEATH OF JOHN COMYN'S MESSENGER

Now, when Robert was nearing the borders of the marches, there met him a messenger whom, when he sighted him afar off, he suspected, both from the fellow's gait and from his dress, to be a Scot. So, when he got nearer, he asked him whence he came and whither he was making his way. The messenger began to pour forth excuses for his sins; but Robert ordered his vassals to search him. Letters, sealed with Robert's seal about the covenant entered into between him and John Comyn, were found addressed to the king of England through this messenger, and were forthwith pulled out. The messenger's head was thereupon struck off, and God very much to be praised for His guidance in this prosperous journey.

CXVI

DEATH OF WILLIAM WALLACE

In the year 1305, William Wallace was craftily and treacherously taken by John of Menteith, who handed him over to the king of England; and he was, in London, torn limb from limb, and, as a reproach to the Scots, his limbs were hung on towers in sundry places throughout England and Scotland.

25

CXVII

JOHN COMYN'S DEATH

The same year, after the aforesaid Robert had left the king of England and returned home, no less miraculously than by God's grace, a day is appointed for him and the aforesaid John to meet together at Dumfries; and both sides repair to the above-named place. John Comyn is twitted with his treachery and belied troth. The lie is at once given. The evil-speaker is stabbed, and wounded unto death, in the church of the Friars; and the wounded man is, by the friars, laid behind the altar. On being asked by those around whether he could live, straightway his answer is:—" I can." His foes, hearing this, give him another wound:—and thus was he taken away from this world on the 10th of February.[3]

CXVIII

CORONATION OF KING ROBERT BRUCE

Now, when a few days had rolled on, after the said John's death, this Robert of Bruce, taking with him as many men as he could get, hastened to Scone; and, being set on the royal throne, was there crowned, on the 27th of March, 1306, in the manner wherein the kings of Scotland were wont to be invested;—and great was the task he then undertook, and unbearable were the burdens he took upon his shoulders. For, not only did he lift his hand against the king of England, and all partakers with him, but he also launched out into a struggle with all and sundry of the kingdom of Scotland, except a very few well-wishers of his, who, if one looked at the hosts of those pitted against them, were as one drop of water compared with the waves of the sea, or a single grain of any seed with the multitudinous sand. His mishaps, flights, and dangers; hardships and weariness; hunger and thirst; watchings and fastings; nakedness and cold; snares and banishment; the seizing, imprisoning, slaughter, and downfall of his near ones, and—even more—dear ones (for all this had he to undergo, when overcome and routed in the beginning of his war)—no one, now living, I think, recollects, or is equal to rehearsing, all this. Indeed, he is reported to have said to his knights, one day, when worn out by such numberless and ceaseless hardships and dangers:—

> Were I not stirred by Scotland's olden bliss,
> Not for earth's empire would I bear all this.

Moreover, with all the ill-luck and numberless straits he went through with a glad and dauntless heart, were any one able to rehearse his own struggles, and triumphs single-handed—the victories and battles wherein, by the Lord's help, by his own strength, and by his human manhood, he fearlessly cut his way into the columns of the enemy, now mightily bearing these down, and now mightily warding off and escaping the pains of death—he would, I deem, prove that, in the art of fighting, and in vigor of body, Robert had not his match in his time, in any clime. I will, therefore, forbear to describe his own individual deeds, both because they would take up many leaves, and because, though they are undoubtedly true, the time and place wherein they happened, and were wrought, are known to few in these days. But his well-known battles and public exploits will be found set down below, in the years wherein they took place.

BATTLE OF METHVEN

The same year, on the 19th day of June, King Robert was overcome and put to flight, at Methven, by Odomar of Valence, who was then warden of Scotland on behalf of the king of England, and was staying at the then well-walled town of Perth, with a great force of both English and Scots who owed fealty and submission to the king of England. Now, though the foresaid king did not lose many of his men in this struggle, yet, because of the bad beginning, which is often crowned by an unhappy ending, his men began to be disheartened, and the victorious side to be much emboldened by their victory. Then, all the wives of those who had followed the king were ordered to be outlawed by the voice of a herald, so that they might follow their husbands; by reason whereof, many women, both single and married, lurked with their people in the woods, and cleaved to the king, abiding with him, under shelter.

CONFLICT AT DALRY, IN THE BORDERS OF ARGYLE

The same year, while this king was fleeing from his foes, and lurking with his men, in the borders of Athol and Argyle, he was again beaten and put to flight, on the 11th of August, at a place called Dalry. But there, also, he did not lose many of his men. Nevertheless, they were all filled with fear, and were dispersed and scattered throughout various places. But the queen fled to Saint Duthac in Ross, where she was taken by William, Earl of Ross, and brought to the king of England; and she was kept a prisoner in close custody, until the battle of Bannockburn. Nigel of Bruce, however, one of the king's brothers, fled, with many ladies and damsels, to Kyndrumie [Kildrummie] Castle, and was there welcomed, with his companions. But, the same year, that castle was made over to the English through treachery, and Nigel, and other nobles of both sexes, were taken prisoners, brought to Berwick, and suffered capital punishment. The same year, Thomas and Alexander of Bruce, brothers of the aforesaid king, while hastening towards Carrick by another road, were taken at Loch Ryan, and beheaded at Carlisle —and, thus, all who had gone away and left the king, were, in that same year, either bereft of life, or taken and thrown into prison.

SUNDRY TROUBLES WHICH FELL UPON KING ROBERT

The Earl of Lennox and Gilbert of Haya, alone among the nobles, followed the aforesaid king, and became his inseparable companions in all his troubles. And though sometimes, when hard pressed by the pursuing foe, they were parted from him in body, yet they never departed from fealty and love towards him. But, soon after this, it came to pass that the aforesaid king was cut off from his men, and underwent endless woes, and was tossed in dangers untold, being attended at times by three followers, at times, by two; and more often he was left alone, utterly without help. Now passing a whole fortnight without food of any kind to live upon, but raw herbs and water; now walking barefoot, when his shoes became old and worn out;

now left alone in the islands; now alone, fleeing before his enemies; now slighted by his servants; he abode in utter loneliness.   An outcast among the nobles, he was forsaken; and the English bade him be sought for through the churches like a lost or stolen thing.   And thus he became a byword and a laughing-stock for all, both far and near, to hiss at.   But when he had borne these things for nearly a year alone, God, at length, took pity on him; and, aided by the help and power of a certain noble lady, Christiana of the Isles, who wished him well, he, after endless toils, smart, and distress, got back, by a roundabout way, to the earldom of Carrick.   As soon as he had reached that place, he sought out one of his castles, slew the inmates thereof, destroyed the castle, and shared the arms and other spoils among his men.   Then, being greatly gladdened by such a beginning after his long spell of ill-luck, he got together his men, who had been scattered far and wide; and, crossing the hills with them in a body, he got as far as Inverness, took the castle thereof with a strong hand, slew its garrison, and levelled it with the ground.   In this very way dealt he with the rest of the castles and strongholds established in the north, as well as with their inmates, until he got, with his army, as far as Slenach [Slaines].

CXXII

ROUT AT SLENACH

In the year 1307, John Comyn, Earl of Buchan, with many nobles, both English and Scots, hearing that Robert, king of Scotland, was, with his army, at Slenach, marched forward to meet him and give him battle.   But when they saw the king, with his men, over against them, ready for the fray, they halted; and, on Christmas Day, overwhelmed with shame and confusion, they went back, and asked for a truce, which the king kindly granted.   After the truce had been granted, the king abode there, without fear, for eight days; and he there fell into a sickness so severe, that he was borne on a pallet whithersoever he had occasion to be moved.

CXXIII

DEATH OF EDWARD I., KING OF ENGLAND

The same year died Edward I., king of England, on the 5th of April, at Burgh-upon-Sands.   This king stirred up war as soon as he had become a knight, and lashed the English with awful scourgings; he troubled the whole world by his wickedness, and roused it by his cruelty; by his wiles, he hindered the passage to the Holy Land; he invaded Wales; he treacherously subdued unto him the Scots and their kingdom; John of Balliol, the king thereof, and his son, he cast into prison; he overthrew churches, fettered prelates, and to some he put an end in filthy dungeons; he slew the people, and committed other misdeeds without end.   He was succeeded by his son Edward II., who was betrothed to Elizabeth, daughter of Philip, king of France.

CXXIV

ROUT AT INVERURIE

In the year 1308, John Comyn and Philip of Mowbray, with a great many Scots and English, were again gathered together, at Inverurie.   But when King Robert heard of this, though he had not yet got rid of his grievous sickness, he arose from his pallet, whereon he was always carried about, and commanded his men to arm him and set him on horseback. When this had been done, he too, with a cheerful countenance, hastened with his army against the enemy, to the battle-ground—although, by reason of his great weakness, he could not go upright, but with the help of two men to prop him up. But when the opposing party saw him and his ready for battle, at the mere sight of him they were all sore afraid and put to flight; and they were pursued as far as Fivy, twelve leagues off. So when the rout was over, and the enemy were overthrown and scattered, King Robert ravaged the earldom of Buchan with fire; and, of the people, he killed whom he would, and, to those whom he would have live, he granted life and peace. Moreover, even as, from the beginning of his warfare until the day of this struggle, he had been most unlucky in the upshot of every battle, so, afterwards, there could not be found a man more fortunate in his fights. And, from that day, the king gained ground, and became ever more hale himself; while the adverse party was daily growing less.

CXXV

VICTORY OVER THE GALWEGIANS AT THE RIVER DEE

The same year, at the Feast of Saint Peter and Saint Paul, Donald of the Isles gathered together an imposing host of foot, and marched up to the river Dee. He was met by Edward of Bruce, who overcame the said Donald and all the Galwegians. In this struggle, Edward slew a certain knight named Roland, with many of the nobles of Galloway; and arrested their leader, the said Donald, who had taken to flight. After this, he burnt up the island.

CXXVI

CONFLICT OF KING ROBERT WITH THE MEN OF ARGYLE

The same year, within a week after the Assumption of the blessed Virgin Mary, the king overcame the men of Argyle, in the middle of Argyle, and subdued the whole land unto himself. Their leader, named Alexander of Argyle, fled to Dunstafinch [Dunstaffnage] Castle, where he was, for some time, besieged by the king. On giving up the castle to the king, he refused to do him homage. So a safe-conduct was given to him, and to all who wished to withdraw with him; and he fled to England, where he paid the debt of nature.

CXXVII

In the year 1310, so great was the famine and dearth of provisions in the kingdom of Scotland, that, in most places, many were driven, by the pinch of hunger, to feed on the flesh of horses and other unclean cattle.

CXXVIII

In the year 1311, the aforesaid King Robert, having put his enemies to flight at every place he came to, and having taken their fortresses, and levelled them with the ground, twice entered England, and wasted it, carrying off untold booty, and making huge havoc with fire and sword. Thus, by the power of God, the faithless English nation, which had unrighteously racked many a man, was now, by God's righteous judgment, made to undergo awful scourgings; and, whereas it had once been victorious, now it sank vanquished and groaning.

CXXIX

THE TOWN OF PERTH TAKEN BY KING ROBERT

On the 8th of January, 1312, the town of Perth was taken with the strong hand by that same King Robert; and the disloyal people, both Scots and English, were taken, dragged, and slain with the sword; and thus,—

> Fordone, they drained the gall themselves had brewed.

The king in his clemency, spared the rabble, and granted forgiveness to those that asked it; but he destroyed the walls and ditches, and consumed everything else with fire. The same year, the castles of Buth, Dumfries, and Dalswinton, with many other strongholds, were taken with the strong hand and levelled with the ground. The same year, the town of Durham was, in great part, burnt down by the Scots; Piers de Gaveston was killed by the Earl of Lancaster; and Edward, the first-born of the king of England, was born at Windsor.

CXXX

ROXBURGH CASTLE TAKEN BY JAMES OF DOUGLAS

On Fasten's Even, in the year 1313, Roxburgh Castle was happily taken by the Lord James of Douglas, and, on the 14th of March, Edinburgh Castle, by the Lord Thomas Randolph, Earl of Moray; and their foes were overcome. The same year, the king entered the Isle of Man, took the castles thereof, and victoriously brought the land under his sway.

CXXXI

CONFLICT AT BANNOCKBURN

Edward II., king of England, hearing of these glorious doings of King Robert, and seeing the countless losses and endless evils brought upon him and his by that king, gathered together, in revenge for the foregoing, a very strong army both of well-armed horsemen and of foot—crossbowmen and archers, well skilled in warcraft. At the head of this body of men, and trusting in the glory of man's might, he entered Scotland in hostile wise; and, laying it waste on every side, he got as far as Bannockburn. But King Robert, putting his trust, not in a host of people, but in the Lord God, came, with a few men, against the aforesaid king of England, on the blessed John the Baptist's day, in the year 1314, and fought against him, and put him and his to flight, through the help of Him to whom it belongeth to give the victory.[4] There, the Earl of Gloucester and a great many other nobles were killed; a great many were drowned in the waters, and slaughtered in pitfalls; a great many, of divers ranks, were cut off by divers kinds of death; and many—a great many—nobles were taken, for whose ransom not only were the queen and other Scottish prisoners released from their dungeons, but even the Scots themselves were, all and sundry, enriched very much. Among these was also taken John of Brittany, for whom the queen and Robert, bishop of Glasgow, were exchanged. From that day forward, moreover, the whole land of Scotland not only always rejoiced in victory over the English, but also overflowed with boundless wealth.

CXXXII

EDWARD CROSSES INTO IRELAND

Edward of Bruce, King Robert's brother, entered Ireland, with a mighty hand, in the year 1315; and having been set up as king there, he destroyed the whole of Ulster, and committed countless murders. This, however, some little time after, brought him no good. In the year 1316, King Robert went to Ireland, to the Southern parts thereof, to afford his brother succor and help. But, in this march, many died of hunger, and the rest lived on horse-flesh. The king, however, at once returned, and left his brother there. In the year 1317, the cardinals were plundered, in England, by Robert of Middleton, who was, soon after, taken, and drawn by horses, in London.

CXXXIII

THE TOWN OF BERWICK TAKEN

In the year 1318, Thomas Randolph, Earl of Moray, destroyed the northern parts of England; and, on the 28th of March of the same year, the Scots took the town of Berwick, which had been, for twenty years, in the hands of the English. On the 14th of October of the same year was fought the battle of Dundalk, in Ireland, in which fell the Lord Edward of Bruce, and a good many Scottish nobles with him. The cause of this war was this: Edward was a very mettlesome and high-spirited man, and would not dwell together with his brother in peace, unless he had half the kingdom to himself; and for this reason was stirred up in Ireland, this war, wherein, as already stated, he ended his life.

CXXXIV

BERWICK BESIEGED BY THE KING OF ENGLAND

In the year 1319, on the day of the finding of the Holy Cross, Edward, king of England, besieged the town of Berwick; but, meeting with no success, he quickly retreated in great disorder. The same year, the Earl of Moray burnt up the northern parts of England, as far as Wetherby; and, at the end of the month of August, he pitched his tents at Boroughbridge.

CXXXV

TREACHERY OF WILLIAM OF SOULIS AND HIS ADHERENTS

In the beginning of the month of August, 1320, Robert, king of Scotland, held his parliament at Scone. There, the lord William of Soulis and the Countess of Stratherne, were convicted of the crime of high treason, by conspiring against the aforesaid king; and sentence of perpetual imprisonment was passed upon them. The lords David of Brechin, Gilbert of Malerb, John of Logie, knights, and Richard Broune, esquire, having been convicted of the aforesaid conspiracy, were first drawn by horses, and, in the end, underwent capital punishment. The lords Eustace of Maxwell, Walter of

Barclay, sheriff of Aberdeen, and Patrick of Graham, knights, Hamelin of Troupe, and Eustice of Retreve [Rattray] esquires, were accused of the same crime, but were not found guilty in any way.   It so happened, also, at the same time, that when Roger of Mowbray had been released from the trammels of the flesh, his body was taken down thither, and convicted of conspiracy; whereupon it was condemned to be drawn by horses, hanged on the gallows, and beheaded.   But the king had ruth, and was stirred with pity: so he yielded him up to God's judgment, and commanded that the body of the deceased should be handed over for burial by the Church, without having been put to any shame.   The same year, on the 17th of March, our lord the Pope's legates came to the king of Scotland, at Berwick.

CXXXVI

In the year 1321, there was a very hard winter, which distressed men, and killed nearly all animals.   The same year, the Earl of Moray destroyed the northern parts of England, and the bishopric of Durham, with famine, fire, and sword.

CXXXVII

THE KING OF SCOTLAND CROSSES INTO ENGLAND, AND THE KING OF ENGLAND INTO SCOTLAND

On the 1st of July, 1322, Robert, king of Scotland, entered England with a strong hand, and laid it waste for the most part, as far as Stanemore, together with the county of Lancaster.   The same year, on the 12th of August, Edward II., king of England, entered Scotland with a great army of horse and foot, and a large number of ships, and got as far as the town of Edinburgh; for he sought to have a struggle and come to blows with the aforesaid king.   But the king of Scotland, wisely shunning an encounter for the nonce, skilfully drew away from his army all animals fit for food.   So, after fifteen days, Edward being sore pressed by hunger and starvation, went home again dismayed, having first sacked and plundered the monasteries of Holyrood in Edinburgh, and of Melrose, and brought them to great desolation.   For, in the said monastery of Melrose, on his way back from Edinburgh, the lord William of Peebles, prior of that same monastery, one monk who was then sick, and two lay-brethren, were killed in the dormitory by the English, and a great many monks were wounded unto death.   The Lord's Body was cast forth upon the high altar, and the pyx wherein it was kept was taken away.   The monastery of Dryburgh was utterly consumed with fire, and reduced to dust; and a great many other holy places did the fiery flames consume, at the hands of the aforesaid king's forces.   But God rewarded them therefor, and it brought them no good.   For, the same year, on the 1st of October, King Robert marched into England in hostile wise, and utterly laid it waste, as far as York, sacking the monasteries, and setting fire to a great many cities and towns.   But Edward II., king of England, came against him at Biland, with a great force, both of paid soldiers from France, and others hired from a great many places, and of natives of the kingdom itself; but he was put to flight at the above-named place, in the heart of his own kingdom, not without great slaughter of his men, and in no little disorder.   Out of his army, John of Brittany, Henry of Stibly [Sully], and other nobles, not a few, fled to the monastery of Rivaulx, and were there taken; and they were afterwards ransomed for sums untold. Thus, the king of Scotland having gained a gladsome victory, went home again, with his men, in great joy and honour.   The same year, on the 1st of October, Andrew of Barclay was taken, and, having been convicted of treachery, underwent capital punishment.

CXXXVIII

AMBASSADORS SENT BY THE KING OF SCOTLAND TO THE POPE AND THE KING OF FRANCE

In the year 1325, ambassadors were sent by Robert, king of Scotland, to treat for a renewal of the friendship and alliance formerly struck up between the kings of France and Scotland; and to restore them in force forever, that they might last for all time unto them and their successors; and also that he might be at one, and come to a good understanding, with the Holy Roman Church, which had, through the insinuations of enemies, been somewhat irritated against the king and kingdom.   So when all this business had been happily despatched, these messengers sped safely home again.   In that year —on Monday, the 5th of March, to wit, in the first week of Lent—David, King Robert's son, and the heir of Scotland, who succeeded his father in the kingdom, was born in the monastery of Dunfermline, after complines.

CXXXIX

THE QUEEN OF ENGLAND BRINGS HIRED SOLDIERS INTO ENGLAND

In the year 1326, the lady Elizabeth, queen of England, brought a great many hired soldiers from sundry parts of the world; and, after having taken her husband, King Edward, and thrown him into prison, she bade Hugh de Spensa [Spencer] and his father, be hanged on the gallows, and be torn limb from limb.   Because of this outbreak, a bishop was beheaded in London; and a great many earls, barons, and nobles were everywhere condemned to a most shameful death.   The same year, Edward III., then fifteen years old, on his father being thrown into prison, was, though unwilling, crowned king of England, at Candlemas.   That year, moreover, was, all over the earth, beyond the memory of living man, fruitful and plentyful in all things, to overflowing.   The same year, the whole Scottish clergy, the earls and barons, and all the nobles, were gathered together, with the people, at Cambuskenneth, and, in the presence of King Robert himself, took the oaths to David, King Robert's son and heir,—and to Robert Stewart, the aforesaid king's grandson, in case that same David died childless.   There, also, Andrew of Moray took to wife the lady Christina, that king's sister.

CXL

MESSENGERS SENT TO THE KING OF SCOTLAND BY THE ENGLISH

In the year 1327, the English sent messengers to the king of Scotland, under a show of wishing to treat for a secure peace.   But though they met together more than once, they made no way.   At length their double-dealing was laid bare, and the Scots entered the northern parts of England, with a strong hand, on the 15th of June, and wasted it with fire and sword.   The same year, in the month of August, the earl of Moray and James of Douglas, with many Scottish nobles, invaded England, with arms in their hands, and after having brought great loss upon the English, pitched their tents in a certain narrow place named Weardale; while, over against them, and at the outlet of the road, as it were, over 100,000 English troops were posted round the Scots.   There the armies lay, for eight days, in sight of each other, and daily harassed one another with mutual slaughter; but they shunned a hand-to-hand battle.   At length, however, the Scots, like weary warriors, sought an opportunity of saving themselves; and, having struck down in death many of the foe, and taken a great many English and Hainaulters, they returned home sound and safe, by a roundabout road, by night.

CXLI

The same year, a few days after their retreat, the king of Scotland besieged Norham Castle, and, soon after, Alnwick Castle, one after the other; and, in that siege of Norham, William of Montealt, knight, John of Clapham, and Robert of Dobery, were killed through their own want of skill. The same year, on the 17th of March, ambassadors were sent by the king of England to the king of Scotland, at Edinburgh, to arrange and treat for a firm and lasting peace, which should abide for all time.   So, after sundry negotiations, and the many and various risks of war incurred by both kingdoms, the aforesaid kings there came to an understanding together about an indissoluble peace; and the chiefs and worthies of either kingdom tendered their oaths thereto, which were to last unshaken for all time, swearing upon the soul of each king faithfully to keep all and sundry things, as they are more fully contained under certain articles of the instruments thereof, drawn up on either side as to the form of the peace.   And, that it might be a true peace, which should go on without end between them, and between their respective successors, the king of Scotland, of his own free and unbiassed will, gave and granted 30,000 merks in cash to the king of England, for the losses he himself had brought upon the latter and his kingdom; and the said king of England gave his sister, named Joan, to King Robert's son and heir, David, to wife, for the greater security of peace, and the steady fostering of the constancy of love.

CXLII

ESPOUSAL OF KING DAVID—DEATH OF WILLIAM OF LAMBERTON, BISHOP OF SAINT ANDREWS

On the 17th of July, 1328, David, King Robert's son and heir, was, to the unspeakable joy of the people of either kingdom, married to Joan, sister of Edward III., king of England, at Berwick, in presence of Elizabeth, the girl's mother, then queen of England.   The same year died William of Lamberton, bishop of Saint Andrews.

CXLIII

DEATH OF KING ROBERT OF BRUCE

On the 7th of June, 1329, died Robert of Bruce, of goodly memory, the illustrious King of Scots, at Cardross, in the twenty-fourth year of his reign. He was, beyond all living men of his day, a valiant knight.

CXLIV

DEATH OF JAMES OF DOUGLAS

On the 26th of August, 1330, James of Douglas and the king of Spain gathered together the hosts which were flocking from different parts of the world, in aid of the Holy Land, and warred down the Sultan, and number-less Saracens with him; and when these had been overcome and put to flight, after a great many of them had been killed, and the booty had been shared, the said king went back safely, with his army. But the aforesaid James, alas! kept a very few with him, as his army; and as this was by no means hidden from another Sultan, who was lurking in ambush, the latter, with his men, started out from his hiding place, and challenged James to battle. No sooner had the said James recognized his army and banners afar off, than, in his fearlessness, he dashingly charged them with his men. A great many Saracens were there slain; and James himself ended his days there in bliss, while he and his were struggling for Christ's sake. With him, a certain William of St. Clair, and Robert Logan, knights, and a great many others, lost their lives. This James was, in his day, a brave hammerer of the English; and the Lord bestowed so much grace upon him in his life, that he everywhere triumphed over the English.

CXLV

CORONATION OF KING DAVID

On the 24th of November, 1331, David, son and heir of King Robert, was anointed King of Scots, and crowned at Scone, by the lord James Bennet, bishop of Saint Andrews, specially appointed thereunto by a Bull of the most holy father John XXII., then sovereign Pontiff. We do not read that any of the kings of Scotland, before this David, were anointed or with such solemnity crowned. The same day, John Stewart, Earl of Angus—Thomas Randolph, son and heir of Thomas Earl of Moray—and other nobles of the kingdom of Scotland, received the order of knighthood.

NOTES TO CHAPTER XXIV

[1] By examining the dates of instruments in Prynne and Rymer, we may, with tolerable exactness, ascertain the progress of Edward during this fatal year : At Rokesburgh, 21st May, 1303 ; Edinburgh, 4th June ; Linlithgow, 6th June ; Clackmannan, 12th June ; Perth, 28th June–10th July ; An instrument in Fœdera, t. ii. p. 934, is dated Perth, 10th June, 1303 ; but this is a mistake instead of 10th July, as will appear from comparing it with a relative instrument (*ibid.*), Aberdeen, 24th August ; Kinlos in Moray, 20th September–10th October ; Dundee, 20th October ; Kinros, (erroneously printed Kinlos,) 10th November ; Dumfermline, 11th December. Hence we may conclude that Edward crossed the Forth near Clackmannan, and that the siege of the castle of Brechin happened in the interval be-tween 10th July and 24th August. As Edward was at Aberdeen 24th August, and at Kinlos in Moray 20th September and 10th October, there is a probability, at least, that he never marched his army into Caithness. While residing in Moray, he had a view of the coast of Caithness. He may, perhaps, have crossed over in a ship, from curiosity. This may account for the expression of historians, "that Edward went as far north as Caithness." The truth is, that, at that time, the country to the north of Ross-shire was of small account in the political system of Scotland—Hailes, *Annals of Scotland*, vol. i., p. 303.

² " Posterity ought to remember the chief associates of Bruce in his arduous attempt to restore the liberties of Scotland.

" They were, William of Lambyrton, Bishop of St Andrew's ; Robert Wisheart, Bishop of Glasgow ; the Abbot of Scone ; the four brothers of Bruce, Edward, Nigel, Thomas, and Alexander ; his nephew, Thomas Randolph of Strathdon ; his brother-in-law, Christopher Seaton of Seaton ; Malcolm (5th) Earl of Lennox ; John of Strathbogie (10th) Earl of Athole ; Sir James Douglas ; Gilbert de la Haye of Errol, and his brother Hugh de la Haye ; David Barclay of Cairns of Fife ; Alexander Fraser, brother of Simon Fraser of Oliver Castle ; Walter de Somerville of Linton and Carnwath ; David of Inchmartin ; Robert Boyd ; and Robert Fleming ; Randolph, afterwards Earl of Moray ; Seaton, ancestor of the Duke of Gordon, Earl of Winton, Earl of Dunfermline, and Viscount Kingston ; De la Haye, of Earl of Errol ; Fraser of Lord Lovat and Lord Salton ; Somerville, of Lord Somerville ; Inchmartin, of Earl of Findlater, Earl of Airley, and Lord Banff ; Boyd, of Earl of Kilmarnock ; Fleming of Earl of Wigton. Matth. Westm., p. 452, adds Alan Earl of Mentieth. Nigel Campbell, the predecessor of the Duke of Argyle, etc., and Fraser of Oliver Castle, were also engaged in the cause ; but it does not appear that they assisted at the coronation of Robert I.—To this list David Moray, Bishop of Moray, might be added. The English asserted that he preached to the people of his diocese, ' that it was no less meritorious to rise in arms for supporting the cause of Bruce, than to engage in a crusade against the Saracens.' "—Hailes, *Annals of Scotland*, vol ii., pp. 2, 3.

³ " Bruce repaired to Dumfries, where Comyn happened at that time to reside. Bruce requested an interview with him in the convent of the Minorites. There they met before the great altar. Bruce passionately reproached Comyn for his treachery. 'You lie,' cried Comyn. Bruce stabbed him instantly. Hastening out of the sanctuary, he called ' To horse.' His attendants, Lindesay and Kirkpatrick, perceiving him pale, and in extreme agitation, anxiously enquired, how it was with him ? ' Ill,' replied Bruce, 'I doubt I have slain Comyn.' ' You doubt ? ' cried Kirkpatrick ; and rushing into the church, fixed his dagger in Comyn's heart (10th February 1306).

" Sir Robert Comyn generously attempted to defend his kinsman, and shared his fate.

" The justiciaries were holding their court at Dumfries when this strange event happened. Imagining their lives to be sought, they barricaded the doors. Bruce ordered the house to be fired. They surrendered. He permitted them to depart out of Scotland unmolested.

" Such is the account of this unhappy catastrophe delivered by our writers. The English relate its circumstances in a different, but not more probable manner. I think that the historians of both nations have erred in their accounts, and that the real nature of this fatal quarrel is still unknown."—Hailes, *Annals of Scotland*, vol i., pp. 320, 321.

⁴ " March 26. Edward II. made great preparations for the relief of the castle of Stirling. He invited many Irish chiefs to his aid ; and he summoned his English subjects in Ireland to join the army under the command of the Earl of Ulster.

" May 27. He ordered a great army to be assembled for the succour of the castle of Stirling.

" Bruce assembled his army at Torwood, between Falkirk and Stirling ; and he chose the ground on which he was to combat the English.

" June 23. Edward II., with his army, came in sight of the Scots, who were posted between Stirling and the stream called Bannockburn. There were skirmishes, this day, in which the Scots had the advantage. Bruce slew Henry de Bohun in single combat.

" June 24. The two nations fought. The English were totally routed. Edward II. fled sixty miles without halting. The Earl of March threw open the gates of his castle of Dunbar to Edward, and conveyed him by sea into England,

" The castle of Stirling surrendered according to treaty. Moubray, the governor, entered into the service of Scotland.

" The castle of Bothwell was besieged. The Earl of Hereford, who had taken refuge there after the rout at Bannockburn, capitulated.

" Edward Bruce, and Douglas, wasted Northumberland, laid the bishopric of Durham under contribution, penetrated to Richmond in Yorkshire, burnt Appleby, etc., and returned home loaded with plunder.

" August 1. Edward II. summoned a parliament at York, in order to concert measures for the public security.

" August 10. He appointed the Earl of Pembroke, late guardian of Scotland, to be guardian of the country between Tweed and the Trent.

" September 18. Bruce having made overtures for peace, Edward II. appointed commissioners to treat with the Scots.

" October 17. The Scots again invaded England, and levied contributions.

" John Baliol died, leaving his son Edward heir to his fatal pretensions."—Hailes, Anno 1314.

CHAPTER XXV

FROM BRUCE TO FLODDEN

KING ROBERT BRUCE was succeeded by his son David, then a boy seven years of age, who was crowned at Scone November 24, 1331. Randolph, Earl of Moray, became regent, in accordance with King Robert's settlement. He died, however, in July, 1332, and was followed in the regency by the Earl of Mar, a man of vastly inferior ability.

During his rule, Edward Baliol, a son of the deposed King John, secured the assistance of England and laid claim to the Scottish throne for himself. He landed in Fifeshire with an army of 4400. Through the inefficiency of the regent and his associates, the Scotch armies failed to oppose this invader, and Baliol was actually crowned as king, at Scone, less than two months later. Seven years of civil war followed his usurpation, largely fomented and encouraged by the English king, Edward III., who, during this time, made four successful invasions of Scotland.

Sir Andrew Moray, of Bothwell, succeeded to the regency in 1334. He was an honest and successful leader, and in 1335 defeated and killed the Earl of Athole in Aberdeenshire. After a long struggle against his country's enemies, he died in 1338, and was succeeded by the Steward of Scotland, a son of King Robert Bruce's daughter Marjory, and of Walter, the sixth Steward. In 1337, Edward III. advanced his claim to the throne of France. Baliol, being left to his own resources, became an object of suspicion and hatred among the Scotch. In 1339, he fled to and became a pensioner of England.

The Steward thereupon laid siege to Perth, where Baliol's forces were quartered, and in August, 1339, it capitulated. During that year, Stirling and all the northern castles were recovered, but those of Edinburgh, Roxburgh, Jedburgh, Berwick, and others remained in the hands of the English. Edinburgh Castle was retaken in April, 1341.

In 1346, King David assembled an army at Perth, and, marching south of the Border, fought the English near Durham on October 17th. In this battle the Scots were defeated, and most of their leaders captured — the King among the number; but the Steward escaped with a portion of his army. The prisoners were taken to London, where the Earl of Menteith was executed as a traitor.

King David continued a prisoner in England until 1357, when he was permitted to return, the Scotch having agreed to pay the English for his ransom the sum of 100,000 merks. David II. had had no children by his wife. His long residence in England, together with the natural weakness of his character, brought him readily under English influence, and led him, in 1363, to suggest to the Scottish Parliament that it should choose as his successor one of the sons of the king of England. Parliament rejected this proposition with contempt, as well as a later one inimical to Scottish independence which was submitted by David in 1366.

David died in 1371, and was succeeded by his nephew, the Steward, who was crowned at Scone, March 26, 1371, as Robert II. During the next ten or twelve years the Scots succeeded in driving the English invaders completely out of the kingdom. The Ancient League between Scotland and France was renewed in 1371. In 1385 the French sent a force of 2000 men to Scotland to assist the Scots in an invasion of England. The French and Scottish ideas of politeness and methods of warfare differed so widely, however, that their leaders soon became involved in disputes, and the French returned to their own land.

A truce was concluded with England in 1389 by the Scots and French, which continued for ten years.

Robert II. died in April, 1390, and was succeeded by his oldest son, John, who was crowned under the title of Robert III. A younger son of Robert II. was the Earl of Fife, afterwards known as the Duke of Albany, who had acted as regent during the later years of his father's reign, and retained his power under the name of Governor of the Kingdom, after his brother came to the throne. A third brother, the Earl of Buchan, known in history as the Wolf of Badenoch, ruled the northern provinces, and became notorious for his cruelty. The king was of too timid and peaceful a nature to restrain the lawlessness of his nobles. Indeed, he found it necessary to enter into bonds with many of them for the protection of himself and his heirs, and to purchase immunity and allegiance from them by grants of money. The Duke of Albany, Lord Stuart of Brechin, Lord Murdoch Stuart, Sir William Lindsay, Sir John Montgomery, and many others were parties to bonds of this character with the King.

In 1398, by reason of the infirmity or imbecility of King Robert III., Parliament appointed his oldest son, the Duke of Rothesay, as regent for three years, under the title of Lieutenant of the Kingdom. Rothesay's uncle, the Duke of Albany, plotted to destroy that prince, and in 1401 had him seized and imprisoned in the castle of Falkland, where he died of starvation. Albany then resumed his former position as Governor of the Kingdom.

The king's second son, James, then fourteen years of age, was sent to France for safety. He sailed in March, 1405, but his vessel was captured by an English ship, and he was carried to London and imprisoned in the Tower. Robert III. died April 4, 1406. Albany was elected as regent and continued to rule the kingdom until his death, in September, 1419. His son, Murdoch Stuart, then succeeded to the office of Governor.

King James remained a prisoner in England until 1424, when, Scotland having agreed to pay for his ransom the sum of 40,000 pounds, he was permitted to return.

James I. entered Scotland on April 1, 1424, and was crowned king at Scone on the 21st day of the following month. He immediately began to lay plans for breaking the power of the nobles, and within a year proceeded to carry them into execution.

He assembled a Parliament at Perth, March 12, 1425. For eight days it was engaged in passing laws designed to restrain the nobles. On the ninth day the Duke of Albany was seized and imprisoned, with many of the chief nobles. A court was held at Stirling on the 24th of May. Walter Stuart, the eldest son of the Duke of Albany, was accused of robbery, convicted, condemned, and beheaded. The next day, Albany himself, with his second son and the Earl of Lennox, was tried, convicted, sentenced to death, and executed.

In 1427, James, having restored order in the Lowlands, proceeded north to Inverness, where he summoned the Lord of the Isles and fifty of the Highland chiefs to attend his Parliament. They attended, were instantly seized and imprisoned, and many of them were executed. The Lord of the Isles, having made submission, was released. But immediately after the departure of the king he revolted, and attacked Inverness. The king returned, fought and defeated him in Lochaber, and kept up such a vigorous warfare against him that the insurgent was obliged to surrender. In 1429 he was imprisoned in the castle of Tantallon.

James sought to restrain his nobles from oppressing the people, to make them more dependent upon the Crown, and to rule the kingdom through Parliament. In his short reign Parliament was assembled fifteen times and over one hundred and sixty statutes were passed, many of them dealing with the reform of the administration of justice.

In 1431, James, continuing his purpose of reducing the power of the nobles, appropriated to the Crown certain lands which had been alienated by Albany; and in 1435 confiscated the estates of the Earl of March, whose title was tainted on account of his father's treason. The dispossessed earl and his family retired to England.

About this time, Duncan Stuart, Earl of Mar, died, and his estates were seized by the Crown, on the ground of his illegitimacy. The Scottish nobles were now alarmed and enraged at the proceedings of the king. They formed a plot to murder him. The chief actor in the conspiracy was one Sir Robert Graham. He had once proposed in open Parliament that the king be seized and put into confinement; and he suffered the loss of all his lands as a punishment. Graham's partners in this plot were Walter Stuart, Earl of Athole, a son of Robert II., and Robert Stuart, a grandson of Athole's, who was then chamberlain to the king.

The Court had gone to hold Christmas at Perth, in the Monastery of the Dominicans, or Black Friars. Here, about midnight, on February 20, 1437, the king prepared to retire to rest. He was standing at the fire in his gown, talking with the queen and the other ladies, who had not yet withdrawn.

Stuart, the false chamberlain, had removed the bolts of the doors, which made communication in the interior of the building easy.

When about to retire, James "harkyned and hard grete noise without, and grete clateryng of harnych, and men armyd, with grete sight of torches. . . . And, sodenly, the Quene, with all the other ladis and gentilwomen, rane to the chaumber dure, and fonde hit opyne; and they wold have shutt hit, but the lokes wer so blundrid that thay nethir cowth ne myght shutt hit." The king besought the women to obstruct all entrance as long as they were able. Running to the window he found that it was too strongly barred by iron rods to permit of egress. He then seized the fire tongs, pried up a flag-stone, and descended to a private vault beneath the floor. The assassins rushed through the halls, fearing their victim had escaped. But one, Thomas Chambers, who was familiar with the building, remembered the vault, and going to the place, saw that the floor had been newly broken. Raising the flagging and holding his torch down into the vault, he descried the king. Sir John Hall, knife in hand, leaped down into the vault, and was followed by his brother, but the king overpowered them both by main strength, and threw them beneath his feet. Sir Robert Graham followed the Halls, with drawn sword. The king, now much weakened by his struggles with the others, begged for mercy, or at least for a confessor. Graham denounced him as a tyrant, and passed his weapon through the king's body, adding, "Thou shalt never have other confessor but this same sword." The two Halls then stabbed him repeatedly as he lay prostrate. Thus perished the ablest and best king of all the Stuart line.

Within forty days from the time of James's death, his murderers were all captured and barbarously executed. Athole's punishment was continued for three days. On the first day, he was put into a cart containing a high crane, with ropes passing through pulleys and tied to his body; so that being hoisted up, and suddenly allowed to fall, without reaching the floor of the cart, he was racked with intolerable pains. Then he was placed in a pillory, and a red-hot iron crown was set upon his head. The next day, he was bound upon a hurdle, and drawn at a horse's tail through the principal streets of Edinburgh. The third day, he was bound upon a plank in a conspicuous place, and his bowels being cut out whilst he was yet alive, were cast into a fire and burned before his face; as was also his heart. Then his head was taken off and exposed to public view, being set upon a pole in the highest part of the city. Robert Graham, the actual murderer, was carried in a cart through the town of Stirling, his right hand nailed to a gallows post that had been set up in the cart. Then the hangman took Graham's sword, and with it cut off the offending hand. Stripped naked and still fastened to the gallows, he was again driven through the streets, accompanied by two executioners, who continually ran red-hot iron spikes into his thighs, shoulders, and other least vital parts, and with red-hot pincers burned and tore the flesh until his body was a mass of charred and bleeding wounds. Be-

26

fore being permitted to die, his son was disembowelled, living, before his eyes.

After the death of James I., his son, a boy of eight years, succeeded to the throne, and was crowned at Holyrood as James II. on March 25, 1437. The Earl of Douglas was appointed Lieutenant of the Kingdom. He died in 1439. His son and successor having been murdered by the heads of the rival families of Crichton and Livingston, the son's uncle, James Douglas, assumed the title. He died in 1443, and his son, William Douglas, succeeded. William was a man of energy and ambition. His power soon became enormous. Having obtained custody of the king, by a compact with Livingston, he assumed the title and power of Lieutenant of the Kingdom. He divorced his wife, and married his cousin, the "Fair Maid of Galloway," thus reuniting the domains of his house. In 1449 the king married, and began to show energy and ability in affairs of state. The Livingston family, who had enriched themselves at the expense of the Crown, were seized and imprisoned, and the heir to the title executed.

In February, 1452, Douglas was invited to visit the king at Stirling Castle, and he complied. After dining and supping with the royal party, the king took him aside for a private interview. During their conversation the subject of Douglas's bonds with the Earls of Crawford and Ross was discussed. The king insisted that Douglas should break these secret bonds, but this the latter declined to do. At last the king drew his dagger, exclaimed, " This shall! " and twice stabbed his guest. The nobles at hand then rushed upon the bleeding man and killed him outright.

Civil war at once broke out in the kingdom of Scotland. The new Earl of Douglas and his brothers defied and scorned the king's authority, and burned and wasted the country. After many fruitless efforts the king managed to muster an army, and advanced in person against Douglas, entering his territory, and proceeding through Peeblesshire, Selkirk Forest, Dumfries, and Galloway. Douglas Castle was captured, and peace was concluded in August, 1452.

But the head of the house of Douglas once more united the territories of his family by marrying his brother's widow. He conspired against the king, and sought to overthrow the Stuart dynasty. The king raised an army and marched again into the lands of Douglas, besieging and capturing the castle of Abercorn and other strongholds. Douglas was defeated at Arkinholm, one of his brothers was killed, and another captured and beheaded. Douglas himself fled to England, and the estates of the earldom were forfeited to the Crown. The Earl of Angus, himself a Douglas, had stood by the king and rendered him important service in this formidable contest. On him James conferred the title and estates of the house, and it passed into a saying that " the Red Douglas had put down the Black."

The Scottish army laid siege to Roxburgh Castle, at Berwick, which was still retained by the English. It finally capitulated; but in 1460 King James was accidentally killed while witnessing the firing of one of the large cannon used in the siege. He was struck by an iron wedge used in tightening one of the bands about the gun, which was forced out during its firing.

He was succeeded by his son, James III., also a boy of eight years at the time of his father's death. For several years the government was conducted by Bishop Kennedy, who died in 1466. Lord Boyd then seized the king's person, and assumed supreme control of the kingdom. In 1467, his eldest son was created Earl of Arran and married to the king's sister. But the rule of the Boyds was of short duration. In 1469 they were tried for treason and convicted. The head of the house fled to England, where he soon afterwards died. His brother Alexander was executed at Edinburgh. The Earl of Arran was forced to flee, and was soon stripped of his royal wife by a divorce. She afterwards married the head of the Hamilton family, and that house subsequently attained a high position in the kingdom.

James III. was a prince of cultivated tastes but feeble character. He shrank from the rude society of his peers, and surrounded himself with artists of humble origin, whose influence and accomplishments excited the scorn and animosity of the illiterate nobles. In 1482, many of the king's favorites were murdered by the Earl of Angus and his associates at Lauder Bridge, and James himself was imprisoned in Edinburgh Castle for a season.

During the next half-dozen years, the nobles continued to plot against their king, and finally resolved to dethrone him. For this purpose, James's son, a youth of sixteen years, was encouraged to rise in rebellion against his father. With the assistance of the southern nobles, he raised an army, and taking the field against the king was met by the latter in battle. They fought on June 28, 1488, at a small brook, called Sauchie Burn, in the vicinity of Stirling. The engagement was fiercely contested. The king fled from the field. His horse stumbled, throwing its rider, and some of the rebels came up and killed him.

A few days after, James IV. was crowned king at Scone. Warned by his father's fate, he kept on good terms with the nobility. Instead of letting them dwell apart in their gloomy castles, he attracted them to the Court by its gay festivities. Free and affable in manner, he possessed a charm which made him the best-beloved king, by both great and small, that Scotland ever had. His reign covered the period of the discovery of America. The king took an interest in shipbuilding, and the nation made some progress as a naval power. The relations of Scotland became more and more interwoven with the other kingdoms of Europe. Spain, then in the zenith of her glory and power, kept an ambassador at the Court of Scotland, one Don Pedro de Ayala. This minister sent to the Spanish king, his master, an interesting description of the Scottish ruler, his subjects, and his country, which has been preserved in the archives of Simancas, and of which Bergenroth has made an abstract in his *Calendar of Spanish State Papers*. This account, it should be remembered, is the work of a foreigner, who had no motive of flattery; who wrote what James was never to see; and who happened to be removed from Scottish influence when he penned his despatch, which bears date, London, 25th July, 1498, and reads as follows:

The King is twenty-five years and some months old. He is of noble stature, neither tall nor short, and as handsome in complexion and shape as a man can be. His address is very agreeable. He speaks the following foreign languages—Latin, very well; French, German, Flemish, Italian, and Spanish; Spanish as well as the marquis, but he pronounces it more distinctly. He likes very much to receive Spanish letters. His own Scottish language is as different from English as Aragonese from Castilian. The King speaks, besides, the language of the savages who live in some parts of Scotland and on the islands. It is as different from Scotch as Biscayan is from Castilian. His knowledge of languages is wonderful. He is well read in the Bible and in some other devout books. He is a good historian. He has read many Latin and French histories, and profited by them, as he has a very good memory. He never cuts his hair or his beard. It becomes him very well.

He fears God and observes all the precepts of the Church. He does not eat meat on Wednesdays and Fridays. He would not ride on Sundays for any consideration, not even to mass. He says all his prayers. Before transacting any business he hears two masses. After mass he has a cantata sung, during which he sometimes despatches very urgent business. He gives alms liberally, but is a severe judge, especially in the case of murderers. He has a great predilection for priests, and receives advice from them, especially from the Friars Observant with whom he confesses. Rarely, even in joking, a word escapes him that is not the truth. He prides himself much upon it, and says it does not seem to him well for kings to swear their treaties as they do now. The oath of a king should be his royal word, as was the case in bygone ages. He is neither prodigal nor avaricious, but liberal when occasion requires. He is courageous, even more so than a king should be. I am a good witness of it. I have seen him often undertake most dangerous things in the last wars. I sometimes clung to his skirts, and succeeded in keeping him back. On such occasions he does not take the least care of himself. He is not a good captain, because he begins to fight before he has given his orders. He said to me that his subjects serve him with their persons and goods, in just and unjust quarrels, exactly as he likes; and that, therefore, he does not think it right to begin any warlike undertaking without being himself the first in danger. His deeds are as good as his words. For this reason, and because he is a very humane prince, he is much loved. He is active and works hard. When he is not at war he hunts in the mountains. I tell your highness the truth when I say that God has worked a miracle in him, for I have never seen a man so temperate in eating and drinking, out of Spain. Indeed, such a thing seems to be superhuman in these countries. He lends a willing ear to his counsellors, and decides nothing without asking them; but in great matters he acts according to his own judgment, and in my opinion he generally makes a right decision. I recognise him perfectly in the conclusion of the last peace, which was made against the wishes of the majority in his kingdom.

When he was a minor he was instigated by those who held government to do some dishonourable things. They favoured his love-intrigues with their relatives, in order to keep him in their subjection. As soon as he came of age, and understood his duties, he gave up these intrigues.   When I arrived he was keeping a lady with great state in a castle.   He visited her from time to time.   Afterwards he sent her to the house of her father, who is a knight, and married her.   He did the same with another lady by whom he had had a son.   It may be a year since he gave up, so at least it is believed, his love-making, as well from fear of God, as from fear of scandal in this world, which is thought very much of here.   I can say with truth that he esteems himself as much as though he were Lord of the world.   He loves war so much that I fear, judging by the provocation he receives, the peace will not last long.   War is profitable to him and to the country.

Another view of the character of James IV. is to be found in the first book of John Knox's *History of the Reformation in Scotland*.   This account is doubly interesting from the light it throws on the religious condition of Scotland at that period.   From Knox's history, it will be seen that Protest-antism in Scotland originated in Ayrshire and the other counties of the west —ever the most enlightened and progressive part of the kingdom.   Knox's account is as follows (the italics are his):

Albeit that in the days of King James II. and III., we find small question of religion moved within this realm; yet, in the time of King James IV., in the sixth year of his reign, and in the twenty-second of his age, which was in the year of God 1494, were summoned before the King and his great council, by Robert Blackater, called Archbishop of Glasgow, the number of thirty persons remaining, some in Kyle-stewart, some in Kingkyle, and some in Cunningham; among whom were George Campbell of Cessnock, Adam Reid of Barskyming, John Campbell of Newmills, Andrew Schaw of Polke-mac, Helen Chalmer, Lady Pokelie, Isabel Chalmer, Lady Stairs.
These were called the Lollards of Kyle: they were accused of the articles following, as we have received them out of the register of Glasgow.
I. That images are not to be had, [*in the kirk*,] nor to be worshipped.
II. That the reliques of saints are not to be worshipped.
III. That laws and ordinances of men vary from time to time, and that by the pope.
IV. That it is not lawful to fight for the faith, nor to defend the faith by the sword, [*if we be not driven to it by necessity*,] which is above all law.
V. That Christ gave power to Peter, [*as also to the other apostles*,] and not to the pope, his pretended successor, to bind and loose within the kirk.
VI. That Christ ordained no priests to consecrate, as they do in the Romish church these many years.
VII. That after consecration in the mass, there remains bread; and that there is not the natural body of Christ.
VIII. That tithes ought not to be given to ecclesiastical men, as they were then called, [*viz.* wholly; *but a part to the poor, widow, or orphans, and other pious uses*].
IX. That Christ at his coming hath taken away power from kings to judge.   [*This article we doubt not to be the venomous accusation of the enemy, whose practice hath ever been to make the doctrine of Jesus Christ subject to kings and rulers, as if God thereby would deprive them of their royal seats; while, on the contrary, nothing confirms the power of magistrates more than doth God's truth.   But to the articles.*]

X. That every faithful man or woman is a priest, [*in that sense that they are called by the apostle St. John, Apoc. i. 6. and v. 18. and xx. 6*].

XI. That the unction of kings ceased at the coming of Christ. [*And truly it was but late since kings were anointed, namely in Scotland, for Edgar was the first anointed king in Scotland, about the year* 1100.]

XII. That the pope is not the successor of Peter, but where he said, "Go behind me, satan."

XIII. That the pope deceives the people by his bulls, and his indulgencies.

XIV. That the mass profiteth not the souls, who in those days are said to be in purgatory.

XV. That the pope and the bishops deceive the people by their pardons.

XVI. That indulgencies ought not to be granted to fight against the Saracens.

XVII. That the pope exalts himself against God, and above God.

XVIII. That the pope cannot remit the pains of purgatory.

XIX. That the blessings of the bishops [*of dumb dogs they should have been stiled*] are of no value.

XX. That the excommunication of the kirk is not to be feared [*if there be no true cause for it*].

XXI. That in no cause it was lawful to swear, [*viz. idly, rashly, and in vain*].

XXII. That priests may have wives, according to the constitution of the law, [*and of the primitive Christian church*].

XXIII. That true Christians receive the body of Jesus Christ every day by faith.

XXIV. That after matrimony is contracted and consummate, the kirk may make no divorcement.

XXV. That excommunication binds not, [*if unjust*].

XXVI. That the pope forgives not sins, but only God.

XXVII. That faith should not be given to miracles, [*to such namely as the Romish were then, and are to this day*].

XXVIII. That we should not pray to the glorious Virgin Mary, but to God only, [*since he only hears us, and can help us*].

XXIX. That we are no more bound to pray in the kirk than in other places.

XXX. That we are not bound to believe all that doctors of the kirk have written.

XXXI. That such as worship the sacrament in the kirk [*we suppose they meant the sacrament of the altar*] commit idolatry.

XXXII. That the pope is the head of the kirk of antichrist.

XXXIII. That the pope and his ministers are murderers of souls.

XXXIV. That they which are called princes and prelates in the church, are thieves and robbers.

By these articles, which God of his merciful providence caused the enemies of his truth to keep in their registers, may appear how mercifully God hath looked upon this realm, retaining within it some spark of his light, even in the time of greatest darkness. Neither ought any man to wonder albeit that some things be obscurely, and some things doubtfully spoken; but rather ought all the faithful to magnify God's mercy, who, without public doctrine, gave so great light. And further, we ought to consider, that seeing that the enemies of Jesus Christ gathered the foresaid articles, thereupon to accuse the persons aforesaid, that they would deprave the meaning of God's servants, so far as they could; as we doubt not but they have done, in the heads of excommunication, swearing, and of matrimony; in the which it is no doubt but the servants of God did condemn the abuse only, and not the right ordinance of God: for, who knows not that the excommunication in those days was altogether abused; that swearing abounded, without punishment or remorse of conscience; and that divorcement was made, for such causes as worldly men had invented ? But to our history. Albeit that the accusation of the bishop and his accomplices was very grievous, yet God so assisted his servants, partly by inclining the King's heart to gentleness, (for divers of them were his great familiars,) and partly by giving bold and godly answers to their accusators, that the enemies in the end were frustrate of their purpose: for, while the bishop, in mockage, said to Adam Reid of Barskyming, " Reid, believe ye that God is in heaven ? " He answered, " Not as I do the sacraments seven." Whereat the bishop thinking to have triumphed, said, " Sir, lo, he denies that God is in heaven." Whereat the king wondering, said, "Adam Reid, what say ye ? " The other answered, " Pleaseth your majesty to hear the end betwixt the churl and me": and therewith he turned to the bishop, and said, " I neither think nor believe, as thou thinkest, that God is in heaven; but I am most assured, that he is not only in heaven, but also in the earth; but thou and thy faction declare by your works, that either ye think there is no God at all, or else, that he is so set up in heaven, that he regards not what is done upon the earth; for, if thou firmly believedest that God were in heaven, thou shouldest not make thyself check-mate to the King, and altogether forget the charge that Jesus Christ, the Son of God gave to his apostles, which was, to preach his gospel, and not to play the proud prelates, as all the rabble of you do this day." " And now, Sir," said he to the King, " judge ye, whether the bishop or I believe best that God is in heaven." While the bishop and his band could not well revenge themselves, and while many taunts were given them in their teeth, the King, willing to put an end to further reasoning, said to the said Adam Reid, " Wilt thou burn thy bill ? " He answered, " Sir, and the bishop and ye will." With these, and the like scoffs, the bishop and his band were so dashed out of countenance, that the greatest part of the accusation was turned to laughter.

On August 8, 1502, James IV. was married to Margaret Tudor, daughter of Henry VII. of England, and sister to Henry VIII. A hundred years later, the issue of this marriage united the crowns of the two kingdoms. In 1509, Henry VII. died, and Scotland lost a quiet neighbor. Soon after the accession of Henry VIII. to the throne, England engaged in a war with France, and Scotland, under the terms of the league subsisting between that country and France, took the side of her old-time ally. In 1513, the Scottish army, with the king at its head, marched to the Border, and crossed the Tweed on August 22d. The battle of Flodden was fought September 9, 1513. The Scots were defeated, with a loss of upwards of eight thousand. Among the slain was the king, together with the flower of his nobility.

CHAPTER XXVI

THE BEGINNING OF THE REFORMATION

IN October, 1513, James IV.'s son, an infant of three years, was crowned at Scone, under the title of James V. His mother was named as regent. This arrangement continued until her marriage in the following year with young Archibald Douglas, Earl of Angus. The Duke of Albany was then recalled from France, and arriving in Scotland in May, 1515, was made regent. He began his government with bold measures, designed to reduce the arrogance and power of the nobles. Offenders of the highest rank were seized, imprisoned, and executed. But these proceedings failed to produce their intended effect, and after a short time Albany discovered the hopelessness of attempting to secure order in the kingdom. He repeatedly returned to France to be free from the turmoil; and after a fluctuating rule of eight years, his regency ended in 1524.

The Earl of Angus now returned, and with the concurrence of the Earl of Arran and others, he became guardian of the king, and assumed the office of chancellor of the kingdom; having obliged Archbishop Beaton to resign that post. The latter, in 1528, organized a conspiracy, by means of which King James effected his escape from the Douglases, and took refuge in the castle of Stirling. "This sudden reaction," says Buckle, "was not the real and controlling cause, but it was undoubtedly the proximate cause of the establishment of Protestantism in Scotland. For the reins of government now passed into the hands of the Church."

James appointed the Archbishop of Glasgow, chancellor ; the Abbot of Holyrood, treasurer; and the Bishop of Dunkeld, keeper of the privy seal. The most influential of the nobles were persecuted, and some of them driven from the kingdom. Thus excluded from the government, the nobles began to show a leaning toward the doctrines of the Reformation. Hating the clergy, they became enraged at the ecclesiastical influence over the king; and as time passed they grew firmer in their adherence to the principles of the Reformation.

They were stripped of their honors and their wealth, and many became outcasts, traitors, and beggars. But while their political power was gone, their social power remained. The real foundation of their authority was unshaken, because that authority was based on the clan spirit and the affections of the people. The desire of the nobles for revenge gave rise to a deadly contest between the Scottish aristocracy and the Scottish Church. This conflict lasted without interruption for thirty-two years, and was finally concluded by the triumph of the nobles, who, in 1560, completely overthrew the Church, and destroyed the whole of the Scottish hierarchy. It is a noteworthy fact in connection with the history of the Reformation in Scotland that most of its leaders and armies came from the western Lowlands, chiefly from those districts in which Wallace and Bruce had lived and raised their armies more than two centuries before. Especially interesting is this fact to him who studies the history of the transplanted Scot in Ireland and America; for most of the Scottish emigrants to those countries emigrated from that part of Scotland.

In 1525, Parliament prohibited the importation of Luther's books. In 1527, Patrick Hamilton, who had been a disciple of Luther in Germany, returned home, and began to promulgate his teachings. Early in the following year, he was seized and imprisoned in the castle of St. Andrews, where he was tried, convicted, and burned for heresy on February 29, 1528. In 1534, Gourly, a priest, and Straiton, a layman, were both condemned for heresy, and hanged and burned.

In 1537, James married Magdalen, daughter of the king of France. She died a few months after her arrival in Scotland, and in the following year, he married Mary, daughter of the Duke of Guise. In 1542, Henry VIII. proclaimed war against Scotland; but, while two armies were raised and disbanded, the only engagement which took place was that known as the panic of Solway Moss, where the English leader surprised and scattered the Scots, capturing a number of prisoners.

James died on December 14, 1542, leaving a seven-days-old daughter who afterwards became known to history as Mary Stuart. James Hamilton, Earl of Arran, being next heir to the throne, was elected regent. Henry VIII. of England intrigued for a match between his son, Edward, and the infant queen. A treaty of alliance between England and Scotland was concluded, subject only to ratification by the Scottish Parliament. The clergy, however, headed by Cardinal Beaton (who, on the death of his uncle in 1539, had first become Archbishop of St. Andrews), were very much opposed to the scheme. There was much diplomatic wrangling, but in the end the cardinal triumphed. In December, 1543, Parliament repudiated the treaties, and, in presence of the French ambassadors, renewed the Ancient League with France.

Henry declared war, and avowed his intention of taking the infant queen by force. In April, 1544, he instructed his commander, the Earl of Hertford, to invade Scotland, "there to put all to fire and sword, to burn Edinburgh town . . . sack Holyrood House, and towns and villages about Edinburgh . . . sack Leith, and burn and subvert it, and all the rest, putting man, woman, and child to fire and sword without exception when any resistance should be made." This done, he was to "pass over to the Fife land, and extend like extremities and destructions in all towns and villages whereunto he might reach conveniently, not forgetting amongst all the rest . . . the cardinal's town of St. Andrews . . . sparing no creature alive within the same." Hertford carried out his king's instructions, leading two expeditions into Scotland, one in May, 1544, and another in September.

Meanwhile Cardinal Beaton continued his persecution of the Protestants. He held a court at Perth in January, 1544, and many persons were there convicted of heresy. A number were banished; and four men and one woman were condemned to death—James Randalson, James Hunter, William Anderson, Robert Lamb, and the latter's wife. The men were hanged, but the woman, who had an infant at her breast, was drowned.

George Wishart, a popular reformed preacher, returned from England into Scotland near the end of the year 1544. On the 16th of January, 1546, Wishart, accompanied by John Knox, was preaching in Haddington. That same night, he was apprehended at Ormiston, conveyed to Edinburgh, and shortly after to St. Andrews. Here he was tried for heresy on February 28th, condemned by Cardinal Beaton, and burned to death by his order on the 11th of March. The martyrdom of this man roused a deep feeling of indignation in the popular mind, which was encouraged by many of the nobles; and not long after Cardinal Beaton paid for Wishart's life with his own.

Early on the morning of May 29, 1546, Norman Leslie, son of the Earl of Rothes, with two other men, secretly gained admission to the castle of St. Andrews, where Beaton was then living. They were followed by James Melville and three others, who asked an interview with the cardinal. Immediately afterwards, Kirkaldy, Laird of Grange, approached, with eight armed men. They aroused the suspicion of the porter at the gate, but he was instantly stabbed and cast into the ditch. A few minutes later the party was within the walls of the castle. Its defenders and the workmen on the ramparts were turned out with surprising alacrity, and all the gates shut and guarded. The unusual noise aroused the cardinal from his bed, but he had taken only a few steps when his enemies entered the room and ruthlessly murdered him. Meanwhile the alarm was raised in the town. The common bell was rung. The cry running through the city that the castle was taken, the cardinal's friends came rushing forward to scale the walls and rescue him. "What have ye done with my Lord Cardinal?" they cried. "Where is my Lord Cardinal? Have ye slain my Lord Cardinal? Let us see my Lord Cardinal." They that were within bade them go home, for the cardinal had received his reward and would trouble the world no more. The crowd still insisted on seeing him, and the cardinal's body was brought to the blockhouse head and lowered over the battlements by means of sheets tied to an arm and a leg. The terrified citizens recognized their master, and dispersed to their homes.

The determined band of conspirators who had slain the cardinal, joined by one hundred and fifty of their friends, succeeded in holding the castle of St. Andrews against the regent for more than a year. No attempt was made to reduce it until three months had passed, and then Arran laid siege to the castle. After several weeks' unavailing effort, he raised the siege and departed. John Knox joined the garrison about ten months after the cardinal's death. In the end of June, 1547, a number of French galleys appeared off the coast, and the attack on the castle was renewed from the seaward side. This soon brought the defenders to submission. The garrison surrendered to the French commander, and were conveyed to France. A number, including the principal gentlemen, were distributed among various French prisons. The remainder, of whom John Knox was one, were confined on board the galleys. Here Knox, chained to his oar, lived and rowed as a galley slave for nearly two years. In 1549, he obtained his liberty, came to England, and preached at Berwick and Newcastle. He was appointed one of King Edward VI.'s chaplains in 1551. In March, 1554, he left England, and passed to Geneva.

Henry VIII. died in England in January, 1547, but his policy was continued after his death. As previously stated, he had wished for the betrothal of the infant queen of Scotland with his own son, Edward VI. Lord Hertford, Duke of Somerset, therefore proceeded with the invasion of Scotland which his master had begun in 1544. The Scots were reduced to great extremities. In September, 1547, the battle of Pinkie was fought near Edinburgh, which resulted in the disastrous defeat and rout of the Scottish army. Fourteen thousand Scots were slain in the pitiless carnage of this retreat. The next year, however, a French army of seven thousand men arrived to assist the Scotch. The young queen was sent to France, and thus one object of the war was removed. After many severe struggles, the Scots and French drove the English out of the castles, and recovered the southern part of the kingdom. Peace was finally concluded in 1550.

Toward the end of the summer of 1550, Adam Wallace, a man of humble rank from Ayrshire, was accused of heresy, condemned, and burned at Edinburgh. In England the period of persecution under Mary Tudor and Philip of Spain caused many Scotsmen who had formerly fled across the Border to return home. Knox also came back from Geneva in September, 1555, and preached zealously against the mass. Amongst the hearers who approved his doctrines were the Prior of St. Andrews, afterwards known as the Regent Moray, the Earl of Argyle (then Lord Lorne), and others.

The Romanists were alarmed, and Knox was summoned to appear at Edinburgh on May 15, 1556. He determined to appear, but when Erskine and other nobles who professed the new doctrines met in Edinburgh in force, the citation of Knox was abandoned. On the day that he should have appeared in court, he preached in Edinburgh to a larger audience than had ever listened to him. Soon after he was called to preach to the English congregation at Geneva, and returned to that place. After his departure the bishops again summoned him, and on Knox's failure to appear, they caused him to be burned in effigy at the Cross of Edinburgh.

But the reformed doctrines continued to spread. Among their most active advocates at this time were William Harlaw, John Willock, a native

of Ayrshire, John Douglas, Paul Methven, and others.   In December, 1557,
a number of the nobles came out on the side of the Reformation movement,
and joined in a bond, known as the First Covenant, by which they agreed
to assist each other in advancing the reformation of religion, in "maintaining God's true congregation, and renouncing the congregation of Satan."
Among those who subscribed this document were Archibald Campbell, Earl
of Argyle, and his son Archibald (Lord Lorne), Alexander Cunningham,
Earl of Glencairn, James Douglas, Earl of Morton, and John Erskine of
Dun.   The leaders of this movement came to be known as "the Lords of
the Congregation."

In April, 1558, Walter Mill, an old man of over eighty years, formerly a
priest, was accused of heresy, and imprisoned at St. Andrews.   He was
tried before a gathering of bishops, abbots, and other Romish dignitaries,
and condemned to be burned.   They sought to make him recant by brutal
threatenings.   "I will not recant the truth," he said, "for I am corn, and
not chaff; I will not be blown away by the wind nor burst by the flail, but
will abide both."   This old man's heroic attitude in his extremity forms a
marked contrast with that of Archbishop Cranmer, who was also an old man
when he was burned in England some two years before.   The people of St.
Andrews heaped a cairn of stones on the spot of Walter Mill's martyrdom,
" in testification," says John Knox, " that they would his death should abide
in recent memory.   The bishops and priests, thereat offended, caused once
or twice to remove the same, with denunciation of cursing, if any man should
there lay any stones; but in vain was that wind blown; for still was the heap
made, till the priests stole away by night the stones to build their walls."

As a result of the preaching of William Harlaw and others in Edinburgh,
some of the young men of that city took the image of St. Giles and threw it
into the North Loch.   It was afterwards drawn out and burned.   This affair
made a great sensation.   Through the influence of the bishops with the
queen regent, four of the chief preachers were cited to appear before the
justiciary court at Stirling, on May 10, 1559.   The preachers resolved to
answer the summons, but first appeared in Edinburgh.   With them came
their Protestant friends from the West, composed largely of the followers of
the Campbells from Argyle and the Cunninghams and Douglases from Ayrshire, Dumfries, and Galloway.   At the instigation of a shrewd counsellor in
the bishops' party, proclamation was made by the regent that all who had
come to town without requisition by the authorities should proceed to the
Borders, and there remain fifteen days, to take their tours of frontier duty.
The Protestants felt that such a thing was not to be considered, as it would
leave their preachers at the mercy of the bishops.   Accordingly, some of
the leaders made their way into the chamber where the queen regent was
sitting in council with her bishops.   James Chalmers of Gadgirth, one of
the Western barons, a bold and zealous man, stood forth and spoke.
" Madam," he said, " we know that this is the malice of the bishops.   We

vow to God we shall make a day of it. They trouble our preachers, and would murder them and us. Shall we suffer this any longer? No, madam, it shall not be." Forthwith, every man put on his steel bonnet. The regent promised to withdraw the citation; but she broke her word. The accused preachers were summoned, and failing to appear, were proclaimed rebels.

Meanwhile, shortly before St. Giles's day, the bishops gave an order to the town council of Edinburgh that they should either recover the old image of St. Giles, or make a new one. The council answered, that " nowhere in God's word could they find commandment given to set up images, though in several places they did find commandment to break them down." The priests thereupon borrowed an image from the Grey Friars, which they set upon a shoulder-high barrow. Priests, friars, canons, and their followers then formed a procession, which was led by the queen regent herself. The crowd soon began to jostle the saint's bearers, and caused the image to wobble on its barrow. A cry arose, " Down with the idol! Down with it! " and it was pulled down. A man in the crowd took hold of the saint by the heels and battered the head to splinters on the cobble-stones.

John Knox had landed at Leith on May 2d, and proceeded to join his friends. On the eleventh of May, after Knox had preached a vehement sermon against the mass in the parish church of Perth, a priest was so imprudent as to uncover an altar in order to say mass. A youth exclaimed at the top of his voice: " This is intolerable, that when God, by His Word, hath plainly damned idolatry, we shall stand and see it used in despite." The priest gave him a blow. He threw a stone at the priest, which struck the tabernacle and broke one of the images. Instantly the people began to cast stones, to tear down the altars and images, and to destroy every vestige of the ornaments of the church. The mob then proceeded to sack the monasteries of Grey Friars, Black Friars, and Charterhouse. Such was the destruction that " within two days," says Knox, " the walls only did remain of all these great edifications." This example was followed in other places, and in a short time most of the religious houses in the kingdom were despoiled of their altars, images, and monuments.

When the queen regent learned of the riot at Perth, she threatened to destroy the town, " man, woman, and child, to burn it with fire, and salt it in sign of perpetual desolation." The Reformers who were assembled in the town accordingly called upon their friends for assistance. Letters were written to their western brethren in Cuningham and Kyle. These are the two districts of Ayrshire which afterwards furnished so much of the Scottish population of Ulster. The people of Kyle met at the kirk of Craigie, to hear the letters read. Some were faint-hearted, and hesitated. Alexander Cunningham, Earl of Glencairn, standing before the congregation, said, "Let every man serve his conscience. I will, by God's grace, see my brethren in St. Johnstown [Perth]; yea, although never man should accompany me, I will go, if it were but with a pike on my shoulder; for I had rather die with that company than live after them.'' These brave words so stirred his hearers that they immediately set forth for Perth. Twelve hundred mounted men and as many more on foot was the number that reached there. With them were Glencairn, Lords Ochiltree and Boyd, and brave James Chalmers of Gadgirth — the same who had forbidden the queen regent to harm the preachers.

The Lords of the Congregation were now supported by a considerable force. The regent's French troops marched upon Perth and advanced as far as Auchterarder. Here an arrangement was made by which the queen regent bound herself to allow the people of Perth the free exercise of their religion. But later she again broke faith. The Lords, proceeding rapidly, invaded St. Andrews. The primate fled. The regent's army then approached; another treaty was made; and this she also failed to keep. She was expecting reinforcements from France, and parleyed for delay. Failing to obtain peace, the Congregation took more vigorous measures. One division of its army entered Perth on June 25th; another, under Argyle and the Prior of St. Andrews (who meanwhile had joined the Reformers), took possession of Edinburgh on the 29th. The regent proceeded to Dunbar. The Protestant army demolished the monasteries of the capital, and seized the coining irons of the mint.

CHAPTER XXVII

THE DAYS OF KNOX

THE queen regent retreated to Leith. During August and September a number of French troops disembarked and began to fortify that port. The Lords of the Congregation had already laid siege to the town, but the Frenchmen soon made the fortifications so strong that the siege was raised, and the Protestants returned to Edinburgh. Skirmishing immediately began between the two armies, in which the French were generally victorious. The Scots were forced out of Edinburgh, and retired to Stirling.

At John Knox's suggestion, negotiations were now opened with England for the despatch of reinforcements, and in January, 1560, a treaty was concluded at Berwick between the Protestants and the English. Within a few weeks an English fleet, with from six to eight thousand men, appeared in the Firth of Forth. The united Scotch and English forces then besieged Leith, and on the sixth of July that city capitulated. An arrangement was made which resulted in the withdrawal of the French and English forces from Scotland, with the agreement that the Scottish monarch should not make peace or war except with the consent of the Estates of the Kingdom; that none of the high offices of the realm should be deputed to aliens; that churchmen should not hold the offices of treasurer and comptroller; and that a Parliament should assemble in August. Peace was proclaimed on July 8, 1560, and a few days after the French and English troops departed. Meantime, the death of the queen regent had taken place on the tenth of June.

Parliament assembled in August. Among its enactments were measures abolishing the jurisdiction of the pope in Scotland; prohibiting the mass, and adopting a Confession of Faith for the Reformed Church.

Francis II. of France, husband of the young Queen of Scots, died in December, 1560. In the following August, Mary returned from France to Scotland. Four days after her arrival, arrangements were made for the celebration of mass in the queen's chapel. Such an outcry arose amongst the people that the chapel door had to be guarded, and order was with difficulty preserved. On the following Sunday John Knox declaimed against the mass. Mary took him to task for stirring up her subjects against their ruler, and for teaching sedition. Knox appeared before the queen. The following is his account of their interview:

Whether it was by counsel of others, or of the Queen's own desire, we know not, but the Queen spake with John Knox, and had long reasoned with him; none being present, except the Lord James [brother to Mary]; two gentlemen stood in the one end of the room. The sum of their reasoning was this: The Queen accused him, that he had raised a part of her subjects against her mother and herself; that he had written a book against her just authority (she meant the treatise against the regiment of women), which she had, and would cause the most learned in Europe to write against; that he was the cause of great sedition and great slaughter in England; and that it was said to her, that all that he did was by necromancy.

To the which the said John Knox answered: " Madam, it may please your majesty patiently to hear my simple answers: and first," said he, " if to teach the word of God in sincerity; if to rebuke idolatry, and to will a people to worship God according to his word be to raise subjects against their princes, then cannot I be excused . . . but, madam, if the true knowledge of God and his right worshipping, be the chief causes which must move men to obey their just princes from their heart (as it is most certain that they are), wherein can I be reprehended ? . . ."

" But yet," said she, " you have taught the people to receive another religion than their princes can allow; and how can that doctrine be of God, seeing that God commandeth subjects to obey their princes ? " " Madam," said he, " as right religion took neither original nor antiquity from worldly princes, but from the eternal God alone, so are not subjects bound to frame their religion according to the appetite of their princes; for oft it is, that princes are the most ignorant of all others, in God's true religion. . . . If all the seed of Abraham should have been of the religion of Pharaoh, to whom they had been a long time subjects, I pray you, madam, what religion should there have been in the world ? Or if all men in the days of the apostles, should have been of the religion of the Roman emperors, what religion should have been upon the face of the earth ? . . . and so, madam, ye may perceive that subjects are not bound to the religion of their princes, albeit they are commanded to give them obedience."

" Yea," quoth she, " none of these men raised their sword against their princes." " Yet, madam," quoth he, " ye cannot deny but they resisted; for those that obey not the commandments given, in some sort resist." " But yet," said she, " they resisted not by the sword."

" God," said he, " madam, had not given them the power and the means." " Think you," said she, " that subjects, having power, may resist their princes ? " " If princes do exceed their bounds," quoth he, " madam, and do against that wherefore they should be obeyed, there is no doubt but they may be resisted, even by power; for there is neither greater honor, nor greater obedience to be given to kings and princes than God hath commanded to be given to father and mother; but so it is, that the father may be stricken with a frenzy, in the which he would slay his own children; now, madam, if the children arise, join themselves together, apprehend the father, take the sword or other weapon from him, and, finally, bind his hands, and keep him in prison till that his frenzy be overpast, think ye, madam, that the children do any wrong ? Or, think ye, madam, that God will be offended with them that have staid their father from committing wickedness ? It is even so, madam, with princes that would murder the children of God, that are subject unto them. Their blind zeal is nothing but a very mad frenzy; and therefore, to take the sword from them, to bind their hands, and to cast them into prison, till that they be brought to a more sober mind, is no disobedience against princes, but just obedience; because that it agreeth with the word of God."

At these words, the Queen stood, as it were, amazed, more than a quarter of an hour; her countenance altered, so that the Lord James began to intreat her, and to demand, "what hath offended you, madam ? " At length, she said, " Well, then, I perceive that my subjects shall only obey you, and not me; and shall do what they list, and not what I command; and so I must be subject unto them, and not they to me." " God forbid," answered he, " that ever I take it upon me to command any to obey me, or yet to set subjects at liberty to do whatsoever please them; but my travail is, that both princes and subjects obey God. . . ."

" Yea," quoth she, " but ye are not the church that I will nourish; I will defend the church of Rome; for I think it is the true church of God."

George Gordon, fourth Earl of Huntly, and ruler of the Highland chieftains, rebelled against the Government in the summer of 1562, during the visit of Mary to his territories. The Forbes, Fraser, and Mackintosh clans, and others, who had been under Huntly, now that they had the opportunity deserted his standard and joined the queen. The gates of the castle of Inverness were closed against her, but the castle was soon taken, and the garrison hanged. When the royal party returned to Aberdeen, Huntly and his retainers followed them. An engagement ensued at Corrichie, in which Huntly was defeated and slain.

On July 29, 1565, Mary married her cousin, Henry Stuart, Lord Darnley, eldest son of the Earl of Lennox. Darnley was a Roman Catholic, and, like Mary, had been bred on the Continent. The marriage was made against the wishes of Queen Elizabeth of England, and Mary's natural brother, James Stewart, Prior of St. Andrews and Earl of Moray, himself a Protestant, did his utmost to prevent it. Moray and his party met at Stirling on the 15th of July, to consult on the project of rebellion; but the queen ordered a general muster of the Crown vassals on the 22d. The intended marriage was proclaimed, and on the 29th it took place at Holyrood.

Moray and his associates — the Duke of Chatelherault, the Earls of Argyle, Glencairn, Rothes, and other barons—having mustered a thousand of their followers, were proclaimed rebels. They were unable to face the royal forces, and retired to Dumfries. Afterwards they disbanded and fled to England.

Mary's marriage proved extremely unhappy. Her husband was a vain man, of weak character; while the Queen was a proud, licentious woman, who quickly wearied of her new toy, and sought to discard it. Their domestic quarrels soon became notorious.

The French Court of the time of Catharine de' Medici, in which Mary Stuart was reared, " is known," says Swinburne, " to readers of Brantome as well as that of imperial Rome at its worst is known to readers of Suetonius or Petronius,—as well as that of papal Rome at its worst is known to readers of the diary kept by the domestic chaplain of Pope Alexander VI. Only in their pages can a parallel be found to the gay and easy record which reveals without sign of shame or suspicion of offence the daily life of a Court compared to which the Court of King Charles II. is as the Court of Queen Victoria to the society described by Grammont. Debauchery of all kinds,

27

and murder in all forms, were the daily matter of excitement or of jest to the brilliant circle which revolved around Catharine de' Medici.''

It is not surprising, therefore, that Mary's code of morals should have been to some extent moulded after the fashion of her mother-in-law, a woman whose main instrument of policy was the corruption of her own children. Some two years before her marriage to Darnley she had caused the execution of one of her French lovers, Pierre de Boscosel de Chastelard, for the offence or the misfortune of a second *detection* at night in her bedchamber.

Little more than a year after her marriage, Mary was heard to say that unless she could be freed of her husband in some way, she could have no pleasure in living, and if she could find no other remedy, she would take her own life. The queen had several foreigners in her service, and one, named David Rizzio, acted as her foreign secretary, being also the secret agent in Scotland of the papal court. He was the son of a musician of Turin, and, having accompanied the Piedmontese ambassador into Scotland, gained admission to the queen's circle by his skill in music. He soon became an object of the queen's favor, and her French secretary happening to return at that time to his own country, Rizzio was given his place. He now began to make a figure at Court, and it became apparent that the best way to gain the successful issue of a suit was through '' Davie,'' the Queen's secretary. Soon he equalled the greatest and most opulent subjects in the richness of his dress, and the number of his attendants. He studied to display the whole extent of his favor. He affected to talk often and insolently with the queen in public. Through his assistance Mary was married secretly to Darnley, some four months before the date of their public marriage.

Sometime after the marriage the queen caused to be made an iron seal bearing Darnley's signature, and this she gave to Rizzio, in order that state papers requiring the king's name might be signed by her secretary. In this way, it soon became a common saying at Court that '' Davie is he that worketh all.'' His apparel, household, and equipages exceeded those of the king himself, and soon the people began to say the same of his privileges. On one occasion, hearing that Rizzio had entered the queen's bedchamber, Darnley came to a private door, the key to which he always carried, and for the first time found it bolted on the inside.

According to one account, Darnley privately assured his uncle, George Douglas, of his wife's infidelity; he had himself, if he might be believed, discovered the secretary in the queen's apartments at midnight under circumstances yet more unequivocally compromising than those which had brought Chastelard to the scaffold. Darnley accordingly entered into a bond with Lord Ruthven and other Scottish nobles who were incensed against Rizzio, by the terms of which they agreed to despatch the Italian favorite. The plot was well matured, and everything prepared for its realization. On the evening of March 9th, Earl Morton, with one hundred and sixty men, took possession of the inner court of the royal palace, and guarded the gates.

Darnley ascended to the queen's apartments, accompanied by Lord Ruthven. They found their victim sitting with the queen in her boudoir. After a short struggle, he was dragged out into an adjoining room and killed.

The following day the rebellious nobles who had been exiled returned to Edinburgh, and, with a view to making the Earl of Moray king, seized the city. Mary escaped to Dunbar, taking Darnley along. Here she raised an army, and returning in force obliged the rebels to flee. Morton and Ruthven escaped to England, others fled to the Highlands, and some of them retired to their own estates. After a short time the queen pardoned Moray and his associates; but she declined to pardon those directly implicated in the murder of Rizzio, and began secretly to plot for the destruction of her own husband, for whom she now conceived the most bitter hatred. Some time before she had become very much infatuated with James Hepburn, Earl of Bothwell. After the death of Rizzio, Bothwell's influence over Mary became unbounded. At Court he arranged everything according to his own pleasure. The queen loaded him with honors, and bestowed on him vast grants of Crown and Church lands. Mary finally left Holyrood Palace and took lodgings at the Chequer House, adjoining Bothwell's residence, the two houses being connected by a passageway in the rear.

In June, 1566, Mary retired into the castle of Edinburgh, and there, on the 19th day of that month, James VI. of Scotland and I. of England was born. Much sympathy has been lavished upon the unfortunate and guilty queen of Scotland for her sufferings in after life, and the sad ending of her troubles. Sympathy has not been lacking, also, for the unhappy Rizzio, who perished because he was the queen's favorite. No doubt in their untimely deaths they both expiated many of their crimes against society of their own day. But the death of many Marys would not atone for the long and grievous burden of oppression, persecution, and murder inflicted upon humanity during the next century by the progeny of that ill-fated woman.

After the birth of James VI., the queen became reconciled with the rebellious nobles, and though Huntly (the fifth earl) and Bothwell remained at the head of the government, Moray, Argyle, Glencairn, and others were readmitted to a share in its administration. In December, the baptism of the infant prince took place at Stirling. All the preparations for the ceremony were committed to Bothwell. Darnley was not present at the baptism. He was in Stirling during the festivities, but kept his own apartment.

Toward the end of the year, Darnley visited his father at Glasgow, where he was taken ill with a disease resembling the smallpox, brought on, says Buchanan, by a dose administered by the queen. When nearly recovered, Mary visited him, and induced him to return with her to Edinburgh. Here, instead of lodging Darnley in the palace, she had him placed in a small house in the suburbs, belonging to one of Bothwell's followers.

Meanwhile, a plot for the murder of Darnley had been concocted. Sir James Balfour, the friend and attorney of Bothwell, drew up a bond for

Darnley's destruction, which was signed by the Earls of Huntly, Argyle, Morton, and others who took part in the conspiracy. The queen joined in the plot, and was the chief instrument in luring her husband to his death. During Darnley's convalescence she appeared very attentive to him, and for several nights slept in a room below the one he occupied. By means of duplicate keys, which Bothwell had caused to be made, the latter's agents had free access to the house. A barrel of powder was sent for to Bothwell's castle of Dunbar, and a large quantity placed in the queen's room, directly under Darnley's bed in the room above. On Sunday night, February 9th, the queen passed from Holyrood and joined her husband. There was some conversation between them, and then Mary recollected that she had promised to attend the ball to be held that night in honor of the marriage of two of her servants. She bade Darnley farewell, and departed with Bothwell and Huntly. Before the powder train was finally set off, Darnley and his servant seem to have discovered their danger and attempted to escape, but were caught and strangled to death in the garden. Bothwell, with a company of his followers, returned from Holyrood about midnight, and joined the two conspirators, Hepburn and Hay, who had already lighted the train. The explosion shook the earth for miles around, and aroused the citizens of Edinburgh. Bothwell hurried back to the palace, and after drinking some wine, retired to his apartments. A short time later, when news of Darnley's assassination was brought to him, he sprang up, crying out, "Treason! Treason!" Gordon, his brother-in-law, and others, rushed into his room in alarm, and together they sought the queen and told her of the consummation of the crime.

The murder caused great excitement, and printed bills were posted on the door of the Parliament House, naming Bothwell, Balfour, and others as the murderers. Rumors arose that Bothwell would marry the queen. The Earl of Lennox insisted that the parties accused should be brought to trial. A jury trial was finally had April 12, 1567. On that day Bothwell had three thousand of his armed retainers in the streets of Edinburgh. The court met. Bothwell appeared, but no witness dared to face him, and he was acquitted. He then challenged to single combat any one who would affirm that he was guilty of Darnley's murder.

Eight or nine days after the trial, the queen visited her infant son at Stirling. On her return, when within a few miles of Edinburgh, she was met by Bothwell, at the head of eight hundred horsemen, and, taking her bridle-rein, he conducted Mary to his castle of Dunbar. Soon after, Bothwell escorted the queen to Edinburgh, where preparations for their marriage were hastened. Previous to the seizure of Queen Mary, Bothwell's wife, Lady Jane Gordon, sister to the Earl of Huntly, had sued for a divorce. This was granted on May 7th; and on the 15th of the same month Bothwell and the queen were married at Holyrood.

For a brief season after the marriage, Mary and her new husband seemed happy. But Bothwell's temper soon led him into bitter quarrels with his wife; and once in the hearing of the French ambassador, their quarrel was so wild that Mary screamed for a knife with which to stab herself.

Some weeks before the marriage, a league to punish Bothwell for his crimes had been formed by some of the nobles, among whom were Kirkaldy of Grange, Lethington, Morton, Mar, Ruthven, Lindsay, Hume, Herries, Glencairn, Cassilis, and Eglinton. Within a few weeks after the marriage, these men were ready to execute their scheme.

Bothwell and the queen left Edinburgh on the seventh of June, and passed to Borthwick (or Botherwick) Castle, about ten miles south of the capital. Morton and Hume, with eight hundred of their Borderers, appeared before Borthwick, and the guilty couple escaped with difficulty to the castle of Dunbar. The nobles seized Edinburgh. The queen mustered about three thousand men, and marched upon the capital. The forces confronted each other at Carberry Hill near Musselburgh, where, after a day spent in parleying, Mary surrendered to the nobles, and Bothwell was allowed to ride off in the direction of Dunbar. The queen was taken to Edinburgh on the 15th of June, and on the 17th she was conveyed a captive to Lochleven Castle, which stood on an island in the lake. On the 23d, she was forced to sign her abdication of the throne, and to confirm the appointment of Moray as regent, to govern during the minority of her son.

In the parish church of Stirling, James VI., a baby of thirteen months, was crowned king on July 29, 1567. On the following day, the king's authority was proclaimed, and the reign of Queen Mary ceased. Moray assumed the office of regent, August 22d.

Through the assistance of the Duke of Hamilton and his brother, the Archbishop of St. Andrews, Mary escaped from Lochleven Castle after more than ten months' captivity. One of her partisans, young George Douglas, half-brother to the regent, had bribed some of the servants at the castle, and gained them to the queen's interest. One evening in May, 1568, a page who served at the table managed to purloin the key of the outer gate from the keeper of the castle while he was at supper. The page carried the key to the queen; they gained the gate unperceived, locked it behind them, and crossed the lake in a boat which had been left for the garrison. Lord Seton and a party of Mary's friends were waiting on the shore, and when the queen landed they mounted her on horseback and rode off to Hamilton town.

Many of the nobility and barons who were unfavorable to the regent now repaired to the queen, with offers of support and service. At Hamilton she soon had around her a camp of six thousand men. Her chief adherents, besides the Hamiltons, were Argyle, Huntly, Rothes, Seton, Cassilis, Harris, Livingston, Fleming, and Claud Hamilton.

The regent was at Glasgow, only eight miles distant from Hamilton, when news of the queen's escape reached him. Within ten days, he had mustered four thousand men, marched from Glasgow, and on May 13th fought Mary's forces at the village of Langside. The battle lasted less than three quarters of an hour; "then the queen saw her troops swept down the hill, broken and scattered in defeat, the Macfarlanes, with leaps and yells and flashing claymores, cutting and hewing among the wretched fugitives." Mary fled toward the Border, and found refuge in the abbey of Dundrennan on the shore of Solway Firth, sixty miles from the field of battle. Here she remained for three days, then crossed over into England, and threw herself upon the protection of Queen Elizabeth. Elizabeth committed her to the custody of the Earl of Shrewsbury. After twenty years imprisonment, Mary was beheaded on the 8th of February, 1587.

When Bothwell was separated from Queen Mary at Carberry Hill on the day of her surrender to the lords, he repaired to Dunbar Castle, and thence fled to Orkney. Before leaving Dunbar, he sent George Dalgleish, his servant, to the castle at Edinburgh, instructing him to bring back a certain silver casket which Bothwell had left in a desk in his apartment. This casket had been given to Mary by her first husband, Francis II., and she had afterwards presented it to Bothwell. Sir James Balfour, governor of the castle, delivered the box to Dalgleish, but privately informed the earl of Morton that he had done so. In consequence, the messenger was intercepted on his return.

The silver casket was opened and found to contain a number of letters and sonnets written by Mary to Bothwell. There were eight letters in all, and these letters contained such incontestible proof of the queen's participation in Darnley's murder that the nobles had little difficulty in persuading Mary to sign her abdication at Lochleven. The letters were laid before Parliament a few months later, and unanimously declared, many of the queen's partisans being present, to have been "written wholly with Mary's own hand." They were afterwards placed in evidence against the queen at her trial in England; and though in her time, as in later years, labored attempts were made to prove the letters forgeries, Mary's known character and subsequent behavior afforded convincing proof of her guilt.

One of the letters reveals the queen's knowledge of, and assent to, Bothwell's plan of carrying her off to Dunbar Castle by a pretended show of force after Darnley's murder. The Earl of Huntly had been let into the secret, and tried to dissuade the queen from carrying out the design. Mary wrote to Bothwell, "He preached unto me that it was a foolish enterprise, and that with mine honor I could never marry you, seeing that being married, you did carry me away. . . . I told him that, seeing I had come so far, if you did not withdraw yourself of yourself no persuasion, nor death itself, should make me fail of my promise."

Two days after Mary's arrival at Glasgow, when she had gone there with the purpose of decoying Darnley back to Edinburgh, she wrote a long letter to Bothwell, one of the eight found in the casket. In this letter from Glasgow, Mary said:

Being departed from the place where I had left my heart, it was easy to be judged what was my countenance, seeing that I am no more than a body without a heart. . . . He [Darnley] said that he was like one dreaming, and that he was so glad to see me, he thought he would die of joy. . . . You never heard him speak better or more humbly. If I had not known from experience that he has a heart as soft as wax, and if mine had not been of diamond, into which no dart can enter but that which comes from your hands, I could have pitied him. However, fear nothing. . . . We are coupled [referring to her own husband and to Bothwell's wife] with two false races: the Devil sunder us, and God unite us forever, for the most faithful couple that ever he tied. . . . Cursed be this pocky fellow that troubleth me so much. . . . You make me dissemble so much that I am afraid thereof with horror, and you make me almost to play the part of a traitor. Remember, that if it were not for obeying you, I had rather be dead. My heart bleedeth for it. To be short, he will not come but with condition that I shall promise to be with him as heretofore at bed and board, and that I shall forsake him no more. . . . Send me word what I shall do, and whatsoever happens to me, I will obey you. Think also if you will not find some invention more secret by medicine, for he is to take medicine at Craigmillar. . . . Burn this letter, for it is too dangerous. . . . Now if it please you, my dear life, I spare neither honor, conscience, hazard, nor greatness whatsoever; take it, I pray you, in good part, and not after the interpretation of your false brother-in-law, to whom, I pray you, give no credit against the most faithful lover that ever you had, or ever shall have. See not her [Bothwell's wife] whose feigned tears should not be so much esteemed as the true and faithful labors which I sustain to merit her place, for the obtaining of which against my nature I betray them that may hinder me. God forgive me.

CHAPTER XXVIII

JAMES STUART, SON OF MARY

JAMES STEWART, Prior of St. Andrews and Earl of Moray, known in Scottish history as the "Good Regent," was the natural son of James V. by Lady Margaret Erskine, daughter of the fifth Earl of Mar, who afterwards married Sir Robert Douglas of Lochleven. He was born in 1533, and in his infancy was placed under the care of George Buchanan. James Stewart accompanied his half-sister, the young Queen Mary, when she went to France for her education. When the Reformation began, although at first adhering to the party of the queen regent, later (1559), he joined the Lords of the Congregation and soon became the leader of the Protestant nobles.

Moray was in Paris when he heard of the revolution which had dethroned Mary, and of his own nomination to the regency. He returned home at once, and taking the reins of government into his own hands, soon proved his ability to perform the work to which he had been called. After the battle of Langside and the flight of his sister into England, the regent continued his efforts to maintain order. But it was a difficult undertaking, as he had many enemies and his position tended to multiply them. Sir William Kirkaldy of Grange, governor of Edinburgh Castle, and Maitland of Lethington, now joined the queen's party, and a period of civil war ensued. For some years the factions of the regent and the queen kept the kingdom in incessant turmoil. Early in the year 1570, during a period of civil strife, Moray marched his army to Stirling. While returning through Linlithgow, on January 23d, he was shot by Hamilton of Bothwellhaugh, and died within a few hours.

Six months later, Matthew Stewart, Earl of Lennox, father of the murdered Darnley, was elected regent, and assumed the government. His ablest supporters were John Knox and James Douglas, Earl of Morton. The regent summoned a Parliament to meet at Edinburgh in May, 1571; but the queen's party held possession of the capital, and the meeting was adjourned, to reconvene at Stirling. It met there in August; at the same time, the opposing party held its Parliament in Edinburgh. From that city, a company of the queen's adherents, under the Earl of Huntly and Lord Hamilton, marched against Stirling, surprised the lords who were there assembled, and killed the regent. John Erskine, Earl of Mar, was then chosen regent; but he died on the 28th of October, 1572.

The regency now devolved upon the Earl of Morton. In the spring of 1573, he concluded an arrangement with England by which nearly two thousand English troops entered Scotland and assisted in the reduction of the castle of Edinburgh. The castle was surrendered toward the end of May. Its governor, Kirkaldy of Grange, and his brother, were hanged at the Cross of Edinburgh.

John Knox died at Edinburgh on November 24, 1572, in the sixty-seventh year of his age.

Early in 1578, Morton resigned the regency. He had never been popular, and his treatment of the Reformed Church lost him the support of its clergy. When the Roman Church was abolished at the time of the Reformation, the bishops and other prelates of that establishment were allowed to receive, during their lives, two thirds of the ecclesiastical revenues, the Protestant Church receiving for its maintenance one third. As the prelates began to die, their offices were filled by clerical agents of Morton and some of the other nobles. These agents being ministers, assumed the titles and were allowed a small part of the revenues of their positions, but handed the bulk of the receipts over to the patrons who had secured their appointment. The Scotch people called them straw bishops, or *tulchans* — tulchan being the name applied to a stuffed calf, which at milking time was set in position as if to suck the cow, the cow thus being deceived into giving her milk freely.

Alexander Erskine, keeper of Stirling Castle, and guardian of the young king, held a secret meeting with some of the dissatisfied nobles, in 1578, at which the twelve-year-old James was present. At this meeting the king was advised to take the reins of government into his own hands. Knowledge of the meeting having come to Morton's ears, he tendered his resignation as regent, which James accepted.

The government was then committed to a council of twelve members; and a competition between the rival factions in Scotland began for the possession of the juvenile king's favor. In 1579, Esme Stewart, Lord D'Aubigne, nephew of the Regent Lennox, and cousin to James, arrived in Scotland from France, where he had been brought up. This unworthy nobleman soon became a favorite of the king. He was first created Earl, then Duke of Lennox, and was appointed High Chamberlain and governor of the castle of Dumbarton. Captain James Stewart, second son of Lord Ochiltree, and brother-in-law to John Knox, was another of the king's favorites. He was elevated to the rank of Earl of Arran in 1581.

In December, 1580, Captain Stewart entered the king's council chamber, Earl Morton being present, and accused the latter of having taken part in the murder of Darnley. Two days later, the ex-regent was imprisoned in Edinburgh Castle, and was tried on the 1st of June, 1581. Almost every man upon the jury was his known enemy. Morton was condemned and beheaded on June 2d. Before his death he acknowledged that Bothwell had told him of the plot, and tried to induce him to join in the conspiracy. When asked why he had not revealed the intended crime, he replied "To whom could I have revealed it? To the queen? She was the doer of it

To Darnley? I durst not for my life; for I knew him to be such a child, that there was nothing told him but he would reveal it to her again."

In the spring of 1581, the king ratified Craig's *Confession of Faith*, which thus became the first National Covenant of Scotland. About this time Boyd, Archbishop of Glasgow, having died, the Privy Council granted to the Duke of Lennox the revenues of the archbishopric. But as Lennox was not able to draw them in his own name, he had recourse to a bishop of straw, according to the tulchan system. He found a minister of Stirling, named Robert Montgomery, who consented to play the part of his tulchan; and the king sought to impose this puppet upon the General Assembly of the Church of Scotland.

In 1582, the Assembly met at St. Andrews determined to prevent the settlement of Montgomery as Archbishop of Glasgow. The Government, understanding what they were about to do, sent a messenger-at-arms, who entered the Assembly hall and forbade them to proceed against Montgomery, under penalty of being treated as rebels. Notwithstanding this threat, the Assembly, after serious deliberation, declared that " No man could pretend to ecclesiastical functions, office, promotion, or benefice, by any absolute gift, collation, or admission by the civil magistrate or patron "; and that Montgomery, by accepting an ecclesiastical function at the hands of the State, had incurred the double penalty of deposition and excommunication.

Montgomery, in alarm, appeared before the Assembly, acknowledged that he had offended God and His Church, humbled himself before them, and promised to give up the archbishopric. But he was induced by Lennox to retain his post and soon after entered with a band of soldiers into the hall in which the Presbytery of Glasgow had met, to whom he presented an order from the king. The Presbytery refused to comply with this order, which they regarded as null and void in an ecclesiastical matter. The moderator was dragged from his chair, insulted, beaten, and thrown into prison.

The excommunication of Montgomery was announced from the pulpits. An Extraordinary Assembly met and drew up an address to the king in these terms :

That your Majesty, by device of some councillors, is caused to take upon you a spiritual power and authority, which properly belongeth unto Christ, as only King and Head of the Church, the ministry and execution of which is only given unto such as bear office in the ecclesiastical government in the same. So that in your Highness' person, some men press to erect a new popedom, as though your Majesty could not be full King and head of this commonwealth, unless as well the spiritual as temporal sword be put into your Highness' hands — unless Christ be bereft of his authority, and the two jurisdictions confounded which God hath divided, which directly tendeth to the wreck of all true religion.

It now remained to present this spirited address to the king. A deputation, at the head of which was Andrew Melville, repaired to Perth, where the king was residing. The Court was indignant at the boldness of the Assembly, the two favorites exclaimed loudly against it, and all were apprehensive that the ministers would answer for their audacity with their lives. They were warned against appearing before the king ; but notwithstanding all solicitations and menaces, the deputies on the following day proceeded to the palace.

Melville and his associates entered, and the king in council received them, sitting on his throne, surrounded with the splendor of his Court. Melville stepped forward and gravely read the remonstrance. But hardly had he finished, when the Earl of Arran, who was standing near the throne, frowning angrily on those around him, exclaimed in a threatening voice, " Who dare subscribe these treasonable articles ? "

" We dare," replied Melville calmly; and then advancing to the table which was before the king, he took a pen from the hand of the secretary of the Council, and signed his name below the articles. The other deputies immediately followed his example. Every one present was filled with amazement, and none dared to interrupt them.

Arran, overawed, was silent; Lennox addressed some conciliatory words to the deputies; the king yielded. Montgomery retired; and the jurisdiction of the Church, in regard to the calling and deprivation of ministers, was thus sanctioned anew.

The unworthy favorites of James, having disposed of Morton, their most dreaded rival, now became supreme in the Council of the king. Naturally, they abused their power, and before long a conspiracy was formed against them by many of the noblemen and gentry. The boy king was invited to Ruthven Castle, in Perthshire, for a season of hunting. Here he was to be entertained by the Earl of Gowrie. On the night of James's arrival, the earl and his friends assembled a thousand men and surrounded the castle. The next morning the king was told that he must remain as a prisoner. The Earl of Arran was seized and imprisoned, and the Duke of Lennox ordered to leave the kingdom. This plot is known in history as " The Raid of Ruthven."

Soon after, the king was removed to Stirling, and in October, 1582, he was conveyed to Holyrood Palace. He succeeded in escaping from the Ruthven party in June, 1583, and most of the parties to the plot immediately fled to England. The Earl of Gowrie was seized, tried for treason, condemned, and beheaded at Stirling in May, 1584. Andrew Melville, the leader of the Reformed clergy, was apprehended, but managed to escape, and fled to Berwick.

The Earl of Arran was reinstated as royal favorite, Lennox meanwhile having died in France. The former bestowed on himself the highest offices, became governor of Edinburgh, Blackness, Dumbarton, and Stirling Castles, four of the most important strongholds in the kingdom, and was made Chancellor and Lieutenant-General of Scotland.

In May, 1584, James convened a Parliament, which met with closed doors, and in which Montgomery sat as Archbishop of Glasgow, and Adamson, a still baser character, as Archbishop of St. Andrews. These two prelates, leagued with the unworthy favorites of James, inaugurated the most despotic measures.

At this Parliament were passed those acts, infamous in the history of Scotland, known as the Black Acts, which decreed that the king and his Council were competent in all matters; that all judgment, spiritual or temporal, which had not been approved by the king and his Parliament, should be of no force; and that the bishops and ecclesiastical commissioners appointed by the king might rule in all that concerned the Church.

Thus was the State set up to rule over the Church; and under the State, bishops were commissioned who were naturally its servile agents. These proceedings practically annihilated the Scottish Church, and left her neither liberty nor independence.

The Black Acts were proclaimed at the Market-Cross of Edinburgh. In vain did a few ministers read at the same place, in presence of the people, a protest against this legislation, which was a death-blow to the Church. The will of Arran prevailed, and more than twenty ministers were obliged to fly for safety into England. The king and his party, having obtained ample recognition of their supreme power, resolved to crush the rebellious preachers and nobles. Parliament was re-assembled in August. A process of treason was passed against the banished nobles, and their lands were forfeited. An act was passed commanding all ministers, and masters of colleges and of schools, to sign and humbly promise to observe the acts of the last Parliament; and they were ordered to obey the bishops appointed to rule over them.

Lord Maxwell had been for many generations the leading nobleman in Dumfries and its neighborhood; but the king at this time ventured to encroach upon his local supremacy in the election of a provost. Maxwell thereupon made war against James, and mustered a thousand men. The banished nobles saw their opportunity, and joined him. In November, 1585, they returned, collected their adherents, and met Maxwell at Selkirk. Thence with an army of eight thousand men they marched on Stirling. The king and Arran were in Stirling when the army approached. Arran fled to the Highlands, and the king had no alternative but to receive the proffered homage of his rebellious nobles and to pardon them. Most of the exiled ministers returned with the nobles, and resumed their functions. After a severe struggle with the Crown, the Presbyterian party prevailed.

On October 22, 1589, the King sailed for Norway, where he was to marry the Princess Anne of Denmark. Before starting he appointed Robert Bruce, one of the ministers of Edinburgh, as a member of his Privy Council, declaring that he trusted to him more than to all his nobles to preserve peace in the country.

On his return, James appeared delighted with the services rendered to him by the Presbyterian ministers. He called a General Assembly in August, 1590, and whether moved by dissimulation, or by a transient fit of enthusiasm, there pronounced that eulogy on the Church of Scotland which afterwards became famous: "I thank God that I was born in such a time as the time of the light of the Gospel; to such a place, as to be king in such a kirk, the sincerest kirk in the world. The Church of Geneva keepeth Pasch and Yule. What have they for them? They have no institution. As for our neighbor kirk in England, it is an evil said mass in English, wanting nothing but the liftings. I charge you, my good people, ministers, doctors, elders, nobles, gentlemen, and barons, to stand to your purity, and to exhort the people to do the same; and I, forsooth, so long as I brook my life and crown, shall maintain the same against all deadly enemies."

How soon and how completely James forgot these words will shortly appear. In the meantime they produced their effect. In 1592, Parliament passed a bill, abolishing all "acts contrary to the true religion," and ratifying the acts of the general assemblies. This has ever since been regarded as the charter of the Church of Scotland.

Notwithstanding James's professions there were still rumors of plots and designs of the Jesuits, and the clergy were annoyed at the lenity of the King to the Catholic nobles, Huntly, Errol, and Angus. In 1593, James made a demonstration against the Catholic earls, and they retired to Caithness. Later, they rebelled, and the Earl of Argyle was commissioned to march against them. He met them in battle at Glenlivet, on October 13, 1594. After a severe engagement, Argyle was completely defeated, and his followers fled in confusion. The king then marched with an army into Aberdeenshire, where Huntly fled before him. The latter's castle, together with that of the Earl of Errol, were dismantled; and in March, 1595, the Catholic earls left Scotland.

They returned in the summer of 1596, and the king seemed inclined to restore them to favor. Desirous of securing his succession to the English throne, James was rapidly declining from Presbyterianism, which he knew to be distasteful to the English Court. Being aware that in the domain of Elizabeth there existed a powerful Romanist party, he even attempted to conciliate them. Therefore, those Scottish nobles who were inclined to Catholicism having returned home, the government was intrusted by the king to eight councillors, the majority of whom were avowed or disguised Roman Catholics, and whose actions soon justified all the fears of the Reformers.

The commissioners of the General Assembly resolved to send a deputation to the king, to avert the evils with which their country was threatened, and appointed as their speaker James Melville, nephew of Andrew Melville. He was selected on account of his courteous manners, and because he was in favor with the sovereign. The commissioners were granted an interview, but scarcely had Melville begun to speak, when the king interrupted him, accusing the Presbyterian ministers of sedition. As the petitioner was beginning a reply, couched in the mildest terms, Andrew Melville, the uncle, finding that the occasion demanded a full and uncompromising statement of first principles, quitted the subordinate position which he had been willing for the time to occupy, and confronting the king, began to address him. James endeavored authoritatively to command the elder Melville to silence; but his high spirit was roused, and could not be overborne. Seizing the king's robe by the sleeve, in the earnestness of his mind and action, and terming him "God's silly vassal," Andrew Melville addressed him in a strain such as few kings have had the privilege of hearing.

"Sire," said he, "we will always humbly reverence your Majesty in public; but since we have this occasion to be with your Majesty in private, and since you are brought in extreme danger of your life and crown, and along with you the country and the Church of God are like to go to wreck, for not telling you the truth and giving you faithful counsel, we must discharge our duty, or else be traitors both to Christ and you. Therefore, Sire, as divers times before I have told you, so now again I must tell you, there are two kings and two kingdoms in Scotland: there is King James, the head of the commonwealth, and there is Christ Jesus, the King of the Church, whose subject James the Sixth is, and of whose kingdom he is not a king, nor a lord, nor a head, but a member."

James then declared the Catholic lords had returned without his previous knowledge, and pledged his word that the proposals which they had made to the Privy Council should not be received until they left the kingdom, and that even then he would show them no favor before they satisfied the Church.

This solemn pledge of the king was soon broken, however, and steps for restoring the conspirators succeeded one another with rapidity. Mr. David Black, minister of St. Andrews, delivered a sermon in which he assailed the king and his nobles as false to their pledges. He was immediately summoned before the Privy Council, and appeared, but declined its jurisdiction. He was tried, and sentenced to confinement beyond the Tay. The commissioners of the Assembly addressed a protest to the king, but were answered by a royal proclamation declaring their powers illegal, and ordering them to leave Edinburgh. An act of Council was also passed, requiring the ministers, before receiving payment of their stipends, to subscribe a bond, by which they promised to submit to the judgment of the king and the Privy Council as often as they were accused of seditious or treasonable doctrine; and commanding all magistrates in burghs and noblemen and gentlemen in country parishes, to interrupt and imprison any preachers whom they should hear uttering such language from pulpits.

On the 17th of December, a rumor spread that the Earl of Huntly had been at the palace of Holyrood. One Balcanquhal referred to this in his sermon preached at Edinburgh on that day. At its close, he called on the barons present not to disgrace their names and their ancestors, but to meet the ministers immediately in the little church. Here a crowd collected, and the minister pointed out to them the consequences to the Reformed Church if the Catholic earls should be reinstated.

A deputation waited on the king, who was in Council, to lay before him the dangers which threatened religion. "What danger see you," said the king, "and who dares to assemble against my proclamation?" Lord Lindsay replied, "We dare do more than that, and will not suffer religion to be overthrown." The clamor increasing, the king became alarmed, and ordered the doors of the palace to be closed. The next day he left Edinburgh for Linlithgow, where he issued a proclamation which ordered the courts of law to be removed from the capital. The provost was commanded to imprison the ministers, and the tumult was declared a treasonable riot. Eventually the provost and magistrates were severely punished, and a fine of 20,000 merks imposed on the capital.

On the 5th of August, 1600, an event occurred which has become known in Scottish history as the Gowrie Conspiracy. John Ruthven, third Earl of Gowrie, was the son of that Gowrie who took part in the Raid of Ruthven during James's minority, and grandson of Lord Ruthven, who acted a leading part in the killing of David Rizzio. This third Earl of Gowrie led the opposition in Parliament against the levying of a tax which James wished to impose, and in consequence the king's project was defeated. He accordingly became very much incensed against Gowrie. Robertson suggests that James had a more serious grievance against the Ruthvens. It was whispered about that there was an estrangement between the king and his wife due to the discovery of an *amour* between the queen and Gowrie's brother, Alexander Ruthven. On the morning of the fifth of August the king left his palace of Falkland on a hunting expedition, accompanied by some twenty of his courtiers. Later in the day he rode with his attendants towards Perth, and drew up at Gowrie House. No preparations had been made for entertaining the king, but after some delay dinner was prepared and served. When the repast was finished, the king and Alexander Ruthven had some whispered conversation together, and then both withdrew to an upper chamber of the mansion. Some of the courtiers, accompanied by the Earl of Gowrie, passed out of the house into the courtyard. While there, the king's voice rang out from a turret window above crying, "Treason! treason! Help! I am murdered!" Those who were without entered the house and ran up the stairs to the king's chamber. The servants below heard the sounds of a fierce struggle going on overheard. When it ceased and they had made their way to the scene, the Earl of Gowrie was found dead in the picture gallery, having been stabbed from behind. His brother lay dead on the turnpike stair, his sword unsheathed. Some of the servants ran into the street and announced to the citizens that their master, the earl, had been murdered.   An alarm was raised, and soon a large crowd assembled under the windows of Gowrie House, and a great outcry was raised against the king. " Come down! " they shouted; " come down, thou son of Signor Davie! thou hast slain a better man than thyself! "   It was some time before the tumult could be allayed, and then the king and his party mounted their horses and rode back to Falkland.

About a month afterwards, the king published his account of this murder, which was to the effect that he was decoyed to Gowrie House by Alexander Ruthven, who promised to divide with him a pot of gold that he had stolen; that when the king left the chamber where he had dined, he was led into a room and there locked in with an armed man; that Alexander Ruthven retired, but soon returned and tried to bind the king ; that the king overpowered him and thrust him out of the chamber, the armed man never interfering; that one of the royal train then came up and stabbed Ruthven twice or thrice with his dagger; that the Earl rushed in when the tumult rose, with some armed servants at his back, and after a sharp fight was stricken dead with a stroke through his heart.   Such was the king's story.   The courtiers who had been with him on the day of the tragedy testified to its correctness; but the majority of the people disbelieved it and the opinion became general that the Gowrie Conspiracy was a contrivance of the king to murder Gowrie.

CHAPTER XXIX

THE WISEST FOOL IN CHRISTENDOM

QUEEN ELIZABETH died on March 24, 1603, and the same day James VI. was proclaimed her successor. He began his progress southward on the fifth of April, and on May 6, entered London, greeted by the shouts of his English subjects.

James had a fixed aversion to a Presbyterian Church, and as fixed a love for a Church on the Episcopalian plan. A Presbyterian Church, he had found, could not be easily induced to do royal bidding. All its ministers being equal in power, nothing could be done except by the voice of the majority. This required public assemblies and free discussions — things which despots cannot bear. It was quite different with the Episcopacy. There the minister was merely the subject of the bishop, and the bishop of the archbishop. The king appointed both the bishops and the archbishops, so that the whole fabric hung at the royal girdle.

The removal of the Court from Edinburgh to London proved for a time disastrous to the trade and prestige of the Scottish capital. James was followed South by many of the nobility and gentry; and there soon began from Scotland an exodus which carried thousands of her sons to all quarters of the world. They repaired in such swarms to London that the king issued a proclamation forbidding any of his countrymen from leaving Scotland without a passport from the Privy Council. Walter Scott, in his *Fortunes of Nigel*, gives an interesting account of the Court of James I. in London, to which flocked so many thousands of his needy countrymen in search of place or preferment. In the beginning of James's reign the emigration from Scotland to Ulster began; and about the time of the English settlement of Virginia hundreds of enterprising Scots were crossing the Irish channel to build themselves homes and communities in Down and Antrim.

Besides these many went to the continent and served under foreign princes. A strong brigade of Scots fought with much glory in the armies of Gustavus Adolphus, King of Sweden; while others entered the service of Austria and the Italian states. But the great majority of these soldiers of fortune made their way to France, where they had been favored visitors ever since the beginning of the Ancient League between that country and Scotia. There was a "Scotland Street" in Paris as early as 1313, so-called from the number of Scottish students living thereon. Dieppe and Orleans, also, had its "Scottish Quarter." The Scots College was founded at Paris by David, Bishop of Moray, in the year 1326, and it was usually filled with Scotch students. In Bruce's day there were Scotch colonies at Metz and at Clermont-sur-Oise. " Scotch holy bread " (fat of beef), " Haughty as a Scot," " Through to daylight like a Scotch dagger " were some French proverbs of that time.

28

The " Scots Guard," organized in France by Charles VII. about 1425, was the most trusted of all the royal troops, and the king's person was virtually placed in its care. It continued to be called the Scots Guard even after there had ceased to be any Scotchmen in it. In his story of *Quentin Durward*, Scott gives a fascinating description of the life these Guards led at Court and in the field. When Joan of Arc began her heroic struggle the Scottish soldiers warmly devoted themselves to her service; and in all the work of the recovery of France from England the Scots took a prominent part, until the throne of Charles VII. was secure. During the defence of Orleans the bishop of that See was a Scot named Kirkmichael, and while the siege lasted the bishop and the Scottish residents greatly distinguished themselves by their valor. When Joan of Arc made her way to the beleaguered city, she was accompanied by Sir Patrick Ogilvy and a large number of Scottish soldiers. One soldier, Walter Bowe, returned to his native land and became a monk at Inch Colm, where he continued Fordun's *Chronicle*, and commemorated the deeds of Joan of Arc, " whom," he writes, " I saw and knew and in whose company I was present to her life's end."

James was not long master of the English throne before he applied himself to his cherished design of putting down the Presbyterian and setting up an Episcopal Church in Scotland. Before doing this, he first proceeded to tear down the Presbyterian party in England. How James went about this work may be gathered from the account of his Hampton Court Conference, which was ordered to assemble at that palace in the early part of January, 1604, at which the king announced, he would hear arguments for and against the bishops. The account of this conference was published by Dr. Barlow, the Dean of Chester, in 1604. It was reprinted in 1638, and again in a collection of tracts called *The Phœnix*. The following extracts are taken from a reprint made by Thomas Fuller in his *Church History of Britain*, published at London in 1655 (Oxford edition, 1845, vol. v., pp. 266 to 304):

First Day, Jan. 14, 1604:
KING JAMES.—" For blessed be God's gracious goodness, who hath brought me into the promised land, where religion is purely professed, where I sit amongst grave, learned, and reverent men; not as before, elsewhere, a king without state, without honor, without order, where beardless boys would brave us to our face. . . ."
Second Day, Monday, January 16th:
KING JAMES.—" I approve the calling and use of bishops in the church, and it is my aphorism, ' No BISHOP, No KING,' nor intend I to take confirmation [away] from the bishops, which they have long enjoyed, seeing as great reason that none should confirm, as that none should preach, without the bishop's license. . . ."
MR. KNEWSTUB [regarding the use of the cross in baptism].—" Put the case, the Church hath power to add significant signs, it may not add them where Christ hath already ordained them, which is as derogatory to Christ's institution as if one should add to the Great Seal of England."

KING JAMES.—" The case is not alike, seeing the sacrament is fully finished before any mention of the cross is made therein."

MR. KNEWSTUB.—" If the Church hath such a power, the greatest scruple is, how far the ordinance of the Church bindeth, without impeaching Christian liberty."

KING JAMES.—" I will not argue that point with you, but answer as kings in Parliament, *Le roy s'avisera.* This is like Mr. John Black, a beardless boy, who told me the last Conference in Scotland that he would hold conformity with his majesty in matters of doctrine, but every man for ceremonies was to be left to his own liberty. But I will have none of that; I will have one doctrine, one discipline, one religion, in substance and in ceremony. Never speak more to that point, how far you are bound to obey."

DR. REYNOLDS.—" I desire, that, according to certain provincial constitutions, the clergy may have meetings every three weeks:

" i. In rural deaneries, therein to have prophesying, as Archbishop Grindall and other bishops desired of her late majesty.

" ii. That such things as could not be resolved there might be referred to the arch-deacon's visitations.

" iii. And so, the episcopal synod, where the bishop with his presbytery shall determine such points before not decided."

KING JAMES.—" If you aim at a Scottish Presbytery, it agreeth as well with monarchy as God and the devil. Then Jack and Tom, and Will and Dick, shall meet and censure me and my Council. Therefore, I reiterate my former speech, *Le roy s'avisera.* Stay, I pray, for one seven years before you demand; and then if you find me grown pursy and fat, I may perchance hearken unto you, for that government will keep me in breath and give me work enough. I shall speak of one matter more, somewhat out of order, but it skilleth not. Dr. Reynolds, you have often spoken for my supremacy, and it is well; but know you any, here or elsewhere, who like of the present government ecclesiastical, and dislike my supremacy ? "

DR. REYNOLDS.—" I know none."

KING JAMES.—" Why, then I will tell you a tale. After that the religion restored by King Edward the Sixth was soon overthrown by Queen Mary here in England, we in Scotland felt the effect of it; for thereupon Mr. Knox writes to the Queen Regent, a virtuous and moderate lady, telling her that she was the supreme head of the Church; and charged her as she would answer it at God's tribunal, to take care of Christ's evangel in suppressing the popish prelates who withstood the same. But how long, trow you, did this continue ? Even till by her authority the popish bishops were repressed; and Knox, with his adherents, being brought in, made strong enough. Then began they to make small account of her supremacy, when, according to that more light wherewith they were illuminated, they made a farther reformation of religion. How they used the poor lady, my mother, is not unknown; and how they dealt with me in my minority. I thus apply it: My lords, the bishops, I may thank you that these men plead thus for my supremacy. They think they cannot make their party good, but by appealing unto it; but if once you were out and they were in, I know what would become of my supremacy; for, No BISHOP, No KING. I have learned of what cut they have been, who, preaching before me since my coming into England, passed over with silence my being supreme governor in causes ecclesiastical. Well, Doctor, have you anything else to say ? "

DR. REYNOLDS.—" No more, if it please your Majesty."

KING JAMES.—" If this be all your party hath to say, I will make them conform themselves, or else I will harry them out of the land, or else do worse. . . ."

Third Day:

THE ARCHBISHOP OF CANTERBURY.—" Undoubtedly, your Majesty speaks by the special assistance of God's Spirit. . . ."

THE BISHOP OF LONDON.—" I protest, my heart melteth with joy, that Almighty God, of his singular mercy, hath given us such a king, as, since Christ's time, the like hath not been."

Three events, of greater or less relative importance, characterize the reign of King James after his accession to the English throne. The first of these was a new translation of the Bible into English. This was suggested to the king at the Hampton Court Conference by the same Dr. Reynolds whose Puritan party the royal bully had threatened to harry out of his kingdom. James caught at the idea at once. To be the patron of such a work of learning exactly suited his vanity. Accordingly, though opposed by the Bishop of London, the proposition was sanctioned by the king. In July, 1604, he wrote a letter intimating the appointment of fifty-four scholars for the preparation of the version, and instructing the bishops that whenever " a living of twenty pounds " became vacant, they should inform his Majesty of the circumstance, in order that he might recommend one of the translators to the patron. Seven of those who were appointed died, or declined the task. The remaining forty-seven were divided into six groups. Two groups sat at Westminster, two at Oxford, and two at Cambridge. They agreed upon their method of operation, made a division of the work, and completed their task within four years. The expenses seem to have been borne by Barker, the printer and patentee, who paid the sum of £3500.

The second event for which the reign of James will be forever memorable was his confiscation of the estates of the banished Catholic earls of Ulster, the eviction of the native Irishry from these estates, and their subsequent plantation and acquisition by Scottish and English " undertakers," in accordance with the king's plans.

The third event was James's persecution of the Independents in England, and the oppression of the Presbyterians in Scotland. As a result of these persecutions, John Robinson's Pilgrim followers were compelled to seek a refuge in Holland, and later in America, where they founded the Puritan Commonwealth; while many of the bravest and most independent spirits in Scotland crossed over to the new settlements in Ulster, where they likewise helped to build up democratic communities and families that later added such a large and influential element to the Anti-Jacobite population of America.

The additional power which his position as King of England gave him soon led James to attempt the substitution of Episcopacy for Presbyterianism in Scotland. He first attempted to deprive the Scottish Church of its General Assemblies by proroguing their meetings; for he knew that so long as these bodies could meet in freedom, bishops could never get authority in Scotland.

On the 2d of July, 1605, notwithstanding the king's prorogation, nineteen ministers met in Assembly at Aberdeen. While they were sitting, a messenger-at-arms entered and charged them in the king's name to dismiss or incur the penalty of rebellion. The Assembly did dismiss, but appointed to meet again in three months. The wrath of the king, when informed of the meeting of this Assembly, knew no bounds. The ministers were forthwith arrested, and fourteen were sent to prison. Eight of these were banished to the remotest parts of the kingdom. The other six, among whom were John Forbes, the moderator, and John Welsh, son-in-law to John Knox, were confined in dungeons in the castle of Blackness, and after suffering fourteen months' imprisonment, were banished to France.

In the summer of 1606, letters were sent by the king to six of the most distinguished of the ministers who had not been already seized on account of the Aberdeen Assembly, ordering them to appear at the English Court in September. These ministers were Andrew and James Melville, William Scott, John Carmichael, William Watson, James Balfour, Adam Colt, and Robert Wallace. The king's aim was to engage the ministers and the English bishops in a conference touching the superior merits of Episcopacy; and every endeavor was used to draw the Scottish ministers into the use of language which might furnish a plausible pretext for instituting proceedings against them. James commanded them to attend a course of sermons preached by four English divines—on the bishops, the supremacy of the Crown, and the absence of all authority for the office of lay elders. The Scots heard the bishops' sermons with silent contempt; but Andrew Melville was accused of having caricatured the service in a Latin epigram which came under the notice of the Privy Council. For this he was summoned to answer before that tribunal, and was brought to trial as guilty of a treasonable act. Melville, in a moment of passion, when delivering a vehement invective against the hierarchy during the course of his examination, seized and shook the white sleeves of Bancroft, the Archbishop of Canterbury, at the same time calling them "Romish rags." For this offence he was imprisoned in the Tower of London four years, and afterwards banished to Sedan, in France, where he died. His nephew, James Melville, was also imprisoned and prohibited from returning to Scotland. The other four ministers were banished to remote parts of Scotland.

Free meetings of the Assembly having now been suppressed, the king proceeded to call together from time to time packed assemblies, and at one of these held at Glasgow, June 8, 1610, Episcopacy was restored; the right of calling and dismissing assemblies was declared to belong to the royal prerogative; the bishops were declared moderators of diocesan synods; all presentations to benefices were appointed to be directed by bishops; and the power of excommunicating and absolving offenders was conferred on them.

James now sought to introduce five articles of his own into the Church discipline, known as the *Five Articles of Perth*. These articles were kneeling at the communion, the observance of holy days, episcopal confirmation, private baptism, and the private administration of communion. They were adopted by an Assembly which met at Perth in August, 1618, and ratified by a Parliament which met at Edinburgh three years later. Meanwhile, the king had set up an engine of tyranny called the Court of High Commission, with the Archbishop of St. Andrews at its head. This Scottish Inquisition had power to summon before its bar any individual whatever, to examine into his life, conversation, and opinions on matters of religion, and to fine, imprison, or banish at discretion.

James insisted that his articles should be enforced on the people. He was always exhorting and threatening in vain; nonconforming ministers were imprisoned and banished without effect; and in spite of all his efforts many of the conforming ministers' churches began to be deserted, and they were left to declaim against schism and rebellion to empty pews.

James's natural timidity made him constantly wear on his fat body a dress stuffed and padded thick enough to resist the stroke of a dagger. Nevertheless, he was vindictive to a degree, and susceptible to the grossest flattery. He was extremely conceited — a weak feature of his character much fed by the fulsome adulation of his English bishops. Of his kingly prerogatives he had the most extravagant ideas. In literature he was a pedant. He died March 27, 1625, at the age of fifty-nine.

That is not wholly a fanciful argument which is used by some who believe James to have been the son of Rizzio, basing their belief on the theory of hereditary transmission of parental foibles. The carping pettishness and vanity of his character, manifested in the importance which he gave to the minutest details of ecclesiastical formalities, is certainly more in keeping with that of the Italian agent of the Papal Court, who became the secretary, confidante, and favorite of James's mother, than it is with those traits which distinguished the family of his mother's lawful spouse.

CHAPTER XXX

SCOTLAND UNDER CHARLES I.

JAMES VI. was succeeded by his son, Charles I., who began his reign at the age of twenty-four. Like his father, he held erroneous ideas concerning the royal prerogative, and like some of his father's descendants who rule in the present day, was firmly convinced that he had been taken into partnership by the Almighty for the purpose of remodelling the universe. It has been said that Charles was incapable of distinguishing between his moral and political rights; possibly an inherited tendency led his narrow Jesuitical mind to assume and to maintain that his political position gave him an unquestionable right to dictate to his subjects the form of their worship. Hating Presbyterianism as intensely as his father had hated it, he was determined on establishing Epispopacy in Scotland and was delayed in this project only by the lack of money. To procure this, in October, 1626, he issued a revocation of all grants of lands by the Crown since the Reformation. This was intended for the benefit of the bishops and clergy, but it naturally aroused feelings of resentment among the nobles whose interests it threatened to invade, many of whom had received grants of Church lands from the Crown. Charles sent the Earl of Nithsdale to propose his plans to the Scottish Parliament, with promises of kingly favor to those who should submit, and threats of rigorous proceedings against those who might refuse.

The Convocation of nobles, though usually servile enough, resisted this proposition with all its power. The barons and gentry composing that body, while ever willing to assist the king in subverting the civil and religious rights of his subjects, became violently enraged when their own property rights were threatened. A secret meeting was held, at which the interested nobles resolved among themselves to destroy the king's emissary and all his supporters, in case the detested measure should be pressed. When the day of meeting came, therefore, the conspirators entered the Parliament House carrying arms concealed about their persons for the purpose of killing Nithsdale and his party in the open convention. That nobleman in some way became aware of the temper of the barons, and prudently deferred presenting the measure until it could be submitted to Charles for modification. The king accordingly found it necessary to limit the scope of his demands, and raised processes to reduce the grants on legal grounds. Finally, a deputation from the nobles visited London to treat with the king and a compromise was effected. The church lands and the property in dispute were permitted to remain in the hands of those who held them, under the condition of paying a proportion as rental to the Crown, while the Crown also insisted on a right of feudal superiority, whereby additional dues would fall to the public revenue; an arrangement was also effected by which the lands became chargeable for tithes for the benefit of the clergy.

Many of the nobles only surrendered their full claims to the church lands with a grudge which long embittered their minds, and predisposed them to join in the struggle against the king which subsequently ensued.

Charles visited Scotland in 1633, and was crowned at Holyrood on June 18th. He brought with him a little, square-faced, dark-eyed man, who afterwards became notorious as Archbishop Laud, of whom it has been said, "He came in like a fox, reigned like a lion, and died like a dog." Charles was eager to complete the scheme of church polity which his father had begun, and during his presence in Scotland preparations were made for composing a new book of canons and a liturgy. Bishops and archbishops had been for some thirty years forced upon the Church of Scotland. The king and his archbishop thought the time had now come for making the Scots use the Episcopal forms of worship also, thus completing the uniformity between the churches of the two kingdoms. Accordingly, they caused a liturgy or service-book to be prepared for use in Scotch congregations. It was framed by the bishops of Ross and Dunblane on the pattern of the English prayer-book, and submitted to Laud for his approval. It came back with numerous alterations. The canons, as finally revised by Laud and the bishops of London and Norwich, were ratified by the king in May, 1635, and promulgated by him in 1636. They bore little resemblance to any Scottish ecclesiastical rules subsequent to the Reformation. Charles also signed a warrant to the Privy Council on the 18th of October, 1636, which contained his instructions concerning the introduction of the new liturgy, and the Council in December issued a proclamation ordering all the people to conform to the same. The royal proclamation ordered the new service-book to be observed in all the churches on Easter day, 1637, but, on account of popular opposition, the authorities postponed the date of its introduction. This postponement merely served to heighten the feeling against it.

The 23d of July, 1637, was the day finally set for the introduction of the new service. In the cathedral church of St. Giles at Edinburgh, the two archbishops and other bishops, the members of the Privy Council, and the magistrates in their robes, attended in the forenoon to grace the proceedings. The Bishop of Edinburgh was to preach, and the Dean to read the service. A great crowd filled the church. The Dean, attired in his surplice, came from the vestry, and passed to the reading-room amid a deep silence. He had scarcely begun to read when confused cries arose. As he proceeded, the clamor became louder, and the prayers could not be heard. An old woman, named Janet Geddes, who kept a cabbage-stall at the Tron, grasped the little folding-stool on which she sat, and threw it at the Dean's head, crying, "Out! thou false thief, dost thou say mass at my lug?" The Dean, forgetful of his dignity, dodged the missile, and it flew by his head without harming him. The people now started to their feet, and the church became a scene of wild uproar. The voices of the women were loudest; some cried, "Woe, woe me!" others shouted that they were "bringing in Popery," and a number of stools were thrown at both bishop and dean. Several of the more vehement rushed towards the desk, to seize upon the object of their indignation. The dean, terrified by this sudden outburst of popular fury, tore himself out of their hands and fled, glad to escape, though with the loss of his sacerdotal vestments. The bishop of Edinburgh himself then entered the pulpit, and endeavored to allay the wild tumult, but in vain. He was instantly assailed with equal fury, and was with difficulty rescued by the interference of the magistrates. When the most unruly of the rioters had been thrust out of the church, the dean attempted to resume the reading, but the din of the mob on the outside, shouting aloud their hostile cries against "Popery," breaking the windows, and battering the doors, compelled him to terminate the service abruptly. When the bishops came out of the church the multitude attacked Bishop Lindsay, and he narrowly escaped with his life.

At a meeting of the Glasgow Synod, John Lindsay preached, after being warned by some of the women in the congregation that " if he should touch the service book in his sermon, he should be sent out of his pulpit." William Annan, minister of Ayr, in a sermon preached before the same Synod, defended the liturgy. Afterwards, on leaving the church, he was assailed with cries and reproaches; which were repeated whenever he appeared on the streets. Returning one night from the bishop's residence, he was surrounded by some hundreds of persons, most of whom were women, and assailed with neaves, staves, and peats. " They beat him sore," says the old chronicle, " his cloak, ruff, and hat were torn. However, on his cries, and lights set out from many windows he escaped all bloody wounds." At Brechin, the bishop of that district armed himself with pistols, and entering the church with his family and servants, bolted and barred the doors, and read the service to his followers. On coming out, he was set upon by the people, nearly killed by their treatment, and obliged to leave the place and give up his bishopric.

The excitement spread over the country like wild-fire. The liturgy was everywhere spurned. Petitions from all parts were poured in upon the Privy Council, and that body wrote a mild letter to the king, advising him of the serious crisis which the attempt to enforce the book had brought on. On the 4th of August, the Council was commanded by the king to punish all the persons concerned in the disturbance, and to support the bishops and clergy in establishing the liturgy. In violation of the chartered rights of the burghs, the king also ordered them to choose no persons as their magistrates except such as would conform. The Council resolved that another attempt should be made to use the liturgy on Sunday, the 13th of August; but when that day came, none could be found in Edinburgh who were willing to officiate as readers.

Meanwhile, the king's letter to the Privy Council tended to increase the popular excitement. In the course of a few days, twenty-four noblemen, many barons, about a hundred ministers, commissioners from sixty-six parishes and also from a number of the principal burghs, with large numbers of the gentry and commoners from the counties of Fife, Stirling, Lothian, Ayr, and Lanark, arrived in Edinburgh, all resolved to defend the purity and freedom of their national religion. This multitude crowded the streets; when lodging failed they camped at the gates and beneath the walls of the city. They came to petition the king, through his Council, against the service-book and the change in public worship. Their petitions were received, and a promise was given that they should have his Majesty's answer on October 17th.

In the middle of that month a greater number of people than before met in Edinburgh, to await the king's answer. Fresh petitions from two hundred parishes were presented. On the 17th of October, the king's answer was announced in the shape of three proclamations by the Council, which were to the effect that nothing would be done that day touching religious matters; that the petitioners should leave Edinburgh within twenty-four hours, under pain of rebellion; that the government and courts of law should remove to Linlithgow; and that all copies of a certain popular book, entitled *A Dispute against the English Popish Ceremonies Obtruded upon the Church of Scotland*, should be brought to the Council and publicly burned.

The petitioners resolved at once to disobey the summons, and, instead of acting merely on the defensive, to become themselves the assailants. They accordingly laid before the Privy Council a formal complaint against the prelates, accusing them directly of being the cause of all the troubles that disturbed the nation, by their lawless and tyrannical attempts to force the book of canons and the liturgy upon an unwilling Church and people. They complained also of the arbitrary nature of the proclamation commanding them to leave the town, while they were peaceably waiting for an answer to their supplication. They pointed out some of the pernicious characteristics of the books of common prayer and canons, as being subversive of the discipline established in the Scottish Church; and concluded by declaring the belief of the petitioners that all these wrongs had been committed by the bishops, and craving that these matters might be brought to trial, and decided according to justice.

This important document was subscribed by thirty-eight of the nobility, several thousand gentlemen, nearly all the ministers of the kingdom, and all the commissioners of the burghs.

The morning following the proclamations of the Council, while the bishop of Galloway was proceeding to the Council House, a mob attacked him and pursued him to the door. The crowd then surrounded the Council House, and demanded that the obnoxious lords should surrender. A part of the mob also gathered around the Town House, and, entering the lobbies, threatened that, unless the magistrates joined the citizens in opposing the liturgy, they would burn the building. When this became known to the Council, the Treasurer and the earl of Wigton forced their way to the Town House, where they held a brief consultation with the magistrates as to the best means of dispersing the mob. The magistrates accordingly announced to the multitude without that they had acceded to the demands of the people. But the moment the Treasurer and his friends attempted to return to the Council House, they were assailed with hootings and jeers. Then a rush was made, and the Treasurer was thrown to the ground; his hat, cloak, and staff of office were torn from him, and it was with difficulty he escaped being trodden to death. He was rescued by his companions, however, and finally carried to the Council House. Here, in a short time, the magistrates joined the Council, and all of them were beset by the crowds. Many trembled for their safety, and at last it was resolved to send for the nobles who were opposed to the liturgy. By their persuasions, the crowds were dispersed, and the counsellors managed to reach their homes in safety.

Before separating, the Presbyterians agreed to meet again on the 15th of November. In the interval they exerted themselves to the utmost to secure a large meeting of the people to await an answer to their former petitions. On the appointed day, the Presbyterians assembled in the capital again, in still larger numbers. The Privy Council held a conference with their leaders, and requested the nobles to use their influence with their friends to induce them to return quietly to their homes. The nobles on the side of the petitioners maintained their right to meet and to present their grievances; but, to obviate all cause of complaint, they agreed for their party that it should act through representatives. To this the Council assented, and the petitioners accordingly appointed four permanent committees, the first consisting of as many nobles as pleased to join the party ; the second, two gentlemen from every county ; the third, one minister from every presbytery ; and the fourth, one burgess from every burgh. These representatives formed a general commission, representing the whole body of the Presbyterians. A smaller committee was then chosen by the general commission, the members of which were to reside at Edinburgh, watch the progress of events, and be ready to communicate with the whole body on any emergency. This smaller committee was composed of sixteen persons—four noblemen, four gentlemen, four ministers, and four burgesses; and from the circumstance of their sitting in four separate rooms in the Parliament House, they were designated " The Four Tables." A member from each of these constituted a chief Table of last resort, making a supreme council of four members. At first, the Tables only took charge of the petitions, and urged them on the attention of the government; but they shortly began to form proposals for the party, to assume the functions of government, and the control of affairs ultimately passed into their hands.

On December 21, 1637, the committee of the Tables demanded of the Privy Council that their petitions should be heard. John Campbell, Earl of Loudon, boldly stated their grievances, and protested against the bishops, who were the chief delinquents, sitting as judges in their own cases. In

January, 1638, the Earl of Traquair, Lord Treasurer of Scotland, was called to London by the king, and returned to Scotland with Charles's instructions, which were soon made public. They appeared in the form of a proclamation, which declared that " the bishops were unjustly accused as being authors of the service-book and canons, seeing whatever was done by them in that matter was by his Majesty's authority and order." The proclamation further condemned all meetings and petitions against the use of the books, prohibiting all such proceedings under pain of rebellion; and ordaining that no supplicant should appear in any town where the Council was sitting under pain of treason. Traquair attempted to have this proclamation issued at Stirling before the Presbyterians could publicly protest against it; thus shutting them off from the only legal method by which the dispute could be brought before Parliament. But when the members of the Privy Council appeared in Stirling to publish the proclamation, they were met by the Lords Home and Lindsay, who read a protest, and affixed a copy of it on the market-cross beside that of the proclamation, thus preserving the constitutional right of the petitioners to appeal to Parliament. In this protest, they claimed that they should still have the right to petition the king; stated that they would not recognize the bishops as judges in any court ; that they should not incur any loss for non-observance of such canons and proclamations as were contrary to the Acts of Parliament and of the General Assembly; and that if any disturbance should arise, it should not be imputed to them.

These proceedings hastened on the crisis. The Presbyterians now realized fully the extent to which the king was willing to go in supporting the bishops. At the same time, it became apparent that there was needed a closer organization and more permanent bond of union among them than that afforded by the Tables, if they expected to undertake a forcible resistance to the policy of Charles. Under these considerations it was suggested by Alexander Henderson and some of his brother ministers, that the Presbyterians should in a public manner renew their acceptance of the National Covenant. On the 26th of February the subject was openly mentioned in the churches, and it was found that there was a general desire on the part of the nation that the Covenant should be newly taken. Accordingly, Alexander Henderson and Johnstone of Warriston, an advocate, were appointed to frame an instrument to suit the present conditions, and Lords Rothes, Loudon, and Balmerino were selected to revise it. This new National Covenant consisted of three parts—the first was a copy of the negative confession, or old Covenant of 1581; the second contained a summary of the Acts of Parliament which condemned Roman Catholicism and ratified the Acts of the General Assembly establishing the Reformed Church; and the third part—written by Henderson—was the New Covenant, by which the subscribers swore in the name of the " Lord their God," that they would remain in the profession of their religion; that they would defend it to the utmost of their power from all errors; that they would stand by the king's person in support of the true religion, the liberties, and the laws of the kingdom; and that they would stand by each other in defence of the same against all persons.

The 28th of February, 1638, was the day chosen for the signing of the Covenant. By daybreak all of the commissioners were met. The Covenant was read over to them, and each proposition discussed and agreed to. The meeting for the signing of the Covenant had been appointed for the afternoon, and crowds of people soon gathered in the Greyfriars' Church and churchyard. From all parts of the kingdom some sixty thousand people assembled; and before the commissioners appeared the church and grounds were densely filled with multitudes of Scotland's bravest and wisest sons and daughters. When the hour of two approached, Rothes, Loudon, Henderson, Dickson, and Johnstone entered, bearing a copy of the Covenant prepared for signatures. The Earl of Loudon then stood forth and spoke to the people. He made an eloquent and patriotic address touching the preservation of their religion, their duty to God, and to their country. He voiced the nation's defiance of tyrannous threatenings in these memorable words: " We know no other bands between a king and his subjects than those of religion and the laws; and if these are broken, men's lives are not dear to them. Threatened we shall not be. Such fears are past with us." After he had ceased speaking, Johnstone of Warriston unrolled the vast sheet of parchment and read the Covenant. Opportunity was then given for those who might have objections to offer to do so, but no objections were offered. An aged nobleman, the earl of Sutherland, was the first to sign the bond, and then name followed name in quick succession until all within the church had affixed their signatures. The parchment was then carried out to the churchyard, and placed on a flat gravestone for additional signatures. Here the scene became still more impressive. The emotions of many became irrepressible. Some wept and cried aloud; some burst into a shout of exultation; some, after their names, added the words "till death"; and some, opening a vein, subscribed with their own blood. As the space became filled, they wrote their names in a contracted form, limiting them at last to the initial letters, till not a spot remained on which another letter could be inscribed. On the next day, copies of the Covenant were circulated in Edinburgh, and carried throughout the kingdom, that by being universally signed it might become indeed a National Covenant. Before the end of April there were few parishes in Scotland in which the Covenant had not been signed by nearly all of competent age and character. " Some men of no small note," wrote Henderson, " offered their subscription, and were refused, till time should prove that they joined from love of the cause and not from the fear of man." Gentlemen, ministers, citizens, laborers, assembled in crowds to swear it and sign it. In less than two months, Scotland was banded together under the Covenant.

Word of the state of affairs in Scotland was quickly sent to King Charles by the Council, and in April several members of that body were called to London, where in consultation with some of the bishops, the situation was thoroughly discussed by the king.   His Majesty finally called to his cabinet the archbishops of Canterbury and of St. Andrews, the bishops of Galloway, Brechin, and Ross, and the marquis of Hamilton; and this council proceeded to devise measures of repression.   Charles appointed Hamilton as High Commissioner, ordered him to proceed to Scotland, and among other numerous instructions gave him the following : "If you cannot, by the means prescribed by us, bring back the refractory and seditious to due obedience, we do not only give you authority, but command all hostile acts to be used against them, they having deserved to be used in no other way by us but as a rebellious people."

Lord Hamilton accordingly returned to Scotland in June, but dared not publish the royal proclamation, as he was entirely without means to enforce it.   This being the case, he corresponded with his master, and it was agreed between them that he should parley with the Presbyterian party and soothe them with fair promises while the king was getting together an army.   After some months spent in fruitless negotiation and quibbling with the Scots, the King finally consented to call an Assembly, just as they were getting ready to convene one for themselves.   This Assembly met in the cathedral of Glasgow on November 21, 1638.   It consisted of one hundred and forty ministers, freely chosen by their presbyteries, and ninety-eight ruling elders. Seventeen of the elders were noblemen, nine were knights, twenty-five were landed proprietors, and forty-seven were burgesses of good position.   The marquis of Hamilton was present as the king's commissioner, instructed, as the king's correspondence shows, to use every endeavor to divide the Assembly by sowing jealousy between the clergy and laity.   On no account was he to permit them to interfere with the bishops.   Before it should come to that, he was to dismiss the Assembly.   Notwithstanding Hamilton's persistent opposition, Alexander Henderson was elected as moderator by his associates, and Johnstone of Warriston appointed clerk of the Assembly. Hamilton offered a paper in the name of the bishops, protesting against the authority of the Assembly.   He then argued on the subject, and parts of it were debated.   The moderator then put the question, whether the Assembly found itself a competent judge of the bishops ?   Before a vote could be taken, Hamilton, aware of the temper of the meeting, arose, in the king's name dissolved the Assembly, and departed.   But a protest was read against the arbitrary order of the king, a vote taken, and the Assembly continued its sittings; going on with its business of trying the bishops for their usurpation and tyranny over the Church, and for serious moral offences besides. The proceedings lasted an entire month.   Bishops, and the whole fabric of prelacy, were solemnly condemned and swept out.   The Reformed Church of Scotland was restored in its entirety and purity.   All that had been done by the bishops in the name of the Church since 1605 was annulled.   The book of canons, the liturgy, the High Commission, and Episcopacy itself were condemned. The bishops, who had always allied themselves with the despotic tendencies of the Crown, and to the utmost limits of their power had been the mere tools of the king and the pliant instruments of the royal will and pleasure, were convicted and condemned. Acts were passed relating to education and other important subjects. The Assembly closed its work by appointing its next meeting to be held at Edinburgh in July, 1639.

Civil war now became inevitable. General Alexander Leslie was therefore appointed leader of the Covenanting army. He soon organized a force and equipped it for the field. The Covenanters seized the castles of Edinburgh, Dumbarton, and other strongholds; and before the king arrived at York, the whole of Scotland was in the hands of the Presbyterians. In the beginning of May, the king's fleet of twenty warships, and several smaller vessels, with 5000 troops on board, sailed into Leith Roads. But both sides of the Firth were so well defended that not a boat could land. Before long, the crowded condition of the transports, miserably victualled and watered, caused disease to break out, and many victims were carried off by death.

Meanwhile, the king, having mustered his army at York in the beginning of April, 1639, advanced to the Border, and encamped on Birks plain in the valley of the Tweed, about three miles above Berwick. The Covenanters, about twelve thousand strong, advanced to fight the king, and encamped June 1st on Dunse Law, a low hill lying near the Border town of Dunse, about six miles distant from the camp of the royal forces, and on the opposite side of the Tweed. In a few days, reinforcements increased the Presbyterian army to more than twenty thousand men. Around the sides of the hill were pitched the tents of the army, each regiment forming a cluster. The top of the hill was surmounted by forty cannon. A banner-staff was planted at each captain's tent-door, from which floated the Scottish colors, displaying not only the national arms, but also this inscription in golden letters—" For Christ's Crown and Covenant." The army was chiefly composed of Scotland's thoughtful and high-souled peasantry. Nearly a score of noblemen were present, mostly in the command of regiments, and each regiment had its minister — some of them ready and determined to take an active part in the fight against the bishops. One minister, Rev. Robert Baillie of Kilwinning, was accompanied by " half a dozen good fellows," furnished with pike and musket out of his own pocket. His servant rode after him, with a broadsword at his side. The minister himself bore a sword, and carried a brace of pistols at his saddle-bow.

When the king found a force confronting him larger than his own, he decided that it would be safer for him to treat with his subjects than to attempt forcibly to coerce them. A messenger having intimated as much to the Scottish leaders, the earl of Dunfermline was sent to negotiate with the king. Following this, an arrangement was made, by which the religious matters in dispute were to be referred to the General Assembly and to Parliament. Peace was therefore proclaimed, on June 18th, and two days later the Scots burned their camp on Dunse Law and disbanded their army. They were shrewd enough, however, to retain their principal officers in readiness to assemble the army again if occasion should arise.

It soon became evident that the king's promises had been made only to enable him to gain time to raise a larger army. He had determined to chastise the Scots, and summoned his English Parliament, which met in April, 1640. A majority of the Parliament refused to grant supplies until they obtained the redress of the grievances under which England up to that time had been meekly suffering. Rather than yield, the king dissolved the House of Commons, and then set himself to raise the necessary funds by every means in his power. In the month of July he was enabled to take the field at the head of 19,000 foot and 2000 cavalry, and marched again for the North, to engage in what his own soldiers called a "Bishops' War."

Meanwhile, the Scotch Parliament met in June. After repealing all the acts which permitted churchmen to sit and vote in Parliament, it enacted that a Parliament should meet every three years, and appointed a permanent committee of members to act when Parliament was not sitting. During the spring and summer another Covenanter army also was organized, and it rendezvoused again at Dunse Law, 22,000 foot and 3000 horse, and again under command of General Alexander Leslie. This time the Scots decided not to wait and be invaded, but to march into England. Leaving Dunse Law, they advanced to Coldstream, where they crossed the Tweed. Marching slowly through Northumberland, they came to Newburn on the Tyne, about five miles above Newcastle. Here a crossing was forced, the English retreating to York, where the King's main army lay. On August 30th, the Scots took possession of Newcastle, of all Northumberland, and of Durham, and very peaceably made their abode in those parts for about the space of a year. The Covenanters again petitioned the king to listen to their grievances, and at the same time a number of English nobles petitioned him to summon a Parliament. Unable to fight the Covenanters, he finally offered to negotiate with them, and also summoned the English Parliament to meet at Westminster on the 3d of November — a meeting which afterwards became famous as the Long Parliament. To this English Parliament the Londoners sent in a petition bearing fifteen thousand names, craving to have bishops and their ceremonies radically reformed. Seven hundred clergy of the Church of England sent in a petition and remonstrance to the same effect. An immense agitation against the bishops and the arbitrary course of the king now arose, and all England became inflamed.

Peace between the king and the Scots was concluded in August, 1641; and soon after Charles visited Scotland, and attempted with fair promises to mollify its people and discourage their sympathetic interest in the struggle that had already begun in England between King and Parliament. In this year the hideous affair of the Irish rebellion and massacre threw its horrors into the excitement which already convulsed the public mind. The king had issued commissions to certain Irish leaders authorizing them to rise in arms in his behalf, and the native Irish seized the opportunity to begin a general massacre of their Protestant neighbors, without regard to age, sex, or condition. For six months the work of butchery continued unchecked; and in that time was poured out on the heads of the settlers in Ulster and elsewhere the accumulated wrath and hatred of generations. Parents were obliged to watch the dying agonies of their children and then follow them in death. Men were hung up by the arms and gradually slashed to death to see how much a heretic could suffer before he died.

Charles seems to have imagined that he would be able to overcome the English if he could pacify the Scots. The breach between him and his English subjects was constantly widening. He returned from Edinburgh to England in November. In the spring of 1642, he was forced to leave London, and removed his court to York. On August 23d, near Nottingham, Charles's herald read the king's proclamation calling his subjects to arms, and the war between King and Parliament began.

Communications passed between the English Parliamentary party and the Covenanters. In August four English commissioners appeared before the general assembly which had convened at Edinburgh on the 2d. They expressed their appreciation of what the Covenanters had already done for the cause of liberty, and said they desired the same work might be completed in England, where they had already abolished the High Commission and Episcopacy, and expelled the bishops from the House of Lords. Therefore, they entreated the Covenanters to assist their oppressed brethren in England. After much discussion and largely through the influence of Johnstone of Warriston and his associates, it was agreed to assist the leaders of the Long Parliament. The English leaders proposed a civil league, but the Scots would listen to nothing but a religious covenant. The English suggested that toleration should be given to the Independents, but the Scots would tolerate nothing but a Presbyterian or democratic form of church government in either kingdom. After a long debate, the Solemn League and Covenant was placed before the Assembly, which met at Edinburgh in August, 1643, and unanimously adopted. All the parties to this Covenant bound themselves to preserve the Reformed religion in Scotland and to do their utmost to further its extension in England and Ireland; to endeavor to extinguish popery and episcopacy; to preserve the rights of the Parliament and the liberties of the three kingdoms; and to preserve and defend the king's person.

In England, the Long Parliament had summoned together the ever-memorable Westminster Assembly of Divines, by an enactment entitled, "An Ordinance of the Lords and Commons in Parliament, for the calling of an Assembly of learned and Godly Divines and others, to be consulted with by Parliament, for the settling of the Government and Liturgy of the
29

Church of England, and for vindicating and clearing of the Doctrine of the said Church from false aspersions and interpretations.'' Under this act, one hundred and twenty-one divines were summoned, with ten lords and twenty commoners as laymen. The Scottish Church being invited to send commissioners to assist in the deliberations of this Assembly, sent Alexander Henderson, Samuel Rutherford, Robert Baillie, and George Gillespie, ministers, with the earl of Cassilis, Lord Maitland, and Sir Archibald Johnstone of Warriston. The Assembly continued to sit for more than five years, from 1643 to 1648. The Scotch commissioners took a distinguished part in the labors and debates, but they had no vote. A copy of the Solemn League and Covenant was carried from Edinburgh to London. On September 22, 1643, the members of the House of Commons, the House of Lords, and the Westminster Assembly of Divines all signed it; and afterwards it was signed by many in every county of England. Its immediate effect was that a Scotch army of eighteen thousand foot and three thousand horse, under Leslie, crossed the Tweed, marched south, and joined the Parliamentary army near York. On Marston Moor, four miles from York, they faced the king's army July 2, 1644. At seven in the evening the battle began. By ten o'clock the king's army was shattered and broken in pieces, and the allies stood victorious in a field strewn with four thousand dead.

From this time on, the king's cause began to go down, except for some brief successes attained by the earl of Montrose, a renegade Covenanter, who had raised a small army of Irish and Highlanders and committed many unspeakable outrages on the inhabitants of the counties of Aberdeen, Perth, and Stirling. After the battle of Naseby, June 15, 1645, in which the royal army was almost annihilated by the Parliamentary forces, Charles became a fugitive. In May of the following year, he evaded Cromwell's pursuit at Oxford, rode to the north, and surrendered to the Scottish army at Kelham, near Newcastle.

After remaining in the Scots' camp for eight months, the king was delivered to the Long Parliament, upon a promise from that body that no harm should come to his person. Charles returned to London, where a series of negotiations began again between himself and the Parliament; and after a fresh instance of treachery on the part of the king, he was condemned to death as a tyrant, murderer, and enemy of his country, and beheaded January 30, 1649.[1]

NOTE TO CHAPTER XXX

[1] From the restoration of Charles II. the 30th of January was observed in the Church of England with special religious services as the day of *King Charles the Martyr*. This commemoration, offensive to the great majority of Britons, was abolished by Act of Parliament only so recently as 1859, though the day is still observed by many High Church Episcopalians in London and elsewhere.

CHAPTER XXXI

SCOTLAND UNDER CHARLES II. AND THE BISHOPS [1]

THE news of the execution of Charles I. reached Edinburgh five days afterwards, and on February 5, 1649, his son, Charles II., was proclaimed king. Commissioners were despatched to Holland, where the conditions under which the Scots were willing to receive him as their ruler were proposed to the young king. These conditions had been formally set forth in an Act of Parliament, which declared that before Charles should be accepted as king he should sign and swear the National Covenant and the Solemn League and Covenant; that he should consent to the Acts of Parliament enjoining these Covenants; and that he should never attempt to change any of them; that he should dismiss the counsel of all those opposed to the Covenants and religion; that he should give satisfaction to Parliament in everything requisite for settling a lasting peace; and that he should consent that all civil matters should be determined by Parliament, and ecclesiastical matters by the General Assembly.

Charles had given the earl of Montrose a commission authorizing him to raise troops and subdue the kingdom by force of arms; so he temporized with the commissioners and protracted the negotiations, urging Montrose to make him independent of the Presbyterians. But when the rising was crushed and Montrose hanged, Charles eagerly threw himself into the arms of the Covenanters, agreed to the terms of Parliament, embarked for Scotland, and landed near the mouth of the Spey on June 24, 1650. Although he had previously embraced Romanism, Charles now solemnly swore that he " would have no enemies but the enemies of the Covenant—no friends but the friends of the Covenant."

Cromwell, as captain-general of the English forces, marched against him with an army of 16,000 men. Leslie, who commanded the Scots, by skilful manœuvring compelled Cromwell to retreat from Edinburgh to Dunbar. Thither Leslie followed, and against his own better judgment left a position of advantage, descended to the plain, and offered battle to Cromwell. The Scots were defeated and Edinburgh taken. Notwithstanding this disaster, Charles was crowned at Scone. The Scots then acted on the defensive, and Cromwell might have failed in conquering the northern parts of the kingdom, had not Charles marched to England, in the vain hope of being joined by the people. He was swiftly followed by Cromwell, and on the 3d of September, 1651, completely defeated at Worcester. He then fled from the kingdom, and Cromwell's power became supreme.

On the 20th of April, 1653, the Protector led three hundred men to the English House of Commons, ejected the members, and locked the doors.

After that date, although he sometimes consulted an assembly called a Parliament, which consisted of members from the three kingdoms, Oliver Cromwell remained, until his death, virtually dictator of Great Britain. He died September 3, 1658, and his son Richard was proclaimed as his successor.

For a brief time Richard Cromwell seemed firmly placed in his father's position. He summoned a Parliament, by which he was recognized as First Magistrate of the Commonwealth. But the army began to plot against their new master, and soon compelled him to dissolve Parliament. The Parliament was dismissed by Richard, and Richard in turn was dismissed by the officers of the army. The old " Rump " Parliament was again brought into power, and declared that there should be no First Magistrate; but its members were soon dispersed by the army. Moved by fear, an alliance was then formed between the Royalists and Presbyterians. George Monk, who commanded the Parliamentary army in Scotland, now marched into England, and on the third of February, 1660, entered London. On his invitation, the expelled Presbyterian members returned to the House of Commons and became the majority. By orders of Monk, writs were issued for a Convention, and of this body the Presbyterians formed a majority. Having first saved the nation from the tyranny of Charles, they now saved it from the tyranny of the army; but unfortunately they again put their trust in the house of Stuart.

A letter, sent by Charles to the Commons, from Breda, contained his celebrated Declaration, in which he promised a general pardon and liberty of conscience as conditions of his recall. The excesses of the Baptists and Independents had produced such a reaction in England that even Puritans were willing to try the king without the Covenant, rather than be ruled by officers like Lambert, or by legislators like Praise-God Barebone. The promises of Charles were accepted by the Convention, which invited him to return, without placing any legal limit on his acknowledged prerogatives. Recalled by a Presbyterian Convention, he soon became distinguished as a persecutor of those to whom he owed his throne; and, while some of the political liberty for which the people and the Parliament had fought was maintained, the religious liberty which they had won was entirely lost.

In Ireland, Coote declared for Charles, took Dublin Castle, and by Presbyterian support became master of that kingdom. A Convention was called, which, in February, 1660, met in Dublin. A majority consisted of Episcopalians. Yet, until the wishes of the king were known, they seemed to favor Nonconformists, and the Rev. Samuel Cox, a Presbyterian, was chosen chaplain. Sir John Clotworthy was deputed to treat with Charles, but the rapid march of events prevented any results for good. The Convention deprived Anabaptist ministers of their salaries, but gave to the Presbyterian pastors, and to about a hundred others reported to be orthodox, a right to the tithes of the parishes in which they were placed.

Charles, although he cared little for any religion, preferred Roman

Catholicism, to which faith he had been already reconciled in secret. Although Presbyterians were ready to accept of the king with the Covenant, Charles preferred the Episcopalians, who hated the Covenant as strongly as they loved the king. His desire for power was more likely to be gratified by a Church whose ministers taught that he had a divine right to do wrong, rather than by a Church which advocated limitations to his authority. He therefore lent his influence to re-establish Prelacy, as more lenient to his faults, more hopeful for his ambition, and more like the form of worship he preferred.

In the South the Convention was succeeded by a Parliament. Episcopacy again became the established religion of England, as the act by which it was formerly abolished had never been signed by the king. But there was not yet any law to exclude from the Established Church those ministers who had not been episcopally ordained, and until such was passed they still remained in their charges.

The Episcopalians, being supreme in the Parliament, soon began to act with intolerance. They ordered the Covenant to be burnt and the liturgy to be used without modification; and, for the first time, episcopal ordination was made necessary for holding the position of a clergyman in the Established Church.

An Act of Uniformity was passed (1662), which required every clergyman, if not episcopally ordained, to submit to ordination by a bishop, abjure the Covenant, and renounce the principle of taking up arms against the king under any pretence. It was made a crime under heavy penalties to attend a Nonconformist place of worship. Ministers who refused to submit were deprived of their livings and prohibited from coming within five miles of the town in which they formerly resided, or of any town which was governed by a corporation, or which returned a member to Parliament.

Two thousand clergymen who refused to conform were driven out of their parishes, and subjected to all the penalties permitted by law.

During the administration of Cromwell the Scottish Church had prospered. At the Restoration it is said that, except in some parts of the Highlands, every parish had a minister, every village a school, and every family a Bible. But the Church was now to enter a fiery furnace of persecution. The very Restoration had itself a bad effect, and caused many scenes of dissipation. The nation was drunk with joy. Even so rigid a Presbyterian as Janet Geddes gave her shelves, forms, and the chair on which she sat to make a bonfire in honor of the king's coronation.

The first Scottish Parliament was summoned to meet in January, 1661, and the most shameless bribery was employed in carrying out the wish of Charles to obtain a majority for overthrowing Presbyterianism. Many circumstances favored the king's design. The Presbyterian Church condemned vices which the sons of the nobility loved dearly. All who were given to dissipation wished to see a Church established by law from which they might not fear any ecclesiastical censure. The king ruled the aristocracy, and the aristocracy in reality nominated almost all the members of the Commons. Both Houses of Parliament, according to custom, sat together in the same chamber; and, in violation of law, the members did not subscribe the National Covenant. Several sittings of this Parliament had to be adjourned because Middleton was too drunk to keep the chair; and many of the other members were often in a similar state of intoxication. This Assembly, ready to do anything the king desired, set about its work at once. All legislation for reformation, between 1638 and 1650, was declared treasonable, although the acts in question had been duly sanctioned by the sovereign. The government of the Church was now left entirely in the hands of the king, who soon exercised that power to overthrow Presbyterianism. Then arose the most merciless persecution ever endured by any Church in Great Britain.

The marquis of Argyle, who, in 1651, had placed the crown on the head of Charles, was arrested, tried, and executed without the shadow of a crime proved against him. But he incurred the animosity of the king in being one of those who had formerly compelled him to take the Covenant as a condition of their support; and now the monarch had his revenge.

The Rev. James Guthrie, minister of Stirling, who, in 1650, pronounced sentence of excommunication on Middleton, was the next victim. He was arrested, tried for high treason, condemned, and executed as a traitor. Archibald Johnstone of Warriston followed soon after. On the 4th of October, 1662, the Council issued a proclamation to the effect that every minister admitted since 1649, when patronage was abolished, would be banished from his parish unless he had obtained a presentation from his patron and spiritual induction from his bishop before the 1st of November. Middleton did not expect more than fifteen or twenty would refuse conformity, but, to his great astonishment, about four hundred preferred to resign rather than submit to an unscriptural system of church government and doctrine. These ejected ministers were succeeded by raw youths, generally called curates, although they were parish ministers.

The Rev. James Sharp had been sent by his brethren from Scotland to London, in 1660, to manage the interests of the Scottish Church, and maintain its liberties. But he basely betrayed the cause which he had been selected to uphold and had sworn to defend. As a reward for his treason, he received the bishopric of St. Andrews and the Primacy of Scotland. Together with Sharp, three others,—namely, Fairfoul, Hamilton, and Leighton, —after having been duly ordained deacons and then priests, were consecrated bishops. Of these renegades, Leighton alone possessed any religious principles.

The ejected Scottish ministers now began to preach in the fields. But an act was passed, in 1663, making it unlawful to attend conventicles, as these field meetings were called; and Sir James Turner, a drunken mercenary, with a body of troops, was sent to the West to scatter the people who attended them. Every person not attending at the Episcopal church in his own parish was made liable to excessive fines, and " such corporal punishment as the Privy Council shall see proper to inflict."

This act, called the *Bishops' Drag-Net*, was enforced in Galloway by Turner and his soldiers. Under its operation, the Episcopal curate of each parish was accustomed, after sermon, to call the roll of those living in his parish and to make a list of all who were absent. This list was afterwards handed to the commanding officer, who proceeded to levy and collect enormous fines from the absentees. The fines were generally appropriated by the soldiers, and if a tenant or householder were unwilling or unable to pay, a party of soldiers was quartered upon him until many times the value of the fine was exacted and the victim " eaten up." After all the food in the house was gone, the cattle and goods of the owner were sold for a trifle, and the man utterly ruined.

In 1664, at the instigation of Sharp, a Court of High Commission, or Inquisition, was established in Scotland. Its chief object was to carry out the ecclesiastical laws and to punish all who opposed the government of the Church by bishops. Its powers were absolutely unlimited. All troops and all officers of the law must obey its orders. Its members could call before them whomsoever they chose. They examined no witnesses; they allowed no defence. They punished mercilessly by fines, by imprisonment, by banishment. By this court ministers were imprisoned, women publicly whipped, boys scourged, branded, and sold as slaves to Barbadoes or North America.

In October, 1666, the Council issued a fresh proclamation, which, under severe penalties, required masters to oblige their servants, landlords their tenants, and magistrates the inhabitants of their boroughs to attend regularly the Episcopal churches. Many were thus driven from their homes, their families dispersed, and their estates ruined. In the following November, Mr. Allan of Barscobe, and three other fugitives, who had been forced to seek a hiding-place in the hills of Galloway, ventured from their retreat and came to the Clachan of Dalry to procure some provisions. Here they encountered some soldiers who were about to roast alive an old man whom they had seized because he was unable to pay his church fines. Aided by some of their friends from the village, the Covenanters overpowered the soldiers, and rescued their victim. In the melée one of the soldiers was killed, and another wounded. The Covenanters, realizing that their lives were forfeited in any event, determined to remain in arms, and being joined by MacLellan, Laird of Barscobe, and some other gentlemen of the neighborhood, they soon mustered about fifty horsemen. Proceeding to Dumfries, they surprised and captured Sir James Turner himself. Others of the oppressed people joining them, they marched into Ayrshire. The greater part of the Covenanters, however, were poorly armed. Their most common weapon was a scythe set straight on a stave. With Colonel Wallace at their head the insurgents marched against Edinburgh, nine hundred strong. General Dalziel was sent to oppose them, at the head of a force of three thousand troops. At last, after a desperate struggle, the Presbyterians were overcome at a place called Rullion Green, among the Pentland Hills. About fifty were killed, including Mr. Crookshanks and Mr. McCormick—two ministers from Ireland. Nearly eighty prisoners were taken, either on the field of battle, or afterwards, and of these about thirty-five perished on the scaffold. At the suggestion of the bishops, Mr. John Neilson of Corsack, and Mr. Hugh McKail, minister, were tortured with an instrument called "the boot." It consisted of four pieces of wood in which a leg of the victim was confined. These pieces were then driven together by wedges, which caused them to press so tightly as to make the marrow leave the bone. Before the executions were finished, a letter came from the king to Sharp, as president of the Council, ordering no more lives to be taken. But the archbishop kept back the order until McKail had been executed.

After the Duke of Lauderdale, in 1667, had obtained the chief management of affairs in Scotland, there was a temporary cessation of persecution. A Presbyterian at heart himself, he did not at first proceed to so great cruelties as had been previously practised; and some of the most notorious persecutors were dismissed. By order of the king, an Act of Indulgence was passed by the Council, in 1669, more with the object of creating divisions than of affording relief. A limited liberty of preaching was given by this enactment to ministers who refrained from speaking against the changes in Church and State. Some accepted of this indulgence, and others refused; but those who accepted the relief it afforded were called "king's curates" by the zealous Covenanters, and were by them regarded as little better than the "bishops' curates." Other ministers, who refused this indulgence, began to preach in the fields. To them the people resorted in crowds. Sermons delivered under such circumstances produced a great effect. Many converts were made, and the zeal of the people went up to a high pitch of enthusiasm. Driven to madness by persecution, they came to these meetings fully armed. Watchmen were placed on the hills around. The preacher, with a Bible in his hand and a sword by his side, warned the people to fear spiritual more than temporal death. These appeals rendered them regardless of danger, and many bloody encounters took place between the soldiers and the Covenanters.

Accordingly, the field meetings, or conventicles, became more frequent, and were often attended by such large numbers that the soldiers dared not molest them. But the bishops did not in the least desist from their persecutions. They made it a capital crime for a minister to preach in the fields, or to any assemblage unless it should be housed within four walls. Any one attending a conventicle incurred the penalty of fine, imprisonment, or transportation to the Barbadoes or Virginia. Some seventeen thousand persons were thus punished in a single year for that offence. "Letters of Intercommuning" were issued against many prominent and upright citizens—both men and women—who had been driven from their homes by the persecution. By this means they were outlawed and placed under a ban, death being the penalty to any person who should offer them food, comfort, or succor. Wodrow (vol. i., p. 394) mentions the names of some of these sufferers, as follows: "David Williamson, Alexander Moncrief, William Wiseheart, Thomas Hogg in Ross, George Johnstone, Robert Gillespie, John McGilligan, John Ross, Thomas Hogg in Stirlingshire, William Erskine, James Donaldson, Andrew Anderson, Andrew Morton, Donald Cargill, Robert Maxwell, elder and younger, James Fraser of Brea, John King; and with these a good many ladies and gentlemen were joined, besides many of lower rank, altogether upwards of one hundred persons."

In 1671 the Bass Rock, off the coast of Scotland, was purchased by the Crown, and made a prison for the confinement of prisoners of state. In 1672 the fines became more oppressive, and the ejected ministers were hunted from place to place like wild beasts. Many of them were imprisoned on the Bass the next year.

It was finally determined to crush the Western Presbyterians, or Whigs, as they were sometimes called, by armed force, and for this purpose a body of eight or ten thousand half-savage Highlanders was mustered, and quartered in the western Lowlands for a period of three months, accompanied by a force of regular troops, with field-pieces for attack, shackles for the prisoners, and thumb-screws for torture. This horde of clansmen was given full license and encouraged to rob, kill, torment, and outrage the Presbyterians at will. These Highlanders, the very scum of the country, savage in their natures and cruel in their dispositions, now spread over the Southwest, where they plundered and ravaged without hindrance. On information from the curates they would visit the houses of the Covenanters, empty their oats into the water, tramp their food into the dunghill, and set fire to their belongings. They robbed all whom they met, and those whom they suspected of having property concealed were forced to discover it by being held over a fire. To the defenceless women their behavior was unspeakable.

Notwithstanding the barbarous oppression of the Highland Host, the people would have nothing to do with Episcopacy, and the conventicles multiplied. Thereupon Sharp devised a measure of such crushing severity that it was with difficulty he got it carried in the priest-ridden Council. He drew up the draft of a new edict, giving power to kill every man going armed to or from a conventicle. Any officer, even the meanest sergeant, was authorized to shoot on the spot any man who, as he chose to think, was either going to or returning from a conventicle. But Archbishop Sharp's bloody course was well-nigh run. Regarding Presbyterians with the animosity of an apostate, he had become notorious among their persecutors. In 1668, he had been fired at by a man named Mitchell, who was not captured for six years afterwards. When taken, there was no legal proof of his guilt. Sharp swore with uplifted hand that the prisoner's life would be spared in case he confessed his crime. Notwithstanding this promise, Mitchell, on confessing, was placed in confinement, and afterwards barbarously executed. But before many years the archbishop himself met a fate as horrible as that to which he had been the means of sending so many others. On the 3d of May, 1679, twelve Presbyterians were near St. Andrews, watching for one of Sharp's agents, named Carmichael, who had rendered himself particularly obnoxious as a persecutor by placing lighted matches between the fingers of women and children. Failing to meet the servant, they happened to encounter the archbishop himself, who with his daughter was driving from Edinburgh to St. Andrews. They surrounded the carriage, disarmed the servants, and told Sharp to prepare for his death. He earnestly begged for mercy, promised to lay down his office of bishop, and offered them money if only they would spare his life. Refusing his offers with contempt, they again ordered him to prepare for death. But he still shrank from engaging in prayer, and continued his abject petitions for mercy. They now discharged their pistols at him and, thinking he was dead, turned away. But overhearing his daughter say to herself that there was still life, they returned and found Sharp unhurt. He then got out of the carriage, and going down on his knees cried for mercy, directing his petitions chiefly to David Hackston of Rathillet, who declined to interfere. The others told him to ask for mercy from God and not from them, and afterwards put him to death with their swords. They then returned thanks to God for what had been accomplished, and succeeded in escaping. Presbyterians generally disapproved this awful deed, although they regarded it as a judgment from God on one who first betrayed and then persecuted his brethren.

For many years after Sharp's death, when Presbyterians were apprehended, they were usually asked, whether or not they considered the archbishop's assassination murder. Should they truthfully answer in the negative, or refuse to reply, death was the immediate penalty.

Among the persecutors, none obtained a greater reputation for cruelty than John Graham of Claverhouse. Under a soft exterior he concealed a daring spirit, regardless of danger and death. He had therefore no hesitation in condemning others to what he could face with courage himself.

On the 29th of May, 1679, Mr. Robert Hamilton and some of his friends published a declaration at Rutherglen against all the persecuting acts of the Council and Parliament. Graham of Claverhouse, hearing of this, marched in search of those by whom the declaration was published. Hamilton, with one hundred and seventy foot and forty horse, came up to Claverhouse at a place called Drumclog. After a short preliminary engagement, Balfour with the horse and William Cleland with the infantry crossed a morass and attacked the dragoons, who were soon put to flight. The Covenanters killed forty on the field, and rescued Mr. John King, with about fourteen other prisoners.

Claverhouse fled to Glasgow, where he was pursued by the Covenanters. Failing to capture the city, they retreated to the town of Hamilton. Here they were joined by many country people, and all organized against the common enemy. But they were sadly lacking in arms and training; and through the ill advice of Mr. Hamilton it was determined not to admit into their ranks any one who would not condemn the Indulgence. This action caused a division, and prevented the Presbyterians from being able to raise an army of more than about four thousand men.

The duke of Monmouth, a natural son of King Charles, commanded the royal army sent to subdue this rebellion. The Covenanters awaited his approach on ground gently rising from the left bank of the Clyde, opposite Bothwell. Here a bridge, only twelve feet wide, spanned the river, which winds round the base of the hill on which the village is built. Monmouth occupied Bothwell and the level plain below, and, on the 22d of June, 1679, commenced the attack. Hackston of Rathillet, with three hundred men, placed among cottages and behind barricades, defended the bridge for some time with courage and success. At last their ammunition was expended, and Hamilton, when asked to send a fresh supply, ordered Hackston to withdraw from his position, "leaving the world to debate whether he acted most like a traitor, coward, or fool." Hackston obeyed, the royal army passed the bridge and charged the main body of the Covenanters, who were completely defeated and about twelve hundred taken prisoners. The soldiers then scoured the country and shot a great number suspected of being concerned in the rising.

Although Monmouth was devoid of religion, he was not bloodthirsty, and tried to restrain the cruelty of his army. . But he failed to prevent others who were in power from carrying on their bloody work. Many of the prisoners taken at Bothwell were executed. Among these were some who had refused to take part in the rebellion or to preach to the insurgents. The other prisoners were brought to Edinburgh, almost naked. For five months they were kept in Greyfriars' Churchyard. During almost all this period they had to remain in the open air. At night they slept on the cold ground without shelter from the rain; and if any one, to ease his position, raised his head a little, he was shot at by some of the soldiers. After a lengthened period of suffering a few escaped, some were liberated through the intercession of friends, some were executed, and upwards of two hundred and fifty were condemned to transportation. Placed on board ship, they were crowded together under deck, where there was so little space that most had to stand in order to give more room to the dying. Many fainted, and were nearly suffocated. So little food or water was supplied to them that they had to endure the torments of hunger and thirst. The greater part of fourteen thousand merks, collected for their relief in Edinburgh, was appropriated by their persecutors. The ship sailed from Leith on the 27th of November, 1679, and on the 10th of December it was caught in a storm off

Orkney. The prisoners begged to be put on shore, where they agreed to remain in prison; but the shipmaster refused, and locked the hatches. That night the ship was driven on a rock and broken in the middle. The crew easily escaped by means of a mast laid from the vessel to the shore. The prisoners were left to their fate. Some of them, with the energy of despair, burst open the hatches and made good their way to land; but the crew pushed many of them down the rocks into the sea. Only about forty escaped, who were afterwards sent to New Jersey and Jamaica, where they had to work under a burning sun in company with negro slaves. But few of these remained alive until 1689, when the Revolution brought them liberty.[2] The captain who had so cruelly murdered his prisoners was never brought to trial.

The effect of these persecutions was to cause many of the Presbyterian laity to disown the authority of the civil as well as of the ecclesiastical rulers and form themselves into societies. But Messrs. Donald Cargill and Richard Cameron were the only ministers who now identified themselves with this party. On the June 22, 1680, about twenty of these men met at Sanquhar, and issued a declaration in which they disowned " Charles Stuart " and declared war against him as a tyrant and usurper. Cameron had been an Episcopalian, but having given up Prelacy he became a preacher to those who renounced the civil authority. After many marvellous escapes, he was at last killed in an engagement at Ayr's Moss. David Hackston of Rathillet, the slayer of Archbishop Sharp, was captured at the same engagement, and soon afterwards put to death under circumstances of unparalleled barbarity. His right hand was cut off, and after a little time his left hand. Afterwards, he was hanged up with a pulley, and when half suffocated let down. The executioner then cut open his breast and tore out his still moving heart, into which he stuck his knife, and holding it up said, " Here is the heart of a traitor."

Cargill was now the only minister left alive among the Cameronians. He preached to vast crowds at field conventicles. In September, 1680, he pronounced sentence of excommunication on the king, the duke of York, and the other chief persecutors. But the next year he was captured and executed. The Cameronians then remained without a minister until the return of Mr. James Renwick, who had gone to Holland for ordination. The extreme position taken up by these societies caused the Government to proceed against the other Presbyterians with greater severity.

During the five or six years following Bothwell Bridge the persecution was at its fiercest. The Duke of York—afterwards James II.—now came to Scotland, to urge on the work of murder. " There would never be peace in Scotland," he said, " till the whole of the country south of the Forth was turned into a hunting field." It seemed to give this particular Stuart great pleasure to watch the torments of tortured Covenanters. The country was laid under martial law, and neither age nor sex was spared. Prisoners were tortured until they were compelled to accuse themselves of crimes they had never committed, and were then executed on their own confessions. The years 1684 and 1685 went far beyond the rest in cruelty and murder. They have since been known in Scotland as the " Killing Time." The bishops' soldiers were sent out over the country empowered to kill all Covenanters. Those whom they met were required to answer the following questions: " Was Bothwell Bridge rebellion ?   Was the killing of the archbishop of St. Andrews murder ?   Will you pray for the king ?   Will you renounce the Covenant ? "   As a great majority of the western Lowlanders could not truthfully answer any of these questions in the affirmative, and a negative answer involved immediate death, the defenceless people were slaughtered by thousands.

Almost every burial-place in the western Lowlands of Scotland contains the graves of Scottish martyrs who refused to perjure themselves when these questions were put to them.   Thousands of men, women, and children were thus sacrificed to the malignant fury of the bishops.[2]

Charles died on the 6th of February, 1685, having previously received absolution from a priest of the Church of Rome.   He was succeeded by James, Duke of York, an avowed Roman Catholic, who had even more vices and fewer virtues than his brother.

The new king on his accession promised to maintain the Episcopal Church, and he submitted to be crowned in Westminster Abbey by the archbishop of Canterbury.   A party, made up of the more zealous Protestants and the more determined Whigs, rightly fearing that he would prove a tyrant and a persecutor, began a feeble insurrection.   The earl of Argyle landed in Scotland to call the Covenanters to arms.   The duke of Monmouth, the natural son of Charles II., careless of religion but desirous of a crown, also raised the standard of insurrection in England.   These attempts were both abortive.   Argyle was captured and executed.   Monmouth, defeated at Sedgemoor, suffered the same penalty, notwithstanding his relationship to the king.   Many of his followers were butchered by Colonel Percy Kirke, who scoured the country with his " lambs."   The prisoners, tried by Jeffreys at the " Bloody Assizes," were executed in such numbers as to excite terror and consternation throughout the kingdom.   This judge declared that he could " smell a Presbyterian forty miles," and boasted that he had hanged more traitors than all his predecessors since the Conquest.

The accession of James brought no immediate relief to the persecuted Covenanters of Scotland.   An Episcopal farmer named Gilbert Wilson had two daughters—Agnes, aged thirteen, and Margaret, aged eighteen. These girls attended conventicles, and had become Presbyterians.   Arrested and condemned to death, their father succeeded in procuring the pardon of the younger on paying £100 sterling.   But the elder daughter and an old woman named Margaret MacLaughlan were bound to stakes on the seashore that they might be drowned by the rising tide.   After the old woman was dead, and the water had passed over Margaret Wilson's head, the latter was brought out, restored to consciousness, and offered life if she would take the abjuration oath. But she said, "I am one of Christ's children, let me go." She was then once more placed in the sea, and her sufferings ended by death.

At Priest Hill, in Lanarkshire, lived a man named John Brown, noted for his piety, and void of offence to the world. On the 1st of May, 1685, while engaged in cutting turf, he was seized by Claverhouse, and condemned to death for being a Presbyterian. His wife was present, holding one child by the hand, and exhibiting proof that she would soon again become a mother. With difficulty, Mr. Brown received permission to engage in prayer. By his prayer he so moved the soldiers that not one of them would act as executioner. Thereupon Claverhouse, with his own hand, shot the prisoner dead. His wife, in her sorrow, then turned round to the murderer and told him that his own day of reckoning would soon come. "To men," he replied, "I can be answerable. As for God, I'll take Him into mine own hand."

A change now took place in the policy of King James. Doubtless he would have preferred still to persecute all classes of Puritans, while favoring Roman Catholics. But he felt that it would appear inconsistent in the eyes of the world to give Roman Catholics permission to do the very same things for which his soldiers were shooting down Presbyterians. He also hoped to obtain valuable political aid from Nonconformists in support of the power he claimed, to dispense with those laws by which they, as well as Roman Catholics, were persecuted. Moved by these considerations, he published on the 4th of April, 1687, a Declaration of Indulgence, in which, by his own authority, without any sanction from Parliament, he suspended the penal laws against Nonconformists and Roman Catholics. But, while the ordinary Presbyterian services were permitted and Roman Catholic services encouraged, the regulations against field conventicles were continued in full force. Presbyterians in general deemed it their duty to take advantage of this Indulgence; but the Cameronians refused to comply with the conditions by which liberty might be obtained, and, contrary to law and contrary to the Indulgence, they continued to meet in field conventicles.

The Rev. James Renwick, a young man of five-and-twenty, minister of the persecuted Cameronian societies, had preached with great power against those who took advantage of the Indulgence. But his career was short; for, on the 17th of February, 1688, having been apprehended, he suffered the penalty of death. Renwick was the last of the Scottish martyrs. David Houston came very near to obtaining that honor. Arrested in Ireland, he was brought to Scotland to be tried. On the 18th of June, near Cumnock, in Ayrshire, his military escort was attacked and defeated by a body of Covenanters. Mr. Houston was released, and evaded recapture until King James was driven from his throne.

The persecution in Scotland was now soon to end. About eighteen thousand Presbyterians had been punished by the law or had perished of hardships. Nearly five hundred had been murdered in cold blood, and three hundred and sixty-two had been executed. Nevertheless, after twenty-eight years of persecution the Presbyterian Church stood as firmly as ever in the affections of the Scottish people. Threats, confiscation, torture, and death itself in its most cruel forms had failed to compel them to use a liturgy.

The king issued a second declaration granting further indulgences to the Roman Catholics and Presbyterians. This he ordered to be read in all the churches and chapels of the kingdom. Seven bishops of the English Episcopal Church on petitioning his Majesty to withdraw this obnoxious order, were committed to prison and brought to trial. But all the influence of the court, exercised to procure their conviction, failed to frighten the jury, and the prelates were acquitted. The spirit of the whole nation was now aroused. Tory parsons who had maintained the divine right of kings to do wrong, who, so long as only Nonconformists were persecuted, preached the duty of passive obedience under the most cruel sufferings which his gracious Majesty chose to inflict, were horrified to see their own bishops standing accused before a legal tribunal, and commenced to modify in practice what they held in theory. The great majority of Tories and Churchmen began now to desire a deliverer as earnestly as Whigs and Puritans. All, with singular unanimity, turned their eyes to William Henry, Prince of Orange, grandson of Charles I., nephew and son-in-law of James, and First Magistrate of the Dutch Republic. William was now thirty-eight years of age. When little more than a boy he had contended with honor in the field against the ablest generals of the age. Although defeated in bloody battles, he contrived to reap the fruits of victory and deliver his country from destruction. A Calvinist in religion, he was regarded as head of the Protestant interest on the Continent, and even his enemies admitted that he was the ablest statesman in Europe.

William undertook to free Britain from the tyranny of his father-in-law. With a fleet of six hundred vessels, having on board fifteen thousand soldiers, he arrived at Torbay, in the south of England, on the 5th of November, 1688. There he unfurled his standard with its memorable inscription, " I will maintain the liberties of England and the Protestant religion." James, wholly unable to oppose him, had soon to seek safety in flight. William, and Mary his wife, were then, by a Convention Parliament, elected king and queen of England.

In Scotland, the country people, who had borne with the curates for six-and-twenty years, could now endure them no longer. Without waiting for the Parliament to re-establish Presbyterianism, they drove many of these parsons from their parishes. " The time of their fall," says Patrick Walker, " was now come. Faintness was entered into their hearts, insomuch that the greater part of them could not speak sense, but stood trembling and sweating. I enquired at them what made them to tremble; they that had been teachers and defenders of the prelatic principles, and active instruments in many of our national mischiefs ? How would they tremble and sweat if they were in the Grassmarket going up the ladder with the rope before them, and the lad with the pyoted coat at their tail ! But they were speechless objects of pity.''

In March, 1689, a Convention of the Estates was held in Edinburgh, William, by his own power, dispensing with the laws which deprived Presbyterians of their votes. The Covenanters, in order to protect the members who belonged to their party, assembled in arms, many of them carrying the weapons they had used at Bothwell Bridge. Conspicuous among these brave men was William Cleland, who when only seventeen years of age had led the infantry to victory in the charge at Drumclog. Distinguished as a poet and a mathematician, he was brave even to recklessness. Now he sought to meet Graham of Claverhouse, Viscount Dundee, in mortal conflict. But Dundee, finding that the majority of the Convention could neither be forced nor flattered to support the claims of the House of Stuart, and fearing to be cut in pieces by Cleland, left Edinburgh, and fled to the Highlands. There the mass of the population professed a religion which was a strange mixture of paganism and popery. They had no love for either king or country, but were loyal to their clans and attached to their chieftains, who ruled them as petty sovereigns. Some of these chieftains, fearing they might now be called on to restore what they held of the confiscated estates of the martyred Argyle, were ready to rebel against the authority of William. Thus Dundee was easily able to raise an army of Highlanders. He took the field at once, and defeated General Mackay, on the 27th of July, at Killiecrankie, but was himself slain in the battle. He was succeeded as commander-in-chief by Colonel Canon, who continued the rebellion.

A regiment of Covenanters, under William Cleland, now lay not far off at Dunkeld, placed there among their enemies by some traitor, that they might be cut to pieces. They had been deserted by the cavalry, had been supplied with a barrel of figs instead of gunpowder, and were in all only seven hundred strong; while Canon led to the attack five thousand Highlanders, who had scented blood and were flushed with victory. Cleland drew up his men with great skill behind some walls near a house which belonged to the marquis of Athol. Although surrounded on all sides, the Covenanters repulsed repeated attacks of the enemy. Again and again the Highlanders came on with fearful fury, but the Presbyterians fought with the energy of despair. When their bullets were gone, they used bits of lead cut off the roof of Athol's house. Galled by the fire of the enemy, who shot at them from some dwellings in the vicinity, they sallied out, secured the doors, and set these buildings on fire, so that many of their occupants perished in the flames. After a fearful conflict, the Highlanders at length retreated, and the Covenanters sang a psalm of triumph. The war was now ended, and the power of William supreme throughout Scotland.   But the victory was dearly bought, for the gallant Cleland had fallen.

Meanwhile the Convention had given the crown of Scotland to William and Mary, had abolished all the persecuting laws, and had re-established Presbyterianism as the national religion.   Then in the words of Defoe, "not a dog wagged his tongue against the Presbyterian establishment, not a mouth gave a vote for Episcopacy."

NOTES TO CHAPTER XXXI

[1] The greater part of this chapter is condensed from Latimer's *History of the Irish Presbyterians*.

[2] See Vol. II., p. 252.

[3] See Appendix R (The Scottish Martyrs).   The Privy Council on May 6, 1684, published a list of the fugitives who had been outlawed but not yet apprehended.   This list, containing upwards of 1800 names, is reprinted by Robert Wodrow in his *History of the Sufferings of the Church of Scotland*, bk. iii., ch. viii.

30

THE SCOT IN NORTH IRELAND

NOTE.—A large part of the following account of the Scots in Ireland was written by Dr. W. T. Latimer, and is condensed, by permission, from that writer's valuable *History of the Irish Presbyterians* (James Cleland, Belfast, 1893) and from Mr. John Harrison's monograph on *The Scot in Ulster* (William Blackwood & Sons, Edinburgh, 1888).

CHAPTER XXXII

IRELAND UNDER THE TUDORS

IT has been said of Henry VIII. that the world gained more benefit from his vices than from his virtues. His failure to persuade the Pope to grant him a divorce from Catherine of Aragon led to the downfall of the Roman Church as the State religion of England. In its stead, Henry erected the Church of England, and in 1531 caused Parliament to declare him the supreme head of the Church. Three years later his Church was completely separated from that of Rome, the people accepting their new pope without demur. As has already been pointed out, the change of law produced in England a change of religion, which assumed the Protestant form not so much through the influence of the principles of the Reformation, as through the determination of Henry to make Anne Boleyn his wife. As the result of the Reformation in Scotland, a change of religion produced a change of law and of government; and the Scotch reformers purged their Church from its obvious errors, and stripped her of all forms and ceremonies. In England the form of the new religion arose from a silent compromise, the English Church being left as much like the Romish as possible, in order to get the people to acquiesce in the supremacy of the king. Hence it has never been as successful as the Church of Scotland in throwing off the bonds of feudalism.

In Ireland, it was not until 1537 that the king was declared head of the Church and appeals to Rome were forbidden. But the Irish hated the English as oppressors, and they became more firmly attached to their religion when ordered to lay it aside by their enemies. For this reason, Protestantism made but little progress amongst the native Irish, even within the English Pale. The Irish language was proscribed by the Government, which thus refused to employ the only means by which the people could be made to understand the reformed faith, or be led to adopt the religion of England and become reconciled to her rule.

The first preacher of the Protestant faith in Ireland was George Browne, whom Henry, in 1535, appointed Archbishop of Dublin. By his orders, the " Staff of Jesus " was consigned to the flames. This celebrated crozier, supposed to possess the power of working miracles, had for seven hundred years been regarded with the utmost veneration; and every adherent of the ancient faith was horrified by its destruction.

In Ulster, Con O'Neill, incited by the Pope, made war on the English, but, being defeated in 1539, he promised to acknowledge Henry as head of the Church. Cromer, the Roman Catholic Archbishop of Armagh, made a similar submission; and throughout the Pale the clergy generally took the oath of supremacy. But these submissions were merely nominal. Neither then nor afterwards did any large proportion of the Irish priests or people consent to give up a religion they loved, to please a people whom they hated.

King Henry himself cannot be considered a reformer. In England he beheaded as traitors those who were for the Pope, and burned as heretics those who were against the Pope. At this time there was no persecution in Ireland. But the Reformed faith could not make progress when it was considered a crime to teach the people in the only language which they understood.

Henry died in 1547, and was succeeded by his son, Edward VI., who, although not ten years of age, soon manifested a leaning towards Protestantism. During his reign the English liturgy was read in a few of the Irish cities and towns, but, not being understood by the natives, made only a slight impression. Several bishops favorable to the Reformed faith were now appointed. Of these the most celebrated was Bale, who attempted to instruct the people by dramatic representations of scriptural events. Even he could do but little, as he was opposed by an ignorant clergy who were Romanists in everything but name.

Edward died in 1553, and was succeeded by his sister Mary, an ardent Roman Catholic, who soon re-established the ancient faith in both England and Ireland. Hugh Curwin was appointed Archbishop of Dublin, and others, supposed to be staunch Romanists, were nominated to the sees left vacant by the Protestant bishops, who were driven from the country. Bale remained for about two months; but five of his servants were killed, and he had to make his escape by night, lest he should be torn to pieces by a furious mob.

A Parliament met, which restored the supremacy of the Pope, and enacted that heretics should be burnt for the terror of others. But there were few in Ireland firmly attached to the Reformed faith, and the viceroy was not anxious to appear as a persecutor. Accordingly, that country became a place of refuge for the Protestants persecuted in England, where Latimer and Ridley and many other distinguished leaders perished at the stake.

Elizabeth, daughter of Henry VIII., ascended the throne in 1558. Fearing that the supremacy of the Pope would interfere with her own ambitious schemes, she inclined to the faith which permitted her to rule both Church and State. In one session, without violence or tumult, the religion of the English nation was again changed. The people, ever ready to mould their moral principles according to the will of the sovereign, became Protestants for Elizabeth as readily as they had become Catholics for Mary. Attached to the old forms, yet hating the old abuses, they were ready to accept whatever religion it pleased their rulers to establish. In this case the will of one vain woman determined the future faith of the English race.

In Ireland, the Earl of Sussex, who had been reappointed viceroy, caused the litany to be sung in English. The Romanists raised a report that an image of Christ in the cathedral had begun to sweat blood, to show the wrath of God against those who were trying to reform the Church. But Curwin, who had determined to again embrace Protestantism, found that a sponge soaked in blood had been placed behind the crown of thorns, on the head of the image. Those guilty of the trick had to do public penance. Like Cranmer in England, Curwin, the Archbishop, then once more changed his religion to preserve his position. In the presence of King Henry, he had preached against Frith, who was then in prison, for denying purgatory and transubstantiation, thus using his influence in favor of Frith's martyrdom. A Protestant under Edward VI., Curwin later became zealous for the Old Faith in the reign of Mary. His zeal under Elizabeth was now transferred to the religion which he had a few months previously labored to destroy. Curwin is the connecting link in the chain of Apostolic succession, which is supposed to join the Episcopal Church in Ireland with the ancient Church of St. Patrick. Of the bishops, only Curwin and Field embraced Protestantism, and only Curwin assisted at the consecration of newly appointed bishops. He had been himself consecrated at London House by English bishops, under the presidency of the bloody Bonner, whose orders can be traced step by step to Halsay, Bishop of Leighlin in Ireland. Halsay was an Englishman, who had been ordained at Rome.

In 1570, Pope Pius V. excommunicated Queen Elizabeth, declared her deprived of the kingdom, and absolved the people from obedience to her commands. His Bull, although regarded with contempt in England, was the means of strengthening the opposition to Elizabeth in Ireland; but the government was administered with vigor, and every rebellion subdued.

Con O'Neill, who ruled a large portion of Ulster, had, in 1542, accepted the earldom of Tyrone from Henry VIII., subject to the principles of English succession, and not according to the Irish custom of *Tanistry*, by which the most worthy of the tribe was, during the lifetime of the head, chosen as his successor. The new-made earl promised to give up calling himself " The O'Neill," to recognize Henry as head of the Church, and to compel his tribe to make a similar submission. His illegitimate son Matthew (supposed to be in reality the son of a blacksmith named Kelly) was created Baron of Dungannon, and recognized as his successor. But another son called Shane, or " John the Proud," refused to assent to this compact, made war on his father, and killed Matthew. Old Con did not live long afterwards, and Shane, despising an English title, was proclaimed " The O'Neill." As Protestantism was the religion of his enemies, he preferred the Roman Catholic faith. Fired with the ambition of being king of Ulster, he imagined that through the influence of the Pope he would procure aid from the Catholic sovereigns of the Continent to accomplish his designs. Having carried on a successful war against the English for a long period, he was at last defeated, and in 1567 slain in a drunken carousal by the Mac-Donnells, at Cuchendun.

The condition of Ulster in Shane O'Neill's time is shown by the following report relating to the state of Ireland, written May 8, 1552. (Harl. MSS. Brit. Mus. No. 35, fol. 188 v.–194 v.)

The Chancellor of Ireland to the Duke of Northumberland, relating to the state of Ireland:

Next to Breany [Cavan] is M'Mahon's country, called Oriell, wherein be three captaynes, the one in Dardarye, the other in Ferny, and M'Mahon in Leightie. These countryes [parts of Monaghan and Armagh] are lardge, fast, and stronge; amonge whome there contynued intestine warre before tyme, whereby the most parte of the countrye was made waste, neverthelesse they be tall men of the number of lxxx. horsemen, cc Kearne,[1] iv[xx] [four score] galloglas, [*i.e.*, armed soldiers or servants of a chief] and all these for the most parte doe occupie husbandrye except the Kearne, and yett some of them doe occupie likewise: and nowe of late before Easter, by appointmente of my lorde deputye, I resorted to them to see their countryes ordered; and they all assemblinge before me, I caused them not onlye to finde, at their own chardges yearlie vi[xx] [six score] galloglasses to serve the kinge, and to attende uppon an Englishe captayne of the Englishe Pale, which hath the order of the countrye committed unto hym for the keepinge of the king's majestie's peace, the maintenance of the good and the punishmente of the evell. But alsoe I caused them to putt in their pledges to my handes, as well for the findeinge of the galloglas, as for the due performance of the orders which I tooke betwixt them; which thinge was done without force or rigor, and they as people most gladde to lyve in quyett, applyed to the same, which is great towardnes of obedience. Besides this, they have and yealde to all sesses to the souldiers of Moynehan [Monaghan] and in other places, beeves and carryadge, like as others in the English pale doe.

The next countrye betwene that and M'Gynnose's [Magennis's] countrye called Iveache, is O'Hanlon's countrye called Orres. The same O'Hanlon is an honest man, and he and his countrye lyeth readye to obaye all commandements.

The next to O'Hanlon, is M'Gynnose his countrye afforesaid, wherein the Myorie [Moira] Mr. Marshall fermer, is situated. The same M'Gynnose is a civell gentleman and useth as good order and fashion in his house, as any of his vocacion in Ireland: and doth the same Englishe like. His countrey is obedyent to all sesses and orders; the same Iveache hath been parcell of the countie of Downe, and he beinge made sheriffe thereof, hath exercysed his offyce there as well as any other sherriffe doth; soe as with them there lackes noe honest obedyence.

The next to that countrie is M'Cartan's countrye, a man of small power, wherein are noe horsemen, but Kearne; which countrye is full of bogges, woodes, and moores, and beareth with the captayne of Lecaille.

The next to that countrie is the Duffreyn, whereof one John Whight [White] was landlorde, whoe was deceiptfully murthered by M'Ranills Boye his sonne, a Scott; and sithence that murther he keepeth possession of the saide landes; by meanes whereof, he is able nowe to disturbe the next adjoyneinge on every side, which shortly by Godes grace shal be redressed. The same countrye is noe great circuyte, but small, full of woodes, water and good lande, meet for English men to inhabitte.

The next countrye to the same eastwardes is Leicaille, where Mr. Brereton is farmer and captyne; which is a handsome playne and champion countrye of ten myles length, and fyve myles bredeth, without any woode groweinge therein. The sea doth ebbe and flowe rounde that countrye, soe as in full water noe man cann enter therein uppon drye lande, but in one waye which is lesse than two myles in length; and the same countrye for Englishe free-houlders, and good inhabitants is as civile as few places in the Englishe pale.

The next countrye to that, the water of Strangeforde, is Arde Savage his countrye, which hath bene meere Englyshe, both pleasuant and fayer by the sea; of length about xii myles and iiii. myles in breadeth, about which countrye the sea doth ebbe and flowe; which countrye is now in effecte for the most parte voyde.

The next countrye to Arde Savage is Clanneboy, wherein is one Morier-taghe Cullenagh, one of the O'Neils, whoe hath the same as captayne of Clanneboy. But he is not able to maintayne the same. He hath viii. tall gentlemen to his sonnes, and all they cannot make past xxiiii. horsemen. There is another captyne in that countrye of Phelim Backagh his sonnes, tall men, which take parte with Hughe M'Neile Oge, till nowe of late certayne refused him, and went to Knockfergus.

The same Hughe M'Neile Oge, as your grace hath hearde, was prayed by Mr. Marshall, whoe hath made prayes uppon others of those confynes for the same, soe as he is noe looser, but rayther a gayner by his paynes. He sought to have his matter hearde before my lord deputye and councell, wheruppon a daye was prefixed for the same till Maye; and nowe lately I repayred to his countrye, to talke further with him, to tracte the tyme till grasse growe: for before then the countryes being so barren of victuall and horsemeate, noe good may be done to destroye him, whereby I perceyved that he was determined as he saythe to meete me, and conclude a further peace. Yett he hearinge of the arryval of certayne Scotts to the Glynnes refused to come to me, contrarye to his wryteinge and sendinge; and went to calle M'Connill, whoe landed with vi. or vii.ˣˣ [six or seven score] bowes, as was reported, and thought to bringe them with him to warre uppon his next neighboures; soe as there is no greate likelyehoode in him of any honest conformetye: and perceyveing the same in escheweinge his countrye, I ap-poynted, and planted in the countrye a bande of horsemen and footmen for defence thereof against the Scotte yf they doe come; and upon the as-semblinge of the councell which shal be within these iiii. dayes, God willinge, suche good conclusions shal be taken for the defence of the kinge's majesties subjects in those quarters, and for the revenge uppon the rebells, as yf the Scotte did come, they shall rather repent their prosperitye by their cominge.

This countrye of Clanneboy is in woodes and bogges for the greatest parte wherein lyeth Knockfergus, and soe to the Glynne's where the Scotte doe inhabitt. As much of this countrye as is neare the sea is a champion countrye, of xx. myles in length, and not over iiii. myles in breadeth or little more. The same Hughe hath two castles: one called Bealefarst [Belfast] an oulde castle standinge uppon a fourde that leadeth from Arde to Clan-neboye, which being well repayred, being nowe broken, would be a good defence betwixt the woodes and Knockfergus. The other called Castell-rioughe [Castlereagh] is fower myles from Bealfarst, and standeth uppon the playne, in the middest of the woodes of the Dufferin; and beinge repayred with an honest companye of horsemen, woulde doe much good for the quyett and staye of the countrye there about; havinge besides a good bande of horsemen in Lecaille contynuallie to resorte and doe servyce abroade upon everye occasion; then such men of small power as Hughe is, must be con-tent to be at commandement; for which purpose, there be devises a making which, by God's grace, with haste shall take effecte.

Next to the Glynnes where the Scotte resorte, M'Quoillynes [M'Quillan's] countrye is, adjoyneinge by the sea, and soe to the Banne; a countrye of woodes and most parte waste, by their owne warres and the exacions of the Scotte, and maye not make past xii horsemen. But they were wonte to make lxxx. When the Scotte doe come, the most parte of Clanneboy, M'Quoil-lynes and O'Cahan, must be at their comaundemente in findinge them in their countrye, and harde it is to staye the comeinge of them, for there be soe many landinge places betwene the highe lande of the Raithlandes and Knockfergus; and above, the Raithlandes [Rathlin island] standeth soe farr from defence, as it is verye harde to have men to lye there continuallie, beinge so farre from healpe.

The water of Banne cometh to Loghe Eaughnaie [Lough Neagh] which severeth Clanneboy and Tyroon and M'Quoillynes and O'Cahan's countrye.

O'Cahan's countrye [Derry] is uppon the other side of the Banne, and is for the most parte waste. His countrye joyneth by the sea and is not past xx myles in length, and most parte mountayne lande. They obeye the Baron of Dongannon, but what the Scotte take against their will.

The next countrye to that, on the other side of the Banne is Tyroon, where the Earle of Tyroon hath rule; the fayrest and goodliest countrye in Irelande, universallei, and many gentlemen of the O'Neills dwellinge therin. The same countrye is at least lx. myles in length, and xxiiii. myles in breadeth. In the middest of the countrye standeth Ardnaght pleasantlye situated, and one of the fayrest and best churches in Ireland; and rounde aboute the same is the bishop's landes; and thoroughe occasion of the Earl and Countesse his wyffe, they made all that goodlie countrye wast. For whereas the countrye for the most parte within this iii. years was inhabited, it was within this xii. moneth made wast, thoroughe his makeinge of prayes uppon his sonnes, and they uppon him, soe as there was noe redresse amongst them, but by robbinge of the poore, and takeing of their goodes; whereby the countrye was all waste. Whereuppon my lord deputye appoynted a bande of men, being Englishe souldiers, to lie in Ardnaghe; and left the Baron of Dongannon in commission with other to see for the defence of the countrye and quyett for the poore people, whereby the countrye was kept from such raven as before was used ; and the Earle and Countesse brought to Dublyn, there to abyde untill the countrye were brought in better staye. And they perceyveinge the same, and that they could not retourn, they sent to the Irishe men next to the Englishe Pale, and soe they did to other Irishe-men, that they shoulde not truste to come unto my lorde deputye nor councell. This was reported by part of their owne secrett frindes.

By reason whereof O'Railye, O'Karrol, and divers other, which were wonte to come in withoute feare, refused to come unto us: Whereuppon I went to meete O'Railye to knowe his mynde what he meant. He declared he feared to be kepte under rest as the earle was. And then I toulde him the cause of his retayner was both for the wastinge and destroyenge of his countrye; and for that he said, he woulde never care for the amendinge of the same for his tyme, and yf there were but one ploughe goeinge in the countrye he would spende upon the same, with many other undecent wordes for a captyne of a countrye to saye. And O'Railye hearinge the same, saide, that he deserved to be kepte, and soe did he, yf he had done the like. Soe saide O'Karroll, and other of his countrye. And then Shane O'Neill, the earle's youngest soune came to Dongannon, and tooke with him of the earle's treasure viii[c] [800] lbs. in goulde and silver; besides plate and stuffe, and retayneth the same as yett; whereby it appeareth that he and she were content with the same. For it coulde not bee perceyved that they were greatlye offended for the same. Shane, being at peace till Maye, hearinge of the arryval of the Scotte, did send to them to give them entertaynmente; and soe he sent to divers other Irishe men to joyne with him, and promysed to devyde his goodes with them, which they, for the most parte, refused to doe; but some did. And I hearinge the same, one Maye daye, went to him with suche a bande of horsemen and Kerne of my frinds, to the number of ccc. men, and did parlye with them, and did perceyve nothinge in him but pryde, stubbornes, and all bent to doe what he coulde to destroye the poore countrye. And departing from me, beinge within iiii. myles to Dongannon he went and brent the earle's house; and then perceyveing the fyer, I went after as fast as I coulde, and sent light horsemen before to save the house from breakinge: and uppon my comeinge to the towne, and findinge that a small thinge woulde make the house wardeable, what it wanted I caused to be made upp, and left the baron's of Dongannon's warde in the castle. And having espyed where parte of his cattle was, in the middest of his pastures, I took from him viiᶜ kynes, besides garranes; and they sessed in the countrye cc. galloglas, and joyned all the gentlemen and souldiers of the countrye with the baron; wherewith all they were contented and pleased, and swore them all to the kinge's majestie: soe as I trust in God, Tyron was not soe like to doe well as within a shorte tyme I trust it shal be: and doe trust, yf a good presedent were there, to see good orders established amongst them, and to putt them in due execution, noe doubte but the countrye woulde prosper.

Next to that countrye is O'Donnell's countrye, named Tyreconell [Donegal], a countrey both large, proffitable, and good, that a shipp under sayle maye come to fower of his howses. And bemeane of the warre which was betwene him and his father, the countrye was greatlye ympoverished and wasted, soe as he did banishe his father at last, and tooke the rule himselfe. And nowe the like warre was betwene him and the Callough O'Donnell, so as the warres did in effect waste the whole countrye. And I beinge sent thether to pacifie the same, did bring them to Dublyn, where order was taken betwene them. But as yett they keepe the kinge's peace, and performe orders.

The next countrye to O'Donnell is Ferranaghe [Fermanagh], M'Guyer [Maguire], his countrye; a stronge countrye, and M'Guyer that is nowe a younge handsome gentleman, and maye make cc. kerne, and xxiii horsemen. And he, the Calloughe O'Donnell, Tirraghe Lynnaghe O'Neyll, Henri M'Shane, and all the rest be joyned with the Baron of Dongannon to serve the kinge's majestie, and all these be younge men, and of most power in the North, soe as yf the earle and O'Donnell were at such libertye as ever they were, without those they had noe power. And so by Gode's grace the thinge well followed, as I trust in God it shall, this summer will make a quyett Irelande.

Irishemen be soone brought nowe to obedyence, consideringe that they have no libertye to praye and spoyle, whereby they did maintayne their men, and without that they woulde have but fewe men. And the pollecye that was devysed for the sendinge of the Earles of Desmond, Thomonde, Clanricarde, and Tyroon, and the Baron of Upper Ossorie, O'Carroll, M'Guyres, and others into England, was a greate helpe of bringinge all those countryes to good order. For none of them that went to England committed harme uppon the kinge's majestie's subjects. The wynninge of the Earle of Desmond, was the wynninge of the rest in Mounster with small chardges. The makeinge of O'Brian, earle, made all that countrye obedyent. The makeinge of M'William, Earle of Clanricarde, made all his countryes dureinge this tyme quyett and obedient as it is nowe. The makeinge of Fitzffadricke Baron of Upper Osserye hath made his countrye obedient; and the haveinge of their landes by Dublyn, is such a gag uppon them as they will not forfayte the same throughe willfulle follye. And the gentlenes my lorde deputye doth use amonge the people, with wisdome and indifference, doth profitt, and make suer the former civilletye. Soe as presidents in Mounster, Connaghe, and Ulster, by Gode's grace, will make all Irelande, beinge made shire lande, that the lawe may take the right course, and yll men throughe good perswacion brought to take their landes of the kinge's majestie to them and their heyres for ever after. And preachers appoynted amongst them to tell them their dutyes, towardes God and their kinge, that they maye knowe what they ought to doe. And as for preachinge, we have none, which is our lack, without which the ignorante cann have noe knowledge, which were verye needfull to be redressed.

Hugh O'Neill, son of Matthew and reputed grandson of Earl Con O'Neill, had been brought up at the English court, and was recognized as Earl of Tyrone. In the war with Desmond he commanded a troop of horse for the English. When in Tyrone he was a Roman Catholic, but when in England he conformed to the Established religion. After the death of his wife he fell in love with and married Mabel, sister of Sir Henry Bagnal. For her accommodation he began to build a new castle at Dungannon. The house in which he resided was thatched with heather, and he procured a large quantity of lead to roof the new building. Before the walls were finished he had risen in revolt, and the lead was melted into bullets, of which one afterwards found its way into the brain of his brother-in-law.

At first this Irish chief was successful in his rebellion. Where the Battleford Bridge now stands, two miles from Eglish, and the same distance from Benburb, he inflicted, in 1597, a severe defeat on the lord deputy, who afterwards died of his wounds. On the fifteenth of August, 1598, he completely overthrew Bagnal at the Yellow Ford, between Armagh and Blackwatertown. Bagnal was killed, and 1700 of his men were left dead on the field of battle. But afterwards the English prosecuted the war with more vigor, and, notwithstanding Spanish assistance, Hugh O'Neill was defeated by Mountjoy. He then submitted to the English Government, and received a pardon.

The following description of the counties of Ulster was written by Marshal Sir Henry Bagnal in 1586, and is reprinted from the *Ulster Journal of Archeology*, First Series, vol. ii., pp. 137–60. Another transcript of a portion of the same report, relating to the counties of Down and Antrim, and varying somewhat from the following, has been printed in Dubourdieu's *Statistical Survey of Antrim* (Dublin 1812):

[From the State Paper Office. Endorsed: "Description of Ulster, 20th December, 1586 ; with some interlineations by Lord Burghley."]

The Province of Ulster lieth in the further part north of the realme. It is divided from Meath with the ryver Boyon uppon the southeast parte and with the Breny, which is Orelye's countrey, on the south part, and uppon the southwest parte it bowndeth uppon Conaght, namelie, uppon Orurke's countrey, and Oconohuor Sligah ; the rest is altogether environed with the sea. It conteyneth in it 9 counties, that is to saie, 3 of auncient and olde making, and 6 made (or rather to be made) newe ; the names of them are these :   Old—Louth, Downe, Antrim—3 ; Newe—Manachan, Farnemagh, Tirone, Dungale, Colraine, Armaghe—6.

Lowth.—The Countie of Lowthe lieth betwene the ryver of Boyn and the haven of Carlingford. . . . . .

Monachan.—The Countie of Monachan conteyneth these countreis: Iriell, Dartrey, Loghtie, and Trow. The chife Capten therof is one Sir Rory McMahon, who hath ben sometyme contributory to Tur. Oneyle, and nowe is left to the government of the Earle of Tyron, yet of himselfe is very desirous to yeld onlie to the Quene, and to be governed after the Englishe manner. He is able to make of his owne nation, and other his followers, 100 horsmen and 400 footemen. Buildings in his countrey are none, save certaine old defaced manasteries.

Farnmanagh.—The Countie of Farnmanaghe conteyneth all Farmanaghe, Tyrmingraghe, and Tyrmyn Omungan. The Capten of all this Countie is Sir Conohour McGwyre, left alwaies to the commandment and rule of Tur-[logh] Oneyle, and yet he very desirous to depend on the Quene. He is able to make (and most of his owne nation) 80 horsmen, 240 shot, and 300 kerne. His countrey for the most part is very strong of wood and bogge, especially nere the great lake called Earne, wherein is divers ilands, full of woodes. Buildinges in this countrey, non of importance.

Tyron.—The Countie of Tyron conteyneth all the land from Blackwater to Liffer ; the chife Capten there is Tur. Oneyle, [save] that of late the halfe thereof and more, by a composition made by the nowe Lord Deputie, is let to the Erle of Tiron for certen yeres, for which he shold paie to Tur. a 1000 marckes by yeare, which hath ben deteyned by the said Erle. Where through it is like that some troble will arise betwene them or it be longe. Turloghe desireth from Her Matie to his sonne that porcion of Tyron wherein he dwellethe, and is the remotest part from th' Englishe Pale-ward. The graunting hereof, in my opinion, were very expedient, especially for 2 respects ; the one, for extinguishinge their barborous costome of Tanetship, which is th' occasion of much mischife and disorder ; th' other, that by this division it will weeken the force and greatnes of such as succede, whereby they shall not be of power to do the hurt they were wont. The principall septes of this countrey are these : first, the Oneyles, who most ar all horsmen ; the Clandonelles, all galloglas ; the Odoonelles, a very strong sept, and much affected to Shane Oneyle's sonnes ; the Hagans ; and the Quyns: so as the whole force of this countrey may make 300 horsmen and 1500 footemen. But it is to be considered that allwaies the strengthe and greatnes of the Oneyles stoode chiffest uppon bandes of Scottes, whom they caused their Uriaghes to victuall and paie. Buildinges uppon Tur. parte is the Castle of Straban, wherein he most comonlie dwelleth, and the Newe Castle. Uppon the Earle's part is Donganon, and a defaced castell built by Shan Oneyl uppon the Blackwater, called Benburbe.

Dunegall.—The Countie of Donnegall conteyneth all Terconell, which is all the landes belonginge unto O'Donell and that sirname, and all Odohertie's countrey. Odonell is Capten and Governor of Tirconnell, the chife strengthe of whome standeth most uppon two septes of people called the Ogallochelles and McSwynes, who are all galloglas for the most parte. He is able to make above 200 horsmen and 1300 footemen. Betwene him and Oneyl hath ben contynuall warres for the Castell of Lyffer and the landes there aboutes, lienge betwene bothe their countreis bordringe uppon Lough Foyle, which by meane of their dissention is kepte altogether waste and uninhabited, neither is there any dwellinge in the Castle.

O'Doghertie's Countrie is a promontory, almost environed with the sea, namlie, Lough Swylie on the south parte, and Lough Foile on the northe. It is governed by a Capten called Odoghertie, who beinge not of power able to defend himself, is forced to contribute bothe to Oneyle and Odonell, and (*alterius vicibus*) to serve them both. His countrey, lienge uppon the sea, and open to the Isles of Ila and Uura in Scotland, is almost yearlie invaded by Scotes, who take the spoile of it at their pleasures; whereby Odoghertie is forced allwaies to be at their devocions. He is able of his owne nation and other, his followers, to make 60 horsmen and 300 footemen. Buildinges in his countrey are the Dery, which is defaced, and Greencastle and [   ], which ar wardable.

Colran.—The Countie of Colrane conteyneth all Ocahan's countrey, and lieth betwene Lough Foyle and the Bann; the Capten thereof is one Rory Ocahan, allwaies left to the government and rule of Tur. Oneile, and therefore contributethe to him. The chife strengthe of this man is his owne nation, who are able to make 140 horsmen and about 400 footemen. Yet, because he borderethe so nere the Scotte, he is much affected to them, and at all tymes doth yelde them great relife and succor. He hath buildinges in his countrey uppon Loughfoyle side, two strong castles, th' one called Anaghe, and th'other, Lymbevadie, and uppon the Bann, nere the samon fishinge, 2 castles, th' one called the Castle of Cobran, somewhat defaced, yet wardable, th' other, Castle Rooe, wherein Turloghe Oneyl kepeth a constable and a warde, to receve his parte of the fishing.

Ardmaghe.—The Countie of Ardmache conteyneth these countreis, viz: Oriragh, which is Ohanlon's countrie, Clanbrasell, Clancan, Clanawle, Mucknoe, Tireaughe, Fues, and Oneylan; most of these have severall Captens, to whom these countreis do apperteine, but ar of late made all contributaries to the Erle of Tyron, th' them selves be desyrous to take their land of the Quene. Ohanlon's countrey reacheth from the Newry, and from Dundalk, to Armache. It is for the most parte without wood, but full of hills and boggs; it is able to make nere 40 horsmen and 200 footemen.

Clanbrasell is a very woodie and boggie countrey, uppon the great Loghe's side called Eaghe; it hath in it no horsmen, but is able to make 80 kerne.

Clancan is a very stronge countrey, allmost all wood and deep bogg; it is invironed on th' one side with the aforesaid great Loghe, and on th' other side with a greate bogge and 2 deepe ryvers, th' one called the Blackwater, and th' other, the little Bann, both which in this countrey do fall into the foresaid Loghe. In this countrey are no horsmen, but about some 100 kerne who lyve for the most parte uppon stealthes and roberies.

Clanawle is a pece of countrey which of right apperteinethe to the Archebushop of Ardmache and his freeholders, and lieth betwene Ardmache and the Black Water. There is in it, nere to the ryver, much under woodes and boggs, but the rest, being toward Ardmache, is champion and fertill. Uppon

parte of this lande is the bridge and fort of Blackwater built.   Turloghe
Bresolache holdethe this portion of land from the Erle of Tyron, to whom he
paiethe his rents and service.   The said Tur., with his sonnes, now is able to
make 30 horsmen and 80 footemen.

Muckno and Tireawh lie betwene Ardmache and McMahon's countrey,
not long since apperteyning to him, but now possessed by the Erle of Tyron
who hath placed there certen of his own waged followers, that yield their
rents and services only unto him.

Fewes bordereth upon the English Pale, within three miles of Dundalk;
it is a very stronge countrey of wood and bogg, peopled with certen of the
Neyles, accustomed to lyve much uppon spoile of the Pale.   It was of late
appointed to contribute to the Erle of Tyron.   They are able to make some
30 horsmen and 100 footemen.

Oneylan is likewise a woode land, lienge betwene Ardmache and Clancan; this th' Erle of Tyron hathe, and claymeth to be his enheritance.   He
hath placed there some of the Quins and Hagans, who fostered him, and
sometymes he dwellethe him selfe amongest them there, in a little iland
called Loch Coe.

Buildings in the Countie of Ardmache, none, save the fort at Blackwater,
most needful to be repaired and better fortified ; and Ardmaghe, a small
villadge, having the church and other the Frieries there, for the most part,
broken and defaced.

Downe.—The Countie of Downe conteyneth these countreis : the Lordship of the Newrie and the Lordship of Mowrne, Evagh, otherwize called
Maginis' countrey, Kilulto, Kilwarlyn, Kinalewrty, Clainbrasel McGoolechan, Lecahull, Diffrin, Little Ardes, Great Ardes, and Southe Clandeboy.

The Lordships of Newrie and Mowrne [in ye county of Down] are the
inheritance of Sir Nicholas Bagnoll, who at his cominge thither founde them
altogether waste, and Shane Oneil dwellinge within less than a mile to the
Newrie, at a place called Fedom, suffringe no subject to travell from Dundalk northward.   But sithence the fortifications and buildinges made there
by the said Sir Nicholas Bagnoll, all the passages are made free, and much
of the countreis next adjacent reduced to reasonable civilitie.

Evaghe, otherwise called McGynis' countrey [in ye County of Down], is
governed by Sir Hugh McEnys, the cyvilest of all the Irishrie in those parts.
He was brought by Sir N. B. from the Bonaght of the Onels to contribute to
the Q., to whome he paiethe an anuall rente for his landes, which he hath taken
by letters patentes ; to holde after the Englishe manner for him and his
heires males, so as in this place onelie [amongest the Irishry of Ulster] is the
rude custom of Tanestship put awaie.   Maginis is able to make above 60
horsmen and nere 80 footemen ; he lyveth very civillie and Englishe-
like in his house, and every festivall daie wearethe Englishe garmentes
amongest his owne followers.

Kilultoe is a very fast countrey, full of wood and bogg ; it bordereth upon
Loghe Eaghe and Clanbrasell ; the Capten thereof is one Cormock McNeil,
who likewise was brought by Sir N. B. from the bondage of the Oneils to
yeld to the Quene.   He is able to make 20 horsmen and 100 kerne.   This
countrey (afore the Barons wars in England) was possessed and enhabited
by Englishe men, and there dothe yet remayne an olde defaced castle, which
still berethe the name of one Sir Miles Tracie.

Kilwarlyn, boundinge uppon Kilultagh, is a very fast woodland, the
Capten thereof by sirname is a McGenis, called Ever McRorie, and sometymes did contribute and yeld to Clandeboye, but nowe reduced to have

dependance onlie uppon the Quene.   He is able to make some 12 horsmen and 80 footemen.

Kinalewrtie, otherwise called McCartan's countrey, is likewise a wood-land, and boggy ; it lieth betwene Kilwaren and Lecahull.   In tymes past some interest therein was geven to Sir N. Malbie, but never by him quietlie enjoyed ; now the Capten thereof is called Acholie McCartan, and doth yeld onlie to the Quene.   He is able to make aboute 60 footemen, but no horsmen.

Clanbrasell McGoolechan is a very fast countrey of wood and bogg, inhabited with a sept called the Kellies, a very savage and barborous people, geven altogether to spoile and roberies, greatlie affected to the Scott, whom they often drawe into their countreis for the spoilinge of the subject.   They do contribute (but at their own pleasure)to the Capten of South Clandeboy. They can make no horsmen, but some 120 kerne and shott.

Lecahull is the enheritance of th' Erle of Kildare, geven to his father and his mother by Quene Marie ; it is almost an island, and without wood.   In it is the Bushop's Sea called Downe, first built and enhabited by one Sir John Coursie, who brought thither with him sondrie Englishe gentlemen, and planted them in this countrey, where some of them yet remayne, thoughe somewhat degenerate, and in poore estate ; yet they holde still their freeholdes.   Their names are Savages, Russells, Fitzsimons, Awdleis, Jordans, and Bensons.

Diffrin, sometymes the enheritance of the Maundevilles, and now apper-teyninge to one White, who is not of power sufficient to defend and manure the same ; therefore it is usurped and inhabited for the most parte by a bastard sorte of Scottes [the Islanders], who yeld to the said White some smale rent at their pleasure.   This countrey is for the most parte woody, and lieth uppon the Loghe which goeth out at the haven of Strangford.   There are of these bastard Scottes dwellinge here some 60 bowmen and 20 shott, which lyve most uppon the praie and spoile of their neighbors.

Little Ardes lieth on the north side of the river of Strangford, a fertile champion countrey.   It is the enheritance of the Lord Savage, who hath now for certain yeares farmed the same to Capten Peers.   There are besides dwellinge here certaine auncient freeholders of the Savages and Smithes, able to make amongst them all some 30 horsmen and 60 footemen.   They are often harrowed and spoyled by them of Clandeboye, with whom the borders of their landes do joine.

Great Ardes is that countrey which was undertaken by Mr. Smithe ; it is almost an island, a champion and fertile land, and now possessed by Sir Con McNeil Oge, who hath planted there Neil McBrian Ferto,[2] with sondry of his own sirname.   But the auncient dwellers there are the Ogilmers, a riche and stronge sept of people, alwaies followers of the Neils of Clande-boye.   The force of the enhabitants nowe dwellinge her is 60 horsmen and 300 footemen.

Southe Clandeboy is for the most parte a woodland, and reacheth from the Diffrin to the river of Knockfergus ; the Capten of it, Sir Con McNeil Oig Onele, who, in the tyme that the Erle of Essex attempted this countrey, was prisoner in the castle of Dublin, together with his nephewe, Hughe McPhelim, Capten of North Clandeboy, by meane whereof Sir Brian McPhelim (younger brother to Hughe) did then possesse bothe the countreis. The southe parte is now able to make 40 horsmen and 80 footemen.[3]

Antrim.—Antrim, stretchinge from the haven of Knockfergus to the going out of the Bann, conteyneth these countreis : North Clandeboy, Island Magye, Brian Caraghe's Countrey, Glynnes, and the Rowte.

North Clandeboye is for the most parte a plaine countrey, lienge in

lengthe from the river of Belfarst and Knockfergus to the Rowte, and in
bredthe from the Glinnes to the great Loghe called Eaghe. All this land is
geven by letters patentes to Sir Brian McPhelim's sonnes, the Quene's
pensioners, notwithstandings, by a newe division, latlie made by the now
Lord Deputie, the one moitie thereof is allotted to the rule of Hugh
McPhelim's sonnes, whereby great dissension doth depende betwene them,
and great slaughter on both partes often commytted. The principall followers in this countrey are these : the McGies, McOnulles, Onulchalons,
Durnam, and Tarturs. The force which they are able to make is 60 horsmen and 300 footemen, but by meane of their domestique dissention the
countrey is for the most parte waste and depopulate ; so as it is able to yeld
little or nothing to Her Ma$^{tie.}$

Iland McGye is a portion of land within three miles of Knockfergus,
almost environed with sea ; the headland thereof makethe the haven of
Olderfleete. It is five miles longe, but little more then a mile brode, all
plaine, without any wood, very fertile. It is almost all waste ; suche as be
there be the McGyes, and contribute to the Lord of Clandeboy, but doth of
right belong unto the Quene's Castle of Carikfergus.[4]

Brian Caraghe's countrey was a portion of Northe Clandeboy, won from
it by a bastard kinde of Scottes, of the sept of Clandonells, who entred the
same and do yet holde it, beinge a very stronge pece of land lienge uppon the
north side of the Band. The name of the nowe Capten thereof is Brian
Caraghe, who possessethe likewise another pece of a countrey of Tyron side
uppon the Band, for which he doth contribute to Onele, and for his landes
on the north side, to them of Clandeboy. By reason of the fastnes and
strentghe of his countrey, having succour and friendes on each side of the
Band, it [he] is so obstinate and careless as he never yet would appear before
any deputie, but yeldeth what relife he can to the Scottes. His force in
people is very small ; he standethe only uppon the strentghe of his countrey,
which indeed is the fastest ground of Ireland.

The Glynnes, so called because it is full of rockie and woodie dalles ; it
stretchethe in lengthe 24 miles (on the one side beinge backed by a very
steepe and bogie mounteyne, and on th' other parte with the sea) ; on
whiche side there are many small creekes betwene rockes and thickets, where
the Scottishe gallies do commonlie land ; at either end are very narrow
entries and passages into this countrey, which liethe directlie opposite to
Cantire, from which it is 18 miles distant. The Glynnes conteyne 7
Baronyes, whereof the Ile of Raghlin is counted half a Barony ; the
names of the Baronies are these : Larne, Park, Glanarm, Redbaye [Dubour-
dieu's account adds : "where Randall, now lord of the country, has his
residence], Lade, Cary, and Mowbray. These were sometime the inheritance
of Baron Myssett [Biset], from whom it is discended to a daughter, who was
married to one of the Clandonells in Scotland, by whom the Scottes nowe
make their clayme to the whole, and did quietlie possesse the same for many
yeares, till nowe of late (beinge spoyled of their goodes) they were banished
into Scotland ; but agane the countrey, by instructiones from her Ma$^{tie.}$, is let
to be helde from Her Highnes to Agnus McKonell, Lord of Cantire in
Scotland, and to his uncle, Sorlie Boye. The force of this countrey is un-
certaine, for that they are supplied, as neede requireth, from Scotland, with
what numbers they list to call, by makinge of fiers upon certeine steepe rockes
hanginge over the sea. The auncient followers of the countrey are these—
the Myssetts, some fewe remaininge, but in poore estate, the MacKayes, the
Omulrenies, the Mac y Gilles, the MacAwnleys, the MacCarnocks, and the

Clanalsters [Dubourdieu's account adds : " who are by original Scottish "],
who are most desirous to lyve under the Scottes, because they do better
defende them and less spende them then the Irish Lorde doth.

The Route, a pleasant and fertile countrey, lyinge betwene the Glynnes
and the ryver of Band, and from Clandeboye to the sea. It was sometymes
enhabited with the Englishe (for there remaineth yet certaine defaced castles
and monastaries of their buildinges).   The now Capten that maketh clayme
thereto is called McGwillim [the posterity, as is thought, of a Welshman—Dubourdieu's account]; but the Scott [Sir James MacSurley] hath well nere ex-
pulsed him from the whole, and dryven him to a small corner near the Bann,
which he defendeth rahter by the mayntenaunce of Turloch Oneil than his
owne forces; and the said Scottes did inhabite the rest, which is the best parte,
till likewise they were by her Ma^{tie's} forces, banished as aforesaid; but nowe
come back and possesse all in usurped manner as before. The chiefe auncient followers of this countrey are—the O'Haryes and the O'Quyns, who
dwell upon their lands and yelde rent and service to the Scott [the aforesaid James].   They are able to make 60 stronge and well furnished horsmen
and about 200 footemen.

Castles wardable are onelie Belfast, Edenduchar, and Olderfleete; and
castles defaced are these : Portmucke, in Iland Magy, Glanarme and
Redbaye, in the Glyns, and Castle Martyn, in the Rowte.

[Dubourdieu's account adds: " The chiefe house is called Dunluce,
standing upon a rock in the seashore, where the said Sir James hath his
residence.

" Carickfergus is the only town in the shire, upon the river, three miles
broad over against the towne, walled partly with stone, and partly with
sodds.   There are in it two wards: the one in the castle, in the south ende
of the towne; the other in the abbye, in the north end thereof. This towne
is governed by a mayor and two sheriffs; and at this day there are but 16
freemen of this towne.

" Castles wardable at this day: Belfast, eight English miles up the river
from Carrickfergus, where the passage is over the river at low water; Eden-
duffee Carrick, near Lough Eagh. Castles defaced: Olderfleet, Glanowre,
Castle Marteen, in the Route."]

It may easlie be perceaved, by this slender and brief description of
Ulster, what hath ben and ar the reasons why this Province hath ben from
tyme to tyme more chargeable to Her Matie then any other, as namlie :

1. The want of good townes and fortified places, wherewith other places
are better replenished.

2. And next, the sufferance of the Oneils to usurp the government of
the severall Captens and freeholders, and by little and little to excede the
bowndes of their owne, and so encrease uppon the possessions of other;
whereby they were made stronger then otherwise they colde have ben, and
abled thereby to wage and mainteine the greater number of Scottes.

3. Thirdlie, the confininge so nere to the Iles of Scotland, and the
contynuall comerce which the Irishry have with the people of those partes,
occasionethe the often cominge in of them, to the greate hurt of this Province
and the subjects which dwell there.

4. Fourthlie, and lastlie, the want of due exercises of religion and
justice, of sacred and civill instructions, is the occasion of much impietie
and barboresnes; which two are the mother and nurse of all their disobedience, disorder, and disloyaltye.

REMEDIES

1. For a remedie to the first: thoughe it be a thing greatly to be wished, that the example were folowed by K. Henry the Second, of K. John and of others since their tyme, of famous memorye, who, havinge great desire to reforme that countrey, did make sondrey fortifications, as well there as in other places of the realme; yet, considering Her Maties excessive charge nowe bestowed, as well for the defence of this her realme as in other partes beyond the seas, for the necessarie strengtheninge of her whole dominion, it is not convenient to desier Her Maties greater expense; but onlye that such revenues as this Province may be made to yelde Her Matie may be employed uppon fortyfications in places most needful for certaine yeres.

2. And to the second: lyke as in former tyme of good government it was a thing most regarded in all treaties to weaken the force of the Oneiles by withdrawing from them their Uryaghes, as was done by K. H. th' Eighthe with Con O'Neil, who, when he had made him Earle of Tyron, gave him no more by patent than the bare countrie of Tyrone, and spec- yalle provided that he should not intermedle with anie on this side the Blackwater; soe is it most needful to take the opportunitie which now the people and the time doth better offer then it did then. Thearfore, the way is, to aportionate both to Tur. Lenoghe and the Earle of Tyron [beinge of one sirname] landes on the north side of Blackwater, to them and their heirs males, indyfferently bounded by some well acquainted with those countries, whearwith they should only deale, and medle no further, but leave the governemente of the rest for Her Matie to the cheef commissioner, or other Her Highnes' offiycers in that Province.

3. To the therd: as there is noe way soe good as to fortifie the coast neere their landing place, soe me thinketh that will seeme too chardgeable, and thearfore will not lyke Her Matie soe well. In which respect a second way should be thought uppon, and that may be this:

It is evidente that the people which most anoy us from Scotland are the Clandonells, who are ever in contynuall warre with another secte of people of the Iles, named McAlans. And yf on McAlan Her Matie would bestow some convenient pension, he will, I thincke, undertake to kepe the Clandonells soe contynually occupied as the shalbe hable to sende none of their people to disturbe Her Highnes' subjectes in Ulstar, whearof will aryse to Her Ma^rie a treble commoditie with a single chardge; for she shall bothe prevente the myscheef which is now wrastled with rather then redressed, and save the chardge, which is almost yeerelie, in this frutelesse labour spente, amountinge oft to above ten thousand powndes a yeere, together with the loss of manie men's lyves, and also assure herself of a good frend and instrumente in the backes of the Scottes, to afflicte them and worke diversion of their forces when they shalbe aboute to attempte anythinge against us.

4. As for the fourth: it might doubtlesse be remedied yf these countreis weare as well broughte to the nature as to the names of Sheeres; that is, that the Sheeres being perfectly bonded, Sheryffes of Englysh education may be appointed in everye countie, and in certaine convenient places some preachers and free schooles. And for the whole Province, a Counsaile weare established, of the wysest, gravest, and best disposed, dwellinge within the same, havinge some other joyned with them that were not possessyoners therein. That alsoe, assizes, quarter sessions, and such other lyke tymes should duely and orderly be in every countie observed; which

all require not soe great chardge and travaile in the beginninge as they yeld both proffitt and honour in the ende.

Since the writing of the premises I doe perceave, by letters lately receaved out of Ireland, that the Earle of Tyron hath taken upon hym the rule of Sir Hugh McEnys, Sir Con McNeyle Oge, the Capten of Kilwarlyn, and sundry others, who, at my cominge thence, depended only upon the Quene.

Queen Elizabeth died in 1603, and was succeeded by James VI., King of Scotland. In Scotland, the Protestant Reformation had produced a vast effect on its inhabitants. John Knox, a man of learning, eloquence, and fearless courage, had led the reformers to victory. A system of education was provided for the people. The principles of Protestantism sank into their hearts and changed the habits of their lives. In two generations men of clay were transformed into men of iron. An ignorant and changeable people became the foremost race in the world, possessed of all the qualities necessary to render the Celts of Ireland subject to the authority of England. Hitherto, English colonists had been absorbed by the Irish. But now another description of colonist was to settle in Ulster, capable of holding the Celt in subjection, and keeping the " back door " of access to England closed against all her enemies.

After James became King of England, he appointed as Lord Deputy of Ireland, Sir Arthur Chichester, who desired to see the country colonized with men of his own race and religion.[5] It was reported that he intended to seize the earl of Tyrconnell and the earl of Tyrone, both of whom had been in rebellion against the Government. But these two chieftains, with many of their friends, fled from the country in 1607, and never returned. All their estates, embracing the six counties of Colerain (now Londonderry), Tyrone, Armagh, Cavan, Fermanagh, and Donegal, were immediately confiscated by the Crown, and became available for purposes of plantation.

NOTES TO CHAPTER XXXII

[1] A *kern* was one of the old Irish irregular light-armed infantry, carrying only a sword and javelin; corresponding to the *cateran* of the Scottish Highlands, and distinguished from the heavier-armed *galloglass*.

[2] The transcript of this passage printed in Dubourdieu's *Statistical Survey of Antrim* (Dublin, 1812) reads as follows: "Great Ardes is almost an island, a champion and fertile land, and now possessed by Neil MacBryan Flain," etc.

[3] Dubourdieu's transcript of Bagnal's description of county Down gives the following in addition:

" Townes in the County of Downe, viz., The Newrie, Downe, Ardglass, all unwalled, and without any privileges of a corporation.

" Castles of the said County: Green Castle, near the barr of Carlingford, upon the sea. Dondrom, in the bottom of the bay that divideth Le Cahel from Eveagh. The castle of Narrow-water, which keepeth the river that goeth to the Newrie passable. Strangford, Ringhaddy, Scattery, Castle Reagh, within the isles of Lough Coyne.

''This countie hath the sea to the east, the county of Armagh to the west, the haven of Carlingford and that river to the south, the countries of Brasilogh, Clancan, and Lough Eagh to the north.''

⁴Dubourdieu's transcript adds: '' It is granted in lease by the Queen to one Savage, one of the Earl of Essex, his men.''

⁵Sir Arthur Chichester was the second son of Sir John Chichester of Raleigh, in Devonshire. He commenced his public career by robbing one of the Queen's purveyors, for which offence he was compelled to retire to France, where he soon became distinguished as a soldier. Queen Elizabeth pardoned him, probably because she thought that she had as much need for his military services as Henry IV. of France. (Lodge, *Peerage of Ireland*, edited by Archdall, vol. i., p. 318 ; Granger, *Biographical History of England*, vol. ii., p. 98.) On Chichester's return, he was sent to Ireland to assist in the suppression of Tyrone's rebellion, and proved himself a willing and effective instrument in carrying out Mountjoy's ruthless policy of extermination against the native Irish. English writers, and among them old Fuller, delight to tell how Chichester was so instrumental in ploughing and breaking up the barbarous Irish nation, and then sowing the soil with the '' seeds of civility.'' The preparatory process consisted simply in the remorseless and wholesale destruction of human life, and all kinds of property. He proceeded on the conviction that the sword, even when wielded against helpless women and children, was not sufficiently destructive, and therefore called to his work all the horrible agencies of famine and pestilence. Describing a journey which he made from Carrickfergus, along the banks of Loughneagh, into Tyrone, Chichester says: '' I burned all along the lough, within four miles of Dungannon, and killed 100 people, sparing none of what quality, age or sex soever, besydes many burned to death ; we kill man, woman, and child ; horse, beast, and whatsoever we find.'' On another occasion, after his return from a similar expedition into the Route, he writes : '' I have often sayd and wrytten that it is famine that must consume them ; our swordes and other indeavoures worke not that speedie destruction which is expected.'' (See an interesting contribution by William Pinkerton, Esq., in *Ulster Journal of Archæology*, vol. v., p. 209, and note.) Thomas Gainsforde, the writer of *The True, Exemplary, and Remarkable History of the Earl of Tirone*, already quoted, refers to the dire calamity inflicted at that period on the helpless inhabitants of Ulster. '' For the sword-men,'' says he, '' perished with sicknesse and famine the next yeere following, and the poore calliots [old women] devoured one another for mere hunger, and showed us the lamentable effects of a calamitous warre and afflicted country'' (p. 37). The writer expresses his gratification on the advancement of Chichester to the chief-governorship as follows : '' By this time is Sir Arthur Chichester lord deputy, who watched these parts of the North more narrowly than any other before him. First, because of his long experience and residence amongst them, as being governor of Knogfergus, and a laborious searcher of Logh Con [Strangford Lough] with all the territories adjacent '' (p. 47).— Hill, *Montgomery Manuscripts*, p. 48.

CHAPTER XXXIII

THE SCOTTISH PLANTATION OF DOWN AND ANTRIM

COLONISTS from North Britain had already possessed themselves of large portions of Down and Antrim, the two counties lying nearest to Scotland, some years before the inception of King James's " Great Plantation." The history of these early settlers in county Down has been preserved to some extent in the recently published *Montgomery Manuscripts* and *Hamilton Manuscripts*,[1] which both come very close to being contemporary records of the periods of which they treat ; and in the *Macdonnells of Antrim* the Rev. George Hill gives a great deal of information about the Scottish colonization of that county. The most important parts of these manuscripts are reprinted as appendices to this volume. The main points of the story may be outlined in a few paragraphs.

At the beginning of the seventeenth century, the north half of county Down, known as the Upper Clannaboye country, was ruled by one of the cadets of the great O'Neill family, who bore the name, Con McNeale Mc-Bryan Feartagh O'Neill, and lived in the old mansion house of Castlereagh, two or three miles distant from Carrickfergus Castle (now Belfast). Toward the end of the year 1602, Con happened to be entertaining some relatives in his halls of Castlereagh, when his wine gave out. A fresh supply, which he had ordered from Spain, had been brought as far as Belfast, but was detained on its arrival there by the queen's exciseman, until Con should pay a lately imposed duty, concerning which he neither knew nor understood anything. The old chieftain's blood arose, and he ordered some of his retainers to proceed to Belfast and bring the wine by force. There his servants had an encounter with some English soldiers, and in the melee one of the soldiers was killed. O'Neill was therefore accused of " levying war against the queen," and lodged in Carrickfergus Castle. Sir Arthur Chichester proposed to hang him, as an example, and for a time it looked as if Con's praiseworthy desire to supply his relatives and friends with a proper amount of " drink " would result in the host's losing his head.

In this extremity, Con's wife communicated with a friend in Scotland, one Hugh Montgomery, who was the Laird of Braidstane, in Ayrshire. He had been looking for an eligible " settlement " in the north of Ireland, and kept himself posted as to what went on there through relatives who traded to Ireland from the port of Irvine. In consideration of the cession to himself of one-half of Con's lands in county Down, he now agreed with the latter's wife to assist the prisoner to escape, and entrusted the carrying out of the enterprise to his relative, Thomas Montgomery, who was the owner of a sloop which sometimes traded with Carrickfergus. The latter accordingly began by making love to the daughter of the keeper of Carrickfergus Castle. Being admitted to the castle, Thomas managed to so ingratiate himself with the prison guards, and to supply them so generously with drink, that it was not difficult for him to obtain their consent for the admission to Con's quarters of a large cheese which had been sent by the latter's wife, ostensibly for the purpose of replenishing the prisoner's larder. This cheese was hollowed out, and contained a long rope, by means of which, when night came, Con managed to escape from the castle. Letting himself out of his window, he found Thomas Montgomery's sloop in waiting, and within a few hours he was carried across the Irish channel to Braidstane and safety.

There Con entered into an agreement with Hugh Montgomery, by which he ceded to that gentleman half his lands in Clannaboye, on condition that the latter should obtain for him a free pardon from King James, and get him permission to kiss the king's hand. This Montgomery proceeded to do, but, finding his own influence at Court not sufficient, he was obliged to have recourse to a brother Scot, whose word had more weight with the king. This man was James Hamilton, who had been employed by James I. as his political agent in Dublin. With his assistance, Con received a free pardon, was admitted to the king's presence, and permitted to return to his house of Castlereagh. During the negotiations at Court, it had become necessary for Con to increase his promised recompense to Montgomery by making it sufficiently large to satisfy James Hamilton also. So, when the patent was finally issued under the Great Seal, April 16, 1605, " on the humble petition of Conn McNeale McBryan Feartagh O'Neale and of Hugh Montgomery, Esq., and of James Hamilton, Esq.,'' it granted to the said James Hamilton all the lands in the Upper Clannaboye and the Great Ards which had been possessed by Con, or by his father, Bryan Feartagh O'Neale, in his lifetime. Hamilton had previously entered into an agreement with Montgomery and O'Neill as to what portion he should retain and what portion Montgomery should receive. He reconveyed to O'Neill one-third of the estate; and that third as well, in the course of a few years, was run through with and dissipated by the convivial and generous Con.

Both Hamilton and Montgomery, as soon as their patents were passed by the Irish Council, crossed into Scotland to call upon their whole kith and kin to aid them in the plantation of their vast estates. Both were Ayrshire men, from the northern division of the county. Hamilton was of the family of Hamilton of Dunlop, while Montgomery was of the great Ayrshire family of that name, sprung from a collateral branch of the noble house of Eglinton, and sixth Laird of Braidstane, near Beith. The king had granted Con's land to Hamilton on the express condition that he should " plant " it with Scottish and English colonists. Hamilton seems to have received the hearty support of his own family, for four of his five brothers aided his enterprise and shared his prosperity. From them are descended numerous families in Ulster, and at least two Irish noble families.

Hamilton founded the towns of Bangor and Killyleagh, in county Down, and there is no doubt that he did "plant" the land which he had acquired with Scottish tenants, the most of them evidently from the same counties in Scotland—Ayr, Renfrew, Wigtown, Dumfries, and Kirkcudbright—as the men who followed Montgomery. The names of some of those who held farms from the Hamilton estates in 1681 and 1688 appear on rent-rolls of those years as follows (*Hamilton Manuscripts*, pp. 108–111, 125–131), the majority of these residing in and near the towns of Bangor and Killyleagh:

John Adair, Thomas Aiken, Widow Alexander, William Alexander, Robert Allan, Andrew Anderson, James Anderson, James Anderson's widow, Robert Anderson, James Aniston, William Armstrong, David Aul, James Aule, Alexander Baillie, Alexander Baily, Edward Baily, James Bailie, John Baily, Esq., William Barclay, James Beatty, —— Beatty's executors, William Beers, James Biglam, James Black, James Blackwood, John Blackwood, John Bleakly, Sr., James Blakely, John Blakely, Jr., James Blany, David Boid, Widow Boid, William Bole, David Boyd, John Bredfoot, Thomas Bradin, Thomas Bradly, Gilbert Brakenrig, Thomas Bradley, Alexander Browne, George Browne, James Browne, Widow Browne, Samuel Browne, William Brown, George Byers, James Byers, Widow Byers, William Byers, John Camlin, John Campbell, Michael Campbell, Robert Campbell, Widow Campbell, James Carmuheall (Carmichael?), M. Carr, Henry Carse, James Caul, James Chambers, Andrew Clarke, James Clarke, John Cleland, Patrick Cleland, Widow Cleland, John Clugston, Widow Cochran, Richard Coney, Thomas Cooper, Widow Cooper, John Corey, Joseph Corsby, Thomas Costbes, Thomas Coulter, A. Cowden, William Cowden, Widow Cowey, William Crafford, James Cringle, Hugh Criswill, James Criswill, Sr., William Criswell, Robert Cudbert, John Cumin, Robert Cunningham, Widow Danison, John Davison, John Daziell, John Delop, Andrew Dixon, James Dixon, John Doblin, Alexander Dobby, William Donnelson, Widow Dowy, David Duffe, David Duggan, Widow Duggan, James Dunlap, John Dunlap, George Dunn, John Espy, John Fairiss, Captain Fairly, Hugh Fairly, William Fairly, Alexander Ferguson, Hugh Ferguson, Thomas Ferguson, Andrew Finlay, Hans Finlay, John Finlay, Robert Finlay, Nathaniel Forgy, George Forman, George Forrest, James Forrest, Nathaniel Forsythe, William Fullerton, John Gamble, William Gastle, John Gay, Hugh Gervin, Alexander Gibony, John Gibbon, Widow Gibson, William Gibson, John Gilmore, John Gilpatrick, James Gordon, John Gowdy, schoolmaster, William Gowdy, Widow Greer, Widow Gregg, Hugh Hamil, Esq., Alexander Hamilton, Archibald Hamilton, Arthur Hamilton, Captain Gawen Hamilton, Lieut. Gawin Hamilton, Hugh Hamilton, James Hamilton, John Hamilton, Patrick Hamilton, Robert Hamilton, Robert Hamilton, tailor, Robert Hamilton, merchant, Widow Hamilton, William Hamilton, William Hamilton, Esq., Thomas Hamington, Patrick Hannah, Lodk. Harper, John Harris, Widow Hawthorne, John Hay, John Henderson, John Henry, James Heron, Widow Heron, David Heslip, John Francis Hewart, James Hewitt, William Hewitt, William Hillhouse, William Hogg, —— Holhouse, John Hollan, David Holland, William Holliday, William Hollyday, —— How, Gilbert How, John Hui, John Hunter, Alexander Hutchison, Henry Inch, John Ireland, James Irwin, John Irwin, Sr., Robert Irwin, John Jackson, John Jenkin, George Johnston, John Johnston, William Johnson,

Edmond Kelly, James Kelly, William Kelton, David Kennedy, George
Kennedy, Doctor Hugh Kennedy, James Kennedy, John Kennedy, Andrew
Kernochan, Robert Kindsay, Widow Laggan, Widow Laughlin, Widow
Lead, Archibald Lenox, Widow Lenox, James Lenzy, John Leslie's execu-
tor, Samuel Lewes, James Lindsay, John Lindsay, Elizabeth Lockert, John
Lockert, Richard Lockart, Robert Loggan, John Long, Robert Long,
Widow Lowdan, James Lowdon, John Lowdon, John Lowdon, Jr., Thomas
Lowry, John Luke, James Luthersdale, Janet Lyon, Alexander McAmt,
John McBride, Andrew McCaldon, Andrew McCalla, Joseph McCan, John
McCardy, James McCarly, Thomas McCarly, Widow McCarly, Alexander
McCartney, William McClurgh, W. James McCo, Janet McComb, Caghtry
McConnell, James McConnell, John McConnell, William McCormick, Adam
McCrea, Matthew McCrea, Robert McCreery, Robert McCrery, James
McCullam's widow, Thomas McCullen, Widow McCullin, James McDowell,
John McDowell, Patrick McDowell, Widow McDowell, John McDoran,
Andrew McFerran, Thomas McFerran, Archibald McGibbon, John McGill,
Revd. Jackson McGuire, Widow McIlduffe, Thomas McIlrath, John McHoll,
Alexander McKee, John McKee, Thomas McKee, Ninian McKelvy, Thomas
McKelvy, Widow McKelvy, Joseph McKitrick, John McLaughlin, Alice Mc-
Mehan, James McMechan, John McMechan, Patrick McMechan, Widow Mc-
Mechan, William McMechan, William McMorlan, Eneas McMullen, Hugh
McMullan, James McMunce, James McMurray, James McNaght, John
McNarry, John McNeily, James McNily, Alexander McRobins, Alexander
McTeer, James McWilliam, James Macumson, John Mahaule, George
Mally, John Malley, —— Mant, John Matthew Marshall, Matthew Marshall,
Finlay Martin, Joseph Martin, William Martin, John Mathy, Alexan-
der Maxwell, George Maxwell, James Maxwell, Robert Maxwell, Philip
Mayers, Josias Milton, James Mitchell, Robert Mitchell, David Montgomery,
Hugh Montgomery, Nathaniel Montgomery, William Montgomery, Widow
Montgomery, John Moorhead, William Moorhead, Widow Moorhead, Arcibald
Moore, Captain Moore, Hugh Moore, James Moore, Jane Moore, John Moore,
Robert Moore, Widow Moore, James Morell, Captain Morrow, David Morrow,
Samuel Mossman, Widow Murray, Mrs. Neill, Widow Nelson, John Nesbit,
Thomas Nesbitt, George Newell, Hugh Nicholson, James Oghterson, Thomas
Oliver, Patrick Orr, Tomas Orr, Janet Paradine, Alexander Parker, Gawin
Patterson, John Patterson, Robert Patterson, William Patterson, James
Peticrue, John Petticrew, William Petticrew, Widow Petticrew, John Patton,
George Pollock, Thomas Pottinger, Randulph Price, Esq., Widow Purdy,
—— Ramsey's heirs, Hugh Rea, James Rea, Widow Rea, Alexander Read,
John Read, Mrs. Richison, Mrs. Ritchison, Alexander Ritchy, Archibald
Richy, Widow Ritchy, George Ringland, Alexander Robb, John Robb,
John Robinson, George Ross, James Ross, Esq., John Ross, Robert Ross,
William Rowan, Gawen Russell, William Russell, Hugh Savage, James
Savage, Esq., John Savage, Esq., John Scott, Margaret Scott, Widow Scott,
John Shannon, John Shaw, William Shaw, Esq., Widow Shearer, James
Sim, Gilbert Simpson, Robert Simpson, Widow Simpson, Mr. Sloan, ——
Sloane, James Sloan, James Sloans, James Smith, John Smith, Robert
Smith, Alexander Spittle, James Spotswood, James Stanus, James Steele,
James Steel, Jr., Robert Sterlin, Hans Stevenson, James Stevenson, John
Stevenson, Alexander Stewart, John Stewart, William Stewart, James
Sumers, John Sumers, Widow Sumers, John Swadlin, John Swaline's
executors, John Syers, Ninian Tate, Thomas Taylor, Thomas Tailor,
James Thompson, John Thompson, Robert Thompson, Widow Thompson,

John Throw, Robert Tod, —— Trail, Mrs. Trail, Patrick Vance, George Wallace, Hugh Wallace, Thomas Wallace, William Wallace, Widow Wallace, Archibald Wardlaw, Widow Wardon, John Warnock, Robert Warnock, Widow Warnock, John Watson, Valentine Watson, George Watt, John Watt, William Watt, Edward Weaver, St. John Webb, David Welsh, James Whitla, Widow Whitla, David White, Hugh White, Widow White, Captain Williamson, Widow Williamson, Hugh Wilson, Widow Wilson, Alexander Wily, John Wily, Jr., Adam Woods, Andrew Woods, Widow Woods, James Worrell, Samuel Wright, John Wyly, Sr., William Young.

To Hamilton fell the western portion of North Down, to Montgomery the eastern, and both seem to have added to their estates when Con O'Neill was forced to sell the third which he had reserved for himself.

In the *Montgomery Manuscripts* is preserved a careful account of how Hugh Montgomery " planted " his estate, the country around Newtown and Donaghadee, known as the " Great Ards." Montgomery belonged to a family having numerous connections throughout North Ayrshire and Renfrewshire, and to them he turned for assistance. His principal supporters were his kinsman, Thomas Montgomery, who had done the successful wooing at Carrickfergus; his brother-in-law, John Shaw, younger son of the Laird of Wester Greenock; and Colonel David Boyd, of the noble house of Kilmarnock. With their help, Montgomery seems to have persuaded many others of high and low degree to try their fortunes with him in Ireland.

The names of the emigrants are intensely Scottish. They began to cross in May, 1606. Persons of substance generally took out letters of denization soon after they came to Ireland, and sometimes before leaving Scotland. The following received such letters of denization in 1617 (*Calendar of Patent Rolls, James I.*, pp. 326, 339), the majority of them having settled on Sir Hugh Montgomery's estates probably ten years prior to that date:

Gilbert Adare of Ardehine, Andrew Agnewe of Carnie, Thomas Agnew, Gray Abbey, John Aickin of Donoghdie, Patrick Allen of Ballydonane, David Anderson of Castle Canvarie, John Barkley of Ballyrolly, David Boyde of Glasroche, Thomas Boyde of Crownerston, Robert Boyle of Drumfad, Nynnan Bracklie Newton of Donoghdie, William Caderwood of Ballyfrenzeis, James Cathcart of Ballirogane, James Cowper of Ballichosta, Michael Craig of the Redene, William Crawford of Cuningburn, Claud Conyngham of Donoghdie, David Cunyngham of Drumfad, Hugh Cunyngham of Castlespick, John Cuningham of Rinchrivie, William Cuninghame of Donoghdie, Charles Domelston of Proveston, John Fraser of Donoghdie, John Harper of Ballyhay, John Harper of Donoghdie, Robert Harper of Provostoun, Thomas Harvie of Newton, Thomas Kelso of Ballyhacamore, David Kennedy of Gortivillan, Walter Logane of Logane, Uthred McDowgall of Ballimaconnell, David McIlveyne of Ballelogan, James McMakene of Donoghdie, John Martin of Dunnevilly, James Maxwell of Gransho, John Maxwell of Ballihalbert, Hugh Montgomery of Granshaghe, John Montgomery of Ballymacrosse, John Montgomery of the Redene, Matthew Montgomery of Donoghdie, Patrick Montgomerie of Ballycreboy, Robert Montgomery of Donoghdie, William Montgomery of Donoghdie, Hector

Moore of Donan, John Moore of Donoghdie, Quintene Moore of Aughneill, William Moore of Milntowne, William Moore, preacher at Newton, John Mowlen of Mowlen, Patr., Thomas Nevin of Ballicopl, John Peacocke of Ballidonan, Andrew Sempill of Ballygrenie, Alexander Speire of Grayabbey, Patrick Shaw of Balliwalter, William Shaw of Ballykilconan, John Thompson of Blackabbey, James Williamson of Clay, Allen Wilson of Newton, Robert Wilson of Newtowne, John Wyly of Ballyhay, William Wymis of Newtowne.[2]

The success of the settlements made by Hamilton and Montgomery was immediate; for four years after the foundation of the colony—in 1610—Montgomery alone was able to bring before "the king's muster-master a thousand able fighting men to serve, when out of them a militia should be raised."[3] Four years later we have again specific information of the progress of the Scottish colonies under Hamilton and Montgomery. It is contained in a letter from the earl of Abercorn to John Murray, King James's Secretary of State. He writes: "They have about 2000 habile Scottis men weill armit heir, rady for his Majestie's service as thai sall be commandit. . . . Sir Hew Montgomery is in building ane fyin houese at the Newton, quhairof ane quarter is almost compleit, an Sir James hes buildit at Killilarche ane very stronge castill, the lyke is not in the northe." This muster of 2000 men able to bear arms of course represented an emigration of at least 10,000 souls.

Meantime, across the river Lagan, in county Antrim, a "plantation" had been made which, although not at first peculiarly Scottish, was soon to become so. During almost the whole of James's reign probably the most powerful man in Ireland was Sir Arthur Chichester, who in 1604 became lord deputy, an office which he held until 1616.

In 1603, Chichester obtained a grant of "the Castle of Bealfaste or Belfast, with the appurtenants and hereditaments, spiritual and temporal, situate in the Lower Clandeboye"; while in the years immediately succeeding he acquired the lands along the north shore of what was then called Carrickfergus Bay almost to Lough Larne. Belfast is in reality, from its very foundation, not an Irish, but an English and Scottish town. The survey of 1611 tells us how this settlement was progressing: "The town of Belfast is plotted out in a good forme, wherein are many famelyes of English, Scotch, and some Manksmen already inhabitinge, and ane inn with very good lodginge, which is a great comforte to the travellers in these partes." The settlement commissioners passed along the north shore of Belfast Lough, finding everywhere houses springing up, and in every part of the lord deputy's lands "many English famelies, some Scottes, and dyvers cyvill Irish planted." At Carrickfergus the commissioners found a pier and townwall being built, and all through South Antrim—in Island Magee, at Templepatrick at Massereene, and along the shores of Lough Neagh to Toome —settlements of English and Scots, and houses and "bawns" being erected.*

* Benn's *History of Belfast*, pp. 674–76.

The Rev. John Dubourdieu, in his *Statistical Account of Antrim*, written in 1812, states :

  The earliest English settlers of whom anything is known here, were those who came over to Carrickfergus on the first invasion, in the reign of Henry II. ; but what attended their descendants, if they left any, we are ignorant of ; their number was small, and as they were soldiers, probably few survived. But from that time there were many arrivals in the different reigns, until the numerous colonies came in the reigns of Queen Elizabeth and of James I. Those who settled about Carrickfergus were in the latter reign, and brought from Devonshire by Sir Arthur Chichester. Their descendants retained some of the customs of their ancestors, within the memory of persons still [1812] alive ; amongst these was the Devonshire mode of conveying grain in the straw and hay, in bundles on the backs of horses, instead of carriages. . . . The load or bundles of hay were called trusses, and hay is there still computed by that name. The narrow causeways and immense divisional ditches are also supposed to have had a Devonshire origin. Another part of this colony settled in the district of Malone, or Milone, adjoining to Belfast, where their descendants are still to be distinguished by their looks and manners, but particularly by the air of comfort about their dwellings, and a fondness for gardens and orchards. Near Belfast was likewise a colony of Lancashire and Cheshire men, settled there, as it is said, by Sir Moyses Hill ; but from Malone to Lisburn, and thence over the greatest part of the barony of Massereene, and the south part of the barony of Antrim, but especially towards the west, the country is mostly occupied by the descendants of English settlers, and some Welsh, who came over in the reign of Elizabeth in great numbers, and also in the beginning of that of James I.; with the different great families that at different times obtained grants of lands here. Upper Massereene was colonized by the Seymours, Lords Conway, and Sir George Rawdon ; part of Lower Massereene also ; the remainder, and part of the Barony of Antrim by the Skeffingtons, Langfords, and Nortons, which last came in the reign of Elizabeth.

  While South Antrim was thus "planted" mainly by English settlers, the northern half of the county was opened up for settlement, without the violent transference of land from Celt to Saxon which was carried out in other parts of Ulster.

  The northeast corner of Ireland had been long held by the Macdonnells, a clan which also peopled the island of Jura, and Cantyre on the mainland of Scotland. We have already seen, from Marshal Bagnal's description of Antrim, that this clan had acquired a foothold in the Route and the Glens some years before the settlement of Montgomery and Hamilton in county Down. The story has been told at length by the Rev. George Hill in his *Macdonnells of Antrim*. In a scarce work entitled *The Government of Ireland under Sir John Perrott, Knight*, etc. (London, 1626, p. 136), the author states that about 1584, "the Deputy received intelligence of the approach of a thousand Scottish islanders, called Redshanks, being of the septs or families of the Cambiles [Campbells], Macconnells [Macdonnells], and Magalanes, drawne to invade Ulster by Surleboy,' one of that nation, who had usurped, and by power and strong hand, possessed himself of the Mac-quilies' [McQuillans'], and other men's lands in Ulster, called the Glinnes and the Route; meaning to hold that by force, which he had gotten without right, by violence, fraud, and injury.''

Some of the details of the conquest of Antrim by the Macdonnells may be learned from the following notes on the Scottish settlement of North Antrim, taken from the MacAdam manuscripts.   These notes were made by James Bell, who lived near Ballymoney, county Antrim, about 1850, where he formed a large collection of Irish antiquities, a catalogue of which is given in the MacAdam manuscripts, and many of which may be seen in the Town Hall at Ballymoney.   Mr. Bell writes :

The town of Ballymoney is said to be of considerable antiquity, but as no written records of its origin are now known to exist, and very few tradi-tional accounts of its early history are preserved by the inhabitants, little is now known on the subject beyond the recollection of the present generation, who would appear not to be descended from the original or earliest inhabi-tants, but from strangers, and therefore all the early records and traditions are lost.   A battle is said to have been in Ballymoney, at a very early period, between the inhabitants and strangers ; and the tradition says that the in-habitants were defeated with great slaughter, the survivors flying to the county of Derry and the Glens of Antrim.   The town was burnt down, so that, according to this account, " one might walk on the walls from the head to the foot of the town."   The probability is that these strangers were from Scotland, and the reasons for such a supposition are—the Irish language was never remembered to have been spoken or even understood in the town or neighborhood, neither are the names of the inhabitants Irish, but almost all Scotch ; and the proprietors of the town and formerly of all the lands in the neighborhood, the Earls of Antrim, are of known Scotch descent.
It has always been admitted that the parts of Scotland opposite to Ulster were invaded or colonized from Ireland, and that a constant intercourse, either of friendship, trade, or war, has ever since existed between the two nations, which may in the end have led to the final settlement of the Scotch in that part of the country.   A manuscript still in existence, shows that the Scottish clan of MacDonnell, who by an intermarriage, got footing in Ire-land, established themselves, by the powerful support they received from Cantyre and the Western Isles, in a tract of country forty miles in length. The people of those days generally followed the fortunes of their chiefs. The greater part of the native Irish who survived these bloody scenes trans-planted themselves elsewhere, while the Scots remained possessors of the field ; hence the old traditions, language, and customs of the country were gradually lost.   In proof of the Scottish origin of the present inhabitants, a short extract is here given from the manuscript above alluded to :—
" About the year 1580, Coll MacDonnell came with a parcel of men from Cantyre to Ireland to assist Tyrconnel against great O'Neill, with whom he was then at war.
" In passing through the Root of the county of Antrim, he was civilly re-ceived and hospitably entertained by MacQuillan, who was the lord and master of the Root.
" At that time there was a war between MacQuillan and the men beyond

the river Bann ; for the custom of this people was to rob from every one, and the strongest party carried it, be it right or wrong.

"On the day when MacDonnell was taking his departure, MacQuillan, who was not equal in war to his savage neighbors, called together his militia, or Galloglaghs, to revenge his affronts over the Bann, and MacDonnell, thinking it uncivil not to offer his services that day to MacQuillan, after having been so kindly treated, offered his service in the field.

"MacQuillan was right well pleased with the offer, and, with the Highlanders, went against the enemy ; and where there was a cow taken from MacQuillan's people before, there were two restored back ; after which Mac-Quillan and MacDonnell returned with a great prey, and without the loss of a man.

"Winter then drawing nigh, MacQuillan invited MacDonnell to stay with him at his castle until the spring, and to quarter his men up and down the Root. This MacDonnell gladly accepted, and in the meantime seduced Mac-Quillan's daughter and privately married her, on which ground the Scots afterwards founded their claim to MacQuillan's territories.

"The men were quartered two and two through the Root ; that is to say, one of MacQuillan's Galloglaghs and a Highlander in every tenant's house. It so happened that the Galloglagh, according to custom, was entitled to a *mether* of milk as a privilege.   This the Highlanders considered an affront, and at length one of them asked his host—'Why do you not give me milk as you give the other ?'   The Galloglagh immediately made answer—'Would you, a Highland beggar as you are, compare yourself to me or any of Mac-Quillan's Galloglaghs ?'   A combat ensued, which ended in the death of the Galloglagh.   MacQuillan's Galloglaghs immediately assembled to demand satisfaction, and in a council which was held it was agreed that each Gallo-glagh should kill his comrade Highlander by night, and their lord and master with them ; but Coll MacDonnell's wife discovered the plot and told it to her husband, so the Highlanders fled in the night time and escaped to Raghery.   From this beginning the MacDonnells and MacQuillans entered on a war, and continued to worry each other half a century, till the English power became so superior in Ireland that both parties made an appeal to James I., who had just then ascended the throne of England.   James favored his Scotch countrymen, the MacDonnells, to whom he made over by patent four great baronies, including along with other lands, all poor MacQuillan's possessions.   However, to save some appearance of justice, he gave to Mac-Quillan a grant of the great Barony of Inisowen, the old territory of O'Dogherty, and sent to him an account of the whole decision by Sir John [Arthur] Chichester.

"MacQuillan was extremely mortified at his ill-success, and very discon-solate at the difficulties which attended the transporting of his poor people over the river Bann and the Lough Foyle, which lay between him and his new territory.   The crafty Englishman, taking advantage of his situation, by an offer of some lands which lay nearer his old dominions, persuaded him to cede his title to the Barony of Inisowen ; and thus the Chichesters, who afterwards obtained the title of Earls of Donegal, became possessed of this great estate, and honest MacQuillan settled himself on one far inferior.

"One story more [says the MS.] of MacQuillan.   The estate he got in exchange for the Barony of Inisowen was called Clanreaghurkie, which was far inadequate to support the old hospitality of the MacQuillans.   Bury Oge MacQuillan sold this land to one of Chichester's relations, and having got [the value of] his new granted estate in one bag, was very generous and hospitable as long as the bag lasted ; and so was worthy MacQuillan soon exhausted."

These facts may in some measure account for the total absence of everything ancient, or truly Irish, within the town or in the neighborhood of Ballymoney, and indeed in the greater part of the Root of county Antrim.

According to tradition, the ground now occupied by the town of Ballymoney comprised two distinct but very small villages ; and as the origin of all villages and even towns arose from their connection with some great house or castle, we have evidence of this in the names still attached to the town-parks, those at the north end being called the Castlebarr fields and those at the south end the Castle Crofts. No vestige of either of these castles now remains, nor are they remembered by any person living ; neither is there any account or tradition existing with regard to Castlebarre ; but the castle at the south end of Ballymoney is said to have been built or inhabited by a person called Stewart. This account is probable, as the person who was agent to the Earl of Antrim about the year 1641 was named Archibald Stewart, and belonged originally to Ballintoy. The last inhabitant of the castle is said to have been a Captain Butler. . . .

A house of worship for Presbyterians stood at an early period on the site of the present meeting-house of the first Presbyterian congregation, but no records are known to show the date of its erection.⁵

The chief of the Scoto-Irishmen in Antrim at the beginning of the seventeenth century was Randall Macdonnell. After Tyrone's rebellion, he resolved to throw in his lot with the Government, and turn loyal subject. He persevered in this course, notwithstanding many trials to his loyalty, and as reward he received a grant of the northern half of county Antrim, from Larne to Portrush, and the honor of knighthood. He set himself ardently to the improvement of his lands, " letting out to the natives on the coast, and also to the Scottish settlers, such arable portions of his lands as had been depopulated by the war, for terms varying from 21 to 301 years." These leases seem to have been largely taken advantage of by the Scottish settlers, who allowed the natives to keep the " Glynnes " or Glens—that district so much visited now for its splendid coast scenery—and themselves took possession of the rich land along the river Bann, from Lough Neagh to the town of Coleraine near its mouth. So Macdonnell and his property prospered ; and in 1620, when King James raised him to the dignity of Earl of Antrim, the patent conferring the honor, after enumerating the faithful services which Macdonnell had rendered to the Crown, specially mentioned " the fact of his having strenuously exerted himself in settling British subjects on his estates." Thus county Antrim, from north to south, became nearly as Scottish as the portion of county Down north of the Mourne mountains.

NOTES TO CHAPTER XXXIII

¹ See Appendix S (*The Montgomery Manuscripts* and *The Hamilton Manuscripts*).

² Additional names are printed in five numbers of Thomas Allen Glenn's *American Genealogist* for 1899, vol. i.

³ The muster-master was an officer commissioned in each district to discover the number of able-bodied men therein, together with the available arms possessed by them. He

was further required carefully to enroll the men and arms in a book, to be consulted when troops might be needed for active service. From this statement of the author it is evident that a large number of settlers had come with Sir Hugh Montgomery to the Ards during the first four years of his colonization. It is to be regretted that no list of these original settlers can now be found. Among them were several named Orr, who appear to have originally settled in the townlands of Ballyblack and Ballykeel, and were the progenitors of a very numerous connection of this surname throughout the Ards. The earliest recorded deaths in this connection, after their settlement in the Ards, were those of James Orr of Ballyblack, who died in the year 1627, and Janet McClement, his wife, who died in 1636. The descendants, male and female, of this worthy couple were very numerous, and as their intermarriages have been carefully recorded, we have thus fortunately a sort of index to the names of many other families of Scottish settlers in the Ards and Castlereagh. Their descendants in the male line intermarried with the families of Dunlop, Gray, Kennedy, Coulter, Todd, M'Birney, M'Cullough, Campbell, Boyd, Jackson, Walker, Rodgers, Stevenson, Malcomson, King, Ferguson, M'Quoid, Cregg, Barr, M'Munn, Bryson, Johnson, Smith, Carson, M'Kinstry, Busby, M'Kee, Shannon, M'Garock, Hamilton, Cally, Chalmers, Rea, M'Roberts, Creighton, M'Whirter, M'Kibben, Cleland, Abernethy, Reid, Agnew, Wilson, Irvine, Lindsay, M'Creary, Porter, Hanna, Taylor, Smyth, Carson, Wallace, Gamble, Miller, Catherwood, Malcolm, M'Cleary, Pollok, Lamont, Frame, Stewart, Minnis, Moorehead, M'Caw, Clark, Patterson, Neilson, Maxwell, Harris, Corbet, Milling, Carr, Winter, Patty, Cumming, M'Connell, M'Gowan. Nearly an equal number of Orrs married wives of their own surname. These numerous descendants, bearing the surname of Orr, resided in Ballyblack, Clontinacally, Killinether, Ballygowan, Ballykeel, Munlough, Ballybeen, Castleaverie, Conlig, Lisleen, Bangor, Gortgrib, Granshaw, Killaghey, Gilnahirk, Ballyalloly, Ballyknockan, Ballycloughan, Tullyhubbert, Moneyrea, Newtownards, Ballymisca, Dundonald, Magherascouse, Castlereagh, Bootin, Lisdoonan, Greyabbey, Ballyrea, Ballyhay, Ballywilliam, Saintfield, Ballymacarrett, Craigantlet, Braniel. The greatest number of the name lived in Ballykeel, Clontinacally, and Ballygowan. The descendants in the female line from James Orr and Janet M'Clement of Ballyblack intermarried with the families of Riddle of Comber, Thomson of Newtownards, Moore of Drummon, Orr of Lisleen, Orr of Ballykeel, Murdock of Comber, Irvine of Crossnacreevy, M'Creary of Bangor, Hanna of Conlig, Orr of Bangor, Orr of Ballygowan, M'Munn of Lisleen, Barr of Lisleen, Davidson of Clontinacally, Jamieson of Killaghey, Martin of Killynure, Martin of Gilnahirk, Matthews of ——, Watson of Carryduff, Shaw of Clontinacally, Todd of Ballykeel, Jennings of ——, Davidson of ——, M'Kibbin of Knocknasham, M'Cormick of Ballybeen, M'Cullock of Ballyhanwood, M'Kee of Lisleen, Patterson of Moneyrea, Dunwoody of Madyroe, Barr of Bangor, M'Gee of Todstown, Burgess of Madyroe, M'Kinning of Lisnasharock, Gerrit of Ballyknockan, Pettigrew of Ballyknockan, M'Coughry of Ballyknockan, Yates of ——, Shaw of ——, Stevenson of Ballyrush, M'Kibbin of Haw, Piper of Comber, Blakely of Madyroe, Orr of Ballyknockan, Stewart of Clontinacally, Hamilton of Ballykeel, Dunbar of Slatady, Orr of Ballygowan, Malcolm of Bootan, Porter of Ballyristle, M'Connell of Ballyhenry, Kennedy of Comber, Malcolm of Moat, Orr of Ballykeel, Martin of Ballycloughan, Reid of Ballygowan, Lewis of ——, Orr of Clontinacally, Orr of Florida, M'Creary of ——, Miller of Conlig, Lowry of Ballymacashan, Harris of Ballymelady, Orr of Ballyknockan, M'Quoid of Donaghadee, Appleton of Conlig, M'Burney of ——, Hanna of Clontinacally, Johnson of Rathfriland, Orr of Ballykeel, Stewart of Clontinacally and Malone, Patterson of Moneyrea and Lisbane, Black of Gortgrib, Hill of Gilnahirk, Murdock of Gortgrif, Kilpatrick of ——, Gregg of ——, Huddlestone of Moneyrea, M'Culloch of Moneyrea, Steel of Maghrescouse, Erskine of Woodburn, Campbell of ——, White of ——, Clark of Clontinacally, M'Fadden of Clontinacally, Hunter of Clontinacally and Ravarra, Orr of Castlereagh, M'Kean of ——, M'Kittrick of Lisleen, Frame of Munlough, Garret of Ballyknockan, Kennedy of Tullygirvan, Orr of Munlough, Dickson of Tullygirvan, M'Clure of Clontinacally, Porter of Beech-hill, Dinwoody of Carrickmadyroe, Strain of Newtownards, Burns of Cahard, Kennedy of Tullygirvan, M'Calla of Lisdoonan, M'Bratney of Raferey, Harrison of Holywood, Piper of Moneyrea, MacWilliam of Ednaslate, Patterson of Tonachmore, Wright of Craigantlet, Boden of Craigantlet, Henderson of Ballyhaskin, Morrow of Belfast, M'Quoid of Braniel, M'Lean of Ballykeel, Neilson of Ravara, Crawford of Carrickmadyroe, M'Gown of Cross-nacreevy, Orr of Ballybee (MSS. Genealogy of the Family of James Orr of Ballyblack, drawn up from inscriptions on tombstones, by the late Gawin Orr of Castlereagh).—Rev. George Hill, *Montgomery Manuscripts*, p. 66.

⁴ Surly Boy (Charles the Yellow) was the Gaelic or Irish name of the chief of the Macdonnells.

⁵ *Ulster Journal of Archeology*, new series, vol. iii., pp. 148–152.

32

CHAPTER XXXIV

THE GREAT PLANTATION OF ULSTER

A T the beginning of James I.'s time, although Elizabeth had waged fierce and devastating wars against the Ulster chiefs during most of her long reign, English authority was scarcely recognized in the North of Ireland. It was represented by the commanders of the ten districts into which Ulster was divided, but their rule was little more than a military one, and scarce extended beyond the buildings which composed their military posts ; and by the bishops of the Episcopal Church, who had probably even fewer followers in spiritual things than the district governors had in temporal. The country still enjoyed its native laws and customs — still obeyed its native chiefs. There were no towns in Ireland to play the part which the English and Scottish burghs had done in the Middle Ages, to be the homes of free institutions, the centres from which civilization might spread. Belfast scarcely existed even in name, and Derry and Carrickfergus consisted but of small collections of houses round the English forts. The whole country, like the Scottish Highlands, was inhabited by clansmen, obeying tribal laws and usages, and living in some measure on agriculture, but mainly on the produce of their herds and flocks. The land was held by the chiefs nominally for the clans, but really for their own benefit.

The plantations in county Down and county Antrim, thorough as they were as far as they went, were limited in scope in comparison with the "Great Plantation of Ulster," for which James I.'s reign will be forever remembered in Ireland. It is extremely difficult to make out the circumstances which led up to this remarkable measure, or to understand the action of the Ulster chiefs, who, to all appearance, played so thoroughly into the hands of the Government. Which side first was false to the peace, it is impossible now to say. One party declares that the chiefs began to conspire against the Government ; the other, that the Government drove the chiefs to conspire in self-defence. The Ulster chiefs began to correspond with Spain once more, as if in preparation for a new outbreak ; the Government intercepted the letters, and O'Neill, earl of Tyrone, and O'Donnell, earl of Tyrconnel, confessed, if not guilt, at least fear of punishment, by leaving their country, and sailing from Lough Swilly along with a number of adherents, on the 3d September, 1607. In 1608, Sir Cahir O'Dogherty perished in rebellion, and his lands were confiscated. Mulmorie O'Reilly, whose father died fighting for the English at Yellow Ford, and whose mother was a niece of the duke of Ormond, had to accept a "proportion" of his lands. Other native chieftains, against whom there was no accusation of disloyalty, were compelled to surrender a large part of their property, and a vigorous attempt was now made to plant the country with Protestants.

It is asserted by Hill, that as a result of the flight of the earls and of an act of Parliament known as the 11th of Elizabeth, no less than 3,800,000 acres in Tyrone, Derry, Donegal, Fermanagh, and Cavan were placed at the disposal of the Crown, and made available for plantations.   The earls had now rebelled against the king and been proclaimed traitors, and their lands were therefore " escheated " to the Crown.   Estates were constantly changing hands in this way in Scotland during the sixteenth century.   The more important of the chiefs had gone into voluntary exile with Tyrone ; against the rest it was not difficult for the Crown lawyers to find sufficient proof of treason.   Thus all northern Ireland—Londonderry, Donegal, Ty-rone, Cavan, Armagh, and Fermanagh—had passed at one fell swoop into the hands of the Crown ; while, as we have seen, Down and Antrim had been already, to a great extent, taken possession of and colonized by English and Lowland Scotch.   The plan adopted by King James for the colonization of the six " escheated" counties was to take possession of the finest portions of this great tract of country, amounting in all to nearly four millions of acres ; to divide it into small estates, none larger than two thousand acres ; and to grant these to men of known wealth and substance.   Those who accepted grants were bound to live on their land themselves, to bring with them English and Scottish settlers, and to build for themselves and for their tenants fortified places for defence, houses to live in, and churches in which to worship.   The native Irish were assigned to the poorer lands and less accessible districts ; while the allotments to the English and Scots were kept together, so that they might form communities and not mix or inter-marry with the Irish.   The errors of former Irish " plantations " were to be avoided—the mistakes of placing too much land in one hand, and of allowing non-resident proprietors.   The purpose was not only to transfer the owner-ship of the land from Irish to Scot, but to introduce a Scottish population in place of an Irish one ; to bring about in Ulster exactly what has happened without design during the last half-century in New Zealand, the introduction of an English-speaking race, the natives being expected to disappear as have perished the Maori.

The English Council requested the Scottish Privy Council to draw up a list of Scotsmen willing to settle in Ulster.   The king seems to have taken the duty of selecting the Scottish undertakers into his own hands, the men who got grants being of higher social standing and wider influence than those who first offered.   A second and more careful survey having been made in 1609, the commission proceeded, in the summer of 1610, to divide up the land.   This second survey may have been better than the first, but it was very inaccurate after all, as it mapped out for division only 500,000 acres of land suitable for " plantation," out of a total acreage of 3,800,000 con-tained in the six counties.[1]   Fifty-nine Scotsmen were chosen, and to them 81,000 acres were allotted in estates scattered over the five counties, London-derry being reserved for the city of London.   A careful examination of the list of Scottish undertakers enables us to see the plan which was finally adopted for securing proper colonists.   There was, of course, as was always the case at this time, a certain number of the hangers-on about the Court who got grants, which they at once sold to raise money.   But as a whole, the plan of distribution was thoroughly well conceived and well carried out.

James seems to have seen that the parts of Scotland nearest Ireland, and which had most intercourse with it, were most likely to yield proper colonists. He resolved, therefore, to enlist the assistance of the great families of the southwest, trusting that their feudal power would enable them to bring with them bodies of colonists.   Thus grants were made to the duke of Lennox, who had great power in Dumbartonshire ; to the earl of Abercorn and his brothers, who represented the power of the Hamiltons in Renfrewshire. North Ayrshire had been already largely drawn on by Hamilton and Montgomery, but one of the sons of Lord Kilmarnock, Sir Thomas Boyd, received a grant ; while from South Ayrshire came the Cunninghams and Crawfords, and Lord Ochiltree and his son ; the latter were known in Galloway as well as in the county from which their title was derived.   But it was on Galloway men that the greatest grants were bestowed.   Almost all the great houses of the times are represented,—Sir Robert Maclellan, Laird Bomby as he is called, who afterwards became Lord Kirkcudbright, and whose great castle stands to this day ; John Murray of Broughton, one of the secretaries of state ; Vans of Barnbarroch ; Sir Patrick McKie of Laerg ; Dunbar of Mochrum ; one of the Stewarts of Garlies, from whom Newtown-Stewart in Tyrone takes its name.   Some of these failed to implement their bargains, but the best of the undertakers proved to be men like the earl of Abercorn and his brothers, and the Stewarts of Ochiltree and Garlies ; for while their straitened means led them to seek fortune in Ireland, their social position enabled them without difficulty to draw good colonists from their own districts, and so fulfil the terms of the " plantation " contract, which bound them to " plant " their holdings with tenants.   With the recipient of two thousand acres, the agreement was that he was to bring " forty-eight able men of the age of eighteen or upwards, being born in England or the *inward* parts of Scotland."   He was further bound to grant farms to his tenants, the sizes of these being specified, and it being particularly required that these should be " feus " or on lease for twenty-one years or for life.   A stock of muskets and hand weapons to arm himself and his tenants was to be provided.   The term used, " the inward parts of Scotland," refers to the old invasions of Ulster by the men of the Western Islands.   No more of these Celts were wanted ; there were plenty of that race already in North Antrim ; it was the Lowland Scots, who were peace-loving and Protestants, whom the Government desired.   The phrase, " the inward parts of Scotland," occurs again and again.

These lands were now granted to three classes of proprietors.   The first were English and Scottish undertakers, who were to plant with tenants from

England or Scotland, and conform themselves in religion according to his Majesty's laws. The second were " servitors," or military undertakers, who were permitted to take Irish tenants ; and the third were native Irish who obtained grants. The first paid a yearly rent of £5 6s. 8d., the second of £8, and the third of £10 13s. 4d. for every thousand acres. But if the servitors planted part of their estates with English or Scotch tenants, their rents for all the lands thus colonized would be the same as was paid by the first class.

In 1609, the forfeited lands were surveyed by commissioners, many grants were made to undertakers and servitors, and all things prepared for planting Ulster with another race, professing another religion. The Episcopal Church received a large proportion ; Trinity College was not forgotten ; and the great part of county Derry was given to the Corporation of London, on condition of building and fortifying Londonderry and Coleraine, and thus spending twenty thousand pounds on the property. A committee of the Corporation, called the Irish Society, was formed, whose duty was to carry out the plantation of their estates.

Next year, the first settlers began to arrive. Some came from England, but most were from Scotland. The English settled in the southern part of the province ; while the Scots occupied the north and centre, including Londonderry—and Coleraine, as well as Tyrone, " the fayrest and goodliest countrye in Ireland universallie." Among these settlers were so many who left their country for their country's good, that it became a proverb regarding any one not doing well, to say that his latter end would be " Ireland." But the great body of colonists were earnest and industrious. Succeeding bands were even more earnest and more industrious, while the most worthless among them were, in every mental and moral quality, far above the Irish by whom they were surrounded.

At first these settlers erected their rude, rush-thatched huts near the landlord's castle for protection, and every night they had to place their flocks within the " bawn," or walled enclosure by which that castle was surrounded, for fear of the Irish driving them off in the darkness. But, afterwards, as the settlers became more numerous, they ventured to build their houses here and there in little clusters called towns. This caused each farmer's land to be divided into lots, separated one from another, and mixed up with the lots of others.

Many of the natives, driven to the mountains or woods, were known as woodkernes, and lived by plunder. But woe betide the unfortunate woodkerne when taken in theft ! Small crimes were punished by death. Bloodhounds were kept for tracing these outlaws, who, when taken, were often shot without trial. If tried, they were generally found guilty, and, when sentenced, halters were immediately put round their necks ; they were then led through the principal streets of the town to the places of execution, and hanged in the most barbarous manner. But woodkernes were not the only enemies of the settlers. Large flocks of wolves roamed about by night, and often made sad havoc among their cattle. The land was unfenced and undrained. Much of it was covered with woods, affording refuge to the outlaws.[2] But on the other hand, rents were low and labor did not cost much. The laws were repealed which made it criminal to have any dealings with the native Irish, who were now employed by the settlers as domestic servants. The wages of a ploughman was six shillings and eightpence a quarter. A servant maid got ten shillings a year. Laborers received twopence, and tradesmen sixpence a day. A cow was worth about a pound, and a horse four pounds. But money was then more available than now, and purchased more of the necessaries of life. In the past, Irishmen had thought labor a disgrace. Old Con O'Neill had cursed those who sowed wheat as well as those who learned English. Their chief sustenance came from cattle, and their food was milk and butter and herbs, such as " scurvy grass." But the colonists drained the swamps, cut down the woods, sowed wheat, and planted the potato—an article of food lately brought from America. Barley was also cultivated extensively, and was prepared for use by pounding in those round stone troughs still to be seen at old farmhouses, and preserved as curiosities.

Even then a trade in linen had taken root in the country. Existing before the foot of a Saxon had been placed on its free soil, it was now carried on with vigor and success. The colonists sowed flax, spun the flax into yarn, and wove the yarn into linen cloth. The cloth when sold produced much of the money they obtained. There was also woollen cloth manufactured. Both commodities were easily conveyed over bad roads to the seaports for exportation ; and were highly esteemed abroad.

With their lands at a nominal rent, their clothing and their tools manufactured by themselves, with linen and woollen cloth, cattle and horses, to sell, the colonists soon began to thrive. As the woods were cut and the marshes drained, a larger proportion of the country was cultivated. The land, after its long rest, brought forth abundantly. The success of the settlers induced many of their friends from Scotland to follow. The vacant parts of the country were occupied. The woodman's axe rang in the forests, and the husbandman's plough turned up the fruitful soil in the plains. Notwithstanding a difference of race and religion, a common humanity was often sufficient to establish a feeling of friendship between the settlers and the more civilized of the Irish. The woodkernes were subdued or exterminated, and prosperity began to reign in Ulster.

The settlement made by Hugh Montgomery and James Hamilton in 1606 opened up the county of Down to Scottish emigrants. They took possession of the whole of the north of the county, but they were satisfied with the arable lands which they found there, and did not intrude on the hill-country of the southern baronies, which therefore remained Irish and Roman Catholic. To the west of the county the Scots were met by the English colony which

Chichester had founded at Belfast, and which spread up the river Lagan, along both its banks, towards Hillsborough, on the county Down side, and far into county Armagh on the west. Their common Puritanism formed a bond of union between these English and Scottish colonists. It made them unite and form into communities wherever they met, whether on the banks of the Lagan or northward throughout the length and breadth of county Antrim, when it was opened up to settlers by Sir Arthur Chichester along the shores of Belfast Lough, and by Macdonnell northward to the Giant's Causeway. The only district of this county not thoroughly colonized was the highlands along the northeast shore. Then came James's great scheme of colonization in 1610, which threw open the other six counties, for English and Scottish settlers. In some of these counties, and in some parts of them, the settlements were successful ; in others they failed to take root. In Armagh, the British colony took firm hold, because, as soon as the county was opened up, settlers flocked into it across the borders from Down, and in even greater numbers from the English colony in Antrim. On the other hand, the " plantation " of Cavan was, comparatively speaking, a failure. In county Tyrone, the British settlers did not invade the mountainous country on the borders of Londonderry county, but contented themselves with the finer lands in the basin of the Mourne, and on the shores of Lough Neagh, and along the streams which flow into it. Londonderry county was during the early years of the settlement left very much to itself by the " Irish Society of London, " which kept its contract largely in the direction of drawing its rents—an operation which is still performed by the London Companies, the valuation of the Londoners' property being stated in the Government return for 1887 at £77,000 per annum. At the mouths of the two rivers which drain the county, however, the London Society founded the towns of Londonderry and Coleraine, and these as time went on became ports by which emigrants entered and spread all over the fertile lands of the county. In Donegal the British only attempted to colonize the eastern portion ; while in Fermanagh the Scots seemed to be so little at home that they handed over their lands to the English, who here established a strong colony, from which have sprung some of the best-known names among the English in Ireland. Into these districts of Ulster both English and Scottish emigrants, but especially the latter, continued to stream at intervals during the whole of the seventeenth century.

The progress of the colonies in the different counties is very accurately described in a series of reports by Government inspectors, and in the letters of Chichester himself. Of the Scottish undertakers, and of the manner in which they were doing their work, there is a special report ; and, on the whole, Chichester is favorably impressed with them. "The Scottishmen come with greater port [show], and better accompanied and attended, but, it may be, with less money in their purses."

For two or three years after the "great settlement" of 1610, the colony went on increasing; and then its progress was checked by rumors of a great plot among the natives to sweep away the foreign settlers. Such a conspiracy did actually exist, and was certainly a thing which might be expected; but it was discovered and suppressed in 1615, before it came to a head. In 1618 the Irish Government instructed Captain Nicholas Pynnar to inspect every allotment in the six "escheated" counties, and to report on each one, whether held by "natives" or "foreign planters." The report presents a very exact picture of what had been done by the settlers in the counties inspected —Londonderry, Donegal, Tyrone, Armagh, Cavan, and Fermanagh. Pynnar points out that many of the undertakers had altogether failed to implement the terms of their agreement. On the other hand, he reports the number of castles, "bawns," and "dwelling-houses of stone and timber built after the English fashion," and mentions the number of tenants, and the size and conditions of their holdings. He states that "there are upon occasion 8000 men of British birth and descent for defence, though a fourth part of the lands is not fully inhabited." Of these, more than half must have been Scots; and if there be added the great colonies in Down and Antrim, there must have been an imigration from Scotland of between 30,000 and 40,000 in these ten years.

The only county in which the Scottish settlers failed to take firm root was Fermanagh, for there, by 1618, when Pynnar reported, a large number of the Scottish proportions had been sold, and were held by Englishmen. The result is seen in the small number of Presbyterians in comparison to Episcopalians to be found at the present day in county Fermanagh.

The north of Ireland is now very much what the first half of the seventeenth century made it. North Down and Antrim, with the great town of Belfast, are English and Scottish now as they then became, and desire to remain united with the countries from which their people sprang. South Down, on the other hand, was not "planted," and it is Roman Catholic and Nationalist. Londonderry county too is Loyalist, for emigrants poured into it through Coleraine and Londonderry city. Northern Armagh was peopled with English and Scottish emigrants, who crowded into it from Antrim and Down, and it desires union with the other island. Tyrone county is all strongly Unionist, but it is the country around Strabane, which the Hamiltons of Abercorn and the Stewarts of Garlies so thoroughly colonized, and the eastern portion, on the borders of Lough Neagh, around the colonies founded by Lord Ochiltree, that give to the Unionists a majority; while in eastern Donegal, which the Cunninghams and the Stewarts "settled" from Ayrshire and Galloway, and in Fermanagh, where dwell the descendants of the Englishmen who fought so nobly in 1689, there is a great minority which struggles against separation from England. Over the rest, even of Ulster, the desire for a separate kingdom of Ireland is the dream of the people still, as it was three centuries ago. In many parts of Ireland which were at one time and another colonized with English, the colonists became absorbed in the native population; but in Ulster, where the Scottish blood is strong, this union has not taken place, and the result is the race difference which is so apparent in the electoral statistics of the present day. It is perhaps the stern Calvinism of these Scots, which still survives, that has prevented the colony from mixing with the surrounding people, and being absorbed by them, as the Jews of the northern kingdom became merged in the surrounding " heathen." The history of the Presbyterian Church is therefore an important part of the story of the Scot in Ulster; in fact, for many years the history of Ulster, as far as it has a separate history, is chiefly ecclesiastical.[3] It must be so; for this is a story of Scotsmen and of the first half of the seventeenth century, and at that time the history of Scotland is the history of the Scottish Church. Church polity, Church observance, Church discipline, fill all the chronicles, and must have formed the public life of the people.

NOTES TO CHAPTER XXXIV

[1] See Appendix T (Conditions of the Ulster Plantation).

[2] This state of desolation was the result, in a great measure, of Mountjoy's ruthless policy, as carried out against the natives by Chichester and his officers, especially in the county of Down. The following extract from Fynes Moryson's *Itinerary* is an awful record of the condition to which the hapless natives were reduced: " Now because I have often made mention formerly of our destroying the Rebels Corne, and using all meanes to famish them, let me by two or three examples show the miserable estate to which the Rebels were thereby brought. Sir Arthur Chichester, Sir Richard Moryson, and the other Commanders of the Forces, sent against Bryan Mac Art aforesaid, in their return homeward, saw a most horrible spectacle of three children (whereof the eldest was not above ten yeeres old), all eating and knawing with their teeth the entrals of their dead mother, upon whose flesh they had fed twenty dayes past, and having eaten all from the feete upward to the bare bones, rosting it continually by a slow fire, were now come to the eating of her entralls in like sort roasted, yet not divided from the body, being as yet raw. . . . Capt. Trevor and many honest Gentlemen lying in the Newry can witness, that some old women of those parts used to make a fire in the fields, and divers little children driving out the cattel in the cold mornings, and comming thither to warme them, were by them surprised, killed and eaten, which at last was discovered by a great girle breaking from them by strength of her body, and Captaine Trevor sending out souldiers to know the truth, they found the childrens skulles and bones, and apprehended the old women, who was executed for the fact. The Captains of Carrickfergus, and the adjacent Garrisons of the Northern parts can witnesse that upon the making of peace, and receiving the rebels to mercy, it was a common practise among the common sort of them (I meane such as were not Sword-men), to thrust long needles into the horses of our English troopes, and they dying thereupon to bee readie to teare out one another's throate for a share of them. And no spectacle was more frequent in the Ditches of Townes, and especiallie in wasted Countries, then to see multitudes of these poore people dead with their mouths all coloured greene by eating nettles, docks, and all things they could rend up above ground."—Part ii., book iii., chap., i. p. 271.

[3] See Appendix V (Early Presbyterian Congregations in Ireland). Also, Reid and Killen's *History of the Presbyterian Church in Ireland.*

CHAPTER XXXV

THE ULSTER PLANTATION FROM 1610 TO 1630

THE allotments of lands by King James to the Scottish, English, and native "undertakers" in the six escheated counties of Tyrone, Armagh, Cavan, Londonderry, Fermanagh, and Donegal are shown in the tabulations given below. Where transfers or reconveyances of the estates were made prior to 1620, that fact is also noted.

The following were the precincts or baronies set apart for the Scottish undertakers, and the allotments to each individual, for nearly all of which grants were issued in 1610.

COUNTY OF ARMAGH: PRECINCT OF FEWES—6000 ACRES

1. 2000 acres to Sir James Douglasse [or Douglas], Knt., of Spott, Haddingtonshire. Sold in 1611 to Henry Acheson, who afterwards sold it to Sir Archibald Acheson.
2. 1000 acres to Henry Acheson, gent., Edinburgh. Sold to Sir Archibald Acheson in 1628.
3. 1000 acres to Sir James Craig, Knt. Sold to John Hamilton in 1615.
4. 1000 acres to William Lawder, gent., of Belhaven. Sold to John Hamilton in 1614.
5. 1000 acres to Claude Hamilton, gent., of Creichnes.

COUNTY OF TYRONE: PRECINCT OF MOUNTJOY—9500 ACRES

1. 3000 acres to Andrew Stewart, Lord Ochiltree, Galloway.
2. 1000 acres to Robert Stewart, gent., of Hilton, Edinburgh. Transferred to Andrew Stewart, Jr., before 1620.
3. 1500 acres to Sir Robert Hepburne, Knt., of Alderston, Haddingtonshire.
4. 1000 acres to George Crayford [or Crawford], Laird of Lochnories, Ayrshire. Transferred to Alexander Sanderson before 1620.
5. 1000 acres to Bernard Lindsey of Lough-hill, Haddingtonshire. Transferred to Alexander Richardson before 1620.
6. 1000 acres to Robert Lindsey of Leith, Edinburghshire.
7. 1000 acres to Robert Stewart of Robertown, Ayrshire. Transferred to Andrew Stewart, Jr.

COUNTY OF TYRONE: PRECINCT OF STRABANE—13,500 ACRES

1. 3000 acres to James Hamilton, Earl of Abercorn, Renfrewshire.
2. 2000 acres to Sir Claude Hamilton, Knt., of Lerleprevicke (brother of James), Renfrewshire.

3. 2000 acres to James Clapen [or Claphame], gent.   Transferred to Sir Robert Newcomen, Knt., before 1620.

4. 1500 acres to Sir Thomas Boyd, Knt., of Bedlay [or Bonehawe], Renfrewshire.   Transferred to James Hamilton before 1620.

5. 1500 acres to Sir George Hamilton, Knt. (brother of James), Renfrewshire.

6. 1000 acres to Sir John Dromond [or Drummond], Knt., of Mentieth, Perth.

7. 1500 acres to James Haig, gent.   Transferred to Sir William Stewart in 1613.

8. 1000 acres to Sir George Hamilton, Bynning, Renfrewshire.

COUNTY OF DONEGAL: PRECINCT OF PORTLOUGH (PART OF THE BARONY OF RAPHOE)—12,000 ACRES

1. 3000 acres to the Duke of Lennox (Ludovic Stuart), Dumbartonshire.

2. 1000 acres to Sir Walter Stewart, Knt., Laird of Minto, Roxburghshire.   Transferred before 1620 to Sir John Colquhoun, Laird of Luss, Dumbartonshire.

3. 1000 acres to Alexander McAula of Durlin, gent., Dumbartonshire.

4. 1000 acres to John Cuningham of Crafield [or Crawfield], Ayrshire.

5. 1000 acres to William Stewart, Laird of Dunduff, Maybole, Ayrshire.

6. 2000 acres to James Cuningham, Laird of Glangarnocke, Ayrshire.

7. 1000 acres to Cuthbert Cuningham of Glangarnocke, Ayrshire.

8. 1000 acres to James Cuningham, Esq., of Glangarnocke, Ayrshire.

9. 1000 acres to John Stewart, Esq.

COUNTY OF DONEGAL: PRECINCT OF BOYLAGH—10,000 ACRES.

1. 2000 acres to Sir Robert Maclellan, Laird of Bomby, Kirkcudbrightshire.

2. 1500 acres to George Murraye, Laird of Broughton, Whithorn, Wigtonshire.

3. 1500 acres to William Stewart, Esq., Wigtonshire.

4. 1000 acres to Sir Patrick Mackee of Laerg, Knt., Minnigaff, Wigtonshire.

5. 1000 acres to James McCullough [or M'Culloch], gent., of Drummovell, Wigtonshire.

6. 1000 acres to Alexander Dunbar, gent., of Egirnes, Wigtonshire.

7. 1000 acres to Patrick Vans of Libragh, gent., Kirkinner, Wigtonshire.

8. 1000 acres to Alexander Coningham of Powton, gent., Sorbie, Wigtonshire.

Few of these eight undertakers having made settlement of their lands in 1620, the entire 10,000 acres were patented to John Murray.

COUNTY OF FERMANAGH: PRECINCT OF KNOCKNINNY—9000 ACRES

1. 3000 acres to Michael Balfoure [or Balfour], Lord Burley, Pittendreich, Fifeshire.   Transferred to Sir James Balfour.

2. 1500 acres to Michael Balfoure, his son, Fifeshire. Transferred to Sir Stephen Butler.

3. 1500 acres to Sir John Wishart [or Wisehart], Knt., Laird Pettaro, Forfarshire. Transferred to Sir Stephen Butler.

4. 1000 acres to Thomas Monepenny [or Moneypenny], Laird of Kinkell, or Kinalle, Fifeshire. Transferred to Thomas Crichton.

5. 1000 acres to James Trayle, Esq., Fifeshire. Sold to Sir Stephen Butler, 4th August.

6. 1000 acres to George Smelhome [or Smailholme], Leith, Edinburgh-shire. Sold to Sir Stephen Butler, 26th August, 1618.

COUNTY OF FERMANAGH: PRECINCT OF MAGHERIBOY—9000 ACRES

1. 2000 acres to Sir John Home [or Hume], Knt., Manderston, Berwickshire.

2. 1500 acres to Robert Hamilton (son of Gilbert Hamilton of Raplock). Portions sold to Archibald Hamilton, 1st December, 1614, and balance to Malcolm Hamilton.

3. 1000 acres to James Gibb (son of John Gibb). Conveyed to John Archdale by James Hamilton, 26th February, 1617.

4. 1000 acres to Jerome Lindsey, Esq., Leith, Edinburghshire. Sold to Sir William Cole, 16th October, 1612.

5. 1500 acres to William Fowler, Esq. Sold to John Home, 26th July, 1615.

6. 1000 acres to Alexander Home (brother of John), Berwickshire. Sold to Sir John Home.

7. 1000 acres to John Dunbarr, Esq., of Mochrum, Wigtonshire.

COUNTY OF CAVAN: PRECINCT OF TULLOCHONCO (NOW TULLYHUNCO)— 6000 ACRES

1. 2000 acres to Sir Alexander Hamilton of Endervicke in Scotland, Knt., Renfrewshire. Granted to Sir Francis Hamilton (grandson of Alexander), 20th July, 1621.

2. 1000 acres to Sir Claude Hamilton (his son), Knight, Renfrewshire.

3. 1000 acres to Alexander Achmootie (or Achmouty), Fifeshire (probably). Sold to James Craig, 14th August, 1610.

4. 1000 acres to John Achmootie (brother of said Alexander). Sold to James Craig, 6th August, 1610.

5. 1000 acres to John Browne of Gorgeemill, gent. Sold to Archibald Acheson about 1612.

COUNTY OF CAVAN: PRECINCT OF CLANCHY (NOW CLANKEE)—6000 ACRES

1. 3000 acres to Esme Stuart, Lord Aubigny (son of Esme Stewart, the first Duke of Lennox), Dumbartonshire. Sold to Sir James Hamilton, 30th July, 1611.

2. 1000 acres to William Baillie, Esq.

3. 1000 acres to John Raleston, Esq. Sold to John Hamilton, 11th June, 1613.

4. 1000 acres to William Downbarr. This proportion seems to have been transferred to William Hamilton.

The following were the precincts or baronies set apart for English undertakers only, with the allotments to each individual, for most of which grants were issued in 1610.

COUNTY OF ARMAGH: PRECINCT OF ONEILAN—16,500 ACRES

1. 1000 acres to Richard Rolleston, clergyman, Staffordshire.
2. 2000 acres to Francis Sacheverell, Leicestershire.
3. 1500 acres to John Brownlowe, Esq., Nottinghamshire.
4. 1000 acres to James Matchett, clergyman, Norfolk. Sold before 1620.
5. 2000 acres to William Powell, "one of the equerries of the King's Stable." Sold in 1610.
6. 1500 acres to John Dillon, Esq., Staffordshire.
7. 1000 acres to William Brownlowe, gent., Nottinghamshire.
8. 1500 acres to William Stanhowe, Norfolk.
9. 2000 acres to John Heron, gent.
10. 3000 acres to Sir Anthony Cope, Knt., of Cope Castle.

COUNTY OF TYRONE: PRECINCT OF CLOGHER—12,500 ACRES

1. 2000 acres to Sir Thomas Ridgewaie, Knt., Treasurer-at-War.
2. 2000 acres to John Leigh, gent.
3. 1500 acres to Walter Edney, Esq., and Thomas Edney, his brother.
4. 1000 acres to George Ridgeway, gent., Devonshire (brother to Sir Thomas Ridgeway).
5. 1000 acres to William Parsons, Dublin.
6. 1000 acres to William Turvin. Sold before 1620.
7. 2000 acres to Edward Kingswell. Sold in 1616.
8. 2000 acres to William Glegge. Sold before 1612.

COUNTY OF TYRONE: PRECINCT OF OMAGH—11,000 ACRES

1. 3000 acres to George Tuchet, Lord Audley.
2. 2000 acres to Sir Marvin Tuchet, Knt., son of George Tuchet.
3. 2000 acres to Sir Ferdinand Tuchet, Knt., son of George Tuchet.
4. 2000 acres to Edward Blunte, Esq., Derbyshire. Sold before 1620.
5. 2000 acres to Sir John Davys, Knight, son-in-law of George Tuchet.

COUNTY OF DONEGAL: PRECINCT OF LIFFER (BARONY OF RAPHOE)—
15,000 ACRES

1. 1500 acres to Henry Clare, Norfolk.
2. 2000 acres to William Willson, Suffolk.
3. 1500 acres to Edward Russell, Esq., London. Sold before 1612.

4. 1500 acres to Sir William Barnes, Knt. Sold in 1610.
5. 1000 acres to Capt. Ralph Mansfield.
6. 2000 acres to Sir Thomas Cornewall, Knt., baron of Burford, Shropshire.
7. 2000 acres to Sir Thomas Remyngton, Knt. Sold before 1620.
8. 2000 acres to Sir Maurice Barkeley, Knt., Somersetshire. Sold before 1620.
9. 1500 acres to Sir Thomas Coach [Coates], Knt.

COUNTY OF FERMANAGH: PRECINCT OF CLANCALLY—5000 ACRES

1. 1000 acres to Sir Hugh Wirrall, Yorkshire and Middlesex.
2. 1000 acres to Robert Bogas, Suffolkshire. Sold before 1620.
3. 1000 acres to Robert Calvert, gent. Sold before 1620.
4. 1000 acres to John Sedborough, Esq.
5. 1000 acres to Thomas Flowerdewe, Esq., Norfolk.

COUNTY OF FERMANAGH: PRECINCTS OF LURG AND COOLEMAKERNAN— 9000 ACRES

1. 1000 acres to Thomas Flowerdewe, Esq.
2. 2000 acres to Thomas Blenerhassett, Esq., Norfolk.
3. 2000 acres to Sir Edward Blenerhassett.
4. 1000 acres to John Archdale, Suffolk.
5. 1000 acres to Edward Warde, gent. Sold in 1611.
6. 1000 acres to Thomas Barton, Norfolk. Sold before 1620.
7. 1000 acres to Henry Honynge [or Hunings], Suffolk. Sold before 1620.

COUNTY OF CAVAN: PRECINCT OF LOUGHTEE—13,260 ACRES

1. 2000 acres to Sir Richard Waldron, Knt.
2. 2000 acres to John Fishe, Esq., Bedfordshire.
3. 2760 acres to Sir Stephen Butler, Bedfordshire.
4. 2000 acres to Sir Nicholas Lusher, Knt., Bedfordshire.
5. 1500 acres to Sir Hugh Wyrrall, Knt., Middlesex.
6. 1500 acres to John Tailor, gent., Cambridgeshire.
7. 1500 acres to William Snow. Transferred to Peter Ameas.

The following were the precincts or baronies set apart for servitors (Scottish and English) and for natives, with the allotments to each individual, for which grants were issued in 1610:

COUNTY OF ARMAGH : PRECINCT OF ORIER—6620 ACRES

1. 1000 acres to Sir Gerald Moore, Knt., Mellifont, Privy Councillor.
2. 1500 acres to Sir Oliver St. John, Wiltshire, Master of Ordnance.
3. 500 acres to George Tuchet, Lord Audley.
4. 1000 acres to Sir Thomas Williams, Knt.
5. 1000 acres to John Bourchier, Esq., former Master of Ordnance.
6. 1000 acres to Francis Cooke, Esq., Norwich.

7. 200 acres to Charles Poynts, gent., Gloucestershire.
8. 120 acres to Marmaduke Whitechurch, Esq.
9. 300 acres to Capt. Henry Adderton.

COUNTY OF TYRONE : PRECINCT OF DUNGANNON—7320 ACRES

1. 1320 acres to Sir Arthur Chichester, the Lord Deputy for Ireland.
2. 2000 acres to Sir Thomas Ridgeway, Vice Treasurer.
3. 2000 acres to Sir Richard Wingfield, Knt., Marshal of the Army, Suffolkshire.
4. 1000 acres to Sir Toby Caulfield, Knt., Oxfordshire.
5. 1000 acres to Sir Francis Roe, Knt., Essex.

COUNTY OF DONEGAL : PRECINCTS OF DOE AND FAWNETT (NOW KILMAC-RENAN)—11,696 ACRES

1. 1000 acres to William Stewart, Esq., Wigtonshire.
2. 1000 acres to Patrick Crawford, Esq., of Lifford.
3. 1000 acres to John Vaughan, Esq.
4. 1000 acres to John Kingsmill, Hampshire
5. 1000 acres to Basill Brooke, Esq.
6. 1000 acres to Sir Richard Hansard, Knt.
7. 300 acres to Thomas Perkins and George Hilton.
8. 500 acres to Sir Thomas Chichester, Knt., brother of Arthur.
9. 1000 acres to Henry Hart, Esq., London.
10. 1128 acres to Sir Ralph Bingley, Knt.
11. 400 acres to Edward Ellis, gent.
12. 1000 acres to Henry Vaughan, Esq., brother of John.
13. 500 acres to Sir Richard Bingley, Knt., Westminster, brother of Sir Ralph.
14. 100 acres to George Gale, gent.
15. 240 acres to Charles Grimsditche, gent., London.
16. 528 acres to Thomas Browne, Esq.

COUNTY OF FERMANAGH : PRECINCT OF CLINAWLY—2246 ACRES

1. 1500 acres to Sir John Davys, Knt., Attorney-General.
2. 500 acres to Samuel Harrison, Esq.
3. 246 acres to Peter Mostin, gent., Flintshire (Wales).

COUNTY OF FERMANAGH : PRECINCTS OF COOLE AND TIRCANNADA—4500 ACRES

1. 1500 acres to Sir Henry Folliott, Knt.
2. 1000 acres to Roger Atkinson.
3. 1000 acres to William Cole, Esq.
4. 1000 acres to Paul Goore, London.

COUNTY OF CAVAN : PRECINCT OF TULLAGHAH—5900 ACRES

1. 2000 acres to Sir George and Sir Richard Graeme [Graham], Knts.
2. 1500 acres to Huge Coolme, Devonshire, and Walter Talbott.
3. 1000 acres to Nicholas Pynnar.
4. 1200 acres to Edward Rutlidge and Bryan McPhilip O'Reyly, gents.
5. 200 acres to Thomas Johnes, gent.

COUNTY OF CAVAN: PRECINCT OF CLONMAHONE—4500 ACRES

1. 2000 acres to Sir Oliver Lambert, Knt., Privy Councillor, London.
2. 1500 acres to Joseph Johnes, gent.
3. 500 acres to John Russon, gent.
4. 500 acres to Anthony Atkinson, gent.

COUNTY OF CAVAN: PRECINCT OF CASTLE RAHEN—3900 ACRES

1. 400 acres to Sir John Elliot, Knt., Baron of the Exchequer.
2. 1000 acres to John Ridgeway, Esq. [brother of Sir Thomas].
3. 1000 acres to Sir William Taaffe, Knt., Louth.
4. 500 acres to Roger Garth.
5. 1000 acres to Sir Edmund Fettiplace, Knt.

COUNTY OF CAVAN: PRECINCT OF TULLAGHGARVY—4250 ACRES

1. 750 acres to Sir Thomas Ashe, Knight, and John Ashe, gent., Meath.
2. 1500 acres to Archibald and Brent Moore, gents., Kent.
3. 2000 acres to Capt. Richard Tirrell.

NATIVES
COUNTY OF ARMAGH: PRECINCT OF ORIER

1. 2000 acres to Arte McBaron O'Neile [half-brother to the Earl of Tyrone] and his wife.
2. 1500 acres to Henry McShane O'Neale.
3. 140 acres to Tirlagh Groome O'Hanlon.
4. 100 acres to Shane McShane O'Hanlon.
5. 100 acres to Shane McOghie O'Hanlon, gent.
6. 240 acres to Oghie Oge O'Hanlon's two sons, Felim and Brian.
7. 120 acres to Rorie McFerdoragh O'Hanlon, gent.
8. 120 acres to Shane Oge McShane Roe O'Hanlon, gent.
9. 360 acres to Carbery McCan, gent.
10. 80 acres to Donell McCan, gent.
11. 120 acres to Patrick McManus O'Hanlon and Ardell Moore O'Mulchrewe.
12. 60 acres to Redmond McFardoragh O'Hanlon.
13. 360 acres to Con McTirlagh [O'Neill], gent.
14. 240 acres to Brian McFelin Roe McDonell, Hugh McCarbery O'Neale, and Shane McTirlagh O'Neale.

15. 240 acres to Mulmory McDonell, Arte McTirlagh O'Neale, and Neale McTirlagh O'Neale.
16. 100 acres to Felim Oge McDonell, gent.
17. 100 acres to Donough Reogh O'Hagan, gent.
18. 120 acres to Calvagh McDonell, gent.
19. 120 acres to Laughlin O'Hagan, gent.
20. 80 acres to Edmond Groome McDonell.
21. 83 acres to Alexander Oge McDonell.
22. 100 acres to Brian Oge O'Hagan, gent.
23. 120 acres to Colla McArte McDonell, gent.
24. 180 acres to Donough Oge McMurphie.
25. 540 acres to Donnell McHenry O'Neile, Felim McTirlagh Brassilagh [O'Neill], and Eugene Valley [Owen Ballagh] O'Neyle, and Edmund Oge O'Donnelly.
26. 240 acres to Owen McHugh O'Neale, gent.
27. 240 acres to Hugh McTirlagh O'Neale, Art McTirlagh O'Neale, and Henry McTirlagh O'Neale.
28. 120 acres to Rorie McPatrick McCan, gent.
29. 60 acres to Brian, son of Melaghlin, son of Art O'Neale, gent.
30. 120 acres to Patrick Moder, gent.
31. 120 acres to Cormack McTirlagh Brassilagh, gent.
32. 60 acres to Tirlagh Oge McTirlagh Brassilagh, gent.
33. 120 acres to Neece Quin.
34. 120 acres to Hugh McGilleduffe, gent.
35. 100 acres to Felim O'Quin.
36. 100 acres to Cahier O'Mellan, gent.
37. 80 acres to Hugh McBrian McCan.
38. 160 acres to Carberie Oge McCan and Toole McFelim McCan.
39. 80 acres to Ardill McFelim O'Hanlon, gent.

COUNTY OF TYRONE: PRECINCT OF DONGANON

1. 3330 acres to Tirlagh O'Neale of Caslane, Esq.
2. 800 acres to Neal O'Neale, Esq. [brother of the above].
3. 370 acres to Bryan O'Neale, gent. [brother of the two preceding grantees].
4. 2620 acres to Catharine Ny Neale, wife of the late Terence or Tirlagh Oge O'Neale, and now [1613] wife of Robert Hovenden, gent.
5. 400 acres to Tirlagh Oge O'Neale, gent. [brother of Felimy Roe, aforesaid].
6. 200 acres to Neal Roe O'Neale.
7. 1500 acres to Bryan O'Neale, gent.
8. 200 acres to Neale O'Neale.
9. 360 acres to Henry O'Neale, gent.
10. 300 acres to Charles O'Neale.

33

11. 1160 acres to Con Boy O'Neale.
12. 120 acres to Hugh O'Neale.
13. 140 acres to Robert Hovenden, gent.
14. 60 acres to Donill McShane [surnamed] Mallatas, gent.
15. 120 acres to Con Boy O'Neale, gent
16. 60 acres to Hugh McDonell O'Neale, gent.
17. 60 acres to Cormock McNemee, gent.
18. 60 acres to Tirlagh Oge McBrian [O'Neale], gent.
19. 60 acres to Rorie O'Gormeley, gent.
20. 60 acres to Jenkin O'Devin, gent.
21. 60 acres to Henry Oge O'Neale, gent.
22. 60 acres to Bryan O'Neale and Neale Roe.
23. 60 acres to Art McRowrie O'Neale, gent.
24. 60 acres to Hugh Groome O'Hagan, gent.
25. 60 acres to Art McArte O'Neale, gent.
26. 60 acres to Felim McAmallan, gent.
27. 60 acres to Shane McDonell Groome O'Donnilly, gent.
28. 60 acres to Shane Roe O'Neale, gent.
29. 60 acres to James McGunchenan, gent.
30. 120 acres to Henry McNeal McArte [O'Neale], gent.
31. 120 acres to Edmond Oge O'Haggan, gent.
32. 120 acres to Murtagh O'Quin, gent.
33. 60 acres to Fardoragh O'Haggan, gent.
34. 60 acres to Hugh Groome O'Mulchallane, gent.
35. 60 acres to Felim Boy O'Haggan, gent.
36. 60 acres to Neale O'Quin, gent.
37. 60 acres to Teige McEdmond Oge O'Hagan.
38. 120 acres to James Sheale, gent.
39. 140 acres to Owen Roe O'Quin, gent.
40. 120 acres to Bartholomew Owen, gent.
41. 120 acres to Gillaspick McDonnell, gent.
42. 60 acres to Shane McLaughlin O'Donilly, gent.
43. 120 acres to Owen O'Corr, gent.
44. 120 acres to Brian O'Develin, gent.
45. 60 acres to Fardoragh McCahir O'Mallen, gent.
46. 60 acres to Caragh O'Donilly, gent.
47. 60 acres to Owen O'Hagan, gent.
48. 120 acres to Owen Oge O'Hagan McOwen McEvistan, gent.
49. 60 acres to Shane McHugh McAderany O'Donilly, gent.
50. 60 acres to Con McTirlagh O'Neale, gent.
51. 60 acres to Felim Groome McFelimy McNeale [O'Neale], gent.
52. 60 acres to Fardoragh McBrian Carragh O'Neale, gent.
53. 60 acres to Felim Oge O'Mulcreve, gent.
54. 120 acres to Laghlen O'Hagan, gent.

55. 60 acres to Randall McDonnell, gent.
56. 60 acres to Hugh McCawell, gent.
57. 60 acres to Hugh McHugh Mergagh O'Neale, gent.
58. 120 acres to Mary Ny Neal [daughter of Sir Cormack].
59. 60 acres to Tirlagh Oge O'Gormeley, gent.
60. 1000 acres to Bryan Crossagh O'Neale [son of Sir Cormack].

COUNTY OF DONEGAL: PRECINCTS OF DOE AND FAWNETT (NOW KILMACRENAN)

1. 896 acres to Walter McLaughlin McSwyne, gent.
2. 2000 acres to Donald McSwine Fawnett, gent.
3. 64 acres to Manus McNeale McSwyne.
4. 2000 acres to Sir Mulmory McSwyne na Doe, Knt.
5. 2000 acres to Donough McSwyne Banagh, gent.
6. 596 acres to Nene Duffe Neene James [Ineen dubh, daughter of James Macdonnell], widow of Hugh, son of Manus O'Donnell.
7. 403 acres to Honora Bourk, widow of —— O'Boyle [lord of Boylagh].
8. 2000 acres to Tirlagh O'Boyle, gent. [son of the preceding grantee].
9. 128 acres to Neale Garrow McRowrie [O'Donnell], gent.
10. 128 acres to Caffer McHugh Duffe O'Donnell, gent.
11. 128 acres to Hugh Boy McQuin, gent.
12. 128 acres to Donell McQuin, gent.
13. 128 acres to Hugh Boy McSwine, gent.
14. 128 acres to Patrick Crone McCree, gent.
15. 128 acres to Neale McMulmorie McSwine and Tirlagh Carragh Mc-Swine, gents.
16. 128 acres to Owen McGillpatrick, gent.
17. 64 acres to Farroll Hugh O'Galchor, gent.
18. 64 acres to Donnell Groome McArte.
19. 128 acres to Grany Ny Donnell.
20. 774 acres to Murtagh O'Dowgan, Owen Modder McSwine, Owen Mc-Morphy, Donell O'Deveney, Donough O'Seren, Calvagh McBryan Roe McSwine, and Neale McSwine.
21. 1000 acres to Hugh McHugh Duffe [O'Donnell], gent.
22. 960 acres to Donell Ballagh O'Galchor, Dowltagh McDonell Ballagh, Edmond Boy O'Boyle, Tirlagh, Oge O'Boyle, Irrel O'Boyle, Cahir Mc-Malcavow, Shane McTirlagh, Dowaltagh McGillduffe, Farrell Mc-Tirlagh Oge, Loy O'Cleary, and Shane O'Cleary.
23. 128 acres to Owen Oge McOwen and Owen McOwen Edegany.

COUNTY OF FERMANAGH : PRECINCT OF CLINAWLY

1. 100 acres to Cormock O'Cassida, gent.
2. 300 acres to Donell dean Magwire and James McDonough Magwire, gents.
3. 150 acres to Rorie McAdegany Magwire, Owen McCoconaght Magwire, and Donell Oge O'Muldoon, gents.

4. 100 acres to Donough Oge Magwire, gent.
5. 190 acres to Felim Oge Magwire, gent.
6. 100 acres to Cahell McGilleduffe Magwire, gent.
7. 190 acres to Redmond McGillpatrick Magwire, gent.
8. 350 acres to Shane McHugh, gent.
9. 50 acres to Donell McCormock, gent.
10. 50 acres to Coconaght McHugh, gent.
11. 50 acres to Donough Oge McHugh, gent.
12. 145 acres to Donough Oge McDonaghy Magwire, gent.
13. 50 acres to Felim McAwly, gent.
14. 145 acres to Bryan Oge Magwire, gent.
15. 50 acres to Donough McRorie, gent.
16. 100 acres to Rorie Magwire, gent.
17. 120 acres to Thomas McJames McDun Magwire, Bryan McJames Mc-
    Dun Magwire, and Hugh McJames McDun Magwire, gents.
18. 300 acres to Tirlagh Moyle Magwire, gent.
19. 220 acres to Bryan McThomas [Magwire], gent.
20. 120 acres to Patrick McDonell, gent.
21. 130 acres to Shane McEnabb [or McCabe], gent.
22. 140 acres to Patrick McHugh Magwire, gent.
23. 120 acres to Bryan O'Corcoran, gent.
24. 140 acres to Edmund McBryan McShane, gent.
25. 100 acres to Felim Duffe McBrien, gent.
26. 100 acres to Cormocke McDonell, gent.
27. 100 acres to Connor McTirlagh, gent.
28. 240 acres to Bryan McMulrony, gent.
29. 140 acres to John Magwire, gent.
30. 150 acres to Donell Groome McArte, gent.
31. 192 acres to Hugh O'Flanegan, gent.
32. 390 acres to Oghy O'Hossy, gent.
33. 180 acres to Cormac Oge McHugh, gent.
34. 60 acres to Shane McDenett, gent.
35. 120 acres to Shane McDonell Ballagh and Brian O'Skanlan.
36. 96 acres to Shane Evarr Magwire, gent.
37. 96 acres to Cormock McBryan Magwire, gent.
38. 144 acres to Cormock McCallo Magwire, gent.
39. 48 acres to Conogher Glasse Magwire, gent.
40. 48 acres to Henry McElynan, gent.
41. 48 acres to Felim McElynan, gent.
42. 50 acres to Melaghlin Oge McCorr, gent.
43. 100 acres to Connell McWorrin, gent.
44. 100 acres to Moriertagh O'Flanegan, gent.
45. 96 acres to Hugh Boy Magwire, gent.
46. 50 acres to Patrick McHugh, gent.

47. 190 acres to Rorie McDonough Magwire and Pat. Ballagh Magwire, gents.
48. 100 acres to Tirlagh Mergagh Magwire and Felim Duffe McRorie Magwire, gents.
49 60 acres to Garrett Magwire and John Magwire, gents.

COUNTY OF FERMANAGH : PRECINCTS OF COOLE AND TIRCANNADA

1. 1500 acres to Con McShane O'Neale, gent.
2. 2000 acres to Bryan Maguyre, gent.
3. 500 acres to Tirlagh Magwire, gent. [brother of the preceding grantee].
4. 120 acres to John Magwire, gent.
5. 120 acres to Richard Magwire, gent.

COUNTY OF CAVAN : PRECINCT OF TULLAGHAH.

1. 300 acres to John and Connor O'Reily, gents.
2. 100 acres to Cahir McOwen, gent.
3. 300 acres to Cahell McOwen O'Reyly, gent.
4. 150 acres to Donell McOwen, gent.
5. 200 acres to Owen O'Shereden, gent.
6. 100 acres to Cahill McBrien O'Reily, gent.
7. 1000 acres to Felim McGawran, gent.
8. 300 acres to Mulmore McHugh McFarrall O'Rely, gent.
9. 175 acres to Cormacke McGawran.
10. 75 acres to Donough Magauran, gent.
11. 150 acres to Hugh McManus Oge Magauran, gent.
12. 200 acres to Breene Oge Magauran, gent.
13. 200 acres to Mulmorie McTirlagh O'Reily, gent.
14. 200 acres to Felim, Brian, and Cahir, sons of Hugh O'Reyly, late of Ballaghaneo.
15. 150 acres to Tirlagh McHugh McBryan Bane O'Reylie.
16. 400 acres to Bryan McKernan, gent.
17. 100 acres to Donnell McFarrall Oge McKernan, gent.
18. 150 acres to Callo [Calvagh] O'Gowne, gent.
19. 200 acres to Shane McCabe, gent.
20. 100 acres to Wony [Una] McThomas McKernan.
21. 200 acres to Donill Backagh McShane O'Reyly, gent.
22. 300 acres to Bryan McShane O'Reyly, gent.

COUNTY OF CAVAN : PRECINCT OF CLONMAHONE.

1. 2000 acres to Mulmorie McHugh Connelagh O'Rely, gent.
2. 475 acres to Gerald Fleming, Esq.
3. 100 acres to Hugh McBrien O'Reyly, gent.
4. 162 acres to Edward Nugent, gent.
5. 450 acres to Christopher Nugent, gent.
6. 200 acres to Edward Nugent, gent.

7. 300 acres to Philip McTirlagh Bradie, gent.
8. 50 acres to Richard Fitz-Simons.

COUNTY OF CAVAN : PRECINCT OF CASTLE RAHEN

1. 2300 acres to Walter, Thomas, and Patrick Bradie, gents.
2. 300 acres to Cahire McShane O'Reily of Cornegall, gent.
3. 150 acres to Barnaby Reily of Nacorraghes, gent.
4. 475 acres to Shane McHugh O'Reily of Ballaghana, gent.
5. 50 acres to Thomas McJames Bane of Kilmore, gent.
6. 300 acres to Philip McBrien McHugh O'Reily, gent.
7. 200 acres to Owen McShane O'Reily, gent.
8. 400 acres to Bryan O'Coggye O'Reily.
9. 200 acres to Mulmorie McOwen O'Reily.
10. 200 acres to Hugh Roe McShane O'Reily.
11. 300 acres to Philip and Shane O'Reily, brothers.
12. 900 acres to Shane McPhilip O'Reily, gent.
13. 50 acres to Shane Bane O'Moeltully, gent.
14. 100 acres to Edward Nugent, gent.
15. 500 acres to Owen McMulmorie O'Reily, gent.
16. 100 acres to Hugh McGlasney, gent.
17. 25 acres to Shane McPhilip O'Reily.

COUNTY OF CAVAN : PRECINCT OF TULLAGHGARVY

1. 3000 acres to Mulmorie Oge O'Reylie, gent.
2. 1000 acres to Mulmorie McPhilip O'Reilie, Esq.
3. 1000 acres to Hugh O'Reilie, Esq.
4. 150 acres to Terence Braddy, gent.
5. 300 acres to Morish McTully, gent.
6. 150 acres to Thomas Braddy, gent.
7. 150 acres to Connor McShane Roe [O'Bradie], gent.
8. 262 acres to Henry Betagh, gent.

In the *Carew Manuscripts, 1603–1624*, published by the British Government, may be found a series of reports made by commissioners who were appointed by the king at different periods to visit the various landlords in Ulster to whom allotments had been made, and take account of their progress. The first party to make such an inspection consisted of five commissioners, among whom was the Lord Deputy for Ireland, Sir Arthur Chichester, who had himself been allotted the district now occupied by the city of Belfast. This visit was made in the summer of 1611, and the commissioners' report is as follows :

A Relation of Works done by Scottish Undertakers of Land in the Escheated Counties of Ulster certified by the Governors, Sheriffs and others; and some seen and surveyed by us in one journey into that Province begun the 29th July, 1611.

Precinct of Portlough [County of Donegal]. Duke of Lennox, chief undertaker of 2000 acres. Sir Aulant Aula, Knight, his agent, resident, with some British families; no preparation for building, save some timber trees felled and squared. Sir Walter Stewart, Knight, Laird of Minto, 1000 acres; hath taken possession in person, the summer 1610; returned into Scotland, has done nothing. John Crawford, Laird Kilberry, 1000 acres; not appeared nor any for him, and nothing done. Alexander McAula of Durlinge; 1000 acres; appeared not, nothing done. Sir James Cunningham, Knight, Laird Glangarnoth, 2000 acres; took possession but returned into Scotland; his agent, Robert Younge, resident, built one Irish barn of coples; he hath 44 head of cattle, one plow of garrons, and some tillage last harvest. Three families of British resident on his proportion, preparing to build; as yet, no estate passed to them. John Cunningham of Crawfield, 1000 acres; resident with one family of British; is building a bawn, and preparing materials; hath a plow of garrons, and thirty head of cattle. Cuthbert Cunningham, 1000 acres; resident with two families of British; built an Irish house of coples, and prepared materials to re-edify the castle of Coole McEctrean; hath a plow of garrons, and 80 head of cattle in stock. William Stewart, Laird Dunduffe, 1000 acres; his brother was here for him the summer 1610, and returned into Scotland; left a servant to keep stock, being 2 mares and 30 head of cattle. James Cunningham of Horomilne, 1000 acres; was here the summer 1610, returned into Scotland; left six servants to keep cows; nothing done, nor preparation made for building.

Precinct of Boylagh [County of Donegal]. Sir Robert Maclellan, Knt., Laird of Bombey, chief undertaker of Rosses, 2,000 acres; took possession in the summer 1610, returned into Scotland; his agent, Andrew Johnson, resident, hath prepared no material for building. George Murrye, Laird Broughton, 1500 acres; took possession summer 1610, returned into Scotland. His brother came with two or three others, and 30 or 40 cows; no preparation for building. William Steward, brother to Gartlesse [Lord Garlies], 1500 acres; took possession in the summer, 1610, returned into Scotland; six families of British upon his proportion. He is building a mill and other houses; agent John Stewart, resident, materials provided for building. Sir Patrick McKee, Knight, 1000 acres, not appeared; agent resident; nothing done. Alexander Cunningham, of Ponton Elder, 1,000 acres; not appeared; agent resident; making winter provisions; no materials for building. James McCullogh, 1000 acres; not appeared; agent resident; nothing done. Alexander Downebar, 1000 acres; resident in person; nothing done. Patrick Vans, 1000 acres; has not appeared. Six quarters of his land let to English and Scotchmen for four years; nothing done.

Precinct of Knockninny. Lo. Burley, 3000 acres, in the county of Fermanagh; took possession in the summer 1610, returned into Scotland, left as agent, Captain Meldrame, who is non-resident. Lo. Burley hath sent over 24 persons, freeholders, tenants, and servants, resident. One large house built of 14 rooms; oaks felled and squared, and preparations for building; 60 barrels of barley and oats sown and reaped last harvest; 70 cows brought out of Scotland which belong to the tenants; and a boat of eight tons built for his lordship's use. Sir John Wyshard, La. Pittaro, 1500 acres; possession taken; returned into Scotland; done nothing. He is since our return from the north arrived and brought with him 15 persons well armed; he hath set up two ploughs sowing wheat and intends to go forward with building. Mr. Balfore, La. Mountwhany, 1500 acres; appeared in person, brought over eight freeholders and lease-holders with four women servants. He felled 200 oaks, provided lime, and brought over a dozen horses and mares for work, with household stuff. La. Kinalle, 1000 acres ; not appeared and none for him ; nothing done. James Trayle, 1000 acres ; took possession, returned into Scotland. Sent over four persons to make freeholders, &c. Some timber and other materials provided, and six horses and mares out of Scotland. George Smolhome, 1000 acres, taken possession, returned into Scotland ; no agent, done nothing.

Precinct of Mageriboy [County of Fermanagh]. Sir John Home, Knight, 2000 acres ; has taken possession, returned into Scotland, nothing done, nor any agent present. Robert Hamylton, 1500 acres ; has been here to see the land, but has not taken possession, and nothing done. But since our return [to Dublin] he is arrived in Fermanagh (as we are informed), with 18 tenants and artificers for planting ; with 60 head of cattle, 10 horses and mares for labour ; is felling timber and providing materials for building. William Fouler, 1500 acres ; taken possession ; returned into Scotland, done nothing. James Gybb, 1000 acres ; the like. Jerhome Lindsey, 1000 acres ; took possession by attorney, did nothing else. Alexander Home, 1000 acres ; the like. John Downebarr, 1000 acres ; taken possession, returned into Scotland, and sent over six persons, whereof two freeholders, one leaseholder, one tenant for years, and two tenants at will ; some building in hand ; eight horses for work brought over, with money to provide materials.

Precinct of Strabane [County of Tyrone]. The Earl of Abercorne, chief undertaker, has taken possession, resident with lady and family, and built for the present near the town of Strabane some large timber houses, with a court 116 foot in length and 87 foot in breadth, the grounsells of oaken timber, and the rest of allor [alder] and birch, which is well thatched with heath and finished. Has built a great brew-house without his court 46 foot long and 25 foot wide. His followers and tenants have, since May last, built 28 houses of fair coples ; and before May, his tenants, who are all Scottishmen, the number of 32 houses of like goodness. Is preparing materials for building a fair castle and bawn, which he means to put in hand for the next spring. There are 120 cows in stock for his own use. Sir Thomas Boyde, Knight, has a proportion of land, is resident with his wife and family ; is providing material for building. Sir George Hamilton, Knight, a proportion of land, resident with his wife and family. Has built a good house of timber for the present, 62 foot long and thirty foot wide. He brought over some families of Scots, who have built them a bawn and good timber houses, 80 cows and 16 garrons among them. Sir John Dumonde [Drummond], Knight, 1000 acres ; appeared in person, took possession, and has one Scottishman, 2 garrons and a mare. James Clapham, 1000 acres ; resident, prepares to people his land, competent store of arms in readiness. James Hayge, 1500 acres ; has not appeared, nor any for him ; nothing done. Sir Claude Hamylton, Knight, 2000 acres ; has not appeared nor any for him ; nothing done. George Hamilton, 1000 acres ; has taken possession, is resident, making provisions for building.

Precinct of Mountjoy [County of Tyrone]. The Lord Uchelrie [Ochiltree], 3000 acres ; being stayed by contrary winds in Scotland, arrived in Ireland (at the time of our being in Armagh, upon our return home), accompanied with 33 followers, gent. of sort, a minister, some tenants, freeholders, and artificers, unto whom he hath passed estates ; and hath built for his present use three houses of oak timber, one of 50 foot long and 22 wide, and two of 40 foot long, within an old fort, about which he is building a bawn.

He has sundry men at work providing materials, and there are in readiness 240 great trees felled, and some squared; and is preparing stone, brick, and lime for building a castle, which he means to finish next Spring. There are two ploughs going upon his demesne, with some 50 cows, and three score young heifers landed at Island Magy [Magee], in Clandeboy, which are coming to his proportion, and some 12 working mares; and he intends to begin residence upon his land the next Spring, as he informeth us. Sir Robert Hepburne, Knight, 1500 acres; sowed oats and barley the last year upon his land, and reaped this harvest 40 hogsheads of corn; is resident; hath 140 cows, young and old, in stock, and 8 mares. Hath 7 householders, being in number 20 persons; is building a stone house 40 foot long and 20 wide, already a story high, and before the end of this season he intends to have it three stories high, and to cover it, and the next Spring to add another story to it; good store of timber felled and squared, and providing materials to finish the work. The Laird Lochnorris, 1000 acres; being diseased himself, as we were informed, had his agent here, Robert O'Rorke; hath some timber felled, and is preparing materials for building against next Spring. Bernard Lendsey and Robert Lendsey, 1000 acres apiece; have taken possession personally in the Summer, 1610, returned into Scotland; agent, Robert Cowties, resident; a timber house is built on Robert Lendsey's portion, who hath three householders, being in number 12 persons. Hath eight mares and eight cows with their calves, and five oxen, with swine and other small cattle, and a competent portion of arms. Robert Stewart of Haulton, 1000 acres; has appeared in person, having brought some people. Timber felled, and providing materials for building. Robert Stewart of Robstone, 1000 acres; has appeared in person, with tenants and cattle; timber felled and squared and is preparing materials for building.

Precinct of the Fewes [County of Armagh]. Sir James Dowglasse, Knight, 2000 acres; George Lawder is his deputy, has done nothing. Claud Hamilton, 1000 acres; is building a stone bawn with round flankers, 24 yards square, and a wall 8 foot high; has raised stone to finish the bawn, and to make a stone house, and has drawn trees to the building; is now building three houses, one 48 feet long. Five families, 16 men and women of British birth, are upon the land, whereof six are masons. Eighty cows and 14 horses and mares in stock. William Lawder, 1000 acres; Alexander Lawder, resident agent; certain houses built and repaired, where are ten families and three servants, to the number of 18, residing; 18 horses and mares, and 60 cows; stone raised and timber felled. James Craige, 1000 acres; resident; has begun to build a mill, sown and reaped oats and barley; built some tenements wherein are placed some families of British. Henry Acheson, 1000 acres; resident; has raised stone and felled timber. Has 8 or 9 people; who have 30 cows and 15 horses and mares, with some arms.

Precinct of Tullaghchinko [County of Cavan]. Sir Alexander Hamilton, Knt., 2000 acres in the County of Cavan; has not appeared, his son Claude Hamilton took possession and brought two tenants, three servants and six artificers; is in hand with building a mill, trees felled, hath a minister but not yet allowed by the bishop; has raised stones and hath competent arms in readiness. Besides the above named there are arrived upon that proportion since our return from the journey (as we are informed), twelve tenants and artificers who intend to reside there and to build and plant upon the same. John Auchmothy and Alexander Auchmothy, 1000 acres, have not appeared. James Craige is their deputy for five years, who has brought 4 artificers of divers sorts with their wives and families and

2 other servants.   Stone raised for building a mill and timber felled, a walled house with a smith's forge built, four horses and mares upon the ground with competent arms.   Sir Claude Hamilton, Knt., 1000 acres ; has not appeared, nor any for him, nothing done.   John Browne, 1000 acres , sent an agent to take possession, who set the same to the Irish, returned into Scotland, and performed nothing.

Precinct of Clanchie.   The Lo. Obigny, 3000 acres ; in the county of Cavan ; appeared not nor any for him, nothing done, the natives still remaining.   William Downebarr, William Baylye, and John Rolestone, 1000 acres apiece ; the like.   Since our return from the north, one Mr. Tho. Creighton arrived here and presented himself as the agent for the Lo. Obigney and William Downebarr, William Bayley and John Rolestone, who informed us that he brought with him sundry artificers and tenants, with cattle, horses and household provisions for the planting and inhabiting of that precinct, and is gone thither with intent to provide materials ; and it is said that Downebarr, Bayley, and Rolestone are arrived themselves in the north and gone to their portions.   Likewise, one Mr. John Hamilton arrived and presented himself as agent for Sir Claud Hamilton, undertaker, of 1000 acres in the county of Cavan ; who informed us that he brought with him people to plant and is gone thither with resolution to provide materials to go in hand with buildings upon that proportion.   Likewise, George Murey, Lo. Broughton, undertaker of 1500 acres, in the precinct of Boylagh appeared before us here at Dublin and returned to his land.   Since our return one John Fullerton hath arrived at Dublin, who presented himself before us as agent for James Dowglasse who informed us that he brought 15 families with him to plant upon that land with artificers and workmen.

Signed, Arthur Chichester, G. Carew, Th. Ridgeway, R. Wingfelde, Ol. Lambart.

A Perfect Relation and Report of the Works, Buildings, and Fortifications done by the English, surveyed by us in most places, and the rest certified by the governors, sheriffs, and others employed by us in our journey in the Province of Ulster begun the 29th of July, 1611.

[The report first refers to the town of Colraine, and the buildings, etc., in progress in it.]

Men and labourers employed in Colraine : Carpenters, 41 ; sawyers, 28 ; wheelwrights, 4 ; bricklayers, 11 ; plasterers, 2 ; masons, 11 ; slaters, 10 ; brickmakers, tilemakers, and their men, 20 ; lime burners, 5 ; limestone diggers, 4 ; quarrymen, 10 ; labourers, 40 ; labourers about the fortifications, 50 ; boat and bargemen, 12 ; clerks, 3 ; carters, 11 ; men in the carvel, 7 ; in the woods : shipwrights, 4 ; sawyers, 9 ; timber squarers, 4 ; wainmen, 8 ; timber woodfellers and rafters of timber and wood, 12 ; cottmen from the wood to the Leape, 9 ; lath renders, 20 ; overseers thereof, 3 ; floaters of timber from the Leape, 3 ; English and Irish men employed by Mr. Nugent for the felling, &c., of timber, 32 ; millwrights in Colrayne, 4 ; carters at the Leape and in the woods, 2.   The whole number of workmen at Colrayne and in the woods, 379.

Whole number of horses employed, 37 ; whole number of oxen employed in Colraine and the woods, 37.

A declaration of what is done in the woods of Clanconkeyne in the Barony of Lough Enisholyne granted to the Londoners, in which is a house, wherein Mr. Holliocke dwelleth :

County of Colerayne.   In the county of Coleraine we neither found nor understood of anything done, or in hand to be done, by the Londoners, towards the performance of the Articles of the Plantation. Their agents receive the rents there, and in the barony of Lough Enish O'Lyn [Lough-insholin], from the natives, and seek not to remove them, which makes the said natives to conceive that they shall not be displanted ; which is a great hindrance to the plantation of that county and ill example to their neighbours.

The Castle of Lemavady. Sir Thomas Phillips, Knight, hath erected a watermill at Lemavady, unto which he drew water a mile, in a sluice or pond, 12 foot broad and 5 foot deep ; he hath put in good forwardness an Inn, builded English fashion, for the relief of passengers passing that way, containing in length 46 foot, and in breadth 17 foot, two stories high. Timber is for the most part ready there, and brought with very great difficulty out of the woods of Glenconkeyne, over very great bogs and mountains 12 and 14 miles distant from him, which hath and will be very chargeable. He hath towards the building of the castle of Lemavady, and other buildings, felled and squared in the woods good store of timber ; and hath raised store of stone out of the ditch, adjoining the castle, being a very hard Rock, whereby he intends to make some good work for the defence of the country.

Dungiven. Captain Edward Doddington hath builded at Dungiven a castle of 22 foot broad, four stories high, whereof some part of the walls were standing before, and is now by him well finished and slated. He hath built a house adjoining to the castle of 43 foot long and 18 broad, the walls whereof some parts were standing, but now very well and handsomely slated and finished. He hath repaired a bawn of lime and stone about the castle and the house, with flankers of sufficient strength for defence. Towards the building of the castle and the bawn he had 200£ from the King, upon which and the rest of his building he hath bestowed 300£ as he affirmeth.

Derry. Next we come to Derry, where we saw the church well slated and repaired. Two fair houses of stone, two stories high, slated and finished with cellars to each house. A store house covered and walled with deal boards, with a place to work dry in. A thatched house wherein Mr. Wray dwelleth. A saw pit covered with deal boards. A fair large smith's forge, with a dwelling-house to the same. Two fair lime-kills. A fair wharf of 300 foot long, and about 14 broad, and 8 or 9 foot high. Two heads of wharfs at the ferry-places on both sides the river. A bark building of 70 or 80 tons, with provisions of plank and other timber for her, &c., &c.

Town of Lyffer. A good and strong fort built of lime and stone, with bulwarks, a parapet, and a large ditch of good depth cast about it on the river side, with a storehouse for victuals and munition, a gatehouse with a drawbridge. This fort was built by Sir Richard Hansard, towards which the King allowed him 200£ English. There is another small fort in the town rampiered and ditched, about which are certain houses built of good timber after the English manner which serve for the use of a gaoler, and to keep the prisoners. Sir Richard Hansard, Knight, being appointed by the now Lord Deputy to be at Lyffer with his Company in 1607, found but one house in that town. Upon view of the town we found it [1611] well furnished with inhabitants of English, and Scottish, and Irish, who live by several trades, brought thither by Sir Richard, who built 21 houses for tenants who are to give entertainment to passengers. Thirty-seven houses were built by others.

Precinct of Lyffer. Sir Henry Doewra, Knight, undertaker of 2000 acres, has by allowance of the Council, passed over his portion of land to William Wylson of Clarye, in Suffolk, who has letters patent in his own name. The said Wylson had his agent, Chris. Parmenter, resident, who appeared before us. There are some families of English resident, who brought over good store of household stuff, and have stock 21 cows and oxen, 9 mares, one service horse, and some small cattle. Sir Morris Barkley, Knight, undertaker of 2000 acres ; has not been here nor any agent for him, nothing done. Sir Robert Remyngton, Knight, 2000 acres ; the like. Sir Thomas Cornwall, Knight, 2000 acres ; his agent, Edward Littleton, took possession, and is resident ; has built nothing, nor provided any materials yet. Sir William Barnes, Knight, 1500 acres ; sold his proportion to Captain Edward Russell, who is possessed, but has done nothing. Sir Henry Clare, 1500 acres ; has an agent, resident, named William Browne, nothing done. Sir Thomas Coache, Knight, 1500 acres ; is a resident, has built a large timber house adjoining to the Castle of Skarfollis, and is providing materials for re-edifying the Castle. Four families of British upon his land, to whom he intends to pass estates. Captain Edward Russell, 1500 acres ; is resident, and his son with him. There are two English houses of timber framed ; stock, four horses, six English cows, and a bull ; three or four English labourers, but no tenants. Captain Mansfield, 1000 acres ; is resident, has no inhabitants, nothing done.

Town of Donegal. We found a fair bawn built with flankers, a parapet, and a walk on the top fifteen foot high. Within the bawn is a strong house of stone, built by Captain Bassill Brooke, towards which the King gave him 250£ English. Many families of English, Scottish, and Irish are inhabiting in the town, who built them good copled houses after the manner of the Pale. About two miles from thence Captain Paul Goare [Gore] has erected a fair stone house out of the ruins of O'Boyle's old castle upon the sea-side, which he has by direction of the Lords of the Council delivered up to Laird Broughton, undertaker of those lands ; he demands some consideration for his charges, which we think him worthy of.

Fermanagh. Precincts of Clancally and Lurg and Coolemakernan. Thomas Flowerdew, 2000 acres ; is resident, has brought over two free-holders and five fine copyholders ; he cast a trench about an old Rath, and is building an English house, of 50 feet long and 22 broad, providing materials. Edward Warde, 1000 acres ; has not appeared, nor any for him ; nothing done. Thomas Plumsteed has made over his portion to Sir Hugh Worrall ; nothing done. Thomas Chiney, 1000 acres ; has not appeared, nor any one for him ; nothing done. Henry Gunning [Honynge], 1000 acres ; has taken possession, but nothing done. John Sedborough, 1000 acres ; is resident with his wife and family ; has brought over two free-holders, one leaseholder, and three copyholders ; felled timber, raised stones, set up an oven, and two chimneys in his house, and intends to go in hand with his bawne. Robert Calvert, 1000 acres ; is resident ; has built a house after the English manner. Has two families of English, unto whom he will give estates. Six other families have promised to come unto him at May next. Robert Bogas, 1000 acres ; has not appeared, nor any for him ; nothing done. John Archdale, 1000 acres ; the like.

Enishkellin. There is a fair and strong wall newly erected of lime and stone, 26 foot high, with flankers, a parapet, and a walk on the top of the wall, built by Captain William Colle [Cole], constable thereof, towards which he had 200£ sterling from the King. A fair house begun upon the foundation of the old castle, with other convenient houses for store and munition, which, besides the laying out of the Captain's own money, will draw on some increase of charge to the King. The bawn is ditched about with a fair large ditch and the river on one side, with a good drawbridge. The King hath three good boats there ready to attend all services. A large piece of ground adjoins the fort with a good timber house, after the English fashion, built by the captain, in which he and his family now dwell.

Tyrone. Precinct of Clogher. Sir Thomas Ridgway, vice-treasurer and treasurer at Wars in Ireland, undertaker for 2000 acres, has appeared in person. His agent is Emanuel Ley, resident this twelve month, who is to be made a freeholder under him. Sir Thomas brought from London and Devonshire, the 4th May, 1610, twelve carpenters, mostly with wives and families, who have since been resident, employed in felling timber, brought by Patrick McKenna of the Trugh [Trough], county Monaghan, none being in any part of the Barony of Clogher, or elsewhere nearer him, viz., 700 trees, 400 boards and planks, besides a quantity of stone, timber for tenements, with timber ready for the setting up of a water-mill. He is erecting a wardable castle and houses, to be finished about the next Spring. Ten masons work upon the castle, and two smiths. One Mr. Farefax, Mr. Laughton, Robert Williams, Henry Holland, and three of said carpenters are to be made freeholders. Other families are resident wherewith he will perform all things answerable to his covenants.

Edward Kingswell, 2000 acres ; has appeared at Dublin and taken possession personally ; returned into England to bring over his wife and family ; has freeholders, tenants, and workmen ; his agent, William Roules, has money imprested for providing materials to set forward all necessary works. Sir Francis Willoughby, Knight, 2000 acres ; has taken possession personally ; William Roules and Emanuel Ley, in his absence, employed in providing materials for buildings ; 200 trees felled and squared. George Ridgway, 1000 acres ; took possession in person ; his agent is resident since March last ; some materials ready in place. Intends to go forward with building his bawn. Some freeholders and tenants to inhabit, but no work done. William Parsons, the King's surveyor, 1000 acres ; took possession personally ; his brother, Fenton Parsons, his agent, resident since March last ; has provided materials for building ; has two carpenters and a mason, and expects four Englishmen with their families to come over shortly ; no work done. William Clegge, 2000 acres ; has not appeared nor any for him. It is reported that he passed his land to Sir Anthony Cope, whose son came to see the same and returned into England ; nothing done. But by letter he desires to be excused, promising to go on thoroughly with his plantation next Spring. Captain Walter Ednye, 1500 acres ; took possession personally ; his son-in-law resident since March last. Provision made for building a house, the foundation laid. Six families of English in the kingdom that will come to plant and settle next Spring. William Turven, 1000 acres ; took possession in person ; his brother resident since March last ; has provided materials for buildings. Agreed with four families to come out of England the next Spring to plant, who promised to bring other five families. Intends to go shortly in hand with building a bawn and a house, but nothing done yet.

Precinct of Omye. The Lord Audley, 3000 acres ; has not appeared, nor any for him ; nothing done. Sir Marvin Audley, Knight, 2000 acres ; the like. Sir Ferdinando Audley, Knight, 2000 acres ; the like. Sir John Davys, Knight, the King's Attorney General, 2000 acres ; possession taken by his agent, William Bradley, resident, who is preparing materials for building a stone house or castle with a bawn, which materials will be ready before Allhallowtide next ; at this instant the walls of the castle are 22 foot high, and in breadth between the walls 19 foot, and in length 36 foot. Already four fee farmers, one leaseholder, and a carpenter, with their families, are ready to be estated on portions, which they could not receive until now, for that five quarters of the best of the said lands were in controversy, and some of it not yet cleared. The said Sir John intends to finish his works next Spring, and to plant and people his lands according to the articles.

The Fort of the Omye. Here is a good fort fairly walled with lime and stone, about 30 foot high above the ground with a parapet, the river on one side and a large deep ditch about the rest, within which is built a fair house of timber after the English manner. All begun by Captain Ormond [Edmond] Leigh, and finished by his brothers John and Daniel Leigh, at their own charges upon the lands of the Abbey of Omye, at which place are many families of English and Irish, who have built them good dwelling houses, which is a safety and comfort for passengers between Donganon and the Liffer. The fort is a place of good import upon all occasions of service and fit to be maintained.

The Castle of Mountjoy, upon Loch Chichester, beside the old fort, wherein are many inhabitants, both English and Irish, together with Sir Francis Roe's foot company. Here is a fair castle of stone and brick, covered with slate and tile, begun in the late Queen's time, and finished by his Majesty. It is compassed about by a good strong rampier of earth, well ditched and flanked with bulwarks. In this castle Sir Francis Roe, the constable, and his family dwell.

The Forte of Deserte Martyne, a place in Glanconkeyne, is thought fit for the King's service and the serving of travellers between Colraine and all parts of Tyrone and Armagh, to be laid out with 300 acres for a fort, to be erected for lodgings for a constable and wardens. The London agents have agreed to the place and number of acres, but in regard that Deserte Martine, on which the fort is to be erected, is the Bishop of Derry's land and a quarter adjoining, we think fit that the Londoners should give him so much in exchange thereof of their own land, and we think it not amiss that the King should give 200 £ towards erecting the fort, and the constable to pay the overplus, if any.

Armagh, Precinct of Onellan. The Lord Saye and Seale, 3000 acres ; has made over his portion to Sir Anthony Cope, Knight, who has sent over a very sufficient overseer named William Pearson, with another to assist, who are resident. They have begun a fair castle of free-stone, and other hard stone, 14 or 15 workmen, and 9 carpenters employed. Great part of the free-stone for the coynes and windows are prepared 4 or 5 miles beyond Armagh. Two English carts or teams with horses and oxen attend the drawing of materials. There are 20 muskets and cavaliers, with competent furniture ready upon all occasions. The way for carriage of timber, which is five miles, is made passable, and so is the way to the freestone, which is 8 miles from the place. Two of the principal workmen are to be made freeholders, the rest are to have land upon reasonable terms. Sixteen mares and horses employed in carriage of materials. John Brownlow, 1500 acres, and his son William Brownlow, 1000 acres ; both resident, and dwelling in an Irish house. Have brought over six carpenters, one mason, a tailor and six workmen ; one freeholder and six tenants upon their land. Preparations to build two bawns. Some muskets and other arms in readiness. Mr. Powell, 2000 acres ; has put over his land to Mr. Roulstone. No freeholders nor artificers are drawn upon it, nor work done, save the building of two bays of a house. When we were in the north, one William Banister, presented himself before us as agent for Powell, and said that preparations were being made for building a house and bawn, that divers Englishmen had promised to come over and inhabit his land.

The preceding part certified by Sir Toby Calfield and the Sheriff before we went our journey.

Francis Secheverell, 2000 acres ; is resident ; has brought over three masons, one carpenter, one smith, nine laborers and two women ; four horses and a cart ; no freeholders or other tenants. Has drawn stone and other materials to the place where he intends to build. Certified by Sir Toby Calfield and the Sheriff before we went the journey, but upon our coming into the country, Secheverell adds to his certificate that he has built three houses and placed tenants in them, and is building a stone house, and has competent arms in his house. Mr. Stanhawe, 1500 acres ; was here, took possession, and returned into England. His son, Stephen Stanhawe, overseer in his absence, has done nothing.' Mr. James Matchett, 1000 acres ; his eldest son, Daniel Matchett, aged 24 years, agent, resident since Michaelmas, 1610. Two freeholders upon the land, but no tenants or laborers. Certified by Sir Toby Calfield and the Sheriff before our journey, since which time he added to his certificate that he has begun a bawn, and intends to finish it before Allhallowtide, and to effect what is required by the articles. Has provided materials for buildings ; has 9 horses and other beasts ready to draw the same to his work ; has arms for 10 men. Mr. John Dyllon, 1500 acres ; is resident with his wife, children and family. Brought over 22 Englishmen, with their wives, children and servants, with 52 English cows, 15 horses for work, 6 carpenters, 3 masons, 7 labourers, and 2 women servants. Has felled oaks, small and great. All this was certified by Sir Toby Calfield and the Sheriff ; but, at our being in the north, Dyllon adds that he has built a strong bawn, with houses for lodgings and to keep provisions in, and is well stored with arms and munition. Mr. Roulston, 1000 acres ; is resident ; has timber buildings after the English fashion. There are three men of good sort resident, who shall be freeholders, whereof one has built a house of stone and clay. Seven poor Englishmen, with their wives, children and some servants, who are to be tenants. They have four English cows, and eight horses for ploughing among them all.

The Moyrye Castle. A pretty castle upon the park of the Moyrye, built in the time of the late Earl of Devonshire's government here, at the Queen's charge ; where Captain Anthony Smith is constable, and has a ward of 12 men. Has drawn some families of British to dwell upon the lands thereunto adjoining, which is a good relief to passengers between Dundalke and Newrye.

The Fort of Charlemont. A good fort built, fairly ditched, with a strong palisade and bulwarks. Within the fort are good houses, built after the English fashion, for lodgings and to keep the King's store of victual and provision. Sir Toby Calfield, constable there, has 60£ ster. from the King towards this building. A very fair garden without the rampier, etc. The town is replenished with many inhabitants both English and Irish, who have built them good houses of coples after the best manner of the English.

The Fort of Mount Norris. A good fort well rampiered, with bulwarks, and a palisade, and a fair deep ditch. Within this fort Captain Anderton has built a fair cage-work house, and others to keep victual and munition in. Some inhabitants of English and Irish, who have settled themselves, have built good houses after the manner of the Pale, which is a great relief and comfort for passengers between the Newrye and Armagh.   It is a place of special import upon all occasions of service, and fit to be maintained.

Cavan, Precinct of Loughtie.   Sir John Davys, Knt., 2000 acres ; has made over his proportion to Mr. Richard Waldron who sold his estate to Sir Nicholas Lusher, Knt., nothing done.   Sir Hugh Worrall, Knt., 1500 acres ; was here in the summer [1610] took possession and returned into England.   His lady and family came over about the 20th of July last.   Three freeholders resident, 1 is building on his freehold ; 20 artificers and servants, or thereabout, resident, most of whom lived there all last winter.   He has built a fair house at Bealturberte after the English manner, and three other dwelling houses, with a smith's forge.   Between Sir Worrall and Mr. Stephen Butler were built at Bealturberte five boats of several burthens, one of them will carry 12 or 14 tons.   Timber prepared for building.   Arms for 10 men of all sorts, and burnt by mischance in a house as much as would furnish 12 more.   John Taylor, 1500 acres ; came over in the summer of 1610, took possession and remained most part of the following winter, went into England about Shrovetide last, left his deputy with some 7 or 8 tenants. Came back about May last with provisions, but went back again and is not yet returned.   Brought over 3 freeholders, whereof 2 are gone into England for their wives and families, the other, resident, is Taylor's deputy.   One copyholder placed upon the land and 8 artificers, able men and servants.   A timber house with a chimney furnished where he means to erect his dwelling house.   Materials for building ready, but not drawn home.   Competent arms of all sorts to furnish 12 men.   John Fish, 2000 acres ; came over in the summer, took possession, went back again, and left his deputy here, returned with his wife and family about May last.   Brought with him 4 freeholders, 2 whereof returned for their families, none of them yet settled.   Brought with him artificers and servants of all sorts, 33 or thereabout.   [Preparations for building detailed.]   Two English teams of horses, with English carts continually employed in drawing materials, oaks felled and carpenters employed in the woods of Fermanagh, felling more.   Arms of all sorts for 35 men or thereabout, a barrel of powder with match and lead proportionable.   William Snow, 1500 acres ; never came, nor any for him.   Passed over his proportion to William Lusher, son to Sir Nicholas Lusher, done nothing.   Since our return from the North, William Lusher, son to Sir Nicholas, who bought William Snowe's proportion of 1500 acres in that precinct, came over with his father, took out warrants of possession, and is gone down to his land.

Edward Littleton, agent for Sir Thomas Cornwall, undertaker of 2000 acres in the precinct of Lyffer arrived here since our return from the North, and is gone down to his proportion.

The Lo. Audley and Mr. Blunte, undertaker in the precinct of the Omye, came out of England since our return from the North, and went to see their proportions.

A Relation of the proceedings of the Servitors and Natives in their buildings upon the proportions of land allotted to them on the distribution of the escheated counties of Ulster :

Precinct of Kilmacrenan.—Captain Will Stewart has built upon the proportion of 1000 acres allotted him as a servitor in the Barony of Kilmacrenan, a fort or bawn of lime and stone with two flankers. [Described.] Under one is a room either for a mountain house or a prison, and upon that a court of guard, and above that an open "freight" and in the outmost part thereof a sentinel house, one curtain 16 foot high, and 2 others 12 foot high, and the other 8 foot high, whereupon he intends to erect a stone house. Has built three houses English fashion and is in hand for three more which will serve for tenants. The rest of the servitors have done nothing by reason of the wildness of the land, being the worst in all the country, insomuch that the natives are unwilling to come to dwell upon it until they be forced to remove. Servitors are providing materials, and purpose to perform their covenants by the time prescribed. [The natives have performed no works, but two of them providing materials ; none others removed to portions assigned.]

County Fermanagh. — [Servitors to whom lands were assigned are providing materials for buildings, but have done nothing. Two natives have removed to portions assigned them and built great copelled houses, where they dwell. No other natives of that county are yet removed, nor is any work done.]

County Tyrone.—Sir Arthur Chichester now Lo. Deputy, has 600 acres about Donganon, as a servitor, where he intends to build a castle or strong house of lime and stone, and to environ the same with a good and substantial stone wall and a deep ditch with a counter scarfe of stone to hold up the earth. Has now masons and workmen to take down such remains of the decayed ruins of the old castle as are yet standing. [Preparations detailed.] Town to be made a corporation, and there are families of English and other civil men, who for the present have built houses of coples, but are bound to build of cagework or stone after the English, and make enclosures about the town. Sir Thomas Ridgeway, Treasurer at Wars, 2000 acres in precinct of Donganon, as servitor, has carpenters providing timber &c., for building next spring. Sir Richard Wingfield, Knight Marshel of the Army, 2000 acres as servitor, has great store of timber for buildings, and will have other materials ready by the beginning of spring. Sir Toby Calfield, Knt., 1000 acres as servitor, is providing materials for building. [Detailed.] Will be ready to build next spring. Sir Francis Roe, Knt., 1000 acres as servitor, is providing materials for building. William Parsons, his Majesty's Surveyor, 1000 acres as servitor, preparing to forward buildings next spring. Francis Ansley, 400 acres, as servitor, had made a bawn of earth and sods with convenient ditch and flankers and provided timber to build a substantial English house within it. Captain Tyrlagh O'Neale, one of the natives of Tyrone, has removed and dwells on his lands in the precinct of Donganon, has no preparation for building but an Irish house. None of the rest are removed nor have made any preparations for building.

County Armagh.—Lo. Audley, 2000 acres in reversion of Arte McBarron, and 500 acres as servitor in precinct of Oryer in co. Armagh. The 500 acres set out but no preparation for building. Sir Oliver St. John, Knt., Master of the Ordnance, 1500 acres as servitor, is making preparations for building. Sir Gerrott Moore, Knt., 1000 acres as servitor, is providing timber, &c. for building. Sir Thomas Williams, Knt., 1000 acres as servitor, has let the most part to Captain Anthony Smith, who has promised to perform the conditions required. Sir John Bourchier, Knt., and Captain Francis Cooke, 1000 acres apiece as servitors. Sir John Bourchier is providing materials for building. Lieutenant Charles Poynts, 200 acres as servitor, has provided timber and materials for buildings.

[Condition of natives' proportions detailed.]

County of Cavan.—Sir Oliver Lambert, 2000 acres as servitor in Clanmahon, is providing materials but has built nothing.   Captain William Lyons and Lieut. Joseph, 1500 acres as servitors, have done no work.   Lieut. Atkinson and Lieut. Russen, 500 acres apiece, have done nothing but taken possession.   Sir William Tathe, Knt., 1000 acres as servitor in B. Castle Rame, has taken possession, but done nothing.   Sir Edmond Fetiplace, 1000 acres, has taken possession, done nothing else.   Captain John Ridgway, 1000 acres.   [Preparations described.]   120 great oaks have been brought from Fermanagh 30 miles from here, and more ready framed, being 280 garron loads from Bealturbert ; has made a watercourse for mill in stormy and rocky ground which cost him 25 £ as he says.   Has agreed for 500 barrels of lime in Meath to be brought him upon demand.   Has removed five Irish houses near his castle and built two other Irish houses in the Great Island.   Has an English millwright, smith, and farrier with their wives and families and necessary tools, and an English and Irish house carpenter with their wives and families, 2 or 3 other families of several trades, and has contracted at Bealturbert for a boat for use at Lough Rawre.   Lieut. Carth, 500 acres as servitor, and has taken possession, but done nothing else.   Sir Thomas Ashe, Knt., and his brother John, 750 acres in the Barony of Tullaghgarvy are building a bawn of sods and earth with a good large ditch at a place called Dromhyle, and intend to draw water from the lough adjoining to compass the same ; have drawn a watercourse two miles long to a place where they purpose to make a mill.   Have made preparations for building a good house, and will have their materials ready next spring.   Mr. Brent Moor and Mr. Arthur Moor, 1500 acres ; have taken possession but done nothing. Sir George Græmes and Sir Richard Græmes, 1000 acres apiece in the Barony of Tolehagh as servitors, have taken possession but done nothing.   Captain Hugh Colme and Walter Talbot, 1500 acres as servitors, have built a strong timber house and two other wattled houses, felled 40 timber trees, no other work.   [Progress of natives in County Cavan detailed.]

The servitors being charged by us with backwardness in having done so little, answered for the most part that they had not taken out their patents until the end of Candlemass term last, and that by reason the British do yet retain natives (who ought to be their tenants) they are disabled to put things forward as otherwise they would, but they will go roundly in hand with their works this next spring as they have promised us.

Signed Arthur Chichester, G. Carew, Th. Ridgway, R. Wingfield, Ol. Lambart.

A note how the Plantation goes forward in Farmanoch, and what the Undertakers have done there, and their proceedings.

(1). Barony of Lorge.—First, Sir Edward Blennerhassett, whose son as agent for his father is there, and with him six persons, of which two have their wives, but whether they are to be leaseholders or freeholders he knoweth not until his father's coming.   They are all well armed.   They have made one English house, with three rooms beneath, a chimney and an oven with a loft, and part of the house is already thatched; some boards are already sawed for the loft and about fifteen trees felled and squared.   For cattle they have four mares and a horse, and have brought a dozen head of cattle or thereabout.   For lime and stone I see none.

(2). Thomas Blennerhassett has with him six persons, one a joiner, another a carpenter, and three other workmen with one tenant.   He has built a boat, and has broken stones for lime and some burnt; and thirty trees felled; some squared and sawed; a fair large Irish house, with windows and rooms after the English manner, wherein is a new kitchen with a stone chimney, and an oven.   For cattle three horses, a mare and some thirteen head of other cattle.

(3). Barony of Clankelly.—Thomas Flowerdew, has with him six persons one a carpenter, others freeholders or lease-holders; has built an Irish house with a chimney at the end, made of wattles, contrived in two rooms, and a frame for a timber house of birch, most part of it to be set up within a Danes fort.   He has a plow of mares and garrons, two English horses, an English mare, one cow, with some three or four bullocks for their provision, and some few arms.

(4). Sir Hugh Worral has his brother there taking up his rent, but as yet, nothing else goes forward.

(5). Mr. Sudborough has with him eight men well armed, including two sons, and one, Mr. Stookes a lease-holder; he has contrived an Irish house into three rooms, and built a wattled chimney in it.   He has one plough of mares and garrons, an English horse and mare, and 20 head of cows.

(6). Robert Culvert has with him six persons furnished well with pieces and pikes, and one leaseholder ; has built an Irish house in three rooms and a wattled chimney in the end.   He has a plough of garrons and three English horses, and about fifteen cows ; twenty trees felled towards building.

(7). Barony of Knockninny.—Lord Burleigh.   His agent, Mr. Mildron, has 20 men well furnished with pikes and pieces ; has a house built with six couples, the ends with a double chimney in the middle ; 108 trees felled, and two kilns of lime burnt of the stones of Castleske.   Cattle: 40 cows and two ploughs of garrons and horses.

(8). Sir John Wisherd, is newly come over with some 15 persons well arrived ; has two ploughs, is now sowing wheat ; and likeliest to go forward of any of the undertakers.

(9). Barony of Terlagh.—Sir John Hume's man is there receiving his rent and duties, but nothing done.

(10). Mr. Hamleton has come lately, and with him 10 people, with 14 garrons and horses, and is buying cattle daily; is about to set up a plow or two instantly.   As yet nothing built.

(11). Mr. Dunbar's brother is there taking up his duties and rent, but doth nothing else that I see.

For all the rest some of them came and saw the land and went their ways, and what order they took I know not, and what is above written is all that I have seen.

Witness my hand,

22nd September, 1611.   PHILLIP GATISFETH.

A second commission was appointed to visit the settlements a few years after Chichester's inspection in 1611, but its members performed their duties in such an unsatisfactory manner that in 1618 Captain Nicholas Pynnar was appointed to visit all the "undertakers," and make a detailed report of the number of men and houses found in each settlement, the nature and extent of the improvements made, and the provisions for defence available to the British settlers in case of an armed uprising on the part of the native Irish. This work was performed by Captain Pynnar in the following year, and from his exhaustive report on the same the following abstract has been in part prepared (see *Carew Manuscripts, 1603-1624*, pp. 392-423; also, Harris's *Hibernica*):

ABSTRACT OF NICHOLAS PYNNAR'S SURVEY IN 1619

I.—SCOTCH UNDERTAKERS

COUNTY OF ARMAGH: PRECINCT OF FEWES

1. 2000 acres, Archibald Acheson (grantee from Sir James Douglas): stone bawn built; castle begun; 4 freeholders, 20 lessees, 5 cottagers, 7 houses, total 29 families who, with their undertenants, are able to produce 144 men with arms; also built the town of Clancarny containing 29 British tenants.

2. 1000 acres, Henry Acheson: stone bawn and house built; 2 freeholders, 17 lessees and a great number of other tenants; able to produce 30 men with arms.

3. 1000 acres, John Hamilton (grantee of James Craig): stone bawn built; 2 freeholders [Henry and Ralph Grindell and John Courtiouse], 6 lessees [among them Robert Elliott], 12 cottagers ; able to produce 30 men with arms.

4. 1000 acres, John Hamilton (grantee of William Lawder): stone bawn built, with house; 2 freeholders, 5 lessees, 10 cottagers, 7 houses; able to produce 30 men with arms.

5. 500 acres, John Hamilton (grantee of Claude Hamilton, who had been obliged to give up 500 acres of his original proportion to the Dean of Armagh): stone bawn and six houses near; 1 freeholder, 4 lessees, 5 cottagers; able to produce 22 men with arms. [John Hamilton's tenants in 1617 were: William Hope, John Grane, Edward Irwinge, Matthew Gamble, Cornelius McKernan, Andrew Bell, David Arkles, John Hamilton, John Davidson, Alexander Sym, Patrick Ritchie, Fergus Fleck, Eliza Grier, John Hamilton the elder, Cuthbert Grier, Robert Gilmore, Adam Rae, David Leetch, Robert Hamilton, Archibald Grame, John Willie, William Bell, Robert Hamilton, Henry Grindall, John Hamilton the elder of Dromanish, and his son John, Adam Colte, John Johnstone, Patrick Graunton, George Parker, Henry Hunter, John Deans, John Trumble, John Kirk, Francis Carruthers, James Moffat, Raulfe Grindell, Thomas Courtiouse, Henry Grindell, Gilbert Kennedy, Laurence Shirloe, Robert Ferguson, John Browne, John Ferguson, Thomas Pringle, Archbauld Grier, John Hall, George Gamble, Owen O'Corr, Cormack O'Corr, Robert Elliott, Alexander Grier, Robert Allen, John Allen, and Bryanbane O'Neale.]

This made a total in Fewes precinct of 11 freeholders, 52 lessees, 32 cottagers; able to produce, with their undertenants, 256 men with arms.

COUNTY OF TYRONE: PRECINCT OF MOUNTJOY

1. 3500 acres, Andrew Stewart: castle thatched ; 7 freeholders, 12 lessees; able to produce, with their undertenants, 80 men with arms. [In 1628 portions were sold to Gilbert Kennedy and John Collis. Christopher Harrison was the first purchaser from the landlord.]

2. 1000 acres, Andrew Stewart, Jr. (transferred from Robert Stewart): building bawn and castle; 2 freeholders, 8 lessees; able to produce 32 men with arms.

3. 1800 acres, Robert Heyborne (Hepburne): stone house and bawn; 6 freeholders, 3 lessees, 10 houses; able to produce 26 men with arms. [In 1620, portions of this land were sold to Thomas Averell, John Lyford,

Michael Lawrence, Robert Edmonston, John Coulson, Henry Clarke, and William Ploughman; and later, before 1629, the remainder was conveyed to Henry Stewart.]

4. 1000 acres, Alexander Sanderson (transferred from George Crawford): stone bawn and house; 5 freeholders, 4 lessees, 7 cottagers; able to produce 36 men with arms. [His son, Archibald, sold a portion of this estate to John Madder in 1639.]

5. 1000 acres, Alexander Richardson (transferred from Bernard Lindsey): stone bawn and timber house; 2 freeholders, 4 lessees, 11 cottagers; able to produce 39 men with arms.

6. 1000 acres, Robert Lindsey's widow: earth bawn, timber house, 2 freeholders, 8 lessees, 12 cottagers; able to produce 30 men with arms.

7. 1000 acres, David Kennedy: stone bawn containing timber house; 2 freeholders, 5 lessees, 9 cottagers, 12 houses; able to produce 36 men with arms. [Sold to John Syminton before 1630.]

Total in Mountjoy Precinct, 28 freeholders, 52 lessees, 39 cottagers; able to produce 311 men with arms.

COUNTY OF TYRONE : PRECINCT OF STRABANE

1. 3000 acres, James Hamilton, Earl of Abercorn : a strong castle built ; and about it a town of 80 houses containing 120 families ; 12 freeholders, 20 lessees, 53 townsmen ; able to produce 286 men with arms. [An inquisition taken at Strabane, 16 August, 1693, mentions the following tenants as having holdings in the town of Strabane, viz., Anne Newburgh, William Henderson, James and Patrick Hamilton, Oliver McCasland, Samuel Lawes, Robert Robinson, John Anderson, Andrew Parke, Walter McFarland, John Love, James McGee, and Thomas Holmes.]

2. 2000 acres, Claude Hamilton's estate : stone bawn containing a good castle ; 6 freeholders, 14 lessees, 6 houses ; able to produce 50 men with arms.

3. 2000 acres, Sir Robert Newcomen, Knt. (transferred from James Clapen): castle and bawn being built, and town of 14 houses ; 4 freeholders, 9 lessees, 12 cottagers ; able to produce 48 men with arms.

4. 1500 acres, James Hamilton, Earl of Abercorn (transferred from Sir Thomas Boyd) : bawn and large strong castle begun ; 3 freeholders, 10 lessees ; able to produce 100 men with arms.

5. 2500 acres, Sir George Hamilton : a bawn of stone, and village of 10 houses on 1000 acres ; bawn, house, and village of 30 houses on 1500 acres ; 6 freeholders, 25 lessees, 12 townsmen ; able to produce 93 men with arms.

6. 1000 acres, Sir John Drommond, Knt. : a stone bawn containing a timber house ; village of 10 houses and water-mill near ; 30 British men. [Among these were John Grime, John McGowan, William Reade, William Sharpe, Patrick Smythe, John Crosby, William Crosby, William Munteeth, John Wood, Thomas Gryme, Patrick Brum, Thomas Beane, John McAulay.]

7. 1500 acres, Sir George Hamilton, and Sir William Stewart (transferred from James Haig) : no improvements, but said to be 8 British families on the estate.

Total in Strabane Precinct, 31 freeholders, 78 lessees, 95 cottagers and townsmen ; able to produce 607 men with arms.

COUNTY OF DONEGAL : PRECINCT OF PORTLOUGH

1. 3000 acres, Duke of Lennox : a very strong castle, built of lime and stone, but no freeholders. The land well inhabited and full of people.

2. 1000 acres, Sir John Colquhoun, Laird of Luss (transferred from Sir

Walter Stewart) : stone bawn, with a poor house ; 2 freeholders, 3 lessees, 5 cottagers ; able to produce 26 men.   [This estate was held in 1662 by Humphrey and Robert Galbraith who sold it back in 1664 to Sir John Calhoun, son of the Laird of Luss.]

3. 1000 acres, Alexander McAula : stone house and bawn ; 2 freeholders, 9 lessees ; able to produce 30 men with arms.

4. 1000 acres, John Cunningham : a stone bawn and house ; village of 26 houses and water-mill ; 2 freeholders, 12 lessees ; able to produce 50 men with arms.   [On November 1, 1614, John Cunningham leased several parcels of his lands to the following persons : James Robbin, Robert Hunter, John Martin, William Boyle, James Patterson, Alexander McKilchany, John Plowright, John Molsed, Robert Allane, John Fyeff, Donnell McKilmun, John Wilson, Bernard Coningham, James Boyl, John Bryce, William Sare, Donnell Gillaspick, John Fleminge, Donnell McEvene, William McCassack, Alexander Colewell, John Wigton, John Ramsay, Stephen Woolson, Andrew Calwell, William Coningham, Andrew Coningham, Robert Boyl, Donnell Connell. (*Inquisitions of Ulster, Donegal, 5, Car. I.*).]

5. 1000 acres, William Stewart, Laird of Dunduff : stone bawn and house, 2 freeholders, 8 lessees ; able to produce 40 men with arms.   [On the 10th of June, 1614, William Stewart, Laird of Dunduff, set off several portions of his lands to the following persons : Archibald Thomson, John Coningham, John Hood, James Dunsayer, William Fullerton, Gilbert Kennyday, John MacKay, John Smyth, Alexander Lokard, Alexander Hunter, James Sayre, Walter Stewart, William Smelley, Thomas Lodge, Hugh O'Douherty, Con O'Donnell, Arthur Stewart, James Maghan, Dermont O'Brallaghan, Shane O'Brallaghan, Killegroome O'Derny, Anthony Stewart, gent., Toole McVegany, Michael McLoghery, Owen Macintire. (*Inquisitions of Ulster, Donegal, 9, Car. I.*).]

6. 2000 acres, Sir James Cunningham, Laird of Glangarnocke : there is built here a little bawn of lime and stone and a small house in it ; near to the bawn there is a small village, consisting of 12 houses inhabited with British tenants ; no Irish on the land ; said to be able to produce 40 men.

7. 1000 acres, Cuthbert Cunningham : nothing built by him ; 6 freeholders, 9 lessees, 15 cottagers, able to produce 80 men with arms.

8. 1000 acres, James Cunningham : stone house and bawn ; 2 freeholders, 6 lessees, 15 cottagers ; able to produce 42 men with arms. [On the 1st of May, 1613, James Coningham, or Cunningham, set out a large quantity of his lands to the persons whose names are underwritten : Alexander Dunne, John Dunne, Donnell McKym, John Dunne, junior, John Younge, William Hendry, Alexander Grynney William Stewart, William Valentyne, Hugh Moore, William Moore, David Kennedy, John Watson, Robert Paterson, William Ekyn, George Blacke, Andrew Smythe, James Gilmore, William Gaate [Galt], George Peere [Pery], John McKym, Andrew Browne, William Sutherland, William Rankin, John Smythe, John Purveyance, John Harper, Hugh Lokard, Thomas Scott, John Browne, John Roger, William Teyse, [Teese], Donnell McEredy, David Kennedy, William Valentyne, William Arnett, Andrew Arnett, John Alexander, John Hutchine, Peter Stevenson, John Hamilton, Edward Homes, George Leich. (*Inquisitions of Ulster, Donegal, 5, Car. I.*).]

9. 1000 acres, Sir John Stewart : neither castle nor bawn built, but the land well inhabited with British tenants.

Total in Portlough Precinct, 16 freeholders, 47 lessees, 35 cottagers ; able to produce 268 men.

[But slight improvements having been made by the original undertakers, the whole 10,000 acres of this precinct was patented to John Murray, afterwards Earl of Annandale, in 1620].

1. 2000 acres, John Murray (transferred from Robert Maclellan) : a bawn and small castle ; leased to Captain Thomas Dutton who had recently arrived, with 6 English families.

2. 1000 acres, John Murray (transferred from George Murray) : nothing built, and all the land inhabited with Irish.

3. 1500 acres, John Murray (transferred from William Stewart) : leased to James Toodie and others ; 11 lessees ; said to be 30 families on the land ; able to produce 40 men with arms.

4. 1000 acres, John Murray (transferred from Patrick McKee) : a bawn of stone ; 23 families planted on this land, all of British birth ; able to produce 40 men.

5. 1000 acres, John Murray (transferred from James McCullogh) : leased to James McCullogh ; very few British on the land.

6. 1000 acres, John Murray (transferred from Alexander Dunbar): leased to Rowland Cogwell ; a stone bawn and castle ; 2 leaseholders, having under them 10 British families.

7. 1000 acres, John Murray (transferred from Patrick Vans) : leased to William Hamilton and others ; a stone bawn and very strong castle ; 28 families of British birth said to be on the land ; able to produce 50 men with arms.

8. 1000 acres, John Murray (transferred from Alexander Cunningham) : leased to Alexander Cunningham : strong stone bawn ; very few British tenants, but many Irish ones.

Total in Boylagh Precinct, 56 tenants ; able to produce 130 men with arms.

1. 3000 acres, Sir James Balfour (transferred from Michael Balfour, father of James) : great number of men at work building a castle and bawn ; schoolhouse built ; church under way ; town of 40 houses near the castle, all inhabited with British tenants ; able to produce 82 men with arms.

2. 1500 acres, Sir Stephen Butler (transferred from Michael Balfour, Jr.): 12 lessees, able to produce 15 men with arms.

3. 1500 acres, Sir Stephen Butler (transferred from Sir John Wishart) ; a stone house and bawn ; 17 lessees, able to produce 66 men with arms.

4. 1000 acres, George Adwick, guardian of David Crichton, son of Thomas Crichton, deceased (transferred from Thomas Moneypenny) : bawn of stone enclosing a poor thatched house ; 6 freeholders, 4 lessees.

5. 1000 acres, George Adwick, agent for Sir Stephen Butler (grantee of James Trayle) : no British tenants.

6. 1000 acres, Sir Stephen Butler (grantee of George Smelhome) : stone house and bawn ; 3 lessees ; [Richard Buckland, Robert Montgomerye, Charles Waterhouse] ; able to produce 15 men.

Total in Knockninny Precinct, 6 freeholders, 76 lessees; able to produce 178 men with arms.

1. 2000 acres, Sir John Home : castle and bawn ; a village near containing 24 families ; 4 freeholders, 9 lessees, 11 cottagers ; able to produce 30 men with arms.

2. 1500 acres, Malcolm Hamilton (grantee of Sir Robert Hamilton) : a strong castle, but no bawn; 3 freeholders, [Robert Weire, Gabriel Coningham, and James Somerville] ; 11 lessees, [Daniel Elliott, Gabriel Coningham, Jr., Alexander Coningham, Matthew Chambers, David Cathcart, Gilbert Lainge, John Watson, William Crawford, John Hall, George Deinbane, John Greer, William Hall and Thomas Cranston] ; able to produce 77 men with arms.

3. 1000 acres, John Archdale (grantee from James Gibb) : stone bawn and house ; 6 freeholders, 5 lessees, 3 cottagers; able to produce 26 men with arms.

4. 1000 acres, Sir William Cole (grantee of Jerome Lindsay) : stone castle and bawn ; windmill ; 2 freeholders, 11 lessees ; able to produce 34 men. [Among William Cole's grantees in 1613 were Thomas Shaw of Enniskillen, Clinton Ogle, and Richard Orme.]

5. 1500 acres, Sir John Home or Hume (grantee of William Fowler) : nothing built ; 3 freeholders, 12 lessees ; able to produce 30 men.

6. 1000 acres, George Home, agent for his father, Sir John Home (grantee of Alexander Home) : stone bawn ; 3 lessees.

7. 1000 acres, John Dunbar : stone bawn and 2 water-mills ; 2 freeholders, 7 lessees ; able to produce 60 men with arms.

Total in Magheriboy Precinct, 20 freeholders, 58 lessees, 14 cottagers ; able to produce 257 men.

COUNTY OF CAVAN : PRECINCT OF TULLOHONCO

1. 2000 acres, Jane Hamilton, guardian of Francis Hamilton (grandson of Sir Alexander Hamilton) : strong castle and bawn built ; 6 freeholders [in 1629 George Griffin, Francis Cofyn, Stephen Hunt, and Richard Lighterfoote were among the freeholders] ; 25 lessees. [The inquisition of 1629 names four of these : Stephen and Susan Hunt, Adam Maunderson, John McVittye, and John Acheson.]

2. 1000 acres, Jane Hamilton, widow of Sir Claude Hamilton : no castle built, but a town consisting of 22 houses.

3. 1000 acres, } James Craig (grantee of Alexander and John Ach-
4. 1000 acres, } mootie) : stone castle and bawn ; 5 freeholders, 7 lessees, 21 cottagers ; able to produce 100 men.

5. 1000 acres, Archibald Acheson (grantee of John Brown) : stone bawn ; 2 freeholders, 19 lessees ; able to produce 28 men.

Total in Tullohonco Precinct, 13 freeholders, 51 lessees ; able to produce 180 men.

COUNTY OF CAVAN : PRECINCT OF CLANCHY

1. 3000 acres, Sir James Hamilton (grantee of Esme Stuart) : a very large, strong castle 28 x 50, five stories high, and stone bawn 80 feet square ; 8 freeholders [Richard Hadsor, John Kennedie, John Hamilton, Richard Lighterfoote, Edmond Stafford, and three others] ; 8 lessees [Edward Bailie, John Hamilton, John Loch, William Price, George Steele, James Stewart, and two others] ; 25 cottagers ; able to produce 80 men with arms.

2. 1000 acres, William Baillie : stone bawn ; castle building ; 2 freeholders [Edward and James Baillie], 4 lessees [in 1629 they were John Steivinson, John Baillie, James Teate, David Barbour, Gilbert Cuthbertson, John Hamilton, William Rae, and Walter Miller], 4 cottagers ; able to produce 28 men with arms.

3. 1000 acres, John Hamilton (grantee of John Ralston) ; stone house

and 2 bawns, one 100 feet square ; village of 8 houses ; water-mill with 5 houses adjoining ; 2 freeholders [David Barber and David McCullagh], 6 lessees [Alexander Davyson, 1618 ; Alexander Anderson [Henderson] 1619 ; John Wyllie, 1627 ; John Musgrave, 1618 ; John and Patrick Fenlay (Finlay), 1620 ; Robert Taillor, 1619 ; John Deanes, 1620 ; Oliver Udney, 1621], 7 cottagers ; able to produce 40 men with arms.

4. 1000 acres, William Hamilton : stone house and bawn ; village of 5 houses ; 2 freeholders, 6 lessees, 6 cottagers ; able to produce 30 men.

Total in Clanchy Precinct, 14 freeholders, 24 lessees, 42 cottagers ; able to produce 178 men.

II.—ENGLISH UNDERTAKERS

COUNTY OF ARMAGH : PRECINCT OF ONEILAN

1. 1000 acres, Richard Roulstone : bawn of sods containing small house ; village of 9 houses ; 2 freeholders, 8 lessees ; able to produce 24 men with arms.

2. 2000 acres, Francis Sacheverill : 3 freeholders, 18 lessees ; able to produce 50 men with arms.

3. 1500 acres, William Brownlow (son of John Brownlow, deceased) : house of brick and stone ; timber bawn ; 3 mills ; town built, containing 42 houses, all inhabited with English families ; 5 freeholders, 52 lessees ; able to produce 100 men with arms. [This report also includes William Brownlow's original proportion of 1000 acres.]

4. 1000 acres, Sir Oliver St. John (grantee of James Matchett) : 2 timber bawns containing houses ; village of 5 houses ; 5 freeholders, 8 lessees, 4 cottagers ; able to produce 30 men with arms.

5. 2000 acres, Michael Obbyns (grantee of William Powell) : bawn of sods and boards, with brick house ; 4 houses near ; 5 freeholders, 15 lessees ; able to produce 40 men with arms.

6. 1500 acres, John Dillon : brick house half built ; no bawn ; two villages ; 3 freeholders, 26 lessees ; able to produce 40 men with arms.

7. 1000 acres, William Brownlow : a strong stone house. [See also proportion No. 3 above.]

8. 1500 acres, William Stanhowe : nothing built ; not above three or four poor Englishmen upon the land. All inhabited with Irish.

9. 2000 acres, John Heron : two small bawns of earth ; several houses ; 1 freeholder, 12 lessees ; able to produce 26 men with arms.

10. 3000 acres, Sir Anthony Cope : bawn of stone ; two watermills and one windmill ; 6 freeholders, 34 lessees, 7 cottagers ; able to produce 80 men with arms. [Symon Gevers, George Bridge, and John Adams were among these.]

Total in Oneilan Precinct : 30 freeholders, 173 lessees, 11 cottagers ; able to produce 390 men with arms.

COUNTY OF TYRONE : PRECINCT OF CLOGHER

1. 2000 acres, Sir Thomas Ridgeway : stone castle and bawn ; a town built containing 15 houses ; 2 freeholders, 18 lessees ; able to produce 56 men with arms.

2. 2000 acres, John Leigh : a house and bawn of stone built ; small village containing 8 houses ; 8 freeholders, 12 lessees, 21 cottagers ; able to produce 48 men with arms.

3. 1500 acres, Walter Edney and Thomas Edney : stone house and

bawn (60 x 140) built; castle begun; 5 freeholders, 10 lessees, 4 cottagers; able to produce 60 men with arms.

4. 1000 acres, George Ridgeway: a bawn of stone but no house in it; 1 freeholder, 10 lessees; able to produce 26 men with arms.

5. 1000 acres, William Parsons: large stone house and bawn; a village containing 9 houses; 2 freeholders, 9 lessees, 4 cottagers; able to produce 38 men with arms.

6. 1000 acres, Sir Gerrard Lowther, Knight (grantee of William Turvin): bawn of stone; leased to Mr. Pringle living in a poor cabin, who claims to have twenty tenants.

7. 2000 acres, Sir William Stewart, Knight (grantee of Edward Kingsmill): castle and large bawn (120 x 240) of stone building; a village with 9 houses built; 5 freeholders, 9 lessees, 8 cottagers; able to produce 64 men with arms.

8. 2000 acres, Sir William Cope (transferred from William Glegge): a stone bawn built 80 feet square, and a small house within; but no English settler on the land.

Total in Clogher Precinct: 23 freeholders, 68 lessees, 37 cottagers; able to produce 292 men with arms.

COUNTY OF TYRONE: PRECINCT OF OMAGH

1. 3000 acres, Lady Audley (widow of George Tuchet, Lord Audley): neither castle nor bawn on the land; 8 lessees, 3 cottagers; able to produce 11 men.

2. 2000 acres, Sir Marvin Tuchet: nothing built; said to have 64 tenants on this and his other estates.

3. 2000 acres, Sir Marvin Tuchet (grantee of Sir Ferdinand Tuchet): nothing built.

4. 2000 acres, Sir Marvin Tuchet (grantee from Edward Blunte) : stone house; rent-roll shows 64 British tenants on this and two preceding proportions.

5. 2000 acres, Sir John Davys: no bawn; two strong stone castles; 4 freeholders, 12 lessees; able to produce 30 men.

Total in Omagh Precinct: 4 freeholders, 20 lessees; able to produce 41 men.

COUNTY OF DONEGAL: PRECINCT OF LIFFER

1. 1500 acres, Peter Benson (conveyed from Henry Clare) : stone house and bawn; water-mill; village containing 10 houses; 5 freeholders, 19 lessees; able to produce 68 men with arms. [Among these tenants in 1616 were Robert Kilpatterick, James Kilpatterick, Archibald McMathe, James Maxwell, James Tate, John Ewart, Thomas Watson, George Newton, Ludovic Stubbins, Toole McDevitt, George Hilton, George Bailie, Richard Roper, James Read, Henry Preston, Thomas Preston, Donnell McKecoge, Charles Atkinson, Richard Babington, Edward Catherall, John Kilpatterick.]

2. 2000 acres, William Willson: large bawn and castle; a village of 10 houses; 6 freeholders, 14 lessees, 50 undertenants; able to produce 106 men.

3. 1500 acres, Sir John Kingsmill (grantee of Edward Russell): a stone house and bawn; village of 30 houses; 5 freeholders, 8 lessees; able to produce 36 men with arms.

4. 1500 acres, Sir John Kingsmill and William Willson (grantee of Sir

William Barnes) : strong bawn and house ; 6 freeholders, 6 lessees, 5 cottagers ; able to produce 46 men with arms.

5. 1000 acres, Captain Ralph Mansfield : stone house and bawn ; a village of 9 houses ; 2 freeholders, 16 lessees ; able to produce 46 men with
arms.

6. 2000 acres, Robert Davis (grantee from Sir Thomas Cornwall) : stone
house and bawn ; several small villages ; 4 freeholders, 28 lessees ; able to
produce 54 men with arms.

7. 2000 acres, Sir Ralph Bingley (grantee of Sir Thomas [or Robert]
Remyington) : a strong castle ; 4 freeholders, 17 tenants ; able to produce
60 men with arms.

8. 2000 acres, Sir Ralph Bingley (grantee of Sir Maurice Berkeley) :
stone house ; brick bawn ; mill ; a village of 6 houses ; 7 freeholders, 12
lessees, 10 cottagers ; able to produce 64 men with arms.

9. 1500 acres, Sir Thomas Coates : brick ready for building house and
bawn ; village of 6 houses ; 4 freeholders, 9 lessees, 6 cottagers ; able to
produce 56 men with arms.

Total in Liffer Precinct : 43 freeholders, 129 lessees, 21 cottagers ; able
to produce 536 men with arms.

COUNTY OF FERMANAGH : PRECINCT OF CLANCALLY

1. 1000 acres, Sir Hugh Wirrall : a bawn of stone built 60 feet square ;
and small stone house within, standing waste ; no tenants.

2. 1000 acres, Edward Hatton (grantee of Robert Bogas) : strong stone
house and bawn ; water-mill ; village of 10 houses ; 2 freeholders [Nicholas
Willoughby was one of these in 1629], 5 lessees, 8 cottagers ; able to produce
20 men with arms.

3. 1000 acres, George Ridgeway (grantee of Robert Calvert) : a stone
bawn building ; 1 freeholder, 7 lessees ; able to produce 12 men with arms.

4. 1000 acres, John Sedborough : a poor sod bawn ; 6 lessees, said to
be 12 more ; able to produce 24 men. [The names of several British tenants are mentioned in the *Inquisitions of Ulster, Fermanagh (40 and 55)*,
Car. I., as occupying lands on this proportion about the year 1630 : Hugh
Stokes, Clinton Maunde, Robert Allen, Faithful Teate, Christopher Gas-
coine, Robert Newcomen, William Stamers, Stephen Allen, Randulph Daye,
John and Thomas Tybbals, Toby Vesie, Joseph Dickinson.]

5. 1000 acres, Thomas Flowerdewe : small stone house and large stone
bawn ; a village of 6 houses ; 2 freeholders, 14 lessees ; able to produce 40
men.

Total in Clancally Precinct : 5 freeholders, 44 lessees, 8 cottagers ; able
to produce 96 men with arms.

COUNTY OF FERMANAGH : PRECINCT OF LURG AND COOLEMAKERNAN

1. 1000 acres, Thomas Flowerdewe : nothing built.

2. 2000 acres, Thomas Blenerhassett ; stone bawn and house ; church
in building ; village of 6 houses ; 4 freeholders, 3 lessees ; able to produce
26 men.

3. 2000 acres, Sir Edward Blenerhassett : stone house and strong
stone bawn ; village of 9 houses ; 4 freeholders, 22 British families ; able to
produce 40 men with arms.

4. 1000 acres, John Archdale : bawn and house ; water-mill ; 2 villages
containing 8 houses each ; 6 freeholders [in 1629 they were William and

Thomas Lawton, William Johnson, Owen Griffith, Thomas Clarke, Edward Moore, Thomas Moore, David Byas], 10 lessees, 4 cottagers; able to produce 42 men with arms.

5. 1000 acres, Sir Gerard Lowther (grantee through Harrington Sutton of Edward Warde): stone house and bawn; water-mill; village of 10 houses; 2 freeholders, 12 lessees; able to produce 28 men with arms.

6. 1000 acres, Sir Gerard Lowther (grantee of Thomas Barton): stone bawn, but no house; 5 freeholders, 1 lessee.

7. 1000 acres, Edward Sibthorp and Henry Flower (conveyed from Henry Honyng): stone bawn, standing waste and used as a pound for cattle; a village containing 14 houses; 2 lessees.

Total for Lurg and Coolemakernan: 21 freeholders, 28 lessees, 4 cottagers; able to produce 136 men with arms.

COUNTY OF CAVAN : PRECINCT OF LOUGHTY

1. 2000 acres, Thomas Waldron (heir to Sir Richard Waldron, deceased): bawn of sods, stone castle, windmill; town of 31 houses; 5 freeholders, 17 lessees, 31 cottagers; able to produce 82 men with arms.

2. 2000 acres, John Fish: very strong castle and bawn; 2 villages of 10 houses each, built of stone; 4 freeholders, 18 lessees, 14 cottagers; able to produce 60 men with arms.

3. 2760 acres, Sir Stephen Butler: very strong castle and bawn; one fulling mill; two corn mills; the town of Belturbet building; 15 freeholders, 76 lessees; able to produce 139 men with arms.

4. 2000 acres, Sir George Mainwaring (grantee of Sir Nicholas Lusher): brick house, stone bawn; village of 7 houses; 3 freeholders [Henry Chesman, 1612; John Taylor, 1613; Walter Bassett, 1615,] 21 lessees [Nicholas Lysley, 1622; Thomas Jackson, 1616; Robert Gamble, 1617; Richard Castledine, 1618; Edward Lockington, 1618; Thomas Guye, 1627; John Broadhurst, 1616; Richard Nutkin, 1616; John Reley, 1616; Robert Newton, 1616; Bartholomew Jackson, 1616; Roger Moynes, 1629]; able to produce 48 men.

5. 1500 acres, Sir Hugh Wyrrall: stone house, no bawn; 3 freeholders, 5 lessees, 8 cottagers; able to produce 26 men.

6. 1500 acres, John Taylor: castle and bawn built; village of 14 houses; 7 freeholders, 7 lessees, 10 cottagers; able to produce 54 men with arms.

7. 1500 acres, Peter Ameas: stone house and bawn; a village of 7 houses; 4 freeholders, 7 lessees; able to produce 30 men.

Total for Loughty Precinct: 41 freeholders, 101 lessees, 63 cottagers; able to produce 439 men with arms.

III.—THE LONDONERS' PLANTATION

Londonderry: 92 houses, containing 102 families.

Colerane: Town so poorly inhabited that there are not men to man a sixth part of the walls.

3210 acres, Goldsmiths' Hall: John Freeman, lessee; stone bawn (100 x 100) and castle; 12 houses, 6 freeholders, 24 lessees; able to produce 90 men with arms.

3210 acres, Grocers' Hall: Edward Rone had this but died; bawn building; 8 houses, for most part inhabited with Irish.

3210 acres, Fishmongers' Hall: James Higgens, agent for the Company;

stone bawn (125 x 125) and house ; 15 houses and church ; 6 freeholders, 28 lessees ; able to produce 40 men with arms.

3210 acres, Ironmongers' Hall : George Cammynge, agent for the Company ; brick bawn, strong castle ; 8 houses, an infinite number of Irish who give such great rents that the English cannot get any lands.

3210 acres, Mercers' Hall : Mr. Varnon, agent for the Company ; stone castle and bawn (120 x 120) ; 6 houses ; 46 town lands let to Irish of the sect of Clandonnells, the wickedest men in all the country.

3210 acres, Merchant Tailors' Hall : Valentine Hartopp, lessee ; strong castle, no bawn ; church ; 7 stone houses ; 6 freeholders, 18 lessees, 5 cottagers ; able to produce 40 men with arms.

3210 acres, Haberdashers' Hall : Sir Robert McLellan, lessee ; strong castle, no bawn ; able to produce 80 men with arms.

3210 acres, Clothworkers' Hall : Sir Robert McLellan, lessee ; stone castle ; all inhabited with Irish.

3210 acres, Skinners' Hall : Lady Dodington, widow of Sir Edward Dodington, deceased, lessee ; 2 strong castles and stone bawns ; 2 villages of 12 houses each ; 7 freeholders, 8 lessees, 12 cottagers ; able to produce 80 men with arms.

3210 acres, Vintners' Hall : Baptist Jones, lessee ; brick bawn and 2 good houses within ; 10 houses, all inhabited with English ; 76 men with arms.

3210 acres, Drapers' Hall : William Russell, agent for the Company ; stone bawn and castle ; 12 houses ; the tenants have no estates.

3210 acres, Salters' Hall : Hugh Sayer, lessee ; stone bawn, castle building ; 7 houses near bawn, 9 houses at Salters' Town inhabited by British families, but none have estates.

Total : 31 freeholders, 99 lessees, 17 cottagers ; able to produce 406 men with arms.

IV.—SERVITORS

COUNTY OF ARMAGH : PRECINCT OF ORIER

1. 1000 acres, Sir Gerald Moore : a stone bawn and small house, inhabited by an Irishman.

2. 1500 acres, Sir Oliver St. John : castle and stone bawn ; a town of 35 to 40 houses built [Ballymore], inhabited with English tenants.

3. 500 acres, Sir John Davies (grantee of Lord Audley) : nothing built ; no English tenants.

4. 1000 acres, Captain Anthony Smith (transferred from Sir Thomas Williams) : stone house and bawn building.

5. 2000 acres, Henry Bourchier (transferred from John Bourchier) : stone bawn and house built.

6. 200 acres, Charles Poyntz : a new brick bawn and house being built.

COUNTY OF TYRONE : PRECINCT OF DUNGANNON

1. 1640 acres, Sir Arthur Chichester : a stone fort built, 120 feet square ; 3 houses, inhabited by Englishmen ; also a town built containing a church and 21 houses inhabited by British tenants ; 30 English families.

2. 2000 acres, Sir Thomas Ridgeway : stone bawn, 160 feet square, timber house ; 3 English families.

3. 2000 acres, Sir Richard Wingfield : stone bawn and 2 houses ; church building ; 28 English families ; able to produce 30 men with arms.

4. 1000 acres, Sir Tobey Caulfield : very large and fine stone castle ;

water-mill; a town built near the bawn containing 15 English families; able to produce 20 men with arms.

5. 1000 acres, Sir Francis Roe : earth bawn, house of brick and stone ; 17 houses inhabited by British tenants.

6. 1000 acres, William Parsons : stone bawn and house ; one English family.

7. 480 acres, Sir Francis Ansley : sod bawn.

COUNTY OF DONEGAL : PRECINCT OF DOE AND FAWNETT
(NOW KILMACRENAN)

1. 1000 acres, Captain Paul Gore : a stone bawn and timber house built ; inhabited by an English family.

2. 1000 acres, Sir George Marburie (transferred from Patrick Crawford): stone bawn ; a town built [Letterkenny] containing 40 houses all inhabited by British tenants ; able to produce 50 men.

3. 1000 acres, John Wray (grantee of John Vaughan) : stone bawn and house ; some English families.

4. 1000 acres, John Kingsmill : stone bawn built, but no English on the land.

5. 1000 acres, Basil Brooke : a stone bawn and house and one Englishman.

6. 1000 acres, Sir William Stewart (transferred from Sir Edward Hansard) : stone house and bawn ; 8 British families ; able to produce 20 men with arms.

7. 172 acres, Lieut. Thomas Perkins : nothing built.

8. 1000 acres, Sir Thomas Chichester: clay bawn built, but fallen to waste.

9. 1256 acres, Henry Hart : a stone fort and house in which is an English family.

10. 1000 acres, Sir William Stewart (transferred from Sir Richard Hansard) : stone castle and bawn ; water-mill; church ; has built the market town of Ramelton containing 45 houses and 57 families.

11. 400 acres, Nathaniel Rowley (transferred from Lieut. Edward Ellis): nothing built.

12. 1000 acres, John Vaughan (transferred from Henry Vaughan) : a bawn built containing a stone house inhabited by an English gentleman.

13. 500 acres, Captain Sanford (transferred from Sir Richard Bingley) : stone castle and bawn ; 4 English families.

14. 108 acres, William Lynn (transferred from Lieut. George Gale) : nothing built.

15. 240 acres, William Lynn (transferred from Charles Grimsditche) : nothing built.

16. 528 acres, Nathaniel Rowley (transferred from Thomas Browne) : nothing built.

17. 1000 acres, Arthur Terrie : stone bawn and good house ; 6 English families : able to produce 10 men with arms.

COUNTY OF FERMANAGH : PRECINCT OF CLINAWLY

1. 1500 acres, Sir John Davys : a fair stone house built on the abbey lands, but no bawn.

2. 500 acres, Captain Samuel Harrison's widow ; nothing built.

3. 300 acres, Peter Mostin : nothing built.

COUNTY OF FERMANAGH :   PRECINCT OF COOLE AND TIRCANNADA

1. 1500 acres, Sir Henry Folliott : stone house and bawn ; water-mill ; a town of 11 houses inhabited with Scottish and English families.

2. 1000 acres, Captain Roger Atkinson : stone house and bawn ; water-mill, tucking-mill ; 2 freeholders.

3. 1000 acres, Sir William Cole : stone bawn ; water-mill : 7 lessees ; able to produce 18 men with arms.

4. 1000 acres, Captain Paul Gore : stone bawn and house ; 8 British families.

COUNTY OF CAVAN : PRECINCT OF TULLAGHAH

1. 2000 acres, Sir George and Sir Richard Grimes : a stone bawn built, containing a little house.

2. 1500 acres, Captain Hugh Culme and Walter Talbott : a strong bawn built, surrounding a stone castle.

3. 1000 acres, William Parsons : no buildings.

COUNTY OF CAVAN : PRECINCT OF CLONMAHONE

1. 2000 acres, Sir Oliver Lambert : stone house and large stone bawn ; 1 English family.

2. 1000 acres, Sir Oliver Lambert (grantee of Joseph Jones) : stone bawn 200 feet square ; small house ; 4 English families.

3. 500 acres, Captain Fleming : a stone bawn and house built, very strong.

4. 1000 acres, Archibald Moore (grantee of John Russell and Anthony Atkinson) : a strong sod bawn built containing an Irish house.

COUNTY OF CAVAN : PRECINCT OF CASTLE RAHEN

1. 400 acres, Sir John Elliott : stone bawn and small house; all inhabited by Irish.

2. 1000 acres, Captain Hugh Culme (grantee of John Ridgeway) : stone house and bawn ; town of 8 houses ; 12 English families.

3. 1000 acres, Sir Thomas Ashe (grantee of Sir William Taaffe) : an old castle new mended ; all the land inhabited by Irish.

4. 500 acres, Sir Thomas Ashe (grantee of Roger Garth) : sod bawn ; all inhabited by Irish.

5. 1000 acres, Sir Thomas Ashe (grantee of Edmund Fettiplace) : stone bawn ; all inhabited by Irish.

COUNTY OF CAVAN : PRECINCT OF TULLAGHGARVY

1. 750 acres, Sir Thomas Ashe and John Ashe : bawn of clay and stone ; all inhabited by Irish.

2. 1500 acres, Archibald Moore and Captain Hugh Culme (grantee of Brent Moore) : bawn and house ; 4 English families.

3. 2000 acres, Captain Richard Tirrell : strong stone bawn built.

Pynnar's *Brief of the General State of the Plantation for Persons Planted in the Several Counties.*

COUNTY OF CAVAN

Freeholders	68
Lessees for lives	20
Lessees for years	168
Cottagers	130
Families	386
Bodies of men	711

COUNTY OF FERMANAGH

Freeholders	59
Lessees for lives	10
Lessees for years	117
Cottagers	75
Families	321
Bodies of men	645

COUNTY OF DONEGAL

Freeholders	59
Lessees for lives	25
Lessees for years	217
Cottagers	46
Families that have no estates	70
Families in all	417
Bodies of men	1,106

COUNTY OF TYRONE

Freeholders	84
Lessees for lives	26
Lessees for years	183
Cottagers	154
Families	447
Bodies of men	2,469

COUNTY OF ARDMAGH

Freeholders	39
Lessees for lives	18
Lessees for years	190
Cottagers	43
Families	290
Bodies of men	642

COUNTY OF LONDON-DERRY

Freeholders	25
Lessees for years	78
Cottagers	16
Families	119
Bodies of men	642

THE WHOLE CONTENT OF THE SIX COUNTIES

Freeholders 334
Lessees for lives 99
Lessees for years................................. 1,013

Families....................................... 1,974
Bodies of men with arms [1].................... 6,215

May it please your Lordships,—I have in the book before written, set down all the particulars I find of the State of the Plantation of his Majesty's escheated Lands in Ulster now to stand.

And, First, it appears by the particulars, that in the Brittish Families within mentioned, there are 6,215 Bodies of Men ; but I may presume further to certify, partly by observing the Habitation of these Lands, and partly by conferring with some of knowledge among them, that upon occasion, there be found in those Lands at least 8,000 Men of Brittish Birth and Descent, to do his Majesty's Service for Defence thereof, though the fourth part of the Land is not fully inhabited.

Secondly,—It appears by the particulars, that there are now built within the Counties of Ardmagh, Tyrone, Donagall, Fermanagh, Cavan, and London-Derry, 107 Castles with Bawnes, 19 Castles without Bawnes, 42 Bawnes without Castles or Houses, and 1897 Dwelling Houses of Stone and Timber, after the English manner in Townreeds, besides very many such Houses in several parts which I saw not; and yet there is great want of Buildings upon their Lands, both for Townreeds and otherwise.   And I may say, that the abode and continuance of those Inhabitants upon the Lands is not yet made certain, although I have seen the Deeds made unto them.   My reason is, that many of the English Tenants do not yet plough upon the Lands, neither use Husbandrie, because I conceive they are fearful to Stock themselves with Cattle or Servants for those Labours.   Neither do the Irish use Tillage, for that they are also uncertain of their Stay upon the Lands; so that, by this means, the Irish ploughing nothing, do use greasing [2] ; the English very little; and were it not for the Scottish Tenants, which do plough in many places of the Country, those Parts may starve ; by Reason whereof the Brittish, who are forced to take their Lands at great Rates, do lie at the greater Rents, paid unto them by the Irish Tenants, who do grease their Land ; and if the Irish be put away with their Cattle, the Brittish must either forsake their Dwellings, or endure great distress on the suddain.   Yet the combination of the Irish is dangerous to them, by robbing them, and otherwise.   I observe the greatest number of Irish do dwell upon the Lands granted to the City of London ; which happeneth, as I take it, two ways.   First, There are five of the Proportions assigned to the several Companies, which are not yet estated to any Man, but are in the Hands of Agents ; who, finding the Irish more profitable than the Brittish Tenants, are unwilling to draw on the Brittish, perswading the Company that the Lands are mountainous and unprofitable, not regarding the future security of the whole ; Secondly, The other seven of the Proportions are leased to several persons for 61 years, and the Lessees do affirm that they are not bound to plant English, but may plant with what people they please ; neither is the City of London bound to do it by their Patents from his Majesty, as they say; and by these two actions, the Brittish that are now there, who have many of them built houses at their own charges, have no estates made unto them, which is such Discouragement

35

unto them, as they are minded to depart the Land; and without better Settlement will seek elsewhere, wherein it is very fit the City have Direction to take a present Course, that they may receive their assurances; and this being the Inconveniency, which in this Survey I have observed, further than what was set down formerly by Sir Josias Bodley's last Survey,[3] I have thought good to make the same known to your Lordships, submitting the further Consideration thereof to your Lordships' deep judgment.

NICHOLAS PYNNAR.

Besides the foregoing reports of Chichester and Pynnar the following brief muster returns have been preserved, which indicate the growth of the British settlements in Ulster during the first twenty years of the "plantation." George Alleyne was appointed Muster Master of Ulster, July 10, 1618, and the summary of his muster of men between the ages of eighteen and fifty made in that year is given in the *Calendar of State Papers for Ireland, 1615–1625*, pp. 220–230:

There be in the six escheated counties 197,000 acres. There appeared in all 1964 men. There ought to have appeared, according to the proportion or rate of 24 men to every 1000 acres within these six escheated counties 4728 as follows: Armagh, population 528—number appearing 238; Tyrone, population 1116—number appearing 393; London-derry, population 864—number appearing 610 (county 410; city, 100; Colerain, 100); Cavan, population 588—number appearing 539; Fermanagh, population 744—number appearing 184; Donegal, population 888—number appearing 0.

A muster of the city of Londonderry was taken by Sir Thomas Phillips and Richard Hadsor, the King's commissioners, on Sep. 20, 1622, of all the inhabitants with their servants residing in the city of Londonderry, with their several arms (*Calendar of State Papers for Ireland, 1615–1625*, p. 391). The list of names is printed in the *Ordnance Survey for the County of Londonderry*, p. 89, with the following summary:

The whole number of masters and servants very well armed are 100; 23 carslets; 60 muskets; 27 halberts.

A muster of the town of Coleraine was taken also on the same day, of which the following is a summary:

41 shott; 22 halberts; 25 armed men; 12 unarmed men.

Sir Thomas Phillips, writing from Limavady under date of July 17, 1617, (probably to the Lord Deputy) says, referring to the London planters who established the town of Londonderry:

When they had dispended some £15000 they offered to lose all so they might be freed of it and were earnest with me to bring them off as well as I had brought them on. They cannot justly say they have sent over any but their workmen, while some few will stay in the country, others are wrangling bankrupts that cannot stay in England.

Again, on November 8, 1630, the same writer addressed a memorial to the King setting forth, "that the London Plantation in Ulster proves now through their misplanting the danger of the whole kingdom. Instead of 30,000 British in the escheated counties, there are not 7,000."

Peter Heylin, the celebrated champion of the English Church, thus laments over the progress of Puritanism at this period in Ireland while, at the same time, he unconsciously bears testimony to the exemplary care of the Presbyterians in maintaining the public preaching of the Gospel wherever they settled. (*History of the Presbyterians from 1536 to 1647*, p. 393, Oxford, 1670) :

Hereupon followed the plantation of Ulster, first undertaken by the city of London, who fortified Coleraine and built Londonderry, and purchased many thousand acres of land in the parts adjoining. But it was carried on more vigorously, as more unfortunately withal, by some adventurers of the Scottish nation, who poured themselves into this country as the richer soil ; and, though they were sufficiently industrious in improving their own fortunes there, and set up preaching in all churches wheresoever they fixed, yet whether it happened for the better or for the worse, the event hath showed. For they brought with them hither such a stock of Puritanism, such a contempt of bishops, such a neglect of the public liturgy, and other Divine offices of this Church, that there was nothing less to be found amongst them than the government and forms of worship established in the Church of England.

NOTES TO CHAPTER XXXV

[1] This included all men of British descent between the ages of 16 and 60 belonging to the 1974 families, together with their tenants and servants.

[2] Grazing.

[3] Made in 1615.

CHAPTER XXXVI

STEWART'S AND BRERETON'S ACCOUNTS OF THE PLANTA-
TION OF ULSTER

THE Rev. Andrew Stewart, or Stuart, was minister of Donaghadee in county Down from 1645 to 1671. His father, who was also the Rev. Andrew Stewart, was a man of eminent piety. He was minister of Done-gore, near Antrim, from 1627 to 1634. The author of the following short portion of the *History of the Church of Ireland*, was only ten years of age at the time of his father's death. The family were left in straitened circum-stances; but the wants of the widow and her children were graciously sup-plied. When little more than twenty-one years of age, young Andrew was ordained to the pastoral charge of Donaghadee, where he labored a quarter of a century. Fleming, in his *Fulfilling of the Scriptures*,—the first part of which was published in 1674,—speaks of him as a worthy clerical brother, with whom he corresponded. " Mr. Andrew Stewart, minister of Dona-ghadee," says he, " was a great observer of confirmations of the truth, whom I cannot mention without sorrow at the remembrance of the late removal of so eminent and useful a minister of Jesus Christ."

In the early part of 1670, Mr. Greg of Newtownards was requested by his brethren " to endeavour the composing a History of the Beginning and Progress of the Gospel" in the North of Ireland; but he died in the July of the same year, and the task seems to have then devolved on Mr. Stewart. Kirkpatrick, in his *Presbyterian Loyalty*, speaks of both these gentlemen in terms of high commendation. " Mr. John Greg, Presbyterian minister in Newton, and Mr. Andrew Stewart, Presbyterian minister in Donaghadee, were" says he, " men of great sagacity, judgment, and veracity, as many yet alive can testify." Mr. Stewart's work is divided into three chapters, and is entitled, " A Short Account of the Church of Christ as it was (1) Among the Irish at first ; (2) Among and After the English entered ; (3) After the Entry of the Scots." The author, as is plain from various intima-tions, intended the third chapter to be the principal portion of his work ; but his death, in the beginning of the year 1671, prevented the completion of his design. The first and second chapters, though constituting by far the greater portion of the manuscripts, are of little historical importance, and some of the materials are gathered from very doubtful authorities. All the lights of modern investigation have failed to illustrate satisfactorily the dark period to which they relate. The fragment of the third chapter, which is here published in full, supplies very valuable information.

The copy from which the following fragment has been taken is deposited among the *Wodrow Manuscripts* in the Advocate's Library, Edinburgh.

The subjoined letter from the Rev. Andrew Craford, minister of Carn-money, will explain how the historian of the *Sufferings of the Church of Scotland* happened to obtain the transcript. It may be proper to add that Mr. Livingston, mentioned in this communication, was the minister of Tem-plepatrick, and the correspondent of Wodrow.

CARNMONEY, NIGH BELFAST, September 7, 1724.

REV. AND DEAR SIR:

The Papers which come along with this are a copy of some papers which were left by my uncle, the Rev. Andrew Stewart, minister of Donagadee, in the County of Down, and North of Ireland. The original was written with his own hand. I could have no greater assurance that it is his writing, ex-cept I had seen him write it, having carefully compared the writing with many other manuscripts of his, from the great respect I did justly bear to him, and found it a valuable performance. I took an exact copy some years ago for my own use; but the original itself being not now in my cus-tody, I have transcribed this from my own copy with the greatest care and with my own hand which, though it is not as fair as I could wish—as multi-tude of business would not allow me the necessary time a fair draught would require—yet, I nothing doubt you will find it legible.

My near relation to the deceased author renders it improper for me to give you an ample character of him; but if you desire any further informa-tion concerning him, some care shall be taken to obtain it from more proper hands. His father was minister in Dunagor, in the county of Antrim, be-fore the rebellion of the Irish in the year 1641, and among the first Presby-terian ministers who laboured in these parts after the Reformation; and my uncle, being then a young man, had the opportunity of being an eye witness to some of the most remarkable passages which he has inserted in these papers; which, if they give you any satisfaction in the reading, or can serve you in any of the good purposes you have in view, it will be my great satisfac-tion. However that be, you may depend on the exactness of the copy which I now send you by the influence and at the earnest desire of my dear brother, the Rev. William Livingston, who appears very solicitous to serve you, and joins with me in desiring the favour that you would allow it a place among your valuable Collection which you have made, and are still making for the service of the church.

I hope you will proceed in your exemplary industry; and that the Lord may assist and give you success in all your labours, is the fervent prayer of, rev. and dear sir, your most affectionate brother and humble servant,

AND. CRAFORD.

For Rev. Mr. Wodrow.

Of the English, Mr. Stewart states, not many came over to Ireland:

For it is to be observed, that being a great deal more tenderly bred at home in England, and entertained in better quarters than they could find here in Ireland, they were very unwilling to flock hither, except to good land, such as they had before at home, or to good cities where they might trade, both of which in these days were scarce enough here. Besides that the marshiness and fogginess of this island was still found unwholesome to English bodies, more tenderly bred and in a better air; so that we have seen, in our time, multitudes of them die of a flux called here the country disease, at their first entry. These things were such discouragements, that the new English came but very slowly, and the old English were become no better than the Irish.

He then adds :

The King had a natural love to have Ireland planted with Scots, as being, beside their loyalty, of a middle temper, between the English tender and the Irish rude breeding, and a great deal more like to adventure to plant Ulster than the English, it lying far both from the English native land and more from their humour, while it lies nigh to Scotland, and the inhabitants not so far from the ancient Scots manners ; so that it might be hoped that the Irish untoward living would be met both with equal firmness, if need be, and be especially allayed by the example of more civility and Protestant profession than in former times had been among them.

The progress of the plantation is thus described :

The Londoners have in Lagan a great interest, and built a city called Londonderry, chiefly planted with English. Coleraine, also, is built by them, both of them seaports, though Derry be both the more commodious and famous. Sir Hugh Clotworthy obtains the lands of Antrim, both fruitful and good, and invites thither several of the English, very good men, the Ellisses, Leslies, Langfords and others. Chichester, a worthy man, has an estate given him in the county of Antrim, where he improves his interest, builds the prospering mart Belfast, and confirms his interest in Carrickfergus, and builds a stately palace there. Conway has an estate given him in the county of Antrim, and builds a town, afterwards called Lisnegarvy, and this was planted with a colony of English also. Moses Hill had woodlands given him, which being thereafter demolished, left a fair and beautiful country, where a late heir of the Hills built a town called Hillsborough. All these lands and more were given to the English gentlemen, worthy persons, who afterwards increased and made noble and loyal families in places where formerly had been nothing but robbing, treason, and rebellion. Of the Scots nation, there was a family of the Balfours, of the Forbesses, of the Grahames, two of the Stewarts, and not a few of the Hamiltons. The Macdonnells founded the earldom of Antrim by King James's gift, the Hamiltons the earldoms of Strabane and Clanbrassil, and there were besides several knights of that name, Sir Frederick, Sir George, Sir Francis, Sir Charles his son, and Sir Hans, all Hamiltons ; for they prospered above all others in this country after the first admittance of the Scots into it.

The writer then gives the following account of the settlement in the county of Down, of the Hamilton and Montgomery families, who proved the most successful promoters of the Scottish plantation, and were intimately connected with the subsequent vicissitudes of the Presbyterian Church in Ulster :

Therefore the lords having a good bargain themselves, make some of their friends sharers, as freeholders under them. Thus came several farmers under Mr. Montgomery, gentlemen from Scotland, and of the names of the Shaws, Calderwoods, Boyds, of the Keiths from the North. And some foundations are laid for towns, and incorporations, as Newton, Donaghadee, Comber, Old and New, Grey-Abbey. Many Hamiltons also followed Sir James, especially his own brethren, all of them worthy men ; and other farmers, as the Maxwells, Rosses, Barclays, Moors, Bayleys, and others whose posterity hold good to this day. He also founded towns and incorporations, viz., Bangor, Holywood and Killileagh, where he built a strong castle, and Ballywalter. These foundations being laid, the Scots came hither apace, and became tenants willingly and sub-tenants to their countrymen (whose manner and way they knew), so that in a short time the country began again to be inhabited.

The remainder of Stewart's *History* reads as follows:

The Third and Chiefly Intended Part of the History of the Church of Ireland as the Gospel Began, was Continued and Spread in this Island under our Lord Jesus Christ, after the Scots were naturalized.

I have given some account before, how the entry of the Scots was into this Island, and upon what political grounds it was established. I am now to show what course and prosperity the word of God had amongst them ; but, before I come to this, I must show a little further what was done in the entry of King Charles I. Yet, let it still be remembered, that from the days of King James, and from the aforesaid Act made in his time, the North of Ireland began to be planted with Scots inhabitants, but they were so few at first and so inconsiderable, that they were not much noticed nor heard of almost, till after King James died and King Charles succeeded ; in whose days the Scots began to be noticed, and yet they were not at first noticed by Charles himself, till the days of his deputy, or Lieutenant Wentworth—commonly called the Earl of Strafford.

King Charles, therefore, appointed him to be Lord Lieutenant of Ireland —a man of mighty state, but exceeding perverse against all godliness and the professors thereof. Under him the King held a Parliament in Ireland (commonly called *decimo Caroli*), in which some things concerning the church were enacted—yet such as need not be much stuck upon—in regard, the most remarkable thing was the clergy giving to the King eight entire subsidies, which fell to be about the year 1634, at which time Ussher was Primate of all Ireland ; yet, they did not this for nothing, for afterwards they obtained a lart Act to enable restitutions of impropriations and tythes, and other rights ecclesiastical to the clergy, with a restraint of alienating the same, and this is to be seen at large in the 10th and 11th *Caroli*. But, leaving these things, I intend with a straight course to carry on the History of propagating the Gospel among the new plantation of Scots, and to declare how it began, and by what instruments the Lord did it.

Whereas, I said before, King James had prepared a place and liberty in Ireland for them, and having given some lands to some men whom he had nobilitated, these men sought tenants for their lands ; and from Scotland came many, and from England, not a few, yet all of them generally the scum of both nations, whom, for debt, or breaking and fleeing from justice, or seeking shelter, came hither, hoping to be without fear of man's justice in a land where there was nothing, or but little, as yet, of the fear of God. And in a few years there flocked such a multitude of people from Scotland that these northern counties of Down, Antrim, Londonderry, etc., were in a good measure planted, which had been waste before ; yet most of the people, as I said before, made up a body (and it's strange, of different names, nations, dialects, tempers, breeding, and, in a word, all void of godliness), who seemed rather to flee from God in this enterprise than to follow their own mercy.[1] Yet God followed them when they fled from him — albeit, at first it must be remembered that they cared little for any church.   So God seemed to care as little for them, for the strangers were no better entertained than with the relics of Popery served upon a ceremonial service of God under a sort of anti-Christian hierarchy, and committed to the care of a number of careless men whom the law calls priests, who were only zealous to call for their gain from their quarter—men who said " come ye, I will bring wine ; let us drink, for the morrow shall be as this day, and much more abundant " ; and thus it fared with the people at first towards the end of King James' and beginning of King Charles' reign, for, in very deed, it was such people, such priests.

In those days, because the plantation was of Scots, the King appointed Scotsmen to be bishops where they dwelt, so Echlin was made bishop of Down, and after him Leslie ; Knox, Bishop of Raphoe, and after him John Leslie ; and other bishops were made from among the Scots — as Maxwell, Adair, and afterwards Baily.   But, these seeking to ingratiate themselves with the King, and to be sure that they, being strangers, should come behind in nothing, ran before all in violent carrying forward the breeding of their country-men to kindly conforming to the English order of doctrine, discipline worship, and government.   Only the Scots, who had estates and lands given them appeared forward ; the rest, as I said, cared little what profession was uppermost, and yet thought it a scorn to be hurled against their will into a sudden change of what they had been bred to ; and, therefore, though they had not the feeling of things from any principle of grace in their hearts, yet the very pride of their heart and sort of nationality biased them to scorn con-forming, though they joined with it, because it was the King's will and the law of the land.

Thus, on all hands Atheism increased, and disregard of God — iniquity abounded, contention, fighting, murder, thieving, adultery, etc. — as among people, who as they had nothing within them to overawe them, so their min-isters' example was worse than nothing, for, from the Prophets of Israel, pro-faneness went forth to the whole land.   And verily at this time the whole body of this people seemed ripe, and soon ripe for the manifestation, in a greater degree of God's judgments or mercy than had been seen for a long time ; for their carriage made them to be abhorred at home in their native land, insomuch that going for Ireland was looked on as a miserable mark of a deplorable person—yea, it was turned to a proverb, and one of the expres-sions of disdain that could be invented to tell a man that Ireland would be his hinder end.   While thus it was, and when any man would have expected nothing but God's judgment to have followed the crew of sinners, behold the Lord visited them in admirable mercy, the like whereof had not been seen anywhere for many generations.   For among them who had been permitted to preach by the bishops, there was one Mr. Glendinning, a man who never would have been chosen by a wise assembly of ministers, nor sent to begin a reformation in this land, for he was little better than distracted — yea, after-wards did actually distract—yet this was the Lord's choice to begin the admirable work of God, which I mention on purpose that all men may see how the glory is only of the Lord's in making a holy nation in this profane land, and that it was not by might nor by power, nor by man's wisdom, but by my Spirit, says the Lord.   This Mr. Glendinning had been bred at St. Leonard's College, in St. Andrews, and finding little place in Scotland when things were so carried as to satisfy laudable order in the church, he runs to Ireland with the rest, and having been ordained a minister, is placed in a parish near to Antrim, called Oldstone.

Mr. Robert Blair was come to Bangor, and began to found a blessed work there before Mr. Glendinning went to Oldstone, or anything of that nature did appear in his ministry ; for he, coming first to Carrickfergus and there beginning to preach, Mr. Blair came over from Bangor upon some business, and occasionally hearing Mr. Glendinning to preach, perceived some sparkles of good inclinations in him, yet found him not solid, but weak, and not fit for a public place and among the English ; on which Mr. Blair did call him, and using freedom with him, advised him to go to some place in the country among his countrymen—whereupon he went to Oldstone, and was there placed, where God made use of him to awaken the consciences of a lewd and secure people thereabout, his preachings being threatening ; and being of a forward zealous temper according to his light (this passage I had from Mr. Blair among divers other things relating to that time), this man, seeing the great lewdness and ungodly sinfulness of the people, preached to`them nothing but law, wrath, and the terrors of God for sin ; and in very deed for this only was he fitted, for hardly could he preach any other thing ; but behold the success ! for his hearers, finding themselves condemned by the mouth of God speaking in his word, fell into such anxiety and terror of con-science that they looked on themselves as altogether lost and damned, as those of old who said, " Men and brethren, what shall we do to be saved ? " and this work appeared, not in one single person only, or two, but multitudes were brought to understand their way and to cry out, " What shall we do ? "

I have seen them myself stricken, and swoon with the Word—yea, a dozen in one day carried out of doors as dead, so marvellous was the power of God smiting their hearts for sin, condemning and killing ; and some of those were none of the weaker sex or spirit ; but indeed some of the boldest spirits, who formerly feared not with their sword to put a whole market town in a fray ; yea, in defence of their stubbornness, cared not to lie in prison and in the stocks, and being incorrigible, were as ready to do the like the next day. Yea, I have heard one of them, then a mighty strong man (now a mighty Christian), say that his end in coming to church was to consult with his companions how to work some mischief, and yet at one of those sermons was he so catched, that he was fully subdued. But why do I speak of him ? We knew, and yet know multitudes of such men who had no power to resist the word of God ; but the heart being pricked and smitten with the power of God, the stubborn, who sinned and gloried in it, because they feared not man, are now patterns of sobriety, fearing to sin because they fear God ; and this spread through the country to admiration, so that, in a manner, as many as came to hear the word of God, went away slain with the words of his mouth, especially at that river (commonly called Six-Mile Water),—for there this work began at first—thereafter at Larne by Mr. Dunbar. For a short time this work lasted as a sort of disease for which there was no cure, the poor people lying under the spirit of bondage ; and the poor man who was the instrument of it, not being sent, it seems to preach the Gospel so much as law, they lay for a time in a most deplorable condition, slain for their sin, and knew of no remedy. The Word they could not want, and yet the more they heard it, the more they could not abide it, as Paul says.

But the Lord, who said to Israel after they had been two years at Mount Sinai, " Ye have dwelt long enough about this mount," did so to those afflicted consciences ; for the report of this harvest flying abroad, brought over several zealous, godly men, who most of them were young men who could not be admitted in Scotland unless they would conform, and they, hoping that God would accept their labours in Ireland, where an effectual door seemed to be opened, came to this land, and in a short time came those memorable persons to the County Antrim :

1. Mr. Josias Welsh, son to the famous Mr. John Welsh ; he pitched at Templepatrick, as chaplain to Captain Norton, so he was next neighbor to the Oldstone.

2. Mr. George Dunbar, who had been once minister in Ayr in Scotland, but being ousted by the bishop came to Ireland, and laboured with great effect.   After he was put from Ayr, he was for a time prisoner at Blackness, and in Ireland first preached at Carrickfergus, but having no entertainment there, stayed a while at Ballymena, then came to Larne, or Inver, by whose means all that country heard the Word, and were first gathered unto the Lord.

3. Mr. Robert Cunningham at Holywood, in the County of Down, had been one of them who, before the coming of the rest were like to have conformed, but proved a most excellent minister in the Lord's work.

4. Mr. James Hamilton, that worthy man who died minister at Edinburgh.   After he had been famous there, he was at this time minister at Ballywalter, in the Ards, County of Down.

5. Mr. John Livingston, son to the very worthy Mr. William Livingston, who had been minister at Lanark, in Scotland.   He was minister of Killinchy, in the County of Down.

6. Mr. Robert Blair, who was a star of the first magnitude and appeared eminent in the Lord's work before the rest came, was from being Professor of Philosophy in Glasgow, invited hither by Sir James Hamilton, and embraced the charge of Bangor, by whose means also not only was his neighbour, Mr. Robert Cunningham, like another Apostle, instructed in the way of God more perfectly, but his spiritual wisdom and learning was a great ornament and help to the beginnings of this church.

At this time of people gathering to Christ, it pleased the Lord to visit mercifully the honourable family in Antrim, so that Sir John Clotworthy and the lady, his mother, and his own precious lady, did shine in an eminent manner in receiving the Gospel, and offering themselves as first fruits of their honourable families to the Lord, and did worthily in cherishing these beginnings, whose example instantly other gentlemen followed, such as Captain Norton, and others, of whom the Gospel made a clear and cleanly conquest, and by their means some more godly ministers were added, as we shall hear afterward.

Now, remember what fever the whole country was in, and hear how it was allayed ; for God sending Mr. Welsh upon that water side, the first of the work began, God gave him the spirit to preach the Gospel, and to bring the Word to heal them whom the other by his ministry had wounded, so that the slain were breathed upon and life came into them, and they stood up as men now freed from the spirit of bondage ; then did love enter instead of fear ; the oil of joy for the spirit of heaviness, and withal, strong desire of knowledge, peace of deeply exercised consciences, a full walking, and a great desire in many to walk in the ways of God.   Indeed, the joy and spirit of that time in this place can't by words be well expressed.

Then, those that feared the Lord spake often one to another, and the Lord hearkened and heard, and put them (as it were soon) among His jewels, if He have any jewels in any part of the earth.   This is much to be observed when you consider what stuff He had to make them of, and when you think again that, without law or liberty sought or obtained of the rulers, Christ entered upon that work at His own hand, and strengthened His kingdom in Ireland by putting it in the hearts of a people who had been rebels all their lives long.

When, therefore, the multitude of wounded consciences were healed, they began to draw into holy communion, and met together privately for edification (a thing which in a lifeless generation is both neglected and reproved); but now the new life forced it upon the people who desired to know what God was doing with the souls of their neighbours who (they perceived) were wrought on in spirit, as they had been.

There was a man in the parish of Oldstone called Hugh Campbell, who had fled from Scotland, for he had killed a man there. Him God caught in Ireland, and made him an eminent and exemplary Christian until this day. He was a gentleman of the house of Duket Hall. After this man was healed of the wound given to his soul by the Almighty, he became very refreshful to others who had less learning and judgment than himself, and, therefore, invited some of his honest neighbors who fought the same fight of faith to meet him at his house on the last Friday of the month, where, and when beginning with a few, they spent their time in prayer, mutual edification, and conference of what they found within them, nothing like the superficial and superfluous worship of some cold and old idle-hearted professors who afterwards made this work a snare to many ; but these new beginners were more filled with heart exercise than with head notions, and with fervent prayer rather than conceity gifts to fill the ear,—yea, the Lord sent down the fire of love, real affection, and fervency among them, to declare that He accepted their sacrifice as a sweet savour to the Lord.

This meeting as I said, began with a very few ; but still, as they truly increased, so did this meeting for private edification increase, and still at Hugh Campbell's house on the last Friday of the month—at last they grew so numerous that the ministers who had begotten them again to Christ thought fit that some of them should be still with them to prevent what hurt might follow.

The following account of Scotland and Ireland during the time of the great emigration to Ireland is taken from Sir William Brereton's account of his *Travels in Holland the United Provinces, England, Scotland, and Ireland, 1634-5*. (Chetham Society, Manchester, 1844) :

In this kingdom [of Scotland] the clergy of late extend their authority and revenues. Archbishoprick of St. Andrewes is Lord Chancellor of Scotland and Regent here. And, as I was informed by some intelligent gentlemen, it is here thought and conceived that they will recover so much of that land and revenues belonging formerly to the Abbeys, as that they will in a short time possess themselves of the third part of the kingdom. The Duke of Lennox and Marquis Hamilton are possessed of the largest proportion of Church-land: it is expected that they should resign and deliver up their interests and rights therein to the Church, whose example it is thought will induce the rest of the nobility to do the like. And to the end that they may carry some sway in Parliament, it is now endeavoured (as some herein informed me, Mr. Calderwood and Dr. Sharpe) to restore abbots, and to invest them in the revenues and seats of abbeys : hereof they say there are forty-eight which are intended to be established, who are all to sit and carry voices in Parliament; which, if it can be effected, then there will be always in the parliament-house so strong a party for the king, considering those officers that have an immediate dependance upon him and the bishops and abbots, as that they will be able to sway the whole house. Divers of the clergy incline this way, and many also are mighty opposite and averse hereunto.

This city [Edinburgh] is placed in a dainty, healthful, pure air, and doubtless were a most healthful place to live in, were not the inhabitants most sluttish, nasty, and slothful people. I could never pass through the hall, but I was constrained to hold my nose ; their chambers, vessels, linen, and meat, nothing neat, but very slovenly ; only the nobler and better sort of them brave, well-bred men, and much reformed.

Many Highlanders we observed in this town in their plaids, many without doublets, and those who have doublets have a kind of loose flap garment hanging loose about their breech, their knees bare ; they inure themselves to cold, hardship, and will not diswont themselves ; proper, personal, well-complectioned men, and of able men ; the very gentlemen in their blue caps and plaids.

The discipline of the Church of England is much pressed and much opposed by many pastors and many of the people. The greatest part of the Scots are very honest and zealously religious. I observed few given to drink or swearing, but if any oath, the most ordinary was, " Upon my soul." The most of my hosts I met withal, and others with whom I conversed I found very sound and orthodox, and zealously religious. In their demands they do not so much exceed as with us in England, but insist upon and adhere unto their first demand for any commodity. . . .

July 1 —Hence I departed from Falkirk, and about twelve miles hence there is a town called Cuntellen. . . .

There is very little or no timber in any of the south or west parts of this kingdom, much less than in England. I have diligently observed, but cannot find any timber in riding near one hundred miles ; all the country poor and barren, save where it is helped by lime or sea-weeds. Limestone is here very plentiful, and coals, and where there are no coals, they have abundance of turves. Poorest houses and people that I have seen inhabit here ; the houses accommodated with no more light than the light of the door, no window ; the houses covered with clods ; the women only neat and handsome about the feet, which comes to pass by their often washing with their feet.

We lodged in Glasgow, in Mr. David Weymes' house ; his wife's name is Margarett Cambell (the wives in Scotland never change, but always retain, their own names). . . .

— I came from Glasgow about eight hours, and came to Erwin about twelve hours, which is sixteen miles. We passed through a barren and poor country, the most of it yielding neither corn nor grass, and that which yields corn is very poor, much punished with drought. We came to Mr. James Blare's in Erwin, a well affected man, who informed me of that which is much to be admired ; above ten thousand persons have within two years last past left the country wherein they lived, which was betwixt Aberdeen and Ennerness, and are gone for Ireland ; they have come by one hundred in company through this town, and three hundred have gone hence together shipped for Ireland at one tide ; none of them can give a reason why they leave the country, only some of them who make a better use of God's hand upon [them], have acknowledged to mine host in these words : " that it was a just judgment of God to spew them out of the land for their unthankfullness."

This country was so fruitful formerly, as that it supplied an overplus of

corn, which was carried by water to Leith, and now of late for two years, is
so sterile of corn as they are constrained to forsake it.   Some say that, these
hard years, the servants were not able to live and subsist under their masters, and therefore, generally leaving them, the masters being not accustomed, nor knowing how to farme, to till, and order their land, the ground
hath been untilled ; so as that of the Prophet David is made good in this
their punishment : " a fruitful land makes He barren, for the wickedness of
them that dwell therein ; " for it is observed of these, that they were a most
unthankful people : one of them I met withal and discoursed with at large,
who could [give] no good reason, but pretended the landlords increasing
their rents : but their swarming in Ireland is so much taken notice of and
disliked, as that the Deputy hath sent out a warrant to stay the landing of
any of these Scotch that came without a certificate.   Three score of them
were numbered returning towards the place whence they came, as they
passed this town.   Some of them complain of hard years (the better to colour
and justify this their departure) but do withal acknowledge that corn is as
cheap with them as in this town ; but in the distraction and different relation
of themselves, there may be observed much matter of admiration ; and,
doubtless, *digitus Dei* is to be discerned in it.

Hence we came to Aire, which is eight miles upon the sea coast, a most
dainty pleasant way as I have ridden, wherein you leave the sea on your
right hand.   .   .   .   Coming late to Aire, we lodged in one Patrick Mac-
kellen's house, where is a cleanly neat hostess, victuals handsomely cooked,
and good lodging, eight ordinary, good entertainment.   No stable lodging
to this inn ; we were constrained to seek for a stable in the town, where we
paid 8d. a night for hay and grass for an horse, and 1s. a peck for base oats.
This also is a dainty, pleasant-seated town ; much plain river corn land
about it ; and better haven, there being a river, whereon it is placed, which
flows much higher than the bridge, which is a great and fair neat bridge, yet
nevertheless it is but a bare naked haven, no pier, no defense against the
storms and weather.   Better store of shipping than at Erwin.   Most inhabiting in the town are merchants trading unto and bred in France. [Flemings.]

Enquiring of my hostess touching the minister of the town, she complained much against him, because he doth so violently press the ceremonies, especially she instanced in kneeling at the communion ; whereupon,
upon Easter day last, so soon as he went to the communion-table, the people
all left the church and departed, and not one of them stayed, only the pastor
alone.   .   .   .

July 6.—At Belfast my Lord Chichester hath another dainty stately
house (which is indeed the glory and beauty of that town also), where he is
most resident, and is now building an outer brick wall before his gates.
This not so large and vast as the other, but more convenient and commodious, the very end of the Loch toucheth upon his garden and backside;
here also are dainty orchards, gardens, and walks planted.   Near hereunto,
Mr. Arthur Hill (son and heir to Sir Moyses Hill) hath a brave plantation,
which he holds by lease, which still is for thirty years to come ; the land is
my Lord Chichester's, and the lease was made for sixty years to Sir Moyses
Hill by the old Lord Chichester.   This plantation is said doth yield him a
£1000 per annum.   Many Lankashire and Cheshire men are here planted;
with some of them I conversed.   They sit upon a rack rent, and pay 5s. or
6s. an acre for good ploughing land, which now is clothed with excellent
good corn.   From Bellfast to Linsley Garven is about seven mile, and is a
paradise in comparison of any part of Scotland.   Linsley Garven is well

seated, but neither the town nor country thereabouts well planted, being almost all woods, and moorish until you come to Drom-moare.   This town belongs to my Lord Conoway, who hath there a good, handsome house, but far short of both my Lord Chichester's houses, hereabouts ; my Lord Conoway is now endeavouring a plantation, though the lands hereabouts be the poorest and barrenest I have yet seen, yet may it be made good land with labour and charge.

From Linsley Garven to Drom-more is about seven mile.   Herein we lodged at Mr. Haven's house, which is directly opposite to the Bishop of Drom-more his house, which is a little timber house of no great state nor receipt. . . .

In this diocese, as Mr. Leigh, his chaplain reported, this is the worst part of the kingdom, and the poorest land and ground, yet the best church livings, because there are no impropriations.

July 7.—We left Drome-more and went to the Newrie, which is sixteen miles.   This is a most difficult way for a stranger to find out.   Herein we wandered, and being lost, fell amongst the Irish towns.   The Irish houses are the poorest cabins I have seen, erected in the middle of the fields and grounds, which they farm and rent.   This is a wild country, not inhabited, planted, nor enclosed, yet it would be good corn if it were husbanded.

NOTE TO CHAPTER XXXVI

[1] This account is also confirmed by Blair, who says : " Although amongst those whom Divine Providence did send to Ireland, there were several persons eminent for birth, education and parts ; yet the most part were such as either poverty, scandalous lives, or, at the best, adventurous seeking of better accommodation had forced thither, so that the security and thriving of religion was little seen to by those adventurers, and the preachers were generally of the same complexion with the people."

CHAPTER XXXVII

CHURCH RULE IN IRELAND AND ITS RESULTS

THE founders of the Presbyterian Church in Ireland were ministers who had taken refuge in Ulster, driven from Scotland and England by King James's persecutions of the Presbyterians and Puritans. The southwest of Scotland, from which the Ulster settlers largely came, was during this whole period intensely Presbyterian. It was the district from which came a large part of the army and leaders who first confronted the tyrannical Charles. In the succeeding generation, it furnished the "Westlan Whigs," who fought at Bothwell Bridge ; and it also produced the martyrs whose graves are still visited at Wigtown, and in the quiet upland kirkyards of Galloway and the "clachan" of Dalry.

Although more than three-fourths of the seventeenth-century settlers in Ulster were Presbyterians, an effort was soon made to include them in the Episcopal Establishment. In the early part of his reign, the "British Solomon" had expressed a great love for the Church in which he had been educated. How James belied these youthful protestations has already been told in the account of his treatment of the Scottish Church. After he had succeeded Elizabeth, in 1603, as ruler of England, he became as much a persecutor of the Puritans in the South as he had been of the Presbyterians in the North. Those who suffered from these oppressions, both pastors and people, accordingly began to look elsewhere for a place of refuge. The Presbyterians of the South emigrated in large numbers to Holland and to America. Those of the North went principally to Ireland, although the laws there against nonconformity were annoying, and the local authorities in some places inclined to press them. The Corporation of Belfast had arranged a scale of fines for parties above the age of thirteen who might absent themselves from public worship, as by law established, on Sundays or on holy days. The amount for a householder was five shillings ; for a married woman, two and sixpence ; for a servant, one shilling, and for a child, tenpence. In these penalties, however, the Irish Episcopal Church was more moderate than the Puritans of Massachusetts. Indeed, the Irish Church in many of its principles was so similar to that of Scotland, that many Scottish Presbyterians who left their country rather than submit to Episcopacy, did not hesitate to unite themselves with the more evangelical Episcopal Church in Ireland.[1]

Of the Presbyterian ministers in the Irish Established Church, the most celebrated was Robert Blair, "a man of majestic appearance, deep piety, great learning, and persuasive eloquence." He resigned his position as professor in Glasgow University rather than submit to the prelatic form of despotism which James was forcing on the Scottish Church. Invited by Sir James Hamilton, lately created Lord Claneboy, Blair proceeded to Bangor in 1623, and was ordained one of his Lordship's vicars.

At that time, many of the rectors in the Episcopal Church were laymen. One of these was Lord Claneboy, who was rector of a number of parishes. Being a Presbyterian himself, he made Presbyterians his vicars. To them he gave one-third of the Church revenues of the parishes in which they officiated. This secured to each of them about twenty pounds per annum, which, it is probable, was supplemented by a few pounds yearly from the people. Blair was ordained in the Presbyterian form, Bishop Echlin consenting to officiate as a presbyter. In 1626 Josias Welsh, son of John Welsh, of Ayr, and grandson of John Knox, likewise resigned his professorship at Glasgow, and settled at Templepatrick in Antrim, being ordained by his kinsman Knox, who had succeeded Montgomery as bishop of Raphoe. In 1630 he was followed by John Livingston, minister at Torpichen, who had been " silenced " in 1627 by Archbishop Spottiswoode. Like Blair, he was ordained by a bishop (Knox) who became a " presbyter " for the time being.

King James had died in 1625, and was succeeded by his son Charles, a monarch as faithless, tyrannical, and selfish as his father, but one of a less cowardly spirit. It has been said that while the arrogant assumptions of James excited the rage of his subjects, his cowardice caused their contempt. Conditions in Great Britain at the end of James's reign were in a state where it was necessary that they should become worse before they could become better. Charles lost no time in making them worse. James's doctrine of the divine right of kings to do wrong was carried by Charles to its logical conclusion. In the Established Church of England he found a willing supporter of his pretensions, and used it to carry out his designs.

In 1633 William Laud was made archbishop of Canterbury, and persecution was carried on with renewed vigor. Under his leadership, a new party rapidly acquired power in the Church of England. Like the English Ritualists of the present day, they imagined a nation might as well be without a church as a church without Apostolic orders, and that Roman Catholics who preserved these orders were nearer the truth than Presbyterians who rejected them. In religion, they fought the doctrines of Calvinism, regarding the Presbyterian as a stubborn schismatic, whose theology was dangerous to the Church, and whose politics were dangerous to the state. Their enmity towards the Puritans within their own Church was greater than their enmity to the Roman Catholics without it. In politics, they firmly believed in the divine right of the king to do as he pleased.

The rulers of the Irish Church now adopted the policy of their brethren in England. Echlin, bishop of Down, was the first who exhibited a disposition to compel his clergy to conform to the ceremonies as well as to subscribe to the Articles of the Episcopal Church. Moved by the prevailing party in Ireland, he suspended from the ministry in September, 1631, Messrs. Blair, Welsh, Dunbar, and Livingston. Archbishop Usher, on being informed of the matter by Blair, wrote Echlin to relax his "erroneous" censure. This order was obeyed, and the ministers returned to their work. But Echlin's agent hurried to London and, through Laud, persuaded the king to order the Lords Justices to direct Echlin to have these Presbyterian ministers tried as fanatical disturbers of the peace. After another effort on the part of the bishop who tried to induce the ministers to conform, Messrs. Blair, Welsh, Dunbar, and Livingston were, in May, 1632, again suspended. Usher expressed his sorrow at being unable to interfere, as the order for trial had come from the king. Blair appealed to the king, who referred him to Thomas Wentworth, then lord deputy of Ireland. Blair proceeded to Dublin and presented the king's letter; but Wentworth, refusing to remove the sentence, began to upbraid the petitioner, and to revile the Church of Scotland.

At this period, high rents in Scotland were driving the people to Ulster at the rate of four thousand a year, just as the same cause, a century later, drove them from Ulster to America. The wave of colonization moved westwards from Antrim and Down, and southwards from Derry. Had this movement continued, the loyal population would soon have been so numerous as to fear no rebellion of the natives. But Presbyterians, being then firmly attached to their faith, were not inclined to settle in a country where they would be deprived of Gospel ordinances. The persecution in Ireland soon checked immigration from Scotland, and prevented the growth of that part of the Irish population which was joined to Britain by the ties of race and religion.

The lord deputy, Wentworth, had become very unpopular with the Ulster landlords, on account of looking sharply into the way in which they had fulfilled the contracts of plantation, by which they held their estates. He now thought it better to allay their fears for a time until he should obtain from Parliament some necessary supplies. This opportunity was turned to the best account in favor of the suspended ministers by Lord Castle-Stewart, who was himself a Presbyterian. He represented to the lord deputy that it would be expedient to restore the deposed ministers, in order to soothe the feelings of the Northern Scots. Wentworth fell in with the suggestion, and, by his orders, Echlin, in May, 1634, withdrew for six months his sentence of suspension on the four clergymen.

So soon as the six months were expired, Wentworth, at the request of Bishop Bramhall, caused Echlin to renew his suspension of Blair and Dunbar. When the bishop was about to pronounce sentence, Blair summoned him to appear before the tribunal of Christ to answer for his evil deeds. This is said to have produced such an effect on the prelate that he died in great distress of mind soon after.

Wentworth now effected such changes in the constitution of Trinity

36

College as to effectually exclude Puritans from places of power or profit in that institution ; and he determined to make a similar change in the Church. Nothing in the Irish Church was so obnoxious to him as its Puritanism ; and that Puritanism he determined to extinguish. Both he and Charles considered that the great object of a church was to render men obedient to royal authority ; and therefore they determined to exclude from its pale all who preferred to serve God rather than to obey the king.

A convocation of the Church was summoned to meet, that this design might be accomplished. Bramhall ruled the Upper House, and Wentworth himself, through Leslie and other creatures of his own, guided the proceedings of the Lower House. One hundred canons were framed and adopted. By these, the thirty-nine Articles of the English Church were approved, and its various rites and ceremonies adopted. Wentworth succeeded in persuading Archbishop Usher and the members of Convocation that to approve of the English Articles would not interfere with the authority of the Irish Articles. But this was a mere trick ; for afterwards the government regarded the Irish Articles as abolished, because they had not been formally approved by any of the canons.

Wentworth now exercised the power of a dictator in the State, and of a pope in the Church. A court of High Commission was established in Dublin which could deal with the life and property of every individual in the kingdom, and from which there was no appeal. The Deputy prevented Parliament passing certain " graces," which, in return for a large sum of money, the king had promised to all his Irish subjects, but chiefly to the Roman Catholics.

Echlin was succeeded as bishop of Down by Henry Leslie, a Scotchman by birth, a bigoted Episcopalian, and a willing persecutor. In November, 1635, he deposed Livingston, and caused Melvin, minister of Downpatrick, to pronounce on him sentence of excommunication. But both Blair and Livingston continued to preach in private, at the risk of severe punishment.

It was now determined to make all clergymen conform to the new canons, and conduct worship according to the strictest Episcopal forms. At a visitation held by Leslie, in 1636, he required his clergy to sign these canons. Many consented with reluctance, and afterwards failed to carry out what they had promised. But Brice of Broadisland or Ballycarry, Colvert of Oldstone, Cunningham of Holywood, Hamilton of Ballywater, and Ridge of Antrim, refused to sign, although urged by the bishop in private. Leslie then determined, by advice of Bramhall, to depose these faithful ministers. To carry out his decision, he held a meeting of his clergy on the 10th of August, 1636, in the Episcopal church at Belfast, and after a long discussion he passed sentence of perpetual silence, within his diocese, on the accused ministers.

Blair, Livingston, Hamilton, and several others had now determined to emigrate with their friends and families to New England. They secured a ship of one hundred and fifty tons burden built near Belfast. In this frail bark, named *The Eagle's Wing*, one hundred and forty Presbyterians set sail from Loch Fergus, on the 9th of September, 1636, ready to encounter the winds and the waves, that they might have freedom from persecution in the new world. Among the emigrants were Blair, Livingston, Hamilton, and McClelland. Mrs. Livingston accompanied her husband. The voyage turned out disastrously. Storms arose, and contrary winds drove them into Loch Ryan. But again they sailed westward, till they were nearer America than Ireland. Then they encountered fearful storms of wind and rain from the northwest. The swellings of the sea rising higher than mountains hid the midday sun. Their rudder was broken and their sails torn. Leaks were sprung which required them to be constantly pumping. Huge waves broke over the deck and tore up the planks, till at last they concluded it was the Lord's will that they should return. Having changed their course homewards, they made good progress, and on the 3d of November came to anchor in Loch Fergus.

The deposed ministers remained for only a short time in Ireland. Blair and Livingston, hearing that warrants for their apprehension were issued, fled to Scotland. The other deposed ministers sought refuge in the same country. They were followed by many of their faithful people, who preferred to leave their homes rather than be deprived of hearing the Gospel preached. Others who remained in Ireland were accustomed to visit their ministers at communion seasons, to the number of five hundred at a time. On one occasion Livingston, who settled at Stranraer, baptized as many as twenty-eight children brought from Ireland.

Meanwhile, in Scotland the attempt of the king to impose the liturgy on the people met with most determined opposition. Starting with the Janet Geddes riot in St. Giles's Cathedral, in 1637, the opposition grew, and it was not long before the Scots had an army in the field confronting the royal tyrant.

The Irish Presbyterians, strongly opposed to the forms of prelacy, sympathized with their brethren in Scotland ; and even the clergy of the Established Church failed to carry out the provisions of the canons they had signed. Bishop Leslie complained that they cut down the liturgy to the lessons and a few collects ; and that while these were being read, the people walked about in the churchyards, and then came rushing in to hear the sermon.

Wentworth seems to have feared a rising of the Scots ; for in a letter to Coke, the English Secretary of State, he states that there are 13,092 British men between sixteen and sixty in Ulster, but congratulates himself on the fact that they are badly armed. At the suggestion of Charles he determined, in 1639, to compel all the Ulster Scots above sixteen years of age to swear that they would obey all the king's "royal commands." This declaration became known as the "Black Oath." Commissions were issued to the northern magistrates to administer it in their districts. It was to be publicly read to the people, who were to take it on their knees. Scots who professed to be Roman Catholics were exempted. Troops sent to compel Presbyterians to swear, executed their orders with ruthless severity. Even Lord Claneboy deserted the principles of his youth and became a persecutor himself. The Ulster Scots, horrified at the idea of declaring they would obey commands which were certain to be contrary to the laws of God and injurious to the liberties of the country, refused obedience, at the risk of being committed to prison. Many were seized and brought to Dublin, where some were kept for years in confinement. A man named Henry Stewart was fined five thousand pounds, his wife the same amount, and his daughters and servant two thousand pounds each. Unable to pay the fines they were committed to prison. Many thousands of Presbyterians fled to Scotland, and although they then felt banishment grievous, they afterwards blessed God for permitting them to be driven out of a country where they might afterwards have perished in the great rebellion.

Wentworth was created earl of Strafford, and became lord lieutenant of Ireland. In order to assist the king in his war with Scotland, he collected an army of nine thousand men, largely composed of Irish natives, which he stationed at Carrickfergus. His object was, by military force, to aid Charles in carrying out a scheme he called the "thorough"; which in reality was the establishing of an absolute monarchy. Finding that a large proportion of the Ulster Scots were prepared to give up their lives rather than take the obnoxious oath, and that those who swore could not be depended upon, he formed the design of removing them all out of the country. But events in England now demanded his presence, and he left Ireland never to return.

Charles having failed in his plans of raising money to carry on war with the Scots, summoned another English Parliament, which met on the 3d of November, 1640, and is known as the Long Parliament. It abolished the courts of Star Chamber and of High Commission, and released those imprisoned for nonconformity. Strafford and Laud were arrested, and both paid the penalty of death for their numerous crimes. The Irish Presbyterians, through Sir John Clotworthy of Antrim, member for the English borough of Malden, petitioned this Parliament for redress of their many grievances. They recounted the persecutions they had endured; they complained that their "learned and conscionable" ministers had been banished, and the care of their souls committed to illiterate hirelings, who received only five or ten pounds a year; that the rectors through connivance of their bishops were non-resident, and the people perished from want of spiritual food; and that all this time masses were publicly celebrated "to the great grief of God's people, and increase of idolatry and superstition." They prayed Parliament to redress their grievances, and especially to restore their banished ministers.

The government of Ireland was now committed to Sir John Parsons and Sir John Borlase, both Puritans. Under their guidance, the Parliament abolished the court of High Commission, and religious liberty was practically re-established.   Roman Catholics and Nonconformists became members of Parliament, judges, and magistrates.   The exiled Presbyterians began to return, until shortly after 1640 there were thirty regular congregations in Ulster, and it seemed as if peace and prosperity were about to reign in Ireland.   Yet this was the dawn of the darkest day in the history of the country.

Certain descendants of the northern chieftains whose estates had been confiscated at the beginning of the century, and others who had themselves gone away when very young, lived now at the Courts of Rome and Madrid. These exiles, thinking the English were fully occupied with their own disputes, formed a plan with their friends in Ireland for expelling the settlers of the English race, and overthrowing Protestantism in the country.   When this plot was almost ripe for execution, Charles, thinking he had gained Scotland by lately made concessions, opened a correspondence with some Irish Roman Catholic leaders.   He promised them many civil and religious advantages, including a legal establishment of the Roman Catholic faith in Ireland, if they would take up arms in his behalf, and disarm all Irish Protestants except the Ulster Scots, whom the king imagined he could unite with their kinsmen in Scotland.   Reilly asserts that the scheme originated with Charles, who sent his instructions to Ormond and Antrim.   But the leaders of the old Irish, hearing of this design, determined to begin the rebellion at once, to anticipate the Anglo-Norman families who were gained by Charles, and to rob and murder for their own advantage rather than for the advantage of the king.   They determined to seize as many fortified places as possible, especially Dublin Castle, where there was a large store of arms.   These designs were frustrated by a follower of the Clotworthy family named Owen O'Connolly, a native Irishman who had turned Protestant and become an elder in the Presbyterian Church.   O'Connolly having obtained information concerning the plot from his foster-brother, Hugh Oge Mac-Mahon, came late in the evening of the 22d of October, 1641, to the Lord Justice Parsons, whom he informed of the projected insurrection.   The Council was summoned, and means taken to defend the town and castle. Next day the rebellion broke out all over Ulster.   The native Irish, who hated work, and who loved plunder more than they feared danger, sprang to arms on the first summons of their leaders.   Charlemont was surprised by Sir Phelim O'Neill, who told Lord Caulfield that he had authority for what he was doing, probably referring to the king's commission.   Almost everywhere throughout Ulster the castles were taken ; but Derry, Enniskillen, Belfast, Carrickfergus, and Coleraine were saved.

At first, the rebels acted with comparative moderation.   They contented themselves with robbing the Protestants, stripping them naked, and sending them off defenceless.   But they soon abandoned this moderation, and aimed at murdering the entire native Protestant population.   Neither woman nor infant was spared.   The brains of the children were dashed out before the eyes of their mothers, some were thrown into pots of boiling water, and some were given to the pigs that they might be eaten. A Protestant minister was crucified. Many had their hands cut off or their eyes put out before their lives were taken. Others were promised protection on condition of their becoming the executioners of their own nearest and dearest relations ; but if they accepted these terms, they themselves were afterwards murdered. Many were promised their lives on condition of conforming to popery, but any who recanted were told that, being now in the true Church, they must be killed at once lest they might afterwards fall from the faith. Various calculations have been made of the number who perished, and it probably reached more than ten thousand.

As a body, the Presbyterians suffered less than other Protestants. Their leading ministers had been driven out of the country. Many of the people had followed. The few months of liberty which intervened between the execution of Strafford and the beginning of the rebellion were not sufficient to enable many to return. The bishops who had banished both pastors and people to Scotland saved them from destruction.

At first, the king's orders were obeyed and the Scots suffered no injury. Many of them succeeded in escaping ; but some perished by being too confident. Mr. R. Stewart, of the Irry, near Stewartstown, whose wife was granddaughter to the earl of Tyrone, had armed six hundred Scots. Assured, however, by his Irish relatives, that none of his people would be injured, he disbanded his forces. But the night these men reached their homes, most of them were murdered. Many Protestants fled for safety to the woods, where some perished of hardships, and others were devoured by wolves. At Oldstone, near Antrim, " about twenty women, with children upon their backs and in their hands were knocked down and murdered under the castle wall ; and about three-score old men, women, and children, who had license to go unto Larne or Carrickfergus, were that day or next, murdered by The O'Hara's party, within a mile-and-a-half of the said castle."

On the 15th of November, 1641, Sir Phelim O'Neill obtained possession of Lurgan by capitulation ; but on the 28th of the same month, he was repulsed from Lisburn. In December, he captured Strabane, which was defended by the widow of Lord Strabane. He fell in love with his fair captive, and married her soon afterwards. Augher, Castlederg, Omagh, and Newtownstewart were saved from the enemy. An arrangement for the protection of the Irish Protestants was now made between the English and the Scottish Parliaments. A Scotch army of ten thousand was to be sent for the relief of Ireland, and as Ireland was a dependency of England, the English Parliament was to provide for its support.

A detachment of these forces, under General Robert Monro, arrived in April, 1642, and at once marched against the enemy, whom they defeated on their way to Newry. Having captured this town, they put the garrison to the sword. Monro now marched against O'Neill, who occupied Armagh ;

but before he could arrive, the Irish general burned the town, murdered the Protestants, and retired to Charlemont.   Sir John Clotworthy built a number of boats, by means of which he captured the vessels of the enemy on Lough Neagh.   His forces put the Irish to flight near Moneymore, and saved the lives of about one hundred and twenty Protestant prisoners who were about to be murdered.   In the northeast, Sir William and Sir Robert Stewart defeated the enemy on several occasions and Strabane was retaken. These vigorous proceedings restored comparative security to the greater part of Ulster.

The Scottish forces were accompanied by their chaplains.[2]   Many of their officers were elders.   The Episcopal clergy had been generally driven out of the country, and their people preferred the simple rites of Presbyterian worship.   When four sessions had been organized in the army it was determined to form a presbytery.

On the 10th of June, 1642, the first regular presbytery of the Church in Ireland was constituted at Carrickfergus.   It consisted of five ministers and four ruling elders.   The ministers were Mr. Hugh Cunningham, who about 1646 was installed at Ray, county Donegal ; Mr. Thomas Peebles, who in 1645 became minister of Dundonald and Holywood ; and Mr. John Baird, who in 1646 was installed in The Route ; also Mr. John Scott and Mr. John Aird, who returned to Scotland.   Mr. Peebles was appointed clerk, which position he held until his death nearly thirty years afterwards.   Mr. James Simpson and Mr. John Livingston, although in Ireland, were prevented by distance from being present.

When it was known that this court had been established, applications began to be received from many districts for preaching of the Gospel.   Sessions were erected in Antrim, Ballymena, Ballywalter, Bangor, Belfast, Cairncastle, Carrickfergus, Comber, Holywood, Donaghadee, Newtown-Ards, and other localities, where it was determined to place pastors as soon as possible.

Bangor and Ballywalter petitioned the Church of Scotland to restore to them Messrs. Blair and Hamilton, their former ministers.   A general petition from Presbyterians in Down and Antrim was presented to the same Assembly, requesting the restoration of those pastors whom " persecution of the prelates " had driven out of the country, and asking them to " superadd " other able men to lay " the foundation of God's house according to the pattern."

As the supply of ministers in Scotland was then limited, on account of previous persecution, the Assembly could not send any to settle permanently in Ireland ; but they ordered Messrs. Blair, Hamilton, Ramsay, McClelland, Baillie, and Livingston—six of their most popular preachers—to go there for a limited time.

Meanwhile, the king had come to an open rupture with his Parliament. In August, 1642, the royal standard was erected at Nottingham ; and many followed their monarch to fight for the institutions by which they were themselves oppressed.   At first, success seemed about to smile on the cause of

Charles; but after a time, all was changed. Oliver Cromwell arose to power. The army was remodelled. Respectable, God-fearing men, who hated prelacy as strongly as they loved truth, became soldiers, and received pay sufficient to provide, without plunder, the necessaries of life. With this army the tide of war was soon rolled backwards. The forces of Charles were defeated in several bloody battles, and the authority of Parliament became supreme.

A correspondence had been opened between the Scotch Assembly and the English Parliament regarding a uniformity of religion between the nations. As a result, an assembly of divines met at Westminster, which compiled the Confession of Faith, the Catechisms, and the Directory for Public Worship. This assembly commenced its sittings on the 1st of July, 1643, although forbidden to meet by a proclamation of Charles. It was to consist of one hundred and twenty divines, with ten lords, and twenty commoners as lay-assessors, and seven Commissioners from the Scots. Among the lay-assessors was Sir John Clotworthy of Antrim, who represented Malden in the Long Parliament. As almost all the members were English Puritans, it is incorrect to regard the Confession and Catechisms prepared by this Assembly as Scotch in their origin.

In the same year, as a result of negotiations carried on between the English Parliament, the Scottish Convention of Estates, and the General Assembly, a religious bond called "The Solemn League and Covenant" was drawn up by Alexander Henderson, and submitted to these bodies. Those who signed this document pledged themselves to maintain the Reformed religion, to extirpate Popery and Prelacy, to preserve the liberties of the kingdom, and to lead holy lives themselves.

This solemn bond was accepted by the General Assembly, by the Convention of Estates in Scotland, and by the English Parliament. On the 25th of September, in St. Margaret's Church, Westminster, the assembly of divines, the Scottish Commissioners, and the members of the Commons, with uncovered heads and uplifted hands, swore to its provisions. A few weeks afterwards it was taken by the Lords, and an order was issued that it should be administered to every person in England above eighteen years of age. A similar course was pursued in Scotland. The Covenant was solemnly received by commissioners representing the Church, State, and the kingdom of England. It was sent to the moderators of the presbyteries, and its provisions were to be subscribed to by "all of understanding" throughout the country.

Meanwhile the operations of Monro's little army in Ireland were sadly hampered for want of supplies. It is doubtful whether his force ever reached the stipulated number of ten thousand, although it is certain that four thousand men joined it in the autumn of 1642. The arrangement between the two Parliaments had been that the English should pay the Scottish troops; but by the autumn of 1642, England was plunged in civil war, and the money which had been raised for the war in Ireland was seized to carry on war against Charles. The Scottish regiments, therefore, fared very badly, and at times seem to have been driven to live on the country in which they were settled. The campaign of 1643 was not a brilliant one, although ground was recovered. The winter found the troops very discontented ; they had received almost no pay since they landed, and when news came of the proposed expedition into England in support of the Parliament, three of the regiments were no longer to be held back, but returned to Scotland against orders. The Ulster settlers were greatly alarmed at the prospect of being left unprotected should the rest of the Scottish troops also go ; but fortunately a supply of money and of provisions arrived at Carrickfergus in April, 1644—a portion of the food being a free gift of three thousand bolls of meal from the shire of Ayr. About the same time, too, the Dutch showed their sympathy with the cause of Protestantism in Ireland by making a collection in all the churches of Holland by order of the States-General ; they transmitted to Ulster four shiploads of provisions and clothing, which were distributed among both people and soldiery.

On the 4th of November, 1643, Owen O'Connolly was sent by Parliament to the commanders in Ulster, to make preparations for administering the Covenant in Ireland. For this purpose, the Rev. James Hamilton and three other clergymen came over the next spring. On the 1st of April, 1644, they presented their commissions to the Presbytery, and soon afterwards began the work of receiving signatures. The regiments took the Covenant from their own chaplains, or if they had none, from the Scottish commissioners. Major Dalzell, who was afterwards noted as a great persecutor, was the only person connected with the army who refused to swear. Then came in crowds the people near the places where the regiments were stationed. They all joined willingly, except a few Episcopal ministers and some "profane and ungodly persons ; so that there were more of the country become swearers than were men in the army." Those who had taken the Black Oath were compelled to renounce it publicly before being admitted to the Covenant.

The commissioners appointed went from town to town to preach and explain the provisions of the document they carried. Having administered it in several places in Antrim and Down where troops were stationed, they set out for the extreme North. " From Ballymena they went with a guard of horse toward Coleraine, under one William Hume, of General Leslie's regiment. They went the next day (being Thursday) to the Church, and few being present except the soldiers of the garrison, they explained the Covenant to them, and left it to their serious thoughts till the next Sabbath, being also Easter day. On this Lord's day the convention was very great from town and country. They expounded more fully the Covenant, and, among other things, told the people that their miseries had come from those sorts of people who were there sworn against, and specially from the Papists. The righteous hand of God had afflicted them for going so near the Papists in their former worship and government in the Church; and, whereas, the Episcopal party endeavored peaceableness with the Papists, by symbolizing with them in much of their superstition; the Sovereign Holy Lord had turned their policy to the contrary effect, for their conformity with idolaters —going on in a course which had a tendency at least that way."

In this manner was the Covenant taken by the people throughout the greater part of Ulster. The Commissioners rode along accompanied by an escort of cavalry to protect them from parties of the enemy roaming about. But their progress was slow on account of the badness of the roads, which went straight through deep bogs and over hills so steep that it was difficult to ride either up or down; while in the valleys the horses sank deep, and even the higher mountain roads were often continual morasses. As there were but few bridges, most of the rivers had to be crossed by fords, often impassable after rain.

But, notwithstanding all impediments, the Commissioners proceeded diligently with their work. From Coleraine they went to Derry, and from Derry to the Presbyterian parts of county Donegal. They ventured even as far as Enniskillen without meeting any armed band of rebels. In some places the natives fled at their approach, having a superstitious fear of their power, and imagining that it was by the sword Covenanters were determined to "extirpate" popery.

In Ulster, the Covenant was taken by about sixteen thousand persons besides the army. It was given only to those "whose consciences stirred them up." But if we suppose it was taken by one-half of the adults it would indicate that there was still a Protestant population of seventy thousand in that province after all who had perished in the rebellion.

For some time the work of settling ministers in congregations proceeded but slowly. In 1642, Mr. John Drysdale was ordained in Portaferry, and Mr. James Baty in Ballywalter. Three years afterwards Mr. David Buttle was ordained in Ballymena, and Mr. Archibald Ferguson in Antrim; but from that time the work of settlement proceeded with great rapidity. In 1647, upwards of twenty congregations had permanent pastors and several others had sessions and occasional supplies of preachers.

The power of the Irish rebels had been almost overthrown by the victories of Monro, when in 1642 the celebrated Owen Roe O'Neill arrived in Ireland. He was great-grandson of Matthew O'Neill, baron of Dungannon, and had been distinguished in the Spanish and Imperial services. Placed in command of the rebels, he determined to conduct the contest according to the rules of civilized warfare, and to punish all concerned in murder.

A General Assembly of the confederate Catholics, lay and clerical, met at Kilkenny on the 24th of October, arranged for carrying on the war, and performed the functions of a parliament. They handed over the endowments of the Episcopal Church to the Church of Rome. But, ere long, they began to negotiate with the king through the marquis of Ormond, the Protestant head of the great Anglo-Norman family of Butler. Charles concluded these negotiations through the earl of Glamorgan ; and, having conceded almost everything demanded by the confederate Roman Catholics, received from them in return the promise of troops to assist him against his English subjects.

In October, 1643, the earl of Antrim escaped from Carrickfergus Castle, where he had been imprisoned by Monro, and made his way to the king at Oxford. He promised to send two thousand Irish troops to assist the royalist chieftains in the Highlands, who, through jealousy of Argyle, rather than through love of Charles, were ripe for rebellion against the authority of the Parliament.

The first party of Antrim's Irish, under Alaster MacDonnell (sometimes called " Coll-Kittagh," or left-handed Coll, after his father), passed over to Scotland protected by a frigate. They captured, on the 2d of July, 1644, Messrs. Weir and Hamilton, who were returning to Scotland. These gentlemen were kept a long time in prison, and endured such hardships that Mr. Weir died. Mr. Hamilton was at last exchanged, and had a successful ministry at Dumfries and at Edinburgh.

The marquis of Montrose, at the head of the Highland royalists and their Irish allies, now took the field and gained many victories. Having captured Aberdeen, his Irish forces were there distinguished for their great cruelty. They compelled those whom they killed to strip previously, lest their clothes, spoiled in the act of murder, might be rendered less serviceable to the murderers. " The wyf durst not cry nor weep at her husband's slauchter befoir her eyes, nor the mother for the son, nor the dochter for the father ; which, if they war heard, then war they presently slayne also." Formerly, when acting for the Covenanters, Montrose oppressed Aberdeen because it inclined to the royal cause; now he murdered its inhabitants because they supported the very principles he had formerly punished them for opposing.

But the overthrow of Charles at Naseby, in 1645, enabled the regular Scotch army under Leslie to return. Montrose was completely defeated at Philiphaugh, and fled from the kingdom. Afterwards he returned, was captured, and on the 21st of May, 1650, executed.

The war in Scotland drove many to Ulster, and was rather an advantage to the Presbyterians in Ireland. The Parliament, now completely victorious over Charles, sent three commissioners to Ulster, lest the Presbyterians might be induced to join Ormond and the king in opposition to the Sectaries, now rising into power. These commissioners acknowledged the acts of the Presbytery, ordered the Covenant to be tendered at places where it had not been received previously, and " they also did give a right of tithe of parishes to as many of the new entrants as did apply to them."

In 1646 the confederate Catholics concluded a treaty with King Charles, to which the papal nuncio was strongly opposed.   In this opposition he was supported by Owen Roe O'Neill, who, afterwards, got so many of his own creatures returned to the Assembly that he was able to control its actions.

O'Neill, with about five thousand foot and five hundred horse, now made a descent on Ulster.   General Monro, with an army fully as numerous, took the field to oppose him, and marched to Hamilton's Bawn.   Colonel George Monro, son-in-law of the general, at the head of a detachment, was coming from Coleraine to join the main body ; while O'Neill, stationed at Benburb, was between these two divisions of the Protestant army.   Fearing lest Colonel Monro might be overwhelmed by the enemy on his march, General Monro, on the morning of the 5th of June, 1646, advanced from Hamilton's Bawn to Benburb, with the intention of crossing the river to attack O'Neill.   But the old castle, with its four towers, stood in majestic grandeur on a cliff one hundred feet high, which overhung its base above the Blackwater at the very spot where a ford rendered the passage possible.   Monro, having viewed the position from a ridge of rugged hills just opposite to the castle, abandoned his intention of crossing there, and marched along the Armagh bank of the river, eight miles to Caledon.   Even now there is but a narrow path which leads in the direction the Scots marched.   They had, therefore, to toil over numerous bramble-covered hills, and through the bogs which lay between them, dragging their cannons with immense labor. Then, having crossed at Caledon, they left their baggage there with a guard of fifteen hundred men, and marched back towards Benburb, along the Tyrone side of the river — over hills and through the fearful quagmires which then existed on the left bank of the Blackwater, from Knocknacloy to Tullygiven.   They drove before them a party of Irish, under O'Ferral, who tried to obstruct their progress.   Late in the evening, after a march of more than twenty-five miles, ready to faint with fatigue, they came in front of O'Neill, who occupied an advantageous position at Drumflugh, near Benburb, with the Blackwater on the left.   The Irish army was placed on a range of hills, with valleys between them.   O'Neill then addressed his men, telling them to behold the enemies of God and of their souls, exhorting them to fight valiantly against those who had deprived them of their chiefs and their children, who sought for their spiritual and temporal lives, who had taken their lands, and rendered them wandering fugitives.

Monro opened fire with his cannons, and the enemy replied.   At first the Scots made some progress, but, being soon checked, they began to lose ground.   O'Neill then advanced to the attack, and Monro ordered his cavalry to charge.   But these were only Irish under English officers, and they retreated in disorder through the foot, making room for the enemy's horse to follow.   Then another squadron of cavalry was hurled against the Irish ; but they, being hard pressed, got mixed up with the foot, and all fell into disorder. O'Neill now charged with his pikemen, and the Protestant ranks gave way. At this critical moment a detachment of Irish cavalry approached from the north, returning from Dungannon, where they had engaged Colonel George Monro with doubtful success. This reinforcement enabled O'Neill to turn General Monro's left, while the charge of his pikemen had divided the Scottish army in two. One part was driven down the gently sloping hill from Derrycreevy and Carrowbeg to where the Battleford Bridge now crosses the Blackwater. Thistle Hill, steep and impassable, was before them, the Irish behind and on their right, while to their left was the river, dark and deep, even in the midst of summer. Into this river the fugitives— horse and foot — were driven in one surging mass. The waters rose high above those struggling in the stream for life. Yet the Scots pressed madly onwards, rushing in on the top of the dead and dying, in a vain effort to escape. It was at last possible to cross the river on the bodies of the dead, yet very few succeeded in getting over. Those behind were slain by the enemy, and it is admitted by O'Mellon that even the wounded were butchered as they lay on the field of battle.

The second and smaller division of Monro's army endeavored to retreat backward to Caledon. But it is stated that many of them were drowned in Knocknacloy Lough. This is exceedingly probable, as a marsh between the lough and the river was then impassable, and the cavalry who came from Dungannon would prevent the Scots retreating in the direction of Brantry, on the other side of the lough. Caught as in a net, most of the fugitives must have perished.

Many accounts of this engagement are contradictory, each of the other, and are inconsistent with local traditions and the positive assertion of O'Mellon that the battle began at Drumflugh. Besides, the statement made by Carte, and all the historians who follow Carte, that O'Neill had the Blackwater on his right, is untrue ; as, in that case, he would have drawn up his men with their backs to the advancing Scots. Immense numbers of leaden bullets have been found in the very spot where the battle took place. There also graves can still be pointed out ; while no relic of the engagement has been found on the banks of the Oona, where some imagine it was fought.

More than three thousand of Monro's troops lay slain on the field of battle. The general himself, without either hat or wig, escaped with diffi- culty, and Sir James Montgomery's regiment alone retreated in order ; but Lord Montgomery of Ards was taken prisoner. O'Neill had only seventy killed and two hundred wounded. He captured fifteen hundred horses and two months' provisions for the Scottish army. Having proceeded to Tandragee, which he was about to attack, the nuncio summoned him south to counteract the influence of the party who had made peace with the king. O'Neill obeyed, and marching to Kilkenny, threw away all the fruits of the greatest victory which the Irish ever gained over their Saxon masters.

The Presbytery was grieved at this sudden calamity ; but it did not in- terfere with its labors in spreading the Gospel, and several congregations now obtained pastors. On the 7th of May, 1646, Mr. Patrick Adair was ordained minister of Cairncastle, near Larne, and for a lengthened period occupied a distinguished position among his brethren in the Church. Mr. Thomas Kennedy was in the same year ordained at Donaghmore, two miles from Dungannon. Mr. Kennedy was elder brother of Mr. Gilbert Kennedy of Dundonald, and nephew of John, sixth earl of Cassilis, one of the lay-assessors of the Westminster Assembly. About the same time Mr. Anthony Shaw was settled in Belfast, Mr. Thomas Hall in Larne, and Mr. Robert Cunningham in Broadisland. The work of supplying vacant congregations went on with rapidity. Presbyterians in great numbers now came from Scotland, and Ulster seemed about to enter on a new career of prosperity.

The marquis of Ormond still held Dublin for King Charles. But despairing of being able to gain the Scots, or to rule the Kilkenny confederates, he agreed to surrender the city to commissioners of the English Parliament. These commissioners reached Dublin in June, 1647, and one of their first acts was to substitute the Directory for the Prayer-Book, as prelacy had been previously abolished in England. But as a body, they favored the Independents, and were hostile to the Scotch influence in Ireland. On the 16th of July, the English regiments in Ulster, which were hitherto under Monro, were placed by Parliament under Colonel George Monk, one of the most renowned time-servers mentioned in history. Monro still kept the Scotch forces together, but next year he was surprised in Carrickfergus by Monk, and sent a prisoner to England.

The majority of the Long Parliament were Puritans, who desired to reform the Church on the basis of Presbyterianism. But several sects of enthusiasts had of late sprung up in England. Of these the most powerful were the Independents, who held that every congregation was a self-governing community, owning no subjection to either bishop or presbytery. Their chief leader was Oliver Cromwell, and they were as powerful in the army as Presbyterians in the Parliament. In political matters they aimed at a " root and branch " reformation, desiring to establish a commonwealth on the ruins of monarchy, while the Presbyterians desired to merely limit the king's power.

The Independents failed to prevent Parliament resolving to establish Presbyterianism as the national religion of England, but they succeeded in preventing that resolution from being carried into effect, and the Presbyterian system was not established anywhere except in Middlesex and Lancashire. Without organization it had no chance of surviving at the Restoration.

Meanwhile, Charles tried to negotiate with both parties at the same time, in order to extirpate " the one and the other." But failing in these attempts, he surrendered himself to the Scottish army before Newark. The Scots having received payment for their services in England, gave up the king to commissioners of the English Parliament, lest it might be thought a breach of faith to bring him to Scotland. In June, 1647, he was seized by the English army. The Parliament condemned this act and determined to continue negotiations with his Majesty. But the Parliament itself was overthrown by the force which had rendered it supreme. Colonel Pride, with a detachment of soldiers, seized the Presbyterian members, or forced them to flee from London. After "Pride's purge," the remainder, called the "Rump," were controlled by the army and the Independents. The king was brought to trial, condemned, and on the 30th of January, 1649, beheaded at Whitehall. The Commons now abolished the House of Lords and the monarchy itself.

Meanwhile the Irish Catholics, disgusted with the insolence of Rinuccini, the papal nuncio, had driven him from power. Ormond, who returned in September, 1648, had made a treaty with the confederates, and was soon at the head of an Irish army in the interest of the king. But Monk in the east and Coote in the west of Ulster, held the greater part of that province for the Parliament.

The Presbytery, although in the power of these generals, protested against the execution of Charles and the "insolent and presumptious practices" of the sectarian party in England. This representation evoked the wrath of John Milton, who although he had sworn to the Covenant, was angry with the Westminster Assembly for condemning his dangerous doctrine of divorce. He published a reply to the Presbyterian protest so full of scurrility as to be unworthy of the greatest Englishman of the age. He calls Belfast a "barbarous nook of Ireland," and accuses the Presbytery of exhibiting "as much devilish malice, impudence, and falsehood as any Irish rebel could have uttered," and declares that by their actions he might rather judge them to be "a generation of Highland thieves and red-shanks."

For some time there had been five distinct political parties in Ireland : (1) the extreme Catholics under the leadership of Owen Roe O'Neill, who wished for the utter destruction of Protestantism; (2) the moderate Catholics, who had made peace with Ormond ; (3) the royalists, who supported the king "without the Covenant"; (4) the Presbyterians who upheld "the king and the Covenant"; and (5) the republicans, represented by Coote and Monk.

Monk now left the country, and Coote, with about one thousand men, the only republican force in Ulster, remained in occupation of Londonderry. Sir Alexander Stewart, with the Presbyterian troops of the Lagan, sat down before that city in March, 1649, and until August it was closely blockaded. Sir Robert Stewart, uncle of Sir Alexander, joined the besiegers with a party of Royalists, and Sir George Monro, who had a commission from Charles, came with a number of Highlanders and Irishmen. These commanders were afterwards joined by Lord Montgomery.

Montgomery had formerly pretended to be a zealous Presbyterian ; and when taken prisoner at Benburb, the Scotch Assembly used their influence to procure his release. He had been lately chosen general by the Council of the Presbyterian army in Ireland, to oppose the republicans. But meanwhile, through Ormond, he received a commission from Charles II. to be commander-in-chief of the Royalist forces in Ulster, and he determined to betray the principles he had sworn to defend.   By his orders Sir George Monro left the other generals to conduct the blockade of Derry, and, capturing Coleraine, came to attack Belfast, which was held by Colonel Wallace for the Presbyterians.   Montgomery now hurried up his forces, as if to defend the town from Monro, and they were admitted on the 27th of June. He then threw off the mask, "produced his commission from the king, and discharged Wallace of his trust."   Lord Montgomery and Monro now captured Carrickfergus, and on the 11th of July, Monro again joined the beseigers of Londonderry.   Montgomery followed with a considerable force, and for some time the seige was vigorously prosecuted.

The Presbytery now finding that Montgomery was for the king without the Covenant, drew up, on the 7th of July, a declaration warning their people against serving in the royalist army.   And very many Presbyterians immediately withdrew from the beseigers of Londonderry, exhibiting a readiness to obey the admonitions of their Church seldom shown in later days.

To the amazement of both friends and foes, Owen Roe O'Neill, in consequence of a private treaty with Coote, came on the 7th of August to relieve the city.   Montgomery was compelled to raise the siege and return to his quarters in Antrim and Down.   O'Neill became ill before he left the neighborhood, and soon afterwards died in county Cavan.

Oliver Cromwell having rendered the Parliament supreme in England, and the independents supreme in the Parliament, now came to Ireland to act as lord lieutenant.   On the 15th of August, 1649, he landed at Dublin.   On the 3d of September he invested Drogheda, which had been garrisoned by the best of Ormond's soldiers, most of whom were English.   A summons to surrender being rejected, Cromwell took the town by storm on the 11th, and put the garrison with many defenseless inhabitants to the sword.   At Wexford he exercised the same severity.   Other towns opened their gates when summoned.   Venables, sent north to co-operate with Coote, met him at Belfast, which was taken on the 30th of September.   On the 6th of December these generals gained a great victory over Lord Montgomery, not far from Lisburn.   Heber M'Mahon, bishop of Clogher, at the head of the Irish, was defeated near Letterkenny with great slaughter, and his head placed on one of the gates of Londonderry.   The long contest was over.   Ireland, for the first time in her history, was completely subdued.

During all this time the Irish Presbyterians were closely watched lest they might espouse the interest of Charles.   By a council of war, an act of banishment was pronounced against their ministers.   Many of them fled from the country, and others, in the dress of farmers, travelled through their parishes and preached in private houses, or in the fields, at the risk of imprisonment.   The "engagement" was now pressed on the occupants of public offices, and heavy penalties inflicted on those who refused to swear.

But after Charles left the kingdom, the government of Ireland seemed less inclined to persecute Presbyterians, although the Roman Catholic faith was repressed with great severity. Cromwell, when in the country, had been asked by the governor of Ross for a promise of religious liberty as a condition of surrender. In reply, he declared he did not meddle with any man's conscience ; but if a liberty to " exercise " the mass was meant, that would not be permitted where the Parliament of England had power.

During the period of Episcopal ascendancy, the practice was to press with full force against Presbyterians the penal laws seldom enforced against Catholics. The Romanist was pardoned, and the Presbyterian punished for violating the provisions of the same enactment. But now the republicans began to permit Presbyterian pastors to exercise the functions of their office, although Roman priests were punished with great severity. Through the intercession of Lady Clotworthy, mother of Sir John Clotworthy, Mr. Ferguson got leave to return to his work, and others came back about the same time. Even the Episcopal Church was treated tenderly. Some of the bishops received small pensions, and several of the clergy lectured in private.

The Great Protector died on the 3d of September, 1658, and his son Richard was proclaimed his successor. Henry Cromwell was promoted to be lord lieutenant of Ireland, and continued to rule the country with wisdom and vigor. In the five years of his government more progress was made in reducing Ireland to subjection than in fifty years under the Stuarts. Rebellion had been subdued. Life and property had been rendered safe. Liberty of conscience for almost all classes of Protestants had been established. Many settlers from England and Scotland had been " planted " in the Celtic districts of the South and West. In Ulster, marshes had been drained, woods cut down, and farmhouses built. Landlords had now begun to reap the advantages of higher rent. The Presbyterian colonists had not been absorbed or modified by the Irish as their Anglo-Norman predecessors had been in the past. The Celts themselves were beginning to learn the language and to adopt the custom of their conquerors. Presbyterianism made rapid progress. Congregations were established not only in Antrim, Down, and Derry, but in Tyrone, Armagh, and other counties. As the wave of colonization flowed onwards, ministers went along with their countrymen. There were now in Ireland about seventy Presbyterian clergymen, having under their care eighty congregations, and nearly one hundred thousand people. The Presbytery had become so large that it was sometimes called a Synod.

In 1641, less than one-third of the landed property in Ireland was owned by Protestants. But after Cromwell's conquest, as a result of vast confiscations, they became owners of three-fourths of the whole country. What remained to Roman Catholic landlords in Ulster, Leinster, or Munster had to be exchanged by them for an equivalent in Connaught. Many grants

37

were made to soldiers of Cromwell, and on these lands Protestant settlements were established.   Every popish priest was banished, and the celebration of the rites of Roman worship repressed with ruthless severity.   But the rule of the Protector did not last long enough to firmly establish Protestantism in the South and West ; unfortunately it lasted long enough to make that religion detested by the Celts ; and the " curse of Cromwell " has ever since been a proverb.

NOTES TO CHAPTER XXXVII.

[1] The following were the first Calvinistic ministers established in Ulster : Edward Brice, (from Stirlingshire), Broadisland, Antrim, 1613 ; Robert Cunningham, Holywood, Down, 1615 ; John Ridge (from England), Antrim, Antrim, 1619 ; ———— Hubbard (from England),Carrickfergus, Antrim, 1621; Robert Blair (from Glasgow), Bangor, Down, 1623 ; James Hamilton (from Ayr), Ballywalter, Down, 1625 ; Josias Welsh (from Ayr), Templepatrick, Antrim, 1626 ; Andrew Stewart, Donegore, Antrim, 1627 ; George Dunbar (from Ayr), Larne, Down, 1628 ; Henry Colwort (from England), Oldstone, Down, 1629 ; John Livingston (from Torpichen), Killinchy, Down, 1630 ; John McClelland, Newton-Ards, Down, 1630 ; John Semple, Enniskillen in Magheriboy and Tyrkennedy.

[2] See Appendix U (The Adair Manuscripts).

CHAPTER XXXVIII

LONDONDERRY AND ENNISKILLEN

AT first, Cromwell's government pressed hardly on the Ulster Presbyterians, and many of the settlers were scheduled for transportation into Leinster and Munster on account of their having opposed the army of the Commonwealth.[1] Cromwell relented, however; the orders for transportation were not carried out, although lands seem to have been found for some of the Commonwealth soldiers in the northern counties. The great majority of these, however, settled in the South.[2] Government allowances were made to the Presbyterian clergy; and under Cromwell's strict rule the North of Ireland seems to have recovered steadily from the terrible blow of the Rebellion of October, 1641.

With the Restoration ceased the intimate connection which had existed between Scotland and her colony in Ulster; they had been kept together in very great measure by their common religion, and now in both the Presbyterian Church fell on evil days, and had to fight a long fight for very existence. In Ireland the Scottish Church had not to wait long before it received its quietus. Charles II. landed at Dover on the 25th of May, 1660; his restoration brought back Episcopacy as a matter of course; but if the Irish bishops had been wise men it need not have brought any persecution of the Northern Presbyterians, for it was insanity for the two parties of Protestants to quarrel in face of the enormous mass of opposing Catholics. There was no Archbishop Usher now to restrain the bishops, so they went to work with a will; and within a year of the Restoration every Presbyterian minister, save six or seven who recanted, were driven from their churches; they were forbidden to preach, baptize, marry, or exercise any function of the ministry. The old Scottish writer, Wodrow, in his *History of the Sufferings of the Church of Scotland*, gives a list of the ejected clergy. The numbers show approximately how the Scottish colony had recovered from the effects of the Rebellion of 1641, and grown in strength during the nine quiet years of Cromwell's government. There were in 1660 sixty-eight Presbyterian ministers in Ireland, all save one in Ulster, and of these sixty-one left their churches, and seven conformed to the Established Church.[3] Woodrow gives his reason for quoting the list: "Because I have always found the elder Presbyterian ministers in Ireland reckoning themselves upon the same bottom with and, as it were, a branch of, the Church of Scotland." The Presbyterian Church in Ireland, although it soon got back its liberty to some extent, did not entirely recover from the blow of 1661 until the next century was nearly run out. The number of Presbyterian churches in Ulster gives some indication of the population of Scottish origin, although a moiety of the Presbyterians were English. The extent of the emigration from Scotland is, however, more exactly given by Sir William Petty in his *Political Survey of Ireland in 1672*. He takes the total population of the country at 1,100,000, and calculates that 800,000 were Irish, 200,000 English, and 100,-000 Scots—of course the English were scattered all over Ireland, the Scots concentrated in Ulster. Petty divides the English into " 100,000 legal Protestants or Conformists and the rest are Presbyterians, Independents, Anabaptists, and Quakers." He states distinctly that a very large emigration had taken place from Scotland after Cromwell settled the country in 1652. The pov⌐ ⊃f the Scots must, indeed, have been so considerable, and so much feared as to be greatly exaggerated, for it was asserted in Parliament in 1656 that they " are able to raise 40,000 fighting men at any time." *

Charles II.'s reign brought many remarkable changes, which had much effect on Ulster, as well as on the rest of Ireland. It saw the beginning of the "Regium Donum," the State grant to the Presbyterians. The persecution did not continue as hotly as it was begun in 1661 ; gradually the Presbyterians recovered a portion of their freedom ; gradually their ministers returned. In 1672 the Presbyterian clergy approached the king directly. The good-natured monarch received them kindly, and granted them from the Irish revenues a sum of £1200, to be given annually towards their support. It was the beginning of the State aid to the Irish Presbyterian Church, which continued with a slight interval until put an end to by the Disestablishment Act of 1869. The other and deeper mark made on Irish history was the beginning of that repression of Irish industries which was to come into full force in Queen Anne's time. The first blow struck was an act which forbade the exportation of cattle from Ireland to England ; the second when, by the fifteenth of Charles II. (1675), Ireland, which up to this time in commercial matters had been held as part of England, was brought under the Navigation Acts, and her ships treated as if belonging to foreigners.

The Revolution of 1688 was accomplished almost without bloodshed in England ; in Scotland the struggle really finished at Killiecrankie ; in Ireland it was long and bloody. Once more it was the old race difference—a cleavage in race made more bitter by that terrible land question : the creation of the great settlements of Elizabeth and James's time, and of the yet more violent settlement of Cromwell. The Revolution in England of necessity brought civil war to Ireland. The greater portion of Ireland remained loyal to James II.; the North at once declared for William II. The Protestants of Ulster universally took arms, but their raw militia had little chance against the army which Tyrconnel, the lord deputy, had got together in support of James II. Rapidly he overran Ulster, until only at two points was the cause of Protestantism and of William of Orange upheld,—at Enniskillen and at Londonderry.

The Irish Presbyterians heard with delight of William's success. Dr.

Duncan Cumyng, on the part of their leaders, proceeded to London to congratulate the prince on his arrival, and to point out the danger in which Irish Protestantism was placed.

At that time, Ireland was prosperous, and provisions were cheap.   The native Irish lived on potatoes, beans, pounded barley, and oaten bread. Unless on festival days, they seldom tasted beef or eggs.   Yet their craving for flesh was strong ; for when they chanced to light on a carrion, " dead or drowned," they gladly ate it even when in loathsome decay.   As to clothing they wore neither shirts or shifts, and all the members of the family slept together on straw or rushes strewed on the ground, in the same apartment with their cattle and their swine.   Of 200,000 houses in Ireland only 16,000 had more than one chimney, 24,000 had just one chimney, and 160,000 had neither fixed hearth nor windows.   Almost the entire population lived in the country.   Belfast in 1666 contained not much more than a thousand inhabitants, and when William arrived could not have had much above two thousand at the highest calculation.   Besides Belfast, there were not half a dozen places in Ulster better than mere country villages.   The religious bigotry of the people was in proportion to their ignorance and rudeness of manners.   The Roman Catholics regarded their priests with feelings of superstition ; and believing they possessed miraculous power, feared to disobey their commands.

The authority of James had been more firmly established in Ireland than in any other part of the kingdom.   The lord deputy, Tyrconnel, himself a Roman Catholic, had placed Romanists in all important positions of civil and military power.   Protestants were dismissed from the army and their arms given to Roman Catholics before their eyes.   This process was continued until very few except Irish Celts were left in the force.   Every Catholic who could speak a little English, and had a few cows or horses, set up for a gentleman, wore a sword, and got into some employment to the exclusion of a Protestant.   Even the judges were distinguished more for their " brogue and their blunders " than for any knowledge of the law they were supposed to administer.   Arms were supplied to the Irish peasants, with which they committed many outrages on their Protestant neighbors.   The houses of the aristocracy were ransacked, the furniture smashed, and the plate carried off.   About a million of cattle were taken by force from their Protestant owners, or killed in sheer wantonness.   The Irish, who formerly lived on potatoes, oaten bread, and buttermilk, now feasted on raw beef or mutton ; and it is calculated that, in all, they destroyed property belonging to Protestants which was valued at upwards of £5,000,000 sterling.

On the 3d of December, 1688, a letter addressed to the earl of Mount-Alexander was found on the street of Comber, county Down.   This letter asserted that a massacre of Protestants had been arranged for the 9th of the same month.   And although there was no truth in this statement, it was generally believed.   Men still in the vigor of manhood remembered the fearful massacre of forty-seven years before; and they feared that the scenes of 1641 would be re-enacted immediately. Tyrconnel declared to representatives of the Dublin Protestants that the report was untrue; and when they refused to credit his assertions, he threw his wig into the fire, and assailed them with a volley of oaths. But his lordship's imprecations did not convince them that "Lying Dick Talbot" had learned to speak truth. Some of the ruling caste now fled from the kingdom; but the majority, not possessing the means of residing in another country, retired to the nearest place of safety in their own land.

The chief Protestant strongholds were Londonderry and Enniskillen, and to these towns most of the northern colonists fled for protection. Londonderry was then one of the chief towns in Ulster, and contained two or three thousand inhabitants. Enniskillen was an unwalled village of eighty houses, situated on an island in the river which joins the two sheets of water known as Lough Erne. Early in December, the inhabitants of this little town were thrown into a state of consternation on hearing that a party of Roman Catholic soldiers were coming to remain with them as a garrison. Captain Corry, an Episcopal landlord of the neighborhood, wished to admit the soldiers. The Rev. Robert Kelso, the Presbyterian clergyman, strongly urged resistance, and the townsmen adopted his advice, although they could muster only eighty men fit to carry arms, and though their munitions of war consisted of but twenty firelocks and ten pounds of gunpowder. Mr. Kelso labored both in public and in private to animate "his hearers to take up arms and stand upon their own defence; showing example himself by wearing arms, and marching in the head of them when together."

But the forces of the Enniskillen men were soon augmented by friends of the same race and religion, who had fled from the murderous attacks of Roman Catholics in the South or West. Thus reinforced they marched out of Enniskillen, and having proceeded about four miles, encountered a large party of Irish soldiers, whose officers were at that very moment dining with Captain Corry, the Episcopal landlord who had wished to admit them to the town. The Irish, left without leaders, fled at the first onset. This speedy victory silenced all in Enniskillen who opposed resistance to the power of James. Gustavus Hamilton was elected governor; an army of Protestants was raised, and from that time till the end of the war, the men of Enniskillen carried on a vigorous and successful campaign.

But Londonderry was the chief Protestant stronghold in Ireland. It was built on the slope and summit of a hill rising one hundred and twenty feet above the level of the river, and was surrounded by a wall, which is now fifteen feet high. This wall was defended by a number of cannons, presented to the town by some of the wealthy London guilds. The French generals of James might regard these fortifications with contempt, but behind them were seven thousand of the bravest men in Europe, with their wives and their children, for whom they were determined to fight to the last.

Early in December, the inhabitants of Derry were alarmed to hear that a Catholic regiment under Lord Antrim was about to be placed in their town as a garrison, and that these troops were actually on their march. This alarm was strengthened by a sermon preached to the Roman Catholics of Derry, showing how dangerous it was to spare even one of those whom God had devoted to destruction. On the 7th of December, when a copy of the letter addressed to Lord Mount-Alexander was received by Alderman Tomkins, the people concluded that Lord Antrim was coming to murder the inhabitants. A fearful scene of excitement ensued, and many determined to fight rather than admit the king's forces. Dr. Hopkins, the Episcopalian bishop of Derry, pointed out the sin of disobeying James, the " Anointed of the Lord," but the people could not comprehend that it was " a crime to shut the gates against those whom they believed sent thither to cut their throats." Nine out of every ten being Presbyterians, they were the more inclined to reject a policy they condemned, because it was advocated by a man whose office they despised. But when the Rev. James Gordon, Presbyterian minister of Glendermot, strongly advised resistance, they were easily persuaded to adopt the course they desired, when urged by one who held the same religious principles as themselves. The spirit of the Derry Presbyterians now rose high. Lord Antrim's soldiers were drawing near. No time was to be lost. Thirteen young men, since known to history as the " 'Prentice Boys of Derry," drew their swords, ran to the gate, and locked it, when the Irish were only sixty yards distant. Their names were: William Cairns, Henry Campsie, William Crookshanks, Alexander Cunningham, John Cunningham, Samuel Harvey, Samuel Hunt, Alexander Irwin, Robert Morrison, Daniel Sherrard, Robert Sherrard, James Spike, James Steward. The other gates were secured and the magazine seized. The Irish soldiers remained outside until they heard a man named James Morrison shouting, "Bring about a great gun here," when they retired in haste and recrossed the river. Bishop Hopkins now addressed the multitude, telling them that in resisting James, who was their lawful king, they were resisting God Himself. But this speech had no effect, and he soon left the town to those whom he called " the disloyal Whigs."

Roman Catholics were now excluded, and by the advice of David Cairns, a Presbyterian gentleman from Tyrone, six companies of Protestants were raised and armed.' Cairns now set out for London to try to obtain the supplies necessary for defending the town. When Tyrconnel heard that the gates of Derry had been closed in face of the royal army he was inflamed to madness. He cursed and swore and threw his wig into the fire as usual. But as almost all the great towns in England had already declared for William he began, when his rage cooled, to affect moderation. He now proposed to garrison Derry with Protestants, and sent thither Lord Mountjoy and Colonel Robert Lundy, with six companies, to reduce the town to submission. Mountjoy was a Protestant and his regiment was one of the few which contained a large proportion of the same religion. The inhabitants of Derry, not being certain of William's ultimate success, and in the meantime wishing to absolve themselves from "tincture of rebellion" against James, permitted Lundy, who was a Scottish Episcopalian, with two troops of Protestant soldiers, to enter the town. The inhabitants meanwhile were to have liberty to keep their own companies under arms.

After the Prince of Orange had overthrown all opposition in England, he sent Richard Hamilton to offer terms to Tyrconnel, who seemed inclined to submit. But his hesitation was probably to gain time. When Hamilton arrived in Dublin he failed to persuade Tyrconnel to betray James, but was himself easily induced to betray William and accept of a command in the Irish army. Tyrconnel, finding that Mountjoy's presence was troublesome, sent him with Baron Rice on a mission to France. Mountjoy was told to inform James that it would be useless to try the fate of war in Ireland. But Rice was instructed to get his companion placed in prison, and to urge James to come over at once with a French force. Should he refuse, then Rice was to offer Ireland to Louis of France. This message was faithfully delivered, and Mountjoy was placed in prison, where he was detained for more than three years.

Tyrconnel now began to raise troops and occupy all the passes leading to the North. Protestants were ordered to deliver up their arms, but no attempt was made to disarm the native Irish, who everywhere, except in Ulster, carried on their work of destruction. They embraced with ardor the cause of King James, since it would give them an opportunity of robbing and murdering their Protestant neighbors. To obtain that privilege they would as willingly have fought against James as for him.

The arrest of Mountjoy in France created consternation among all the Protestants of Ireland, and most of them fled from their homes for safety. The Protestant leaders formed a council at Hillsborough, and put themselves in a position of defence. But on the 21st of February, 1689, their forces were defeated in an unsuccessful attempt to surprise Carrickfergus Castle, and the government of James afterwards treated them as rebels.

On the 13th of February, William and Mary, having accepted the crown, were proclaimed king and queen in London. Similar proclamations were afterwards made in those towns of Ulster where the Protestants were supreme. On the 12th of March, James landed at Kinsale and was warmly received by the native Irish and by the Episcopal clergy. We are told in *Ireland's Lamentation* that the king was so greatly annoyed by "rude country Irish gentlewomen" who persisted in kissing him that he ordered them to be kept at a distance. His progress was slow, as he rode on horseback over miserable roads, and it was the 24th of the month before he reached Dublin. Here he called a parliament which met at Dublin May 7th.[*]

Tyrconnel had already sent a Presbyterian minister — the Rev. Alexander Osborne, of Dublin — to the Protestant gentry in arms, with an offer of favorable terms of surrender. These proposals Mr. Osborne communicated to Sir Arthur Rawdon, but, at the same time, conveyed a private warning that the lord deputy could not be trusted, as he had broken " all such capitulations " made with Protestants in the South and West. The council, therefore, rejected the deputy's terms, and began to prepare for resisting the renegade, Richard Hamilton, who was on his march with troops to reduce them to submission. At a meeting of the Protestant leaders on the 14th of March, nine Presbyterian clergymen offered to raise forces to fight for William and Mary. This offer was gladly accepted ; but it was too late. Hamilton had arrived at Newry before it was thought that he had left Dublin. And on the very day this offer was made, the Protestants, under Sir Arthur Rawdon, were, at the first onset, completely defeated by Hamilton in an engagement commonly known as "The Break of Dromore." Some of the colonists now submitted to James, and took protection ; but the majority fled northwards, or left the country altogether. Unable to carry their household furniture with them, they smashed it to bits, and threw their provisions into the ditches lest they should fall into the hands of the enemy. Some Protestants took refuge in Coleraine, where, on the 27th of March, they repelled an attack of Hamilton. But they had to contend with the treachery of pretended friends, as well as with the open hostility of enemies.

When Mountjoy withdrew from Derry, he was succeeded by Lundy, who soon afterwards submitted to William, that he might retain his authority and have an opportunity of betraying the town. On the 21st of March, he and other officers of the army, with several leading citizens, signed a declaration by which they all bound themselves to oppose "the Irish enemy." ' On that same day, Captain James Hamilton arrived at Derry, from England, with arms, ammunition, and five hundred and ninety-five pounds of money. He carried a commission for Colonel Lundy to be governor of the city, which was given to him after he had taken the oath of fidelity to King William. Having now obtained an official position of authority, Lundy began to use all the power attached to that position to advance the cause of James. Although he had five hundred barrels of powder in his stores, he refused to send ammunition to towns that wished to resist the enemy ; and although provisions were so plenty that a goose could be bought for three pence, forty-five eggs for a penny, and a quarter of beef for four shillings, he made no attempt to lay up a necessary store. He ordered all garrisons of Ulster to withdraw to Derry on the plea that he had plenty of provisions there, and soon afterwards proposed to surrender that city on the plea that his provisions were insufficient.

On the 10th of April, Counsellor Cairns returned from London to Londonderry. He brought a letter from King William to Lundy, containing promise of speedy assistance ; but it produced no effect on the governor, whose object was to betray the city.   Nevertheless, he signed an agreement with his officers to stand by his post to the last.[8]

Richard Hamilton now marched towards Londonderry.   Unable to cross the river at Waterside, he directed his course to Strabane, where the Mourne and Finn unite to form the Foyle.   A few resolute men there might have prevented his passage, but Lundy had arranged everything so that he might cross in safety.   Several regiments were ordered to guard the river at Clady and Lifford, but they were neither sent in time nor supplied with sufficient ammunition.   The Irish crossed the Mourne without opposition, and early on the fifteenth came to the Finn at Clady, where the bridge had been broken down.   The main body of the Protestants had not arrived, and their infantry, who guarded the ford, were easily routed ; but Captain Murray with about thirty cavalry disputed the passage till they had exhausted the three rounds of ammunition with which each man had been supplied.   The Irish then crossed without difficulty.

Meanwhile the main body of the Protestant army, numbering nearly ten thousand men, were concentrating nearer Derry ; but finding the enemy had crossed, they fled without resistance.   Lundy had not set out for the scene of conflict until the Irish had made good their passage.   Meeting his own troops retreating before the enemy, he never attempted to rally them, but returned to the city as quickly as he could, and closed the gates on many of the Protestant fugitives who were forced to remain outside, in danger of being attacked by the Irish.   That very day, Colonel Cunningham and Colonel Richards arrived in Lough Foyle with two regiments which King William had despatched to assist the townsmen.   Lundy and a few of his friends on whom he could depend held a council of war with Cunningham, Richards, and some of their officers.   He represented that the provisions in Derry could not last more than eight or ten days, and that the place was not tenable against such an army as now marched to the assault.   Therefore he advised that the two regiments be sent back, and the townspeople permitted to make terms with the enemy.   This proposition was opposed by Richards, who said that "quitting the town was quitting of a kingdom "; but Lundy carried his point, and the troops were sent back to England without being permitted to land.

King James had travelled northwards to join his army.   On the 14th of April, he reached Omagh.   The inhabitants had fled to Derry, and, before leaving, had destroyed what they could not carry with them.   The houses were without windows, and the country without provisions.   The roads were bad and the weather unfavorable.   But the hopes of a speedy victory through Lundy's treachery impelled James to proceed to Derry, which, on the seventeenth, he summoned to surrender.

Within the walls, the Protestants were, meanwhile, beginning to discover the true state of affairs.   Lundy's action in having the two regiments sent back to England convinced them of that treachery which they previously had only suspected. They now became mutinous, and, in their rage, fired on some officers who were escaping from the city, killing one and wounding another. Meanwhile Lundy was still proceeding with his plans for surrender. In answer to the summons of James, he sent Archdeacon Hamilton and two other gentlemen to see what terms his Majesty would grant. But when Hamilton and his companions returned, they were refused admission by the citizens.

On the eighteenth, King James advanced with his army to the walls, expecting the influence of Lundy to prevent active opposition to his admission. But those who guarded the gates, contrary to the express orders of the governor, fired on the advancing soldiers, and killed an officer at the king's side. His Majesty now retired to a safe distance, and awaited the result of his negotiations.

The people, finding they were betrayed, became fearfully excited. They threatened to kill Colonel Whitney, whom Lundy sent to order them not to fire at the Irish army, and they wanted nothing but a leader to depose the traitor within, and resist the enemy without. At that moment Adam Murray arrived from Culmore with a party of cavalry. Murray was a Presbyterian. His ancestors lived at Philiphaugh, in Scotland, and he himself resided at Ling, on the Faughanwater. After the defeat at Cladyford, he retired to Culmore. But just as King James was seeking admission to the city he approached at the head of a large party of horsemen. Lundy and his council were then sitting to arrange a surrender. The arrival of Murray filled them with alarm, as they knew his entrance would destroy their design. Accordingly, they sent him word to withdraw his cavalry to the back side of the hill, out of sight of all those who occupied the walls. Astonished at these orders, he questioned the messenger, a relative of his own, and from him found out that the governor was then negotiating a surrender. Murray now hastened to the town with all speed, but found the gates closed and admission refused. After some parley, the Rev. George Walker, acting on behalf of the council, offered to permit Murray himself to be drawn up the wall by a rope, and admitted, on condition that his troops should be excluded. But this offer was refused with disdain, and " in opposition to the orders of Lundy and the exertions of Walker," the gates were opened by Captain Morrison. Murray and his men were received with enthusiasm, and the city saved from surrender.

Meanwhile the council had agreed to capitulate. But, alarmed when they found Murray had entered, they summoned him to appear before them. He came accompanied by his friends, with the air of one in authority, and refused with indignation to sign the terms of surrender. He openly accused Lundy of treachery, and told him that his neglect to guard the fords at Strabane was the cause of their present difficulties. He then left the council and began to make preparations for defending the city. Lundy now tried to persuade some Presbyterian ministers to advise Murray and his followers, who were nearly all of the same faith, to agree to the terms of surrender. But the ministers refused to give an advice contrary to their convictions.

The position of affairs in Derry now suddenly changed. Murray was master of the town. He compelled the captain of the guard to deliver up the keys, and placed on the walls men in whom he could trust. He was then requested to become governor himself, but unfortunately refused, declaring that his talents were rather for the field than for "conduct or government in the town." A council met to choose a governor. Baker, Mitchelburn, and Johnston were nominated, but Baker, having the majority, was selected. The new governor then asked permission to have an assistant to manage the department of "stores and provisions." This being granted, he selected the Rev. George Walker, rector of Donaghmore, near Dungannon. Lundy, disguised as a soldier, escaped from the town, made his way to Scotland, and afterwards, together with his dupes, Cunningham and Richards, was dismissed from his Majesty's service.

There were now about twenty thousand people within the walls of Derry, of whom seven thousand were able to bear arms. The fighting men were divided into eight regiments, each under a colonel; but Murray was "general in the field upon all sallies." James now sent the earl of Abercorn to offer the town favorable terms of surrender. The citizens would all receive a free pardon, and Murray a thousand pounds for himself and a colonel's commission. Abercorn was met at the gate by Murray, who, refusing to betray his race and his religion for any personal advantage, rejected these proposals with disdain.

When King James found that the town could not be taken unless by a regular siege, he returned to Dublin, leaving the command to Maumont, who now surrounded the city, and began to throw in shells from Waterside. On the 21st of April a large party of the garrison made a sally. Colonel Murray at the head of the cavalry charged through the enemy. Three times he met their commander, General Maumont himself, who, at the final encounter, was killed.

By the death of Maumont, Richard Hamilton again became commander-in-chief of the Irish army.

In this encounter the Protestants did not lose more than a dozen men, while the enemy lost about two hundred. But this advantage was more than counterbalanced two days afterwards when the besiegers, by capitulation, obtained possession of Culmore Fort, situated four miles north of Derry, commanding the entrance to the Foyle, and rendering relief from the sea exceedingly difficult. Encouraged by their success in the field, the Protestants sallied out on the twenty-fifth in the direction of Pennyburn. There was a series of skirmishes that day, with varying success, but the garrison lost only two men killed and a dozen wounded. On the side of the enemy the loss was considerable. The earl of Abercorn had his horse killed, and escaped with difficulty, leaving behind his saddle and his scarlet cloak.

Late on the night of the 5th of May, the besiegers, under Brigadier-General Ramsay, made an attack on Windmill Hill, a little to the southwest of the city. They drove back a few men who were guarding the place, and, taking advantage of some old ditches, began to throw up earthworks. Their object was to retain this place for a battery, and thereby attack the walls with better hope of success. Governor Baker, having determined to drive the enemy from this position so dangerous to the garrison, ordered ten men to be selected from each company to make an attack. But before his arrangements were complete, a great number of the soldiers, having become impatient, rushed out at Bishop's gate and Ferry-quay gate, under the leadership of some inferior officers, and made a furious attack on the enemy. Both parties fought hand to hand, as if the fate of the town depended upon the event of that summer morning. From daylight till noon the bloody conflict continued. So close were the combatants engaged that often they struck one another with the butts of their muskets. After a fearful struggle, the citizen soldiers were victorious. With a loss of only four killed and twenty wounded, the enemy were put to flight, Ramsay and two hundred of his men were slain, and five hundred wounded. Lord Netterville, Sir Gerard Aylmer, Lieutenant-Colonel Talbot, and Lieutenant Newcomen were taken prisoners. The Protestants then fortified Windmill Hill and retained possession of it afterwards in spite of the enemy.

The siege now became a blockade. Sixteen forts erected round the city prevented any possibility of obtaining provisions by sudden sallies ; and the enemy hoped to conquer by famine men whom they had failed to subdue by the sword. It soon became well known that Murray was the moving spirit among those by whom the town was defended.

Hamilton now determined to try whether filial love would be more powerful than bribery to induce Murray to make the town surrender. Accordingly he seized the Colonel's father, an old man of eighty, who resided a few miles from Derry, and threatened to hang him unless he would induce his son to capitulate. The old man went into the town as desired, but, regardless of consequences, advised his son to hold out to the last. Murray refused to yield. His father returned to the camp, and Hamilton, to his credit, permitted him to go home unmolested.

On Saturday, the 18th of May, Captain John Cunningham and Captain Noble, with about a hundred men, made an attack on a fort which stood on the hill above Creggan. At first they seemed likely to succeed ; but a party of the enemy's cavalry got between them and the city. With all the energy of despair, they cut their way back through the opposing horsemen, but Captain Cunningham and about sixteen others were killed.

Towards the end of May, the Rev. George Walker, assistant governor, was strongly suspected of embezzling the stores and endeavoring to surrender the city. Besides, he was accused of certain " personal vices," which from statements of Dr. Davis and Mackenzie were in all probability habits of drunkenness. Colonels Murray, Hamil, Crofton, and Monro, together with upwards of a hundred other officers, "subscribed a resolution to prosecute him" on these charges. But Governor Baker got the matter settled by the appointment of a council of fourteen, whom the governors were bound to consult on every matter of importance. All the colonels had seats in this council, and besides there were representatives of the town and of the country. Each member had to swear that he would not treat with the enemy without the "knowledge and order" of that council in its collective capacity.

Meanwhile the cannonade continued. Day by day the great guns of James played on the town, and the great guns on the wall and on the flat roof of the cathedral replied. New batteries were erected and the city was assailed from every side. At first the shells used by the besiegers were small, but afterwards they were so large that they tore up the streets and often killed the inhabitants in their houses, and even in their cellars, to which they had fled for safety. The pavements were now dug up that the bombs might sink into the soft earth where they fell.

Although Presbyterians constituted a very great majority of the Protestant inhabitants of Derry, they had been compelled to erect their meeting-house outside the walls. It had been lately destroyed, and within the city there was no place of worship except the cathedral. This building was used during the siege by both denominations of Protestants. In the morning it was occupied by those who used the liturgy, but then there was only a thin attendance. In the afternoon it was at the disposal of dissenters, but it was not sufficient to contain the numbers who desired to worship according to the more simple form. It was therefore necessary to have four or five other places of meeting. We learn from Mackenzie's journal, that on Tuesday, the 21st of May, "the Nonconformists kept a solemn fast, and had sermons in two places of the city besides the cathedral, where there were considerable collections made for the poor." The Episcopal ministers in the town were maintained from the stores, or had a weekly allowance of money. The other clergymen received nothing from any public source. During the siege there were eight Presbyterian and eighteen Episcopal ministers in the town. Mackenzie acted as chaplain for Walker's regiment, who were almost all Presbyterians. Although the governors and a large proportion of the superior officers were Episcopalians, more than ninety out of every hundred of the rank and file were Scotch Presbyterians. They in reality saved the town for Ireland and Ireland for the kingdom.

On Tuesday, the 4th of June, the enemy made a most determined attempt to recapture Windmill Hill. They came on from different directions with both infantry and cavalry. The cavalry advanced by way of the Strand, wearing armor under their clothes, and carrying faggots before them with which to fill up the trenches. The garrison, finding that their balls struck these men without result, aimed at their horses. The assailants, thrown into confusion, were attacked by a large party under Captains James and John Gladstanes. Most of the enemy were killed or driven into the river, and their commander, Captain Butler, taken prisoner. Meanwhile their infantry had made an attack between the windmill and the river, and had assailed some forts at the Bogside. They advanced in face of a fearful storm of shot, for the garrison, drawn up in three lines, were enabled, by discharging successively, to maintain an almost continual fire. The women supplied their husbands with food, drink, and ammunition, and, when the enemy drew near, assailed them with volleys of stones, which did considerable execution. But still the Irish advanced. They came up to the very works, when some of them were pulled over by the hair of their heads. Failing to force an entrance, the survivors at length retreated, carrying bodies on their backs as a protection from the volleys of shot sent after them. The enemy had about four hundred killed and wounded, and besides some were taken prisoners, while the citizens lost only five or six men. That night many bombs were thrown into the city. Of these one weighed two hundred and seventy-three pounds and was charged with seventeen pounds of powder. The garrison now began to stand in need of balls themselves, and they used bricks cased in lead, which answered their purpose very well.

The defence of Derry had excited the admiration and sympathy of England. In order to relieve the city, the Government sent an expedition under the command of Major-General Kirke, notorious for the cruelty with which he treated the unfortunate country people concerned in Monmouth's rebellion. Kirke arrived in Lough Foyle early in June, and on the eighth, one of his ships, in attacking Culmore Fort, ran aground and was considerably injured by the enemy's cannon before the rising tide enabled her to float. For some days afterwards nothing more was attempted, but on the thirteenth, the sentinels on the cathedral tower saw thirty vessels in Lough Foyle. Soon the news spread throughout the city, and a thrill of joy excited the hearts of the brave men who held the town when they saw the approach of assistance.

The Irish, now fearing lest relief might be conveyed up the river to the besieged city, made a boom of wood, bound with iron and secured by chains, which they placed in a narrow part of the river between Culmore and the town. This boom, constructed of materials which were too heavy, sank and was broken. Another was made with fir beams bound with chains. One end was secured by a bridge, and the other by woodwork and masonry. It floated on the water and was considered sufficiently strong to prevent the passage of any ship up the river.

During this time the fleet lay idle, and the citizens began to grow impatient. Disappointed in obtaining speedy relief by sea, they turned their thoughts to the Enniskillen men, who, a few days before, had marched as far as Omagh. Colonel Murray, with about twenty men, embarked, during the night of the 18th of June, in a lately constructed boat, hoping to land two boys at

Dunnalong Wood, about four miles up the river, from whence it was hoped they might make their way to Enniskillen. But the boat was soon discovered by the enemy, and nearly struck by one of their numerous cannon-shots. Having arrived at the wood, the boys were so much frightened that no persuasion could force them to land. The party now turned back, and the first light of a summer morning enabled them to discover that they had been followed by two of the enemy's boats which, manned by dragoons, were now in their way as they returned. A fearful engagement ensued. Both sides fired until they had exhausted their shot. One of the enemy's boats then came close, and the dragoons tried to board, but Murray's men killed a lieutenant and three of the soldiers with their weapons, and threw others into the water. The remainder surrendered, and the occupants of the second boat, seeing that the other had been captured, made off as quickly as possible. Murray, with his prize, now returned to the city amidst a fearful fire from the shore. A ball hit him on the helmet and bruised his head, but he was the only one of his party struck, and the thirteen prisoners were landed in safety.

On the very day Murray returned from this expedition, the question of relieving the city was discussed by the officers of the fleet at a council of war held on board the *Swallow*. It was determined that, since the garrison were not pressed by the enemy or by want of provisions, they would wait until such forces arrived from England as would make it possible by land to raise the siege ; or until they would receive word that the condition of affairs was desperate in the city. Accordingly Kirke made no attempt to send supplies up the river, although the wind was favorable, but lay inactive in the lough.

While there, he succeeded in communicating with the garrison. A man named Roche, who was afterwards a captain in William's army, and a companion named Cromie, made their way from the fleet up the bank of the river until they were opposite the town. Roche then undressed, swam over, and got four guns fired from the cathedral tower as a sign of his safe arrival. But Cromie, being unable to swim, had to remain behind, and was taken by the enemy. Roche on his return went to the place where he had previously left his clothes, but was discovered by the Irish and pursued for three miles as he ran naked through the woods torn by brambles. At last, he was overtaken by the enemy and his jaw broken by a blow from a halbert. But he succeeded in plunging into the river, and, notwithstanding many wounds, made his way, amid a storm of bullets, back to the city. Afterwards, a man named M'Gimpsy volunteered to Colonel Murray to swim to the fleet. He carried a letter in a small bladder tied round his neck. In the bladder were also two bullets, so that, if pursued, he could, by breaking the string allow all to sink to the bottom. But M'Gimpsy was drowned in the river, and the letter describing the desperate condition of the citizens was found by the enemy.

On the 28th of June, the arrival of young Lord Clancarty with his regiment, to reinforce the besiegers, created great enthusiasm among the Irish, as they firmly believed in the truth of an old prophecy that Clancarty would one day knock at the gates of Derry. The very night of his arrival he made a vigorous attack on the bulwarks at Butcher's gate. But the defenders fired furiously from the walls. A party under Noble sallied out, and after a hard contested fight drove off the assailants. Clancarty may be said to have knocked at the gates, but he failed to enter, although he came nearer than any other who had led an attack on the town.

A dispute had previously arisen between Governor Baker and Colonel Mitchelburn. They had drawn their swords on one another, and Mitchelburn by orders of Baker, had been placed in prison. Not long afterwards the governor was seized with fever, when, notwithstanding this quarrel, a council of officers by his advice selected Mitchelburn to act as his deputy. Baker died on the 30th of June, and Mitchelburn continued to act as governor without any confirmation of his authority by the council.

The failure of Hamilton to capture the city had caused him to be superseded by General Conrad de Rosen, a Livonian by birth, a man of savage manners, barbarous speech, and cruel disposition. Angry at the successful resistance made by untrained countrymen, he raved and swore and threatened. He would demolish the town ; he would bury it in ashes ; he would spare neither age nor sex, if it had to be captured by storm.

First, he determined to offer favorable terms of surrender, accompanied with terrific threats. Imagining that if the common soldiers knew the nature of his proposals they would compel their officers to submit, he caused a dead bomb to be thrown into the town containing his conditions, signed by Hamilton, and followed by a letter of his own, indicating the penalties of a refusal. If they surrendered, all would obtain protection, liberty of conscience, and a restoration of what they had lost by the war. If they held out, then the old men and women left in the country would be driven to Derry, and starved to death outside the walls, if not admitted by the garrison, Rosen's idea being that, if admitted, the remaining provisions would be speedily consumed.

This plan failed ; for, although supplies were now growing scarce and the mortality had become great, the rank and file were more determined than even their officers to resist to the bitter end. Accordingly Rosen's conditions were refused and his threats defied. Driven to madness, he now sent out many parties of soldiers, who collected thousands of Protestants—old men, women, and children—that had been left at home, and drove them at the point of the sword to the city walls. But admission was refused, and even the poor captives themselves, with stern determination, acquiesced in the resolution by which they were excluded.

The garrison now threatened as a reprisal to hang their prisoners of war. For this purpose they erected a gallows on the wall, in sight of the enemy's camp. They requested Rosen to send priests to shrive those who were to suffer. The prisoners were in a state of terrific fear. They wrote to the Irish commanders that they were all to be hanged the next day, unless the Protestants without the walls were permitted to return home. Rosen was at

38

first inflexible. He meant what he said. He would let the prisoners without perish from hunger if not admitted by their friends within. Hamilton and some of his officers remonstrated, and at last the non-combatants who survived were permitted to return ; but many had previously perished from their hardships. Some able-bodied men who were among them remained in the town, and a few in the town who were useless succeeded in getting away with the crowd ; but others, known by their sickly appearance, were turned back. King James himself was angry when he heard of Rosen's cruelty, and said it would not have been thought of by any but a barbarous Muscovite. Rosen was now recalled and Richard Hamilton left once more in command.

Meanwhile the siege had been prosecuted with vigor. Trenches were extended near to the town, and cannon placed in commanding positions. There was even an attempt made to mine the walls, but fortunately the attempt was a failure. The supply of water within was insufficient, and the garrison were often exposed to great danger when they went to Columbkille's well without. But the want of food had begun to be more keenly felt than the want of water. Some of the more lukewarm deserted to the enemy. Day by day provisions became more scarce, until, at last, rats and mice, fattened on the blood of the slain, were eagerly devoured. A brave soldier named John Hunter states in his journal :

" I myself would have eaten the poorest cat or dog I ever saw with my eyes. The famine was so great that many a man, woman, and child died for want of food. I myself was so weak from hunger that I fell under my musket one morning as I was going to the walls ; . . . and yet when the enemy were coming, as many a time they did, . . . then I found as if my former strength returned to me. I am sure it was the Lord that kept the city, and none else."

A stench arose from the slain, and sickness became more fatal than the weapons of the enemy. The garrison, which at first numbered upwards of seven thousand fighting men, was reduced to four thousand three hundred, of whom many had contracted diseases from which they afterwards died. And yet there were some professing Protestants who had but little sympathy for these sufferings. A certain clergyman, on hearing of how many thousands died in Derry, fighting for the Protestant religion and the liberties of the country, remarked that it was " no matter how many of them dy'd, for they were but a pack of Scots Presbyterians."

Kirke had gone to the island of Inch by way of Lough Swilly. There he threw up entrenchments ; and he appeared determined to attempt by land to relieve the city. But, overestimating the strength of the enemy, who could not then have had more than six or seven thousand men before Derry, he remained inactive. In vain the garrison exhibited signals of distress, and used every means in their power to urge him to do what might have been done, with less difficulty, before the boom was erected.

Everywhere throughout Ulster, Presbyterian farmers exhibited courage

sadly wanting in some of the professional soldiers.   When it was known that
provisions were scarce in Londonderry, Mr. James Knox, who resided
near Coleraine, with the assistance of his two sons, brought a herd of
cattle to Lough Foyle opposite Culmore, and, on a dark night, drove
them along the slob, made them swim across the river, and introduced them
into the city by the " water-gate."

On the 10th of July, Hamilton again offered favorable terms of
surrender, embracing the fullest civil and religious liberty.   Commissioners
appointed by both parties arranged the preliminaries.   When this proposition
came before the council, Walker strongly advocated the policy of capitulat-
ing.   But the majority carried a resolution not to submit, unless Hamilton
would send hostages to the ships, in security of fulfilling the promised conditions, and extend the time of surrender till the 26th of July.   These terms
were refused, and hostilities were continued.   A few days afterwards Colonel
Murray led out a small party to attack the enemy who were in trenches near
Butcher's gate.   But, unfortunately, he was shot through both thighs, near
the body, and his wounds were not healed until four months afterwards.

When provisions were almost exhausted, Mr. James Cunningham discovered a plan of making pancakes out of starch mixed with tallow.   This food
acted as a medicine for the sick and it enabled the town to hold out a week
longer.

On Thursday, the 25th of July, the garrison made a sally with the object
of capturing some cows then grazing behind the enemy's lines.   At first, the
attempt seemed likely to succeed.   The Irish were driven out of their
trenches and sixty of them killed ; but meanwhile the herders chased their
cattle away, and the object of the attack was not accomplished.   Next day,
the garrison took one of their last cows outside the walls, tied her to a stake,
covered her with tar, and set her on fire, thinking that her roaring would
cause some of the enemy's cattle to run to her relief.   But the poor animal,
maddened by pain, succeeded in breaking loose from the stake, and had to
be shot to prevent her from running into the Irish lines.

On the 27th of July, all their cows, dogs, and available horses were
killed.   Ash wrote in his journal that Wednesday would be their last day, if
relief did not previously arrive.

The Rev. James Gordon, Presbyterian minister of Glendermot, now paid
a visit to Kirke, and pointed out to him that it would be possible to sail up
the river, cut down the boom, and, in this way, relieve the city.   Whatever
might be the motive which determined Kirke,— whether the advice of Gordon or orders received from Schomberg,—he now did what could have been
much more easily done when he first arrived.

On the evening of Sunday, the 28th of July, the wind turned towards
the north.   Shortly before sunset, the sentinels on the tower saw three ships
spread their sails and direct their course towards the Foyle.   Two of these
were merchant vessels with provisions, the third was the *Dartmouth*, frigate

of war, commanded by Captain Leake. Sailing right before the wind, they soon arrived at Culmore. Leake then ran his frigate close to the fort and engaged its guns, while the provision ships passed on, accompanied by the *Swallow's* long-boat " barricadoed and armed with seamen to cut the boome." The wind now sank to a calm ; but the tide was rising fast, and bore the relieving vessels onwards, amid a storm of balls from great guns along the banks of the river, which here was only five hundred feet wide. All went well till the ships reached the boom, against which the *Mountjoy* was driven with all her force. The huge barricade cracked and yielded, but did not give way, while the ship, by force of the rebound, was stuck fast in the sand. From all sides the enemy set up a shout of triumph, which passed from man to man until it arose around the city walls and caused the hearts of their brave defenders to feel the agony of despair. The Irish now fired their cannons, manned their boats, and prepared to board. At that moment two regiments of their horse came galloping up, but when the first ranks were within a pike's length of the ship, she discharged at them her cannons loaded with partridge shot. Many of the enemy were killed, while the rebound of the guns drove the vessel into deep water. Meanwhile the crew of the long-boat were cutting the boom. The ship, afloat once more ran against the barricade, forcing it to give way with a tremendous crash. Just then her gallant master, Captain Browning, was shot through the head and fell in the moment of victory. The obstruction was passed. The rising tide brought the vessels toward the town. To hasten their speed the long-boat took them in tow. Other boats met them on the way and rendered similar assistance. At ten o'clock they reached the quay in safety, and, with a loss of only five men killed, brought relief to the city. Now from man to man along the walls arose a cheer of triumph. The joy-bells rang loudly. The cannons thundered from the tower. Presbyterians had won what they thought was liberty, but what was in reality the privilege of being persecuted by a prelatic aristocracy rather than by a Roman Catholic democracy.

A rampart of barrels filled with clay was thrown up in haste to protect those engaged in unloading. This work was accomplished with such rapidity that every family had a plentiful supper that night before retiring to rest. For two days longer the army of James continued to fire at the town ; but on the morning of the 1st of August their camp was vacant, their tents destroyed, and the line of their retreat southwards marked by many houses in flames. At Strabane, hearing of Macarthy's defeat near Newtown-Butler, they were so frightened that they burst some of their great guns ; and although the winds blew and the rain fell in torrents they retreated with precipitation, by way of Dungannon, to Dublin.

The garrison of Derry had lost about two thousand eight hundred men during the siege. Of these the vast majority died from sickness, as only about eighty were slain in battle. But of the non-combatants it is probable that more than seven thousand perished. The Irish army lost about nine thousand, of whom a large proportion fell in the field. When the siege was raised, their blockading force probably did not exceed six thousand men.

James was greatly disappointed by the result ; and he said that if there had been as many Englishmen in his army as there were of others, they would before then have brought him Derry stone by stone. The stand made by this city prevented him from reinforcing Dundee, who, on the 27th of July, was slain at the battle of Killiecrankie.

In the meantime the men of Enniskillen had fought many battles, and in almost all had been victorious. On the 11th of March, 1689, they proclaimed William and Mary. Soon afterwards, when ordered by Lundy to fall back on Londonderry, they refused obedience. Joined by many refugees from places farther south, they determined to submit only when conquered.

The Irish, under Lord Galmoy, had laid siege to Crom Castle, which belonged to Captain Crichton. But two hundred men, sent from Enniskillen, succeeded in entering the place. Thus reinforced, the garrison made a furious attack on Galmoy, beat his men out of the trenches, and compelled him to retreat to Belturbet. On his arrival there he proposed to exchange one of his prisoners, Captain Dixie, son of the dean of Kilmore, for Captain Brian Maguire, who had been captured by the Protestants. This proposal was accepted and Maguire sent to Belturbet. But Galmoy, instead of liberating Dixie, ordered him and another prisoner named Charleton to be tried by court-martial for making war against King James. Having been found guilty and sentenced to death, they were offered their lives on condition of becoming Roman Catholics. This proposition they rejected with disdain, and consequently were both hanged from a sign-post in Belturbet. Their heads were afterwards cut off, and, having been first " kickt about the streets for foot-balls," were fixed on the market-house. Maguire, who had been set at liberty, was so disgusted with Galmoy's perfidy that he refused to remain any longer in the service of King James.

About the end of March, Governor Hamilton sent a detachment of cavalry to obtain a share of the arms and ammunition which had arrived in Derry. But Colonel Lundy gave the party a " very cold welcome," and they succeeded in obtaining only five barrels of powder out of five hundred then in store, and sixty old muskets without stock or lock ; though these were afterwards fitted up so as to be serviceable.

A party under the command of Lloyd, whom Witherow terms "the Murray of Enniskillen," drove the enemy from Trillick, and made successful raids in many different directions. They burned Augher Castle, and brought home such a large quantity of provisions and cattle that a cow could be bought in Enniskillen for two shillings, while the inhabitants of Londonderry were dying with famine.

The Protestant garrison of Ballyshannon, commanded by Captain Folliott, was now besieged by a strong party of the enemy, and Lloyd advanced to their relief. At Belleek, three miles from Ballyshannon, he encountered the

Irish, drawn up in a narrow pass barricaded in front, a bog on one flank, and Lough Erne on the other.   But Lloyd was shown a pass by which his men advanced safely.   The enemy, fearing that they were about to be flanked, fled from a position they had thought impregnable, leaving behind them three hundred killed, wounded, or prisoners.   Thus the siege of Ballyshannon was raised.

About the end of May, Lloyd set out with fifteen hundred men on another expedition.   He captured Ballinacarrig Castle, and advanced to Kells, within thirty miles of Dublin, where he created great consternation.   Having captured five hundred horses, five thousand "black cattle," the same number of sheep, and a large store of arms, he returned, without the loss of a single man.   All this time, Sarsfield was encamped at Manor-Hamilton, sixteen miles west of Enniskillen.

Emboldened by their victories, the men of Enniskillen now determined to try the possibility of relieving Derry by marching past Omagh, capturing the Irish position at Waterside, and, from thence, carrying supplies to the town across the Foyle.   Against the wishes of the whole army, Governor Hamilton determined to take the command, leaving the ever-victorious Lloyd in charge of Enniskillen.   On the 10th of June he set out with two thousand men.   Having marched as far as Omagh, he found there a party of the enemy fortified in the house of Captain Mervin, and before they could be compelled to surrender, he heard from prisoners that Lord Clancarty with three regiments was approaching on his march to Derry.   Under these circumstances Hamilton thought it wiser to retreat to Enniskillen.

Lloyd now started with a large force to attack Brigadier Sutherland, who was gathering stores at Belturbet.   But Sutherland, frightened by exaggerated reports of his enemy's strength, beat a hasty retreat, leaving behind a garrison which surrendered to Lloyd on his arrival.   Three hundred prisoners, seven hundred muskets, with ammunition and provisions, were thus obtained without losing the life of a single man.

The duke of Berwick, an illegitimate son of King James by Arabella Churchill, was sent, at the head of a large detachment of Irish, to prevent raids between Derry and Enniskillen, and to maintain communication with Dublin.   On the 13th of July he advanced from Trillick towards Enniskillen.   Unfortunately Lloyd was absent, as he had been sent to communicate with Kirke, through the captain of the *Bonaventure*, then in Killybegs.   Governor Hamilton, with one hundred infantry and a party of cavalry, met the enemy a very short distance from the town.   He ordered Lieutenant MacCarmick to make a stand with the infantry, promising that he would be supported by the cavalry and that reinforcements would be sent immediately.   MacCarmick did as he was told, although suspecting he would be left to his fate.   Hamilton then returned to Enniskillen, and, notwithstanding that the way along which he went back was full of "armed men," neglected to send relief to the gallant few who had dared to encounter an army.   At last, when urged by Lieutenant Campbell and Captain Webster, he ordered a company on the other side of the lough, two miles away, to be sent; but they failed to arrive in time.

The enemy with six hundred dragoons on foot and two troops of horse, made a furious attack on MacCarmick. But his infantry stood so firmly and fired with such execution that the enemy began to retreat. The Protestant cavalry, under Montgomery and King, instead of rendering assistance, turned, without firing a single shot, and fled from the field. The dismounted dragoons of the enemy immediately charged. Just then, two troops of their horse coming up surrounded the Protestant infantry and cut them to pieces. MacCarmick's son was killed at his side, and he himself was taken prisoner. Of his whole force only about thirty escaped. Among these was a brave soldier named James Wilson. Surrounded by a number of dragoons, he was assailed by all at once. Some of them he stabbed, others he struck down with his musket, and several he threw under the feet of their own horses. At last, wounded in twelve places, his cheeks hanging over his chin, he fell into a bush. There a sergeant struck through his thigh with a halbert; but Wilson, exerting all his strength, pulled it out, and ran it through the sergeant's heart. By the assistance of this halbert he walked back to Enniskillen. He was afterwards cured of his wounds and survived for thirty years.

This engagement was fought within cannon-shot of the town. Berwick did not venture to draw nearer to the fort, but withdrew from the neighborhood, and continued to keep open the communication of the army before Derry with the capital.

On the 12th of July, commissioners from Enniskillen conferred with General Kirke, who, in compliance with their request, sent the town a large supply of arms and ammunition, and also some officers under command of Colonel Wolseley. These officers arrived in Enniskillen on the very day that Derry was relieved. Before they were many hours in the town it was reported that General Macarthy had made an attack on Crom Castle, and that he intended to place a garrison in Lisnaskea, which was only ten miles from Enniskillen. Wolseley immediately sent Colonel Berry with a large party of cavalry and infantry to take possession of Lisnaskea Castle before it could be occupied by the enemy. But finding it in ruins, he then marched to oppose Macarthy. Taking up a strong position with a bog in front, he sent to Wolseley for reinforcements, and awaited the enemy. The Irish soon appeared, and under Anthony Hamilton, "the most brilliant and accomplished of all who bore the name," advanced to the attack along a road in front. But the Enniskillen men opened a furious fire. Hamilton was wounded, and his second in command killed. The Irish retreated, and their retreat soon became a flight. Berry followed them a mile beyond Lisnaskea, but finding himself nearing the front of their main body, he stopped the pursuit.

Meanwhile Wolseley had arrived with strong reinforcements, who in their hurry had forgotten to bring provisions. Compelled therefore, either to fight at once or retreat, Wolseley put it to the men themselves, whether to advance or to retire, and they unanimously determined to advance. The battle-word was then given, "No Popery," and the Protestants, twenty-two hundred strong, marched to attack Macarthy who was at the head of some thirty-five hundred men. As Wolseley advanced, the Irish retreated, until they came to a hill near Newtown-Butler, where they tried to make a stand. But the Protestants came on with such fury that Macarthy withdrew from his position, burned Newtown-Butler, and, about a mile beyond the village, placed his army on a hill with a bog in front, through which passed a narrow road completely commanded by his artillery. Wolseley began the attack immediately. His cavalry tried to pass along this road, but were brought to a stand by the fierce fire of the enemy's guns. Lloyd on the left and Tiffin on the right now passed on with the infantry through the bog and up the hill. They killed the gunners who were firing the cannon, and then rushed against the main body of the enemy. The Protestant cavalry dashed along the road and charged up the hill. The Irish horse retreated, and the foot, seeing the others flee, fled themselves. Being ignorant of the country, most of them took the direction of Lough Erne. The cavalry escaped; but the infantry, with the lough before and the Protestants behind, had only a choice between death in the lake or by the sword. About five hundred took to the water and were all drowned, except one man, who swam across. Macarthy himself was wounded and taken prisoner. In all, the Irish lost about two thousand slain, five hundred drowned, and four hundred prisoners. This battle was fought on the 31st of July, and that very night the army of James raised the siege of Londonderry.

The Enniskillen men next resolved to attack Sarsfield, who lay near Bundoran; but he retreated on hearing of the defeat at Newtown-Butler. They then determined to give battle to the duke of Berwick, but immediately afterwards heard that the army of James had passed Castlecaulfield on the way to Dublin. It was then too late to follow.

Lieutenant-Colonel Gore, by orders of Colonel Tiffin, went with three troops of horse and one hundred and fifty infantry to reconnoitre in the direction of Sligo. Gore, by means of a spy, succeeded in making Sarsfield believe that his foes were only the advance-guard of a large army, and the Irish general evacuated the town without firing a shot. A few hours afterwards, Gore entered and captured a large quantity of arms and provisions.

After Derry was relieved, Kirke assumed despotic authority in the city, and he refused to send soldiers through the country to protect the lives and property of Protestants from marauding parties of the enemy. In consequence of this neglect, Limavady was burned the week after Derry was delivered. Under pretense of making provisions cheap, he seized the cattle of many Protestant farmers in the neighborhood, pretending they belonged to the enemy, and sold them to the butchers. By a process of amalgamating regiments, many officers were dismissed, and some who had themselves purchased arms for their men were placed under the command of others who had not for this purpose expended a single penny. He took away Murray's horse, seized the saddles his horsemen had bought at their own expense, and in every way treated the people of Derry as if they had been enemies he had conquered rather than friends he had relieved.

The sick received no provisions from the stores, and many of them, trying to regain their homes, died by the way. One brave soldier who lived near Lifford had left his wife and family of young children at home when he went to Derry. In his absence, an Irish soldier, who had formerly been his own servant, came to rob his family. On entering, he at once asked his former mistress where her money was kept. She replied that he knew very well himself, handing him the key of a large oaken chest. The soldier opened the lock, raised the weighty lid, and stooped down to secure the money within. Then the lady, watching her opportunity, dashed the lid with terrific force on the soldier's neck, jumped on the top herself, and held it down with her weight till she was sure the robber was dead. Afterwards, in the silence of the night, she and her servant-maid buried the body in a neighboring field.

The treatment which the defenders of Derry received from the Government was quite as bad as the treatment they had received from Kirke. A committee, appointed by the English House of Commons, admitted that a sum of £195,091 was due to the Derry and Enniskillen regiments for arrears of pay, of which only £9806 had been paid. Besides this, a sum of £138,000 was expended by the officers and soldiers on their own maintenance, and on horses, arms, and accoutrements which were made use of by the Government, without any recompense or allowance to the owners.

Although the just claims of these gallant soldiers were admitted, the debt was never discharged. On the other hand, Walker, who had tried to induce the council to surrender, received the recompense of a hero; and Captain Corry, who had threatened to put in prison anybody who took arms to defend Enniskillen, got two thousand pounds and an estate as his reward. Poor Mitchelburn failed to get even the arrears of his pay, was refused the governorship of Culmore fort, and, being unable to discharge his debts, was placed in prison.

After Derry was relieved, Kirke sent the Rev. George Walker to present King William with an address signed by the chief defenders of the town. Walker set out on the 9th of August, 1689. He went by way of Scotland, and was presented with the freedom of Glasgow and Edinburgh. In London the king received him with favor, and the public with acclamations. He published an account of the siege, which had a large sale and ran through several editions. In this work he alluded to himself as the governor, and to the governor as Colonel Mitchelburn. He claimed to have led the garrison in several desperate conflicts, to have performed many daring deeds of valor, and to be in reality the person who saved the town. But these deeds of valor are recorded by himself alone. We have it on the best authority, that during the siege he was a man of peace, and that the only blood he shed was "the blood of the grape." Although Walker knew well that the Rev. Alexander Osborne, a Dublin clergyman, was the person who first informed the Ulster Protestants of Tyrconnel's deceptive designs, he had the audacity to assert that Osborne was a spy of the lord deputy. He conveyed to his readers the impression that Mr. David Houston, a Covenanting preacher, had raised divisions among the Protestants in Derry, although Houston was not in the neighborhood at the time. He concealed the fact that on the 18th of April Murray prevented the surrender of the town. He gave the Presbyterians no credit for their defence of the city, although they were nine out of every ten of the rank and file, and he told a deliberate lie in stating he did not know the names of the Presbyterian clergymen in the town during the siege, although a correct list of them had been given to him before his book was published. Mackenzie had been chaplain to his own regiment, and when in Edinburgh Walker was able to mention them by name to Mr. Osborne, whom he hastened to asperse. But his great object was to make the world believe that the Presbyterian defenders of Derry were a miserable minority, and that he, who had never headed a sally or repulsed an attack, was a great military hero, entitled to all the rewards due for saving the town he had tried to surrender. Such was Walker. Yet his story, having got the start, was believed by the world, and some even to this day have magnified this meddling Munchausen into a military genius and a hero.

In London there was at first nobody to contradict his assertions, and he was taken at his own estimate of himself. The world thought he had saved the city. Crowds followed him when he appeared in public. He received five thousand pounds, the thanks of Parliament, and the promise of a bishopric, while the real defenders of the town were left in starvation.

Walker's account had not been long issued when an anonymous pamphlet, entitled *An Apology for the Failures Charged on the Rev. Mr. George Walker's Printed Account of the Late Siege of Derry*, was published, in which a few of his mistakes were pointed out and his assumptions exposed. Some friends of Mr. Walker replied, and before the end of 1689 Walker himself published a vindication of his *True Account*. In this he practically admits many of the charges by not attempting to refute them. Early in 1690, the Rev. J. Boyse, of Dublin, published his *Vindication* of the Rev. Alexander Osborne from the accusation made by Walker that he was a spy of Tyrconnel. In this pamphlet the "Governor of Derry" was absolutely crushed, and neither he nor any of his friends ventured to reply.

In order to give the world a true account of the defence of Derry, the Rev. John Mackenzie, minister of Cookstown, the chaplain of Walker's own regiment, published *A Narrative of the Siege of Londonderry*. Before publication it was read over to Colonel Murray, Colonel Crofton, Lieutenant-

Colonel Blair, Captain Saunderson, and Captain Samuel Murray, who gave their assent to its contents. This fact is certified by Sir Arthur Rawdon, Sir Arthur Langford, Colonel Upton, Mr. David Cairns, and several others who at the same time had been present, and had concurred in Mackenzie's statements. This narrative may therefore be regarded as the united account of all these gentlemen. It related many circumstances not told by any other historian. It did justice to Murray and Noble, put Walker in his proper position, and proved the falsehood of his *True Account* and his *Vindication.* Walker did not venture to reply. A friend of his, supposed to be Bishop Vesey, published a pamphlet entitled *Mr. John Mackenzie's Narrative a False Libel.* In this he printed some certificates from officers who had lost their property during the siege, and who thought the influence of Walker would be useful in recovering what they sought. But even they dealt in generalities and did not venture to contradict the main charges. Mackenzie then published *Dr. Walker's Invisible Champion Foyl'd,* to which crushing reply neither Walker nor any of his friends ventured to rejoin.

It is not necessary to recount further the war by which William III. regained Ireland in 1690, save to regret that the great Dutchman's broad-minded scheme of religious toleration was not carried out and the disgraceful repressive measures of the next reign rendered impossible. One lasting benefit William III. conferred on Ulster—he did his best to encourage the linen manufacture, especially by inducing colonies of French Protestant refugees, driven from France by the revocation of the Edict of Nantes, to settle in northeast Ireland, with Lisburn as their centre. These Huguenots seem to have been men of skill and enterprise, many of them of rank and education. They received inducements to settle, their churches having special privileges, even when in the next reign the most severe laws were passed against dissent.

One strange memorial of this reign we have,—the list of the survivors of the brave men who defended Londonderry, and who signed an address to William and Mary on the 29th of July, 1689, immediately after the siege was raised. The names are so strikingly familiar to Scotsmen that the list might be taken from an Edinburgh directory. Of course there are many good English names, like that delightful surname which Thackeray has made beloved as long as the English language lasts,—Dobbin ; but the Scottish surnames are very numerous. There are five Hamiltons, and three Stewarts, and three Cunninghams, and three Mansons, besides representatives of very many Lowland Scottish surnames. One very Scottish name, too, is that of Gladstone, spelled in the old Scottish way " Ja. Gledstanes." [2]

NOTES TO CHAPTER XXXVIII.

[1] By the decisive battle of Worcester in 1651, which compelled Charles the Second to abandon the kingdom and seek safety on the continent, Cromwell's popularity and influence became almost unbounded.

The news of this unexpected revolution reached Carrickfergus on the day on which the members of the Presbytery appeared before the Commissioners. The intelligence entirely disconcerted their plans, the power from which they derived their authority being at an end. No other alternative remained than to exhort the ministers to a peaceable conduct, and dismiss them to their parishes without delay. The Commissioners in Dublin, however, having cheerfully submitted to the new Council of State, and the commissions of the subordinate courts having been renewed throughout the kingdom, the original design of removing " all the popular Scotts " out of Ulster was immediately resumed. A proclamation was published by " the Commissioners for the settling and securing the Province of Ulster," specifying the conditions on which it was proposed to transplant the leading Presbyterians in the counties of Down and Antrim to certain districts in Munster. This proclamation was accompanied with a list of two hundred and sixty persons—including all those who, by their known attachment to monarchical and Presbyterian principles, and by their station and influence, were most obnoxious to the reigning faction—who were required, within a specified time and under certain penalties, to embrace the terms now offered.

Declaration by the Commissioners for the settling and securing the Province of Ulster ; dated at Carrickfergus, the 23d of May 1653.

A list of the names of such as are to remove according to the foregoing Declaration :

COUNTY OF ANTRIM.

Belfast and Malone Quarters :
Lieutenant Thomas Corston, Corporal Thomas MacCormick, Hugh Doke, Robert Cluxton, George Martin, Alexander Lockard, Robert King, Quintin Catherwood.

West Quarters of Carrickfergus :
John Murray, John Russel, John Reid, John Young, John Donnelson, John Hanna, James Reid, James Patterson, William Kiggard, George Russel, John Holmes, George Gibson, Robert Tikye, John Clark, sen., Patrick Martin, Nicholas Campbell, Andrew Read, sen., Andrew Read, jun., Quarter-master Archy Crawford.

Broadisland and East Quarters of Carrickfergus :
Gilbert Eccles, John Dowglesson, Captain Edmonston, David MacClee, David Harpur, John M'Kerger, Walter Hutchinson, Thomas MacColpin, Matthew Logan.

Islandmagee, Magheramore, and Ballynure Quarters :
Captain Robert Kinkead, Hugh Hume, James Lawder, Captain James MacCullogh, John Blair, William Agnew, John Agnew.

Six-Mile-Water Quarters :
Captain George Welsh, Mr. William Shaw, Captain Ferguson, Lieutenant Huston, Lieutenant Robert Ferguson, Alexander Pringle, Andrew Taggart, Quintin Kennedy, James Cutberd [Cuthbert ?], John Wilson, Teague O'Munts, William Crawford, William Sloane, Mr. Arthur Upton, John Crawford, Mr. Francis Shaw, Gilbert MacNeilly, Lieutenant Samuel Wallace, George Young, John Wilson.

Antrim Quarters :
Captain Henry Sibbalds, Captain John Williams, Captain John Fisher, Captain John Macbride, Quarter-master Mitchell, Major Clotworthy, David Mitchell, Ensign John Cormick, John Waugh, merchant, Robert Shannon, John Whyte, Quarter-master Ferguson, Captain James Campbell, Lieutenant James Lindsay, Lieutenant James M'Adam.

Shane's Castle, Largy, and Toome Quarters :
Lieutenant-Colonel Walter Stewart, Lieutenant Andrew Adair, Henry Verner, William MacCullogh, Cornet John Shaw, Lieutenant James Dobbin, Ensign John Bryan, Thomas

Collock [Pollock?]—Matthew Hamill, Laird of Rockwood, Captain Robert Huston, Captain Jackson, Lieutenant MacNally, Lieutenant Robert Carre, Lieutenant James Pont, Lieutenant Hamill, Lieutenant Grimsills, Ensign Dobbin, Lieutenant Alexander Cunningham, Ensign Robert Cunningham, Lieutenant Martin, Robert Porter, William Collock.

Braid, Kevit, and Clonoghorty Quarters :
    Thomas Adair, Corporal James MacCollogh, William Hamilton, John Spratt, Lieutenant Paul Cunningham, Captain William Huston, Sir Robert Adair, Captain Thomas Fairborn, Captain David Johnson, Lieutenant Auchmuty, Lieutenant William Johnson, Major Alexander Adair, Cornet James Brown, Cornet John Stewart, Adam Johnson, James Ewart, Kingham Dunbarr, Halbert Gledston.

Killileagh and Kilmakevit Quarters :
    David Kennedy, Lieutenant Campbell, Captain Henry Langford, William Norris, William Cunningham, George Campbell, John Gordon of Borsheagh, Lieutenant Erwin, Lieutenant Antony Ellis, Lieutenant MacElroy.

Glenarm Barony :
    Mr. James Shaw, Captain John Shaw, Mr. Donnelson, John Berry, Patrick Agnew, John Shaw, James Cromie, Francis Agnew, William Greg, Randal Buttle, James Donnelson, Captain-Lieutenant James Hume, James Fenton.

Route Quarters :
    Major John Stewart, Lieutenant-Colonel Robert Kennedy, Captain James Stewart, Captain Alexander Stewart, Fergus MacDougall, John MacDougall, John Boyle, John Getty, Alexander Stewart, sen., James Maxwell, Captain Marmaduke Shaw, John Henry, Cornet Robert Knox, Mr. William Hutchin, Robert Henry, Alexander Scott, Lieutenant James Moncrief, Robert Harrute, Andrew Rowan, Thomas Boyd, Samuel Dunbarr, Alexander Delap, Adam Delap, Anthony Kennedy, Major Hugh Montgomery, Cornet John Gordon, Captain John Huston, Lieutenant-Colonel Cunningham, John Bell, Mr. Adam Boyd, John Reid, Lieutenant Arch. Campbell, Mr. John Peoples, Mr. Cathcart, Captain Arch. Boyd, Captain John Robinson, Lieutenant Thomas Stewart, Quarter-master Robert Stewart.

Coleraine Quarters :
    John Johnson, Thomas Abernethy, Edward M'Clelland, James Johnson, Col. Gilbert M'Philip, David Wilson, Robert Hutton, Major Robert Blair, Ensign Andrew M'Adam, Ensign Robert Mills, Ensign Alexander M'Cann, Ensign Donald M'Ferson.

COUNTY OF DOWN.

Castlereagh, Kilwarlin, and Lisnegarvy Quarters :
    Corporal Gilbert Matthews, John Strain, John Cowtard, Robert Graham, James Graham, John Cowan, Thomas Rea, Captain James Manson.

Lord of Ards' Quarters :
    The Lord Ards, Captain Charles Campbell, Captain William Buchanan, Lieutenant Hugh Dundas, Captain John Keith, John Montgomery of Movill, Lieutenant James Nowell, James MacConkey, William Catherwood, William Shaw, Fergus Kennedy, Captain Hugh Montgomery, Mr. Hugh Montgomery, Lieutenant John Wilson, Lieutenant And. Cunningham, Lieutenant M'Dowell of Cumber.

Little Ards, Greyabbey, and Lisburnagh Quarters :
    Gilbert Heron, Robert Maxwell, Robert Ross, John Park, Lieutenant John Monipenny.

Lord Claneboy's Quarters:

The Lord Claneboy, Lieutenant Gawn Hamilton, Captain John Boyle, Lieutenant Hugh Wallace, James Ross, sen., William Hamilton, Mr. George Ross, John Hamilton of Bally-macgormack, Patrick Allen, Gawn Hamilton, Captain Alexander Stewart, William Hamilton, jun., John Stevenson, Ninian Tate, Lieutenant Edward Baillie, Francis Purdy, Captain James Stevenson, John Barclay, Quarter-master Edward Magee, Ensign James Cooper, Lieutenant Robert Cunningham, Lieutenant Carr, Captain Matthew Hamilton, Captain Colin Maxwell, David Williamson, James Ross, jun.

Lecale Quarters:

Lieutenant Hugh Montgomery, Lieut. Launcelot Greece [Gracey], Lieutenant Thomas Lindsay, Lieutenant Woodney, Lieutenant John Reynolds, Captain John Wooll, James Stewart, John Dunbarr, John Tenant, James Porter, Stephen Masor [Mercer?], John M'Dowell.

[2] The following extract is from a letter written in 1679, addressed to the King and forwarded to the Duke of Ormond by Lionel Jenkins, Secretary of State (Report VII., *Historical MSS. Commission*, part ii., pp. 742–743).

"I landed in Ireland 27 Sep., 1679. . . . . . Now I much and many times have wondered at one thing, that all the Lieutenants of Ireland have continued or rather confirmed and settled such commands of military forces upon those that were notoriously known to be Oliver's only creatures, and his immediate officers. . . . . . These are the prime leaders and rulers in that county [Waterford] who backed with infinite of their sect keepe a due correspond with those of the north of Ireland, who are most Scotts and Scotch breed and are the northern Presbyterians and phanatiquies, lustly, able-bodyed, hardy, and stout men, where one may see three or four hundred at every meeting-house on Sundays, and all the north of Ireland is inhabited with these, which is the popular place of all Ireland by farr. They are very numerous and greedy after land."

[3] The "List of Ejected Ministers in Ulster" (1661) is published by Dr. Reid, in his *History of the Presbyterian Church in Ireland* vol. ii., pp. 253–255, taken by him from Wodrow's list (vol. i., pp. 324, 325), with the addition by Dr. Reid of the places where the deposed ministers officiated. It is as follows (the names of those who survived the Revolution of 1688 being indicated by a star):

Presbytery of Down—Andrew Stewart, Donaghadee; Gilbert Ramsay, Bangor; John Greg, Newtown Ards; William Reid, Ballywalter; John Drysdale, Portaferry; James Gordon, Comber; Thomas Peebles, Dundonald; Hugh Wilson,* Castlereagh; Michael Bruce,* Killinchy; William Richardson, Killileagh; John Fleming, Downpatrick; Alexander Hutchinson,* Saintfield; Henry Livingston,* Drumbo; Henry Hunter, Dromore; James Campbell, Rathfriland; Andrew McCormick, Magherally.

Presbytery of Antrim—William Keyes, Belfast; James Shaw, Carnmoney; Robert Cunningham,* Broadisland; Thomas Hall,* Larne; Patrick Adair, Cairncastle; James Fleming, Glenarm; Gilbert Simpson, Ballyclare; Anthony Kennedy,* Templepatrick; Thomas Crawford, Donegore; Robert Hamilton, Killead; Robert Dewart, Connor; John Shaw, Ahoghill; James Cunningham, Antrim; John Cathcart, Randallstown.

Presbytery of Route—David Buttle, Ballymena; William Cumming, Kilraughts?; John Douglass, Broughshane; Robert Hogsyard, Ballyrashane; Gabriel Cornwall, Ballywillan?; Thomas Fulton, Dunboe?; William Crooks,* Ballykelly; Thomas Boyd,* Aghadoey; James Ker, Ballymoney; John Law, Garvagh.

Presbytery of Tyrone—Robert Auld, Maghera?; Archibald Hamilton, Donaghhendry; George Keith, Dungannon; Thomas Kennedy,* Donoughmore; Thomas Gowan, Glasslough; John Abernethy,* Minterburn; Alexander Osborn,* Brigh; James Johnston, Lisnaskea?.

Presbytery of Lagan—Robert Wilson,* Strabane; William Moorcraft, Newtown-

Stewart; John Wool, or Will, Clondermot; William Semple, Letterkenny; John Hart, Taughboyne; John Adamson, Omagh?; John Crookshanks, Raphoe; Thomas Drummond, Ramelton; Robert Craighead,* Donoughmore; Hugh Cunningham, Ray; Hugh Peebles, Lifford; Adam White,* Fannet; William Jack, Bullalley, Dublin.

The ministers who conformed to the Episcopal requirements were as follows : Andrew Rowan, Dunaghy or Clough, Antrim; George Wallace, Holywood, Down; Mungo Bennett, Coleraine; —— Caldwell; Robert Rowan; —— Brown of Bellaghy; William Mill, or Milne; James Fleming; Alexander Dunlop, Kilmore, Down; Andrew Nesbitt, Glenarm, Antrim.

⁴ The following conjectures and statements cover about all the information at the present time available from which we can estimate the population of Ulster during the seventeenth century.

In 1619 . . . an accurate Government Survey was made of the state of every family of the Plantation. There were not quite 2000 families in all (exact 1974), and in these 6215 were between sixteen and sixty, fit to bear arms. In 1633, on a similar inquiry, 13,092 were the numbers returned as capable of bearing arms. See *State Letters of the Earl of Stafford*, vol. i., folio, London.—Prendergast, *Cromwellian Settlement of Ireland*, chapter ii.

Ulster was at this time [1641] very thinly populated, and it was estimated that its whole population consisted only of about 100,000 Scotch, and 20,000 English. This is the estimate of Carte (*Life of Ormond*, pp. 177-178). It appears from a Government Survey that in the confiscated counties alone there were in 1633, 13,092 men capable of bearing arms.—Lecky, *England in the Eighteenth Century*, book ii., chapter vi.

Sir William Petty computes the British (including therein both English and Scotch) to be before the rebellion in proportion to the Irish as two to eleven; at which rate there were about two hundred and twenty thousand British in the whole kingdom. Now, it is certain that the great body of the English was settled in Munster and Leinster, where few murders were committed (1641); and that in Ulster, which was the dismal scene of the massacre, there were above an hundred thousand Scotch, who before the general plantation of it had settled in great numbers in the counties of Down and Antrim, and new shoals of them had come over upon the plantation of the six escheated counties; and they were so very powerful therein that the Irish either out of fear of their numbers, or for some other politic reason spared those of that nation (making proclamation on pain of death, that no Scotchman should be molested in body, goods or lands), whilst they raged with so much cruelty against the English. There were none of these latter nation settled in Ulster before the plantation; there were (as I see by Lord Chichester's book) but fifty English undertakers concerned in carrying on that work; and it was not so easy for these to bring from England, a rich, plentiful, and quiet country, any considerable number of husbandmen and artificers to a strange country, wasted, inhabited by a wild, savage, turbulent, and rapacious people, whose language they knew not, as it was for the Scotch to undertake to bring numbers from Scotland, where half the nation spoke the Irish tongue and where they were to remove to a country naturally more fertile than their own, and wherein they had multitudes of friends, relatives, and countrymen, to assist and instruct them in those methods of improving land and enriching themselves which they had practised before them with success. It cannot therefore reasonably be presumed that there were at most above twenty thousand English souls of all ages and sexes in Ulster at this time.—Thomas Carte, *Life of Ormond* (1735), pp. 177, 178.

The following enumeration of the population of Ulster was reprinted in *Transactions of the Royal Irish Academy*, vol. xxiv. The date of this census is not certainly known but it is supposed to have been taken about 1658, or a few years before the Restoration : County Antrim, Scotch and English, 7074; Irish, 8965; total, 16,039. Armagh, Scotch and English, 2393; Irish, 4355; total, 6748. Cavan, Scotch and English, 6485; Irish, 8218; total, 14,703. Donegal, Scotch and English, 3412; Irish, 8589; total, 12,001. Down, Scotch and English, 6540; Irish, 8643; total, 15,183. Fermanagh, Scotch and English, 1800; Irish, 5302;

total, 7102. Londonderry, Scotch and English, 4428 ; Irish, 5306 ; total, 9734. Monag-han, Scotch and English, 434 ; Irish, 3649 ; total, 4083. Tyrone, Scotch and English, 8085 ; Irish, 10,245 ; total 18,330.   Total, Scotch and English, 40,651 ; total, Irish, 63,-272 ; total, Ulster, 103,923.

The war ended at last in 1652.   According to the calculation of Sir W. Petty, out of a population of 1,466,000, 616,000 had in eleven years perished by the sword, by plague, or by famine artificially produced.   504,000, according to this estimate, were Irish, 112,000 of English extraction.   A third part of the population had been thus blotted out, and Petty tells us that according to some calculations the number of the victims was much greater. Famine and the sword had so done their work that in some districts the traveller rode twenty or thirty miles without seeing one trace of human life, and fierce wolves—rendered doubly savage by feeding on human flesh—multiplied with startling rapidity through the deserted land, and might be seen prowling in number within a few miles of Dublin.   Liberty was given to able-bodied men to abandon the country and enlist in foreign service, and from 30,-000 to 40,000 availed themselves of the permission.   Slave-dealers were let loose upon the land, and many hundreds of boys and of marriageable girls, guilty of no offence whatever, were torn away from their country, shipped to Barbadoes, and sold as slaves to the planters. Merchants from Bristol entered keenly into the traffic.   The victims appear to have been for the most part the children or the young widows of those who were killed or starved, but the dealers began at length to decoy even Englishmen to their ships, and the abuses became such that the Puritan Government, which had for some time cordially supported the system, made vain efforts to stop it.   How many of the unhappy captives became the prey of the sharks, how many became the victims of the planters' lusts, it is impossible to say.   The worship which was that of almost the whole native population was absolutely suppressed.—Lecky *Ireland in the Eighteenth Century*, vol. i., pp. 104, 105.

For some years after the Revolution, a steady stream of Scotch Presbyterians had poured into the country [Ireland], attracted by the cheapness of the farms, or by the new openings for trade, and in the reign of Anne, the Nonconformists boasted that they at least equalled the Episcopalian Protestants in Ireland, while in the Province of Ulster they immensely out-numbered them. (Killen's *Ecclesiastical Hist. of Ireland*, ii., p. 242.) In 1715, Archbishop Synge estimated at not less than fifty thousand the number of Scotch families who had settled in Ulster since the Revolution. (Synge's *Letters*, British Museum, Add. MSS., 6117, p. 50.)   Three years later Bishop Nicholson, writing from Londonderry, states that this parish, —which extended far beyond the walls,—though one of the most Episcopalian in the province, contained eight hundred families of Protestant Nonconformists, and only four hundred of Conformists, while in some of the parishes in his diocese there were forty Presbyterians to one member of the Established Church. (Nicholson's *Letters*, British Museum, Add. MSS., 6116, p. 127.)   But the political power of the Dissenters, even before the imposition of the test, was by no means commensurate with their number, for they were chiefly traders and farmers and very rarely owners of the soil.   In the House of Lords they were almost unrep-resented.   In the House of Commons they appear to have seldom, if ever, had more than twelve members.   When the Test Act expelled them from the magistracy only twelve or thirteen were deprived.   In the Province of Ulster, Archbishop Synge assures us that there were not in his time more than forty Protestant Dissenters of the rank of gentlemen, not more than four who were considerable landowners, and according to Bishop Nicholson they had not one share in fifty of the landed interest in that province. (Archbishop Synge's *Letters*, p. 35, British Museum, Add. MSS., 6117.   Nicholson's MSS. *Letters*, p. 157.) Abernethy gave a higher estimate in 1751.   He says :   " The Protestant Dissenters in Ireland are half of its Protestant inhabitants in the province of Ulster.   As appears by authentic accounts lately sent from it, there are about 50,000 families of Dissenters, and consequently about 216,000 souls.   In three counties (Down, Antrim, and Tyrone), there are about sixty Dissenting gentlemen who possess estates from £200 to £1400 a year." (Abernethy's *Scarce Tracts*, p. 61.)—Lecky, *Ireland in the Eighteenth Century*, vol. i., pp. 423, 424.

There were in 1660, sixty-eight Presbyterian ministers in Ireland, all save one in Ulster, and of these sixty-one left their churches, and seven conformed to the Established Church. . . . The number of Presbyterian Churches in Ulster gives some indication of the population of Scottish origin, although a moiety of the Presbyterians were English. The extent of the emigration from Scotland is, however, more exactly given by Sir William Petty in his *Political Survey of Ireland in 1672*. He takes the total population of the country at 1,100,000, and calculates that 800,000 were Irish, 200,000 English, and 100,000 Scots,—of course the English were scattered all over Ireland, the Scots concentrated in Ulster. Petty divides the English into " 100,000 legal Protestants or Conformists, and the rest are Presbyterians, Independents, Anabaptists and Quakers." He states distinctly that a very large emigration had taken place from Scotland, after Cromwell settled the country in 1652. The power of the Scots must, indeed, have been so considerable and so much feared as to be greatly exaggerated, for it was asserted in Parliament in 1656, that they " are able to raise 40,000 fighting men at any time."—Harrison, *The Scot in Ulster*, p. 83.

It is probable that the population of Ireland during the first half of the eighteenth century remained almost stationary. For many years after the rebellion of 1641, the country had been extremely underpopulated, and the prevailing habit of early and prolific marriages would naturally have led to very rapid multiplication, but famine, disease, and emigration were as yet sufficient to counteract it. Unfortunately our sources of information on this subject are very imperfect. No census was taken; our chief means of calculating are derived from the returns of the hearth-money collectors, and the number of cabins that were exempted from the tax, as well as the great difference in different parts of the country in the average occupants of a house, introduce a large element of uncertainty into our estimates. It appears, however, according to the best means of information we possess, that the population in the beginning of the century was not far from two millions, and that it increased in fifty years to about 2,370,000. (See a collection of statistics on this subject in Nicholls' *Hist. of the Irish Poor Law*, p. 11., and Newenham on *Population in Ireland*.) Dobbs in his *Essay on Irish Trade*, pt. ii., p. 9 (published in 1731), calculating the average of families at 4.36, estimates the population at that time as low as 1,669,644, but adds, " I don't insist upon this as a just computation ; I am apt to believe it is rather within the truth." The proportion of Roman Catholics to Protestants is also a question of much difficulty. In the reign of Charles II., Petty had estimated it at eight to three. In a return, based on the hearth-money collection, which was made to the Irish House of Lords in 1731, it was estimated at not quite two to one (1,309,768 to 700,453). It is probable, however, that the inequality was considerably understated. The great poverty of many of the Catholics, and the remote mountains and valleys in which they lived, withdrew them from the cognizance of the tax-gatherer, and Primate Boulter, in 1727, expressed his belief that there were in Ireland at least five Papists to one Protestant. (Boulter's *Letters*, vol. i., p. 210.) In another letter, dated December, 1731, he says : " The Papists, by the most modest computation, are about five to one Protestant, but others think they cannot be less than seven to one" (vol. ii., p. 70). Newenham gives more credit to the return of the House of Lords. It must be remembered that at this time Connaught was exclusively Catholic, while in Munster, Berkeley estimated the Catholics as seven to one. Coghill, a very intelligent Irish politician and member for Trinity College, however, in a letter to Southwell, dated November, 1733, said he was firmly persuaded that Papists did not outnumber the Protestants by more than three to one. The whole population he estimated at rather below two millions (British Museum, Add. MSS., 21,122). Abernethy, one of the best Presbyterian authorities, wrote about 1751 : " The number of Papists in this kingdom exceeds that of Protestants of all denominations in the proportion, some have said, of eight to one, others of six to one, but the lowest computation which deserves any regard is that of three to one." (Abernethy's *Scarce Tracts*, p. 59.) Archbishop King, writing in 1727, said : " The Papists have more bishops in Ireland than the Protestants have, and twice (at least) as many priests." (Mant. vol. ii., p. 471.) Boulter adds a statement which, if it be unexaggerated, furnishes an extraordinary example of the superiority of Catholic zeal in the midst of the penal laws, and at a time when Protestantism enjoyed all the advantages of an almost universal monopoly. He says : " We have incumbents and curates to the number of about 800, whilst there are more than 3,000 Popish priests of all sorts here." (Boulter's *Letters*, vol. i., p. 210.)—Lecky, *England in the Eighteenth Century*, vol. ii., pp. 277, 278.

Sadler's *State of Ireland*, p. 393, etc., gives the total population of Ireland in 1733 as 2,015,229, of which number 505,395 were inhabitants of Ulster. In 1767 the population of Ireland was 2,544,276. Edward Wakefield in his *Statistical and Political Account of Ireland* (London, 1812), vol. ii., p. 684, fixes the total number of families living in Ulster, in the year 1733, at 101,079, of whom 62,620 were estimated to be Protestant families, and 38,459 Catholic families. The same author estimates that for the year 1792, the proportion of Catholics to Protestants in County Armagh was as three to one ; of the Protestants a very great majority are classed as Dissenters from the Established Episcopal Church, and these Dissenters were chiefly Presbyterians. In Antrim, for the same year, the Catholic and Protestant population was about equal ; of the Protestants a very great majority were Dissenters, chiefly Presbyterians. In Cavan, the proportion of Catholics to Protestants was as five to one ; of the Protestants a very great majority were Presbyterians. In Donegal the proportion was six to one, the Protestants being almost all Presbyterians. In Down the proportion was as one to one, the Protestants nearly all Presbyterians. In Fermanagh the proportion was as three to one, with few Dissenters. In Londonderry the proportion was as two to one, with a great majority of the Protestants Presbyterians. In Monaghan the proportion was as five to one, with the Dissenters nearly all Presbyterians. In Tyrone the proportion was six to one, with few Protestants but Presbyterians.

[5] December 10, 1688, six companies of foot were formed with the following officers : First Company—captain, Samuel Norman ; lieut., William Crookshanks ; ensign, Alexander Irwin. Second Company—captain, Alexander Leckey ; lieut., James Lennox ; ensign, John Harvey. Third Company—captain, Matthew Crocker ; lieut., Henry Long ; ensign, Francis Hunt. Fourth Company—captain, Warham Jemmet ; lieut., Robert Morrison ; ensign, Daniel Sherrard. Fifth Company—captain, John Tompkins ; lieut., James Spaight ; ensign, Alexander Cunningham. Sixth Company—captain, Thomas Moncrieff ; lieut., James Morrison ; ensign, William Mackey.—Mackenzie's *Narrative*.

[6] The Parliament called in Dublin by King James, 7th May, 1689, had no representatives from the counties of Derry, Donegal or Fermanagh ; and as many Protestants from those counties were engaged in the defence of Londonderry, they are described in the Act as of Donegal and Derry. In the subjoined abstract from it, are the names and addresses of such of the attainted persons as appear in the Corporation Minutes or any of the Derry diaries, as participators in the defence of Derry, Sligo, or of the Passage of the Bann. Of course many more are in the Act than we can identify as being the same persons mentioned in those diaries.

" An Act for the Attainder of Divers Rebels, and for Preserving the Interest of Loyal Subjects.

" WHEREAS a most horrid invasion was made by your Majesty's unnatural enemy the Prince of Orange, invited thereunto and assisted by many of your Majesty's rebellious and traiterous subjects ; and having likewise raised, and levied open rebellion and war in several places in this Kingdom and entered into association, and met in conventions, in order to call in and set up the said Prince of Orange, and the said rebels and traitors, having the impudence to declare for the Prince and Princess of Orange against your sacred Majesty, BE IT

ENACTED, that the Persons hereafter named, viz. :—Hugh Montgomery, Earl of Mount Alexander ; John Skeffington, Viscount Massareene ; William Caulfield, Viscount Charlemont ; William Stewart, Viscount Mountjoy ; Ezekiel Hopkins, Lord Bishop of Derry ; Henry Lord Blaney, of Monaghan ; Sir Arthur Royden, of Moyra, Bart. ; Sir Francis Hamilton, of Castlehamilton, Bart. ; Sir William Francklin, of Belfast, Bart. ; Sir Tristrum Beresford, of Ballykally, Bart. ; Sir John Magill, of Gill-Hall, Knt. ; Samuel Morrison, Gent. ; all late of the CITY OF DUBLIN. Robert Rochford, Esq., of WESTMEATH. Henry Baker, of Dumagan, Esq ; James Brabazon, of Carrstown, Gent. ; Christopher Fortescue, of Dromiskin, Esq. ; all of the COUNTY OF LOWTH. George Vaughan, of Buncrana, Esq. ; John Forward, of Coolemackiltraine, Esq. ; Hugh Hamill, of Lifford, Esq ; William Groves, of Castleshannaghan, Esq. ; Kilmer Braizier, of Rath, Esq. ; Major Gustavus Hamilton, of Rusogile ; John Wigton, of Raphoe, Gent. ; John Cowen, of St. Johnstown, Gent. ; Chas. Calhoone, of Letterkenny, Gent. ; James Fisher, of Derry, Gent. ; and Captain Jervis Squire, of Donaghmore, all of the COUNTY OF DONEGAL AND LONDONDERRY. David Kearnes, of Askragh, Esq. ; Audley Meryn, of Trilick, Gent. ; George Walker, of Donoughmore, Clerk ; William Stewart of Killemoon, Gent. ; all of the COUNTY OF TYRONE. John Knox, of Glasslogh, Clerk, of the COUNTY OF MONAGHAN. Clotworthy Skeffington, of Antrim, Esq.; Col. Robt. Adaire, of Ballymena ; Arthur Upton of Templepatrick, Esq. ; Lieutenant-Colonel William Shaw, of Gemeway ; Captain William Shaw, of Bash ; Lieutenant-Colonel Robert Hueston, of Cregg ; Captain William Adare of Ballymena ; all of the COUNTY OF ANTRIM. Daniel Mac Neale, of Dundrum, Gent., of the COUNTY OF DOWN. Major Joseph Strowde, of Lisburne, in the COUNTY OF ARMAGH. Alex. Stewart, Esq., son of the Lord Mountjoy ; Warham Jemett, Collector ; Capt. Alexander Lecky, Capt. Samuel Norman, Capt. Matthew Cockins, Capt. Alex. Tomkins, Capt. John Tomkins, Capt. Thomas Moncrieff, Capt. James Lennox, Capt. Horace Kennedy, Lieut. Wm. Crookshanks, Lieut. Jas. Spicke, Lieut. Danl. Sherrard, Lieut. Edward Brooks, Lieut. Henry Long, Lieut. William Macky, Lieut. Robert Morrison, Lieut. Wm. Newton, Lieut. Henry Campsy, Lieut. Henry Thompson, Col. George Philips, of Newtownlimavady ; Lieut.-Col. Edward Carry, of Dungivin ; Capt. Stephen Heard, Capt. James Strong, Capt. Thomas Ash, Capt. Samuel Hobson, Captain Abraham Hilhouse, of Ballycastle ; Col. George Canning, of Garvagh ; Capt. Wm. Church, Capt. Miller, Capt. Adam Downing, of Bellaghy ; Captain Samuel Wright, Lieutenant-Colonel Robert Lundy, and David Rosse, of Londonderry, Gent. ; all of the COUNTY OF LONDONDERRY. Capt. Chidley Coote, of Voughtershire, ROSCOMMON. Henry Nickleson, of Ballanagargine, Gent. ; Adam Ormsby, of Comine, Gent. ; Francis Gore, of Sligo, Gent. ; Charles Nicleson, of Larrass, Gent. ; all of the COUNTY OF SLIGO. Major Owen Vaughan of Carrowmore, MAYO, whether dead or alive, or killed in open rebellion, or now in arms against your Majesty, and every one of them shall be deemed, and are hereby declared and adjudged traitors, convicted and attainted of high treason, and shall suffer such pains of death, penalties, and forfeitures respectively, as in cases of high treason are accustomed. And whereas Robert Lindsay, of Manor Lindsay, Esq., of TYRONE, and Francis Annesley, jun., of Cloghmagherycatt, Gent., of DOWN, have absented themselves from this Kingdom, since the Fifth of November last, they shall suffer such pains of death, and other forfeitures and penalties as in cases of high treason are accustomed."

This abstract of the Act, is taken from a copy published in *The State of the Protestants of Ireland under the late King James's Government*, written by William King, who was Chancellor and Dean of St. Patrick's, Dublin, during the Revolution, and afterwards Bishop of Derry.

⁷ Declaration of Union, March 21, 1689—

" Whereas, for various reasons, rumors etc., are spread abroad among the vulgar, that the Right Honorable the Lord Blaney, Sir Arthur Rawdon, Lieutentant-Colonel Maxwell, and other gentlemen and officers of quality, are resolved to take protections from the Irish,

and desert the general service for defence of the Protestant party in this Kingdom, . . .
For wiping off which aspersion and clearing the minds of all Protestant friends wheresoever,
from all suspicions . . . it is hereby unanimously declared, protested and published to
all men, by Colonel Robert Lundy, Governor of Derry, the said Lord Blaney, Sir Arthur
Rawdon, and other officers and gentlemen, subscribing hereunto, that they and their forces
and soldiers are entirely united among themselves, and fully and absolutely resolved to oppose
the Irish enemy with the utmost force, and to continue the war against them to the last, for
their own and all Protestants' preservation in this Kingdom.   And the committee of Londonderry do hereby declare and publish to all men that they are heartily and sincerely united
with the said Colonel Robert Lundy *et al.* and all others that join in this common cause, and
with all their force and power will labor to carry on the said war.   And if it should happen
that our party should be so oppressed by the Irish enemy, that they should be forced to retire
into this city for shelter against them (which God forbid) the said Lord Blaney, Sir Arthur
Rawdon, and their forces, and all other Protestant friends, shall be readily received into this
city, and as much as in us lies, be cherished and supported by us.—Dated at Londonderry the
21st of March, 1688–89.   [Signed]   Robert Lundy, Blaney, William Stewart, Arthur Raw-
don, George Maxwell, James Curry, John Forward, Hugh MacGill, William Ponsonby, H.
Baker, Chris. Fortescue, James Brabazon, John Hill, Samuel Norman, Alexander Tomkins,
Mathew Cocken, Horas Kennedy (Sheriff), Edward Brook (Sheriff), Alexander Lecky,
Francis Nevill, James Lennox, Fredrick Cowsingham, John Leslie, Henry Long, William
Crookshanks, Massareene, Clot. Skeffington, Arthur Upton, Samuel Morrison, Thomas Cole,
Francis Forster, Edward Cary, John Cowan, Kilner, Brasier, James Hamilton, John
Sinclare."

[8] The officers who signed the agreement to stand by their posts April 10, 1689, were:
Paulet Phillips, Hugh Magill, Richard Crofton, John Hill, George Hamilton, Arthur Upton,
Robert Lundy, [Henry] Blaney, Arthur Ralston, William Shaw, Richard Whaley, James
Hamilton, Nicholas Atchison, Hugh Montgomery, Thomas Whitney, William Ponsonby,
Richard Johnson, John Forward, George Squire, J. Blainey, John Tubman, Daniel McNeill.
Among other officers who took part in the defence of Londonderry were, William Stuart,
Francis Hamilton, Francis White, John Hamilton, John Barry, Walter Dawson.

[9] The Address of the defenders of Londonderry is printed in Walker's history of the
siege.   The caption and signers of the Address are as follows :

To the most Excellent Majesty of William and Mary, King and Queen of England, Scot-
land, France, and Ireland, Defenders of the Faith, etc. :   The humble Address of the
Governors, Officers, Clergy, and other Gentlemen in the City and Garrison of
Londonderry, etc.

Oliver Apton, Adam Ardock, Thomas Ash, William Babbington, Andrew Bailly, John
Bailly, Robert Bayley, Thomas Baker, James Barrington, Robert Bennet, Bartholomew
Black, James Blair, Francis Boyd, Robert Boyd, Thomas Brunett, John Buchanan, John
Campbell, William Campbell, Henry Campsie, James Carr, George Church, William Church,
Michael Clanaghan, Matthew Clarke, Dalway Clements, John Clements, John Cochran,
Matthew Cocken, Thomas Conlay, Richard Cormack, George Crofton, John Crofton, Richard,
Crofton, John Cross, William Cross, David Mons Cuistion, James Cunningham, John Cun-
ningham, Michael Cunningham, Edward Curling, Henry Cust, Edward Davyes, Robert
Dennison, John Dobbin, William Dobbin, Adam Downing, Philip Dunbarr, Richard Fane,
Daniel Fisher, James Fleming, Richard Fleming, John Fuller, Ralph Fullerton, James
Galtworth, George Garnet, James Gledstanes, Stephen Godfrey, Warren Godfrey, Joseph
Gordon, James Graham, Andrew Grigson, William Grove, Thomas Gughtredge, James
Hairs, Albert Hall, John Halshton, Hugh Hamill, Andrew Hamilton, Arthur Hamil-
ton, John Hamilton (2), William Hamilton, . . . Hannston, John Hering, Abraham

Hilhouse, James Huston, John Humes, Richard Islen, Christopher Jenney, Joseph Johnston, Thomas Johnston, Thomas Key, Charles Kinaston, Robert King, Alexander Knox, Frederick Kye, Henry Lane, Thomas Lane (2), Robert Lindsie, John Logan, James Mc Carmick, James McCartney, John McClelland, Matthew McClellany, Archibald McCulloch John Maghlin, Robert Maghlin, James Manson, Theophilus Manson, William Manson, John Michelborn, Henry Monry, William Montgomery, James Moore, Robert Morgan, Patt Moore, Adam Morrow, Bernard Mulhollan, David Mulhollan, John Mucholland, Thomas Newcomen, Arthur Noble, Francis Obre, Thomas Odayre, Henry Pearce, Dudley Phillips, Alexander Rankin, Alexander Ratcliff, Edmund Rice, Richard Robinson, Robert Rogers, Michael Rullack, Alexander Sanderson, Archibald Sanderson, Robert Skinner, Thomas Smyth, Gervase Squire, Alexander Steward, Marmaduke Stewart, William Stewart, James Stiles, William Thompson, James Tracy, George Walker (2), Robert Walker, Robert Wallace, George White, Nicholas White, Thomas White, Benjamin Wilkins, Frac. Wilson, James Young, Henry ——verett.

The foregoing list is also printed in Thomas Witherow's *Derry and Enniskillen*, as well as the following names of signers to a similar " Humble Address of the Governors, Officers, Clergy, and other Inhabitants of your Majesties' Town of Enniskillen," which was also forwarded to William and Mary from that city in 1689.

Alexander Acheson, Francis Aldrich, Daniel Armstrong, John Armstrong, Martin Armstrong, Thomas Armstrong, John Ballard, Claudius Bealy, Ambrose Bedel, William Birney, Hugh Blair, William Blashford, James Browning, John Browning, William Browning, Marcus Buchanan, Theodore Bury, James Campbell, William Campbell, Christopher Carleton, George Cashell, Allan Cathcart, Hugh Cathcart, James Cathcart, Malcome Cathcart, William Charleton, Robert Clark, Isaac Collyer, George Cooper, George Corry, Hugh Corry, James Corry, John Corry, Arnold Cosbye, Edward Cosbye, Laurence Crow, John Crozier, Edward Davenport, Thomas Davenport, John Dean, Paul Dean (Provost), James Delap, James Devitt, Edward Dixy, Cor. Donellan, George Drury, Robert Drury, Au. Ellis, Edward Ellis, Francis Ellis, Hercules Ellis, James Ewart, Francis Folliott, Samuel Forth, Daniel French, John Frisell, William Frith, All. Fulton, John Fulton, Hugh Galbraith, John Galbraith, Bar. Gibson, Francis Graham, James Graham, William Gore, Edward Gubbin, John Hale, Andrew Hamilton, Gustavus Hamilton (Governor), George Hammersley, George Hart, Morgan Hart, Thomas Hart, Jason Hazard, Daniel Hodson, Povey Hookes, Henry Howel, H. Hughes, Thomas Hughes, William Jivine, Henry Johnston, James Johnston (2), Robert Johnston (2), Thomas Johnston, William Johnston, Charles King, F. King, James King, John King, William Kittle, Thomas Leturvel, Matthew Lindsay, Thomas Lloyd, John Lowder, James Lucy, Robert McConnell, William McCormick, Charles McFayden, James Matthews (2), James Mitchell, Andrew Montgomery, Hugh Montgomery, Robert Moor, Toby Mulloy, John Neper, Richard Newstead, Thomas Osborn, William Parsons, John Price, John Rider, John Roberts, James Robison, Robert Robison, Thomas Roscrow, William Ross, George Russell, Ninian Scot, Thomas Scot, John Sheriffe, Thomas Shore, Ichabod Skelson, William Slack, Henry Smith, W. Smith, Aylet Sommes, Robert Starling, Robert Stevenson, Richard Taylor, Robert Vaughan, Robert Ward, George Watson, Matthew Webster, Robert Wear, Thomas White, Roger Wilton, William Wiseheart, Edward Wood, John Woodward, Matthew Young (2), Thomas Young.

CHAPTER XXXIX

THE EMIGRATION FROM ULSTER TO AMERICA

WE now come to two groups of measures which were to mould the history of Ireland during the eighteenth century, and the baneful effects of which are still felt in that country — the repression of her woollen manufactures, and the penal laws in matters of religion.

The end of the seventeenth century probably saw the last of the emigration of Scots into Ulster; while for the years that were to follow, the Scots were to leave Ulster in thousands for America. For some time after the Revolution a steady stream of Scotch Presbyterians had poured into the country, attracted by the cheapness of the farms and by the new openings for trade. In 1715, Archbishop Synge estimated that fifty thousand Scotch families had settled in Ulster since the Revolution.

The commerce of Ireland, after two devastating civil wars, cannot have been extensive, or of a magnitude which ought to have excited the envy or fear of England; but in the end of the seventeenth century the state of England was not a prosperous one, and her woollen manufacturers imagined that competition from Ireland was injuring them. The consequence was that in 1698, Parliament petitioned William III. to have laws enacted for the protection of the English woollen manufacture by the suppression of the Irish; and accordingly, the next year the Government passed an Act through the Irish Parliament, which was utterly subservient, forbidding any exportation of Irish woollens from the country. It was afterwards followed by Acts forbidding the Irish to export their wool to any country save England—the English manufacturers desiring to get the wool of the sister kingdom at their own price.

The penal laws against Roman Catholics and Presbyterians are the special glory of Queen Anne's time; hers was essentially a High Church régime, and in the Irish Parliament the High Church party ruled supreme. The Acts against Roman Catholics denied them the exercise of their worship, and laid the great body of the people of Ireland under pains and penalties so cruel and degrading that the laws could not in reality be put in force to their full extent. Those against Presbyterians were not so severe, but were sufficiently galling, and strangely unreasonable, as being applied against the very men who had been the stoutest bulwark of Protestantism not twenty years before. The blow against the Protestant dissenters was delivered through a Test Act, which compelled all serving in any capacity under the Government, all practising before the law courts, all acting in any town council, to take the communion of the Established Church. The Act at once emptied the town councils of the Ulster towns; it deprived of their commissions many who were serving as magistrates in the counties.   It drove out of the Corporation of Londonderry several of the very men who had fought through the siege of 1689.   A strange commentary on the Test Act was given in 1715, when Scotland was in ferment owing to the Jacobite Rebellion, and trouble was feared in Ireland.   The services of the Presbyterians were accepted for the militia, and then the Government passed an Act of Indemnity to free them from the penalties they had incurred by serving their country and breaking the Test Act.

The Irish Presbyterian Church had, in 1688, five presbyteries, above eighty ministers, eleven probationers, and about one hundred congregations. In the northern counties, Bishop Leslie calculated that Presbyterians were then fifty to one of the Episcopalians.   After Schomberg's arrival, in 1689, presbyteries began to meet as usual, but as many ministers were still in Scotland, there was difficulty in procuring supplies for the vacant charges. Several houses of worship had been destroyed, and the people greatly suffered from the ravages of war.

The English Parliament, which met towards the end of 1691, enacted that no person could sit in the Irish Parliament, or hold any Irish office, civil, military, or ecclesiastical, or practise law or medicine in Ireland, until he had taken the oaths of allegiance and supremacy, and had subscribed the declaration against Transubstantiation.   This Act — contrary to the Treaty of Limerick — was only one of the many persecuting laws by which Irish Roman Catholics were afterwards oppressed, but Presbyterians were not yet asked to make any declaration to which they could object.   They were, therefore, eligible for public offices in Ireland, although a minister was liable to three months' imprisonment in the common jail for delivering a sermon, and to a fine of a hundred pounds for celebrating the Lord's Supper.   In England, an Act of Toleration protected them in their worship, while by the Test Act they were excluded from office.

Although William often tried to persuade the Irish Parliament to pass an Act permitting dissenters to worship God according to the dictates of their conscience, his influence failed to overcome the power of bishops who controlled the House of Lords.   These efforts were always met by attempts to impose a Test Act, rendering it necessary for all who held places of power or profit under the Government to partake of the Lord's Supper in the Episcopal Church.   The bishops induced the Lords' committee on religion, of the Irish Parliament which met in 1692, to pass a resolution declaring that there should be no toleration of dissenters unless all public officials were compelled to communicate three times a year in their parish churches, and that severe penalties ought to be inflicted on any dissenting minister who ventured to preach against the Episcopal Church.

Several circumstances prevented Presbyterians from obtaining Parliamentary influence sufficient to save them from persecution.   The aristocracy, at the Restoration, went over to prelacy, which they had sworn to extirpate. By that aristocracy, both Houses of the Irish Parliament were completely controlled. The House of Lords belonged to them altogether, and they returned most of those supposed to represent the people in the Commons. The county members were elected by the freeholders; and freeholders were manufactured by the landlords to suit their own purposes.

There were then no large cities by which the power of the Episcopal oligarchy might be restrained. Dublin, with a population of thirty thousand, was by far the largest place in the kingdom. There was not a single town in Ulster with a population of five thousand. Yet villages like Augher, Charlemont, and St. Johnston each returned two members. In these places the landlords were as supreme as in their own castles. A burgess, on his election, had often to swear that he would obey all the proprietor's commands and boroughs could be bought or sold like any other commodity. Even in the large towns the people had no right to elect their representatives. The mayor, or " sovereign," and burgesses returned the members; but when a burgess died or resigned, his successor was elected by the other burgesses. And thus there was no real representation of the people in Ireland.

Besides all this, Presbyterians were confined to the Province of Ulster, while Episcopalians were scattered over the country. The fact that Presbyterians constituted almost the entire population in parts of the North, was of no avail in the South, where they were a small minority of the Protestants. Accordingly, Presbyterians having no political power, had to submit to political persecution. But they had also to endure a social persecution. The feudal system which transferred the ownership of the soil from the tribe to the landlord was one of the many evils introduced by the power of England. The Presbyterian farmer was a serf who had to submit to the will of his landlord, and in elections, when he had a vote, was obliged to support the enemies of his country, his class, and his creed.

In 1695 a new Parliament was summoned. Soon after it met, the earl of Drogheda brought before the House of Lords a bill for " ease to dissenters." But of forty-three Peers who were present, twenty-one were bishops, and a resolution postponing the consideration of the bill was carried without difficulty. The same measure of relief was proposed in the Commons, but was so strongly opposed that the Government was unable to carry it through. Lord Capel, the firm friend of toleration, died in 1696, and during several years Ireland was governed by Lords Justices. For a considerable period the leading spirit among these was Henri de Ruvigny, Earl of Galway, a French Protestant, who sympathized with Presbyterians in their struggles for freedom.

The Government, conscious of its weakness, made no attempt to pass a Toleration Bill in the Parliament of 1697, but succeeded in obtaining an Act by which legal protection was continued and extended to foreign Protestants, and provision made for carrying out a promise of the king to give salaries to their ministers.

Under the enlightened government of William, the Presbyterian Church made progress, notwithstanding the frowns of landlords and the rage of prelates. Many thousands of Presbyterians came to Ireland between the years 1690 and 1698 to occupy farms laid waste by the ravages of war. New congregations were established, and old congregations became large. In the neighborhood of Derry there were few ministers but had one thousand " examinable " persons, while many clergymen of the Established Church in the same district would not have more than a dozen to attend their services. Even now, after two hundred years of persecution, Presbyterians in these districts form a large majority of the Protestant population.

In March, 1702, Presbyterians lost a friend and protector by the death of King William. This monarch had always done his best to save them from persecution; but he was surrounded by an aristocracy who hated both himself and his principles, and it was with difficulty he retained by favor the crown he had won by the sword.

William was succeeded by Anne, daughter of James. She was at heart a Tory and a Jacobite. From her Presbyterians had much to fear and little to expect. However, the power of the Whigs during a great part of this reign saved dissenters from much they might have suffered had Tories been in office.

The congregations of the Irish Presbyterian Church, which now numbered nearly one hundred and twenty, were, in 1702, rearranged, and placed under the nine presbyteries of Belfast, Down, Antrim, Coleraine, Armagh, Tyrone, Monaghan, Derry, and Convoy; the three sub-synods of Belfast, Monaghan, and Lagan; and one general synod, which held a yearly meeting in June.[1]

The English Parliament, in 1703, extended to Ireland the provisions of a previously existing law, by which all persons in civil, military, or ecclesiastical offices were required to take the Oath of Abjuration, declaring that the son of King James had no right to the crown. Only six Irish Presbyterian ministers refused to make this declaration. These non-jurors considered that the oath was so worded as to bind them to declare that the Pretender was not the son of King James. Accordingly, they refused to swear, although as Whigs they were all opposed to the claims of the Stuarts. Among these Presbyterian non-jurors the Rev. John McBride, of Belfast, was particularly obnoxious to the prelatic party. Several attempts to obtain his arrest having failed, at last one of those clerical magistrates, who were so particularly zealous as persecutors, issued a warrant for his apprehension; and the accused had to fly from the country, although Lord Donegal offered to secure him to the value of his estate.

After the accession of Anne, the grant of Royal Bounty had been renewed, and its payment was continued, although the Irish House of Commons resolved, in October, 1703, that this " pension " was an unnecessary branch of the fiscal establishment. But a proposition involving greater danger and more disastrous consequences soon came before the Parliament in Dublin.   In direct violation of the Treaty of Limerick, a bill was introduced " to prevent the further growth of Popery."   This bill contained many clauses directed especially against Roman Catholics, and, with the approval of the Queen, another clause was introduced by the authorities in England, to the effect that all public officers in Ireland must take the Sacrament according to the rites of the Episcopal Church.   Presbyterians seemed confounded, and made but little resistance.   Few of them had seats in Parliament, and these few were powerless to prevent the bill passing.   The Roman Catholics were heard by counsel.   Their advocate in his speech upbraided the Government for now proposing to inflict pains and penalties on Presbyterians — the very men who had saved Ireland.   But all was in vain. The bill passed, and on the 4th of March, 1704, received the royal assent. Presbyterians were excluded from the magistracy, customs, excise, post-office, courts of law, and municipal offices.   Throughout Ireland, the Presbyterian magistrate was deprived of his position of power, and the Presbyterian postmaster of his means of support.   As a reward for their services, Presbyterians were declared incapable of filling the most humble office under that Episcopal Government for which they preserved Derry to Ireland and Ireland to Great Britain.

In Londonderry, ten aldermen and fourteen burgesses—about two-thirds of the entire corporation—preferred their Presbyterian faith to their official position.   In Belfast, the sovereign and a majority of the twelve burgesses were Presbyterians; and for some time the minority of the corporation did not attempt to exclude them.   But on the 7th of August, 1707, the death of Mr. William Cairns caused a vacancy in the Parliamentary representation of the borough.   In the contest which followed, only four burgesses took part, as the Presbyterian members of the corporation did not attempt to exercise their franchise.   This matter was reported to the House of Commons, and, by a majority of sixty-five to fifty-three, they declared that the office of burgess was vacated whenever its occupant did not qualify by becoming a Conformist.   The Presbyterian members were now excluded from the Belfast corporation.   Presbyterians lost their power in this and every other Parliamentary borough, and the representation of places, where they were then almost the entire population, was, by this means, transferred to a miserable minority of persecuting prelatists.

In 1704, some Presbyterians residing at Lisburn were excommunicated by Episcopal authority for the crime of being married by ministers of their own Church.   The Government, however, refused to issue the writs necessary for seizing excommunicated persons, and the offenders escaped imprisonment. The next year a bill was brought into the Irish Parliament containing clauses which would have rendered Presbyterian marriages illegal.   But Mr. Broderick, the Speaker, managed to get these clauses stricken out.

The judge on a northern circuit, having heard that several Presbyterians had been summoned to give evidence in a court of their own Church, denounced the custom, and charged grand juries to prosecute all concerned in holding such illegal meetings.

But notwithstanding these persecutions, and the fact that Presbyterians were compelled to pay tithes for the support of rectors whose sermons they never heard and whose doctrines they did not believe, while in addition they had to support their own clergymen, their Church grew and prospered with the growth of the country.

A Tory ministry having obtained power in 1710, the government of Ireland was again committed to the duke of Ormond, who appointed the primate and the commander of the forces to be Lords Justices until his arrival. A lately-passed Act had given any two magistrates the power of inflicting severe penalties on parties refusing to take the Abjuration Oath, and this Act was used by many Episcopal justices of the peace to oppress the Irish Non-conformists.

In 1713, the Rev. Alexander McCracken, of Lisburn, one of the Presbyterian non-jurors, was arrested, without a warrant, by Mr. Westerna Waring, High Sheriff of Down, who was then sunk in debt and was afterwards expelled from the Irish House of Commons. Mr. McCracken was fined five hundred pounds and condemned to six months' imprisonment. This imprisonment he suffered, but his sufferings were not supposed to expiate his crime. Being still under the obligation of taking the Oath, he again refused, and, consequently, was kept in jail until George I. was nearly two years on the throne. During all this time Roman Catholic priests were not molested for refusing to swear the same oath, notwithstanding they were mostly Jacobites, while the Presbyterians were loyal to the Protestant succession. Evil days now seemed to draw nigh. By an "Act against Schism," passed by the English Parliament, every Presbyterian schoolmaster became liable to imprisonment for three months if he discharged the duties of his office. The Royal Bounty was now definitely withdrawn, and all over Ulster there was an outburst of Episcopal tyranny. The doors of the Presbyterian churches in Downpatrick, Antrim, and Rathfriland were "nailed up," and a storm of persecution seemed about to burst on the devoted heads of all Protestant Nonconformists.

For some time the Queen's health had been failing, and it was now plain that her death was near. In common with almost all Tories, she favored the Pretender's claims; and a plot was formed to place him on the throne. The Whigs now began to take measures of self-defence. It was ascertained that fifty thousand Irish Presbyterians were prepared to carry arms in defence of the Protestant succession, and a Huguenot clergyman was sent with this news to Hanover. The Queen died on the 1st of August, 1714, before the Tories had their plans fully matured, and King George succeeded to the throne without opposition.

The new king regarded all Tories as Jacobites, and dismissed them from office. The Nonconformists had now a protector ready to exercise his power of pardon to save them from the consequences of laws made by his enemies to punish his friends.

As it was feared that an attempt would soon be made by the Pretender to gain the throne by his sword, the Lords Justices called out the militia in Ireland. Although Presbyterians exposed themselves to severe penalties for receiving pay from the crown, without taking the Test, they immediately offered their services to the Government. This offer was gladly accepted, and a promise was given that no Presbyterian would be punished for taking up arms to defend the Protestant religion and the House of Hanover.

The death of the Queen had caused a dissolution of the Irish Parliament. In 1715, a general election took place, and a few Presbyterian candidates were successful in northern constituencies. Clotworthy Upton and Sir Arthur Langford were returned for the county of Antrim, Hugh Henry for Antrim borough, George Macartney for Belfast, Archibald Edmonston for Carrickfergus, and Hercules Rowley for county Derry. A desperate effort was made to keep out Colonel Upton, but, notwithstanding the fury of the territorial aristocracy, he was supported by a majority of the Presbyterian freeholders.

When the Irish Parliament met, it was found that the Whigs had a majority in the Commons, and a bill was passed through the Lower House indemnifying Presbyterians for all time to come from penalties incurred by serving in the militia, and, for ten years, from penalties incurred by serving in the army. But even this small measure of relief met with such opposition in its subsequent stages that it had to be abandoned; and the only people in Ireland upon whom the king could depend were refused permission to carry arms in defence of his crown. But the Commons passed resolutions to the effect that any person who would prosecute a dissenter for accepting a commission in the army or militia was an enemy of King George and a friend to the Pretender.

On the 6th of September, 1715, the earl of Mar raised the standard of the Stuarts in Scotland. The duke of Argyle marched against the rebels at once, and after a desperate battle at Sheriffmuir, remained master of the field. Although the victory was not decisive, the clans were so much discouraged that they returned home, and the arrival of the Pretender himself did not prevent the rebellion coming to a speedy termination.

Meanwhile, Presbyterians remained exposed to the persecutions of their enemies. Four members of Tullylish congregation were, in 1716, delivered over to Satan by Episcopal authority, for the high crime of being married by their own minister, the Rev. Gilbert Kennedy.

In 1717 there were 130 ministers, 140 congregations, 11 presbyteries, and nearly 200,000 people in connection with the Synod of Ulster. These people were scattered over a wide district, and it was difficult for so few ministers to attend to their spiritual wants. Stipends were small, but money had a large purchasing power. In 1721 the people of Omagh erected the church in which the descendants of those who formed the first congregation still worship.

The Government now determined to make another attempt to pass their long promised Toleration Bill. But the Tories, fearing that the proposed enactment might be too favorable to Nonconformists, introduced a bill of their own, which granted them mere toleration. Even this measure of relief was considered far too much by many Episcopalians, and it passed through the Lords by a majority of only seven votes. This Act delivered Protestant dissenters from penalties for absence from religious services in their parish churches; and it permitted Nonconformist ministers to discharge all the functions of their office without incurring the former penalty of one hundred pounds. An Act of Indemnity was also passed to protect civil or military officers, who were Nonconformists, from the consequences of having in the past received pay from the crown without taking the Test But they were not protected from the consequences of similar acts in future, and no attempt was made to repeal the Test Act itself.

These various repressive measures fashioned the history of Ireland during the first seventy years of the eighteenth century. The country was utterly wretched, and broken-hearted. Its agriculture was miserable, and chronic scarcity alternated with actual famine; it had little commerce, and no manufactures, save the slowly increasing linen manufacture of Ulster.

There are two outstanding facts in the history of Ulster at this time besides the rise of the linen manufacture—the steady emigration, and the rise of the Secession Church. The latter is a strong proof of the kinship to Scotland, the former is, perhaps, even a stronger proof of the blood which was in her sons, for they left Ulster, as their forefathers had come to it, in search of a more kindly home across the seas. The emigration from Ulster is one of the most striking features of Irish history, and one which had a most marked effect on the vital force of the United States of America, which drew so much of its best blood from the Presbyterians of the north of Ireland. There was nothing to induce the active-minded men of the North to remain in Ireland, and they left in crowds, going away with wives and children, never to return. In 1718, there is mention of " both ministers and people going off." In 1728, Archbishop Boulter states that " above 4200 men, women, and children have been shipped off from hence for the West Indies, within three years." In consequence of the famine of 1740, it is stated that for " several years afterwards, twelve thousand emigrants annually left Ulster for the American plantations "; while from 1771 to 1773, " the whole emigration from Ulster is estimated at thirty thousand, of whom ten thousand were weavers." Thus was Ulster drained of the young, the enterprising, and the most energetic and desirable classes of its population. They left the land which had been saved to England by the swords of their fathers, and crossed the sea to escape from the galling tyranny of the bishops whom

England had made rulers of that land. They came to a new and a better land, and here they founded their homes, built their churches, established their communities, and again set up their religion. And here, also, in the end, the sons were obliged to draw their swords in order that they might save to themselves from England the land which they had won.

A writer in the *Dublin University Magazine* for 1832 (vol. i. pp. 476, 477), in speaking of the Protestant emigration to America, says:

> The long interval of calm which followed the Revolution [of 1688] liberalized the feelings of the generation which came after that event, and led the Proprietary into a system of setting their lands, which has been followed by the most disastrous consequences in the emigration of their Protestant tenantry. That system is thus described by a writer who published his pamphlet in 1745: " Popish tenants are daily preferred, and Protestant rejected, either for the sake of swelling a rental or adding some more duties which Protestants will not submit to. . . . The Protestants being thus driven out of their settlements, transport themselves, their families, and effects to America, there to meet a more hospitable reception from strangers to their persons, but friends to their religion and civil principles."

The Lord Primate Boulter, who had come from England, and been appointed one of the Lord Justices, in 1728, wrote a letter on the subject of the emigration from Ireland,[2] to the ministry in England, in which he says: " The whole North is in a ferment at present, and the people are every day engaging one another to go next year to the West Indies [*i. e.*, to North America]. The worst is, that it affects only Protestants, and reigns chiefly in the North, which is the seat of our linen industry."

The extent in numerical amount to which this emigration went is far beyond what would be supposed; but it appears on the clearest evidence that from the year 1725 to 1768 the number of emigrants gradually increased from 3000 to 6000 annually, making altogether about 200,000 Protestants. By the returns laid before Parliament in 1731, the total number of Protestants in Ireland was 527,505. Now, of these 200,000 emigrated; so that, making ample allowance for the increase of population between the years 1731 and 1768, we shall still find that one third of the whole Protestant population of Ireland emigrated within that disastrous period.

Arthur Young, who visited Ireland in 1776, published the result of his observations in 1780, under the title, *A Tour in Ireland*. In writing of the causes which led to the emigration of the Ulster Scots from 1772 to 1774, he says:

> The spirit of emigrating in Ireland appeared to be confined to two circumstances, the Presbyterian religion and the linen manufacture. I heard of very few emigrants except among manufacturers of that persuasion. The Catholics never went; they seem not only tied to the country, but almost to the parish in which their ancestors lived. As to emigration in the North, it was an error in England to suppose it a novelty, which arose with the increase of rents. The contrary was the fact; it had subsisted perhaps forty years, insomuch that at the ports of Belfast, Derry, etc., the passage trade,

as they called it, had long been a regular branch of commerce, which employed several ships, and consisted in carrying people to America. The increasing population of the country made it an increasing trade; but when the linen trade was low, the passenger trade was always high. At the time of Lord Donegal's letting his estate in the North [about 1772], the linen business suffered a temporary decline, which sent great numbers to America, and gave rise to the error that it was occasioned by the increase of his rents.

NOTES TO CHAPTER XXXIX

[1] See Appendix V (Early Presbyterian Congregations in Ireland).
[2] For Boulter's letters see Appendix L.

END VOL. L

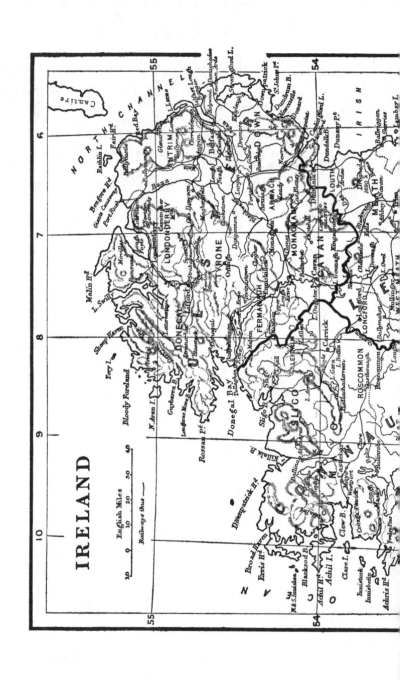

IRELAND

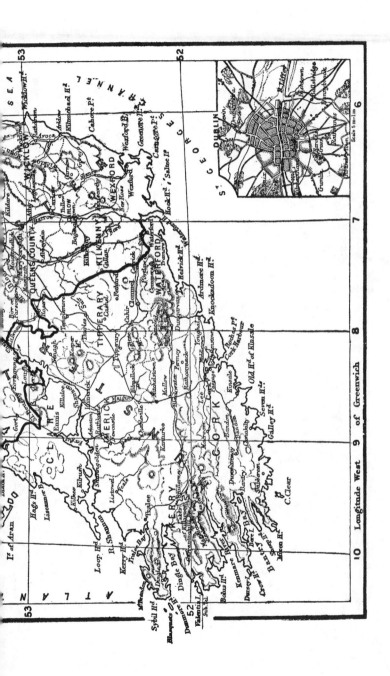